Rocky Mountains

Nicko Goncharoff
Kimberley O'Neil
Marisa Gierlich
Eric Kettunen

LONELY PLANET PUBLICATIONS
Melbourne • Oakland • London • Paris

Rocky Mountains

2nd edition

Published by
Lonely Planet Publications
Head Office: PO Box 617, Hawthorn, Vic 3122, Australia
Branches: 150 Linden St, Oakland, CA 94607, USA
                 10A Spring Place, London NW5 3BH, UK
                 1 rue du Dahomey, 75011 Paris, France

Printed by
Colorcraft Ltd, Hong Kong
Printed in China

Photographs by

James Blank	Ric Ergenbright	Ray Hillstrom	John Mock
Maxine Cass	Lee Foster	Eric Kettunen	Kimberley O'Neil
Michael Clark	Marisa Gierlich	Abrahm Lustgarten	Robert Raburn
John Elk	Djon Good	Bill McRae	Tony Wheeler

Front cover: ©Tom Till, cabin in historic mining town, San Juan Mountains, Colorado

First Published
October 1995

This Edition
February 1999

ISBN 0 86442 536 8

text & maps © Lonely Planet 1999
photos © photographers as indicated 1999
climate chart compiled from information supplied by Patrick J Tyson, © Patrick J Tyson, 1999
illustration on page 792 from *Trails Plowed Under* by Charles M Russell, copyright 1927, is used by
permission of Doubleday, a division of Random House, Inc.

Nicko Goncharoff

Born and raised in New York, Nicko went to the University of Colorado, where he learned about the outdoors, partying and how to get a degree. He then left for a short stint in Asia that ended up lasting about eight years. After trying his hand at magazines, newsletters and a financial news wire, Nicko came to Lonely Planet in 1994. He wrote the *Hong Kong* city guide and coauthored guides to China, Japan, and Thailand's islands and beaches before returning to research the Rocky Mountains. He now lives in San Francisco.

Kimberley O'Neil

Kimberley has over 12 years of professional experience in adventure travel and tourism. As a former Director of Asian Operations for a North American tour operator, she designed and operated trekking and mountaineering trips throughout the Himalaya and Karakoram. She has been a consultant on ecotourism for the World Conservation Union – Pakistan, and also works as a computer software instructor. Kimberley and her husband John Mock are coauthors of LP's *Trekking in the Karakoram & Hindukush* and live in Northern California.

Marisa Gierlich

Marisa was born and raised in Hermosa Beach, CA. Thanks to adventurous parents, she began traveling at age seven and hasn't stopped for more than eight months since. She did manage to earn an English degree at the University of California, Berkeley, where she began writing for *The Berkeley Guides* – an employ that took her to France, Sweden, Italy and Alaska – and she has worked on the first editions of Lonely Planet's *Rocky Mountain States* and *California & Nevada* guides. When not writing guide books, Marisa leads hiking and biking tours for Backroads, and runs, skis and surfs with her husband Paul.

Eric Kettunen

After graduating from the University of Michigan, Eric spent four years at a New York art book publisher before being 'saved' by Tony and Maureen Wheeler and delivered to LP's California office in 1988, first as sales and marketing manager and later as the US general manager. When the 2nd edition of *The Rocky Mountains* came around, he gallantly volunteered to take on the grueling task of updating central Colorado, including Aspen, Vail, Breckenridge and some even tougher travel destinations.

From the Authors

From Nicko Colorado is a big place for one person to handle, and dozens of people helped me project my coverage and make my research both easier and more pleasant. Jennifer at Colorado Mountain School gave me some good tips and a quiet place to work. The information department staff at Rocky Mountain National Park were both helpful and fun. Special thanks to my Fort Collins buddies, Anita and Vince, for their outstanding hospitality. A tip of the hat also to John and Gina Petty for letting me stay in their beautiful home, and to my Grand Junction mountain bike guides, John, Jim and Clint. Also thanks to Curt Lane at the Bike Peddler for great info on mountain biking in western Colorado. In Paonia, Barbie at Rocky Mountain Inn was a particularly kind host. Jamie Meyer, Edward and Lynn Calloway, Mary Jo Somrak, Chris Cottrell and Ali all helped me figure out the magic of Crested Butte in record time. Art and Barbara Gould gave me a fabulous roof to stay under in Telluride, while in Creede, Christine and Lindsay gave me a great cup of coffee and a fine start to my day. Special thanks go to Caroline, who showed up just in time to help me keep my sanity. My deepest gratitude to Mike, Nan, Tom, Debbie, Mary, Steven, Steve, Ken and my other Boulder friends: I don't know how I would have done this book without you folks. And last, thanks to Wayne Bernhardson and Robert Raburn, who wrote the first edition of this book and thus did a hell of a lot of legwork.

From Kimberley Many thanks to the hundreds of people across Idaho and Wyoming who shared their wisdom – from the chambers of commerce and NPS and USFS rangers to hotel clerks. Heartfelt thanks to the OARS family who enabled a memorable descent of the Main Fork of Idaho's Salmon River: Russell Walters, General Manager of OARS in Angels Camp, CA; Curt Chang, manager of OARS Boatland in Lewiston, ID; and river guides extraordinaire Eric Hudelson, Dan Sorcinelli, Chris Quinn, Willow Nelson, Jeff Wallach and especially Remony Burlingame. Thanks also to Olivia James, president, and Erasmo Paolo, managing director, of the River Company, Stanley, ID, for a fun outing on the Upper Salmon River. Thanks to Ruth Harris at the Asotin Museum in Asotin, WA, for sharing her knowledge of the history of the Clearwater and Snake rivers. Special thanks to old friends who offered hospitality and support during 9000 miles of research: Melanie Stafford, acting president of the Denver NOW chapter, for her input on women travelers; Regina and Jim Bock; camping and rafting pal Mary Carlson; Al Read, president of Exum Mountain Guides, Thomas Turiano, and Kelly Rich for their climbing expertise; and especially Andy and Betsy Olerud for a memorable kayaking trip in the Winds and their infinite enthusiasm for the Tetons. None of this would have been possible without the support of my loving husband, John Mock.

From Marisa First of all, many thanks to the team that made this the bionic book – Nicko for his thoughtful and strong coordination, Kim for her exemplary organization, Eric for, well, just for being Eric, and Carolyn Hubbard for keeping the faith and pulling us all together. Alex and Bart are the patient and precise cartographers who made mapping a relative breeze.

Joan and Jim transcended the boundaries of ordinary generosity when they provided meals, accommodation, knowledge of the area, comfort and friendship while I was in Glacier Country. Everyone who has such people in their lives is blessed! Thanks to Ernie and Gail at Missoula's Birchwood Hostel (a veritable home-away-from-home), and to Jim and Peggy Oury who welcomed me at Montana's finest accommodation.

Susan and Bobby of The Sanders B&B were a joy to visit and provided great tips on outdoor activities in the Helena area. Verna Pontrelli's aunt and uncle offered a great tour and insider information on the Eureka area. Kelly and Melissa, besides being terrific playmates and awesome cooks, were super-helpful in covering West Yellowstone and the Madison and Gallatin valleys. And thanks to Vandy, Fernando and Kevin Rebholtz – Red Lodge will never be the same.

Also, the interpretive specialist at Glacier National Park's headquarters deserves a big thanks for the time and energy he spent on the Glacier National Park section. And last, but not even close to least, Paul, my folks, and the Burgins, the kindest, most loving and understanding family ever.

From Eric As general manager of Lonely Planet's US office I don't get out much, and updating most of Colorado's Western Slope has given me a better appreciation for the hard work and professionalism of our authors and in-house staff. Thanks to Nicko Goncharoff for his advice and encouragement – but especially for letting me update Aspen! Thanks also to Carolyn Hubbard and Alex Guilbert for pointing me in the right direction before I left for Colorado and Sue Peters for keeping me on track through the editing stage.

In Colorado, thanks to Mick Kelly and Tom Sullivan at The Minturn Inn who provided a wealth of information about the region and for making sure I wouldn't get lost in the Holy Cross Wilderness Area, the guys from the bikeshop at Winter Park who showed me firsthand why the resort is 'Mountain Bike Capital USA,' and to all the helpful staff at the USFS stations, tourist offices and chambers of commerce throughout the state who provide accurate information and good advice to travelers every day.

A special thanks to Ingrid, Kirstin, Barb and David Klein who shared with me their favorite places in and around Aspen and also their beautiful home on the Frying Pan River.

From the Publisher

This book is the product of many people's energies and input. Tom 'Wild Bill' Downs and Calamity Sue Peters were the project editors, roped in by style-rustler and senior editor Carolyn Hubbard. Maureen Klier also lent a hand and a rhyme or two. The cabal of fastidiousness (copyeditors and proofreaders) was comprised of Julie Connery, Marianne Dresser and Andrew Nystrom, with Paige Penland fine-tuning a chapter as well. The numerous marvelous maps are the handiwork of cartographers Alex Guilbert, Dion Good and Bart Wright, who drew and corrected ad infinitum with hardly a whimper, with greatly appreciated help from Amy Dennis, Guphy, Patrick Huerta, Rini Keagy, Jenny King, Beca Lafore, Margaret Livingston and Henia Miedzinski. Hayden Foell headed a pack of illustrators which included Hugh D'Andrade, Rini Keagy, John Fadeff and Jim Swanson. Rini Keagy was the cover-artiste. Production czar Scott Summers was aided and abetted by the able team of Dion Good, Margaret Livingston, Richard Wilson, Shelley Firth and Emily Douglas. Further thanks goes to valiant multitaskers Joslyn Leve, Sacha Pearson and Josh Schefers.

This Book

This 2nd edition was produced at Lonely Planet's US offices. Nicko Goncharoff was the coordinating author and wrote parts of Colorado, Kimberley O'Neil wrote Idaho and Wyoming, Marisa Gierlich wrote Montana, and Eric Kettunen wrote parts of Colorado. Veteran LP author Wayne Bernhardson and Robert Raburn contributed to the 1st edition. Bill McRae contributed to the Idaho chapters, originally published in Lonely Planet's *Pacific Northwest*.

Thanks

Many thanks to the travelers who used the last edition and wrote to us with helpful hints, useful advice and interesting anecdotes. Their names are:

Alice Ackrill, Liam Barrett, Sherry Benson, Morris Biggins, Cheryl Carruth, Darcy Coale, Raffa Deganutti, Bob Everhart, Chris Gibb, Mark L Goodman, Sarah Hakimoglu, Nigel Henderson, Lee Hendricks, Marian Holder, Brendon Keane, Wendy Lee, Lisa Leu, Matthew and Stephanie Lewis, Prue Lygo, John Masterson, Jenny McRae, Sarah Medcalf, Barbara S Miller, Todd and Joby Moore, Mike and

Vana O'Brien, Lori Olivier, Thomas L Radinsky, Jennifer Schnakenberg, Tim Searle, Gill Shears, Jenna Shearstone, Barry Shine, Bernard Van de Walle de Ghelcke, Kevin Vaughan, BJ Wakefield, Johan Wiberg.

Warning & Request

Things change – prices go up, schedules change, good places go bad and bad places go bankrupt – nothing stays the same. So, if you find things better or worse, recently opened or long since closed, please tell us and help make the next edition even more accurate and useful.

We value all of the feedback we receive from travelers. A small team reads and

acknowledges every letter, postcard and email, and ensures that every morsel of information finds its way to the appropriate authors, editors and publishers. All readers who write to us will find their names in the next edition of the appropriate guide and will also receive a free subscription to our quarterly newsletter, *Planet Talk*. The very best contributions will be rewarded with a free Lonely Planet guide.

Excerpts from your correspondence may appear in new editions of this guide, in *Planet Talk* or in the Postcards section of our website (www.lonelyplanet.com) – so please let us know if you don't wish to have your letter published or your name acknowledged.

Contents

SOUTHERN MOUNTAINS 332

WESTERN COLORADO 408

EASTERN PLAINS 448

WYOMING 465

FACTS ABOUT WYOMING 466

SOUTHERN WYOMING 469

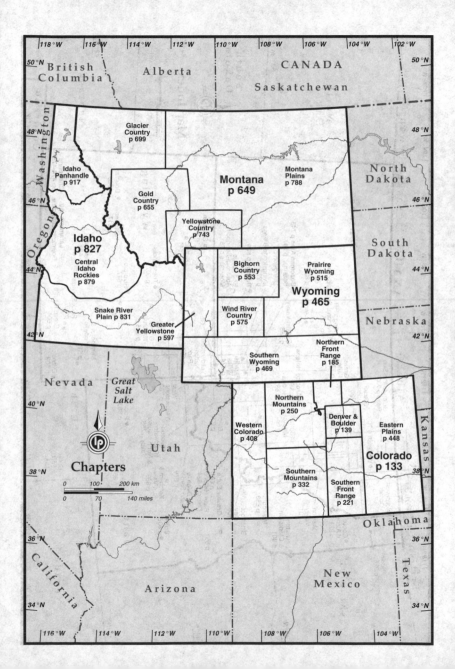

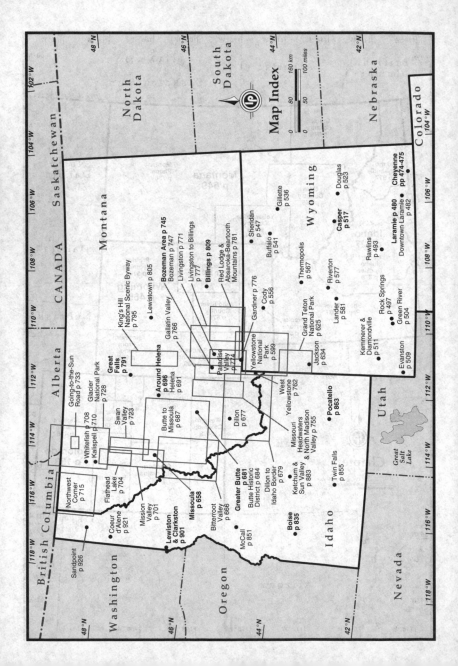

Map Index

0   80   160 km
0   50   100 miles

British Columbia
Alberta
Saskatchewan
CANADA

Washington
Montana
North Dakota
South Dakota

Oregon
Idaho
Wyoming
Nebraska

Nevada
Utah
Colorado

Sandpoint p 926
Northwest Corner p 715
Going-to-the-Sun Road p 733
Whitefish p 708
Kalispell p 710
Glacier National Park p 728
Flathead Lake p 704
Coeur d'Alene p 921
Mission Valley p 701
Swan Valley p 723
King's Hill National Scenic Byway p 795
Lewistown p 805
Great Falls p 791
Butte to Missoula p 687
Around Helena p 696
Helena p 691
Lewiston & Clarkston p 901
Missoula p 558
Bitterroot Valley p 666
Greater Butte p 681
Butte Historic District p 684
Dillon to Idaho Border p 679
Dillon p 677
Gallatin Valley p 766
Paradise Valley p 771
Bozeman Area p 745
Bozeman p 747
Livingston p 771
Livingston to Billings p 777
Billings p 809
Red Lodge & Absaroka-Beartooth Mountains p 781
Gardiner p 776
Sheridan p 547
Gillette p 536
Buffalo p 541
McCall p 851
Boise p 835
Ketchum & Sun Valley p 883
Dillon to Idaho Border p 679
Missouri Headwaters & North Madison Valley p 755
West Yellowstone p 762
Yellowstone National Park p 599
Cody p 556
Thermopolis p 567
Grand Teton National Park p 625
Lander p 577
Riverton p 577
Casper p 517
Douglas p 523
Wyoming
Pocatello p 863
Twin Falls p 855
Jackson p 634
Kemmerer & Diamondville p 511
Rock Springs p 497
Green River p 504
Rawlins p 493
Laramie p 480
Downtown Laramie p 482
Cheyenne pp 474-475
Evanston p 509
Great Salt Lake

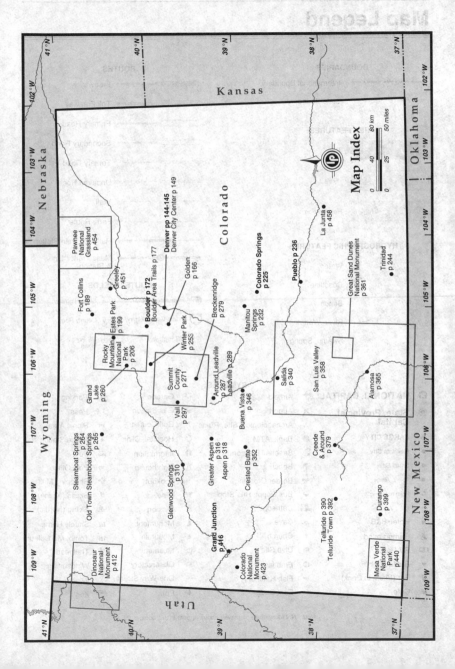

Map Index

Kansas

Colorado

Wyoming

Nebraska

Utah

New Mexico

Oklahoma

Pawnee National Grassland p 454

Fort Collins p 189

Greeley p 451

Estes Park p 199

Rocky Mountain National Park p 206

Grand Lake p 260

Boulder p 172
Boulder Area Trails p 177

Denver pp 144-145
Denver City Center p 149

Golden p 166

Winter Park p 253

Breckenridge p 279

Summit County p 271

Around Leadville p 287
Leadville p 289

Vail p 297

Buena Vista p 346

Manitou Springs p 232

Colorado Springs p 225

Pueblo p 236

La Junta p 458

Salida p 340

San Luis Valley p 358

Great Sand Dunes National Monument p 361

Alamosa p 365

Trinidad p 244

Steamboat Springs p 264
Old Town Steamboat Springs p 265

Glenwood Springs p 310

Greater Aspen p 316
Aspen p 318

Crested Butte p 352

Creede & Around p 379

Grand Junction p 416

Colorado National Monument p 423

Telluride p 390
Telluride Town p 392

Durango p 399

Dinosaur National Monument p 412

Mesa Verde National Park p 440

0   40   80 km
0   25   50 miles

Map Legend

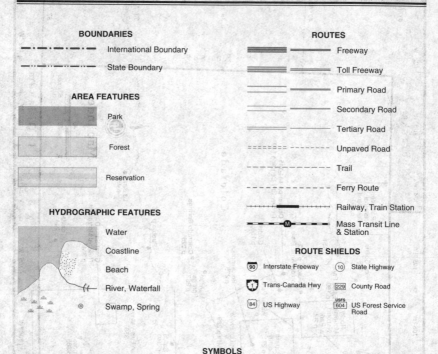

BOUNDARIES

– ·· – ·· – ·· – International Boundary

– ·· – ·· – ·· – State Boundary

AREA FEATURES

Park

Forest

Reservation

HYDROGRAPHIC FEATURES

Water

Coastline

Beach

River, Waterfall

Swamp, Spring

ROUTES

Freeway

Toll Freeway

Primary Road

Secondary Road

Tertiary Road

Unpaved Road

Trail

Ferry Route

Railway, Train Station

Mass Transit Line & Station

ROUTE SHIELDS

(90) Interstate Freeway

Trans-Canada Hwy

(84) US Highway

(10) State Highway

229 County Road

USFS 604 US Forest Service Road

SYMBOLS

✪ NATIONAL CAPITAL
◉ State, Provincial Capital
● LARGE CITY
● Medium City
● Small City
● Town, Village
○ Point of Interest

■ Hotel, B&B
▲ Campground
⇆ RV Park
▼ Restaurant
♟ Bar (Place to Drink)
☕ Cafe

✈ Airfield
✈ Airport
∴ Archaeological Site, Ruins
Ⓢ Bank, ATM
⌂ Baseball Diamond
⌐ Beach
⚹ Border Crossing
● Bus Depot, Bus Stop
✚ Cathedral
∩ Cave
† Church
◂ Dive Site
Q Embassy
⌐ Fish Hatchery
⤜ Foot Bridge

❖ Garden
⛽ Gas Station
⌐ Golf Course
○ Hospital, Clinic
ⓘ Information
⚸ Lighthouse
✳ Lookout
⛏ Mine
⚐ Mission
⚑ Monument
▲ Mountain
⛫ Museum
⛪ Observatory
— One-Way Street
▲ Park

◻ Parking
)(Pass
⋔ Picnic Area
★ Police Station
⊟ Pool
✉ Post Office
❖ Shopping Mall
⚡ Skiing (Alpine)
⚐ Skiing (Nordic)
Ⅲ Stately Home
▣ Tomb, Mausoleum
⚐ Trailhead
◣ Windsurfing
⚘ Winery
🐘 Zoo

Note: Not all symbols displayed above appear in this book.

Introduction

With its towering peaks and lush mountain valleys, the magnificent Rocky Mountain range is home to some of the USA's most stunning natural beauty. Millions of people flock to these awesome mountains and their nearby plains each year to enjoy the scenery, outdoor recreation, historical sites and some of the world's best skiing. In addition to the nature, there are also countless small towns and villages throughout the region – a legion of charming, friendly stopovers for visitors making their way from one impressive site to the next.

The Rockies, acting as North America's spine, split the USA along the Continental Divide. Eastward flowing rivers cross the plains to join the great Mississippi, and the arid western drainage snakes through imposing mountain ranges to reach the Pacific via the mighty Columbia River or to dwindle away on the sands of the southern Colorado Desert.

A fascinating range of topography awaits travelers visiting the Rocky Mountain region. In addition to the peaks themselves, some of which reach above 14,000 feet, there are fertile river valleys, sprawling reaches of semi-desert, high Alpine plateaus, plunging canyons, even massive sand dunes. This variety means that often the trip to a destination is just as rewarding as seeing the place itself. As with much of the USA, public transportation is sadly limited, and by far the best way to explore the region is by private car, or if you have the time, by bicycle.

Early Spanish explorers were the first to reach the area, but rugged mountain men

17

and fur traders pioneered the European exploration of the northern Rockies. The Rockies soon became identified with the 'Wild West' of brawling, rough and ready mining camps, long-distance cattle drives and gunfighters.

Western settlement displaced or supplanted the native peoples who had inhabited the region for millennia, leaving them socially sidelined and impoverished. Despite this grim, unfortunate history, the indigenous presence has not disappeared and, in some ways, is now more visible – Native Americans are being voted into public office and powwows are popular community events.

Colorado is the region's economic powerhouse and Denver, Colorado's capital, is the only true metropolis in the four states. Idaho, Montana and Wyoming, almost exclusively rural, are among the least populated states in the country.

This book does not cover the entirety of the Rocky Mountains, which transcend state and national boundaries – see also Lonely Planet's *The Southwest* for Utah, New Mexico and Arizona and *Canada* for the northern reaches.

Facts about the Rocky Mountains

HISTORY

Nearly 20,000 years ago, when the accumulated ice of the great polar glaciers of the Pleistocene Epoch lowered sea levels throughout the world, the ancestors of American Indians crossed from Siberia to Alaska via a land bridge over the Bering Strait. Over millennia, subsequent migrations distributed the population southward through North and Central America and down to the southern tip of South America.

The first inhabitants of North America were nomadic hunter-gatherers who lived in small bands, and this type of society existed on the continent even into very recent times. In the northern plains, from about 16,000 years ago, the early Clovis complex consisted of hunters who eventually exterminated megafauna like mammoths and *Bison antiquus*, forerunner of the modern buffalo by about 12,000 years. The slightly later Folsom complex, discovered near the Colorado-New Mexico border, occupied rather larger sites.

Late Paleo-Indian artifacts of the Cody cultural complex indicate reliance on the modern bison, while around 7500 years ago some peoples switched to hunting smaller game – a likely indicator of human population pressure on the declining bison. Petroglyphs along the canyon walls of Central Idaho's mighty rivers testify to over 8000 years of human habitation. The most complex societies in North American antiquity, however, were the agricultural pueblos of the Colorado Plateau, where Anasazi cliff dwellers left behind impressive ruins in areas like Mesa Verde near Cortez, Colorado.

Native Americans at Contact

Many different Native American groups occupied the Rocky Mountain region at the time of European contact. In the harsh landscapes of Oregon and Idaho's southern desert, nomadic tribes like the Shoshone and Paiute became fearsome warriors and hunters after the 18th century, when horses – stolen from Spanish California – gave them easy mobility. With horses, the Shoshone-Bannocks quickly became one of the dominant Indian groups in the West, ranging across the Rockies onto the Great Plains to hunt buffalo and onto the Columbia Plateau to trade and plunder.

The Shoshone were most amenable to the foreign presence. Numbering about 2000 in 1800, they were concentrated in the western Wyoming drainage of the Green, Snake, Bear and Columbia rivers; their population fell from a peak of 3000 in 1840 to only 800 by 1900. Staple foods included bison, elk, beaver, mule deer, fish, berries and wild roots. Most Shoshone now reside on the Wind River Reservation in central Wyoming, but smaller numbers live at Fort Hall, Idaho, and at Duck Valley, which straddles the Idaho-Nevada border.

Also friendly to traders were the Crow or Absaroka who lived at the headwaters of the Yellowstone, Powder, Bighorn, Platte and Wind rivers. They numbered about 4000 in 1800. The Blackfeet, by contrast, resented and resisted the European invaders to their territory in the upper Missouri, Milk and Marias rivers and the Judith Basin. Their population peaked at about 30,000 before the smallpox epidemic of 1837.

The Utes consisted of six eastern bands in Colorado and five western bands in Utah; their Colorado territory stretched from the Uinta Mountains and the Yampa River in the north to the San Juan River in the south, and as far east as the Front Range. They are now confined to the Ute Mountain Indian Reservation in southern Colorado and northern New Mexico, the Southern Ute Indian Reservation adjacent to it in southern Colorado, and the Uintah-Ouray Reservation in northern Utah. The Utes accommodated trappers, even attending the

William Clark   Meriwether Lewis

The Lewis & Clark Expedition

When Jefferson made the decision in 1803 to explore the western part of the country to find a water passage to the Pacific, he enlisted his young protégé and personal secretary, Meriwether Lewis, to lead an expedition. Lewis, then 29, had no expertise in botany, cartography or Indian languages and was known to have bouts of 'hypochondriac affections' – a euphemism for schizophrenia – but he couldn't resist the opportunity. Lewis in turn asked his good friend William Clark, already an experienced frontiersman and army veteran at the age of 33, to join him. In 1804, they left St Louis, MO, and headed west with an entourage of 40, including 27 bachelors, a dog and Clark's African American servant, York.

They traveled some 8000 miles in about two years, documenting everything they came across in their journals with such bad spelling that it must have taken historians a few extra years just to sort out what they wrote. In an almost biblical fashion they named some 120 animals and 170 plants, including the grizzly bear and the prairie dog. While Clark's entries are the more scientific, Lewis was known to explore alone and write pensive, almost romantic, accounts of the journey.

Despite encountering hostilities, the group faired quite well, in part because they were accompanied by Sacagawea, a young Shoshone woman who had been married off to a French trapper. Her presence, along with her child's, and her ability to liaise between the explorers and the Indians eased many potential conflicts. York also eased tensions between the group and the locals – his color and stature of six feet and 200 pounds being both fascinating and intimidating to the Indians.

Lewis and Clark returned to a heroes' welcome in St Louis in 1806 and were soon appointed to high offices. In 1808 Lewis was appointed governor of the Louisiana Territory, but died a year later, purportedly during a 'fit' in which he either committed suicide or was murdered. Clark dealt with his new fame a bit better, and was appointed superintendent of Indian Affairs in the Louisiana Territory and governor of the Missouri Territory. He died at the age of 68. ■

various rendezvous, but eventually came into conflict with settlers on the Western Slope. The Nez Percé, while based in what is now Idaho, also participated in the fur trade and rendezvous in present-day Wyoming.

Exploration & Settlement

The first Europeans to see the Rocky Mountain area were Spaniards moving north from Mexico. They founded the city of Santa Fe at the end of the 16th century, and established land grants as far north as the Arkansas River in present-day Colorado. In the search for overland routes to California, the Domínguez-Escalante Expedition of 1775-76 explored the Colorado Plateau well into northern Colorado, but concentrated on what is now Utah.

In the early 18th century, French explorers and fur traders converged on the northern plains from eastern Canada, but by the early 19th century Spanish influence extended throughout the western half of present-day Colorado, the southwestern corner of Wyoming, and even shared, at least formally, occupation of parts of Montana with the British. Virtually all of New Mexico, Arizona, California, Utah and Nevada were under Spanish authority, but another player in the imperial game would soon supersede them.

In 1803, the upstart USA, under the presidency of Thomas Jefferson, took advantage of a surprising French proposal to purchase an ill-defined area known as the Louisiana Purchase, including the coveted port of New Orleans. The area also included virtually all of present-day Montana, nearly three quarters of Wyoming, and the eastern half of Colorado. Shortly after the 830,000-sq-mile purchase, which guaranteed that the USA would come into conflict with Spain, Jefferson took steps to assess the resources of this enormous acquisition by inviting army captain Meriwether Lewis to command an expedition intended to learn what the United States had acquired; Lewis in turn invited his older colleague William Clark to serve as co-commander.

The official rationale for Lewis and Clark's Corps of Discovery was to benefit American commerce by seeking a 'Northwest Passage' to the Pacific Ocean, but Jefferson made it clear that the expedition was to make serious scientific observations on flora, fauna, climate and the inhabitants of the region. (See the sidebar on Lewis and Clark for details.)

Lewis and Clark's was the most successful of early US expeditions to the west; others ended in disaster. After a foray into Colorado in 1806-07, Zebulon Pike was arrested in New Mexico by Spanish police, perhaps because of machinations of General James Wilkinson, the Governor of Louisiana Territory who took Spanish money in exchange for information on US troop movements. (Pike, who was described by historian Herman J Viola as 'a poor explorer with a knack for getting lost,' never climbed the famous peak that bears his name.)

Major Stephen Long attempted to organize an expedition to establish a fort on the Yellowstone River in 1819, but failed miserably because of a series of logistical bungles – among other problems, the steamboats carrying their supplies were unable to ascend the shallow Missouri. Long did manage to explore the Front Range of the Rockies, and others in his party even scaled Pikes Peak, but like Pike he produced incomplete and misleading accounts that described the West as a 'Great American Desert,' discouraging settlement for decades.

The Fur Trade & the Emigrant Trails

As knowledge of the American West grew, so did interest in its exploitable resources. One of these resources was the beaver, whose pelts became fashionable hats favored by European gentlemen. For a brief time, the fur trade made a contribution to the settlement of the West. The first white explorers in southern Idaho were fur trappers. The first European to explore the Idaho Panhandle was David Thompson, a fur trader and cartographer who crossed the Rocky Mountains and in 1809 established

Women on the Trail

Between 1840 and 1870, around 250,000 people crossed the USA to claim free land in the Oregon and California territories and to try their luck at mining. It was generally the men who made the initial decision to embark on the overland journey, and once a woman's husband, father or brother decided to go, there was little recourse for her to stay at home.

While historians and feminists idealize the sense of liberation on the trail, the majority of first-hand accounts tell of resentment of being thrust into an unfamiliar world. Women often clung to their traditional roles as the only bastions of civility in the wild. As Nannie Alderson writes in her memoirs, *A Bride Goes West*, 'I believe we stuck all the more firmly to our principles of etiquette, because we were so far from civilization. We could still stand on ceremony though our floors were dirt.'

The journey often entailed six to eight months of travel in a rickety wagon on a bumpy trail. Typically, women washed the clothes, prepared meals and attended the children, while men drove the team, garnered the meat for meals and tended the herd. Yet in order to survive along the trail, women often found themselves performing tasks traditionally reserved for the men.

Undoubtedly the heaviest burden women bore on the trail was child-rearing. Pregnant women were often without assistance, and many women died during childbirth. Lillian Schlissel reports in *Women's Diaries of the Westward Journey* (Schocken Books, 1989), 'One out of every five women was seized by some stage of pregnancy, and virtually every married woman traveled with small children.' Children were especially prone to illness and disease, and were often injured in accidents such as falling out of the wagon or getting lost in a herd.

Male pioneers mostly wrote of the ferocity and danger of Native Americans, while women often found them friendly and even helpful. Women's diaries question the value of sacrifices made along the way and describe the personal struggle.

Some women found the trail a welcome break from the boredom of everyday life. Susan Perrish wrote that 'we were a happy carefree lot of young people, and the dangers of hardships found no resting place on our shoulders. It was a continuous picnic and excitement was plentiful.' For others it was a horrible trip. Elizabeth Smith Greer wrote of her 1847 journey from Indiana to Oregon:

> It rains and snows. We start this morning around the falls with our wagons . . . I went ahead with my children and I was afraid to look behind for fear of seeing the wagons turn over into the mud . . . there was not one dry thread on one of us – not even my babe . . . I have not told you half we suffered. I am not adequate to the task. ■

Kullyspell House on Lake Pend Oreille, where he traded with and maintained friendly relations with the tribes.

Another pioneer fur trader in the Rocky Mountains was Manuel Lisa, a Spaniard who built a fort at the mouth of the Bighorn River and recruited John Colter, who had split off from the Lewis and Clark Expedition (with permission) to explore the Yellowstone region and was, arguably, the first of the legendary 'mountain men.' Colter and others like Kit Carson, Jim Bridger, Jim Beckwourth (a free African American) and Thomas Fitzpatrick knew the Rockies backcountry better than anyone except the Indians, with whom many of the mountain men had good relationships.

Their annual summer rendezvous, attended by suppliers, Indians and even early tourists, were celebrations of the year's accomplishments.

But the romantic image of the mountain man is an exaggeration; rather than rugged individualists selling their catch to the highest bidder, most of the trappers were company men who were on salary and sometimes advanced a year's supplies. In 1823, for example, William Ashley of St Louis advertised for 100 men to trap beaver in the Rocky Mountains for $200 a year. The trade collapsed by 1840, as silk hats replaced beaver in urban American and European fashion.

The lasting contribution of the mountain men was their local knowledge of the terrain and of routes through and across the mountains, which paved the way for later emigrants all the way to Oregon and California. Their close relations with the Native Americans were another plus – many mountain men married, or at least fathered children by, Native American women, and could pass freely through areas where strangers might draw suspicion. After the fur trade failed, Jim Bridger (who had a Shoshone wife) opened a trading post and guided emigrants over South Pass in south central Wyoming and across the Great Basin.

Even into the 20th century, hundreds of thousands of emigrants followed the Oregon Trail up the Missouri River to the North Platte and across the Continental Divide to South Pass, where they split up to various destinations, including Oregon, California and Utah. The latter was where the Mormons, persecuted in New York and the Midwest, found a place to practice their religion. In the late 1860s, completion of the Transcontinental Railroad across southern Wyoming slowed, but did not halt, the inexorable march of wagon trains.

At the same time, explorers continued to seek other routes across the mountains. The ambitious John C Frémont, who became known as the Great Pathfinder, spent much of the 1840s wandering the West for the Corps of Topographical Engineers, thanks in part to the political influence of his father-in-law, Senator Thomas Hart Benton of Missouri. While Frémont's effort at mapping the best route to Oregon and his shadowy attempt at undermining Mexican rule in California were successful, two expeditions to find a route across the southern Rockies failed miserably, costing the lives of many of his men. Nevertheless, Frémont was a political suc-

cess, becoming a senator from California and the Republican nominee for President in 1856.

Dismantling Mexico

The exploration of the American West had major political consequences, most notably with Mexico, which had gained independence from Spain in 1821. That same year, the USA acknowledged Mexico's hegemony over most of the West, as far north as the present-day northern state lines of California, Nevada and Utah, including southwestern Wyoming, perhaps three quarters of Colorado, Arizona, New Mexico, Texas and even small parts of Kansas and Oklahoma.

Mexico's independence led to an active settlement strategy in which the Mexican government offered land grants in the southern area to civilians and retired military personnel. In 1822, trade caravans began to travel along the Santa Fe Trail, which stretched between St Louis and Santa Fe (then part of Mexico). William Bent's fort on the Arkansas River provided an important outpost for this commerce from 1833 to 1849. The 1843 land grant to fur traders Cornelio Vigil and Ceran St Vrain, between the Purgatoire and Arkansas rivers, attracted the likes of Jim Beckwourth, Kit Carson, Thomas Boggs and William Bent. In 1851, Mexican settlers founded San Luis – Colorado's oldest community – on the Sangre de Cristo Grant.

The fledgling Mexican state, however, was weak and unable to hold Texas as Anglo settlers moved into the territory; as early as 1836 Texas had declared independence. The continued movement of American settlers into Mexican territory, and the later warfare over border placement at the Rio Grande, led to huge territorial gains in the Mexican cession of 1848. This land grab expanded US boundaries almost to their present size and incorporated Native American and Spanish-speaking peoples into the Union. Especially in southern Colorado, these communities have proven resilient and culturally distinct.

Mexico was not the only power to lose territory to the expanding USA. After some complex diplomatic maneuvering and threats of war, in 1846 the British and US governments agreed to divide the Oregon Country, an area of land from the Pacific Ocean to the Rocky Mountains that had been under joint occupancy, along the 49th parallel. Sections of Montana and Wyoming were included in the part that became US territory.

The Fate of the Native Americans

In contrast with Hollywood's depiction of wagon trains being regularly ambushed by Native Americans, most crossings of the Oregon Trail were relatively uneventful; the heavily laden emigrants frequently had to abandon many of their prized possessions on the side of the trail, a far more common trauma than Indian attacks. The region's first inhabitants certainly viewed the passing travelers with skepticism, though sometimes reactions were more violent. Seeing increasing numbers of white emigrants treading upon their homeland, the Shoshone and Bannock mounted bolder and bloodier attacks during the 1850s. In response, the US Army built a number of military forts along the Oregon Trail, including a new Fort Hall and Fort Boise. In one engagement in 1863, US Army cavalry units ambushed and slaughtered some 400 Shoshone near Preston. Shortly thereafter, the Shoshone and Bannock were confined to Fort Hall Indian Reservation.

The US government also signed an endless series of treaties to defuse Native American objections, promising that white settlers would not venture beyond certain homeland boundaries, such as Wyoming's North Platte River. These treaties established huge reservations, such as the Shoshone's on Wyoming's Wind River, and a system of government rations to compensate Native Americans for their loss of hunting territory. Under pressure from miners and other emigrants, the federal government continually reduced the reservations' size and even shifted them to less desirable areas.

On the northern plains, gold miners' incursions into Native American territory en route to gold fields in Montana and the Black Hills, exacerbated by the US Army's building a string of forts along the Bozeman Trail, ignited a series of wars against the Lakota (Sioux), Cheyenne, Arapaho and others. As the centennial year of 1876 approached, the Lakota and their allies stunned the country by obliterating Lieutenant Colonel George Armstrong Custer's 7th Cavalry at the Little Bighorn valley (in Montana), but the army's logistical superiority eventually prevailed – their virtually unlimited supplies arrived by rail, while the Lakota had to hunt the declining bison to get their families through the winter.

Catastrophic for the Indians, the near extinction of the bison was a function of several interrelated factors. The most direct was uncontrolled hunting, as the government implemented a deliberate policy of eliminating the most important subsistence resource on the continent. Professional riflemen took more than 4 million hides on the southern plains in the early 1870s; incompetent skinners wasted many of these, and nearly all the meat rotted. Facilitated by the arrival of the railroad, the same history recurred on the northern plains in the 1880s, but bison numbers had fallen even before this slaughter because of drought, habitat destruction, competition from introduced livestock like horses and cattle, and new diseases like tuberculosis and brucellosis. All of these elements contributed to the marginalization of the peoples who depended on them for their livelihood.

In Colorado, Ute territorial sovereignty survived a bit longer due to the tribe's isolated mountain domain. But with the influx of silver miners west of the Divide in the 1870s, Chief Ouray had little option but to sign a series of treaties relinquishing traditional hunting grounds. In 1879, the White River Band of Utes attacked federal troops and White River Indian Agent Nathan Meeker and his family near the present-day town of

Meeker. All Utes suffered from the vicious American reaction. By 1881, Utes not removed to forsaken lands in Utah were left with a narrow 15-mile-wide strip of plateau land in southwestern Colorado.

Water & Western Development

While Oregon filled with settlers and the California Gold Rush faded, Americans began to think of occupying the area between the coasts, rather than viewing it

The Real Wild West

The romantic notion of the Wild West, one of the most misleading images in US history, suggests a principled universe of law and order opposing chaos and anarchy, good guys confronting bad guys, cowboys versus Indians and progress against reaction. These oversimplifications conceal a more complex and interesting reality.

The Wild West is traditionally linked to individuals who stood their ground against challenges to their honor, even against overwhelming odds, such as the hero of Owen Wister's landmark novel *The Virginian*. Wister's protagonist, who tamed the frontier against the anarchy represented by his unsavory adversary, Trampas, was the fictional counterpart to real-life figures like Wyatt Earp, Doc Holliday and Wild Bill Hickok, who faced their enemies in the street.

While these battles often – but not always – took place between individuals or small groups of men, they represented something much greater and more notable: a struggle over control of Western resources between incompatible sectors of society. The hired guns of merchants, mining czars and cattle barons conflicted with the outcast champions of little guys like homesteaders, mineworkers and mavericks – the latter were also called 'rustlers' by those who claimed the unmarked calves they branded. Walter van Tilburg Clark's famous novel *The Ox Bow Incident* tells the story of powerful men who mistakenly hang an accused but innocent rustler.

Figures like the legendary Butch Cassidy, whose Wild Bunch audaciously robbed the Union Pacific Railroad that dominated Wyoming political and economic life, proved difficult or impossible to apprehend because many ordinary citizens admired or sympathized with their exploits, and protected them from authority. It may or may not be true that Cassidy once rode 120 miles in a bitter winter to obtain medicine for a sick child, or that he tipped bartenders with $20 gold pieces, but persistent accounts of such generosity imply the high regard in which local people held an individual widely admitted to be a rustler.

The Hollywood legacy of cowboys and Indians, imitated for decades by children everywhere, shows how one-sided American interpretation of history can be. It's only recently been acknowledged that cowboys were invaders on Native American lands as cattle herds replaced bison on plains and prairies. The same is true of the US Army: romantically viewed as heroic defenders of pioneer emigrants and settlers, the ill-trained or vengeful enlistees were often responsible for butchery like the notorious 1861 Sand Creek Massacre, in which the 3rd Colorado Volunteers attacked, slaughtered and mutilated at least 150 sleeping Cheyenne men, women and children.

Of course, Native Americans also committed atrocities, often in response to military or settler provocations. Even though they were viewed as a unity against the invaders, they were, in fact, a variety of peoples often no more similar than Spaniards and Swedes, and were often bitter rivals. The Pawnee, for instance, often served as US Army scouts against their traditional Lakota enemies. Nor were these the only ethnic conflicts: others took place between whites and Hispanics, Mormons and non-Mormons and between the Chinese and European miners, the former used as strikebreakers by manipulative mining companies. All these disputes embodied ethnic components not usually acknowledged in traditional histories of the West.

Revisionist historians have effectively presented such analyses in recent years, and even popular culture has begun to take a more discriminating view of the Wild West. ■

simply as a transit corridor. Mining attracted only transitory residents, while extensive land uses like ranching could support only a small population. The lingering image of the Great American Desert, a myth propagated by explorers like Pike and Long who used the humid East as a standard of comparison, deterred agricultural settlers and discouraged urban development.

Water was a limiting factor as cities like Denver and Cheyenne began to spring up at the base of the Front Range and utopians like Horace Greeley, who saw the Homestead Act of 1862 as the key to agrarian prosperity, planned agricultural experiments on the nearby plains. This act envisioned the creation of 160-acre family farms to create a rural democracy on the Western frontier. These plots of land were subdivided based on the General Land Survey which created a checkerboard pattern of sq-mile sections of land still visible from the air today.

Government agents encouraged settlement and development in their assessments of the region, but differed on how to bring it about. Two of the major figures in this process were Frederick V Hayden of the United States Geological Survey (USGS) and John Wesley Powell, first of the Smithsonian Institution and later of the USGS. Hayden, who surveyed the Yellowstone River area and played a major role in its declaration as a national park, was so eager to promote economic development in the West that he exaggerated the region's agricultural potential on the optimistic but mistaken assumption that 'rain follows the plow' – that is, that planting and cultivating could change the climate. Unlike Pike and Long, who saw no potential in the plains, Hayden saw too much.

Powell, a great figure in Western and American history, made a more perceptive assessment of the potential and limitations of the region. Famous as the first man to descend the Colorado River through the Grand Canyon, Powell knew that the region's salient feature was aridity, that its limited water supply depended on the

snowpack that fell in the Rockies and could vary dramatically from year to year, and that the 160-acre ideal of the Homestead Act of 1862, devised in the humid East and liable to corruption and manipulation, was inappropriate to the terrain and environment of the West. His masterful *Report on the Lands of the Arid Regions of the United States* challenged the tendency toward unbridled exploitation of the region's minerals, pastures and forests, and proposed classifying and distributing the land according to its suitability for irrigation.

Powell's report recommended the construction of dams, canals and ditches to create an integrated, federally sponsored irrigation system administered by democratically elected cooperatives. Unfortunately, his vision collided with the interests of influential cattle barons, who wanted to maintain their access to lands and water. Nor did it appeal to boosters and real estate speculators who seemed convinced that the West could absorb an unlimited number of farmers from an overpopulated East. These interests united to undermine Powell's blueprint; what survived was the idea that water development was essential to the West.

It took time to create the technology, but 20th-century development took the form of megaprojects like the mammoth Glen Canyon Dam on the Colorado River, and water transfers from Colorado's Western Slope to the Front Range and the plains via a tunnel under the Continental Divide. These, in turn, provided subsidized water for large-scale irrigators and electrical power for users far from their source – effectively inverting Powell's goals and creating a landscape of dams, reservoirs, canals, tunnels and hydroelectric facilities that would characterize the region as much as, if not more than, its dwindling wildlands.

Statehood
Colorado American expansion in the West spread to Colorado with the discovery of gold in the mountains west of Denver in 1859. In 1861, the boundaries of Colorado

Cattle Barons & the 'Cowboy State'

The removal of the Native American 'threat' opened Wyoming's plains to ranchers who pastured cattle where enormous bison herds once roamed. Wyoming later became the 'Cowboy State,' but it was really the cattle barons' state, as the powerful Wyoming Stock Growers Association (WSGA) controlled the politicians in Cheyenne.

The cattle barons lived in luxury in Cheyenne or even back east while their employees did the hard work of running unsustainable numbers of cattle on the arid prairies. The ferocious winter of 1886-87 killed much of their stock and made them vulnerable to small-time ranchers, whom they accused of being rustlers, and to homesteaders, who were known pejoratively as 'nesters.'

While the cattle barons remained a powerful factor in Wyoming politics – even passing legislation excluding the smaller ranches from acquiring stock except on WSGA approval – the disaster of 1886-87 marked a turning point. The WSGA's foolish attempt to drive out Powder River homesteaders with a mercenary Texan army in 1892 largely discredited the organization, though it never entirely disappeared. The unsuitability of most of Wyoming for homesteading allowed relatively large cattle ranches to return in some areas.

The cowboy was more an icon than a reality. Rather than the independent, self-reliant individual depicted in romantic literature, he was an ordinary employee of large enterprises like the legendary Swan Land and Cattle Company, which controlled hundreds of thousands of acres of pasture land. The few lucky enough to establish their own herds emulated the men for whom they had worked. ∎

Territory were defined, and President Lincoln appointed William Gilpin the first governor.

In 1870 two sets of railroad tracks reached Denver, ending Colorado's isolation: the Denver Pacific connected Denver with the Union Pacific's transcontinental line at Cheyenne, Wyoming, and the Kansas Pacific arrived from Kansas City, Missouri. That same year, General William Palmer began planning the Denver & Rio Grande's narrow-gauge tracks into the mountain mining camps. The mining emphasis shifted from gold to silver during the 1870s as mountain smelter sites, like Leadville and Aspen, developed into thriving population centers almost overnight.

National political expedience led to Colorado statehood in 1876, the centennial of United States independence. The rest of the country scoffed at the premature statehood for the fledgling territory. One Pennsylvania editor even sneered, 'Colorado consists of Denver, the Kansas Pacific Railway and scenery. The mineral resources of Colorado exist in the imagination. The agricultural resources do not exist at all.'

Wyoming Construction of the Transcontinental Railroad in the 1860s really opened up the Wyoming territory, which had its boundaries officially designated in 1868. The impetus behind this came from the Union Pacific Railroad (UP), whose westward progress demanded a closer and more responsive government. Cheyenne became the territorial capital, and the powerfully paternalistic and politically influential UP acquired the nickname 'Uncle Pete.'

Wyoming's first legislators enacted an extraordinary statute in 1869 granting all women 21 years of age and older the right to vote and hold office. Unprecedented in its time, Wyoming's action drew praise from Susan B Anthony, the great women's suffrage crusader, and when it obtained statehood in 1890, it became known as the 'Equality State.' In fact, Wyoming may not have deserved quite the credit it got. While some legislators saw it as an issue of principle, others voted for it because Wyoming had so few women. They thought the resulting publicity would attract more emigrants: in the 1870 census, men over the age of 21 outnumbered women six to one.

Montana Gold was discovered in Bannack's Grasshopper Creek in 1863, just as rushes in California, Nevada, Colorado and Idaho were petering out. The intense population increase and large sums of money flowing out of Bannack (which was part of Idaho Territory) caused Sidney Edgerton, Chief Justice of Idaho Territory, to petition Congress for a new territory east of the Rocky Mountains. On May 26, 1884, Montana became a territory and Edgerton its first territorial governor.

Gold strikes continued – notably in Last Chance Gulch (Helena) and Alder Gulch (Virginia City). Just as electricity was becoming available to the public and creating an enormous demand for copper wire, Marcus Daly struck the world's largest and purest vein of copper in Butte, which would continue to be mined for the next 100 years. Montana was obviously here to stay, and in 1889 became the 41st state of the Union.

Idaho Real settlement of Idaho did not come until gold was discovered at Pierce on Orofino Creek in 1860; the following year, gold was discovered in the Boise basin. Miners rushed to the Idaho mountains, establishing gold camps and trade centers like Lewiston and Boise. By 1863, Idaho was declared a US territory.

Rich silver and lead veins spurred the growth of communities such as Wallace, Mullan and Kellogg, which boomed as smelters lined the banks of the river and railroads competed to transport the region's mineral wealth. By 1890 Idaho was granted statehood, and 10 years later the homesteading boom brought more permanent settlers to central Idaho valleys.

The Contemporary Rockies

In all four states, the extractive industries of mining, grazing and timber played a major role in economic development. These highly capitalized industries, with low labor requirements, encouraged the growth of cities and towns to provide financial and industrial support. They also subjected the region to boom and bust cycles as they exhausted those resources in an unsustainable manner, and left a legacy of environmental disruption not likely to disappear any time soon.

From its earliest days the West was, and still is, the country's most urbanized region; when Colorado became a state in 1876, more than a third of its residents lived in Denver. Even though Wyoming Montana and Idaho are much less urbanized than fast-growing Colorado, most residents of those states live in cities or small towns amidst a very thinly populated countryside.

In part, this urbanization was a function of the tourist economy, as Americans, who had flocked to the national parks during the economic boom after WWII, began to appreciate the Rockies as a place to live rather than just to visit. The federal government played a role by providing employment, thanks in large part to investment in Cold War military installations like NORAD, a Dr Strangelove-like facility near Colorado Springs, and Warren Air Force Base, the command center for a series of dispersed missile silos near Cheyenne, Wyoming. Urbanization accelerated as the wealthy beneficiaries of the economic policies of the Reagan era built opulent vacation homes in Aspen, Sun Valley and similarly prestigious resort areas. Others relocated to once remote towns like Telluride, Colorado, as the communications and information revolution decentralized some sectors of the economy.

Development and urbanization had beneficial effects as well, as increasingly well-educated locals and emigrants shared the environmental concerns of the late 1960s and early 1970s. Practices such as strip mining, overgrazing and clear-cutting came under scrutiny from local chapters of influential environmental organizations like the Sierra Club, Friends of the Earth and the Wilderness Society, as well as from regional groups like the Greater Yellowstone Coalition and the Wyoming Outdoor Council. Military facilities like the Rocky

Mountain National Arsenal near Colorado Springs and the Rocky Flats nuclear weapons facility near Denver came under attack by activists concerned with environmental contamination, and were declared priority cleanup sites under the federal Environmental Protection Agency's Superfund program.

Tourism is now an economic mainstay in the Rockies. While the region's natural attractions have drawn curious visitors since the establishment of Yellowstone National Park in 1872, for most of that time only wealthy travelers with time and money could see the backcountry. But after WWII, general prosperity and the improvement of roads brought larger numbers of middle-class tourists into the national parks.

Colorado, which had also been luring tourists since the late 19th century, wasted little time in tapping this new source of revenue. Promoters offered auto routes over the Royal Gorge, up Pikes Peak and Mt Evans and across the Alpine tundra of Rocky Mountain National Park. Skiing started to draw adherents in 1927 when the opening of the Moffat Tunnel brought Winter Park within easy reach of Denverites traveling on the D&RG Railroad. More distant ski resorts had to wait for air service or the opening of the Eisenhower Tunnel on I-70 to bring the crowds to them. To keep the rooms filled during the off-season, Aspen initiated its widely mimicked cultural festivals in the late 1940s.

In 1936, a group of investors associated with the Union Pacific developed a European ski resort near the old smelter town of Ketchum, Idaho. Called Sun Valley, the resort was soon another early recreational foothold in the region and it became the playground of Hollywood stars and the wealthy elite.

However, Idaho, along with Montana and Wyoming, didn't feel the full effects of tourism until the 1980s. Now that it's begun there seems little chance of turning back. Small towns once known as lumber or agricultural centers are now filled with mountain bike and raft shops, and a new generation of ranchers scrambles to entice outsiders to fish or float on their property – a far cry from the isolationist ethic of yesteryear.

GEOGRAPHY

While complex, the physical geography of the Rocky Mountain region divides conveniently into two principal features: the Rocky Mountains proper and the Great Plains. Extending from Alaska's Brooks Range and Canada's Yukon Territory all the way to the Mexican border, the Rockies trend northwest to southeast, sprawling from the steep escarpment of Colorado's Front Range westward to Nevada's Great Basin. Their towering peaks and ridges form the Continental Divide: to the west, waters flow to the Pacific Ocean; to the east, toward the Atlantic Ocean and the Gulf of Mexico.

At the eastern base of the Rockies, the plains extend over 2500 miles from the delta of Canada's Mackenzie River, draining into the Arctic Ocean, to the coast of southern Texas on the Gulf of Mexico. Towards the east, the plains stretch for hundreds of miles toward the Mississippi River valley and the Great Lakes.

Colorado Colorado's total area of 103,730 sq miles makes it the eighth largest state in the USA. Its lowest point is 3400 feet above sea level where the Arkansas River flows into Kansas; at 14,433 feet above sea level, Mt Elbert near Leadville is the other extreme. Overall, Colorado has more than 1000 peaks of elevations over 2 miles and 54 of the nation's 69 summits over 14,000 feet.

Colorado is divided into three general landform provinces: the Eastern Plains, the Rocky Mountains and the Colorado Plateau on the west. Each of these north-south strips is interrupted by local landform variations. In southwestern Colorado, the San Juan Mountains are thrust up from plateau lands and are out of key with the mountain and plateau provinces typified by high, flat mesas. The mountain province is interrupted by broad, flat, high-altitude valleys: North Park centered on Walden, South Park surrounding Fairplay in the center of the state and the immense San Luis Valley.

Wyoming Wyoming's total area of 97,105 sq miles makes it the ninth-largest state, and it ranges in elevation from the Belle Fourche River (3100 feet) in the Black Hills to Gannett Peak (13,804 feet) in the Wind River Range.

The Eastern Plains region includes the Powder River and North Platte River basins, the Black Hills, and the Laramie and Medicine Bow mountains, near the Wyoming-Colorado state line. Western Wyoming has high desert basins west of the Continental Divide, including the huge Green River Basin and the smaller Great Divide and Washakie basins. Along the Utah and Idaho state lines, the Overthrust Belt is a zone of jumbled sedimentary features. The granitic Teton Range and Jackson Hole line the Wyoming-Idaho state line, with the Yellowstone Plateau in the northwest, the Wind River Range and its expansive basin to the south, and the Bighorn Basin and Mountains trending south from the Wyoming-Montana state line.

Montana With a total area of 145,556 sq miles, Montana is the fourth largest state in the USA. The lowest point in Montana, 1820 feet, is on US 2 at the Montana-Idaho border, the highest is Granite Peak in the Beartooth Range at 12,799 feet.

Montana's three geographic zones are: the plains, which stretch across the eastern two-thirds of the state; the Middle Rocky Mountains, which include part of the Yellowstone Plateau and the Absaroka and Beartooth ranges; and the Northern Rocky Mountains, which make a 200-mile-wide band of northwest-southeast trending ranges from Glacier National Park to Yellowstone National Park.

Montana's main river is the Missouri, which drains from the eastern side of the Continental Divide and eventually flows to the Gulf of Mexico and the Atlantic. Rivers on the western side of the Divide flow into the Pacific via the Clark Fork and Kootenai rivers.

Idaho Idaho's total area of 82,751 sq miles places it 11th on the state size roster. Its highest point is the 12,662 foot Borah Peak; at the other end of the spectrum is Lewiston at 783 feet.

There are essentially two different geographic areas to Idaho. The Rocky Mountains dominate the Panhandle area – the narrow arm squeezed between Washington and Montana – and the deep mountain canyons of central Idaho. As the mountains rise higher, approaching the central spine of the Continental Divide, just across the border in Montana more rainfall is wrung out of the prevailing easterly airflows, supporting both deep forests and mighty rivers. Much of central Idaho is comprised of the highly contorted Salmon and Clearwater river drainages. These rivers both drain directly into the Snake River in its famed Hells Canyon, the deepest gorge in North America.

Nearly all of the broad southern base of Idaho is part of the arid Snake River basin. Although the Snake River rises in Yellowstone National Park, the majority of the river's traverse of Idaho is across a relentless lava plateau. Most of the land paralleling the river through the bottom third of the state is flat and dusty, while to the south rise mirage-like fault block mountains thinly clad with vegetation.

GEOLOGY

In the late Cretaceous Period, about 65 million years ago, tectonic movements known as the Laramide Revolution disturbed the broad sediments of western North America. This uplift, accompanied by volcanic activity and subsequent folding and faulting, created the mountainous landscape of much of modern Colorado, Wyoming, Montana and Idaho. The granitic peaks of the Front Range rise nearly 10,000 feet above the adjacent plains; the highest point is Colorado's 14,433-foot Mt Elbert. The sedimentary peaks farther

Dinosaurs & Their Habitat

The sparse grasslands and fierce winters of Wyoming and western Colorado seem an improbable setting for a diverse subtropical region. But 150 million years ago, this area was covered with shallow lakes and marshes where the great dinosaurs roamed, feeding on aquatic plants, ferns, rushes, cattails – and sometimes on each other. As the climate changed, or, according to other accounts, after a catastrophic meteor struck the planet, these beasts disappeared, but the sediments in which they died preserved their skeletons and over time fossilized them. The resulting sandstones and shale were eventually exposed at the earth's surface by erosion.

Since the 1878 discovery of Como Bluff, near Rawlins, the region has been one of the most important areas for dinosaur research in the world. Further discoveries, like the one at Green River in what is now Dinosaur National Monument, have been numerous. Over time, dinosaurs have worked their way into the popular consciousness, so much so that the Wyoming legislature recently asked school children to choose an official state dinosaur (as opposed to merely a state fossil) from among *Triceratops, Apatosaurus* (brontosaurus), *Diplodocus* and *Megalosaurus*. They chose *Triceratops*.

The fossil record of dinosaurs is biased toward size, so that the remains of relatively small animals like the ostrich-like *Coelurosaurs*, which walked upright and left bird-like tracks, deteriorated more rapidly and may be underrepresented. This was less the case with Carnosaurs, the large, upright meat eaters like *Tyrannosaurus Rex*; Prosauropods, forerunners of the four-footed vegetarian behemoths like *Apatosaurus* and *Brachiosaurus*; Stegosaurs (plated dinosaurs); Ankylosaurs (armored dinosaurs); three-toed Duckbills and Hadrosaurs; and Ceratopseans (horned dinosaurs).

Dinosaur enthusiasts visiting the Rocky Mountain states have a host of sites and museums to indulge their interests, including Dinosaur National Monument in northwestern Colorado, the Dinosaur Valley Museum and several other quarry sites in and around Grand Junction, Como Bluff near Rawlins, Wyoming, Western Wyoming College in Rock Springs and the University of Wyoming Geological Museum in Laramie. Visitors intending to explore the dinosaur country of western Colorado might obtain Walter R Averett's *Guidebook for Dinosaur Quarries and Tracksites Tour: Western Colorado and Eastern Utah* (Grand Junction Geological Society, 1991).

One good general source for further reading is Ron Stewart's *Dinosaurs of the West* (Missoula, Montana: Mountain Press, 1988). For some of the more controversial ideas on dinosaurs, including the notion that dinosaurs were social animals, see Robert T Bakker's *The Dinosaur Heresies: New Theories Unlocking the Mystery of the Dinosaurs and Their Extinction* (Morrow, 1986).

Finally, be wary of people selling jewelry made of dinosaur fossils; recently people have been blasting the sites where there are fossils in order to collect the pieces. In no way should this be encouraged. ∎

north are slightly lower, but their clearly defined strata add color and variety to the landscape.

Behind the Front Range lie several scattered mountain ranges and broad plateaus; their most notable geological feature is the spectacular Rocky Mountain Trench, a fault valley 1100 miles long that crosses northern Montana into Canada. The Colorado Plateau, in the southwestern part of the state near the borders with Utah, New Mexico and Arizona, has been heavily eroded by the Colorado River and its tributaries (like the Gunnison). Active vulcanism also distinguishes the region, notably in Wyoming's Yellowstone National Park, where earthquakes are quite common. Ancient lava flows cover many other areas, punctuated by extinct volcanos like the Spanish Peaks of southwestern Colorado.

Successive glaciations also altered the face of the land. The Laurentide Ice Sheet, which covered most of eastern North America, scoured much of the Great Plains as far south as Nebraska and westward to the foothills of the Rockies, leaving deep sediments as it receded into the Arctic during the warming of the Quaternary Era. A separate Cordilleran System of glaciers formed at higher altitudes in the Rockies, covering the uplands but leaving many moraines, lakes, cirques and jagged Alpine landforms as they melted. Remnants of these glaciers survive only at the highest elevations; at the same time, the rivers formed by their melting deposited extensive sediments on the piedmont, at the base of the Front Range.

CLIMATE

The climate of the Rocky Mountain states depends on two major factors: elevation and topography. Nearly all of Colorado, Wyoming and Montana consists of relatively high terrain more than a mile above sea level. (Idaho, which has more varied terrain, is somewhat different.) Distant from the warming influence of the oceans and at latitudes mostly above 40° N, such elevations may enjoy warm summer days but almost always experience cool nights (and sometimes frosts). Winters can be truly severe in the semidesert areas east of the Rockies, which are vulnerable to dry polar continental air masses that bring subzero temperatures and occasional blizzards. Chinooks are powerful seasonal winds that lose their moisture on crossing the mountains and heat up as they descend, and they bring occasional relief from even the coldest weather. Refer to the charts in the back of the book for more statistics.

The cordillera of the Rockies blocks or slows the penetration of relatively warm, damp air masses from the northern Pacific Ocean; by the time Pacific storms reach the Rockies, they have already passed over several mountain ranges and have lost much of their moisture, and the snow that falls on the western slopes and other favored locations is often the dry champagne powder so favored by skiers. Because of the Rockies' fragmented terrain, there can be great local variation in temperature and precipitation, depending on factors like orientation to the sun and wind. In most areas the brief growing season lasts only from June to September, although a few favored microclimates experience a slightly longer period. Most of the region is subject to brief but violent summer thunderstorms.

Colorado Colorado's climate is influenced by two major factors. First, its mid-continental location accounts for a wide variation in daily and seasonal temperatures and the overall semiarid character of the state. Most of Colorado averages between 10 to 18 inches of precipitation per year – often arriving as sudden summer thunderstorms. Second, the Rocky Mountains act as a barrier that intercepts much of the moisture that arrives from the west – particularly on the higher western slopes that receive an average of 220 inches of snowfall each year. Temperatures drop with gains in altitude, and weather in the mountain areas is highly unpredictable.

Wyoming Most of Wyoming is high desert country where extremes are the rule – summer temperatures can exceed 100°F but nighttime temperatures can fall below freezing, and July snowstorms in Yellowstone National Park are not unusual. One characteristic of Wyoming's climate is the nearly incessant wind. Chinooks often melt the snow and relieve the winter chill on the plains.

Montana Montana's weather can bring anything at anytime, but summer temperatures usually hover in the 80s west of the Rockies, in the 100s on the Eastern Plains. In winter (which can begin in October and last until May) temperatures stay in the 20s, though tremendous winds often bring them down below zero in the east. The plains receive much less precipitation than the mountainous west, and they are targeted by winds coming unchecked from the north across the Canadian plains. January temperatures average 11° to 22°F, July temperatures are 64° to 93°F with thunderstorms most afternoons. The coldest

Rocky Mountain Wildlife

Top Left: Buffalo
Bottom: Elk

Top Right: Golden eagle
Middle Right: Mountain goat

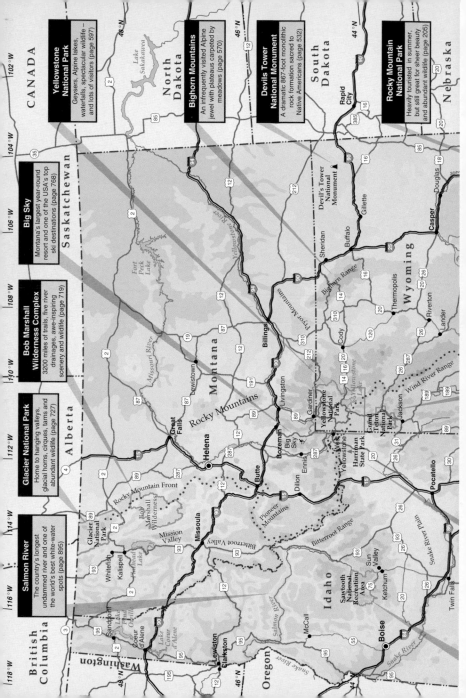

Yellowstone National Park
Geysers, Alpine lakes, waterfalls, spectacular wildlife – and lots of visitors (page 597)

Bighorn Mountains
An infrequently visited Alpine jewel with plateaus carpeted by meadows (page 570)

Devils Tower National Monument
A dramatic 867-foot monolithic rock formation sacred to Native Americans (page 532)

Rocky Mountain National Park
Heavily touristed in summer, but still great for sheer beauty and abundant wildlife (page 205)

Big Sky
Montana's largest year-round resort and one of the USA's top ski destinations (page 768)

Bob Marshall Wilderness Complex
3200 miles of trails, five river drainages, awe-inspiring scenery and wildlife (page 719)

Glacier National Park
Home to hanging valleys, glacial horns, cirques, tarns and abundant wildlife (page 727)

Salmon River
The country's longest undammed river and one of the world's best white-water spots (page 895)

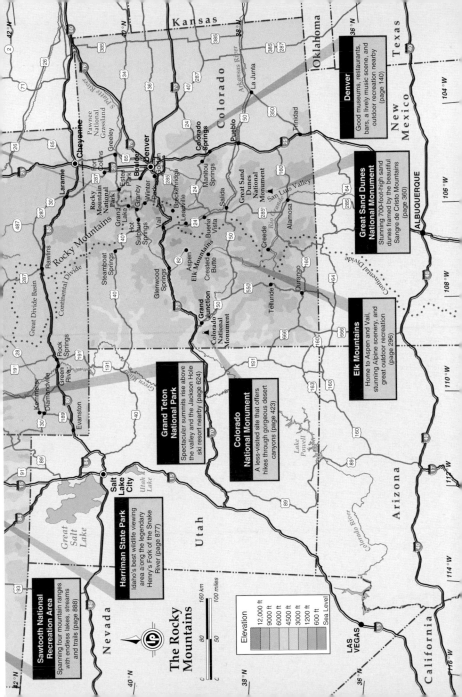

Denver
Good museums, restaurants, bars, a lively music scene, and outdoor recreation nearby (page 140)

Great Sand Dunes National Monument
Stunning 700-foot-high sand dunes framed by the beautiful Sangre de Cristo Mountains (page 360)

Elk Mountains
Home to Aspen and Vail, stunning Alpine scenery, and great outdoor recreation (page 296)

Grand Teton National Park
Spectacular summits rise above the valley and the Jackson Hole ski resort nearby (page 624)

Colorado National Monument
A less-visited site that offers hikes through gorgeous desert canyons (page 423)

Harriman State Park
Idaho's best wildlife viewing area along the legendary Henry's Fork of the Snake River (page 877)

Sawtooth National Recreation Area
Spanning four mountain ranges with endless lakes, streams and trails (page 888)

The Rocky Mountains

Elevation
12,000 ft
9000 ft
6000 ft
4500 ft
3000 ft
1200 ft
600 ft
Sea Level

ABRAHM LUSTGARTEN

LEE FOSTER

ROBERT RABURN

ABRAHM LUSTGARTEN

The Great Outdoors

Top: Glacier Gorge, Rocky Mountain National Park, CO
Bottom Left: Salmon River, ID

Middle Right: Lake Fork of the Gunnison River, CO
Bottom Right: Black Canyon of the Gunnison National
Monument, CO

Chinook Winds

Chinook is a regional term for the warm, dry *föhn* wind which can occur on the leeward side of a mountain anywhere in the world. As air masses descend the Front Range of the Rockies, warming and compressing with the decreased elevation, the result is a hot, dry wind that can cause temperatures to rise as much as 50°F in less than an hour. In 1980 a chinook caused the temperature in Nevada City, MT, to rise 47°F in seven minutes.

To ranchers, farmers and cowboys of the Eastern Plains, chinook winds have a special significance. When a chinook blows down from the Rockies in the dead of winter, it brings temperatures that liberate the land, cattle and people from a substantial blanket of snow and ice. Cattle can graze and ranchers can increase the animals' feed rations for the rest of the winter. In an area that needs all the climatic help it can get, chinook winds are a boon, a blessing and a mysterious friend. However, for tourists an unexpected chinook can mean the start of the mud season. ■

temperature ever recorded in the USA was in 1954 at Rogers Pass, near Helena, when it dropped to -70°F.

Idaho In southern Idaho's Snake River Plain, winters tend to be milder than in the north. Winter low temperatures hover in the teens, but even in winter most days are sunny. Summer weather can be oppressively hot, especially when combined with the humidity from the irrigation projects. Temperatures can exceed 100°F for days at a time in July and August when evening temperatures rarely drop below 80°F. Early summer is a bit cooler. Rainfall is scant in southern Idaho. In the valley bottom, rainfall can be as low as eight inches annually; Boise, set against the foothills, receives 12 inches.

Rain and snowfall is greatest in the deep forests of the Panhandle, where upwards of 60 inches of precipitation are possible.

The weather during summer is usually clear and balmy, with highs above 90°F. In winter, storms surge down out of Canada, blanketing the area with snow and low temperatures. Temperatures below 0°F are not unusual.

The mountains and canyons of central Idaho experience much the same cold, winter weather as the north, but summer temperatures are notably warmer. In the steep canyons of the Snake and Salmon rivers, summer days can be airless and oppressively hot. Lewiston in August can see daily highs near 100°F, but by evening, temperatures tend to drop.

ECOLOGY & ENVIRONMENT

Though each state can point to its own particular issues and conflicts, all four face the same basic quandary: how the balance the need to live off the land with the need to preserve for current and future generations.

The spectacular environmental bounty of the Rocky Mountains states is coveted by numerous competing interests. Timber and mining companies have drawn enormous wealth from the land, while farmers must partly thank dams on the mighty rivers for increasingly greater harvests. Ranchers are proponents of 'open space,' but only when it's being grazed by their cattle. Facing this coalition of 'mixed-use' supporters are those who call for no more exploitation of natural resources: leave the land to animals and low-impact humans, like hikers.

Obviously a balance needs to be struck: humans may like the idea of untouched wilderness, but they also enjoy having food, fossil fuels and small conveniences, like cars. None would be possible without farms, oil wells or mines. In the Rockies, a series of debates, verbal altercations and compromises may be defining ways that Americans can utilize the land without losing it.

Already there has been a marked drop in traditional methods of exploiting natural resources. Removing ill-conceived dams, slowing clear-cutting and road building, and limiting open-pit mining are some of the efforts now underway. While it's obvious that society is dependent on mining, anyone who has seen the catastrophe that was the Climax mining operation in Leadville, CO, knows that stricter rules need to be put into effect.

But although the dangers of unregulated mining are widely known in Colorado, debate still runs hot in Montana, which was built on the industry. When Atlantic Richfield shut down Butte's Berkeley Pit mine in 1980, it left an 800-foot deep, mile-long, half-mile wide pit that filled heavy-ore and cyanide contaminated groundwater. Although Butte's rate of birth defects has since risen tremendously, and its water supply is on the brink of contamination, a similar mine is being proposed for McDonald Meadows near the headwaters of the Blackfoot River. Downstream at Rock Creek (20 miles east of Missoula), the American Smelting and Refining Co wants to drill 9000 feet down to make one of the largest copper/silver mines in the USA. The issue may not be so much whether these operations proceed, but whether the operators can be persuaded to keep environmental damage to the minimum amount possible.

Other debates focus on the role of the US Forest Service. Is it here to protect, or develop, the land it regulates? In Colorado and Montana, the forest service has tried repeatedly to sell off parcels of land to timber or energy firms, and in many cases had been caught between powerful business interests and extremely vocal, and angry, environmental groups. The agency has yet to define its mission. In a recent case, after a 1997 public opinion poll revealed that Montanans opposed energy resource development along the Rocky Mountain Front by a two-to-one margin, the Lewis and Clark National Forest announced that the Front would be off-limits to federal oil and gas leasing for the next 15 years. Each division of the USFS, however, is at its own discretion to lease (or not lease) their land. Two months later, the Helena National Forest, which has jurisdiction of the southern end of the

Front, was negotiating a proposal for exploratory drilling in Upper Alice Creek, which runs from the Continental Divide into the Blackfoot River.

Wildlife issues are also highly controversial. Reintroduction of grizzly bears in Montana's Selway-Bitterroot Wilderness and of gray wolves in Yellowstone National Park has kindled debate between animal rights activists and ranchers. Local recreationists, who have neither political nor economic stake in the debates, are generally divided between those who want to see the animals in their original habitats and those who fear the potential harm to humans.

FLORA & FAUNA
The natural environments of the Rocky Mountain states consist of high mountains, plateaus and plains, each with its own distinctive biota. Many of these lands enjoy varying levels of protection from various local, state and federal agencies. See the National Parks & Outdoor Activities chapter for information on the agencies.

Flora
The vegetation of the Rocky Mountain region is closely linked to climate, which in turn depends on rainfall and elevation. Vegetation at certain altitudes varies depending on exposure and availability of water.

Sparse piñon-juniper forests cover the Rockies' lower slopes from about 4000 to 6000 feet above sea level, while ponderosa pines indicate the montane zone between 6000 and 9000 feet, where alders, aspens, willows and the distinctive blue spruce flourish in damper areas. In the sub-Alpine zone above 9000 feet, Engelmann spruce largely replace pine (though some stands of lodgepoles grow higher) while colorful wildflowers like columbine, marsh marigold and primrose colonize open spaces. In the Alpine zone above 11,500 feet, Alpine meadows and tundra supplant stunted trees, commonly known by the German term *krummholz*, which can only grow in sheltered, southern exposures.

East of the Rockies, the Great Plains are an immense grassland of short and tall grasses, interrupted by dense gallery forests of willows and cottonwoods along the major rivers. Those arid zones closest to the Rockies consist of shorter species like wheatgrass, grama, and buffalo grass, which grow no higher than about 3 feet.

Fauna

Like the flora, the fauna of the Rockies divides into characteristic assemblages correlated with elevation, but the relative abundance of the more mobile animals varies seasonally. In the alpine zones, for instance, small rodents like pikas inhabit rockfalls throughout the year, but larger mammals like Rocky Mountain elk (*Cervus elaphus*) and bighorn sheep are present only in summer. The Great Plains have their own singular fauna, like pronghorn antelope and prairie dogs that rarely enter the mountains, while species like mule deer and coyotes range over a variety of zones from the plains to the peaks. The solitary, lumbering moose, *Alces alces shirasi,* prefers riparian zones.

The most famous animal of the plains, of course, was the magnificent buffalo or bison that grazed the prairies in enormous herds until its near-extinction. The bison survives in limited numbers, but some ambitious conservationists have proposed the elimination of domestic livestock and the restoration of a 'Buffalo Commons' where up to 60 million of this distinctive species may once again graze.

The swift pronghorn *Antilocarpa americana* grazes short-grass plains nearest the mountains, while the prairie dog neither inhabits the prairies, nor is it a dog: related to the squirrel, it lives in sprawling burrows known as prairie dog 'towns.' Prairie dog towns, which once covered hundreds of sq miles of short-grass plains, have been reduced as human settlers killed off prodigious numbers of the once-abundant rodent. Another casualty of the war against the prairie dog was the black-footed ferret *Mustela nigripes*, which preyed on prairie

Bison (aka buffalo)

dogs, but now exists only in tiny, isolated colonies.

Probably the most notorious animal in the Rockies is the grizzly bear, *Ursus arctos horribilis*, whose notoriety may be inversely proportional to its numbers. The smaller, less aggressive black bear, *Ursus americanus,* is far more widespread.

GOVERNMENT & POLITICS

The USA has a federal system with a President and a bicameral Congress, consisting of the 100-member Senate and the 435-member House of Representatives. Each of the 50 states has two senators and a number of congressional representatives in proportion to its population. The thinly populated Rocky Mountain states consequently wield disproportionate power in the senate, but this is diluted in the larger House. Colorado, the largest of the four states populationwise, has eight representatives in addition to its two senators. Idaho has two representatives, while Montana and Wyoming, with their very small populations, have the minimum single representative.

The head of each state's government is the governor, who presides over a bicameral legislature consisting of a senate and a house delegation.

The Rocky Mountain West is generally conservative in its politics, usually supporting the Republican party in presidential elections, but there are enclaves of liberal and even radical politics. Colorado is the most diverse and liberal, but its voters nevertheless approved the overtly discriminatory anti-homosexual Amendment 2 (since overturned by the Colorado Supreme Court); conservative Montana paradoxically sent liberal Democratic Senator Mike Mansfield to Washington for decades.

Political battles are often influenced by powerful business interests supporting natural resource development, such as large-scale agriculture, mining, energy and ranching. This impact is particularly powerful in the less populous states, where business and political ties run deep. For example, Idaho's conservative Republican governor Phillip Batt is former president of the Idaho Food Producers and the Idaho Hop Grower's Association. Along with land use, water is another contentious issue. The controversial eastward diversion of the Colorado River for the benefit of Denver and other Front Range cities is part of a much larger struggle over the region's most precious resource.

In recent years, political groups outside the mainstream have drawn more than their share of media attention. Northern Idaho has become notorious for its enclaves of neo-Nazis, white supremacists and the militia movement preparing for what it sees as an inevitable war against the federal government. In Montana the Freemen militia group invited a government siege that sparked a media quest to document every quirky, radical group in the state: there was plenty of material. Even Colorado, long considered fairly mainstream, has now become the base for numerous right-wing groups promoting some rather extreme agendas. That none of these radical organizations has taken root in the heavily developed east and west coasts of the US suggests that they don't enjoy widespread support or sympathy, just enough adherents to make the average American a bit nervous about which direction the country may be heading.

Colorado's Conservative Core

While Colorado is generally a politically conservative state, it's home to some groups that have expanded the boundaries of the right wing. Extremists opposed to civil rights for minorities, gays and women have all set up shop in Colorado during the 1990s and their activities may have influenced general opinion. In 1992 Colorado voters passed the controversial Amendment 2, forbidding local governments from enacting laws protecting homosexuals from discrimination in employment and housing, provoking a nationwide economic boycott against the state. Arguing that the amendment denied gays equal protection under the state and federal constitutions, the State Supreme Court struck down the law in 1994.

Colorado Springs in particular appeals to groups and individuals that espouse everything from white supremacy to book censorship. Particularly active are conservative Christian groups ostensibly created to promote a 'return to family values': this slogan often masks highly focused right-wing political agendas. Other controversial organizations, such as the People for the West, which generally promotes development of natural resources over preservation, find strong support in Colorado Springs. Gun control is also not a big favorite here: the local interpretation of the Constitutional right to bear arms permits citizens to carry concealed handguns. Many feel this positive attitude towards guns helped encourage Springs local Francisco Duran, who in October 1994 sprayed the White House with bullets from a machine gun purchased under the city's relaxed gun laws.

Of course not all Christian groups harbor political aims, and advocates of 'mixed-use' of land are often equally concerned with protecting their environment as well as their livelihood. But the extreme groups are the ones that grab headlines. As a result, mentioning Colorado, and the Springs in particular, can send shivers down the spines of anyone who tries to steer clear of the far right. ■

ECONOMY

The economies of Colorado, Wyoming and Montana have many features in common, mostly their dependence on natural resources like minerals and energy, soils and pasture, and extensive forests. Gold, of course, spurred early settlement in the 19th century, but silver and copper soon superseded it as corporations replaced the individualistic miner – the cheaply worked open-pit copper mines of Montana drove those of Michigan out of business by the 1880s.

The copper pits have mostly closed, but lesser minerals like lead, zinc and coal remain important. The region's petroleum and natural gas fields are also very productive. While oil shale resources drew considerable attention in the early 1970s, the energy crisis associated with the OPEC oil embargo and falling oil prices has since made their exploitation economically impractical.

The region's marked aridity limits agricultural possibilities, which include limited areas of irrigated farming, mostly along the upper Colorado River and its tributaries, and extensive cattle and sheep ranching, both in the mountains and on the plains. Some cattle and sheep ranchers use irrigation to improve pasture in lands of otherwise low productivity. With more than 100,000 sq miles in national forests and commercial timberland, the four states also have an important timber industry.

Water has been a major factor in limiting plains agriculture. The eastern part of the Great Plains, comprising the wheat, corn and cotton growing areas of the upper Missouri-Mississippi River drainage, are well-watered, but 'Beyond the 100th Meridian' (to use the title of Wallace Stegner's book), rain-fed agriculture becomes very risky. The irrigated Colorado Piedmont, at the base of the Front Range, benefits from eastward water diversions from the Rockies, but the rest of the plains is remote from water sources except for aquifers, which have been overexploited.

The region's spectacular mountain scenery and, in some areas, its equally appealing cultural resources, have contributed to a flourishing tourist industry. Summer is the peak season, but the winter ski season is also a major attraction. Tourism, which is becoming one of the top earners in each state, may be one way the region can avoid the constant boom-and-bust cycles that afflict economies based heavily on natural resources.

Denver, the region's only sizable city, has become an important business and manufacturing center, and, as a transport hub, it benefits from its central location at the base of the Front Range. It has also been at the forefront of Colorado's development into a center of high-tech and service industries. The Front Range is host to a wide array of computer, software and telecommunications ventures, leading some to liken it to a smaller version of California's Silicon Valley. This, along with a boom in service industries related to finance, retail and tourism has helped make Colorado's economy one of the fastest growing in the US during the 1990s.

Wyoming's economy is less diverse, depending mainly on mining, tourism, and agriculture, including ranching. As the unsustainability of massive harvesting and extraction of natural resources grows more apparent, Wyoming, like other Rocky Mountain states, is working to halt the erosion of its greatest natural resource – its breathtaking beauty – by promoting both tourism and recreation.

Tourism is now Montana's number one industry, followed by real estate. Ranchers are finding it increasingly profitable to divide their holdings and sell them, parcel by parcel, to developers. Over the four years between 1993 and 1997, property values rose 43%. Property taxes increased accordingly, but with a Grandfather Clause thrown in to protect the property owners who have been here the longest. Mining is still important, though Canadian companies now control most of Montana's mining operations, the largest being Pegasus Inc which has the Zortman and Landusky gold mines in the Little Rocky Mountains. Surveys suggest a wealth of minerals remain below Montana's surface, but environmental concerns have stifled most mining proposals over the past decade.

Agribusiness is by far the largest segment of the Idaho economy, and the state produces one-third of the nation's potatoes and most of its peas, onions and processed vegetables. But high-technology employment has doubled in the last 10 years, and now accounts for twice the number of jobs as the once huge timber sector and almost as many jobs as agriculture. Employment in agriculture, timber and mining continues to decline, while employment in the hotel and lodging sector is growing at more than 10% each year.

POPULATION & PEOPLE

While the Rockies are thinly populated in contrast to much of the rest of the country, the region is growing rapidly. Colorado, with the area's only truly metropolitan population (in and around Denver and the Front Range), is by far the largest of the four states in population. Idaho and Montana are also growing quickly, but Wyoming is the second least populated state in the country.

Colorado also has the broadest ethnic mix in the region, thanks to a large Hispanic population concentrated in Denver and the San Luis valley, an African American population mostly in Denver, and substantial numbers of Native Americans. Colorado's population of 3,822,676 (as of 1996) is still largely white, though Hispanics have long held significant influence in the state – particularly in the south – and make up 14% of the overall population. African Americans represent 4.3% and Native Americans and Asian are both under 1% of the total. More than half the state's population is concentrated in the Denver Metro area, and about another half million are spread up and down along the Front Range.

Wyoming's 1998 population is projected to be 495,930, of which 94% are white, 2.2% Native American and a mere 0.8% and 0.6% African American and Asian,

respectively. Growth into the 21st century is projected at less than 1% annually. Wyoming's largest city is Cheyenne; of the other cities, only Casper and Laramie have more than 20,000 inhabitants. Nearly 60% of the population lives in communities of fewer than 10,000 people. Indicative of a transitory population, more than 20% of the state's housing units are mobile homes or trailers.

According to the 1996 census, there are 879,372 people living in Montana – about six persons per square mile. Montana's population today reflects the makeup of its early northern European settlers. Along with the dominant white population are Native Americans (6%), Hispanic (1.5%), Asian (0.5%) and African American (0.3%). Most minorities live in Billings. Over half of the population lives in urban centers, with Billings' population of 85,000 being the largest. Great Falls, Helena, Missoula and Kalispell are close behind (in that order) with Bozeman making fast strides.

Idaho's population was 1,189,251 in 1996; 94% white, 5% Hispanic, and 1% Native American. Idaho's average annual state growth rate is 3%, the third highest in the US. Boise with a 3.4% annual growth rate is the fastest growing US city. Most people live in the Snake River Plain, although 43% of the population lives on farms or in rural districts.

EDUCATION

Colorado, Wyoming, Montana and Idaho all have state universities, the most prestigious of which is the University of Colorado at Boulder. State universities are tax-supported and generally less expensive than private colleges, many of which are church-affiliated. Other major institutions of higher learning in Colorado are Colorado State University in Fort Collins, the University of Northern Colorado in Greeley and the privately run Denver University. The state is also home to the interesting Colorado Mountain College in Gunnison, which focuses on natural sciences specifically related to Alpine environments. Another esoteric university is the Colorado School of Mines in Golden which draws students from around the globe for its top rated geology and mineral research curriculum.

Wyoming's only major school is the University of Wyoming in Laramie. Other institutes of higher learning include Casper College in Casper and Central Wyoming College in Riverton.

Montana's two biggest universities are the University of Montana in Missoula, whose forestry and creative writing programs are among the USA's best, and Montana State University in Bozeman, which is known for its strong agri-business department. Montana College of Mineral Science and Technology (Montana Tech) in Butte has an important mining technology school and mineral science research center. Dillon is home to Western Montana College, which educates about 80% of the teachers in the state.

Idaho's major school is the University of Idaho, located in Moscow. Others include Boise State University, Idaho State University in Pocatello and College of Southern Idaho in Twin Falls.

ARTS

Underestimated because of its isolation and small population, the West has nevertheless inspired generations of artists and writers. The earliest, of course, were the Native American peoples who left petroglyphs and pictographs in the canyons of the Colorado Plateau and other regions. Artists accompanied the early expeditions of Lewis and Clark and Stephen Long, and even attended the fur traders' rendezvous of the early 19th century, leaving records that were not just historically valuable but artistically enduring.

During the Great Depression of the 1930s, the federal government built many new public buildings, usually post offices and courthouses, which became architectural landmarks. Many show distinctive exterior friezes and interior murals that are well worth a stop; these are mentioned in the text.

In recent years, resort towns like Jackson, Aspen and Cody have become centers for the arts, though much of the work sold or exhibited is not by local artists. On the other hand, Grand Junction, Colorado, has an Art on the Corner program displaying sculptures by local artists, while nearby Delta and Paonia have some extraordinary murals of local and regional significance. Casper, Wyoming, remodeled a power plant and lumber yard into a delightful facility for local and traveling art exhibitions.

The performing arts have also made progress. Denver and Boulder, Colorado have gained national recognition for their performing arts programs. But the spread of culture has gone further afield. Gillette, Wyoming, best known for open-pit coal mining, is one of several unlikely sites, with modern music and theater venues.

Music Country & western music, which actually originated in the South, is the most widespread musical style in the Rocky Mountain states. Bluegrass is popular, and there are some good local bluegrass scenes, particularly in Colorado. Country music influences can include rhythm and blues, gospel and, increasingly, rock music. The traditional C&W sound is typified by the twang of a steel guitar and lyrics that describe heartache, religion, poverty, trucks, guns or prison life. Nationally recognized C&W stars include the late Hank Williams, Patsy Cline, Willie Nelson, Johnny Cash and his daughter Rosanne Cash, Loretta Lynn, Merle Haggard, Clint Black, Dwight Yoakum and Garth Brooks.

Classical and contemporary music also make themselves heard in the Rockies. This is in part a legacy of the ostentatious opera houses built in mining camps by wealthy silver barons. The tradition of performing arts in the isolated mountain communities is maintained by today's ski resorts – in part as a strategy to attract visitors during the summer off-season. Telluride's film festival and bluegrass festival draw visitors from around the world. Breckenridge, Aspen and Vail have strong summer schedules featuring renowned classical and jazz artists. Steamboat Springs offers a summer chamber music series. In Wyoming, Jackson's Grand Teton Music Festival attracts classical performers from throughout the country and around the world. Idaho summers see music festivals come to Sandpoint and Boise, and the National Fiddlers contest is held in Weiser.

Literature Fiction, both literature and pulp, established characters that would be parodied in numerous television films and motion pictures. Owen Wister, a Pennsylvanian, first drew attention to the region with *The Virginian* in 1902. Zane Grey followed suit with *Riders of the Purple Sage* in 1912, which became hugely popular and paved the way for the formula Western novel. Readers would soon come to expect rough and rugged characters who demonstrate an unwieldy sense of independence and who also know how to handle their liquor, their horses and their guns.

The dime novel of the early 20th century helped create the epic myths and legends that now haunt the tourist towns of the Rocky Mountain states. Louis L'Amour (1908-1988) once supported himself as a deputy sheriff in North Dakota and wrote very popular pulp fiction; his first Western novel, *Hondo*, published in 1953, was an instant success. He went on to write 80 more, including *How the West Was Won* and *The Quick and the Dead*.

Colorado mining camps inspired writers like Anne Ellis to write her biographical account of hardships among the working class in *The Life of an Ordinary Woman*. Telluride native David Lavender recounts the transition from ranching to uranium mining in the Colorado Plateau in *One Man's West*. Colorado's dean of nature writing, Enos Mills, published 16 books of careful natural observation from his cabin near Estes Park before his untimely death in 1922. His *Adventures of a Nature Guide* contains an excellent sampling of his work.

Black Elk, born in Wyoming's Powder River Basin, is famous for *Black Elk Speaks: The Life Story of a Holy Man of the Oglala Sioux*, an autobiographical clas-

sic still widely read in university courses. Caroline Lockhart, transplanted from Illinois, became a newspaper editor in Cody and wrote several novels with local settings; most notably *Lady Doc*. Novelist and essayist Gretel Ehrlich, originally from California, is probably the state's best known contemporary writer.

Idaho claims Ezra Pound, the poet, born in Hailey in 1885, and Ernest Hemingway, who made his home in Ketchum. Vardis Fisher, a novelist and essayist chronicled Idaho during the 1930s and '40s and is remembered for *Idaho: A Guide in Word & Picture*, the WPA guide to Idaho.

The Big Sky (1947), by AB Guthrie, Jr, gave Montana its most popular nickname. Dorothy Johnson's *A Man Called Horse* (1953) includes the story 'The Man Who Shot Liberty Valance' – the epitome of early Western literature. Spike Van Cleve captured the essence of cowboy curmudgeonry and story-telling in *A Day Late and a Dollar Short*.

Other modern writers, like Wallace Stegner, Ivan Doig, Thomas McGuane and Gretel Ehrlich, have taken Western literature in very different directions, avoiding the stereotypes and breaking the myths. (McGuane's *Something to Be Desired* is a good contemporary choice.) In this realm, Montana's literary tradition has always enjoyed a position of respect. The University of Montana (U of M), in Missoula, continually produces gifted writers. In 1988 the Montana Committee for the Humanities and Montana Historical Society published *The Last Best Place* (University of Washington Press, 1991), edited by Annick Smith and William Kittredge. The 1200-page anthology encompasses the entire range of Montana literature, from Native American stories to journal entries of early homesteaders to excerpts of works by popular contemporary writers.

Visual Arts Colorado's spectacular landscapes have attracted many talented painters and photographers, but few Colorado natives have national fame in their own backyard. Denver's Art Museum is the state's foremost

Cowboy Poetry

That such a thing as cowboy poetry even exists is a small puncture in the media stereotype of the American cowboy. Always portrayed as the strong, silent type, the typical Western hero (or heroine) is not the sort you picture reciting Shakespeare as s/he rides off into the sunset.

Cowboy poetry, regular in meter and simple in rhyme, tells stories of what they knew and what surrounded them: unruly cattle, wide-open spaces, dramatic weather and incurable isolation. The poetic language, riddled with shur-nuffs, buckaroos and yonder's, reflects their subject matter and poetic intent completely. Unlike their contemporaries, original cowboy poets had no literary training (usually no education at all), no mentors to copy and no styles to duplicate. Their easily memorized poems were obviously meant to be recited and repeated. Take Allen McCanless's *The Cowboy's Soliloquy* first published in 1885:

> All day o'er the prairie alone I ride
> Not even a dog to run by my side
> My fire I kindle with chips gathered round
> And boil my coffee without being ground.
> Bread lackin' leaven' I bake in a pot
> And sleep on the ground for want of a cot
>
> I wash in a puddle, and wipe with a sack
> And carry my wardrobe all on my back.
> My ceiling the sky, my carpet the grass
> My music the lowing of herds as they pass
> My books are the brooks, my sermon the stones
> My parson's a wolf on a pulpit of bones.

Cowboy poetry made its first major public appearance in 1908 in Howard (Jack) Thorp's *Songs of the Cowboys* and in 1910 in John Lomax's *Cowboy Songs and other Frontier Ballads*. In the 1970s and '80s, a cowboy poetry revival began to brew and has been gaining popularity ever since. In 1985 the first Cowboy Poetry Gathering met in Elko, Nevada, and drew a crowd of 10,000. Today there are over a hundred similar gathering spread throughout the country, and the Elko event now draws crowds of up to 50,000 people.

Modern cowboy poets, however, are an entirely different breed: while they may write with the sky overhead and earth below, they can't re-create the sense of space and isolation that is lost in today's world. One of the most talented poets is Baxter Black, a frequent contributor on National Public Radio's *Morning Edition*. His recordings, such as *Live at the Grange*, are always amusing and reveal modern urban and rural life in the West.

Several good anthologies of cowboy poetry have been published, including *Cattle, Horses, Sky, and Grass* (Northland Publishing, 1994), edited by Warren Miller, and *Cowboy Poetry: A Gathering* (Gibbs M Smith Inc, 1985). ■

gallery. The Colorado Springs Fine Arts Center houses an excellent collection, and its Taylor Museum is the most noted display of Native American and Hispanic work in the state. Denver's Museum of Western Art and the AR Mitchell Gallery in Trinidad both excel in Western themes. The Pioneer Museum in Colorado Springs offers representative works by noted photog-

raphers, painters and cartographers – it also showcases Van Briggle pottery. Ute tribal crafts are featured at the Pino Nuche Ute Center in Ignacio and the Ute Museum in Gunnison. La Junta's Koshare Indian Museum displays outstanding art from tribes throughout North America.

Painters and photographers have found Wyoming fertile ground for their crafts ever since Alfred Jacob Miller accompanied Scottish nobleman William Drummond Stewart to the Green River Rendezvous in 1837. Albert Bierstadt, Thomas Moran, Frederic Remington, Carl Rungius and others all interpreted Wyoming landscapes, wildlife and people on canvas, while photographers William Henry Jackson and Charles J Belden both left memorable legacies depicting the state's wild landscapes and peoples. Cody-born abstract painter Jackson Pollock is undoubtedly the best known artist to hail from Wyoming.

But Charles M Russell is undeniably Montana's most celebrated artist. His oil paintings, watercolors and illustrated stories portray virgin Montana scenes – early encounters between Indians and explorers, buffalo on the plains and cowboys with their herds. Although reproductions of his work are emblazoned on everything from greeting cards to pillow cases, the bulk of his original work is in Great Falls and Helena.

SOCIETY & CONDUCT

By reputation and ideology, the West is the most individualistic region of an individualistic country. It is also a socially conservative area. That conservatism is heightened by constant change and threats to the 'old way of life.' Even in the most progressive cities of the Rocky Mountain states you will encounter people whose lives depend (now or generations hence) on mining, logging, and ranching. Change is coming quickly through younger generations, yet these are still the traditional cornerstones of the region's economy and need to be accepted if not necessarily agreed with. Just because people subscribe to different views than your own doesn't mean they can't be considerate and hospitable. In fact, visitors to the rural areas of the Rockies often find the locals extremely friendly and polite.

You're most likely to encounter strong conservatism in rural areas, especially in areas that rely on agriculture, oil, ranching or logging. While gay and lesbian travelers will probably feel quite comfortable in the bigger cities, they can expect plenty of stares and giggles in small towns and cowboy-style bars. T-shirts emblazoned with slogans like 'Earth First!,' 'Save the Trees' and 'Vegetarian for Life' should probably be left in your luggage.

Visitors should also try to be aware of local political issues – don't broadcast your animal rights convictions in a bar full of hunters or denounce clear-cutting in a mill town, for example, without having some idea of your audience and their experiences and upbringing.

While most conservatives are simply averse to the changes they see occurring in their sacred wide-open spaces, you may run across those ignorant few who believe that anyone sympathetic to the environment is a 'tree-hugger' communist, that being gay is 'against the Lord' and people of color should go 'back to where they came from.' Indeed, some locals will take advantage of outsiders or foreigners to declare their own strong opinions, which you may find repellent. While there's not much you can do to save these misguided souls, you can spare yourself by finding a way to diplomatically disengage yourself from the conversation.

Car Culture

Foreign visitors will soon realize that, for better or worse, the automobile is more than just transportation. It's impossible to overstate the impact of the automobile on American life, a topic that has become the subject of many books.

In the Rocky Mountain states, where public transportation is underdeveloped or nonexistent, an automobile is a necessity, but it can also be a symbol of mobility, social class and economic status. For Hispanic teenagers, for instance, the car represents independence, as they crowd the streets of towns like Trinidad and Pueblo, Colorado, with their low riders (classic cars so modified that they nearly scrape the pavement). For urban cowboys, the pickup truck has replaced the traditional horse.

Recycling & Littering

Traveling in a car seems to generate large numbers of cans and bottles. If you'd like to save these for recycling, you'll find recycling centers in the larger towns. Materials accepted are usually plastic and glass bottles, aluminum and tin cans and newspapers. Some campgrounds and a few roadside rest areas also have recycling bins next to the trash bins so look out for those.

Even better than recycling is to reduce your use of these products. Many gas stations and convenience stores sell large plastic insulated cups with lids which are inexpensive and ideal for hot and cold drinks. You can usually save a few cents by using your cup to buy drinks.

Despite the trashed appearance of many large cities, littering is frowned upon by most Americans. Travelers need to respect the places they are visiting even though it may seem that some locals think it's OK to trash their territory. Some states have implemented anti-littering laws (which impose fines for violation) to try to curb the problem. When hiking and camping in the wilderness, take out everything you bring in – this includes *any* kind of garbage you may create.

RELIGION

The oldest religions in North America are Native American religions, greatly modified since contact with Europeans; some, like the Native American Church, which uses hallucinatory peyote buttons as a sacrament, are in part pan-Indian responses to encroachment by the Judeo-Christian culture. Scattered throughout the region, sacred sites like Devils Tower and the Medicine Wheel (both in Wyoming) draw worshippers from Native American enclaves throughout the region.

The oldest European religion in the Rockies is Roman Catholicism, the legacy of early Spanish incursions into New Mexico and the San Luis Valley of southwestern Colorado. Catholicism and various Protestant denominations are the most important religions in numbers of adherents.

Both Catholic and Protestant missionaries accompanied early fur traders and traveled the Oregon Trail to evangelize among Native American peoples. Many Indians nominally converted to Christianity, or a hybrid form of it. One key

The Hutterites

In the 17th century many brotherhoods of Hutterites (a brethren descended from the Moravian Anabaptists) lived in Moravia, but persecution drove them east to resettle in Russia. Facing further persecution, a group of Hutterites, along with Russian Mennonites, emigrated to the USA in 1874. President Grant offered them sizable land grants in South Dakota, agreeing to their proposal that they pay land tax, but not go to war. They eventually moved west and north to settle also in Montana and Canada. Once these groups had settled, more Hutterites emigrated from Russia. Similar in many ways to the Mennonites in Canada, they live simply and practice both pacifism and communism.

Hutterite communist principles are based on Acts 4:32-35 in the Bible, which say 'neither said any of them that ought of the things which he possessed was his own; but they had all things in common.' The theory that an individual is to be subordinated to the will of the community *(Gelassenheit)* is reinforced in their educational system. Because of their strong faith and community orientation, they have stayed together (few venture away to join the modern ways) – a rare feat among religious communities.

Unlike the Mennonites or Amish, the Hutterites accept farm machinery and vehicles and invite technical improvements. They have always been very efficient farmers and continue to buy more land. Such practices have not sat well with the people of the prairie states, angered that these noncommunicative neighbors buy up the land but don't support the economy through consumerism. Apathy, however, seems to be the main reaction to these communities. When asked about their Hutterite brethren, local Montanans generally give a passive 'I don't know or really care' shrug, and move on to another topic of conversation. ■

symbol of a settled community, as opposed to a roughshod frontier town, was construction of a permanent church.

Throughout the Rockies are outliers and enclaves of the Church of Jesus Christ of Latter Day Saints (LDS), more commonly known as the Mormons. Though their strongest influence is in neighboring Utah, Mormons are numerous in communities like Wyoming's Star Valley and Powell, near the Wyoming-Montana state line. The Mormon church is also one of Idaho's largest organized religions, and is concentrated in the southeast. Mormon strictures on activities like gambling and alcohol consumption are very influential in these areas, and it is unquestionably the most cohesive religious group in the region.

The most recent religious development in the region is the growth of New Age communities like Crestone, Colorado (home of actress Shirley MacLaine), which has a Zen Center, Ashram Temple and Spiritual Life Institute. In Montana, where Jesuit missionaries and Lutheran ministers once dominated, one can now go to Buddhist meditation groups and Hindu-based Sidda Yoga meetings, especially in Missoula, Bozeman, Hamilton and Kalispell.

Darker variants of this new spiritualism are millennial groups like Elizabeth Claire Prophet's Church Universal and Triumphant, a heavily armed cult occupying a fortress compound near Gardiner, Montana (the northern entrance to Yellowstone National Park). Paramilitary groups, some of whom rationalize their beliefs on religious grounds, also inhabit some rural areas, but visitors are unlikely to come in contact with them.

Facts for the Visitor

PLANNING

When to Go

For many travelers, the Rocky Mountains are a summer destination, but the winter ski season also draws large numbers of visitors. Some prefer the fall, when the aspens flaunt their autumn gold, or the spring wildflower season.

It starts to feel like summer in the Rocky Mountains around June, and the warm weather lasts until about mid-September. While winter weather doesn't usually settle in until late November, snow storms can start hitting the mountain areas as early as September. Winter usually lasts until March or early April.

Due to the mountain terrain, high altitude and dry climate, the one constant in the weather is that it can always change quickly. Colorado's Front Range often sees warm sunny days in February, while mountain areas anywhere in the four states can be hit by snow or hail storms in July. The trick is to be prepared and keep an eye on weather conditions in the area you're traveling to. Below are phone numbers you can call to check on road conditions in each state:

Colorado	☎ 303-639-1111 (west)
	☎ 303-639-1234 (east)
Wyoming	☎ 307-733-9966
Montana	☎ 800-332-6171
Idaho	☎ 208-336-6600

In nearly all parts of the Rockies summer is the high season, which means more crowds and often higher lodging rates. In areas where winter recreation is well established (mainly ski resorts) peak season rates and conditions also apply. Lodging rates can increase by as much as 30% during peak seasons, depending on where you are. Seasonal rate variations are detailed in this book's destination chapters.

Traveling in the off-season can be rewarding since you don't have to contend

with crowded roads, shops and visitors centers, and many high-end places to stay offer more affordable room rates. The downside is that information centers often close, tours and guided activities have limited schedules if they function at all, and restaurants are often vacant, or shut for the season. The best off-season time is mid-September through October, as the weather usually stays warm and services aren't yet totally shut-down. You may not get the lowest lodging rates, but prices are almost always lower than during peak season. For details on weather and temperatures in the four states, see the Climate section in Facts about the Rocky Mountains.

Maps

Good maps are widely available in the US, making it easy to find your way around. In addition to the suggestions below, the relevant destination chapters have information on maps specific to each area, including those designed for activities such as hiking and mountain biking.

Highway Maps The American Automobile Association (AAA) issues the most comprehensive and dependable highway maps, which are free with AAA membership (see 'Useful Organizations') and available for a reasonable price to nonmembers. These range in scope from national, regional and state maps to very detailed maps of cities, counties and even relatively small towns.

Topographic Maps The US Geological Survey (USGS), an agency of the federal Department of the Interior, publishes very detailed topographic maps of the entire country, at different scales up to 1:250,000. Maps at 1:62,500, or approximately 1 inch:1 mile, are ideal for backcountry hiking and backpacking. Some private cartographers are producing updated versions of old USGS maps at 1:62,500. Many bookstores and outdoor equipment specialists carry a wide selection of topographic maps.

Atlases Visitors spending any significant amount of time in the USA should try to acquire the appropriate state volume of the DeLorme Mapping series of atlases and gazetteers, which contain detailed topographic and highway maps at a scale of 1:250,000. Available in some bookstores, these are especially useful off the main highways and cost about $20 each. For overall, more general highway maps, the *Rand McNally Road Atlas* ($8) is good. It covers all 50 US states, as well as Canada and Mexico, and has some useful additional features such as driving time and distance charts, and details on state driving laws.

What to Bring

The Rocky Mountain region is mostly temperate, mid-latitude country whose climate resembles that of northern Europe (but at generally higher elevations). Carry seasonally appropriate clothing, but be prepared for changeable weather, including flash thunderstorms and frosts even in midsummer. In the summer heat of southern Colorado and Idaho, you will want lightweight cottons.

Excellent outdoor gear and clothing is available at reasonable prices throughout the region, but the selection is better and prices are generally lower in large cities. The Denver/Boulder area in Colorado is especially good in terms of both choice and cost. If you're bringing your own camping gear, be sure to include an all-weather tent and warm sleeping bags: even in summer temperatures in the mountains can drop to freezing at night.

Personal preference largely determines the best way to carry your baggage. A large zip-up or duffel bag with a wide shoulder strap is convenient for buses, trains and planes. Obviously if you're planning to do a lot of camping or hiking, a backpack will be what you carry. Internal frame packs, with a cover which protects the straps from getting snagged in storage on buses or planes, offer both convenience on the road and comfort on the trail.

Don't overlook essentials like a Swiss Army knife, needle and thread, a small pair of scissors, contraceptives, sunglasses and swimming gear. Basic supplies like toothbrushes, toothpaste, shaving cream, shampoo and tampons are readily available everywhere. Due to the high altitude, sunblock should be carried, even in winter: it only takes 20 minutes to get a sunburn on a sunny day in the mountains. See National Parks & Outdoor Activities for a more detailed list of what to bring on hikes and outdoor trips.

HIGHLIGHTS

Without doubt, the main reason to visit the Rockies is to soak in the magnificent natural beauty, which comes in a stunning array of color, terrain and atmosphere. From the desert canyons of western Colorado to the lush Alpine splendor of Glacier National Park, this region offers visitors almost unrestricted access to breathtaking nature, the type that defies verbal description and makes one thankful to be part of this amazing world.

But the Rockies' appeal is not limited to natural sights. The region's generally friendly residents and wealth of historical, well-preserved 19th-century towns also add to the visitor's experience. The rural nature of most areas can mean running into some provincial or rigidly conservative attitudes, and in towns near national parks and other tourist zones travelers may find locals indifferent, or even rude. But generally people are happy to take a bit of extra time to help out or converse with visitors, and hospitality, rather than hostility, is the norm.

Below are some of the authors' choices for best things to see and do in the various states. While these include sights that would make any tourist brochure, there are a few places where you'll find you're mixing mostly with the locals.

Colorado

Arapahoe Basin With some of the best, and latest, steep skiing in Colorado, this bare-bones ski area still manages to ward off the glitz and haughtiness that has invaded Aspen, Telluride and Vail.

Boulder Hanging out on the rooftop deck of the West End Tavern, having a beer and watching the sun set behind the Flatirons is one of the better ways to 'passively' observe this town's beautiful setting and lively atmosphere.

Colorado National Monument This underappreciated unit of the National Park System, featuring stunning polychrome sandstone canyons, is one of the most rewarding side trips possible off an interstate highway.

Fruita Just west of Grand Junction, the area around this small town offers some of the best mountain bike trails since Moab was 'discovered' in the late 1980s.

The Peak to Peak Hwy Stretching from Nederland (west of Boulder) to Estes Park, this highway passes the beautiful Indian Peaks Wilderness, the massive 14,255-foot Long's Peak, and numerous national forest trails, access roads and campgrounds.

San Luis With one of the few 'commons' in the USA, Hispanic culture and the meaning of community is evident in Colorado's oldest permanent settlement against the backdrop of the Sangre de Cristo Mountains.

Wyoming
Devils Tower One of the most imposing landmarks on the globe, and a popular challenge for rock climbers, this national monument (and Native American sacred site) is well worth the long drive.

Fort Laramie National Historic Site The last chance for resupply on the Oregon Trail during the 19th century, eastern Wyoming's Fort Laramie still retains its frontier atmosphere, thanks to timely efforts at restoration and preservation.

Grand Teton National Park The Tetons may be the most photographed mountain range in the country, for good reason. Don't be content to shoot at a distance, though: walk the trails.

Laramie Spend the afternoon wandering this gracious city's historic district and wind up with a fine meal at Jeffery's Bistro.

Medicine Wheel This Native American sacred site atop the Bighorn Mountains has breathtaking views over the Bighorn Basin and superb nearby camping.

Sinks Canyon State Park According to one survey, this small reserve, where the Popo Agie River disappears into limestone bedrock and resurfaces half a mile lower, is one of America's top 50 state parks, and is home to a wide range of wildlife.

Snowy Range Just west of Laramie, the Snowy Range is frequented mostly by locals. This high but accessible mountain range offers scenic hiking and spectacular views.

Wind River Range Accessed from Pinedale, Lander or Dubois, Wyoming's highest mountain range has a superb network of trails along and across the Continental Divide.

Yellowstone National Park Despite its troubles, the world's first national park is still one of Wyoming's top sights, but get out of your car and onto the trails.

Montana
Abasaroka-Beartooth Hwy Much less traveled than Glacier National Park's Going-to-the-Sun Rd, the Absaroka-Beartooth Hwy traverses stark tundra-covered plateaus, and passes jagged granite peaks and glacial lakes. Excellent hiking trails lead into this wilderness from Red Lodge and Paradise Valley.

Big Hole Battlefield National Monument The flight of Chief Joseph and the

Nez Percé Indians is chronicled by historic markers throughout the state, but the Big Hole Battlefield National Monument gives the most thorough explanation of that sad episode in US history.

Bitterroot Range The glacially formed Bitterroot Range, in the southwest corner of Montana, has 29 canyons that are lined with excellent trails, many of which end up at high mountain lakes.

Glacier National Park After the first week in November, Going-to-the-Sun Rd is closed to car traffic, and runners and skiers take over.

Makoshika State Park The stunning badlands scenery here offers solitude and great views.

Missoula Spend the morning at the Second Thought cafe or (in summer) outside at Bernice's Bakery.

Museum of the Rockies Despite the hordes of tourists that visit each summer, Bozeman's Museum of the Rockies has Montana's best natural history exhibits, with dinosaur replicas built by the man behind the creatures that looked so real in the film *Jurassic Park*.

Red Lodge A fine place to go bar-hopping.

Idaho
Boise A hip, lively city that offers a nice mix of cultural activity and nightlife; also a good jumping off point for exploring the rivers and lakes of southwestern Idaho.

Henry's Fork of the Snake River This area is mythic at hatch time, with trout leaping everywhere you look and swans gracefully circling in the eddies.

Salmon River White-water enthusiasts can enjoy a day trip on the Lower Salmon near Riggins, or a classic multiple-day run down its Middle Fork, ranked one of the world's top 10 white-water rivers.

Sawtooth National Recreation Area With four mountain ranges, four major rivers, 42 peaks over 10,000 feet, 1000 lakes, 100 miles of streams, and 700 miles of trails, the Sawtooths offer something for everyone.

Sun Valley With a touch of old-world grandeur and new world glitter, this resort also offers some of the country's fluffiest, deepest powder skiing.

TOURIST OFFICES
Information on state tourist offices can be found in the introductory chapters for each state. Local tourist offices are listed under the relevant destination.

The USA currently has no government affiliated tourist offices in other countries. For region-specific information, ask your travel agent.

VISAS & DOCUMENTS
All foreign visitors (other than Canadians) must bring their passport. All visitors should bring their driver's license and any health-insurance or travel-insurance cards.

You'll need a picture ID to show that you are over 21 to buy alcohol or gain admission to bars or clubs (make sure your driver's license has a photo on it, or else get some other form of ID). It's a good idea to make a photocopy of your passport and international ID to carry around instead of the original. There's nothing worse than losing your identity on a trip.

Canadians must have proper proof of Canadian citizenship, such as a citizenship card with photo ID or a passport. Most visitors are also required to get a US visa.

The US State Department's Bureau of Consular Affairs website (travel.state.gov) has excellent info on visa, passport and customs requirements.

Visas
Apart from Canadians, and those entering under the Visa-Waiver Pilot Program (see below), all foreign visitors need to obtain a visa from a US consulate or embassy. In

most countries the process can be done by mail or through a travel agent.

Your passport should be valid for at least six months beyond your intended stay in the USA, and you'll need to submit a recent photo (37 x 37 mm) with the application. Documents of financial stability and/or guarantees from a US resident are sometimes required, particularly for those from developing countries.

Visa applicants may be required to 'demonstrate binding obligations' that will ensure their return back home. Because of this requirement, those planning to travel through other countries before arriving in the USA are generally better off applying for their US visa while they are still in their home country – rather than while on the road.

The most common visa is a Non-Immigrant Visitors Visa, B1 for business purposes, B2 for tourism or visiting friends and relatives. A visitor's visa is good for one or five years with multiple entries, and it specifically prohibits the visitor from taking paid employment in the USA. The validity period depends on what country you're from. The length of time you'll be allowed to stay in the USA is ultimately determined by US immigration authorities at the port of entry. If you're coming to the USA to work or study, you will probably need a different type of visa, and the company or institution which you're going to should make the arrangements. Allow six months in advance for processing the application.

Visa Waiver Pilot Program

Citizens of certain countries may enter the USA without a US visa, for stays of 90 days or less, under the Visa Waiver Pilot Program. Currently these countries are Andorra, Argentina, Australia, Austria, Belgium, Brunei, Denmark, Finland, France, Germany, Iceland, Ireland, Italy, Japan, Liechtenstein, Luxembourg, Monaco, the Netherlands, New Zealand, Norway, San Marino, Spain, Sweden, Switzerland, and the UK. Under this program you must have a roundtrip ticket that is nonrefundable in the USA and you will not be allowed to extend your stay beyond 90 days. Check with the US embassy in your home country for any other requirements.

Visa Extensions & Re-Entry

If you want, need, or hope to stay in the USA longer than the date stamped on your passport, go to the local INS office (or call ☎ 800-755-0777, or look in the local white pages telephone directory under US Government) *before* the stamped date to apply for an extension. Anytime after that will usually lead to an unamusing conversation with an INS official who will assume you want to work illegally. If you find yourself in that situation, it's a good idea to bring a US citizen with you to vouch for your character. It's also a good idea to have some verification that you have enough money to support yourself.

Travel Insurance

No matter how you're traveling, make sure you take out travel insurance. This should cover you not only for medical expenses and luggage theft or loss, but also for cancellations or delays in your travel arrangements. Everyone should be covered for the worst possible case, such as an accident that requires hospital treatment and a flight home. Coverage depends on your insurance and type of ticket, so ask both your insurer and your ticket-issuing agency to explain the finer points. Ticket loss is also covered by travel insurance. Make sure you have a separate record of all your ticket details – or better still, a photocopy of it. Also make a copy of your policy, in case the original is lost. STA Travel and Council Travel offer travel insurance options at reasonable prices.

Buy travel insurance as early as possible. If you buy it the week before you fly, you may find, for instance, that you're not covered for delays to your flight caused by strikes or other industrial action that may have been in force before you took out the insurance.

If you're planning to travel a long time, the insurance might seem very expensive, but if you can't afford it, you certainly won't be able to afford a medical emergency in the USA.

International Driving Permit

An International Driving Permit is a useful accessory for foreign visitors in the USA. Local traffic police are more likely to accept it as valid identification than an unfamiliar document from another country. Your national automobile association can provide one for a small fee. They're usually valid for one year.

Hostel Card

Most hostels in the USA are members of Hostelling International/American Youth Hostel (HI/AYH), which is affiliated with the International Youth Hostel Federation (IYHF). You can purchase membership on the spot when checking in, although it's probably advisable to purchase it before you leave home. Most hostels allow nonmembers to stay but will charge them a few dollars more.

Student & Youth Cards

If you're a student, get an international student ID or bring along a school or university ID card to take advantage of the discounts available to students.

Seniors' Cards

All people over the age of 65 get discounts throughout the USA. All you need is ID with proof of age should you be carded. There are organizations such as AARP (see Senior Travelers) that offer membership cards for further discounts and extend coverage to citizens of other countries.

Automobile Association Membership Cards

If you plan on doing a lot of driving in the USA, it would be beneficial to join your national automobile association. See Useful Organizations for information.

EMBASSIES & CONSULATES

US diplomatic offices abroad include the following:

Australia
  21 Moonah Place, Yarralumla ACT 2600
  (☎ 2-6270-5000)
  Level 59 MLC Center 19-29 Martin Place,
  Sydney NSW 2000 (☎ 2-9373-9200)
  553 St Kilda Rd, Melbourne, Victoria
  (☎ 3-9526-5900)
Canada
  100 Wellington St, Ottawa, Ontario K1P
  5T1 (☎ 613-238-5335)
  1095 W Pender St, Vancouver, BC V6E
  2M6 (☎ 604-685-4311)
  1155 rue St-Alexandre, Montreal, Quebec
  (☎ 514-398-9695)
France
  2 rue Saint Florentin, 75001 Paris
  (☎ 01 42 96 12 02)
Germany
  Deichmanns Aue 29, 53170 Bonn
  (☎ 228-33-91)
Ireland
  42 Elgin Rd, Ballsbridge, Dublin
  (☎ 1-687-122)
Israel
  71 Hayarkon St, Tel Aviv (☎ 3-517-4338)
Japan
  10-5 Akasaka 1-chome, Minato-ku, Tokyo
  (☎ 3-3224-5000)
Netherlands
  Lange Voorhout 102, 2514 EJ The Hague
  (☎ 70-310-9209)
  Museumplein 19, 1071 DJ Amsterdam
  (☎ 20-310-9209)
New Zealand
  29 Fitzherbert Terrace, Thorndon,
  Wellington (☎ 4-722-068)
Norway
  Drammensveien 18, 0244 Oslo
  (☎ 22-44-85-50)
Sweden
  Strandvagen 101, S-115 89 Stockholm (☎ 8-
  783-5300)
Switzerland
  Jubilaumsstrasse 93, 3005 Berne
  (☎ 31-357-70 11)
UK
  5 Upper Grosvenor St, London W1
  (☎ 0171-499-9000)
  3 Regent Terrace, Edinburgh EH7 5BW
  (☎ 31-556-8315)
  Queens House, 14 Queen St, Belfast BT1
  6EQ (☎ 232-328-239)

Embassies in the USA

Addresses and phone numbers of foreign diplomatic representatives can be found in

HIV & Going Through Customs

Everyone entering the USA who is not a US citizen is subject to the whim and authority of the Immigration & Naturalization Service (INS), regardless of whether that person has legal immigration documents. The INS can keep someone from entering or staying in the USA by excluding or deporting them. This is especially relevant to travelers with HIV (Human Immunodeficiency Virus). Though being HIV positive is not a ground for deportation, it is a 'ground of exclusion' and the INS can invoke it to refuse to admit visitors to the country.

Although the INS doesn't test for HIV at customs, they may try to exclude anyone who answers yes to this question on the non-immigrant visa application form: 'Have you ever been afflicted with a communicable disease of public health significance?' INS officials might also stop people if they seem sick, are carrying AIDS/HIV medicine or even if the officer happens to think the person looks gay, though sexual orientation is not legally a ground of exclusion. Because the INS can refuse or delay admission to anyone they suspect of being HIV positive, your best protection is not to tip them off.

It is imperative that visitors know and assert their rights. Immigrants and visitors should avoid contact with the INS until they discuss their rights and options with a trained immigration advocate. For legal immigration information and referrals to immigration advocates, contact The National Immigration Project of the National Lawyers Guild (☎ 617-227-9727), 14 Beacon St, Suite 602, Boston, MA 02108, or Immigrant HIV Assistance Project, Bar Association of San Francisco (☎ 415-267-0795), 685 Market St, Suite 700, San Francisco, CA 94105. ■

the yellow pages telephone directory under 'Consulates.' Most nations' principal diplomatic representation is in Washington, DC. To find out the telephone number of your embassy or consulate in DC, call ☎ 202-555-1212.

In the Rockies, Denver is the only city that has foreign consulates. For a complete listing refer to the Denver & Boulder chapter.

CUSTOMS

US Customs allows each person over the age of 21 to bring one liter of liquor and 200 cigarettes duty free into the USA. US citizens are allowed to import, duty free, $400 worth of gifts from abroad, while non-US citizens are allowed to bring in $100 worth.

Currency Regulations US law permits you to bring in, or take out, as much as $10,000 in US or foreign currency, traveler's checks or letters of credit without formality. Larger amounts of any or all of the above – there are no limits – must be declared to customs.

MONEY

Costs

Costs in the Rocky Mountain states are fairly reasonable, especially when compared to expensive US destinations like New York or California. The exception is Colorado, where the steady flow of tourists allows motels, hotels and restaurants in the more traveled areas to jack up prices, even during non-peak seasons.

Cost for accommodations varies seasonally, between the cities and the countryside, and between resorts and everywhere else. Generally rates are higher in summer, between Memorial Day and Labor Day, when prices can be anywhere from 10 to 50% higher than during the off-peak times of late winter or late fall. The cheapest motel rates will usually be in the $20 to $30 range, and a few places have inexpensive hotels as well. Again, in Colorado motel rates in places like Boulder, Durango or Vail may start as high as $40 for a basic room.

Camping on national or state land is generally inexpensive, between $5 to $10 per night, while private sites offering facilities like hot showers and laundry charge anywhere from $10 to $20.

Winter rates at ski resorts are often ridiculously high, with average motel rooms starting at $70, and upscale hotel rooms at around $180! Ski-accommodation-airfare packages can help bring costs down though.

Food is affordable. The occasional splurge at a first-rate restaurant will cost anywhere between $25 and $50 depending on where you are, but good restaurant meals can be found in almost any town or city in the region for $10 – half that for some lunch specials. If you purchase food at markets you can get by even more cheaply.

Except for within cities, public transportation is generally both expensive and limited. In many areas a car is the only way of getting around; fortunately rentals are fairly inexpensive in large cities, and gasoline costs a fraction of what it does in Europe and most of the rest of the world. For more information on purchasing and operating a car, see the Getting Around chapter.

Carrying Money

Carry your money (and only the money you'll need for that day) somewhere inside your clothing (in a money belt, a bra or your socks) rather than in a handbag or an outside pocket. Put the money in several places. Most hotels and hostels provide safekeeping, so you can leave your money and other valuables with them. Hide or don't wear any valuable jewelry. A safety pin or key ring to hold the zipper tags of a daypack together can help deter theft.

Cash & Traveler's Checks

Though carrying cash is more risky it's still a good idea to travel with some for the convenience; it's useful to help pay all those tips and some smaller, more remote places may not accept credit cards or traveler's checks. A big advantag of traveler's checks is they offer greater protection from theft or loss and in many places can be used as cash. American Express and Thomas Cook are widely accepted and have efficient replacement policies.

Keeping a record of the check numbers and the checks you have used is vital when it comes to replacing lost checks. Keep this record separate from the checks themselves.

You'll save yourself trouble and expense if you buy traveler's checks in US dollars. The savings you *might* make on exchange rates by carrying traveler's checks in a foreign currency don't make up for the hassle of exchanging them at banks and other facilities. Restaurants, hotels and most stores accept US-dollar traveler's checks as if they were cash, so if you're carrying traveler's checks in US dollars, the odds are you'll rarely have to use a bank or pay an exchange fee.

Take most of the checks in large denominations. It's only towards the end of a stay that you may want to change a small check to make sure you aren't left with too much local currency.

ATMs

ATMs are a convenient way of obtaining cash 24 hours a day from a bank account back home (within the USA or from abroad). The number of these machines has soared in recent years, and even small-town banks in the middle of nowhere have ATMs. They are common in most shopping areas.

There are various ATM networks and most banks are affiliated with several. Exchange, Accel, Plus and Cirrus are the predominant networks. An insidious practice adopted by US banks is to levy a $1 to $2 fee for using a 'non-web' ATM, that is one not directly run by your own bank. For travelers, this means virtually every ATM, so you may wish to withdraw somewhat larger amounts less frequently.

For a nominal service charge, you can also withdraw cash from an ATM using a credit card or a charge card. Credit cards usually have a 2% fee with a $2 minimum, but using bank cards linked to your personal checking account is usually far cheaper. Check with your bank or credit card company for exact information.

Credit & Debit Cards

Major credit cards are accepted at hotels, restaurants, gas stations, shops, and car rental agencies throughout the USA. In fact, you'll find it hard to perform certain transactions such as renting a car or purchasing tickets to performances without one.

Even if you loathe using credit cards and prefer to rely on traveler's checks and ATMs, it's a good idea to carry one for emergencies. If you're planning to primarily use credit cards it would be wise to have either a Visa or MasterCard in your deck, since other cards, such as American Express, aren't as widely accepted.

Places that accept Visa and MasterCard may also accept debit cards. Unlike a credit card, a debit card deducts payment directly from the user's checking account. Instead of an interest rate, users are charged a minimal fee for the transaction. Be sure to check with your bank to confirm that your debit card will be accepted in other states – debit cards from large commercial banks can often be used worldwide.

Carry copies of your credit card numbers separately from the cards. If you lose your credit cards or they get stolen, contact the company immediately. Following are toll-free numbers of the main credit card companies for reporting lost or stolen cards. Contact your bank if you lose your ATM card.

American Express	☎ 800-992-3404
Diners Club	☎ 800-234-6377
Discover	☎ 800-347-2683
MasterCard	☎ 800-826-2181
Visa	☎ 800-336-8472

International Transfers

You can instruct your bank back home to send you a draft. Specify the city, bank and branch to which you want your money directed, or ask your home bank to tell you where a suitable one is, and make sure you get the details right. The procedure is easier if you've authorized someone back home to access your account.

Money sent by telegraphic transfer should reach you within a week; by mail allow at least two weeks. When it arrives it will most likely be converted into local currency – you can take it as cash or buy traveler's checks. This type of transfer carries higher fees than sending a bank draft.

You can also transfer money by American Express, Thomas Cook or Western Union, though the latter has fewer international offices.

Currency

The US dollar is divided into 100 cents (¢). Coins come in denominations of 1¢ (penny), 5¢ (nickel), 10¢ (dime), 25¢ (quarter), and the seldom seen 50¢ (half dollar). Quarters are the most commonly used coins in vending machines and parking meters, so it's handy to have a stash of them. Notes, commonly called bills, come in $1, $2, $5, $10, $20, $50, and $100 denominations – $2 bills are rare, but perfectly legal. There is also a $1 coin that the government has tried unsuccessfully to bring into mass circulation; you may get them as change from ticket and stamp machines. Be aware that they look similar to quarters.

Currency Exchange

Outside the cities, most banks throughout the Rocky Mountain region will probably not have facilities for exchanging exchange cash or traveler's checks in major foreign currencies. So it's best to take care of this before heading out to the outlying areas. Thomas Cook, American Express, and exchange windows in airports offer exchange (although you'll get a better rate at a bank).

At press time, exchange rates were:

Australia	A$1	=	US$0.58
Canada	C$1	=	US$0.66
France	FF10	=	US$1.80
Germany	DM1	=	US$0.60
Hong Kong	HK$10	=	US$1.30
Japan	¥100	=	US$0.74
New Zealand	NZ$1	=	US$0.49
United Kingdom	UK£1	=	US$1.69

Tipping

Tipping is expected in restaurants and better hotels, and by taxi drivers, hairdressers and baggage carriers. In restaurants, wait staff are paid minimal wages and rely upon tips for their livelihoods. Tip 15% unless the service is terrible (in which case a complaint to the manager is warranted) or 20% if the service is great. Never tip in fast-food, take-out or buffet-style restaurants where you serve yourself.

Taxi drivers expect 10% and hairdressers get 15% if their service is satisfactory. Baggage carriers (skycaps in airports, attendants in hotels) get $1 for the first bag and 50¢ for each additional bag. In budget hotels (which don't have attendants anyway) tips are not expected.

Special Deals

The USA is probably the most promotion-oriented society on Earth. Though the bargaining common in many other countries is not generally accepted in the US, you can work angles to cut costs. For example, at hotels in the off-season, casually and respectfully mentioning a competitor's rate may prompt a manager to lower the quoted rate. Artisans may consider a negotiated price for large purchases. Discount coupons are widely available – check circulars in Sunday papers, at supermarkets, tourist offices, or chambers of commerce.

Supermarkets also run specials on tickets for local attractions, especially 'family' attractions, like amusement parks or professional sporting events (usually baseball). If there is skiing within a two-hour drive, cheap lift tickets are often available at supermarkets as well.

Taxes & Refunds

Almost everything you pay for in the USA is taxed. Occasionally, the tax is included in the advertised price (eg, plane tickets, gas, drinks in a bar, and entrance tickets for museums or theaters). Restaurant meals and drinks, accommodations, and most other purchases are taxed, and this is added to the advertised cost. When inquiring about hotel or motel rates, be sure to ask whether taxes are included or not. Sales and service tax rates are set by state and local governments, and thus vary from place to place.

Unless otherwise stated, the prices given in this book don't reflect local taxes.

POST & COMMUNICATIONS
Postal Rates

Postage rates increase every few years. Currently, rates for 1st-class mail within the USA are 32¢ for letters up to 1 ounce (23¢ for each additional ounce) and 20¢ for postcards.

International airmail rates (except to Canada and Mexico) are 60¢ for a half-ounce letter, $1 for a 1-ounce letter and 40¢ for each additional half ounce. International postcard rates are 50¢. Letters to Canada are 46¢ for a half-ounce letter, 52¢ for a 1-ounce letter and 40¢ for a postcard. Letters to Mexico are 40¢ for a half-ounce letter, 46¢ for a 1-ounce letter and 35¢ for a postcard. Aerogrammes are 50¢.

The cost for parcels airmailed anywhere within the USA is $3 for 2 pounds or less, increasing by $1 per pound up to $6 for 5 pounds. For heavier items, rates differ according to the distance mailed. Books, periodicals and computer disks can be sent by a cheaper 4th-class rate.

Sending Mail

If you have the correct postage, you can drop your mail into any blue mail box. However, to send a package 16 oz or larger, you must bring it to a post office. If you need to buy stamps or weigh your mail, go to the nearest post office. The addresses of each town's main post office is given in the text. In addition, larger towns have branch post offices and post office centers in some supermarkets and drug stores. For the address of the nearest, call the main post office listed under 'Postal Service' in the US Government section in the white pages of the telephone directory.

Usually, post offices in main towns are open weekdays from 8 am to 5 pm, and Saturday 8 am to 3 pm, but it all depends on the branch.

Receiving Mail

You can have mail sent to you c/o General Delivery at any post office that has its own zip (postal) code. Mail is usually held for 10 days before it's returned to sender; you might request your correspondents to write 'hold for arrival' on their letters. Alternatively, have mail sent to the local representative of American Express or Thomas Cook, which provide mail service for their customers.

Telephone

All phone numbers within the USA consist of a three-digit area code followed by a seven-digit local number. If you are calling locally, just dial the seven-digit number. If you are calling long distance either from within the United States or from another country, dial 1 + the three-digit area code + the seven-digit number. To call Canada, simply dial 1 + the area code.

For local directory assistance dial ☎ 411. For directory assistance outside your area code, dial ☎ 1 + the three-digit area code of the place you want to call + 555-1212. For example, to obtain directory assistance for a toll-free number, dial ☎ 1-800-555-1212.

Area codes for places outside the region are listed in telephone directories. Be aware that due to skyrocketing demand for phone numbers (for faxes, cellular phones, etc), some metropolitan areas are being divided into multiple new area codes. These changes might not be reflected in older phone books. When in doubt, ask the operator.

The 800 or 888 area code is designated for toll-free numbers within the USA and sometimes from Canada as well. These calls are free. (If you are dialing locally, the toll-free number is sometimes not available.) It's common for organizations and businesses to change their 800 numbers, so if you try a number that's no longer in service or that has been picked up by another company, call ☎ 800-555-1212 and request the company's new number.

The 900 area code is designated for calls for which the caller pays at a premium rate – phone sex, horoscopes, jokes, etc.

Local calls usually cost 25¢ at pay phones, although occasional private phones may charge more. Long-distance rates vary depending on the destination and which telephone company you use – call the operator (☎ 0) for rate information. Don't ask the operator to put your call through, however, because operator-assisted calls are much more expensive than direct-dial calls. Generally, nights (11 pm to 8 am), all day Saturday and from 8 am to 5 pm Sunday are the cheapest times to call (60% discount). Evenings (5 to 11 pm, Sunday to Friday) are mid-priced (35% discount). Weekday calls from 8 am to 5 pm are full-priced calls within the USA.

Many businesses use letters instead of numbers for their telephone numbers in an attempt to make it snappy and memorable. Sometimes it works, but sometimes it is difficult to decipher the letters on the keys. If you can't read the letters, here they are: 2 – ABC; 3 – DEF; 4 – GHI; 5 – JKL; 6 – MNO; 7 – PRS; 8 – TUV; 9 – WXY. The number 1 has no letters assigned it, and there are no Qs or Zs on the keys.

International Calls To make an international call direct, dial 011, then the country code, followed by the area code and the phone number. You may need to wait as long as 45 seconds for the ringing to start. International rates vary depending on the time of day and the destination. Call the operator (☎ 0) for rates. The first minute is always more expensive than extra minutes.

Hotel Phones Many hotels (especially the more expensive ones) add a service charge of 50¢ to $1 for each local call made from a room phone and they also have hefty surcharges for long-distance calls. Public pay phones, which can be found in most lobbies, are always cheaper. You can pump in quarters, use a phone credit card, or make collect calls from pay phones.

Phone Debit Cards A new long distance alternative is phone debit cards, which allow purchasers to pay in advance, with access through a toll-free number. In amounts of $5, $10, $20 and $50, these are available from Western Union, machines in some supermarkets, convenience stores and some other sources.

When using phone credit cards, be cautious of people watching you dial in the numbers – thieves will memorize numbers and use your card to make phone calls to all corners of the Earth.

TTY Teletypewriter (TTY) telephones consist of a keyboard and a visual display, and are designed for those who are deaf, hearing impaired or who have speech disabilities. More and more government agencies (including national parks) are operating TTY numbers, although there is unfortunately no national directory assistance service. However, local phone books usually list TTY numbers where available and detail area services in the front pages that deal with phone services. TTY is also sometimes referred to as TDD, telephone device for deaf people.

In the Rocky Mountain states, several telecommunications relay services help TTY callers, relaying calls between persons using TTY and ordinary phone users. These agencies can also usually handle queries about TTY facilities in the area.

Colorado Vocational Rehabilitation Services
   ☎ 303-894-2650
Wyoming Telecommunications Relay Service
   ☎ 307-777-5634, 800-452-1408
Montana Telecommunications Access Program
   ☎ 406-444-1335, 800-833-8503

Fax, Telegraph & Email

Fax machines are easy to find in the USA, at shipping companies like Mail Boxes Etc, photocopy services and hotel business service centers, but be prepared to pay high prices (over $1 a page). Telegraphs can be sent from Western Union (☎ 800-325-6000). Email is quickly becoming a preferred method of communication; however, unless you have a laptop and modem that can be plugged into a telephone socket, it's difficult to get online.

Hotel business service centers may provide connections, and trendy restaurants and cafes sometimes offer Internet service as well. Cheaper motels often only allow credit or phone card long-distance calls, which can be a hassle if your internet access number is not local – some dial-up software does allow for making credit card calls however.

BOOKS

The western USA has long been a popular subject for writers. In recent years, the focus has shifted from cowboys and Indians stereotypes to more complex and sophisticated assessments of the region and its place in national history and politics. Such topics as women's history, urban development and environmental degradation through mining, forestry and agriculture have crept into the forefront.

Many of the books below are widely available throughout the region, in commercial bookstores as well as those associated with the NPS, the USFS and museums.

Geography, Environment & Natural History

The Great Gates is a comprehensive geographic history of Rocky Mountain passes by one of Western America's best storytellers, Marshall Sprague.

Rocky Mountain Plants by Ruth Ashton Nelson is a good source on Rocky Mountain flora.

Rocky Mountain Mammals is a definitive work by David M Armstrong.

From Grassland to Glacier is an indispensable introduction to Colorado's ecosystems, authored by Cornelia Fleischer Mutel & John C Emerick.

Roadside Geology of Colorado, part of a popular series, is written by Halka Chronic, and makes an easy to read guide for amateur rockheads.

For Everything There Is a Season: The Sequence of Natural Events in the Grand Teton-Yellowstone Area by Frank G Craighead, Jr, offers an interpretive naturalist's account of Greater Yellowstone and its environment.

The Greater Yellowstone Ecosystem: Redefining America's Wilderness Heritage, an edited collection by Robert B Keiter and Mark S Boyce, tackles controversial issues like fire ecology and environmental policy, and wildlife conservation and reintroduction.

Yellowstone Wildlife: A Watcher's Guide is by Todd Wilkinson.

Roadside Geology of Wyoming by Dave R Lage-
son & Darwin R Spearing is a good companion on the highway.

Rising from the Plains by John McPhee deftly
interweaves the narrative of a pioneer woman's journal with the achievements and ideas
of her geologist son to offer a highly read-
able account of the Wyoming landscape's
evolution.

Idaho Wildlife Viewing Guide by Leslie Benjamin Carpenter is an outstanding field guide.

Roadside Geology of Idaho by David D Alt &
Donald W Hyndman is a guide to the complex geology of the Gem State.

History

The Oxford History of the American West, edited
by Clyde Milner II, Carol A O'Connor &
Martha A Sandweiss, critically reevaluates
the stereotyped Western experience of cowboys and Indians, and provides new perspectives in topics like environmental and labor
history, Western literature and popular
culture.

It's Your Misfortune and None of My Own: A
New History of the American West is another
revisionist view of the modern West, by
Richard White.

Exploring the West by Herman J Viola traces the
routes and recounts the experiences of Lewis
and Clark, Pike, Frémont, Powell, King and
many others.

A Colorado History by Carl Ubbelohde, Maxine
Benson & Duane A Smith is a comprehensive work that follows a familiar chronological outline.

One Man's West sees Colorado's preeminent historian, David Lavender, look to his own
cowboy past as well as that of the state.

The Magnificent Mountain Women: Adventures
in the Colorado Rockies, by Janet Robertson
(who herself has climbed all 54 of Colorado's 14,000-foot peaks), provides a broad-
ranging account of pioneer women and
includes plenty of good photographs.

Ski Tracks in the Rockies by Abbot Fay recounts
the history of skiing in Colorado, beginning
with pioneers using 'Norwegian snowshoes'
to move about in mountain mining camps.

Wyoming by TA Larson is the standard history of
the state.

The Yellowstone Story (2 volumes) by Aubrey L
Haines is a history of our first national park.

Montana: An Uncommon Land is a well-
rounded, easy to follow history book by K
Ross Toole, a professor at U of M who is

considered Montana's foremost contemporary historian.

This House of Sky, Ivan Doig's family saga that
rides a fine line between fact and fiction, is
the best portrayal of Montana's history, attitude and perspective.

A Traveler's Companion to Montana History by
Carroll Van West, is a good roadside read.

Idaho for the Curious by Cort Conley is the
single best guide to the history of Idaho.

River of No Return by Johnny Carrey & Cort
Conley is a history of settlement in the
Salmon River valley.

Native Americans

Indian Country is a modern classic by one of
America's most eloquent writers on Native
American issues, Peter Matthiessen.

Indian Tribes of the Northern Rockies by Adolf
& Beverly Hungry Wolf is a small but interesting collection of narratives and tales.

Roads to Center Place by Kathryn Gabriel
explains how Colorado's Ancestral Puebloan
sites like Chimney Rock, Mesa Verde and
Hovenweep were related to a broader Native
American culture in the Southwest.

West of the Divide: Voices from a Ranch and a
Reservation recounts life amid the Ute
mountain tribe as observed by reporter Jim
Carrier.

The Arapaho by famed anthropologist Alfred
Kroeber and The Northern Shoshone by
Kroeber's colleague Robert Lowie offer
classic ethnographies of the Native Americans living on the Wind River Reservation.

Idaho Indians: Tribal Histories by the Native
American Committee, Idaho Centennial
Commission, is written for a youthful audience, but is still a good brief source of information on regional Native America.

Travel Guides

The Smithsonian Guide to Historic America: The
Rocky Mountain States, by Jerry Camarillo
Dunn, is rich in detail and awash with color
photographs; it covers Colorado, Wyoming,
Montana and Idaho.

The Traveler's Guide to the Oregon Trail by
Julie Fanselow is worth consideration for
those following the historical pathways
across the region.

The Complete Guide to Colorado's Wilderness
Areas by Mark Pearson with color photos by
John Felder, has details about the state's
extensive backcountry opportunities.

100 Hikes In Colorado by Scott S Warren includes day hikes and backpack trips for casual or serious hikers.

8000 Miles of Dirt: A Backroads Travel Guide to Wyoming by Dan Lewis is good for those who want to leave the highways completely behind.

Guide to the Wyoming Mountains & Wilderness Areas is a good guide for backcountry travelers by Orrin H & Lorraine G Bonney.

The Hiker's Guide to Montana written by Bill Schneider and researched by 30 veteran hikers, makes travel through some of the more remote regions of the state worthwhile.

Bitterroot to Beartooth by Ruth Rudner is a must for hikers who want to explore southwest Montana.

Bookstores

Previously only large cities like Denver and university towns like Boulder and Laramie had good bookstores, but in recent years many small towns have acquired better outlets, in part because of increased interest in Western history and related topics. Noteworthy bookstores are listed in this book under the Information heading for each town or city.

Many NPS, USFS and BLM visitor centers and offices now carry excellent selections of books and maps on flora, fauna, and local and regional subjects. The nonprofit Rocky Mountain Nature Association, Rocky Mountain National Park, Estes Park, CO 80517 (☎ 970-586-0108), carries a comprehensive selection of maps, hiking guides and books on animals, plants, geology and natural history. They operate retail outlets at popular USFS, NPS and State Park offices. If considering purchases over $100, you should spend $15 to join the RMNA – members receive a 15% discount on book orders.

ONLINE SERVICES

The state governments and tourist offices all have websites, usually with hyperlinks allowing you to access more specific and detailed information on destinations, accommodations, attractions, etc. In addition, each state has hundreds of sites and homepages, run by local chambers of commerce, resorts and small businesses.

Since websites tend to come and go, we've limited the selection in this book to those which look likely to stay around and be kept up to date. The site addresses are listed with the destination or organization.

If you want to do some predeparture research or planning on the World Wide Web, the best way to start would be to log on to one of the various search engines (Yahoo! seems to be one of the best for recreation and tourism) and do a keyword search for your destination or activity. Remember that combining terms to narrow your search (eg, Breckenridge+mountain biking) can prevent you from facing a list of several hundred search items, some of which may only be marginally related to your area of interest.

FILMS

Though most westerns have been filmed in the dramatic canyon and desert scenery of Utah, many productions have been shot farther north. In recent years the Rockies have served as locations for a range of films that step out of the Western, and sometimes even Hollywood, mold.

Anthony Mann's *The Naked Spur* (1953) tells the tale of an embittered Civil War veteran who joins up with two dubious partners on a bounty hunt for a murderer. Nominated for an Oscar for best writing, the film was shot in Durango and stars Jimmy Stewart, Janet Leigh and Robert Ryan. Filmed in Montrose and Durango, Nery Hathaway's *True Grit* (1969) stars John Wayne as the gruff Rooster Cogburn, who aids a young girl in her search to find the man who killed her father. Moving to more contemporary Hollywood offerings, Ridley Scott's *Thelma & Louise* (1991), starring Susan Sarandon and Geena Davis as two small-town women who trade in their domestic lives for an odyssey of adventure and violence on the road, includes a good amount of Colorado scenery. Stanley Kubrick directed *The Shining* (1980) based on Stephen King's bestselling novel. Starring Jack Nicholson, this horror classic was filmed largely at Estes Park's famed Stanley Hotel. Veering a bit away from the mainstream, *Things to Do in Denver When You're Dead* (1995), directed by Gary Fleder, is a well-made film noir/gangster flick that chooses the unlikely setting of Colorado's capital, and stars Andy Garcia, Christoper Walken and Treat Williams.

George Steven's *Shane* (1953), starring Alan Ladd, is a classic tale of an embattled gunfighter defending homesteaders from an evil cattle baron. Shot around Jackson Hole, it may now seem a bit clichéd, but it's beautifully filmed and still holds its place as a classic Western. Steven Spielberg's *Close Encounters of the Third Kind* (1977) surmises on Earth's first contact with aliens, but prominently features Wyoming landmark Devils Tower. Richard Lang's *Mountain Men* (1980), starring Charlton Heston and Brian Keith, is a rather dull film about trappers and Indians, but gives a good feel for the beauty of the Grand Tetons. For a look at Wyoming's 'alien' landscape, check out the high-budget (but sometimes silly) *Starship Troopers*, Paul Verhoeven's 1997 sci-fi film about war between humans and interstellar insects that was shot in Hell's Half Acre, near Casper.

The influence of Montana on the national popular imagination extends even to Hollywood, and directors have turned many a tale of the Old West into showcases for Jimmy Stewart or John Wayne. Thomas McGuane's comic novel *Rancho Deluxe* (1975), about modern-day rustlers, was made into a film starring Jeff Bridges and Harry Dean Stanton. A more offbeat Western is Arthur Penn's delightful *Little Big Man* (1970), starring Dustin Hoffman as Jack Crabb, who at age 100 recounts his life as Indian captive, gunslinger and scout for General George Custer at Little Big Horn. In the past few years, fishing poles have replaced guns and Montana's rivers have replaced Main St as the site of the final showdown. Robert Redford directed a 1992 film adaptation of Norman Maclean's short story *A River Runs Through It*, which exposed the deep-seated truth that fishing is intertwined in all facets of Montana's existence, including the arts. *The River*

Wild (1994, director Curtiss Hanson) highlights a rather dangerous version of whitewater rafting. *Powwow Highway* (1989), directed by Jonathan Wacks, takes a sometimes hard-edged look at the challenges of Native Americans trying to preserve their cultural identity in modern America. Though also shot in New Mexico and Sheridan, WY, the story is set (and was partially filmed) on Montana's Northern Cheyenne Reservation.

King Vidor's *Northwest Passage* (1940), starring Spencer Tracy, Robert Young and Walter Brennan, is a typical cowboys and Indians story, filmed in and around McCall. While the clichés may be offensive, the cinematography (which won an Oscar in 1941) is excellent. Clint Eastwood's 1985 *Pale Rider* somewhat redresses the cultural imbalance with its revisionist look at frontier mining life. Though set in California, some filming was done in the Sawtooth National Recreation Area. Gus Van Sant's 1991 film *My Own Private Idaho*, an offbeat tale of two young male hustlers starring River Phoenix and Keanu Reeves, was shot in the state and was popular with fans of arty, non-mainstream film.

PHOTOGRAPHY & VIDEO
Film & Equipment

Print film is widely available at supermarkets and discount drugstores. Color print film has a greater latitude than color slide film; this means that print film can handle a wider range of light and shadow than slide film. However, slide film, particularly the slower speeds (under 100 ASA), has better resolution than print film. Like B&W film, slide film is rarely sold outside of major cities and when available is expensive.

Film can be damaged by excessive heat, so don't leave your camera and film in the car on a hot summer's day and avoid placing your camera on the dash while you are driving.

It's worth carrying a spare battery to avoid disappointment if your camera dies in the middle of nowhere. If you're buying a new camera for your trip do so several weeks before you leave and practice using it.

Drugstores are a good place to get your film cheaply processed. If you drop it off by noon, you can usually pick it up the next day. A roll of 100 ASA 35mm color film with 24 exposures will cost about $6 to get processed.

If you want your pictures back right away, you can find one-hour processing services listed in the yellow pages under 'Photo Processing.' The prices tend to creep up past $10, so be prepared to pay. Many one-hour photo finishers operate in the larger cities, and a few can also be found near tourist attractions.

Video Systems

The USA uses the National Television System Committee (NTSC) color TV standard, which is not compatible with other standards (PAL or SECAM) used in Africa, Europe, Asia and Australia unless converted.

Restrictions

About the only places you'll find limits on photography are military installations and at Native American rituals. In the case of the former you really needn't worry unless there are specific warning signs: if not, go ahead and snap a shot of that missile silo or jet fighter taking off. If you wish to photograph or videotape Native American pow-wows and ceremonial dances special permits often must be obtained from a local tribal council office.

Airport Security

All passengers on flights have to pass their luggage through X-ray machines. Technology as it is today doesn't jeopardize lower speed film, so you shouldn't have to worry about cameras going through the machine. If you are carrying high speed (1600 ASA and above) film, then you may want to carry film and cameras with you and ask the X-ray inspector to visually check your film.

NEWSPAPERS & MAGAZINES
Colorado

Although the *Denver Post* is generally acknowledged to be the most influential

paper in the region, the tabloid-format *Rocky Mountain News* is Colorado's oldest newspaper, founded in 1859 by William Byers. Articles in both are remarkably similar: occasionally one finds examples of good local reporting, while news beyond state lines come strictly from the wire services. The *Post's* 'Ski & Snow' supplement offers plenty of skiing bargains, making the bulky mid-November Sunday issue especially worthwhile. Both papers are available statewide.

Neither of Denver's staid dailies can match *Westword*, a free weekly, for witty information on events and entertainment. Their annual 'Best of Denver,' published in late June, is a fat listing of favorite places to eat, drink and be merry. It leaves no stone unturned – how about the 'Best Gay Bar for Porn-Star Wannabes' or the 'Best Rattlesnake' menu offering or the 'Best Way to Tick Off Coloradans for Family Values'?

Wyoming

Wyoming's only statewide newspaper is the influential *Casper Star-Tribune*, which enjoys a wide distribution in part to its home city's central location. It does a good job of covering the state, especially in its 'Border to Border' section, and can be critical of politicians. The next largest newspaper is the Cheyenne-based *Wyoming Tribune-Eagle*.

Montana

Montana has three large-circulation newspapers: the *Billings Gazette*, *Great Falls Tribune* and the *Missoulian*. Each has an opinionated following. Billings' paper reflects the conservative attitudes of ranchers and oil industry leaders, as does the Great Falls daily, though the former does a better job of covering national and international events. The *Missoulian*, influenced by the city's progressive university community, has been labeled 'eco-facist' by its eastern counterparts, and is known for its good state news coverage.

Published quarterly, *Big Sky Journal* features articles by Montana natives covering history, art, wildlife and modern problems facing Montanans. It's sold ($6) at good newsstands, bookstores and airports.

Idaho

The Boise-based *The Idaho Statesman* is the mainstream daily newspaper.

RADIO & TV

All rental cars have car radios and travelers can choose from hundreds of stations. Most radio stations have a range of less than 100 miles, and in and near major cities scores of stations crowd the airwaves with a wide variety of music and entertainment. In rural areas, be prepared for a predominance of country & western music, local news and talk radio.

National Public Radio (NPR) features a more level-headed approach to discussion, music and sophisticated news on the FM band. NPR's *Morning Edition* and its afternoon *All Things Considered* are both genuinely informative news programs. Public radio stations carrying news-oriented National Public Radio (NPR) can usually be found in the lower numbers of the radio band.

All the major TV networks have affiliated stations throughout the USA. These include ABC, CBS, NBC, FOX and PBS. Cable News Network (CNN), a cable channel, provides continuous, if rather shallow, news coverage.

TIME

Colorado, Wyoming and Montana are all on Mountain Standard Time, seven hours behind GMT/UTC. Most of Idaho also lies within the Mountain time zone except for most of Northern Central Idaho and the Panhandle, which are on Pacific time, eight hours behind GMT/UTC. All four states switch to Mountain Daylight Time (or Pacific Daylight Time) one hour later, from the last Sunday of April to the last Saturday of October.

ELECTRICITY & MEASUREMENTS

In the USA voltage is 110V and the plugs have two (flat) or three (two flat, one

National Public Radio

National Public Radio covers most of the Rocky Mountain states region, thanks to repeater transmitters in mountainous areas.

Colorado NPR Stations

Alamosa	KRZA, 88.7 FM
Aspen	KAJX, 91.5 FM
Boulder	KGNU, 88.5 FM
Carbondale (Glenwood Springs)	KDNK, 90.5 FM
Colorado Springs	KRCC, 91.5 FM
Cortez	KSJD, 91.5 FM
Crested Butte	KBUT, 90.3 FM
Denver	KCFR, 90.1 FM
	KUVO, 89.3 FM
Grand Junction	KPRN, 89.5 FM
Greeley	KUNC, 91.5 FM
Ignacio	KSUT, 91.3 FM
Paonia	KVNF, 90.9 FM
Telluride	KOTO, 91.7 FM
Vail	KPRE, 90.1 FM

Wyoming NPR Stations

Jackson	KUWJ, 90.3 FM
Laramie	KUWR, 91.9 FM
Rock Springs	KUWZ, 90.5 FM

Montana NPR Stations

Billings	KEMC, 91.7 FM
Bozeman	KBMC, 102.1 FM
Fort Belknap	KGVA, 88.1 FM
Great Falls	KGPR, 89.9 FM
Havre	KNMC, 90.1 FM
Miles City	KECC, 90.7 FM
Missoula	KUFM, 89.1 FM

Idaho NPR Stations

Boise	KBSU, 90.3 FM
	KBSX, 91.5 FM
McCall	KBSM, 91.7 FM
Moscow	KRFA, 91.7 FM
Rexburg	KRIC, 100.5 FM
Twin Falls	KBSW, 91.7 FM

round) pins. Plugs with three pins don't fit into a two hole socket, but adapters are easy to buy at hardware or drugstores.

Distances are in feet (ft), yards (yds) and miles (mi). Three feet equals one yard (.914 meters); 1760 yards or 5280 feet are one mile. Dry weights are in ounces (oz), pounds (lbs) and tons (16 ounces are one pound; 2000 pounds are one ton), but liquid measures differ from dry measures. One pint equals 16 fluid ounces; two pints equals one quart, a common measure for liquids like milk, which is also sold in half gallons (two quarts) and gallons (four quarts). Gasoline is dispensed by the US gallon, which is about 20% less than the Imperial gallon. Pints and quarts are also 20% less than Imperial ones. Refer to the chart on the inside back cover to make conversions to metric measurements.

LAUNDRY
There are self-service, coin-operated laundry facilities in most towns of any size and in better campgrounds. Washing a load costs about $1.50 and drying it another $1.50 to $2. Some laundries have attendants who will wash, dry and fold your clothes for you for an additional charge. To find a laundry, look under 'Laundries' or 'Laundries – Self-Service' in the yellow pages of the telephone directory. Dry cleaners are also listed under 'Laundries' or 'Cleaners.'

HEALTH
For most foreign visitors no immunizations are required for entry, though cholera and yellow fever vaccinations may be required of travelers from areas with a history of those diseases. There are no unexpected health dangers, excellent medical attention is readily available, and the only real health concern is cost: a collision with the medical system can cause severe injuries to your financial state.

Hospitals and medical centers, walk-in clinics and referral services are easily found throughout the region.

In a serious emergency, call ☎ 911 for an ambulance to take you to the nearest hospital's emergency room. But note that ER charges in the USA are incredibly expensive.

Predeparture Preparations
Make sure you're healthy before you start traveling. If you are embarking on a long

trip, make sure your teeth are in good shape. If you wear glasses, take a spare pair and your prescription. You can get new spectacles made up quickly and competently for $100 to $200, depending on the prescription and frame you choose. If you require a particular medication, take an adequate supply and bring a prescription in case you lose your medication. In the US just going to a doctor for a new prescription is costly, as is medication.

Health Insurance A travel insurance policy to cover theft, lost tickets and medical problems is a good idea, especially in the USA, where some hospitals will refuse care without evidence of insurance. There are a wide variety of policies and your travel agent will have recommendations. International student travel policies handled by STA Travel and other student travel organizations are usually a good value. Some policies offer lower and higher medical expenses options, and the higher one is chiefly for countries like the USA with extremely high medical costs. Check the fine print.

Some policies specifically exclude 'dangerous activities' like scuba diving, motorcycling and even trekking. If these activities are on your agenda, avoid this sort of policy.

You may prefer a policy that pays doctors or hospitals directly, rather than your having to pay first and claim later. If you have to claim later, keep *all* documentation, and check to see what type of details your insurance provider will require, which sometimes includes proof of the currency exchange rate on the day of your medical visit. Some policies ask you to call back (reverse charges) to a center in your home country for an immediate assessment of your problem.

Check whether the policy covers ambulance fees or an emergency flight home. If you have to stretch out, you will need two seats and somebody has to pay for it!

Medical Kit If you're going off the beaten path, it's wise to take along a small, straightforward medical kit. This should include:

- Aspirin, acetaminophen or Panadol, for pain or fever
- Antihistamine (such as Benadryl), which is useful as a decongestant for colds; to ease the itch from allergies, insect bites or stings; or to help prevent motion sickness
- Kaolin preparation (Pepto-Bismol), Immodium or Lomotil, for stomach upsets
- Antiseptic, mercurochrome and antibiotic powder or similar 'dry' spray, for cuts and grazes
- Calamine lotion, to ease irritation from bites or stings
- Bandages, for minor injuries
- Scissors, tweezers and a thermometer (note that airlines prohibit mercury thermometers)
- Insect repellent, sunscreen lotion, lip balm and water purification tablets

Food & Water
Care in what you eat and drink is the most important health rule; stomach upsets are the most common travel health problem but the majority of these upsets will be relatively minor. American standards of cleanliness in places serving food and drink are very high.

Bottled drinking water, both carbonated and noncarbonated, is widely available in the USA. Tap water is almost always OK to drink; ask locally.

Everyday Health
Normal body temperature is 98.6°F or 37°C; more than 4°F or 2°C higher indicates a 'high' fever. The normal adult pulse rate is 60 to 80 per minute (children 80 to 100, babies 100 to 140). You should know how to take a temperature and a pulse rate.

Respiration (breathing) rate is also an indicator of illness. Count the number of breaths per minute: between 12 and 20 is normal for adults and older children (up to 30 for younger children, 40 for babies). People with a high fever or serious respiratory illness (like pneumonia) breathe more quickly than normal. More than 40 shallow breaths a minute usually means pneumonia.

Climate-Related Problems
Altitude Sickness This is something to particularly watch out for in this region. Acute mountain sickness (AMS) occurs at high altitude and can be fatal. In the thinner atmosphere of the high mountains, lack of oxygen causes many individuals to suffer headaches, nausea, nose bleeds, shortness of breath, physical weakness and other symptoms that can lead to very serious consequences, especially if combined with heat exhaustion, sunburn or hypothermia. Most people recover within a few hours or days. If the symptoms persist it is imperative to descend to lower elevations. For mild cases, everyday painkillers such as aspirin will relieve symptoms until the body adapts. Avoid smoking, drinking alcohol, exercising strenuously or eating heavily.

There is no hard and fast rule as to how high is too high: AMS has been fatal at altitudes of 10,000 feet, although it is much more common above 11,500 feet. It is always wise to sleep at a lower altitude than the greatest height reached during the day. A number of other measures can also prevent or minimize AMS:

- Ascend slowly – have frequent rest days, spending two to three nights at each rise of 1000m. If you reach a high altitude by trekking, acclimatization takes place gradually and you are less likely to be affected than if you fly directly to high altitude.
- Drink extra fluids. Mountain air is dry and cold and you lose moisture as you breathe.
- Eat light, high-carbohydrate meals for more energy.
- Avoid alcohol, which may increase the risk of dehydration.
- Avoid sedatives.

Heat Exhaustion Dehydration or salt deficiency can cause heat exhaustion. This can especially be a problem during the dry, hot summer in the Rocky Mountain region, particularly the lower elevations.

Take time to acclimatize to high temperatures and make sure that you get enough liquids. Salt deficiency is characterized by fatigue, lethargy, headaches, giddiness and muscle cramps. Salt tablets may help. Vomiting or diarrhea can also deplete your liquid and salt levels. Anhydrotic heat exhaustion, caused by the inability to sweat, is quite rare; unlike the other forms of heat exhaustion it is likely to strike people who have been in a hot climate for some time, rather than newcomers. Always carry and use a water bottle on long trips.

Heat Stroke Long, continuous periods of exposure to high temperatures can leave you vulnerable to this serious, sometimes fatal, condition, which occurs when the body's heat-regulating mechanism breaks down and body temperature rises to dangerous levels. Avoid excessive alcohol intake or strenuous activity when you first arrive in a hot climate.

Symptoms include feeling unwell, lack of perspiration and a high body temperature of 102° to 105°F (39° to 41°C). Hospitalization is essential for extreme cases, but meanwhile get out of the sun, remove clothing, cover with a wet sheet or towel and fan continually.

Hypothermia Changeable weather at high altitudes can leave you vulnerable to exposure: after dark, temperatures in the mountains or desert can drop from balmy to below freezing; likewise, a sudden soaking and high winds can lower your body temperature too rapidly. If possible, avoid traveling alone; partners are more likely to avoid hypothermia successfully. If you must travel alone, especially when hiking, be sure someone knows your route and when you expect to return.

Seek shelter when bad weather is unavoidable. Both woolen clothing and synthetics, which retain warmth even when wet, are superior to cottons. A quality sleeping bag is a worthwhile investment, although goose down loses much of its insulating qualities when wet. Carry high-energy, easily digestible snacks like chocolate or dried fruit.

Get hypothermia victims out of the wind or rain, remove their clothing if it's wet and replace it with dry, warm clothing. Give them hot liquids – not alcohol – and high-calorie, easily digestible food. In advanced stages it may be necessary to place victims in warm sleeping bags and get in with them. Do not rub victims but place them near a fire or, if possible, in a warm (not hot) bath.

Sunburn In the Rocky Mountains' high altitude areas it can take as little as 10 minutes to get a painful sunburn: longer exposure can lead to more serious burns. Be sure to take along a powerful sunscreen and apply to any exposed areas before hiking, biking, skiing or engaging in any outdoor activities. A hat is also a good idea, and zinc cream offers extra protection for your nose and lips.

Infectious Diseases

Diarrhea A change of water, food or climate can cause the runs; diarrhea caused by contaminated food or water is more serious, but it's unlikely in the USA. Despite all your precautions you may still have a mild bout of traveler's diarrhea from unfamiliar food or drink. Dehydration is the main danger with any diarrhea, particularly for children, who can dehydrate quite quickly. Fluid replacement remains the mainstay of management. Weak black tea with a little sugar, soda water or soft drinks diluted 50% with water are all good. With severe diarrhea a rehydrating solution is necessary to replace minerals and salts. Such solutions, like Pedialyte, are available at pharmacies.

Giardiasis Commonly known as Giardia, and sometimes 'Beaver Fever,' this intestinal parasite is present in contaminated water. Giardia routinely contaminates apparently pristine rushing streams in the backcountry, so avoid drinking from them unless you have an advanced filter system: it's just not worth the risk.

Symptoms are stomach cramps, nausea, a bloated stomach, watery, foul-smelling diarrhea and frequent gas. Giardia can appear several weeks after exposure to the parasite; symptoms may disappear for a few days and then return, a pattern which may continue. Tinidazole, known as Fasigyn, or metronidazole (Flagyl) are the recommended drugs for treatment. Either can be used in a single treatment dose. Antibiotics are useless.

Hepatitis Hepatitis is a general term for inflammation of the liver. There are many causes of this condition: poor sanitation, contact with infected blood products, drugs, alcohol and contact with an infected person are but a few. The symptoms are fever, chills, headache, fatigue and feelings of weakness and aches and pains, followed by loss of appetite, nausea, vomiting, abdominal pain, dark urine, light-colored feces and jaundiced skin. The whites of the eyes may also turn yellow. Hepatitis A is the most common strain. You should seek medical advice, but there is not much you can do apart from resting, drinking lots of fluids, eating lightly and avoiding fatty foods. People who have had hepatitis should avoid alcohol for some time after the illness, as the liver needs time to recover. Viral hepatitis is an infection of the liver, which can have several unpleasant symptoms, or no symptoms at all, with the infected person not knowing that they have the disease.

HIV/AIDS HIV, the Human Immunodeficiency Virus, develops into AIDS, Acquired Immune Deficiency Syndrome, which is a fatal disease. Any exposure to blood, blood products or body fluids may put the individual at risk. The disease is most often transmitted through sexual contact or from dirty needles – vaccinations, acupuncture, tattooing and body piercing can be potentially as dangerous as intravenous drug use.

Fear of HIV infection should never preclude treatment for serious medical conditions. A good resource for help and information is the US Center of Disease Control AIDS hotline (☎ 800-342-2437, 800-344-7432 in Spanish). AIDS support groups are listed in the front of phone books.

Cuts, Bites & Stings
Bites & Stings Bee and wasp stings and nonpoisonous spider bites are usually painful rather than dangerous. Calamine lotion will give relief, and ice packs will reduce the pain and swelling. Bites are best avoided by not using bare hands to turn over rocks or large pieces of wood.

Cuts & Scratches Skin punctures can easily become infected in the backcountry, especially if you're sweating or getting dirty. Treat any cut with an antiseptic such as Betadine. When possible avoid bandages, which can keep wounds wet.

Poison Oak Just brushing past this plant while on a hike can cause a blistery and extremely itchy rash on bare skin, which should be washed with a strong soap (Fels Naptha is a recommended brand) immediately after exposure. Cortisone creams can lessen the itching in minor cases. Poison oak, related to poison ivy, is a tall, thin shrub with shiny three-part leaves that grows in shady, moist areas in the western USA, including the Rocky Mountain states.

Rattlesnakes Rattlesnakes are common in the desert, the plains and even in some elevated forest areas. To minimize chances of being bitten, always wear boots, socks and long trousers when walking through undergrowth where snakes may be present. Keep your hands out of holes and crevices, and be cautious when collecting firewood.

Though painful, rattlesnake bites do not cause instantaneous death, rarely kill healthy adults under any circumstances, and antivenin is usually available. Keep the victim calm and still, wrap the bitten limb tightly, as you would for a sprained ankle, and then attach a splint to immobilize it. Seek medical help; tourniquets and sucking out the poison are now discredited.

Ticks Ticks are a parasitic arachnid that may be present in brush, forest and grasslands, where hikers often get them on their legs or in their boots. Always check your body for ticks after walking through a high grass or thickly forested area. The adults suck blood from hosts by burying their head into skin, but they are often found unattached and can simply be brushed off. However, if you try to brush one off but leave the head in your skin, it increases the likelihood of infection or disease, such as Rocky Mountain spotted fever or Lyme disease.

If you do find a tick on you, remove it immediately. Using a pair of tweezers, grab it by the head and gently pull it straight out – do not twist it. (If no tweezers are available, use your fingers, but protect them from contamination with a piece of tissue or paper.) Do not touch the tick with a hot object like a match or a cigarette – this can cause it to regurgitate noxious gut substances or saliva into the wound. And do not rub oil, alcohol or petroleum jelly on it. If you get sick in the next couple of weeks, consult a doctor.

Colorado Tick Fever This is a virus spread by the Rocky Mountain wood tick, which, despite the name of the disease, may be found outside of Colorado. Anywhere from one to 300 cases are reported each year. The sickness has a three- to five-day incubation period and lasts five to 10 days on average for those ages eight to 30, and to three weeks for those over 30.

Symptoms include head and body aches, lethargy, nausea and vomiting, sensitivity to light, abdominal pain and a skin rash (rare). There is no vaccine, treatment is by antibiotics and 20% of cases require hospitalization if lasting to three weeks.

Rocky Mountain Spotted Fever This disease is rare in Colorado, but may be found in outlying areas and is caused by *Rickettsia rickessii* bacteria carried by the Rocky Mountain wood tick. Only the adult wood tick will bite, and it has to have been feeding six to 10 hours to transmit the disease.

A two- to four-day incubation period will result with symptoms like fever, spotted rash on the wrists, ankles or waist that may spread over the entire body, headache, nausea, vomiting and abdominal pain. All symptoms but fever may or may not occur, and muscle cramping is also possible.

More severe problems can develop. Treatment consists of doses of antibiotics and 20% of cases left untreated end in death. If after 12 hours of being in the woods symptoms appear, seek medical attention immediately.

Lyme Disease This disease is also spread by tick bites. It's extremely rare in the Rocky Mountain states, and more common in the Northeastern states.

WOMEN TRAVELERS
Women often face different situations when traveling than men do. Women, especially those traveling alone, need a little extra awareness of their surroundings.

The US is such a diverse and varied country that it is impossible to give advice that fits every place and every situation. People are generally friendly and happy to help travelers, and women travelers usually have a wonderful time unmarred by dangerous encounters. To ensure that this is the case, consider the following suggestions.

Exercise more vigilance when in large towns and cities than in rural areas. Try to avoid unsafe or 'bad' neighborhoods or areas. If you are unsure if an area is safe or unsafe, ask at your hotel or call the tourist office for advice. When you must go into or through unsafe areas, it is best to travel in a private vehicle (eg, car or taxi). Traveling is more dangerous at night, but in the worst areas daytime crimes occur. Carry the best available maps and familiarize yourself with them. Tourist maps can sometimes be deceiving, compressing areas that are not tourist attractions and making distances look shorter than they are. Always look confident and act like you know where you are going.

The threat of sexual assault exists in cities and, to a lesser degree, in rural areas. By avoiding vulnerable situations such as drinking, using drugs or traveling alone, you can reduce your chances of becoming a victim. While there may be less to watch out for in rural areas, men who are unaccustomed to seeing women traveling alone may still harass them. Try to avoid hiking or camping alone, especially in unfamiliar places.

To further reduce your risk of sexual assault, exercise common sense and communicate honestly, assertively, and clearly. Look people in the eye instead of looking down, letting them know you are aware of their presence. Watch for people who invade your personal space, ignore you, or try to isolate you.

Men may interpret a woman drinking alone in a bar as a bid for male company, whether a woman intends it that way or not. If the company is unwelcome, most men respect a firm, but polite, 'No thank you.' Be aware of Rohypnol or 'roofies,' a drug that can be slipped into drinks causing blackouts. Rohypnol has been used nationwide in sexual assault cases.

Do not hitchhike alone, and do not pick up hitchhikers when driving alone. If you get stuck on the road and need help, it is a good idea to have a premade sign to signal for help. Avoid getting out of your car to flag down help. Stay inside, lock the doors, turn on the hazard lights, and wait for the police to arrive. Carry the telephone number for AAA emergency road service if you are a member. When traveling in remote areas where help may not be readily available, you may want to carry a cellular telephone, if this option is available to you. If using public transportation, make sure to check the times of the last bus or train before you go out at night.

To deal with potential dangers, many women protect themselves with a whistle, mace, cayenne pepper spray, or some sort of self-defense training. Remember to have a 'get-away' plan in your head at all times. If you decide to carry a spray, contact the local police to find out about regulations and training classes. Laws regarding sprays vary from state to state, so know the laws for the region through which you are traveling. Airlines do not allow sprays on board; carrying them is a federal felony because of their combustible design.

If despite all precautions you are assaulted, call the police or ☎ 911, which connects you with the emergency operator for police, fire and ambulance services. In some rural areas where ☎ 911 is inactive, call ☎ 0 for the operator. Larger towns and cities usually have rape crisis centers and women's shelters that provide help and support. Check the telephone directory for listings or ask the police for referrals.

Resources & Organizations

The headquarters for the National Organization for Women (NOW; ☎ 202-331-0066), 1000 16th St NW, Suite 700, Washington, DC 20036, is a good resource and can refer you to state and local chapters. NOW's fully-staffed offices are in New York, Washington, DC, and Los Angeles. Dedicated volunteers run NOW's other nationwide chapters; callers to these chapters are likely to reach voicemail. Calls may be returned within a day or two. Planned Parenthood (☎ 212-541-7800), 810 7th Ave, New York, NY 10019, gives referrals to their nationwide clinics and offers advice on medical issues. Alternatively, check the yellow pages under 'Women's Organizations & Services' for local telephone numbers and additional resources.

GAY & LESBIAN TRAVELERS

In US cities and on both coasts it is easier for gay men and women to live their lives with a certain amount of openness. As you travel into the middle of the country it is much harder to be open. Gay travelers should be careful, *especially* in the rural areas where holding hands might get you bashed.

With the conservatism that prevails in the Rockies, attitudes towards gay people can sometimes be rather primitive. There are no laws prohibiting public displays of affection between same-sex couples, but don't be surprised if you're stared at, hassled and asked to leave an establishment. Bar crowds in small agricultural towns may look oddly upon two men entering together (gay or not) if they don't fit the cowboy image or have local license plates on their pickup. Even in Colorado, in many ways the most progressive of the four states, civil rights advocates had to put up a fierce fight against the anti-gay rights state Amendment 2, which threatened to strike down anti-discrimination ordinances in Denver, Boulder and Aspen. In 1994, Colorado's Supreme Court ruled that amendment unconstitutional.

Gay and lesbian groups are still targeted by conservative groups in Colorado, especially right wing religious organizations. But at the same time awareness and attitudes have improved, especially in the Denver area, which is home to a vibrant gay community and several well-run gay and lesbian groups.

You may search in vain for gay bars in Wyoming, Montana or Idaho, but you will find meetings and events hosted by gay, lesbian and bisexual groups. These are often associated with universities, so you're most likely to find such groups in college towns like Laramie, Bozeman and Missoula, and Moscow and Boise. These are also good places to pick up information on gay-friendly businesses, such as motels or B&Bs, in the area.

Resources & Organizations

The Women's Traveller with listings for lesbians and *Damron's Address Book* for men are both published by Damron Company (☎ 415-255-0404, 800-462-6654), PO Box 422458, San Francisco, CA 94142-2458. *Ferrari's Places for Women* and *Ferrari's Places for Men* are also useful. These can be found at any good bookstore as can guides to specific cities. Another useful resource is the *Gay Yellow Pages* (☎ 212-674-0120), PO Box 533, Village Station, NY 10014-0533, which has a national edition and also regional editions.

In Denver you can pick up copies of the lesbian and gay *Pink Pages* which lists gay supportive businesses in the state. Distributed around the city, you can also get a copy from the publisher's Denver office (☎ 303-433-8135), 2785 Speer Blvd, Suite 202, Denver, CO, 80211. Another business directory for the gay friendly community is

the *Rainbow List*, published by Rainbow Planet Inc (☎ 303-443-7768), PO Drawer 2270, Boulder, CO 80306-2270. These publications have handy index sections at the back with numbers for gay organizations, businesses and entertainment venues.

For further information on gay rights and lifestyles in Colorado and the Rocky Mountain region contact the Gay, Lesbian & Bisexual Community Services Center of Colorado (☎ 303-831-6268), 1245 E Colfax Ave, Suite 125, PO Box 18E, Denver, CO 80218-0140. They also have a website (tde.com/glbcscc). Another good group is Equality Colorado (☎ 303-839-5540), PO Box 300476, Denver, CO 80203 (website: www.tde.com/~equality). Equality Colorado is more political in nature, and administers the Anti-Violence Project, aimed at curbing both domestic abuse and hate crimes.

PRIDE, the national gay and lesbian organization, has offices in Helena (☎ 442-9322, 800-610-9322; PRIDE123@aol .com), PO Box 755, Helena, MT 59624, and Bozeman (☎ 406-388-1481), PO Box 7380, Bozeman, MT 59771. Gay Montana, part of the national Lambda Organization, is geared mostly towards men. Its headquarters (☎ 406-994-4636) are in the Strand Union Bldg of MSU in Bozeman.

DISABLED TRAVELERS

Public buildings (including hotels, restaurants, theaters and museums) are required by law to be wheelchair accessible and to have available restroom facilities. Public transportation services (buses, trains and taxis) must be made accessible to all, including those in wheelchairs, and telephone companies are required to provide relay operators for the hearing impaired. Many banks now provide ATM instructions in Braille and you will find audible crossing signals as well as dropped curbs at busier roadway intersections.

Some government agencies and organizations, including the National Park Service, have TTY telephone services for deaf or speech-impaired persons. For more information, see the Post & Communications section above.

Larger private and chain hotels have suites for disabled guests. Many car rental agencies offer hand-controlled models at no extra charge. All major airlines, Greyhound buses and Amtrak trains allow service animals to accompany passengers and frequently sell two-for-one packages when attendants of seriously disabled passengers are required. Airlines will also provide assistance for connecting, boarding and deplaning the flight – just ask for assistance when making your reservation. (Note: Airlines must accept wheelchairs as checked baggage and have an onboard chair available, though some advance notice may be required on smaller aircraft.) Of course, the more populous areas are generally more likely to have facilities for the disabled; it's always important to call ahead to see what is available.

For more information on transportation considerations, see the Getting There & Away chapter.

Organizations & Resources

A number of organizations and tour providers specialize in the needs of disabled travelers:

Mobility International USA – Advises disabled travelers on mobility issues. It primarily runs an educational exchange program. PO Box 10767, Eugene, OR 97440 (☎ 541-343-1284, fax 541-343-6812; miusa@igc.apc.org)

Moss Rehabilitation Hospital's Travel Information Service – 1200 W Tabor Rd, Philadelphia, PA 19141-3099 (☎ 215-456-9600, TTY 215-456-9602)

Society for the Advancement of Travel for the Handicapped (SATH) – 347 Fifth Ave, No 610, New York, NY 10016 (☎ 212-447-7284)

Twin Peaks Press – A quarterly newsletter; also publishes directories and access guides. PO Box 129, Vancouver, WA 98666 (☎ 360-694-2462, 800-637-2256)

Web pages – A good website worth finding is www.access-able.com.

SENIOR TRAVELERS

Though the age where the benefits begin varies with the attraction, travelers from 50 years and up can expect to receive cut rates and benefits. Be sure to inquire about such rates at hotels, museums and restaurants.

Visitors to national parks and campgrounds can cut costs greatly by using the Golden Age Passport, a card that allows US citizens aged 62 and over (and those traveling in the same car) free admission nationwide and a 50% reduction on camping fees. You can apply in person for any of these at any national park or regional office of the USFS or NPS or call the National Park reservation service at ☎ 800-365-2267 for information and ordering.

Organizations

Some national advocacy groups that can help in planning your travels include the following:

American Association of Retired Persons (AARP) – This is an advocacy group for Americans 50 years and older and a good resource for travel bargains. US residents can get one-year/three-year memberships for $8/20. Citizens of other countries can get same memberships for $10/24. 601 E St NW, Washington, DC 20049 (☎ 800-424-3410)

Elderhostel – This is a nonprofit organization that offers seniors the opportunity to attend academic college courses throughout the USA and Canada. The programs last one to three weeks and include meals and accommodations, and are open to people 55 years and older and their companions. 75 Federal St, Boston, MA 02110-1941 (☎ 617-426-8056)

Grand Circle Travel – This group offers escorted tours and travel information in a variety of formats and distributes a free useful booklet, 'Going Abroad: 101 Tips for Mature Travelers.' 347 Congress St, Boston, MA 02210 (☎ 617-350-7500, fax 617-350-6206)

National Council of Senior Citizens – Membership in this group (you needn't be a US citizen to apply) gives access to added Medicare insurance, a mail-order prescription service and a variety of discount information and travel-related advice. Fees are $13/30/150 for one year/three years/lifetime. 1331 F St NW, Washington, DC 20004 (☎ 202-347-8800)

TRAVEL WITH CHILDREN

The biggest problem you're likely to encounter traveling the Rockies is keep the kids occupied during those long drives or bus rides. The tourist and visitor market in the four states, especially Colorado, has long been used to catering to families. As a result, there are plenty of 'family style' restaurants that don't frown upon vocal youngsters and offer children's menus. Even the smaller motels are generally equipped with extra beds and sometimes cribs, and some of the larger places even have daycare facilities.

Most sights and attractions in the region discount admission for children. During winter, all ski resorts offer children's lift tickets (still fairly expensive), group lessons for kids and, in some of the larger places, good daycare facilities.

There isn't much of a break for transportation, although most airlines allow kids under 2 years of age to fly free if they sit on a parent's lap. Car rental agencies are not required by law to provide car seats, but if you're traveling with infants, renting them is highly recommended. Seats cost around $7 to $10 per day.

Please note that some bars and restaurants serving alcohol may only allow entry to those age 21 and over. The same applies to most casinos.

For information on enjoying travel with the young ones, read *Travel With Children* (1995) by Lonely Planet cofounder Maureen Wheeler.

USEFUL ORGANIZATIONS

For information on state-specific groups, check under the information section of the relevant state chapters.

American Automobile Association

For its members AAA ('Triple A') provides great travel information, distributes free road maps and guide books, and sells American Express traveler's checks without commission. The AAA membership card will often get you discounts for accommodations, car rental, and admission charges. If you plan to do a lot of driving – even in a rental car – it is usually worth joining the AAA. It costs around $60 for the first year and $40 for subsequent years.

Members of other auto clubs like the Automobile Association in the UK are entitled to the same services if they bring their membership cards and/or a letter of introduction.

AAA also provides emergency roadside service to members in the event of an accident, breakdown, or locking your keys in the car. Service is free within a given radius of the nearest service center, and service providers will tow your car to a mechanic if they can't fix it. The nationwide toll-free roadside assistance number is ☎ 800-222-4357. All major cities and many smaller towns have a AAA office where you can start membership.

Nature Conservancy

With a mission to protect the rarest living things for future generations, the Nature Conservancy has purchased many Rocky Mountain properties with unique natural attributes. Most of the sites are accessible to visitors and offer organized field tours. The Colorado office for the Nature Conservancy (☎ 303-444-2950) is at 1244 Pine St, Boulder, CO 80302. The Wyoming Field Office (☎ 307-332-2971) is at 258 Main St, Suite 200, Lander, WY 82520. In Montana (☎ 406-443-0303) they are at 32 S Ewing, Helena, MT 59601. The Idaho Field Office (☎ 208-726-3007) can be reached at PO Box 165, Sun Valley, ID 83353.

DANGERS & ANNOYANCES
Personal Security & Theft

Although street crime is a serious issue in large urban areas, visitors need not be obsessed with security. Taking a few sensible precautions should help ensure your safety and prevent theft.

Always lock cars and put valuables out of sight, whether you are in a town or in the remote backcountry, even if you're leaving the car for just a few minutes. Rent a car with a lockable trunk. If your car is bumped from behind in a remote area, it's best to keep going to a well-lit area or service station.

Be aware of your surroundings and who may be watching you. Avoid walking on dimly lit streets at night, particularly when alone. Walk purposefully. Avoid unnecessary displays of money or jewelry. Divide money and credit cards to avoid losing everything. Whenever possible, use ATM machines in well-trafficked areas.

In hotels, don't leave valuables lying around your room. Use safety-deposit boxes or at least place valuables in a locked bag. Don't open your door to strangers – check the peephole or call the front desk if unexpected guests try to enter.

Street People The USA has a lamentable record in dealing with its most unfortunate citizens, who often roam the streets of large cities in the daytime and sleep by store fronts, under freeways or in alleyways and abandoned buildings.

This problem is less acute in the Rocky Mountain states compared with urban areas on both coasts, but it is certainly not absent. Street people and panhandlers may approach visitors in the larger cities and towns; nearly all of them are harmless. It's an individual judgment call whether it's appropriate to offer them money or anything else. Some Americans, if they decide to give, choose to offer food to ensure their donation won't be spent on drugs or booze.

Guns The USA has a widespread reputation, partly true but also propagated and exaggerated by the media, as a dangerous place because of the availability of firearms. It is true that many rural residents in the Rocky Mountain states carry guns (sometimes displayed on a rack mounted inside the rear window of their pickup truck), but they most often target animals or isolated traffic signs, rather than humans, so don't be too alarmed. However, care should be taken when hiking during the hunting season (see below).

Recreational Hazards
In wilderness areas the consequences of an accident can be very serious, so inform someone of your route and expected time of return.

Wildlife As more and more people spend time in the backcountry or impinge on wildlife habitat, attacks on humans and pets are becoming more common especially in Colorado, where tourism and immigration are both booming. Black bears, grizzly bears and pumas (mountain lions) are the most serious hazards, but seemingly placid and innocuous beasts like bison and mule deer are equally capable of inflicting serious injury or even fatal wounds on unsuspecting tourists. Some carry rabies. Keep your distance from all wild animals – even prairie dogs and squirrels, both of which can transmit disease.

Mining Ruins Many recreational areas, including parts of some national parks, were once mining sites and may contain a variety of hazards, including but not limited to open mine shafts, deadly gases, decayed timbers, hazardous chemicals and radioactivity. Such hazards are usually, but not invariably, posted against trespass. Err on the side of caution.

Hunting One needs to be extra alert when heading into the backcountry during hunting season, generally between late September and early December. During this time hunters from all across the country descend on the Rocky Mountain states to hunt, mainly for deer and elk. While locals are usually quite skilled, visiting hunters who get out only once a year can be jumpy, and less selective in their targets than one might hope. There are also some irresponsible and dangerous people who drink while toting their guns.

Most hunting takes place on national forest or BLM land. During hunting season always wear bright colors when in the backcountry, and be sure to check with the local forest ranger to see if there are any areas best avoided.

Natural Hazards
Flash floods are a serious hazard in the desert backcountry and even on paved highways. If bad weather is threatening,

Bears

Travelers in the Rocky Mountain states need to beware of the presence of bears, which can be unpredictable and potentially dangerous when humans invade their habitat. Whether camping in a developed site or hiking in the backcountry, visitors to this region need to avoid contact with both black and grizzly (brown) bears.

It can be helpful to learn the difference between brown bears and black bears since the two do not behave in exactly the same way (adult grizzlies, for example, can't climb trees very well, but black bears can). You can't rely on color alone – black bears also come in various shades of brown and some brown bears look almost black. Instead, look for the distinguishing hump on the grizzly's shoulder as well as long claws and the wide, dish-shaped face. Grizzlies also tend to be quite a bit bigger than black bears.

The main causes of human-bear conflict arise from the animal's instinctual protection of its young, the presence of food and surprise encounters.

Bears do not see well. However, they have an extremely keen sense of smell and are attracted not just to food, but to other potentially pungent items such as toothpaste, lotions, perfumes and deodorants. When camping, clean up and pack out garbage and spilled food, use bear-proof canisters for storage, and 'bear-bag' your food and toiletries by suspending them from a tree limb away from your sleeping area, at least 10 feet from the ground and 4 feet from the trunk. In some national parks and USFS wilderness areas, there are simple food and meat storage facilities – usually a pole between two trees that backpackers can use to hang food. Backpackers should carry a 50-foot length of cord or rope in order to take advantage of these facilities. Some developed campgrounds provide barrels or bear-resistant metal boxes, but in other areas campers should always lock their food safely within the car.

Bears live a sedentary life and will typically avoid contact if given sufficient warning of approaching individuals. Make noise, stay out of prime habitat and always make every effort to avoid placing yourself between a sow and her young. The largest bear populations are found in areas of Gambel oak and aspen and near chokecherry and serviceberry bushes, whose berries are well liked by bears.

With the increasing popularity of mountain biking, the odds of surprising a bear are that much greater. Bear bells have been the favorite noisemaking deterrent for many years, but rangers report that the human voice is also effective (show tunes seem to work especially well).

There are several theories, none of them guaranteed, as to what to do if you encounter a bear. Back away slowly out of the bear's path, avoiding eye contact, and wave your hands

seek high ground away from watercourses, which can fill instantly with runoff. Wait for low water before you attempt to cross any swollen stream. If your vehicle becomes stuck under such conditions, abandon it rather than risk drowning.

While the Rocky Mountain region is less famous for seismic activity than California, earthquakes are not unknown so visitors should not be surprised should the ground rumble beneath them. Montana's 1959 Hebgen Lake quake, which altered many of the main thermal features in Yellowstone National Park, measured a powerful 7.5 on the Richter scale.

Avalanches The Rocky Mountain region, particularly Colorado, witnesses dozens of avalanches every winter. Even if you've had avalanche training and are equipped with locator beacons, chances of surviving a big slide are minimal. Check with local authorities and the forest service before heading out to do any backcountry skiing, snowshoeing or camping.

Lightning Electrical storms are common in the Rocky Mountain high country, especially in summer. Lightning strikes humans fairly rarely, but in exposed terrain, such as the treeless tundra or the open dunes of

above your head slowly (humans are the only creatures, besides apes, able to do this) to let the bear know you aren't another animal.

Another tactic is to leave something on the ground (a hat, backpack, water bottle) between you and the bear to distract it if it charges. If a bear does charge, do not run (bears can sprint up to 40 mph for short distances), and *do not scream* (that may frighten the bear, making it more aggressive). Drop to the ground and crouch into a ball, covering the back of your neck with your hands, and your chest and stomach with your knees. Do not resist the bear's inquisitive pawing- it may get bored and go away.

If a bear comes to your camp at night or any other time move your camp immediately. Climbing a tree is one alternative, but remember that black bears and young grizzlies can climb trees too, and adult grizzlies can manage a few branches, so it may be necessary to climb very high.

Red pepper spray (or capsicum) is sold as a mace-like self-defense weapon against bears. How to use it is currently being reconsidered. While it may give backcountry campers a sense of security and will irritate the bear if sprayed into its eyes and nose, it should not be sprayed on tents, the ground or anywhere else, nor test-sprayed in areas where people will be. A USGS researcher recently reported seeing brown bears rolling on ground that had been sprayed with pepper spray in what looked like some sort of catnip-like glee. And not long ago, a forest ranger in Alaska found a pepper spray can on a trail in brown bear country that had been chewed up like a nice big wad of tangy metallic chewing gum.

The above guidelines are by no means complete and cannot cover every possible bear situation. For more information, contact the NPS or the USFS. ■

Colorado's San Luis Valley, it is still a very serious hazard, and often claims several lives each year. When in exposed areas, always keep an eye on the weather to see if any storms are developing, and bear in mind the distance and route to more sheltered terrain. In summer electrical storms usually hit in mid-afternoon.

EMERGENCY

Throughout most of the USA dial ☎ 911 for emergency service of any sort; in large cities or areas with substantial Hispanic populations, Spanish-speaking emergency operators may be available, but other languages are less likely. This is a free call from any phone. A few rural phones might not have this service, in which case dial 0 for the operator and ask for emergency assistance – it's still free. Each state also maintains telephone numbers for traffic information and emergencies, including the following:

Colorado State Patrol	☎ 303-239-4501
Colorado Road Report	☎ 303-639-1234
Wyoming State Patrol	☎ 800-442-9090
	☎ 307-777-4321
Wyoming Road Report	☎ 307-733-9966
Montana State Patrol	☎ 800-525-5555
Montana Road Report	☎ 800-226-7623

Idaho State Patrol   ☎ 208-334-2900
Idaho Road Report   ☎ 208-336-6600

Lost or Stolen Documents

Carry a photocopy of your passport separately from your passport. Copy the pages with your photo and personal details, passport number and US visa. If it is lost or stolen, this will make replacing it easier. In this event, you should call your embassy. You can find your embassy's telephone number by dialing ☎ 202-555-1212 (directory inquiries for Washington, DC).

Similarly, carry copies of your traveler's check numbers and credit card numbers separately. If you lose your credit cards or they get stolen, contact the company immediately. (See Money, earlier, for company phone numbers.) Contact your bank if you lose your ATM card.

LEGAL MATTERS

If you are stopped by the police for any reason, bear in mind that (except for a few states) there is no system of paying fines on the spot. For traffic offenses, the police officer will explain your options to you. Attempting to pay the fine to the officer is frowned upon at best and may compound your troubles by resulting in a charge of bribery. Should the officer decide that you should pay up front, he or she can exercise their authority and take you directly to the magistrate instead of allowing you the usual 30-day period to pay the fine.

If you are arrested for more serious offenses, you are allowed to remain silent. There is no legal reason to speak to a police officer if you don't wish, but never walk away from an officer until given permission. All persons who are arrested are legally allowed (and given) the right to make one phone call. If you don't have a lawyer or family member to help you, call your embassy. The police will give you the number upon request.

Drinking & Driving Laws

Each state has its own laws and what is legal in one state may be illegal in others.

Some general rules are that you must be at least 16 years of age to drive (older in some states). Speed limits are 65 and 75 mph on interstates and freeways unless otherwise posted. Speed limits on other highways are 55 mph or less, and in cities can vary from 25 to 45 mph. You can drive five mph over the limit without much likelihood of being pulled over, but if you're doing 10 mph over the limit, you'll be caught sooner or later. In small towns, driving over the posted speed by any amount may attract attention. Watch for school zones, which can be as low as 15 mph during school hours – these limits are strictly enforced. Seat belts and motorcycle helmets must be worn in most states.

The drinking age is 21 and you need an ID (identification with your photograph on it) to prove your age. You could incur stiff fines, jail time and penalties if caught driving under the influence of alcohol. During festive holidays and special events, road blocks are sometimes set up to deter drunk drivers. Any peace officer is allowed to ask for a preliminary alcohol screening test (walking a straight line, etc) and a chemical test. Refusal to comply results in driver's license suspension for one to six months.

For details on speed limits and drinking and driving limits for specific states, see the Road Rules section in the introductory chapter for each state.

For more information on car rental, insurance and other automobile related concerns, see Getting Around.

Trespassing

Most land owners will enforce their own trespassing laws without getting the police involved. If you refuse to leave their land it's another story. Fines for trespassing usually don't exceed $500 and imprisonment in the county jail for the offense will not be longer than six months, but usually you'll just get fined $100 and escorted out of the county.

Land owners are required by law to mark no-trespassing zones by posting a notice or painting in fluorescent paint on a post, structure or natural object.

BUSINESS HOURS

Businesses stay open from 9 am to 5 pm, but there are certainly no hard and fast rules. In some large cities, a few supermarkets and restaurants are open 24 hours. Shops are usually open from 9 or 10 am to 5 or 6 pm (often until 9 pm in shopping malls), except Sundays when hours are noon to 5 pm (often later in malls).

Post offices are open weekdays from 8 am to 4 or 5:30 pm, and some are open from 8 am to 1 pm on Saturday. Banks are usually open weekdays from either 9 or 10 am to 5 or 6 pm. A few banks are open from 9 am to 2 or 4 pm on Saturdays. Basically hours are decided by individual branches, so if you need specifics call the relevant branch.

HOLIDAYS

National public holidays are celebrated throughout the USA. Banks, schools and government offices (including post offices) are closed and transportation, museums and other services are on a Sunday schedule. Holidays falling on a weekend are usually observed the following Monday.

January
New Year's Day, January 1

Martin Luther King, Jr, Day, 3rd Monday of the month
February
Presidents' Day, 3rd Monday of the month
April
Easter, on a Sunday usually in early April, sometimes in late March
May
Memorial Day, last Monday of the month
July
Independence Day, July 4
September
Labor Day, 1st Monday of the month
October
Columbus Day, 2nd Monday of the month
November
Veterans' Day, November 11

Thanksgiving Day, 4th Thursday of the month

December
Christmas Day, December 25

Public offices, schools, banks and some businesses close on Colorado Day, the first Monday in August, in commemoration of Colorado's admission to the Union as the 38th state.

Cultural Holidays Besides the above public holidays, the USA celebrates a number of other events linked to culture, religion or society. Here are some of the most widely observed ones:

February
Valentine's Day, February 14. Lovers and spouses celebrate romance with greeting cards, gifts and romantic dinners.
March
St Patrick's Day, March 17. The patron saint of Ireland is honored by all those who feel the Irish in their blood, are inclined to don green garb or down beer.
April
Passover, either in April or March, depending on the Judaic calendar. Families join to honor persecuted forebears and partake in the symbolic seder dinner.
May
Cinco de Mayo, May 5. The day the Mexicans wiped out the French Army in 1862 is now occasion for Americans to eat Mexican food and drink margaritas.
October
Halloween, October 31. Kids and adults dress in costumes: the former go 'trick-or-treating' for candy, the latter to parties to act out their alter egos.
November
Day of the Dead, November 2. Mexicans honor dead relatives.

Election Day, 2nd Tuesday in November.
December
Hanukkah, spans eight days of the month as set by Judaic calendar. Also called 'The Feast of Lights.'

Kwanzaa, December 26 to 31. African-American celebration to give thanks for the harvest.

New Year's Eve, December 31. Some folks ring in the new year by dressing up and drinking champagne, while others stay home and watch the festivities on TV. The following day people stay home to nurse their hangovers and watch college football on TV.

SPECIAL EVENTS

Throughout the year, but especially in summer, residents of the Rockies celebrate a variety of local and regional cultural festivals. Some of the more worthwhile are listed here.

Dates for the following events may vary from year to year – local tourist information offices will have exact dates. For details on each event, see individual geographical entries.

Colorado

January
The *Ullr Fest* and the *International Snow Sculpture Championship* are held in Breckenridge. The *National Western Stock Show & Rodeo* takes place in Denver.

February
Steamboat Springs Winter Carnival takes place in Steamboat Springs.

March
The *American Ski Classic* is held in Vail

April
Taste of Vail happens in Vail.

May
The *Kinetic Conveyance Parade and Challenge* takes place in Boulder. *Cinco de Mayo* festivities happen in Denver, Fort Collins, Grand Junction, Greeley, Pueblo and Trinidad. The *Iron Horse Bicycle Classic* is held in Durango. *Fiesta del Rio Bluegrass Festival* occurs in Pueblo.

June
June is a busy month, with the *Aspen Music Festival* in Aspen, the *Colorado Brewers Festival* in Fort Collins, the *Colorado Stampede Rodeo* in Grand Junction, the *Greeley Independence Stampede* in Greeley, *FIBArk Boat Race* in Salida, the *Telluride Bluegrass Festival* in Telluride, and the *Santa Fe Trail Festival* in Trinidad.

July
Mid-summer events include *Dance Aspen* in Aspen; the *Colorado Shakespeare Festival* in Boulder; the *Breckenridge Festival of Music* and *Jazz in July* in Breckenridge; *Aerial Weekend* and *Fat Tire Bike Week* in Crested Butte; *Pikes Peak International Hill Climb* (an auto race) in Colorado Springs; *Steamboat Cowboy Roundup Days* and *Steamboat Springs Rainbow Weekend* in

Steamboat Springs; and *Bravo! Colorado Music Festival* in Vail.

August
Events held in August include *Pikes Peak or Bust Rodeo* in Colorado Springs, *New West Fest* in Fort Collins, *Mesa County Fair* in Grand Junction, *Boom Days Celebration* in Leadville, the *Rockygrass Bluegrass Festival* in Lyons; *Pikes Peak Marathon* in Manitou Springs, *Jazz in the Sangres* in Westcliffe, the *Colorado State Fair* in Pueblo, *Steamboat Vintage Auto Race* in Steamboat, and the *Telluride Jazz Celebration* in Telluride.

September
Summer winds down with the *Aspen Filmfest* in Aspen, the *Breckenridge Festival of Film* in Breckenridge, *A Taste of Colorado* in Denver, and the *Colorado Mountain Winefest* in Grand Junction. *Oktoberfest* festivities begin in Breckenridge, Fort Collins and Glenwood Springs.

October
Oktoberfest is celebrated in La Veta.

Wyoming

June
Bozeman Trail Days, are held in Ft Phil Kearny State Historical Site. *Jackalope Days* takes place in Douglas.

July
Summer events include the *1838 Mountain Man Rendezvous* and the *Hot Air Balloon Rally* in Riverton; *Cheyenne Frontier Days* in Cheyenne; the *Cody Stampede* in Cody; *Desert Balloon Extravaganza* in Rock Springs; the *Grand Teton Music Festival* at Teton Village; the *Green River Rendezvous* in Pinedale; the *International Climbers' Festival* in Lander; and *Laramie Jubilee Days* in Laramie.

August
Buffalo Bill Festival takes place in Cody. The *Central Wyoming Fair & Rodeo* is held in Casper. The *Gift of the Waters Pageant* is in Thermopolis. The *Wyoming State Fair* is held in Douglas.

September
Events include the *Fort Bridger Rendezvous* at Fort Bridger State Historic Site, and the *Jackson Hole Fall Arts Festival* in Jackson.

Montana

April
The *International Wildlife Film Festival* takes place in Missoula.

May
:   The *Miles City Bucking Horse Sale* is a highlight in Miles City.

June
:   The *Lewis and Clark Festival* comes to Great Falls, and *Little Bighorn Days* happens in Hardin.

July
:   Events include *Libby Logger Days* in Libby, the *Miles City Hot Air Balloon Round-Up* in Miles City, and *Bannack Days* in Bannack.

August
:   The *Festival of Nations* takes place in Red Lodge. The *Montana Cowboy Poetry Gathering* comes to Lewistown.

Idaho

June
:   The *National Old Time Fiddlers Contest* is held in Weiser.

July
:   The *Idaho International Folk Dance Festival* takes place in Rexburg. The *San Inazio Basque Festival* is in Boise.

August
:   Events include the *Festival at Sandpoint* in Sandpoint, the *Shoshone-Bannock Indian Festival* on the Fort Hall Indian Reservation, and the *Western Idaho Fair* in Boise.

September
:   The *Lewiston Roundup* takes place in Lewiston.

WORK

Seasonal work is possible in national parks and other tourist sites, especially ski areas; for information, contact park concessionaires or local chambers of commerce.

Seasonal work is relatively easy to come by as long as you show up early. Ski resorts do most of their hiring in early to mid-November; summer resorts like to have a full staff by July 1st. Jobs are generally limited to restaurants or retail unless you have experience skiing, guiding or know someone with a farm or dude ranch (they generally hire family or family friends). Some of the best places to hunt for work in the Rockies are the larger resort towns (like Aspen, CO, Big Sky, MT, Jackson Hole, WY, and Sun Valley, ID) and gateway towns to the big national parks, such as Estes Park, CO, West Yellowstone, MT,

and Whitefish, MT. The US minimum wage is $5.15, though restaurant wait staff often earn less than that, as they're expected to make up the difference in tips.

If you're not a US citizen, you'll need to apply for a work visa from the US embassy in your home country before you leave. The type of visa varies depending on how long you're staying and the kind of work you plan to do. Generally, you'll need either a J-1 visa, which you can obtain by joining a visitor-exchange program, or a H-2B visa, which you get if you are sponsored by a US employer. The latter is not easy to obtain (since the employer has to prove that no US citizen or permanent resident is available to do the job); the former is issued mostly to students for work in summer camps. Although in practice many foreigners get work in the US illegally, be forewarned that if caught the penalties can be quite severe: deportation at the very least, and possibly a stiff fine as well.

The Colorado State Labor and Employment Department operates a number of Job Service Centers throughout the state, including in some of the resort towns. These local offices can provide information about temporary, part-time and full-time employment (and in some cases they can help arrange it). The service centers are listed in local phone books, or you can contact the main office (☎ 303-620-4200), 1515 Arapaho St, Tower 2, Suite 400, Denver, CO 80202, to get addresses and phone numbers for centers in the area you're headed to.

In Wyoming, the state's Department of Employment (☎ 307-777-7672), 122 W 26th St, Cheyenne, WY 82002, lists work opportunities in all sectors.

The Montana Job Service has listings of service and non-service industry jobs that you can access by filling out a State of Montana employment application and paying $10 (good for four months). There are offices in Billings, Bozeman, Flathead, Great Falls, Helena and Missoula. Contact the Job Services Division (☎ 406-444-3555) of the Department of Labor & Industry, 1327 Lockey St, Helena, MT 59601, for the phone numbers and addresses of the local offices, which can in turn tell you about job opportunities in their area. You can also check job listings posted on their Internet site (jsd.dli.mt.gov/).

The Idaho Department of Labor Job Service (☎ 208-334-6200), 219 Main St, Boise, ID 83735, lists both public and private employment opportunities throughout the state. Listings can also be found on their website (www.labor.state.id.us).

ACCOMMODATIONS

The spectrum of accommodations in the Rockies ranges from campgrounds and hostels to simple motels, B&Bs and five-star luxury hotels, as well as that uniquely Western institution, the 'guest' or 'dude' ranch. You should be able to find something reasonable in most areas.

Camping

Camping is the cheapest, and in many ways the most enjoyable, approach to a vacation. Visitors with a car and a tent can take advantage of hundreds of private and public campgrounds and RV parks at prices of $10 per night or even less.

Public Campgrounds These are on public lands such as national forests, state and national parks, BLM lands, etc (see Useful Organizations above).

Free dispersed camping (meaning you can camp almost anywhere) is permitted in many public backcountry areas. Sometimes you can camp right from your car along a dirt road, especially in BLM and national forest areas. Obviously, in this situation there are no facilities. In other places, you can backpack your gear into a cleared campsite.

Information and detailed maps are available from many local ranger stations or BLM offices (addresses and telephone numbers are given in the text) and may be posted along the road. Sometimes, a free camping permit is required, particularly in national parks, less so in forests and BLM areas.

When camping in an undeveloped area choose a camp site at least 200 yards

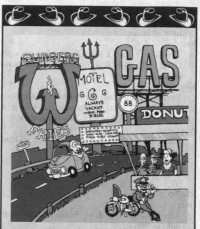

Gas, Food, Lodging
When coming into a city on the highway you will notice signs that say 'Gas Food Lodging' followed by something like 'Next Three Exits.' Don't assume these exits will lead you directly into the city center – they won't. You'll end up traveling along strips of chain motels, fast-food restaurants and gas stations with small grocery stores. If you have no intention of staying in town, but would rather catch a few hours' sleep and head out early on the road, these establishments do provide a cheap alternative to downtown and a bit of true Americana. ■

(approximately 70 adult steps) from water and wash up at camp, not in the stream, using biodegradable soap. Dig a six-inch deep hole to use as a latrine and cover and camouflage it well when leaving the site. Burn toilet paper, unless fires are prohibited. Carry out all trash. Use a portable charcoal grill or camping stove; don't build new fires. If there already is a fire ring, use only dead and downed wood or wood you have carried in yourself. Make sure to leave the campsite as you found it.

Developed areas usually have toilets, drinking water, fire pits (or charcoal grills) and picnic benches. Some don't have drinking water. At any rate, it is always a good idea to have a few gallons of water when camping. These basic campgrounds usually cost about $5 to $7 a night.

Some areas have showers or RV hookups and often cost $8 to $10. National forest and BLM campgrounds are usually less developed, while national park and state park campgrounds are more likely to have more amenities. The less-developed sites are often on a 'first-come, first-served' basis, so plan on an early arrival, preferably during the week, as sites fill up fast on Fridays and weekends. More developed areas may accept or require reservations; details are given in the text.

Costs given in the text for public campgrounds are per site. A site normally accommodates up to six people (or two vehicles). If there are more of you, you'll need two sites. Public campgrounds often have seven- or 14-night limits.

Private Campgrounds These are on private property and are usually close to or in a town. Most are designed with RVs in mind; tenters can camp but fees are at least several dollars higher than in public campgrounds. Fees given in the text are most often for two people per site with a fee of $1 to $3 for each additional person. Some places just charge per vehicle. In addition, state and city taxes apply. However, they may offer discounts for week or month stays.

Facilities can include hot showers, coin laundry, swimming pool, full RV hookups, games area, a playground and a convenience store. Kampgrounds of America (KOA) is a national network of private campgrounds with sites usually ranging from $12 to $20, depending on hookups. Some people like these places, others regard them as the McDonalds of campgrounds. You can get the annual directory of KOA sites by calling or writing: KOA (☎ 406-248-7444), PO Box 30558, Billings, MT 59114-0558. There is a $3 charge.

Reservations During peak months of June through September reservations are a good idea, especially at popular national parks like Grand Teton, Rocky Mountain or Yellowstone. To make a reservation, you must pay with Visa, MasterCard or Discover Card. For sites in national forests call ☎ 800-280-2267. For sites in national parks call the National Park Reservation Service at ☎ 800-365-2267.

Hostels
The US hostel network is less widespread than in Canada, the UK, Europe and Australia and is predominately in the north and coastal parts of the country. Not all of the hostels are directly affiliated with Hostelling International/American Youth Hostels (HI/AYH). Those that are offer discounts to HI/AYH members and usually allow nonmembers to stay for a few dollars more. Dormitory beds cost about $10 to $15 a night. Rooms cost $20 to $30 for one or two people.

HI/AYH hostels expect you to rent or carry a sheet or sleeping bag to keep the beds clean. Dormitories are segregated by sex and curfews may exist. Kitchen and laundry privileges are usually available in return for light housekeeping duties. There are information and advertising boards, TV rooms and lounge areas. Alcohol may be banned.

Several Rocky Mountain towns sport hostels, mostly in Colorado. Not all those listed below are affiliated with HI/AYH.

Colorado – Breckenridge, Colorado Springs, Conejos River, Crested Butte, Denver, Durango, Estes Park, Glenwood Springs, Grand Junction, Grand Lake, Nederland, Pitkin, Silverthorne
Wyoming – Jackson, Teton Village
Montana – Bozeman, Cooke City, East Glacier Park, Kalispell, Missoula, Polebridge, St Ignatius, West Yellowstone
Idaho – Gooding, Kellogg, Naples

Reservations Reservations are accepted and strongly advised during the high season – there may be a limit of a three-night stay then. You can call HI/AYH's national office (☎ 202-783-6161) to make reservations for any HI/AYH hostel, or use their code-based reservation service at ☎ 800-909-4776 (you need an access code

Dude Ranches

In his book *Dude Ranches and Ponies*, Lawrence B Smith applies the term 'dude' to 'an outsider, city person, or tenderfoot; one who came from another element of society; in short, a stranger as far as the American West and its ways are concerned.' Most people (men and women) who visit dude ranches today are 'dudes' in the truest sense, looking for an escape from a fast-paced, high-tech world.

Dude ranch history dates back to the late 19th century, when the Eaton brothers established a hay and horse ranch near Medora, ND, 80 miles east of Glendive, MT. Family and friends who came from the East by train stayed for months at a time and helped in all of the everyday ranch chores and cattle activities. When one guest asked if he could pay for his room and board, the Eatons saw the potential for a business venture. In 1904 they moved the first dude ranch to the mountains of Wolf, WY, where Eatons' Ranch is currently run by third, fourth and fifth generation family members.

Soon other ranchers got wind of the Eatons' success, and dude ranches sprang up all over the West. President Theodore Roosevelt helped popularize stays; the expansion of the railroads and the opening of Yellowstone National Park also factored into the development of dude ranches in the Rocky Mountain states – most of the earliest ranches were near one of the two. By the 1920s, many Western ranchers made more money on Eastern visitors than on livestock, and soon two groups were formed: the Dude Ranchers' Association and in 1924 the Colorado Dude & Guest Ranch Association. These associations are still going strong.

Guests continue to outnumber cattle at most of the 40 top-end 'ranches' listed in the associations' catalogue. You can find anything from a working-ranch experience (smelly chores and 5 am wake-up calls included) to a Western Club Med. Typical week-long visits

to use this service, available from any HI/ AYH office or listed in their handbook).

Motels

Motel accommodations in the Rocky Mountain states run from basic to very comfortable, with a wide range of prices. It's not impossible to find acceptable motel accommodations for as little as $20 per night in towns along I-80 in southwestern Wyoming, but in tourist destinations like Aspen or Jackson even the normally budget Motel 6 chain charges nearly $60 per night. In general, summer is the peak season and prices can be as much as double, though the major ski resorts are also expensive in winter. Special events and conventions can fill up a town's motels quickly, so call ahead to find out what will be going on. The chamber of commerce is always a good resource.

In general expect to pay $30 to $50 for a double room in most locations; this will usually include telephone with cable TV (with one premium channel showing un-

interrupted movies), and a private bathroom with shower or bathtub. Some places may even have swimming pools and hot tubs. Mid-range motel chains include Super 8, Days Inn and Econo Lodge. At the top end of the motel range are chains like Comfort Inn, Sleep Inn and Rodeway Inn. Best Western and Holiday Inn often have decent restaurants and additional amenities like hot tubs, but usually cost more than they're worth.

Bargain motel chains like Motel 6 are usually clean and comfortable, but notably devoid of character. In smaller towns cheap rooms are basically acceptable 'mom & pop'-type places which can be quite pleasant, but in larger towns, the cheap motels may be in more dodgy areas. Don't leave valuables out in your car and exercise caution.

Regardless of your choice of accommodations, beware of making phone calls directly from your room. Some places charge around 75¢ for local calls versus 25¢ at a pay phone. Long-distance rates

start at over $100 per person per day, including accommodation, meals, activities and equipment. A few B&Bs offer dude-ranch experiences, often allowing shorter stays at considerably lower rates than the association members.

Accommodations range from rustic log cabins to cushy suites with whirlpools and cable TV; meals range from family-style spaghetti dinners to four-course gourmet meals. Often, authentic cowhands are scarcer than a snowstorm in July – look for college students and others with riding proficiency and a knack for Western wear to cater to dude-ranch guests.

While the centerpiece of dude ranch vacations is horseback riding, many ranches feature swimming pools and have expanded their activity lists to include fly-fishing, hiking, mountain biking, tennis, golf, skeet-shooting and cross-country skiing.

In his book *Ranch Vacations* (John Muir Publications, 1994), considered the bible of ranch vacation guides, Gene Kilgore suggests questions to ask when screening a dude ranch: Are the rates all-inclusive? Does the ranch provide airport/train/bus pick-up/drop-off? Is there a minimum stay? Will the ranch cater to special diets? Does the ranch provide equipment and fishing licenses? Is child care provided, and to what extent? Are riding lessons available? Are laundry services available? Is liquor provided or allowed? Is smoking permitted?

For listings, descriptions and contact information for dude ranches throughout the Rockies, try the Dude Ranchers' Association (☎ 970-223-8440; fax 970-223-0201), PO Box 471, Laporte, CO 80535. Listings are also available through their website (www.dude-ranch.org). For ranches within Colorado, contact the Colorado Dude & Guest Ranch Association (☎ 970-887-3128), PO Box 300, Tabernash, CO 80478. Also check out their website (www.coloradoranch.com). ∎

are often surcharged by 100 to 200%! Be prepared to add room tax to prices. Children are often allowed to stay free with their parents, but rules for this vary. Some places allow children under 18 to stay free with parents, others allow children under 12 and others may charge a few dollars per child. Call and inquire if traveling with a family.

Hotels & Lodges

The best hotel accommodations are in large cities and resort areas, where they are more often called lodges, with upscale prices. Amenities include restaurants and bars, swimming pools, Jacuzzis, exercise rooms, saunas, room service and concierges.

In some smaller towns in the Rocky Mountain states hotels tend to be disreputable flophouses, though, of course, there are exceptions.

In national parks, accommodations are limited to either camping or park lodges. Lodges are often rustic looking but usually quite comfortable. Restaurants are on the premises and tour services are often available. National park lodges are not cheap, with most rooms going for close to $100 for a double during the high season, but they are your only option if you want to stay inside the park without camping. Many lodges are fully booked months in advance, especially during the high season and around holidays, so make a reservation as soon as your plans are set.

B&Bs

European visitors should be aware that North American B&Bs aren't usually the casual, inexpensive sort of accommodations found on the Continent or in Britain. While they are usually family-run, many B&Bs in the Rocky Mountain states require advance reservations, though most will be happy to oblige drop-in guests if they have space.

B&B prices include breakfast, usually substantial, American-style meals, but lighter Continental breakfasts are not unheard of. The cheapest establishments, with rooms in the $30s and $40s, may have clean but unexciting rooms with a shared bathroom.

Pricier places have rooms with private baths and sometimes fireplaces, balconies and dining rooms with enticingly grand breakfasts and other meals. They may be in historical buildings, quaint country houses or luxurious urban townhouses. Most B&Bs fall in the $50 to $100 price range, but some go over $100. The best are distinguished by a friendly attention to detail by owner/hosts who can provide you with local information and contacts and a host of other amenities.

A large majority of B&Bs prohibit smoking, if not entirely at least in guests' rooms.

Long-Term Rentals

This refers to houses or condominiums that can be rented anywhere from two days to two months. This type of lodging is most often found in resort areas and almost always includes kitchens and living rooms. While condominiums and houses are often very expensive, several people can lodge for the same price and they can be more economical than motels or hotels on a per person basis for a larger group, especially since you can cook your own food. The chambers of commerce in resort towns like Vail, Aspen, Jackson or Steamboat Springs will have information on condominium listings and can give advice on renting.

Reservations

The cheapest budget places may not accept reservations, but at least phone from the road to see what's available; even if they don't take reservations they'll often hold a room for an hour or two.

Chain hotels will all take reservations days or months ahead. Normally, you have to give a credit card number to hold the room. If you don't show and don't call to cancel, you will be charged the first night's rental. Cancellation policies vary – some let you cancel at no charge 24 hours or 72 hours in advance, while others are less forgiving. Find out about cancellation penalties when you book.

Also make sure to let the hotel know if you plan on a late arrival – many motels will give your room away if you haven't arrived or called by 6 pm. Motel and hotel chain central reservation systems might not be aware of local special discounts. Booking ahead, however, gives you the peace of mind of a guaranteed room when you arrive.

Some places, especially B&Bs and some cabins, won't accept credit cards and want a check as a deposit before they'll reserve a room for you.

See the appendix at the back of the book for a list of toll-free motel and hotel reservation numbers.

FOOD
Mealtimes

Usually served between about 6 am and 10 am, American breakfasts are large and filling, often including eggs or an omelet, bacon or ham, fried potatoes, toast with butter and jam and coffee or tea.

Lunch is available from 11 am to 2 pm. One strategy for enjoying good restaurants on a budget is to frequent them for lunch, when fixed-price specials for as little as $5 or slightly more are common.

Dinners, served anytime between about 5 and 10 pm, are more expensive but often still reasonably priced; portions are usually large. Some of the better restaurants will require reservations.

Restaurants in the USA frequently close on Mondays; phoning ahead is a good idea.

Regional

Outside urban areas and tourist centers, much of the Rocky Mountain region is a culinary desert dominated by greasy spoon cafes and monotonous chain restaurants. Montana and Wyoming, in particular, are cattle country, where vegetarians may have to hire a detective to find anything besides conventional meat and potatoes.

Dominant cooking methods are grilling, baking, and most of all, frying. A regional favorite is 'chicken-fried steak,' a slab of steak breaded and then deep-fried. Even the delicate meat of freshwater trout is

Vegetarians in Cattle Country

If you plan on sticking to a strict vegetarian diet while traveling in the Rocky Mountain states, you'll have to get used to two things: grudging looks from local ranchers and baked potatoes. Cattle ranching constitutes much of this area's economy, and if all at once the world turned vegetarian, many family ranches – in operation for multiple generations – would be left high and dry.

Because most people in the eastern plains were raised on beef, they often don't understand vegetarianism. If you ask for a menu item to be made without meat, a server may look at you quizzically, then suggest something like chicken strips or fish as a 'meat-free' alternative. Terms like 'tofu' and 'tempeh' are as foreign to eastern plains folk as the soy bean products they describe. In big cities, and the western part of the Rocky Mountain states where tourists and college students shed an alternative light on the culinary scene, the options are more plentiful.

Pizza parlors are always a good standby, since most offer vegetable pizza toppings.

When a restaurant's menu revolves around beef, often the only option for a vegetarian is to order a melange of side dishes: salad (ie, a heap of iceberg lettuce topped with a few cherry tomatoes and croutons), potatoes, fried mushrooms, coleslaw. Most soups contain beef or chicken stock, so be sure to ask before laying into a bowl. The sure-fire dish, available at most restaurants, full of carbohydrates and low in fat (if you refrain from using heaps of butter and sour cream), is the all-American baked potato. People won't even look at you weirdly if that's all you order. ∎

often subjected to breading and pan frying. Boiled vegetables are relegated to a position of nutritional necessity. Most foreign visitors will find the fare quite bland. If so, stop by a Mexican restaurant for a dose of spice, or order up a bowl of chili – a stewed mixture of Western staples: beef, pinto beans and dried chili powder that can be found at nearly any cafe or diner.

Another regional alternative to traditional 'Western fare' is the Indian or Navajo taco, a variant on the Mexican variety in which the traditional ingredients of ground beef, cheese, lettuce, tomato and salsa rest on reservation-style fry bread rather than on a tortilla. Another regional specialty, Rocky Mountain oys-

ters, is an 'appetizer' may cause some men to squirm upon learning precisely what a castrated bull has contributed to this dish.

Buffalo (bison) meat is an increasingly popular alternative to beef for several reasons, one of which is unquestionably its novelty and tourist appeal. At the same time, the bison is a native range animal well adapted to the prairies and plains, as opposed to ecologically exotic beef cattle. Its fat and cholesterol content is also lower than that of beef, making it a healthier dietary choice.

Ethnic Fare

A benefit to the great melting pot of the USA is a diversity of ethnic cuisine.

Mexican food, of course, long predates the US Constitution, and Chinese restaurants have long served the region, but Thai, Vietnamese and other Asian alternatives are more recent arrivals. Italian food is common, while French and similar Continental cuisines are available in some areas.

The most diverse fare is to be found in large cities like Denver and resorts like Jackson, Steamboat Springs and Aspen, but there are many surprises in unexpected places.

Mexican & Southwestern The Hispanic influence – particularly in southern Colorado, in the large cities and in the agricultural areas that attract itinerant Mexican labor – is responsible for a vibrant, flavorful cuisine termed either Mexican, Tex-Mex or Southwest. It is not uncommon to find a selection of Mexican entrees in many restaurants.

There are many Mexican cuisines, but the most popular dishes in the Rocky Mountains are derived from the Mexican interior – with a few Southwestern adaptations. One sure indicator of authentic Southwest cuisine are sopaipillas served with honey in lieu of tortillas. Flan pudding with a caramel sauce is a simple, yet delicious dessert treat.

Another indicator of authenticity is the query, 'red or green?' referring to whether you want red- or green-chile sauce to smother your meal. This sauce is not to be confused with the above mentioned western chili containing beans. Many diners are unaware that the same pepper plant produces either red or green peppers – with color depending on ripeness – and think that the pepper's color indicates spiciness.

Green peppers are roasted and peeled to impart the fresh vegetable's flavor, whereas red peppers are dried and chefs add the crushed remains to a tomato-based sauce. The ingredient in a pepper that imparts spiciness is capsicum: jalapeños are loaded with it, the mild bell has almost none, and Anaheims and poblanos are moderately spicy. Since any pepper plant can be harvested green or left on the vine to turn red,

it is the type of pepper used in a recipe and the quantity – not color – that determines spiciness.

The vegetarian diner should always inquire if a meatless sauce is available, since many green-chile recipes include small quantities of pork. For 40 days from Ash Wednesday to Easter during the observance of Lent, religious penitence leads many Hispanic-run restaurants to offer special vegetarian menu items.

Mexican vegetarian dishes such as chiles rellenos (typically, roasted Anaheim peppers, stuffed with rice and cheese, and sometimes with ground meat, then fried), bean burritos or tacos or cheese enchiladas are available in many restaurants. Without causing too much trouble, a diner can usually request particular entrees to be made substituting beans and rice for meat. Beware of refried beans, which can be made with animal fat – if given a choice, ask for pinto or black beans.

Fruit
Fresh local fruit is a summer and autumn treat. Because of the high altitude and ferocious winters, hardy fruits like apples and pears are most common, but the more temperate Grand Valley and surrounding areas on the western Colorado Plateau produce excellent peaches, grapes, apricots and cherries.

Self-Catering
Nearly every town of any size has a supermarket with a wide variety of fresh and prepared foods at reasonable prices; these are good places to stock up on supplies for camping trips, rather than outlying convenience stores which may inflate prices.

Some towns have produce or farmers' markets that offer a good selection of fresh fruits and vegetables at very reasonable prices. The location and frequency of these markets are indicated in the text.

DRINKS
Alcohol Drinks
Parts of the Rocky Mountain states were formerly 'dry' and in some Colorado coun-

ties only relatively weak 3.2% beer is available. In Wyoming, only bars or liquor stores may sell alcohol; supermarkets may not legally sell beer or wine. Beer is the most widely consumed alcoholic drink in the region. The usual hard liquors (spirits), like whisky and gin, are widely available at both bars and liquor stores.

Beer In the past decade the Rocky Mountain States, Colorado in particular, have played an active role in the revival of small breweries and brewpubs. Colorado alone boasts some 30 to 40 of these operations, but 'craft-brewed' beers are also found in Wyoming, Montana and Idaho. Foreign visitors who still think all American beer is watery brew like Budweiser or Miller should take the time to try some of these microbrews. The variety and quality on offer is truly refreshing: pale ales, bitters, wheat beers, stouts and porters, among others. Many breweries try to use local ingredients, and all look to their area's natural sights and other attractions when choosing clever names for their various creations. Brewpubs nearly always have full kitchens as well as bars, so you may find them listed in this book either under the Places to Eat or Entertainment section.

Wine Colorado is the only Rocky Mountain state to boast a substantial wine industry, with wineries in and around the town of Palisade, in the Grand Valley, near the city of Grand Junction.

Alcohol & Drinking Age Persons under the age of 21 (minors) are prohibited from consuming alcohol in the USA. Carry a driver's license or passport as proof of age to enter a bar, order alcohol at a restaurant, or buy alcohol. Servers have the right to ask to see your ID and may refuse service without it. Minors are not allowed in bars and pubs, even to order nonalcoholic beverages. Unfortunately, this means that most dance clubs are also off-limits to minors, although a few clubs have solved the underage problem with a segregated drinking area. Minors are, however, welcome in the dining areas of restaurants where alcohol may be served.

ENTERTAINMENT
Bars & Nightclubs
The distinction between bars and nightclubs can be academic, but in general a bar is an establishment that serves alcohol (beer, wine and spirits) and may offer live music on occasion, while a nightclub is a more formal venue that depends on live entertainment (often but not necessarily music) for its economic viability. In cities, bars and nightclubs present a variety of performers ranging from rock 'n' roll and country & western (C&W) bands through lounge singers and standup comedians. In rural areas the regular attraction will be a local dance band, playing a variety of styles, but one can usually expect either C&W or rock-and-roll.

Cinema
While the video revolution has certainly driven some movie theaters out of business, towns as small as Paonia, CO (population 1400), have managed to keep their cinemas open. The widest selection of movies, however, is available in large cities like Denver and resorts like Jackson; some of them offer afternoon matinees that are at discount prices.

Theater
The most diverse theatrical productions are staged in Denver and in university towns like Boulder. Tourist destinations like Jackson, WY, and Creed and Central City, CO, have small local companies and may support summer repertory groups.

SPECTATOR SPORTS
Baseball The Denver-based Colorado Rockies debuted in the National League in 1993; in 1995, they moved into Coors Field, a downtown baseball-only park. The regular season lasts from early April to early October, followed immediately by intra-league playoffs and the World Series

Rodeo: A Western Ritual

Rodeo, from the Spanish word meaning roundup, began with the cowboys of the Old West. As they used to say, 'There was never a horse that couldn't be rode – and never a rider that couldn't be throwed.' Naturally, cowboys riding half-wild horses eventually competed to determine who was the best. The speed with which they could rope a calf also became a competitive skill.

Rodeo as we know it today began in the 1880s. The first rodeo to offer prize money was held in Texas in 1883, and the first to begin charging admission to the event was in Prescott, AZ, in 1888. Since then, rodeo has developed into both a spectator and professional sport under the auspices of the Professional Rodeo Cowboys Association (PRCA).

For the first-time spectator, the action is full of thrills and spills but may be a little hard to understand. Within the arena, the main participants are cowboys and cowgirls, judges (who are usually retired rodeo competitors) and clowns. Although the clowns perform amusing stunts, their function is to help out the cowboys when they get into trouble. During the bull riding, they are particularly important if a cowboy gets thrown. Then clowns immediately rush in front of the bull to distract the animal, while the winded cowboy struggles out of the arena.

While men are the main contenders in a rodeo, women also compete, mainly in barrel racing, team roping and calf roping.

Each rodeo follows the same pattern, and once you know a few pointers, it all begins to make sense. The first order of the day is the grand entry, during which all contestants, clowns and officials parade their horses around the arena, raise the US flag and sing the national anthem. The rodeo then begins, usually including seven events, which are often in the following order.

Bareback Bronc Riding Riders must stay on a randomly assigned bucking bronco (a wild horse) for eight seconds, which from the back of a crazed horse can seem like an eternity. The cowboy holds on with one hand to a handle strapped around the horse just behind its shoulders. His other hand is allowed to touch nothing but air, otherwise he's disqualified. His spurs must be up at the height of the horse's shoulders when the front hooves hit the ground on the first jump out of the chute, and he must keep spurring the horse during the ride. Two judges give 25 points each to the horse and the rider, for a theoretical total of 100. A good ride is one in which the horse bucks wildly and the rider stays on with style – a score of over 70 is good.

Calf Roping This is a timed event. A calf races out of a chute, closely followed by a mounted cowboy with a rope loop. The cowboy ropes the calf (usually by throwing the loop over its head, although a leg catch is legal), hooks the rope to the saddle horn, dismounts, keeping the rope tight all the way to the calf. A well-trained horse will stand still and hold the rope taut to make the cowboy's job less difficult. When he reaches the calf, the cowboy throws the

between the champions of the National and American leagues.

Minor league baseball, the Major Leagues' training ground, is also popular. Colorado Springs Sky Sox, the Rockies' top minor league affiliate, play in the Class AAA Pacific Coast League, while several Major League organizations field teams in the short-season Pioneer League, which consists entirely of first-year professionals. Four of the Pioneer League's eight franchises are in Montana: Butte, Billings, Great Falls and Helena. In many ways, the small, intimate parks provide an ideal environment for viewing the sport and seeing future stars on the way up.

Basketball America's most popular international sports export is organized at the professional level as the National Basketball Association (NBA), which has a prolonged season lasting from late

animal down, ties three of its legs together with a 6-foot-long 'piggin string' and throws up his hands to show he's done. A good roper can do the whole thing in just a few seconds.

Saddle Bronc Riding This has similar rules to the bareback event and is scored the same way. In addition to starting with the spurs up above the horse's shoulders and keeping one hand in the air, the cowboy must keep both feet in the stirrups. Dismounting from the saddle of a bucking bronco is not easy – watch the two pickup men riding alongside to help the contestant off. This demands almost as much skill as the event itself.

Steer Wrestling In this event (also called bull-dogging), a steer that may weigh as much as 700 pounds runs out of a chute, tripping a barrier line, which is the signal for two cowboys to pursue the animal. One cowboy – the hazer – tries to keep the steer running in a straight line, while the other cowboy – the wrestler – rides alongside the steer and jumps off his horse trying to grip the steer's head and horns – this at speeds approaching 40 miles per hour! The wrestler must then wrestle the steer to the ground. The best cowboys can accomplish this in under five seconds.

Barrel Racing Three large barrels are set up in a triangle, and the rider must race around them in a clover shape. The turns are incredibly tight, and the racer must come out of them at full speed to do well. There's a five-second penalty for tipping over a barrel. Good times are around 15 to 17 seconds.

Team Roping A team of two horseback ropers pursues a steer running out of the chute. The first roper must catch the steer by the head or horns and then wrap the rope around the saddle horn. The second team member then lassos the steer's two rear legs in one throw. Good times are as low as five seconds.

Bull Riding Riding a bucking and spinning 2000-pound bull is wilder and more dangerous than bronc riding, and it is often the crowd's favorite event. Using one heavily gloved hand, the cowboy holds on to a rope that is wrapped around the bull. And that's it – nothing else to hold on to, and no other rules apart from staying on for eight seconds and not touching the bull with your free hand. Scoring is the same as for bronc riding.

For a full overview on rodeo, consult Kristine Fredriksson's *American Rodeo from Buffalo Bill to Big Business* (Texas A&M University Press, 1985), Clifford P Westermeier's *Man, Beast, Dust: The Story of Rodeo* (University of Nebraska Press, 1987; originally published in 1948), Teresa Jordan's *Cowgirls: Women of the American West* (University of Nebraska Press, 1992) and Mary Lou LeCompte's *Cowgirls of the Rodeo: Pioneer Professional Athletes* (University of Illinois Press, 1993). ■

October to mid-June. The region's only NBA team is the Denver Nuggets, but university and high school teams attract many spectators in local communities. The Colorado Xplosion, the state's professional women's basketball team, is a member of the newly formed American Basketball League.

Football American football draws enormous crowds in the fall. The Denver Broncos of the National Football League (NFL) have the region's largest and most fanatical following, which became even more maniacal after the Broncos won the Superbowl after the 1997 season. The University of Colorado at Boulder is a major college power and other state universities in Colorado, Wyoming, Montana and Idaho also field teams. Like basketball, high school football is extraordinarily popular in local communities.

Hockey The Colorado Avalanche, based in Denver, is one of the top-ranked teams in the National Hockey League (NHL), having captured the Stanley Cup by winning the championship the end of the 1995 season. As a result they have developed an almost frightening loyalty among Colorado fans. Despite their more northern climes and chillier winters, the other Rocky Mountain states have yet to field professional hockey teams, though most universities participate in the sport.

Soccer The Colorado Rapids is the region's major league soccer team. They are also based in Denver.

National Parks & Outdoor Activities

The national parklands, forests and wilderness areas of the Rockies offer some of the world's best opportunities to enjoy natural beauty. Though many national parks and national forests occupy lands that were once settled, most are now protected from major development, allowing native flora and wildlife a chance to thrive in environments approaching their original condition.

Of course, as interest in outdoor recreation and 'adventure vacations' continues to increase, so does the threat to the backcountry. While responsible hikers and campers are fairly low-impact, outdoor sports such as mountain biking, horseback riding, skiing, and any motorized activity can potentially wreck havoc on Alpine, high plains and desert ecosystems. The degree of damage is largely determined by how you play: a bit of consideration and respect for the environment can help ensure that more people benefit from the beauty of the outdoor without spoiling it for themselves and others.

This chapter gives an introduction to the national parks in the region, and explains other federally regulated areas like national forest and Bureau of Land Management (BLM) lands. Following that is a list of the major outdoor activities that can be enjoyed in this amazing part of the USA.

National Parks, Forests & Other Federal Lands

Many visitors find the USA's national parks a major reason for visiting the country. The now global idea of setting aside large, scenic natural areas for posterity dates from the creation of Wyoming's Yellowstone National Park in 1872.

The National Park Service (NPS), an agency of the Department of the Interior, administers several categories of reserves with differing degrees of protection: national parks, national monuments, national recreation areas and national historic sites.

Created only by acts of Congress, national parks are generally large areas that often surround spectacular natural features and cover hundreds of square miles. Commercial activities and development within national parks are, in theory, severely restricted. National monuments, by contrast, may be created by presidential order, but do not enjoy the same level of protection as national parks; mining and grazing are allowed within them, though such activities are usually regulated. National recreation areas are usually sites with exceptional natural features that have been severely altered, usually by dam projects and large reservoirs. National historic sites are places of special cultural and historical significance, also administered by the NPS.

Travelers with little hiking experience will appreciate the well-marked, well-maintained trails in national parks, often with restroom facilities at either end and interpretive displays along the way. The trails give access to the parks' natural features, and usually show up on NPS maps as nature trails or self-guided interpretive trails. These hikes are usually no longer than 2 miles. Expect them to be fairly crowded unless you are visiting during non-tourist season (before Memorial Day and after Labor Day).

Another way to escape the crowds, and also see the best of what the parks have to offer, is to head into the backcountry for several days. Most national parks require overnight hikers to carry backcountry permits, available from visitor centers or ranger stations, which must be obtained 24 hours in advance and may require you to

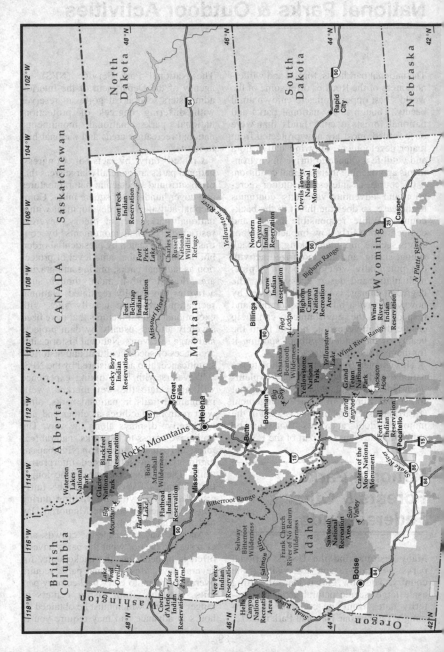

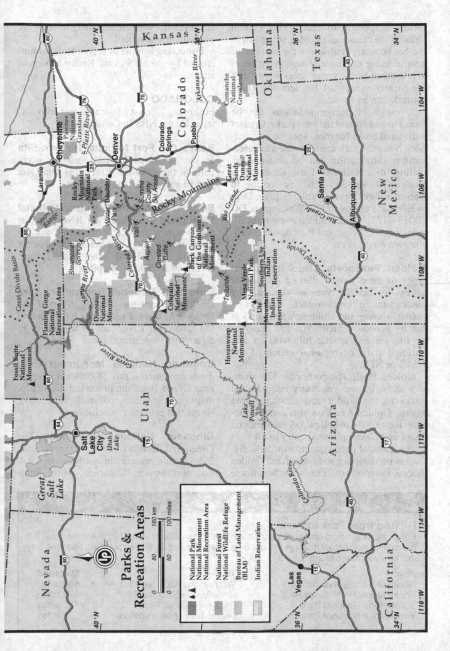

follow a specific itinerary. This system reduces the chance of people getting lost in the backcountry and limits the number of people using one area at any given time. While some backcountry areas see a lot of use, nearly every park has sections where solitude can be found.

A range of accommodations can be found in and around national parks. Contact individual parks for more specific information. National park campground and reservations information can be obtained by calling the National Park Reservation System (☎ 800-365-2267) or writing to National Park Service Public Inquiry, Dept of Interior, PO Box 37127, Washington, DC 20013-7127. Online information is available at the US National Park Service website (www.nps.gov).

Golden Passports There are several types of these passes offering discounted access for certain types of visitors. The passes admit a private vehicle, or the passholder, spouse and children when entry is not by private vehicle. You can apply in person for any of the following at any national park or regional office of the USFS or NPS.

Golden Eagle Passports cost $25 annually and offer one-year entry into national parks to the holder and accompanying guests. Golden Age Passports carry a one-time fee of $10 and allow US residents 62 years and older unlimited entry to all sites in the national park system, with 50% discounts on camping and other fees. Golden Access Passports offer the same benefits to

US residents who are clinically blind or are permanently disabled.

Following is a list of scenic areas administered by the NPS in the Rocky Mountain states.

COLORADO
Following is a list of scenic areas administered by the NPS in Colorado.

Bent's Old Fort National Historic Site In southeastern Colorado, on the north bank of the Arkansas River, this small site was an early prairie trading post.

Black Canyon of the Gunnison National Monument The Gunnison River cut this deep, narrow and scenic western Colorado gorge nearly 2500 feet below the adjacent plateau. Its 13,000 acres also feature forests of ancient piñon pines.

Curecanti National Recreation Area Upstream from the Black Canyon of the Gunnison, several reservoirs have flooded the Gunnison River and its tributaries to create this recreational area.

Colorado National Monument Once dinosaur country, this 18,000-acre reserve near Grand Junction, in western Colorado, displays the most colorful, distinctive forms that erosion can achieve.

Dinosaur National Monument The Green and Yampa rivers flow through this 298-sq-mile reserve, in northeastern Utah and northwestern Colorado, where dino-

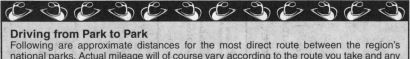

Driving from Park to Park
Following are approximate distances for the most direct route between the region's national parks. Actual mileage will of course vary according to the route you take and any detours you make along the way.

From	To	Distance
Rocky Mountain National Park	Yellowstone National Park	600 miles
Rocky Mountain National Park	Mesa Verde National Park	478 miles
Yellowstone National Park	Glacier National Park	426 miles
Yellowstone National Park	Grand Teton National Park	8 miles

saur fossils lie in impressive quarries. Equally impressive Native American petroglyphs embellish nearby scenic canyons.

Florissant Fossil Beds National Monument Volcanic ash covered this former lake bed in the mountains west of Colorado Springs, preserving 6000 acres of fossil flora and fauna, including petrified sequoias.

Great Sand Dunes National Monument In south central Colorado's San Luis Valley, near the south end of the Sangre de Cristo range, the shifting sand dunes at this 56-sq-mile monument are the highest in the country, rising up to 800 feet.

Hovenweep National Monument In southwestern Colorado and southeastern Utah, this 300-acre monument protects the ruins of defensive fortifications which once protected a vital water supply for pre-Columbian inhabitants.

Mesa Verde National Park In southwestern Colorado, covering 80 sq miles, this park is primarily an archaeological preserve. Its elaborate cliffside dwellings are relics of Ancestral Puebloans who evolved a complex social structure that lasted for centuries until their mysterious abandonment of the dwellings around 1300 AD.

Rocky Mountain National Park Only a short hop from Denver, this Front Range park straddles the Continental Divide offering 395 sq miles of Alpine forests, lakes, and tundra covered by summer wildflowers and grazed by bighorn sheep. Unlike the Tetons, most of its high peaks can be reached by hikes.

WYOMING
Following is a list of scenic areas administered by the NPS in Wyoming.

Big Horn Canyon National Recreation Area In southeastern Montana and north central Wyoming, the Yellowtail Dam

drowned the Bighorn River to create the reservoir known as Bighorn Lake, the centerpiece of this 188-sq-mile area.

Devil's Tower National Monument This solitary, massive sheer-sided rock tower, sacred to many Native Americans, rises 1200 feet above the plains in northeastern Wyoming.

Flaming Gorge National Recreation Area The red canyon walls of the Green River gorge gave this area its name. Northern Utah's Flaming Gorge Dam has submerged the Green River for 90 miles north into Wyoming to create this national recreation area.

Fort Laramie National Historic Site At the confluence of Wyoming's North Platte and Laramie rivers, this 836-acre site contains several restored structures from its days as a frontier army post.

Fossil Butte National Monument Once the site of an enormous lake, freshwater fish fossils over 50 million years old are the prime attraction of this 820-acre high desert reserve.

Grand Teton National Park The most dramatic peaks in the region, the granite spires of the Tetons tower 7000 feet above nearby Jackson Hole. Created in 1929, the park offers 148 sq miles for hiking, climbing, viewing wildlife and other recreational activities. Its highest point is 13,766-foot Grand Teton.

Medicine Wheel National Historic Landmark On a high plateau in the Bighorn Mountains east of Lovell, this 70-foot diameter sacred medicine wheel is revered by all the region's Native American peoples.

John D Rockefeller Jr Memorial Parkway Rockefeller purchased and then donated over 55 sq miles of land to Grand Teton National Park. In recognition of his contribution, the US Congress declared the

7½ miles of road between Yellowstone and Grand Teton national parks as the John D Rockefeller Jr Memorial Parkway.

Yellowstone National Park The world's first national park is a wonderland of volcanic geysers, hot springs, Alpine lakes, forested mountains, waterfalls and the most spectacular wildlife in North America outside the Arctic. All of which make Yellowstone National Park the region's single most popular tourist destination.

MONTANA
Following is a list of scenic areas administered by the NPS in Montana.

Bighorn Canyon National Recreation Area In southeastern Montana and in northern Wyoming, the Yellowtail Dam drowned the Bighorn River to create the reservoir known as Bighorn Lake, the centerpiece of this 188-sq-mile area.

Big Hole National Battlefield In western Montana, near the town of Wisdom, this historical site covers 655 acres where in 1877 the US Army surprised an encampment of Nez Percé, starting a bloody battle that lasted two days.

Custer Battlefield National Monument In southeastern Montana, on the Crow Reservation, this 765-acre monument memorializes a confrontation that sent shock waves throughout the USA: on the eve of the nation's centennial in 1876, the Lakota Sioux took charge of their territory by wiping out General George Armstrong Custer's 7th US Cavalry.

Glacier National Park Montana's only national park (excluding a sliver of Yellowstone), Glacier comprises 1558 sq miles of high sedimentary peaks, Alpine lakes and small glaciers, and imposing fauna, including the grizzly bear. Canada's Waterton Lakes National Park adjoins it to the north.

Grant-Kohrs Ranch National Historic Site Near Deer Lodge, this was the center of one of the largest open-range ranches in the country.

IDAHO
Following is a list of scenic areas administered by the NPS in Idaho.

City of Rocks National Reserve Remote, clean granite spires attract mostly climbers to this reserve, but these evocative spires fascinate all who visit, including Oregon Trail pioneers, who left their names on Register Rock.

Craters of the Moon National Monument Otherworldly barren black basalt, cinder cones and lava tubes at Craters of the Moon National Monument give a glimpse of volcanic activity that ceased only 2000 years ago.

EBR-1 National Historic Landmark Electricity from splitting the atom first became a reality here and nearby Arco was the world's first atomic-powered community, almost 50 years ago. If you are interested in where the dream of atomic energy is going, you will want to see EBR-1 National Historic Landmark, where it all began.

Hagerman Fossil Beds National Monument The world's best upper Pliocene-era fossil beds, from when this was a marsh-covered grassland, are close to I-84 near Twin Falls. Guided tours begin from the comprehensive Hagerman Fossil Beds National Monument visitor center.

Hells Canyon National Recreation Area The Snake River carves the deepest canyon in North America through Hells Canyon. Most people see it from the river via rafts or jet boats, rather than making their way to Heavens Gate Lookout on the rim for the stunning view down into the canyon.

Nez Percé National Historic Park The tragic story of the dramatic flight for freedom of the Nez Percé, and their marvelous creation myth, are embodied in the vast landscape of the Nez Percé National His-

National Park Services & Activities

This chart includes accommodations, services and activities available within park boundaries. Though not included here, other options are often close by at gateway towns. In addition to facilities listed, all parks have visitor centers and handicapped accessible toilets.

National Park	Accommodations	Food	Activities
Glacier	camping, chalets, lodges	restaurants, food market	biking, fishing, hiking, riding, cross-country skiing
Grand Teton	camping, cabins, lodges	restaurant, food market	biking, boating, climbing, fishing, hiking, riding, cross-country skiing
Mesa Verde	camping, lodges	restaurant, food market	nature hikes, NPS guided tours
Rocky Mountain	camping	restaurant	biking, climbing, fishing, hiking, riding, cross-country skiing
Yellowstone	camping, cabins, lodges	restaurant, food markets	biking, boating, fishing, hiking, riding, cross-country skiing

toric Park, adjacent to the Nez Percé Indian Reservation.

Sawtooth National Recreation Area In the heart of Idaho, this recreation area centers on the granite Sawtooth Mountains, with fabulous Sun Valley to the south and the meadows, forests, lakes and rivers of the Stanley Basin to the east and north.

NATIONAL FORESTS

The US Forest Service (USFS) is under the US Department of Agriculture and administrates the use of forests. Many of the most scenic areas in the Rocky Mountains are under USFS jurisdiction. National forests are less protected than parks, being managed under the concept of 'multiple use,' which includes timber cutting, watershed management, wildlife management and recreation. Critics have accused the USFS of promoting unsustainable forestry practices at the expense of conservation.

Current information about national forests can be obtained from ranger stations, listed in the text. National forest campground and reservation information can be obtained by calling ☎ 800-280-2267, TTY 800-879-4496. Callers need to know the name of the national forest and the name of the campground. An $8.65 service charge applies regardless of the number of nights reserved. You can also get info from the USFS website (www.fs.fed.us/).

WILDERNESS AREAS

If you want to leave the 'civilized world' behind, these wilderness areas, which are inaccessible to mechanized travel, are the places to go. The Federal Wilderness Act of 1964 established certain places 'where the earth and its community of life are untrammeled by man, where man himself is a visitor who does not remain.' This pioneering legislation has since been used to prohibit and limit development of roadless areas throughout the country, in the interest of preserving biological diversity, protecting valuable watersheds and offering recreational escapes from urban areas. While national park and national forest areas differ slightly in their management, the general philosophy behind them is to 'take only photographs, leave only footprints.'

All motorized transport is prohibited. Only about 1.8% of the land in the lower 48 states (excluding Alaska and Hawaii) enjoys wilderness designation.

The NPS, USFS and BLM all manage wilderness areas in the Rocky Mountain states. The majority of these designated areas are on USFS land, but while the BLM is a relative latecomer to the concept, some of its wilderness areas are among the best in terms of sheer solitude. Many people hike and backpack in the Rocky Mountain wilderness areas, though some also enter on horseback. The NPS, USFS and BLM impose restrictions on some wilderness areas by requiring entry permits, limiting group size, limiting or even prohibiting campfires in some areas and regulating camping sites and length of stay. Many wilderness areas have no developed campsites.

Some of the most hikable USFS wilderness areas are the Indian Peaks, Flat Tops and Maroon Bells in Colorado, the Bridger-Teton, Popo Agie and Cloud Peak in Wyoming and the Bob Marshall, Anaconda-Pintler and Selway-Bitteroot in Montana.

BUREAU OF LAND MANAGEMENT
The BLM, as it is commonly called, manages public use of federal lands. This is no-frills camping, often in untouched settings (most of BLM's holdings are in the Southwest desert). There are few restrictions on activity in BLM lands, which means one can often camp, hike or bike wherever one chooses. A downside to this for those who seek quiet is this laissez-faire approach also beckons off-road drivers and motorcyclists.

Each state has a regional office located in the state capital. Look in the blue section of the local white pages directory under US Government, Interior Dept or call the Federal Information Center (☎ 800-688-9889).

FISH & WILDLIFE SERVICE
Each state has a few regional Fish & Wildlife Service (FWS) offices that can provide information about viewing local wildlife. Their phone numbers appear in the blue section of the local white pages directory under US Government, Interior Dept, or you can call the Federal Information Center (☎ 800-688-9889).

STATE PARKS
Each of the Rocky Mountain states maintains its own system of parks, wildlife areas and reserves which are generally smaller and less diverse than those in the federal system. However, they can contain some surprisingly beautiful scenery, and often make for good camping options. For details, see individual state chapters.

Outdoor Activities

HIKING & BACKPACKING
There is perhaps no better way to appreciate the beauty of the Rocky Mountain states – their lofty glacial peaks, peaceful dense forests, remote mountain meadows and high Alpine lakes – than on foot and on the trail. Leaving the highway for a few days (or even a few hours) to explore the great outdoors can refreshen road-weary travelers and give them a heightened appreciation of the scenery which goes whizzing past day after day. Some travelers will experience one good hike and decide to plan the rest of their trip around wilderness or hiking areas.

One important thing to remember is that once you get into the backcountry, much of the scenery looks the same throughout the Rocky Mountain region, so unless you are longing specifically to see the Tetons, time is better spent out of the car on the trail than in the car trying to get to a certain trail in a certain area. Hiking in one of Wyoming's wilderness areas may be much more rewarding, just as beautiful and half as crowded as hiking in Yellowstone National Park.

Safety
The major forces to be reckoned with while hiking and camping are the weather (which

is uncontrollable) and your own frame of mind. Be prepared for the Rockies' unpredictable weather – you may go to bed under a clear sky and wake up to two feet of snow, even in mid-August. Carry a rain jacket and a light pair of long underwear at all times, even on short afternoon hikes. Backpackers should have a pack-liner (heavy-duty garbage bags work well), a full set of rain gear and food that does not require cooking. A positive attitude is helpful in any situation. If a hot shower, comfortable mattress and clean clothes are essential to your well-being, don't head out into the wilderness for five days – stick to day hikes.

Highest safety measures suggest never hiking alone, but solo travelers should not be discouraged, especially if you value solitude. The important thing is to always let someone know where you are going and how long you plan to be gone. Use sign-in boards at trailheads or ranger stations. Travelers who are looking for hiking companions can inquire or post notices at ranger stations, outdoors equipment stores, campgrounds and youth hostels.

Fording rivers and streams is another potentially dangerous but often necessary part of being on the trail. In national parks and along maintained trails in national forests, bridges usually cross large bodies of water (this is not the case in designated wilderness areas, where bridges are taboo). Upon reaching a river, unclip all of your pack straps – your pack is expendable, you are not. Avoid crossing barefoot – river cobbles will suck body heat right out of your feet, numbing them and making it impossible to navigate. Bring a pair of lightweight canvas sneakers for this purpose, to avoid sloshing around in wet boots for the rest of your hike.

Although cold water will make you want to cross as quickly as possible, don't rush things: take small steps, watch where you are stepping and keep your balance. Using a staff for balance is helpful, but don't rely on it to support all your weight. Don't enter water higher than mid-thigh; once higher than that your body gives the current a large mass to work against.

If you should get wet, wring your clothes out immediately, wipe off all the excess water on your body and hair and put on any dry clothes you (or your partner) might have. Synthetic fabrics and wool both retain heat even when they get wet, but cotton does not.

People with little hiking or backpacking experience should not attempt to do too much, too soon, or they might end up being non-hikers for the wrong reasons. Know your limitations, know the route you are going to take and pace yourself accordingly. Remember, there is absolutely nothing wrong with turning back or not going as far as you originally planned.

What to Bring

Equipment The following is meant to be a general guideline for backpackers, not an 'if-I-have-everything-here-I-will-be-fine' checklist. Know yourself and what special things you may need on the trail;

Treading Lightly

Backcountry areas are composed of fragile environments and cannot support an inundation of human activity, especially insensitive and careless activity.

A code has evolved to deal with the growing numbers of people in the wilderness. Most conservation organizations and hikers' manuals have their own backcountry codes that outline the same important principles: minimizing the impact on the land, leaving no trace and taking nothing but photographs and memories. Above all, stay on the main trail, stay on the main trail, and, lastly, even if it means walking through mud or crossing a patch of snow, *stay on the main trail*. Shortcutting causes severe erosion: even if it doesn't feel like you're doing any damage, that quick hike through the hillside brush could be the first step toward killing the flora that keeps that slope from sliding down to destroy the habitat below. ■

consider the area and climatic conditions you will be traveling in. Note that this list is inadequate for snow country or winter.

- Boots – light to medium are recommended for day hikes, while sturdy boots are necessary for extended trips with a heavy pack. Most importantly, they should be well broken in and have a good heel. Waterproof boots are preferable.

- Alternative footwear – thongs or sandals or running shoes for wearing around camp (optional) and canvas sneakers for crossing streams.

- Socks – heavy polypropylene or wool will stay warm even if they get wet. Frequent changes during the day reduce the chance of blisters, but are usually impractical.

- Subdued colors are recommended, but if hiking during hunting season, bright blaze orange is a necessity.

- Shorts, light shirt – for everyday wear; remember that heavy cotton takes a long time to dry and is very cold when wet.

- Long-sleeve shirt – light cotton, wool or polypropylene. A button-down front makes layering easy and can be left open when the weather is hot and your arms need protection from the sun.

- Long pants – heavy denim jeans take forever to dry. Sturdy cotton or canvas pants are good for trekking through brush, and cotton or nylon sweats are comfortable to wear around camp. Long underwear with shorts over them is the perfect combo – warm but not cumbersome – for trail hiking where there is not much brush.

- Wool or polypropylene or polar fleece sweater or pullover – essential in chilly or cold weather.

- Rain gear – light, breathable and waterproof is the ideal combination. If nothing else is available, use heavy-duty trash bags to cover you and your packs.

- Hat – wool or polypropylene is best for cold weather, while a cotton hat with a brim is good for sun protection. About 80% of body heat escapes through the top of the head. Keep your head and neck warm to reduce the chances of hypothermia.

- Bandanna or handkerchief – good for a runny nose, dirty face, unmanageable hair, picnic lunch and flag (especially a red one).

- Small towel – one which is indestructible and will dry quickly.

- First-aid kit – should include self-adhesive bandages, disinfectant, antibiotic salve or cream, gauze, small scissors and tweezers.

- Knife, fork, spoon and mug – a double-layer plastic mug with a lid is best. A mug acts as eating and drinking receptacle, mixing bowl and wash basin. Bring an extra cup if you like to eat and drink simultaneously.

- Pots and pans – aluminum cook sets are best, but any sturdy one-quart pot is sufficient. True gourmands who want more than pasta, soup and freeze-dried food will need a skillet or frying pan. A pot scrubber is helpful for removing stubborn oatmeal, especially when using cold water and no soap.

- Stove – lightweight and easy to operate is ideal. Most outdoors stores rent propane or butane stoves; test the stove before you head out, even cook a meal on it, to familiarize yourself with any quirks it may have.

- Water purifier – optional but really nice to have; water can be purified by boiling for at least 10 minutes though even then some hardy microbes may remain.

- Matches or lighter – waterproof matches are good and having several lighters on hand is smart.

- Candle or lantern – candles are easy to operate, but do not stay lit when they are dropped or wet and can be hazardous inside a tent. Outdoors stores rent lanterns; as with a stove, test it before you hit the trail.

- Flashlight – each person should have his or her own and be sure its batteries have plenty of life left in them.

- Sleeping bag – goose-down bags are warm and lightweight, but worthless if they get wet; most outdoors stores rent synthetic bags.

- Sleeping pad – this is strictly a personal preference. Use a sweater or sleeping bag sack stuffed with clothes as a pillow.

- Tent – make sure it is waterproof, or has a waterproof cover, and know how to put it up *before* you reach camp. Remember that your packs will be sharing the tent with you.

- Camera and binoculars – don't forget extra film and waterproof film canisters (sealable plastic bags work well).

- Compass and maps – each person should have his/her own.

- Eyeglasses – contact-lens wearers should always bring a back-up set.

- Sundries – toilet paper, small sealable plastic bags, insect repellent, sun screen, lip balm, unscented moisturizing cream, moleskin for foot blisters, dental floss (burnable and good when there is no water for brushing), sunglasses, deck of cards, pen or pencil and paper or notebook, books and nature guides.

Food Keeping your energy up is important, but so is keeping your pack light. Backpackers tend to eat a substantial breakfast and dinner and snack heavily in between. There is no need to be excessive. If you pack loads of food you'll probably use it, but if you have just enough you will probably not miss anything.

Some basic staples are packaged instant oatmeal, bread (the denser the better), rice or pasta, instant soup or ramen noodles, dehydrated meat (jerky), dried fruit, energy bars, chocolate, trail mix (gorp – raisins and peanuts mixed with various other goodies like sunflower seeds, M&Ms or dried fruit), and peanut butter or honey or jam (in plastic jars or squeeze bottles). Don't forget the wet-wipes, but be sure to pack them out.

Books
There are quite a few good how-to and where-to books on the market, usually found in outdoors stores, or bookstores' Sports & Recreation or Outdoors sections. Chris Camden's *Backpacker's Handbook* (Ragged Mountain Press, 1992) is a beefy collection of tips for the trail. More candid book is *A Hiker's Companion* (The Mountaineers, 1992), written by Cindy Ross & Todd Gladfelter, who hiked 12,000 miles before sitting down to write. *How to Shit in the Woods* (Ten Speed Press, 1994) is Kathleen Meyer's explicit, comic and

Wilderness Camping
Camping in undeveloped areas is rewarding for its peacefulness, but presents special concerns. Take care to ensure that the area you choose can comfortably support your presence, and leave the surroundings in better condition than on arrival. The following list of guidelines should help:

- Camp below timberline, since Alpine areas are generally more fragile. Good campsites are found, not made. Altering a site shouldn't be necessary.

- Camp at least 200 feet (70 adult steps) away from the nearest lake, river or stream.

- Bury human waste in cat holes dug 6 to 8 inches deep, at least 200 feet from water, camp or trails. The salt and minerals in urine attract deer; use a tent-bottle (funnel attachments are available for women) if you are prone to middle-of-the-night calls by Mother Nature. Camouflage the cat hole when finished.

- Use soaps and detergents sparingly or not at all, and never allow their residue to enter streams or lakes. When washing yourself (a backcountry luxury, not a necessity), lather up (with biodegradable soap) and rinse yourself with cans of water 200 feet away from your water source. Scatter dish water after removing all food particles.

- Carry a lightweight stove for cooking and to use a lantern instead of a fire.

- If a fire is allowed and appropriate, dig out the native topsoil and build a fire in the hole. Gather sticks no larger than an adult's wrist. Do not snap branches off live, dead or downed trees. Pour wastewater from meals around the perimeter of the campfire to prevent the fire from spreading, and thoroughly douse it before leaving or going to bed.

- Establish a cooking area at least 100 yards away from your tent and designate cooking clothes to leave in the food bag, away from your tent.

- Burn cans to get rid of their odor, remove them from the ashes and pack them out.

- Pack out what you pack in, including all trash – yours *and* others'. ■

useful manual on toilet training in the wilderness. For more books, including state specific guides, see the Facts for the Visitor chapter.

Maps

A good map is essential for any hiking trip. Both NPS and USFS ranger stations usually stock topographical maps that cost about $2 to $6. In the absence of a ranger station, try the local stationery or hardware store.

Longer hikes require two types of maps: USGS Quadrangles and US Department of Agriculture Forest Service maps. To order a map index and price list, contact the US Geological Survey, PO Box 25286, Denver, CO 80225. Also good is the Trail Ways series, which have clearly marked, easy to read topo maps for many popular hiking areas.

For more general information on maps, see that entry in Facts for the Visitor; for information regarding maps of specific forests, wilderness areas or national parks, see the appropriate geographic entry.

Getting to the Backcountry

Getting to the backcountry can often be a trying tangle of switchback roads and unmarked forest service roads. For this reason it is recommended that you obtain a topographic map and a USFS map of the area you intend to traverse.

You can reach backcountry areas in southern Colorado by taking either the Cumbres & Toltec Scenic Railroad from Antonito, CO, to Chama, NM, or the Durango & Silverton Narrow Gauge Railroad. These lines allow access to wilderness areas, including the Continental Divide National Scenic Trail, at their water stops (see relevant geographic entries in the Colorado chapters for more information).

ROAD & MOUNTAIN BIKING

Bike-friendly cities where you can ditch the car and ride to museums and other attractions on a network of routes include Missoula, Denver, Boulder, Fort Collins, Durango, Pueblo, and to a limited degree,

Colorado Springs. Denver-Boulder buses offer bicycle access. Colorado's Summit County features a great system of bike routes and bike-friendly buses that link its towns. Buses between Aspen and Glenwood Springs also carry bikes. In Telluride, you will find 'community bicycles' available for anyone to use for local cruising.

The Rockies are a mecca for mountain bikers. Crested Butte, CO, shares the mantle with California's Marin County for developing the mountain bike, beginning with a rugged tour over Pearl Pass to Aspen in 1976. Each July, Crested Butte hosts Fat Tire Bike Week and celebrates mountain bike pioneers and innovations at their Mountain Bike Museum and Hall of Fame. The mountains around Aspen and Crested Butte, the hills of the northern Front Range and trails near Fruita are among the top spots for mountain biking in the region.

Multiple-day mountain bike tours are available using the San Juan Hut System that extends from Telluride across the Colorado Plateau to Moab, UT. Campers can travel the 500-mile Colorado Trail. Current plans are to create the Great Divide Mountain Bike Route, running 3000 miles from Canada to Mexico along the spine of the Rocky Mountains.

Mountain biking is becoming increasingly popular in Montana. Big Sky and the Big Mountain (Whitefish) offer lift-serviced trails, while West Yellowstone has an excellent network of trails both in and outside Yellowstone National Park. There are also good single tracks in the Absaroka and Gallatin ranges accessible from the Paradise Valley. Bozeman is the state's mountain biking hub, largely due to its young and fearless population. *Fat Trax Bozeman* (Falcon Press, 1996) is available at sport shops around town.

Idaho's Taft Tunnel Bike Trail follows a converted rail line through mountain tunnels and over high railway trestles, across the state line to Montana. The centerpiece of the trail is the 8771-foot-long Taft Tunnel, constructed in 1909.

Information

Descriptions of off-road bike trails in national forests are generally available by contacting the forest supervisor's office in the area. DeLorme publishes a topographic *Atlas & Gazetteer* for each state. These are good tools for planning trail rides.

Dennis Coello's *Mountain Bike Rides of the West: Twenty Classic Tours* (Northland Publishing, 1989) describes trips in and around Dinosaur National Monument, Rocky Mountain National Park, Greys River (WY), Hovenweep, Telluride, the Tetons and Yellowstone, Durango, Crested Butte and Glacier National Park.

Colorado *Bicycle Colorado Magazine* is glossy magazine that explains popular road rides and mountain biking at some of the state's ski resorts. It's published annually by the nonprofit Bicycle Colorado (☎ 970-536-0051), PO Box 698, Salida, CO 81201. It's usually available in bike shops and larger visitors centers.

The Colorado Bicycle Pedestrian Program Manager (☎ 303-757-9982) at the Colorado Department of Highways, 4201 E Arkansas Ave, No 225, Denver, CO 80222, sells maps of suggested touring routes. Their slender 'Colorado Bicycle Manual' is a handy summary of state laws, bicycle resources and guide books.

Information about state parks with off-road trails is available from Colorado State Parks (☎ 303-866-3437), 1313 Sherman St, No 618, Denver, CO 80203. The Colorado State Parks office also publishes a free 'Colorado Trails Guide' showing bike routes and off-road trails in three areas of the state: North Front Range, South Front Range and the Western Slope and Mountains. Larger visitors centers may have a copy of this map.

One of the few comprehensive guides to the state is the *Mountain Biker's Guide to Colorado* (Menasha Ridge Press, 1996) by Linda Gong and Gregg Bromka, which details 66 rides. Although it doesn't have any topo maps, information on elevation is included. Otherwise stop by a local bike shop for books and maps. Laura Rossetter has written several guides to mountain trails in various parts of Colorado. Both Latitude 40 and Trail Ways publish maps that can be used for both road and mountain biking.

Wyoming The Wyoming Department of Transportation (☎ 307-777-4719), 5300 Bishop Blvd, PO Box 1708, Cheyenne, WY 82003, publishes the 'Wyoming Bicycle Guidance Map,' which shows state-wide routes, significant grades, prevailing winds, the average daily summer traffic volume, designated mountain bike routes, campsites, elevations and towns with bike shops. This compact, easy-to-read map is a vital planning tool for cyclists.

For eastern Wyoming, obtain D Horning and H Marriott's *A Mountain Biker's Guide to Wyoming East of the Divide* (Poorperson's Guidebooks, 1989).

Montana General vehicle traffic-volume maps of the state are available for $2 from the Bicycle/Pedestrian Coordinator (☎ 406-444-6118), Montana Department of Transportation, 2701 Prospect St, Helena, MT 59620.

Adventure Cycling (☎ 406-721-8791), 150 E Pine St, Missoula, MT 59801, publishes maps and guides to favorite rides in and around Montana. One popular route is from Missoula up through the Swan Valley (Hwy 83) to Glacier National Park. Backroads (☎ 800-462-2848; www.backroads.com), leads organized bike tours with camping and inn options ($500 to $1500) through Glacier and Yellowstone national parks.

Laws & Regulations

Throughout the Rocky Mountains, bikes are restricted from entering designated wilderness areas and national park trails, but may otherwise ride on national forest and BLM single-track trails. Trail etiquette requires that cyclists yield to other users. Helmets should always be worn to reduce the risk of head injury, but they are not mandated by law.

Cyclists may use about 80% of Colorado's rural interstate routes, all but a few short urban sections in Wyoming and on the broad shoulders of all interstate highways in Montana. Montana's incomparable Going-to-the-Sun Rd, through Glacier National Park, has midday bicycle access restrictions.

SKIING & SNOWBOARDING

The Rocky Mountain states, Colorado in particular, are home to some of the USA's most popular ski destinations. High mountains and reliable snow conditions have attracted investors and multi-million dollar ski resorts, equipped with the latest in chair lift technology, snow-grooming systems and facilities. Along with the big-name places like Aspen, Vail, Jackson Hole, Big Sky and Sun Valley, are small operations with a handful of lifts, cheaper ticket prices and terrain that is often as challenging as their glitzier neighbors (after all, the smaller ones are in the same mountain ranges).

In addition to downhill skiing, there are ample opportunities for cross-country and backcountry skiing. The USFS often maintains summer hiking trails as cross-country trails during the winter, offering great opportunities to experience wilderness areas that teem with people in the summer. Many places specialize in cross-country skiing and offer weekend or week-long packages that include lodging, meals and equipment rentals. Downhill areas also frequently have cross-country areas, and in the winter golf courses often have terrain suited to beginners.

Snowboarding has recently swept the nation's ski culture and taken on a following of its own and growing numbers of snowboarders are seen on Rocky Mountain slopes. While snowboarders originally bore an image as outsiders, set apart by their youth, baggy pants and funky hats, their ranks have expanded to include people of all ages, including a lot of ex-skiers! Ski mountains are starting to dedicate terrain to snowboarders, developing halfpipes and snowboard parks.

Ski areas are often well equipped with places to stay, places to eat, shops, entertainment venues, child-care facilities (both on and off the mountain) and transportation. In fact, it is possible to stay a week at some of the bigger places – Snowmass, Vail, Big Sky, Sun Valley – without ever leaving the slopes.

In areas where the developer owns everything, items tend to be more expensive, whereas ski areas built near pre-existing towns, like Winter Park or Crested Butte, CO, have more variety in facilities and prices. One thing is guaranteed – you can save at least $5 a day by buying food at a grocery store and packing your own lunch. Lodges are equipped with lockers so you don't have to tote your food around all day and worry about falling on your sandwich.

All ski areas have at least one comfortable base lodge with a rental office, ski shop and lockers. There are also cafeterias and lounges or bars, where non-skiers, tired skiers and cold skiers can relax in warmth in front of a bay window looking out onto the skiers outside. You do not have to buy a lift ticket or pay to enjoy the base lodge.

At major ski areas, lift tickets cost anywhere from $35 to $58 for a full day and $17 to $35 for a half-day which usually starts at 1 pm. Three-day or week-long lift passes are usually more economical, especially if they do not need to be used on consecutive days.

Equipment rentals are available at or near even the smallest ski areas, though renting equipment in a nearby town can be cheaper if you have the capacity to transport it to the slopes; basic rentals, including skis, boots and poles, cost from $12 a day. Basic snowboard packages include board and boots and also start around $12. For anywhere from $20 to $40 you can rent 'demo' equipment, allowing you to try the newest equipment on the market. This is especially useful if you're in the market for your own skis or snowboard, and want to see what's available.

Visitors planning on taking lessons should rent equipment on the mountain since the price of a group lesson, around $35 for a half-day (more at the larger resorts), usually includes equipment rentals, with no discount for having your own gear. Children's ski schools are popular places to stash the kids for a day, offering lessons, day-care facilities and providing lunch for around $40 to $50 per child.

Downhill Skiing & Snowboarding

The Rockies offer some of the USA's most skiable downhill terrain. Colorado alone boasts 26 ski resorts and there are significant ski mountains in Wyoming, Montana and Idaho.

Colorado Colorado's 26 ski areas dominate the nation's ski scene and attract 11 million skiers and snowboarders annually.

Convenient access counts: the center of Colorado's ski industry lies about 80 miles west of Denver in Summit County. This is North America's most popular ski destination with four ski areas – Breckenridge, Arapahoe Basin, Keystone and Copper

Mountain – that offer something for everybody, from families at Keystone to extreme skiers at A-Basin.

The *Denver Post*'s special Ski & Snow section appears on the second Sunday of November; it surveys the nation's skiing experts (readers and editors from *Ski Magazine*, *Skiing* and *Snow Country*) about their personal favorites. Vail is repeatedly chosen as the nation's 1st- or 2nd-favorite resort due to its variety of terrain that guarantees you'll never get bored. (The town's haughtiness is another matter.) If you have only one day to ski in Colorado, most agree that Vail is the place to go. Aspen and Crested Butte follow in the voting.

Nightlife is lively at Aspen, Telluride and Breckenridge – all historic mining towns with ski slopes. Crested Butte deserves mention as another scenic mining town with a good nighttime scene and some of the most challenging terrain in the state. Winter Park's renowned bumps and unique access from Denver on the Ski Train give it a special appeal as a day trip. Families appreciate the beginner and intermediate slopes at Snowmass and Buttermilk, plus the large corps of instructors that teach the kids while mom and dad slip away on the bus to more difficult slopes at nearby Aspen. When snow is in short supply, or you want to extend your ski season into late spring, head for Steamboat Springs which receives deep snows annually. A-Basin's high elevation on the Continental Divide makes it another late-season favorite.

Most resorts offer introductory snowboarding lessons – Aspen's Buttermilk is gaining an excellent reputation for its guaranteed learn-to-snowboard lessons. There are bargain half-day courses at Loveland Basin available for $30, and Purgatory offers free lessons to first-time snowboarders with the purchase of a lift ticket.

Information on 23 of Colorado's 26 mountains is available from Colorado Ski Country USA (☎ 303-837-0793), 1560 Broadway, Suite 2000, Denver, CO 80202 (www.skicolorado.org/).

For a report of snow conditions at resorts across the state, call the Snow Report (☎ 303-825-7669).

Wyoming Jackson Hole Mountain Resort in Teton Village is the largest resort in Wyoming, offering a world-class variety of skiing. Other nearby resorts are the Snow King Resort in Jackson and Grand Targhee Ski & Summer Resort in Alta.

Montana Big Sky is Montana's premier resort, 33 miles south of Bozeman. With a tram, gondola, nine chair lifts, 4180 feet of vertical drop and ever-increasing resort developments at the foot of the slopes, Big Sky beats Montana's other ski hills hands down. However there are other areas near towns where you can soak up some real Western color at night. The Big Mountain has a full resort at its base but is only 11 miles from the lively town of Whitefish, and is also close to Glacier National Park. Red Lodge Mountain is increasing in popularity; besides being next to a great party town, it has a good network of cross-country trails nearby.

Bridger Bowl is where Bozeman locals and MSU students go. It's humble in both size and amenities but has some great chutes and bowls above the area served by the lift. Locals tend to head toward Bridger Bowl near Bozeman and Snowbowl near Missoula.

Idaho Idaho's finest skiing is at Sun Valley Resort, where powder-dry snow and steep descents have been attracting celebrity skiers for decades to Bald Mountain and Dollar Mountain. In Idaho's Panhandle, Schweitzer Mountain Resort near Sandpoint and Silver Mountain Resort near Kellogg offer great facilities. Southwestern Idaho's best areas are Bogus Basin, close to Boise, and Brundage Mountain, near McCall.

Cross-Country & Backcountry Skiing

Cross-country or Nordic skiing offers a chance to get exercise, experience natural beauty at close quarters and save a few dollars by not needing to buy a downhill lift ticket. National parks, notably Yellowstone, close their roads during the winter and maintain cross-country trails into the parks' interiors.

The relatively new sport of backcountry skiing takes its roots from its Nordic cousin. The difference lies in the equipment and the terrain. Special telemark bindings, boots and skis now allow winter skiers to not only travel cross country but also tackle steep slopes or bowls that lie along their path. This is one of the most difficult types of skiing to learn, and the best place to first try it is probably at a ski resort or local snow slopes – not deep in the wilderness. Although some bindings allow skiers to lock down their boots, à la Alpine skiing, you really should have strong downhill telemarking skills before heading into the backcountry.

Modeled after European and Scandinavian traditions, yurt or hut systems have made their way into the USA's backcountry landscape. Huts are placed three to four hours (about 15 miles) apart from each other, and provide beds, cooking utensils, stoves, firewood and plenty of camaraderie and conversation. The idea is to ski from hut to hut, spending the night at each one, to make a complete loop of five to 10 days. People with less time or energy can ski into a hut from the initial trailhead, spend the night and ski out again the next day. Most huts enforce a two-night maximum and take reservations up to one month in advance. Each hut system, usually with at least three huts, operates independently.

The Environmental Impact of Skiing

Over the past decade, the impact of skiing on the environment has started receiving more attention. Most early ski hills consisted of a tow rope run on a generator from the back of a pickup truck, or a well-worn path to the top of a treeless slope – hardly an environmental threat. In fact, many ski pioneers were environmental enthusiasts who simply wanted a way to enjoy the outdoors during the winter.

However, skiing has turned into a consumer-driven industry, and some ski resorts have evolved into self-contained micro-cities that are actually bigger than many towns in the Rocky Mountain states. With a few big investors behind it a pre-planned resort community can descend on a pristine valley almost overnight. But while profit is almost certain for its investors, the project often leaves the environment decaying under its weight.

For example, a proposed East Fork Ski Resort would have developed 4 sq miles of private forest and 7 sq miles of the San Juan National Forest in Colorado's East Fork Valley, near the town of Pagosa Springs (population 1600). The planned resort, a joint venture between a Chicago developer and Balcor, a subsidiary of American Express, would have had 2700 housing units to accommodate 16,700 residents, and a ski mountain with eight lifts and a gondola to facilitate 13,500 skiers per day. Considering that the main inhabitants in the East Fork Valley are currently elk, wolverines and peregrine falcons, these figures are staggering.

With housing units come wood-burning stoves, sewage systems, two-car garages, parking lots and roads. Ski runs require clear-cutting and snowmaking equipment (which uses thousands of gallons of water each day). One study predicted that the resort would destroy nearly 70 acres of wetlands, consume 95% of the valley's elk calving grounds and dump more than 1 million gallons of sewage per day into the East Fork of the San Juan River.

The permit for the project was terminated in July 1994, and an appeal by the developers was denied in March 1995. A similar project targeting the wilderness around Vail and Beaver Creek was also shut down by government regulators, and fierce debate surrounds Crested Butte's plans to expand into a neighboring mountain. Of course, Colorado would not be Colorado without its ski resorts, and schussing down a ski slope is not meant to be a guilt-ridden experience. But with 26 areas already in the state, and a ski industry that is by no means threatened, when does recreation become 'wreck-creation'? ■

Often terrain between huts can be challenging and may require some strong backcountry skiing skills, so check with hut operators to see what you might be facing.

NPS, USFS, BLM and private lands support hundreds of miles of cross-country trails, some operated under special-use permits by private industries. The following is a list of some of the more popular areas.

Colorado Although many resorts in Colorado offer cross-country facilities adjacent to Alpine slopes, most Nordic skiers prefer to avoid the downhill crowds by visiting dedicated Nordic areas and backcountry trails on public park and forest lands. Perhaps the premier scenic skiing opportunities

are available at Rocky Mountain National Park, Mesa Verde National Park and Black Canyon of the Gunnison National Monument. Among the better, uncrowded cross-country centers are Twin Lakes between Leadville and Aspen, Red Feather Lakes northwest of Fort Collins and also the Fairplay Nordic Ski Center. The Frisco Nordic Center features an exclusive trail area on a peninsula jutting into Dillon Reservoir in Summit County.

Backcountry tourists can set off from high-altitude trailheads at Montezuma. Ashcroft Ski Touring near Aspen offers groomed trails, plus backcountry trails over Pearl Pass to Crested Butte, where Big Mine Park offers groomed trails, lessons and backcountry guides. Near Vail Pass, Shrine Pass Road is a popular touring route with a nearby restaurant.

The ultimate backcountry touring is available using the system of 12 huts strategically located along trails in the Aspen-Leadville-Vail area by the renowned 10th Mountain Division Hut Association. Near Lake City, the Hinsdale Haute Route offers three huts along the Continental Divide leading to Creede. Also in the Colorado Plateau, the San Juan Hut System is set up in the vicinity of Telluride, Ridgway and Ouray on the Mt Sneffles Wilderness border. Details and contact information for these hut systems can be found under the relevant destination entries. For a complete list of Colorado's huts, check out Brian Litz's *Colorado Hut to Hut* listed in Books, below.

Wyoming Yellowstone National Park provides excellent backcountry access. One fun trip is taking a snow coach to the Snow Lodge near Old Faithful and spending a few days skiing around geyser basins, the Grand Canyon of the Yellowstone and up Mt Washburn. The Snowy Range Ski Area, near Centennial, also has Nordic facilities and the White Pine Recreation Area, near Pinedale, is an area that's not overrun with tourists in the winter. Almost all of Jackson Hole is also skiable.

Montana Most of Montana's groomed cross-country trail systems are on national forest land and maintained by local ski clubs. For this reason there's usually no fee, nor any amenities. The best of these are Rendezvouz Cross-Country Ski Trails (West Yellowstone), Chief Joseph Cross-Country Trails (on the Montana-Idaho border at the southern end of the Bitteroot Valley), Silver Crest Ski Trails (between Great Falls and Livingston), Seeley Lake Ski Trails (in the Swan Range near Seeley Lake and the Bob Marshall Wilderness Complex), Blacktail Ski Trails (on the west shore of Flathead Lake) and MacDonald Pass Trail System (15 miles west of Helena).

One of the most charming cross-country ski places is the Izaak Walton Inn (in Essex, near Glacier National Park) where trails start from an old railroad lodge; there's a good restaurant here and old railroad cars have been made into cozy accommodations. Chico Hot Springs (in the Paradise Valley) is another spot where the lodge atmosphere is as good as the skiing. The Lone Mountain Ranch (at Big Sky) is similar, but less isolated.

Bohart Ski Ranch, near Bozeman, is an old log cabin that acts as a base lodge for an excellent 18-mile trail system. There are also good back-country trails into Glacier National Park.

Idaho Sun Valley and Galena Lodge in Sawtooth National Recreation Area are the most popular cross-country ski areas. On the west side of the Grand Tetons, near Victor, Rendezvous Ski Tours operates three huts accessible to backcountry skiers at elevations ranging from 8000 to 8800 feet. All can be reached via 4-mile trails that are skiable for anyone with basic cross-country skills. See Teton Valley in the Idaho Snake River Plain chapter for details.

Books & Magazines
In *Rocky Mountain Skiing*, Claire Waller gives information on ski resorts, accommodations and special ski programs for the four states covered in this book, as well as New Mexico, Utah and Alberta and British Columbia, Canada.

Brian Litz's *Colorado Hut to Hut* covers backcountry skiing, hiking and mountain biking around Colorado's extensive hut systems. Another good resource is Richard DuMais' *Fifty Colorado Ski Tours*, which caters more to Nordic skiers. The same author has also written *Fifty Ski Tours in Jackson Hole & Yellowstone*.

Another guide to this excellent Nordic ski area is *Cross-country Skiing Yellowstone Country* by Ken and Dena Olsen and Steve and Hazel Scharosch.

'Ski Touring Trails,' a brochure available from the USFS Northern Region, PO Box

7669, Missoula, MT 59807, provides a general overview of cross-country and backcountry possibilities in Montana's national forests and the 'Montana Winter Guide,' available from Travel Montana, PO Box 200533, 1424 9th Ave, Helena, MT 59620-0533, gives a place-by-place description of all of Montana's ski areas, downhill and cross-country.

Ski and *Skiing* are both year-round magazines available in most newsstands, airports and sporting goods stores. They feature travel articles, how-to advice and equipment tests; try to get a copy of the October or November issues for general information. *Snow Country* magazine ranks ski areas throughout the USA on the basis of categories, including terrain, ski school, night life, lodging and dining; Colorado resorts like Vail, Snowmass and Steamboat Springs always rank high on its lists.

ROCK CLIMBING & MOUNTAINEERING

Opportunities for rock climbing and mountaineering are almost unlimited in the Rockies – Colorado alone has 54 peaks over 14,000 feet above sea level, more than the rest of the USA combined. In 1868, the year before his celebrated descent of the Colorado River, the legendary John Wesley Powell with publisher William Byers became the first to sit atop one of these 14ers when they scaled 14,255-foot Longs Peak. In 1916, when Albert R Ellingwood and Eleanor S Davis climbed 14,294-foot Crestone Peak in the Sangre de Cristo Mountains, the last of the 14ers had been conquered.

Some of the world's great mountaineers have learned or polished their skills in the Rockies, most notably Paul Petzoldt, the founder of the National Outdoor Leadership School (NOLS) in Lander, WY. Petzoldt first climbed the Grand Teton at age 16 and more recently failed in a game attempt to repeat the achievement at age 86. He was also a member of the US Army's famed 10th Mountain Division, whose WWII training in the Rockies made

it possible to startle unsuspecting German troops in rugged positions the Germans thought unassailable.

Climbing and mountaineering are demanding activities requiring top physical condition, an understanding of the composition of various rock types and their hazards, other hazards of the high country and familiarity with a variety of equipment, including ropes, chocks, bolts, carabiners and harnesses. Many climbers prefer granite, like that found in the Teton Range, because of its strength and frequent handholds, but some climbers prefer limestone

US Climbing Ratings

In the US, climbing and mountaineering routes are generally classified using the Yosemite Decimal System (YDS), which has five classes. Class 1 is hiking, while Class 2 involves climbing on unstable materials like talus and may require use of the hands for keeping balance, especially with a heavy pack. Class 3 places the climber in dangerous situations, involving exposed terrain (the Sierra Club uses the example of a staircase on a high building without handholds – scary but not difficult), with the likely consequences of a fall being a broken limb. Ideally one should have climbing rope on hand, just in case.

Class 4 involves steep rock, smaller holds and great exposure, with obligatory use of ropes and knowledge of knots and techniques like belaying and rappelling; the consequences of falling are death rather than injury. Class 5 divides into a dozen or more subcategories based on degree of difficulty and requires advanced techniques, including proficiency with rope.

For serious climbers from outside the US, following are some comparisons of US Class 5 ratings with those of other international systems.

System	Rating	
YDS	5.2 – 5.9	5.10 – 5.14a+
UIAA	I – VI	VI+ – X+
Australian	11 – 18	19 – 33
French	1 – 6a	6a+ – 8c ∎

for a challenge. Some sedimentary rock is suitable for climbing, but crumbling volcanic rock can be very difficult.

The Access Fund, PO Box 67A25, Los Angeles, CA 90067, is a nonprofit organization working to keep climbing areas open to the public by purchasing or negotiating access to key sites.

Safety

Climbing is potentially a hazardous activity, though serious accidents are more spectacular than frequent; driving to the climbing site can be more dangerous than the climb itself. Nevertheless, climbers should be aware of hazards that can contribute to falls, serious injury or death.

Weather is an important factor, as rain makes rock slippery and lightning can strike an exposed climber; hypothermia is an additional concern. In dry weather, lack of water can lead to dehydration.

Environmental Concerns

To preserve the resource on which their sport relies, many climbers are now following guidelines similar to those established for hikers. These include concentrating impact in high-use areas by using established roads, trails and routes for access; dispersing use in pristine areas and avoiding the creation of new trails; refraining from creating or enhancing handholds; and eschewing the placement of bolts wherever possible. Climbers should also take special caution to respect archaeological and cultural resources, such as rock art, and refrain from climbing in such areas. Some climbers also use chalk that's specially colored to blend in with the rock in the area they're climbing.

Sites

So much of the Rocky Mountain region offers superb climbing that entire books are devoted to relatively small areas around climbers' meccas like Jackson Hole and Estes Park, the access points to Grand Teton and Rocky Mountain national parks.

There are good Colorado spots at Penitente Canyon near La Garita in the San Luis Valley, Taylor Canyon near Crested Butte, Greenhorn Reservoir in Summit County and the Gore Range near Kremmling. Lesser known but locally popular areas include Eldorado Canyon State Park and the Flatirons near Boulder, the Snowy Range sites along the Wyoming-Colorado border and Vedauwoo Rocks near Laramie, WY.

Wyoming's Wind River Range, especially the Cirque of the Towers, is another exceptional choice for both general mountaineering and rock climbing. The nearby Lander region attracts climbers with its world-class rock. Devils Tower National Monument, in the Black Hills of northeastern Wyoming, is a popular stop on the summer climbing circuit.

The stable rock and many uncharted climbs of Hyalite Canyon, near Bozeman, makes it a rock and ice climbing mecca. Pine Creek, in the Paradise Valley, is known for the Blue and Green Gullies – featured in Yvon Chouinard's book *Climbing Ice*. Another good spot that is less developed is Humbug Spires, south of Butte; it takes an hour or so on the trail to reach the spires. For mountaineering many people head to the Bob Marshall Wilderness Complex, which has many great one-day peak climbs. Glacier National Park also offers good peak climbing but routes are much less documented and thus require advanced trip research and good map and compass skills. For nontechnical peaks, head to the Bitterroot Range or the Gallatin Valley where trails are well-marked.

Idaho's Sawtooth Mountains offer great mountaineering and high-quality rock like Elephant Perch. Remote City of Rocks south of Burley is a fun place to climb.

Books

A good general introduction to climbing can be found in *Mountaineering: The Freedom of the Hills* by the Mountaineers in Seattle, WA.

For Colorado, Stewart M Green's *Rock Climbing Colorado* covers some 1500 climbing routes throughout the state. For hitting the big peaks, there's Walter R

Borneman's & Lyndon J Lampert's *A Climbing Guide to Colorado's Fourteeners*.

Titles for Wyoming include *Teton Classics: Fifty Selected Climbs in Grand Teton National Park* by the prolific climbing writer Richard Rossiter, *Sinks Canyon Rock Climbs 1994* by Greg Collins and *Free Climbs of Devils Tower* by Dingus McGee.

Falcon Press (Helena, MT) publishes *Rockclimbing Montana* and *The Climber's Guide to Glacier National Park*, both widely available in the western half of the state. *Big Sky Ice* by renowned Montana climber Ron Brunckhorst, is the state's definitive guide to ice climbing (it's available at sport stores in Bozeman).

HORSEBACK RIDING & PACK TRIPS

Given the American West's cowboy heritage, horseback riding is naturally a very popular summer activity throughout the Rockies, usually, but by no means always, associated with guest (dude) ranches. Visitors enjoying guest-ranch vacations will often enjoy unlimited access to riding and may even join in cattle drives à la *City Slickers*, the popular film starring Billy Crystal.

More casual riders will find rides expensive, as visitors during the short summer tourist season end up paying for the cost of feeding these hay burners over the winter: rates for recreational riding start around $15 per hour or $25 for two hours, though the hourly rate falls rapidly thereafter and full-day trips usually cost around $75 with a guide. Guided trips usually require a minimum of two persons. Backcountry pack trips, again with a guide, cost upwards of $100 per person per day, and usually involve some related activity, such as fly-fishing. A new variation on this theme is the llama pack trip, which substitutes the less predictable horse with these more docile South American animals.

Stables are almost ubiquitous throughout the West, but most numerous near major resort areas like Aspen, Estes Park and Grand Lake, CO; Jackson and Yellowstone National Park, WY; and Glacier National Park, MT. Experienced riders may want to let the owners know, or else you may be saddled with an excessively docile stable nag. Another option you may come across is a llama.

WHITE-WATER RAFTING

The Rocky Mountains offer a myriad of alternatives for one of the most exhilarating outdoor activities possible. Commercial outfitters in all four states provide white-water experiences ranging from inexpensive half-day trips to overnight and multiple day expeditions; those on NPS, USFS and BLM lands operate under permits from the appropriate agency, but individuals and groups with their own equipment do not need permits. Those not ready for white-water excitement can try more sedate float or tube trips.

River trips are classified on a scale of one to six, according to difficulty; Class I is virtually placid enough for an inner tube, while Class VI is 'unraftable.' On any given river, classifications can vary over the course of the year, depending on the water level. Higher water levels, usually associated with spring runoff, can make a river trip either easier or more difficult, by covering up hazards or increasing the velocity of the river, while lower water levels can expose hazards like rocks and whirlpools, making the river more exciting. Some, if not most, rivers depend on water releases from upstream dams.

White-water trips take place in either large rafts seating 12 or more people, or smaller rafts seating 6; the latter are more interesting and exciting because the ride over the rapids can be rougher and because everyone participates in rowing. For multiple day trips advance reservations are almost always essential. Full-day trips usually run anywhere from $50 to $90 depending on where you are, while overnights can cost $100 to $200. Trips in Colorado are generally more expensive than in the other states.

White-water trips can involve any of a variety of different boats, depending on the type of trip you want and the equipment used by the operator. The smallest craft are

Rafting River Ratings

The US rapid rating system, similar to that used in Europe, is:

Class I – very easy
  small regular waves and riffles; few or no obstacles, little maneuvering required

Class II – easy
  small waves with some eddies, low ledges, and slow rock gardens; some maneuvering required

Class III – medium
  numerous high and irregular waves, strong eddies, narrow but clear passages that require expertise in maneuvering; shore scouting necessary

Class IV – difficult
  long rapids with powerful, irregular waves, dangerous rocks and boiling eddies; precise maneuvering and shore scouting imperative

Class V – very difficult
  long rapids with wild turbulence and extremely congested routes that require complex maneuvering

Class VI – limits of navigation ■

one- or two-person inflatable or fiberglass kayaks. For group trips, there's the paddle raft (usually 14 feet long and carrying four to eight passengers paddling), the rear-mounted oar raft with guide and passengers paddling, and the center-mounted oar rafts, in which the guide paddles and passengers just ride. These latter are usually 16 feet long: there are 18- to 22-foot models, but these can take the ride out of rapids. The opposite of these is the dory – a hard-hulled (wood or steel) boat rowed by a guide that gives a surprisingly fun 'roller-coaster' ride on the white-water.

While white-water trips are not without danger, and it's not unusual for participants to fall out of the raft in rough water, serious injuries are rare and a vast majority of trips are without incident. All participants are required to wear US Coast Guard approved life jackets, and even nonswimmers are welcome. All trips have at least one river guide trained in lifesaving techniques.

National Wild & Scenic Rivers

Congressional legislation establishes certain criteria for the preservation of rivers with outstanding natural qualities; many of these are the best places for white-water rafting and canoeing. Wild rivers are, simply speaking, free-flowing and remote, while scenic rivers enjoy relatively natural surroundings and are free of impoundment, but have better access by road. Recreational rivers are more developed and usually have roads close by.

Rivers

In Colorado, good choices are the Arkansas River between Buena Vista and Cañon City, the undammed Yampa River west of Steamboat Springs, the Lake Fork of the Gunnison River, the Rio Grande near Creede and the Cache la Poudre and North Platte rivers near the Wyoming border.

Popular Wyoming rivers include the Snake River between Hoback Junction and Alpine south of Jackson, Shoshone River west of Cody and the Wind River south of Thermopolis.

Just outside the Yellowstone National Park boundary near Gardiner, MT, the Yellowstone River is the longest free-flowing river in the entire country. The Gallatin and Stillwater rivers in Montana are also popular choices. The stretch of the Clark Fork River that goes through Alberton Gorge, 35 miles west of Missoula, is considered Western Montana's best white-water with Class III and IV rapids.

Popular Idaho rivers include the Upper Salmon River east of Stanley, Upper Salmon River near the towns of Salmon and North Fork, Lower Fork Salmon River near Riggins, Moyie River and St Joe National Wild & Scenic River in the Panhandle, the Snake River (near Twin Falls, through the Snake River Birds of Prey Natural Area, through the Hagerman Valley, and near Boise), and the Payette River.

Books & Maps

Each of the Rocky Mountain states has a guide to white-water and float trips, including Doug Wheat's *The Floater's Guide to*

Colorado, Dan Lewis' *Paddle & Portage: The Floater's Guide to Wyoming Rivers*, Curt Thompson's *Floating & Recreation on Montana Rivers* and Hank Fischer's *Floating Guide to Montana*. Maps are more useful for the actual trip. Maps of wild and scenic rivers are usually available at USFS offices and some bookstores for $6; these provide very detailed description of rapids and historic/cultural sites along way, and they're also waterproof.

CANOEING

While white-water rafting is the most popular water sport in the Rocky Mountain states, many raft-laden rivers are just as good for canoeing. The problem lies in obtaining the proper equipment if you don't happen to have a canoe strapped to your vehicle. The best canoe rental resources are often small operations that usually double as campgrounds and summer resorts on the shore of a calm body of water.

Montana's tranquil waters offer some good canoeing opportunities. Swan and Seeley lakes both have a handful of lakeside lodges with canoe rentals. The Red Rock Lakes National Wildlife Refuge (near West Yellowstone) has a canoe trail connecting several marshy lakes, though rental equipment is nonexistent. The historic Missouri River Breaks, near Fort Benton, MT, offers nearly 160 miles of this federally designated wild and scenic river suitable for canoe travel. The section of the river near Great Falls is a good destination for canoeists with limited experience.

FISHING

Native fish populations throughout the Rocky Mountains have been devastated by indiscriminate planting of introduced species, overfishing and water pollution. In mining regions like the upper Arkansas River, pollution from abandoned mines in the Leadville, CO, area have so severely poisoned the river that fishery biologists rarely find brown trout over three years old. Construction of the Flaming Gorge Dam on the Green River cooled the river's water temperature, pushing native species toward extinction. Artificial planting of sport fish represents the only way that fish populations can be maintained in polluted or dammed rivers. As a result of competition with introduced species, native cutthroat trout have suffered throughout the region.

A relatively small number of undisturbed streams now attract a growing number of anglers. (In the mid-1990s thousands of novices were drawn to the sport of fly-fishing after watching Robert Redford's popular motion picture, *A River Runs Through It*, set on Montana's Blackfoot River.) A homespun yet informative fly-fishing website is www.montana.com/flyfishing.

In Colorado, about 170 miles of the state's 9000 miles of trout streams are designated as Gold Medal Waters. For a river to qualify for Gold Medal status – defined by the density and number of big fish in a unit of water – the native populations must not be overfished, and these areas have strict catch and tackle restrictions. Other streams are managed as Wild Trout Waters, in efforts to reestablish trout raised entirely in a natural environment. Fish watching sites, established in Yellowstone National Park and a few other federal lands, encourage natural population variety by limiting harvest.

Colorado

Colorado's fishing season is year round and no more than eight cold-water sport fish may be taken per day or in possession at any time. Special regulations apply to many waters in the state. An annual

resident license costs $20 (nonresidents pay $40). Both residents and nonresidents can purchase either a one-day license ($5.25) or a five-day license ($18). Free fishing without a license is allowed on the first full weekend of June. For licensing information contact the Colorado DOW (☎ 303-297-1192, 303-291-7230), 6060 Broadway, Denver, CO 80216.

Wyoming
With local exceptions on a few lakes, Wyoming offers year-round fishing. Anglers may take no more than six trout or most other cold-water sport fish per day. Fishing licenses cost $6 a day ($3 for Wyoming residents) and $65 a year ($15 for Wyoming residents). Licenses and regulations are available from the Wyoming Game & Fish Department (☎ 307-777-4600), 5400 Bishop Blvd, Cheyenne, WY 82006-0001.

Montana
Most Montana lakes and reservoirs are open year round, but the stream and river sport fishing season runs from the third Saturday in May to the end of November. Daily catch limits in the popular west and central regions are five trout. Special regulations apply to many waters in the state. You can buy a Montana fishing license at any Fish Wildlife and Parks office, most ranger stations, sporting goods shops and general stores (in remote spots, try a drug store, gas station or bar).

To get a license you must first have a $5 Conservation License (good for the rest of your life), available where fishing licenses are sold. A seasonal license costs $45 and is good for one year; a two-day stamp costs $10. Regulations vary according to the area and season and are available from any licensing agent. For more information contact the Department of Fish, Wildlife & Parks, Fisheries Division (☎ 406-444-4720), PO Box 200701, Helena, MT 59620-0701.

Idaho
The Idaho Department of Fish and Game (☎ 208-334-3700), 600 S Walnut, Boise,

ID 83707-0025 and local vendors issue fishing licenses. A fishing license costs $7.50 plus $3 per day; for the full season it costs $52 ($17 for Idaho residents). A three-day (two-fish limit) salmon/steelhead permit costs $32. Other permits include salmon ($6.50), steelhead ($6.50) and sturgeon ($1.50).

GOLF
Recent decades have seen a proliferation of golf courses throughout the Rocky Mountain states. Even many small towns have nine- or 18-hole courses open to the public at reasonable prices, while the more established resorts have deluxe courses with very high green fees.

WINDSURFING
It's tempting to write that there's plenty of wind but no surf, but one of the few benefits offered by the massive water projects of the Rocky Mountain states is the opportunity for this sport, especially in blustery Wyoming. Most of Wyoming's state parks, like Buffalo Bill State Park near Cody, Pathfinder Reservoir near Rawlins and Glendo State Park near Douglas, are centered around artificial reservoirs, as are Flaming Gorge and Bighorn Canyon. (Flaming Gorge is partly in Utah and Bighorn Canyon is mostly in Montana,

but both are accessible from Wyoming.) Along Colorado's Northern Front Range, Horsetooth Reservoir in Ft Collins is another spot where you can take to the wind-blown waters.

CAVING

Experienced spelunkers can explore caves in several areas of limestone bedrock, mostly but not exclusively in Wyoming. The highest altitude limestone cave in North America is Colorado's Marble Cave, 11,000 feet above sea level in the Sangre de Cristo Wilderness of the San Isabel National Forest. The main cave sites in Wyoming are around Bighorn Canyon National Recreation Area, near Lovell, Sinks Canyon State Park near Lander and Shoshone Cavern on Cedar Mountain (Spirit Mountain) near Cody. Montana's Azure Cave, south of the Fort Belknap Indian Reservation on BLM land in the Little Rocky Mountains between Zortman and Landusky, is another possibility. For more details, see individual geographical entries.

Two limestone cave areas are open to casual visitors for guided tours, without need of equipment or experience: Lewis & Clark Caverns State Park, near Whitehall, MT and the tacky commercial Cave of the Winds, near Manitou Springs, CO.

Because of the delicate and tightly circumscribed subterranean environments, cavers must make special efforts to respect the ecosystem and its inhabitants by leaving no trace of human presence, avoiding contact with sensitive formations and refraining from disturbing bats and other animals. Cavers should also travel in groups, with a minimum of three persons. Hazards associated with caving that you might encounter include poisonous gases and dangerous spores.

A useful resource for cavers is Chris Hill, Wayne Sutherland and Lee Tierney's *Caves of Wyoming* (University of Wyoming, 1976), a publication of the 'Bulletin of the Geological Survey of Wyoming.' Cave maps are available from the Wyoming Geological Survey, PO Box 3008, University Station, Laramie, WY 82070. For more information refer to the relevant destination chapters.

HOT-AIR BALLOONING

Floating above the Rockies has its attractions, given the scenery, but it's not cheap at the relatively few locations that offer it commercially. At Jackson, WY, and Steamboat Springs, CO, figure about $80 for a half-hour flight above the mountains, $150 to $200 for an hour or a bit longer. The views are incomparable. Balloon flights that take in the vistas of Glacier National Park are available out of Whitefish, MT.

For enthusiasts with their own equipment, the region's biggest event is early July's Hot-Air Balloon Rally in Riverton, WY; Rock Springs, WY, holds a similar one around the same time. Grand Junction and Crested Butte, CO, and Miles City, MT, also sponsor hot-air balloon festivals.

Getting There & Away

This chapter focuses on getting to transport hubs in the Rocky Mountain states from key US ports of entry and other parts of the world. Because there are so many routes into, out of, and within the USA, along with constant changes in routings and ticket prices, much of this information is general.

A reminder: before you set out on your journey, make sure you take out travel insurance. For details, see the Visas & Documents section of the Facts for the Visitor chapter.

AIR

US domestic air fares vary tremendously depending on the season you travel, the day of the week you fly, the length of your stay and the flexibility the ticket allows for flight changes and refunds. Still, nothing determines fares more than demand, and when things are slow, regardless of the season, airlines will lower their fares to fill empty seats.

While airlines don't maintain set low- and high-season rates, prices rise from mid-June to mid-September (summer), when 90% of Americans go on vacation. It's also expensive to travel around Thanksgiving (the last Thursday in November) and the busy one week before and after Christmas.

Airports

Denver International Airport (DIA) is the only major airport in the region and is the principal gateway for the Rockies, as well as one of United Airlines' two US hubs. From here you can get flights to destinations in Colorado, Wyoming, Montana and Idaho. Salt Lake City, UT, is the only other airport in the region that sees a large amount of national traffic and offers connections to western Colorado, Wyoming, Montana and Idaho. Rapid City, SD, also has connections to Wyoming. Most Montana and Idaho air connections run east-west, between major international airports at Minneapolis-St Paul, MN, to the east and Seattle, WA, and Portland, OR, to the west.

Airlines

Flights into Denver International Airport from major international airports are usually reasonably priced, especially as round-trips, but short hops to destinations like Jackson or Steamboat Springs on commuter lines like United Express or Continental Express are disproportionately expensive. If you are arriving from overseas or another major airport in the USA, it is usually much cheaper to buy a through ticket to small airports as part of your fare rather than separately, unless your travel plans are too spontaneous to do so.

Domestically, ticket prices to Denver are unfortunately often expensive. High airport-use taxes imposed upon the airlines (and passed on to you) and the dominance of United Airlines on Denver routes often makes budget fares hard to find. For example, low fares on the regional Frontier Airlines are limited to a few smaller airports like Albuquerque, NM, and El Paso, TX. Another start-up, Vanguard Airlines, offers discount fares on flights to Dallas (via Kansas City, MO). The Chicago and San Francisco markets are more competitive, and smaller airlines like America West, Frontier and Vanguard sometimes force the larger carriers to match fares.

For several years Western Pacific Airlines offered great budget fares from Denver and Colorado Springs to a wide range of destinations across the country. But fierce price wars with the major carriers hit the airline hard, and at the time of writing it had declared bankruptcy. It may yet be bailed out, but it would require investors willing to take on behemoths like United Airlines.

For a list of toll-free phone numbers for major US domestic carriers (including regional airlines), please see the appendix at the back of the book.

Buying Tickets

Rather than just walking into the nearest travel agent or airline office, it pays to do a bit of research and shop around. If buying tickets within the US, the *New York Times*, *Los Angeles Times*, *Chicago Tribune*, *San Francisco Examiner* and other major newspapers all produce weekly travel sections with numerous travel agents' ads. Council Travel (☎ 800-226-8624, cts@ciee.org) and STA (☎ 800-777-0112) have offices in major cities nationwide. The magazine *Travel Unlimited* (PO Box 1058, Allston, MA 02134) publishes details of the cheapest air fares and courier possibilities.

Those coming from outside the US might start by perusing travel sections of magazines like *Time Out* and *TNT* in the UK, or the Saturday editions of newspapers like the *Sydney Morning Herald* and *The Age* in Australia. Ads in these publications offer cheap fares, but don't be surprised if they happen to be sold out when you contact the agents: they're usually low-season fares on obscure airlines with conditions attached.

The plane ticket will probably be the single most expensive item in your budget, and buying it can be intimidating. It is always worth putting aside a few hours to research the current state of the market. Start shopping for a ticket early – some of the cheapest tickets must be bought months in advance, and some popular flights sell out early. Talk to other recent travelers – they may be able to stop you from making some of the same old mistakes. Look at the ads in newspapers and magazines, consult reference books and watch for special offers.

Phoning a travel agent is still one of the best ways to dig up bargains. However, airlines have started to cater more to budget travelers, and can sometimes offer the same deals you'll get with a travel agent. Airlines often have competitive low-season, student and senior citizens' fares. Find out not only the fare, but the route (Is it direct or are there lots of stops?), the duration of the journey (How long are the layovers?) and any restrictions on the ticket.

You can also use the Internet to hunt for low fares. For example, Cheap Tickets (www.cheaptickets.com) and Travelocity (www.travelocity.com) are two services that can help. To buy a ticket via the web you'll need a credit card. Also, while some find this a convenient way to purchase budget tickets, other travelers have reported long wait times and disconnections, or have found that the online services' fares can't always match those of travel agents or the airlines themselves.

Some airlines now offer specials deals on the Internet. United Airlines offers e-fares, a program in which tickets for selected routes and dates are released every Wednesday at substantial discounts. These tickets are snapped up almost as soon as they are released, so you'll need to log on to United's website (www.ual.com) early Wednesday. To purchase these tickets you'll need to register with United and also be a member of its Mileage Plus frequent flyer program (call ☎ 605-399-2400 to sign up). Ticket conditions are highly inflexible, so read the directions and requirements carefully.

Cheap tickets are available in two distinct categories: official and unofficial. Official ones have a variety of names including advance-purchase fares, budget fares, Apex and super-Apex. Unofficial tickets are simply discounted tickets that the airlines release through selected travel agents (not through airline offices). The cheapest tickets are often nonrefundable and require an extra fee for changing your flight. Many insurance policies will cover this loss if you have to change your flight for emergency reasons. Return (roundtrip) tickets usually work out cheaper than two one-way fares – often *much* cheaper.

Use the fares quoted in this book as a guide only. They are approximate and based on the rates advertised by travel agents and airlines at press time. Quoted airfares do not necessarily constitute a recommendation for the carrier.

Air Travel Glossary

Apex – Apex, or 'advance purchase excursion' is a discounted ticket that must be paid for in advance. There are penalties if you wish to change it.

Bucket Shop – An unbonded travel agency specializing in discounted airline tickets.

Bumping – Just because you have a confirmed seat doesn't mean you're going to get on the plane – see Overbooking.

Cancellation Penalties – If you must cancel or change an Apex ticket there are often heavy penalties involved, but insurance can sometimes be taken out against these penalties. Some airlines impose penalties on regular tickets as well, particularly against 'no-show' passengers.

Check In – Airlines ask you to check in a certain time ahead of the flight departure (usually two hours on international flights). If you fail to check in on time and the flight is overbooked, the airline can cancel your booking and give your seat to somebody else.

Confirmation – Having a ticket written out with the flight and date you want doesn't mean you have a seat until the agent has checked with the airline that your status is 'OK' or confirmed. Meanwhile you could just be 'on request.'

Discounted Tickets – There are two types of discounted fares – officially discounted (see Promotional Fares) and unofficially discounted. The lowest prices often impose drawbacks like flying with unpopular airlines, inconvenient schedules or unpleasant routes and connections. A discounted ticket can save you other things than money – you may be able to pay Apex prices without the associated Apex advance booking and other requirements. Discounted tickets only exist when there is fierce competition.

Full Fares – Airlines traditionally offer 1st class (coded F), business class (coded J) and economy class (coded Y) tickets. These days there are so many promotional and discounted fares available from the regular economy class that few passengers pay full economy fare.

Lost Tickets – If you lose your airline ticket an airline will usually treat it like a travelers' check and, after inquiries, issue you another one. Legally, however, an airline is entitled to treat it like cash and if you lose it then it's gone forever. Take good care of your tickets.

No-Shows – No-shows are passengers who fail to show up for their flight. Full-fare passengers who fail to turn up are sometimes entitled to travel on a later flight. The rest of us are penalized (see Cancellation Penalties).

On Request – An unconfirmed booking for a flight; see Confirmation.

Open Jaws – A return ticket where you fly to one place but return from another. If available this can save you backtracking to your arrival point.

Overbooking – Airlines hate to fly empty seats and since every flight has some passengers who fail to show up they often book more passengers than they have seats. Usually

If traveling from the UK, you will probably find that the cheapest flights are being advertised by obscure bucket shops whose names haven't yet reached the telephone directory. Many such firms are honest and solvent, but there are a few rogues who will take your money and disappear, to reopen elsewhere a month or two later under a new name. If you feel suspicious about a firm, don't give them all the money at once – instead leave a deposit of 20% or so and pay the balance once you receive the ticket. If they insist on cash in advance, go elsewhere. And once you have the ticket, call the airline to confirm that you are booked on the flight.

the excess passengers balance those who fail to show up but occasionally somebody gets bumped. If this happens guess who it's most likely to be? The passengers who check in late.

Promotional Fares – Officially discounted fares like Apex fares which are available from travel agents or direct from the airline.

Reconfirmation – At least 72 hours prior to departure time of an onward or return flight you must contact the airline and 'reconfirm' that you intend to be on the flight. If you don't do this the airline can delete your name from the passenger list and you could lose your seat. You don't have to reconfirm the first flight on your itinerary or if your stopover is less than 72 hours. It won't hurt to reconfirm more than once.

Restrictions – Discounted tickets often have various restrictions on them – advance purchase is the most usual one (see Apex). Others are restrictions on the minimum and maximum period you must be away, such as a minimum of 14 days or a maximum of one year. See Cancellation Penalties.

Standby – A discounted ticket where you only fly if there is a seat free at the last moment. Standby fares are usually only available on domestic routes.

Tickets Out – An entry requirement for many countries is that you have an onward or return ticket, in other words, a ticket out of the country. If you're not sure what you intend to do next, the easiest solution is to buy the cheapest onward ticket to a neighboring country or a ticket from a reliable airline which can later be refunded if you do not use it.

Transferred Tickets – Airline tickets cannot be transferred from one person to another. Travelers sometimes try to sell the return half of their ticket, but officials can ask you to prove that you are the person named on the ticket. This is unlikely to happen on domestic flights, but on an international flight tickets may be compared with passports.

Travel Agencies – Travel agencies vary widely and you should ensure you use one that suits your needs. Some simply handle tours, while full-service agencies handle everything from tours and tickets to car rental and hotel bookings. A good one will do all these things and can save you a lot of money but if all you want is a ticket at the lowest possible price, then you really need an agency specializing in discounted tickets. A discounted ticket agency, however, may not be useful for things like hotel bookings.

Travel Periods – Some officially discounted fares, Apex fares in particular, vary with the time of year. There is often a low (off-peak) season and a high (peak) season. Sometimes there's an intermediate (shoulder) season as well. At peak times, when everyone wants to fly, not only will the officially discounted fares be higher but so will unofficially discounted fares, or there may simply be no discounted tickets available. Usually the fare depends on your outward flight – if you depart in the high season and return in the low season, you pay the high-season fare. ■

You may decide to pay more than the rock-bottom fare by opting for the safety of a better-known travel agent. Established firms like STA Travel, which has offices worldwide, Council Travel in the USA or Travel CUTS in Canada are valid alternatives and they offer good prices to most destinations.

Once you have your ticket, remember to write down its number, together with the flight number and other details, and keep the information somewhere separate but still accessible. That way, if the ticket is lost or stolen, having this information readily available will help you get a replacement ticket.

Special Fares for Foreign Visitors
Almost all domestic carriers offer Visit USA passes to non-US citizens. The passes are actually a book of coupons – each coupon equals a flight. Typically, the minimum number of coupons is three or four and the maximum is eight or 10, and they must be purchased in conjunction with an international airline ticket anywhere outside the USA except Canada and Mexico. Coupons cost anywhere from $100 to $160, depending on how many you buy. Most airlines require you to plan your itinerary in advance and to complete your flights within 60 days of arrival, but rules can vary between individual airlines. A few airlines may allow you to use coupons on standby, in which case you should call the airline a day or two before the flight and make a 'standby reservation.' Such a reservation gives you priority over all other travelers who just appear and hope to get on the flight the same day.

Round-the-World Tickets Round-the-World (RTW) tickets have become very popular in the last few years. Airline RTW tickets are often real bargains and can work out to be no more expensive or even cheaper than an ordinary return ticket. Your best bet is to find a travel agent that advertises or specializes in RTW tickets. Prices start at about UK£850, A$1800 or US$1300. These are for 'short' routes such as Los Angeles, New York, London, Bangkok, Honolulu, Los Angeles. As soon as you start adding stops south of the equator, fares can go up to the US$2000 to $3000 range.

The official airline RTW tickets are usually put together by a combination of two airlines, and they permit you to fly anywhere you want on their route systems as long as you do not backtrack. For example, Qantas flies in conjunction with either American Airlines, British Airways, Delta Air Lines, Northwest Airlines, Canadian Airlines, Air France or KLM. Canadian Airlines links up with KLM or South African Airways, among others. Continental Airlines flies with either Malaysia Airlines, Singapore Airlines or Thai Airways.

Other restrictions are that you must usually book the first sector in advance and cancellation penalties apply. There may be restrictions on the number of stops permitted, and tickets are usually valid from 90 days up to a year. An alternative RTW ticket is one put together by a travel agent combining discounted tickets.

Although most airlines restrict the number of sectors that can be flown within the USA and Canada to four, and some airlines black out a few heavily traveled routes (like Honolulu to Tokyo), stopovers are otherwise generally unlimited. In most cases a 14-day advance purchase is required. After the ticket is purchased, dates can be changed without penalty and tickets can be rewritten to add or delete stops for around $50 each.

Getting Bumped
Airlines routinely overbook and count on some passengers canceling or not showing up. Occasionally, almost everybody does show up for a flight, and then some passengers must be 'bumped' onto another flight. Getting bumped can be a nuisance because you have to wait around for the next flight, but if you have a day's leeway, you can turn this to your advantage.

On oversold flights, the gate agent will first ask for volunteers to be bumped in return for a later flight plus compensation of the airline's choosing. (If there aren't enough volunteers, some passengers will be forced onto a later flight. Each airline has its own method of choosing who will be bumped.) When you check in at the airline counter, ask if the flight is full and if there may be a need for volunteers. Get your name on the list if you don't mind volunteering. Depending on how oversold the flight is, compensation can range from a discount voucher toward your next flight to a fully paid roundtrip ticket or even cash. Be sure to confirm a later flight so you don't get stuck in the airport on standby. If you have to spend the night, airlines frequently foot the hotel bill for their bumpees. You don't have to accept the airline's first offer and can haggle for a better deal.

However, be aware that, due to this same system, being just a little late for boarding could get you bumped with none of these benefits.

Travelers with Special Needs

If you have special needs of any sort – a broken leg, dietary restrictions, dependence on a wheelchair, responsibility for a baby, severe fear of flying – you should let the airline know as soon as possible so that they can make arrangements accordingly. You should remind them when you reconfirm your booking (at least 72 hours before departure) and again when you check in at the airport. It may also be worth ringing round the airlines before you make your booking to find out how they can handle your particular needs.

Airports and airlines can be surprisingly helpful, but they do need advance warning. Most international airports can provide escorts from check-in desk to plane where needed, and there should be ramps, lifts, accessible toilets and reachable phones. Aircraft toilets, on the other hand, are likely to present a problem; travelers should discuss this with the airline at an early stage and, if necessary, with their doctor.

Guide dogs for the blind will often have to travel in a specially pressurized baggage compartment with other animals, away from their owner, though smaller guide dogs may be admitted to the cabin. Guide dogs are not subject to quarantine as long as they have proof of being vaccinated against rabies.

Deaf travelers can ask for airport and in-flight announcements to be written down for them.

Children under two travel for 10% of the standard fare (or free, on some airlines), as long as they don't occupy a seat. (They don't get a baggage allowance either.) 'Skycots' should be provided by the airline if requested in advance; these will take a child weighing up to about 22 lbs. Children between two and 12 can usually occupy a seat for half to two-thirds of the full fare, and do get a baggage allowance. Strollers can often be taken on as hand luggage.

Baggage & Other Restrictions

On most domestic and international flights you are limited to two checked bags, or three if you don't have a carry-on. There could be a charge if you bring more or if the size of the bags exceeds the airline's limits. It's best to check with the individual airline if you are worried about this. On some international flights the luggage allowance is based on weight, not size or numbers of bags; again, check with the airline.

If your luggage is delayed upon arrival (which is rare), some airlines will give a cash advance to purchase necessities. If sporting equipment is misplaced, the airline may pay for rentals. Should the luggage be lost, it is important to submit a claim. The airline doesn't have to pay the full amount of the claim, rather they can estimate the value of your lost items. It may take them anywhere from six weeks to three months to process the claim and pay you.

Smoking Smoking is prohibited on all domestic flights within the USA. Many international flights are following suit, so be sure to call and find out. Many airports in the USA also restrict smoking.

Illegal Items Items that are illegal to take on a plane, either checked or as carry-on, include aerosol cans of polishes, waxes, and similar products; tear gas and pepper spray; camp stoves with fuel; and scuba diving tanks that are full.

Within the USA

Buy domestic air tickets in the USA as early as possible, since this is the main way to get the cheapest fares. The lowest priced tickets are 21-day advance purchase, followed by 14-day advance purchase. Tickets between major destinations (like New York to Denver) that are purchased within seven days of departure are ridiculously expensive, usually ranging from $1000 to $1300. This compares to $250 to $500 if you buy three weeks in advance.

For information on where to hunt down bargain fares and buy tickets, see the preceding Buying Tickets section. Following are some sample roundtrip fares (based on 21-day advance purchase), and approximate direct flying times between major US airports and Denver International Airport (DIA), the hub for air travel to the Rockies region. Note that direct flights often cost more, so if you get a bargain ticket you may be facing one or more stopovers and thus a longer flight.

	Fare	Duration
Chicago	$250	2¼ hours
Los Angeles	$200	2½ hours
Miami	$500	3¾ hours
New York	$300	3½ hours
San Francisco	$200	2¾ hours

Canada

Travel CUTS (☎ 888-838-2887, 416-977-2185 in Toronto) has offices in all major cities. The Toronto *Globe and Mail* and *Vancouver Sun* carry travel agents' ads.

The UK & Ireland

Check the ads in magazines like *Time Out*, plus the *Evening Standard* and *TNT*. Also check the free magazines widely available in London – start by looking outside the main railway stations.

Most British travel agents are registered with the ABTA (Association of British Travel Agents). If you have paid for your flight to an ABTA-registered agent who then goes out of business, ABTA will guarantee a refund or an alternative. Unregistered bucket shops are riskier but sometimes cheaper.

London is arguably the world's headquarters for bucket shops, which are well advertised and can usually beat published airline fares. Good, reliable agents for cheap tickets in the UK are Trailfinders (☎ 0171-937-5400), 194 Kensington High St, London, W8 7RG; Council Travel (☎ 0171-437-7767) 28a Poland St, London, W1, and STA Travel (☎ 0171-937-9971), 86 Old Brompton Rd, London SW7 3LQ. The Globetrotters Club (BCM Roving, London WC1N 3XX) publishes a newsletter called *Globe* that covers obscure destinations and can help you find traveling companions.

Sample Fares from International Cities

City	Low-Season	High-Season
Toronto to:		
DIA	C$1474	C$1503
Vancouver to:		
DIA	C$1883	C$1902
London to:		
LA	£467	£259
NYC	£305	£168
DIA	£550	£330
Paris to:		
LA	2400FF	4070FF
NYC	1650FF	3217FF
DIA	2550FF	4383FF
Frankfurt to:		
LA	DM1599	DM1119
NYC	DM 979	DM599
DIA	DM1099	DM1029
Sydney to:		
LA	A$1349	A$1799
NYC	A$1599	A$2049
DIA	A$1650	A$1850
Auckland to:		
LA	NZ$1730	NZ$1880
NYC	NZ$2120	NZ$2270
DIA	NZ$2120	NZ$2270
Tokyo to:		
LA	US$860	US$1040
	¥125,474	¥151,736
NYC	US$900	US$1185
	¥131,310	¥172,891
DIA	US$1050	US$1185
	¥153,195	¥172,891

Continental Europe

In Amsterdam, NBBS (☎ 624 09 89) at Rokin 38 (and several other locations throughout the city) is a popular travel agent. In Paris, Council Travel (☎ 01 44 55 55 44) is at 22, rue des Pyramides, 75001. For great student fares, contact USIT Voyages (☎ 01 42 34 56 90) at 6, rue de Vaugirard, 75006 Paris.

The most common route to the Rocky Mountain states from Europe is west via New York, but other gateway cities like

Miami and Atlanta are alternatives. If you're interested in heading east with stops in Asia, it may be cheaper to get a Round-the-World ticket instead of returning the same way.

Australia & New Zealand

In Australia and New Zealand, STA Travel and Flight Centres International are major dealers in cheap air fares; check the travel agents' ads in the Yellow Pages and call around. Qantas flies to Los Angeles from Sydney, Melbourne (via Sydney or Auckland) and Cairns. United flies to San Francisco from Sydney and Melbourne (via Sydney) and also flies to Los Angeles.

The cheapest tickets have a 21-day advance-purchase requirement, a minimum stay of seven days and a maximum stay of 60 days. Flying with Air New Zealand is slightly cheaper, and both Qantas and Air New Zealand offer tickets with longer stays or stopovers, but you pay more.

Asia

Hong Kong and Bangkok are the region's two best spots to buy discount airplane tickets, but their bucket shops can be unreliable. Ask the advice of other travelers before buying a ticket. STA Travel, which is dependable, has branches in Hong Kong, Tokyo, Singapore, Bangkok and Kuala Lumpur. Flights to the USA may go via Anchorage, Alaska, Honolulu, Hawaii, or Tokyo.

Of all the carriers serving the US from Asia, United Airlines has the largest number of routes and flights, including twice-daily runs from both San Francisco and Los Angeles to Hong Kong and Tokyo. Other Japan destinations include Nagoya and Osaka. United's fares aren't always the cheapest, but it's worth checking as they sometimes drop to compete with other carriers. Northwest Airlines also serves Hong Kong and Tokyo. Some of the lowest fares are often offered by Malaysia Airlines and Korean Airlines, which serve respectively serve southeast and northeast Asia as well as Hong Kong.

Central & South America

Most flights from Central and South America go via Miami, Houston or Los Angeles, though some fly via New York. Most countries' international flag carriers (like Aerolíneas Argentinas and LAN-Chile) as well as US airlines (like United and American) serve these destinations, with onward connections. Continental has flights from about 20 cities in Mexico and Central America, including San Jose, Guatemala City, Cancún and Mérida.

Arriving in the USA

Even if you are continuing immediately to another city, the first airport that you land in is where you must carry out immigration and customs formalities. Even if your luggage is checked from, say, London to Denver, if your flight first lands in New York, you will have to take your bags through customs there. For more information on customs requirements and limits look under Customs in Facts for the Visitor.

If you have a non-US passport, with a visa, you must complete an Arrival/Departure Record (form I-94) before you approach the immigration desk. It's usually handed out on the plane, along with the customs declaration. It's a rather badly designed form, and lots of people take more than one attempt to get it right. Some airlines suggest you start at the last question and work upwards. Answers should be written *below* the questions. For question 12, 'Address While in the United States,' give the address of the location where you will spend the first night. Complete the Departure Record too (the lower part of the form), giving exactly the same answers for questions 14 to 17 as for questions 1 to 4.

The staff of the Immigration & Nationalization Service (INS) can be less than welcoming. Their main concern is to exclude those who are likely to work illegally or overstay, so visitors will be asked about their plans, and perhaps about whether they have sufficient funds for their stay. If they think you're OK, a six-month entry is usually approved.

It's a good idea to be able to list an itinerary that will account for the period for which you ask to be admitted, and to be able to show you have $300 or $400 for every week of your intended stay. These days, a couple of major credit cards will go a long way towards establishing 'sufficient funds.' Don't make too much of having friends, relatives, or business contacts in the USA – the INS official may decide that this will make you more likely to overstay.

Departure Taxes
Airport departure taxes are normally included in the cost of tickets bought in the USA, although tickets purchased abroad may not have this included. There's a $6 airport departure tax charged to all passengers bound for a foreign destination. However, this fee, as well as a $6.50 North American Free Trade Agreement (NAFTA) tax charged to passengers entering the USA from a foreign country, are hidden taxes added to the purchase price of your airline ticket.

LAND
Unless you're one of the few who travel by train, you'll probably be using one of several interstate highways to reach the Rockies by land. Interstates 70 and 80, both of which run nearly the entire length of the USA, respectively pass through central Colorado and southern Wyoming. Interstate 25 runs north-south from New Mexico through Colorado and ends at a junction with I-90 in northern Wyoming. I-90 in turn runs north and then heads west to span most of southern Montana before continuing on through northern Idaho and on to Seattle, WA. Southern Idaho is linked to Portland, OR by I-84 while I-15 connects southeast Idaho and western Montana with Salt Lake City, UT, and Las Vegas, NV.

Bus
Greyhound, the only nationwide bus company, has reduced local services considerably, but still runs cross-country buses between San Francisco and New York via Wyoming, Denver and Chicago; between Seattle and New York via Minneapolis-St Paul and Chicago; and between Los Angeles and New York via Las Vegas, Denver and Chicago. There are also bus services from other eastern seaboard cities like Philadelphia and Washington, DC, and southern cities like Atlanta, GA, and Miami.

Because buses are so few, schedules are often inconvenient, fares are relatively high and bargain air fares can undercut buses on long-distance routes; in some cases, on shorter routes, it can be cheaper to rent a car than to ride the bus. However, very long-distance bus trips are often available at bargain prices by purchasing or reserving tickets three days in advance. For more details, see the Bus entry in the Getting Around chapter.

Train
Amtrak (☎ 800-872-7245, TTY 800-523-6590) provides cross-country passenger service between the West Coast and Chicago; travelers to or from the East Coast must make connections in Chicago. Because routes are limited, fares can be expensive and trains often run behind schedule, probably only dedicated train travelers will care to take on the adventures of Amtrak travel. The train is an even worse option for getting around within the Rocky Mountain states (as opposed to getting to them); due to service cutbacks, Amtrak trains only serve a few destinations besides Denver.

The northernmost route is the daily *Empire Builder*, which runs from Seattle through northern Montana to Minneapolis and Chicago. This train makes 12 stops in Montana (including East Glacier and Whitefish) and one stop in Idaho at Sandpoint.

The daily *California Zephyr* from San Francisco (Emeryville, California), passes through Colorado en route to Denver and Chicago. Stops in Colorado include Denver, Fraser-Winter Park, Glenwood Springs and Grand Junction.

The *Southwest Chief* goes from Los Angeles via Albuquerque and the southern

Colorado towns of Trinidad, La Junta and Lamar, to Kansas City and Chicago. There is no passenger train service in Wyoming or southern Idaho.

Amtrak tickets may be purchased aboard the train without penalty if the station is not open 30 minutes prior to boarding; otherwise there is a $7 penalty. Rail travel is generally cheaper by purchasing special fares in advance. Roundtrips are the best bargain, but even these are usually as expensive as air fares, if not more so.

The best value overall is their All Aboard America fare. This costs $318 for adults and enables you to travel anywhere you want. There are limitations, however. Travel must be completed in 45 days, and you are allowed up to three stopovers. Additional stopovers can be arranged at extra cost. Your entire trip must be reserved in advance and the seats are limited, so book as far ahead as possible. Travel between mid-June and late August costs $378. These tickets are for reclining seats; sleeping cars cost extra. If you want to travel in just one region, the eastern, central or western parts of the country, All Aboard America fares are $198/228 low/high. The cost for two regions is $258/318.

Another travel package is Amtrak Air Rail, a partnership with United Airlines that allows you to take the train one-way, and travel the other way by air. It's a bit limited for travelers, as you must start and end your journey from the same city. Prices ranges from $223/259 (low/high season) for West Coast travel to $455/517 for a transcontinental ticket.

For non-US citizens, they offer a USA Rail Pass which comes in three types and must be purchased outside the US (check with your travel agent): National pass, 15 days at $285/425 (low/high season) or 30 days at $375/535. Regional passes vary: 30 day passes cost $240/310 for travel in the far western region; $255/310 for the eastern region; or $260/395 for the western region. Last are the East or West Coastal passes which cost $225/275 low/high. Sleeping accommodations are an extra charge. Advanced booking is rec-

ommended, especially during the peak season.

For further travel assistance, call Amtrak or ask your travel agent. Note that most small train stations don't sell tickets; you have to book them with Amtrak over the phone. Some small stations have no porters or other facilities, and trains may stop there only if you have bought a ticket in advance.

Car
Drivers of cars and riders of motorbikes will need to have the vehicle's registration papers, liability insurance and an international drivers permit in addition to their domestic license. Canadian and Mexican driver's licenses are accepted. Customs officials along the entry points between Canada and Montana can be strict and wary of anything that doesn't look straight-laced. To avoid unnecessary conflicts, dress well and be cordial when driving between countries.

For information on buying or renting a car, or using a drive-away (driving a car for someone else) see the Getting Around chapter.

ORGANIZED TOURS
Tours of the USA are so numerous that it would be impossible to attempt a comprehensive listing; for overseas visitors, the most reliable sources of information on the constantly changing offerings are major international travel agents like Thomas Cook and American Express. Probably those of most interest to the general traveler are coach tours that visit the national parks and guest ranch excursions; for those with limited time, package tours can be an efficient and relatively inexpensive way to go.

Try Gray Line Tours for standard package bus tours of Rocky Mountain sights. The company has operations in Colorado (☎ 800-348-6877), Wyoming (☎ 800-443-6133) and a special branch for Yellowstone National Park (☎ 800-523-3102). Discover Colorado Scenic Tours (☎ 303-425-3586) offers more personalized service, allowing you to map out your own route. They offer one-day or multiple-day trips and costs are around $60 per person per day for a party of two, not including accommodations or meals.

Green Tortoise (☎ 415-821-0803, 800-867-8647), 494 Broadway, San Francisco, CA 94133, offers alternative bus transportation with stops at places like hot springs and national parks. Meals are cooperatively cooked and you sleep on bunks on the bus or camp. This is not luxury travel, but it is fun. The 16-day National Parks Loop from San Francisco (which covers Yellowstone, the Grand Tetons and Dinosaur National Monument as well as several national parks in Utah) runs from June through August. The cost is $499 plus $141 toward the food fund.

Trek America (☎ 973-983-1144, 800-221-0596, fax 973-983-8551), PO Box 189, Rockaway, NJ 07866, offers roundtrip camping tours to different areas of the country. In England, they are at 4 Water Perry Court, Middleton Rd, Banbury, Oxon OX16 8QG (☎ 01295-256777, fax 01295-257399), and in Australia contact Adventure World 75 Walker St, North Sydney, NSW 2060 (☎ 9955-5000, fax 9954-5817, www.Trekamerica.com). These tours last from one to nine weeks and are designed for small, international groups (13 people maximum) of 18- to 38-year-olds. Tour prices vary with season, with July to September being the highest. Some side trips and cultural events are included in the price, and participants help with cooking and camp chores. Tours including food and occasional hotel nights start at $606 for a 10-day tour to $2566 for their nine-week Trailblazer tour of the entire country. The company also runs a three-week Rocky Mountain High Tour from Seattle, WA, to Los Angeles that includes a stay at a Montana ranch and visits to Yellowstone, Grand Teton, Rocky Mountain and Mesa Verde national parks.

Similar deals are available from Suntrek (☎ 707-523-1800, 800-786-8735, fax 707-523-1911), Sun Plaza, 77 West Third St, Santa Rosa, CA 95401. Suntrek also has offices in Germany (☎ 089 480 2831, fax 089 480 2411), Sedanstrasse 21, D-81667, Munich; and Switzerland (☎ 1-462 6161, fax 1-462 6545), Birmensdorferstr 107, CH-8036, Zurich. Their tours are for the 'young at heart' and attract predominantly young international travelers, although there is no age limit. Prices range from about $1050 for the three-week trek to about $3850 for their 13-week around America treks.

Road Runner USA/Canada (☎ 800-873-5872), 1050 Hancock, Quincy, MA 02169, organizes one- and two-week treks in conjunction with Hostelling International to different parts of the USA and across country. They also have offices in England (☎ 01892-512700), 64 Mt. Pleasant Ave, Tunbridge Wells, Kent TN1 1QY. Prices start at $499 for one week to $1199 for three weeks. AmeriCan Adventures (☎ 800-864-0335) offers seven- to 42-day camping trips to different parts of the USA. Itineraries are flexible usually following a theme like Route 66 or Wild West. Prices start at $419 for seven days to $1739 for 42 days. Their Rocky Mountain Adventure tour lasts 21 days and takes in sights in both the Canadian and US Rockies, including Glacier and Yellowstone national parks, Craters of the Moon and the Oregon Trail.

Specialized Tours

In addition to traditional package tours, there are some study and environmental tours to the Rocky Mountain states. The University of California Research Expeditions Program (☎ 510-642-6586), at the University of California, Berkeley, CA 94720-7050, runs work/study expeditions assisting scholars in the field with research projects, some of which occasionally take place in the Rocky Mountain region. For details of what's planned call them or check out their website (www.mip.berkeley.edu/urep).

Elderhostel (☎ 617-426-8056), 75 Federal St, Boston, MA 02110, is a nonprofit organization offering international educational programs and active trips for those ages 55 and above, and has programs throughout the West.

Outdoor Adventure River Specialists (OARS; ☎ 209-736-4677, 800-346-6277), PO Box 67, Angels Camp, CA 95222, runs river rafting and kayak trips on Wyoming's Snake River, Jackson Lake and Yellowstone Lake, as well as Colorado's Dolores, Yampa and Green rivers near the border with Utah.

Bicycling, hiking and walking, cross-country skiing, running and multi-sport tours are another possibility. One good company for this kind of activity is Backroads (☎ 510-527-1555, 800-462-2848), 801 Cedar St, Berkeley, CA 94710.

WARNING

The information in this chapter is particularly vulnerable to change: prices for international travel are volatile, routes are frequently introduced and canceled, schedules change, special deals come and go, and rules and visa requirements are amended. Airlines and governments seem to take a perverse pleasure in making price structures and regulations as complicated as possible. You should check directly with the airline or a travel agent to make sure you understand how a fare (and ticket you may buy) works. In addition, the travel industry is highly competitive and there are many lurks and perks.

The upshot of this is that you should get opinions, quotes and advice from as many airlines and travel agents as possible before you part with your hard-earned cash. The details given in the chapter should be regarded as pointers and are not a substitute for your own careful, up-to-date research.

Getting Around

The Rocky Mountain states are fairly well-connected by commuter flights, although the cost may deter most travelers from using this option more than once or twice during their visit. On the ground, public transportation in the region leaves much to be desired and travelers without their own vehicles need to be patient and flexible to take advantage of the limited possibilities.

AIR

Denver International Airport is the main air hub for the Rockies, and from here you can get flights to destinations in all four states covered in this book. For information on the airport itself see Getting There & Away under the Denver section of the Denver & Boulder chapter.

Most of the short flights within the region carry high price tags: it can cost as much as $300 to fly from Denver to Telluride depending on the time of year. The best way to cut down the cost is to link your regional flight to your flight into Denver or Salt Lake City, UT, in which case the commuter connection is often a fraction what it would cost to book it separately.

Airports

Colorado Colorado has commercial airports at Alamosa, Aspen, Colorado Springs, Cortez, Durango, Fort Collins, Grand Junction, Gunnison (near Crested Butte), Lamar, Montrose, Pueblo, Telluride, Vail (Eagle County) and Yampa Valley (serving Steamboat Springs). All of these destinations are served by flights out of Denver, although Grand Junction also has flights to Salt Lake City. During ski season, the resort airports offer direct flights to major cities around the country.

Wyoming Wyoming airports are at Casper, Cheyenne, Cody, Gillette, Jackson Hole, Laramie, Riverton, Rock Springs, Sheridan, and Worland. Most of Wyoming's airports are not connected to each other, but are instead served by flights out of Denver.

Montana Montana has commercial airports at Billings, Bozeman, Glacier National Park (between Whitefish and Kalispell), Great Falls, Helena, Lewistown, Missoula, West Yellowstone, and Miles City. Most airports are connected with out-of-state destinations like Salt Lake City or Seattle, WA, and some instate flights, such as Helena-Great Falls or Missoula-Kalispell.

Idaho Idaho's main airport is Boise. Airports at Challis, Hailey, Lewiston, McCall, Salmon, and Stanley have connections to Boise. Idaho Falls, Pocatello, and Twin Falls airports have flights to Boise, Denver, and Salt Lake City.

Airlines

The dominant carrier in the region is United Express, the commuter airline arm of United Airlines. It's reach has grown since it absorbed Mesa Airlines (although you'll still see aircraft sporting Mesa colors, nearly all their ticketing is now handled by United). United Express serves all four states covered in this book, mainly out of Denver International Airport, and has a near monopoly on Colorado destinations. In winter some Colorado ski resorts are served by other airlines such as Delta Airlines and its commuter operation, SkyWest/Delta Connection, Northwest Airlines, and American Airlines.

United Express and SkyWest/Delta Connection are the main airlines serving Wyoming, and also fly to destinations in Montana and Idaho. Other carriers serving Montana are Big Sky Airlines, Horizon Air and Northwest Airlines. The latter two also serve Idaho, along with Southwest Airlines.

Toll-free numbers for these airlines can be found in the 800-number appendix at the back of this book.

BUS

Since Americans rely so much on their cars and usually fly long distances, bus transport is less frequent than is desirable, but some good deals are available. Greyhound (☎ 800-231-2222), the main bus line for the region, has extensive fixed routes and its own terminal in most central cities (often in undesirable parts of town). However, the buses are comfortable, the company has an exceptional safety record and it usually runs on time. Don't look for excitement however: some travelers who have sampled the worst bus rides that developing countries can dish out still contend that there's nothing worse than the mind-numbing boredom of a long Greyhound ride.

Greyhound has reduced or eliminated services to smaller rural communities. In other small towns it no longer has its own terminals, but merely stops at a given location, such as fast-food restaurants like McDonald's (which may be the only choice for meal stops – bring your own food if burgers and fries are unappealing). At these unlikely stops, boarding passengers usually pay the driver with exact change.

Other regional bus lines operate in the area. TNM&O (Texas-New Mexico & Oklahoma Coaches Inc) is affiliated with Greyhound and serves the same lines through Colorado and parts of Wyoming. (For information, call Greyhound.) Powder River Coach USA primarily serves eastern Wyoming, but it also goes to Denver, Billings, MT, and Rapid City, SD. Rim Rock Stages serves Montana destinations. Check the appendix at the back of this book for contact phone numbers.

Greyhound Fares

Tickets can be bought over the phone with a credit card (American Express, MasterCard or Visa) and mailed if purchased 10 days in advance or picked up at the terminal with proper identification. Discounts apply to fares bought 14 or 21 days in advance. Greyhound terminals also accept American Express, traveler's checks and cash. Note that all buses are nonsmoking, and reservations are made with ticket purchases only.

Special Fares Greyhound occasionally introduces a mileage-based discount fare program that can be a bargain, especially for very long distances, but it's a good idea to check the regular fare anyway. As with regular fares, these promotional fares are subject to change.

Ameripass Greyhound's Ameripass is potentially useful, depending on how much you plan to travel, but the relatively high prices may impel you to travel more than you normally would simply to get your money's worth. There are no restrictions on who can buy an Ameripass; it costs $199 for seven days of unlimited travel year-round, $299 for 15 days and $409 for 30 days. Children under 11 travel for half price. You can get on and off at any Greyhound stop or terminal, and the Ameripass is available at every terminal.

International Ameripass This can be purchased only by foreign tourists, students and lecturers (with their families) staying less than one year. Prices include $119 for a four-day pass for unlimited travel Monday to Thursday, $179 for a seven-day pass, $269 for a 15-day pass, $369 for a 30-day pass and $539 for a 60-day pass. The International Ameripass is usually bought abroad at a travel agency or can be bought in the USA through the Greyhound International depot in New York City (☎ 212-971-0492) at 625 8th Ave at the Port Authority Subway level, open Monday to Friday from 7 am to 4 pm (Fridays until 7 pm) and Saturday from 7 am to 3 pm. New York Greyhound International accepts American Express, MasterCard and Visa, traveler's checks and cash, and allows purchases to be made by phone.

Greyhound will also allow travelers to buy 14-day and 21-day advance fare tickets for travel between specific destinations, which can be mailed either to the buyer's home overseas or to a designated address in the USA.

To contact Greyhound International in order to inquire about regular fares and routes, call ☎ 800-246-8572, or check out their website (www.greyhound.com) Those buying an International Ameripass must complete an affidavit and present a passport or visa (or waiver) to the appropriate Greyhound officials.

There are also special passes for travel in Canada that can be bought only through the New York City office or abroad.

TRAIN

Rail service within the Rocky Mountain region is very limited. Amtrak's long-distance trains are few and serve only a few destinations. For more information, see the Train entry in the Getting There & Away chapter.

Tourist trains, which are essentially day trips, include the weekend *Ski Train* from Denver's Union Station to Winter Park, CO; the Durango & Silverton Narrow Gauge Railroad in southern Colorado; the Georgetown Loop out of Georgetown, CO; the Cumbres & Toltec Scenic Railroad from Antonito, CO, to Chama, NM; and the Pike's Peak Cog Railway in Manitou Springs, CO. Although they are tourist trains, the Durango and Cumbres lines allow backpackers and anglers access to wilderness areas at their water stops. In Montana, Rockies Rail Tours runs luxury trips between Billings or Bozeman and Sandpoint, ID (with bus transfer onto Spokane, WA), as well as trips that go through Livingston, the Paradise Valley and Yellowstone National Park.

On many of these trains it's imperative that you make reservations or buy advance tickets. For regional fares and specifics on tourist trains, check the destination listing in the text.

CAR & MOTORCYCLE

The US highway system is extensive, and, since distances are great and buses can be infrequent, auto transport is worth considering despite the expense. Foreigners will need an International or Inter-American Driving Permit to supplement the national driver's license, but US police are more likely to want to see the national, provincial or state driver's license.

Rental

Major international rental agencies like Avis, Budget, Hertz and National have offices throughout the region, but there are also local agencies. To rent a car, you must have a valid driver's license, be at least 25 years of age and present a major credit card or else a large cash deposit.

Many rental agencies have bargain rates for weekend or week-long rentals, especially outside the peak summer season or in conjunction with the purchase of an airline ticket. Prices vary greatly in relation to region, season and type or size of the car you'd like to rent. Rental agencies sometimes offer discounts in tandem with national motel chains. Since the deregulation of the US airline industry, airlines have been jockeying to provide the most appealing premiums for potential flyers. If you belong to any frequent-flyer programs, ask what discounts they entitle you to.

Basic liability insurance, which will cover damage that you may cause to another vehicle, is required by law in some states, in which case it is included in the

---

Mileage Chart

Following are distances between major cities in the Rocky Mountain states:

Denver to	
Salt Lake City	512 miles
Grand Junction	246 miles
Cheyenne	100 miles
Cheyenne to	
Jackson	436 miles
Sheridan	329 miles
Sheridan to	
Bozeman	269 miles
Bozeman to	
West Yellowstone	89 miles
Kalispell	324 miles
Missoula	201 miles
Missoula to	
Coeur d'Alene	168 miles
Coeur d'Alene to	
Boise	454 miles
Boise to	
Denver	814 miles

price of renting the car. In other states you have the option of whether or not to purchase liability insurance, which is also called 3rd-party coverage. While it can cost you an extra $10 per day, it may be well worth it: the fee is nothing compared to what a lawsuit in the litigation-happy USA could do to your finances. However, some credit cards, such as the MasterCard Gold Card, will already cover liability insurance if you rent for 15 days or less and charge the full cost of rental to your card. If you opt to do that, you'll need to sign a waiver declining the rental agency coverage. Check with your credit card company to see, as often car rental agency staff won't know which card covers what.

Collision insurance, also called the Collision Damage Waiver (CDW), is optional; it covers the full value of the vehicle in case of an accident, except when caused by acts of nature or fire. For a mid-size car rented out of Denver, the cost for this extra coverage is around $15 per day. You don't need to buy this waiver to rent the car. If you have collision insurance on your personal auto insurance policy, this may also cover rental cars. Again, check with your insurance company to find out.

Agencies also tack on a daily fee per each additional driver in the car, which is usually around $5 per day.

Be aware that most major rental agencies in noncompetitive markets (most of the Rocky Mountain states) only offer unlimited mileage if you specifically ask for that rate. This may cost a bit more, but should still be cheaper in the long run if you're driving long distances (hard to avoid in this region).

Purchase

If you're spending several months in the USA, purchasing a car is worth considering; a car is more flexible than public transport and likely to be cheaper than rentals, but buying one can also be very complicated and requires plenty of research.

It's possible to purchase a viable car in the USA for about $1500, but you can't expect to go too far before you'll need

some repair work that could cost several hundred dollars or more. It doesn't hurt to spend more to get a quality vehicle. It's also worth spending $50 or so to have a mechanic check it for defects. Some American Automobile Association (AAA) offices have diagnostic centers where they can do this on the spot for its members and those of foreign affiliates. You can check out the official valuation of a used car by looking it up in the *Blue Book*, a listing of cars by make, model and year issued and the average resale price. Local public libraries have copies, as well as back issues of *Consumer Reports*, a magazine that annually tallies the repair records of common makes of cars.

If you want to purchase a car, the first thing to do is contact AAA (☎ 800-222-4357) for some general information. Then contact the state's Department of Motor Vehicles to find out about registration fees and insurance, which can be very confusing and expensive. If this is the first time you have registered a car in the USA, you'll have to fork over some money first (about a few hundred dollars) and then a few hundred more for general registration.

Inspect the title carefully before purchasing the car; the owner's name that appears on the title must match the identification of the person selling you the car. If you're a foreigner, you may find it very useful to obtain a notarized document authorizing your use of the car, since the motor vehicle bureau in the state where you buy the car may take several weeks or more to process the change in title.

Insurance While insurance is not obligatory in every state, all states have financial responsibility laws and insurance is highly desirable; otherwise, a serious accident could leave you a pauper. (Liability insurance is mandatory in the four states covered in this book). In order to get insurance, some states request that you have a US driver's license and that you have been licensed for at least 18 months. If you meet those qualifications, you may still have to pay anywhere from $300 to $1200 a year for insurance, depending on the state and where the car is registered. Rates are generally lower if you register it at an address in the suburbs or in a rural area, rather than in a central city. The minimum term for a policy is usually six months, but some insurance companies will refund the difference on a prorated basis if the car is sold and the policy voluntarily terminated. Collision coverage has become very expensive, with high deductibles, and is generally not worthwhile unless the car is somewhat valuable. Regulations vary from state to state but are generally becoming stringent throughout the USA.

Obtaining insurance, however, is not as simple as walking into an agency, filling out a form and paying for it. Many agencies refuse to insure drivers who have no car insurance (a classic Catch-22!); those who will do so often charge much higher rates because they presume a higher risk. Male drivers under the age of 25 will pay astronomical rates. It is advisable to shop around.

Holders of foreign driver's licenses may also have difficulty finding insurance firms that will sell them a policy. However, AAA

may be able to help. For example, the Colorado branch (☎ 800-283-5222 in Colorado) works with several firms that offer policies to non-US citizens.

Drive-Aways
Drive-aways are cars that belong to owners who can't drive them to a specific destination but are willing to allow someone else to drive it for them. For example, if somebody moves from Boston to Denver, they may elect to fly and leave the car with a drive-away agency. The agency will find a driver and take care of all necessary insurance and permits. If you happen to want to drive from Boston to Denver, have a valid license and a clean driving record, you can apply to drive the car. Normally, you have to pay a small refundable deposit. You pay for the gas (though sometimes a gas allowance is given).

You are allowed a set number of days to deliver the car – usually based on driving eight hours a day. You are also allowed a limited number of miles, based on the best route and allowing for reasonable side trips, so you can't just zigzag all over the country. However, this is a cheap way to

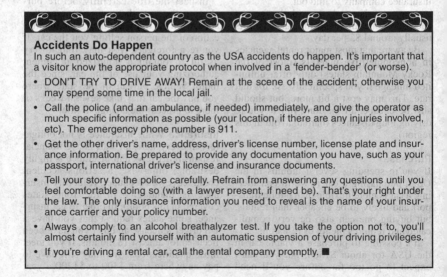

Accidents Do Happen
In such an auto-dependent country as the USA accidents do happen. It's important that a visitor know the appropriate protocol when involved in a 'fender-bender' (or worse).

• DON'T TRY TO DRIVE AWAY! Remain at the scene of the accident; otherwise you may spend some time in the local jail.

• Call the police (and an ambulance, if needed) immediately, and give the operator as much specific information as possible (your location, if there are any injuries involved, etc). The emergency phone number is 911.

• Get the other driver's name, address, driver's license number, license plate and insurance information. Be prepared to provide any documentation you have, such as your passport, international driver's license and insurance documents.

• Tell your story to the police carefully. Refrain from answering any questions until you feel comfortable doing so (with a lawyer present, if need be). That's your right under the law. The only insurance information you need to reveal is the name of your insurance carrier and your policy number.

• Always comply to an alcohol breathalyzer test. If you take the option not to, you'll almost certainly find yourself with an automatic suspension of your driving privileges.

• If you're driving a rental car, call the rental company promptly. ∎

get around if you enjoy long-distance driving and meet eligibility requirements.

Drive-away companies often advertise in the classified sections of newspapers under 'Travel.' They are also listed in the yellow pages of telephone directories under 'Automobile Transporters & Drive-away Companies.' You need to be flexible about dates and destinations when you call. If you are going to a popular area, you may be able to leave within two days or less, or you may have to wait over a week before a car becomes available. The routes most easily available are coast to coast, although intermediate trips are certainly possible.

Safety

Drivers should be aware that much of the Rocky Mountain region is open-range country in which cattle and, less frequently, sheep forage along the highway. A collision with a large animal (including game animals like deer or moose) can wreck a car and severely injure or kill the driver and passengers, not to mention the animal, so pay attention to the roadside – especially at night. Seat belts are obligatory for the driver and all passengers in all four states.

Many roads in the Rockies are two-lane highways, which means cars rush past each other at speeds often exceeding 120 miles per hour. On these roads it's a good idea to keep your headlights on even in daytime, just to give other drivers that much more time to be aware of your presence.

During winter months, especially at the higher elevations, there will be times when tire chains are required on snowy or icy roads. Sometimes roads will be closed to cars without chains or 4WD. So it's a good idea to keep a set of chains in the trunk. (Note that some rental car companies specifically prohibit the use of chains on their vehicles, so you are responsible for any damage caused by them.) Roadside services might be available to attach chains to your tires for a fee (around $20). Other cold-weather precautions include keeping a wool blanket, warm clothing, extra food, a windshield ice-scraper, a snow shovel,

flares and an extra set of gloves and boots in the trunk for emergencies.

Some states have motorcycle helmet laws. Colorado doesn't, but Wyoming stipulates that riders under the age of 19 must wear helmets, while Montana and Idaho require helmets on those under 18. Use of a helmet is highly recommended regardless of your age.

Weather is a serious factor throughout the Rocky Mountain states, especially in winter. All four states provide road and travel information as well as state highway patrol information by telephone; for these numbers, see the Emergency entry in the Facts for the Visitor chapter and under Information for each state.

To avert theft, do not leave expensive items, such as purses, compact discs, cameras, leather bags or even sunglasses, visibly lying about in the car. Tuck items under the seat, or even better, put them in the trunk and make sure your car does not have trunk entry through the back seat; if it does, make sure this is locked. Don't leave valuables in the car overnight.

TAXI

Taxis or minivans connect some popular tourist areas, like Denver and Winter Park, CO, or Jackson and Pinedale, WY. Taxis are especially expensive for long distances, but aren't so outrageous if shared among two or three people. Check with the service before setting out regarding fares per-person, return-trip fees and taxes. Check the yellow pages under 'Taxi' for phone numbers and services. Drivers often expect a tip of about 10% of the fare.

BICYCLE

Cycling is an interesting, inexpensive and increasingly popular way to travel in the USA, and in the Rocky Mountain states especially. Roads are good, shoulders are usually wide and there are many good routes for mountain bikes as well. The changeable weather can be a drawback, especially at high altitudes where thunderstorms are frequent. In some areas the wind can slow your progress to a crawl (traveling west to east is generally easier than east to west), and water sources are far apart. Cyclists should carry at least two full bottles and refill them at every opportunity. Spare parts are widely available and repair shops are numerous, but it's still important to be able to do basic mechanical work, like fixing a flat tire, yourself.

Bicycles can be transported by air. You *can* disassemble them and put them in a bike bag or box, but it's much easier simply to wheel your bike to the check-in desk, where it should be treated as a piece of baggage. You may have to remove the pedals and front tire so that it takes up less space in the aircraft's hold; check all this with the airline well in advance, preferably before you pay for your ticket. Be aware that some airlines welcome bicycles, while others treat them as a decidedly undesirable nuisance and do everything possible to discourage them.

Motorists are generally courteous to cyclists, though they often drive too fast. Cyclists may encounter the occasional arrested-development imbecile who likes to harass cyclists to show off, however. Some cities require helmets, others don't, but they should always be worn.

For more on the details, see the Road & Mountain Biking entry in the National Parks & Outdoor Activities chapter.

HITCHHIKING

Hitchhiking is never entirely safe in any country in the world, and we don't recommend it. Travelers who decide to hitch should understand that they are taking a small but serious risk. You may not be able to distinguish a rapist, murderer, thief, or even a driver who's just had too much to drink, before you get into the vehicle. People who do choose to hitchhike will be safer if they always travel in pairs and let someone know where they are planning to go.

Because public transport is so limited in parts of the Rocky Mountain states, especially in Wyoming, Montana and Idaho, some visitors may be tempted to hitchhike to areas where access is difficult. Should you hitch, keep a close watch on your possessions; there have been instances of 'friendly' drivers absconding with an innocent hitchhiker's possessions while the latter visited the toilet during a gasoline stop.

In Colorado, hitchhiking is illegal and pedestrians on the highway must walk in the opposite direction of traffic. It is legal in Montana and Wyoming, though restricted in areas near state prisons in Montana. Hitchhiking in Idaho is illegal on interstate highways, though it's allowed on all other roads.

Colorado

ABRAHM LUSTGARTEN

Facts about Colorado

The best known of the Rocky Mountain States, Colorado owes its fame to the mountains which soar to majestic heights and create unrivaled vistas and recreation opportunities. Colorado lays claim to 54 of the country's 69 summits over 14,000 feet. This wealth of Alpine scenery means that during the peak summer season when millions of tourists flood the state, visitors can still find solitude at a remote mountain lake or meadow or atop a craggy summit. Even Rocky Mountain National Park, the state's premier attraction, offers dozens of back-country hikes and campsites that see few visitors. The hiking, climbing and mountain biking found in Colorado's high country are among the best in the US. During the winter, these areas are also home to some of the world's most famous ski resorts.

But there is more than just mountains. Western Colorado has beautiful desert canyons and mesas, and areas like the sprawling San Luis Valley that open up to reveal farms and ranchlands. Rivers, including the Arkansas, Colorado and Rio Grande, snake throughout the state, offering outstanding white-water rafting, kayaking and canoeing. East of the Rockies the prairie lands of the Eastern Plains stretch far beyond the horizon. While there's not a great deal to do out here, it makes an interesting contrast from life in the rest of the state.

Colorado's urban attractions are mostly located along the Front Range, the foothills that mark the eastern edge of the Rocky Mountains. Running from Fort Collins in

Colorado's Casino Casualties

In 1991, a ballot proposal was passed that allowed gambling in the twin historic towns of Central City and Black Hawk in the hope this could revive economies that sporadic tourism had failed to support. The result was a sudden transformation from backwater to 'boomtown': busloads of punters swarmed through town, filling the casinos, bars and restaurants, parting with most of their money in the process. However, locals weren't sharing in the feast: most of the money went to the national 'gaming' corporations, and what profits did remain in town couldn't make up for the lost charm and reasonable costs of living. The story is similar in Cripple Creek, another mining town turned gambling haven, located in the mountains southwest of Denver.

Local residents have mostly regretted the ballot decisions to allow casinos into their towns. Coloradans' disenchantment with mountain gambling in general was apparent in 1995, when a proposal to allow gambling in the southern town of Trinidad was soundly defeated across the state. With all the beautiful small towns Colorado has to offer, there's no need to endure visiting these gambling towns, which is why they aren't covered in this book. However, if you're keen on gambling, plenty of information on transport, accommodation and casinos is available from nearly any Colorado tourist office. ■

the north to Trinidad in the south, this corridor is the most densely populated section of Colorado, particularly the area around the capital, Denver. Long derided as a glorified cowtown, Denver developed into a lively city with good entertainment, dining and cultural offerings. Nearby the university town of Boulder draws visitors with its beautiful natural setting and progressive intellectual atmosphere. Moving south along the rapidly developing Front Range, Colorado Springs is none too interesting as cities go, but still lures hordes of visitors with a glut of tourist traps that have sprung up around the more worthwhile sites of Pikes Peak and Garden of the Gods.

Though not as homogeneous as Montana, Colorado is not very socially diverse. However, visits to the southern section of the state, particularly the San Luis Valley, reveal some nearly intact preserves of Hispanic culture. Some Native Americans still live in the Ute Mountain and Southern Ute Indian reservations in southwest Colorado, which lie near the fascinating ruins of Mesa Verde National Park. Native American tribes used to inhabit large areas of the state until they were pushed back by European settlers in the late 19th century. Signs of these 'frontier days' are readily found throughout the state, particularly in historic mining towns such as Telluride, Creede and Crested Butte.

INFORMATION
State Tourist Offices
The Colorado Travel & Tourism Authority (☎ 303-296-3384), PO Box 3524, Englewood, CO 80155, publishes a useful state vacation guide and offers regional information packages. It also operates Colorado Welcome Centers at the entry points of Burlington, Cortez, Dinosaur, Fruita, Julesburg Lamar and Trinidad, where you'll find excellent (and free) state highway maps and a wealth of other travel information covering the entire state. Call the authority's toll-free number (☎ 800-265-6723) to have a vacation guide sent to you. You can also visit them online at their website (www.colorado.com). Another site worth checking out is run by the Colorado Adventure Guide (www.coloradovacation.com), which has information on destinations, accommodations and suggested itineraries.

For information from the statewide Colorado Division of Wildlife (DOW), 6060 Broadway, Denver, CO 80216, call ☎ 303-297-1192. For USFS information on the state, call ☎ 303-275-5350 or write PO Box 25127, Lakewood, CO 80225. This USFS office is at 740 Simms St in Golden. For information about state parks or state-run recreation areas, call ☎ 303-866-3437; the address is 1313 Sherman St, Room 618, Denver, CO 80203.

To check on road conditions in the state call ☎ 303-639-1234.

Useful Organizations
The Colorado Endowment for the Humanities (☎ 303-573-7733), 1623 Blake St, Denver, CO 80205, sponsors first-rate traveling museum exhibits and public presentations that visit various communities.

Most of the many environmental and conservation groups in Colorado belong to the Colorado Environmental Coalition (☎ 303-837-8701), 777 Grant St, suite 606, Denver, CO 80203. CEC's achievements over the past 30 years include passage of the 1983 and 1990 wilderness bills; stopping the proposed Two Forks Dam in the South Platte River's Cheesman Canyon; protection of untold acres of old-growth forest; and saving BLM lands and Anasazi ruins from oil and gas development.

Since 1931, the grand dame of Colorado conservation organizations, the Rocky Mountain Nature Association, has focused on educating park and forest visitors – they now offer maps, books and guides at 40 visitors centers throughout the Rocky Mountain region. Members receive a discount on publications – contact the RMNA (☎ 303-586-0108), Rocky Mountain National Park, Estes Park, CO 80517.

Area Codes
Originally covering the entire state, the telephone area code 303 now includes only the metropolitan Denver, Boulder and

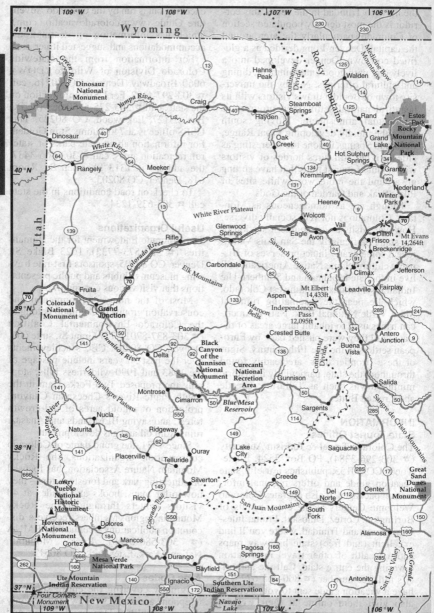

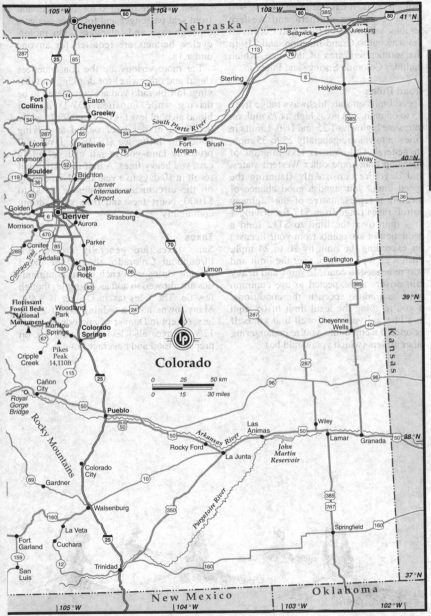

Colorado

0   25   50 km

0   15   30 miles

Golden areas. It has been replaced by 970 in the expansive northern and western regions, which stretch from Fort Collins all the way out to Grand Junction, and 719 in the southeastern area of the state, which includes Colorado Springs and Pueblo.

Road Rules

Speed limits on state highways range from 55 to 65 mph, and go as high as 75 mph on interstate highways I-25 and I-70. Limits in cities in towns are generally 25 to 35 mph. In general, Colorado is less tolerant of speeding than some other Western states, and if you're consistently flaunting the speed limits you stand a good chance of meeting a representative of the highway patrol. Fines range from $17 for driving 1 to 4 mph over the limit to $112 (and a deduction of six points from your license) for exceeding the limit by 20 to 24 mph. Push it 25 mph or more over the limit and you're headed to court. In snow and heavy rain drivers are expected to use common sense and adjust speed to the conditions: if you're going the legal limit of 65 mph in a blizzard you could well find yourself ticketed if a cop thinks you're endangering other drivers (which you would be).

Seat belts are required for the driver and front seat passenger and for all passengers on highways and interstates. On motorcycles, helmets are required for anyone under 18.

Far more serious are the consequences (legal and otherwise) for drinking and driving. In Colorado you are considered to be driving while impaired (DWI) if your blood alcohol level is 0.51 to 0.99%, while 0.10% or higher is classified as driving under the influence (DUI). A DWI will probably land you in jail and definitely earn you heavy fines. A first-time DUI will result in 10 days to a year in jail depending on the circumstances, fines of $100 to $1000, court fees and time spent doing community service.

Taxes

Sales taxes are generally around 3% throughout Colorado, though the exact amount varies with each town: communities are allowed to add as 4% more, though few do. The sales tax in Denver is 3.8%. Many towns have a lodging tax of 2% or less, except in Denver where lodging tax is 12%. Denver also levies a dining tax on prepared food and beverages of 4%.

Denver & Boulder

More than half of Colorado's population is clustered around this hub on the Front Range that extends from Boulder in the north, south through the multitude of suburbs surrounding Denver and west to the Continental Divide. Once separated by farms and fields, Denver and Boulder are now linked by an endless sprawl of suburban housing. During the 1990s, population growth in this area has exploded, with as many as 2000 people moving in each week, nearly doubling the population in less than 10 years.

The lure is the foothills and eastern peaks of the Rocky Mountains that comprise the Front Range. Forming a beautiful western backdrop to the Denver region, this is the area's outdoor playground. The ski areas of Eldora and Loveland Basin are enticingly close to Boulder and Denver, respectively. Road access to the summit of Mt Evans, a 14er (a peak over 14,000 feet) south of Idaho Springs, is only an hour

away from the Denver skyscrapers, as are many of the Denver Mountain Parks. South of Golden, Red Rocks Park and Amphitheater is one of the world's best music and performance venues, although the acts are often less stellar than the scenery.

All of this makes the Denver/Boulder area a great place to live, as well as visit. But of course its draw may well lead to its demise. Traffic congestion, air pollution, water shortages and skyrocketing real estate prices are just some of the social problems that have accompanied the Denver boom. As in many US cities, lower and middle-class wage-earners are being pushed out of their original neighborhoods as rents soar beyond their reach. Many of the historic mining towns west of the city have also been hit: those along the narrow Clear Creek and I-70 resemble noisy truck stops, making vacation relaxation difficult. However, state and local governments work to protect and preserve the area's

HIGHLIGHTS

- Denver Museum of Natural History – some of the USA's best wildlife, geological and dinosaur exhibits

- Lodo – lower downtown Denver, a surprisingly lively restaurant and nightlife hub

- 16th St Mall – stroll past a wide array of shops, cafes, bars and good restaurants

- Mt Evans – amazing views from this 14,264-foot summit, one hour's drive west of Denver

- Boulder – at the foot of the Rockies, this hip college town offers culture and excellent hikes in its mountain parks

- Peak to Peak Hwy – the slowest and prettiest route between Boulder and Estes Park

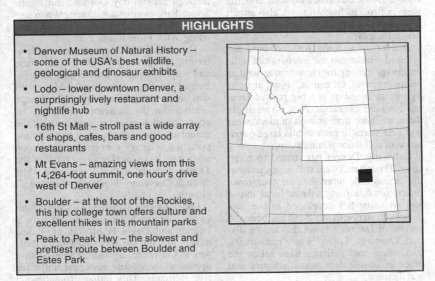

mountain parks and wilderness areas, no simple task considering many are only an hour's drive from the cities.

Denver

Denver's 'Mile High City' moniker is more than mere symbolism – one of the steps to the State Capitol is exactly 5280 feet above sea level. While the population of the city proper is only 497,000, Metro Denver (population 2,152,000) represents an economic realm that extends beyond Colorado's borders throughout the Rocky Mountain region. Denver harbors the corporate headquarters for mining, oil and rail-transportation firms, plus regional offices for nearly every branch of the federal government. It is the major air terminal for the region as well.

Visitors will find an array of museums and galleries, including some of national stature, such as the Denver Museum of Natural History and the Denver Art Museum. Professional sports teams, including the Colorado Rockies baseball team and the Denver Broncos football team, also attract a loyal following whose enthusiasm borders on mania.

Denver is a town for the outdoor-oriented. Flat terrain and a network of trails encourage cycling for recreation as well as utility purposes. Of course, skiing at nearby mountain resorts is a big part of Denver's winter character. Not surprisingly there are more than enough outdoor wear and gear stores to cater to this large population of recreational enthusiasts.

Culturally, Denver has started to come alive. Though many are still happy to label the city as little more than an overgrown prairie town, a fairly vibrant local music and art scene has developed in the past decade. In step with this trend has been the revival of Denver's lower downtown district, known as 'LoDo,' where restaurants, bars, shops and galleries have taken the place of obsolescent manufacturers and warehouses.

History

When the gold seekers began flocking to the South Platte River Valley in 1859, Arapaho and Cheyenne buffalo hunters already occupied hundreds of camps in the area. Urban development threatened the wilderness resources that Native Americans relied upon and the new arrivals had little concern for the rights or welfare of the prior inhabitants.

General William H Larimer made a shameless attempt to sway Kansas Territorial Governor James W Denver into granting Larimer and his partners a township at the confluence of Cherry Creek and the South Platte River by proposing to name the new town Denver. It worked, and the Denver City Township Company was set up in late 1859. On the west bank of Cherry Creek, another party had already laid out Auraria in 1858. Nevertheless, local claims of mineral riches were greatly exaggerated by the land promoters and many gold-seekers became 'go-backers,' proclaiming the Pikes Peak gold claims to be nothing but humbug. New discoveries in 1859 on Clear Creek, west of Denver, which flows through present-day Golden, and in the South Park interior area, brought a resurgence of people in the human tide accumulating at the Front Range.

The gold rush led to increased overland freight and passenger business via horse and wagon, focusing on Denver. Its position at the foot of the Rocky Mountains was as convenient as any Front Range location for the shipments and financial operations that served mining areas in the mountains. But without water or rail transportation, Denver's overnight rise soon stagnated. Its isolated position south of the Transcontinental Railroad, opened in 1869 through Cheyenne, threatened to curtail all growth.

Local bigwigs, including Governor John Evans, Walter S Cheesman, William J Palmer and David H Moffat, Jr, raised money to build the 106-mile Pacific Railway to Cheyenne. By 1881, Union Station opened to consolidate passenger traffic for five railroads. This Italian Romanesque

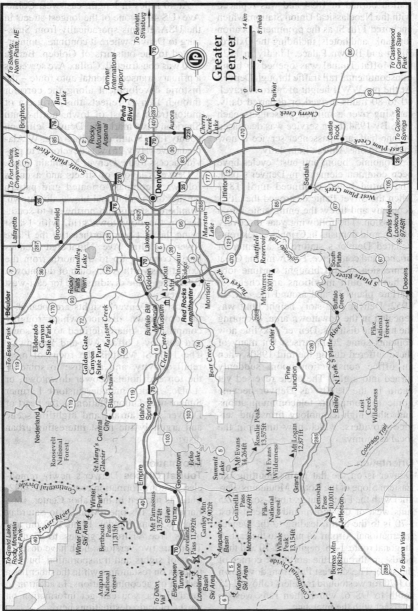

station burned in 1894 and was replaced with the Neoclassical Union Station, which anchored 17th St as the prominent location for banks and hotels, including the Oxford, Barth and Brown Palace. Finally in 1928 the Moffat Tunnel was opened to bring transcontinental rail traffic through Denver. At the pre-WWII height of railroad travel, 60 to 80 trains arrived or departed daily, carrying over a million passengers each year. By 1954, train service was decreased by one-half, and passenger service is now limited to one Amtrak train daily.

Economic 'boom and bust' cycles have been common elements in Denver's past. The initial boom continued until 1893 when the Silver Panic destroyed the city's economy and threw the entire state into a depression. The following year discovery of rich gold deposits in Cripple Creek rejuvenated Denver's stature as a center of finance and commerce. Following the Great Depression, WWII brought wartime jobs at hastily built munitions and chemical warfare plants in and around the city. In 1952, Denver's 12-story height limit was repealed in the downtown area, excepting the historic districts. Denver's skyline now contains some 20 highrises, but many of these suffered during the mid-1980s when an office construction boom suddenly turned into a glut. The cycle reversed yet again in the 1990s, as Denver became home to computer, telecommunications and other high-technology firms and service providers, which now underpin the local economy.

Orientation

Denver is on the flat plains abutting the Eastern Slope of the Rocky Mountains. Parallel with the Front Range, north-south I-25 runs west of downtown and the east-west I-70 is to the north, leading to the Denver International Airport 24 miles to the east. A diagonal route, I-76, begins at I-70 and then heads up through the northeast corner of the state. The shortest link from downtown to I-70 for westbound travelers follows I-25 south to US 6, which then runs west to intersect with the interstate.

At 40 miles in length, east-west Colfax Ave (US 40) is one of the longest streets in the USA. It runs sporadically from Strasburg to Denver where it continues uninterrupted to the outskirts of Golden. Before I-70 was constructed, Colfax Ave served as a primary transcontinental auto route – the historic development along the corridor through Denver reflects this early era of motor travel. West of town, north-south Sheridan Blvd marks the Denver-Jefferson county line. South of Colfax Ave, W Alameda Ave (Hwy 26) was developed to provide access to the Denver Mountain Parks.

Denver's layout of streets and avenues follows a compass-oriented grid pattern outside of the diagonal blocks downtown. Numbered streets run northwest to southeast in the downtown grid, with 1st St being the first road northeast of the Platte River at Colfax Ave. Numbered avenues begin counting up to the north from the axis at Ellsworth Ave, south of downtown. Broadway is the dividing line for east-west avenues.

Most of Denver's sights are located in the downtown district, which roughly comprises a square defined to the south and east by Colfax Ave and Broadway. The 16th St Mall is the focus of most retail activity, and is close to some of the top end hotels. Lower downtown, or 'LoDo,' which includes historic Larimer Square near Union Station, is the heart of Denver's restaurant and nightlife scene and arguably the most interesting urban district.

Information

Tourist Offices Denver's newly remodeled visitor information center (☎ 303-892-1112) is located in the Tabor Center, 1668 Larimer St. It's open Monday to Saturday 8 am to 5 pm, Sunday 10 am to 2 pm and offers free visitors' guides to Denver. There are two versions: both have descriptions of sights and transportation, but one focuses on restaurants while the other has a section on accommodations. In addition to local sights, you can get information on most Colorado destinations here.

Money As a financial center for the Rocky Mountain states, Denver naturally offers plenty of banking services. Among the larger banks with downtown offices and numerous branch offices are: Bank One Colorado NA (☎ 303-759-0111), at the corner of 17th and Lawrence Sts; Norwest Bank (☎ 303-861-8811), 1740 Broadway; and Firstbank (☎ 303-623-2000), at the corner of 16th and Tremont Sts, which offers Saturday morning service at its branches in King Soopers stores; one is at the corner of 9th and Corona Sts (☎ 303-237-5000).

For foreign currency exchange, head to Thomas Cook Currency Services at (☎ 303-571-0808) 1625 Broadway, or American Express (☎ 303-298-7100), 555 S 17th St.

Post & Communications The Denver downtown post office at 951 20th St is open weekdays; the zip code is 80201. For fax services or package shipping in the downtown area, try the Packaging Store (☎ 303-830-1092; fax 303-830-1093), 1092 Broadway. Kinkos Copies offers numerous 24-hour outlets with fax service in Denver; near downtown try the location at 1509 Blake St (☎ 303-623-3500) or 555 W 17th St (☎ 303-298-8610).

Consulates & Representatives Of the offices listed below, only the Mexican, Netherlands and Thai consulates can actually issue visas. The Korean Consulate also issues visas, but only to US passport holders. The others, most of which are honorary consuls, can offer assistance to their respective citizens traveling in the US, answer visa and other travel-related queries and provide applications for visas and passports. Many offices are only staffed part-time and some are located outside the city center, so it's a good idea to call ahead for information.

Australia
    999 18 St (☎ 303-297-1200)
Denmark
    1777 S Harrison St (☎ 303-692-9090)
France
    1420 Ogden St (☎ 303-831-8616)

Germany
    350 Indiana St (☎ 303-279-1551)
Italy
    16613 W Archer Ave (☎ 303-271-1429)
Mexico
    48 Steele St (☎ 303-331-1110)
Netherlands
    5560 S Chester Ct (☎ 303-770-7747)
Norway
    370 17th St (☎ 303-592-5930)
Sweden
    4242 E Amherst Ave (☎ 303-758-0999)

Travel Agencies AAA Colorado (☎ 303-753-8800), 621 17th St, offers maps and guides for members, and full travel services for nonmembers. American Express Travel (☎ 303-298-7100) is at 555 17th St. Council Travel (☎ 303-571-0630), 900 Wazee St, is a good place for cheap air tickets.

International Passport Visas (☎ 303-753-0424) is a private firm that specializes in helping both Americans and foreign nationals obtain visas and passports. The standard service charge for a visa is $85, plus the fee charged by the respective country. While it seems expensive, it saves you the time and hassle of contacting consulates in other cities and arranging for express mailing of your passport and application. The fee is lower for visas which can be obtained locally.

Bookstores Johnny's Newsstand (☎ 303-825-6397), in the basement level at 1555 Champa St (below the McDonald's restaurant), carries a selection of foreign newspapers plus hard-to-find environmental papers such as *High Country News*.

Just north of the Cherry Creek Shopping Center, four floors of shelves contain an awesome array of new volumes at Tattered Cover Bookstore (☎ 303-322-7727), 2955 E 1st Ave. Weekend browsers from throughout the western USA and Plains states congregate to make this one of the most popular bookstores on the planet. Check it out on a weekday to enjoy one of the comfy reading chairs or get personal assistance from one of the store's 300 employees. A branch in LoDo (☎ 303-436-1070), 1628 16th St at

COLORADO

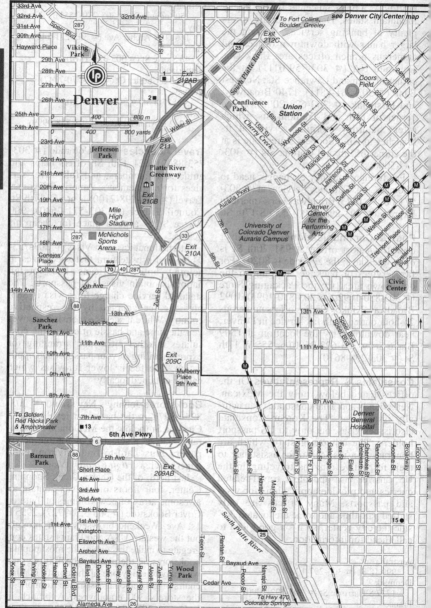

see Denver City Center map

To Fort Collins,
Boulder, Greeley

Exit
212C

33rd Ave
32nd Ave
31st Ave
30th Ave
Hayward Place
29th Ave
28th Ave
27th Ave
26th Ave
25th Ave
24th Ave
23rd Ave
22nd Ave
21st Ave
20th Ave
19th Ave
18th Ave
17th Ave
16th Ave
Conejos Place
Colfax Ave
14th Ave

Speer Blvd
287
32nd Ave

Zuni St

Viking
Park

Denver

Jefferson
Park

Water St

Exit
211

Platte River
Greenway

Exit
210B

Mile
High
Stadium

McNichols
Sports
Arena

BUS
70 40 287

Exit
212AB

1

2

287

Confluence
Park

South Platte River

15th St

Cherry Creek

Union
Station

Wynkoop St
Wazee St
Blake St
Market St
Larimer St
Lawrence St
Arapahoe St
Curtis St
Champa St

Aurari Pkwy

7th St

University of
Colorado Denver
Auraria Campus

33

Exit
210A

5th St

Denver
Center
for the
Performing
Arts

Coors
Field

Welton St
Glenarm Place
Tremont Place
Court Place
Cleveland Place

Broadway

Civic
Center

4th St
23rd St
22nd St
21st St
20th St
19th St
18th St
17th St
16th St

400   800 m

400   800 yards

88

4th Ave

13th Ave

Holden Place

Sanchez
Park

12th Ave
11th Ave
10th Ave
9th Ave
8th Ave

To Golden,
Red Rocks Park
& Amphitheater
7th Ave

13

6th Ave Pkwy

Barnum
Park

88

5th Ave
Short Place
4th Ave
3rd Ave
2nd Ave
Park Place
1st Ave
Irvington
Ellsworth Ave
Archer Ave
Bayaud Ave

Knox St
Julian St
Irving St
Hazel St
Grove St
Hooker St
Federal Blvd
Elliot St
Decatur St
Clay St
Bryant St
Alcott St
Zuni St
Yuma St

Wood
Park

Alameda Ave

6

26

Zuni St

Exit
209C

Mulberry
Place
9th Ave

Exit
209AB

14

Denver
General
Hospital

8th Ave

13th Ave

11th Ave

8th Ave

Speer Blvd
Speer Blvd

Osage St
Quivas St
Navajo St
Mariposa St
Lipan St

Santa Fe Drive

Kalamath St
Inca St
Galapago St
Fox St
Elati St

Bannock St
Cherokee St
Delaware St

Acoma St
Broadway

Lincoln St

15

South Platte River

Tejon St
Raritan St
Pecos St

Bayaud Ave

Cedar Ave

To Hwy 470,
Colorado Springs

25

COLORADO

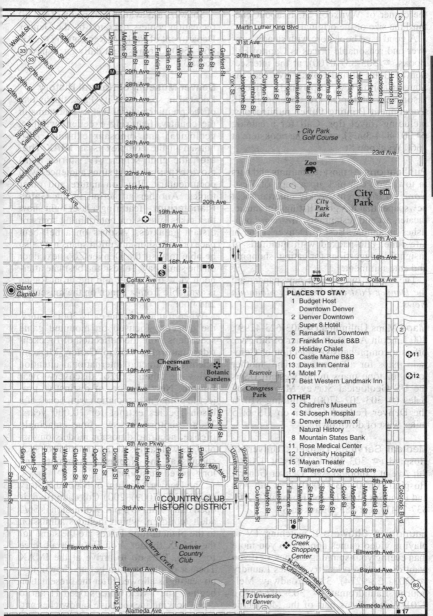

Martin Luther King Blvd
31st Ave
30th Ave
29th Ave
28th Ave
27th Ave
26th Ave
25th Ave
24th Ave
23rd Ave
22nd Ave
21st Ave
20th Ave
19th Ave
18th Ave
17th Ave
16th Ave
Colfax Ave
14th Ave
13th Ave
12th Ave
11th Ave
10th Ave
9th Ave
8th Ave
7th Ave
6th Ave Pkwy
5th Ave
4th Ave
3rd Ave
1st Ave
Ellsworth Ave
Bayaud Ave
Cedar Ave
Alameda Ave

City Park Golf Course
Zoo
City Park Lake
City Park
Cheesman Park
Botanic Gardens
Reservoir
Congress Park
State Capitol
COUNTRY CLUB HISTORIC DISTRICT
Denver Country Club
Cherry Creek
Cherry Creek Shopping Center
N. Cherry Creek Drive
S. Cherry Creek Drive
To University of Denver

BUS 70 40 287

PLACES TO STAY
1 Budget Host Downtown Denver
2 Denver Downtown Super 8 Hotel
6 Ramada Inn Downtown
7 Franklin House B&B
9 Holiday Chalet
10 Castle Marne B&B
13 Days Inn Central
14 Motel 7
17 Best Western Landmark Inn

OTHER
3 Children's Museum
4 St Joseph Hospital
5 Denver Museum of Natural History
8 Mountain States Bank
11 Rose Medical Center
12 University Hospital
15 Mayan Theater
16 Tattered Cover Bookstore

the corner of Wynkoop St, is about one-third the size of the original store.

A good used bookstore with steady turnover and reasonable prices is Capitol Hill Books (☎ 303-837-0700), at the intersection of Grant St and Colfax Ave near the State Capitol. A surprisingly diverse assortment of topics are covered in US Government Printing Office publications, including travel tips. Call for a catalog (☎ 303-844-3964), or visit the bookstore at 1660 Wynkoop St.

Publications At most restaurants and bars in town you can pick up a copy of *Westword*, an irreverent weekly entertainment newspaper that has great listings for music, theater, art and restaurants. *Westword* publishes an annual 'Best of Denver' issue in late June, jam-packed with hundreds of insightful suggestions for eating, shopping and entertainment.

The state's two largest newspapers are the *Denver Post* and the *Rocky Mountain News*.

Maps Maps Unlimited (☎ 303-623-4299), 800 Lincoln Ave at the corner of 8th Ave, offers a comprehensive selection of Colorado maps for all purposes. The 'mother lode' for topo maps in the western US is the US Geological Survey Map & Book Sales (☎ 303-202-4700), Building 810 in the Denver Federal Center on US 6, 5 miles west of downtown.

Medical Services Denver's University Hospital (☎ 303-399-1211) is at 4200 E 9th Ave at Colorado Ave. Denver General Hospital (☎ 303-436-6000) is at 6th Ave and Bannock St. St Joseph Hospital (☎ 303-837-7111) is at 1835 Franklin St.

Laundry & Showers If watching TV or playing video games appeals to you more than eyeing your spinning clothes, or if you want drop-off service, try Cycles Laundry (☎ 303-722-9274), 320 Broadway. Melbourne Laundromat (☎ 303-292-6386), 2201 Welton St, is part of the Melbourne Hostel, convenient if you're staying there.

Showers are available at many of the 30 recreation centers operated by the Denver Department of Parks & Recreation (☎ 303-964-2500). Nonresident daily guest passes cost $3.

Denver Museum of Natural History

Located in spacious City Park, this is one of the premier natural history museums in the country, featuring excellent wildlife, geological and dinosaur exhibits. Also housed in the complex is an **IMAX Theater**, the giant-screen (4½ stories high) movie experience that stuns audiences with documentary films on nature and other topics. Another attraction is the **Gates Planetarium** – featuring a laser light show that takes guests on entertaining tours of distant galaxies. Visitors on a hell-bent pace or with short attention spans may also be able to visit the Denver Zoo next door on the same day. To rest, the best late afternoon view of Denver and the Front Range is available from a bench on the museum's 2nd floor.

When founded in the early 20th century, the museum focused on mounted game specimens from the collection of Breckenridge naturalist Edwin Carter. Museum scientists attracted international attention following their 1926 discovery near Folsom, New Mexico, of distinctive projectile points in association with bones of a bison species extinct for 10,000 years. Today visitors can see some amazingly lifelike, accurate dinosaur models on display, as well as fossils and remains of such species as the Nebraska mammoth and long-jawed mastodon.

The Denver Museum of Natural History (☎ 303-322-7009), 2001 Colorado Blvd, is open daily 9 am to 5 pm. Admission is $6/4 adults/children, which includes admission to the planetarium. Prices are the same for the IMAX theater. You can visit all three for $9/6. Be sure to arrive at the IMAX Theater or planetarium before showtime – no seating is allowed after the presentation begins. The T-Rex Cafe is open 11 am to 2 pm, serving inexpensive sandwiches and tasty hot meals such as spaghetti for around

$5; there's also a deli that serves sandwiches all day.

To get to the museum from downtown, take eastbound bus Nos 20 or 32 from 17th and Blake Sts.

Denver Zoo

In the event you do not see bighorn sheep in the wild, the Denver Zoo (☎ 303-331-4100), in City Park at 2300 Steel St, is the next best place to go.

Founded in 1896 after the mayor was presented with a bear cub, the Denver Zoo continued to feature bears until Johnny and Jenny – among the last grizzly bears in Colorado – died in 1925 and 1936 from causes related to their captivity. Other native species have had greater success. The Denver Zoo's turn-of-the-century efforts have helped reestablish small commercial bison herds in the Rocky Mountain and Plains states, where the 19th-century bison slaughter still represents the greatest environmental transformation caused by humans on earth.

Also featured are other indigenous species like Rocky Mountain goats, elk, moose and a new wolf exhibit. About 600 species from around the world are also represented – the 'Tropical Discovery' exhibit is a major attraction. The zoo is open daily 9 am to 6 pm April to October, 10 am to 5 pm October to April. Admission costs $6/3 adults/children.

Eastbound bus No 20 connects the zoo with downtown Denver (17th and Blake Sts).

Denver Art Museum

Resembling a modern high-rise jail, the Denver Art Museum (☎ 303-640-4433), 100 W 14th Ave, houses one of the largest Native American art collections in the USA, displaying work from tribes throughout the country. Works are arranged geographically and reflect New World art from thousands of years ago to the present.

Among the Post-Columbian displays are *santos*, Hispanic religious paintings and carvings. American Western artists are also featured, and European masters are well-represented. The museum is open Tuesday to Saturday 10 am to 5 pm, noon to 5 pm on Sunday. Admission is free on Saturday,

Pu at Rocky Flats

In 1989 Rocky Flats, a 10-sq-mile site 15 miles west of Denver, employed over 7000 workers to build plutonium triggers for nuclear weapons. The Cold War ended the following year and other military facilities are now undergoing a 'swords to plowshares' transformation, but Rocky Flats is a hopeless mess that will long remain a toxic site.

Rocky Flats now employs over 7000 workers (as well as several high-priced private sector environmental consulting firms) to monitor, study and plan ways to clean up the land, water and facilities contaminated by 50 tons of radioactive plutonium – the element Pu, with a nuclear half-life of 24,000 years. There is no known way to safely handle or transport the extremely toxic plutonium, and even optimistic plant officials admit that cleanup is decades away.

Above the deadly vaults containing the plutonium, a few wind-powered generators represent a relatively feeble attempt by the US Department of Energy to show that conversion is progressing. Don't expect public tours anytime soon, and if one is offered, you might consider the account of a woman with a Geiger counter who participated in a public group tour in 1993. In supposedly safe areas of the facility, the monitoring device registered radioactivity 10 times the level found outside the plant.

It will take 10 half-lives, or 250,000 years, before the toxic, radioactive and explosive properties of the plutonium are rendered harmless. As yet, the US Department of Energy does not have a definitive plan for disposal. However, for various reasons, they have rejected several disposal alternatives including disposal in space, underground detonation of surplus weapons and ocean or seabed disposal. ■

otherwise $4.50/2.50 adults/students and seniors. The museum café is open 8 am to 6 pm, on Sunday 11 am to 6 pm. A sizable selection of books on art and Western Americana is offered in the gift shop.

Colorado History Museum

Unlike the myriad local museums throughout the state displaying bedpans, you won't find the Colorado History Museum a tedious experience. There are beautiful exhibits of Native American rugs, mostly from Pueblo tribes to the south and New Mexico. Technological innovations in mining and transportation are also displayed in life-size exhibits.

The Colorado History Museum (☎ 303-866-3682) is in the Civic Center at 1300 Broadway. It's open Monday to Saturday 10 am to 4:30 pm, Sunday noon to 4:30 pm. Admission is $3/1.50 adults/children.

Byers-Evans House & Denver History Museum

William Byers, publisher of the *Rocky Mountain News*, built the two-story brick mansion at 1310 Bannock St in 1883. It was sold in 1889 to another Denver scion, William Gray Evans. The Colorado Historical Society offers tours of the house, featuring period furnishings, and shows a short film about the two families. Admission to the adjacent Denver History Museum, with interactive videodisks about the city as well as exhibit cases and drawers filled with city artifacts, is included in the $3 admission. The Byers-Evans House (☎ 303-620-4933) is open 11 am to 3 pm Tuesday to Sunday.

State Capitol

It took only 200 ounces of gold to replace the original copper dome of the 1886 State Capitol (☎ 303-866-2604), at the corner of Broadway and E Colfax Ave. In many aspects, especially the large rotunda, its layout mimics the national capitol. Drop by the governor's reception room on the 1st floor. Access to public galleries for the House and Senate chambers are on the 3rd floor. Don't miss the stained-glass portraits

honoring pioneers like Barney Ford, the former slave who influenced the state's Constitution to protect minority civil rights. These are in the **Colorado Hall of Fame** near the top of the dome which also offers great views. The State Capitol is open weekdays 7:30 am to 5:30 pm; free 45-minute tours are offered between 9:30 am and 3 pm. Meet tour guides at the north (Colfax) entrance. Reservations are advised.

United States Mint

In 1869, the federal government opened the Denver Mint, a branch of the US Mint, to transform Colorado's mineral riches into bullion. However, no coining was done until 1906, two years after the present building was completed. The Denver Mint (☎ 303-405-4761), 320 W Colfax Ave, is one of three gold depositories in the USA. Six gold bars, each weighing 400 troy ounces, are on display there, and it produces over 5 billion coins each year. Free 20-minute tours are offered on a first-come, first-served basis weekdays 8 am to 2:45 pm (9 am on Wednesdays).

Molly Brown House Museum

Although on a first-name basis with Eastern society, Molly Brown was snubbed in Denver. A social climber, she prospered with her husband James from the Leadville mining boom. However, she was not acknowledged by Denver high society until her good deeds toward poor immigrant women on a lifeboat following the 1912 sinking of the *Titanic* brought her acclaim as a heroine.

The hit musical from the 1960s, *The Unsinkable Molly Brown*, immortalized her rags-to-riches story. In 1894 the Browns moved to the elaborate sandstone-trimmed Victorian home at 1340 Pennsylvania St. Costumed guides (Molly liked big hats) give tours and serve an afternoon tea. The museum (☎ 303-832-4092) is open Monday to Saturday 10 am to 4 pm, Sunday noon to 4 pm; from September to June it's closed Mondays. Admission is $5/1.50 adults/children (six to 12).

Denver City Center

PLACES TO STAY
10 Oxford Hotel
20 Melbourne HI/AYH
25 Westin Inn/Tabor Center
29 Denver Marriot City Center
33 Executive Tower Inn
35 Standish Hotel
38 Comfort Inn
39 Brown Palace Hotel
41 Adam's Mark Denver
43 YMCA of Metro Denver-
   Central Branch
46 Denver HI/AYH
48 Hostel ot the Rocky Mountains
51 Royal Host Motel
60 Capitol Hill Mansion B&B
62 Broadway Plaza Motel

PLACES TO EAT
8 La Casa de Manuel
11 McCormick's Fish House
13 Delhi Darbar
15 Old Spaghetti Factory
19 Mercury Cafe
21 Pizza Colore Cafe
27 Brasserie Z
28 Rocky Mountain Diner
44 Walnut Cafe
45 Taki's Golden Bowl
58 Cherokee Bar & Grill
59 Dozens
63 Denver Buffalo Company

OTHER
1 Breckenridge Brewery
2 Broadway Brewing
   Company
3 Black History Museum
4 Forney Transportation
   Museum
5 Wyncoop Brewing
   Company
6 Wazoo's
7 El Chapultepec
9 Postal Annex
12 Kinko's Copies
14 RTD Market Street
   Station
16 Denver Bus Terminal
17 Post Office
18 Federal Building
   & Courthouse
21 Market St Lounge
22 St Marks Coffeehouse
24 Convention
   & Visitors Bureau
26 Rock Bottom Brewery
31 Johnny's Newsstand
32 Varton's Jazz Club
   & Restaurant
33 Student Union
34 Robert Waxman
   Camera & Video
36 Paramount Theater
37 Eastern Mountain Sports
40 Norwest Bank
42 RTD Civic Center
   Bus Station
47 Odgen Theatre
49 US Mint
50 Capitol Hill Books
52 Police Station
53 Denver Art Museum
54 Byers-Evans House
   & Denver History
   Museum
55 Denver Public Library
56 Colorado History Museum
57 Molly Brown House
61 Post Office Annex
64 Gart Brothers
   Sporting Goods

COLORADO

Black American West Museum & Heritage Center

'We tell it like it was' is the motto of the Black American West Museum & Heritage Center (☎ 303-292-2566), north of downtown in the Five Points neighborhood at 3091 California St. Although a few notable African American pioneers arrived with the onset of Colorado's mining boom in the early 1860s, it was after the Civil War that most black professional and working-class people arrived in the state. Black cowboys were particularly important – almost a third of the Western range workers were African American.

The museum, dedicated to correcting former versions of history, is housed in the home of Dr Justina Ford, Denver's first black physician. Take the light rail to the stop at 30th and Downing Sts. The museum is open Wednesday to Friday 10 am to 2 pm, Saturday and Sunday noon to 5 pm. Admission costs $3/1 adults/children (12 to 17).

Forney Transportation Museum & Platte Valley Trolley

Next to Confluence Park, the cluttered Forney Transportation Museum (☎ 303-433-3643), 1416 Platte St, is like a wrecking-yard display of 450 vintage wagons, locomotives – including the world's largest steam engine – trolleys, aircraft, farm equipment and cars. All but the most avid transportation buffs should skip the museum itself (admission $4) and hop aboard the Platte Valley Trolley (☎ 303-458-6255) at the museum for a half-hour ride along the South Platte River to the children's museum. The trolley operates daily 11 am to 4 pm (weekends only in winter months) and costs $2/1 adults/seniors and children. From I-25, take exit 211 (23rd Ave) then go east on Water St. Or catch the westbound bus Nos 28, 32 or 44 from 15th and Blake Sts downtown.

Children's Museum of Denver

Hands-on exhibits at the Children's Museum of Denver (☎ 303-433-7444), across from Mile High Stadium at 2121

Crescent Drive, include a mini television studio, a supermarket and a bank. Kids are guaranteed to have a ball in the 'ballroom' filled with 80,000 balls. It's open 10 am to 5 pm Tuesday to Sunday. Admission is $5. From 15th and Blake Sts downtown, take bus No 10.

Museo de las Americas

Located southeast of downtown Denver, this new museum (☎ 303-571-4401), 861 Santa Fe Dr, focuses on Latino art and history and Latinos' contribution to the southwest US. It's a good way to appreciate the extensive role played by Latino culture in the development of this part of the country, which has often been obscured or 'written out' by traditional white historians. The surrounding neighborhood is mostly Latino and offers many chances to sample authentic Mexican and Latin American cuisine.

From downtown Denver catch the light rail to Osage St, walk four blocks east on 10th Ave to Santa Fe, then turn right and head another block to the museum.

Denver Botanic Gardens

A quiet respite from urban sounds and hard-edged terrain is available east of downtown at the Denver Botanic Gardens (☎ 303-331-4000), 1005 York St. In addition to indigenous plants in the Plains Garden and Xeriscape Demonstration Garden, imported species are featured in the Tropical Conservatory, Water Garden and Japanese Garden. It's open daily 9 am to 5 pm. Admission to the serene pathways and trails cost $3/1 adults/children (6 to 15).

From 17th and Blake Sts, take the eastbound No 20 bus to Yorkshire St, then change to the No 24, which takes you to the gardens.

Road Biking

Denver's flat terrain and wide streets make utilitarian bicycle trips easy, but you can also find plenty of easy recreational trails. Especially popular trails follow the Platte River Greenway and Cherry Creek from **Confluence Park**. The Colorado Division of Parks and Recreation (☎ 303-866-3437)

A Shaky Scheme

Northeast of Denver on the plains grassland lies an immense tract of seemingly undeveloped land that was once used by the military for manufacturing and storing deadly chemical weapons. When conceived during WWII, military planners intended the large area to act as a natural barrier to protect Denver residents in the event of an explosion or chemical accident. Most of the modifications to the site did not disturb the surface which is, ironically, dotted with small lakes that provide habitat for a large bird population and will soon be designated as a National Wildlife Area.

While the prairie surface was left intact, experiments with deep-well disposal of waste during the 1960s really shook things up. Using large pumps to inject tremendous quantities of an as yet unidentified toxic waste material deep into the earth's crust, the Army Corps of Engineers embarked on a scheme that would later be literally reconstituted as a fiendish plot for a James Bond film.

Engineers operated the 1200-foot well from 1962 to 1965, inadvertently lubricating the shear zone between the ancient Precambrian basement rocks and the younger Fountain formation – the very fault zone responsible for the displacement that formed the Rocky Mountains!

Denver residents began noting minor then more substantial earthquakes (5.3 on the Richter scale). Scientists from the Colorado School of Mines discovered that there was a direct relationship between the amount of fluid pumped and the magnitude of the tremors. Pumping stopped soon afterward.

Weapons are no longer made or stored at the former arsenal. In 1992 Congress set aside the 27-sq-mile site as the Rocky Mountain Arsenal National Wildlife Refuge, although official designation is contingent upon the area being cleaned up. Unlike the former nuclear weapons plant at Rocky Flats, this cleanup will not take millennia. Free bus tours are offered on by the US Fish and Wildlife Service from the West Gate at E 72nd Ave and Quebec St. Call the USFWS (☎ 303-289-0232) for times and other information. Closed-circuit television cameras allow viewing of bald eagles in their winter roost, attracted by the large prairie dog population. You can also see hawks, owls, deer and coyote and learn about the environmental cleanup at the arsenal. ∎

publishes a useful map and trail guide for the Denver Metro Area that is usually available from the Denver visitors center.

Golf

The Denver Department of Parks & Recreation (☎ 303-964-2563) runs a few courses: City Park Golf Course (☎ 303-295-4420), 2500 York St; Evergreen Golf Course (☎ 303-674-4128), 29614 Upper Bear Creek Rd; the par 3 Harvard Gulch Golf Course (☎ 303-698-4078), 660 E Iliff Ave; JF Kennedy Golf Course (☎ 303-751-0311), 10500 E Hampden Ave; Overland Golf Course (☎ 303-698-4975), 1801 S Huron St; Wellshire Golf Course (☎ 303-692-5636), 3333 S Colorado Blvd; and Willis Case Golf Course (☎ 303-458-4877), 4999 Vrain St.

Nonresident green fees cost around $19 for 18 holes, $13 for 9 holes, $6.50 for the par 3 Harvard Gulch and $8.50 for JF Kennedy.

Special Events

Kicking off the new year in mid-January is the two-week **National Western Stock Show & Rodeo** (☎ 303-297-1166), held at Brighton Rd and I-70 exit 275B; this is the largest show of its kind in the country. Mexico's victory at the Battle of Puebla is celebrated with two days of festivities at the 16th St Mall during **Cinco de Mayo**. The first weekend in July is the **Cherry Creek Arts Festival** at Cherry Creek North, one of the country's largest arts and crafts shows. Bring a healthy appetite to **A Taste of Colorado**, a showcase of the region's top restaurant talent held on Labor Day weekend in September at the Civic Center Park.

Places to Stay

Denver has dozens of places to stay, especially when it comes to upper-end hotels. The following is a selection of places that we consider good value for money. If you need further help booking accommodations, you can call Denver Metro Convention and Visitors Bureau Area Reservations (☎ 800-462-5280).

Places to Stay – budget

City Center Denver has three hostels, all of which offer fairly convenient access to downtown. The basic but clean *Melbourne International Hotel & Hostel* (☎ 303-292-6386) is at 607 22nd St east of the bus terminal and Union Station. Dorm beds cost $10 for HI/AYH members, $13 for nonmembers. There are private rooms with shared bath for $21/27, and with private bath for $24/30. Pluses include bicycle storage, a coin laundry and a separate six-bed dorm with its own bathroom room for female guests. Guests are limited to a three-day stay, and reservations are necessary between April and September. The laundry on the bottom floor serves as the day office, but there's someone to help with check-in until midnight. The cheapest beds in town by far are at the *Denver International Hostel* (☎ 303-832-9996), 630 E 16th Ave. More than 100 beds are distributed through dorms with a maximum of six beds each, for the amazing price of $7.60. Linen rental is $1 per day. Separate dorm rooms for females, couples and families are available, and there's also a library, game room and coin laundry. The office is open from 8 to 10 am and 5 to 10:30 pm.

The relatively new *Hostel of the Rocky Mountains* (☎ 303-861-7777), located a bit farther east from the Denver International Hostel at 1530 Downing St, has 80 beds divided into two- and four-bed dorm rooms. Each bed costs $11; private rooms with shared bath are available for $25. Each room comes equipped with microwave oven, refrigerator and cable TV. A laundry and bike rentals are available. Office hours are 8 am to 12 pm and 5 to 10 pm. The hostel also offers free pickup from the bus and train stations.

It may not look too impressive on the outside, but the *Standish Hotel* (☎ 303-534-3231), 1530 California St, is cheap and convenient to the 16th St Mall. Singles/doubles with shared bath are $26/28 for, $34 with private bath.

Also centrally located is the *YMCA of Metro Denver – Central Branch* (☎ 303-861-8300), 25 E 16th Ave, where rooms with common bath cost $25. For $29 you can get a room that shares a bath with only one other room; rooms with private bath are $34. Weekly rates are available, and reservations are strongly advised.

East of downtown, the 1890s Victorian *Franklin House B&B* (☎ 303-331-9106), 1620 Franklin St, offers singles/doubles with shared bath for $25/35, or rooms with private bath for $45/55. Staff at the European-style Franklin House are fluent in German, French and Spanish and, unlike most other B&Bs, smoking is permitted.

Metro Area One of the closet places to camp near Denver is *Denver North Campground* (☎ 303-452-4120, 800-851-6521), 16700 N Washington in Broomfield, a suburb north of the city. Tent sites are fairly steep at $18 in winter (more in summer); RV sites with water and electric hookup are $22. There is a pool and a convenience store on the grounds. Take 1-25 north to exit 229 and turn right. You can also camp in the Denver Mountain Parks at Genesse Mountain in the *Chief Hosa Campground* (☎ 303-526-0364), reached from I-70 exit 253. Tent sites cost $16 and the campground is closed in winter.

While there are lots of trucker and budget motels scattered outside the city, most are too far away to be of practical value for visiting Denver. A few exceptions include the *Motel 7* (☎ 303-592-1555), 930 Valley Hwy at 8th Ave at the intersection of US 6 and I-25 exit 209 C; basic singles/doubles are $32/40. South of Hwy 6 at 480 Wadsworth Blvd, *Motel 6 Denver-Lakewood* (☎ 303-232-4924) offers singles/doubles for $34/40.

Airport Area There is no budget accommodation right next to Denver International Airport, but there are a couple places in the nearby suburb of Aurora near the junction of Colfax Ave and I-225, about 20 minutes' drive from DIA. The *Heaven on Earth Inn* (☎ 303-364-2671), 13650 E Colfax Ave, has clean singles/doubles for $35/41 and an indoor pool. It's run by members of the Maharishi religious group, so if meditating guests are not your style you may want to skip this place. Nearby the *Family Motel* (☎ 303-344-9150), 13280 E Colfax, has rooms with full kitchens for $39/$49 as well as a hot tub and swimming pool. Neither place offers shuttle service to the airport, but shuttle vans and taxis are easily arranged.

A slew of hotels and motels were left high and dry when Stapleton Airport closed to make way for DIA. Some of them still bill themselves as 'airport hotels,' and their claim is helped by a free shuttle service run from the Stapleton area to DIA, 14 miles away. In the budget range there's *Motel 6 Denver East* (☎ 303-371-1980), next to Peoria St at 12020 E 39th Ave, which offers spartan singles/doubles for $35/40. Similar rooms at the *Travelers Inn* (☎ 303-371-0551), 3850 Peoria St, are $40/45.

Places to Stay – middle
City Center One of the few places that's truly mid-range in price is the newly revamped *Broadway Plaza Motel* (☎ 303-893-3501), 1111 Broadway, where singles/doubles go for $39/51. A recent remodeling hasn't completely erased the place's dingy feel, but it is reasonably close to city center attractions and restaurants.

To get a similar rate, head 1 mile northwest of downtown to the ambitiously named (but quite mundane) *Denver Downtown Super 8 Hotel & Conference Center* (☎ 303-433-6677), 2601 Zuni St west of I-25 exit 212AB. Standard singles/doubles cost $35/43 during the week, $40/47 on weekends. Facilities include a restaurant and a swimming pool. On the other side of Speer Blvd, *Budget Host Downtown Denver* (☎ 303-447-6229), 2724 Wyandot St, has

singles/doubles from $33/36, though these prices can vary with time of year and occupancy levels.

In the 1980s, portions of E Colfax Ave near downtown had a tawdry reputation that the *Royal Host Motel* (☎ 303-831-7200), 930 E Colfax Ave, inadvertently nourished with a sign that displayed only the letters 'Ho' in the word Host. Singles/doubles cost $39/44. The nearby *Ramada Inn Downtown* (☎ 303-831-7700, 800-542-8603), 1150 E Colfax Ave, isn't a bad off-season deal at $55/60 for singles/doubles, though summer rates increase to $70/75.

Near the upper end of the mid-range category is the high-rise *Comfort Inn Downtown* (☎ 303-296-0400), 401 17th St, where rooms start at $85/90. At these rates you're really just paying for location and may want to consider spending just a bit more for one of the more affordable top-end spots.

Another option is the weekend special at *Executive Tower Inn* (☎ 303-571-0300, 800-525-6651), 1405 Curtis St. Rooms that normally cost $135 are offered for $85 Friday to Sunday and include access to the health club. However, any savings are lost if you must pay for parking during your stay.

Metro Area Two miles west of downtown is the *Ramada Inn Denver Downtown West* (☎ 303-433-8331, 800-388-5381), 1975 Bryant St west of I-25 exit 210B. Recently remodeled rooms are not a bad deal at $67/77 when you throw in the free shuttle to downtown, fitness center and swimming pool. A bit more downmarket is *Days Inn Central* (☎ 303-571-1715), 620 Federal Blvd on US 6 west of downtown. Average singles/doubles cost $39/45 during the week, but jump to $59/69 on weekends.

One place worth trying east of downtown is *Holiday Chalet* (☎ 303-321-9975), 1820 E Colfax Ave. This mansion built in 1896 features bright rooms with private bath and full kitchen starting at $74/79; suites with sunrooms go for $100.

South of the Cherry Creek Shopping Center, rooms start at $69 at *Best Western Landmark Inn* (☎ 303-388-5561), 455 S

Colorado Blvd. Rates vary with season and occupancy so call ahead to check. Overall it's not a bad spot, with an indoor pool, fitness room and hot tub and some rooms have nice mountain views.

Airport Area There are only two hotels genuinely located next to Denver International Airport, both offering comfortable, upscale rooms. The *Fairfield Inn DIA* (☎ 303-576-9640, 800-228-2800), 6851 Tower Rd, has rooms from $80. Singles/doubles at the nearby *Hampton Inn DIA* (☎ 303-371-0200), 6290 Tower Rd, are $79/89. Both places offer free Continental breakfasts and 24-hour airport shuttles.

Nearby along the hotel row near the defunct Stapleton Airport, *Quality Inn & Suites* (☎ 303-320-0260, 800-677-0260), 4590 Quebec St just north of I-70, offers singles/doubles for $54/59, along with an outdoor pool, fitness center and a free airport shuttle that runs 5 to 12 am. In Aurora, *Best Western Executive Hotel* (☎ 303-373-5730), 4411 Peoria St near I-70 exit 281, has newly remodeled large rooms for $79, and also offers a swimming pool and airport shuttle service.

Places to Stay – top end
City Center The recently opened *Adam's Mark Denver* (☎ 303-893-3333), 1550 Court Place, boasts a great location for seeing downtown Denver and offers high-end amenities including a fitness room, sauna, heated outdoor pool, full business center and two restaurants. Rooms are a good value at $105.

Capitol Hill Mansion B&B (☎ 303-839-5221, 800-839-9329), 1207 Pennsylvania St, features balconies and fireplaces on the upper floors of this turreted red sandstone mansion. Listed in the National Register of Historic Places, this is one of the top-rated B&Bs in the country. All rooms offer private baths and range in price from $90 to $165, the latter including an in-room Jacuzzi and either balcony or fireplace.

Denver's oldest hotel, the luxurious *Oxford Hotel* (☎ 303-628-5400, 800-228-5538) opened in 1891. This longtime fixture at 1600 17th St near Union Station has gone through many changes, most notably the addition of the renowned Cruise Room Bar following Prohibition and a costly renovation in 1983 that retained the beautiful wrought-iron staircase and added the lobby fireplace and Italian bronze chandeliers. Rooms start at $155, though weekend specials can lower the price to $119 (except in summer). Another excellently maintained historic landmark is the famous *Brown Palace Hotel* (☎ 303-297-3111, 800-321-2599), 321 17th St, where rooms range from $195 for a standard double to $275 for a junior suite. Though not equipped with as many modern touches (health clubs, etc), the hotel consistently retains its four-star rating for its outstanding atmosphere, decor and service.

For a more modern place, the *Westin Inn/Tabor Center* (☎ 303-572-9100), 1672 Lawrence St, is probably your best bet for decor, service, location and facilities including a very attractive heated indoor/outdoor pool. Rates range from $125 to $198 depending on season and occupancy. Another option is the conveniently located *Denver Marriot City Center* (☎ 303-297-1300), 1701 California St, which also has a full range of guest facilities, though it's probably not quite up to Westin standards. Rooms cost $152.

Metro Area *Castle Marne B&B* (☎ 303-331-0621, 800-926-2763), near E Colfax Ave at 1572 Race St, is a stunning three-story masonry mansion listed on the National Register of Historic Places. It offers nine elegant rooms, all with private bath, ranging from $85 and $200, the latter featuring an in-room hot tub and private balcony.

South of the Cherry Creek Shopping Center, the isolated black tower of *Lowes Giorgio Hotel* (☎ 303-782-9300), 450 E Mississippi Ave, is in an unlikely (noncentral) location for a luxury hotel catering to business travelers. Elaborate Italian decor resembles Milan's finest lodgings. Rooms cost $199, but $99 weekend rates are a relative bargain.

Places to Eat

City Center Downtown Denver is overrun with restaurants of all types, some quite good. In addition to those listed below, you might want to check the places listed in the 'Café' section of the *Westword* weekly, which has dozens of informative restaurant mini-reviews. One of the free Denver visitor guides also has restaurant listings, but these are more akin to advertisements.

For breakfast, *Dozens* (☎ 303-572-0066), 236 13th Ave south of the capitol, offers egg breakfasts for about $6 or fresh muffins and cinnamon rolls in a smoke-free dining room south of downtown. The nearby *Cherokee Bar & Grill* (☎ 303-623-0346), 1201 Cherokee St, is a favorite with courthouse employees, whose sketches grace the walls. Try the Acoma omelet with roasted chiles or the 'Verdict Burger' with cheddar and bacon for lunch, both about $6. Another popular breakfast and lunch spot is *Walnut Cafe* (☎ 303-832-5108), 338 E Colfax Ave.

If all you need is a caffeine fix, espresso is available on many corners – you shouldn't have to look hard to find a coffee shop. One spot catering to both locals and Larimer Square visitors is *St Mark's Coffeehouse* (☎ 303-446-2925), 1416 Market St. High tea is served daily from noon to 4 pm in the atrium lobby at the *Brown Palace Hotel* (☎ 303-293-9204), 321 17th St. Prices range from $16 to $21 depending on what you eat and whether you opt for champagne.

For cheap lunches, it's hard to beat *Taki's Golden Bowl* (☎ 303-832-8440), 341 E Colfax Ave, where you can get generous rice bowls, yakisoba or udon soup for $3 to $5. The veggie-loaded miso soup for 98¢ is one of the best deals in town. On the other side of town, *Mercury Cafe* (☎ 303-294-9281), 2199 California St, offers what *Westword* magazine perfectly describes as 'healthy hippie fare,' including vegetarian enchiladas for $5 or tofu, meat, fish or fowl dinners for up to $10.

Adding a nice touch of Old West style to the corner of 18th and Stout Sts is *Rocky Mountain Diner* (☎ 303-293-8383), 1800 Stout St, a comfortable Western-style diner with a modern menu including such items as buffalo meatloaf and roast duck enchiladas along with more traditional fare. Portions are quite large and the breakfasts are also good. Lunch with drinks runs around $10 per person.

If you want to really go Western, *Denver Buffalo Company* (☎ 303-832-0880), a few blocks south of the capitol at 1109 Lincoln St, specializes in lean buffalo burgers, steaks and sausage from their own Colorado ranch. The experience doesn't come cheap however: lunches generally range from $10 to $15, dinners from $15 to $35 for buffalo filet.

Reasonably priced Italian meals in a casual atmosphere are available at a few downtown establishments. *Pizza Colore Cafe* (☎ 303-534-6844), 1512 Larimer St, is open late with ample outdoor seating and serves delicious vegetarian lasagna with a cream sauce for $8. *The Old Spaghetti Factory* (☎ 303-295-1864), in the former cable-car building at 1215 18th St, offers large plates of spaghetti with sauces such as clam and mizithra cheese for $7.

If you're looking for Mexican food, locals reckon *La Casa de Manuel* (☎ 303-295-1752), 2010 Larimer St, is one of the better choices. Authentic tacos, fresh guacamole and green chile help spice up the menu; full dinners go for under $10. Indian food fans should enjoy *Delhi Darbar* (☎ 303-595-0680), 1514 Blake St, another popular spot with Denverites. The $6 lunch buffet is definitely a good deal.

McCormick's Fish House (☎ 303-825-1107), in the handsome iron-front building at 1659 Wazee St, offers fresh oysters – not the Rocky Mountain variety, but extremely fresh ocean harvests from around the globe. The menu changes daily to reflect what's available. As you might expect, fresh seafood several thousand miles from the ocean doesn't come cheap, but they do a good job with it here.

Brasserie Z (☎ 303-293-2322), 815 17th St, is unique in that it offers good American nouvelle cuisine at affordable prices, especially for lunch. Hamburger fans might want to try the 'Heavenly Burger' ($5.25), said to be the best in town by *Westword*'s food critics.

If you're really in the mood to splurge, head to what many still feel is Denver's finest restaurant, the *Palace Arms* (☎ 303-297-3111) in the Brown Palace Hotel at 321 17th St. The menu is an interesting mix of East-West fusion and traditional European fare. The interesting range of appetizers go for $9 to $15, and entrees range from $25 to $65 for Beef Tenderloin Wellington.

Entertainment

To find out what's happening in music, theater and other performing arts, pick up a copy of the weekly *Westword*, distributed each Wednesday, which has capsule movie reviews. The Friday morning editions of the *Denver Post* or *Rocky Mountain News* contain complete cinema showings. *Passport to the Arts*, published by the *Denver Post*, is a comprehensive listing of dance, music, opera, theater, science and nature events and special museum programs.

To get the lowdown on rock, alternative and jazz gigs, stop by Wax Trax (☎ 303-831-7902), on the 600 block of E 13th Ave, Denver's leading music store – it's really four stores specializing in CDs, jazz and oldies and new and used records. Let the staff know what you like to hear and they can help identify the local talent and upcoming headline performers you might enjoy.

There are two biweekly gay newspapers, *Out Front* and *H Inc*, which carry informative articles about the local scene as well as entertainment listings. They can be found in most gay bars, some straight bars and in coffee shops around the Capitol Hill area.

Denver Center for the Performing Arts

Denver's regional leadership in cultural events is undeniable. Occupying almost four city blocks south of 14th St between Arapahoe and Champa Sts, the Denver Center for the Performing Arts complex (☎ 303-893-4300) is the nation's second largest, following only New York City's

Lincoln Center in seating capacity. With the large *Auditorium Theatre* and *Buell Theatre*, plus four smaller theaters in the *Helen Bonfils Complex*, it hosts the resident Denver Center Theater Company (☎ 303-893-4000), the Colorado Ballet (☎ 303-837-8888) and touring Broadway shows. In addition, the *Boettcher Concert Hall*, offering in-the-round performances, hosts the Colorado Symphony Orchestra (☎ 303-986-8742) and Opera Colorado (☎ 303-986-8742). For tickets to all events at the complex, contact the Denver Center Box Office (☎ 303-893-4100).

Cinemas Denver has more than enough mega-multiplex movie chains, which you can find through the local papers. However, it might be more fun to check out the *Mayan Theater* (☎ 303-744-6796), 110 Broadway, for good old, garish moviehouse atmosphere. It has three screens showing first-run films.

Don't miss the 4½-story-tall *IMAX* screen in the Denver Museum of Natural History (☎ 303-370-6300).

Brewpubs Denver claims to be the largest brewing city in the USA, but the figures are skewed by the existence of the Coors brewery in nearby Golden. Nonetheless, there are several good spots to choose from, all of which offer fine beer and usually good food as well.

Denver's first brewpub, *Wyncoop Brewing Company* (☎ 303-623-9518), opened at the corner of 18th and Wyncoop Sts in 1988 and is probably the most lively spot. The 2nd floor is littered with billiards tables, and it's a hopping scene on weekend nights. Another place that sees a lot of action on weekends is *Rock Bottom Brewery* (☎ 303-534-7616), 1001 16th St, which generally draws a 'prettier' crowd than the other brewpubs. The beer is good and the patio seating on the pedestrian mall is a plus.

Broadway Brewing Company (☎ 303-292-2555), 2441 Broadway, is a great place to sample Colorado beers: they make beer for the Wynkoop as well as for Aspen's Flying Dog Brewery, so you're never lacking for a choice of excellent brews. It's a bit more laid back than some of the other places as well. Near Coors Field baseball stadium, *Breckenridge Brewery* (☎ 303-297-3644), 2200 Blake St, has some outstanding selections: try their famed 'Avalanche' amber ale. It has an outdoor patio and is the place to be before a Colorado Rockies baseball game.

Denver, Boulder and Fort Collins all have dedicated breweries (as opposed to smaller-scale brewpubs). If you're interested in expanding your horizons, an excellent way to tour some of these facilities is with Foam on the Range Brewery & Pub Tours (☎ 970-224-2435) a small outfit based in Fort Collins that takes suds fans on tours of Front Range breweries in a specially fitted bus. Tours from Denver leave for Boulder and Fort Collins, and there are also departures from Boulder and Fort Collins. (See Brewery Tours in the Fort Collins section of the Northern Front Range chapter.)

Bars The brewpubs mentioned above are some of Denver's most popular bars, but for variety take a stroll through Larimer Square, where there are bars to suit about any personality.

The Art Deco *Cruise Room Bar* (☎ 303-628-5400) in the Oxford Hotel was designed to resemble the 1st-class bar on the Queen Mary. Not only is this a neon-lit architectural treasure – even the bathrooms are special – but the mementos in the hallway add to its attraction.

Cigar or scotch aficionados may want to stop by the *Churchill Bar* in the Brown Palace Hotel. Like everything else here, the prices are steep, but the selection of 37 single malt scotch whiskeys and a full menu of cigars are truly impressive. After a couple of scotches you won't even feel the pain in your wallet.

If you're looking for a younger, more raucous atmosphere, *Wazoo's* (☎ 303-297-8500), 1819 Wazee, fits the bill. It's a cavernous place with pool tables, a huge beer selection and televised sports coming at you from every corner.

Live Music & Clubs There's always some musician playing somewhere in Denver's surprisingly lively music scene. *Westword* is probably your best guide.

To check out local bands, the small *Cricket on the Hill* (☎ 303-830-9020), 1209 E 13th, is a good choice. *Herman's Hideaway* (☎ 303-777-5840), 1578 S Broadway, started as a neighborhood bar and also books plenty of local bands, as does *Market Street Lounge* (☎ 303-893-6754), 1417 Market St. Occasional headliners such as Warren 'Werewolves of London' Zevon appear at the *Ogden Theatre* (☎ 303-830-2525), 935 E Colfax Ave.

Grunge fans will appreciate *Seven South* (☎ 303-744-0513), 7 S Broadway. An eclectic mix of performers, ranging from Cajun to Blues to Big Band swing, play weekends at the *Mercury Cafe* (☎ 303-294-9281), 2199 California St.

El Chapultepec (☎ 303-295-9126), near the ballpark at 1962 Market St, is a cozy venue for top jazz performers; music begins nightly at 9 pm with no cover charge. More sedate is *Varton's Jazz Club and Restaurant* (☎ 303-399-1111), 1800 Glenarm Pl. Denver's *Botanic Garden Amphitheater* (☎ 303-331-4000), 1005 York St, hosts a summer evening series of classical, jazz and world music concerts.

In town, the main venue for national acts is the *Paramount Theater* (☎ 303-534-8336), 1631 Glenarm Place. East of downtown at 3317 E Colfax, the *Bluebird Theater* (☎ 303-322-2308) also gets the occasional big-name performer along with good local bands.

From May to September, *Fiddler's Green Amphitheater*, 6350 Greenwood Plaza Blvd, hosts headline performers such as Steely Dan, Elton John and Santana. It's not a very friendly place and a lot of locals don't like it, especially since its opening relegated the wonderful *Red Rocks Amphitheater* to mainly hosting second-tier performers such as John Tesh and Electric Light Orchestra. Denver's largest venue for rock music is *McNichols Arena* near Mile High Stadium. It mainly functions as a sports stadium so the acoustics are horrible, but when big acts like the Rolling Stones or Eric Clapton come to town, this is where they play. Performances at all three venues are controlled by Barry Fey Productions, and information on events is available by calling ☎ 303-640-7330. Most concert tickets are also available from Ticketmaster (☎ 303-830-8497).

For Country &Western entertainment, head for *Grizzly Rose* (☎ 303-295-2353), 5450 N Valley Hwy, where headliners like Marshall Tucker, the Charlie Daniels Band and Jerry Lee Lewis helped earn the club an award from the Country Music Association as the best venue in the nation.

Spectator Sports

At the time of writing, the Ascent Group, which owns the Denver Nuggets and the Colorado Avalanche sports teams, planned to build a new arena to be called the Pepsi Center, a testament to the shameless commercialization of US sports. Though disputes with the Denver City government derailed the construction schedule, the new project site located south of Coors Field will probably be home to the new arena by the time you read this. A similar situation exists with the Denver Broncos' Mile High Stadium: the team's owner has asked that Denver taxpayers foot more than 50% of the bill for a new stadium. The city initially balked at the request, reasoning that it came from one of the National Football League's most successful franchises. At the time of writing the issue had yet to go to Denver voters, so if you want to catch a game in town check around to see who's playing where.

Baseball National League baseball expansion in 1993 led to the Colorado Rockies Baseball Club joining the Western Division. Their comfortable new ballpark is widely admired and always sold out, even when the Rockies are in a slump (an all-too-common occurrence). It's a great place to take families, with $5 center field bleacher seats. From April to early October, the facility hosts 81 league games and has a 50,000-person capacity, though there

is parking for fewer than 5000 vehicles. Ten different RTD RockiesRide (☎ 303-299-6000) routes serving Boulder provide direct service to the ballpark, or take the free shuttle from the 16th St Mall. Night games can be very pleasant, but always be prepared for afternoon thundershowers at day games. For information, tickets and schedules call ☎ 800-388-7625.

Basketball The Denver Nuggets are in the National Basketball Association's Midwest Division and play 41 home games at McNichols Sports Arena (☎ 303-572-4703), 1635 Clay St, between October and April. For information, tickets and schedules call ☎ 303-893-6700. At the time of writing the Nuggets had been cannon fodder for most other NBA teams, so tickets should be easy to get for the foreseeable future.

The Colorado Xplosion (☎ 303-832-2225) is the state's newly created professional women's basketball team. A lack of national television coverage has hampered the development and popularity of women's basketball in the US, but the level of play is high and definitely worth watching. Games are played at McNichols Sports Arena and the nearby Denver Coliseum.

Football The Denver Broncos attract some of the most fanatic, rabid fans in the National Football League, who were rewarded in January 1998 when their team captured the 'world' championship at Superbowl XXXII. Mere mortals usually can't get tickets: the waiting list for season tickets is longer than a decade! Individual game tickets are usually scooped up by well-connected people and corporations. Games are played at Mile High Stadium, west of downtown at the corner of 20th and Bryant Sts. For ticket information to the eight home games call ☎ 303-649-9000. RTD's BroncoRide (☎ 303-299-6000) takes fans to the stadium from 29 locations, including Boulder.

Hockey Almost as popular as the Broncos is the Colorado Avalanche, a top-rated team that capped its 1995 season by winning the National Hockey League's top prize, the Stanley Cup. Tickets are expensive but not always impossible to get, but most fans reckon the action is worth the expense. Games are played at McNichols Arena; call ☎ 303-893-6700 for ticket information.

Soccer The Colorado Rapids, a major league team, struggles for fans like most US soccer teams but does better than many due to Denver's obsession with spectator sports. The Rapids play at Mile High Stadium; for ticket info call ☎ 303-299-1570.

Shopping
The Denver Visitors Center will happily supply you with shopping guides to nearly every corner of the city. Following is a brief summary of the main areas where consumers cluster.

Cherry Creek Mall Anchored by Neiman-Marcus and Saks Fifth Avenue, the Cherry Creek Mall, 3000 E 1st Ave, is Denver's single largest attraction, drawing shoppers from throughout the Rocky Mountains and Eastern Plains. Along with top-end comparison-shopping opportunities at 125 specialty shops and restaurants plus an eight-screen cinema, the Tattered Cover Bookstore is nearby (see Bookstores above). The mall is open weekdays 10 am to 9 pm, Saturday 10 am to 7 pm and Sunday noon to 6 pm.

Larimer Square Although the idea of outlining renovated turn-of-the-century buildings with a multitude of 'decorative' lights sounds tacky, the 1400 block of Larimer St presents an appealing array of boutiques, galleries, restaurants and nightclubs, making up a vibrant activity center. Most businesses in Larimer Square (☎ 303-534-2367) are open weekdays 10 am to 7 pm, Saturday 10 am to 6 pm and Sunday noon to 5 pm. Restaurants can get you started in the morning, and the clubs let you wind down from a day of shopping and exploring the historic district.

16th St Mall Denver's 16th St Mall, the primary retail street downtown, has been sensibly redesigned to accommodate pedestrians, not cars. The mix of shops – upscale, downscale, you name it – makes for a nice change from most pedestrian malls, though the upper-end curio and accessory shops seem to be gaining the upper hand. Be sure to stop and admire the restored clock mechanism in the **D&F Tower** at Arapahoe St. Free shuttle transit operates between the RTD Civic Center bus terminal on Broadway and the RTD Market St Station at the north end.

About 65 upscale specialty shops and a dozen-plus restaurants are in the two-block glass-enclosed **Tabor Center** (☎ 303-572-6866), next to 16th St at the north end between Larimer and Arapahoe Sts. **Writer Square** (☎ 303-628-9056), 1512 Larimer St, is yet another city block of frivolous boutiques and restaurants near the north end of the 16th St Mall.

Film & Photography Robert Waxman's Camera & Video (☎ 303-623-1155), in the historic Denver Dry Goods Building at 1545 California St, at the corner of 15th St, is the largest store of its kind in the world. It sells everything from amateur $9 plastic cameras and film to the most sophisticated professional outfits and darkroom supplies.

Sporting Goods Denver is a sporting goods bazaar with many giant stores offering a multitude of gear for every imaginable recreational activity. Among the most amazing is Gart Brothers Sporting Goods Company (☎ 303-861-1122), 1000 Broadway, a retail sports palace housed in a handsome Neo-Gothic style three-story building, built as an auto dealership in 1925 (check out the old Franklin and Studebaker car showroom on the same block). The rooftop tennis courts are reached by golf carts that cruise up the interior ramp past loads of merchandise. On Labor Day the 'Sniagrab' ('bargains') sale on ski equipment is a Denver happening. Another good place is Eastern Mountain Sports

Dealing with DIA

The nation's newest airport since Dallas-Fort Worth inaugurated its inconvenient design in 1974, Denver International Airport opened in 1995 amid criticism and controversy. The project suffered repeated delays, cost overruns in the billions of dollars and a state-of-the art automated baggage handling system that seemed capable only of mangling luggage. The project's woes were even enough to make international news, putting immense pressure on Denver Mayor Wellington Web, city authorities and the contractors. Pundits happily predicted that DIA users would fare no better than the luggage used in the early baggage system tests.

Three years later media critics are largely silent, though many users still grumble about DIA. The main drawbacks are its distance from the city – 24 miles, or about 40 minutes in Denver's heavy traffic, compared to 15 minutes for Stapleton – and its vast size, which requires passengers to spend more time walking from the parking lots and taking the automated train to the distant gate concourses. Another justifiable gripe is the high airport-use fee imposed on airlines, which translates into higher airfares. The fees prompted Continental Airlines to abandon Denver as a major hub and kept bargain-fare leader Southwest Airlines from entering the market. As a result, premium-priced United Airlines is the dominant carrier with over two-thirds of the airport traffic, though competition periodically forces United to lower its fares.

Compared with many US airports, however, DIA is in many ways quite pleasant. It's clean, generally efficient, well laid-out and staff are usually friendly. Its five runways and widely separated gate concourses help keep delays down: in 1996 DIA had the second-best on-time record of all US airports. And if your flight is delayed or if you have a long wait for a connection, there are plenty of restaurants, bars, artwork and exhibits to help you pass the time. The white tent-roofed terminal has several outdoor style cafés that are pleasant places to sip a beer and grab a snack.

Here are a few tips to help make your trip through DIA smoother.

Arrival Be prepared to walk. The gate concourses are quite long and you'll usually face a fairly long hike to the concourse center, where you'll find the subway that takes you to baggage claim. Automated sidewalks help make the walk a bit faster.

(☎ 303-446-8338), 1616 Welton St, which also boasts a wide selection and often has sales offering good bargains.

Western Wear Even drugstore cowboys who have never been closer to a cow than a T-bone steak can get duded-up and look the part at Miller Stockman Western Wear (☎ 303-825-5339), 1600 California St. The store offers over 400 pairs of shit-kickers and has been in business since 1918.

Getting There & Away

Airport Information Denver International Airport (DIA), which opened in 1995 on 53 sq miles of former grasslands and prairie dog burrows, is among the nation's 10 busiest airports. The $4.9 billion facility is the first big airport built in America in more than 20 years. It has five full-service runways that allow simultaneous landings – even during the foul weather that plagued the former Stapleton Airport with delays. (Stapleton closed when DIA opened.)

Located 24 miles from downtown, DIA is connected with I-70 exit 238 by the 12-mile-long Peña Blvd. The new facility has an automated subway that links the terminal to three concourses and 94 gates. Concourse C is almost a mile from the terminal, hence the need for automated transport of people and baggage.

Information on airline connections, schedules, ground transportation and parking is available from DIA (☎ 303-342-2000, 800-247-2336). Tourist and airport

If someone is picking you up at the airport, have them meet you at the baggage claim about 15 to 20 minutes after your flight arrives. This saves them the walk and train ride to the gate, and TV monitors all around the baggage claim area make it easy to figure out which carousel will be handling your flight's baggage.

If you're taking a shuttle van to Denver, the Front Range or the mountains, go to the counter first before you pick up your bags. Some vans run only once an hour and fill up quickly, so the sooner you buy your ticket, the better your chance of getting a seat on the next departure. If you are traveling with a friend or two, one person can head to baggage claim while the other arranges transport.

Departure Arrive early – after checking in you'll still need around 25 minutes to get to your gate. Allow enough time so that you won't have to avoid stress out and rush. Also, many airlines give away booked seats if they're not claimed 20 minutes prior to departure. If you've rented a car, you should be back at the rental car lot 90 minutes prior to take-off. The lots are 5 miles from the airport and you'll need to turn in your car and catch a shuttle bus to the terminal. DIA is not a bad place to wait for a little while, so err on the side of caution.

The west parking garage, dedicated to United Airlines, is often full. Use the eastern one unless you have a lot of luggage; once you're in the terminal it's a fairly short walk to the west side and the United check-in counters.

Give yourself plenty of time to reach the airport. Traffic is often heavy on I-25, I-270 and I-70, the highways most people use to reach DIA. From downtown Denver allow at least 40 minutes to an hour to reach the airport. From I-70 exit 284 it's another 12 miles along Peña Blvd before you reach the terminal and parking garages.

Coming or Going Avoid the airport during major holidays like Thanksgiving and Christmas. Despite its size and modern facilities, DIA gets overloaded just as any other airport, and traffic along Peña Blvd can really get backed up. Overbooked seats, flight delays and general mix-ups also loom larger – these are the times your bags are most likely to head off to New York just as you board a flight to San Francisco. ∎

information is available 6 am to midnight from a booth located at the north end of the terminal's central hall, near the exit top of the escalators from the subway train. Information on ground transport is available from a booth at the south end of the hall.

Pick up the *Denver International Airport Visitor's Guide* for information on the airport's art displays, the rotating exhibits from the Denver Museum of Natural History and the many shops, including ski and golf outlets.

Airlines DIA is served by about 20 airlines, connecting it to nearly every major US city. But most flights are run by United Airlines, which has made Denver one of its two main US hubs. For more

information, see the Getting There & Away chapter.

Refer to the 800-number appendix at the back of this book for airline telephone numbers.

Bus Greyhound and affiliate TNM&O offer frequent buses on routes along the Front Range and on transcontinental routes. All buses stop at the Denver Bus Terminal (☎ 303-293-6555) at the corner of 19th and Arapahoe Sts in downtown Denver north of the capitol. It's not the city's most charming spot, so if you're facing a long wait it's worth walking a few blocks to hang out at the Mercury Cafe or another restaurant or bar in the area. The terminal is open 6 am to midnight.

Powder River Coach USA (☎ 800-442-3682), which offers twice-daily service north to Cheyenne, WY, and on to Montana and South Dakota, also runs from the Denver Bus Terminal.

Train Amtrak's *California Zephyr* runs daily between Chicago and San Francisco (Emeryville) via Denver. Trains arrive and depart from Denver's **Union Station** at the corner of 17th and Wyncoop Sts. Westbound departures are around 9 am, eastbound around 8:30 pm. The Amtrak ticket office (☎ 303-825-2583) at the station is open 7 am to 9 pm. For recorded info (updated daily) on arrival and departure times, call ☎ 303-534-2812. Amtrak agents (☎ 800-872-7245) can also provide schedule information and train reservations.

Denver's *Ski Train* (☎ 303-296-4754) to Winter Park operates on weekends throughout the ski season, leaving Union Station at 7:15 am and departing Winter Park at 4:15 pm. The scenic trip takes two hours and crosses the Continental Divide via the Moffat Tunnel. Advance-purchase roundtrip coach tickets cost $35 to $40; seats in the 1st-class Club Car, which includes breakfast and après-ski snacks, are $60.

Car At the intersection of I-70 and I-25, Denver is pretty hard to miss: even the poorest navigators should have no trouble finding this place.

Auto Driveaway Co (☎ 303-757-1211), 5777 E Evans Ave, may be able to provide free transportation in exchange for vehicle delivery – get a drive-away just like Jack Kerouac did in *On the Road*! Be prepared to post a substantial deposit that will be forfeited if you damage the car (as Kerouac did). Willingness to be flexible about your travel destination and to forego sight-seeing to meet a rigid time allowance will improve your chances of landing a car.

Also check the ride boards at the hostels (see Places to Stay) or at the north wing of Driscoll University Center at the University of Denver, which is connected to the main campus by the pedestrian walkway over E Evans Ave.

Getting Around

To/From the Airport A complete Ground Transportation Center is centrally located on the 5th level of DIA's terminal, near the baggage claim. All transportation companies have their booths located here and passengers catch vans, shuttles and taxis outside the 5th-level doors.

Complimentary hotel shuttles represent the cheapest means of getting to/from the airport. Several of the hotels located at the closed Stapleton Airport, 15 miles from DIA, and elsewhere offer service to and from DIA. Courtesy phones for hotel shuttles are available in the Ground Transportation Center.

RTD (☎ 303-299-6000, 800-366-7433) buses are available outside door 506 on the East Terminal and door 511 on the West Terminal. The AF express route serves DIA-Downtown Denver hourly 6:45 to 12:45 am, with stops at the Stapleton Transfer Station and the Denver Bus Terminal, before arriving at the Market St Station a few blocks from Amtrak's Union Station. Downtown-DIA buses operate hourly 3:25 am to 10:25 pm. Travel time is typically under an hour and fares cost $6, or $10 roundtrip – exact fare only.

Buses (routes AS, AF and AB) run every 15 minutes between DIA and Stapleton Airport, providing access to lodging and budget parking ($2 per day). The fare is $4.

For DIA-Boulder travelers, route AB buses leave daily 6:15 am to 11:15 pm. From Boulder, buses run 3:20 am to 9:15 pm. Fares for the 1½-hour trip cost $8, $13 roundtrip.

There are a number of airport shuttle van and limousine services. The Denver Airporter (☎ 303-227-0000), Super Shuttle (☎ 303-370-1300, 800-258-3826) and Denver Express Shuttle (☎ 303-342-3424, 800-448-2782) all offer frequent van service to downtown hotels for $15. If you need door-to-door service, try Shuttle King (☎ 303-363-8000), which charges $18 to $20 for rides to destinations in downtown Denver, more for outlying suburbs.

Airport shuttles to the Front Range and Mountain areas are also not hard to come by (see To/From the Airport for the relevant destination).

Taxi service to downtown Denver costs a flat fare of $35, excluding tip.

Bus The Regional Transit District (RTD; ☎ 303-299-6000) provides public transportation throughout the Denver and Boulder area. Local fares cost $1.25 during peak weekday hours (6 to 9 am, 4 to 6 pm), 75¢ during off-peak hours. Free shuttle buses operate along the 16th St Mall, closed to automobile traffic since 1980. Local buses also offer expanded service to baseball and football games for $2.

Buses to Boulder (route B) carry bicycles in the cargo compartment and offer frequent service from the Market St Station at the corner of 16th and Market Sts. The Denver to Boulder one-way RTD fare is $3. If you wish to visit Golden, take the Nos 16 or 16L buses that stop at the corner of 15th and California Sts in downtown Denver. The fare is $1.25.

From April to early September, visitors to the Museum of Natural History, the Zoo, Larimer Square, the Botanic Gardens and other attractions can board the RTD's special **Cultural Connection Trolley** with the purchase of an all-day ticket for $3. Self-guided tours aboard the trolley provide an excellent orientation that takes less than an hour. The trolley leaves the Denver Center for the Performing Arts at 14th and Curtis Sts every half-hour 9:30 am to 5:30 pm.

Light Rail RTD's light rail line serves 14 stations on a 5-mile route that passes through downtown; NB (northbound) trains run on California St, while SB (southbound) trains follow Stout St. The northern end of the line follows Welton St through the Five Points neighborhood to the Black American Western Museum & Heritage Center at the corner of 30th and Downing Sts. The southern end passes the Auraria Campus before reaching the Gates Rubber plant at the intersection of I-25 and Broadway. Trains operate between 4:30 and 1:30 am and run every five minutes during peak periods. Fares are the same as for local buses. Bikes may board during off-peak hours with permit only.

Car Nearly all the major car rental firms have counters in the baggage claim level at DIA – the cars, however, are 5 miles away. Complimentary shuttle buses for all rental car companies drop off patrons on both sides of the Ground Transportation/Commercial Vehicle Level (level 5) of the main terminal and load at their designated stop on each side. Refer to the 800-number appendix at the back of the book for car rental firm phone numbers.

A few agencies also have offices in downtown Denver, including: Avis (☎ 303-839-1280), 1900 Broadway; Budget (☎ 303-341-2277), 1980 Broadway; Enterprise (☎ 303-293-8644), 2255 Broadway, and Hertz (☎ 303-297-9400), 2001 Welton St.

If you don't have a credit card, there are also a few local firms that accept cash deposits. Affordable Rent-A-Car (☎ 303-617-8696) will arrange to pick you up and accepts drivers under 21. A-Courtesy Rent A Car (☎ 303-733-2218, 800-733-2218) also accepts cash deposits, but their vehicles cannot be driven outside of Colorado.

Taxi Three taxi companies offer door-to-door service in Denver: Metro Taxi (☎ 303-333-3333), Yellow Cab (☎ 303-777-7777) and Zone Cab (☎ 303-444-8888).

DENVER MOUNTAIN PARKS & SOUTH PLATTE RIVER

In 1912, Denver voters approved spending public money to acquire the distant Mountain Parks land. That same year, Frederick Law Olmstead, the esteemed planner of New York City's Central Park, recommended the purchase of **Genesse Mountain** and construction of a road up **Lookout Mountain** west of Golden. The system currently includes 27 parks, beginning 15 miles west of Denver at an elevation of 5700 feet and rising to **Echo Lake** and **Summit Lake** on the flank of 14,264-foot Mt Evans – 60 miles from Denver. Red Rocks Park was acquired in 1927; the stage and seating were completed in the natural amphitheater in 1941. The skiers' playground at Winter Park, west of the Continental Divide over Berthoud Pass, was acquired in 1933 (see Winter Park in the Northern Mountains chapter). Camping is available in Genesse Mountain Park at the *Chief Hosa Campground* (☎ 303-526-0364), reached from I-70 exit 253.

Morrison

Morrison (population 460), is a National Historic District 32 miles southwest of Denver on Hwy 8, set amid spectacular upturned red rocks on the banks of Bear Creek. Excavations of what is called the Morrison Formation began in 1877 and have yielded fossils of over 70 dinosaur species. You can view dinosaur footprints by taking a self-guided tour of **Dinosaur Ridge** (☎ 303-697-3466), located about 2 miles north of Morrison along Hwy 26. A visitor's center, open 9 am to 4 pm, is located on the east side of the ridge near the C-470 highway.

Morrison's restaurants are popular destinations for cyclists following the Bear Creek Greenway and Platte River Greenway from downtown Denver. A former drugstore and soda fountain is now a fun Mexican restaurant, the *Morrison Inn* (☎ 303-697-6650), 301 Bear Creek Ave. Historic photos of early Morrison line the restaurant walls. Dishes such as spinach enchiladas cost $7 and fajitas are $10. In the evenings the bar is crowded with a young outdoor-oriented crowd.

Red Rocks Park & Amphitheater

Red Rocks Park is a 600-acre section of Denver's Gateway Mountain Parks. Located north of Morrison, it's open daily 5 am to 11 pm. From 1936 to 1941, members of the Civilian Conservation Corps worked on constructing the outdoor amphitheater, set between 400-foot-high red sandstone rocks with splendid natural acoustics, which has since featured a variety of concert performances. Climbing on the stunning formations is prohibited. However, 250-plus steps lead to the top of the 9000-seat theater, offering views of the park and Denver miles in the distance off to the east.

Geologists from the nearby Colorado School of Mines make regular forays with students to study unique exposure of the earth's structure in the vicinity of the park. At a **Geologic Overlook** north of the amphitheater off Tunnel Rd, a plaque describes the tumultuous sequence of events leading to the upheaval that formed the Rocky Mountains and created the 'hogback' ridges from the formerly horizontal sandstone formations in the foothills.

South Platte River

Pressure from nearby urban populations is evident everywhere you look in this part of the Pike National Forest southwest of the Chatfield Reservoir. Maps and information are available at the USFS South Platte Ranger Station (☎ 303-275-5610), located on US 285, 6.5 miles west of the exit from highway C-470 and about 5 miles from Morrison.

Colorado Trail Starting at Chatfield Reservoir, the 500-mile-long Colorado Trail (USFS Trail 1776) enters the Rocky Mountains along the South Platte River on its way to Durango. It crosses eight mountain ranges, seven national forests, six wilderness areas and five river systems. The lower section of the trail through Platte Canyon to Strontia Springs Reservoir is used heavily during the day.

The Colorado Trail Foundation (CTF), PO Box 260876, Lakewood, CO 80226-0876, offers maps and books that describe the trail. Proceeds support the CTF's generous volunteer work to create and maintain the trail. Their official guide is Randy Jacobs' *The Colorado Trail*, a 240-page paperback available for $15.50 (plus 4.3% sales tax for Colorado residents). Jan Robertson's *Day Hikes on the Colorado Trail* is a 48-page pocket guide ($6.25). A complete set of 29 waterproof topographic maps is $20. With large color plates photographed by John Fielder, *Along the Colorado Trail*, with text by John Fayhee, will have to remain at home while you are on the trail – it's available for $22 softbound, $33 hardbound.

Buffalo Creek Mountain Bike Area The USFS South Platte Ranger District (☎ 303-275-5610) offers about 40 miles of bike trails, including the Colorado Trail, in the Buffalo Creek Mountain Bike Area. There are two access points: the busiest is 3½ miles south of Buffalo Creek where Jefferson County Rd 126 (S Deckers Rd) intersects the Colorado Trail. Another option is the Miller Gulch trailhead reached from Bailey by taking Park County Rd 68 for 5 miles, then veering left on Park County Rd 70 for another mile before taking a left on USFS Rd 553. Miller Gulch Rd (USFS 554) will be on your right within half a mile. The USFS South Platte Ranger District can provide you with a free pamphlet outlining some of the rides.

Devil's Head Lookout Southwest of Denver, on the highest summit in the forested Rampart Range, is Devil's Head Lookout (elevation 9748 feet). Although the area offers USFS campsites ($9), they are typically full and sometimes noisy. Picnics and day hikes, however, are highly recommended. In a little over a mile, you can climb almost 1000 feet to the fire lookout which offers a commanding view of Spanish Peaks to the south, Mt Evans to the north, South Park to the west and the Eastern Plains. To get there from Denver, follow US 85 south to Sedalia then take Hwy 67 for 10 miles west to Rampart Range Rd, which leads 9 miles to the Devils Head National Recreation Trail and picnic grounds.

Greater Denver Area

GOLDEN
Golden (population 15,000) has earned a place on the map largely due to the Coors Brewery, which calls the town home. While this fact attracts many visitors, it deters those who are understandably unimpressed with the watery beer or its controversial manufacturer. But there's a bit more to Golden than brewery tours. The town has a small historic district, a few interesting museums and the highly regarded Colorado School of Mines. Some may find Golden an interesting day trip but it probably doesn't warrant on overnight stay, particularly since accommodations are fairly expensive.

Golden was founded in 1859 at the mouth of Clear Creek Canyon, after prospectors discovered gold in the stream that flows through town. From 1862 to 1867, Golden served as the Colorado Territorial capital. You can win plenty of bar bets with visitors who assume Golden is named for the glinting yellow mineral – the seat of Jefferson County was named for Thomas L Golden who camped near the creek in 1858.

Information
The Golden Chamber of Commerce/Visitor Center (☎ 303-279-3113, 800-590-3113), at the corner of 10th and Washington Sts, is open 8:30 am to 5 pm weekdays, 10 am to 4 pm weekends. In addition to maps and museum and hotel info, they can provide you with a walking tour guide to the 12th St historic district, which includes the 1867 Astor House Hotel Museum.

Norwest Bank (☎ 303-279-4563) has a 24-hour ATM at 1301 Jackson St. The post office is at 619 12th St; the zip code is 80402.

The laundry at 804 10th St is open daily 7 am to 10 pm. If you've just come down from camping in the Denver Mountain Parks, you can get a shower (and swim, sauna and workout if you wish) at the Golden Recreation Center (☎ 303-384-8100), located at the west end of 10th St. Admission is $4.

Bins for recycling paper, glass and metal are located opposite the Safeway supermarket at the corner of 18th and Jackson Sts.

Buffalo Bill Memorial Museum & Mountain Parks
Four and a half miles west of Golden on Lookout Mountain Rd, **Lookout Mountain**

COLORADO

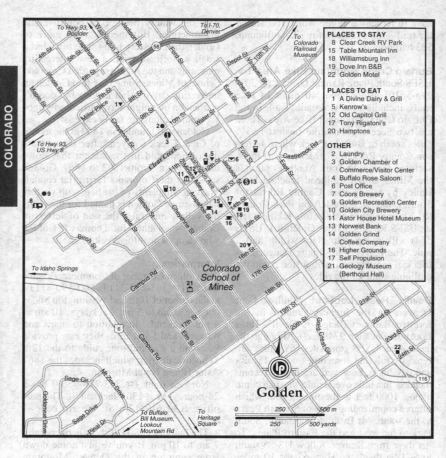

PLACES TO STAY
8   Clear Creek RV Park
15   Table Mountain Inn
18   Williamsburg Inn
19   Dove Inn B&B
22   Golden Motel

PLACES TO EAT
1   A Divine Dairy & Grill
5   Kenrow's
12   Old Capitol Grill
17   Tony Rigatoni's
20   Hamptons

OTHER
2   Laundry
3   Golden Chamber of
     Commerce/Visitor Center
4   Buffalo Rose Saloon
6   Post Office
7   Coors Brewery
9   Golden Recreation Center
10   Golden City Brewery
11   Astor House Hotel Museum
13   Norwest Bank
14   Golden Grind
     Coffee Company
16   Higher Grounds
17   Self Propulsion
21   Geology Museum
     (Berthoud Hall)

Golden

Park is the gateway to the Denver Mountain Park system. The summit offers great views of Golden and Denver and features the Buffalo Bill Memorial Museum (☎ 303-526-0747) near the site where Buffalo Bill Cody was buried in 1917.

Like Buffalo Bill's 19th-century Wild West Show, the museum is an engaging presentation. It's open daily 9 am to 5 pm in the summer; admission is $3/1 adults/children (five to 16).

Short trails through scenic wildflower meadows and ponderosa forest are nearby at the **Lookout Mountain Nature Center**

(☎ 303-526-0594), part of the Jefferson County Open Space Parks, about 2 miles west of the museum. The center is open 10 am to 4 pm Tuesday to Sunday.

Continuing west on Lookout Mountain Rd from the museum, turn right onto US 40 and follow the road west to the I-70 overpass (exit 254) leading to Denver's **Genesee Park**, a favorite place to view elk and bison herds. In the late summer and early fall it's common to hear the elk bulls bugling or see them pair off to tangle their great antlers while putting on a display of bucking and fighting.

Colorado Railroad Museum

A surefire winner for the railroad buff, this museum housed in an old depot provides a comprehensive history of Colorado railroads and street rail companies. Indoor exhibits and model trains, some 50 locomotives and cars, comprise the impressive collection of 'railroadania.'

The Colorado Railroad Museum (☎ 303-279-4591) is 2 miles east of Golden at 17155 W 44th Ave; take 10th St from downtown. It's open daily 9 am to 5 pm; extended hours to 6 pm June to September. Admission is $3.50/1.75 adults/children.

Colorado School of Mines Museum

Set below the giant 'M' on Mt Zion, the School of Mines, founded in 1874, is the nation's second institution devoted to minerals. On the 2nd floor of Berthoud Hall at the corner of 16th and Maple Sts, the school's geology museum (☎ 303-273-3823) features mining exhibits and mineral and fossil displays. It's open Monday to Saturday 9 am to 4 pm, Sunday 1 to 4 pm. In summer, hours vary according to volunteer help. Admission is free.

Coors Brewery Tour

Water – now pumped from below ground rather than drawn from the roiling muddy waters of Clear Creek – is what Coors claims makes its beer distinctive. Tours of the brewery cover the history of Adolph Coors after his arrival in the USA from Wuppertal, Germany, in 1847, though it omits his family's reported links to fascist groups earlier in this century. Adolph founded the Golden Brewery in 1873, changing the name to Coors in 1880. The company survived Prohibition in Colorado from 1916 to 1933 by making malted milk, butter and near-beer. With only one brewery and a nonpasteurized product with a short shelf life, Coors limited distribution to the West, giving it a cachet among the other virtually indistinguishable American beers. Any regional distinction is now lost as Coors is distributed nationwide and another plant on the East Coast assists in production.

The great copper vats are impressive, as is the scale of the entire operation. The plant visit, however, only accounts for 30 minutes of the 1½-hour tour; the rest is little more than a tedious promotion following by tastings (for adult visitors only).

The Life & Times of a Legend

William F 'Buffalo Bill' Cody gained his colorful sobriquet while working as a buffalo hunter for the Kansas Pacific Railroad in 1867. Prior to that he'd been a Pony Express rider and received the Medal of Honor as an Indian Scout.

At his famous Wild West Show, which opened in 1883, Cody presented a cast of performers demonstrating shooting, riding and acting skills. His cast reflected racial and ethnic diversity not found in today's rodeo events (also see Cody in the Bighorn Country chapter of the Wyoming section). A featured performer was sharpshooter Miss Annie Oakley. Native Americans, including Chief Sitting Bull, were presented as proud and honorable people in re-enacted battles. Russian cossacks and Mexican vaqueros were also part of the program.

'If Cody hadn't lived, we would've had to invent him,' joked Bill Carle, the park concessionaire whose family operated the Pikes Peak summit store from 1893 to 1992 and the Mt Evans Crest House from 1956 to 1979. ■

Free tours are offered daily every 15 minutes 10 am to 4 pm. Tours in Spanish are available on Saturdays. To arrange tours in other languages, call ☎ 303-277-2552.

From Washington Ave, Coors Brewing Company (☎ 303-277-2337) is only three blocks east on 12th St; walk past the hops growing on the plant fence to the giant copper kettle at the entrance, where tours begin.

Road & Mountain Biking
Nearby parks offer plenty of opportunities for off-road rides, and road riders will find a number of loops beginning in Golden. Immediately south of I-70 along Hwy 26, **Matthews/Winters Park** has trail access to the Mt Vernon townsite, which in 1859 was the capital of the provisional Territory of Jefferson. East of Matthews/Winters Park and Hwy 26, the Dakota Ridge Trail follows the spine of Hogback Park south for 2 miles before crossing Hwy 26 near Morrison to Red Rocks Trail, which returns to Matthews/Winters Park.

If you're in good shape and don't mind a steep climb, try **White Ranch Open Space Park**, which has miles of challenging single-track and fire road rides. There are two trailheads: one just off of Hwy 93 on the way to Boulder, the other 15 miles up Golden Gate Canyon Rd en route to Golden Gate Canyon State Park.

The best place to get a map and information on bike trails and road loops is Self Propulsion (☎ 303-278-3290), 1212 Washington St, where free friendly advice as well as bicycle rentals are offered.

Places to Stay
As the name suggests, *Clear Creek RV Park* (☎ 303-278-1437), only a few blocks west of downtown on 10th St, caters mainly to vehicle camping, but does have six tent sites which are little more than patches of grass and dirt next to a chain-link fence. Sites are pricey at $17, but include access to showers. Far nicer campsites are available 16 miles out of town at *Golden Gate Canyon State Park* (☎ 303-582-3707), featuring 19 sq miles of camp-

ing and hiking among beautiful rocky peaks and aspen-filled meadows. Back-country sites cost $3 to $5, while the more than 150 developed sites with showers and laundry cost between $7 to $12, the latter having electricity access. For site reservations (advisable) call ☎ 303-470-1144 or ☎ 800-678-2267. From Hwy 93, a half-mile north of Golden, turn left on Golden Gate Canyon Rd and continue 15 miles to the visitors center. Daily park fees are $4 per vehicle.

The friendly *Dove Inn B&B* (☎ 303-278-2209), 711 14th St, a handsome Victorian home built between 1878 and 1886, offers rooms with private bath and TVs with VCRs from $70 to $90.

The cheapest motel lodgings reasonably near the Golden downtown area are at *Golden Motel* (☎ 303-279-5581), 24th and Ford Sts. The owners wouldn't reveal their rates, but locals estimated that the modest rooms cost around $40.

Rooms at the *Williamsburg Inn* (☎ 303-279-7673), 1407 Washington Ave, are more expensive at $65/70 for singles/doubles, but the furnishings are cozy, the rooms clean and the owners amiable. *Table Mountain Inn* (☎ 303-277-9898, 800-762-9898), 1310 Washington Ave, is an upscale Santa Fe-style hotel with rooms for $89/94.

Places to Eat
For an eye-opening caffeine jolt, check out the patio overlooking Golden at *Higher Grounds* (☎ 303-271-9998), 803 B 14th St at the corner of Washington Ave. Don't miss the three-story cobblestone Armory Hall, built in 1913, now housing the *Golden Grind Coffee Company* at the corner of 13th and Arapahoe Sts. *Kenrow's* (☎ 303-279-5164), 718 12th St, offers an all-you-can-eat breakfast for $3 and lunch specials for $5 to $6. Another bargain spot is *A Divine Dairy & Grill* (☎ 303-278-7311), 720 Arapahoe St, where you can get burger and sandwich lunches for under $3. Freshly made soup, breads, Mexican dishes, pasta and salads are part of the $6 all-you-can-eat lunch buffet at *Hamptons* (☎ 303-279-8151), 1518 Washington Ave.

The *Mesa Bar & Grill* (☎ 303-277-9898), in the Table Mountain Inn at 1310 Washington Ave, offers fine Southwest cooking. For breakfast try the relleno omelet; for lunch, the vegetarian Navajo flatbread pizza ($7) or the tequila- and lime-cured Rocky Mountain trout ($9) are good.

Located at the site of the former Territorial Capitol, *Old Capitol Grill* (☎ 303-279-6390), 1122 Washington Ave, features pleasant 'modern Old West' decor. Lunch sandwiches are about $6 and Old West platters like chicken-fried steak are $8 to $10.

Tony Rigatoni's (☎ 303-277-9020), 710 14th St, has an appealing menu of pizza and pasta items; lunch specials go for about $6 and dinner items range from $7 to $12.

Entertainment
Featuring retro-rock acts such as Leon Russel, Edgar Winter and Dr Hook, *Buffalo Rose Saloon* (☎ 303-279-5190), 1119 Washington Ave, is one of the more entertaining venues in Colorado for the genre. The balding crowd at a recent performance of Iron Butterfly doing 'In-A-Gadda-Da-Vida' gives new meaning to the term 'skinheads.'

Dwarfed by Coors, *Golden City Brewery* (☎ 303-279-8092), in a Victorian doctor's home at 920 12th St, is proud to be the number-two brewery in Golden. It offers half-gallon jugs of its various ales, bitters and stouts for $7. The front section houses a mini-brewpub where light lunches are available along with pints of beer for $2, one of the best bargains you'll find anywhere in Colorado.

Getting There & Away
RTD (☎ 303-299-6000) bus routes No 16 and 16L connect Golden with downtown Denver (at the corner of 15th and California Sts). The easiest route by car from Denver is to I-25 north to I-70, then I-70 to exit 265 where you can catch Hwy 58 west into town. From downtown Denver to Golden is about 16 miles.

IDAHO SPRINGS & GEORGETOWN
Just west of Denver along I-70, Idaho Springs (20 miles west of Denver) and Georgetown (15 miles farther west) were founded as mining towns in the 19th century and still have an historical feel about them. Both towns have a spread of antique shops, galleries and restaurants as well as the dramatic backdrop of the rising Rocky Mountains.

Indian Springs Resort
Once advertised as Radium Hot Springs, later Soda Creek, the dowdy Indian Springs Resort (☎ 303-989-6666), south of I-70 at 302 Soda Creek Rd, features geothermal caves, an enclosed pool and Club Mud. Rates are reasonable and it's open 7:30 am to 10:00 pm year-round (see Places to Stay & Eat below).

Argo Gold Mill
In 1910 a 22,000-foot-long tunnel was completed by Samuel Newhouse connecting Idaho Springs with Central City. It was used to transport ore to the Argo Mill (☎ 303-567-2421), 2350 Riverside Drive, where it was processed to recover gold. Half-hour tours cost $10. Note the boulder filled with holes at the entrance, which was used in a drilling contest.

Georgetown Loop Railroad
From late May to early October you can ride an historic steam engine train through the mountains from Georgetown to the town of Silver Plume and back. The trip takes 70 minutes and costs $11.95/7.50 adults/children under 15. Trains leave from the Old Georgetown station (☎ 303-569-2403, 800-691-4386), 1106 Rose St (exit 228 off I-70).

St Mary's Glacier
If you like the idea of skiing year-round, head to this 11,000-foot, 10-acre permanent snowfield. Take I-70 exit 238 2 miles west of Idaho Springs and follow the Fall River Rd for 12 miles to the trailheads at the glacier.

Places to Stay & Eat
Built in 1882, *The Lodge* (☎ 303-278-9294), 1601 Colorado Blvd, with its handsome

rough-hewn exterior of quarter-sawn logs and leaded glass on the Colorado St entry, is a Victorian gem listed on the National Register of Historic Places. The recently restored rooms are comfortable but still maintain their historic feel. Singles/doubles with shared bath are $55, rooms with private bath are $65/75. The large bar is a great place to sit back and enjoy a beer. *Indian Springs Resort* (☎ 303-989-6666), 302 Soda Creek Rd in Idaho Springs, has doubles for $45 to $75.

Pasta and burger meals cost about $8 at *Pittsburgh Mining Co* (☎ 303-567-4591), 1600 Main St in Idaho Springs. Georgetown's *Red Ram Restaurant & Saloon* (☎ 303-569-2300), 606 6th St, has a more upscale menu, including slow-cooked prime rib.

MT EVANS

The pinnacle of many visitors' trips to Colorado is a drive to the Alpine summit of Mt Evans (elevation 14,264 feet) – less than an hour west of Denver's skyscrapers. In 1930, the state added a new meaning to the term 'highway' when it opened the Mt Evans Hwy. From I-70 exit 240 at Idaho Springs, Mt Evans Hwy takes you through a 6725-foot elevation change. Near the exit in Idaho Springs, the USFS Clear Creek Ranger Station (☎ 303-567-2901), open daily 8 am to 5 pm, offers information and a good selection of books and topo maps of the area. The lower portion of the road travels through a montane ecosystem for 13 miles to **Echo Lake**, where the University of Denver's High Altitude Lab is situated in the sub-Alpine ecosystem at 10,700 feet. Reservable USFS campsites at *Echo Lake Campground* (☎ 800-280-2267) get plenty of use and cost $9, plus the $8.65 reservation fee. Freezing temperatures can be experienced here throughout the year – the lab once recorded a low of –52° F.

The last vestiges of forest before ascending to the Alpine tundra, the gnarly bristlecone pine, can be visited on foot at the **Mt Goliath Natural Area**. Four miles above Echo Lake, take the Alpine Gardens trail for just over a mile downhill and back. Continuing on the road past Summit Lake, which freezes solid in the winter, you are likely to encounter Rocky Mountain goats and bighorn sheep. From the end of the highway it's a 200-foot scramble to the summit.

The onset of cold temperatures returns Mt Evans' slopes to their rightful inhabitants. The area is typically open from Memorial Day to Labor Day.

EMPIRE

I-70 now carries most of the traffic toward the Continental Divide, while Empire (population 431) sits astride US 40, the historic route toward scenic 11,315-foot Berthoud Pass. When dedicated in 1938, US 40 was the first hard-surfaced transcontinental route. Summer traffic bound for Granby or Winter Park on the Western Slope over Berthoud Pass continues to follow US 40, and in the winter Empire plays host to many skiers returning from Winter Park. (Drivers take heed: Empire is a prime hideout for the highway patrol ready to ambush those who flout the town's 35-mph speed limit.)

Top-end dining and lodging is offered at *Peck House* (☎ 303-569-9870), 83 Sunny Ave. Established in 1862, it's the oldest hotel in Colorado. The lunch menu features a sausage and cheese platter for $7, while dinners cost between $14 and $19. Shared-bath doubles are $45; most rooms with private baths are $70 to $80.

Rocky Mountain goats live just an hour from Denver.

LOVELAND SKI AREA

Loveland Basin Ski Area (☎ 303-571-5580) is set against the Continental Divide above the I-70 Eisenhower Tunnel bores, 56 miles west of Denver. Convenient access to Denver and $35 lift tickets make Loveland a popular day trip. Its base elevation is 10,600 feet and the summit is 12,280 feet. About half of the 836 skiable acres are intermediate, while the remainder of the trails are evenly divided between beginner trails and expert runs such as Avalanche Bowl and Tigers Tail, served by the No 1 lift. Loveland averages around 340 inches of snow a year, and some glorious powder days can be had here. It also has a cozy, unassuming atmosphere that makes for a nice change from some of Colorado's snobbier resorts.

Snaking around and above the ski area, Hwy 6 crosses Loveland Pass and offers access to some outstanding backcountry runs. Avalanches are a serious danger here, however, so consult with someone at the local resort or ski shop before you hit the powder.

Loveland is only 56 miles from Denver on I-70. Be sure to take I-70 exit 216 or you will have to travel through the Eisenhower Tunnel into Summit County to turn around.

Boulder

Boulder (population 90,900) has traditionally been considered Colorado's most unique community. In a largely conservative state, Boulder has long been a bastion of liberal politics, alternative lifestyles and progressive social attitudes. While most other towns in postwar Colorado worried about boosting their economies, the City of Boulder focused more on quality of life issues, spending money to aquire mountain parks and other open space areas and putting caps on business growth. This is reflected in the human scale of the Pearl St Mall, Boulder's excellent network of bicycle routes and the surrounding greenbelt that has preserved a place for people to enjoy the natural environment near their homes, a successful model for other cities and counties.

Boulder was also an intellectual and cultural center long before Denver started to shed its cowtown status. This was mainly due to the presence of the University of Colorado-Boulder, or 'CU,' Colorado's premier public university with an enrollment of 20,000. The university draws students and professors from all across the US and the world.

Unfortunately, crowds flocking to Boulder in search of the good life have driven up property and retail prices and created some truly nasty traffic congestion. Business executives are moving in to replace the hippies and artists who can no longer afford Boulder rents, and demand for consumer services is threatening the town's original goal of putting living standards ahead of economic growth. Despite local resistance, more national chain stores and restaurants are coming to town, forcing homegrown merchants out of business. Boulder is beginning to look like just another rich white suburb, albeit with a beautiful mountain backdrop.

One thing that hasn't changed is Boulder's mania for outdoor recreation, kept alive by the large student population, Boulder's location at the foot of the Front Range and the excellent open space system. Tenderfoot hikers struggling up the slopes to the Flatirons are humbled by joggers who breeze by, seemingly unaffected by steep slopes or rarefied atmosphere. Some of the nation's top track and cycling athletes have chosen Boulder as a year-round home and training center. Especially in summer it seems as if half the town has taken the day off to bike, hike, run or climb a mountain. For visitors, Boulder is a good jumping-off point for day trips into the Boulder Mountain Parks or excursions to mountain destinations such as the Indian Peaks Wilderness and Rocky Mountain National Park.

History

Before Boulder was established as a small mining center in 1858, Chief Niwot and

COLORADO

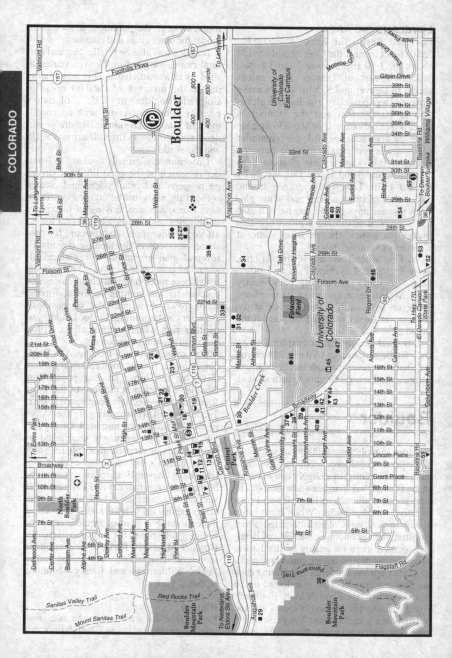

COLORADO

PLACES TO STAY		36	Flagstaff House	17	Boulder Theatr
4	Hotel Boulderado	38	Dot's Diner	19	Boulder Station
5	Boulder Victoria Historic B&B	43	Illegal Pete's	20	Post Office
25	Best Western Golden Buff Lodge	44	Prufrock's	22	Boulder Army Store
		51	Chautauqua Dining Hall	24	Wild Oats Vegetarian Market
29	Foot of the Mountain Motel	52	May Wah Cuisine	26	AAA Colorado
30	University Inn			27	Eads News & Smokeshop
31	Econo Lodge	**BARS**		28	Crossroads Mall
33	Briar Rose	9	West End Tavern	32	Naropa Institute
35	Boulder Marriot	10	Round Midnight	34	Changes in Latitude
40	Boulder HI/AYH	13	Oasis Brewery	37	Boulder Mountaineer
49	Lazy L Motel	14	The Foundry	39	Full Cycle
50	Super 8 Motel Boulder	15	Walnut Brewery	41	Fox Theatre
54	Best Western Boulder Inn	21	Mountain Sun Pub & Brewery	42	Council Travel
				45	University of Colorado Museum
PLACES TO EAT		**OTHER**		46	Macky Auditorium
2	Eddie Lubin's Magic Diner	1	Boulder Community Hospital	47	University Memorial Center
3	Cafe Gondolier			48	Fiske Planetarium
7	Nancy's	6	Boulder Convention & Visitors Bureau	53	Kinko's Copies
12	Abo's Pizza	8	University Bicycles	55	USFS Boulder Ranger District Office
18	Rocky Mountain Joe's	11	Trident Booksellers & Cafe		
23	Harvest Restaurant & Bakery	16	Norwest Ban		

the Southern Arapaho tribe frequented the artesian springs at the mouth of Eldorado Canyon. Other nomadic plains tribes, including the Cheyenne, Comanche and Kiowa, were also noted by the few explorers and fur trappers who entered the area. English-speaking Chief Niwot intercepted Thomas Aikens and a party of gold-seekers at the mouth of Boulder Canyon in 1858. Niwot's request that the miners leave Arapaho land was rebuffed and he was helpless in stopping the advance of the armed intruders. Subsequently, Chief Niwot is said to have placed a curse on Boulder – anyone who sets eyes on the place will be so enamored with it that leaving is not possible. In turn, overpopulation will result in the area's demise.

In 1875 the state legislature offered the city $15,000 for the construction of a university, on the condition that Boulder's citizens contribute an equal amount. Construction of Old Main followed and two teachers initiated instruction at the University of Colorado in fall 1877. In 1898, a group of Texas teachers selected Boulder as the spot to emulate the summer cultural haven for music and art at Lake Chautau-

qua in New York. A year later, Texado Park (now called Chautauqua Park) opened.

Construction of the Boulderado Hotel in 1909 capitalized on the growing popularity of tours to the mountains west of town. Boulder set out to make itself a destination and soon the system of Mountain Parks was growing through private donations and purchases from federal and state agencies.

Boulder's growth accelerated after WWII, as GI loans helped to swell the student population. After 1951, Chief Niwot's curse began to take seed when the 27-mile Denver-Boulder turnpike (now US 36) opened, making metropolitan commuting feasible. Now some 140 years later, many believe Niwot's curse has finally become reality.

Orientation

Central Boulder is bordered by the mountains to the west, 28th St to the east, Baseline Rd to the south and Valmont Rd to the north. Numbered streets are aligned roughly north-south; street numbering begins at the foothills with 3rd St.

Boulder's two major districts of interest to the visitor are the Pearl St Mall downtown and the University Hill district that rises to the south. The two areas are separated by east-west Boulder Creek, a 9-mile corridor for pedestrians and bicyclists. Canyon Blvd (Hwy 119), which intersects 28th St heads, west to skirt the southern edge of downtown before entering Boulder Canyon and continuing to Nederland and the Eldora Ski Area. The University Hill area is adjacent to the main CU campus.

Information
Tourist Offices The Boulder Convention & Visitors Bureau (☎ 303-442-2911), at 2440 Pearl St at Folsom St, offers maps, brochures and assistance weekdays 9 am to 5 pm. An information cart is also located toward the east end of Pearl St Mall near the courthouse. Motorists arriving from Denver on US 36 can stop at the Davidson Mesa Information Center a few miles south of town to pick up brochures and maps. This spot gives a great view of Boulder, the Flatirons and on a clear day the Rocky Mountains.

For information and self-guided tour maps of the CU campus, head to the reception desk at University Memorial Center, on campus at the intersection of Broadway and Euclid Ave. The desk is open 7 am to midnight, and also runs guided campus tours at 10:30 am and 2:30 pm daily. For tour info call ☎ 303-492-6301.

For information about the Arapaho and Roosevelt national forests, stop by the USFS Boulder Ranger District Office (☎ 303-444-6600), 2995 Baseline Rd.

Money An ATM is in the downstairs lobby of the building at the corner of 13th St and College Ave on University Hill. There's also an ATM at University Memorial Center, on campus at Broadway and Euclid Ave. Just one block south of the Pearl St Mall on 13th St is a Norwest Bank ATM. The bank branch itself (☎ 303-442-0351), 1242 Pearl St, offers complete banking services.

Post & Communications The central post office is at 1905 15th St; the zip code

---

The Flatirons: Boulder's Beautiful Backdrop
Boulder's most distinguishing physical feature is the Flatiron Rock Formation. Lending a strong scenic emblem to the town, the Flatirons are part of the Fountain formation seen at Denver's Red Rocks Park and Colorado Springs' Garden of the Gods. With the uplift of the Rocky Mountains beginning about 65 million years ago, the Fountain formation sediments were tilted upward. Subsequent erosion has carved the broken edges of the strata into jagged ridges. Over the past 1.5 million years, cooling has resulted in glaciers scouring the deep U-shaped canyons in the terrain above the Flatirons. The general warming trend over the past 10,000 years has caused the glaciers to retreat to the highest ridges on the Continental Divide. One of these, Arapaho Glacier, is owned by the City of Boulder to provide water, considered by many (mostly Boulderites) to be the tastiest in the country.

In addition to providing a stunning scenic backdrop to the town, the Flatirons are popular with hikers and climbers. Trails up and around the Flatirons lead to nice views of the Eastern Plains and to the west the gorgeous peaks of the Continental Divide. The first and second Flatirons can be attempted without ropes, though serious accidents have resulted when some free-climbers got too careless. Free-climbing the third Flatiron is not a wise idea at all. ■

---

is 80304. Near the south end of campus at 2616 Baseline Rd (near the corner with Broadway), Kinko's Copies (☎ 303-494-2622; fax 303-494-0879), can handle fax and copy needs 24 hours a day. There's another branch at 2795 Pearl St (☎ 303-449-7100; fax 303-449-7805).

Travel Agencies Boulderites are the most worldly travelers in Colorado, and there are plenty of travel agents to help them make their plans. On University Hill,

American Youth Hostels-Hostelling International (HI/AYH; ☎ 303-442-1166), 1310 College Ave, can issue a membership card and help you plan your itinerary. AAA Colorado (☎ 303-753-8800), 1933 28th Ave, offers travel planning services for members and the general public. Council Travel (☎ 303-447-8101), 1138 13th St, caters to student and budget travelers. Among the larger companies is Boulder Travel Agency (☎ 303-443-0380), 1655 Folsom St.

Bookstores The Boulder Bookstore (☎ 303-447-2074), 1107 Pearl St Mall, has a great selection of books and an adjacent coffee shop. Among the many used book dealers are Stage House (☎ 303-447-1433), 1039 Pearl St, and The Bookworm (☎ 303-449-3765), 2850 Iris Ave. Boulder is home to several issue-specific bookshops that exclusively stock books dealing with New Age, feminist, spiritual and other topics. Check the yellow pages for listings.

For travel books and maps check out Changes in Latitude (☎ 303-786-8406), 2416 Arapahoe Ave (in a strip mall between 28th and Folsom Sts). The Boulder Army Store (☎ 303-442-7616), 1545 Pearl St, offers a selection of outdoor books and topo maps. Maps of all types and for all purposes are available at Boulder Map Gallery (☎ 303-444-1406), 1708 13th St.

Newspapers To check on what's happening with Boulder's entertainment and restaurant scene, pick up a copy of the weekly *Boulder Planet* newspaper or the *Boulder Weekly*. Another good resource, aimed more at the college crowd, is the free *Colorado Daily*. Unless you want to delve into small-town politics, don't bother with Boulder's main newspaper, the *Daily Camera*. While not a terrible paper, many feel it has consistently failed to realize its potential, leading some to label it the 'Daily Disappointment.'

Out-of-town and foreign newspapers are available at Eads News & Smokeshop (☎ 303-442-5900), 1715 28th St.

Medical Services Boulder Community Hospital (☎ 303-440-2273) is at 1100 Balsam Ave at N Broadway.

Laundry & Showers Doozy Duds Laundromat (☎ 303-442-6063), on University Hill at 1150 University Ave, is open daily 7 am to 11:30 pm and has coin-op laundry and drop-off service. The three Boulder recreation centers offer swimming and showers for $4.25; call ahead for public swim hours: North Boulder Rec Center (☎ 303-413-7260), 3170 N Broadway; South Boulder Rec Center (☎ 303-441-3448), 1360 Gillespie Drive; and East Boulder Rec Center (☎ 303-441-4400), 5660 Sioux Drive.

Politically Correct – Intellectually Awry

The recent surge in upper middle-class residents and Boulder's history as an outspoken, politically active community has resulted in a strange mix: a town that bickers over petty social issues and gets hung up on what's 'politically correct.' While 'political correctness' – the idea of speaking in a such a way so that no one on earth is possibly offended – has afflicted much of the US, it's put down particularly firm roots in Boulder. An example: in 1995 a local high school band planned to play the Christmas carol 'Silent Night' during the school's holiday festivities. Letters poured into the local *Daily Camera* newspaper, expressing shock that Christian music should be imposed on the community in such a manner. Solutions proposed include that students hum, rather than sing, the tune, so the offensive words wouldn't harm the ears of non-Christians. In this silly debate, the fact that Christmas is by definition a Christian holiday seemed to have been forgotten. Where Boulder once embraced the radical and outspoken, it now seems to have swung in another, less inspiring direction: trying to build a community where no one's feathers get ruffled. ∎

– Nicko Goncharoff

Pearl St Mall

Pearl St Mall, along Pearl St between 11th and 15th Sts, is a welcome change from the conformity of the bland, enclosed shopping malls typically found in US towns. It's more like a European shopping district with crowds of people making up a significant part of the overall show. Sit back on a bench and observe the mix of people, listen to street musicians playing flutes, guitars, and even sitars and catch a whiff of patchouli oil or clove tobacco. While hawkers offer goods and services, including fortune-telling, children clamber over the pedestrian mall's play area. You can sign petitions, listen to soapbox zealots or join groups that work to advance just about any cause imaginable. Panhandling is tolerated, but aggressive demands are not. Posters and bills on public information kiosks list upcoming events. The mall even has that American rarity – public restrooms – at 13th St.

Historic Boulder

Guided and self-guided tours of Boulder's historic homes and downtown buildings are available from the Historic Boulder organization (☎ 303-444-5192) based in the 1877 Arnett-Fullen House at 646 Pearl St. Nearby is Mapleton Hill, home to Boulder's oldest and most magnificent homes. Historic Boulder is open weekdays from 9 am to 4 pm.

University of Colorado Museum

Exhibits in the museum (☎ 303-492-6892), 15th St at Broadway, focus on the geology, biology, human prehistory and native cultures of the Rocky Mountain region. Revolving exhibits have featured 'Jurassic Giants' and Dian Fossey's 'Gorillas in the Lens.' It's open weekdays 9 am to 5 pm, Saturday 9 am to 4 pm and Sunday 10 am to 4 pm. Admission is free, but donations are welcome.

The Naropa Institute

'New Age' is not what this small, Buddhist-inspired institute of higher learning would care to add to its list of attributes, though most people would think of it that way. Instead, The Naropa Institute promotes itself as a fully accredited, nonsectarian liberal arts college that's 'colorful, unconventional and photogenic.' Beat poet Allen Ginsberg and writer Ann Waldman founded Naropa's Jack Kerouac School of Disembodied Poetics, a writing and poetics MFA program.

The institute, established 25 years ago by Chögyam Trungpa Rinpoche to blend Western logic with Eastern intuition, offers traditional degrees as well as continuing education courses. It's held in high regard internationally, and has even played host to the Dalai Lama. The Naropa Institute (☎ 303-444-0202), 2130 Arapahoe Ave, also hosts a number of lectures, performances and workshops throughout the year. To get there, look for the red schoolhouse and the several buildings behind it set back from Arapahoe Ave near 22nd St.

Leanin' Tree Museum of Western Art

Located in an industrial park off the Diagonal Hwy at 6055 Longbow Drive, Leanin' Tree Museum (☎ 303-530-1442), is also the corporate headquarters for Leanin' Tree, publishers of Western-art greeting cards. The upstairs museum features over 200 original Western paintings and 80 bronze sculptures. It's open weekdays 8 am to 4:30 pm, weekends 10 am to 4 pm. Admission is free.

Hiking

Years ago, hikers used to climb to the Crags Hotel, 800 feet above South Boulder Creek in Eldorado Canyon (see Rock Climbing below) and could even flag the D&RG Western train as it passed on its way toward Moffat Tunnel. Nowadays, when the **Rattlesnake Gulch Trail** is not closed to protect raptor nesting sites (February 1 to July 31), you can hike about 1½ miles to the ruins of the hotel and continue another half-mile to wave to passengers on Amtrak's *California Zephyr*. Below the entrance to Eldorado Canyon, the **Mesa Trail** enters the City of Boulder Open Space and the **Towhee Trail** leads through

COLORADO

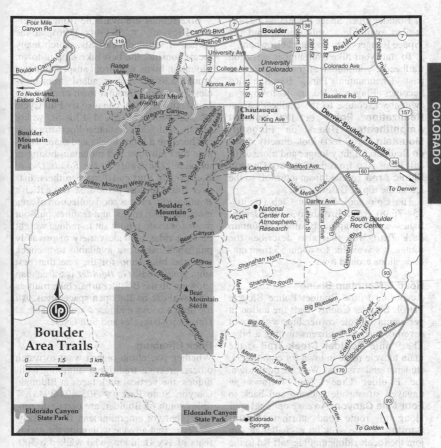

Boulder Area Trails

Four Mile
Canyon Rd

Boulder Canyon Drive

To Nederland,
Eldora Ski Area

Range
View

Boy Scout

Tenderfoot

Ute

Flagstaff Mtn
6960ft

Gregory Canyon

Saddle Rock

Royal Arch

Boulder
Mountain
Park

Flagstaff Rd

Long Canyon

Ranger

Green Bear

Green Mountain West Ridge

The Flatirons

Chautauqua

Bluebell Mesa

McClintock

Enchanted Mesa

NBS

Mesa

Boulder
Mountain
Park

Bear Canyon

Bear Peak West Ridge

Fern Canyon

Bear
Mountain
8461ft

Shadow Canyon

Shanahan North

Shanahan South

Mesa

0   1.5   3 km
0   1   2 miles

Eldorado Canyon
State Park

Eldorado Canyon
State Park

Eldorado
Springs

Canyon Blvd

Arapahoe Ave

University Ave

College Ave

Aurora Ave

Chautauqua
Park

King Ave

University
of Colorado

Boulder

Folsom St

28th St

30th St

Boulder Creek

Foothills Pkwy

Colorado Ave

Baseline Rd

Denver-Boulder Turnpike

Martin Drive

Stanford Ave

Table Mesa Drive

Skunk Canyon

NCAR

National
Center for
Atmospheric
Research

Darley Ave

Lehigh St

Ithaca Drive

Gillespie Dr

Greenbriar Blvd

South Boulder
Rec Center

Broadway

To Denver

Big Bluestem

Big Bluestem

South Boulder Creek

Eldorado Springs Drive

Towhee   Mesa

Homestead

Doudy Draw

To Golden

chokecherry canyon bottoms, frequented by black bears in late summer, before rejoining the Mesa Trail on the uplands where mule deer roam. The relatively easy Mesa Trail continues north for 7 miles to Chautauqua Park, offering access to more difficult routes such as the **Shadow Canyon**, **Fern Canyon** and **Bear Canyon** trails. These three trails lead to the top of Bear Peak (8461 feet), a steep climb that rewards you with spectacular views of the plains to the east and the Rockies to the west.

From the Chautauqua Park area, trails head in many directions. An easy trail that introduces hikers to Boulder's natural environment, the **McClintock Nature Trail** leads to a stunning view of the Flatirons and Boulder from its starting point behind the Chautauqua Amphitheater in the park. By continuing south on the **Enchanted Mesa Trail** and returning on the Mesa Trail, you can hike an easy 2-mile loop. Also at the Chautauqua site is the Boulder Mountain Parks Ranger Cottage (☎ 303-441-3408), open weekdays 8:30 am to 5 pm and irregular hours on weekends, with information on trails leading across the broad sloping meadow to the climbing areas on the First, Second and Third Flatirons. Information about areas of the City of Boulder Open Space (☎ 303-441-4142) is also available at this station, but the 'Space Rangers' are on patrol elsewhere.

To start your hike from higher-elevation trailheads, continue west on Baseline Rd past Chautauqua Park. Baseline Rd becomes Flagstaff Rd as it follows a switchback course to the trailheads from **Realization Point** or the **Summit Amphitheater.** Hikers on **Flagstaff Mountain** (6960 feet) look directly down on Boulder. Slightly longer and more difficult loops start from the **Gregory Canyon Picnic Area**, reached from a turnoff to the left at the top of Baseline Rd.

The Colorado Mountain Club (☎ 303-554-7688), 825 S Broadway, suite 40, publishes a topographic Boulder Mountain Park *Trail Map* that also describes the routes. It's available for about $5 from outdoor shops around town.

Road & Mountain Biking

According to the Boulder Police Bicycle Patrol, Boulder County leads the nation in per-capita bicycle ownership, with about seven of every 10 citizens owning a bike. The 9-mile **Boulder Creek Trail** is the main bicycle route in town for commuters, students and visitors. West of downtown, the Boulder Creek Trail follows an unpaved streamside path up and back to **Four Mile Canyon**. An easy optional spur along this route heads north to **Mount Sanitas**. Those seeking a challenge can join the locals riding up Flagstaff Rd to the top of **Flagstaff Mountain**, a 4-mile ride that should give you more than enough exercise. Don't try this if you're having any difficulties with the altitude.

Most trails in the Boulder Mountain Parks are off-limits to riders; exceptions include intermediate-level trails in **Doudy Draw** near Eldorado Springs and **Marshall Mesa** off Marshall Rd south of town. Far more technically challenging is the 10-mile loop at **Walker Ranch**, located west of Flagstaff Mountain about 10 miles from Boulder along Flagstaff Rd. This is another adventurous route that can be recommended only for the truly fit.

Bike rentals are available from University Bicycles (☎ 303-444-4196), at the corner of 9th and Pearl Sts, which many locals consider the best bike shop in town. Mountain bikes with front suspension cost around $20 per day, standard street bicycles for cruising around town are $15. On University Hill you can also try Full Cycle (☎ 303-440-7771), 1211 13th St, where rentals cost $20/25 standard/performance.

There are a lot of books and maps available for both road and mountain biking in the area. *The Guide to the Roads Out of Boulder*, by Burt and Terry Struthers, lists over 100 road rides in the area. Dave Rich's *Boulder Rides* has a good collection of area mountain bike routes and features pull-out maps for those who want to reduce weight on their rides. A wide variety of privately published maps are available too; check with the bike shop for the one that best suits your needs. *Go Boulder* is a free map showing all the Boulder urban bike trails as well as those on the open space areas. All the above books and maps are available at University Bicycles and Full Cycle.

Rock Climbing

Whether you climb or just want to watch others practice traditional climbing techniques, the vertical rock faces at Eldorado Canyon State Park (☎ 303-494-3943), 7 miles south of Boulder, are certain to provide plenty of entertainment. It's unlikely, however, that anyone will outdo the daring feats of Ivy Baldwin, who walked a 500-foot-long cable stretched between The Bastille, on the south side of the canyon next to the road, to the Wind Tower, 582 feet above South Boulder Creek. Between 1906 and 1926 he crossed the canyon 'for relaxation' 89 times.

This is one of the most popular climbing areas in the country, offering Class 5.6 to 5.9 climbs. Peregrine and Prairie falcons also nest on the walls; be sure to stay 100 yards from any nesting sites. The park is closed from February to August to protect the raptor habitat. The park entrance is on Eldorado Springs Drive 3 miles west of Hwy 93. Admission costs $4 for motor vehicles,

$2 for hikers and cyclists. On summer weekends the narrow canyon typically cannot support excess auto traffic after noon.

No-bolt sport climbing is available on the three Flatirons, reached via hiking trails from Chautauqua Park (see Hiking above).

The Boulder Mountaineer (☎ 303-442-8355), 1335 Broadway, offers gear, books, maps, climbing lessons and guide service. The standard guide to the area is Richard Rossiter's *Boulder Climbs South* (Chokestone Press, 1989).

Special Events

The **Kinetic Conveyance Parade and Challenge** for human-powered vehicles takes place in late April and early May. In early August, the three-day **Rocky Mountain Bluegrass Festival** (also called 'Rockygrass'; ☎ 303-449-6007) is held in Lyons 12 miles north of Boulder. Not everything in Boulder County is hip and groovy – to prove it, check out the tractor pull competition at the **Boulder County Fair & Livestock Show** (☎ 303-772-7170), held each August at the county fairgrounds at 9595 Nelson Rd in Longmont, 10 miles northeast of Boulder.

From June to September, **Chautauqua Summer Festival** (☎ 303-449-2413) performances are held in the Chautauqua Auditorium, a National Landmark. Performers have included guitarist Leo Kottke, Los Lobos, the Cajun group Beau-Soleil and Colorado's talented Mother Folkers. The free **Forum Lecture Series** is held in the Chautauqua Community House on summer weekdays.

Where there's a Will there's a play. From late June to mid-August, the bard's classic plays are presented at the **Colorado Shakespeare Festival** on the CU campus. Contact the Colorado Shakespeare Festival Box Office (☎ 303-492-0554), PO Box 261, Boulder, CO 80309-0261, by mail before mid-May for the best seats. Telephone orders are accepted after mid-May.

Places to Stay

Camping Near town try the *Boulder Mountain Lodge* (☎ 303-444-0882), west of town on Hwy 119 at 91 Four Mile Canyon Rd. The campground offers 25 spaces shaded by pines and cottonwood trees for $14.

Hostels In the University Hill district, the *Boulder International Youth Hostel* (☎ 303-442-0522), 1107 12th St, offers men's and women's dorms with plenty of showers for each. Dorm beds cost $15 with a $1 surcharge for linens. Private rooms with shared bath are available in adjacent buildings for $30, not a great deal though far cheaper than most motel rooms in summer. A laundry, lockers and bicycle storage are also provided. During peak summer months, nearby facilities are used for overflow and there is a three-day stay limit.

B&Bs The 1890s brick *Briar Rose* (☎ 303-442-3007), 2151 Arapahoe Ave, offers nine unique rooms ranging from $119 to $149 in summer, $94 to $134 in winter. The top-end rooms have fireplaces. In addition to a full breakfast, tea and cookie trays are served in the afternoon. The *Boulder Victoria Historic Bed & Breakfast* (☎ 303-938-1300), 1305 Pine St, is a beautifully restored mansion close to downtown. Its seven rooms range from $129 to $189 in summer, $20 to $30 less in winter. Along with breakfast, afternoon tea and evening port are served.

Motels Unfortunately Boulder is an expensive place to stay, especially during the long peak season which lasts from May to October. During winter months you can expect discounts of 15% or more.

Cottages and lodge rooms are available from Memorial Day to Labor Day at *Chautauqua Park* (☎ 303-442-3282), 900 Baseline Rd, a city-owned historic district on 26 beautiful acres at the base of the Flatirons. The late 19th-century Chautauquan movement sought to foster self-improvement for rural Americans. Today the movement offers a summer lecture series and concerts, plus a retreat from everyday life. Rooms in the two lodges cost $52, and cottages start at $58 for efficiencies, $68 for a

COLORADO

one-bedroom unit up to $110 for a three-bedroom. All rooms are subject to a four-night minimum. The rates drop if you reserve and stay for over a week. Reservations are accepted in November for the following year.

North of the CU campus, singles/doubles cost a ridiculous $80/90 at the *Econo Lodge* (☎ 303-449-7550), 2020 Arapahoe Ave. The *University Inn* (☎ 303-442-3830), 1632 Broadway, offers convenient access to the campus plus a laundry; rooms start at $80/87. Neither place is noteworthy, just cashing in on their proximity to CU and downtown.

Near the entrance to Boulder Canyon, cozy (though somewhat small) wood-paneled rooms are available start at $70 at *Foot of the Mountain Motel* (☎ 303-442-5688), 200 Arapahoe Ave. If you want to really be in the mountains, motel-style rooms are $59 ($44 in winter) at *Boulder Mountain Lodge* (☎ 303-444-0882), set in a shady canyon 4 miles west of Boulder at 91 Four Mile Canyon Rd.

There is a string of largely similar motels east of the CU campus on 28th St, including:

Best Western Boulder Inn, 770 28th St
   (☎ 303-449-3800), $83 to $93, pool, sauna, free Continental breakfast
Best Western Golden Buff Lodge, 1725 28th St
   (☎ 303-442-7450), $82, pool, health club, hot tub
Lazy L Motel, 1000 28th St (☎ 303-442-7525), $76, pool, kitchenettes
Super 8 Motel Boulder, 970 28th St
   (☎ 303-443-7800), $64 to $72, pool

Hotels If you're going for a hotel, try the beautifully restored brick *Hotel Boulderado* (☎ 303-442-4344, 800-433-4344), a block from Pearl St Mall at 2115 13th St. First opened in 1909, a new addition was added to the original 42 rooms in 1985. All of the rooms are furnished with antiques and reflect the hotel's original elegance. Single/double rooms cost $134/154. The *Boulder Marriot* (☎ 303-440-8877), at 2660 Canyon Blvd, is the newest high-end

hotel in town, offering modern top-end singles/doubles for $119/129. The double rate includes breakfast.

Places to Eat

Boulder has around 300 restaurants, an enormous number given the population. Below are some selected local favorites, but there are many more places worth trying. For inspiration, check out the *Boulder Planet* and *Boulder Weekly* for restaurant reviews and listings.

A cheap way to get started is to take advantage of the 7 to 9 am early-bird special at *Dot's Diner* (☎ 303-447-9184), 1333 Broadway; eggs, hash browns and toast costs $2.25. For atmosphere, check out Dot's original branch (☎ 303-449-1323) in a converted gas station at 799 Pearl St. In addition to the breakfast special, Dot's does excellent omelets and other egg and waffle treats. Another good breakfast spot is the long-standing *Rocky Mountain Joe's* (☎ 303-442-3969), 1410 Pearl St Mall, where two eggs with two side dishes costs $3.75. This is also a good spot for lunch. For more upscale breakfasts and lunches there's *Nancy's* (☎ 303-449-8402), 825 Walnut St. The omelets are a bit lighter and puffier, the decor more rarefied and prices are higher, but it's still good value for the food and atmosphere. All these places are packed on weekends, when you can expect a wait.

In the University Hill area is *Prufrock's* (☎ 303-443-7461), 1322 College Ave, offering whole-grain baked goods, vegetarian foods and espresso at reasonable prices. You can still see some of the more colorful local characters at a favorite downtown coffee shop, *Trident Booksellers & Cafe* (☎ 303-443-3133), 940 Pearl St.

Many Boulder restaurants have vegetarian menus; among the best is *Harvest Restaurant & Bakery* (☎ 303-449-6223), 1738 Pearl St. Ingredients are always fresh, the food is outstanding and reasonably priced and there's a daily choice of home-made soups and baked goods. Though primarily a vegetarian hangout, carnivores take note: Harvest hamburgers are among the best in town. Lunches and dinners range from $5 to $15.

For tasty food around the clock try *Eddie Lubin's Magic Diner* (☎ 303-440-4340), 1245 Alpine Ave in North Boulder. The menu features fresh soups, sandwiches, hot turkey and roast beef platters ($7) and excellent ice cream desserts. All types of coffees are also on offer, but the varied decor – including a Las Vegas booth where you can spin a 'Wheel of Magic' to win prizes such as a free root beer or a kiss from the chef – should be enough to keep you awake. Up on University Hill, *Illegal Pete's* (☎ 303-444-3055), 1320 College Ave, has won rave reviews from locals for its excellent oversized burritos ($4).

Homestyle Italian pastas and seafood dinners typically run $8 to $12 at *Cafe Gondolier* (☎ 303-443-5015), 2845 28th St near Valmont Rd; on Tuesday and Wednesday, try the all-you-can-eat spaghetti dinner for $3.50. *Abo's*, with branches at 950 Pearl St (☎ 303-443-9113) and on the Hill at 1120 College Ave (☎ 303-443-3199), has the best New York-style pizza in town. Their $4.25 slice, salad and drink special is a good deal.

For Chinese food, one of the best places in town is the *May Wah Cuisine* (☎ 303-499-8225), 2500 Baseline Rd near the corner with Broadway. Their $5 lunch special is guaranteed to leave you full and happy.

All Boulder visitors should experience the *Chautauqua Dining Hall* (☎ 303-440-3776), 900 Baseline Rd at the end of 9th St, built in 1898. Service on the verandah overlooking the expansive grounds features gourmet American cuisine with breakfasts around $8, lunches $10 and dinners $20. The restaurant is open May to October only.

Among the many top-end restaurants in town, the most spectacular is probably *Flagstaff House* (☎ 303-442-4640), located at 1138 Flagstaff Rd. Perched on the north side of Flagstaff Mountain, it offers great views of Boulder and the Front Range

along with excellent Continental dishes and some local game offerings. Another upscale spot definitely worth visiting is the *Red Lion Inn* (☎ 303-442-9368), located about 2.5 miles up Boulder Canyon Dr west of town. Specializing in German fare and wild game, this place oozes with character and warmth. If you get to your table and order before 6:15 pm, you can take advantage of the early bird menu offering full entrees for under $10. Otherwise you're looking at $15 to $30 for anything from excellent wiener schnitzel to wild boar.

Entertainment

Pick up a free copy of the *Boulder Weekly* for the calendar of events. The *Boulder Planet* has an easy-to-read chart of music and other cultural events happening around town in the Arts & Entertainment section.

Bars & Brewpubs Again, there's plenty of these on hand. For billiards and brews, head to *The Foundry* (☎ 303-447-1803), 1109 Walnut St, a cavernous place with nearly a dozen full-size pool tables and a fine selection of draft beer, whiskey and cigars. Bands also play here on weekend nights. At 1005 Pearl St, *Round Midnight* (☎ 303-442-2176) also has a few pool tables but the action centers on the dance floor, which gets packed on weekend nights as DJs keep the crowd happy with a mix of alternative, disco, techno, house and acid jazz. The nearby, *West End Tavern* (☎ 303-444-3535), 926 Pearl St, is unpredictable: some nights it's hopping, others it's dead. The best time to go here is the late afternoon, when you can enjoy a beer and a burger on the rooftop deck and take in the outstanding view of the Flatirons.

Brewpubs are big in Boulder: at last count there were six in town. The pioneer *Walnut Brewery* (☎ 303-447-1345), 1123 Walnut St, has fairly refined decor and attracts an older professional crowd; things usually don't get too rowdy here. The beer is brewed by *Rockies Brewing Company* (☎ 303-444-8448), 2880 Wilderness Place, a major microbrewery in its own right that produces a full selection of Boulder beers. The *Wilderness Pub* at the brewery has a nice outdoor patio, a good place to hang out and continue sampling ales after taking a brewery tour, offered daily at 2 pm.

A bit more lively is *Oasis Brewery* (☎ 303-449-0363), 1095 Canyon Blvd, which has billiards and games and draws a younger, collegiate crowd. Some don't like Oasis beer as much as other local brands, but it's worth trying to see what your taste buds think. Just east of Pearl St Mall, *Mountain Sun Pub & Brewery* (☎ 303-546-0886), 1535 Pearl St, hosts a more down-to-earth crowd: long hair, dreadlocks and tie-dye is the norm here. The beer is generally good, though occasionally inconsistent, and the bar also has a great selection of 'guest beers' from other area breweries. The Mountain Sun often has bluegrass music on Sunday nights.

Live Music In the University Hill Area, headliners such as Merle Saunders, Lyle Lovett and Leftover Salmon appear at the *Fox Theater* (☎ 303-447-0095), 1135 13th St. This also a good place to catch popular local and area bands. Though sometimes it can go for weeks without a performance, the *Boulder Theater* (☎ 303-786-7030), 14th and Pearl Sts, still books major acts such as Dave Brubeck, Leo Kottke and the occasional bluegrass star like Sam Bush. Nearby, the *Catacombs Bar* (☎ 303-443-0486), in the basement of the Hotel Boulderado, often has local blues bands and usually attracts a lively crowd.

The University of Colorado regularly schedules performances of classical music, either at the Gothic *Macky Auditorium* or *Grusin Music Hall* in the Imig Music Building. For concert schedules and info call ☎ 303-492-8008.

Getting There & Away
Public ride boards are posted outside Wild Oats Vegetarian Market, 1825 Pearl St; in the Boulder International Youth Hostel, 1107 12th St; on the CU campus in University Memorial Center; and at the Boulder Mountaineer, 1335 Broadway.

Bus Regional Transit District (RTD; ☎ 303-299-6000) buses (route B) operate between the Boulder Station at the corner of 14th and Walnut Sts and Denver's Market St Station, with additional stops in Boulder along Broadway at Euclid St, Regent St and Baseline Rd. Express buses make the journey in 45 minutes; normal service takes about an hour. All buses carry bikes in the luggage compartment. The one-way fare is $3.

Hostel Hauler (☎ 303-586-3688) offers Boulder-Estes Park (a Rocky Mountain National Park gateway) shuttle service for $15 one-way, $20 roundtrip. It leaves Boulder at about 10 am, picking up passengers at the Boulder hostel and the Boulder Bus Station. Passengers may be dropped at Bear Lake Trailheads in Rocky Mountain National Park, the Estes Park visitors center or the H-Bar-G Hostel, also in Estes Park.

Car Boulder is 27 miles northwest of Denver via I-25 to US 36. If you're arriving from the north on I-25, take the Longmont exit and follow Hwy 119 due west 7 miles to Longmont, then continue another 15 miles southwest on the Diagonal Hwy. US 36 and Hwy 119 converge on north-south 28th St.

Getting Around
To/From the Airport RTD's (☎ 303-299-6000) Skyride bus route AB offers hourly service to Denver International Airport each day for $8 one-way. The bus makes stops at the Boulder Station and along Broadway at Euclid St, Regent St and Baseline Rd. The trip takes about 1½ hours. Frequent door-to-door shuttle service between the Boulder area and Denver International Airport is available from the Boulder Airporter (☎ 303-444-0808) which provides service from Boulder hotels for $14 or from private addresses for $19. Call ahead to book a reservation.

Bus RTD buses provide fairly frequent service in and around Boulder, with many lines running between downtown and the University Hill area along Broadway, and several along Canyon Blvd and Arapahoe Ave serving the motels and shopping malls along 28th St. More useful for visitors, however, is the Boulder 'HOP,' a city-sponsored shuttle bus that makes a circuit through CU, downtown and out to Crossroads Mall on 28th St. Buses run every 15 minutes Monday to Wednesday 7 am to 9 pm; Thursday through Saturday service is extended to 2:30 am. Fares for both RTD and the HOP are 75¢. Bus maps are available in local phonebooks and from the RTD station at 14th and Walnut Sts.

Car Avis (☎ 303-499-1136) is at 4800 Baseline Rd, or Dollar (☎ 303-417-9096), at 30th St and Arapahoe Ave in Crossroads Mall.

Taxi Boulder Yellow Cab (☎ 303-442-2277) operates around the clock.

AROUND BOULDER
Nederland, Eldora Ski Area & Indian Peaks Wilderness Area
Heading west 17 miles up scenic Boulder Canyon will bring you to Nederland, a lively and sometimes gritty town near the base of the Indian Peaks Wilderness Area. For visitors it mainly serves as a gateway to Eldora Ski Area and hiking and camping in Indian Peaks, though the town has a certain charm as well as several good restaurants and bars.

Eldora Ski Area (☎ 303-440-8700), 4 miles west of Nederland, primarily gets day visitors who take advantage of its convenience and inexpensive lift tickets ($32). At the time of writing these rates were scheduled to go up, however. Though a fairly small facility with around 500 skiable acres, some recently opened areas offer interesting terrain, and a few expert trails in the Corona Bowl boast a 1400-foot vertical drop. A new high-speed quad chairlift also makes this place more fun.

Introductory two-hour ski or snowboard lessons include an all-day beginner lift ticket and rental equipment for $46. The Eldora Rossignol Nordic Center offers about 27 miles of machine-set tracks and

some backcountry trails. A lift ticket is required on the Nordic ski trails, with the exception of the public Jenny Creek Trail which is also popular with cyclists and runners in the summer. Nordic lifts tickets cost $10, though they were also set to increase.

Forming the impressive backdrop to Nederland, the Indian Peaks area offers many fine hiking and camping opportunities. Especially nice is the hike up to 12,000-foot **Arapaho Pass**, accessed from the Fourth of July campground. It's a gentle ascent but be prepared to spend the entire day – if the altitude doesn't slow you down, the scenery should. For more information on Indian Peaks check at the Nederland Visitors Center, which has maps and guidebooks. It's located in the center of town diagonally opposite The Village shopping mall. In the mall itself, the Ace Hardware store also sells topographic and USGS maps for the Indian Peaks area and issues camping permits (required June to September 15) as well as hunting and fishing licenses.

Places to Stay & Eat The grubby *Nederland Hostel* (☎ 303-258-7788), 8 W Boulder St in Nederland, offers foam mattresses and one bathroom for two dorms that can house four men and four women. Dorm beds are $15, private singles/doubles cost $25/30. It's a blue and white building across the road from The Village shopping mall. Some guests have reported drunken lodgers and incidents of theft, so be alert if you bunk down here.

The next cheapest option is the *Nederhaus Motel* (☎ 800-422-4629), 686 Hwy 119 S, which has fairly unexciting singles/doubles from $49/59. It's located a half-mile west of the town center, near the turnoff for Eldora Ski Resort.

The only other option in town is the *Best Western Lodge at Nederland* (☎ 303-258-9463, 800-279-9463), 55 Lakeview Drive opposite The Village shopping mall. Nicely appointed rooms cost $75/95.

A good place for breakfast is *Whistler's Cafe* (☎ 303-258-7871), next to the police station and behind the Nederland Visitors

Center. Hearty breakfasts and lunches are a good value at $5 to $10; try their famous Mountain Muffin. It closes around 2 pm, but reopens for dinner some nights of the week. Nearby *Neapolitan's Italian Restaurant* (☎ 303-258-7313), 1 W 1st St, has fairly standard Italian fare, but it's a fun place, the portions are huge and prices start at $6.

The best food in town is served at *Tungsten Grill* (☎ 303-258-9231), 155 Hwy 119 S, diagonally opposite the Nederland Visitors Center. The eclectic menu has an interesting blend of American and European dishes. Lunches cost around $10, dinner around $20.

Entertainment Nederland has in recent years become a small center for live music, mostly of the acoustic variety. One place that regularly books nationally known acts is the *Acoustic Coffeehouse* (☎ 303-258-3209), 95 East 1st St. Most of the music takes place Thursday through Saturday nights; previous performers have included bluegrass heavyweights Peter Rowan and Tim O'Brien and folk legend Norman Blake. It's also a nice place for coffee and a snack during the day.

Moon Time (☎ 303-258-7398) is considerably rowdier, staying open until 2 am every night of the week. They often have live music and nationally known acts roll through from time to time. In addition to a good selection of microbrews, there's Cajun-style bar food on offer.

Getting There & Away Nederland is reached via Hwy 119, also known as Boulder Canyon Drive. If you're relying on public transportation, the RTD (☎ 303-299-6000) bus N from Boulder goes to Nederland and on to the Eldora Ski Area for only $2.

The Peak to Peak Hwy

Stretching some 40 miles between Nederland and Estes Park, this north-south route takes you past a series of breathtaking mountains, including the 14,255-foot Long's Peak, lush valleys and grassy meadows. You can break up the ride by stopping at one of the little towns along the way. These include **Ward**, a center for alternative living and '60s throwbacks, **Peaceful Valley**, notable for the little onion-domed church perched above the village and tiny **Ferncliff** and **Allenspark**, which lie near some stunning mountain vistas.

Just opposite the turnoff for Ward is the road leading up to **Brainard Lake**. The lake itself is tiny but is in a gorgeous setting and there are some great hiking trails leading off from it. If hiking around here works up your appetite, stop in at the *Millsite Inn*, just north of the turnoff to Ward. The food is nothing special but it's an interesting place with plenty of local color for a bite to eat or a beer.

There are places to stay in Peaceful Valley, Ferncliff, Allenspark and south of Estes Park, mostly in the form of lodges, cabins and B&Bs; prices range from $50 to $90. There are also national forest campgrounds near Peaceful Valley and Allenspark, as well as the Long's Peak Campground, which is part of Rocky Mountain National Park.

At the southern end, the Peak to Peak Hwy starts from Nederland as Hwy 72. It then turns into Hwy 7 West just north of Allenspark and continues from there to end at Estes Park.

Northern Front Range

Once a refuge from the rapid growth of Denver and Boulder, the northern reaches of the Front Range are now being targeted for development, particularly the college town of Fort Collins, which is growing as rapidly as its urban neighbors to the south. But the town still retains some of its original charm, and the wonderful peaks, meadows and rivers of the Roosevelt National Forest just to the west remain relatively unspoiled.

The primary attraction of the northern Front Range is Rocky Mountain National Park, worth visiting any time of year, though the summer crowds can be oppressive at the gateway town of Estes Park. If the prospect of hiking into the backcountry sounds appealing you can leave most of your fellow visitors behind. In any case, equally beautiful scenery and outdoor activities can be had both north and south of the park boundaries.

HIGHLIGHTS

- Rocky Mountain National Park – sheer beauty and abundant wildlife abounds despite tourist hordes

- Long's Peak – a strenuous though popular hike that rewards you with views from 14,255 feet

- Fort Collins – entertaining bars and restaurants in Old Town, with fine hiking and biking nearby

- Cache la Poudre River – 75 miles of protected river canyon, home to elk, moose and bighorn sheep

FORT COLLINS

Fort Collins (population 104,000) lies at the northern end of the Front Range on the Cache la Poudre (rhymes with 'neuter') River. This formerly staid farming community has developed into a vibrant city, especially near the Colorado State University campus and the recently refurbished historical buildings of Old Town, with nightly entertainment and brewpubs. In fact, microbrews are one of Fort Collins' main 'exports' and the Colorado Brewers Festival, begun in 1989, is now a major attraction in late June.

Proximity to the Rocky Mountains and 'Poudre' River also contribute to Fort Collins' appeal, and make it a good jumping-off point for wilderness excursions. At night, patrons dance to surprisingly good bands in the clubs; during the day they can be spotted rafting down the Poudre's challenging whitewater. Nearby Horsetooth Mountain Park and Reservoir attracts mountain bikers and day hikers. An extensive network of paths links many of the parks and open space areas, allowing bicyclists and in-line skaters to enjoy the watercourses through town.

History

French trappers traveling north along the Front Range in the winter of 1836 encountered a snowstorm and decided to cache some of their unnecessary gear – primarily gunpowder – by burying it on the banks of what came to be called the Cache la Poudre River.

A branch of the Overland Trail left the South Platte River at its confluence with the Poudre River and turned north toward Wyoming along the path followed by modern US 287. To protect travelers and settlers along the trail, the War Department established Camp Collins in 1862. The first civilians arrived to trade with the military in 1864 – unfortunately the year the post vanished in a flood – and a trickle of agricultural settlers began arriving thereafter.

In 1870, the territorial legislature agreed to establish Colorado Agricultural College on land donated by several citizens, three years before Fort Collins was officially a town. By 1879 classes were being taught in Old Main and the college was eventually designated Colorado State University (CSU). From its agricultural roots, the study of irrigation led to lucrative hydraulic engineering contracts from the US Bureau of Reclamation to design major dam and water projects throughout the western USA.

An agricultural boom doubled the population to over 8000 during the first decade of the 20th century. In 1903 the Great Western Sugar Factory began milling beets which also provided feed for the area's sheep and lambs – the area claimed to be the 'Lamb Feeding Capital of the World.' But many of the workers in the beet fields were poorly paid German or Russian immigrants who enjoyed none of the prosperity that growth brought to earlier arrivals and agricultural corporations. That same role is now played by Latin American itinerant workers, who still live as 2nd-class citizens, US antidiscrimination legislation notwithstanding.

Orientation
College Ave (US 287) is the main north-south artery and primary commercial corridor. North of Mulberry St (Hwy 14) is downtown and Old Town; two blocks south of Mulberry St, on the west side of College Ave, is the CSU campus. Farther south College Ave degenerates into a strip of fast-food outlets, shopping malls and suburban sprawl.

Northeast of College and Mountain Aves, Old Town is a small triangle of streets aligned with the Poudre River and the railroad. Mountain Ave separates north-south street addresses. Continuing north over the river, US 287 makes a broad curve west past Laporte to the junction with Hwy 14, at the mouth of the Poudre River Canyon 10 miles from Fort Collins.

Information
Tourist Offices The Fort Collins Convention and Visitors Bureau operates a Visitor Information Center (☎ 970-482-5821, 800-274-3678) in a restored downtown house at 420 S Howes St. It's open daily 8:30 am to 5 pm and is well-stocked with maps and pamphlets on recreational and cultural activities in the area, as well as information on lodging and restaurants.

For maps and information about CSU, stop by the University Visitors Center (☎ 970-491-4636), 1301 S College Ave at Pitkin St.

The USFS headquarters for the Arapaho and Roosevelt national forests and the Pawnee National Grasslands is at 240 W Prospect Rd and Colorado Blvd. Their information Center (☎ 970-498-2770), 1131 S College Ave, offers maps and trail information for an extensive recreational area. It's open weekdays 8 am to 4:30 pm. Colorado State Parks (☎ 970-226-6641), 3842 S Mason St, has information about access to local recreational areas and campsites.

Money ATM machines are all over downtown and Old Town. An easy-to-spot 24-hour ATM is at the high-rise Key Bank (☎ 970-482-3216), 300 W Oak St.

Post & Communications The main post office (zip code 80525) is at 301 Boardwalk Drive, just east from US 287 near the Foothills Fashion Mall south of downtown. A more convenient location for most visitors is the branch at the corner of W Olive and Howes Sts. Kinko's Copies (☎ 970-221-2679; fax 970-493-4496), 130 West Olive St, has 24-hour fax service.

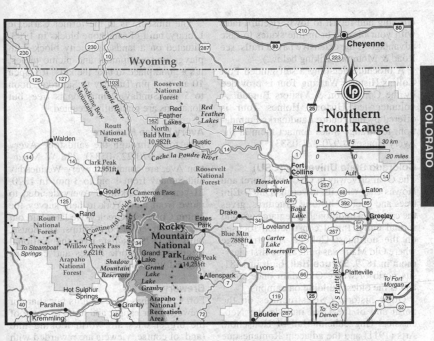

Travel Agencies Among the numerous travel agencies in town, Fort Collins Travel (☎ 970-482-5555), 333 W Mountain Ave, has been around the longest and has a good reputation.

Bookstores The Stone Lion Bookstore (☎ 970-493-0030), 107 N College Ave, has one of the better selections in town. For used and rare books try The Old Corner Book Shop (☎ 970-484-6186), at 216 Linden St next to Linden's Brewing Company.

Newspapers For daily news about local events check the *Fort Collins Coloradoan* newspaper.

Medical Services Poudre Valley Hospital (☎ 970-495-7000), southeast of downtown off Riverside Ave at 1024 S Lemay Ave, has 24-hour emergency care.

Laundry A&B Dry Cleaning and Laundry (☎ 970-482-2406), at 127 W Mulberry St, is open daily from 6 am to midnight. Drop-off service (65¢ per pound) is offered 7 am to 10 pm Monday to Friday; shorter hours during weekends.

Historic Old Town
With many of its buildings restored, this area has become the city's center for restaurants and nightlife, and also makes for a nice stroll during the day. The **City Drug Store**, 261 Linden, was built in 1887 on the former site of 'Old Grout,' the sutler's store built in 1865 to sell provisions to the military. The Sports Station restaurant was once the Union Pacific Railroad Depot, built in 1911. Opposite the depot are the **Vandewark Building** and other brick structures built between 1879 and 1881.

Cross over the Poudre River on Linden St to the 11-acre **Gustave Swanson Nature Area**, a handicap accessible interpretive nature site on your left. To the right, you can follow a section of the **Poudre River Trail** to the Lincoln Ave crossing and return to town. (Return later with your bicycle or in-line skates to take advantage of the extensive paved trails; see Road & Mountain Biking below.)

A brochure detailing a self-guided Fort Collins Historic Walking Tour is provided by the Convention & Visitors Bureau. A volunteer-led Historic Homes Tour is offered by the Poudre Landmarks Foundation; to arrange times contact them at the Avery House (☎ 970-221-0533).

Colorado State University (CSU)

The Oval driveway at CSU, W Laurel and Howes Sts, with its towering Dutch Elm trees and over 20 historic structures, gives the campus a traditional collegiate aura and formal entry. Initial construction focused on the northeast College Ave frontage where Old Main was built as the first classroom in 1879. **Spruce Hall**, built in 1881, sits north of where Old Main once stood and is the oldest building on campus.

Other historic CSU structures on the north end of the Oval include the Neoclassical Guggenheim Hall of Household Arts (1911) and the adjacent Romanesque Mechanical Arts Building, begun in 1885. West of Howes St, the attractive Italian Renaissance-style Ammons Hall opened in 1922.

In response to President Kennedy's 1963 call for US citizens to aid people around the world, researchers in the **Weber Building** on the west side of the Oval developed many of the ideas used in creating the Peace Corps. In 1964, the first Peace Corps volunteers were trained at CSU before being sent to Pakistan.

Fort Collins Museum

Points and scrapers used as tools by Paleo-Indians, excavated in the late 1930s by Smithsonian archaeologists 25 miles north of Fort Collins at the Lindenmeir Ranch, and are now on display at the Fort Collins Museum (☎ 970-221-6738), 200 Mathews St. Other exhibits include an Overland Trail room and a collection of log buildings moved to the grounds, including Fort Collins' first dwelling, built in 1864.

The museum is in the former Carnegie Library, built of sandstone blocks in 1903. Situated on a landscaped city block with playground equipment and picnic tables, it's a good place to take the kids. It's open 10 am to 5 pm Tuesday to Saturday, noon to 5 pm Sunday. Admission is free, but donations are gratefully accepted.

Avery House Museum

Free tours through the sandstone Avery House (☎ 970-223-0533), 328 W Mountain Ave, are conducted every Wednesday and Sunday from 1 pm to 3 pm. In 1870, 21-year-old Franklin C Avery decided to move from New York to help survey the Union Colony at Greeley. He later laid out the wide streets of Fort Collins. The house, built in 1879, is listed on the National Register of Historic Places and contains original furnishings.

Brewery Tours

Fort Collins has more than its fair share of breweries per capita, and tours of some of the bigger ones are worth looking into (and, of course, viewers are rewarded with free samples at the end of their visit).

The **New Belgium Brewing Company** (☎ 970-221-0524), 500 Linden St, has guided tours of its new facility daily at 2 pm. You can also take a walk-through on your own anytime from 9 am to 5 pm. Out at 800 E Lincoln Ave, **Odell Brewing Company** (☎ 970-498-9070) gives ad-hoc tours from 9 am until around 3 pm Monday to Saturday. Both breweries produce outstanding beer and have rightfully become quite successful.

Jumping up in scale (though not necessarily in quality), you can also tour the **Fort Collins Anheuser-Busch Brewery** (☎ 970-490-4691), 2351 Busch Drive. One of 13 Anheuser-Busch breweries in the USA, this is the year-round home of the Clydesdale horses, which were first used by the brewer to draw beer wagons through the streets of St Louis. Complimentary tours of the massive brewery and Clydesdale stables are available daily from 10 am to 4 pm. To get there from town,

COLORADO

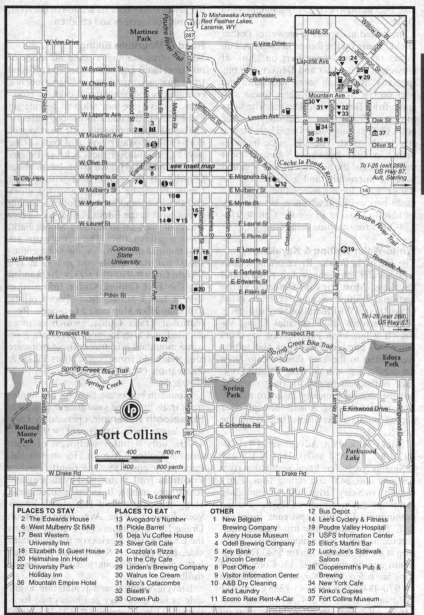

PLACES TO STAY
2   The Edwards House
6   West Mulberry St B&B
17 Best Western
    University Inn
18 Elizabeth St Guest House
20 Helmshire Inn Hotel
22 University Park
    Holiday Inn
36 Mountain Empire Hotel

PLACES TO EAT
13 Avogadro's Number
15 Pickle Barrel
16 Deja Vu Coffee House
23 Silver Grill Cafe
24 Cozzola's Pizza
26 In the City Cafe
29 Linden's Brewing Company
30 Walrus Ice Cream
31 Nico's Catacombs
32 Bisetti's
33 Crown Pub

OTHER
1   New Belgium
    Brewing Company
3   Avery House Museum
4   Odell Brewing Company
5   Key Bank
7   Lincoln Center
8   Post Office
9   Visitor Information Center
10 A&B Dry Cleaning
    and Laundry
11 Econo Rate Rent-A-Car

12 Bus Depot
14 Lee's Cyclery & Fitness
19 Poudre Valley Hospital
21 USFS Information Center
25 Elliot's Martini Bar
27 Lucky Joe's Sidewalk
    Saloon
28 Coopersmith's Pub &
    Brewing
34 New York Cafe
35 Kinko's Copies
37 Fort Collins Museum

take I-25 north to exit 271 (Mountain Vista Drive).

Interested in exploring breweries farther afield? Foam on the Range Brewery & Pub Tours takes avid beer fans on tours of breweries in Boulder and Denver in a bus specially fitted with sofas, armchairs and beer on tap. Tours to all three towns also leave from Boulder and Denver. The tours run every Friday through Saturday, and the point of departure rotates weekly from one city to the next. The $45 price includes visits to four breweries, draught beer served aboard the bus, discounted beer and food at micropubs and a 'Foam on the Range' mug. Ideally reservations should be made two weeks in advance, but you may be able to squeeze in sooner. Call ☎ 970-224-2435 for schedule details.

White-Water Rafting & Kayaking
The Cache la Poudre River offers serious white-water challenges for rafters and kayakers. Most trips on Colorado's first National Wild & Scenic river are rated Class III or IV (difficult or very difficult). 'The Narrows' is a suicidal Class V+ stretch where even experienced kayakers choose to portage. Float trips and tubing are limited to the area downstream from the confluence with the river's North Fork. June is the best month for river running, but the season typically lasts from mid-May to mid-August. A map showing river access points is available free from the USFS.

Rocky Mountain Adventures (☎ 970-493-4005, 800-858-6808), 1117 N US 287 at Shields Ave, offers kayak instruction (two sessions cost $45) and rafting trips. Early season two-day trips ($169 including camping) stay overnight at Rustic, a small community 30 miles upstream from US 287. Their most popular trip features high adrenaline white-water rapids, plus a lunch stop at the Mishawaka Inn for $54. The minimum age on this trip is 13. Comparable trips are offered by Wanderlust Adventure (☎ 970-484-1219, 800-745-7238), and A-1 Wildwater (☎ 970-224-3379, 800-369-4165). All companies offer shorter trips on the lower Class II or III section of the river, suitable for novices and children.

Road & Mountain Biking
Fort Collins maintains some 80 miles of on-street lanes and bike routes and off-road trails that accommodate college students, commuters and recreational cyclists. However, cyclists are not allowed to ride on College Ave, the main north-south artery.

The bike paths provide a pleasant tour of Fort Collins' waterways and parks. One paved path follows the Cache la Poudre River from Taft Hill Rd downstream about 6 miles to the confluence with Spring Creek. From the confluence of the creek and the river, another trail follows Spring Creek west to the Edora Pool & Ice Center and continues on to Rolland Moore Park, about 6 miles farther. The paved paths are also popular routes for in-line skate enthusiasts: half-day rentals cost just $7 at The Wright Life (☎ 970-484-6932), 200 Linden St. The Fort Collins Visitor Information Center has a single-sheet 'Fort Collins, Colorado Bike Map' and a two-page 'Recreational Trails Guide,' which is more detailed and also includes information on some mountain bike trails. These maps are also available from Fort Collins Parks & Recreation (☎ 970-221-6640), at 214 N Howes St.

Mountain bikers can head for the single-track trails in the red sandstone hogbacks at **Horsetooth Reservoir**, operated by Larimer County Parks Department (☎ 970-679-4570), only 4 miles southwest of town from S College Ave on Horsetooth Rd. Park entry costs $5. The 6-mile earthen **Foothills Trail**, maintained by the city and free to the public, links open-space areas along the east side of Horsetooth Reservoir. From College Ave, head west on Drake Rd (bike lanes) for 3 miles toward the CSU 'A' (for Aggies) on the mountainside, turn right on S Overland Trail then left on Larimer County Rd 42-C to the trailhead.

Bicycle supplies and rentals are available at Lee's Cyclery & Fitness two locations: 202 W Laurel St (☎ 970-482-6006)

or 2722 S College Ave (☎ 970-226-6006). Rental rates range from $10 to $30 per day depending on the type of bike.

Hiking & Cross-Country Skiing

The trails around Horsetooth Reservoir provide a convenient getaway for a day hike or climb to the top of Horsetooth Mountain, but you may also make an overnight trek into the Lory State Park backcountry. Excellent cross-country ski opportunities await winter visitors on the trails around the reservoir. (See Mountain Biking above, and Camping below.) Stop by the Mountain Shop (☎ 970-493-5720), 632 S Mason St, for maps and outdoor gear.

Swimming & Ice Skating

The Edora Pool Ice Center (☎ 970-221-6679), 1801 Riverside Ave, offers indoor swimming and ice skating daily for $2.50. Call for specific times. From downtown take the Transfort Route 9 bus, Monday to Saturday; if on foot or bike use the Poudre River Trail.

Golf

Two city-operated courses are available: City Park Nine (☎ 970-221-6650), 411 S Bryan Ave at the west end of Mountain Ave near City Park Lake; and the 18-hole Collindale Golf Course (☎ 970-221-6651), 1441 E Horsetooth Rd.

Special Events

There is something happening at either the CSU campus or in town almost every weekend; contact the Fort Collins Convention & Visitors Bureau (☎ 970-482-5821, 800-274-3678) for a complete schedule.

Suds aficionados assemble in Old Town Square for two days in late June for the **Colorado Brewers Festival,** a major event for microbreweries. The school semester's start in mid-August is marked by a three-day carnival, **New West Fest**, the city's biggest bash with food and craft booths and continuous performances. Yet more celebration of ales, porters and stouts takes place during **Oktoberfest** in mid-September.

During summer, free outdoor concerts are held both day and evening at Old Town Square, CSU and The Lincoln Center.

Places to Stay

Camping The nearest camping is at Horsetooth Reservoir below the landmark Horsetooth Rock (7255 feet), just a few miles west of Fort Collins. Near the south bay of the Horsetooth Reservoir, *Larimer County Parks* (☎ 970-679-4570) operates seven campgrounds with 126 sites for tents or RVs. Camping is included in the $5 daily admission fee. To get there from central Fort Collins, take S College Ave south to W Horsetooth Rd, turn right and head 2 miles, left onto Taft Hill Rd, then right (west) onto Larimer County Rd 38E to the park. Inlet Bay Marina (☎ 970-223-0140) offers fishing and camping supplies. At the northwest end of the reservoir, reached from Bellevue, *Lory State Park* (☎ 970-493-1623) offers a few backcountry campsites by permit ($2) only. Admission to the park costs $4 per vehicle in addition to a camping permit.

KOA (☎ 970-493-9758), 10 miles northeast of Fort Collins at the entrance to the Poudre River Canyon on US 287, provides showers with tent sites ($17) separate from the RV area ($23). It's closed in winter.

B&Bs *Elizabeth Street Guest House* (☎ 970-493-2337), 202 E Elizabeth St near the CSU campus, is a handsomely restored American Four Square-style brick house built in 1905. Singles/doubles with shared bath and a full breakfast cost $45 to $55, rooms with private bath range from $65 to $85.

Rooms at *The Edwards House* (☎ 970-493-9191), 402 W Mountain Ave, feature elegant Victorian-era furnishings and most have a gas fireplace and private bath. Doubles range from $79 to $139, including full breakfast and evening refreshments. This Neoclassical house near Old Town, built in 1904, embellishes on Four Square architecture. *West Mulberry St B&B* (☎ 970-221-1917), 616 W Mulberry St, provides rooms with private bath and a hearty breakfast for $89/99; there is also one single for $56.

Motels A few miles north of the town center, the small *Montclair Motel* (☎ 970-482-5452), 1405 N College Ave, has quiet, clean rooms starting at $28/36. Nearby, the *El Palomino Motel* (☎ 970-482-4555), though close to traffic, has cable TV, laundry and a swimming pool. Singles/doubles are $33/43.

Amid the cluster of lodging 4 miles east of downtown at I-25 exit 269B, the mundane *Motel 6* (☎ 970-482-6466), 3900 E Mulberry St (Hwy 14), has singles/doubles for $30/35.

Across from the CSU campus, the *Best Western University Inn* (☎ 970-484-1984), 914 S College Ave, has rooms starting at $46/50, Continental breakfast included.

Hotels Probably the town's best lodging deal is *Mountain Empire Hotel* (☎ 970-482-5536), 259 S College Ave. Clean singles/doubles with shared bath are only $16/18, $27/29 for singles/doubles with private bath and TV. The hotel gets hot in summer, however; open the door and windows before retiring so that the industrial-strength swamp cooler in the hallway can blow out the stale air. Or just open a window and stay out on a pub crawl until the temperature drops.

At the other end of the price spectrum, the *Helmshire Inn Hotel* (☎ 970-493-4683), 1204 S College Ave, offers modern luxury doubles for $80, including breakfast at a nearby restaurant.

University Park Holiday Inn (☎ 970-482-2626) is south of the CSU campus at 425 W Prospect Rd and Center Ave. It has more than 250 rooms, most of them furnished with double beds, ranging in price from $79 to $125. Farther south on 350 E Horsetooth Rd next to the Foothills Fashion Mall, the *Fort Collins Marriott* (☎ 970-226-5200) has rooms ranging from $79 to $140. Both of these hotels offer full-service amenities, including swimming pools, fitness rooms and room service.

Places to Eat
Old Town's streets are lined with restaurants, many of them quite reasonable. A good budget breakfast and lunch spot is the *Silver Grill Cafe* (☎ 970-484-4656), 218 Walnut, known for its giant cinnamon rolls and noontime dinner plates of standard American 'brown and white' cooking for under $6. *In the City Cafe* (☎ 970-221-0960), 150 N College, doesn't offer much atmosphere but does have great food, including vegetarian dishes. It's open Monday to Saturday 6:30 am to 2 pm. The $6 Florentine Benedict breakfast is the most expensive breakfast item; lunch entrees range from $6 to $10.

For a reasonably priced Italian lunch or dinner in a casual atmosphere, try *Bisetti's* (☎ 970-493-0086), 120 S College Ave. Early-bird dinner specials are available before 6:30 pm. Another good spot is the *Crown Pub* (☎ 970-484-5929), 134 S College, with fresh soups, generous side salads ($1.50) and fairly refined dishes such as chicken with prosciutto and gnocchi ($6.95) The pub also boasts an impressive selection of single malt scotch.

For Cajun food, *Linden's Brewing Company* (☎ 970-482-9291), 214 Linden St, does a reasonably good job and lunch prices are not a bad deal: try the blackened redfish with fried fresh vegetables and rice for $6.95. Their beer and fiery Cajun Marys (spicy Bloody Marys) are also recommended. In the same area, *Cozzola's Pizza* (☎ 970-482-3557), 241 Linden St, gets locals' votes for the best pizza in town (closed Mondays).

The Laurel St area north of campus is a popular student hangout and accordingly offers inexpensive food, beer, exam-strength coffee and entertainment. Get your caffeine fix at *Deja Vu Coffee House* (☎ 970-221-3243), 646½ S College Ave, Monday to Thursday 7 am to 10 pm, until 11 pm Friday and Saturday. Try the soups (a 'trencher' costs $4) or $5 pita sandwiches. The *Pickle Barrel*, at the corner of W Laurel and Mason Sts, serves sandwiches and also has an admirable assortment of microbrews and features occasional entertainment. Just around the corner at 605 S Mason St, *Avogadro's Number* (☎ 970-493-5555) has a varied menu catering to both vegetarians and meat-eaters.

Not everything in Fort Collins is geared to student budgets and tastes. *Nico's Catacombs* (☎ 970-482-6426), 115 S College Ave, doesn't even allow shorts in the dining room! This winner of a *Wine Spectator* award for excellence offers dishes ranging from shrimp parmesan over fettuccine to Dover sole with shrimp, capers, mushrooms and white wine sauce. Dinner for two with wine will run around $50.

Still hungry for dessert? *Walrus Ice Cream* (☎ 970-482-5919), 125 W Mountain Ave, has so many tasty homemade flavors that your hardest task will be choosing. It's open Monday to Friday 11 am to 11 pm, with slightly shortened hours on weekends.

Entertainment

Look for a free copy of the monthly *Scene Magazine* for the latest schedule of arts and entertainment events in Fort Collins.

Pubs Despite of the nearby Busch Brewery and Coloradans' traditionally close affiliation with Coors, the per-capita consumption of microbrew beers in Fort Collins must set some kind of a record. Beer lovers spurn the mass-produced suds in favor of special labels and fruity flavors on tap at many pubs in town. One good example is *Coopersmith's Pub & Brewing* (☎ 970-498-0480), 5 Old Town Square, which offers either beer and pool, or beer

and food in two separate buildings. *Lucky Joe's Sidewalk Saloon* (☎ 970-493-2213), 25 Old Town Square, offers a hefty selection of beers plus live music on weekends and most weekdays.

For a change of pace, try *Elliott's Martini Bar* (☎ 970-472-9802), at 234 Linden. Some 38 different types of martinis are on offer here, ranging from $4 to $5.50 for a single (4 oz). Cigars and other cocktails are also available. The Art Deco decor and curved bar add to the atmosphere.

Music & Dancing *Linden's Brewing Company* has live music nightly and really gets hopping on the weekends. Nearby, the *Sunset Jazz Club* (☎ 970-484-4604), 242 Linden St, proves that 'smokefree' and 'jazz' need not be mutually exclusive. The *New York Cafe* (☎ 970-221-2443), 135 W Oak St, mainly books blues acts, stays open as late as state law allows and is also said to have excellent food. Those looking for a fix of Country & Western music can hit the *Sundance Steak House & Saloon* (☎ 970-484-1600), 2716 E Mulberry St.

About 25 miles west of Fort Collins in the Poudre River Canyon, the *Mishawaka Amphitheatre* (☎ 970-482-4420) can accommodate up to 1200 people to hear top performers like David Lindley, Bela Fleck, Hot Tuna and Leon Russell. Most summer shows (through October) are booked by June. The emphasis is on music rather than alcohol (a wise policy, given the 14 miles of winding Hwy 14), and food is served in the dining room cantilevered over the Poudre River (buffalo burgers are $7). The nearby USFS campgrounds cannot accommodate even a fraction of the concert-goers, so many camp on USFS land in Young's Gulch east of Mishawaka.

Theater *The Lincoln Center* (☎ 970-221-6730), 417 W Magnolia St, offers musicals, plays or symphony performances on most weekends and many weeknights.

Getting There & Away

Air The Fort Collins-Loveland Municipal Airport, southeast of Fort Collins at I-25 exit 259, is served by several daily commuter connections with Denver International Airport. Contact United Express (☎ 970-663-4614) for the latest schedule information.

DIA Shuttle The Airport Express (☎ 970-482-0505) provides hourly service between Denver International Airport and the local University Holiday Park hotel 4 am to 6 pm Monday to Friday. Departures leave every other hour on Saturday, and hourly service resumes on Sunday 5 am to 6 pm. The one-way fare is $15; for an additional $4 to $7 they'll pick you up at your door. Allow about 1½ hours travel time. Another operator, Shamrock Airport Shuttle (☎ 970-686-9999), offers similar service and rates.

Bus TNM&O/Greyhound and Powder River buses connect Fort Collins to Denver with around seven departures daily in either direction. Other destinations include Boulder, Greeley, and Cheyenne and Laramie, WY. The bus terminal (☎ 970-221-1327), 501 Riverside Ave, is open 7:30 am to 1 pm and 2 to 6 pm Monday to Friday, 9 am to 12:30 pm Saturday.

Car Fort Collins is 65 miles northwest of Denver via I-25, and 65 miles south of Laramie via US 287. The city center lies 4 miles west of I-25 (exit 269). Hwy 14 runs east-west through town, where it is known as Mulberry St.

Getting Around
To/From the Airport Shamrock Yellow Cab provides taxi service to the Fort Collins-Loveland Municipal Airport.

Bus Transfort (☎ 970-221-6620) operates buses on nine routes 6:30 am to 6:30 pm weekdays and Saturdays on some routes, particularly during CSU sessions. Maps are available in the phone book and at the Downtown/North Transit Center, Mason and Laporte Sts, or the CSU Transit Center west of the Morgan Library on University Ave. Adult fares are 90¢ and include transfer passes.

Car Cars are available from Econo Rate Rent-A-Car (☎ 970-221-2722), 505 Riverside Ave near the bus depot. In the south area of town near the Marriott, try Avis (☎ 970-229-9115), 344 East Foothills Parkway, and Enterprise (☎ 970-224-2592), 2100 S College Ave.

AROUND FORT COLLINS
Severance
Severence (population 227) is 7½ miles east of I-25 in Weld County, southeast of Fort Collins (exit 265, the Harmony exit). The wild plains bison may be gone but bulls from cattle herds continue to provide a bovine delicacy befitting the Rocky Mountains. *Bruce's* (☎ 970-686-2320) at 345 1st St in the middle of town, specializes in 'bull fries,' or Rocky Mountain Oysters, but squeamish diners may select from a menu of steaks and seafood. Live Country & Western music is performed on weekends.

One might assume the town name has something to do with cutting things off, but actually it was named for Dave Severance.

Red Feather Lakes
Secluded fishing lakes, good hiking and a Nordic recreation area attract year-round visitors to this forested area of the Lone Pine Creek drainage about 50 miles northwest of Fort Collins. Take US 287 north for 21 miles, turn left (west) at Livermore on Larimer County Rd 74E for 24 miles to Red Feather Lakes Ranger Station (☎ 970-881-2937), 274 Dowdy Lake Rd, which is operated by the Roosevelt National Forest. It's open 8:30 am to 5 pm Memorial Day to Labor Day only; in winter contact the USFS in Fort Collins for off-season information. Both offices provide trail maps and information on hiking, biking, cross-country skiing and camping.

About 8 miles from the junction of US 287 and County Rd 74E, on the north side, is the Lone Pine Cherokee Park unit trailhead, offering good single-track mountain biking and equestrian opportunities. It's a pretty trail and mostly moderate, though there are some steep sections and technical areas for bikers.

Pleasant, ambling hikes can be had along the Lone Pine Trail, which passes by North Bald Mountain and ascends Middle Bald Mountain. From the latter you can loop back along a jeep road to come out just west of the trailhead. Maps are available from the USFS. To get to the Lone Pine trailhead, follow 74E west for 6 miles. On the way 74E turns into Red Feather Lakes Rd, then Deadman Rd. If you finish your hike early, catch an even more scenic panorama of the Front Range and the Never Summer Ranges at Deadman Tower (10,710 feet), another 10 miles past the Lone Pine trailhead. Just continue on Deadman Rd to USFS Rd 170, then turn right. The tower is open 8:30 am to 4 pm.

Fishing and lakeside USFS campgrounds are available for $10 at *Dowdy Lake* and *West Lake* (☎ 877-444-6777 reservations). Both campgrounds operate May to September. About 9 miles west along 74E/ Deadman Rd, sites at the *North Fork Poudre Campground* cost $8. It's open June to November.

Nordic ski trails for all abilities offer one-hour to full-day loops at *Beaver Meadows Resort Ranch* (☎ 970-881-2450, 800-462-5870), open daily year-round. A daily ski pass costs $10 for adults and includes use of the ice rink and a snow tubing hill (inner tube provided); other equipment available for rental). Stables supplement the range of activities available here.

The resort also has lodge rooms from $49 and cabins from $86. Package deals including skiing and meals are also available. To get there from the Red Feather Lakes Ranger Station, take 74E west for about 2 miles and turn right (north) on County Rd 73C (gravel) for 5 miles to Beaver Meadows.

CACHE LA POUDRE RIVER

From the mouth of the Cache la Poudre River Canyon at Laporte – site of an Overland Stage Station in 1862 – to Walden 92 miles west, Hwy 14 travels through some of Colorado's most scenic country. Mule deer, elk and bighorn sheep inhabit many parts of the canyon and adjacent wilderness

The regal bighorn sheep

areas. The Wild & Scenic Rivers Act protects 75 miles of the Cache la Poudre River from new dams or diversions. Thirty miles of the river meet the highest standards and are designated as 'wild' for being free of dams and diversions and having undisturbed shorelines; the remaining 45-mile protected section is designated 'recreational.' White-water enthusiasts should check with experienced guide services or the USFS (see White-Water Rafting under Fort Collins) before putting into the river and finding unrunnable rapids, like the frothing Narrows, or a dam looming up ahead.

The village of **Rustic**, 32 miles west of the US 287-Hwy 14 junction, offers services and cabin lodging (see Places to Stay below). The USFS Visitors Center (☎ 970-881-2152), 34484 Poudre Canyon Rd in Rustic, occupies the handsome Arrowhead Lodge, built in 1935 and listed on the National Register of Historic Places. It's open 9 am to 5 pm daily in summer.

Stop at the self-service Cache la Poudre Visitor Information Center, 3 miles west of US 287 on Hwy 14, for information on wildlife viewing and fishing regulations. The Picnic Rock River Access opposite the visitors center offers riverside tables, but there is a $4 parking fee from April 15 to

September 15 on account of its popularity as a raft take-out point. Watch for bighorn sheep on the steep slopes along a 35-mile section of the north bank from Mishawaka to **Poudre Falls**, a series of picturesque roaring cascades. The USFS recently developed a particularly good bighorn sheep viewing site equipped with telescopes and explanatory plaques at **Big Bend**, 41 miles west of the US 287-Hwy 14 junction.

After Hwy 14 branches away from the river it ascends Cameron Pass (10,276 feet), where the stunning 12,485-foot **Nohku Crags** form the northernmost peaks of the Never Summer Range.

Fishing

Two sections of the Poudre River, a 10-mile stretch from Pingree Park Rd upstream to the Hombre Ranch west of Rustic and another section between Black Hollow Creek and Big Bend, are specially managed wild trout waters. Catches are limited to two fish over 16 inches long per person, and anglers are required to use artificial flies and lures. The remaining sections are stocked with rainbow trout.

A few nearby lakes offer unique fishing for distinctive species. Mackinaw up to 20 pounds can be taken in **Chambers Lake** 53 miles up the canyon. You will have to hike about 6 miles to fish for wild brook trout at **Browns Lake** in the Comanche Wilderness. In 1951, a wild early summer-spawning rainbow species (like Arctic grayling), called emerald lake rainbow, was introduced to Zimmerman Lake near Cameron Pass on the border of the Neota Wilderness.

Hiking & Backpacking

Many backcountry activities in the Cache la Poudre, Comanche Peak, Neota and Rawah wilderness areas can be accessed via trailheads from the Poudre River. Trails from the Comanche Wilderness lead into Rocky Mountain National Park. The USFS pamphlet 'Cache La Poudre – A Wild & Scenic River' has a map showing the various trailheads and campsites along the

river. The USFS Fort Collins office can also provide more detailed info on hiking trails.

Nine miles from the US 287-Hwy 14 junction, the **Greyrock National Recreation Trail** climbs about 2000 feet to the summit of Greyrock Mountain, offering spectacular views of the Front Range. From the trailhead 3 winding miles west of the filtration plant at the North Fork, you can choose either a 3½-mile up-and-back route, or add a 2-mile loop through adjoining Greyrock Meadow.

At the other extreme, just east of Cameron Pass, hikers start at an elevation of 9500 feet and continue 5 miles along USFS Trail 959 through sub-Alpine forests to Alpine **Blue Lake** (10,800 feet) in the extensive Rawah Wilderness. The trailhead begins 55 miles west of US 287 on the north side of Hwy 14, opposite the turnoff to Long Draw Reservoir and Rocky Mountain National Park.

Places to Stay

Camping The USFS operates around a dozen primitive campgrounds (pit toilets, no showers) along Hwy 14. All are available on a first-come, first-served basis, except for *Chambers Lake* and *Mountain Park* (☎ 877-444-6777 reservations). The campgrounds are often full in summer, so try and get in early. The USFS *Tom Bennett Campground*, south of of the Poudre Canyon on Larimer Country Rd 63E, is a popular staging point for Comanche Peak Wilderness users. Listed below are the USFS Poudre Canyon campgrounds in order of distance in miles (west) from US 287:

Campground	Miles	Fee	No of Sites
Ansel Watrous	13	$9	19
Stove Prairie	17	$10	9
Narrows	21	$6	9
Mountain Park	22	$12	55
Kelly Flats	26	$9	23
Big Bend	41	$9	6
Sleeping Elephant	45	$9	15
Big South	50	$7	4
Aspen Glen	51	$8	8
Chambers Lake	53	$12	52

The *North Park KOA* (☎ 970-723-4310) at Gould on Hwy 14 72 miles west of US 287 and 20 miles southeast of Walden, offers wooded tent sites for $14 and fresh-baked cinnamon rolls every morning.

Around the area of Gould are also a number of campgrounds run by the Colorado State Forest. Access to the state forest costs $4 per day, and a camping pass is an additional $6.

Cabins Most accommodation is grouped around Rustic. The *Rustic Resort* (☎ 970-881-2179), 31443 Poudre Canyon Rd, has cabins on the river ranging from $45 to $75, tent sites for $9 and RV sites for $13.50. There is a decent restaurant here as well. A bit farther west is the *Poudre River Resort* (☎ 970-881-2139), 33021 Poudre Canyon Rd. One-bedroom cabins are $65, two-bedroom units are $85. There are more cabin operations farther west along the river, all with similar conditions and prices.

Yurts Never Summer Nordic (☎ 970-482-9411) operates a system of Mongolian style yurts, circular tents with an inner frame, within the Colorado State Forest. Each yurt is sited to act as a base for mountain biking, hiking, climbing or fishing in the beautiful Never Summer wilderness, and amenities include a wood-burning stove, a complete kitchen and padded bunks. Visitors supply their own food and sleeping bags. Three of the four yurts sleep six people; one sleeps 10. Getting to most of them requires a hike of a least 1½ miles. There are also trails linking the yurts, allowing you to plan a backcountry excursion. Summer rates for six-person yurts are $49 weekdays, $59 weekends; in winter prices rise to $89/99. Reservations are advised. For more information, write to Never Summer Nordic, PO Box 1983, Fort Collins, CO 80522. Access to the yurts is off of Hwy 14, about 72 miles west of US 287, not far from the North Park KOA Campground.

ARAPAHO NATIONAL WILDLIFE REFUGE

Nearly 200 species of birds frequent the summer sagebrush and wetlands of the USFWS' Arapaho National Wildlife Refuge, 105 miles west of Fort Collins by the Cache la Poudre-North Park Scenic Byway (Hwy 14). The star of the show is the sage grouse and its spring mating ritual, the lek.

Organized Tours

In April, Sage Grouse Tours (☎ 970-723-4600) brings people to view the ritual. There's a self-guided auto tour pamphlet available; look for information at the North Park Chamber of Commerce in Walden (☎ 970-723-4600), 517 Main St, open Monday to Saturday 9 am to 5 pm. You can also contact the Refuge Manager (☎ 970-723-8202), PO Box 457, Walden, CO 80480. Refuge Headquarters is 8 miles south of Hwy 14 via Hwy 125, then 1 mile east on Jackson County Rd 32.

If you are visiting the refuge or its surrounding backcountry, Walden is the nearest town of note. North-south Main St is the principal thoroughfare and business district in Walden, and nearly all the town's motels and restaurants can be found here.

Sage grouse, star of the Arapaho.

Big Thompson Canyon

On July 31, 1976, following a four-hour deluge that dumped 12 inches of water in the upper basin around Estes Park, raging waters from the Big Thompson Canyon swept 145 people to their deaths. The torrential waters scoured narrow stretches of the canyon floor, destroying businesses and homes. US 34 became history. Emergency crews recovered victims from the broad floodplain nearly 23 miles southwest beyond the canyon near Longmont. The subsequent reconstruction of the area is an example of stalwart Western resolve. ■

A good detailed Jackson County road map is available for 50¢ at the North Park Chamber of Commerce.

The USFS Routt National Forest North Park Ranger Station (☎ 970-723-8204), 100 Main St, occupies a brand-new building at the north end of town. It's open 7:30 am to 4:30 pm Monday to Friday and has detailed trail information for hikes and biking in the Routt National Forest, including the eastern side of the Mt Zirkel wilderness. National forest maps are available for $4.

ESTES PARK

The eastern gateway to Rocky Mountain National Park, Estes Park depends on a steady flow of tourists for its economic survival. The town's year-round population of just over 3990 explodes to between 25,000 and 30,000 on any given summer weekend.

The flood of tourism supports countless motels, craft shops, kitschy souvenir stores and restaurants. Visitors expecting immediate views of the pristine beauty of Rocky Mountain National Park may be disappointed to find themselves in bumper-to-bumper traffic on E Elkhorn Ave, the town's artery to both park entrances. However, there are ways to bypass this tourist traverse (see Orientation below).

While most people in Estes Park are quite friendly, some definitely look down on tourists, adopting a stark 'us versus them' mentality. The occasional bumper sticker proclaims, 'Don't bother me, I'm a local.'

On the other hand, Estes Park has a certain charm, especially in the off-season, and has nearly any convenience or service a traveler might need. The soaring peaks that form the town's backdrop also help make up for the mundane spread of motels and mini shopping malls.

Orientation

Estes Park occupies the valley at the confluence of the Big Thompson and Fall rivers, just a few miles east of Rocky Mountain National Park. US 36 follows the Big Thompson River out of town to park headquarters and the Beaver Meadows Entrance Station; US 34 leads upstream to the Fall River Entrance Station. South of town, Hwy 7 provides access to the national park at Lily Lake, Twin Sisters Peaks, Long's Peak and Wild Basin. To the north, MacGregor Ave leads to the historic MacGregor Ranch (see Rocky Mountain National Park later in this chapter) and the national park's Lumpy Ridge hiking and climbing area.

Elkhorn Ave (US 34), the congested main street, is divided at Moraine Ave (US 36) into E Elkhorn (US 34/US 36) and W Elkhorn (US 34) addresses. East of the intersection with Wonderview Ave and US 36, US 34 is also called Big Thompson Ave. To avoid Elkhorn Ave traffic on your way to the park, take either the US 34 bypass that turns toward the landmark Stanley Hotel just off Wonderview Ave, or from Hwy 7 turn west at Mary's Lake Rd to the Beaver Meadows park entrance.

Information

Tourist Offices The Estes Park Visitors Center (☎ 970-586-4431, 800-443-7837), 500 Big Thompson Ave (US 34) just east of the US 36 junction, is accommodations central with a large lighted switchboard identifying any available rooms in town. The staff have phones to help you contact lodgings, but most are booked throughout

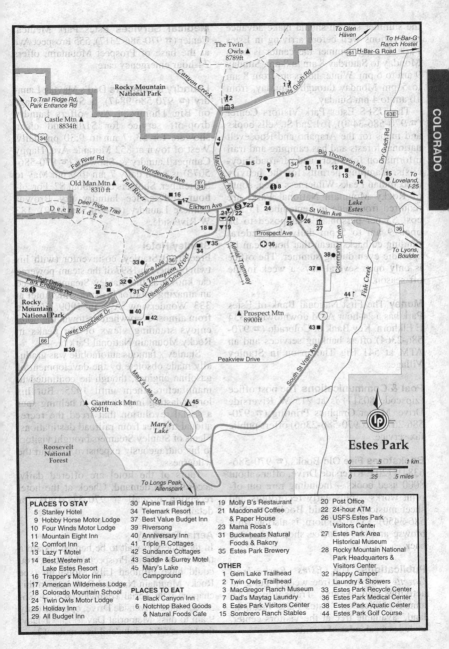

Estes Park

0   .5   1 km

0   .25   .5 miles

PLACES TO STAY
5 Stanley Hotel
9 Hobby Horse Motor Lodge
10 Four Winds Motor Lodge
11 Mountain Eight Inn
12 Comfort Inn
13 Lazy T Motel
14 Best Western at
    Lake Estes Resort
16 Trapper's Motor Inn
17 American Wilderness Lodge
18 Colorado Mountain School
24 Twin Owls Motor Lodge
25 Holiday Inn
29 All Budget Inn

30 Alpine Trail Ridge Inn
34 Telemark Resort
37 Best Value Budget Inn
39 Riversong
40 Anniversary Inn
41 Triple R Cottages
42 Sundance Cottages
43 Saddle & Surrey Motel
45 Mary's Lake
    Campground

PLACES TO EAT
4 Black Canyon Inn
6 Notchtop Baked Goods
    & Natural Foods Cafe

19 Molly B's Restaurant
21 Macdonald Coffee
    & Paper House
23 Mama Rosa's
31 Buckwheats Natural
    Foods & Bakory
35 Estes Park Brewery

OTHER
1 Gem Lake Trailhead
2 Twin Owls Trailhead
3 MacGregor Ranch Museum
7 Dad's Maytag Laundry
8 Estes Park Visitors Center
15 Sombrero Ranch Stables

20 Post Office
22 24-hour ATM
26 USFS Estes Park
    Visitors Center
27 Estes Park Area
    Historical Museum
28 Rocky Mountain National
    Park Headquarters &
    Visitors Center
32 Happy Camper
    Laundry & Showers
33 Estes Park Recycle Center
36 Estes Park Medical Center
38 Estes Park Aquatic Center
44 Estes Park Golf Course

the summer so you should make advance reservations well before arriving in Estes Park. During summer the center is open Monday to Saturday 8 am to 8 pm, Sunday 9 am to 6 pm. Winter hours are from 8 am to 5 pm Monday through Saturday, from 10 am to 4 pm Sunday.

The USFS Estes Park Visitors Center (☎ 970-586-3440), 161 2nd St, sells books and maps for the Arapaho and Roosevelt national forests and has camping and trail information for hikers and off-road bicyclists. Camping permits for the heavily used Indian Peaks Wilderness Area, south of Rocky Mountain National Park, are required from June to September 15 and cost $5 per person. It's supposed to be open 9 am to 5 pm daily, but federal funding cutbacks mean that hours can be sporadic even during summer. The office is only open several days a week in the off-season.

Money The First National Bank of Estes Park has a 24-hour ATM downtown at 334 E Elkhorn. Key Bank of Colorado (☎ 970-586-2364) offers banking services and an ATM at 541 Big Thompson in Stanley Village.

Post & Communications The post office (zip code 80517) is at 215 W Riverside Drive. Master Graphics Printing (☎ 970-586-2679; fax 970-586-2366) offers public fax service.

Bookstores Fine Old Books (☎ 970-586-6384), 120 E Riverside Drive, offers about 8000 used books – including rare out-of-print works – plus early recordings and sheet music. MacDonald Books (☎ 970-586-3450), 152 E Elkhorn, is also worth a browse and has a coffee shop annex out back.

Publications The *Estes Park Trail Gazette* publishes a free weekly guide to activities and events, 'Trails Plus.' An annual publication, 'Estes Park Vacationland,' available free at the visitors center, includes a calendar of events.

Medical Services Estes Park Medical Center (☎ 970-586-2317), 555 Prospect Ave at the base of Prospect Mountain, offers 24-hour emergency care.

Laundry & Showers Dad's Maytag Laundry (☎ 970-586-9847), in Stanley Village on Big Thompson Ave, offers laundry drop-off service for $1/lb and clean showers for $3, 7 am to 9:30 pm daily. West of town at 852 Moraine Ave, Happy Camper Laundry & Showers (☎ 970-586-5073) is open daily 7 am to 9 pm May to September. Showers cost about $2. For 24-hour self-service laundry, try Browns Chinese Laundry (☎ 970-586-6122), 183 W Riverside.

Stanley Hotel

Freelan O Stanley, co-inventor (with his twin brother) in 1897 of the steam-powered car known as the Stanley Steamer, picked an amazing spot for his sprawling hotel at 333 Wonderview Ave in 1909. Visible from almost everywhere in town, the hotel enjoys stunning views of the peaks in Rocky Mountain National Park.

Stanley's famous automobile was gradually made obsolete by the development of gasoline engines, though he continued to manufacture them until 1925. But his longer-lasting impact was in helping spur a social revolution that freed the recreational traveler from railroad destinations. Fleets of Stanley Steamers brought visitors to his outrageously expensive hotel in the wilderness.

Tours of the hotel are offered daily, according to demand. Check at the hotel reception or call ☎ 970-577-1903 for details.

Aerial Tramway

In the time you wait to be herded aboard a tram to the top of Prospect Mountain, you could have climbed Lily Mountain (see Rocky Mountain National Park in this chapter). The Aerial Tramway (☎ 970-586-3675), 420 E Riverside Drive, operates daily 9 am to dusk Memorial Day to Labor Day; the fare is $8/4 adults/children under 12.

COLORADO

Mountain Biking

The USFS Crosier Mountain Trail, a strenuous loop through beautiful meadows near Glen Haven, comes highly recommended by locals. Another favorite is the combination of USFS Pierson Park Rd and Lion Gulch Trail in the vicinity of Homestead Meadows south of Estes Park. Pick up maps and information from the USFS Estes Park Visitors Center. Colorado Bicycling (☎ 970-586-4241), 184 E Elkhorn Ave, rents bikes for $21/28/40 standard/single/dual suspension and can also help with tips on trails in the area.

Golf

Two courses are available: the Estes Park Golf Course (☎ 970-586-8146) offers an 18-hole course at 1080 S St Vrain Ave; or try the nine-hole Lake Estes Executive Golf Club (☎ 970-586-8176 at 690 Big Thompson Ave.

Long's Peak Scottish-Irish Festival

The Long's Peak Scottish-Irish Festival (☎ 970-586-6308 for tickets or information) includes four days of Celtic activities at the fairgrounds in early September. A two-day weekend pass or ticket packages for shows and pub nights cost around $49.

Places to Stay

With the exception of the H-Bar-G Ranch Hostel, expect all lodgings to be filled during the peak July and August period. Do not travel west of Greeley without a reservation during the summer. Off-season rates may be up to one-half summer prices, and many accommodations simply close for the winter. Most of the cheaper motels (which still aren't that cheap) are located east of town along US 34 or Hwy 7.

Camping Tent sites/RV hookups are $19/21 for two persons at the *Estes Park KOA* (☎ 970-586-2888), 1 mile east of Estes Park. *National Park Resort* (☎ 970-586-4563), 3501 Fall River Rd near the Fall River Park Entrance, has wooded tent sites and RV hookups at similar rates. *Mary's Lake Campground* (☎ 970-586-

4411), 2120 Mary's Lake Rd, offers 40 tent sites for $19 for two people as well as RV spaces for $24. Five miles southeast of Estes Park at the end of Hwy 66, near the boundary of Rocky Mountain National Park, *Estes Park Campground* (☎ 970-586-4188) caters to tent campers for $17 for two people per site.

Hostels For more than 25 years Lou Livingston has operated the *H-Bar-G Ranch Hostel* (☎ 970-586-3688; no calls after 9 pm) at 3500 H-Bar-G Rd. The main three-story lodge, built in 1901, offers superb uncluttered views of the Divide – as do most of the cabin porches. Lou runs a tight ship, and his operation has gotten good reviews from travelers. Lodgings are available to HI/AYH members only, but membership cards are available at the hostel for $25. Simple accommodations cost $9 with your own bedding and include access to the common kitchen.

The hostel is open late May to early September. Lou provides free daily shuttle transport from the Estes Park Visitors Center at 5 pm and leaves the hostel to return guests the following morning at 7:40 am. Look for the olive-green army surplus truck. The hostel is 5½ miles north of the visitors center. To get there on your own, travel east on US 34, turn left (north) at the stables on Dry Gulch Rd to the gravel H-Bar-G Rd (Hwy 61) then right (east) to the gate on your right. During the summer there are signs on Dry Gulch Rd to guide you.

Perhaps the best lodging deal in Estes Park is the *Colorado Mountain School* (☎ 970-586-5758), 351 Moraine Ave, close to both the park and town center. Beds with full linen, soap and towels in comfortable, sparkling clean dorm rooms are $20. The price goes down for larger parties: $17 per person for two, $14 for three and over. There's lockable storage and the staff is quite helpful and friendly. The only drawback is when large climbing parties take up the limited number of beds, but the owners are planning to add more beds as well as kitchen facilities.

B&Bs South of Estes Park near Lily Lake at 4900 Hwy 7, the *Baldpate Inn* (☎ 970-586-6181) is a unique lodge and restaurant with 12 modest rooms. Singles or doubles with shared bath cost $70, $85 with private bath, including full breakfast. Built in 1917, the comfortable inn features a rustic, 2nd-story verandah and handmade lodge-pole pine furniture. Guests with bicycles are welcome and the knowledgable staff can offer local trail tips.

Tucked down a dead-end dirt road overlooking the Big Thompson River, the *Riversong* (☎ 970-586-4666) offers nine rooms with private bath in a Craftsman-style mansion for $135 to $250 depending on the room's furnishings and amenities like spa tubs. The minimum stay is two nights. The Riversong is at the end of Lower Broadview Drive; west of town take Moraine Ave, turn onto Mary's Lake Rd then take the first right.

In the same section of town, the *Anniversary Inn* (☎ 970-586-6200), 1060 Mary's Lake Rd, is an 1890s log house with four rooms, each with private bath, ranging from $90 to $140.

Motels Estes Park has more than 40 motels to choose from. There aren't any real bargains, especially during summer. One of the least expensive places is *Lazy T Motel* (☎ 970-586-4376), 1340 Big Thompson Ave. Though not exciting, it has all the amenities, even a pool and sauna! Rooms range from $40 to $65.

Most of the town's motels are remarkably similar: shag carpet and fairly small rooms with television and refrigerator, though some places also boast pools, hot tubs and saunas. Following is a selection of mid-range offerings; rates quoted are for double occupancy during peak season.

All Budget Inn, 945 Moraine Ave (☎ 970-586-3485), $75 to $95, kitchens

Alpine Trail Ridge Inn, 927 Moraine Ave (☎ 970-586-4585), $66 to 86, swimming pool, kitchens

Best Value Budget Inn, 760 S St Vrain (☎ 970-586-4451), $60 to $75, swimming pool, kitchens

Comfort Inn, 1450 Big Thompson Ave (☎ 970-586-2358), $59 to $75, swimming pool, hot tub

Four Winds Motor Lodge, 1120 Big Thompson Ave (☎ 970-586-3313), from $49, swimming pool, hot tub, sauna, kitchens

Hobby Horse Motor Lodge, 800 Big Thompson Ave (☎ 970-586-3336), $60 to $80, swimming pool

Mountain Eight Inn, 1220 Big Thompson Ave (☎ 970-586-4421), $60, swimming pool

Saddle & Surrey Motel, 1341 So St Vrain (☎ 970-586-3326), $60, swimming pool, hot tub, kitchens

Trapper's Motor Inn, 553 W Elkhorn Ave (☎ 970-586-2833), from $46

Twin Owls Motor Lodge, 700 St Vrain Ave (☎ 970-586-4471, $49 to $82, swimming pool

The *Best Western at Lake Estes Resort* (☎ 970-586-3386), 1650 Big Thompson Ave, is simply a single-story motel with a pretentious name. With standard rooms going for $95/110, it's not a great deal. Similarly, the *Holiday Inn* (☎ 970-586-2332, 800-465-4329), 101 S St Vrain Ave at US 36 and Hwy 7, asks at least $100 per room in the summer. It was remodeled in 1996 and has a pool, fitness room and whirlpool, but for the money you're probably better off at a B&B. Still, if everything else is full, try asking here after 10 pm for canceled reservations.

American Wilderness Lodge (☎ 970-586-4403), 481 W Elkhorn Ave, offers better value with nicely appointed rooms from $80. It's walking distance from the town center and includes amenities such as fireplaces, kitchens, sauna, Jacuzzi and an indoor pool.

Cottages Though the facilities can sometimes be basic, cottages generally offer more scenic locations and privacy than motels and are often cheaper as well. One-room cottages cost $45 and larger cabins accommodating four persons are $59 at *Triple R Cottages* (☎ 970-586-5552), 1000 Riverside Drive. Next door, *Sundance Cottages* (☎ 970-586-3922), 960 Riverside Drive, features rustic log exteriors and cable TV; prices range from $65 to $110 for a three-bedroom unit. *Telemark Resort* (☎ 970-586-4343), 650 Moraine Ave, has two-person cottages from $50, most of which are located on the Big Thompson River.

Knotty-pine interiors, full kitchens and a riverside hot tub are among the features of the cabins at *Blackhawk Lodges* (☎ 970-586-6100), 1750 Fall River Rd; prices start at $90. On the boundary of Rocky Mountain National Park, *Glacier Lodge* (☎ 970-586-4401), 2166 Hwy 66, is a lodge/conference center with over 20 meticulously maintained cottages spread over 15 acres. Rates range from $105 to $125.

Hotels The best thing about the landmark *Stanley Hotel* (☎ 800-762-5437), 333 Wonderview Ave, is without doubt the stunning mountain views it commands. Management seemed a bit chaotic when we last visited, perhaps in part due to renovation work that was underway. Things may improve but try and check it out first: with room rates ranging from $159 to $199, you shouldn't settle for anything less than perfection.

Long-Term Rentals Real estate management companies offer cabins and condominiums starting at $400/week for a riverside condo. For weekly or monthly rentals contact Rocky Mountain Realty Company (☎ 970-586-5324, 800-827-8780); Coldwell Banker (☎ 970-586-4425, 800-726-1405); Range Realty (☎ 970-586-2345, 800-748-2433); or Ponderosa Realty (☎ 970-586-3331, 800-324-4149).

Places to Eat
Like lodgings, restaurants in Estes Park often shift to shorter hours, close for several days of the week or shut down all together in the off-season. If you're visiting between September and May it's wise to call ahead.

One of the best spots in town for tasty and healthy food is *Notchtop Baked Goods & Natural Foods Cafe* (☎ 970-586-0272) in Stanley Village. The bread and pastries are delicious and the kitchen also dishes up fine lunches and dinners, including salmon-veggie stir-fry ($11) and the tofu-veggie variation ($8). It's open 7 am to 9 pm most of the year. Just a few doors down, late-risers can try *Mountain Home Cafe* (☎ 970-586-6624), which serves breakfast 7 am to 2 pm.

On the Riverwalk at 152 E Elkhorn, *MacDonald Coffee & Paper House* (☎ 970-586-3450) offers topo maps and guidebooks to examine while you sip a cappuccino. A good place to stock up on trail foods or get freshly made cinnamon rolls, muffins and healthy sandwiches is *Buckwheats Natural Foods & Bakery* (☎ 970-586-5658), 870 Moraine Ave.

Estes Park Brewery (☎ 970-586-5421), 470 E Riverside, serves up some fairly good beers along with its own 'brewery pizza.' Pool tables and a big deck make this a fun spot to go for a snack and a beer.

Despite the 7-mile journey south of Estes Park, a meal at the *Baldpate Inn* (☎ 970-586-6151), 4900 S Hwy 7, is worthwhile. The $10 soup-and-salad buffet is quite good. Customers enjoy outstanding views from the classic lodge dining room furnished with handmade hickory chairs.

Mama Rosa's (☎ 970-586-3330), 338 E Elkhorn Ave, offers outdoor seating and an attentive staff serving family-style Italian lunches and dinners daily. The $9 all-you-can-eat pasta dinner special is a good value, though the food is nothing special. Pasta dishes starting at $9 are also available at *Gazebo Restaurant & Tavern* (☎ 970-586-9564), 225 Park Lane, along with salads and vegetable dishes. Among the wide selection of more expensive entrees offered for lunch and dinner is Khyber chicken or beef, marinated overnight in yogurt and spices.

Molly B's Restaurant (☎ 970-586-2766), 200 Moraine Ave, has hearty, reasonably priced dishes for both vegetarians and carnivores; during summer it's open 6:30 am to 10 pm.

For top-end dining, make a reservation at *Black Canyon Inn* (☎ 970-586-9344), north of town at 800 MacGregor Ave. They specialize in fresh seafood and Italian dishes;

most dinner entrees are priced over $20. The restaurant is closed Mondays.

Entertainment

The *Stanley Hotel* (☎ 970-586-3371) offers summer theater performances, Big Band music and orchestral concerts. Admission generally ranges from $10 to $20. The schedule changes yearly, so check with the hotel.

Getting There & Away

To/From the Airport From Denver International Airport, Charles Tour & Travel Services (☎ 970-586-5151, 800-950-3274) provides six to eight shuttles daily to Estes Park during summer months for $28 one-way. Frequency falls to three trips daily during the off-season.

Bus Hostel Hauler offers an Estes Park-Boulder shuttle service for $15/20 one-way/roundtrip. The eight-passenger van leaves the H-Bar-G Ranch Hostel at 8 am daily. It leaves Boulder at about 10 am, picking up customers at the Boulder hostel and the bus station, offering drop-offs at Bear Lake Trailhead in Rocky Mountain National Park, at Estes Park Visitors Center or at the H-Bar-G Hostel. Call Lou (☎ 970-586-3688) at the H-Bar-G for information. The Hauler runs until late October; after the hostel has closed down for the season call ☎ 303-378-5677 for information.

Car Estes Park is 34 miles west of Loveland via US 34, which you can access from I-25 (exit 257). Many visitors also come up by way of Boulder along US 36, passing through Lyons. A slower but more scenic route is the spectacular Peak to Peak Hwy, which comprises Hwys 72 and 7 and runs north from Nederland to Estes Park. (See Peak to Peak Hwy in the Denver & Boulder chapter.)

Getting Around

Car Raines Motor Company (☎ 970-586-3319), 1211 Woodstock Ave, operates as a Dollar Rent-A-Car outlet.

Taxi Charles Limousine (☎ 970-586-5151) provides taxi service in town and tours of Rocky Mountain National Park.

Bicycle This is a great way to get around the area, though few visitors seem to use this mode of transport (of course the altitude does make for some huffing and puffing). Mountain bikes can be rented from Colorado Bicycle (☎ 970-586-4241), 184 E Elkhorn Ave. Rates are $21/28/40 standard/single/dual suspension.

AROUND ESTES PARK
Enos Mills' Cabin

Enos Mills (1870-1922), a naturalist who led the struggle to establish Rocky Mountain National Park, undoubtedly succeeded due to his infectious enthusiasm and willingness to share nature information. His daughter Enda Mills Kiley continues to share the incredible history of her father with visitors to his tiny cabin, built in 1885. The Mills family maintains an interpretive nature trail leading from the parking lot to the cabin, where news clippings and photographs recount Mills' advocacy to protect nature.

Reprints and vintage copies of many of Mills' books are available for sale at the cabin, in addition to an outstanding collection of his writings edited by Enda Mills Kiley, *Adventures of a Nature Guide* (New Past Press, 1990).

The Enos Mills' Cabin (☎ 970-586-4706), 10 miles south of Estes Park on Hwy 7, is open daily 10 am to 5 pm Memorial Day to Labor Day. Admission is free.

MacGregor Ranch Museum

In 1872 AQ and Clara MacGregor arrived in Estes Park and settled beside Black Canyon Creek near Lumpy Ridge. Their granddaughter Murial MacGregor bequeathed the ranch as an educational trust upon her death in 1970.

The MacGregor Ranch, 1 mile north of Estes Park on Devils Gulch Rd, is a living museum featuring original living and working quarters; the ranch still raises Black Angus cattle. An NPS scenic and conservation easement helps fund the operation (admission is free) and provides trail access to Lumpy Ridge. It's open daily 9 am to 6:30 pm mid-May to mid-September.

Glen Haven
The North Fork of the Big Thompson River flows through Glen Haven, 7 miles east of Estes Park on Devils Gulch Rd. Another scenic approach follows the narrow canyon road for 8 miles northwest from US 34 at Drake, site of the North Fork's confluence with the main channel in Big Thompson Canyon. Handsome picnic grounds at Glen Haven on the narrow banks of the tumbling North Fork beckon travelers to stop. If you forgot to pack a lunch, drop in at the Glen Haven General Store, open daily in summer 9 am to 6 pm, for baked goods and deli items. In winter they're open 'from 9 am to whenever we feel like it!'

The prime attraction, however, is *The Inn at Glen Haven* (☎ 970-586-3897), an effete lair of the English gentry, offering B&B rooms and fine dining. The six top-end rooms cost between $77 (shared bath) and $115 – comments in the guest book about the individually furnished rooms were unanimous in their praise. From May to October, plus winter weekends, the restaurant, open nightly 5:30 to 9:30 pm (closed Tuesday), offers dinner entrees from $17 to $28; steak Escoffier is the most expensive selection.

Rocky Mountain National Park

Rocky Mountain National Park exemplifies the dual – and often conflicting – purposes Congress intended when it established the park in 1915 to promote recreational use while protecting the natural environment for future generations. Federal action to perpetually reserve the park's more than 400 sq miles of scenic wilderness admirably succeeded in replenishing previously decimated populations of elk, bighorn sheep, moose and beaver. Recent efforts have begun to reestablish native greenback and cutthroat trout in 50 of the park's 147 lakes. The NPS has also succeeded at promoting public recreation – almost too well. Some 3 million visitors enter the park each year – many attracted solely to the park's crowded Trail Ridge Rd through spectacular Alpine tundra environments. However, you don't have to hike or camp with everyone else: those who venture on foot in areas away from the road corridor will be rewarded with superlative scenery and wildlife viewing, and even solitude.

HISTORY
Members of the Ute tribe were once numerous throughout Middle Park but they avoided Grand Lake because of its spirits. Legend is that Arapahos and Cheyennes attacked a Ute camp next to Grand Lake, killing many warriors. Before the legendary battle, Ute women and children were placed on a raft and sent out on the lake for safety, but a fierce wind overturned the raft and all aboard drowned. The tale reflects the tragic history of the Arapaho and Cheyenne. After losing their plains hunting grounds to pioneer advances, members of the two tribes were driven into the mountains where they were notorious for their raids on Ute horses grazing in the meadows.

In 1819, Major Stephen H Long's government exploration party on the S Platte River noted 'a high peake was plainly to be distinguished towering above all the others…' but they continued south without entering the area of his namesake summit. Joel Estes arrived with his family in 1860, but left after six years and his cabin was converted to lodge visitors, primarily hunters.

Using hired hands to make fraudulent claims on 160-acre homesteads in his behalf, English earl Lord Dunraven assembled a private hunting estate covering 23½ sq miles of land within a few years of his arrival in 1873. World-famous landscape artist Albert Bierstadt painted *Estes Park* in 1877 and reportedly selected the site for Dunraven to build a hotel.

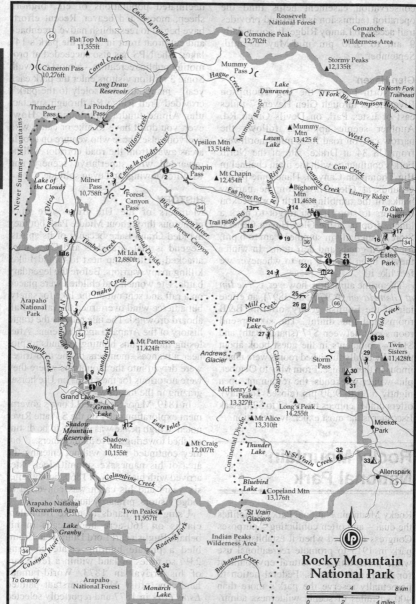

Rocky Mountain National Park

Roosevelt National Forest

Comanche Peak Wilderness Area

Arapaho National Forest

Arapaho National Park

Arapaho National Recreation Area

Indian Peaks Wilderness Area

Flat Top Mtn 11,355ft

Cameron Pass 10,276ft

Comanche Peak 12,702ft

Stormy Peaks 12,135ft

Mummy Pass

Lake Dunraven

To North Fork Trailhead

N Fork Big Thompson River

Long Draw Reservoir

Thunder Pass

La Poudre Pass

Lawn Lake

Mummy Mtn 13,425 ft

West Creek

Lake of the Clouds

Milner Pass 10,758ft

Ypsilon Mtn 13,514ft

Chapin Pass

Mt Chapin 12,454ft

Cow Creek

Lumpy Ridge

To Glen Haven

Forest Canyon Pass

Fall River Rd

Bighorn Mtn 11,463ft

Grand Ditch

Mt Ida 12,880ft

Timber Creek

Trail Ridge Rd

Forest Canyon

Estes Park

Onahu Creek

Mt Patterson 11,424ft

Bear Lake

Twin Sisters 11,428ft

Supply Creek

Andrews Glacier

Storm Pass

Grand Lake

McHenry's Peak 13,327ft

Long's Peak 14,255ft

Glacier Gorge

Meeker Park

Shadow Mountain Reservoir

East Inlet

Mt Alice 13,310ft

Thunder Lake

Allenspark

Shadow Mtn 10,155ft

Mt Craig 12,007ft

N St Vrain Creek

Columbine Creek

Bluebird Lake

Copeland Mtn 13,176ft

Lake Granby

Twin Peaks 11,957ft

St Vrain Glaciers

Roaring Fork

Indian Peaks Wilderness Area

Buchanan Creek

To Granby

Arapaho National Forest

Monarch Lake

0   4   8km
0   2   4 miles

1	Lulu City Ruins	12	East Inlet Trailhead	24	Fern Lake Trailhead
2	Alpine Visitors Center	13	Endovalley Picnic Area	25	Hollowell Park
3	Crater Trailhead	14	Lawn Lake Trailhead	26	Bear Lake Shuttle Bus Parking
4	Colorado River Trailhead	15	Fall River Entrance Station	27	Bear Lake/Glacier Gorge Trailhead
5	Timber Creek Campground	16	Twin Owls Trailhead		
6	Never Summer Ranch	17	Gem Lake Trailhead	28	Lily Lake Visitors Center
7	Onahu Creek Trailhead	18	Hidden Valley Picnic Area	29	Twin Sisters Trailhead
8	Green Mountain Trailhead	19	Many Parks Curve	30	Long's Peak Tent Campground
9	Grand Lake Entrance Station	20	Beaver Meadows Entrance Station	31	Long's Peak Ranger Station
10	Kawuneeche Visitors Center	21	Park Headquarters/Visitors Center	32	Wild Basin Ranger Station
11	Tonahutu/North Inlet Trailheads	22	Moraine Park Museum	33	Olive Ridge Campground
		23	Moraine Park Campground	34	Arapaho Bay Campground

COLORADO

Construction of the hotel and road building into the park prompted Enos Mills to begin his campaign in 1909 to protect the area from 'unrestricted tourist development' as the Estes National Park and Game Preserve. In his own words, 'for six years there was not a day that I failed to work or plan for it.' Mills' allies in advocacy included John Muir, the great naturalist of the Sierra Nevada; J Horace McFarland, President of the American Civic Association; and George Horace Lorimer of the *Saturday Evening Post*. Strong opposition to the plan came from private grazing and timber interests. Mills noted that the USFS was a particular foe to the formation of national parks.

After devoting years to the campaign, Mills emerged victorious when Congress approved the bill creating Rocky Mountain National Park in early 1915. To reach the celebration and tribute to Mills held on January, 26, 1915, attendees from the west side of the newly created park arrived in Estes Park after hiking across the Continental Divide in snowshoes.

Workers completed Fall River Rd over the Divide in 1920, and the Trail Ridge Rd opened in 1932 to provide an alternative route traversing 10 miles of treeless Alpine tundra.

GEOGRAPHY & GEOLOGY
The Rocky Mountain's spine cleaves its namesake park from north to south only 25 miles from the Eastern Great Plains.

Dozens of peaks over 12,000 feet still support small relict glaciers. Long's Peak is the highest peak in the park – its 14,256-foot crest acts as a sentinel to travelers on the plains. West of the Continental Divide, the Colorado River begins its southwestward journey to the Gulf of California while the headwaters of the Cache la Poudre and Big Thompson rivers originate in the Alpine peaks on the east side.

Most light-colored granite peaks in the park were exposed during a regional geologic uplift that began 60 million years ago and ended 5 to 7 million years ago. Volcanic activity during the past 30 million years added other distinctive features to the park: the conical Estes Cone, massive flat-topped lava cliffs along Trail Ridge Rd and the Never Summer Mountains.

Upon this rocky pallet, water and ice carved the jagged peaks, cutting canyons and depositing debris on the plains and great mountain parks and meadows. The most remarkable of these erosive forces were the Ice Age glaciers that receded to their present lofty positions only about 10,000 years ago. As the glaciers receded they deposited material carried from higher elevations, forming moraines. Terminal moraines at the foot of the glacier often formed natural dams, as at Grand Lake. Along the margins of the glaciers, moraines formed substantial parallel ridges, as seen in Horseshoe and Moraine parks. Hikers climbing a glacial trough will typically encounter a steep head wall and semi-circular basin containing a cirque lake – these are remnants of the glacier's steady excavation.

CLIMATE

Weather in the park – as in all mountainous areas – is variable. Summer days often reach 70° to 80°F, yet a sudden shift in the weather can bring snow to the peaks in July! Nevertheless, the climate follows broad predictable patterns based on season, elevation, exposure and location east or west of the Continental Divide. Strong winds are common above treeline. July thundershowers typically dump two inches of rain on the park, while January is the driest month – Bear Lake (9400 feet) normally has a January snow base of 25 inches. The Continental Divide causes a pronounced rain-shadow effect: Grand Lake (west of the Divide) annually averages 20 inches of moisture, while Estes Park receives only about 13 inches yearly.

Roaring Floods

In contrast with the gradual geologic forces, occasional catastrophic events, most commonly avalanches and floods, bring sudden change to the park's landscape. On July 15, 1982, the failure of Lawn Lake Dam, built in 1903, sent a 25-foot-high wall of water racing down the narrow Roaring River Valley. And roar it did! The flood uprooted trees and swept earth and giant boulders 5 miles over Horseshoe Falls, where the incredible mass crashed to the valley floor, damming Fall River. The mass of mud and debris advanced down the valley, covering Elkhorn Ave in Estes Park to a depth of six feet before the floodwaters were absorbed in Lake Estes reservoir almost 3½ hours later. In the process, three campers were killed and the alluvial debris created a lake. Visitors to the alluvial fan climb over boulders weighing as much as 452 tons that were deposited by the flood. ■

FLORA & FAUNA

Both the flora and the fauna of Rocky Mountain National Park are strongly correlated with elevation. The park's west side is notably wetter than the eastern rain shadow; verdant streamside growth, or riparian corridors, cuts through altitudinal zones and provides rich habitat for wildlife. Wet north-facing slopes exhibit markedly different species than drier southern slopes.

Careless campfire habits at the beginning of the 20th century led to major burns in the Bear Lake and Glacier Creek areas. Yet long-term fire suppression has caused the forests to grow dense and more susceptible to great conflagrations, like the one that decimated Yellowstone Park in 1988 (see the Greater Yellowstone Country chapter in the Wyoming section). Controversy followed a park service decision to allow the 1978 Ouzel Fire to burn when it threatened development at Allenspark. It wasn't until 1992 that the park adopted a cautious policy to allow two types of fire: certain lightning-caused fires may burn under careful monitoring, and park staff may prescribe burning in areas that accumulate fuel such as dry underbrush, leaves and such.

Flora

From the park entrances to about 9000 feet, the montane forest ecosystem consists chiefly of yellow-barked ponderosa pine on warmer, drier south-facing slopes and dark-green Douglas fir forests on the moister northern slopes. Both animals and humans tend to enjoy the relatively open forest of the evenly spaced ponderosas, caused by a spreading root system. Good examples occur at Beaver Meadows and Gem Lakes (try shaking hands with the 'friendly fir' to distinguish the species from other evergreen trees by its soft foliage). Aspen and lodgepole pines are pioneering trees in the montane and higher sub-Alpine forests; they are the first to establish themselves following disturbances like fire, timber cutting, avalanche or glacial retreat. The sight and sound of 'quaking' aspen leaves and radiant fall color display – ranging from golden yellow to red – enhance most visits to the area.

The fine-grained bottom soils of the montane meadows inhibit tree growth but form an ideal environment for grasses, herbs and great floral displays. An abrupt junction between the forest and meadow, as at Moraine Park, provides a convenient retreat for the mule deer or elk that venture into the meadow to graze.

Above the montane forests and meadows, between about 9000 and 11,000 feet at treeline, deep lingering snows and a short growing season permit the Englemann spruce and sub-Alpine fir to dominate the sub-Alpine ecosystem.

Toward the upper limit of the sub-Alpine zone, brutal weather stunts tree growth, creating the stark beauty of the *Krummholz*, a German word for 'crooked timber.' In this transition zone from the sub-Alpine forest to treeless Alpine tundra, you can admire how the wind and cold have shaped Englemann spruce, sub-Alpine fir and limber pine into shortened, bizarre forms.

Above treeline is the Alpine tundra. Winter burn effectively prunes woody growth that extends into exposed areas above rocks. With a growing season of less than 40 frost-free days, it is surprising to find over 150 plant species competing for attention during their July burst of color. The hairy leaves of rydbergia – a showy, large yellow sunflower that always faces east – help reduce water loss in the dry climate and enable the plant to survive the years it takes to produce its first and only flower. Avoid trampling nature's fragile carpet – the dwarf clover's pink flowers may be over 200 years old! Stepping on the purple-flowered sky pilot will acquaint you with why it's also called skunkweed. Fall is heralded by the Arctic gentian's late blooming greenish-white trumpet.

Fauna

One of the major attractions at Rocky Mountain National Park is the opportunity to view a diversity and abundance of wildlife rarely encountered outside the park's sanctuary. Policies against hunting, harass-

The bald eagle is making a comeback in Colorado.

ing, feeding or other disturbing activities have helped to save many species from the brink of extinction. Most visitors are attracted to viewing the larger mammals, like elk, bighorn sheep and moose, but the various smaller animals and birds should not be overlooked.

Among the 260 bird species is the white-tailed ptarmigan, which changes color to blend with its seasonal environment. Raptors like the redtail hawk, prairie falcon and the endangered peregrine falcon frequent rocky nest sites in the Twin Owls area of the park. The endangered bald eagle also visits the park – this national symbol is now making a strong comeback in Colorado. The open rocky scree above timberline provides visitors with opportunities to see yellow-bellied marmots, a large rodent also called a 'whistle pig' and the tailless, mouse-like pika.

Bighorn Sheep 'Bighorn Crossing Zone' is not a sign you are likely to encounter anywhere else in the world. From late spring through summer, three or four volunteers and an equal number of rangers provide traffic control on US 34 at Sheep Lakes Information Station, 2 miles west of the Fall River Entrance Station. Groups of up to 60 sheep – typically only ewes and lambs – move from the moraine ridge north of the highway across the road to Sheep Lakes in Horseshoe Park. Unlike the big under-curving horns on mature rams, ewes grow swept-back crescent-shaped horns that only reach about 10 inches in length. The Sheep Lakes are evaporative ponds ringed with tasty salt deposits that attract the ewes in the morning and early afternoon after lambing in May and June. In August they rejoin the rams in the Mummy Range.

As late as 1896, Enos Mills observed similar migrations to the alkaline shores of Mary's Lake, south of Estes Park, but hunters decimated the easy prey in quest of their magnificent horns. Sheep ranchers also moved into the area and their domestic herds introduced diseases like scabies and pneumonia that proved fatal to the bighorn sheep. Only the most isolated wild herds survived to 1915 when Rocky Mountain National Park was established. With disease and hunter predation now under better control, the loss of habitat remains the foremost constraint on fully restoring great herds of bighorns.

To see bighorn sheep on rocky ledges you will need to hike or backpack. The estimated 200 animals in the Horseshoe Park herd live permanently in the Mummy Range. On the west side, an equally large herd inhabits the volcanic cliffs of the Never Summer Mountains. A smaller herd can be seen along the Continental Divide at a distance from the rim of the Crater near Milner Pass. Three miles west of the Alpine Visitors Center on Trail Ridge Rd, Crater Trail follows a steep course for 1 mile to the observation point. Crater Trail is closed during spring lambing from May to mid-July.

Elk One highlight of visiting Rocky Mountain National Park is seeing North American elk, or wapiti, grazing in their natural setting. (The Native American term 'wapiti' means 'white,' a reference to the animal's white tail and rump.) According to NPS surveys about 2000 elk winter in the park's lower elevations, while over 3000 inhabit the park's lofty terrain during summer months. The summer visitor equipped with binoculars or a telephoto lens is almost always rewarded by patiently scanning the hillsides and meadows near the Alpine Visitors Center. Traffic jams up as motorists stop to observe these magnificent creatures near the uppermost Fall River Rd or Trail Ridge Rd. Visitors are repeatedly warned by signs and park rangers not to harass, call to or come in contact with the animals.

Like bighorn sheep, elk were virtually extinct around Estes Park by 1890 – wiped out by hunters. In 1913 and 1914, before the establishment of the park, people from Estes Park brought in 49 elk from Yellowstone. The elk's natural population increase since Congress' 1915 establishment of Rocky Mountain National Park is one of the NPS's great successes, directly attributable to the removal of the human predator.

Mature elk bulls may reach 1100 pounds, cows weigh up to 600 pounds – both have dark necks with light tan bodies. Bulls regenerate their crowning antlers, weighing 25 pounds or more, each year in time to parade before the cows and compete with other bulls for breeding partners during the rut, the fall mating season when deep bugling calls break the forest quiet.

At 1100 pounds, a bull elk can literally stop traffic.

Following rutting season, bull elk shed their antlers and begin growing new ones covered by a soft skin, or 'velvet,' that is lost by late summer as the bony rack reaches a cumbersome five-foot breadth. By this time, the newborn elk calves will be paired with their protective mother cows as the former feed voraciously to add 200 pounds to their 30-pound birthweight before the onset of winter.

During the elk rut in September and October, most large meadows are closed to off-trail travel 5 pm to 7 am.

Beaver The beaver is nature's hydraulic engineer, building dams and hollow island lodges. With four front teeth capable of felling a mature lodgepole pine or aspen, the beaver looks at deciduous woody plants as either food or construction material.

Beavers mate for life, one pair per colony, where offspring born each May or June may stay for two years. A mature beaver can reach 60 pounds – the largest rodent in North America – and is distinguished from the smaller muskrat by its flat hairless tail and bulbous body. Muskrat add to this identity confusion by sometimes living next to a beaver lodge.

Beaver ponds occur throughout the park's lower streams. To see the animal, remember that they rarely wander from their aquatic habitat. Lodges can be found along Mill Creek in Hollowell Park, 2 miles south of the Park Museum.

Other Mammals You are likely to encounter mule deer – the only deer species in the park, so-named for its large mule-like ears – as they browse on leaves and twigs from shrubs at sunny lower elevations. Most moose sightings occur in the Kawuneeche Valley, but don't count on seeing moose without some effort, as this large dark-colored animal can be surprisingly elusive.

Howling coyotes commonly serenade winter campfires – lucky visitors may spy a coyote stalking small rodents in the montane meadows. Other large carnivores like the bobcat and mountain lion are very

rarely seen. Small but ferocious long-tailed weasel hunt near their streamside dens at night; in the winter the weasel's camouflage changes from brown to white, and the animal is called an ermine.

A considerable population of black bears and grizzly bears once inhabited the park area. Only about 30 black bears have survived predation by hunters and 'game management' techniques by federal officials, overanxious to protect visitors and other fledgling species. Two grizzlies were killed in 1951, and the last documented grizzly in Colorado was killed in 1979.

BOOKS
History
Definitely worth reading are the writings of Enos A Mills. Among his 16 books is the short 1917 classic *The Story of Early Estes Park: Rocky Mountain National Park and Grand Lake*; a self-published 5th edition (1980) is available by post from Enda Mills Kiley, Enos Mills Cabin, Long's Peak Route, Estes Park, CO 80517. Isabella L Bird's account of her 1873 climb up Long's Peak in *A Lady's Life in the Rocky Mountains* (University of Oklahoma Press, 1982) is a valuable vignette on that period. For a comprehensive history, turn to Curt Bucholtz's *Rocky Mountain National Park: A History* (Colorado University Press, 1983).

Guidebooks
Kent and Donna Dannen's *Hiking Rocky Mountain National Park – Including Indian Peaks* is the park's most comprehensive guide, now in its 8th edition. Some versions come packaged with a topo map coordinated for use with the guide. Similarly, Jerome Malitz's *Rocky Mountain National Park Dayhiker's Guide* is a handy book of 33 hikes written for use with the Trails Illustrated map of *Rocky Mountain National Park*. Families looking for detailed suggestions on easy and moderate hikes should consult Lisa Gollin Evans' *A Family Guide to Rocky Mountain National Park* (The Mountaineers, 1991).

Technical climbers will be interested in a recent guide by Bernard Gillette, *Rocky*

Mountain National Park: The Climber's Guide (Earthbound Sports Inc, 1993). More detailed is Richard Rossiter's *Rock Climbing Rocky Mountain National Park*, which includes two volumes, one on high peaks and another on crag areas.

The Rocky Mountain Nature Association publishes a series of concise road and trail guides that are authoritative and handsomely illustrated. All are available at visitors centers for only $1 to $2 each. All the pamphlets and books listed here are available at the Park Visitors Center Headquarters bookstore or can be ordered from the Rocky Mountain Nature Association (☎ 970-586-0108).

Maps
Detailed USGS topographical quad maps (1:24,000) and maps of the entire Rocky Mountain National Park (1:62,500) are available for $4 each. Trails Illustrated also offers a waterproof topographical map ($9) of the park at 1:59:000 that indicates backcountry campsites and hiking trails to accompany Malitz's guidebook.

ORIENTATION
Set in Colorado's northern Front Range, Rocky Mountain National Park lies between Comanche Peak and Neota wilderness areas in the Roosevelt National Forest to the north, Indian Peaks Wilderness on the south and between the towns of Grand Lake to the west and Estes Park to the east. (For more on Grand Lake see the Northern Mountains chapter.) The Continental Divide runs northwest to southeast to exit at the south-central end of the park.

Trail Ridge Rd (US 34) is the only east-west route through the park; the US 34 eastern approach from I-25 and Loveland follows the Big Thompson River Canyon. The most direct route from Boulder follows US 36 through Lyons to the east entrances. Another approach from the south, mountainous Hwy 7, passes by the Enos Mills' Cabin and provides access to campsites and trailheads (including Long's Peak) on the east side of the Divide. Winter closure of US 34 through the park makes

access to the park's west side dependent on US 40 at Granby.

There are two entrance stations on the east side, Fall River (US 34) and Beaver Meadows (US 36). The Grand Lake Station (also US 34) is the only entry on the west side. Three of the park's five visitors centers are located outside park entrances: the Park Headquarters Visitors Center is on US 36 between Estes Park and Beaver Meadows Entrance Station, Lily Lake is 6 miles south of Estes Park on Hwy 7 and Kawuneeche is north of Grand Lake on US 34. Year-round access is available through Kawuneeche Valley along the Colorado River headwaters to Timber Creek Campground. The main centers of visitor activity on the park's east side are the Alpine Visitors Center high on Trail Ridge Rd and Bear Lake Rd, which leads to campgrounds, trailheads and the Moraine Park Museum.

North of Estes Park, Devils Gulch Rd leads to MacGregor Ranch and Lumpy Ridge hiking trails. Farther out on Devils Gulch Rd, you pass through the village of Glen Haven to reach the trailhead entry to the park along the North Fork of the Big Thompson River.

INFORMATION
The park has no banking or postal services: for these you'll need to head to either Estes Park or Grand Lake. Public phones are found at visitors centers and all campgrounds except Long's Peak.

Fees & Permits
For private vehicles, the park entrance fee is $10, valid for seven days. Individuals entering the park on foot, bicycle, motorcycle or bus pay $5 each. All visitors receive a free copy of the park's information brochure, which contains a good orientation map and is also available in German, French, Spanish and Japanese.

Backcountry permits ($15) are required for overnight stays outside of developed campgrounds. Reservations by mail or in person are accepted any time after March. Phone reservations can be made only from

March to May 20. The Backcountry Office (☎ 970-586-1242) is in a building reached by a short foot trail east of the Headquarters Visitors Center and is open 7 am to 7 pm daily. For a reservation form and a map of backcountry campsites write: Backcountry Office, Rocky Mountain National Park, Estes Park, CO 80517.

Tourist Offices

The Headquarters Visitors Center (☎ 970-586-1206, TTY 970-586-1319), 2½ miles west of Estes Park on Hwy 36, is the park's main information facility and is open daily year-round. Audiovisual programs are presented in the auditorium and a bookstore is operated by the Rocky Mountain Nature Association. Extended summer hours are 8 am to 9 pm. Other park staff and the library are available weekdays 8 am to 4:30 pm. General park information is broadcast on 1610 AM; for road and weather information, call ☎ 586-1333.

Kawuneeche Visitors Center (☎ 970-627-3471), at the southwest entrance of the park 1 mile north of the town of Grand Lake, is open year-round. It has a small museum, a bookstore, audiovisual programs and issues backcountry permits (see Fees & Permits below) and is open 7 am to 7 pm daily in summer, with varied shorter hours the rest of the year.

Straddling the park boundary with adjacent USFS lands, the Lily Lake Visitors Center, 6 miles south of Estes Park on Hwy 7, offers a small exhibit and a bookstore. It's not worth a special trip unless you plan to stroll around Lily Lake, the park's most recent addition, or take the short hike up Lily Mountain. The center is open 9 am to 4.30 pm daily May to November.

Moraine Park Museum and Visitors Center, 5 miles west of Estes Park on Bear Lake Rd, has natural history exhibits along with park history displays and film presentations (see Museums). Park at the museum and take a shuttle bus to the campgrounds or trailheads along Bear Lake Rd (see Getting Around).

Alpine Visitors Center, 25 miles west of Estes Park on Trail Ridge Rd, has excellent exhibits of Alpine geology and flora and fauna, but the crowds seeking shelter from frequent lightning storms can be overwhelming. From the observation deck visitors can often spot grazing elk on nearby hillsides. It's open 9 am to 5 pm daily June to August, with shorter hours in September and early October; closed in winter which it closes.

Publications

A free seasonal newspaper, 'High Country Headlines,' available at entrance stations and visitors centers, contains current schedules for ranger programs and shuttle buses.

Medical Services

There are no care facilities in the park, but most rangers are trained to give emergency treatment. Emergency telephones (☎ 911, 970-586-1399 at headquarters) are at Long's Peak and Wild Basin ranger stations, as well as at the Bear Lake, Deer Ridge Junction and Lawn Lake trailheads.

Dangers & Annoyances

With the onset of warmer spring weather, hikers should take precautions to avoid bites from wood ticks, which can transmit Colorado Tick Fever. (For more about ticks see Facts for the Visitor.) Once a tick embeds its head in your skin, it is extremely difficult to remove without pulling the blood-engorged body from its head. An easier solution is to avoid becoming a host to this heat-sensing parasite that lurks on the grasses or low brush awaiting warm-blooded mammals. Wear protective clothing and tuck in your shirt and pant legs. Wear light-colored clothing to easily spot ticks, and inspect your clothes, scalp and skin often while hiking. Use a tick repellent on shoes, socks and pant legs.

MORAINE PARK MUSEUM

Built in 1910 as the Moraine Lodge, this structure offers a splendid example of Craftsman-style architecture, intended to blend with nature through the use of native building materials. The park service purchased the lodge during the Depression and it has since served as a visitors center and museum. Featured exhibits portray the park's natural history along with the history of tourism in the park. The geology exhibits provide especially good interpretation of local textbook examples like South Lateral Moraine or the Taylor and Tyndall glaciers visible from the front steps.

The Moraine Museum, 5 miles west of Estes Park on Bear Lake Rd, is open daily 9 am to 5 pm May to mid-October. Admission is free.

NEVER SUMMER RANCH
On the west side of the park, just south of Timber Creek Campground reached by a 1-mile trail, Never Summer Ranch is an early dude ranch now preserved as a cultural landmark. It's open 9 am to 5 pm daily.

SUMMER ACTIVITIES
NPS rangers provide a variety of organized summer activities for visitors, ranging from fireside chats to visitors center lectures and short interpretive hikes which change from year to year. Check a recent issue of 'High Country Headlines,' the free newspaper given to each visitor, or contact the Interpretive Ranger Supervisor (☎ 970-586-1226) for current programs and schedules. Most are free.

Hiking & Backpacking
With over 300 miles of trail, the park offers trails suited to every hiking ability, traversing all aspects of the park's terrain. Families might consider the easy hikes in the Wild Basin to Calypso Falls or to Gem Lakes in the Lumpy Ridge area. At the other extreme is the strenuous hike to Long's Peak, which should only be attempted by those in good physical condition. Spend at least one night at 7000 to 8000 feet prior to setting out to allow your body to adjust to the elevation. Before July, many trails are snowbound and high water runoff makes passage difficult. The following trail descriptions are only a representative selection of the many possible hikes in the park. Dogs and other pets are not allowed on the trails. All overnight stays in the backcountry require permits (see Information above).

A useful organization, the Colorado Mountain Club's local Shining Mountain Group (☎ 970-586-6623) offers some 600 outings each year in the area, many of which are open to the public. To learn more about the group's schedule of activities – and conservation and service work – drop by the Estes Park Public Library at 335 E Elkhorn Ave.

Long's Peak You need not worry about being alone on this 15-mile roundtrip to the lofty summit of Long's Peak (14,255 feet) – one recent Saturday in July a line of over 100 parked cars snaked down the road from the East Long's Peak Trailhead (9400 feet). After the initial 6 miles of moderate trail to the Boulder Field (12,760 feet) the path steepens at the start of the Keyhole Route to the summit, which is marked with yellow and red bulls-eyes painted on the rock. Even superhuman athletes are slowed by the route's ledge system, which resembles a narrow cliffside stairway without a handrail. Scramble the final 'Homestretch' to the summit boulders. The roundtrip hike takes anywhere from 10 to 15 hours.

Remember that safety is more important than the transient goal of reaching the summit. Hikers should immediately turn back in the event of afternoon lightning storms, the first indication of altitude sickness or hypothermia. Many climbers make the trail 'approach' in early predawn hours after overnighting at Long's Peak Campground. The Keyhole Route is generally free of snow mid-July to October – otherwise you will need technical climbing skills and equipment to reach the summit.

The trailhead is at Long's Peak Ranger Station, 11 miles south of Estes Park on Hwy 7; the station is open daily 8 am to 4:30 pm in summer.

Chasm Lake Chasm Lake (11,800 feet) is a cirque fed by Mills Glacier, high on the east side of Long's Peak. At about 3 miles from the start of the East Long's Peak

Trail, a backcountry toilet marks a branch to the south (left) over the Mills Moraine to Columbine Falls and Chasm Lake, 1 mile from the junction. The final part of the trail before reaching Chasm Lake involves traversing a rock ledge.

Twin Sisters Peaks This up-and-back hike provides an excellent warm-up to climbing Long's Peak; in addition, the 11,428-foot summit of Twin Sisters Peak offers unequaled views of Long's Peak. It's an arduous walk, gaining 2300 feet in just 3.7 miles. Erosion-resistant quartz rock caps the oddly deformed rock at the summit and delicate Alpine flowers (plenty of mountain harebell) fill the rock spaces near the stone hut. The trailhead is near Mills Cabin, 10 miles south of Estes Park on Hwy 7.

Lily Mountain One of the easiest climbs in the area, Lily Mountain sits on the park border 6 miles south of Estes Park on Hwy 7. A 1½-mile trail goes up almost 1000 feet to the summit for an outstanding panorama that includes the Mummy Range, Continental Divide, Long's Peak, Estes Park and Estes Cone.

Wild Basin From the Wild Basin Ranger Station, 15 miles south of Estes Park to the turnoff on Hwy 7, easy day hikes lead to cascading waterfalls, beaver ponds and wildflowers in what is also referred to as 'Ouzel country.' Near the trailhead is Copeland Falls, Calypso Cascades appears in less than 2 miles and in another mile you reach Ouzel Falls and a nearby overlook of Long's Peak. Hikers can continue another mile to a junction with the Bluebird Lake Trail that follows Ouzel Creek, or take the north branch to Thunder Lake in the upper St Vrain Creek. Both trails offer campsites and reach timberline at the 6-mile mark.

Fern Lake Forested Fern Lake, 4 miles from the trailhead in Moraine Park, reached by shuttle bus, is dominated by craggy Notchtop Peak. You can complete a loop to the Bear Lake shuttle stop in 8½

miles for a rewarding day hike. With a backcountry camping permit, you can spend more time exploring the countless pristine lakes and waterfalls in the upper Fern Creek drainage before returning by foot via the Mill Creek Basin-Cub Lake routes, or aboard a shuttle from the Bierstadt Lake Trailhead.

Bear Lake Trailhead A sub-Alpine interpretive nature trail circles the lake, and a 1-mile hike takes you past Nymph Lake to beautiful Dream Lake, a small gem surrounded by Englemann spruce below massive Hallett Peak. From here, one trail follows the Tyndall Glacier Gorge, crossing the terminal moraine that separates Dream Lake from Emerald Lake less than a mile upstream. The trail south from Dream Lake passes upstream of Chaos Canyon Cascades and continues to Loch Vale, past Glacier Falls and Alberta Falls, before emerging at Glacier Gorge Junction Trailhead. Bear Lake is served by the Glacier Basin-Bear Lake shuttle. An emergency telephone is located at the trailhead.

Flattop Mountain Trail Surprisingly, this is the only hiking trail in the park to link the east and west sides. Reaching the Divide on Flattop Mountain from the Bear Lake Trailhead entails a strenuous 4½-mile climb, gaining 2800 feet in elevation. From the summit, you have two equidistant options for continuing to Grand Lake: Tonahutu Creek Trail or the North Inlet Trail. Both offer plenty of backcountry campsites on the east side.

Glacier Gorge Junction Trailhead Hikes in this busy area of trails range from the easy stroll to Alberta Falls to more strenuous 5-mile trips up either Glacier Gorge, past Mills Lake and many glacial erratics to Black Lake, or Loch Vale to Andrews Glacier on the Divide. The trailhead is served by the Glacier Basin-Bear Lake shuttle.

Lawn Lake Strenuous hikes into the Mummy Range climb abruptly from the alluvial fan in Horseshoe Park. Although trails to Ypsilon Lake (4½ miles) and Lawn Lake (6 miles) are up and back excursions, it's possible to continue down Black Canyon to Lumpy Ridge.

Gem Lake Easy hikes of about 2 miles in the Lumpy Ridge area lead to Gem Lake from trailheads at either the MacGregor Ranch or below the Twin Owls formations on Devils Gulch Rd, one or 2 miles north of Estes Park respectively.

North Fork Trailhead The North Fork of the Big Thompson River flows from the park through the Comanche Wilderness Area in the Roosevelt National Forest and appeals to families interested in easy hiking along the river, or accomplished backpackers who want a more extensive trail network. The North Fork Trail enters the Comanche Wilderness and follows the riverside path for 4½ miles to the park boundary, eventually reaching Alpine Lost Lake at the 7½-mile mark and Lake Dunraven.

Backpackers can hike a branch trail over Stormy Peaks Pass into the Comanche Wilderness or take a cross-country route to Mummy Pass. To get to the North Fork Trailhead from Estes Park, take Devils Gulch Rd for 9 miles east over the scenic divide through Glen Haven and past some picnic areas along the North Fork to a bridge marked 'Dunraven Forest Access' on your left (east), then proceed 2½ miles to the trailhead.

Milner Pass The Trail Ridge Rd crosses the Divide at Milner Pass (elevation 10,759 feet), where trails head southeast to Mt Ida, the most accessible view peak on the west side of the park. The trail climbs 2000 feet in 4 miles, steeply at first through dense forest before emerging onto an exhilaratingly open tundra zone with fabulous views of the valleys below. At about the 3-mile point the trail peters out, but the route is still easy to follow. Figure about three hours to the summit, and about 2½ hours to return; because the route is so exposed, there is real danger during thunderstorms.

Colorado River Trailhead About 1½ miles north of Timber Creek Campground, this trail follows the Colorado River to the deteriorating ruins of Lulu City, a former mineral boomtown 3½ miles from Trail Ridge Rd. It's possible to make this a loop via the slightly longer Red Mountain Trail.

North Inlet Reached by a short spur from the Kawuneeche Visitors Center, north of Grand Lake on US 34, or from the road near Shadowcliff Lodge in Grand Lake, this trail climbs gradually to Cascade Falls, then more steeply to lakes Nokoni and Nanita. It's possible to continue east across the Divide.

East Inlet At the east end of Grand Lake, in Grand Lake Village, this trail climbs gradually and then steeply toward the Divide, passing several glacial lakes.

Rock Climbing

Many climbers head to **Lumpy Ridge**, a sub-Alpine outcrop of many rock faces only 2 miles north of Estes Park that offers outstanding short climbs and attracts climbers of all abilities. Two trailheads provide access to Lumpy Ridge climbing areas from Devils Gulch Rd: Twin Owls Trailhead begins at the MacGregor Ranch, and about 1 mile east of the ranch is the Gem Lake Trailhead. To protect the nests of birds of prey, some climbing routes are closed mid-April to mid-July.

A quality Alpine face with a short approach is the Englishman's Route up **Hallett Peak** (12,713 feet), the wedge-shaped monolith seen from Bear Lake. This Class 5.8 climb on a sunny, south-facing slope is reached from the **Bear Lake/Glacier Gorge Trailhead**. Another recommended climb is the Sidetrack Route up **Sundance Mountain**, a Class 5.9 climb. Trail Ridge Rd passes over Sundance Mountain and the Fall River Rd follows the glacial valley north of this tremendous glacially carved remnant.

Many of the park's Alpine climbs are long one-day climbs or require an overnight stay on the rock face. Often the only way to accomplish a long climb and avoid afternoon thundershowers is to begin climbing at dawn – this can mean an approach hike beginning at midnight! An alternative is to bivouac at the base of the climb. (A bivouac is defined as a temporary open-air encampment – no tents – established in designated zones between dawn and dusk.) Free bivouac permits are issued only to technical climbers and are mandatory for all overnight stays in the backcountry.

To minimize the environmental impact of backcountry use, the Rocky Mountain National Park Backcountry Office (☎ 970-586-1242) allows only a limited number of people to bivouac at four popular climbing areas. Phone reservations may be made March to May 20 for the following restricted zones: **Long's Peak area**, including Broadway below Diamond, Chasm View, Mills Glacier and Meeker cirque; **Black Lake area** (Glacier Gorge), encompassing McHenry Peak, Arrowhead, Spearhead and Chiefshead/Pagoda; the base of **Notchtop Peak**; and the **Skypond/Andrews Glacier Area**, including the Taylor/Powell peaks and Sharkstooth Peak. Reservations are not needed nor accepted for other bivouacs.

For climbing gear try Colorado Wilderness Sports (☎ 970-586-6548), open daily at 358 E Elkhorn in Estes Park. A small stock of climbing gear is also available from Colorado Mountain School (☎ 970-586-5758), 351 Moraine Ave in Estes Park, where you can also sleep in a dorm for $20, shower after a climb for $2 or enroll in a climbing course. Colorado Mountain School is the only guide service licensed to operate in Rocky Mountain National Park. A one-day climbing workshop, available for all levels of ability, costs about $160, depending on the number enrolled in the course. Advanced expeditions are also available.

Mountain Biking
Mountain biking on park roads is a splendid way to see the park and wildlife, though you are restricted to paved roads and to one dirt road, Fall River Rd.

Climbing the paved **Trail Ridge Rd** has one big advantage over Fall River Rd: you can turn around should problems arise. (Fall River Rd is a 9-mile one-way climb of over 3000 feet.) The pleasant summer weather at lower elevations can suddenly become unmercifully cold at higher altitudes – especially when descending from the park's Alpine peaks. Hypothermia is an emergency experienced by many unprepared bicyclists each month: change into a dry shirt, full gloves and a warm, water-repellent outer shell before you get above treeline and into the wind. The only shelter from lightning is at Alpine Visitors Center. Yet another unpleasantness is the altitude sickness and subsequent dehydration that strikes many people unaccustomed to the 12,000-foot elevation reached on Trail Ridge Rd.

Less daunting climbs and climes are available on the park's lower paved roads. A popular 16-mile circuit is the **Horseshoe Park/Estes Park Loop**. For a bit more of a climbing challenge you can continue to **Bear Lake Rd**, an 8-mile long route that rises 1500 feet to the high mountain basin.

To park your bike and head out for a hike, you'll need a lock long enough to reach around a tree, as there are no bike racks in the park.

If you are not up to climbing either Trail Ridge or Fall River Rds, Colorado Bicycling (☎ 970-586-4241), 184 E Elkhorn in Estes Park, offers tours of Rocky Mountain National Park starting at $45. The tours include brunch during the shuttle ride. The company also rents bikes for $21/40 standard/performance.

Fishing
Fishing is not the primary attraction at Rocky Mountain National Park. Solid freeze and other natural factors at 42 of the 156 lakes in the park limit the number of reproducing populations of fish. In the past, the NPS stocked many lakes and streams with non-native species to appease sport fishing demands, but today only native greenback cutthroat trout and Colorado River

cutthroat trout are stocked. The endangered greenback cutthroat has disappeared from 99% of its original habitat, and the park is a major focal point of restoration efforts. Fishing regulations further encourage replenishment of native fish and removal of exotic species. To abide by these rules, you must be able to identify each species of fish taken. A list of current regulations, open lakes, closed waters and catch-and-release areas is available at park visitors centers and ranger stations.

For supplies, information or fly-fishing classes, stop by the Estes Angler (☎ 970-586-2110), 338 W Riverside Drive in Estes Park. Scot's Sporting Goods (☎ 970-586-2877), 870 Moraine Ave, also offers equipment and guided trips outside park boundaries. (For ice-fishing opportunities, also see Winter Activities below.)

Horseback Riding & Pack Trips

Pack animals are permitted on approximately 80% of the park's trails – mostly outside the heavily used east-side zones. Even so, trails in the vicinity of the YMCA Conference Center and up Twin Sisters Peaks are overcrowded with equestrians. Check the park brochure 'Horses & Other Pack Animals' for trails open to pack animals. The park's Backcountry Guide identifies campsites suited for livestock.

A large number of livery stables rent horses and most have permits for leading trips into the park. Hi Country Stables (☎ 970-586-3244) has facilities within the park at Glacier Creek and Moraine Park. Other operations include Sombrero Ranch Stables (☎ 970-586-4577), 1 mile east of Estes Park, where breakfast rides cost $32 ($38 with steak!), hourly rentals $18; Glen Haven Stables (☎ 970-526-2669), 7 miles northeast of Estes Park at 7408 Larimer Cty Rd 43 in Glen Haven, which has similar rates; and Wild Basin Livery (☎ 970-747-2454) at 12976 Hwy 7 in Allenspark. When booking a ride, bear in mind that tailbones unaccustomed to the saddle tend to ache on rides lasting over two hours. For a complete list of livery operations permitted to lead rides in the park, ask for the 'Concessions/Visitor Services' pamphlet at the Headquarters Visitors Center.

Driving Tours

Most of the park's 3 million annual visitors get no farther than the windshield tour along **Trail Ridge Rd** (US 34) over the Continental Divide, which usually opens in late May and is closed at Many Parks Curve on the east side by mid-October. The ridgetop route, formerly a Ute trail over Milner Pass, was surveyed by federal road builders in 1927 to replace Fall River Rd. Allow at least three hours to travel the 47 miles between Estes Park and Grand Lake, depending on the length of your stops at the short Tundra Nature Trail, Crater Trail, Alpine Visitors Center and various overlook sites.

Have four quarters ready to purchase a guide booklet from a dispenser at the start of **Fall River Rd**, a one-way uphill route near the **Endovalley Picnic Area**. The 9-mile unpaved road looks much as it did when completed in 1920 and usually opens in July. Views are obscured for most of the trip by forested slopes along the Fall River, but Chasm Falls and frequent elk sightings in the tundra near the Alpine Visitors Center are exceptional attractions. Steep grades and a 15-mph speed limit cause many engine problems (overheating) for poorly tuned vehicles. If you're heading up in late September or October check with the visitors center for road conditions: by that point in the season some large ruts can develop.

WINTER ACTIVITIES

The ratio of wildlife to people greatly increases during winter months, though the park is also becoming more popular as a winter destination. Elk, mule deer and bighorn sheep frequent the meadows and plowed roadways. The tracks of coyotes, porcupines, weasels and other small mammals crisscross the blanket of snow. This abundant wildlife further attracts migrating falcons and eagles.

Rangers present weekly Saturday evening programs at the Headquarters Visitors

Center at 7:30 pm in October, 7 pm November to June.

Snowshoeing & Cross-Country Skiing

From December into May, the high valleys and Alpine tundra of Rocky Mountain National Park offer cross-country skiers unique opportunities to view wildlife and the winter scenery undisturbed by crowds. January and February are the best months for dry, powdery snowpack – spring snows tend to be heavy and wet. Most routes follow summer hiking trails, but valley bottoms and frozen stream beds typically have more snow cover and are less challenging. In fact, most of the park should be considered 'backcountry skiing' rather than 'cross-country.' Avalanche hazards are greatest on steep, open slopes in mountainous terrain. Overnight trips require permits, and the USFS NPS will have a list of closed trails.

On the east side, the **Bear Lake** trailheads offer short or long routes suitable for all skiing abilities, from beginner to experienced. The easiest trail for a short one- or two-hour roundtrip leads to Nymph Lake, but experienced skiers can continue to Dream and Emerald lakes. Another beginner trail starts at **Glacier Gorge Junction** and leads to Alberta Falls before continuing as an intermediate route to the Loch Vale-Glacier Gorge trail junction. From here, a snowy stream bed alternative to the summer trail takes you to the Loch trail, an all-day roundtrip.

Other extended tours are possible from the Bear Lake area; for these, you should be equipped for an emergency bivouac. A 10-mile up-and-back tour to **Fern Lake** generally follows Mill Creek after crossing the low divide from Bear Lake on the summer trail. This route is scenic and protected from the harshest winds commonly encountered by skiers on the alternate approach from Moraine Park, which passes the appropriately named Windy Gulch. Likewise, the exposed Trail Ridge Rd (US 34), closed to vehicles west of Many Parks Curve in the winter, is also subject to high winds and blowing snow and makes a poor choice for enjoyable touring.

Rangers lead weekend snowshoe hikes in the east side of the park from January to April, depending on snow conditions. Trailhead locations and times are available from the Headquarters Visitors Center.

NPS visitors centers (see Information above) can provide additional route suggestions. Adventurous skiers planning on overnight backcountry stays also need to obtain free camping permits and information about areas open to overnight stays.

Snowshoe or ski rental costs $10 per day at Colorado Wilderness Sports (☎ 970-586-6548), 358 E Elkhorn in Estes Park.

Winter Hiking

Snow depth to 35 feet on the peaks precludes winter hiking, yet elevations below 8700 feet on the east side are often snow-free. Note that an easy or moderate summer day hike becomes a strenuous affair in deep snow, and roundtrip circuits at lower elevations may be blocked. A few suggestions for up-and-back winter hikes include the **Fern Lake Trail** to The Pool and the **Cub Lake Trail**. Both are reachable from Moraine Park and provide short hikes with opportunities to view wildlife. The closed **Fall River Rd** also beckons foot travel to Chasm Falls. Lumpy Ridge north of Estes Park is another winter hiking area – try the **Gem Lake Trail** from Devils Gulch Rd.

Ice Fishing

Ice fishing is allowed at many of the park's frozen lakes. The same restrictions and regulations apply as in warmer months – check at the visitors center for open waters and suggestions for winter access; monitor ice conditions carefully and take every caution.

PLACES TO STAY

The only overnight accommodations in the park are at campgrounds; the majority of motel or hotel accommodations are around Estes Park and Grand Lake.

Of the park's five formal campgrounds, all except Long's Peak take RVs (no hookups), provide campfire programs, have public telephones and a seven-day limit during summer months. Fees are $14 at Moraine Park and Glacier Basin, during the reservation period, $12 at the others. During the winter there's a $10 fee to camp at Long's Peak, Glacier Basin and Timber Creek.

You will need a backcountry permit to stay outside developed park campgrounds (see Information above). None of the campgrounds features showers, but they do have flush toilets in summer and outhouse facilities in winter. Sites include a fire ring, picnic table and one parking spot.

East Side

Moraine Park and *Long's Peak* campgrounds are open year-round. The location of Long's Peak Campground, 11 miles south of Estes Park on Hwy 7, is intended to provide Long's Peak hikers with an early trail start. It has 30 tent sites available on a first-come, first-served basis for three-day stays. *Aspenglen*, 5 miles west of Estes Park on US 34, also has 56 first-come, first-served sites mid-May to October. Moraine Park (250 sites) and *Glacier Basin* (152 sites) accept reservations at least eight weeks in advance through the National Park Reservation Center (☎ 800-365-2267), PO Box 85705, San Diego, CA 92186-5705. Both campgrounds are served by the shuttle buses on Bear Lake Rd. Glacier Basin is open June to September.

At the southeast boundary of the park near Wild Basin, the USFS *Olive Ridge Campground* (☎ 877-444-6777 reservations) has 56 heavily used sites for $12; it's open from mid-May to November. To reserve a site, you must also pay a non-refundable fee of $9.

West Side

Timber Creek, 7 miles north of Grand Lake, remains open in winter and has 101 sites (no reservations).

GETTING AROUND

Two free shuttle buses provide summer service to campgrounds and trailheads along Bear Lake Rd and its spur routes; the parking area for both is near Glacier Basin Campground.

The Campground Shuttle Route operates hourly between 8.30 am and 12.30 pm and 2 to 5 pm from the Shuttle Bus parking area, with stops at Hollowell Park, Tuxedo Park, Moraine Park Museum (parking available), Moraine Park Campground, Cub Lake Trailhead and Fern Lake Trailhead. The service runs June to mid-August.

The Glacier Basin-Bear Lake Route operates every half-hour between 8:30 am and 5:30 pm, with peak July and August service every 15 minutes. The bus makes intermediate stops at Bierstadt Lake Trailhead and Glacier Gorge Junction. Service ends in late September.

Southern Front Range

A swath of development spreads along the Rockies' eastern edge from Denver down to Colorado Springs, the best-known destination along the southern Front Range. Though one of Colorado's top tourist draws, the Springs gets mixed reviews: some love all the action and attractions, while others find it tawdry and overblown. No one can argue that the views from the 14,110-foot summit of Pikes Peak are stunning, but some may not wish to enjoy the scenery in the company of hundreds of others.

Within Colorado Springs there are some nice hiking and biking trails. But outside the Springs area the crowds thin out and the scenery picks up. To the west, the Florissant Fossil Beds National Monument offers an interesting look at Colorado's ancient past as well as some nice hiking and wildflower viewing. To the south, the industrial city of Pueblo is not too pretty, but farther down Trinidad offers a nice mix of frontier history and Mexican American culture. West of Trinidad, the meadows and Alpine forests around La Veta and Cuchara offer a chance to take a scenic tour that's a bit off the beaten path.

COLORADO SPRINGS

Beneath the famous summit of Pikes Peak, Colorado Springs (population 345,000) is arguably the state's most overrated tourist destination. While there are some interesting sights in and around town, such as the Pioneer Museum, the Pikes Peak Toll Rd (see Around Manitou Springs) and the Garden of the Gods, they have been hyperpromoted and are usually overrun with visitors. Cashing in on the steady crowds are numerous tacky attractions such as the Ghost Town Wild West Museum and the Cave of the Winds, which once may have been beautiful but is now merely a crass walk underground.

The city is pleasant enough, but except for parts of Old Colorado City, the archi-

tecture is nothing special. While some may still enjoy a visit here, it's not a 'must see' destination: Colorado has plenty of other 14,000-foot peaks, hot spring resorts and fine museums in more pleasant, less crowded settings.

Colorado's second-largest city, the Springs is a curious mix of military installations, evangelical conservatives and tourists. It's home to the US Air Force Academy and the North American Aerospace Defense Command (NORAD), which inhabits a 'nuke-proof' tunnel in Cheyenne

HIGHLIGHTS

- Garden of the Gods – spectacular sandstone formations, nestled at the edge of Colorado Springs

- Florrisant Fossil Beds National Monument – a rich collection of flora and fauna dating back 35 million years

- La Veta – scenic splendor and Latino heritage add flavor to this tiny artists' community

- Trinidad – despite a struggling economy, this small city has a wealth of historic sights and a friendly atmosphere

COLORADO

Mountain that conjures up images of Dr Strangelove. Colorado Springs is also home to religious groups such as Focus on the Family and Coloradans for Family Values, which promote right-wing political and social agendas.

From a panoramic perch on the summit of Pikes Peak in 1893, Katherine Lee Bates wrote the lyrics to 'America the Beautiful' – a song that many Americans would gladly adopt as the national anthem. In downtown Colorado Springs at Antlers Park, a statue of Captain Zebulon Montgomery Pike was unveiled November 15, 1906, 100 years after he first saw the peak from the Arkansas Valley, 120 miles away (the air was cleaner then). By November 27, 1806, he had abandoned his attempt to ascend the summit.

Orientation

At the northern border of the city, just west of I-25, is the US Air Force Academy. The interstate bisects the metropolitan area; to the east is the central Colorado Springs business district, and to the west is Old Colorado City, the Garden of the Gods and the town of Manitou Springs. Though Garden of the Gods is part of Colorado Springs, it is outlined in a separate section of this chapter because it is also very close to Manitou Springs accommodations and services.

Referred to as the 'West Side' of Colorado Springs, Old Colorado City stretches along the north side of Colorado Ave just south of 30th St. Originally a separate town, Colorado City was eventually overcome by urban sprawl and was annexed by the Springs in 1917. Its historic district is found along W Colorado Ave between 23rd and 27th Sts.

To get to the cog rail that travels up Pikes Peak, turn west onto Ruxton Ave from Manitou Ave in Manitou Springs. A panoramic view of Pikes Peak with the Garden of the Gods in the foreground is available from Mesa Rd, just off 30th St.

Information

Tourist Offices At the Colorado Springs Visitor Information Center (☎ 719-635-

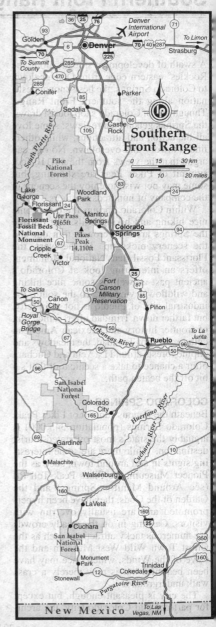

7506, 800-368-4748), on the corner of Cascade and Colorado Aves, you can examine a photo album of B&Bs or stock up on brochures, but the busy assistants can only offer short answers to most questions before they have to tend to the next visitor. Be sure to pick up a copy of the 'Pikes Peak Region & Colorado Springs Official Visitors Guide.' The center is open from 8:30 am to 5 pm daily (weekdays only in winter). It also offers a 24-hour events line recording (π 719-635-1723).

Money There are ATM machines throughout the downtown area. A convenient one is at the Norwest Bank, 90 S Cascade Ave, at the intersection with Colorado Ave, opposite the visitors center.

Post & Communications The post office is at 201 E Pikes Peak Ave; the zip code is 80903. Opposite the post office, Kinkos Copies (π 719-633-6683; fax 633-7046), 214 E Pike Peak Ave, offers fax and copy services.

COLORADO

The Springs' Founders

The soda-water springs at the foot of Pikes Peak were once sacred sites for Native Americans. Each winter, the Utes camped in the Garden of the Gods at Camp Creek in the present Glen Eyrie estate. Their annual migration from the Rocky Mountains to the plains buffalo hunting grounds by the Ute Pass Trail is among the best documented journeys of any Native American group. The Utes created paths that became the mountain highways pioneers would one day follow.

In 1859, Colorado City, then part of Kansas Territory, gained prominence as the supply center for the gold camps of the South Park area using the Ute Pass Trail. This was a center of activity, where miners patronizing the saloons and brothels rubbed shoulders with tuberculosis patients seeking cures from the area's mineral water.

By 1869, General William Jackson Palmer arrived following his release from the Union Army. Palmer envisioned a resort around the springs that wouldn't have the rough character of most early Western towns. His vision was an attempt to coerce his sheltered young Long Island bride, Queen Mellen, to settle with him in Colorado since her father's investment would fund Palmer's D&RG Railroad. In 1871 Palmer founded the Fountain Colony, which struggled at first but was rescued by the unlikely combination of tourists and tuberculosis sufferers. Those partaking in the evils of drink weren't welcomed in Palmer's strict society, but they could easily slake their thirst in nearby Colorado City.

Palmer's infatuation with British customs led to the creation of his Glen Eyrie estate, as well as forming the basis of friendships with several gentlemen from the United Kingdom. Among the first to move to Fountain Colony with Palmer's prompting was Dr William Bell, who founded Villa La Font (now Manitou Springs) around 1872. Another was Dr Samuel Edwin Solly, who promoted the health benefits of smelly, foul-tasting soda water. William Blackmore renamed Villa La Font (Fountain Village) 'Manitou' after the Algonquin spirit of Longfellow's epic poem. Rose Kingsley, the daughter of famed poet Charles Kingsley, also came to reside here.

Americans took on British affectations for formal teas and old-world sports – Fountain Colony began to be called Little London. All this helped Palmer's endeavor to succeed, yet his wife, Queen, remained dissatisfied and returned to the East Coast.

Seeking to improve her health in 1873, author Helen Hunt Jackson was also an early settler in Colorado Springs. In 1881, she published *A Century of Dishonor*, an impassioned appeal for the honorable treatment of the native tribes by the US government. With no improvement in her health, in 1885 she left for the moderate climate of San Francisco, where she died that same year.

In 1911, the elderly Chipeta, widow of Chief Ouray, rode with other tribal members to mark the historic Ute Pass Trail in an event that commemorated Colorado Springs' establishment. ∎

Bookstores The impressive Chinook Bookstore (☎ 719-635-1195), across from Acacia Park at 210 N Tejon St, will brighten the day of any traveler with its fine selection of maps and travel literature, plus its extensive collection of Western Americana. An enormous collection of used books is waiting for readers at Four Corners (☎ 719-635-4514), at 119 E Bijou St, also across from Acacia Park.

Medical Services Memorial Hospital (☎ 719-356-5000), 1400 E Boulder St, offers adult and pediatric trauma care in the Emergency & Trauma Center (☎ 719-365-5221).

Laundry South of downtown at 1536 S Nevada, King's Cleaners & Laundromat (☎ 719-520-5017) is open daily. It has self-service machines, televisions, video games and drop-off service for 90¢ per lb.

Colorado Springs Pioneer Museum

Occupying two floors of the 1903 El Paso County Courthouse, this museum (☎ 719-578-6650), 215 S Tejon St, is well worth a visit. In addition to taking in the fine exhibits (nearly a century in the making), visitors can admire the restored Main Courtroom and ride the Otis 'Birdcage Elevator.'

Displays include maps created by the government-sponsored Western expeditions that followed the Louisiana Purchase from France in 1803 – including those of Captain Zebulon Pike and Major Stephen H Long.

Other displays include an impressive collection of Van Briggle Pottery (see Van Briggle Pottery later in this chapter) and a portion of author Helen Hunt Jackson's home plus accounts of her life and writing in Colorado Springs. The museum is open Tuesday to Saturday from 10 am to 5 pm and is also open Sunday from 1 to 5 pm between May and October. Admission is free.

US Olympic Training Complex

Formerly an Air Defense Command site, since 1978 the training center has evolved to support over half of the 41 sports on the Olympic program, including swimming, cycling, basketball and gymnastics. Visitors may get training schedules to watch the gymnasts and swimmers from large viewing windows.

The visitors center (☎ 719-578-4618), 1750 E Boulder St, offers free video and walking tours of the training complex, Monday to Saturday from 9 am to 5 pm and on Sunday from 10 am to 5 pm. A mile south of the training center, the banked-track velodrome in Memorial Park offers weekday evening bicycle racing thrills under the lights throughout the summer.

Western Museum of Mining & Industry

Much of the historic mining equipment on display at this museum still works and visitors will learn more about mining here from the many exhibits and hands-on displays than by taking every mine tour offered in the state.

The accredited Western Museum of Mining & Industry (☎ 719-488-0880)

Chamber Pots

Careful readers may have noted that museums throughout Colorado are inclined to include an inconspicuous chamber pot or two in their Victorian displays. No such display currently exists at the 1st-class Pioneer Museum, but the amused curators provided a valuable bit of research on the topic by sharing a poem on the porcelain bowl that is not a cookie jar. A brief excerpt from *The Thunder-Mug* written in 1974 by Owen Sanders follows:

When tub and privy moved indoors
To occupy a closet,
The thunder-mug lay silent
And received no more deposit.

Museums that display the chamber pot are the Rosemont Museum in Pueblo, which has a fine example, the Glenwood Springs Frontier Historical Museum and Fairplay's South Park City Museum, among others. ∎

COLORADO

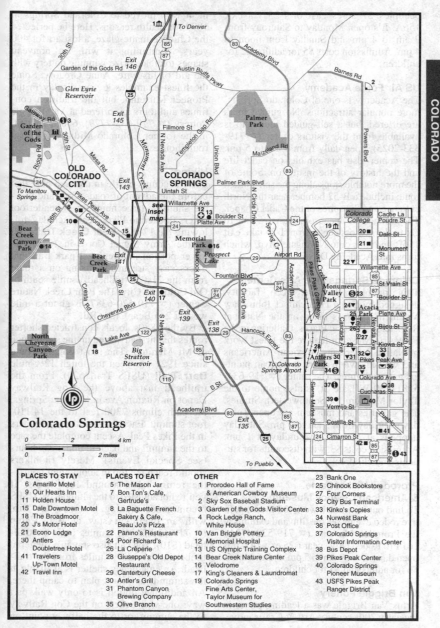

Colorado Springs

PLACES TO STAY	PLACES TO EAT	OTHER	
6 Amarillo Motel	5 The Mason Jar	1 Prorodeo Hall of Fame	23 Bank One
9 Our Hearts Inn	7 Bon Ton's Cafe,	& American Cowboy Museum	25 Chinook Bookstore
11 Holden House	Gertrude's	2 Sky Sox Baseball Stadium	27 Four Corners
15 Dale Downtown Motel	8 La Baguette French	3 Garden of the Gods Visitor Center	32 City Bus Terminal
18 The Broadmoor	Bakery & Cafe,	4 Rock Ledge Ranch,	33 Kinko's Copies
20 J's Motor Hotel	Beau Jo's Pizza	White House	34 Nurwest Bank
21 Econo Lodge	22 Panino's Restaurant	10 Van Briggle Pottery	36 Post Office
30 Antlers	24 Poor Richard's	12 Memorial Hospital	37 Colorado Springs
Doubletree Hotel	26 La Crêperie	13 US Olympic Training Complex	Visitor Information Center
41 Travelers	28 Giuseppe's Old Depot	14 Bear Creek Nature Center	38 Bus Depot
Up-Town Motel	Restaurant	16 Velodrome	39 Pikes Peak Center
42 Travel Inn	29 Canterbury Cheese	17 King's Cleaners & Laundromat	40 Colorado Springs
	31 Phantom Canyon	19 Colorado Springs	Pioneer Museum
	Brewing Company	Fine Arts Center,	43 USFS Pikes Peak
	35 Olive Branch	Taylor Museum for	Ranger District
		Southwestern Studies	

occupies 27 acres east of I-25 via exit 156A. It's open Monday to Saturday from 9 am to 4 pm and Sunday from noon to 4 pm. Admission costs $5 for adults, $2 for children.

US Air Force Academy

The Academy is one of Colorado Springs' more popular attractions. No guided tours are offered, but a self-guided tour map is available from the visitors center (☎ 719-333-2025), open daily from 9 am to 5 pm. The center also has exhibits on cadet life and the history of the institution. Some of the more notable stops along the self-guided route include a B-52 bomber near the North entrance and the spires of the Cadet Chapel. The grounds are open from 9 am to 5 pm. To get to the visitors center from I-25 take exit 156B and turn onto Northgate Blvd, which turns into Academy Drive.

Colorado Springs Fine Arts Center

This pueblo-style Art Deco facility, designed by Santa Fe architect John Gaw Meem in 1936, is listed on the National Register of Historic Places. Galleries in the Fine Arts Museum feature the finest work of Native Americans, Mexican-Americans and well-known Western American painters and sculptures. The center (☎ 719-634-5581), 30 W Dale St, is also home to the Taylor Museum for Southwestern Studies. The galleries and museum are open Tuesday to Friday from 9 am to 5 pm, Saturday it opens at 10 am and Sunday at 1 pm. Admission costs $3, with discounts for students and children.

Prorodeo Hall of Fame & American Cowboy Museum

To find out how ranch work led to competitive rodeo events see the film and exhibits at the Prorodeo Museum (☎ 719-528-4764), 101 Pro Rodeo Drive near I-25 exit 147. It is open daily from 9 am to 5 pm. Admission is $6 for adults and $3 for children.

Van Briggle Pottery

Artus Van Briggle was a leading potter in the early 20th-century Arts & Crafts movement who moved to Colorado Springs in 1899 for health reasons. Here he perfected the Chinese matte glaze, a lost art for 400 years, combining it with art nouveau shapes to create prize-winning pottery with the aid of his wife, Anne Gregory. Some the finest examples are on display in the Pioneer Museum, but the tradition continues and tours are offered at Van Briggle Pottery (☎ 719-633-7729), 600 S 21st St, in the former Colorado Midland Railroad roundhouse.

Hiking

Early accounts of life in the area note that before the advent of roads, cogs and bicycle shuttles, large numbers of tenderfoot hikers flocked to Pikes Peak each day, following the 17-mile **Bear Creek Trail** built by the Army Signal Corps in 1873. The lower portion is a regional park trail that offers easy streamside hiking on a route from the 21st St trailhead, 1 mile south of Old Colorado City. The Bear Creek Nature Center (☎ 719-520-6387) is about a mile west at 245 Bear Creek Rd.

By the 1880s, locals constructed shorter routes that first advanced up the steep slope of Mt Manitou. The most popular route since 1921 has been the tough 12½-mile **Barr Trail** (USFS Trail 620). From the trailhead just above the Cog Railway Depot on Ruxton Ave in Manitou Springs, the path climbs 7300 feet to the 14,110-foot summit. Each August, the top runners in the Pikes Peak Ascent complete the race to the summit and back in under 3½ hours (see Special Events). Merely fit hikers should reach the top in about eight hours – the return takes around four hours. If you're not adjusted to the altitude, the USFS recommends making it a two-day trip, with an overnight stay at Barr Camp (☎ 719-630-3934), 7 miles from the trailhead ($10). You can also stay in a shelter at timberline, about 8½ miles from the trailhead. An emergency shelter is available at the summit, but don't plan to camp there. An additional option is to only walk part way: one-way tickets on the Cog Railway to the summit, or to the halfway point on

Mountain View Trail are available on a limited basis.

For maps and hiking information about the Pike National Forest, which surrounds the Springs and the South Platte River, you should contact the Pikes Peak Ranger District office (☎ 719-636-1602) at 601 S Weber St. If you're serious about exploring the area, you can pick up a copy of Zoltin Maloccsay's *Trail Guide to the Pikes Peak Country*, available at the USFS Pikes Peak Ranger District office for $19.

Road & Mountain Biking

Road bikes are a good means of getting around near the Colorado College campus north of downtown, along Pikes Peak Ave through Colorado City and in Manitou Springs. Also, consider visiting Garden of the Gods (see that section) on a bike – good bike access exists along 30th St on the park's east side and along El Paso Blvd on the south side. Bijou St provides bicycle access over I-25 and Monument Creek.

The 14-mile **Santa Fe Hiking Trail** passes the Air Force Academy and Western Mining Museum on the west side of I-25, north of Colorado Springs between trailheads near Southgate Blvd and Palmer Lake and is accessible on mountain bike. In Colorado Springs, the Pikes Peak Greenway will eventually connect with the Santa Fe Trail to form the 40-mile Spine Trail. For now, the trail follows **Monument Valley Park** north 5 miles from the Bijou St trailhead to Roswell Park near Fillmore St, and south 1 mile to the power plant on Fountain Creek. The hills surrounding Fountain Valley offer a few good trails for mountain bikes to follow, like Bear Creek Trail west of the Bear Creek Nature Center. For more trail information contact volunteers at the nonprofit National Off Road Bicycle Association (☎ 719-578-4596), 1750 E Boulder St.

Colorado Challenge Unlimited (☎ 719-633-6399, 800-798-5954), 204 S 24th St, has led tours all over the world and can provide bikes or guides for local outings – including a 19-mile descent down Pikes Peak Hwy.

Special Events

Every July 4 the Pikes Peak Hwy becomes the course for the **Pikes Peak International Hill Climb**, an auto race that started in 1916. An interesting array of rally cars, trucks, motorcycles and more exotic vehicles shows up at the event, which always draws a slew of gearheads.

In August, the **Pikes Peak or Bust Rodeo** (☎ 719-635-3548) provides 1st-class professional rodeo entertainment. The Triple Crown of Running (☎ 719-473-2625) organizes the **Pikes Peak Ascent**, a 13½-mile run to the summit of Pikes Peak (a climb of 7800 feet) held in August. They also coordinate the **Pikes Peak Marathon** in June, with a course running up and down the peak.

Places to Stay

Rates really get out of hand in summer. For example, the lowly Econo Lodge charges $80 for a very basic single, compared with $35 in winter. Rooms can also be scarce during the peak summer months. In addition to the locally owned motels listed below, Colorado Springs also has representatives from nearly every national motel chain – see the appendix at the back of the book for toll-free phone numbers.

For nearby accommodations in more pleasant surroundings, see Manitou Springs later in this chapter.

Camping *Garden of the Gods Campground* (☎ 719-475-9450, 800-248-9451), 3704 W Colorado Ave (see Manitou Springs map), provides tent/RV spaces for $23/26 in a large, paved area, though a few trees have been thrown in for consolation.

Cabins *Garden of the Gods Campground* (above) has small, basic cabins that sleep four, $35 for two people and $5 per additional person, including bedding. Bathrooms are outdoors, so this could make for a chilly stay in winter. Laundry and showers are available around the clock. Guests may also use the pool and spa. Like the campground, the cabins are closed in winter.

COLORADO

B&Bs The Victorian *Holden House* (☎ 719-471-3980), 1102 W Pikes Peak Ave, has gotten good reviews from travelers and features private baths in all rooms (some with tubs for two); rates are $100 to $110. *Our Hearts Inn* (☎ 719-473-3165, 800-533-7095), 2215 W Colorado Ave, is another Victorian home where all rooms have private bath; some rooms also have fireplaces or jacuzzis. Rates range from $80 to $120.

Motels The *Amarillo Motel* (☎ 719-635-8539), 2801 W Colorado Ave, offers rooms for $45 in summer, $30 in winter. It's on the site of the first cabin in Old Colorado City, replaced in 1862 by the El Paso Hotel. When the hotel burned down in 1890, Charles Stockbridge constructed the present fortress that serves as the motel office, as well as a gun and military souvenir shop.

Rooms at *J's Motor Hotel* (☎ 719-633-5513), 820 N Nevada Ave, are a bit plain, but among the cheapest in town at $43/48 a single/double in summer, about $14 less in winter. Amenities include a heated pool and satellite TV, and the location is convenient to downtown restaurants and sights.

On the south end of downtown, the *Travelers Up-Town Motel* (☎ 719-473-2774), 220 E Cimarron St, and the *Travel Inn* (☎ 719-636-3986), 512 S Nevada Ave, both offer plain singles/doubles for about $50/55 in summer, $30/35 in winter.

Just west of downtown the *Dale Downtown Motel* (☎ 719-636-3721), 620 W Colorado Ave, may not look all that elegant, but it's not a bad value at $46/49 for singles/doubles in summer. There's a heated pool and kitchenette units are available.

The *Maple Lodge* (☎ 719-685-9230), at 9 El Paso Blvd, located near the Garden of the Gods (see Manitou Springs map), has a heated pool, patio area and well-kept rooms starting from $50.

Hotels General Palmer would not recognize the lavish high-rise that replaced 1st-class Antlers Hotel he established in the late 19th century. The rooms at the modern *Antlers Doubletree Hotel* (☎ 719-473-5600, 800-222-8733), 4 S Cascade Ave, cost $150 for a double in summer, $95 in winter.

Resorts At the foot of Cheyenne Mountain, 5 miles southwest of downtown Colorado Springs, *The Broadmoor* (☎ 719-577-5775, 800-634-7711), 1 Lake Circle, ranks among the country's most elite establishments. This amazing complex offers activities like shopping, ice skating, golf, tennis and squash. Tourists come to gawk at the grounds and the 550-room hotel opened by Spencer Penrose in 1918 to rival the Antlers Hotel. Dignitaries like John D Rockefeller helped inaugurate the elaborate palace and it has continued to attract high-ranking officials, including presidents Richard Nixon, Ronald Reagan and George Bush. It would be a shame to simply spend the night without enjoying the spa, movie theater or the grounds, which include a lake and horseback riding and bicycle trails. Doubles ranges from $280 to $375 in summer, and $170 to $260 in winter. Special 'gold,' 'spa' and 'romantic getaway' packages are also available.

Places to Eat
Colorado Springs Metro Area A good health-conscious place to get started is the *Olive Branch* (☎ 719-475-1199), 23 S Tejon Ave. It's a favored breakfast spot offering omelets for $5, or low-fat french toast for $4. Try the fresh fruit smoothie. The lunch and dinner menus are also appealing and include a good selection of salads.

The extremely popular *Giuseppe's Old Depot Restaurant* (☎ 719-635-3111) is housed in a former D&RG train station at 10 S Sierra Madre St, with live tracks in back and an historic steam engine displayed in front. Hearty Italian or American lunches cost between $6 and $8, while dinner prices range from $10 to $20 (filet mignon and lobster tail).

Since the mid-1970s, *Poor Richard's* (☎ 719-632-7721), 324½ N Tejon St, has served vegetarian meals, pizza and beer to a hip crowd that enjoys the selection of alternative press materials and bulletin board advertisements. There are also inter-esting sandwich choices (pecan-crusted chicken breast, grilled eggplant) and four daily soup specials. Prices are a bit steep at $5.25 for a sandwich.

La Crêperie Restaurant (☎ 719-632-0984), 204 N Tejon Ave, is the perfect place for a light treat. It features a mouth-watering selection of dessert crêpes for $3, or you can have a crêpe entree for about $6. On Friday and Saturday nights, the crowd at *Panino's Restaurant* (☎ 719-635-7452), 604 N Tejon Ave, spills out into the street. For $5 you get homemade dough rolled with fillings of cheese, vegetables and beans or lean meats, served with a salad. Favorites include the barbecue panino and a panino smothered in green chile sauce. For inexpensive sandwiches ($3.50), try *Canterbury Cheese* (☎ 719-635-3337), 26 N Tejon. This is a good option if you need items for a picnic lunch.

Take the kids for a handcrafted draft root beer at the *Phantom Canyon Brewing Company* (☎ 719-635-2800), 2 E Pikes Peak Ave, where five to 10 of their fine micro-brews are also on tap. The menu includes some tasty entree salads for around $6 and hearty pub fare, such as shepherd's pie, though more refined items like rainbow trout and paella are also available.

In the Antlers Doubletree Hotel at 4 S Cascade Ave, the lavish *Antler's Grill* (☎ 719-473-5600) offers a fresh and gen-erous breakfast buffet for $10, including a wide array of hot and cold items, juice, coffee and attentive service. The dinner menu includes some regional specialties like pan-seared venison for $19.

Old Colorado City *La Baguette French Bakery & Cafe* (☎ 719-577-4818), 2417 W Colorado Ave, is a bright, spacious eatery that opens at 7 am and serves espresso. Beer and wine are served with inexpensive meals like tortellini with prosciutto in cream sauce or a cheese and fruit plate for under $7. Next door, the historic Thunder & Buttons building houses *Beau Jo's Pizza* (☎ 719-442-0270), 2415 W Colorado Ave. Most people are fond of their creative

pizzas, though hard-core traditionalists (ie, New Yorkers) may balk. *Bon Ton's Cafe* (☎ 719-634-1007), 2601 W Colorado Ave, serves breakfast and lunch to a casual crowd on its large patio for under $6.

The *Mason Jar* (☎ 719-632-4820), at 2925 W Colorado Ave, is so popular that prime-time diners must often wait to be seated, in order to enjoy attentive service and inexpensive American fare for break-fast, lunch or dinner.

Gertrude's (☎ 719-471-0887), 2625 W Colorado Ave, offers a fairly good choice of sandwiches, salads and pastas for lunch and dinner, with a lot of veggie options. It was even voted Colorado Springs' best vege-tarian restaurant by the local newspaper.

Entertainment
Colorado Springs has a fairly lively music and theater scene. The best way to find out what's going on is to pick up a copy of *Go!*, a free entertainment newspaper with theater, dance and music listings. It's published every Friday and can be found at the Colo-rado Springs visitors center and elsewhere.

Spectator Sports
The *Colorado Springs Sky Sox* (☎ 719-597-3000), 4385 Tutt Blvd, is the Triple A minor league farm club for the Major League Colorado Rockies. From April to September the Sky Sox play 72 home games in the Pacific Coast League, against opponents like the Albuquerque Dukes (affiliated with the LA Dodgers), Phoenix Firebirds (San Francisco Giants) and Tucson Toros (Houston Astros).

Sky Sox Baseball Stadium is surrounded by the Sandcreek Community Park in the Stetson Hills northeast of downtown; take I-25 north to exit 146 and travel east on Austin Bluffs Pkwy for 6 miles then turn right on Barnes Rd and continue 2 miles to the park. General admission tickets cost under $4.50 and reserved seats are avail-able for under $7.

Getting There & Away
Air Though not served by as many flights or airlines, the Colorado Springs Airport

(☎ 719-550-1900) offers a viable alternative to Denver International Airport, especially if you're headed to southern Colorado destinations.

America West Airlines offers daily direct flights to Phoenix, AZ. Delta and American Airlines each have daily flights to Dallas-Fort Worth, TX, and Delta offers three more flights to Salt Lake City, UT. United Airlines services Denver and Chicago daily, while Reno Air flies to Las Vegas, NV. United Express provides commuter service to Albuquerque, NM, and Denver.

Other destinations served by direct flights from Colorado Springs include Atlanta, GA (Delta), Houston, TX (Continental), Minneapolis/St Paul, MN (Northwest), and St Louis, MO (TWA). Nearly every other major airport in the country can be reached via connections in these cities, Denver or Chicago.

For the shortest route from the airport to downtown, follow Drennen Rd from the main terminal, turn right on Powers Blvd, then turn left on Fountain Blvd to the central area. From I-25 take exit 139 to reach the airport.

Bus The TNM&O Bus Depot (☎ 719-635-1505) is at 120 Weber St. It's open daily from 5:15 am to 9:30 pm Monday to Saturday, 7:30 am to 9:30 pm Sunday. Eight daily buses travel from Cheyenne to Pueblo via Denver and Colorado Springs.

Car Colorado Springs is in the middle of Colorado, 68 miles south of Denver on I-25, and 44 miles north of Pueblo on the same highway.

DIA Shuttle Colorado Springs Airport Shuttle Service (☎ 719-578-5232) runs five vans daily between Colorado Springs Airport and Denver International Airport, stopping at the city's larger hotels along the way. The fare is $27 per person, one-way.

Getting Around
To/From the Airport Colorado Springs Airport Shuttle Service (☎ 719-578-5232) charges $13 to carry up to two people from

the airport to the Antlers Hotel. The Yellow Cab (☎ 719-634-5000) fare from the Colorado Springs Airport to the Antlers Hotel is approximately $20, and extra passengers are only 50¢ each. American Cab (☎ 719-637-1111) has similar rates.

Bus The City Bus Terminal (☎ 719-475-9733), 127 E Kiowa St, offers schedule information and route maps for all 13 transit lines in the Colorado Springs area. From Monday to Saturday the No 1 bus for Manitou Springs leaves the terminal every 30 minutes until 6:15 pm. The fare to Manitou is $1. You can also use this bus to get to the Garden of the Gods visitors center. Passengers wishing to go to the Olympic Training Center should take the No 1 bus in the North Academy direction.

Car Main rental companies Alamo (☎ 719-574-8579), Avis (☎ 719-596-2751), Budget (☎ 719-574-7401), Hertz (☎ 719-596-1863) and National (☎ 719-596-1519) all rent cars at the Colorado Springs airport.

Taxi Call Yellow Cab (☎ 719-634-5000) for local transportation.

GARDEN OF THE GODS

Author Helen Hunt Jackson referred to these spectacular sandstone formations as 'a supernatural catastrophe.' According to legend, Rufus Cable named them in 1859 when he objected to a proposal to use the area as a beer garden: 'Beer garden! Why this is a fit place for a Garden of the Gods!'

In 1879, Charles Elliot Perkins, head of the Burlington Railroad, purchased the land but kept it in a natural state. Following his death in 1907, his survivors bequeathed 480 acres to Colorado Springs on the condition that the park be established, free of development and open to the public without charge. The park itself is untouched, but is surrounded by housing developments.

Garden of the Gods attracts over 2 million visitors each year and provides a scenic introduction to the geologic history of the Colorado Front Range. The best way to see it and avoid the crowd is to take to one of the park trails, as most visitors prefer the windshield tour.

The Garden of the Gods is northwest of Old Colorado City, about 4½ miles west of downtown Colorado Springs on US 24. To get there take I-25 exit 146 and drive west on Garden of the Gods Rd; turn left (south) on 30th St. Begin your tour at the visitors center (☎ 719-634-6666) on the park's eastern border at Gateway Rd and 30th St. Here you'll see the exhibits on the natural and social history of the rock formations. Special presentations and ranger-led nature walks are scheduled each morning and afternoon. Brochures showing short hiking trails are available in French, German, Japanese and Spanish. During summer months the visitors center is open daily from 8 am to 9 pm; winter hours are from 8:30 am to 5 pm daily.

A one-way loop road through the park begins at Gateway Rd and is well suited for bicyclists (with moderate climbing). Visitors can also choose to leave their cars at the visitors center and take a tram for a small fee. The recent closure of the road passing between Gateway Rocks allows unobstructed viewing of the famous scene toward Pikes Peak, photographed by William Henry Jackson. This route is now a trail that leads to the former Hidden Inn curio shop (rest rooms available), where you will see a stunning view of Cathedral Valley and possibly observe daring rock climbers. An option from the loop route follows Garden Drive past additional formations to another park entrance near US 24 in Manitou Springs. Start in the early morning for the best lighting.

Rock Ledge Ranch
Ornithologist Dr William Slater, author of *History of the Birds of Colorado*, taught at Colorado College and built the Cape Town Dutch-style White House in 1907. Guides at the living history site wear period dress as they show visitors around a restored 1867 homestead, working ranch and blacksmith shop. From the Garden of the Gods visitors center, take Gateway Rd and take the first left onto Ranch Rd. The Rock Ledge Ranch (☎ 719-578-6777) is open from June to Labor Day, Wednesday to Sunday from 10 am to 4 pm. Admission costs $3.

Rock Climbing
The vertical faces of the sandstone formations are not suitable for amateur climbers. Technical climbers must follow established routes and register at the visitors center. Anyone caught climbing, or even scrambling, on the formations without registering is subject to arrest and a $500 fine.

Horseback Riding
Academy Riding Stables (☎ 719-633-5667), on the park's south edge at 4 El Paso Blvd (see Manitou Springs map), offers one-hour rides into the park for $20.

MANITOU SPRINGS
A collection of seven soda-water springs (plus one particularly nasty-tasting sulfur-water spring) is located in Manitou Springs (population 4800). The water has a high mineral content and some locals prefer to drink it by mixing it with lemonade. The downtown area has a nice historical feel to it, but this is usually drowned out by throngs of tourists in summer.

Orientation
Manitou Springs, founded in the narrow canyon of Fountain Creek, sits at the base of Pikes Peak on the southern border of Garden of the Gods, just west of I-25; it's surrounded by Colorado Springs. The core historic district is along Manitou Ave near the intersection with Canon Ave.

Information
The Manitou Springs Chamber of Commerce (☎ 719-685-5089, 800-642-2567), 354 Manitou Ave, offers friendly, personalized service and has well-organized information on local attractions, lodging and restaurants. It's open 9 am to 5 pm daily. Services that aren't available in Manitou Springs can be found in Colorado Springs.

There is an ATM at the Bank One drive-through branch, 484 Manitou Ave.

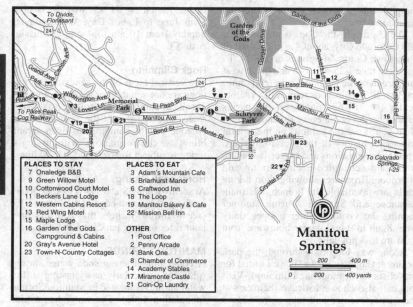

PLACES TO STAY
7 Onaledge B&B
9 Green Willow Motel
10 Cottonwood Court Motel
11 Beckers Lane Lodge
12 Western Cabins Resort
13 Red Wing Motel
15 Maple Lodge
16 Garden of the Gods
    Campground & Cabins
20 Gray's Avenue Hotel
23 Town-N-Country Cottages

PLACES TO EAT
3 Adam's Mountain Cafe
5 Briarhurst Manor
6 Craftwood Inn
18 The Loop
19 Manitou Bakery & Cafe
22 Mission Bell Inn

OTHER
1 Post Office
2 Penny Arcade
4 Bank One
8 Chamber of Commerce
14 Academy Stables
17 Miramonte Castle
21 Coin-Op Laundry

Manitou Springs

0   200   400 m
0   200   400 yards

The Coin-Op Laundry, diagonally oppo-site the town hall at 521 Manitou Ave, is open 24 hours.

Things to See
Community volunteers lead free one-hour tours of the historic mineral springs. You can contact the chamber of commerce (☎ 719-685-5089) for reservations or pick up a map and set out on your own. If you have a bike, consider taking your water bottle along to visit all eight springs on the map.

Don't miss the handsome gazebo at Seven Minute Spring next to Memorial Park, or the **Ute sculpture fountain** at the Ute Chief Spring. Just upstream on Foun-tain Creek is the Ute Pass shelf road to the gold fields, built in 1860, which follows the old Ute Trail. From the switchback on Serpentine Rd, you can follow the old route to **Rainbow Falls**, only a short dis-tance from the paved roadway.

Navajo Springs is in the so-called **Penny Arcade**, where a surprising

number of vintage amusements continue to excite players of all ages. Once the tell-tale marks of a tourist trap, the arcade's skee-ball, Dumbo rides and salt-water taffy are now vestiges of another era. On the north canyon slopes behind the arcade on Park Ave is Jerome Wheeler's *Windermere Summer Home*, an abandoned hotel topped with a five-story turret. In fact, the residen-tial area on upper Canon and Spencer Aves is a good place to compare various styles of turret architecture.

Lower Canon Ave is the main street of the Historic Business District. The **Italian Town Clock** at the intersection of Canon and Manitou Aves was a gift from Jerome Wheeler in 1899.

From the junction of Manitou and Ruxton Aves, it's a stiff climb up Ruxton Ave to the 46-room **Miramonte Castle**, 9 Capital Hill Ave, built in 1892-95 by the wealthy Father Jean Frank Colon – reportedly as a health resort for his ailing mother. Tours of the castle and its exhibits are available for $3.

Pikes Peak Cog Railway

Tourists have been making this trip since 1891, but new Swiss-built trains operate like clockwork on the 3¼-hour roundtrip journey, which includes a 40-minute orientation at the top. Bring a jacket or plan on wasting your time in the summit restaurant and gift shop.

Trains leave the Cog Railway Depot (☎ 719-685-5401), 515 Ruxton Ave, from May to November daily. Ticket prices are $22 for adults and $10 for children. Reservations are essential.

Places to Stay

Many of the small lodgings close for the winter and their rates attempt to make up for it during peak summer months. But prices aren't really higher than those in Colorado Springs and the surroundings are generally more pleasant.

B&Bs Built in 1886, the three-story Queen Anne-style *Gray's Avenue Hotel* (☎ 719-685-1277), 711 Manitou Ave, offers rooms with private or shared bath ranging from $60 to $70, including full breakfasts.

A superior example of well-maintained Craftsman-style architecture, albeit oddly furnished, is *Onaledge* (☎ 719-685-4265, 800-530-8253), 336 El Paso Blvd, where elaborate rooms with private bath cost $95 to $170, for a two-room suite with hot tub and fireplace. Rates are $75 to $140 in winter.

Motels & Cabins The quiet and shady *Beckers Lane Lodge* (☎ 719-685-1866), 115 Beckers Lane, has rooms for $42/50 in summer, though sometimes it only takes weekly rentals. If so, the *Red Wing Motel* (☎ 719-685-5656), at 56 El Paso Blvd, has plain but well-kept rooms from $49 in summer, $30 in winter. If you want to do your own cooking, *Western Cabins Resort* (☎ 719-685-5755), 106 Beckers Lane, has fairly spacious cabins with kitchens available as singles/doubles for $68/78.

The *Town-N-Country Cottages* (☎ 719-685-5427) at 123 Crystal Park Rd are away

from the traffic on Manitou Ave and offer cottage and duplex-style units for $69 ($55 in winter).

There is a slew of motels along the heavily trafficked Manitou Ave. One of the more charming spots is *Cottonwood Court Motel* (☎ 719-685-1312), 120 Manitou Ave. Rooms are a bit small, but most are set back from the road among shade trees. Room rates start at $45 in summer, $30 in winter. A nice summer option is the cozy *Green Willow Motel* (☎ 719-685-9997), 328 Manitou Ave. Cabin style rooms sit back from the road around a grassy courtyard area. Rooms with kitchenettes are available and rates start at $50.

Places to Eat

The *Manitou Bakery & Cafe* (☎ 719-695-5808), in the Historic Landmark District at 729 Manitou Ave, is not a bad spot for a muffin and a latte. Nearby, in a cozy Victorian dining room, *Adam's Mountain Cafe* (☎ 719-685-1430), 110 Canon Ave, offers espresso drinks and a menu of healthy breakfast selections starting at about $3. Dinner prices range from $6 to $10.

Specializing in California-style Mexican dishes, *The Loop* (☎ 719-685-9344), at 965 Manitou Ave, offers a few window seats opening onto the busy sidewalk. Daily lunch specials are a good deal at $4, and dinner combination platters are also not bad value at around $8. The adobe-style *Mission Bell Inn* (☎ 719-685-9089), south of Manitou Ave at 178 Crystal Park Rd, specializes in more traditional Mexican meals. Dinners cost between $8 and $11.

For top-end dining, fish and game entrees range from grilled piñon trout for $14 to exotic caribou for $24 at the *Craftwood Inn* (☎ 719-685-9000), 404 El Paso Blvd. The *Briarhurst Manor* (☎ 719-685-1864), at 404 Manitou Ave, offers outstanding cuisine in a masonry home built in 1876 by Dr William Bell, founder of Manitou Springs The house features a rich wood interior and carved sandstone gables and gargoyles. Dinner prices range from $11 for the pasta primavera to $30 for the rack of lamb.

COLORADO

AROUND MANITOU SPRINGS
Pikes Peak Toll Rd
From the town of Divide, west of Manitou Springs on US 24, you can drive the Pikes Peak Toll Rd to the summit. Built in 1915 by Spencer Penrose, the road is now operated by the City of Colorado Springs. Road conditions and directions are available by calling ☎ 719-635-7506 or 719-684-9383. The road is open from 7 am to 7 pm in the summer, 9 am to 3 pm the rest of the year. The trip costs $6 per person.

Green Mountain Falls
Bypassed by the new US 24 alignment, the town of Green Mountain Falls (population 700) is on the old highway. Its imposing wooden Church in the Wildwood, with a bell tower and elaborate stained glass, dates from 1889 – few wooden structures of such antiquity have avoided fire in this area. A 3-mile loop hike from the small lake, the central focus of the town, leads to **Catamount Falls** and **Crystal Falls**. A trail map is available from a booth at the lake.

Near the lake the *Pine Gables Tavern* (☎ 719-684-2555) has a rustic mountain atmosphere and sometimes offers live blues entertainment. At the upper end of the lake the *Pantry Restaurant* has earned a reputation for good breakfasts. It's conveniently located next to the peaceful *Falls Motel* (☎ 719-684-9745), which has doubles for $50 in summer, $30 in winter. Amenities include an outdoor hot tub and a picnic area.

FLORISSANT FOSSIL BEDS NATIONAL MONUMENT
In 1873, Dr AC Peale, part of the USGS Hayden expedition, was on his way to survey and map the South Park area, when he discovered these ancient lake deposits buried by the dust and ash from a series of volcanic eruptions. Subsequent excavations revealed 1100 insect species, 114 plant species, plus several fish, birds and small mammal species, including the tapir-like oreodont and the mesohippo. In 1969 the triumvirate of renowned paleobotanist Dr Estella Leopold, wildflower authority Dr Beatrice Willard and activist Vim Crane Wright succeeded in gaining national monument protection for the fossils of 35 million-year-old Lake Florissant.

Orientation & Information
The monument is located about 30 miles west of Colorado Springs via US 24. The place to start is the visitors center (☎ 719-748-3253), in the center of the monument on Teller County Rd 1, 2 miles south of US 24. Museum-quality fossil exhibits are on display and rangers provide guides to nearby trails and conduct daily interpretive programs. Special presentations and guided walks are scheduled each summer – call ahead for a calendar of events. The center also sells books on the area's natural history. It's open daily from 8 am to 7 pm from Memorial Day to Labor Day, and the rest of the year from 8 am to 4 pm. Admission is $2 per individual over 16 years of age, or $4 for three or more in a family. The official map and guide given to each visitor is available in French and German.

Hornbeck House
Adeline Hornbeck settled the first 160-acre homestead in the valley in 1878 with her four children. The other outbuildings include a bunkhouse, carriage shed, barn and root cellar. All of the buildings have been restored or rebuilt by the NPS.

Florissant Heritage Museum
The striking old Grange Hall with its bell tower, schoolhouse and outhouse sits in a field of flowers next to US 24 in Florissant. The 'museum' is rarely open, but it really doesn't matter – it's just pretty to look at. Nearby, the mound-shaped rock formation at Fortification Hill was a favorite Ute campsite.

Hiking
The park has more than 10 miles of trails through open meadows and rolling hills – all can be reached on foot from the visitors center. No one should miss the **Walk through Time Nature Trail**, a half-mile

loop. The 1-mile **Petrified Forest Loop** leads to several petrified stumps, including the remains of a giant sequoia measuring 38 feet in circumference. Absolutely no collecting is allowed in the monument. Interpretive brochures are available for both trails.

Signs of deer and elk are often seen along the southeastern segment of the **Hornbeck Wildlife Loop** that crosses the highway in front of the visitors center. After 1 mile it intersects **Shootin' Star Trail** to the Barksdale Picnic area, near Lower Twin Rock Rd. The Shootin' Star features good late afternoon views of Pikes Peak and the possibility of hearing coyotes or catching a glimpse of the resident pair of golden eagles over the quiet, secluded meadows and forests.

Flower Walks Between late June and mid-August, visitors make special trips to Florissant (French for 'blooming') for ranger-guided walks held each Friday at 11:30 am. Admire, but please don't pick.

Places to Stay
No overnight stays are allowed in the monument. The nearest accommodation are in Lake George (4 miles west) and Woodland Park (15 miles east). Both towns are located on US 24. In Lake George the *11 Mile Motel* (☎ 719-748-3931), 38122 US 24, has cabins with mountain views from around $50 in summer, $30 in winter. *Elwell's Cabins* (☎ 719-687-9838), 2220 Lee Circle Drive, Woodland Park, has five cabins spread over 5 acres. Rates start at $55. Also in Woodland Park, *Above the Clouds B&B* (☎ 719-686-0123), 15478 US 24, has rooms with private bath, full breakfasts, a hot tub ranging from $85 to $125. The B&B also has riding stables.

PUEBLO
Once considered the Pittsburgh of the West, Pueblo's smokestack economy waned after WWII. Whereas Pueblo was Colorado's second-largest city during the first half of the 20th century, its present population of 99,400 makes it only the sixth largest. Pueblo hosts the Colorado State Fair from mid-August to Labor Day. Other than that there is little to attract visitors – for most of them Pueblo is just a place to overnight after a long day on the road.

Orientation
Downtown Pueblo's jumbled street pattern is the result of the consolidation of four separate towns. Santa Fe Ave is the north-south commercial artery. From downtown, Union Ave takes a diagonal path southwest across the Arkansas River to the Mesa Junction area.

Information
The Pueblo Chamber of Commerce (☎ 719-542-1704, 800-233-3446), next to the Sangre de Cristo Art Center at 302 N Santa Fe Ave, can provide maps, lodging information and walking tour directions. It's open weekdays from 8 am to 5 pm. Another visitors information center at US 50 and Elizabeth St (I-25 frontage) offers similar information and is open 8 am to 6 pm daily in summer and 8 am to 4 pm Monday to Saturday the rest of the year.

The USFS headquarters office for the Pike and San Isabel national forests (☎ 719-545-8737) is north of US 50 at 1920 Valley Drive. This is a good place to get maps, wilderness hiking gear and camping information for the forests of Colorado's southern Front Range. (Though the Cimarron National Grasslands are in Kansas, this is the place to find information for that as well.)

The Pueblo Bank & Trust (☎ 719-545-1834), in the central district at 301 W 5th St, and the Norwest Bank (☎ 719-544-5090) at 201 W 8th St have ATMs.

The midtown post office is at 1005 W 6 St and the zip code is 81003. Package express and fax services are available at Mail Boxes Etc (☎ 719-543-5800; fax 543-6540), 140 W 29th St.

A good selection of new books, maps and travel guides is available at the Bookery (☎ 719-544-1135), 129 E Abriendo Ave. Tumbleweed Books (☎ 719-544-3420), located nearby at 687 S Union Ave, is a good source of used books.

COLORADO

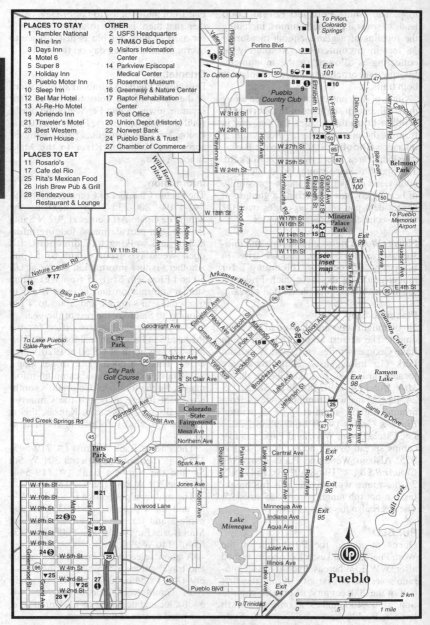

PLACES TO STAY
1 Rambler National Nine Inn
3 Days Inn
4 Motel 6
5 Super 8
7 Holiday Inn
8 Pueblo Motor Inn
10 Sleep Inn
12 Bel Mar Hotel
19 Abriendo Inn
21 Traveler's Motel
23 Best Western Town House

PLACES TO EAT
11 Rosario's
17 Cafe del Rio
25 Rita's Mexican Food
26 Irish Brew Pub & Grill
28 Rendezvous Restaurant & Lounge

OTHER
2 USFS Headquarters
6 TNM&O Bus Depot
9 Visitors Information Center
14 Parkview Episcopal Medical Center
15 Rosemont Museum
16 Greenway & Nature Center
17 Raptor Rehabilitation Center
18 Post Office
22 Norwest Bank
24 Pueblo Bank & Trust
27 Chamber of Commerce

Pueblo

Just north of the central area, Parkview Episcopal Medical Center (☎ 719-584-4000), at 400 W 16th St, provides 24-hour emergency services.

Lady Fair Laundromat (☎ 719-543-0928) is in the central district at 700 W 4th St.

Rosemont Museum

Pueblo's premier historic attraction is the three-story, 37-room Victorian mansion, constructed in 1893 of pink rhyolite stone. It contains elaborate stained glass and elegant, original furnishings. The top floor features an Egyptian mummy and other assorted booty from Andrew McClelland's global travels during the early 20th century.

The Rosemont Museum (☎ 719-545-5290), 419 W 14th St at Grand Ave, is open June to September from 10 am to 2 pm Monday to Saturday and 2 to 3:30 pm Sunday. The remainder of the year, with the exception of January when it's closed

for the entire month, it's open from 1 to 3:30 pm Tuesday to Saturday, and from 2 to 3:30 pm Sunday; it's closed Monday. Admission costs $5 for adults, with discounts for seniors and children.

Greenway & Nature Center

Riverside trails, reptile displays, picnic and playground areas, and a raptor center attract visitors to the Greenway & Nature Center (☎ 719-549-2414), 5200 Nature Center Rd, beneath the cottonwoods on the Arkansas River. Particularly interesting is the Raptor Rehabilitation Center (☎ 719-549-2327), 4828 Nature Center Rd, which was started in 1981 to assist the Department of Wildlife in rehabilitating injured birds of prey.

Visitors are welcome to stop by Tuesday to Sunday from 11 am to 4 pm to see bald eagles, hawks and Mississippi kites. The Nature Center is open Tuesday to Sunday

Battle of Cuerno Verde

Recorded history of the Pueblo area begins with the battle of Cuerno Verde (Green Horn) on September 2, 1779. The Comanche tribe had acquired firearms from French trappers in the first half of the 18th century to strike fear into other tribes as well as the Spanish. In fact, the Ute word *komantica* (Comanche) means 'constant adversary.' Comanche raiders drove the Apache from the plains and battled Utes for horses and control of the Arkansas River basin. In the 1760s New Mexican pueblos and Spanish colonies also suffered from fierce Comanche raids, led by a daring chief the Spaniards called Cuerno Verde.

Juan Bautista de Anza, appointed governor of New Mexico in 1777 after founding San Francisco, vowed to stop the raids. De Anza left Santa Fe in August 1779 with a force of 600 mounted men consisting of some regular soldiers, but mostly Spanish and Pueblo community volunteers. Seeking to surprise, they headed north into the San Luis Valley before turning east toward the Plains. On the way they defeated a small band of Comanche and learned from captives that Cuerno Verde was returning from a raid in New Mexico to a camp south of the Arkansas River, below present Greenhorn Mountain. Ute and Apache warriors anxious to combat the Comanche reportedly joined Anza's corps in ambushing the returning Comanche party. With numerical superiority, the Spaniards killed Cuerno Verde and his son, along with four of his war chiefs, a medicine man and a number of warriors. Although several years passed before the Spanish formally negotiated peace with the Comanche, Anza's work led to a generation of stability.

Accounts differ about how Cuerno Verde was named. One story suggests the Spanish called the leader of the raids Cuerno Verde because he wore a green-painted buffalo-horn headdress. Another legend claims that the young chief earned the name because he was fearless, like the young bull elk when his antlers are still green. His nickname lives on in nearby Greenhorn Mountain and Greenhorn Creek, both named after the battle. ■

COLORADO

from 10 am to 5 pm. The turnoff for Nature Center Rd is 3 miles west of downtown, north of the Pueblo Ave Bridge.

Special Events

Pueblo's major attraction, the **Colorado State Fair**, 1001 Beulah Ave, lasts 17 days from mid-August to Labor Day. Daily admission costs $5. Stroll the carnival area, catch the free entertainment that features everything from Big Band to rock music, or mingle with swine at the livestock exhibit hall and the popular Children's Barnyard. The annual 100-mile **Century Ride** from Salida to Pueblo takes place on the first day of the fair. Additional admission fees are charged for the championship rodeo events and music performances by headliner acts. For grandstand ticket information call ☎ 719-566-0530, or 800-444-3247. From I-25 exit 97A go north one block to Northern Ave; turn left and continue until turning right on Beulah Ave or Prairie Ave where entry gates are located.

Other notable events each year include bluegrass music performances during the **Fiesta del Rio Blue Grass Festival** in May and **Bluegrass on the River** in June. Cinco de Mayo (May 5th) is a lively time to be in town.

Places to Stay

You will need to make a room reservation during the State Fair in late August and early September when rates can soar above those quoted below.

Camping *Lake Pueblo State Park* (☎ 719-561-9320) offers fully developed campsites that include flush toilets, showers and laundry facilities at the Northern Plains campground, accessible from the North Gate entrance and the Arkansas Point campground, off Hwy 96 south of the Pueblo dam. Sites with electric hookups cost $10 and are closed in winter. Primitive sites are also available on the north side for $6. Camping fees do not include the park's daily admission pass of $4. Reservations may be needed in summer and can be made by calling ☎ 800-678-2267. The state park

headquarters is located just north of Hwy 96 (4th St in the city) about 13 miles west of I-25 exit 101.

B&Bs Hang out on the veranda at the elegant *Abriendo Inn* (☎ 719-544-2703), 300 W Abriendo Ave. All seven rooms in this mansion, built in 1906 by the owner of Walter's Brewery, have private baths. Rates start at $59 and increase to $110 for rooms with whirlpool tubs.

Motels Rooms at the *Travelers Motel* (☎ 719-543-5451), near the courthouse at 1012 N Santa Fe Ave, aren't very cheerful, but with rates like $24/29 for singles/doubles, it's hard to beat. If you don't mind the blaring roar of I-25, *Al-Re-Ho Motel* (☎ 719-542-5135), 2424 N Freeway, off W 29th St, offers rooms from $24.

Along US 50 W at the junction with I-25 (exit 101) is a string of national franchise motels, including the ubiquitous *Motel 6*, with singles/doubles for $32/38 at two locations: half a mile west of I-25 at 960 US 50 W (☎ 719-543-8900) or a quarter mile northwest of the I-25 and US 50 junction at 4103 N Elizabeth St (☎ 719-543-6221). Rooms start at $30/35 at the *Rambler National Nine Inn* (☎ 719-543-4173), 4400 N Elizabeth St.

Chain hotels around US 50 W and I-25 include the *Super 8* (☎ 719-543-4104), 1100 US 50 W, with rooms from $38/43; the *Days Inn* (☎ 719-543-8031), at 4201 N Elizabeth ($45/55); and the relatively upscale *Sleep Inn* (☎ 719-583-4000), 3626 N Freeway ($59/69), off Hwy 47. The latter two motels have swimming pools.

Rooms cost $54/59 at the central *Best Western Town House* (☎ 719-543-6530), 730 N Santa Fe Ave. Up in the motel colony on US 50 W, the locally owned *Pueblo Motor Inn* (☎ 719-543-6820), 800 US 50 W, has some rooms facing an inner courtyard, shielding you from the highway noise that afflicts nearly every other motel in town. Pleasant rooms cost $42/49 and there is a heated pool and hot tub on the premises. Just south at 414 W 29th St, the *Bel Mar Motel* (☎ 719-542-3268) is a friendly spot with an outdoor pool and rooms for $40/50, though it is a bit close to I-25.

Hotels Pueblo doesn't really have any top end accommodations, but these hotels hover just above the mid-range category. Rooms at the *Holiday Inn* (☎ 719-543-8050), 4001 N Elizabeth St, are $89/99 during summer, about $20 less in winter. Facilities include a swimming pool and restaurant/bar. Rates are the same at the *Hampton Inn* (☎ 719-544-4700), 4701 N Freeway, reached from I-25 exit 102; a continental breakfast comes with the clean and comfortable, but otherwise utilitarian, rooms.

Places to Eat

Those staying on motel row (US 50 W and I-25) are faced with choosing between various national chain eateries like McDonalds and the more upscale Black-Eyed Pea and Applebee's, among others. However, a short hike down to *Rosario's* (☎ 719-583-1823), 2930 N Elizabeth St, will reward you with an excellent Italian lunch or dinner. Pasta lunches, including salad and fresh bread, range from $6 to $7; while dinner entrees like pasta with shrimp and mussels cost from $8 to $16.

Since 1944 the *Irish Brew Pub & Grill* (☎ 719-542-9974), 108 W 3rd St, has been anything but a traditional Irish pub. Until 11 pm nightly they serve excellent minestrone soup for about $3, in addition to full gourmet meals for $7 to $15. They also brew their own beer on the premises.

If you want to eat where the locals like to go, try the hearty, homestyle meals at *Rita's Mexican Food* (☎ 719-542-4820), 302 N Grand Ave. Their combination platters for around $5 are enormous and heavy and everything is made from scratch (well, OK, maybe not the electric-yellow cheese). This place is for serious eaters who don't need fancy decor or delicate flavors.

For a patio lunch shaded by huge cottonwoods on the Arkansas River, go to the excellent *Cafe del Rio* (☎ 719-549-2009), a Southwest adobe-style restaurant at the end of Nature Center Rd at the Nature Center.

Locals recommend the *Rendezvous Restaurant & Lounge* (☎ 719-542-2247), 218 W 2nd St, for more upscale lunches and dinners. Daily lunch specials are a pretty good value at around $6. The food is a mix of American, Continental and Mexican.

Getting There & Away

Air Pueblo Memorial Airport (☎ 719-948-3355) is 8 miles west of central Pueblo on US 50/Hwy 96. United Express (☎ 719-948-4423) offers daily commuter flights to Denver and Alamosa.

Bus The Greyhound/TNM&O bus depot (☎ 719-544-6295) is at 703 US 50 W, next to the McDonalds, and is open 7 am to 9 pm daily. There are nine buses daily between Pueblo and Denver. There are also southbound buses to El Paso and Dallas, TX; eastbound to Wichita, KS; and westbound to Grand Junction.

Car Pueblo is 112 miles south of Denver at the crossroads of I-25 and US 50. To the west, US 50 follows the Arkansas River for 90 miles past Cañon City to Salida; to the east it heads 64 miles to La Junta and points beyond.

Getting Around

Bus The Pueblo Transit System (☎ 719-542-4306) provides weekday commuter service every 30 minutes on seven routes depicted on a map in the telephone directory. Some routes operate hourly service on Saturdays. Route No 3 operates from downtown at Union Ave and Court St to the State Fairgrounds.

Car Enterprise Rent-A Car (☎ 719-542-6100) has an office in town at 402 W 29th St. At Pueblo Memorial Airport rental cars are available from Avis (☎ 719-948-9665), Budget (☎ 719-948-3363), Hertz (☎ 719-948-3345) and Sears (☎ 719-948-3272).

Taxi City Cab Company (☎ 719-543-2525) provides local transportation.

COLORADO

COLORADO

LA VETA

La Veta (population 780) is the gateway to the Cuchara Valley and the Spanish Peaks' Great Dikes, from which the town takes its Spanish name, meaning 'the vein.' From the streets of this tiny town visitors can admire the scenic Spanish Peaks. Artists and writers have been drawn to La Veta's splendor and their works are featured at the cooperative gallery and in performances by the Spoon River Players.

Orientation & Information

It would take effort to get lost in La Veta – its compass-oriented grid is divided by north-south Main St (Hwy 12). Most businesses are at the north end near the old narrow-gauge railroad. The Cucharas River flows along the western edge of town just a block west of Main St.

The La Veta/Cuchara Chamber of Commerce (☎ 719-742-3676) is housed in an adobe building next to the town park on W Ryus Ave. Visitors are greeted with a display of local artists' work and offered maps and information weekdays from 10 am to 4 pm. The San Isabel National Forest ranger station (☎ 719-742-3681), 103 E Field St, has maps and information on hiking near the Great Dikes of the Spanish Peaks and Culebra Range.

ATMs are available at the First National Bank of Walsenburg (☎ 719-742-3771), 102 E Field St, and the First National Bank of Trinidad booth at the corner of Ryus and Main Sts. The post office is at 117 E Ryus St and the zip code is 81055.

The weekly *La Veta-Cuchara Signature* has a special summer edition with information on lodging, dining and events and is available free from the chamber of commerce.

The Wash House laundromat on W Francisco St is open daily from 8 am to 8 pm. Recycling bins for paper, glass and metal are next to the post office.

Fort Francisco Museum

Partially surrounding the town's original plaza are the Spanish-style adobe fort buildings built in 1862 by John M Francisco and Henry. The adobe buildings form the core of the museum founded in 1957 by the Huerfano County Historical Society. Additional buildings on the museum grounds house coal mining exhibits, a school, a blacksmith shop, a post office and a saloon.

An exhibit on 1914's Ludlow Massacre (see sidebar later in this chapter) shows how mine owners and state militia made life miserable for the foreign-born laborers who came to work in the coal mines. The Hispanic exhibit features a rare display of Penitente carved and painted religious items, known as santos, which provide an opportunity to understand this locally important aspect of Mexican-American culture. From 1851 to 1947 the Catholic Church tried to repress Penitente practices, particularly rituals of penance involving self-abuse. In 1947, Archbishop Edwin Byrne officially recognized the Penitente Brotherhood and together they revised the rituals.

Fort Francisco Museum is open Memorial Day to Labor Day daily from 9 am to 5 pm. A gift shop sells souvenirs and local crafts. Admission is $2 for adults, $1 for children.

The Gallery

Over two dozen artists display paintings, pottery, glasswork and weavings at The Gallery, built in 1983 by the Friends of the Art Guild as a cooperative exhibition space for local artists. It's open June to September, Monday to Saturday from 10 am to 4:30 pm and Sundays from 1 to 4 pm. In May and October it's open on weekends. It's located on E Ryus St, two minutes walk east of the La Veta Inn.

Road & Mountain Biking

Between Walsenburg and north La Veta Pass (9413 feet), Hwy 160 has a good shoulder for bicyclists. Old La Veta Pass is a 4-mile-long alternative that's also worth exploring. From just west of the pass, mountain bicyclists can experience a long descent down Pass Creek Pass north to lodging at Malachite, about 12 miles from Hwy 160. The total La Veta-Malachite distance is 27 miles. From Malachite you can ride to hiking trailheads leading west through the Sangre de Cristo Wilderness to Great Sand Dunes National Monument.

Shorter mountain bike rides near La Veta include a 4-mile trip beside the Cucharas River on Valley Rd northeast of town; a visit to Sulfur Springs and nearby trails, 4 miles southwest of town past the Goemmer Butte volcanic plug on Huerfano County Rd 420; and a climb to the Wahatoya Camp where the trail to the Spanish Peaks begins. To reach Wahatoya Camp, 6 miles south of La Veta, from Hwy 12 south of town, turn left on Huerfano County Rd 361 for 1 mile, turn left on County Rd 360 a short distance across School Creek and turn right 5 miles from the trailhead.

Horseback Riding
Dark Horse Outfitters (☎ 719-742-3652), operated for 20 years by the outgoing Leslie Hicks, offers a $35 'Elk Express' ride including horseback tag games and galloping up to an elk ranch north of La Veta. Half-day/full-day rides into the mountains are also available for $60/100. Be sure to bring your own lunch.

Special Events
During the 4th of July weekend the **Art in the Park** festival includes booths, food and entertainment. Nearby Cuchara holds the **Cuchara Hermosa Art Festival** on the last weekend in July. Another regional art and brewfest, **Octoberfest**, is held in La Veta on the first Saturday in October.

Places to Stay
Camping The congenial owner of *Circle the Wagons* (☎ 719-742-3233), on 124 N Main St at the north edge of La Veta, offers tent sites for $12 and RV hookups for $18. If you just need a shower after a day on the trail, it costs $3. Tent/RV sites cost $10/15 at *Mary's RV Park* (☎ 719-742-3252), 222 W Grand St. Mary's is open from May to late October.

B&Bs *Posada de Sol y Sombra* (☎ 719-742-3159), 113 W Virginia, is a short walk

to the center of activity and offers two home-style rooms with shared bath for $43/49. The owners of *Hunter House* (☎ 719-742-5577), 115 W Grand St, do their best to cater to guests' recreation and dietary needs. They have three rooms starting at $65, a large-screen TV with a selection of video movies available and La Veta's only outdoor fireplace – a nice place to enjoy a brisk fall evening while sipping hot chocolate under the stars.

Motels *Circle the Wagons* (☎ 719-724-3233), 124 N Main St, has singles/doubles for $35/45 in spacious, immaculate double-wide mobile homes. The *La Veta Motel* (☎ 719-742-5303), at the corner of Oak and Field Sts, has cabin-style rooms for $40, though the owners can be hard to find. A few log cabin rooms are available for $50 at the *Log Haven Motel* (☎ 719-742-5757), 228 W Grand Ave.

Hotels The *La Veta Inn* (☎ 719-742-3700), on Main and Ryus Sts, has 15 uniquely decorated rooms with private bath that rent for $65 a double.

Places to Eat
One is reminded of La Veta's small size when looking for a place to eat. The few establishments operate a confusing array of staggered hours so that at least one is open for each meal every day. Call ahead to find out what the latest hours are.

You can get started with an espresso and breakfast of oatmeal and fruit ($3.25) or an omelet ($4.25) at the *La Veta Inn* (☎ 719-742-3700). The inn is also open for lunch and occasionally for dinner during the summer peak season. Hours vary. The neighboring *Ryus Avenue Bakery* (☎ 719-742-3830) has scones, muffins and sandwiches on Tuesday, Thursday and Saturday mornings. Also nearby, the *Covered Wagon Restaurant* (☎ 719-742-5280) features steaks, even on the breakfast menu, but a basic two-egg breakfast with home fries and pancakes is only $3, and hot lunch platters like the hickory smoked brisket for $6 are a pretty good deal. Dinners, mainly steaks, trout and chicken, range from $10 to $16. The restaurant is open from Tuesday to Sunday. Next to Circle the Wagons, *Tugboat Annie's* (☎ 719-742-3743), at N 124 Main St, has a surprising range of seafood dishes for so far inland, like Alaskan king crab legs ($12). Simpler fare like fish and chips, salads, sandwiches and Mexican food is also served. The adjacent dance hall sometimes has live musical performances on weekends.

Entertainment

Since 1979 the Spoon River Players (☎ 719-742-3676) have produced plays in La Veta at the *Fort Francisco Center for the Performing Arts*, a 100-year-old theater. The Players produce three plays per season from June to November. At the time of writing the group was mulling the idea of putting on winter and spring performances as well. Advance booking is recommended in summer.

Getting There & Away

La Veta is 19 miles west of I-25 via US 160 and Hwy 12. The Great Sand Dunes National Monument in the San Luis Valley lies 74 miles east over La Veta Pass via US 160.

AROUND LA VETA

Great Dikes of the Spanish Peaks

The Kapota band of the Ute tribe aptly expressed their infatuation with the striking volcanic Spanish Peaks southeast of La Veta by regarding them as 'breasts of the earth.' Spanish and American travelers relied on these twin sentinels to guide their approach to the Front Range across the eastern Great Plains.

On closer inspection, you'll find hundreds of magnificent rock walls radiating like fins from the peaks. Called dikes, they were formed from fissures surrounding the volcanic core, where molten rock was injected into the earth's crust and cast into solid rock as it cooled. Subsequent erosion has exposed the dikes, leaving a peculiar landscape of abrupt perpendicular rock formations protruding from the earth.

For an opportunity to see wildlife and wildflowers instead of cattle, you can explore the Great Dikes of the Spanish Peaks on foot by following the Wahatoya Trail (USFS Trail 1304) along the saddle between the East and West Spanish Peaks. The trailhead begins at Wahatoya Camp, 6 miles south of La Veta on Huerfano County Rd 360, or from the road over scenic Cordova Pass (11,743 feet), also called Apishapa Pass by former Ute inhabitants. Cordova Pass is on USFS Rd 415, 6 miles east of Cucharas Pass on Hwy 12, 17 miles south of La Veta. Don't miss the opportunity to spot elk in the extensive dry meadows on the slopes immediately south of Cucharas Pass. Trail information, maps and a wildflower brochure are available at the USFS ranger station in La Veta (☎ 719-742-3681).

Cuchara

On Hwy 12, 11 miles south of La Veta, this is an attractive one-street town that comes to life in winter when it serves patrons of the nearby Cuchara Mountain resort. Aside from the post office and a few shops, there's the nicely appointed (and pricey) *Cuchara Inn* (☎ 719-742-3685), with rooms for $85.

Pizza, steaks, booze and occasional live entertainment attract revelers and their dogs to the *Boardwalk Saloon* (☎ 719-742-3450). At the other end of the spectrum, *The Timbers* (☎ 719-742-3838) restaurant is an upscale place somewhat modeled on La Veta's food-art-music theme.

Cuchara Mountain Resort

Originally called the Panadero resort, Cuchara mountain, which is 2 miles west of Cuchara, began attracting skiers in 1982. The slopes get an average of 230 inches of snow. The top elevation is 10,800 feet and the base at Baker Creek Village is 9240 feet. Four chair lifts provide access to 24 trails. Twenty percent of the runs are for expert skiers, and there are also 'extreme expert' ungroomed powder areas boasting a maximum vertical drop of 1560 feet on a trail run of up to 2½ miles. The lifts operate daily from mid-December to early April from 9 am to 4 pm. Full-day adult lift tickets cost $30. During summer and fall outdoor activities include horseback riding and backcountry hiking.

Lodging at *Cuchara Mountain Resort* (☎ 719-742-3163, 800-227-4436) consists of condominiums rented for $95. Peak season reservations must be booked early.

The *Baker Creek Restaurant & Cooking School* is open for lunch and dinner, offering steak and seafood entrees.

Monument Park

Evergreen forests surround Monument Park, 29 miles south of La Veta and 36 miles west of Trinidad on Hwy 12. The park is named for a rock formation rising from the waters of an attractive mountain reservoir. Numerous summer activities are offered, including fishing on the trout-stocked lake, horseback riding and mountain biking. A $4 park entrance fee is charged for each vehicle.

Trailheads at nearby USFS campgrounds lead to Trinchera Peak (13,517 feet). North of Monument Park on Hwy 12 turn left (west) onto USFS Rd 411 to the trailhead at *Purgatoire Campground* (9700 feet), where USFS Trail 1309 leads to the peak about 6 miles away. Another shorter trail from *Blue Lake Campground* (10,500 feet) involves less climbing, reached from USFS Rd 413 north of Cucharas Pass.

The popular *Monument Lake Resort* (☎ 719-868-2226, 800-845-8006) has $10 campsites for RVs and tents, including showers and coin-op laundry. A southwestern adobe-style lodge and cabins were part of a 1930s WPA project, and the resort is now listed on the National Register of Historic Places. Southwestern furnishings distinguish the recently renovated lodge rooms and cabins, which can be rented for $60 a double. The resort's restaurant serves well-prepared, homestyle American food in the dining room and inexpensive burgers and hot dogs on the patio. The *Road to Ruin Bar* features live entertainment and dancing on Friday and Saturday nights. The resort is closed in winter. West of the resort, the San Isabel National Forest (☎ 719-742-3681) offers five primitive campgrounds on the flanks of the Sangre de Cristo range.

Dangers & Annoyances Prior owners of the Monument Lake Resort encouraged black bears to visit for the entertainment of guests. The new owner has stopped this unfortunate practice, but park personnel still carry guns loaded with rubber bullets to ward off problem bears. Don't leave garbage or food out unprotected. Intentional baiting for a photograph of a cute bear quickly weans the animals from a diet of acorns and chokecherries and is a sure death sentence.

TRINIDAD

Trinidad (population 8800) sits on the Purgatoire River where it flows down from the heights of the Sangre de Cristo Mountains out to the Eastern Plains. The town's past is documented in several good museums and on the brick-paved streets in **Corazon de Trinidad**, the 'heart' of downtown that has been designated a National Historic District. Visitors will also find Trinidad a good place to pick up on the outstanding scenery of the upper Purgatoire River and Cucharas Pass (elevation 9994 feet) in the San Isabel National Forest. History buffs might consider spending a day or two to take in the museums, but outdoor enthusiasts will probably want to keep heading west.

Trinidad exhibits a convergence of cultures. A pluralistic society now resides where the trade frontiers of Mexico and the USA once met on the Mountain Branch of the Santa Fe Trail. A vibrant 'car cruising' scene on weekends winds past handsome, well-preserved buildings in the Corazon along Commercial and Main Sts to Trinidad's drive-in restaurants. But despite the renovation efforts, numerous boarded-up buildings and empty storefronts attest to the city's continuing economic woes.

Trinidad is also unofficially credited with being the sex-change capital of the USA. However, you won't find much gender swapping among the local population, only at the local physician's cash-only practices (and even these aren't easy to find).

COLORADO

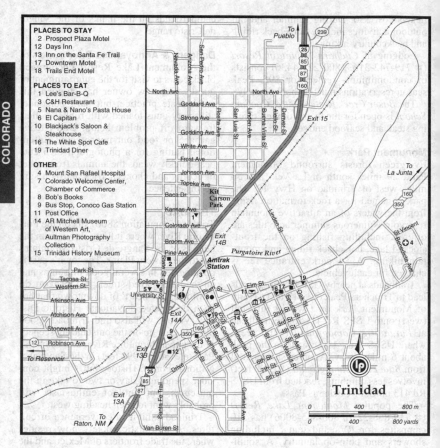

PLACES TO STAY
2   Prospect Plaza Motel
12 Days Inn
13 Inn on the Santa Fe Trail
17 Downtown Motel
18 Trails End Motel

PLACES TO EAT
1   Lee's Bar-B-Q
3   C&H Restaurant
5   Nana & Nano's Pasta House
6   El Capitan
8   Blackjack's Saloon & Steakhouse
16 The White Spot Cafe
19 Trinidad Diner

OTHER
4   Mount San Rafael Hospital
7   Colorado Welcome Center, Chamber of Commerce
8   Bob's Books
9   Bus Stop, Conoco Gas Station
11 Post Office
14 AR Mitchell Museum of Western Art, Aultman Photography Collection
15 Trinidad History Museum

Trinidad

History

From the earliest paleo-Indian peoples to present-day travelers on I-25, humans have converged at this junction between the Plains and Rocky Mountains. The nomadic Comanche and Kiowa plains tribes, as well as the Utes, adopted the site at the confluence of Ratón Creek and the Purgatoire River as an important resting stop along migration paths near hunting grounds.

Spanish explorers, and later foreign trappers, camped on the banks of the Purgatoire River during the 17th and 18th centuries. Spanish expeditions probed the

northern frontier of the empire for metallic riches, which never found.

Mexico's independence from Spain in 1821 opened trade with the USA. William Becknell, who crossed from the Missouri River to Santa Fe over Ratón Pass to establish the Mountain Branch of the Santa Fe Trail, was the first to benefit. (For westbound travelers, Trinidad was the last stop on the Santa Fe Trail before Ratón Pass.) Settlers started arriving in numbers after Texas cattle ranchers began herding longhorn cattle over Ratón Pass on the Goodnight-Loving Trail in 1864. Animosity between sheep and cattle ranchers, as well as those divided by skin color, escalated into the Battle of Trinidad, a riot in 1867 involving about a thousand residents.

The area grew after coal mining began in 1873 and the railroad arrived in 1877. Coal miners were recruited from the influx of poor immigrants, primarily from Italy, Ireland and Greece. Miners spent long hours in hazardous conditions, often laboring to be paid in scrip used to purchase goods from the company store or to rent company housing. These conditions resulted in the violent labor strike of 1913-14 (see the Ludlow Massacre sidebar). Mining peaked in 1928 but as oil and gas fuels replaced

Ludlow Massacre Monument

Cruel tragedy visited the Ludlow coal miners' camp, 12 miles northwest of Trinidad, during the early 20th century. Feudal working conditions in the Huerfano and Las Animas County coal mines led John Lawson and Mary Harris 'Mother' Jones to make demands in Trinidad for union recognition, wage scales and eight-hour workdays. The mine owners refused to meet these demands, prompting workers to call a strike on September 23, 1913, against domination by the Colorado Fuel & Iron Company and others. The mining companies evicted the mostly foreign-born miners from company housing, and the displaced laborers formed large tent colonies. Some 1200 people ended up in the Ludlow tent colony. As the strike wore on, tempers flared into violent clashes between striking workers and mine guards. Governor Elias Ammons called on the Colorado National Guard to help quell the clashes.

Mother Jones

The militia sided with the mine guards. One individual in particular, Lieutenant Linderfelt, openly demonstrated his bitterness and on April 20, 1914, a battle between Linderfelt's troops and strikers erupted, causing Ludlow residents to seek shelter from government machine guns and rifles. The militia ransacked and burned the tent city. While under militia guard, three strikers were killed, including Louis Tikas, leader of the Greek workers. Huddled amid the charred rubble were the bodies of two women and 11 children – victims of asphyxiation.

Inquiries by President Woodrow Wilson's US Commission on Industrial Relations found that the Colorado National Guard had been misused as 'an instrument of suppression maintained for the purpose of intimidating and crushing workmen who go on strike.' In a court-martial, however, Linderfelt was merely demoted in rank. Strikers did not return to work until December and their grievances were still unresolved. However, federal and state legislation eventually led to protection of workers from abuses like those suffered in the southern Colorado coal mines.

The monument at Ludlow, 1 mile west of I-25 exit 27, was dedicated by the United Mine Workers in 1918 to tell the story of this tragic chapter in American labor history. Louis Tikas is immortalized by Zeeze Papanikolas in his book, *Buried Unsung*. Other accounts of the strike have been portrayed in Upton Sinclair's *King Coal* and in Senator George McGovern's *The Great Coal Field War*. ∎

coal Trinidad's population and economy started the decline that still afflicts the town today.

Orientation

The Purgatoire River marks the division between the old Corazon de Trinidad that is south of the river and the grid plan to the north. The railroad and elevated I-25 further accentuate this division. Although the Corazon was established as a grid incorporating the Catholic Church and Santa Fe Trail (now Main St or US 350), the hilly terrain and river together create an interesting – and sometimes confusing – street pattern.

Main St is reached by I-25 exit 13B and is divided between east and west addresses at Commercial St, which crosses the river to the rail depot. A modern shopping center is north of town near I-25 exit 15, while a few freeway lodgings and businesses are 4 miles south at exit 11.

Information

The Trinidad-Las Animas County Chamber of Commerce (☎ 719-846-9285) shares space with the Colorado Welcome Center (☎ 719-846-9512) at 309 Nevada Ave, near I-25 exit 14A; it's open daily from 8 am to 6 pm (5 pm in winter). Guides to the Corazon de Trinidad National Historic District and hundreds of other maps and brochures to help plan your stay or entire Colorado vacation are handed out for free. The Colorado State Highway Patrol (☎ 719-846-9262) provides road information for Ratón Pass south of Trinidad.

An ATM is available at the Trinidad National Bank, 125 N Commercial St.

The post office is at 301 E Main St. Fax services are available at Trinidad Office Supply (☎ 719-846-1041), at 238 N Commercial St.

Bob's Books (☎ 719-846-3672), 249 N Commercial St, is open Monday to Saturday from 9 am to noon and from 1 to 5:30 pm 'most of the time,' as the sign says.

The Mount San Rafael Hospital (☎ 719-846-9213) is south of E Main St (US 350) at 410 Benedicta Ave.

Prospect Plaza Coin-Op Laundry, near the railroad depot north of the river at 416 State St, is open from 8 am to 9 pm daily

Walking Tour

The Corazon de Trinidad National Historic District is a living museum of commercial buildings that will delight architecture buffs.

Start at the Commercial St bridge over the Purgatoire River, following the brick-paved route south. Look at the building behind the neon sign for the Circle Lounge. Here the former **Trinidad Hotel** displays a classic iron-front design and balconies where ladies of yore hailed cowboys as they drove cattle down Commercial St.

At the intersection of Commercial and Main Sts, two outstanding buildings reflect Trinidad's early importance as an economic and transportation hub in the southern Front Range. Presidents Grover Cleveland and Teddy Roosevelt stayed at the **Columbian Hotel**, built in 1879, on the northwest corner. The First National Bank rises five stories on the opposite corner; gargoyles and intricate floral carvings embellish its exterior, built in 1892, while the interior contains elaborate marble work. Also on the south side of the block with the bank are some worthwhile **museums**: the Aultman Photography Collection and the AR Mitchell Museum of Western Art. Continue east on Main St to the adobe Baca House and neighboring Bloom House museums, occupying an entire block.

Head up Walnut St to 3rd, then turn right and continue to the intersection with Maple St, where a garish red metal cupola distinguishes the **Temple Aaron**, Colorado's oldest Jewish synagogue (built in 1883). Walk downhill on Maple St to **Las Animas County Courthouse**, built in 1912, before returning to Main St and walking west past Commercial St.

Turn right (north) onto Animas St and admire the **Trinidad City Hall**, built of local sandstone in 1909. **Carnegie Public Library**, constructed in 1904, is across the street. Turn east onto Church St and walk to Convent St. Before returning to the

Purgatoire River, enter the **Holy Trinity Catholic Church** to view the beautiful stained-glass windows.

Trinidad History Museum

If you're going to pick one museum to visit in Trinidad, make it this one. Two of Trinidad's most prominent families lived in these homes overlooking the Santa Fe Trail and together they are operated by the Colorado Historical Society as a complex called the Trinidad History Museum, which includes the Pioneer Museum.

With wealth gained from large sheep herds, Felipe and Maria Baca moved into the finest house in Trinidad in 1870, a two-story, territorial-style adobe home built the year before. Behind the Baca House is a kitchen garden, an *horno* (outdoor oven) and an adobe building now used as the Pioneer Museum. Judging by his house, Felipe Baca, who served as a territorial representative in the legislature, maintained a relatively modest lifestyle compared to that of his neighbor, cattle baron Frank G Bloom. Bloom applied much of his considerable wealth towards building and furnishing his ostentatious three-story Second Empire-style mansion in 1882.

Informed tour guides will show you through the houses and discuss local history. The museum complex (☎ 719-846-7217), 300 E Main St, is open Memorial Day to Labor Day, Monday to Saturday from 10 am to 4 pm and Sundays from 1 to 4 pm. During the rest of the year call for appointments. Admission is $4 for adults and $2 for children.

AR Mitchell Museum of Western Art & Aultman Photography Collection

Cowboy artist and illustrator Arthur Roy Mitchell contributed to the romantic image of the American West with his leathery cowboy characters created for pulp fiction. During his lifetime (1889-1977), Mitchell painted over 160 covers for Western action and adventure magazines, most during the 1920s and 1930s. Mitchell's illustrations and oil paintings are featured along with works of his contemporaries.

An added highlight is the **Hispanic Folk Art Exhibit**, which includes extremely rare displays of carved and painted religious items, known collectively as santos, used by the Penitente Brotherhood. The Penitente organization served locals well during the violent labor battles fought by coal miners during the early decades of the 20th century.

Oliver E Aultman established his photo studio in Trinidad in 1889. His photos captured the life and struggles of early residents, depicting the broad ethnic diversity that characterized Trinidad from the late 1800s onward.

The AR Mitchell Museum and the Aultman collection (☎ 719-846-4224) are at 150 E Main St. Special exhibits are scheduled through the summer. The museum is open mid-April to October, Monday to Saturday from 10 am to 4 pm. Admission is free.

Firehouse No 1 Children's Museum

Old Firehouse No 1 (☎ 719-846-8220), built in the 1880s at 314 N Commercial St, also housed city officials upstairs and criminals in the dungeon-like jail cells in the basement. Horse-drawn fire-fighting equipment and a fire truck are the museum's highlights. In addition, a model train depicts the railroad system in Las Animas county. The Children's Museum is open from June to September, Monday to Saturday from noon to 4 pm. Admission is free.

Organized Tours

Board the Trinidad Trolley at the Colorado Welcome Center, 309 Nevada St, for a free one-hour introductory tour of the Corazon de Trinidad National Historic District. Tours leave on the hour from 10 am to 5 pm during summer months.

Special Events

A country-music showdown is featured at the **Santa Fe Trail Festival**, held over a weekend in early June. The **Las Animas County Fair** in late August and early September is a week of rodeo, cowboy poetry, music and dancing capped off by the **Labor Day Parade**.

COLORADO

Places to Stay
Trinidad is a popular spot for overnight stays and peak summer rates often remain in effect until October as demand warrants.

Camping *Biggs RV Park* is south of town near the Budget Host Inn (☎ 719-846-3307), 10301 Santa Fe Trail Drive at I-25 exit 11. It offers 7 acres of land with tent sites and RV sites at $15 with all hookups. There is also a restaurant nearby. Showers, toilets and a coin-op laundry are available. Additional campsites are available at Trinidad Reservoir State Recreation Area (see Around Trinidad).

B&Bs In the Corazon, at the intersection of W Main and Animas Sts, the brick *Inn on the Santa Fe Trail* (☎ 719-846-4636) was the residence of Trinidad Mayor Dr Donnelly in the early 1900s. It has been restored according to historic photographs; three of the seven guest rooms have fireplaces and all have private bath. Rooms start at $70.

Motels One of the better choices in town is the *Trails End Motel* (☎ 719-846-4425), 616 E Main St (US 350), which offers convenient access to downtown museums. Recently remodeled rooms with handmade southwestern-style furniture are $33/40. Nearby, the *Downtown Motel* (☎ 719-846-3341), 526 E Main St, has rooms from $40 ($28 in winter). The *Prospect Plaza Motel* (☎ 719-846-4422), 416 State St, charges $34/39 for basic singles/doubles.

South of town, a landmark oil derrick marks the picnic area at the *Budget Host Inn Trinidad* (☎ 719-846-3307), 10301 Santa Fe Trail Drive at I-25 exit 11. It features coin-op laundry and rooms starting at $40/44 in summer ($28/30 in winter).

Near I-25 exit 13B and the foot of W Main St, the *Days Inn* (☎ 719-846-2271) has rooms facing away from the freeway for $65/75 in summer ($20 less in winter). The facilities include a pool, spa, exercise room, restaurant and coin-op laundry. At the *Holiday Inn* (☎ 719-846-4491), south of town off I-25 exit 11, rooms start at

$89/99 in summer. Among the amenities are a heated indoor pool and a hot tub and exercise room.

Places to Eat
The *C&H Restaurant* (☎ 719-846-3851), 443 N Commercial St, is open 6 am to 8 pm Monday to Saturday. If you start the day at 6 am with a veggie omelet for $5, you'll need to burn plenty of calories before returning for lunch to eat a humongous 'All Day Burger.' Good Mexican lunch entrees are also available at very low prices.

Take a step back to the 1950s at the *White Spot Cafe* (☎ 719-846-9957), 500 E Main St (US 350), a refurbished neon-lit roadside diner open for all meals, with your choice of counter seating or vinyl booths. The menu is in the $6 to $8 range. A bit farther out is the *Trinidad Diner*, 734 E Main St, which offers Greek gyros in addition to burgers and sandwiches for under $5. Yet another popular drive-in cafe is *Lee's Bar-B-Q* (☎ 719-846-7621) at 825 San Pedro Ave across from Kit Carson Park. Choose from curb service, inside tables or take-out orders. Grill your own steak or seafood in an 1890 saloon atmosphere at *Blackjack's Saloon & Steakhouse* (☎ 719-846-9501), 225 W Main St.

Italian entrees are featured at *Nana & Nano's Pasta House* (☎ 719-846-2696), 415 University Ave, open for dinner Tuesday to Saturday. Daily pasta specials are under $6. You can choose between Italian or Mexican dishes for lunch and dinner at *El Capitan* (☎ 719-846-9903), 321 State St. A stuffed sopapilla dinner to eat in or take out is under $6.

Getting There & Away
Bus Greyhound/TNM&O buses stop at JR's Travel Shoppe (☎ 719-846-6390), a Conoco gas station near I-25 exit 13B at 639 W Main St. Five northbound buses depart daily at 1:40 and 6:40 am and 12:05, 12:20 and 7:15 pm; southbound buses leave at 3 and 11:55 am and 10:15 pm.

Train Amtrak's *Southwest Chief* passes through Trinidad on its daily Chicago-Los

Angeles route. The westbound train is scheduled to arrive at 10:52 am, the eastbound at 7:16 pm. The Amtrak Depot is north of the river, beneath the freeway on Nevada St.

Car Trinidad is only 14 miles north of the border with New Mexico at Ratón Pass and about 200 miles south of Denver on I-25. The town is a junction between Hwy 12 (designated the Scenic Hwy of Legends) leading into the Sangre de Cristo Mountains, and US 350, the historic Mountain Branch of the Santa Fe Trail.

AROUND TRINIDAD
James M John SWA
Colorado acquired the 128-sq-mile area on top of Fishers Peak Mesa, southeast of Trinidad, for wildlife protection. Trails for hikes and mountain bikes provide the only access to this rich habitat for elk, mule deer and black bear. Local wildlife officers report 53 different bird species in addition to large turkey populations, including a rare acorn woodpecker and a successful peregrine falcon nesting site. Nearby, Lake Dorothy SWA is open for cold water lake and stream fishing with flies or artificial lures. At Lake Dorothy, a trail leads northwest 4 miles to the Fishers Peak Mesa. Camping is permitted, but campsites must be at least 200 yards from the water, except in designated areas with rest room facilities.

To get to James M. John SWA you first must go to Ratón, New Mexico, 23 miles south of Trinidad on I-25. From Ratón, drive 7 miles northeast on New Mexico Hwys 72 and 526, then head north up Sugarite Canyon 12 miles to Lake Dorothy.

Trinidad Reservoir & State Park
Three miles west of the city off of Hwy 12, Trinidad State Park (☎ 719-846-6951) sits on a bluff above the Purgatoire River downstream from the reservoir dam. Facilities here include tent pads, fire rings, rest rooms and drinking water. There are

additional campsites at Carpios Ridge Campground about a mile west of the dam that have flush toilets, showers and coin laundry along with 62 sites for RVs ($12) and tents ($9). Campsites may be reserved in advance (☎ 800-678-2267). Hiking, wildlife viewing, an interpretive nature trail, fishing and boating on the reservoir are available. Vehicle passes cost $4 per day.

Campfire Programs Events at the amphitheater on Carpios Ridge feature local speakers and slide presentations during the summer on weekend evenings, starting between 7 and 8 pm. Check the Friday issue of Trinidad's *Chronicle-News* 'Focus' section for scheduled speakers. Admission is free, but a state park day pass is required for each vehicle entering the park.

Hiking The 5-mile trail from Carpios Ridge to Cokedale National Historic Site (see below) passes a site where Utes once camped and left teepee rings. On the south side of the reservoir, Long's Canyon Watchable Wildlife Area is a good place to view many species, including mule deer, collared lizards, cottontail rabbits, hummingbirds and coyotes. You can reach Longs Canyon by the 2½-mile South Shore trail from the picnic grounds on the south side of the reservoir.

Cokedale National Historic Site
Remnants of 350 coke ovens that once lit the night sky sit beside Hwy 12, 7 miles west of Trinidad. The company town of Cokedale (1906-47) contrasted sharply with other nearby mining camps. Workers paid only $2 per month for tidy houses and were not required to shop at the American Smelting & Refining Company's store. Cokedale is now a National Historic Site that visitors can tour on foot. You can pick up a pamphlet and park your vehicle opposite the baseball diamond at the entrance to town.

COLORADO

Northern Mountains

With some of the state's most impressive Alpine scenery and outstanding ski resorts like Arapahoe Basin, Aspen, Steamboat and Vail, Colorado's Northern Rockies are a mountain-lover's dream. Excellent snow conditions, high elevations and steep vertical drops of up to 4000 feet have drawn skiers to the region for over 60 years.

Wet Pacific storms lose most of their moisture after slamming into the Sierra Nevada in California, leaving the fabled powdery snow that skiers call 'champagne'

- Steamboat – some of Colorado's deepest powder graces this laid-back, attractive ski town

- Winter Park – outstanding mountain bike trails and great, unpretentious skiing

- Arapahoe Basin – no-nonsense, steep, deep skiing for true powder-hounds

- Breckenridge – an historic mining town, now known for partying, skiing and mountain biking

- Elk Mountains – where the glitter of Aspen and Vail are humbled by gorgeous Alpine scenery

to fall on the Rockies. But downhill skiing isn't the only thing that draws travelers to the northern mountains in the winter – backcountry skiing, hut camping and snowshoeing also entice outdoor enthusiasts.

In the spring, summer and autumn hiking and biking in state and national parks, national forests and even the ski resorts continue to bring visitors to the area. There's also fishing on Gold Medal streams (water designated by the Colorado Wildlife Commission as especially good for trout fishing), rafting and kayaking through Class III and IV rapids, weathered ghost towns to explore, horseback riding, camping and touring the mountains until well after autumn turns the aspens to gold.

The Western Slope was once home to Native Americans who hunted and fished among its towering peaks and clear flowing streams. Later, miners and loggers earned their living from the minerals and timber, but now most of the region's population relies on the booming tourist economy centered around the resort areas of Aspen, Steamboat, Summit County and Vail.

Middle Park & Steamboat Springs

Colorado's Middle Park includes parts of Rocky Mountain National Park and other federal lands, among them Arapaho National Forest and Arapaho National Recreation Area. It's main attractions are the Winter Park and Steamboat Springs ski resorts, but this major recreation area is not just a winter destination. Hundreds of miles of Alpine trails offer excellent chances to delve into Middle Park's gorgeous backcountry.

The Ute presence in the area went unchallenged until the 1860s, when local

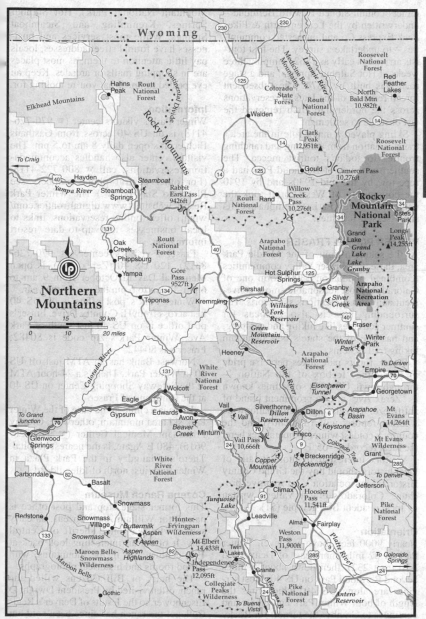

Northern Mountains

Wyoming

Elkhead Mountains

Hahns Peak

Routt National Forest

Continental Divide

Rocky Mountains

Medicine Bow Mountains

Laramie River

Colorado State Forest

Routt National Forest

Roosevelt National Forest

Red Feather Lakes

North Bald Mtn 10,982ft

To Craig

Hayden

Yampa River

Steamboat

Steamboat Springs

Rabbit Ears Pass 9426ft

Walden

Clark Peak 12,951ft

Gould

Cameron Pass 10,276ft

Roosevelt National Forest

Oak Creek

Phippsburg

Yampa

Routt National Forest

Gore Pass 9527ft

Rand

Routt National Forest

Willow Creek Pass 10,276ft

Arapaho National Forest

Rocky Mountain National Park

Grand Lake

Longs Peak 14,255ft

Estes Park

Toponas

Kremmling

Williams Fork Reservoir

Hot Sulphur Springs

Parshall

Granby

Silver Creek

Grand Lake

Lake Granby

Arapaho National Recreation Area

Fraser

Colorado River

Heeney

Green Mountain Reservoir

Blue River

Winter Park

Winter Park

To Denver

Empire

Glenwood Springs

Eagle

Gypsum

Edwards

Wolcott

Avon

Vail

Minturn

Beaver Creek

Vail

Silverthorne

Dillon Reservoir

Dillon

Frisco

Keystone

Arapahoe Basin

Eisenhower Tunnel

Georgetown

Mt Evans 14,264ft

Mt Evans Wilderness

Grant

To Denver

Carbondale

Basalt

Snowmass

Vail Pass 10,666ft

Copper Mountain

Breckenridge

Breckenridge

Colorado Trail

White River National Forest

Redstone

Snowmass Village

Snowmass

Buttermilk

Aspen

Aspen Highlands

Hunter-Fryingpan Wilderness

Turquoise Lake

Climax

Leadville

Hoosier Pass 11,541ft

Alma

Fairplay

Jefferson

Pike National Forest

Maroon Bells-Snowmass Wilderness

Gothic

Maroon Bells

Mt Elbert 14,433ft

Twin Lakes

Independence Pass 12,095ft

Collegiate Peaks Wilderness

Granite

Weston Pass 11,900ft

To Colorado Springs

Platte River

To Buena Vista

N Arkansas R.

Pike National Forest

Antero Reservoir

To Grand Junction

0   15   30 km
0   10   20 miles

miners commissioned Edward Berthoud – underwritten by the Leavenworth & Pikes Peak Express Co and interested communities – to undertake a survey. The first tourists arrived as early as 1862, camping three weeks at Hot Sulphur Springs, and a stage road was built by 1874. The subsequent forced removal of the Utes to reservations across the border into Utah removed the last obstacle to settlement.

Skiing played a major role in the area's transformation from a mining and ranching frontier to today's tourist mecca. The southern gateway of Berthoud Pass had a rope-tow by the mid-1930s and by 1940 the community of West Portal took the name of Winter Park to emphasize its snow-season activities.

WINTER PARK & FRASER

At the southern limit of the Middle Park area, these twin Fraser Valley communities (combined population 1300) form one of Colorado's most reasonable, most convenient and least pretentious ski resorts. The surrounding area is also a focus for summer activities like hiking and camping, and has one of the state's best mountain biking trail systems.

Fraser, for its part, takes perverse pride in being the 'Icebox of the Nation' – through town, US 40 is sometimes known as 'Zerex Ave' after a prominent brand of antifreeze. Travelers perusing nationwide weather reports will frequently find the country's coldest winter temperatures here; the local record is –65°F.

Visitors interested in more details of local history should buy the Grand County Historical Association's informative brochure 'Colorado's Fraser Valley,' written by local resident Bob Temple ($1).

Orientation

Nearly 9000 feet above sea level, Winter Park is 67 miles northeast of Denver via I-70 (exit 232), then north about 8 miles beyond Berthoud Pass on US 40. Most services are along US 40, which runs the length of both Winter Park and Fraser and continues to Granby (the turnoff for Rocky

Mountain National Park), Hot Sulphur Springs, Kremmling and Steamboat Springs. While most services and businesses have formal street addresses, locals pay little attention to them, as most places are in shopping malls or arcades. Keep an eye peeled to find what you're looking for.

Information

Winter Park's visitors center (☎ 970-726-4118) is on US 40 across from Gasthaus Eichler; it's open daily 8 am to 5 pm. The visitors center also handles accommodation reservations; call ☎ 800-722-4118. (For other central phone numbers see Places to Stay below.) The Winter Park Resort website (www.digitalfrontier.com/wpmj) offers online reservations, links to local businesses and up-to-date resort information.

Fraser's visitors center (☎ 970-726-8312), 120 US 40 (Zerex Ave), is open Memorial Day to October from 9 am to 6 pm, 11 am to 6 pm the rest of the year.

Winter Park's post office is on US 40 just across from Hi Country Drive. Fraser's post office is on US 40 just south of Park Ave. Winter Park's zip code is 80482; Fraser's is 80442.

Norwest Bank has an ATM just off US 40 in Winter Park. There's a 24-hour ATM in the Safeway Shopping Center on US 40 at the south end of Fraser.

There is a clinic at the base of the Winter Park ski area mountain; otherwise, Granby Provenant Medical Center (☎ 970-726-9616), 480 E Agate, is the nearest hospital. There's a laundry in the Park Plaza in Winter Park just north of Idlewild Rd.

Cozens Ranch Museum

This former stage stop and post office is named for William Zane Cozens, an early settler who was once sheriff of Central City. It offers an interesting look back at 19th-century life in the mountains, with period rooms and historical photographs.

The heirs of Bill Cozens willed the ranch, often visited by President Dwight D Eisenhower, to the Jesuits of Denver's Regis College; the ranch has since been sold but

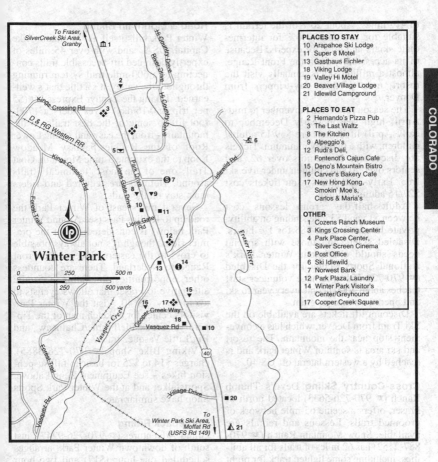

To Fraser, SilverCreek Ski Area, Granby

Winter Park

0   250   500 m
0   250   500 yards

To Fraser, SilverCreek Ski Area, Granby

To Winter Park Ski Area, Moffat Rd (USFS Rd 149)

PLACES TO STAY
10 Arapahoe Ski Lodge
11 Super 8 Motel
13 Gasthaus Eichler
18 Viking Lodge
19 Valley Hi Motel
20 Beaver Village Lodge
21 Idlewild Campground

PLACES TO EAT
2 Hernando's Pizza Pub
3 The Last Waltz
8 The Kitchen
9 Alpeggio's
12 Rudi's Deli,
   Fontenot's Cajun Cafe
15 Deno's Mountain Bistro
16 Carver's Bakery Cafe
17 New Hong Kong,
   Smokin' Moe's,
   Carlos & Maria's

OTHER
1 Cozens Ranch Museum
3 Kings Crossing Center
4 Park Place Center,
   Silver Screen Cinema
5 Post Office
6 Ski Idlewild
7 Norwest Bank
12 Park Plaza, Laundry
14 Winter Park Visitor's
   Center/Greyhound
17 Cooper Creek Square

the Grand County Historical Association placed the museum building on the National Register in 1988. About a mile north of downtown Winter Park, the Cozens Ranch Museum (☎ 970-726-5488) is open daily 11 am to 4:30 pm Memorial Day to October. Admission is $3/1 adults/children.

Skiing
Downhill Skiing Winter Park Resort (☎ 970-726-5514, 800-525-2466), Denver's most convenient world-class ski resort and highly popular among Coloradans, covers over 2 sq miles on four

mountains, with 20 chairlifts, including seven high-speed quads, 121 runs and a total vertical drop of more than 3000 feet. The run called Mary Jane and its famed mogul runs (ranked among the best in the country) attracts a 'rebel' crowd of young (and young at heart) experts, while Winter Park offers groomed runs and glade skiing for all abilities. Opened for the 1997-1998 ski season, Vasquez Cirque has 435 acres of new expert backcountry terrain, including cornices, rock outcroppings and glades. The entire ski area receives a tremendous amount of snow, and some runs can extend to 4½ miles. About 20% of the terrain is suitable for beginners, 40% for intermediate skiers and 40% for experts. Because of its accessibility from the Front Range, almost a million skiers annually visit the resort, most of them day-trippers from Denver.

The season runs from November to mid-April; high season (early December to early April) lift tickets are $39/15 adults/children, with a two-day minimum. Tickets are discounted for seniors over 62, and seniors over 70 and children under five ski free. Early- and late-season tickets cost $27/15 adults/children.

Adult half-day group lessons cost between $15 and $35, depending on ability; private lessons start at $85 for 1½ hours. Disabled skiers and those with special needs should check out Winter Park's National Sports Center for the Disabled (☎ 970-726-5514). A huge volunteer staff teaches about 3000 people every year to ski and operates a race program.

Discount lift tickets are available on the Ski Train from Denver, which has a convenient stop near the mountain. The resort and ski area is south of Winter Park and is reached by a western lateral off US 40.

Cross-Country Skiing Devil's Thumb Ranch (☎ 970-726-5633) located north of Fraser, offers a scenic 65-mile network of groomed trails. Lessons and rentals are available. Snow Mountain Ranch (☎ 970-887-2152) has 62 miles of trails for all abilities, including some lighted track for night skiing and ice-skating.

Equipment Rental Viking Ski Shop (☎ 970-726-8885), at the corner of US 40 and Vasquez Rd in the Viking Lodge in Winter Park, has ski rental packages beginning at $14 per day, up to $25 for high-end gear. (The store also doubles as a bike shop.) Similar rates can be found at Sportstalker (☎ 970-726-8873), across the street in the Cooper Creek Mall, and at Winter Park Sports Shop (☎ 970-726-5554) at the base of the mountain or in the center of town.

Road & Mountain Biking

Winter Park bills itself as 'Mountain Bike Capital, USA,' and with over 45 miles of expertly designed lift-accessible trails connecting to a 600-mile trail system running throughout the valley, it's a title that's well-earned. Taking the Zephyr Express lift ($5 per trip or $16/day) gives riders a 1700-foot lift to some of the best trails on the mountain – from the easy and scenic Lower Roof of the Rockies/Fantasy Meadow Loop to the extreme 3-mile Mountain Goat Trail, one of the most 'technical' trails around. Helmets are required and riders must stay on the trails.

Several miles east of Winter Park the road up to Rollins Pass (see Around Winter Park below) is considered one of the premier rides, though it's not always possible to cross to the eastern slope of the Front Range to Nederland. There are countless other opportunities, including a 5-mile alternative to Fraser that allows cyclists to avoid busy US 40. Visit the Winter Park visitors center for a sketch map of the Tipperary, Creekside/Flume/Chainsaw and Big/Little Vasquez trails.

Viking Bike Shop (☎ 970-726-8885), charges $14 to $25 for basic to full suspension bikes – see Equipment Rental above. Sportstalker and at the Winter Park Sports Shop have similar rates.

Horseback Riding

Grand Adventures (☎ 970-726-9247), just south of downtown Winter Park, arranges scheduled one-hour ($17) and two-hour ($29) horseback rides in Arapaho National Forest, as well as special breakfast and dinner rides throughout the week.

Special Events

Winter Park's first major summer event is the **American Red Cross Fat Tire Classic** held in late June. The annual **Alpine Art Affair** takes place in late July, along with the **Winter Park Jazz Festival**. The annual **Wine & Food Festival** and the **King of the Rockies Mountain Bike Race** happen in early and mid-August, respectively.

Fraser Valley Railroad Days follows in early September, around the same time as the **Famous Flamethrowers High Altitude Chili Cookoff** at Winter Park Resort; for those with real cast-iron stomachs, the latter includes a Jalapeño Eating Contest.

The local **High Country Stampede Rodeo** takes place, rain or shine, 7:30 pm every Saturday in July and August at the John Work Arena in Fraser.

Places to Stay

Winter is the peak season, but relatively reasonable accommodations are available even then. Because most of Winter Park's skiers are commuters from Denver, timeshare or rental condos are abundant, but there are fewer hotels and motels than at other large ski areas.

Winter Park Adventures (☎ 970-726-5701, 800-525-2466) rents a variety of condos in all ranges for as little as $50 with a two-night minimum, though most are considerably more expensive. Winter Park Central Reservations (☎ 970-726-5587, 800-453-2525) is the area's central booking agent.

Camping The USFS *Idlewild Campground* ($8), at the south end of Winter Park just before the Moffat Rd turnoff, is the closest camping area to town. It has only 26 sites, however, and can fill up early. Five miles south of Winter Park, also on US 40, *Robbers Roost Campground* offers another 11 sites.

B&Bs *Engelmann Pines* (☎ 970-726-4632, 800-992-9512), 1035 Cranmer Ave in Fraser, charges $75 to $115 for a double in ski season, $60 to $100 the rest of the year. The *Pines Inn* (☎ 970-726-5416, 800-824-9127), walking distance from Winter Park Ski Resort, offers singles/doubles from $50/85 in summer, $100/110 in ski season.

Motels & Lodges The *Viking Lodge* (☎ 970-726-8885, 800-421-4013), on US 40 between Vasquez Rd and Cooper Creek Way, is one of the best values in town with doubles that range from $35 to $64. This friendly skiers' lodge has a ski/bike shop, hot tub and sauna and offers discounts to HI/AYH members since the town's hostel closed in 1997. *Beaver Village Lodge & Condominiums* (☎ 970-726-5741, 800-666-0281), off US 40 downtown (the lodge is on US 40, the condos on Village Drive), offers hotel rooms and multi-bedroom condos and has a pool and sauna. In summer hotel rooms range from $40 to $70 and a one-bedroom condo goes for $85, but these rates double during winter ski season. For an additional $15 per day, guests can add a meal plan including all-you-can-eat breakfast and dinner buffets.

Doubles at the *Arapahoe Ski Lodge* (☎ 970-726-8222), on US 40 just north of Lions Gate Rd, are $49. The new *Super 8 Motel* (☎ 970-726-8808, 800-541-6130), on US 40 near Lions Gate Rd, has clean doubles starting at $52 in the off-season and up to $125 at Christmas. There's an indoor hot tub and a free Continental breakfast during ski season. The *Valley Hi Motel* (☎ 970-726-4171, 800-426-2094), on US 40 across from the Viking Lodge, has doubles for as little as $65 during peak ski season.

At the *Raintree Inn* (☎ 970-726-4211, 800-726-3340), across from Winter Park Ski Resort, doubles start at $49 in summer, $109 during ski season. The pseudo-Swiss *Gasthaus Eichler* (☎ 970-726-5133, 800-543-3899), 78786 US 40 across from Idewild Rd near Vasquez Creek, has doubles for $59 summer, $149 winter; winter rates include a full breakfast and dinner.

Probably the most luxurious place in town is *Vintage Resort Hotel* (☎ 970-726-8801, 800-472-7017), at Winter Park Resort, where midsummer doubles start at $65 but rise to $180 in the peak Christmas season. The *Iron Horse Resort* (☎ 970-726-8851, 800-621-8190), at the entrance to Winter Park, has lodge rooms and one-bedroom condos for $89/109 in the off-season, $129/269 during regular ski season.

Places to Eat

Winter Park has a wide variety of gourmet food, but Fraser is a bit cheaper and more

COLORADO

down to earth. Many of Winter Park's shopping centers house restaurants.

Winter Park *The Kitchen* (☎ 970-726-9940), on US 40 in the middle of town, warns customers, 'If you're in a hurry, eat somewhere else,' but the breakfast specialties, including a huge plate of huevos rancheros from $6 to $8, are worth the wait. *Carver's Bakery Cafe* (☎ 970-726-8202), 93 Cooper Creek Way, also has superb, reasonably priced breakfasts and lunches with large portions; there's outdoor seating in good weather. *Moffat Bagel Station, Inc* (☎ 970-726-5530), in Park Place Center, offers fresh-baked New York-style bagels, plus sandwiches, soups and salads at good prices.

Deno's Mountain Bistro (☎ 970-726-5332), across the street from the Viking Lodge, is a popular dining and watering hole for skiers and bikers. *Alpeggios* (☎ 970-726-5402), near Lions Gate Rd, is a local favorite for authentic Italian fare. *New Hong Kong* (☎ 970-726-9888), in Cooper Creek Square, features Szechwan and Mandarin dishes made with lighter and healthier ingredients.

Rudi's Deli (☎ 970-726-8955), in the Park Plaza Center on US 40, has excellent sandwiches but is not cheap. *Smokin' Moe's* (☎ 970-726-4700), in Cooper Creek Square, serves up 'darn good Oklahoma-style barbecue,' while *Carlos & Maria's* (☎ 970-726-9674), in the same building, serves Mexican food and has a daily happy hour 3:30 to 6:30 pm. *The Last Waltz* (☎ 970-726-4877), in Kings Crossing Center, features a variety of sandwiches and Mexican and vegetarian specialties. Located at the north end of town, *Hernando's Pizza Pub* (☎ 970-726-5409) serves pizza, pasta and a selection of imported and domestic beers.

Downtown chef-owned *Gasthaus Eichler* (☎ 970-726-5133), 78786 US 40, features an extensive German menu specializing in veal. *Fontenot's Cajun Cafe* (☎ 970-726-4021), in Park Place Center, serves moderately priced sandwiches, pasta and entrees with a Cajun flavor.

Visitors can take the Zephyr Express chairlift (at the base of Winter Park ski resort) to the popular *Lodge at Sunspot* (☎ 970-726-8155), a restaurant/bar high above the resort. The fare is $5/3 adults/children.

Fraser The *Fraser Brazier* (☎ 970-726-8490), at 406 US 40 across from the Crooked Creek, has inexpensive sandwiches, burgers, ice cream and Mexican food.

Entertainment

Crooked Creek Saloon (☎ 970-726-9250), 401 US 40, is a popular local hangout in Fraser. *The Derailer* (☎ 970-726-5514), at the base of Winter Park, is the place where après-ski nightlife begins, with live music during the ski season most nights. *The Slope* (☎ 970-726-5727), between town and the mountain, is another popular après-ski venue.

Getting There & Away

Bus Greyhound (800-231-2222) stops at the visitors center on US 40 in Winter Park and also makes a flag stop in front of Fraser's Crooked Creek Saloon. Departures for Denver are 5:05 am and 6:35 pm; fares are $13 one-way for the 1½-hour trip. Westbound buses from Denver to Salt Lake City, UT, leave Winter Park 10:30 am and 7:30 pm.

DIA Shuttle Home James Transportation Services (☎ 970-726-5060, 800-451-4844) charges $34 per passenger for van rides between Winter Park and Denver International Airport. Schedules and prices may vary seasonally, though there are 10 or more departures in summer and during ski season; reservations are essential.

Train Reservations are required for the scenic *Ski Train* (☎ 303-296-4754), which drops Denver passengers at Winter Park Resort just outside the Moffat Tunnel. It runs Saturdays and Sundays mid-December to early April, Fridays from late December to mid-February; same-day roundtrip fares

Denver

Top: Bucking bronco and a modern skyline
Bottom Left: Suds up at a microbrewery

Middle Right: Paul Stewart, founder of the Black
American West Museum
Bottom Right: Bill Cody's grave

RAY HILLSTROM

ERIC KETTUNEN

LEE FOSTER

Colorado

Top: Headin' to the roundup, near Crested Butte
Bottom Left: Indoor spa, Idaho Springs

Bottom Right: Overlooking the Continental Divide, Loveland Basin Ski Area

are $35 in coach class, $60 in the club car, which includes Continental breakfast, beverages and après-ski snacks. Departure time is 7:15 am from Denver, arriving in Winter Park at 9:15 am; the returning train leaves Winter Park at 4:15 pm and arrives in Denver at 6:15 pm.

Amtrak (☎ 800-872-7245) stops daily in Fraser at the unmanned depot on the corner of Fraser and Railroad Aves. The *California Zephyr* westbound to Emeryville (San Francisco Bay Area) leaves 11:42 am; eastbound to Chicago departure is 4:52 pm.

Getting Around
Winter Park's frequent free shuttle (☎ 970-726-4163) carries skiers around Winter Park and Fraser; it runs every 10 to 15 minutes in winter, hourly in summer. The route starts at Winter Park Ski Area and ends at Fraser's Amtrak depot. The free Smart Shuttle serves local restaurants and bars on Friday and Saturday nights 10:30 pm to 2 am and takes passengers right to their doorstep.

AROUND WINTER PARK
The Moffat Rd & Rollins Pass
In the mid-1860s, JA Rollins established a toll wagon road over this 11,660-foot pass from Nederland/Rollinsville, and early in the 20th century David H Moffat's Denver, Northwestern & Pacific Railway crossed the Continental Divide here. First known as Boulder Pass, then Rollins Pass, it also earned the appellation 'Corona' as railroad workers considered it the crown at the 'top of the world.' Until 1928, when the Moffat Tunnel made the route superfluous, there existed a railroad station, hotel, restaurant and workers' quarters on the summit.

At the south end of Winter Park, just beyond the USFS Idlewild Campground, Moffat Rd (also known as Corona Rd, Rollins Rd and USFS Rd 149) to Rollins Pass is a good dirt road usually open by late June. The upper stretches before Rollins Pass are poorly maintained and a high clearance vehicle is desirable, though 4WD is not necessary. Before driving it, try to find the self-guided auto tour pamphlet

'The Moffat Road,' available for $1 from the chamber of commerce in Winter Park or Fraser. The most interesting roadside attraction is the **Loop Trestle & Tunnel** at the 11-mile point, where the train, emerging from a tunnel, circled 1½ miles to gain just 150 feet in elevation. Take great caution if walking onto the rotting trestle, which has big gaps through which fallen ties littering the slopes below are visible.

From the parking lot at the summit of the pass, the **High Lonesome Trail II**, a segment of the Continental Divide National Scenic Trail, enters the Indian Peaks Wilderness to the north. Offering superb views of the Divide, the trail drops 2000 feet to intersect the High Lonesome Trail, which continues north to Junco Lake, Monarch Lake and beyond to Rocky Mountain National Park.

Another hiking possibility is the **Rogers Pass Trail**, which leaves Rollins Pass Rd near the Loop Trestle; its continuation, the **James Peak Trail**, climbs to 13,294 feet and is named for Dr Edwin James, who made the first recorded ascent of Pikes Peak. The total length is 3½ miles, with the last half-mile largely unmarked.

For maps and guides, go to the USFS Sulphur Ranger District Office (☎ 970-887-3331) in Granby.

SILVER CREEK SKI AREA
Downhill Skiing
The slopes of this family-oriented ski area (☎ 970-887-3384, 800-754-7458), 10 miles north of Fraser and 2 miles southeast of Granby on US 40, are relatively tame by most Colorado standards – the vertical drop, for instance, is barely 1000 feet compared to Winter Park's 3000 feet and Steamboat Springs' 3600 feet. Per-day lift tickets are $32 for adults, $15 for children (six to 12) and $18 for seniors 62 to 69. Seniors over 70 and kids under five ride free.

The ski school offers a full range of lessons with packages for kids including rental tickets, lessons and lunch. Reasonably priced childcare is also available. There's a free shuttle to and from Granby that runs until 10 pm.

Cross-Country Skiing

Over 40 km of trails lead from Silver Creek into the Arapaho National Forest and go through all kinds of different terrain. They connect with the trails of the YMCA of the Rockies (☎ 970-887-2152). Telemarking lessons are available. Rent cross-country skis at the ski shop in the Sterling Base Lodge.

Places to Stay

The 342-room *Inn at SilverCreek* (☎ 970-887-2131, 800-926-4386) has singles/doubles for as low as $45/75, studios ranging from $59 to $129 for a double and one-bedroom units from $79 to $159. It's 1½ miles north of the ski area and offers free shuttle service.

To ski-in, ski-out, stay at the *Mountainside Condo* (☎ 800-223-7677). One-bedroom units with lofts sleep four to six and range from $120 to $195. Two-bedroom units with lofts are $190 to $310 and sleep nine to 11 people.

GRANBY

At the junction of US 40 and US 34, Granby (population 1100) is a crossroads service center convenient to Rocky Mountain National Park and several other nearby recreational and ski areas. The USFS Sulphur District Ranger Office (☎ 970-887-3331) for the Arapaho National Forest is at 62429 US 40 at the east end of town. It has useful hiking brochures for the Continental Divide National Scenic Trail, the Never Summer Wilderness Area and the Winter Park-Fraser-Tabernash area. It is also the place to get permits for backcountry camping in the Indian Peaks Wilderness.

For a quick bite try *Mad Munchies*, 420 E Agate, a local favorite for filling subs, burgers and burritos. *The Longbranch & Schatzi's*, 185 E Agate Ave, has American, German, Greek and Mexican food, with inexpensive lunch specials.

GRAND LAKE

The western gateway to Rocky Mountain National Park, Grand Lake (population 276) was an early mining zone but soon got into the tourist game, establishing a yacht club by 1901. It has since become 'Estes Park West,' a tourist trap with very little to recommend it except a few decent restaurants and one of the cheapest and best accommodation alternatives in the state, the Shadowcliff Lodge hostel. Grand Ave, the main drag, is a jumble of souvenir shops, restaurants and T-shirt stores along a hokey boardwalk. The beautiful lake, however, lives up to its name.

Orientation

On the north shore of its namesake, the largest natural lake in the state, Grand Lake Village is a mile east of the Grand Lake junction of US 34 and W Portal Rd. It is 14 miles north of Granby and only a mile south of the western entrance to Rocky Mountain National Park; US 34 crosses the high tundra of the park as the Trail Ridge Rd. The main drag of the village's compact grid is Grand Ave.

Information

The Grand Lake Area Chamber of Commerce (☎ 970-627-3402, 800-531-1019) is at the junction of US 34 and W Portal Rd; it's open in summer 9 am to 5 pm Monday to Saturday, 10 am to 4 pm Sunday; winter hours are 9 am to 5 pm Friday and Saturday, 10 am to 4 pm Sunday. The downtown information office, upstairs at 928 Grand Ave (enter from the Garfield Ave side), is more helpful. There are no useful maps, not even from the real estate agents whose offices line Grand Ave.

The post office is at 520 Center Drive; Grand Lake's zip code is 80447.

The Mountain Village Laundromat is located on Grand Ave between Broadway and Vine Sts.

Kauffman House Museum

The Ezra Kauffman House, 407 Pitkin St between Lake Ave and Grand Ave, is an 1892 log building that operated as a hotel until 1946. Now on the National Register of Historic Places and operated by the Grand Lake Historical Society (☎ 970-627-3351), it contains period furniture and other artifacts and is open daily 1 to 5 pm in summer.

Mountain Biking

The Grand Lake Metro Recreation District (☎ 970-627-8328) publishes a *Grand Lake Mountain Bike Trail Map* of routes in the Arapaho National Forest west of town; rides are color-coded for difficulty. Rocky Mountain Sports (☎ 970-627-8124), 711 Grand Ave, rents and sells bikes.

Rock Climbing & Mountaineering

Never Summer Mountain Products (☎ 970-627-3642), 919 Grand Ave, carries equipment, clothing and topographic maps.

Hiking

Several Rocky Mountain National Park trailheads are just outside the town limits, including those to the Tonahutu Creek Trail and the Cascade Falls/North Inlet Trail, both near Shadowcliff Lodge.

Horseback Riding

The Sombrero Ranch Stables (☎ 970-627-3514) rents horses right in town at 304 W Portal Rd.

White-Water Rafting

Monarch Guides (☎ 970-627-2409, 888-463-5628) runs half-day, full-day as well as overnight trips on both the upper Colorado and Eagle rivers. Rates are $35 to $100 and include roundtrip transportation.

Snowmobiling

Grand Lake is a popular snowmobile center with hundreds of miles of trails around town and in Rocky Mountain National Park. Snowmobiles can be rented for about $145 a day at Lonesome Dove Cottages (☎ 970-627-8019), 416 Grand Ave; Spirit Lake Rentals (☎ 970-627-9288), 347 W Portal; and Alpine Arctic Cat (☎ 970-627-8866), 902 Grand Ave.

Special Events

Winter's main event is the **Winter Carnival** held in mid-January, while the annual **Ice Fishing Derby** happens in early February.

Grand Lake's annual **Festival of Arts & Crafts** takes place in late June, and in late July boaters clog the waters during the **Grand Lake Regatta**. Throughout the summer, the town sponsors free concerts in the Public Square.

Places to Stay

Since Grand Lake is not a ski resort per se, summer is the high season but seasonal price variations are relatively small.

Camping RVs can park at the vacant city lot at the corner of Park Ave and Hancock St, but it's less than scenic and there are no facilities.

Elk Creek Campground (☎ 970-627-8502, 800-355-2733), on Golf Course Rd (Grand County Rd 48) just west of US 34 and just south of the entrance to Rocky Mountain National Park, stays open year-round. From April to late October, rates are $15 without hookups, $17 for RV sites with water and power, and $19 with full hookups; from November to April, tent or RV sites with power are $19. Camper cabins are $33/doubles. Facilities include a store, laundry and recreation room.

Winding River Resort (☎ 970-627-3215), reached via Grand County Rd 491 opposite the NPS Kawuneeche Visitors Center, has tent sites for $16, sites with water and power for $18, and full hookup sites for $20. It also has cabins from $65 to $85.

Hostels Overlooking the town and the lake from Summerland Park Rd just north of W Portal Rd, the nonprofit *Shadowcliff Lodge* (☎ 970-627-9220), open late May to late September, is one of the best budget alternatives in the state. Along with great lodging, stupendous views and access to Rocky Mountain National Park trails, the lodge offers a congenial environment and supports social causes (it hosts retreats for humanitarian groups such as HIV support organizations, but doesn't obligate casual visitors to participate). Spotless, comfortable hostel accommodations cost $10 for HI/AYH members, $12 for nonmembers, but it also has cabins with kitchens (see

COLORADO

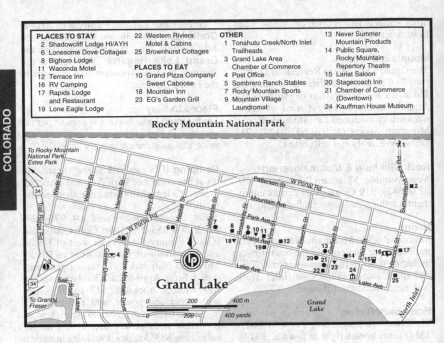

PLACES TO STAY	22 Western Riviera	OTHER	13 Never Summer
2 Shadowcliff Lodge HI/AYH	Motel & Cabins	1 Tonahutu Creek/North Inlet	Mountain Products
6 Lonesome Dove Cottages	25 Brownhurst Cottages	Trailheads	14 Public Square,
8 Bighorn Lodge		3 Grand Lake Area	Rocky Mountain
11 Waconda Motel	PLACES TO EAT	Chamber of Commerce	Repertory Theatre
12 Terrace Inn	10 Grand Pizza Company/	4 Post Office	15 Lariat Saloon
16 RV Camping	Sweet Caboose	5 Sombrero Ranch Stables	20 Stagecoach Inn
17 Rapids Lodge	18 Mountain Inn	7 Rocky Mountain Sports	21 Chamber of Commerce
and Restaurant	23 EG's Garden Grill	9 Mountain Village	(Downtown)
19 Lone Eagle Lodge		Laundromat	24 Kauffman House Museum

Rocky Mountain National Park

Grand Lake

below). Hostel guests should bring sheets or a sleeping bag and, in keeping with the hostel's tradition, must perform a small chore.

B&Bs The *Terrace Inn* (☎ 970-627-3079), 813 Grand Ave downtown, charges $75 for a double.

Lodges, Cabins & Cottages Private singles/doubles at *Shadowcliff Lodge* (☎ 970-627-9220) are $25/30. Shadowcliff also has a limited number of cabins for $60 to $70 for five persons (linen $2 extra per bed); reservations are essential and there is a six-day minimum.

With an ideal setting next to the Tonahutu River, *Rapids Lodge* (☎ 970-627-3707), 209 Rapids Lane, offers cozy, uniquely decorated rooms in an historic building for $50 to $85. *Brownhurst Cottages* (☎ 970-627-3410), on the east end of Grand Ave at Hancock St, has rustic cabins ranging from $50; it's open from mid-May

to early October. *Lonesome Dove Cottages* (☎ 970-627-8019), 416 Grand, has basic cabins that can sleep four to eight starting at $78/doubles.

The historic *Grand Lake Lodge* (☎ 970-627-3967), a National Register of Historic Places landmark, is reached via an eastward lateral half-mile north of Grand Lake junction. It has cabins with views ranging from $69/doubles to $434 for an eight-bedroom cabin with kitchen for up to 25 people. It's open early June to mid-September only.

Motels The *Waconda Motel* (☎ 970-627-8312), 725 Grand Ave, is a good bet with doubles starting at $55, $60 for rooms with a fireplace. *Lone Eagle Lodge* (☎ 970-627-3310, 800-282-3311), 712 Grand Ave, has one- or two-bedroom cabin-style rooms from $50 to $75, while the *Bighorn Lodge* (☎ 970-627-8101, 800-341-8000), 613 Grand Ave, starts at $60. The lakeside *Western Riviera Motel & Cabins* (☎ 970-

627-3580), 419 Garfield St, has economy units for $65; most motel rooms go for $65-plus; cabins with kitchenettes are $100.

Places to Eat
The best dining experience in Grand Lake is at *Rapids Lodge*. With a reasonably priced gourmet Italian menu served in a charming restaurant overlooking the gently flowing rapids of the Tonahutu River, this is a nice place for a romantic dinner. *Caroline's Cuisine at Soda Springs Ranch* (☎ 970-627-9404), 9921 US Hwy 34, is 5 miles south of town but worth the drive. Owners and classically trained chefs Caroline and Jean Claude Cavalera serve up a delicious blend of Continental and American cuisine and offer the most extensive wine list in the area. It's open daily in summer, and from Tuesday through Sunday in winter.

EG's Garden Grill (☎ 970-627-8404), 1000 Grand Ave, has a festive beer garden, serves varied cuisine from interesting salads to seafood and occasionally has live music. The *Grand Pizza Company/Sweet Caboose* (☎ 970-627-8390), 717 Grand Ave, has standard and specialty pizzas (Cajun, for example); it also offers espresso drinks and desserts. The *Mountain Inn* (☎ 970-627-3385), in the historic Humphrey's building at 612 Grand Ave, serves steaks and burgers after 5 pm.

Entertainment
Lariat Saloon (☎ 970-627-9965), 1121 Grand Ave, is the main live music venue in town with shows Wednesday through Sunday. The *Stagecoach Inn* (☎ 970-627-8079), 920 Grand Ave, has occasional live Country & Western bands but always has the best dance floor.

Rocky Mountain Repertory Theatre (☎ 970-627-3421) continues its 30 year-tradition on Grand Ave in the Public Square. The company culls actors from across the USA to present live musicals, comedies and other family entertainment. The season runs June through August; ticket prices are $14/12 adults/children under 12, and family discounts are offered.

Getting There & Away
Home James Transportation Services (☎ 970-726-5060, 800-451-4844) charges $56 per passenger for door-to-airport mini-van service to/from Grand Lake and Denver International Airport. Shuttles from Denver leave at 1 pm, shuttles from Grand Lake to DIA depart at 10 am daily; advance reservations are required.

AROUND GRAND LAKE
Arapaho National Recreation Area
Between Granby and Grand Lake, the USFS-managed Arapaho National Recreation Area (ANRA) abuts Rocky Mountain National Park and Arapaho National Forest's Indian Peaks Wilderness. Part of the Colorado-Big Thompson Reclamation Project, a massive water transfer from the Western Slope to arid northeastern Colorado, the ANRA encompasses several reservoirs, including Lake Granby, pumping stations, canals and the Alva B Adams Tunnel through the Rockies.

The ANRA is largely an uninviting place best left to RVs and motorboaters, but does provide good access to the Indian Peaks Wilderness Area from the Monarch Lake Trailhead at the east end of Lake Granby. Note that backcountry camping in Indian Peaks requires a permit from the USFS at Monarch Lake or in Granby. One interesting crossing of the Front Range is the Cascade Creek Trail over 12,000-foot Pawnee Pass, but the north-south Continental Divide National Scenic Trail also passes through the area. Four major campgrounds within the ANRA cost $10; for reservations call ☎ 877-444-6667).

HOT SULPHUR SPRINGS
Denver Post Editor William Byers first promoted Hot Sulphur Springs as a tourist destination in the 19th century. At one time the rivalry with Grand Lake was so serious that a struggle over which town would be the Grand County seat led to a fatal shoot-out between elected officials; Hot Sulphur Springs prevailed politically, but fortunately it has never suffered the tourist invasion that has made Grand Lake so

COLORADO

ticky-tacky. Of all the hamlets along US 40, Hot Sulphur Springs (population 450) most deserves a stopover.

Orientation & Information
At the foot of 12,804-foot Byers Peak, Hot Sulphur Springs is midway between Granby and Kremmling on US 40 and wedged between Routt National Forest to the north and Arapaho National Forest to the south. It has no formal tourist office, but the Grand County Museum in town is a good source of information.

The post office is at 506 Grand St; zip code 80451.

Grand County Museum
One of the Rockies' better rural museums, the former Hot Sulphur School dates back to 1924. Well-arranged exhibits deal with the evolution of settlement in the area since the time of the Paleo-Indians, the development of area frontier communities, the rise of winter sports, construction of the Moffat Tunnel and German POW camps at Fraser. Outside is a collection of relocated historic buildings, including the original county courthouse, the jail, a blacksmith shop and the Horseshoe Ranger Station.

At 110 Byers Avenue just off US 40 at the east end of town, the museum (☎ 970-725-3939) is open daily 10 am to 5 pm Memorial Day to Labor Day.

Places to Stay
Camping There's no official campground but tent campers and RVs can take advantage of the shade and good fishing at *Pioneer Park* on the north bank of the river, where there's not even anyone to pester you for money. Get drinking and cooking water from the standpipe across from the Riverside Hotel near the bridge; there are portable toilets, but to clean up try the pools at Hot Sulphur Springs Motel (see below).

B&Bs The *Stagecoach Country Inn* (☎ 970-725-3910), 412 Nevava St, is a cozy, well-kept Western-style B&B that has nine comfortable rooms upstairs, a parlor, dining

room and tavern downstairs. Rates range from $50 to $75 and include a full breakfast. Dinners can be arranged on request.

Motels & Hotels *Canyon Motel* (☎ 970-725-3395), 221 Byers Ave, is good value with singles/doubles for $34/38. *Riverside Hotel* (☎ 970-725-3589), in an historic building at 509 Grand St, has rooms for $35/42 and a first-rate restaurant. *Ute Trail Motel* (☎ 970-725-0123, 800-506-0099), 120 E US 40, has rates of $35/40.

Hot Sulphur Springs Resort (☎ 970-725-3306), the town's original spa, has doubles from $48 to $125, which includes use of outdoor pools. The pools are also open daily to nonguests for $6, including access to showers. A full range of massage, body wraps, and facials are available for an additional charge. Open year-round, the resort is two blocks west of town at 5617 County Rd 20 and is so close to the railroad tracks that light sleepers may fear an earthquake when a train passes.

Places to Eat
The *County Seat Cafe* (☎ 970-726-3309), 517 Byers Ave, is Sulphur Spring's most popular eatery, while the rundown looking *M-Bar-Eleven Cafe* (☎ 970-725-9984), 419 Grand Ave, has great steaks at reasonable prices.

Fishing
Riverside Anglers (☎ 970-725-0025) arranges half- and full-day trips on the Colorado River for $100 and $180. There are seasonal locations in both the Ute Trail Motel and the Riverside Hotel.

Getting There & Away
Greyhound (☎ 800-231-2222) will make a flag stop in Hot Sulphur Springs if it's arranged in advance.

KREMMLING
Kremmling (population 1322) is a service center at the junction of US 40 and Hwy 9 about 100 miles west of Denver, 32 miles north of Silverthorne on Hwy 9 and 53 miles southeast of Steamboat Springs. It's

a popular base for hunters and snowmobilers but has recently made efforts to encourage mountain biking.

The USFS Middle Park Ranger District Office (☎ 970-724-9004), at 210 S 6th St (Hwy 9), is open 8 am to 5 pm weekdays in summer but closes at 4:30 pm the rest of the year. Kremmling Memorial Hospital (☎ 970-724-3442), 214 S 4th St, is the only such facility in Grand County.

If you want to spend the night, the *Eastin Hotel* (☎ 970-724-3261, 800-546-0815), 105 S 2nd St, has singles with shared bathrooms from $28; showers are available to nonguests for $5. The best spot in town is *Mountain Breeze B&B* (☎ 970-724-3861, 800-484-2450, ext 4393), 602 Grand Ave. All rooms are $75 and include a full gourmet breakfast.

The *Piece O' Cake Bakery* (☎ 970-724-3412), 104 N 6th St, offers fresh baked goods, sandwiches and decent pizza. *The Wagon Restaurant* (☎ 970-724-9219), 276 Central Ave, is a basic steakhouse.

STEAMBOAT SPRINGS

Steamboat Springs (population 6700) is one of Colorado's more appealing high-class ski resorts. Far from the glitter of Vail and Aspen and despite the sprawling Steamboat Village built to service skiers, the town retains some of its original low-rise character and charm in a delightful natural setting. Many consider it the most laid-back of the major resorts. Away from Lincoln Avenue, the main thoroughfare, the flashiness fades and it's pleasantly residential.

Long before European settlers knew of this area, the Utes summered here to enjoy its warm mineral springs. The story goes that three French trappers first noticed a spring in the Yampa Valley that, accompanied by a chugging sound, reminded them of a steamboat. Since the early 1870s, trappers, guides and miners came to call the future town site Steamboat Springs. The arrival of the railroad in the early 20th century improved access, but Steamboat didn't really take off until construction of the ski area in 1964.

For the last five years, Steamboat has drawn over a million skiers each winter, filling the numerous hotels, motels and condos. Summer is almost as popular with hiking, backpacking, white-water rafting, mountain biking and other outdoor activities. Like similar resorts, it's a fairly pricey destination, but good values are not impossible to find.

Steamboat is also the Routt County seat. Its permanent population of 8000 makes it the largest single community in the county; cattle and sheep ranching and coal mining also make notable contributions to the economy.

Orientation

Steamboat Springs consists of two major areas: the relatively regular grid of central Old Town which straddles US 40, and the newer warren of winding streets at Steamboat Village, centered around the Mt Werner Ski Area at the southeast end of town. US 40 is known as Lincoln Ave through Old Town.

Information

Tourist Offices The Steamboat Springs Chamber Resort Association runs a visitor information center (☎ 970-879-0880, 800-922-2722) at 1255 S Lincoln Ave opposite Sundance Plaza. Staff can help locate a room if accommodations are tight. This is a good place to pick up brochures on lodging, restaurants and recreational activities, as well as coupon books that give discounts at many local businesses.

The USFS Hahn's Peak Ranger Office (☎ 970-879-1870), 925 Weiss Drive, is at the southeast end of town next to the Super 8 motel. It has fairly detailed information on opportunities for hiking, mountain biking, fishing and other activities in the area, including the Mt Zirkel Wilderness. There are also maps for sale. It is open weekdays 8 am to 5 pm year-round; it's also open Saturdays 9 am to 12 pm in summer.

Money Norwest Bank has an ATM located at 320 Lincoln Ave.

COLORADO

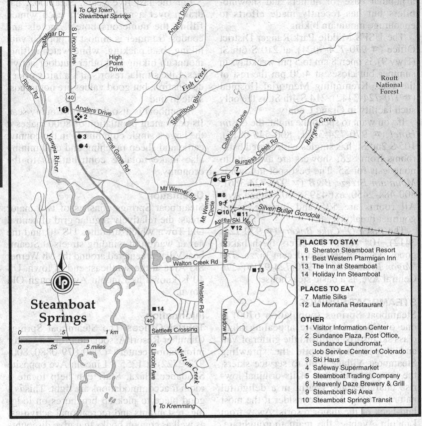

To Old Town
Steamboat Springs

Trafalgar Dr

High
Point
Drive

River Rd

Yampa River

Routt
National
Forest

Anglers Drive

Fish Creek

Steamboat Blvd

Pine Grove Rd

Clubhouse Drive

Burgess Creek

Burgess Creek Rd

Mt Werner Rd

Burgess Creek Rd

Mt Werner Circle

Silver Bullet Gondola

Apres Ski Way

Village Drive

Walton Creek Rd

Whistler Rd

Meadow Ln

Steamboat Springs

0   .5   1 km

0   .25   .5 miles

S Lincoln Ave

Settlers Crossing

Walton Creek

To Kremmling

PLACES TO STAY
8   Sheraton Steamboat Resort
11   Best Western Ptarmigan Inn
13   The Inn at Steamboat
14   Holiday Inn Steamboat

PLACES TO EAT
7   Mattie Silks
12   La Montaña Restaurant

OTHER
1   Visitor Information Center
2   Sundance Plaza, Post Office,
    Sundance Laundromat,
    Job Service Center of Colorado
3   Ski Haus
4   Safeway Supermarket
5   Steamboat Trading Company
6   Heavenly Daze Brewery & Grill
9   Steamboat Ski Area
10   Steamboat Springs Transit

Post & Communications The main post office is at 200 Lincoln Ave; zip code 80477. Pilot Office Supply (☎ 970-879-6450; fax 970-879-1599), at 1025 Lincoln Ave, offers fax and postal services.

Bookstores Off the Beaten Path Bookstore & Coffeehouse (☎ 970-879-6830), 56 7th St, is a great place to browse for books, magazines and newspapers; if you buy something, you can read it over pastries and coffee in the cozy cafe.

Publications Several local publications, most of them giveaways, provide informa-

tion and commercial propaganda, including the daily *Steamboat Today*, the weekly *Steamboat Pilot*, the monthly *Steamboat Springs Review* and the biennial *Steamboat Springs Downtowner*. *The Whistle* is a weekly activities guide.

Medical Services Routt Memorial Hospital (☎ 970-879-1322) is at 80 Park Ave.

Laundry Spring Creek Laundromat (☎ 970-879-5587) is at 35 Lincoln Ave.

Work There are abundant seasonal employment opportunities in this resort community, but low wages and the shortage of affordable housing are drawbacks. Some employers, however, provide free meals and/or ski passes to compensate. For the latest opportunities, contact the Steamboat Springs Chamber Resort Association (☎ 970-879-0880; fax 970- 879-2543) for its monthly *Live Work & Play in Ski Town USA* newsletter, which covers employment, housing and transportation.

Job Service Center of Colorado (☎ 970-879-3075), in Sundance Plaza at 1250 S Lincoln Ave, is a state agency that also helps arrange temporary, part-time and full-time employment.

Trail of the Pioneers Museum
Dedicated to early Steamboat Springs, exhibits in this beautifully maintained Victorian house recreate a period bedroom, kitchen, parlor and dining room, plus a ski gallery, a Western room and a room dedicated to Colorado Utes. The museum (☎ 970-879-2214), 800 Oak St, is open 11 am to 5 pm daily in summer; closed Sunday the rest of the year. Admission is $2.50/1 adults/children.

Mineral Springs
Most of Steamboat's numerous springs are warm rather than hot, and some have been

COLORADO

PLACES TO STAY
1 Mariposa B&B
4 Steamboat Valley Guest House
5 Western Lodge
6 Nordic Lodge Motel
13 Alpiner Lodge
20 Bristol Hotel
25 Nite's Rest Motel
29 Rabbit Ears Motel

PLACES TO EAT
8 Cugino's Pizzeria
9 The Cantina
10 Johnny B Goode's Diner
12 Old Town Pub & Restaurant
14 El Rancho Cafe
21 Mazzola's
24 Winona's
26 Rosie's Cafe
27 Steamboat Brewery & Tavern
30 Steamboat Yacht Club

OTHER
2 Routt Memorial Hospital
3 Eleanor Bliss Center for the Arts
   (Old Railroad Depot)
7 Trail of the Pioneers Museum
11 Buggywhip's Fish & Float Service
15 Norwest Bank
16 Main Post Office
17 Steamboat Springs Health
    & Recreation Center
18 Sore Saddle Cyclery
19 Pilot Office Supply
22 Murphy's Exchange
23 Off the Beaten Path Bookstore
    & Coffeehouse
28 Spring Creek Laundromat
31 Howelsen Ski Area & Jump
32 Steamboat Stables

Old Town
Steamboat Springs

0   250   500 m
0   250   500 yards

damaged by highway construction. Probably the nicest spring is 3 miles from Old Town at Strawberry Park: it's open until midnight and you can actually bathe in it. Most of the others are in the area around 13th St on both sides of the river; look for the map/brochure 'A Walking Tour of the Springs of Steamboat' for more information.

To try the waters in town, head for the Steamboat Springs Health & Recreation Center (☎ 970-879-1828), 135 Lincoln Ave, a modern facility on the site of the old hot springs. It has an Olympic-size swimming pool, hot mineral pools, a water slide, weight room and saunas. It's open daily 6:30 am to 10 pm. The water slide operates daily in summer noon to 6 pm, in winter 4 to 8 pm.

Daily admission to the pool and sauna is $5/3.50/2 adults/teens/children (three to 12) and seniors (62+). The water slide costs an additional $3.50 for 10 rides, and the weight room and exercise classes are also extra.

Gondola Rides
In summer, visitors can take Steamboat Village's Silver Bullet Gondola to the 9080-foot Thunderhead complex for hiking or mountain biking. Service starts at 10 am daily late June to Labor Day; the last lift is usually at 4:30 pm but there are later runs on Friday and Saturday evenings. The one-way fare is $13/7 adults/children (six to 12).

Downhill Skiing
Steamboat Ski Area (☎ 970-879-6111, 800-922-2722), centered around Mt Werner, features 2939 skiable acres, 20 lifts with a capacity of nearly 30,000 skiers per hour and a 3600-foot vertical drop (the second biggest incline in the state). This world-class resort has earned a reputation for having consistently good powder, some of the lightest (and most abundant) in Colorado.

The season starts around Thanksgiving and runs until Easter; lift tickets are $48/28 adults/children, though multiple-day discount tickets can reduce the bite to some degree.

Cross-Country Skiing
The Steamboat Ski Touring Center (☎ 970-879-8180) uses the Sheraton Steamboat Resort Golf Course in winter, but there are many other cross-country sites, such as the Yampa River Trail, Spring Creek Mountain Park and Rabbit Ears and Dunkley passes.

Mountain Biking
The 'Steamboat Trails Map' shows mountain bike routes around town, in Stagecoach and Pearl Lake State Parks and the Mt Zirkel Wilderness. It's available at the visitor information center (see Information above). Steamboat Ski Area (☎ 970-879-6111) promotes biking on Mt Werner, allows bikes on the Silver Bullet Gondola and rents them at the Thunderhead lift. An 'adult with bicycle' gondola ticket costs $20.

Steamboat Trading Company (☎ 970-879-0083), 1850 Ski Time Square, rents mountain bikes for $10/16 half-day/full-day or $28 for two days. Other rental places include Ski Haus (☎ 970-879-0385), 1450 S Lincoln Rd, and Sore Saddle Cyclery (☎ 970-879-1675), 1136 Yampa St, which also offers tours of Routt National Forest.

White-Water Rafting
Buggywhip's (☎ 970-879-8033, 800-759-0343), 720 Lincoln Ave, has half-day trips on the Yampa River from $22, and also offers longer and more challenging excursions on the Yampa, Colorado, Eagle and Arkansas rivers.

Ballooning
Pegasus Activity Group (☎ 970-879-9191, 800-748-2487) runs hot-air balloon flights in both summer and winter, but they're not cheap: $80 per person for half an hour, $150 for an hour. Other ballooning companies include Aerosports Balloonists (☎ 970-879-7433) and Balloons over Steamboat (☎ 970-879-3298).

Horseback Riding

Steamboat Stables (☎ 970-879-2306), southeast of the rodeo grounds, offers one-hour horseback rides for $17, plus breakfast and dinner rides and pack trips.

Special Events

Hardly a winter's day passes without a major ski event, such as mid-January's **Norwest Banks Cowboy Downhill**, in which professional rodeo cowboys slalom down the course before saddling a horse to cross the finish line. The weeklong **Steamboat Springs Winter Carnival** takes place the second week of February.

July 4 sees the annual **Steamboat Cowboy Roundup Days**, while mid-July's **Steamboat Springs Rainbow Weekend** includes a Hot Air Balloon Rodeo and an Art-in-the-Park event. The **Steamboat Springs Pro Rodeo Series** takes place in mid-August. Later in the month peace and quiet give way to the roar of V8 engines when the **Steamboat Vintage Auto Race** kicks off.

Places to Stay

Steamboat Springs' peak season is winter, when skiing is king and lodging rates can triple those summer prices; however, even summer rates skyrocket when demand is high during special events. Spring and fall rates are generally lower; the Christmas and President's Day holidays have the steepest prices. Steamboat Central Reservations (☎ 800-922-2722) is a clearing-house for accommodations, especially condominiums.

Camping While it's not cheap, the *Steamboat Springs KOA Campground* (☎ 970-879-0273), on US 40 about 2 miles west of downtown, is one of the best such facilities in the Rocky Mountain states. For $17, tent campers get the benefit of quiet, shady sites on a small island in the Yampa River, where monster RVs cannot go. Sites with water and power cost $21, sites with full hookups are $23. All guests have access to the hot tub and other facilities. (For other camping options see Around Steamboat Springs below.)

B&Bs At *The Inn at Steamboat* (☎ 970-879-2600, 800-872-2601), 3070 Columbine Drive near Walton Creek Rd, winter rates can range anywhere from $45 in November to $139 during Christmas, depending on the type of room. In Old Town, *Steamboat Valley Guest House* (☎ 970-870-9017, 800-530-3866), 1245 Crawford Ave, is a wooden ski lodge affair with rooms from $80 to $125 during ski season. *Mariposa B&B* (☎ 970-879-1467), 855 Grand St, is a Southwest-style adobe home set back in a quiet residential area. Doubles are $85 to $90 in winter, $75 in summer.

Motels These comprise the 'low end,' a relative term in Steamboat: if you're paying $60 for a room in winter, you're doing great. Steamboat's best value is probably the *Nordic Lodge Motel* (☎ 970-879-0531, 800-364-0331), 1036 Lincoln Ave. The highest winter rates are singles/doubles for $78/92 but during most of the season you should be able to get a room for around $60. The rooms are sparkling clean and amenities include a hot tub, sauna and cable TV. Off-season singles/doubles are as low as $42/48.

Western Lodge (☎ 970-979-1050, 800-622-9200), 1122 Lincoln Ave, is an undistinguished but moderately priced motel at the west end of town; in winter singles/doubles cost around $68/78, about $20 less in off-peak periods. The *Nite's Rest Motel* (☎ 970-879-1212, 800-828-1780), 601

Lincoln Ave, with a good location in the heart of town, has rooms that are a bit dark and small but otherwise not too bad. Singles/doubles are around $80/90 during winter. *Rabbit Ears Motel* (☎ 970-879-1150, 800-828-7702), 201 Lincoln Ave, is a bit nicer and offers discount passes to the Steamboat Springs Health & Recreation Center across the street. Winter rates average around $89/109 for singles/doubles, and dip to $69/89 in the off-season.

Another centrally located 'economy' choice is *Alpiner Lodge* (☎ 970-879-1430), 424 Lincoln Ave, which has winter rates of around $85.

Hotels One of the nicer choices is Old Town's *Bristol Hotel* (☎ 970-879-3083, 800-851-0872), 917 Lincoln Ave, a warm, nicely appointed place that has 22 rooms with either shared or private bath. Winter rates generally range from $69 to $109, though they shoot sharply higher around Christmas.

To be near the slopes, you can't do much better than the *Best Western Ptarmigan Inn* (☎ 970-879-1730), 2304 Apres Ski Way. It's located right next to the Steamboat gondola. Singles/doubles range from $99/109 to $119/129 during ski season (plunging to $59 in summer). Also right on the slopes is *Sheraton Steamboat Resort* (☎ 970-879-2220), 2200 Village Inn Court (you can enter from Mt Werner Circle), probably the most expensive option around. The lowest winter rate of $105 gets you a ground-floor room with no view, and even this modest accommodation will cost $200 or more between December and February. For the money you get luxuries such as a full-size heated pool, private balconies (on the more expensive rooms) saunas, room refrigerators and the like.

Out on Hwy 40, the *Holiday Inn Steamboat* (☎ 970-879-2250), 3190 S Lincoln Ave, charges less than the Sheraton but is also several miles from the slopes and is not as luxurious.

Long-Term Rentals Like all major ski areas, Steamboat has hordes of property management companies offering to rent condominiums for stays ranging from two days to a month. Big Country Management (☎ 970-879-0763, 800-872-0763) offers dozens of choices, nearly all of them in the luxury category. *Ski Inn Condominiums* (☎ 970-879-8000) has units located right at the base of Steamboat ski area at slightly less stratospheric prices.

Places to Eat
Steamboat Springs has such a variety of restaurants that it's hard to give more than a representative sample, but in general the quality is high. One of the best deals in town is dinner at *Johnny B Goode's Diner* (☎ 970-870-8400), 738 Lincoln Ave. A 'belly stuffer' turkey dinner comes with roast turkey slices, mashed potatoes, corn and toast, a very tasty and filling, if starch-heavy, meal for $6.55. Breakfast and lunch are similarly reasonable and Friday nights are a real bargain: $5 gets you a burger, fries and a shake.

Cugino's Pizzeria (☎ 970-879-5805), at 825 Oak St, has an appealing Italian menu and atmosphere. *Mazzola's* (☎ 970-879-2405), at 917 Lincoln Ave, is a little more expensive but is quite popular.

Winona's (☎ 970-879-2483), 617 Lincoln Ave, is a friendly a little deli-bakery with good breakfast and lunch specials; it's open 7 am to 3 pm and again 4:30 to 9:30 pm Monday through Saturday.

The *Old Town Pub & Restaurant* (☎ 970-879-2101), 600 Lincoln Ave, is a lively spot with American food and live music on weekends. Not quite as hopping, the *Steamboat Brewery & Tavern* (☎ 970-879-2233), 5th and Lincoln, has great food and their beer brewed on the premises is excellent. There are some great luncheon items on the menu: try the pan-fried salmon sandwich with pasta salad ($7).

The Cantina (☎ 970-879-0826), 818 Lincoln Ave, has reasonably priced Mexican lunch and dinner specials. Considered the best Mexican-Southwestern place in town, *La Montaña* (☎ 970-879-5800), 2500 Village Drive in Steamboat Village, is considerably more expensive with entrees ranging from $10 to $23.

Mattie Silks (☎ 970-879-2441), 1890 Mt Werner Rd, is one of Steamboat's most highly regarded restaurants for Continental cuisine, steaks and seafood. The *Steamboat Yacht Club* (☎ 970-879-5570), 811 Yampa St, is another well-rated steak and seafood place.

Entertainment
Murphy's Exchange (☎ 970-879-2022), 703 Lincoln Ave, often has live music and can be one of the rowdier spots in town. The *Old Town Pub & Restaurant* (☎ 970-879-2101), 600 Lincoln Ave, also has live music on weekends, including an occasional nationally known act. *Heavenly Daze Brewery & Grill* (☎ 970-879-8080), in the Ski Time Square in Steamboat Village, features live music and home brew.

Getting There & Away
Air Steamboat Springs is served by the Yampa Valley Regional Airport (☎ 970-276-3669) near Hayden, 22 miles west. During the ski season, American, Continental, Northwest, TWA and United Express all fly in to the airport. There are direct flights to and from Denver, Chicago, IL, Cleveland, OH, Dallas/Fort Worth and Houston, TX, Minneapolis/St Paul, MN, and New York/Newark. During the rest of the year United Express has five to six flights daily to/from Denver.

DIA Shuttle Alpine Taxi/Limo (☎ 970-879-2800, 800-232-7433) runs two shuttles daily between Steamboat and Denver International Airport. The one-way fare is $55 ($60 on weekends) and the trip takes around four hours. Steamboat Express (☎ 970-879-3400, 800-545-6050) runs a similar service during ski season only.

Bus Greyhound's US 40 service between Denver and Salt Lake City inconveniently stops at the Phillips 66 gas station about a mile west of town at 30475 Hwy 40. There's a small waiting room next to the station. Buses to Denver leave at 4:20 pm

and 2:25 am, those to Salt Lake at 1:40 and 10:55 pm. There is also an old Steamboat Springs Transit bus stop about 30 feet west of the gas station where you can catch a bus into town.

Car Steamboat Springs is 157 miles from Denver, 196 miles from Grand Junction and 339 miles from Salt Lake City. It lies along US 40 which connects with I-70 to the south, the most commonly used route. There's also an intersection with Hwy 14 which then takes you east to Fort Collins and the Front Range.

Getting Around
To/From the Airport Alpine Taxi-Limo (☎ 970-879-2800, 800-232-7433) and Steamboat Express (☎ 970-879-3400, 800-545-6050) both provide van service to Yampa Valley Regional Airport for $22 one-way.

Bus Steamboat Springs Transit (☎ 970-879-5585) runs a free bus service along Lincoln Ave from 12th St in the west to Walton Creek Rd in the east. It also goes up Mt Werner Rd to the gondola. Approximate hours of service are 6 to 1 am.

AROUND STEAMBOAT SPRINGS
Stagecoach State Park
Sixteen miles south of Steamboat Springs via US 40, Hwy 131 and Routt County Rd 14, Stagecoach State Park (☎ 970-736-2436) is the nearest inexpensive camping to Steamboat Springs; sites cost $7 to $10. There's fishing and a handful of hiking trails.

Mt Zirkel Wilderness
Famed mountaineer Clarence King, first director of the USGS, named 12,180-foot Mt Zirkel for a German petrologist when the two reconnoitered the country in 1874. The most popular entry points to this 250-sq-mile roadless area of the Routt National Forest are in the vicinity of Steamboat Springs, though it's also approachable from Walden or Clark. Detailed maps and information on hiking, mountain biking,

fishing and other activities in this beautiful area are available at the Hahn's Peak Ranger Station (☎ 970-978-1870), 925 Weiss Drive in Steamboat Springs.

Trails Illustrated publishes *Hahn's Peak/Steamboat Lake* and *Clark/Buffalo Pass* maps, while Jay and Therese Thompson describe the walks in *The Hiker's Guide to the Mt Zirkel Wilderness*.

Hahn's Peak

This picturesque quasi-ghost town 27 miles north of Steamboat Springs via Elk River Rd (Routt County Rd 129) was once the terminus of the railroad from Wyoming. It's an unfrequented destination that still has a handful of residents and a couple of interesting junk and crafts shops. Nearby **Steamboat Lake State Park** and **Pearl Lake State Park** (☎ 970-879-3922) are really reservoirs that offer shoreline camping as well as fishing and boating. Camping costs $6 plus a $3 vehicle fee.

Summit County

Locals joke that there are four seasons in Summit County – winter, late winter, Fourth of July and early winter. Reached by I-70 via the Eisenhower Tunnel, this mountain playground is just over an hour's drive from Denver and is home to four ski mountains: Arapahoe Basin Ski Area, Keystone, Breckenridge and Copper Mountain. Skiing was a practical means of travel for miners and early postal workers, but Summit County didn't attract recreational skiers to its lofty slopes (at Arapahoe Basin) until 1947.

During summer months, the 9000-foot altitude provides relief from the heat in the cities along the Front Range, but don't count on swimming in the chilly waters of Dillon Reservoir. On the reservoir's east end, the town of Frisco serves as a convenient hub for most activities in the county, offering moderately priced lodging and visitor information. Below the earthfill dam, Silverthorne is the site of the Arapaho

National Forest Dillon Ranger District offices and visitors center. Breckenridge, a former mining town designated a National Historic District, is an historical highlight of the county.

The growth of Summit County is attributed to the opening of the Eisenhower Tunnel in 1973; from a resident population of 2500 in 1970, the county blossomed to 15,000 by 1995.

SummitNet (www.summitnet.com) is the official website of Summit County and has information on accommodation, restaurants, activities, events, shopping and transportation for all of the towns and resorts within the county and an online reservation service.

The Guide is a seasonal publication covering outdoor activities, the arts, dining and events for all of Summit County. The *Ten Mile Times*, a weekly local newspaper, includes an events calendar.

ARAPAHOE BASIN SKI AREA

Near the Continental Divide where US 6 crosses 11,992-foot Loveland Pass, 6 miles east of Keystone Resort and 90 miles west of Denver, Arapahoe Basin (☎ 970-468-0718, 888-272-7246) is the county's oldest ski area.

Locals call it 'A-Basin' and it's a favorite with experts who enjoy using one lift to get to the good stuff. One look at the steep face of the 2250-foot slope will suggest that 'A' stands for 'awesome,' but if you're looking for high-speed quads and gourmet dining you've come to the wrong place. Arapahoe has some great extreme skiing but there's only four double and one triple chair and the amenities are spartan. This is Colorado's highest ski area with a base elevation of 10,800 feet. Even the unsanctioned 'Nordic activities' on the Loveland Pass roadway are extreme – full-moon parties have been going on for years but are now often interrupted by the state police for illegally blocking the road. Arapahoe is often still open in mid-June, giving it the longest ski season of any Colorado resort.

Lift passes are $39/30/12 for adults/teens/children (six to 12). Children under six and seniors 70 and over ski free. Vail Associates tried to buy Arapahoe Basin along with Breckenridge and Keystone in 1997, but the US Justice Department, ruling that the purchase would give Vail an unfair advantage over competing ski areas, ordered the divestiture of one of the properties. As a result, Arapahoe is now owned by Dundee Realty but lift passes from any Vail-owned resort can be exchanged for an Arapahoe ticket. The ski school has ski and snowboarding lessons for adults and children; a two-hour group lesson without lift ticket or equipment runs $32. Standard ski

rental packages are $17 at the base of the mountain, $32 for top-end gear, and $30 for boards; discount packages combining lift tickets and rentals are available.

Don't look for a 'village' at Arapahoe Basin; the nearest lodging is the Ski Tip Lodge in Keystone. The 'early riser' parking is next to the lifts. Buses arrive from Keystone every 20 minutes.

KEYSTONE SKI RESORT
In operation since 1970, Keystone is a family-oriented resort on the Snake River 5 miles east of Dillon on US 6. It attracts

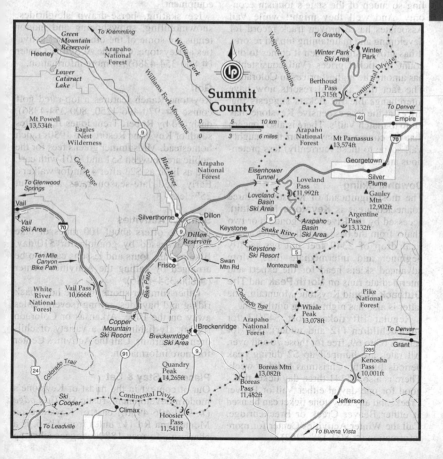

skiers in mid- to late-October, while other ski areas are still waiting for snow. Keystone is definitely a 'resort' in that all the accommodations, restaurants and services are owned and operated by one company. As a result, while the base area lacks the character and variety of real ski towns like Breckenridge and Aspen, Keystone has been well planned and it is easy to book reservations and get information by calling one number (☎ 800-258-9553). Both Keystone and Breckenridge were recently acquired by Vail Associates, which has locals worried about one company controlling so much of the state's tourism economy. And well they might: while Vail Associates has a proven track record for developing and maintaining top ski resorts, it has proven stingy when it comes to discount lift ticket prices (Vail consistently has among the highest prices in Colorado). The fact that all Vail resorts now have interchangeable lift tickets suggests that prices at the less expensive Keystone may jump to match Vail's. There is also concern that the company may export the haughty Vail scene to these (currently) less pretentious areas.

Downhill Skiing

The most significant of Keystone's three connected areas is **Keystone Mountain**, accessed by the River Run gondola or two chairs from the base area. It features a vertical drop of 2340 feet but has mostly beginner and intermediate runs. More advanced skiers head for the expert and intermediate runs on **North Peak** and **The Outback**, behind Keystone Mountain. The latter is also has night skiing until 9 pm.

Regular lift tickets cost $47/17 for adults/children (12 and under); $30 for seniors 65 to 69, free for those 70 and over. All rates are bumped up $2 during peak periods like the Christmas holiday week. There is also a $141 three-day ticket that's good for one day at either Vail or Beaver Creek, and any Keystone ticket can be used at either Beaver Creek or Breckenridge. Call the Winter Activities Center for more information (☎ 800-438-7262).

The Keystone Ski School (☎ 800-255-3715) has a full range of group and private ski/snowboard lessons for adults and children as well as day care programs. For $365 you can even take a three- or five-day ski clinic with personal coaching from Olympic medalists Phil Mahre or Steve Mahre.

Cross-Country Skiing

Keystone has 20 miles of groomed trails accessible for a $9 trail fee, as well as 35 miles of backcountry trails in the Arapaho National Forest. Rentals at the mountain are $18; a $30 Moonlight Tour includes equipment.

Ice skating, horse-drawn sleighrides, snowmobiling, snowshoeing and indoor tennis are some of the other winter activities at Keystone. Call the Activities Center (☎ 800-354-4386) for more information.

Golf

Keystone Ranch features a top-rated golf course (☎ 970-496-4250, 800-354-4386), designed by Robert Trent Jones Jr, 3 miles south of Keystone Resort on a 1930s ranch homestead. Midsummer greens fees for the public are between $51 and $101 with cart, and as little as $23 after 4 pm for walkers. Early- and late-season rates are about 25% less.

Summer Activities

Keystone offers about 100 miles of bike trails accessed by gondola for $10/day. Bike rentals, tours and lessons can also be arranged by calling the Activities Center (☎ 800-354-4386).

Other summer sports include horseback riding and hayrides, rafting (several miles away on the Blue, Arkansas or Colorado rivers), fly-fishing and a variety of children's programs. Call the Activities Center for more information.

Places to Stay & Eat

Out of context in the midst of Keystone's modern development, rustic *Ski Tip Lodge* (☎ 970-496-4950), east of Keystone on Montezuma Rd 1½ miles from US 6, is a charming former 1880s stagecoach stop and a refreshing alternative to the familiar condos. It was converted into a ski chalet in 1946 by Max Dercum while he was developing the lifts for Arapahoe Basin.

Rates range from $60 in the off-season to $150 or $170 for a standard room and as much as $250 for a suite during peak ski season. All rates include breakfast and the least expensive rooms have a shared bath. The lodge is open year-round. Breakfast is open only to guests, but a prix-fixe dinner is open to all. A recent menu included either sweetbreads in puff pastry or salmon with sun-dried tomato as part of a four-course dinner for $49. Llamas graze nearby, waiting to accompany summer visitors on lunch hikes for $27.

Keystone Resort has both hotel and condominium accommodations. Winter rates for two persons range anywhere from $80 to $400, though you'll probably only get the former price through one of the resort's ski-and-stay packages. Fortunately these are usually easy to book. For information call Keystone central reservations at ☎ 800-258-9553.

For a meal to remember, try mountain-top gourmet dining at *Alpenglow Stube*, North America's highest gourmet restaurant, perched near the summit of North Peak at 11,444 feet. It's reached by a 25-minute ride on two gondolas. Don't expect to bump into ski or snowboard bums here: the Alpenglow Stube doesn't allow denim dress and its six-course Bavarian meals featuring wild game and seafood cost $68.

Entertainment
Probably the best live rock music in the county is at the *Snake River Saloon* (☎ 970-468-2788), between Dillon and Keystone at 23074 US 6.

MONTEZUMA
Interested in what life is like in the highest town in the USA? The silver mining town of Montezuma (10,400 feet), 5 miles east of Keystone on Montezuma Rd, has little in common with trendy neighboring resorts. Folks here post homemade signs asking

motorists to slow down, but even at 10 mph a visit to Montezuma (population 69) doesn't take long. Cross-country skiers and mountain bikers will want to explore the nearby trails, especially to the old mining town of Saints John, or up Peru Creek to the huge Pennsylvania Mine or on to Argentine Pass on the Continental Divide.

Places to Stay
For lodging try *Granny's Inn B&B* (☎ 970-468-9297), 5435 Montezuma Rd, which also offers winter sleighrides and summer horseback trips. Singles/doubles cost $60/85 and include breakfast. South of town near the Swan River crossing is the secluded *Paradox Lodge* (☎ 970-468-9445), 5040 Montezuma Rd, owned by George and Connie O'Bleness. You can stay in one of three cabins with a kitchen, or one of four doubles in the main lodge. Rates range from $55 to $120 and include breakfast and use of the wood-fired outdoor hot tub.

DILLON
Dillon (population 640) once served as a roadside stop for travelers heading over Loveland Pass, but the creation of the reservoir flooded the original site in 1964 and since the opening of the Eisenhower Tunnel in 1975, motorists on I 70 barely notice the town as they whiz by. Now it serves mainly as a place for day-skiers to pick up a bag lunch before heading to Keystone or A-Basin. It also offers some (relatively) cheaper accommodation that's still fairly close to the ski areas.

The Dillon Marina (☎ 970-468-5100) rents fishing boats, touring kayaks and sailboats at reasonable rates. Private four-course sunset dinner cruises on either sailboats ($100) or pontoon boats ($65) can be reserved 48 hours in advance. Although steady winds can sweep the reservoir, its cold water is unappealing to windsurfers and swimming is forbidden. Next to the reservoir in Marina Park, the **Dillon Amphitheater** (☎ 970-468-2403) offers Thursday evening nature discussions and Saturday night concerts throughout the summer.

COLORADO

Places to Stay & Eat

The *Best Western Ptarmigan Lodge* (☎ 970-468-2341), 652 Main Street, is the only hotel in the center of Dillon. It's clean, well-maintained and has a pool, sauna and whirlpool. Rates start at $65 in the high season and climb to over $100 during peak holidays. *Spinnaker at Lake Dillon* condominiums (☎ 970-468-8001) offer nightly rates for studios beginning at $50 in the summer and $90 during the winter, use of the pool, sauna and garage included. Each unit has a fully equipped kitchen and laundry.

Arapahoe Cafe & Pub (☎ 970-468-0873), 626 Lake Dillon Drive at W La Bonte St, began in the 1940s as a roadside cafe and motel. In the summer, breakfast – granola, fresh fruit, yogurt and juice for about $6 – and lunch are served on the deck. Dinners of trout, roast duck and vegetarian pasta entrees are served inside and cost between $10 and $15. *Ristorante Al Lago* (☎ 970-468-6111), 240 Lake Dillon Drive, features Italian entrees for $13 to $19, while *Pug Ryan's* (☎ 970-468-2145), at the corner of Lake Dillon Drive and Village Place, is the most popular steakhouse in the area.

Entertainment

Drop by the *Corona Street Grill* (☎ 970-262-1122), 154 Dillon Mall, for occasional live music and a lively happy hour.

Getting There & Away

Dillon is 85 miles west of Denver via I-70 to exit 205, then 1 mile south on US 6. The nearest Greyhound bus stop is in Silverthorne (see below).

SILVERTHORNE

Silverthorne (population 3300) is between Dillon and Frisco north of I-70. The earthfill dam that backs up Dillon Reservoir looms 230 feet above its glitzy clutter of shops. Silverthorne took a turn for the worse when numerous factory outlet stores opened, bringing metropolitan-like congestion and uncharacteristic urban development to the rustic setting at the base of the Gore Mountains.

Information

The USFS visitors center for the Arapaho National Forest's Dillon Ranger District (☎ 970-468-5400), 680 Blue River Parkway (Hwy 9), offers information and books on hiking and camping in the area. The Summit County Chamber of Commerce operates an information booth at the US 6/Hwy 9 junction.

Hiking

Silverthorne is wedged between Eagles Nest Wilderness Area to the west (see Heeney below) and Ptarmigan Peaks Wilderness Area to the east. Both offer backcountry solitude away from vehicles and bikes, but trails directly from Silverthorne are heavily used. The Ptarmigan Wilderness is only a mile wide and 12 miles long, following the treeless ridge of the Williams Fork Mountains. A good day hike in the Ptarmigan Wilderness, with outstanding views of the Gore Range, is the **Ute Pass Trail**, a 4½-mile hike from Ute Pass (9558 feet) to 12,303-foot Ute Peak. To get to the trailhead, follow Hwy 9 north for 12 miles to Ute Pass Rd and continue to the trailhead west of the cattle guard at the pass.

A 'Summer Trailhead Guide,' available from USFS or Summit County Chamber of Commerce, lists suggestions for other hikes. The USFS Dillon District Map is available at the USFS visitors center. Trails in the Eagles Nest Wilderness are shown on topo maps 107 and 108 published by Trails Illustrated.

Rocky Mountaineering Guides (☎ 970-468-9646) offers full-day hiking treks in Summit County for $75. It also offers guided rock climbing and instruction.

Fishing

Don't be surprised to see anglers wading in the Blue River within casting distance of factory-store parking lots and bargain-hunting crowds. Thirty-four miles of the Blue River between Dillon Dam and the Colorado River is designated Gold Medal water, rich for fishing. Excluding the Green Mountain Reservoir, the bag limit is two fish over 16 inches.

For guided fishing trips on the Blue River try Columbine Outfitters (☎ 970-262-0966), 191 Blue River Pkwy. A half-day costs $115; each extra person (up to three) is $25.

Places to Stay & Eat

One thing that Silverthorne does have going for it is the *Alpen Hütte Lodge* (☎ 970-468-6336), 471 Rainbow Drive, one of the best-run HI/AYH facilities in Colorado. Their dorms feature bunks with innerspring mattresses and built-in storage lockers, and the Blue River can be heard from an open window. Beds are $18 through the ski season ($23 during the holidays in December and March) and $12 in the off-season. HI/AYH members receive a $2 per night discount. Guests may rent mountain bikes for $8. There's also the terrific *Silverthorne Recreation Center* (☎ 970-468-0711) directly across the street, with full health club facilities for $6.50/4.50 adults/children.

Other standard chain accommodations can be found along Silverthorne Lane, including: the *Days Inn* (☎ 970-468-8661), the *Hampton Inn* (☎ 800-321-3509), and *Luxury Inns & Suites* (☎ 800-742-1972).

To start the day, the *Blue Moon Baking Company* (☎ 970-468-1472), in the City Market shopping center at 253 Summit Place, offers espresso drinks, smoothies, fresh bagels, apple strudel and stuffed croissants. Their lunch menu of salads and sandwiches on fresh breads is also appealing. *Sunshine Cafe* (☎ 970-468-6663) across from City Market is open daily for breakfast, lunch and dinner and is a local favorite for good food and low prices.

Grill your own steak or seafood dinner at the rustic *Historic Mint* (☎ 970-468-5247), 347 Blue River Parkway. Dinners range from $8 to $16 and the bar offers a good selection of beers. If you feel like kicking up your heels, head for the *Old Dillon Inn* (☎ 970-468-2791), 321 Blue River Parkway, with inexpensive Mexican food and Country & Western music in a rustic decor. *Matteos's* (☎ 970-262-6508), on the north end of town at 122E West 10th and Hwy 9, has a great happy hour and good salads, pasta and pizza by the slice.

Getting There & Away

Greyhound buses (☎ 970-468-1938, 800-231-2222) stop at the Alpen Hütte between Denver and Grand Junction. East-bound buses leave at 8:50 am and 12, 4, 6:25 and 8:45 pm. Westbound buses leave at 9:40 am, 5:10 and 7:55 pm. It's $11/20 one-way/roundtrip to Denver. Use the free Summit Stages buses (☎ 970-453-1339), which carry skis and bikes, to get to Copper Mountain, Keystone or Breckenridge.

Resort Express shuttles (☎ 970-468-0330, 800-334-7433), 273 Warren Avenue, provide one-way ($39) and roundtrip ($78) service to/from Denver International Airport.

HEENEY

Since 1981 the minuscule community of Heeney (population 70), 30 miles north of Silverthorne on the west shore of Green Mountain Reservoir, has staged a Tick Festival on the second Saturday of June. This ridiculous festival reportedly began as a celebration of one man's recovery from tick fever but it has gained popularity with Summit County residents suffering from cabin fever and eager to dance and eat with friends after staging a short parade.

Most visitors arrive in Heeney to fish, camp or hike and climb in the Gore Range. A marina on the Green Mountain Reservoir is also located here. The Blue River is a Gold Medal trout fishery and the reservoir offers kokanee salmon.

The secluded peaks and glacier-carved lakes of the Gore Mountains in the Eagles Nest Wilderness Area, located near Heeney, offer an untrammeled wilderness with only primitive trails – not the place for a novice hiker or map reader. Trailheads begin from Cataract Lake southwest of Heeney at the end of USFS Rd 1725. Mary Ellen Gilliland's *The Summit Hiker* (Alpenrose Press, 1984) is a useful guide to trails and local history.

Places to Stay & Eat

The best fishing in the reservoir is near the churning waters of the outlet slough near the free USFS *Elliot Creek Campground*. Five other campgrounds operated by the

Dillon Ranger District (☎ 970-468-5400) are located around the reservoir: *Davis Springs*, *Willows*, *Cow Creek* and the $8.50 sites at *Prairie Point* and *McDonald Flats*, which has a boat ramp.

For information, food or lodging, the *Green Mountain Inn* (☎ 970-724-3812), 7101 Summit County Rd 30, is the place to go. A couple of modest rooms are offered for $30 to $35 in summer and winter, and they have two rough-looking cabins available. Dinners cost between $8 and $16; there's breakfast on weekends and lunch in summer. They also have the only bar and pool table for miles. Part-owner Scott Astaldi coauthored *High Country Crags: A Rock & Ice Climbing Guide to Summit County*, which is available along with other outdoor guides in a country store at the inn.

FRISCO

This is a convenient base for enjoying Summit County's summer and winter activities. There is a good selection of accommodations, restaurants and shops in a compact area. Copper Mountain, Breckenridge, Keystone and Arapahoe are 20 minutes away, as are some of the country's best white-water rafting, kayaking and fly-fishing waters, and miles and miles of road and mountain biking trails. Frisco (population 2170) is the center of Summit County's extensive bike path network, and in spring, summer and autumn, Main St. is lined with bicycles while cyclists fill the restaurants and cafes. Excellent bike paths lead to surrounding communities; combined with the free Summit Stage transit system, these make it easy to get around any time of year.

Information

Maps of the county and towns are available from the Summit County Chamber of Commerce (☎ 970-668-2051), at 11 S Summit Blvd and Main St. It's open daily from 9 am to 5 pm. The chamber also offers a Summit County guidebook, *The Great Vacation Guide* ($6), which includes information on outdoor activities and restaurants in the area.

Summit County Central Reservations (☎ 970-468-6222, 800-365-6365) arranges lodging, transportation, lift tickets and activities for winter or summer visitors. The Summit County Chamber of Commerce has a guest assistance and referral service (☎ 970-668-0376), located in the Holiday Inn, which provides accommodation, restaurant and activity information for visitors to the county.

The Colorado Community First National Bank (☎ 970-668-3333) is at 1000 N Summit Blvd. The Safeway next door has an ATM. The post office is at 65 W Main St; the zip code is 80443.

Though not very big, the Daily Planet Bookstore (☎ 970-668-5016) offers a good selection of travel guides and local history books, and also sells topo maps. Frisco Medical Center (☎ 970-668-3003) is at the corner of Hwy 9 and School Rd. Frisco's Washtub Laundromat (☎ 970-668-3552), 406 Main St, is perhaps the only business in town with a 'No Bicycles' sign. Recycling bins for glass and aluminum are next to every public trashcan in town.

Frisco Historic Park

Frisco's proliferation of vintage log cabins – many of which are still inhabited – reflects the historical character of this former mining camp. Aficionados of log construction techniques will appreciate the double-dovetail joints at the 1890 Dills Ranch House and the 1895 Bailey House. Inside the Trappers Cabin, visitors will find the kind of pelts that once sustained the area's meager economy prior to mining. Small windows mark the four cells of the 1881 jail next to the Frisco School House Museum (☎ 970-668-3428), 120 Main St. The one-room school, complete with bell tower, is on its original site; it arose in 1890 as a saloon where backwoods chemists practiced fermentation using a copper still. It's open in summer 11 am to 4 pm Tuesday to Sunday, Tuesday to Saturday in winter.

Road Biking

Summit County's network of paved paths provide one of the nation's finest systems for bicycle travel, connecting Frisco with Dillon (5 miles), Breckenridge (10 miles), Copper Mountain (8 miles), Keystone (12 miles) and Ten Mile Canyon over Vail Pass (14 miles). On the Dillon Dam trail is an overlook and telescope to view an osprey nest. From Frisco Historic Park, ride south on 2nd St to Farmers Korner, where trails lead to all destinations except Dillon. Restrooms and water are available at the Blue River inlet to Dillon Reservoir. Cyclists are not the only ones to benefit from the trails – Nordic skiers and skaters also enjoy them in winter.

The gear stores in Frisco can equip you for these outdoor activities and they even rent bike trailers for the kids. Antlers Ski & Sport Shop (☎ 970-668-3152), 900 N Summit Blvd, has fishing and camping supplies, topo maps and bike and ski rentals. Also try Pioneer Sports (☎ 970-668-3668), 842 N Summit Blvd, for ski, bike or skate rentals. Pioneer also offers inline skating lessons for $10 per half-hour.

Cross-Country Skiing

Planned by Olympic silver medalist Bill Koch, the **Frisco Nordic Center** (☎ 970-668-0866) offers about 20 miles of set cross-country ski trails on the Dillon Reservoir peninsula east of Frisco. Lessons and rentals are also available. The main trailhead and parking is off Hwy 9 a mile east of Frisco, or you can reach the center from the Frisco Marina parking area at the foot of Main St. Once the snow arrives, the center is open daily 9 am to 4 pm. Adult passes are $8.

Boating

Whether you want to fish or just cruise Dillon Reservoir, Osprey Adventures (☎ 970-668-5573) at Frisco Bay Marina offers outboard motorboat, canoe and sailboat sales and rentals. A 14-foot sailboat or fishing boat costs $35 for three hours.

Places to Stay

Summit County Central Reservations (☎ 970-468-6222, 800-365-6365) offers condominiums starting at under $50 during summer months and from $100 in winter. Expect higher rates during the busy spring and winter holiday seasons. Also try Summit County Guest Assistance & Referral System (☎ 970-668-0376) in the Holiday Inn.

Camping Four large USFS-run Arapaho National Forest campgrounds (☎ 970-468-5400) line the shores of Dillon Reservoir. 72 pleasant sites are shaded by lodgepole pines can be found at *Heaton Bay*, about a mile east of N Summit Blvd on Dam Rd or reached by the bike path from Frisco; for reservations call ☎ 877-444-6777. Also reservable are the 79 sites at *Peak One*, only a mile east of town on Hwy 9. Fees at both campgrounds are $11.

First-come, first-served sites are available at *Pine Cove*, with 50 sites ($8.50) or *Prospector*, 109 sites ($9.50); both are on the south shore. All rates are for Friday and Saturday nights; other days are $2 less.

B&Bs Built in 1885, Summit County's oldest lodging, *Frisco Lodge* (☎ 970-668-0195), in the center of town at 321 Main St, once served as a railroad inn. Their rustic rooms with shared bath are the cheapest in town and include breakfast. You might elect to stay in one of the inexpensive motel-style rooms if you don't appreciate vintage Led Zeppelin at 11 pm from the downstairs living quarters. Lockable storage for bikes and skis is available. Singles/doubles with shared bath cost $35/40 during summer weekends.

Woods Inn (☎ 970-668-3389, 800-668-4448), 205 S Second one block off Main St, is a great value. It includes a pine-log building constructed in 1938 which was moved from its original site when the Dillon reservoir was filled. It now provides economical B&B accommodation with shared bath, full breakfast and doubles for $45 in summer, $70 in winter. There's also a newer building that has standard rooms and suites with private baths from $70 to $145 in summer, $195 to $410 in winter. Amenities include a cozy living area with a fireplace and a hot tub.

COLORADO

If you're willing to spend a bit more, the *Galena Street Mountain Inn* (☎ 970-668-3224), First Ave and Galena St, is the place to stay. Each of its uniquely decorated 14 rooms has a private bath, cable TV, and phone; the shared amenities include a comfortable living and dining room, a sun deck, hot tub and sauna. Summer rates range from $65 to $120; $85 to $170 in winter.

Also downtown, the modern *Twilight Inn* (☎ 970-668-5009), 308 Main St, offers 12 rooms with a variety of decor, from Victorian frills to Mission-style furnishings, plus an enclosed hot tub, laundry and storage/work area for skis and bicycles. Four 3rd-floor rooms share two bathrooms. A simple buffet breakfast is included with the shared/private rooms that rent for $65/75 during summer, $95/110 in winter.

Motels Singles/doubles cost $40/45 or start at $70 in winter at the unexciting but centrally located *Snowshoe Motel* (☎ 970-668-3444), 521 Main St. A quiet place off the major routes, *Sky View Motel* (☎ 970-668-3311), 305 S 2nd St, offers singles/doubles during summer for $45/50, $88/94 in winter. The *Holiday Inn – Summit County* (☎ 970-668-5000, 800-782-7669), I-70 exit 203, on the shore of Dillon Reservoir, offers rooms starting at $69/89 summer/winter and many resort amenities.

Places to Eat
Butterhorn Bakery & Deli (☎ 970-668-3997), 408 W Main St, is the place to 'carb-up' for a day on the slopes or trails. This bustling locals' favorite serves up a delicious plate-sized breakfast burrito or smoked salmon omelet for $6, as well as homemade breads, bagels and pancakes. For lunch there's a full range of sandwiches from blackened tuna to cool cucumber, and burgers from buffalo to garden, all for under $6.50.

El Rio Cantina & Grill (☎ 970-668-5043), 450 W Main St at the west end of town, features healthy Mexican food with natural ingredients – and the best margaritas in Summit County! Locals fill the El Rio's sunny deck for happy hour every

afternoon. For Italian food head to *Gejos* (☎ 970-668-3308), upstairs at 409 Main St, with good pasta dishes and a lively bar. Vegetarians will want to check out the *Alpine Market* (☎ 970-668-5535), 320 Main Street, for natural foods in bulk, organic veggies and homeopathic and herbal medicines.

Frisco is blessed with a real deli, *Deli Belly's* (☎ 970-668-9255), 275 Main Street, where the mustard is brown and the meats are kosher – all the sandwiches are served with a dill pickle and cost between $3 and $8. For mountain haute cuisine, the award-winning *Uptown Bistro* (☎ 970-668-4728) at 304 Main St is the place. House-cured marinated salmon and grilled crab quesadillas are appetizer specials; for lunch try the spicy peanut noodle salad with sesame-crusted chicken, roasted peanuts and black sesame seeds ($6.50); the main dinner courses include sesame-crusted sterling salmon with Asian stir-fry vegetables ($18).

Getting There & Away
Bus The closest Greyhound bus stop on the way to Frisco is at the Alpen Hütte in Silverthorne.

DIA Shuttle Resort Express (☎ 970-468-7600, 800-334-7433) offers service between Denver International Airport and Summit County for $42/84 one-way/roundtrip. Also try Vans to Breckenridge (☎ 970-668-4566), 741 Ten Mile Drive.

Car From Denver, take I-70 west 95 miles to exit 203. Frisco lies just southeast of the interstate on Hwy 9.

Getting Around
Bus Summit Stage (☎ 970-453-1339) operates 6 am to 11 pm from the Frisco Transit Center, next to the WalMart on N Summit Blvd. Free buses leave Copper Mountain, Keystone, Breckenridge and Silverthorne at the top of the hour and meet in Frisco on the half-hour. The buses carry two to three bicycles on front racks on a first-come, first-served basis.

Car Enterprise (☎ 970-668-1727) is located at 1202 N Summit Blvd.

BRECKENRIDGE

The high point of any visit to Summit County, the small town of Breckenridge (population 1650) is largely a National Historic District. It's also home to Breckenridge Ski Resort, one of the state's more pleasant areas.

In 1859 a party of 54 prospectors led by General George E Spencer of Alabama discovered flecks of gold in the Blue River. The prospectors built a blockhouse for protection against the Utes and named the town after US Vice President John Cabell Breckinridge. After Breckinridge joined the Confederate forces during the Civil War in 1861, ardent Unionists petitioned Congress to change the spelling of the town's name.

More than one gold mining boom altered the landscape around Breckenridge. The initial hand-panning of river gravel soon played out and was replaced by hydraulic mining implemented by wealthy investors who built reservoirs and a system of ditches to supply large water cannons or

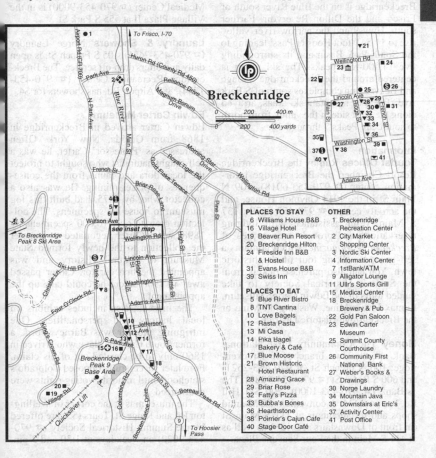

Breckenridge

0   200   400 m

0   200   400 yards

PLACES TO STAY
6   Williams House B&B
16 Village Hotel
19 Beaver Run Resort
20 Breckenridge Hilton
24 Fireside Inn B&B
    & Hostel
31 Evans House B&B
39 Swiss Inn

PLACES TO EAT
5   Blue River Bistro
8   TNT Cantina
10 Love Bagels
12 Rasta Pasta
13 Mi Casa
14 Pika Bagel
    Bakery & Café
17 Blue Moose
21 Brown Historic
    Hotel Restaurant
28 Amazing Grace
29 Briar Rose
32 Fatty's Pizza
33 Bubba's Bones
36 Hearthstone
38 Poirrier's Cajun Cafe
40 Stage Door Café

OTHER
1   Breckenridge
    Recreation Center
2   City Market
    Shopping Center
3   Nordic Ski Center
4   Information Center
7   1stBank/ATM
9   Alligator Lounge
11 Ullr's Sports Grill
15 Medical Center
18 Breckenridge
    Brewery & Pub
22 Gold Pan Saloon
23 Edwin Carter
    Museum
25 Summit County
    Courthouse
26 Community First
    National Bank
27 Weber's Books &
    Drawings
30 Norge Laundry
34 Mountain Java
37 Downstairs at Eric's
41 Post Office

monitors. This destructive method of excavation flushed away the slopes, carrying the runoff through flumes to capture the gold. Waste sand and stone accumulated in the riverbed, burying the original county seat of Parkville in 1882.

In 1887 Tom Groves discovered Tom's Baby, a 135-ounce treasure he reportedly fondled so affectionately that only 103 ounces are left to display in the state's Natural History Museum. It still represents the largest gold nugget ever found in Colorado.

Orientation
Breckenridge is on the Blue River south of Frisco and the Dillon Reservoir. Farther south, Hwy 9 and the narrow river valley rise to 11,541-foot Hoosier Pass, leading to the South Park Basin and its surrounding five 14,000-foot peaks. The ski resort is centered around the Breckenridge Village and Beaver Run complexes south of S Park Ave. The four mountain ski areas, arrayed along the west side of the valley from north to south, are Peaks 7 through 10.

Information
Tourist Offices Run by the Breckenridge Resort Chamber, the Breckenridge information center (☎ 970-453-6018), 309 N Main St in the 1914 Gaymon House, and the activity center (☎ 970-453-5579), 137 S Main, offer assistance with lodging reservations and provide free copies of *Breckenridge Magazine*, which contains a self-guided walking tour of the historic town. You can also purchase tickets from the Summit Historical Society to take guided tours of the Edwin Carter Museum, Lomax Placer Mine, Washington Mine or the Breckenridge Historic District.

Money The Community First National Bank operates two branches in Breckenridge: 106 N French St (☎ 970-453-2521) and 600 S Ridge St (☎ 970-453-9288). The 1stBank (☎ 970-453-1000), 200 Ski Hill Rd, has an ATM. A convenient ATM amid shops and restaurants is at 111 S Main St (in front of Downstairs at Eric's) as well as at 411 S Main in the Four Seasons Plaza.

Post The post office is at 300 S Ridge; the zip code is 80424. Mail Boxes Etc (☎ 970-453-8080) offers package shipping next to City Market shopping center at 400 N Park Ave.

Bookstores Weber's Books & Drawings (☎ 970-453-4723), 100 S Main St, carries a good stock of titles on Colorado history, Native American culture and a very good selection of local and international guidebooks. They also sell topo maps.

Medical Services The Breckenridge Medical Center (☎ 970-453-9000) is in the Village Plaza II at 555 S Park St.

Laundry & Showers Norge Laundry (☎ 970-453-2426), 105 S French St, is open daily and offers drop-off service. The Breckenridge Recreation Center (☎ 970-453-1734), 880 Airport Rd, has showers for $4.

Edwin Carter Museum
Edwin Carter arrived in Breckenridge in 1868 from Oneida, New York. Often addressed as 'Professor' Carter, he was a self-taught naturalist who sought to protect the local flora and fauna from the consequences of placer mining. He was also a collector who, by 1875, had built this log museum to house his specimens. The collection grew to over 10,000 specimens by 1898, when Carter negotiated to transfer the collection to the newly formed State Museum of Natural History and was appointed the first curator. Carter passed away in 1900 before he could take up the appointment.

The museum also includes exhibits on local history and personalities. One intriguing pioneer was Barney Ford, a former South Carolina slave who arrived in 1860 only to be cheated out of his claim. Ford later successfully opposed Colorado's statehood until minority voting rights were guaranteed.

The museum is at the corner of Wellington Rd and Ridge St. Tours ($3) are offered by the Summit Historical Society (☎ 970-453-9022) on weekdays at 1:30 and 3 pm.

Breckenridge Historic District
The Summit Historical Society (☎ 970-453-9022) offers a two-hour walking tour of the well-preserved historic district 10 am Monday to Saturday during the summer. Over 200 historic buildings are in the four-by-four-block district roughly centered on the 1909 **Summit County Courthouse** at 200 E Lincoln Ave. Purchase tickets for $5 at the Breckenridge information center or activities center. Call ahead for other Historical Society tours. A short account of the town's past, including tours of the historic district and nearby ghost towns, is in Mary Ellen Gilliland's *Breckenridge!* (Alpenrose Press, 1988).

Country Boy Mine
This underground tour takes you 1000 feet into the mine where there are working drills and 100-year-old ore carts and dynamite demonstrations. The Country Boy Mine (☎ 970-453-4405), 2 miles northeast of town at 542 French Gulch Rd, is open in summer and winter; admission $10/5 adults/children. Phone ahead for seasonal hours.

Skiing
Downhill Skiing Since 1961, Breckenridge has expanded to a total of four interconnected mountains, making it Summit County's largest ski area in both area and number of visitors. Over 1 million skiers visit the 3 sq miles of skiable terrain each year. Improved snowmaking on Peaks 9 and 10 plus careful grooming all over the area provide quality skiing throughout the season, typically beginning in early November and running well into May. There are four high-speed quad lifts, one triple and nine double chairs and five surface lifts.

The center of attention for experienced skiers is **Peak 8**. Its quad super-chairlift is based about a mile west of town on Ski Hill Rd; free shuttle buses provide service to the Peak 8 lift base and run about every 15 minutes. The lift services a vertical drop of about 1500 feet. The advertised 3398-foot drop includes a hike from the top of the lift to the 12,998-foot summit. An easy 3-mile run from this point, the Four O'Clock

Trail, leads back to town. Most of the 64 trails on Peak 8 are suited to advanced intermediate or expert skiers.

The adjacent **Peak 7** consists of expert terrain accessible by foot and T-bar. **Peak 9** is a beginner-intermediate hill with two quad super-chairlifts, Quicksilver and Beaver Run, which serve the crowded terrain at the backdoor of the enormous resort developments. Morning and afternoon ski classes lining up at the Quicksilver lift add to the congestion. South of Peak 9, the Falcon quad super-chairlift serves the primarily advanced and intermediate trails on the east flank of 11,607-foot **Peak 10**.

The Breckenridge Ski School (☎ 970-453-3250) offers classes for all abilities as well as special courses taught by women for women. Children's Centers (☎ 970-453-3258) offers classes at Peak 8 and Peak 9; child care for infants two months to four years is available at Peak 8 only.

Regular lift tickets costs $47/17 adults/children 12 and under, $30 for seniors 65 to 69. Seniors 70 and over ski free. All fees are bumped up $2 during peak periods like Christmas week. The $141 three-day ticket is good for one day at either Vail or Beaver Creek, and any Breckenridge ticket can be used at Keystone and Arapahoe Basin. For recorded snow information, call ☎ 970-453-6118.

Snowboarding Breckenridge features a 6-acre snowboard terrain park, including a half-pipe, located on Peak 9. Snowboarding lessons are offered through the ski school at the same rates as ski lessons; $38/48 half-day/full-day group lessons.

Cross-Country Skiing Breckenridge Nordic Ski Center (☎ 970-453-9855), at the Whatley Ranch at 1200 Ski Hill Rd, about a half-mile from Peak 8 on the free shuttle route, offers over 17 miles of groomed trails, lessons and equipment rental. A trail pass costs $10 and rental packages are $12 ($18 for high-performance equipment).

Equipment Rental With over 30 locations in most Colorado ski towns it's hard to beat the convenience of the merged Sports Stalker/Christie Sports (☎ 970-453-2455), at 117 S Main St and also the base of Peak 9. Basic packages are $16/day; top-end gear is $28. It's also possible to pick up gear at one location and drop it off at another. Carvers Ski & Snowboard (☎ 970-453-0132), 203 N Main St, offers better rates with basic ski packages at $13, top-end gear for $21. Snowboards and boots are $20 to $26 and all packages are discounted when rented for more than one day.

With several locations in Breckenridge, Rec Sports (☎ 970-453-2194, 800-525-9624) offers basic ski packages starting at

$12, high-end equipment for $24; rentals can be returned at any of the locations.

For Telemark and backcountry packages and snowshoes, Mountain Outfitters (☎ 970-453-2201), 112 S Ridge St, and Great Adventure Sports Center (☎ 970-453-0333), 400 N Park St, are the places to go for equipment, advice and maps. Both have Telemark packages for about $20 and snowshoes for $10 a day.

Hiking
Southwest of Breckenridge, **Quandary Peak** (14,265 feet) offers one of the easier 14er walk-ups if you have a 4WD to reach the trailhead. A 4-mile trail follows an exposed ridgeline to the summit that looks over South Park County and Mt of the Holy Cross. The ranger station in Dillon has maps and directions to the trailhead, as well as suggestions for other routes in the area.

Mountain Biking
There's no shortage of backroads and single-track trails around Breckenridge. A good loop for intermediate riders begins midway between Breckenridge and Frisco at the Gold Hill Trailhead. Take the paved Blue River path down the valley for a warmup; the single-track Gold Hill Trail is on your left (west) immediately after crossing the river. It climbs 3 miles to the Peaks Trail, which takes you 6 miles back to the top of Ski Hill Rd above Breckenridge.

From Breckenridge, the Boreas Pass Rd follows an old railroad alignment and climbs 1925 feet in 11 miles to the 11,482-foot summit. As the gradient does not exceed 5%, however, it's considered 'easy.'

Also consider a loop through Keystone. Use both Keystone Gondolas ($12.50) to get to the top of the mountain, descend 2 miles from North Peak to Keystone Gulch Rd, then ascend about 2 miles up West Ridge Trail and turn left at the Colorado Trail to Tiger Run Rd along the Swan River back to Hwy 9 north of Breckenridge.

The free *Summit County Mountain Bike Guide*, available at bike shops and information offices, covers all of the major biking trails and lists degrees of difficulty. A more descriptive guide is Laura Rossetter's *The Mountain Bike Guide to Summit County Colorado*, available at local bookstores and bike shops. The Breckenridge Fat Tire Society (☎ 970-453-5548) runs a 'Mountain Bike Hotline' (☎ 970-453-4636, ext 3288) with information on ride activities.

Competitive rates on bike and skate rentals are available from Great Adventure Sports Center or Mountain Outfitters (see Equipment Rental above), A Racers Edge (☎ 970-453-0995), 114 N Main St, and Carvers (☎ 970-453-0132), 203 N Main St.

White-Water Rafting
Early-season half-day trips on the Blue River below Silverthorne are not why people come to Summit County. Nevertheless, scenic views of the Gore Range and about 2 miles of Class III whitewater make the convenient trip worthwhile. River trips are offered by Performance Tours (☎ 970-453-0661), 110 Ski Hill Rd, and cost $33/28 adults/children.

Horseback Riding
Breckenridge Stables (☎ 970-453-4438), at the base of Peak 9, offers a two-hour horseback ride with breakfast for $32.

Fishing
Jackson Streit's Mountain Angler (☎ 970-453-4665), 311 S Main St, is a full-service fish and tackle store and Summit County's longest-running fishing guide service. Fly-fishing lessons begin at $100, $35 for each additional person, and full-day fly-fishing trips begin at $175, $50 for each additional person. *Blue River Anglers* (☎ 970-453-9171), 209 N Main Street, offers similar guide services and rates.

Golf
Golfers appreciate the added advantage of the thin air at a 9300-foot elevation. The Jack Nicklaus-designed Breckenridge Golf Course (☎ 970-453-9104) was rated the top public course by *Golf Digest* in 1991. Greens fees during the midsummer high

season run $63 plus $12 for a cart, but a twilight fee of $45, including cart, kicks in after 4 pm. Rates are about 20% less in the low season. The course is on Tiger Run Rd 3 miles north of Breckenridge.

Special Events
In late January the **Ullr Fest**, celebrating the Norse god of winter, is a wild parade and four-day festival featuring a twisted version of the Dating Game, an ice-skating party and a kids concert. Also in January, the **International Snow Sculpture Championship** provides decorations for the River Walk and Bell Tower Mall. A month-long spring skiing celebration in April, **Beach Daze** features BBQs, races and great deals on lift tickets and accommodations after Easter. On the weekend after the Fourth of July, **Jazz in July** (☎ 970-453-6018) features top regional performers at the Maggie Pond in the Village at Breckenridge Resort. The Riverwalk Center hosts over 50 orchestral concerts and chamber recitals each summer in its **Breckenridge Festival of Music** series. For a concert schedule call the Breckenridge Music Institute & National Repertory Orchestra (☎ 970-453-2120). Orchestra tickets cost $20, chamber recitals and the Blue River series on Thursday evenings series run $10.

The 'Kingdom of Breckenridge' was declared after it was discovered that the 1300 sq miles surrounding Breckenridge were not positively part of the USA. The early August **No Man's Land Celebration** celebrates this 'independence' with gold panning and woodcarving contests and historic walking tours. During the third week of September, the **Breckenridge Festival of Film** (☎ 970-453-6200) attracts well-known celebrities, writers and producers to premiere screenings at six theater sites in Summit County. It's followed by a lively **Oktoberfest** with plenty of German beer and oompah music.

Places to Stay
Most of the pillows in Breckenridge are in condominiums. A standard one-bedroom

unit for four costs between $110 and $150 during winter. Breckenridge Resort Central Reservations (☎ 970-453-2918), 311 S Ridge St, can help find a condo. Also try the Accommodations Center (☎ 970-453-7070, 800-821-1365), 321 N Main St.

Rates are highest during winter holidays and spring break, but because of its proximity to the Front Range, Summit County gets considerable weekend traffic. Skiers will find better rates during the early season to mid-December, weekdays in January and February and in the first few weeks of April. The spring 'mud season' and fall are bargain periods. Peak summer months are July through early September.

Hostels The rundown *Fireside Inn B&B and Hostel* (☎ 970-453-6456), 114 N French St, is the only Hostelling International lodging in town. It has four dorm rooms with four beds each and one dorm room with 10 beds for $20 in summer, $23 to 29 in winter; breakfast is available at an additional charge. Private rooms at the Inn range from $50 to $140. Storage for bikes and skis is available and there is a hot tub.

B&Bs The clean and well-run *Swiss Inn* (☎ 970-453-6489), 205 S French St, is the budget traveler's best bet in Breckenridge. A bed in an eight-person mixed-gender dorm costs $25/35 summer/winter, including breakfast. Or you can stay in one of four late 19th-century Victorian rooms that range from $85 to $135 in winter, $57 to $89 in summer. The dormitory is adjacent to a beautiful garden solarium with a hot tub.

Rates for the comfortable rooms with shared bath at *Evans House B&B* (☎ 970-453-5509), 102 S French St, start at $63/86 summer/winter. *Williams House B&B* (☎ 970-453-2975), 303 N Main St, offers antique furnishings in four rooms with private baths starting at $85 in summer and $135 during winter holidays.

Hotels At the base of the Peak 9 lifts, huge top-end resorts dwarf the historic town and are separate, self-contained enclaves offer-

ing deluxe hotel rooms and suites. The *Breckenridge Hilton* (☎ 970-453-4500), 550 Village Rd, has 208 rooms beginning at $85/159 summer/winter. *Beaver Run Resort* (☎ 970-453-6000, 800-525-2253), 620 Village Rd, has over 500 rooms with two queen beds for $105/175 summer/winter or more expensive studios and large suites with spas. Slightly smaller rooms cost $110/165 at *Village Hotel*, part of the enormous *Village at Breckenridge Resort* (☎ 970-453-2000, 800-800-7829), which covers over 18 acres at 655 S Park Ave.

Places to Eat
On the mountain, restaurants can be found on Peaks 8 and 9 and at all the base areas.

Good places to get started with caffeine, muffins, guidebooks and maps are *Mountain Java* (☎ 970-453-1874), 118 S Ridge St, and the *Stage Door Cafe* (☎ 970-453-6964) 213 S Main St, with a full range of coffees plus breakfast burritos and deli sandwiches. Whole-wheat pancakes are a bargain at *Blue Moose* (☎ 970-453-4859), 540 S Main St. The eclectic lunch and dinner menu appeals to vegetarians and seafood lovers, and prices are reasonable. For deli sandwiches and organic bulk goods, stop by *Amazing Grace* (☎ 970-453-1445) at 213 Lincoln Ave across from the courthouse. A bagel fix can be had at *Pika Bagel Bakery & Cafe* (☎ 970-453-6246), 500 S Main St, or *Love Bagels!* (☎ 970-547-1115), 325 S Main St.

Reggae will be playing as you enter the colorful *Rasta Pasta* (☎ 970-453-7467), 411 S Main. They serve up big plates of pasta at $3 to $6.50 for lunch, $5.50 to $10 for dinner. Try the Natural Mystic – pasta with jerk chicken and pineapple curry – but get there early because the place is usually jammin'. For Mexican dinners, try *Mi Casa* (☎ 970-453-2071), 600 S Park Ave. Their adjacent cantina features margaritas by the liter. There's also dynamite Mexican food at the *TNT Cantina* (☎ 970-453-9500), 200 W Washington next to Lone Star Sports.

Blue River Bistro (☎ 970-453-6947), 305 N Main, offers tasty $6 to $9 lunch selections such as pastas, salads, sandwiches and burgers. At *Fatty's Pizza* (☎ 970-453-9802), 106 S Ridge St, you can enjoy pizza and pasta on an upstairs deck. *Bubba's Bones* (☎ 970-547-9942), 110 S Ridge St, is the locals' favorite for real Southern-style BBQ; lunches are around $5 or $6, dinners from $7 to $13.

The Brown Historic Hotel Restaurant (☎ 970-453-0084), 208 N Ridge St, is appealing with its $5 stuffed shrimp with red beans and rice dinner special. Most of the varied menu offerings served in the Victorian dining room, however, cost between $10 and $20. Innovative American cooking is featured at *Hearthstone* (☎ 970-453-1148), 130 S Ridge St, which has starters like grilled portobello mushrooms and smoked seafood, and main courses including rack of elk, crab-stuffed trout and wild mushroom-stuffed chicken for $10 to $22.

Poirrier's Cajun Cafe (☎ 970-453-1877) at 224 S Main has it all, from a simple bowl of 'N'awlins' red beans and rice for $4 to catfish Atchafalaya for $17. They offer special early dinner deals. Elegant to the extreme, the *Briar Rose* restaurant (☎ 970-453-9948), 109 E Lincoln Ave, features steak, game and seafood at top-end prices in an historic building complete with a trophy lounge.

Entertainment

Bars John Wayne would look just right sidled up to the bar at the *Gold Pan Saloon* (☎ 970-453-5499), 105 N Main St, established in the 1870s. In *Downstairs at Eric's* (☎ 970-453-1401), 111 S Main St, you can choose from about 120 beers and swap stories with the mountain bikers and climbers who gather there. Also check out *Breckenridge Brewery & Pub* (☎ 970-453-1550), 600 S Main St, which offers several fine brews made on the premises.

Year-round blues performances by national artists draw crowds to the downstairs club at the *Alligator Lounge* (☎ 970-453-7782), 320 S Main St. *Ullr's Sports Grill* (☎ 970-453-6060), at 401 S Main, offers cheap drinks on Tuesday.

Theater From the month of July to September the *Backstage Theatre* (☎ 970-453-0199), on Maggie Pond in the Village at Breckenridge, presents nightly plays at 8 pm. Tickets cost $10/5 adults/children.

Shopping

The Breckenridge Gallery features original paintings and limited edition bronzes by local and international artists. For locally made sheepskin apparel, stop by the Sheepherder (☎ 970-453-1181), at 211 S Main St. For fine antique Navajo weavings and Western memorabilia, visit the Paint Horse Gallery (☎ 970-453-6813), at 226 S Main. Locally made furniture can be found at High Country Furniture & Gallery (☎ 970-453-2816), 2½ miles north of town at 13217 Hwy 9.

Getting There & Away

Resort Express vans (☎ 800-334-7433) offer service between Denver and Summit County for $39 in summer months; higher rates apply during ski season.

Breckenridge is 104 miles west of Denver via I-70 to exit 203, then Hwy 9 south.

Getting Around

The free Downtown Trolley operates 9 am to midnight June to September and November to April. Free shuttles (☎ 970-453-5000) to the lifts travel in both directions on French St, Lincoln Ave and Park Ave every 15 minutes from 6:40 am to 5:30 pm. Summit Stage buses leave the Bell Tower in Breckenridge at the top of the hour, from the recreation center seven minutes later, arriving at the Frisco Transfer Center on the half-hour.

COPPER MOUNTAIN SKI RESORT

Copper Mountain Resort (☎ 970-968-2882), west of Dillon Reservoir at I-70 exit 195, opened in 1973, the last ski area to crowd into Summit County. Like Keystone, it's a newly developed, self-contained resort. The ski slopes attract weekend skiers from the Front Range as well as 'jet-set' guests staying a week or more at North America's first Club Med.

COLORADO

Skiing

Downhill Skiing Skiers enjoy terrain that is naturally separated into beginner, intermediate and expert areas. Nineteen lifts serve 98 trails covering over 2 sq miles of skiable terrain; another square mile is accessible by snowcat. Trails on the east side of 12,360-foot Copper Peak (16% of the area) suit expert skiers, while intermediate skiers follow trails down the western slope (62% of the area). The total vertical drop is 2600 feet. Beginners hang out on the lower slopes of Union Peak below the main day lodge (22% of the area).

Lift tickets at Copper Mountain cost $47/17 adults/children December 20 though April 12, $29/15 in the early and late seasons; children five and under and seniors over 70 ski free. There's free skiing and snowboarding on K and L lifts at Union Creek (accessing 53 acres of beginner terrain) from January 5 through February 2 (excluding January 18-20), and April 7-20. Call ☎ 970-968-2100 for snow information. It's open 9 am to 4 pm weekdays, 8:30 am to 4 pm weekends from mid-November to late April.

Equipment Rental Ski rentals begin at $17 for the basic package ($14 for children); fully-equipped snowboards rent for $28.

Summer Activities

During summer business is so slow that the resort offers free chairlift rides to a mid-mountain barbecue and USFS ranger-led nature hikes. You can choose between a tundra trek or forest hike that's geared for all abilities and ages; sign up at the activities desk or the welcome center. Also in summer, cyclists can bring their mountain bikes on the lift for $10 per day.

Places to Stay

Rooms at the 600-unit *Copper Mountain Resort* (reservations ☎ 970-968-2882, 800-458-8386) start at $180 in winter. Accommodations range from basic hotel rooms to deluxe suites and condominiums that can sleep up to 10.

Club Med (☎ 970-968-2161, 800-258-2633) offers various seven- and eight-day accommodations and ski packages for $1300 that include a six-day lift ticket and four hours of ski/snowboard instruction a day per person; meals and nightly entertainment are also included.

Getting Around

A free shuttle service in the Village runs every 10 minutes 8 am to 10 pm during ski season. The free Summit Stage shuttle leaves every half-hour from the Mountain Plaza at Copper Mountain and serves Breckenridge and other Summit County destinations.

LEADVILLE

During the 1980s, Leadville's transition from a mining center to tourist town was accepted grudgingly. The loss of mining paychecks from the Climax Molybdenum Company signaled a new economic reality. Residents who recall Leadville's rescue from oblivion (by Climax) after the last smelter closed in 1960 cling to the hope that good times will return.

Nicknamed 'Cloud City' for its 10,200-foot altitude, Leadville attracts visitors curious about the enormous mining operations and characters that once made it Colorado's 2nd-largest city. Poor living conditions make this Colorado's 'Appalachia.' Few would confuse Leadville (population 2600) with other Colorado mountain towns that have readily traded their mining past for resort status.

Visitors who are neither exploring Leadville's bawdy past nor touring the candidate sites for EPA Superfund toxic cleanup are most likely interested in the area's outdoor activities. Quickly scaling the two highest peaks in Colorado is a popular feat. But some may find greater satisfaction by slowly taking in the extensive Alpine environment of the stunning terrain surrounding Leadville.

Orientation

The principal route through town, US 24, follows a dogleg course from Harrison Ave

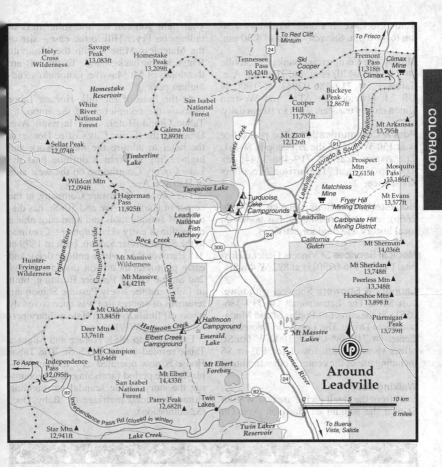

Around Leadville

in the south to E 9th St before continuing north on Poplar St.

Three historic mining areas east of Leadville are easy excursions. Take E 7th St from Harrison Ave to the Fryer Hill mining district, site of the Matchless Mine. This route continues east over 13,186-foot Mosquito Pass (4WD required). The Carbonate Hill district is reached by following E 5th St out to Stray Horse Gulch. To reach California Gulch, where Oro City's mines played out before Leadville's founding, take E 2nd St and turn right on Toledo St to the gulch.

Information

Tourist Offices At the visitors center (☎ 719-486-3900, 800-939-3901), 809 Harrison Ave, you can pick up maps and brochures. The Leadville Chamber of Commerce presents a 30-minute multimedia show, 'The Earth Runs Silver: Early Leadville,' daily at the New Fox Theater (☎ 719-489-0979), 115 W 6th St. The USFS Leadville Ranger Station (☎ 719-486-0749), on the north end of town at 2015 Poplar St, has information, books and topo maps on the Mt Massive Wilderness Area and other forest sites like the crowded

Turquoise Lake. It's open weekdays 7:30 am to 4:30 pm, Saturday 8 am to 4:30 pm.

Money The Commercial Bank of Leadville (☎ 719-482-0420) is at 400 Harrison Ave. Safeway (☎ 719-486-0795), at 1900 N US 24, provides an ATM and Western Union money transfers 7 am to 10 pm daily.

Post & Communications The post office is at 130 W 5th St, the zip code is 80461. The Aspen Leaf (☎ 719-486-3244; fax 719-486-2693), at 711 Harrison Ave, offers fax service.

Bookstores The Book Mine (☎ 719-486-2866), at 502 Harrison Ave, has books on local history and outdoor activities.

Medical Services St Vincent General Hospital (☎ 719-486-0230) is at 822 W 4th St.

Laundry & Showers Showers with towel cost $4 at The Laundromat (☎ 719-486-0551), at the corner of Poplar St and Mountain View Drive. The Leadville Recreation Center (☎ 719-486-0917), 1000 W 6th St, offers showers with towel for $3, or $6 including use of the center's other facilities.

Walking Tour
Start from the small picnic area on W 10th St near the summit of Harrison Ave. On your right you can see the solid mass of tailings on Fryer Hill to the east – site of the Matchless Mine – with the Mosquito Range in the background. To the left are the slopes of Mt Massive, Colorado's 2nd-highest peak.

At the base of the hill, Horace Tabor oversaw the completion of the imposing Tabor Grand Hotel, 711 Harrison Ave. Drop into the (Cloud City Coffee House) at the hotel to admire the marblework and high-ceiling skylight. Continue past the Lake County Courthouse on the west side of Harrison Ave.

The Western Hardware Company, at the corner of Harrison Ave and 5th St, has displays of antique tools and hardware plus a collection of early ski equipment. Continue to the Silver Dollar Saloon, built in 1879 at 315 Harrison Ave, where antique decor and early photographs are on display. On W 2nd St, the vacant Pioneer Building, built in 1892, and the lively Pastime Saloon are remnants of an area that was once so rowdy it was off limits to Camp Hale military personnel during WWII.

From 1877 to 1881, Horace and Augusta Tabor resided at 116 E 5th St. The Tabor House is now operated as a museum displaying the period furnishings and recounting the story of the scandal surrounding Horace's second marriage to 'Baby Doe' ($2 admission).

The Triumphs and Tribulations of Horace Tabor
Horace Tabor arrived in Leadville in 1877 and had the good fortune to grubstake Rische and Hook's successful exploration, receiving half of their discovery for a reported investment of $17. Then he hit the jackpot again by purchasing the Matchless Mine. The millions he made were invested locally and helped launch a political career that eventually led to a US Senate seat.

However, in 1883, while serving in the US Senate, Horace and Augusta Tabor divorced and Horace married a young divorcée, Mrs Elizabeth McCourt Doe, known as Baby Doe. This created a national scandal. The nationwide Silver Panic of 1893 led to widespread mine closures and struck Leadville with a vengeance. Tabor lost his fortune and property holdings, but kept the closed Matchless Mine. From his deathbed in 1899, he instructed Baby Doe to 'Hang on to the Matchless. It will make millions again.'

Like others before and after her, Baby Doe clung to the dream until 1935, when her frozen body was found in a cabin at the mine. ■

RAY HILLSTROM

RAY HILLSTROM

RAY HILLSTROM

ROBERT RABURN

Colorado

op Left: Country road, Vicksburg
ottom: Garden of the Gods, Colorado Springs, with
Pikes Peak in the distance

Top Right: Log cabin carvings
Middle Right: Ghost town

LEE FOSTER

RAY HILLSTROM

ROBERT RABURN

ROBERT RABURN

Colorado

Top Left: Columbine, state flower
Bottom Left: Red Rocks Park & Amphitheater, Denver

Top Right: Georgetown, Breckenridge and Leadville narrow gauge railway
Bottom Right: Square Tower House, Mesa Verde National Park

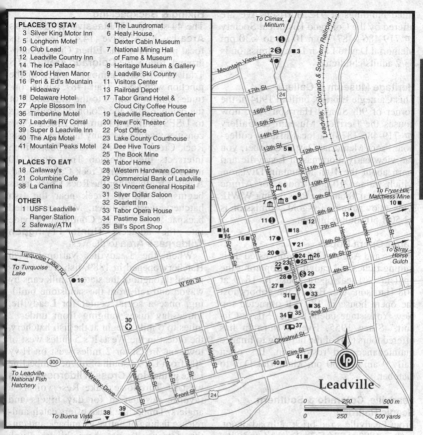

PLACES TO STAY
3 Silver King Motor Inn
5 Longhorn Motel
10 Club Lead
12 Leadville Country Inn
14 The Ice Palace
15 Wood Haven Manor
16 Peri & Ed's Mountain
    Hideaway
18 Delaware Hotel
27 Apple Blossom Inn
36 Timberline Motel
37 Leadville RV Corral
39 Super 8 Leadville Inn
40 The Alps Motel
41 Mountain Peaks Motel

PLACES TO EAT
18 Callaway's
21 Columbine Cafe
38 La Cantina

OTHER
1 USFS Leadville
   Ranger Station
2 Safeway/ATM

4 The Laundromat
6 Healy House,
   Dexter Cabin Museum
7 National Mining Hall
   of Fame & Museum
8 Heritage Museum & Gallery
9 Leadville Ski Country
11 Visitors Center
13 Railroad Depot
17 Tabor Grand Hotel &
    Cloud City Coffee House
19 Leadville Recreation Center
20 New Fox Theater
22 Post Office
23 Lake County Courthouse
24 Dee Hive Tours
25 The Book Mine
26 Tabor Home
28 Western Hardware Company
29 Commercial Bank of Leadville
30 St Vincent General Hospital
31 Silver Dollar Saloon
32 Scarlett Inn
33 Tabor Opera House
34 Pastime Saloon
35 Bill's Sport Shop

Leadville

National Mining Hall of Fame & Museum

The mining museum (☎ 719-486-1229), 120 W 9th St, part of a three-story Victorian schoolhouse built in 1896, is undoubtedly the premier museum in Leadville. The hall of fame on the 3rd floor honors the nation's foremost earth scientists such as John Wesley Powell, famous prospectors like Paddy Martinez, who discovered New Mexico's uranium deposits, and the king-pins of the US mining industry such as the Comstock Lode's Adolf Sutro. The museum is open daily 9 am to 5 pm May to Novem-

ber, weekdays 10 am to 2 pm the rest of the year. Admission is $3.50, with discounts for seniors and children.

Healy House & Dexter Cabin

The salt-box style Healy House (☎ 719-486-0487), 912 Harrison Ave, was built in 1878 by August Meyer, a mining engineer from St Louis. The rough-hewn exterior of the adjacent Dexter Cabin, built by James V Dexter in 1879, relocated from W 3rd St, gives no hint of the sumptuous interior used exclusively by Dexter for entertaining and gambling. Daily tours of these antique-filled buildings at 912 Harrison Ave are offered by the Colorado Historical Society (☎ 719-486-0487) from 10 am to 4:30 pm Memorial Day to Labor Day. Admission is $3/2 adults/children.

Heritage Museum & Gallery
This Carnegie Library, built in 1904 at the corner of 9th St and Harrison Ave, now houses the Heritage Museum & Gallery (☎ 719-486-1878), a local history collection. From Memorial Day to October, you can view early dioramas of Leadville and learn about the 10th Mountain Division, which trained 10,000 troops for Alpine warfare near Tennessee Pass during WWII. Kids enjoy panning for gold. Admission is $2.50/1.50 adults/children.

Tabor Opera House
Horace and Augusta Tabor reinvested their mining riches in Leadville by opening the opulent 880-seat opera house in 1879 at 308 Harrison Ave. Before the Tabors lost the opera house in 1893, it attracted top New York stage talent to the 'Silver Circuit.' Since 1955, Evelyn Furman has offered tours ($4) of the building to finance maintenance and restoration. It's open daily 9 am to 5:30 pm Memorial Day to October.

Leadville, Colorado & Southern Scenic Railroad
From Leadville's red-brick railroad depot, built in 1893 at 326 E 7th St, the Leadville, Colorado & Southern Railroad (☎ 719-486-3936) offers 2½-hour scenic excursions to Fremont Pass. The diesel train and open passenger cars ascend the 21-mile route by backing up past old mines lining the East Fork of the Arkansas River before reaching the giant scar left by the defunct Climax Mine – once the nation's only source for molybdenum. Don't forget your coat, as Climax sees only 35 to 40 frost-free days a year. The train operates daily Memorial Day to early October, with a few special geology and wildflower excursions scheduled each year. Tickets cost $23/13 adults/children four to 12.

Hiking & Backpacking
The 44-sq-mile **Mt Massive Wilderness Area** has Mt Massive (14,421 feet) as its focal point. From the Elbert Creek Campground, follow the **Colorado Trail** (USFS Trail 1776) north almost 3 miles to the junction with USFS Trail 1487, which continues almost 3 miles to the top. South of the campground, the Colorado Trail leads to USFS Trail 1481 up Mt Elbert. Also consider visiting the many high lakes along Rock Creek on USFS Trail 1382, which intersects the Colorado Trail about 10 miles north of Elbert Creek Campground. Another trailhead for the Rock Creek lakes begins at Willow Creek near the fish hatchery west of town. More extended backpack trips cross the Continental Divide into the adjacent **Hunter-Fryingpan Wilderness Area** to the west.

When the Leadville National Fish Hatchery opened in 1889, fish were transported throughout the state in milk cans by wagon and rail from the sandstone building, once a social center for Leadville. Three-day hikes ranging from under 2 miles to 6 miles begin at the fish hatchery, the oldest in the West. It's 5 miles west of town on 3rd St, or 2 miles west on Hwy 300 from US 24 south of town. Timberline Lake in the **Holy Cross Wilderness Area** west of Turquoise Lake Reservoir is a favorite destination for day hikers and anglers. Timberline Lake offers catch-and-release fishing of native greenback and cutthroat trout. To get there, hikers climb about 1000 feet in a little over 2 miles from the trailhead west of the May Queen Campground.

Mountain Biking
Mosquito Pass presents a unique opportunity to ride above 13,000 feet in treeless Alpine scenery. This extremely challenging 7-mile ascent follows E 7th St from Leadville.

Another good destination where you can enjoy panoramic vistas is Hagerman Pass (11,952 feet) west of Leadville. Riders follow a relatively easy railroad grade on USFS Rd 105 for 7 miles to Hagerman

The Rise & Fall of Leadville

In the spring of 1878, August Rische and George Hook established the Little Pittsburg Mine on Fryer Hill, which led to a silver bonanza that eclipsed earlier findings at nearby Oro City. Soon after the ore discovery, Leadville vaulted to a financial position surpassed only by Denver. By 1879 Leadville's character during the silver boom was reflected in its new cultural institutions: four churches, 120 saloons and 188 gambling houses! The 1880 census counted nearly 15,000 residents, five times as many as in Colorado's next largest city, Pueblo. With 15 silver-lead smelters, Leadville could boast that it was the nation's largest smelting center.

As an army of prospectors overturned the mountains in search of ore, speculative investors and profiteers, including Horace Tabor, hauled in exaggerated riches. Others reaped a financial harvest from the sales of staple commodities that they struggled to bring to the isolated mining outpost – often by pack burro. Early freight rates from Denver exceeded the cost of shipping freight from New York to San Francisco around Cape Horn.

Technical innovation focused on the mining district and its accompanying physical isolation. Telephone wires crossed 13,186-foot Mosquito Pass from Fairplay in 1878. The following year, a 'High Line' wagon road over Loveland Pass brought the Georgetown railroad terminal within 60 miles of Leadville. In 1880 the D&RG Railroad entered Leadville from the Arkansas Valley. The UP Railroad opened a connection with the South Park area in 1884 over Fremont and Boreas passes. But the most remarkable accomplishment was the construction of the standard-gauge Colorado Midland Railroad through Arkansas Valley in 1887. Its route followed a difficult alignment avoided by the D&RG.

In 1893 the Silver Panic decimated the mining economy, leaving Leadville to dwindle in importance as the population plummeted to under 4000 by 1930. ■

Pass from the junction on the south bank of Turquoise Lake. On the way you pass *Skinner Hut*, maintained by the 10th Mountain Division Hut Association (☎ 970-925-5775); cyclists and hikers can call for reservations from July to October at the rate of $22 per person per night. The 10th Mountain's system of 12 huts is ideally suited to mountain bike tours as they are all accessible by USFS roads and trails outside the wilderness areas (where mountain biking is prohibited).

An easy ride follows the shoreline trail on the north side of Turquoise Lake for 6 miles between Sugar Loaf Dam and May Queen Campground. Another follows the Colorado Trail north from Tennessee Pass for 2½ miles to Mitchell Creek. For other suggestions, pick up a map from the USFS Leadville Ranger Station.

Daily bike rentals cost $25 at Bill's Sport Shop (☎ 719-486-0739), 225 Harrison Ave, which also sells topo maps.

Skiing

Downhill Skiing Ski Cooper (☎ 719-486-2277), 9 miles north of Leadville, began in 1942 as a ski training center for 10th Mountain Division troops stationed at nearby Camp Hale during WWII. The 460 acres of skiable terrain includes 11,757-foot Cooper Hill with a 1200-foot vertical drop served by one triple and one double chairlift and two surface lifts. About 40% of the 26 trails are intermediate, while the rest are divided between novice and expert runs. There is also a dedicated snowboard terrain park. Lift tickets cost $25/15 adults/children (12 and under) – the lowest regular lift price in the state. Ski Cooper also provides full-day snowcat trips up to 12,606 feet along Chicago Ridge for $125 a day, including lunch. Basic rental packages are $12, high-performance gear is $20 and boarding equipment is $25. You can also rent gear in town at Bill's Sport Shop (see Mountain Biking above), and from

Leadville Ski Country (☎ 719-486-3836), at 116 E 9th St.

Cross-Country Skiing The Ski Cooper/Piney Creek Nordic Center (☎ 719-486-1750) offers 24 km of machine-set tracks for backcountry and cross-country skiing. Full-day trail passes are $8 and rentals are $12. While there you can ski about a mile to the Tennessee Pass Cookhouse for lunch or come back at night for a gourmet five-course meal.

Over 300 miles of backcounty ski trails are served by the 10th Mountain Division Hut Association (☎ 970-925-5775). Their 12 huts sleep 16 each. Membership in the association costs $25 and entitles you to priority reservations.

Organized Tours
Dee Hive Tours & Transportation (☎ 719-486-2339), 506 Harrison Ave, offers a two-hour 4WD tour of old mines and ghost towns for $25.

Boom Days
Refered to as 'Booze Days' by cynical locals, Boom Days is a celebration of Leadville's Wild West history with a parade, street races and mining demonstrations. The highlight of the three-day event in early August is the pack-burro race over a 21-mile course to Mosquito Pass and back.

Places to Stay
Camping The USFS *Halfmoon* and *Elbert Creek* campgrounds in the Halfmoon Creek area 10 miles southwest of Leadville, offer sites for $7.50 with access to stream and lake fishing. The Elbert Creek Campground is a peak-baggers' Shangri-la, located on the Colorado Trail midway between Colorado's tallest peaks – Mt Massive to the north and Mt Elbert to the south. Be sure to get there early as these 10,000-foot sites are available only on a first-come, first-served basis.

Of the six USFS campgrounds on Turquoise Reservoir, you can make reservations (☎ 877-444-6777) for the $10- to

$12-sites at *Silver Dollar*, *Molly Brown*, *Baby Doe* or *Father Dyer* campgrounds. All are within a 2-mile stretch of USFS Rd 104 along the eastern shore. In this same section, near the intersection with Lake County Rd 9, the smaller *Belle of Colorado* has walk-in tent sites for $11. Near the Lake Fork tributary on the reservoir's western tip, *May Queen* has 34 sites available on a first-come, first-served basis for $10.

The private *Sugar Loafin' Campground* (☎ 719-486-1031), 4 miles west of town on Lake County Rd 4, offers tent areas under the trees away from RVs for $19/doubles. The proprietors offer nightly slide presentations and there is a coin-operated laundry. Showers for nonguests cost $4. Or pitch your tent and shower in town for $15 at the *Leadville RV Corral* (☎ 719-486-3111), 135 W 2nd St.

B&Bs The Victorian *Leadville Country Inn* (☎ 719-486-3637, 800-748-2354), 127 E 8th St, offers 10 rooms with breakfast ranging from $57/67 singles/doubles to a top-end room with high-post bed and whirlpool tub for $117/137. All rooms have private bath and guests may use the outdoor hot tub. *Wood Haven Manor* (☎ 719-486-0109, 800-748-2570), 809 Spruce, and *The Ice Palace* (☎ 719-486-8272), 813 Spruce, compete for guests on the same block with rooms from $50 to $125. *Peri & Ed's Mountain Hideway* (☎ 719-486-0716) is around the corner at 201 W 8th; it offers eight cozy rooms for $45 to $75. You can't miss the *Delaware Hotel* (☎ 719-486-1418, 800-748-2004), 700 Harrison Ave. Built in 1886, this Victorian gem was fully renovated in 1985 and features an elegant oak-paneled lobby lit by crystal chandeliers. Its 36 rooms with private bath include breakfast; doubles go for $68 to $103.

The *Apple Blossom Inn* (☎ 719-486-2141, 800-982-9279), 120 W 4th St, features singles/doubles with shared bath for $59/74, while a stay in the former library or fireplace rooms with private bath costs $59/79. If you're on a budget and feeling adventurous try *Club Lead* (☎ 719-486-2202), a few blocks from downtown at 500 E 7th. It's a bit worn down but costs only $20 a night.

Motels The *Alps Motel* (☎ 800-818-2577), 207 Elm St, is the best motel in town with clean, modern rooms for $36/43. *Mountain Peaks Motel* (☎ 719-486-3178), 1 Harrison Ave, advertises 'steam heat' and offers budget singles/doubles for $26/30. Funky trailers form the *Longhorn Motel* (☎ 719-486-3155), 1515 Poplar St, where rooms cost $34/40. If you don't mind lodgings that resemble a 1950s elementary school, the *Timberline Motel* (☎ 719-486-1876), at 216 Harrison Ave, is a better budget choice with rooms for $40/45.

Rooms cost $65/70 at the *Super 8 Leadville Inn* (☎ 719-486-3637), south of town on US 24 at 25 Jack Town Place, which has a sauna. The *Silver King Motor Inn* (☎ 719-486-2610), 2020 N Poplar St, offers laundry facilities and modern singles/doubles for $54/60.

Places to Eat
Loitering is encouraged with gallery exhibits, music and good coffee and food at *Cloud City Coffee House & Deli* (☎ 719-486-1317), 711 Harrison Ave in the Tabor Grand Hotel. The *Columbine Cafe* (☎ 719-486-3599), 612 Harrison, opens at 5:30 am (7 am on weekends) and serves hearty breakfasts and lunches at very reasonable prices.

Callaway's (☎ 719-846-1418), which is in the Delaware Hotel, is an exceptional value and offers simple egg breakfasts for under $4; large charbroiled burgers on the lunch menu cost under $6. Also try the spinach or Caesar salad for under $5. Dinner prices range from $7 to $13 and feature entrees like fettuccine and prime rib specials on weekends.

The Golden Burro Cafe & Lounge (☎ 719-486-1239), at 710 Harrison Ave near the Delaware Hotel, bills itself as a 'Leadville tradition since 1938' and is a favorite family-style restaurant with dinner specialties including steaks, chicken and Mexican dishes.

La Cantina (☎ 719-486-9927), 1 mile south of town at 942 US 24, is the local favorite for authentic Mexican food. *Prospector Restaurant* (☎ 719-486-3955), 3 miles north of town at 2798 Hwy 91, is a more upscale local favorite featuring aged steaks, seafood and Cajun entrees and a fine bar.

Entertainment
The *Pastime Saloon* (☎ 719-486-9986), 20 W 2nd St, is the last saloon on a street that once had 64 bars in Leadville's wilder days. For more historic atmosphere and walls lined with Baby Doe memorabilia, drop into the garish *Silver Dollar Saloon* (☎ 719-486-9914), 315 Harrison Ave. The *Scarlett Inn* (☎ 719-486-9928), 105 E 4th St, a local favorite, is the only joint in town with occasional live music.

Getting There & Away
Denver Shuttle Dee Hive Tours & Transportation (☎ 719-486-2339), 506 Harrison Ave, charges $62 one-way to Denver with a four-passenger minimum.

Car At the northernmost headwaters of the Arkansas River, Leadville is 24 miles south of Summit County and I-70 via Hwy 91 over Fremont Pass. From Vail, Leadville is 38 miles south via I-70 and US 24 over Tennessee Pass.

Getting Around
Shuttle Services Dee Hive Tours & Transportation welcomes hikers, skiers and bicyclists in need of shuttle transportation. Rides to trailheads or ski areas cost $10 to $15 per person for groups of four to six.

Car Rent a car or 4WD vehicle from Leadville Leasing (☎ 719-486-2627), at the airport a couple miles south of town.

FAIRPLAY & AROUND
Flanked by the Mosquito Range to the west and the Tarryall Mountains to the east, the

extensive South Park area is an outdoor paradise. Fairplay's population of 530 represents South Park's only 'urban' center – and the human inhabitants are probably outnumbered by the bison at Hartsel to the south.

In the courthouse square, you will find a small monument to 'Shorty, age 45, 1951'; on Front St there's a memorial to 'Prunes, A Burro 1867-1930.' These revered beasts of burden carried supplies to the mines and returned down the slopes loaded with ore. Since 1949, Fairplay has celebrated **Burro Days** on the last weekend of July, featuring Colorado's only indigenous sport – packburro racing. Racers run beside a loaded burro over a 30-mile course up Mosquito Pass (13,186 feet) and back.

Information
Visitor information is available at South Park Pottery (☎ 719-836-2698), 417 Front St, whose owner is also a member of the South Park Chamber of Commerce (☎ 719-836-3410). Tourist leaflets are also available at the Old Red Barn, 5th and Front Sts. The USFS South Park Ranger Station (☎ 719-836-2031) is open daily 7:30 am to 4:30 pm during summer. Helpful rangers offer plenty of information and maps for wildflower excursions, hiking and biking trails and camping.

The Colorado Community First State Bank (☎ 719-836-2797) at the intersection of US 285 and Hwy 9, has a 24-hour ATM. The post office is at 517 Hathaway St behind the Fairplay Hotel. The zip code is 80440.

The Company Store at South Park City Museum (☎ 719-836-2387), 4th and Front Sts, offers a good selection of books on the area's history.

South Park City Museum
Over 25 relocated historical buildings, and a few still in their original sites, make up fictional South Park City. Each contains an exhibit representing economic or social life during the 1860 to 1900 mining era, including one on burro pack trains.

South Park City Museum (☎ 719-836-2387), 100 4th St on Hwy 9 toward Breck-

enridge near the caboose, is open 9 am to 5 pm May 15 to October 15, until 7 pm during peak summer season. Admission costs $5/2 adults/children and seniors.

Como
The historic railroad town of Como, 8 miles north of Fairplay on US 285, has the feel of an early Clint Eastwood movie with its stark, treeless setting on the slope of Little Baldy Mountain. The **Como Roundhouse**, built in 1881 by the Denver, South Park & Pacific Railroad, features six masonry engine bays that are presently undergoing restoration.

B&B lodging is available between April to mid-November at the old *Como Depot* (☎ 719-836-2594), an interesting architectural design with its symmetrical towers. Singles/doubles start at $30/45; closed Tuesday. It also has a restaurant open 8 am to 8 pm Wednesday to Monday.

Windy Ridge Bristlecone Pines
During the 5th century BC, Colorado's oldest living trees sprouted from seed. By counting and measuring the annual tree rings on the bristlecone pines, dendrochronologists not only know their age but can make inferences about past climatic conditions. The 11,000-foot Windy Ridge grove of limber and bristlecone pines is stunning for the stark beauty of the wind-bent trees against the backdrop of Mt Silverheels across the South Platte River headwaters.

From Alma, 5 miles north of Fairplay, turn left (west) at the Alma Fire House & Mining Museum and continue about 3 miles to the Paris Mine. Turn right on USFS Rd 415 and continue another 3 miles to an old metal ore-loading chute, following a switchback and park. Cross Dolly Varden Creek on foot and continue up the steep road less than a mile to a snake-style rail fence and interpretive sign at the entry to the ridge.

Hiking & Backpacking
The **Buffalo Peaks Wilderness Area**, established in 1993 southwest of Fairplay,

features volcanic terrain that differs from the other glacially carved ranges in the area. From the USFS Weston Pass Campground, USFS Trail 616 follows Rich Creek and leads to the Rough & Tumbling Creek or Fourmile Creek trails, which provide good backcountry hiking loops. Take US 285 11 miles south of Fairplay, turn right (west) onto Park County Rd 22 and continue 12 miles to the trailhead.

In the Tarryall Mountains east of Fairplay, the Colorado Trail passes through the **Lost Creek Wilderness Area**, crossing US 285 at Kenosha Pass. The Brookside-McCurdy trail (USFS Trail 607) is the north-south spine and travels 37 miles through the Lost Creek Wilderness Area, between the Glen-Isle resort in the north and the Twin Eagles trailhead in the south. It intersects with several other trails that can be used to plan loop hikes. The Twin Eagles trailhead is north of Tarryall on Park County Rd 77 near USFS Spruce Grove Campground. Another backcountry trailhead, at the USFS Lost Park Campground, is 20 miles south of US 285 on Park County Rd 56.

Mountain Biking
Many opportunities exist for fat-tire enthusiasts on the USFS roads and nonwilderness trails in the area. Also, Hwy 9 is a signed bike route providing access to the South Platte River's superb fishing sites. From **Hoosier Pass**, 14 miles north of Fairplay on Hwy 9, a moderate ride of under 4 miles heads west to Magnolia Mine then cuts north on single-track trail, descends to Crystal Reservoir and returns to the pass. The railroad grade to **Boreas Pass** from Como is an easy up-and-back 23-mile ride. The **Colorado Trail** west of **Kenosha Pass**, north of Como, is a more challenging 13-mile route to **Georgia Pass**, with a loop option on the 11-mile long West Jefferson Trail (USFS Trail 643). Alternatively, you can continue on the Colorado Trail for 12 miles to Breckenridge.

A bit more difficult is the railroad grade up **Weston Pass** south of Fairplay on Park County Rd 22. From the Rich Creek trailhead (see Hiking & Backpacking below) it's about 6 miles to the scenic summit, where you can choose between continuing to Mt Massive Lakes and Leadville or turning back for an exhilarating descent.

The USFS South Park Ranger Station (☎ 719-836-2031) can provide more details or suggest additional options.

Fishing
Sections of the Middle and South forks of the South Platte River are Gold Medal waters, offering trophy rainbow trout with special catch-and-release restrictions. The South Fork section is south of Fairplay between US 285 and the inlet to Antero Reservoir. The designated section of the Middle Fork is on either side of Hwy 9, past the junction with US 24 at Hartsel and the confluence with the Middle Fork. The Colorado Department of Wildlife (DOW) refers to this section as the Badger Basin Fishing Easement and has developed numerous access points from US 24 in Hartsel and along Park County Rd 439 north of Hartsel. Spinney Mountain Reservoir is also Gold Medal water, harboring huge cutthroat and brown trout. Ice fishing at Antero and Spinney reservoirs is said to often be quite good.

For additional fishing suggestions you can contact the USFS South Park Ranger Station (☎ 719-836-2031) or the Colorado DOW (☎ 719-836-2521), at 16226 Park County Rd 77 near Lake George.

Cross-Country Skiing
You can cross-country ski on 12 miles of groomed trails for $10 per day ($5 for children and seniors) at the Fairplay Nordic Center (☎ 719-836-2658), 2 miles north of Fairplay on Beaver Creek Rd (4th St) – it's well-signed from town. Ski instruction is offered to groups of two to five people for $25 per person. You can rent skis, poles and boots for $10 per day at the base area and warming hut, or go for a package that include trail pass, rentals and ski lesson for $40.

Places to Stay

Camping In town, the *South Park Lodge* (☎ 719-836-3278), 801 Main St, has tent sites for $12, showers included.

Nearby USFS campgrounds are all on a first-come, first-served basis and include *Horseshoe* and *Fourmile*. Drive 1½ miles south of Fairplay via US 285 then turn onto Park County Rd 18 and drive 8 and 9 miles. Campsites cost $7. Only three sites ($5) are available at the USFS *Beaver Creek* campground, about 6 miles east of Fairplay on USFS Rd 659. The USFS campgrounds of *Jefferson Creek* (17 sites), *Aspen* (12 sites) and *Lodgepole* (35 sites) north of Fairplay all cost $7. Above timberline at 12,000-foot elevation *Kite Lake*, 6 miles west of Alma is the highest USFS campground in the country; sites are $3.

Motels & Hotels Budget travelers can try the bunkhouse at *South Park Lodge* (☎ 719-836-3278), 801 Main St, where a clean bed and locker costs $18. Recently renovated singles/doubles are also available for $44/55 in summer, $10 less in winter.

History beckons travelers to the *Fairplay Hotel* (☎ 719-836-2565), 500 Main St, originally established in 1873 but rebuilt after it was destroyed by fire in 1922. A recent $500,000 renovation has further improved conditions, and rooms with private bath are a decent value at $55 in summer. Another pleasant upscale option is the *Hand Hotel* (☎ 719-836-3595), 531 Front St, which offers cozy singles/doubles with modern Western decor for $45/60.

Places to Eat

The *Fairplay Hotel Restaurant* (☎ 719-836-2565) is open for breakfast, lunch and dinner, serving standard American fare. The daily lunch specials are good and generally cost around $6. The *Ranch Restaurant* (☎ 719-836-2789) seems to draw a steady stream of satisfied diners and also has daily lunch specials ($5) as well as a $2.50 breakfast special. Dinners, ranging from $10 to $15, come with soup, a vegetable and a potato.

Getting There & Away

Fairplay is 23 miles south of Breckenridge on Hwy 9 but is most often approached from Denver 90 miles east on US 285, or else from Colorado Springs on US 24 over scenic Wilkerson Pass then north on Hwy 9.

Elk Mountains & Around

This is what most people envision when they think of Colorado. Though the beautiful Elk Mountains make up only a small part of Colorado's Rocky Mountain range, they are home to the of Aspen and Vail ski resorts, easily the state's most famous destinations. Though both towns have gone upscale to the point of snobbery, the influx of unabashed wealth has not diminished the awesome scenery that rewards hikers, bikers and other outdoor enthusiasts.

VAIL

Vail (population 3900) is the nation's largest ski resort. In fact, its nearest rivals in size could easily fit in Vail's back bowls alone. Sparse sagebrush covers the slopes north of I-70, reflecting the semiarid climate, while only the moister north-facing slopes of the Gore Valley can sustain forests. Developments cling to the freeway and frontage roads as the mass of pavement occupies the focal point of the valley floor, and Vail Village gets mixed reviews at best for its 'Instant Tyrolia' design. Although nobody can fault the Village's compact, pedestrian-oriented layout, its slew of high-priced restaurants and fashion boutiques helped inspire the nickname 'Vile.' Some visitors have even found Vail considerably less friendly than other Colorado ski towns, though your experience (hopefully) may well be different.

At any rate, skiing – not architecture and attitude – is what attracts visitors. Even the most ardent Vail critic has to admit that the resort offers some of the best runs in

COLORADO

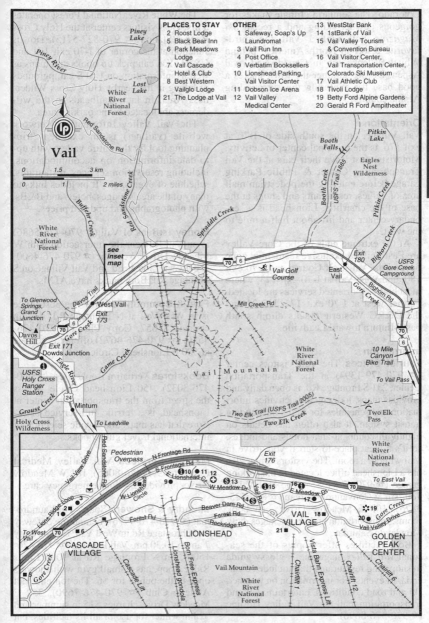

PLACES TO STAY
2 Roost Lodge
5 Black Bear Inn
6 Park Meadows Lodge
7 Vail Cascade Hotel & Club
8 Best Western Vailglo Lodge
21 The Lodge at Vail

OTHER
1 Safeway, Soap's Up Laundromat
3 Vail Run Inn
4 Post Office
9 Verbatim Booksellers
10 Lionshead Parking, Vail Visitor Center
11 Dobson Ice Arena
12 Vail Valley Medical Center

13 WestStar Bank
14 1stBank of Vail
15 Vail Valley Tourism & Convention Bureau
16 Vail Visitor Center, Vail Transportation Center, Colorado Ski Museum
17 Vail Athletic Club
18 Tivoli Lodge
19 Betty Ford Alpine Gardens
20 Gerald R Ford Ampitheater

Vail

Colorado. The semiarid climate makes for gorgeous powder skiing and a recent *Ski Magazine* poll ranked Vail the third-favorite resort in North America, behind Whistler/Blackcomb in Canada and rival Aspen. During summer the town makes a good base for exploring the surrounding Alpine country.

Orientation

Vail Village, on the south side of I-70 at exit 176, is the principal center of activity. Motorists must leave their cars at the Vail Transportation Center & Public Parking garage before entering the pedestrian mall area of lodges, restaurants and shops at the base of the chairlifts. Lionshead is a secondary center and lift about half a mile to the west.

At the extreme ends of the Gore Valley are East Vail, an exclusive residential zone beyond the Vail Golf Course and I-70 exit 180, and West Vail at I-70 exit 173, where most highway-oriented services are located. Farther west at I-70 exit 171, US 24 and the D&RG Western Tracks climb south past Minturn toward Leadville.

Information

Tourist Offices The Vail visitors center (☎ 970-479-1394) at the Transportation Center, 231 S Frontage Rd, is open daily and provides maps, lodging and activities information and schedules for Vail's outstanding transit system. It also often has details on nightly discounts at area hotels and lodges, so it's a great place to start if you arrive in Vail without a room. The visitors center also has a Lionshead office located in the parking garage (☎ 970-479-1385). The Vail Valley Tourism & Convention Bureau (☎ 800-525-3875), 100 E Meadow Drive, can book rooms, transportation and ski packages daily Monday to Saturday.

Both facilities offer copies of the seasonal *Vail Valley* magazine, a glossy guide to shops and restaurants that includes a calendar of events. For information on weather, ski and road conditions, entertainment and transportation, call the Vail Valley Hotline (☎ 970-476-8696).

The White River National Forest operates a first-class visitors center at the Holy Cross Ranger Station (☎ 970-827-5715), Dowds Junction at the corner of I-70 exit 171 and US 24. You can pick up books and maps as well as information on USFS campgrounds or hiking in the nearby Holy Cross Wilderness Area. In fact, trailheads to the wilderness are located in the parking area.

The Vail Valley Information Network website (vail.net) is an excellent trip-planning tool for the entire valley, with up-to-date information on accommodations, including reservation services, restaurants, schedule of events, etc. It includes links to many of the area's lodges, hotels and B&Bs, with photographs and updated prices.

Money 1stBank of Vail (☎ 970-476-5686) is on Vail Rd near the intersection with W Meadow Drive. WestStar (☎ 970-476-4600) is between Lionshead and Vail Village on S Frontage Rd. Both banks have ATMs.

Post & Communications The post office is in West Vail at N Frontage Rd; the zip code is 81657. Copy Plus (☎ 970-476-4556; fax 970-476-4672) offers fax service at 500 E Lionshead Circle.

Bookstores Verbatim Booksellers (☎ 970-476-3032), 450 Lionshead Circle, across the street from the transportation center at Lionshead, is a terrific full-service bookstore that has maps and a wide selection of international travel guidebooks.

Medical Services Vail Valley Medical Center (☎ 970-476-8065), 181 W Meadow Drive, provides 24-hour emergency care.

Laundry & Showers Soap's Up Laundromat (☎ 970-476-4976), behind the Safeway on N Frontage Rd in West Vail, is open daily 7 am to 10:30 pm. Vail Run Inn (☎ 970-476-1500), on N Frontage Rd at 1000 Lions Ridge Loop, has a small gym with showers open to the public for $6. The top-end Vail Athletic Club (☎ 970-476-7690), 352 E Meadow Drive, charges $15 in summer and $28 in winter for use of all its facilities, but cyclists and campers can take showers for $5 if it's not busy. Call ahead.

Colorado Ski Museum & Hall of Fame

Even nonskiers will enjoy this excellent museum. Exhibits depict the history of Colorado skiing, beginning with the utilitarian adoption of the Finnish 'suski,' or snow-glide-shoes, as an early means of transportation in the Rocky Mountains. The museum also details the beginnings or recreational skiing, including the UP Railroad's promotion of Idaho's Sun Valley ski resort in 1936, which brought a touch of glamour to downhill skiing. The installation of ski tows on Colorado slopes before WWII sparked protests that this ruined 'pure skiing.'

The Hall of Fame honors people like Charles Minot Dole, founder of the National Ski Patrol in 1938, who persuaded the War Department of the need to train ski troops. His efforts led to Camp Hale, established on nearby Tennessee Pass to train the 10th Mountain Division troops during WWII. Many recruits were local forest rangers, cowboys and recreational skiers who returned to Colorado to establish a ski industry after tough fighting in northern Italy.

The Colorado Ski Museum (☎ 970-476-1876), level three of the Vail Transportation Center, 231 S Frontage Rd, is open Tuesday to Sunday 10 am to 5 pm. Admission is free but donations are recommended.

Skiing

Downhill Skiing Vail Mountain is so big that skiers never get bored. No matter what your ability, you can always find a new route down the mountain; some say it takes about a week to ski the entire mountain. Vail's four base areas from east to west are Golden Peak, Vail Village, Lionshead and Cascade Village. Before tackling Vail's immense 6¼ sq miles of ski terrain – the largest in the nation – it might be a good idea to take the $20 Vail Mountain Welcome Tour (☎ 970-476-3239), offered daily at 9:15 am at Lionshead and running until noon. Most valuable are the pointers on avoiding long lift lines.

With a vertical drop of 3250 feet and all of that terrain below, it's possible to get in a 3-mile cruiser run (Flapjack to Riva Ridge). For a real endurance test in the bumps try Prima-Pronto-Log Chute – 1500 vertical feet of nonstop moguls. Vail's legendary back bowls – Game Creek, Sun Down, Sun Up, Tea Cup, China, Siberia and Mongolia – often fill with the 'champagne' powder the region is famous for, but if you want a taste of it you'll need to get there early in the day. Hordes of skiers head for the backside on powder days and for 'first tracks' down double-black-diamond terrain, but the back bowls' southern exposure guarantees that snow will soon turn to mush or provide hard spills for intermediate skiers.

Vail upgraded the Lionshead gondola before the 1997-1998 season and added a user-friendly base area with no stairs (tiring in stiff ski boots). The spacious, heated cabins hold 12 passengers comfortably and zip up to the summit in just seven minutes. At the top a new evening activities center has opened, with an ice-skating rink, sledding hill and snowboard park.

With nine on-mountain restaurants, three trailside snack bars and three outdoor barbecues, there is little chance you will go hungry (though you may go broke). *Camp 21*, at the top of Chair 14, is the only budget choice, offering convenience store-type microwave fare. (The nearby upscale *Two Elk Restaurant* was burned down at the end of 1998 by environmental arsonists. At the time of writing, it wasn't certain if the restaurant would be rebuilt.) If you stash your own food on the mountain, you can warm it up in microwaves at Wildwood, Mid-Vail and Eagle's Nest as well as Camp 21.

Lift tickets are $54/35 adults/children. Seniors over 70 ski free and discounts for other seniors are available. Lift tickets can also be used at the Beaver Creek ski area 9 miles west of Vail on I-70, as well as at Breckenridge, Keystone and Arapahoe Basin. For information about tickets call Vail Associates (☎ 970-476-5601).

For a recorded snow condition report, call ☎ 970-476-4888.

Vail offers the world's largest ski school with over 500 instructors. It also has to be one of the most expensive places to take up the sport. A full-day private lesson will cost $430 ($415 if it's booked in advance). All-day beginner group lessons are $85 to $90, lift ticket included. Vail recently introduced the Teen Access lift/lesson pack for $90 all day as well as the Vail Adventure Guide, a full-day small group coaching seminar for advanced and expert skiers. The lift ticket is additional. For children's ski programs call the Golden Peak Center (☎ 970-279-2040); for adult Alpine instruction call ☎ 970-476-3239.

Cross-Country & Backcountry Skiing

The Nordic Center at the Vail golf course (☎ 970-479-4391) at the east end of S Frontage Rd, has 10 km of machine-maintained tracks and is free. Rentals are $17 and you can get there on the free bus from the Transportation Center. At the base of Chair 6, the Golden Peak Center (☎ 970-476-3239) offers backcountry tours combined with gourmet dining. About 15 miles west of Vail, the larger Cordillera Nordic Center (☎ 303-926-5100) has easy, intermediate and expert terrain and packages that include use of their hot tub, pool and sauna as well as guided tours, lessons, moonlight skiing and snowshoeing.

Check with the USFS Holy Cross Ranger Station (☎ 970-827-5715), I-70 exit 171 at US 24, for information on nearby backcountry trails including **Shrine Pass** (see Road & Mountain Biking below), but be aware that many of the nonwilderness routes are infested with noisy snowmobiles. The 10th Mountain Division Hut System (☎ 970-925-5775), 1280 Ute Ave in Aspen, offers a system of trails almost 300 miles long connecting 14 overnight cabins. Paragon Guides (☎ 970-926-5299) uses the 10th Mountain Division's 14 huts between Vail and Aspen for guided three- to six-day trips for all ability levels. Guides provide instruction in telemark, backcountry skiing and winter mountaineering skills.

Equipment Rental You can rent skis at the base of the Vista Bahn lift from Curtin-Hill Sports (☎ 970-476-5337), 254 Bridge St, $16 for a basic package. Also try Buzz's Boots & Boards (☎ 970-476-3320), Mill Creek Court Bldg, 302 East Gore Creek Drive, $16 for basic ski, $19 for basic snowboard packages. Christy Sports/Sports Stalker (☎ 970-476-2244), at 293 Bridge St, has ski packages starting at $16, boards at $28.

Cross-country ski rentals are available at the Vail Nordic Center (☎ 970-476-8366), 1778 Vail Valley Drive at the Vail Golf Course.

Ice Skating

Skaters can practice their skills year-round at the Dobson Ice Arena (☎ 970-479-2271), on W Meadow Drive near E Lionshead Circle. Daily public skating hours are 11 am to 1 pm and evening hours are 7:30 to 9 pm Monday, Wednesday, Friday and Sunday. Admission is $4/3 adults/children. Skate rentals cost $2. You can also skate at the new Adventure Ridge rink at the top of the Lionshead gondola (☎ 970-476-9090) for $8. The rink is open daily noon to 10 pm. Free public skating is available on the outdoor skating rink at The Vail Nordic Center and at the Eagle-Vail Pavilion (☎ 970-949-1504), weather permitting.

Bobsledding

A thrilling 60 seconds of high-speed fun is offered on a 2900-foot course for $12. Vail Bobsled is located just below Mid-Vail near Short Cut Run. Call the Activities Desk (☎ 970-476-9090) for additional information.

Road & Mountain Biking

Bike routes connect the outlying free parking areas with Vail Village. From the West Vail Market you can ride on N Frontage Rd, crossing I-70 at the pedestrian overpass to Lionshead. On the south side of the freeway, a paved bike route extends from W Gore Creek Drive through Cascade Village, Lionshead and Vail Village and continues east on the **10-Mile Canyon Trail** through auto-free road-bike heaven over Vail Pass to Frisco. From the road closure at the east end of Bighorn Rd, 6 miles from Vail Village, it's an 8-mile climb to Vail Pass; there you can turn back or continue 11 miles to Frisco, the hub of Summit County bike trails. Another popular ride, for the hearty rider acclimated to high-altitude exertion, climbs over Tennessee Pass to Leadville on the narrow shoulders of US 24.

Vail Mountain has about 20 well-marked mountain bike trails crisscrossing the ski runs for cyclists of all abilities. They're free – if you're willing to do all the climbing yourself – otherwise an all-day lift pass costs $19 and can be used on the gondola and the Vista Bahn and Wildwood Express quads. Don't be intimidated by Vail's 3330-foot vertical drop: a ride to Mid-Vail is really quite easy along the well-maintained Gitalong Rd, and takes about an hour from the base. From there it's only 10 minutes to Eagle's Nest (the top of the Lionshead gondola) and then – if you need to get to the very top! – a strenuous push to the 11,250-summit via Kloser's Klimb. Pick up a free copy of the 'Biking & Hiking Map' at the information office.

From the Vail Pass Rest Area on I-70 13 miles east of town, **USFS Rd 709** climbs about 3 miles to Shrine Pass. A road to the left leads to the *Shrine Pass Inn* (☎ 970-476-5733), which offers lunch and dinner (by reservation only). From the summit it's 9 miles to Red Cliff on US 24. Along the way there is the Mt of the Holy Cross overlook at about 4 miles from the trailhead.

Mountain bikes are prohibited in wilderness areas, but the USFS offers information on routes that begin in Vail or in the challenging higher altitudes near Camp Hale. From the end of the N Frontage Rd bikeway at the West Vail Market, you can turn on Chamonix Rd to get to the **Davos Trail**, a moderate 4-mile dirt road that leads to the top of Davos Hill overlooking Minturn, with a distant view of Mt of the Holy

Cross. The **Mill Creek Trail** (USFS Rd 710) represents a more difficult up-and-back climb of almost 8 miles (one-way) that begins at the Vista Bahn Express Lift and continues 3½ miles along Mill Creek from the left turn at the fork near the base of Chair 10.

Another option directly from Vail is to ride 12 miles to **Piney Lake**, a moderate climb on the Red Sandstone Rd (USFS Rd 700) which begins at N Frontage Rd about a mile east of the West Vail Market. However, auto traffic on weekends and at midday can be a nuisance. At 5 miles, turn right on a 4WD road to **Lost Lake**; after 1½ miles of descent the road climbs to Indian Meadows, offering views of the Gore Range in the Eagle Mountain Wilderness Area as well as recently logged areas. Bear left at each junction for 4 miles until you reach the single-track trail that covers about one mile to Lost Lake.

A comprehensive guide to area trails, campgrounds and hut systems is the *Vail & Eagle Valley Mountain Biking & Recreation Map* ($8). Also look for Michael Murphy's *Mountain Biking Guide to Vail, Colorado*.

Vail Bicycle Service (VBS), (☎ 970-476-1233), 450 East Lionshead Circle, rents high-end, full suspension bikes for $20 half-day, $35 full-day. Vail Bike Tech (☎ 970-476-5995), 555 East Lionshead Circle, has basic mountain bikes for $15, front-suspension models for $19 and demo bikes for $24. In the village, Christy Sports/Sports Stalker (see Cross-Country & Backcountry Skiing above) has basic mountain bikes for $25, full-suspension models for $30. At Wheel Base (☎ 970-479-0913), front-suspension bikes are $20, full-suspension $30.

Hiking
In 1873 William Henry Jackson discovered and photographed Mt of the Holy Cross (14,005 feet) while with the Hayden Expedition. Along with paintings by Thomas Moran, another member of the expedition, their work symbolized the Colorado

wilderness to millions of 19th-century Americans. Pilgrimages to view the snowy cross on the north face during the late spring and early summer led to the construction of a shelter on Notch Mountain in 1924. The difficult **Notch Mountain Trail** (USFS Trail 2000) climbs almost 3000 feet in 5 miles to 13,100-foot elevation – leaving most tenderfeet gasping for air!

The **Half Moon Pass** (USFS Trail 2009) leads to the cross-country approach up Mt of the Holy Cross. Get an early start to complete in a day the 6-mile climb on this overused trail. From the turnoff to Tigawan Rd (USFS Rd 707), 4 miles south of Minturn, a high-clearance (4WD) vehicle is recommended for the 8-mile journey to both trailheads into the Holy Cross Wilderness Area.

A 2-mile hike to 60-foot **Booth Falls** follows USFS Trail 1885 into the Eagles Nest Wilderness Area from the trailhead off N Frontage Rd west of I-70 exit 180. If you continue beyond the falls on this popular trail, you will encounter meadows filled with wildflowers and views of the Gore Range. The trail continues to Booth Lake, 6 miles from the trailhead, and climbs about 3000 feet.

From the USFS Gore Creek campground, the popular **Gore Creek Trail** (USFS Trail 2015) leads to Gore Lake in the Eagles Nest Wilderness Area. This strenuous 6-mile trail climbs about 2700 feet through spruce and fir forests into the Alpine tundra. Another trail option from near the campground is **Two Elk Trail** (USFS Trail 2005), an 11-mile hike that climbs to Two Elk Pass, passing prime elk habitat before leaving the forest and Vail's back bowls at Cemetery Rd in Minturn. Elk bugling during rutting season is best observed in late summer. This hike can be done in a day or as an overnight trip – consider leaving a vehicle at the Minturn trailhead. The east trailhead is at the gate closing the old US 6 frontage road. Do not park in the campground.

Register for a guided naturalist hike that meets on Tuesdays and Thursdays at the **Vail Nature Center** (☎ 970-479-2291), at 841 Vail Valley Drive. The hikes are 'leisurely in nature' and cost $15. For a short stroll, the four trails at the Nature Center offer excellent interpretive displays on the plants and wildlife along Gore Creek and can be done in under an hour. Shrine Mountain Adventure (☎ 970-827-5363) is a guide service that does not cater to hunters and offers 'alternative backcountry tours.'

Fishing
It's hard to believe that a stream so close to a freeway would be included among Colorado's Gold Medal waters, yet 4 miles of Gore Creek from Red Sandstone Creek to its confluence with the Eagle River is prize trout fly-fishing water. Expect to find rainbow, brook and big brown trout, plus native cutthroat in its tributaries. Regulations permit anglers to take only two fish over 16 inches from the creek. The Eagle River, once too polluted to sustain large mature fish, now yields decent catches, due to EPA Superfund cleanup of the Gilman mill tailings above Minturn. If you're willing to go for a hike, there are nearby mountain lakes and streams offering great fishing opportunities.

Check at the USFS Holy Cross Ranger Station (☎ 970-827-5715) for a complete list of lake and stream fishing opportunities in the district. For tackle and supplies, stop by Gorsuch Outfitters (☎ 970-476-2294), 263 E Gore Creek Drive. They offer a variety of float and wading trips starting at $125 per person as well as a women's clinic for $100. Gore Creek Fly Fisherman, (☎ 970-476-3296), 183 Gore Creek Drive, offers a variety of trips at competitive prices.

White-Water Rafting & Kayaking
The upper Eagle River near Dowd Junction features a kayak slalom course upstream from I-70. Immediately downstream from I-70 is Dowd Chutes, a Class IV white-water rapids. Below Dowd Chutes, the lower Eagle River offers relatively sedate Class II-III floats for about 25 miles. The peak season is in May and wetsuits are necessary. By mid-June the water level is too low for much fun.

Three local companies offer half-day rafting trips that typically cost $60/45 adults/children. Trips through Dowd Chute are limited to adults and cost a bit more. Contact Timberline Tours (☎ 970-476-1414), Nova Guides (☎ 970-949-4232) or Lakota (☎ 970-476-7238).

Alpine Kayak & Canoe (☎ 970-949-3350), 40690 US 6 and US 24 in Avon, is a kayaking school with a full range of programs. A two-day beginner course costs $129, including all gear.

Golf

Heads up! The Jerry Ford Invitational Golf Tournament attracts celebrities and famous golfers each August to the 18-hole par 71 municipal Vail Golf Course (☎ 970-479-2260) at the east end of S Frontage Rd. Greens fees for 18 holes run $70, $45 for nine holes; a cart is additional. The more challenging Eagle-Vail Golf Course is 6 miles west of town with fees of $80, including cart. Next door, the Willow Creek Par 3 course costs $10 for nine holes.

Special Events

Throughout the winter and summer you can expect some activity nearly every weekend. A week of ski celebration takes place in early March during the **American Ski Classic**. Gourmets will enjoy sampling the creations of Vail's chefs at the **Taste of Vail** held on the first weekend in April – don't forget to pack your best blue jeans for the culminating 'Rocky Mountain Formal.' On Memorial Day weekend, a kayak competition on the Eagle River is the main event during the **Jeep White-Water Festival**.

During July and August, free Tuesday night **concerts** begin at 6:30 pm at the Gerald R Ford Amphitheater (☎ 970-476-2918), 530 S Frontage Rd E, featuring popular rock, soul and jazz artists as part of the Hot Summer Nights series. For information contact the Vail Valley Foundation (☎ 970-476-9500).

On July and August weekends, Vail hosts the **Bravo! Colorado Music Festival**, featuring 60 chamber, orchestral and symphonic programs. For schedules and ticket information contact the festival box office, 953 S Frontage Rd, suite 104, at ☎ 970-827-5700.

Places to Stay

Aside from camping, don't expect to find any low-end lodging near Vail. Ski season rates reach their peak during the Christmas and New Year's holidays, when most innkeepers quote rates double to triple the amount charged after the snow melts. Ask at the Vail visitors center about nightly specials, especially during the off-season.

Camping The forested USFS *Gore Creek Campground* at the east end of Bighorn Rd offers 25 campsites for $7 on a first-come, first-served basis. It's only 6 miles from Vail Village by bike route or bus. It's open June to Labor Day weekend and includes seven walk-in tent sites. Reservations are accepted for the 21 sites at the USFS *Camp Hale Memorial Campground* (☎ 877-444-6777), 15 miles south of Minturn on US 24. Campsites at this former training site for the 10th Mountain Division cost $6. It's near the Colorado Trail in a flat, open valley sparsely forested by lodgepole pines.

B&Bs The *Lazy Ranch* (☎ 970-926-3876, 800-655-9343), 0057 Lake Creek Rd, has five rooms in a beautifully restored 100-year-old Victorian about 10 miles west of Vail in Edwards. The comfortable rooms go for $90 to $125 in winter, $60 to $80 in summer and include a big hot breakfast. The contemporary Intermountain (☎ 970-476-4935) has two double rooms and is a couple of miles from town on the free shuttlebus route. Rates are $69/125 winter/summer and a Continental breakfast is included. In West Vail, the log *Black Bear Inn* (☎ 970-476-1304), 2405 Elliot Ranch Rd, features a large streamside deck and 12 rooms with private bath for $95 to $105 in summer, $115 to $215 in winter.

Motels & Lodges Among the least expensive places to stay is the *Roost Lodge*

(☎ 970-476-5451), 1783 N Frontage Rd in West Vail. Its plain contemporary rooms sleep four comfortably. Summer rates are $40 to $99, $60 to $201 in winter. Vail's other 'budget' place, the *Park Meadows Lodge* (☎ 970-476-5598), is on the other side of the freeway at 1472 Matterhorn Circle. They offer 28 one- and two-bedroom condos starting at $54/125 summer/winter. Both offer summer discounts with a certificate available from the visitor information center.

Only one block from four lifts in Vail Village, the small *Tivoli Lodge* (☎ 970-476-5615, 800-451-4756), 386 Hanson Ranch Rd, features a cozy lounge with fireplace, outdoor heated pool, hot tub, sauna and a guest laundry. The Tivoli is like a traditional European ski lodge – the opposite of a sterile condo. Hotel-style rooms with private bath start at $69/119 summer/winter, single or double occupancy, and include Continental breakfast.

Rooms cost $79/220 summer/winter at the *Best Western Vailglo Lodge* (☎ 970-476-5506), 701 W Lionshead Circle, regarded as an elegant small hotel. The *Evergreen Lodge* (☎ 970-476-7810), 250 S Frontage Rd, offers hotel rooms for $120 to $145 in summer, $180 to $205 in winter.

The Vail Cascade Hotel & Club (☎ 970-476-7111, 800-420-2424), 1300 Westhaven Drive, has its own chairlift, two movie theaters and a full indoor athletic facility. Rates range from $109 to $290 in summer, $300 to $1000 in January. At the extreme top end is *The Lodge at Vail* (☎ 970-476-5011), 174 E Gore Creek Drive at the base of the lifts. It has the most convenient location and more amenities than any other lodge in Vail; rates start at $150/420 summer/winter.

It's not much cheaper, but staying in **Avon** 9 miles west of Vail is a good option if you're planning to ski at both Vail and Beaver Creek. There's also the terrific Avon Recreation Center (☎ 970-949-9191), 325 Benchmark Rd, with a pool, sauna, steam and hot tub for $7.50/5 adults/children – the perfect way to unwind after a day on the slopes. Rooms that sleep four

people start at $169 at the *Christie Lodge* (☎ 970-949-7700, 800-551-4326), 47 E Beaver Creek Blvd. *Season's at Avon* (☎ 970-845-3900, 800-859-8242), 134 W Benchmark Rd, has one- and two-bedroom condos for $175 and $235 during ski season – a mere 100 yards from the rec center.

Condominiums Vail Central Reservations (☎ 970-476-1000, 800-525-3875), 100 E Meadow Rd, handles most properties in Vail. Competitive summer rates are available from *Destination Resorts* (☎ 970-476-5031, 800-852-9378), 1031-D S Frontage Rd. A typical medium-priced condominium complex in Vail Village is *Willows & Riva Ridge South* (☎ 970-476-2233), 74 Willow Rd, which offers a good location near the lifts and standard contemporary furnishings. Double occupancy hotel-style rooms cost $89/160 summer/winter; two-bedroom condos suitable for four people run $240/495.

Top-end condos are available at Vail's famous clocktower at the top of Willow Bridge Rd. Hotel-style rooms cost $79/225 summer/winter at the *Lodge Tower* (☎ 970-476-9530), 200 Vail Rd; two-bedroom condos are $230/615.

Places to Eat

At the top of Bridge St, *The Daily Grind* (☎ 970-476-5856) begins serving muffins and coffee at 6:30 am. If you're too tired to make it up the street you can stop for a caffeine fix at *Covered Bridge Coffee* (☎ 970-479-2883). There's a full range of coffees as well as bagels, pastries and hot breakfasts. Lunchtime deli sandwiches are about $5 and include potato chips or fruit. Even if you sleep till noon, you can still start your day at *Blu's* (☎ 970-476-3113), 193 E Gore Creek Drive, which serves breakfast till 5 pm. At night an eclectic menu features upscale dinners along with 'homestyle' staples like chicken-fried steak or liver and onions; prices range from $9 to $17. Or stick with the appetizers, soups and salads and splurge on a bottle of wine.

Pizza slices cost about $3, accompanied by reggae and young locals complaining about high rents and low wages, at *Pazzo's* (☎ 970-476-9026), in Vail Village at Willow Bridge Rd and E Meadow Drive. It's open for breakfast 7:30 am and serves pizza and lasagna ($9) until 11 pm. Locals also drop by for the lunch specials at *Michael's American Bistro* (☎ 970-476-5353) on the 3rd floor of the Gateway Plaza at the corner of S Frontage and Vail Rds.

For Mexican food, *Los Amigos* (☎ 970-476-5847), at the top of Bridge Street facing the mountain, has all the classics as well as fish tacos ($11) and filling vegetarian black bean soup ($5). At *Jackalope Cafe & Cantina* (☎ 970-476-4313) in West Vail you can start off with huevos rancheros or a breakfast burrito (both $6) and come back after skiing for stuffed jalapeño camarones ($10).

May Palace (☎ 970-476-1657), 223 E Gore Creek Drive, offers Chinese lunch specials for $6. All vegetarian dinners are under $10. Don't miss their après-ski chicken wings and buckets of beer. In the same building with patio seating facing Gore Creek is *Up the Creek* (☎ 970-476-8141), offering fresh fruit or burgers and sandwiches for lunch and dinner.

Though it bears no resemblance to a ranch, *KB Ranch Co* (☎ 970-476-1937), in Lionsquare Lodge next to the Lionshead gondola, offers unpretentious dinners with a great salad bar for $10 to $15.

If the kids are howling for something without wild mushrooms and sun-dried tomatoes, head for *The Cafe* (☎ 970-476-7111), in the Vail Cascade Hotel at 1300 W Haven Drive. Ask the waiter and they'll prepare something less intimidating, like a grilled-cheese sandwich or a bowl of spaghetti, while you can choose from grown-up selections ranging from $11 to $19 or sneak off to the top-end *Alfredo's*, also at the Vail Cascade, for a five-course meal of ahi or caribou.

A no-nonsense deli, *Cleaver's Deli* (☎ 970-476-6084), on Hanson Ranch Rd at the top of Bridge St, serves up submarines and regular sandwiches from $3 to $6.75 for a foot-long sub.

The upstairs pizza bar at *Vendetta's* (☎ 970-476-5070), 291 Bridge St, is open till 2 am, one of the few late-night dining options in Vail. You can also enjoy their sunny deck while you dine on minestrone soup for about $3 and traditional antipasta and entree selections for $15 to $25.

Entertainment

Nightclub activity centers on Bridge St from the mountain to the Covered Bridge. At the top of the street, *The Club* (☎ 970-479-0556) is a basement bar featuring rock music. Also at the top of Bridge St, *Nick's* (☎ 970-476-5011), near the bridge, is another nightspot popular with young locals featuring DJ dance music, while the older crowd at *Club Chelsea* (☎ 970-476-5600) dance to blues and piano music.

Hong Kong Cafe (☎ 970-476-1818), 227 Wall St, is small and the crowd spills out onto the patio by late afternoon – the live-music decibel level will either attract you or drive you away. Getting to the bar for a refill of Leinenkugel's (a popular liquor) can be a challenge. In Crossroads Shopping Center you'll find Vail's own Rainbow Trout Stout at the *Hubcap Brewery & Kitchen* (☎ 970-476-5757) and Vail's largest dance floor at *Gartons* (☎ 970-479-0607), which has both DJs and live music.

If you're in Lionshead, *Garfinkel's* (☎ 970-476-3789), next to the gondola, offers live rock music and a 'locals' night' beer bargain on Sunday. Happy hour is 3 to 7 pm every day at *Doolittle's 19th Hole* (☎ 970-479-2911), which is in the Concert Hall Plaza.

It's not convenient, but some of the hottest rock and alternative performers in the area are featured at the *State Bridge Lodge* (☎ 970-653-4444), 14 miles north of Wolcott and I-70 on Hwy 131 at the historic bridge crossing the Colorado River.

Getting There & Away

Air One of the main reasons for Vail's success is the resort's easy access. Most visitors fly into Denver International Airport and continue to Vail on a shuttle van (see DIA Shuttle below). During the December to early April ski season, the Eagle County Airport, 35 miles west of Vail between I-70 exits 140 and 147, offers a surprising amount of jet service.

American Airlines flies to Eagle County Airport twice daily from Dallas/Fort Worth, TX, and daily from Chicago. Northwest Airlines flies nonstop from New York's La Guardia Airport and Minneapolis/St Paul, MN, while Delta flies to Salt Lake City, UT, and United Airlines offers daily flights from Denver.

DIA Shuttle Vans to Vail (☎ 970-476-4467, 800-222-2112) operates frequent shuttle service from Denver International Airport. The approximately three-hour trip costs $54 one-way; $40 in summer.

Bus Greyhound buses stop at the Vail Transportation Center just off the middle I-70 exit for Vail. Three daily buses serve Denver-Grand Junction in each direction, plus an eastbound express bus leaves Vail at 3 pm. The Greyhound ticket office (☎ 970-476-5137) is open Tuesday to Saturday from 7:30 to 11:30 am and from 4:30 to 6:30 pm.

Car Via I-70, Vail is 107 miles west of Denver and 57 miles east of Glenwood Springs. Motorists from Denver cross the 10,666-foot Vail Pass after the town of Frisco. The ski resort is 33 miles north of Leadville via US 24 and I-70.

Getting Around
To/From the Airport From Eagle County Airport the shuttle costs $31. Also try Vail Valley Transportation (☎ 970-476-8008, 800-882-8872).

Bus Vail has fine public transportation – it's free, it goes where you need to go and it operates at short intervals. Travel by bus is thus faster and more convenient than most car trips. The in-town shuttle runs between the base of Golden Peak and Vail Village and Lionshead from 6:15 to 2:15 am at intervals of under 10 minutes. From the Transportation Center, Vail Buses (☎ 970-

328-8143) serves the golf course and Ford Park; West Vail, both North and South; Sandstone; and East Vail. Shuttles and buses stop only at designated stops. Schedules appear in *Vail Valley* magazine.

Car Thrifty (☎ 970-476-8718) rents cars at the Vail Transportation Center. Dollar (☎ 970-476-3919) offers rentals at the Marriott. Also try Enterprise (☎ 970-468-5228) in Avon, and Hertz (☎ 800-654-3131) at the Eagle County Airport.

Taxi Taxi of Vail Valley (☎ 970-476-8294) offers 24-hour local taxi service.

MINTURN

Squeezed between the burgeoning luxury condominium and resort developments of Vail and Beaver Creek, Minturn (population 1130) is a nice respite in the heart of Eagle County. This small railroad town next to the Eagle River was founded in 1887 and the shops and homes retain the coziness and charm of a place that really has been around for awhile. To get there, go 3 miles west of Vail on I-70 then 2 miles south on US 24.

Up until 1997 Minturn was the base for 'helper' engines that assisted heavy freight trains over the 10,242-foot Tennessee Pass tunnel to Leadville, the highest mainline railroad route in the USA. As many as 24 freight trains would pass through town daily. Locals credited these trains with warding developers off Minturn in favor of places farther away from Vail – like Avon and Gypsum – as targets for resort expansion. The line was closed after Union Pacific took over Southern Pacific and opted to run trains via its more efficient rail lines in Wyoming and New Mexico.

Now that the trains are gone the townspeople are getting nervous about Vail's rumored plans of one day connecting Beaver Creek and Vail mountain – via Minturn. Property values have skyrocketed in the last couple of years, so some development looks inevitable. There is also a campaign to turn the rail line into a bike trail as part of the national 'Rails to Trails' program, though nothing was set at the time of writing.

Minturn is gaining a reputation for its galleries and antique stores. Western and Native American art are featured at Woodwind Galleries (☎ 970-827-9232), 151 N Main St. Across the street, Two Elk Gallery (☎ 970-827-5307) features cowboy kitsch and lots of branding-iron and antler-style furnishings and lamps. The owners of Battle Mountain Trading Post (☎ 970-827-4191), 1031 S Main St, lure prospective customers inside by offering cheap ice cream cones, then let the crowded rustic appeal of their costly antiques sell themselves. Bring a truck to haul away such things as barber shop poles, old-fashioned gas pumps or more antler furnishings.

Activities

Minturn and Red Cliff (located about 10 miles farther south on US 24), gateways to the Holy Cross Wilderness Area, offer some of the most spectacular hiking and backcountry skiing in the area. Anyone heading up to the region should first check in with the USFS Holy Cross Ranger District (☎ 970-827-5715), 24747 US 24 at the US 24/I-70 junction. They have free maps of all the area trails and campsites as well as complete information about degree of difficulty and trail conditions. Do not head up to the wilderness area without the proper information from the USFS and the appropriate equipment.

The **Missouri Lakes Trail** is a gorgeous hike beginning about 14 miles south of Minturn on US 24. It's moderately difficult, with 1500 feet of elevation gain to the lakes and another 500 feet to Missouri Pass – 6- and 8-mile roundtrips, respectively. Keen hikers can make this route into a loop by returning via the **Fancy Pass/ Fancy Creek Trail**. Plan on three hours if you're just going to the lakes and back, five hours for the loop. Either way you will get stunning views of rivers, lakes and mountains, especially once you climb above the tree line.

For backcountry mountain biking, hiking, skiing and snowshoeing in the Holy Cross

Wilderness Area, contact Shrine Mountain Adventures (☎ 970-827-5363), 148 Water Street in Red Cliff. Their customized, fully equipped full-day trips run about $90 with lunch, less if you have a large group. Other programs, such as nature hikes and kids' outdoor adventures, are less expensive.

Places to Stay & Eat

The *Minturn Inn* (☎ 970-827-9647), 442 Main St, is a delightful B&B housed in a restored 1915 home along the Eagle River, adjacent to the White River National Forest. All 10 rooms are tastefully furnished and comfortable, from those with shared bath to the 'premier' rooms featuring their own fireplaces, vaulted ceilings and two-person jacuzzis. The friendly owners are longtime residents of both the inn and the town and have a wealth of knowledge about the area. Rates vary for season and room type – anywhere from $65 to $199 – but they are well worth it.

The renovated *Eagle River Inn* (☎ 970-827-5761), 145 N Main St, returned to life as a Santa Fe-style adobe building. Its 12 rooms with tiled baths go for $75 to $98 spring through fall, $100 to $180 during the winter holiday season. Good breakfasts, fresh flowers in each room and nice mountain and river views add to the pleasant atmosphere.

Bonjour Bakers (☎ 970-827-5539), at 474 Main Street just up the street from the Minturn Inn, serves delicious muffins, croissants, bread and desserts baked daily. They'll also make delicious sandwiches to take with you up to the mountains.

The *Turntable Restaurant* (☎ 970-827-4164), 160 Main St, open 5:30 am to 10:30 pm, is on the site of an old railroad engine turntable and the restaurant is decorated with D&RG Western Railroad memorabilia on the walls. Hearty breakfasts cost $4 to $7, while burgers, tacos and burritos range from $4 to $6.

There's no golf course near the *Minturn Country Club* (☎ 970-827-4114), 131 Main St, but you can play shuffleboard after grilling your own food and making a salad. A small New York steak dinner costs just

$9, while the aged 12-oz steak and crab will cost about $15. Empty Chianti bottles left behind by USFS employees decorate the former ranger station now called *Minturno Pasta Palace* (☎ 970-827-9204), 401 Main St, where you choose from six pastas and 11 sauces for $7 to $11. A half-litre of Chianti costs $8 and warm bread with garlic cloves sauteed in olive oil is served with the meal.

For a great selection of bottled and draft beers, including Paulaner, to go with country cooking, try *Booco's Station Smokehouse Barbecue* (☎ 970-827-4224), 455 S Main St, for a pork rib dinner that costs $9 – $13 if you're really gluttonous!

RED CLIFF

About 6 miles south of Minturn on US 24, on the way to the Holy Cross Wilderness Area, the turnoff for Red Cliff (population 300) is just before the big green bridge spanning the Eagle River. This genuine Western town began life as a gold mining center in the mid- to late-1800s before becoming a lumber center. The buildings along Eagle and Water Streets have a definite 'Old West' feel, enhanced by the mountain backdrop. Take a five-minute walk up the switchback trail behind the liquor store for a view of the area, including the hill where the entire town once gathered to defend against a feared Indian attack.

Red Cliff Cafe & Mercantile (☎ 970-827-4223), 166½ Eagle Street, serves as the town's sole restaurant, grocery store and tourist office. It's open 10 am to 9 pm weekdays (closed Wednesdays); 8 am to 9 pm Saturday and 8 am to 1 pm Sunday. Breakfasts won't cost more than $5 and tasty homestyle dinners are about $6.

Next door, the *Red Cliff Lodge* (☎ 970-827-9109) is the only place to stay in town, though it was not yet open at the time of writing. There's a bunkroom for eight and rates were expected to start at $20.

If you're leaving Red Cliff and heading east, consider taking the Shrine Pass road. This 12½-mile dirt road cuts through some remarkable countryside before dropping down to the east side of Vail Pass. Be sure

to stop at the top to check out the view of Mt of the Holy Cross behind you.

BEAVER CREEK

Beaver Creek is an exclusive gated enclave 8 miles west of Vail from its entrance at Avon and I-70. There's something surreal about the sudden appearance of perfectly maintained grounds and neo-Tyrolean buildings that climb before a truly spectacular ski mountain. Though it feels artificial, the skiing is great and accommodations outstanding (though you pay for what you get).

Beaver Creek was initially conceived as part of Vail's scheme to attract the 1976 Winter Olympics, high hopes that were aborted in 1972. Against the environmental objections of the state's voters, the USFS and two governors, Beaver Creek's enterprising proponents finally gained the necessary permits to develop the wooded terrain on the margins of the Holy Cross Wilderness, and the resort opened in 1980.

Beaver Creek boasts a 3400-foot vertical drop, 14 lifts including five high-speed quad chairs and a wide variety of ski terrain for all abilities. Experts will head to the double black diamonds off the Grouse Mountain Express lift or the Westfall lift with runs every bit as challenging as anything at Vail. Beaver Creek is also the first US resort to offer European-style village-to-village skiing from the main village over to Bachelor Gulch and then to the newly acquired Arrowhead Mountain Village several miles west. Can a connection to Vail be far behind? Look out Minturn!

Places to Stay & Eat

Looking for a cheap room at Beaver Creek in the winter? Don't even bother passing through the front gates unless you're prepared to drop at least a couple hundred dollars a night.

The impressive *Hyatt Regency* (☎ 970-949-1234, 800-233-1234) at the base of the mountain has rooms beginning at $360 and topping out at $650 during ski season, $175 to $315 in summer. Across the village at *Embassy Suite's Beaver Creek Lodge*, the rooms run from about $200 to $600, though you can get a double here for under $100 in summer.

At the base of the ski area in the village, *St James Hotel* (☎ 970-845-9300, 800-859-8242) has luxury condominiums with full kitchen, fireplace and all household appliances. There's also a hot tub on the premises. During ski season rates are $475 for a one-bedroom unit, $575 for two-bedrooms; hotel rooms are $250. In summer, the hotel offers backcountry Jeep touring, whitewater rafting and half- and full-day round-up horseback riding.

Even the *Comfort Inn* (☎ 970-949-5511), 0161 W Beaver Creek Blvd (exit 167 off I-70), typically a budget chain, charges $200 for rooms. Amenities include an outdoor heated pool and hot tub and Continental breakfast. They offer shuttles to the Beaver Creek Ski Area, and a shuttle to Vail stops one block east of the hotel.

For a mere $75 to $85 per person, you can dine at *Beano's Cabin* (☎ 970-949-9090) at the Larkspur lift. Guests arrive at the elegant surroundings after a 20-minute sleighride that leaves from the Centennial lift. (It's a far cry from the original log cabin built nearby in 1919 by Chicago lettuce farmer Frank 'Beano' Bienkowski.)

The best restaurant in Beaver Creek is *Mirabelle's* (☎ 970-949-7728), whose elegant French cuisine may warrant a special trip and certainly a lot of cash.

GLENWOOD SPRINGS

Glenwood Springs (population 7620; elevation 5700 feet), next to the Colorado River, has natural hot springs, a mild climate and a range of summer and winter activities. The springs and large outdoor pool are one of Colorado's most popular vacation destinations. Glenwood Springs also represents an inexpensive 'down-valley' winter alternative to Aspen ski areas and is only about 45 minutes west along I-70 from Vail and Beaver Creek, making it a good base for skiing some of Colorado's best mountains.

History
Well before the development of Yampah Hot Springs as a 'Health & Pleasure Resort'

in the 1880s, the Yampa band of Utes took advantage of the vapor caves' curative powers. The original cave, located on the south side of the river, was revealed by the Utes in 1860 to a survey party led by Captain Richard Sopris. Later, the springs appealed to miners seeking respite from the harsh high-elevation camps.

In 1887, the D&RG Railroad sealed over the original cave, leaving the development of the hot springs complex and the vapor caves on the north side of the river up to silver mining magnate Walter Devereux. After being shown the springs by Kit Carson, Devereux envisioned a mountain spa resort with the world's largest naturally heated pool. His stylish hotel and spa covering 10 acres surrounding the hot springs were opened to Colorado's leading entrepreneurs and railroad tycoons in the summer of 1893. President Theodore Roosevelt's appreciation of the natural environment during a brief stay in 1905 helped lead to the establishment of national forest reserves.

Orientation
Since 1896, Grand Ave has crossed the Colorado River and formed the main business street extending due south from the river. The resort spa and pool is north of the river reached by a highway and pedestrian/bicycle bridge. West Glenwood Springs evolved north of the river along US 6, a route now followed by I-70.

Information
Tourist Offices The anteroom visitors center is always open at the Chamber Resort Association (☎ 970-945-6589), at the corner of 11th St and Grand Ave. Helpful staff are available on weekdays 8:30 am to 5 pm, weekends 9 am to 3 pm. USFS headquarters for the White River National Forest (☎ 970-945-2521), 900 Grand Ave, has maps and information about hiking, biking and Nordic skiing. Offices for both the BLM (☎ 970-945-2341) and the Colorado DOW (☎ 970-945-7228) are in West Glenwood Springs at 50633 US 6.

COLORADO

COLORADO

WEST GLENWOOD SPRINGS

To Grand Junction

To Vail

Tunnel

Footbridge

White River National Forest

Devereux Rd

Colorado River

Transfer Trail

Horseshoe Bend

Glenwood Canyon Bike Trail

Colorado River

Bear Creek Scout Trail

White River National Forest

Linden St

W 6th St

Laurel St

Maple St

Pine St

Olive St

Williams St

Two Rivers Park

Exit 115

Red Mountain Trail

Veltus Park

see inset map

8th St

9th St

10th St

11th St

Pitkin Ave

Grand Ave

Blake Ave

Bennett Ave

Palmer Ave

Riverside Dr

Pioneer Cemetery

Colorado Mountain College

Sayre Park

19th St

20th St

23rd St

27th St

Roaring Fork River

Amtrak Station

W 7th St

School St

Pitkin Ave

Colorado Ave

Grand Ave

Cooper Ave

Blake Ave

8th St

9th St

10th St

11th St

PLACES TO STAY

2   Best Western Antlers Motel
3   Glenwood Motor Inn
4   Ramada Inn
5   Hotel Colorado
6   Hot Springs Lodge and Pool
10 Frontier Lodge
12 Hideout Campground & Cabins
15 Hotel Denver
27 Glenwood Springs Hostel
28 Adducci's Inn

PLACES TO EAT

1   The Bayou
8   19th Street Diner
14 Wild Rose Bakery
15 Brew Pub
17 Peppo, Nino, Rick's
18 Italian Underground
19 Daily Bread Bakery & Cafe

OTHER

7   Yampah Spa and Vapor Caves
9   Valley View Hospital
11 Roaring Fork Marketplace, Cajun Laundry
13 BSR Sports
16 BookTrain
20 Summit Canyon Mountaineering
21 Good Health Natural Food Market
22 Post Office
23 Sunlight Sports
24 Bank of Colorado
25 USFS White River National Forest Headquarters
26 Frontier Historical Museum
29 Chamber Resort Association Visitor Center

White River National Forest

S Grand Ave

Midland Ave

Blake Ave

To Aspen

To Ski Sunlight

County Rd 117

White River National Forest

Glenwood Springs

0   .5   1 km

0   .25   .5 miles

Threemile Creek

Money The centrally located Bank of Colorado (☎ 970-945-7422), 9th St and Grand Ave, has a 24-hour ATM. The Alpine Bank, near Glenwood Mall on US 6, offers a convenient ATM for motorists exiting I-70 in West Glenwood Springs, and there are ATMs at the 24-hour Safeway and City Market stores on Grand Ave near 19th St, on the way to Aspen.

Post The main post office is at 113 9th St; the zip code is 81601.

Bookstores For magazines and books on Colorado and the Southwest, stop by Book Train (☎ 970-945-7045), 723 Grand Ave. The gift shop in the Frontier Historical Museum (see below) also sells books. Summit Canyon Mountaineering (☎ 970-945-6994), 732 Grand Ave, has an outstanding collection of outdoor guides and rock-climbing titles in the lower level.

Medical Services Valley View Hospital (☎ 970-945-6535) offers 24-hour emergency care at 1906 Blake Ave, one block east of Grand Ave (Hwy 82) at 20th St.

Laundry Cajun Laundry (☎ 970-945-2351), 3116 Blake Ave in the Roaring Fork Marketplace, has drop-off service at $1/lb. Highlander Laundry (☎ 970-945-0579), 1605 Grand Ave (next to True Value Hardware), has coin machines as well as drop-off service for 90¢/lb ($7 minimum).

Frontier Historical Museum

For the $3 admission you can learn about the history of the town, from coal mining to Doc Holliday to an exhibit on the Native American Utes who once inhabited the area. Period exhibits include furnished rooms – and the ubiquitous porcelain bedpan – in the 1905 house now occupied by the Frontier Historical Museum (☎ 970-945-4448) at 1001 Colorado Ave. Hours are 11 am to 4 pm in summer, 1 to 4 pm in winter; closed Sundays.

Spas

At 709 E 6th St, **Yampah Spa and Vapor Caves** (☎ 970-945-0667) features steam baths and spa treatments including massages, facials and herbal wraps. Admission to the caves costs $6.75, and treatments start at $26 for a back massage. It's open daily 9 am to 9 pm.

The **Hot Springs Lodge and Pool** (see below) includes a therapy pool and massages starting at $35 for half an hour.

Swimming

The **Hot Springs Lodge and Pool** (☎ 970-945-7131), at 401 N River St, is the big tourist draw. Salty water from Iron Mountain's limestone caverns feeds the large 400-by-100-foot open-air pool, created in 1888 and maintained at 90°F.

The Glenwood Springs Fires

Foresters contend that encroaching suburban development has made it even harder to fight forest fires. Suppressing naturally occurring fires interrupts nature's cycle, allowing potential fuel to accumulate and resulting in major conflagrations in places where fires once burned off excess undergrowth with little threat to nature or property.

In 1994, a hot and dry summer prompted Governor Roy Romer to remark 'It's a tinderbox out there' when he banned open fires and fireworks just prior to 4th of July celebrations. At the time of his statement, numerous forest fires were already out of control in Colorado. A performer at an open-air concert in nearby Aspen on July 4, commented on the beautiful red sunset – unaware that it was actually caused by smoke from flames northwest of Glenwood Springs.

On the afternoon of July 6, 14 firefighters died when the blaze suddenly exploded as it was fanned by erratic winds. The nation's worst firefighting tragedy saddened the whole country, but was especially profound for residents of Glenwood Springs, who mourned the loss as if it had been their own families. ■

There's also a smaller therapeutic pool, a children's pool and water slide. Admission is $7.25/4.75 adults/children. Four trips on the water slide cost $3. Admission to the athletic club facilities is $13. It's open daily 7:30 am (9 am in winter) to 10 pm.

Road & Mountain Biking

Narrow Glenwood Canyon once represented an obstacle for bicycles, but now the popular, paved **Glenwood Canyon Trail** follows the Colorado River upstream below the cantilevered I-70 and on the old highway around Horseshoe Bend for 16.2 miles between the Yampah Vapor Caves and Dotsero. There are four modern rest areas along the way with toilets, water and information about the area's history, flora and fauna.

Other local rides, including the 24-mile **Transfer Trail** and the short but serious **Bear Creek/Scout Trail**, are shown on the free topographic 'Glenwood Springs Hiking & Mountain Bicycle Trail Map' from the Chamber Resort Association and USFS headquarters. Bike rentals cost $10 to $20 for a full day, including helmet, at Canyon Bikes (☎ 970-945-8904) in the Hotel Colorado at 319 6th St. For $22 ($10 if you have your own bike), Canyon Bikes will shuttle you and a bike to the end of the Canyon Trail for the long downstream ride through beautiful Glenwood Canyon. Biking and rafting packages are also available.

Both BSR Sports (☎ 970-945-7317), on the river at 210 7th St, and Sunlight Sports (☎ 970-945-9425), 309 9th St at Cooper, rent high-quality front-suspension mountain bikes by the hour ($5), half-day ($12), or full-day ($16).

White-Water Rafting

Glenwood Canyon offers Class III-IV whitewater below the Shoshone Dam 7½ miles east of town. Families with young children can take shorter float trips at the Grizzly Creek turnoff from I-70, or go during low flow. Two Rivers Park, north of the confluence of the Colorado and Roaring Fork Rivers, is the take-out point.

For guided tours, Rock Gardens Rafting (☎ 970-945-6737), east of town on I-70

exit 119 at 1308 Garfield County Rd 129, offers free hot showers after the trip. Also try Blue Sky Adventures (☎ 970-945-6605), 319 6th St (on the ground floor of the Hotel Colorado), or White-Water Rafting (☎ 970-945-8477), west of town at I-70 exit 114. Half-day trips typically cost $32.

Hiking

The relatively low elevations around Glenwood Springs means that there are no Alpine trails above treeline. Numerous trails head north from the Glenwood Canyon Trail, including the 1.2-mile-long **Hanging Lake Trail** which leads to a breathtaking waterfall-fed pond perched in a rock bowl on the canyon wall. It's a strenuous 1½- to 3-hour roundtrip with a 1020-foot elevation gain – but well worth the work! Keep a sharp lookout for bighorn sheep in Glenwood Canyon. Take the Hanging Lake exit 8 miles east of town on I-70, or make a morning or afternoon of it and bike the Canyon Trail 10½ miles to the **Hanging Lake Trailhead**.

A short half-mile hike to the Pioneer Cemetery begins at the corner of 12th and Bennett Sts where **John Henry 'Doc' Holliday** is reportedly buried. At the age of 20, native Georgian Holliday graduated from Baltimore Dental School in 1872, but gained fame as a gambler and gunfighter in the Southwest who participated in the gunfight at the OK Corral with Wyatt Earp and his brothers. In 1887 Holliday died of tuberculosis in Glenwood Springs at the age of 35. A mudslide mixed up the graves, so it's pretty unlikely that Doc is actually buried under the tombstone bearing his name.

For hiking, rock climbing and kayak gear, topographic maps and outdoor books and guides, head for Summit Canyon Mountaineering (☎ 970-945-6994), at 1001 Grand Ave. As with the biking map, the free *Glenwood Springs Trails Guide* is a great resource for hikes which are rated easy, moderate or difficult.

Fishing

Productive Gold Medal water on the Roaring Fork River has large trout and trophy mountain whitefish, averaging two to three pounds, for 12 miles between the Crystal River below Carbondale and the Colorado River. Secluded **Veltus Park**, near W 8th and 9th Sts, is a pleasant picnic area that provides fishing access and a pier on the west side of the river. Also consider contacting a rafting company to float down the river. Drop by Roaring Fork Anglers (☎ 970-945-0180), 2022 Grand Ave, for gear and advice.

Skiing & Snowboarding

Serious skiers head 'up-valley' to Aspen, Aspen Highlands and Snowmass, or east on I-70 to Vail. But **Sunlight Mountain Resort** (☎ 970-945-7491, 800-445-7931), 12 miles south of Glenwood Springs on Garfield County Rd 117, survives by offering good deals to families and intermediate skiers. Sunlight consists of 440 acres of skiable terrain served by four lifts and a 2000-foot vertical drop. Adult lift passes cost $28 – among the least expensive in the state. The cross-country ski area features 18 miles of groomed track and snow-skating trails, plus snowshoeing and ice-skating areas. Packages to ski, swim and stay in Glenwood Springs are offered through Ski Sunlight and start at $50 on weekends; there's free transportation to the hill from the corner of 11th & Grand Sts. Equipment and rentals are available at the mountain or at Sunlight Ski Shop (☎ 970-945-9425), 309 9th St in town. Standard rentals are $14 a day, $20 for high-performance equipment. For snowboard rentals BSR Sports (see Road & Mountain Biking above) has the best rates at $24 per day.

Special Events

Since 1898, residents of Glenwood Springs have celebrated **Strawberry Days** in mid-June, which features artisans, entertainment, a carnival, bike and track events, a parade and free strawberries and ice cream. For two weeks in late June and early July, **Glenwood Springs Dance Festival** features performances, films and open rehearsals. Contact the Glenwood Center for the Arts (☎ 970-945-2414) for specific information. In the summer, free jazz concerts are held every Wednesday night in Two Rivers Park.

Places to Stay

Camping On the way to Ski Sunlight at 1293 Garfield County Rd 117, *The Hideout Campground & Cabins* (☎ 970-945-5621) has shaded tent sites near Threemile Creek for $17, showers included. RV sites are $19 with full hookups, and fully furnished cabins with kitchens are $50 to $135.

Hostels The *Glenwood Springs Hostel* (☎ 970-945-8545), 1021 Grand Ave, has over 40 beds and five private rooms. Discount passes to Ski Sunlight ($20 midweek), the Yampah Vapor Caves and buses to Aspen are also available. Mountain bike rentals are offered to guests for $12 and the hostel provides all-day kayaking trips for just $30. During lulls in the activity, you might check out the owner's collection of over 3000 record albums (heavy on the 1960s). Dorm beds in the house cost $12; $14 in the new section. Private rooms with shared bath run $19 to $26. The hostel is closed between 10 am and 4 pm.

B&Bs *Adducci's Inn* (☎ 970-945-9341), 1023 Grand Ave, is an exceptional value with rates beginning at $28 for rooms with shared bath and up to $75 for the best rooms with private baths; all rates include full breakfast.

On the way to Sunlight Mountain Resort, the *Four Mile Creek Bed & Breakfast* (☎ 970-945-4004), 6471 Country Rd 17, offers a nice escape to the countryside. Housed in a remodeled farmhouse and log cabin next to a pond and stream, this elegant Western B&B has two rooms in the house with shared bath for $85 double, and a cabin for $110 for two, $10 for each additional person (up to four).

Motels There are about 20 motels and hotels in the Glenwood area and those closest to the city center fill up quickly during the summer season, so make reservations well in advance.

COLORADO

South of town, the *Frontier Lodge* (☎ 970-945-5496), 2834 Glen Avenue at Grand, is a great value with doubles starting at $46. Just west of the bridge on the north side of the river in Glenwood Springs, the *Best Western Antlers Motel* (☎ 970-945-8535), 171 West 6th Street, is the nicest motel in town and includes a pool and hot tub. It's also a bit more expensive: high-season rates start at $80, off-season rates drop to $55. Across the street and a bit east, the *Ramada Inn* (☎ 970-945-2500, 800-228-2828), 124 W 6th St, is only a short walk to the resort spa and pool. Doubles start at $75 in summer and go for as little as $35 in the off-season. Directly across from the Ramada, the *Glenwood Motor Inn* (☎ 800-543-5906), 141 West 6th Street, is clean, comfortable and has the best rates close to the center of town, starting at $50 in summer.

If you find yourself without a room in June or July your best bet may be one of the six motels in West Glenwood, 1 to 2 miles from town on US 6. Try *Red Mountain Inn* (☎ 970-945-6353, 800-748-2565), 1.4 miles west of town at 51637 US 6. It features large, modern rooms, a pool and hot tub for about $50/double summer/winter, $35 in the off-season. Just down the road, the *Budget Host* (☎ 970-945-5682), 51429 US 6, offers similar amenities and rates.

Hotels Opposite the railroad depot, at 402 7th St, the 1906 *Hotel Denver* (☎ 970-945-6565, 800-826-8820) is a comfortable and completely renovated hotel in the middle of town. Peak weekend rates for their smaller 'value rooms' start at $65/doubles. A pedestrian bridge crosses the river to the pool.

If you don't mind spending a bit more, the *Hotel Colorado* (☎ 970-945-6511, 800-544-3998), 526 Pine St, is the place to stay. Modeled after the Villa de Medici in Italy, this imposing sandstone resort hotel has been operating for over 100 years and has a rich history that includes presidential guests, gangsters and perhaps a ghost or two! In 1905 President Teddy Roosevelt reportedly returned one day from a bear hunt empty-handed and the hotel maids stitched together a small bear out of scraps of cloth – thus the inception of the famous 'Teddy Bear.' Antique furnishings decorate rooms that range from one double bed to elaborate suites, and the rates remain the same year-round – good value for a place of this caliber, with doubles starting at $80. Make reservations for summer holidays about two months in advance.

The *Hot Springs Lodge and Pool* (☎ 970-945-6571), next door at 415 East 6th, has nice modern rooms starting at $81/doubles in summer. Guests get a slight discount on pool or spa services.

Places to Eat

Vegetarians can go to *Good Health Natural Food Market*, south of the train station at 730 Cooper, for deli items, organic produce, bulk herbs and a complete line of natural foods. Unless you arrive soon after it opens at 7 am, there's usually a crowd waiting for breakfast at the *Daily Bread Bakery & Cafe* (☎ 970-945-6253), 729 Grand Ave. You can also try the *Wild Rose Bakery* (☎ 970-928-8973), across from the train depot at 310 7th St. It's open 7 am to 5 pm and serves delicious muffins, danishes, scones and fresh bread. For bacon, eggs, pancakes and such, try *Rosi's* (☎ 970-928-9186), in the Glenwood Motor Inn at 141 W 6th.

Plan to have lunch in the formal *Devereux Room* at the Hotel Colorado (☎ 970-945-6511). Like the hotel itself, the restaurant offers good value with sandwiches, burgers, pasta and a delicious tortilla soup, each for under $7. The dinner menu is more elaborate and includes fettuccine with seafood and pesto for $18. Meals are served in the lobby next to the massive fireplace during the winter.

The *Brew Pub* (☎ 970-945-1276), at 402 7th, next to the Hotel Denver, has delicious sandwiches and salads as well as a five handcrafted beers on tap. Try Vapor Cave IPA, a premium dry-hopped pale ale – perfect after a day of biking or skiing. Kids can try the homemade root beer. For soda-fountain counter service, check out the *19th Street Diner* (☎ 970-945-9133), 1908 Grand Ave. It serves breakfast all day and traditional blue-plate specials along with contemporary favorites like fajitas.

For bargain carbo-loading you can't beat *Italian Underground* (☎ 970-945-6422), 715 Grand Ave, offering heaping pasta dinners for under $9. *Peppo Nino* (☎ 970-945-9059), 702 Grand Ave, has lasagna or spaghetti dinners for $9 plus more expensive menu items.

Rick's (☎ 970-945-4771), upstairs next to the bridge at 710 Grand, is the spot for an elegant meal, with dishes like shrimp sauté Provençal, portobello and eggplant parmigiani or steak Diane sauté. Entrees are between $8 and $18 and there is a good wine list. Locals head to West Glenwood and the *Fireside Inn* (☎ 970-945-6613), 51701 US 6, for a night out. Their specialties are prime rib, steaks and ribs for $12 to $20; a daily buffet lunch is $6.50.

Adducci's Inn (☎ 970-945-9341), 1023 Grand Ave, serves dishes like ruby trout with capers, shrimp scampi and chicken au madre in its cozy dining room and has a nice selection of French and California wines. For a zanier atmosphere that befits Cajun food, check out the S&M ('swamp and moo') special at *The Bayou* (☎ 970-945-1047), 52103 US 6 in West Glenwood Springs. You can get spicy blackened chicken or even blackened tofu for under $8.

Entertainment

Springs Sports Bar & Grill (☎ 970-945-2388), 722 Grand, has DJ-led hip-hop dancing on the weekends and Country & Western dancing one night a week. *Doc Holliday's* (☎ 970-945-8568), 724 Grand, is a favorite watering hole. For good country music, check out the *Buffalo Valley Inn* (☎ 970-945-6967), 3637 Hwy 82. Free 'Summer of Jazz' concerts are held 6:30 pm each Wednesday at Two Rivers Park.

Getting There & Away

DIA Shuttle Aspen Limo (☎ 970-925-1234, 800-222-2112), at the Glenwood Amtrak Depot, offers service to Denver International Airport for $59 one-way; rates are higher during ski season. Bikes can be loaded in the roof rack for no extra charge.

Bus Greyhound buses between Grand Junction and Denver stop at the Ramada Inn, 124 W 6th St, three times daily in each direction.

Train Amtrak's *California Zephyr* stops daily at the Amtrak Station (☎ 970-945-9563) on South River St. Eastbound trains are scheduled to depart at 1:17 pm and westbound trains leave at 3:32 pm, but expect delays with train travel through the mountains.

Car Glenwood Springs is 159 miles west of Denver and 90 miles east of Grand Junction along I-70.

Getting Around

To/From the Airport Aspen Limo (☎ 970-925-1234, 800-222-2112) serves Aspen airport for $20; higher rates apply during ski season.

Bus Glenwood Trolley buses operate on the half-hour between the W Glenwood Mall and the Roaring Forks Marketplace at the south end of town. Fares cost 50¢. During ski season, free buses serve Ski Sunlight from a stop at 11th St & Grand Ave. Roaring Forks Transit Authority (☎ 970-925-8454) offers bus connections with Aspen from the Glenwood Mall: one-way trips cost $6, or buy a $10 punch ticket good for $20 worth of RFTA rides. Ten up-valley buses operate between 6:05 am and 10:05 pm. Down-valley buses return from Aspen between 7:15 am and 10:15 pm. Call ahead for schedule and stop changes.

Car Enterprise Rent-a-Car (☎ 970-945-8360), at 124 W 6th, is the only major car rental agency in town.

ASPEN

Hedonism reigns in Aspen – the home to 5245 people and host to some of the wealthiest skiers in the world. Instead of mountain-bike mania, you're more likely to see middle-aged men on rented Harley 'hogs,' their thinning hair flying in the breeze, and leather-clad 'mamas' hanging on tight – for

COLORADO

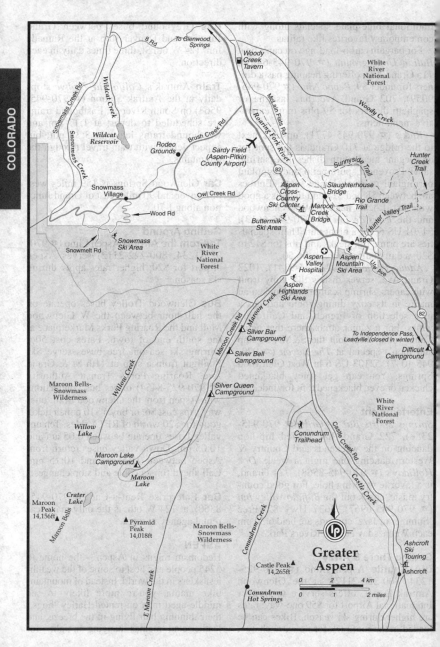

To Glenwood Springs

8 Rd

Woody Creek Tavern

White River National Forest

Woody Creek

Wildcat Creek Rd

Snowmass Creek Rd

Wildcat Reservoir

Rodeo Grounds

Brush Creek Rd

Sardy Field (Aspen-Pitkin County Airport)

McLain Flats Rd

Roaring Fork River

Snowmass Creek

82

Snowmass Village

Owl Creek Rd

Wood Rd

Aspen Cross-Country Ski Center

Sunnyside Trail

Slaughterhouse Bridge

Rio Grande Trail

Maroon Creek Bridge

Hunter Creek Trail

Hunter Valley Trail

Snowmelt Rd

Snowmass Ski Area

Buttermilk Ski Area

Aspen

White River National Forest

Aspen Valley Hospital

Aspen Mountain Ski Area

Ute Ave

82

Maroon Creek Rd

Aspen Highlands Ski Area

Maroon Creek

Willow Creek

Silver Bar Campground

Silver Bell Campground

To Independence Pass, Leadville (closed in winter)

Difficult Campground

Silver Queen Campground

Maroon Bells-Snowmass Wilderness

White River National Forest

Willow Lake

Conundrum Trailhead

Castle Creek Rd

Maroon Lake Campground

Conundrum Creek

Castle Creek

Maroon Lake

Maroon Peak 14,156ft

Crater Lake

Maroon Bells

Pyramid Peak 14,018ft

Maroon Bells-Snowmass Wilderness

Ashcroft Ski Touring

Castle Peak 14,265ft

Greater Aspen

Ashcroft

0   2   4 km
0   1   2 miles

Conundrum Hot Springs

E Maroon Creek

many, Aspen represents a fantasy getaway. For mere mortals not encumbered with payments on one of the private jets parked at Sardy Field, watching the parade of personalities strutting about in garish attire is bit like peeking at a royal court.

To adjust to the flow of Aspen life, relax and take a seat on one of the reclining benches in front of the Paradise Bakery. Whether it's the end of a winter day of skiing or a midsummer evening, an entertaining spectacle is bound to pass by. Aspen police cruise by in Saabs, but one can only wonder if they'd be driving red Cadillac convertibles if 'gonzo journalist' (and Aspen resident) Hunter S Thompson had succeeded in his 1970 campaign to become the local sheriff.

One consequence of Aspen's phenomenal success in attracting the wealthiest individuals on the planet is that property values have skyrocketed and working-class housing is impossible to find. Cooks, maids and other workers commute ridiculous distances, and families live in tents at trailer parks in Carbondale. (So remember to leave tips.) Aspen's stock of Victorian houses was decimated to make room for the monster mansions that sit empty most of the year and the multiple shops downtown. The city council continually grapples with ordinances to limit the size of the enormous vacation castles in an effort to save historic Aspen.

Since 1949, when Walter and Elizabeth Paepcke organized an international Goethe Bicentennial celebration that attracted luminaries like Albert Schweitzer, Aspen's summer festivals have been copied by other resorts. Highbrow cultural activities continue to dominate Aspen's summer schedule, which nurtures artists, musicians, chefs, directors and great minds. Sponsoring organizations are the Institute of Humanistic Studies, which was founded by the Paepckes, the Aspen Center for Physics (late Nobel Laureate and wildcard Richard Feynmann enjoyed Aspen almost as much as Las Vegas), the Rocky Mountain Institute, founded by John Denver, and the Anderson Ranch Arts Center.

Ted Conover looks at the underbelly of Aspen from the perspective of a cab driver and newspaper reporter in *Whiteout: Lost in Aspen*. His raunchy lyrics to John Denver's 'Country Road' will get you thrown out of most karaoke bars!

History

Aspen was called Ute City until an Eastern capitalist named B Clark Wheeler arrived from Leadville on skis in the early months of 1880 to incorporate the town. Although the nearby Smuggler Mountain and Ajax Mountain mines would prove to be steady silver producers, Aspen developed as a supply center for the gold camp at Independence and the silver camp at Ashcroft. As a way-station for the upper camps, Aspen's beauty was not fouled by mine tailings.

When Jerome Wheeler (no relation to B Clark) arrived by stage in 1883, Aspen was a struggling camp. His infusion of capital built a smelter and employed a trained metallurgist, Walter B Devereux. Arrival of the D&RG Railroad in 1887 encouraged mine owners to increase production. By 1891, the Aspen Mining District, led by the Molly Gibson Mine, surpassed Leadville as the largest silver mining district in the state. Aspen was briefly the third largest city in the state after Denver and Leadville. During this euphoric period, Wheeler built the Jerome Hotel and the Wheeler Opera House; both opened in 1889.

Plummeting silver prices in 1893 interrupted the bonanza and Aspen's population dwindled from an estimated 12,000 to 700 by 1930. City lots were available for as little as $5 during the '30s.

Skiing was first proposed by Californian investors at Ashcroft in 1936, but the project floundered. In 1937, Swiss ski expert Andre Roch developed a 'boat tow' on Ajax Mountain. Roch Run was the site of the National Alpine races in 1941. Among the early visitors was Elizabeth Paepcke, who introduced her husband Walter Paepcke to Aspen. He and 10th Mountain Division veteran Friedl Pfeifer started the Ajax Mountain chairlift in 1946.

COLORADO

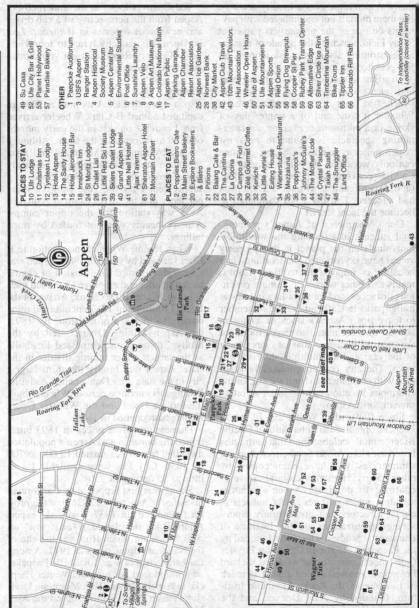

COLORADO

PLACES TO STAY
10 Ulr Lodge
11 Christmas Inn
12 Tyrolean Lodge
13 Hotel Aspen
14 The Sardy House
15 Hotel Jerome/J Bar
18 Innsbruck Inn
26 St Moritz Lodge
38 Little Red Ski Haus
39 Skiers Chalet Lodge
40 Grand Aspen Hotel
41 Little Nell Hotel/
    Ajax Tavern
61 Sheraton Aspen Hotel
62 Mountain Chalet

PLACES TO EAT
2   Poppies Bistro Cafe
19 Main Street Bakery
20 Explore Booksellers
    & Bistro
21 Piñons
23 Baang Cafe & Bar
25 The Cantina
27 La Cocina
30 Campo di Fiori
30 Zélé Gourmet Coffee
32 Kenichi
33 Little Annie's
    Eating House
34 Wienerstube Restaurant
35 Mezzaluna
36 Poppycock's
37 Johnny McGuire's
45 The Mother Lode
44 Crystal Palace
47 Takah Sushi
48 The Smuggler
    Land Office

49 Su Casa
52 Ute City Bar & Grill
53 Planet Hollywood
57 Paradise Bakery

OTHER
1   Paepcke Auditorium
3   USFS Aspen
    Ranger Station
4   Aspen Historical
    Society Museum
5   Aspen Center for
    Environmental Studies
6   Post Office
7   Sunshine Laundry
8   Aspen Velo
9   Aspen Art Museum
16 Colorado National Bank
17 Aspen Public
    Parking Garage,
    Aspen Chamber
    Resort Association
25 Aspen Ice Garden
28 Norwest Bank
38 City Market
42 Aspen Club Travel
43 10th Mountain Division
    Hut Association
46 Wheeler Opera Hous
50 Hub of Aspen
51 Ute Mountaineers
54 Aspen Sports
55 Red Onion
56 Flying Dog Brewpub
58 Cooper St Pier
59 Rubey Park Transit Center
60 Alternative Edge
63 Silver Circle Ice Rink
64 Timberline Mountain
    Bike Tours
65 Tippler Inn
66 Colorado Riff Raft

Orientation

Hwy 82 jogs through town as Main St, intersecting Garmisch St, which divides east-west street addresses. If entering town from down-valley, turn left (north) at Mill St to the Aspen Public Parking Garage (☎ 970-920-5430), 427 Rio Grande Place, where you will also find the visitors center. Driving south on Mill St from the garage will take you past the Hotel Jerome, at the corner of Main St, to the Wheeler Opera House (a secondary visitors center) on Hyman Ave. A pedestrian mall begins on Mill St south of Hyman Ave.

Information

Tourist Offices For seasonal guides, maps and the 'Official Guide to Aspen,' be sure to stop at the Aspen Chamber Resort Association (☎ 970-925-9000, 800-262-7736), housed on the bottom floor of the large Aspen Public Parking Garage on Rio Grande Place near N Mill St. It's open weekdays 8 am 5 pm. On weekends, visitor information is available at the Wheeler Opera House, 320 E Hyman Ave, open 9 am to 5 pm daily.

The White River National Forest's Aspen Ranger Station (☎ 970-925-3445), 806 W Hallam, offers topo maps and information on over 200 miles of trails in the forest and three wilderness areas surrounding Aspen: Hunter Fryingpan, Maroon Bells-Snowmass and Collegiate Peaks. It's open 8 am to 5 pm daily.

The Aspen-Snowmass Interactive website (www.aspenonline.com) has over 3500 pages of information on lodging (including reservations), events, restaurants, museums, outdoor activitities and news. It's a comprehensive and efficient tool for anyone planning a trip to the area.

Money The number of large ATM transactions in Aspen have been known to wipe out the robotic cash supply on long holiday weekends. The Alpine Bank (☎ 970-920-4800), 600 E Hopkins Ave, is open on Saturday and operates an ATM at the base of the Silver Queen Gondola. Also try Colorado National Bank (☎ 970-925-1450), 420 E Main St, or Norwest Bank of Aspen (☎ 970-925-2500), 119 S Mill St.

Post & Communications The main post office is at 235 Puppy Smith St; zip code 81612. Another post office is in Snowmass Village at 1106 Kearns Rd. City Market (☎ 970-925-2590; fax 970-920-2193), 711 E Cooper Ave, offers Western Union and fax services.

Travel Agencies Aspen Club Travel (☎ 970-920-4000), 730 E Durant Ave, is a full-service travel agency that also assists American Express members.

Bookstores Explore Booksellers & Bistro (☎ 970-925-5336), 221 E Main St, is the largest and most comprehensive bookstore in Aspen. Each high-ceiling room in the Victorian house is lined with bookcases, and the store is open daily 10 am to midnight. Aspen Bookstore (☎ 970-925-7427), 665 Durant Ave at the Little Nell Hotel, has a good selection of regional titles.

Publications The *Aspen Daily News'* motto 'If you don't want it printed, don't let it happen' reflects its activist approach to issues confronting the town. The paper includes a weekly Spanish-language insert for the sizable population of Mexican workers who live in Roaring Fork Valley.

Medical Services Aspen Valley Hospital (☎ 970-925-1120) is at 401 Castle Creek Rd near Aspen Highlands, southwest of town.

Laundry & Showers Sunshine Laundry (☎ 970-925-5378), 465 Puppy Smith St, has drop-off service. Showers are $2 at the James E Moore Pool (☎ 970-920-5145), 1 mile south of Hwy 82 at 895 Maroon Creek Rd. It's open weekdays from 8 am to 7:30 pm and 10 am to 6 pm weekends during summer.

Aspen Historical Society Museum

Once the home of silver baron Jerome Wheeler, the faithfully restored Wheeler-

Stallard House, built in 1888, now houses the Aspen Historical Society Museum (☎ 970-925-3721), 620 W Bleeker St. Tours through the three-story home are offered in summer, plus changing exhibits and archives in the Carriage House are open daily 9 am to 5 pm. Admission is $3.

Aspen Center for Environmental Studies

The Aspen Center for Environmental Studies (☎ 970-925-5756) is a 25-acre wildlife sanctuary beside the Roaring Fork River at 100 S Puppy Smith St. Take a self-guided tour of the preserve surrounding Hallam Lake. Anglers will want to study the native cutthroat trout and its food supply in an indoor trout stream. During summer months, the center also conducts guided natural history tours at the top of Aspen Mountain, at Maroon Bells and in Snowmass, as well as Naturalist Field School courses. It's open from 9 am to 5 pm Monday to Saturday. A $2 donation is requested.

Wheeler Opera House

For a brief period after opening in 1889, the 500-seat Wheeler Opera House attracted top talent on the 'Silver Circuit.' This sandstone building (☎ 970-920-7148) at 320 E Hyman Ave reopened after a renovation in 1984. Except during rehearsal for Aspen Music Festival performances, it's open daily for tours from 9 am to 5 pm that cost $2.

Aspen Art Museum

From the Art Park, pedestrians cross a 1911 trestle bridge over the Roaring Fork River to the Aspen Art Museum (☎ 970-925-8050), 590 N Mill St near Red Mountain Rd. Rotating exhibits feature nationally recognized artists. The museum is open 10 am to 6 pm Tuesday to Saturday, noon to 6 pm Sunday. Admission is $3/2 adults/students and seniors.

Maroon Bells

One the most photographed spots in the state overlooks Maroon Lake toward the

Hunter S Thompson – Would you trust this man with your law and order?

pair of 14ers known as the Maroon Bells. Part of the Elk Mountain Range, the Maroon Bells are unique among Colorado's major peaks for their sedimentary composition, giving them their distinctive color, tilted layers and sharp angular forms chiseled by glacial action. To the east, Pyramid Peak is a third 14er in the area. The peaks are part of the Maroon Bells-Snowmass Wilderness Area.

Maroon Creek Rd, a 'cherrystem' into the wilderness, is closed between 8:30 am and 5 pm to cars not using the campgrounds. A guided bus tour is the best way to get to Maroon Lake trailheads. Bicycling the 11-mile Maroon Creek Rd is another option – it climbs 1700 feet. Buses leave Aspen's Rubey Park Transit Center every half-hour from 9 am to 4:30 pm, returning between 9:30 am and 5 pm. Roundtrip fare is $4/2 adults/seniors and children (six to 16).

In summer, the Aspen Center for Environmental Studies offers hourly natural history tours from 10 am to 2 pm. The center's telescope may also help you spot bighorn sheep, elk or eagles on the cliffs above the lake. Inquire at the Maroon Bells bus stop information desk.

Ashcroft

For a scenic excursion, especially during fall, visit the historic mining town of Ashcroft, which was the primary community in the region prior to Aspen's settlement. Check with the Aspen Center for Environmental Studies (☎ 970-925-5756) about guided nature hikes. An admission fee of $2/1 adults/children is charged by the Aspen Historical Society (☎ 970-925-3721), which also offers occasional historical walking tours of the town site. To get there, travel west of town a half-mile on Hwy 82 and go left at the Maroon Creek/Castle Creek turnoff; another sharp left past the hospital puts you on paved Castle Creek Rd. Ashcroft is 11 miles away.

Gondola Rides

The Silver Queen Gondola (☎ 970-925-1220) starts south of Durant St near Hunter St and runs to the top of Ajax Mountain daily 9:30 am to 4 pm during summer and costs $15/12/6 adults/teens (13 to 19)/children (seven to 12). Kids under six and seniors over 70 ride free. There's also a week-long adult pass for $28. At the top, naturalists from the Aspen Center for Environmental Studies lead free guided summer nature walks, leaving the Sundeck restaurant area daily on the hour from 10 am to 2 pm. Two-hour winter snowshoe tours led by a naturalist leave the Sundeck at 10 am and 1 pm and cost $27 if you already have a lift ticket, $35 without a pass. In addition, free classical concerts are offered by the Aspen Music Festival & School at 1 pm most Saturdays.

Skiing

Four ski areas operated by the Aspen Skiing Company dominate daytime activity during winter: Snowmass, 12 miles northwest of Aspen on Hwy 82 (not to be confused with the small town of Snowmass); Buttermilk Mountain, 2 miles west of Aspen; the recently acquired Aspen Highlands, which is about 2 miles southwest of

town; and Aspen (Ajax) Mountain, which overlooks the town. Aspen Mountain is one of the only remaining major ski areas that does not allow snowboards; however, there's plenty of 'shredding' terrain for boarders at Snowmass, Buttermilk and the Highlands.

Lift tickets can be used on all four mountains and cost $59 for adults (28 to 69), $39 for ages 13 to 27 (a great deal), and $35 for children (seven to 12). All others ski free. All the areas are managed by one company, so its numbers (☎ 970-925-1220, 800-525-6200) will connect you with any of the mountains for lift ticket information, accommodations or company run rental shops. Lift tickets are significantly discounted before December 1.

Aspen Mountain One gaze upward will give anyone in town a glimpse of the steep, twisting runs on Aspen Mountain. It's locally known as 'Ajax' after an old mine operation nearby. Andre Roch cut the first run here in 1937, and the mountain quickly developed a reputation among expert skiers. Overall, this is an athlete's mountain, offering over 3000 feet of steep vertical drop from the 11,212-foot summit; beginning level skiers will not find a way down from the top. Most of the expert terrain can be accessed by the base-to-summit Silver Queen gondola that reaches the top in just 14 minutes. Favorite double-black-diamond expert runs include Face of Bell, The Glades, Silver Queen and Zaugg Dump. Aspen has seven other lifts, including one high-speed quad and the country's first high-speed double chair (up Ruthie's Run) – a famous 'intermediate' bump run that would be considered expert terrain at most other resorts.

A free 1½-hour tour of the mountain's 675 acres of challenging trails assembles daily at 10 am and 1:30 pm at the Ski School area at the base of the gondola. One-third of the trails are left ungroomed, offering some great bump runs and glade skiing. The breathtaking America's Downhill World Cup ski race starts at the top of Ruthie's Run and finishes at the bottom of the mountain. Timed NASTAR runs are available on Rip's Run and snowcats provide access to the backside of the mountain on powder days. Contact Aspen Mountain for details.

For ski conditions, call ☎ 970-925-1220. The mountain is open Thanksgiving to mid-April. During the first week of the season, Aspen Mountain hosts **24 Hours of Aspen**, an endurance Alpine skiing marathon.

The Ski School (☎ 970-925-1227) in the gondola building can help adults and children progress to the next level. Chairlifts operate from 9 am to 3:30 pm, except Lift 6, which closes at 3:45 pm. Small group lessons start at $89 for a half-day.

Aspen Highlands Many mourned Aspen Skiing Company's acquisition of scenic Aspen Highlands (☎ 970-925-5300), about 2 miles southwest of Aspen on Hwy 82 on Maroon Creek Rd. Though lift ticket prices have risen to same $59, as at Aspen, Snowmass and Buttermilk, the company has added many long-needed improvements to the mountain. With some of the best extreme skiing found anywhere, breathtaking views from 11,675-foot Loge Peak and the longest vertical drop in Colorado (3800 feet), the 552-acre Highlands naturally developed a strong and devoted following since its opening in 1957.

The Highlands offers challenging terrain for skiers of all abilities on its 80 trails, divided among 20% beginner, 33% intermediate, 17% most difficult and 30% expert only. However, beginners are better off staying at Buttermilk or Snowmass. Reaching the Loge Peak summit used to be a tedious hour-long four-lift ordeal, but now two high-speed quad chairs make the 3635-foot vertical rise trip in about 20 minutes. From the top, you can cruise various intermediate runs all the way down to the bottom. Experts can stay on the Loge Peak lift and ski the extremely challenging and bumped-out Steeplechase until their knees cry 'uncle.' Beginners, however, should not venture above the midway Merry-Go-Round restaurant.

Ski rentals at the mountain run $16 for the basic package, $25 for the performance package and $30 for demos. Snowboard rental runs $25. Discounts kick in when renting for three or more days, and group rates are available. Cross-country ski packages are available for $15.

The mountain is open 9 am to 4 pm daily early December to April 5, and is about 1 mile west of Aspen at 1600 Maroon Creek Rd. Free shuttles to Aspen operate every half-hour 7 to 1:45 am.

Snowmass In 1967, the Aspen Skiing Corporation (now the Aspen Skiing Company) opened Snowmass Village, 12 miles northwest of Aspen on Hwy 82 and down Brush Creek Rd, with five lifts to predominantly intermediate terrain and a village of lodges and condominiums. The Snowmass ski area (☎ 970-923-1220) has since expanded to cover 4 sq miles over several ridgetop peaks served by 18 lifts – seven high-speed quads, two triple and six double chairs and three surface lifts. Eight of the lifts are over a mile in length and the longest run is 4.16 miles. Snowmass recently opened the Cirque surface lift which, in addition to opening up some great extreme skiing, gives the mountain the highest lift-served vertical drop in the country at 4406 feet.

From east to west the lift summits include Elk Camp (11,325 feet), High Alpine (11,775 feet), The Cirque (12,510 feet) Big Burn (11,835 feet) and Sam's Knob (10,630 feet). Elk Camp is exclusively intermediate, and High Alpine features advanced terrain on the Hanging Valley Wall and Glades. Big Burn and Sam's Knob offer a mix of intermediate and advanced trails. The Cirque is mostly expert terrain.

Snowmass also offers a snowboard park featuring a 545-foot-long halfpipe and hosts the American Pro Snowboard series in January. Course offerings from the Snowmass Ski School cater to all abilities and include mogul, powder and style clinics as well as exclusively women's clinics and snowboarding.

Rental equipment is available at Snowmass Sports (☎ 970-923-3567) in the Village Mall. Ski packages run $14 for basic equipment, $18 for performance skis, $25 for demos. If the shop looks busy, check out the multitude of others at the mall.

A free shuttle connects Snowmass with other Aspen ski areas; it picks up and drops off at 15-minute intervals from 8 am to 4 pm at the Snowmass Mall bus stop and at various hotels. From 4 pm to 1 am, RFTA buses to Aspen cost $2. Parking is free at the Rodeo lot, with frequent free shuttles to the lifts. Parking in the base area lots costs $8.

Buttermilk Mountain This mountain (9900 feet on the West Summit), 2 miles west of Aspen on Hwy 82, was developed in 1958 to provide gentle slopes for beginners and intermediate skiers. *Ski* magazine once ranked it as the best place in North America to learn how to ski.

Buttermilk (☎ 970-925-1220) is the smallest of Aspen's ski areas and a great place for families to ski together – 70% of the terrain is groomed nightly and the smaller size makes it easy to meet for lunch at either the Cliffhouse restaurant on top or Bumps at the bottom. Snowboarders can enjoy the halfpipes and parks designed by champion Jimmy Scott.

Among the six chairlifts, the Summit Express quad provides over 1800 feet of vertical rise to East Summit in less than 10 minutes. The only advanced skiing is on the south side of the area on the Upper Tiehack lift. Buttermilk is open mid-December to early April and uses snow-making equipment on about 100 acres.

You can rent skis at the mountain at Buttermilk Sports (☎ 970-925-1220). The following prices are given for per-day peak-season rates; off-peak rates may be lower. Ski rentals run $16 for a basic package, $25 for a performance package and $30 for a demo package. Complete snowboard packages are $25; snowshoes rent for $10. There are discounts for renting for more than three days and also for groups of 20 or more; children's rentals are priced

lower as well. No cross-country rentals are available.

Free shuttles connecting the ski areas run every 15 minutes from about 8 am to 4:30 pm.

Cross-Country Skiing The best cross-country skiing in the area is at Ashcroft (☎ 970-925-1971) in the beautiful Castle Creek Valley. It offers over 20 miles of groomed trails that pass through the ghost town. You can arrange for instruction or guided backcountry day and overnight trips. Be sure to have lunch at the ski-in (or sleigh-in) Pine Creek Cookhouse. The Aspen Cross-Country Ski Center (☎ 970-925-2145) operates 'on the tracks' at the Aspen Golf Course, west of town on Hwy 82. Nordic skiing at Snowmass is available at the Club Cross-Country Touring Center (☎ 970-923-3148), featuring 20 miles of groomed trails.

Backcountry Skiing The 10th Mountain Division Hut Association (☎ 970-925-5775), 1280 Ute Ave, offers a system of trails almost 300 miles long connecting 14 overnight cabins. Nearby huts on the margins of the Hunter-Fryingpan and Holy Cross wilderness areas are available for $22 per person; these huts are popular – especially over weekends – so it's good to reserve space far in advance. Reservations are accepted June 1 for the following winter, and there's a $25 membership fee. These trips do require some backcountry skiing experience, and avalanche training is highly recommended.

The office also has information and takes reservations for the Braun Hut System, which covers Aspen, Vail, Leadville and Hunter Creek. There are six cabins and the terrain is generally remote and challenging, mainly meant for experienced backcountry skiers.

To plan your trip, read the 2nd edition of Lewis W Dawson's *Colorado 10th Mountain Trails*, available at the 10th Mountain Division office for $20. For equipment, proper clothing and some advice about trips into the backcountry, Ute Mountaineers

(☎ 970-925-2849), at 308 S Mill St, and Hub of Aspen (☎ 970-925-7970), at 315 E Hyman, are the best sources.

Equipment Rental Many independent shops in and around Aspen offer rental alternatives to shops run by resorts. For Alpine ski rentals and boards Incline Ski Shop, (☎ 970-920-1038), 555 East Durant, Aspen Sports (☎ 970-925-6331), 408 East Cooper Ave, and Christy Sports/Sports Stalker (☎ 970-925-9237), 428 E Hyman St, have locations in both Aspen and Snowmass, allowing you to rent from one location and drop off at another. Expect to pay around $25 to $30 for a complete basic package and $35 to $40 for top-end skis and boots with poles.

Snowboard rentals and gear are also available at Alternative Edge (☎ 970-925-8272), 555 E Durant Ave, and D&E Snowboard Shop (☎ 970-579 2237), 520 E Durant, for about $25 for board and boots, $30 for high-end equipment.

For snowshoes, cross-country and telemark skis your best bets are Ute Mountaineers (☎ 970-925-2849), at 308 S Mill, The Hub of Aspen (☎ 970-925-7970), 315 E Hyman, and Ajax Sports (☎ 970-925-7662), 635 E Hyman in town. Snowshoes will run around $12 a day, cross-country equipment about $20, and telemark packages around $25.

Ice Skating

Silver Circle Ice Rink (☎ 970-544-0303) has outdoor skating and lessons at Dean and Mill Sts. It's open 9 am to 10 pm; admission is $6/4 adults/children and rentals are $2.50. Check with the rink for public hours, lessons, hockey games and other activities.

The Ice Garden (☎ 970-920-5141), at the corner of S First and E Hyman Sts, is an almost full-size indoor ice rink with public skating, hockey, lessons and skate rentals and a full pro shop. Rates are $4/3 adults/children, rentals are $2. During the Christmas holiday public skating is daily 3 to 5 pm, and 6 to 8 pm, but check with the rink for schedule changes.

Hiking & Backpacking

Aspen is surrounded by three wilderness areas offering plenty of trails that are typically open from July through early fall, when aspen foliage decorates the land. From Lone Pine Rd in Aspen, the **Hunter Valley Trail** (USFS Trail 1992) follows Hunter Creek northeast about 3 miles through wildflower meadows to the **Sunnyside** and **Hunter Creek** trails into the Hunter-Fryingpan Wilderness Area.

From Maroon Lake, the easy **Maroon Creek Trail** (USFS Trail 1982) is a six-mile streamside route that passes beaver ponds and the avalanche area as it follows a downhill path along Maroon Creek to the valley bottom. A 3-mile option ends at East Maroon Portal, where the bus picks up hikers by the roadside. Also from East Portal, the **East Maroon Creek Trail** (USFS Trail 1983) climbs 8½ miles to East Maroon Pass, passing on the east side of Pyramid Peak. Hikers who continue over the divide 6 miles to Gothic can arrange for a shuttle to Crested Butte by Town Taxi (☎ 970-349-5543).

Conundrum Hot Springs, west of Castle Peak (14,265 feet), is the reward for 8½ miles of moderate climbing on the **Conundrum Creek Trail** (USFS Trail 1981). You can continue over Triangle Pass and return on **East Maroon Creek Trail** to catch a bus from Maroon Lake back to Aspen. The trailhead is 5 miles south of the Hwy 82 turnoff for USFS Rd 102, immediately west of town.

Other trails in the Hunter-Fryingpan or Collegiate Peaks wilderness areas east of Aspen tend to be less used than the Maroon Bells-Snowmass area. From Lincoln Creek Rd 11 miles east of Aspen, **New York Creek Trail** (USFS Trail 2182) climbs 4 steep miles to a 12,000-foot-plus pass.

(For more excursions into this wilderness area, see also Leadville, Buena Vista and Crested Butte.)

Mountain Biking

RFTA buses offer racks to carry up to four bikes on a first-come, first-served basis throughout the valley. At Snowmass, bikes are allowed on the Burlingame and Sam's Knob chairlifts. An easy ride for new arrivals is the **Rio Grande Trail** along the Roaring Fork River – it's crowded with joggers, dogs and bicyclists on its 4-mile length on the old railroad grade between Aspen's post office and the Slaughterhouse Bridge.

Mountain bicyclists are restricted from the wilderness trails, but there are still plenty of heavily used routes near town on Aspen Mountain and Smuggler Mountain. Hunter Valley and the **Sunnyside** trails provide a challenging single-track loop north of town. Once you're acclimated to high altitudes, the **Montezuma Basin** and **Pearl Pass** rides offer extreme cycling experiences well above timberline, south of town from Castle Creek Rd. Trails Illustrated publishes the handy topographic *Aspen Bike Map*.

Rentals are $25/65 for standard/full-suspension bikes at The Hub (☎ 970-925-7970), 315 E Hyman Ave, Aspen's oldest bike shop and the sponsor of local cycling events. Colorado Riff Raft (☎ 970-925-5404, 970 925-5405), 555 E Durant, offers standard bikes for $20. Full-suspension bikes rent for $65, $25 for standard bikes, at Ajax Bikes & Sports (☎ 970-925-7662), 635 E Hyman Ave. Aspen Velo (☎ 970-925-1495), 465 N Mill St near the Rio Grande Trail, offers basic bikes for $30 per day, $40 front-suspension, $60 full-suspension.

Bike shuttles to trailheads and guided trips with lunch are available from Aspen Bike Tours (☎ 970- 920-4059), 1435 Sierra Vista Drive, which offers easy trips on pavement along the Roaring Fork and Castle Creek Rd, as well as off-road trips along Hunter Creek and Lincoln Creek. Timberline Mountain Bike Tours (☎ 970-925-3586, 800-842-2453), 516 E Durant Ave across from Rubey Park Transit Center, offers customized tours around Aspen as well as multiple-day hut-to-hut trips using the 10th Mountain Hut System.

Fishing
From McFarlane Creek below the Difficult Campground to upper Woody Creek Bridge, the wild trout water of the **Roaring Fork River** is restricted to fly casting. A catch-and-release program is in effect. Many of the beautiful tributary streams to the Roaring Fork – including Lincoln Creek, Hunter Creek, Castle Creek, Maroon Creek and Snowmass Creek – also offer good fishing. Gold Medal water extends for 14 miles on the Fryingpan River from Ruedi Dam to its confluence with the Roaring Fork River at Basalt.

Fishing gear is available from Aspen Sports (☎ 970-925-6331), 408 E Cooper Ave. Licensed guide services are offered by Aspen Outfitting Company (☎ 970-925-3406), 520 E Cooper Ave, and Oxbow Outfitting Company (☎ 970-925-1505), 675 E Durant Ave. In Basalt, Taylor Creek (☎ 970-920-1128), in the City Market Shopping Center, offers gear, guides and fishing expertise, as does Frying Pan Anglers (☎ 970-927-3441), 6692 Frying Pan Rd.

White-Water Rafting
Whitewater action on the Roaring Fork River does not get a lot of attention, partly because of the short season that typically ends by July, but also because of the difficulty of the river. From Slaughterhouse Bridge in Aspen it's Class V (or higher) during high runoff periods. Extensive experience is necessary to handle upper or lower sections of the river. For equipment and information drop by Ute Mountaineer (☎ 970-925-2849), 308 S Mill St. Colorado Riff Raft (see Mountain Biking above) offers a variety of rafting trips on the Roaring Fork River.

Horseback Riding
T-Lazy-7 Ranch (☎ 970-925-4614), 3129 Maroon Creek Rd, offers hourly horse rentals and breakfast rides. Their menagerie of animals includes llamas and elk. Snowmass Stables (☎ 970-923-3075), 2737 Brush Creek Rd in Snowmass Village, can also put you on an oat-burner or whisk you away on a dinner sleigh ride.

Special Events
There's always something happening in Aspen during the summer months, including

season-long music and dance festivals. Check the calendar in *Aspen Magazine's Traveler's Guide* for a comprehensive list of activities. A lively event is Aspen's **Fourth of July** celebrations which include running and kayak races, music and a parade featuring a 'Wild Bunch' on about 100 Harleys. The **Snowmass Rodeo** (☎ 970-923-3520) takes place every Saturday night in the summer. **Theatre in the Park** (☎ 970-925-9313) features live performances, including musicals and plays most nights at 7:30 pm and a Sunday matinee during the summer next to Rio Grand Park.

The Wheeler and Isis theaters premiere films during the weeklong **Aspen Filmfest** (☎ 970-925-6882) beginning in late September. A four-day January festival ostensibly started by locals in 1951 to shake the winter doldrums, the primary purpose of the **Winterskol** torchlight parade and fireworks is to fill rooms during the mid-January business slump.

Dance Performances Begun in 1969 with performances by Ballet West, the **DanceAspen Festival** is now a six-week festival starting in late June. It presents a variety of renowned choreographic companies, such as the Paul Taylor Dance Company, and solo performers. In addition, student performances and brown-bag discussions with visiting artists take place during the festival. All performances are at the DanceAspen Festival Theater (☎ 970-925-7718), 199 High School Rd. Ticket prices range from $12 to $50. For a schedule or to buy tickets during the season, drop by the Wheeler Box Office (☎ 970-920-5770, 800-933-3820).

Concerts Since 1949, the **Aspen Music Festival** has presented classical concerts. From late June through mid-August, performances are held nightly at the Bayer-Benedict Music Tent, Harris Concert Hall at the north end of 4th St, or the Wheeler Opera House. There are also several afternoon programs. Pick up a schedule or purchase tickets at the Main Box Office

(☎ 970-923-3520) in the Gondola Building on Durant Ave. Tickets cost anywhere from $7 to $48, depending on the performance.

Snowmass Summer of Music (☎ 970-920-4996) presents free outdoor concerts featuring nationally known performers in jazz, rock, blues and world music every Thursday night on Fanny Hill across from the Mall. Shows begin at 6 pm (☎ 970-923-2000). There's also a four-day Labor Day music festival in Snowmass. Recent performers included Ziggy Marley, Los Lobos, the Neville Brothers and Joan Osborne.

Places to Stay

The Aspen Chamber Resort Association (☎ 970-925-9000, 800-262-7736), 425 Rio Grande Place, can set you up with accommodations ranging from hotel rooms to houses to condos. By calling the Aspen Skiing Company (☎ 970-925-1220, 800-525-6200) you can make reservations at any of their complexes. For (not necessarily less expensive) alternatives, try Affordable Aspen (☎ 800-243-9466), a central reservations office that has listings for B&Bs, townhouses and condos all within town.

Winter rates peak during the December to early January holidays, and are at their lowest in fall and spring (late April and May). Prices rise again in summer, but still average around half of winter peak prices.

Places to Stay – budget

Camping The USFS White River National Forest's Aspen Ranger District (☎ 970-925-3445) operates nine campgrounds in the vicinity of Aspen, but only three, *Silver Bar*, *Silver Bell* and *Silver Queen*, all south of Aspen on Maroon Creek Rd, are reservable by calling ☎ 877-444-6777. Together they only account for 14 sites. The fee is $10 plus $7.50 reservation fee.

Nearby *Maroon Lake* offers 44 sites ($12) assigned at the Maroon Valley entrance station. Five miles east of town, *Difficult* campground has 47 sites ($10), but finding a vacant site is difficult. Continuing east on Hwy 82 toward Independence

Pass, the smaller *Weller*, *Lincoln Gulch* and *Lost Man* campgrounds offer a total of 27 sites ($6). A last resort is the free *Portal* campground, 7 miles south of Lincoln Gulch on Pitkin County Rd 23. Dispersed camping is not permitted except along Lincoln Creek 11 miles southeast of Aspen, and a five-day limit is enforced.

Lodges Not only is the 1888 *Little Red Ski Haus* (☎ 970-925-3333), 118 E Cooper Ave, one of Aspen's precious few Victorians remaining in the central area, it's also a budget lodge. Opened as Aspen's first B&B in 1961, it offers dorm-like beds for $42 during winter (including full breakfast), $23 in summer. Another European-style lodge offering dorms with shared baths for $40/25 winter/summer is *St Moritz Lodge* (☎ 970-925-3220), 334 W Hyman Ave. Rates include Continental breakfast. *The Mountain Chalet* (☎ 970-925-7797), 333 E Durant, is the closest budget accommodation to the lifts and town center, with dorm-style accommodation from $28 to $47 during ski season, including a full breakfast. It also offers standard, economy and deluxe rooms from $80 to $200 during ski season, $40 to $100 during summer – and there's a pool, sauna and whirlpool.

Places to Stay – middle

Lodges Since 1952, the *Skiers Chalet Lodge* (☎ 970-920-2037), 233 Gilbert St, has offered no-frills rooms at the base of the Shadow Mountain Lift. Basic rooms with private bath are between $85 and $120 in winter, about half that in the summer.

For couples or groups the *Chalet Lisl* (☎ 970-925-3520), a lodge at 100 E Hyman Ave, is a great deal. Clean, attractive studio apartments with kitchen and one queen and one single bed rent for $114/78 winter/summer. One-bedroom apartments with a twin bed in the living room are $142/90.

If you prefer to stay out of town and want a real Western experience, the *T Lazy Seven* (☎ 970-925-4614), 3129 Maroon Creek Rd, may be the place. It's close to Aspen Highlands, just 3 miles down

Maroon Creek Rd, and offers comfortable rustic wood cabins. Summer or winter prices range from $70 for studios to $280 for five-bedroom cabins that can sleep 10. There are no TVs or telephones but there is a wonderful outdoor heated pool and whirlpool. In the summer there's horseback riding, and sleighrides and snowmobiling in the winter. Advance reservations are strongly advised.

B&Bs A few former motels offer reasonable B&B lodging. At the garish *Christmas Inn* (☎ 970-925-3822), 232 W Main St, singles/doubles cost $86/98 during peak ski season, $58/66 in summer; a simple breakfast is included. The *Ullr Lodge* (☎ 970-925-7696), 520 W Main Street, has standard rooms for $85 to $150 during ski season, $45 to $70 in low season, including a full breakfast in the winter and a Continental breakfast in summer.

The *Heatherbed Mountain Lodge* (☎ 970-925-7077), 1679 Maroon Creek Rd, is directly across the street from Aspen Highlands amid cottonwoods on Maroon Creek. It has a bright common room with fireplace, where complimentary Continental breakfast is served, and big windows overlooking the creek. There's also a heated pool, sauna and hot tub. Standard double rooms are $79 in off-season, $99 during peak ski season and $89 in between. Larger rooms and suites are more.

Hotels The modern *Grand Aspen Hotel* (☎ 970-925-1150, 800-242-7736), 515 S Galena St, is close to the lifts and Rubey Park Transit Center. Its draconian five-night minimum requirement during the regular ski season is balanced with room rates that begin at $139/doubles. During summer, a one-night stay costs around $75, though lower rates may be available.

Places to Stay – top end

The Sardy House (☎ 970-920-2525), 128 E Main, has luxury B&B accommodation in a beautiful, classic Victorian home with pool, sauna, restaurant and bar. Rates range from $370 to $750 during ski season, $85

to $475 the rest of the year. Rooms at the *Hotel Jerome* (☎ 970-920-1000), 330 E Main St, start at $445 during ski season but drop as low as $160 in October. The venerable Jerome underwent a lavish renovation, reopening in 1988 as one of the finest hotels in Colorado. It's only fitting – when the Jerome first opened in 1889, it was Colorado's first hotel with electric lights and indoor plumbing.

Little Nell Hotel (☎ 970-942-4600), 675 E Durant Ave, is a luxury hotel convenient to the slopes that books up fast (it maintains wait-lists for rooms). Room amenities include a wet bar, marble bathroom, TV and VCR, king or two queen beds, a fireplace and a balcony overlooking either the town or Ajax Mountain (mountain views are more expensive). It's Aspen's only five-star, five-diamond hotel; in peak winter season, a basic room goes for between $450 and $600, while the two-bedroom Pfeifer Suite goes for a mere $3500. In summer, rates begin at $275.

Formerly a Ritz-Carlton property, *The Sheraton Aspen Hotel* (☎ 970-920-3300), 315 Dean St, in a beautifully designed red-brick building at the base of Ajax, offers outstanding service, luxury and convenience. Peak winter rates run from $699 to $4000, dropping to as little a $159 in the off-season.

Places to Stay – Snowmass Village

Snowmass central reservations (☎ 970-923-2000, 800-332-3245) will do its best to match your price and quality requirements with one of the many hotel rooms or condos in Snowmass Village, or you can ask for a specific hotel by name.

Snowmass Village is very distinct from Aspen, and it's designed to supply everything a lodger may need. Since all hotels and condos are in one centralized area, there are really no preferred locations among them; the best values will be had by those who make their reservations early.

Snowmass Lodge & Club The benefit to staying at this luxury resort complex (☎ 970-923-5600, 800-525-0710), at 0239 Snowmass Club Circle inside Snowmass Village, is access to the full-service athletic club, outdoor swimming pools, hot tubs and saunas and tennis courts. Accommodations range from rooms and suites to villas. Winter rates for a basic hotel room run $110 to $165 for a junior suite in low season to $349 to $439 during peak winter season. Ski packages, and in summer golf packages, are offered which cover lodging and lift tickets or greens fees.

Places to Eat

Since 1965, the Austrian *Wienerstube Restaurant* (☎ 970-925-3357), 633 E Hyman Ave, has offered reasonably priced no-nonsense meals and efficient service. Breakfasts range from oat-bran pancakes for $4 to egg dishes for about $7. For crêpes and refreshing smoothies try *Poppycocks* (☎ 970-925-1245), at 609 E Cooper Ave. The *Zelle Caffe* (☎ 970-925-5745), at 121 S Galena St, can get you going quickly with fresh juice and pastries.

Budget diners rely on *The Popcorn Wagon* (☎ 970-925-2718), 305 S Mill St, which has outdoor seating and serves tasty crêpes and sandwiches for under $5 until 2 am. *Main St Bakery & Cafe* (☎ 970-925-6446), 201 E Main St, is a good place for dinners such as vegetarian lasagna for $8 or chicken pot pie. *Explore Booksellers & Bistro* (☎ 970-925-5336), 221 E Main St, offers two vegetarian dinner specials each night on their rooftop patio and small dining area on the 2nd floor (next to bookshelves and browsers).

Little Annie's Eating House (☎ 970-925-1078), 517 E Hyman Ave, has a bar and grill atmosphere and offers lunch specials for about $9, dinner for about $11. For a corned beef on rye or an imaginative 'Tahiti' sandwich (ham, bacon, pinneaple, cream cheese and sprouts and mayo!), *Johnny McGuire's Deli* (☎ 970-920-9255), 730 E Cooper Ave, is the place to go. Deli sandwiches come in three sizes: skinny ($4.35), regular ($5.27) and fatty ($8.72).

For lunchtime burgers or more elaborate late-night fare, drop in to the historic *Bentley's at the Wheeler* (☎ 970-920-2240),

328 E Hyman Ave in the Wheeler Opera House, which offers moderately priced dinners and a Victorian bar.

Su Casa (☎ 970-920-1488), 315 E Hyman Ave opposite the Opera House, isn't the most popular Mexican restaurant in town but its lunches and dinners are unpretentious and relatively inexpensive. More popular (and a bit more expensive) is *The Cantina* (☎ 970-925-3663) at 411 E Main St. Also try the New Mexican-style blue corn enchiladas and a bowl of posole at *La Cocina* (☎ 970-925-9714) at 308 E Hopkins Ave.

Crowds flock to *The Mother Lode* (☎ 970-925-7700), 314 E Hyman, where they've been serving pasta since 1959. The place to see or be seen during lunch, dinner or après-ski is *Mezzaluna* (☎ 970-925-5882), 624 E Cooper Ave, which has a menu of northern Italian dishes starting at $13. The $16 basil pesto pizza with shrimp is delicious. Also highly popular is *Campo de Fiori* (☎ 970-920-7717), 205 S Mill St; call ahead or you'll have to sit in the bar and wait for a table. At $15 for risotto and $14 for seafood linguine, the prices are moderate and the food is definitely worth the wait.

As you might imagine, many Aspen restaurants are in the top-end category. In the 1891 Brand Building, *The Smuggler Land Office* (☎ 970-925-8624), 415 E Hopkins Ave, features rack of lamb, seafood and Cajun cuisine served upstairs above the bar. The imposing sandstone Ute City Banque building houses the *Ute City Bar & Grill* (☎ 970-925-4373), 501 E Hyman Ave, a bistro that specializes in wild game, seafood and vegetarian dishes from $17 to $30. Another decent bistro, *Pinons* (☎ 970-920-2021), at 105 S Mill St, offers Colorado cuisine that features elk, ahi and pork tenderloin. The *Little Nell Hotel* restaurant (☎ 970-920-4600, ext 6330) serves various fine cuisines; reservations are recommended.

Baang Cafe & Bar: (☎ 970-925-9969) at 325 E Main St serves Asian food fused with French style and technique with delicious results. Food is served family-style so order lots and share. Try mandarin beef

($26) and calamari salad ($14), or if the prices are too steep, order some appetizers and sit at the candlelit bar.

For sushi in the Rockies, try *Takah* (☎ 970-945-8588), 420 E Hyman, which has an innovative menu and a lively sushi bar, or *Kenichi* (☎ 970-920-2212), 533 E Hopkins St, a popular and upscale restaurant featuring amazing sushi (the spider crab and dynamite shrimp sushi are excellent) and innovative dinner combinations. Sip on a Purple Haze, sake mixed with Chambord. Another innovative restaurant that gets rave reviews is *Poppies Bistro Cafe* (☎ 970-925-2333) in a cozy Victorian home on the west side at 834 W Hallam St. Dinners cost between $20 and $35. Finish the evening with a baked dessert or frozen yogurt at *Paradise Bakery* (☎ 970-925-7585), 320 S Galena Ave, and watch the street activity.

Entertainment

Bars Begin your pub crawl at *Cooper St Pier* (☎ 970-925-7758), 508 E Cooper Ave, a good place to shoot pool or have some pub food before the place gets rowdy – which is early. For a quieter scene, try Hotel Jerome's *J-Bar* (☎ 970-920-1000), Main and Mill Sts, a traditional watering hole where everyone can be comfortable. There's a more historical atmosphere at *Bentley's at the Wheeler* (☎ 970-920-2240), 328 E Hyman Ave. You can round out your history lesson with a visit to Aspen's oldest saloon, *The Red Onion* (☎ 970-925-9043), first opened in 1892 at 420 E Cooper Ave.

Drop in for a Doggie Style Amber Ale and a bite at *Flying Dog Brewpub* (☎ 970-925-7464), 424 E Cooper Ave. The après-ski crowd hangs out at *Ajax Tavern* in the Little Nell Hotel at 675 E Durant Ave. The deck is strictly see-and-be-seen. Just have the valet park your Ferrari as you enter the unreal world of oil sheiks and glamour at *Planet Hollywood* (☎ 970-920-7817), 312 S Galena St, which is also known for its fairly inexpensive fare.

Down-valley about 8 miles, *Woody Creek Tavern* (☎ 970-923-4585), 2 Woody

Creek Plaza, is a 'stuff-on-the-walls' hangout for locals that closes at 11 pm. The popular watering hole of gonzo journalist Hunter S Thompson, it offers cheap beer on tap and pool tables – just like the places back home.

Dancing Top rock and blues performers are occasionally featured at *Double Diamond* (☎ 970-920-6905), 450 S Galena. Near the gondola base at 535 E Dean St, *The Tippler* (☎ 970-925-4977) features late-night DJ dancing, including Tuesday Disco Night – just remember to slip into something polyester. *Club Freedom* (☎ 970-925-6523), 426 E Hyman, is the place for a pulsing technobeat, while *Shooters Saloon* (☎ 970-925-4567), 220 S Galena St, will teach you the intricate moves of the Texas two-step.

Dinner Theater Reservations are essential at the *Crystal Palace* (☎ 970-925-1455), 300 E Hyman, a fun theater and dining experience where, after serving you a delicious meal, the waiters perform an original satirical show. The place was named for the elaborate chandeliers that grace the room and it's been doing business for 40 years. Dinner and the meal run $49 per person, not including appetizers or drinks.

Shopping
Aspen's toney shops will not disappoint even the most materialistic shopper. Probably the only items you won't find here are refrigerator magnets and rubber tomahawks (and the T-shirts here are embroidered with sequins). A vintage gas pump is just the thing for that garage addition project you had in mind.

A courtyard of polished relics forms an irresistible attraction at Waterfall Hope (☎ 970-925-4573). Stars Memorabilia (☎ 970-920-2920), 525 E Cooper Ave, has gallery displays of items that once belonged to the rich and famous, like one of Pete Townsend's smashed guitars. Chepita (☎ 970-925-2871), also at 525 E Cooper Ave, is a grown-up's toy store with one-of-a-kind decorative items like wooden cow-

boys as well as jewelry. Uriah Heep's (☎ 970-925-7456), 303 E Hopkins Ave, has been selling furniture, folk art and rugs in Aspen for over 25 years. With a bronze statue of a biking couple in front, it's tempting to drop into Aspen Harley-Davidson (☎ 970-544-0811) 450 S Galena St, where you can spend either $50,000 on a shiny new 'Hog' or $15 on a cool T-shirt.

For detailed descriptions of galleries, including addresses and phone numbers, pick up a free copy of *Aspen Magazine's* 'Gallery Guide' from the Chamber Resort Association. Most of the galleries are located in the center of town, so it is easy to find them on your own.

Getting There & Away
Air Sardy Field (☎ 970-920-5384), 4 miles north of Aspen on Hwy 82, has to be seen to be believed. Confirming the jet-set appeal of Aspen, it's crammed with the most modern aviation equipment and a fleet of private jets in all shapes and sizes.

For those without their own aircraft, Aspen is serviced by United Express, Frontier, Northwest, Mountain Air Express and Aspen Mountain Air, a feeder for American Airlines. Most flights are to/from Denver, although Northwest had begun nonstop jet service to/from Minneapolis, MN, at the time of writing. United Express (the only other airline flying jets into Aspen) has one direct flight to/from Los Angeles, in addition to about 15 daily Denver flights during peak ski season.

The Eagle County Airport (☎ 970-524-9490) is 70 miles east of Aspen/Snowmass but has an increasing number of jet flights during ski season – and virtually no commercial flights the rest of the year! American, Delta, United, Continental and Northwest Airlines fly Boeing 757s into Eagle from their hubs in Dallas and Houston, TX, Miami, FL, New York, Chicago, Los Angeles, Atlanta, GA, Minneapolis, MN, and Detroit, MI.

DIA Shuttle Colorado Mountain Express (☎ 970-927-9775, 800-525-6363) offers frequent service to Denver International Airport for $89 per person one-way.

Car Aspen is 41 miles south of Glenwood Springs. From Denver, Aspen is 208 miles via I-70 and Hwy 82. During winter months Hwy 82 over 12,095-foot Independence Pass to Leadville is closed.

Getting Around

To/From the Airport RFTA does not operate a designated shuttle to Sardy Field, but the valley buses stop every half-hour about two blocks from the Airport Business Center, and will take you to Aspen for 50¢. In the summer there is direct service to the airport leaving from Rubey Park Transit Center every half-hour from 6:30 am to 6 pm.

High Mountain Taxi (☎ 970-925-8294) will take you to and from Sardy Field for between $10 and $15. Colorado Mountain Express (see DIA Shuttle above) offers frequent service to Eagle Airport (near Vail) for $47 one-way.

Bus The Roaring Fork Transit Agency (☎ 970-925-8484) buses serve Snowmass Village and the valley to El Jebel north of Basalt, on half-hour intervals from 6:15 to 12:15 am. Free in-town shuttles serve the Aspen Highlands Ski Area, Hunter Creek, Mountain Valley, Snowbunny and the Music School on Castle Creek Rd. During music festivals, buses also travel to/from the Music Tent.

Car Agencies with counters at Sardy Field include:

Avis	☎ 970-925-2355, 800-331-1212
Budget	☎ 970-925-2151, 800-527-0700
Eagle	☎ 970-925-2128, 800-282-2128
Hertz	☎ 970-925-7368, 800-654-3131
Thrifty	☎ 970-920-2305, 800-367-2277

If you feel a bit roguish, Magic Carpet Rides (☎ 970-544-0699) can rent you a Harley-Davidson motorcycle.

Taxi High Mountain Taxi (☎ 970-925-8294) operates meter cabs 24 hours a day.

Southern Mountains

The southern reaches of Colorado's Rockies offer some diverse and fascinating terrain. There is plenty of stunning Alpine scenery and some world-class ski resorts, like Crested Butte and Telluride. But there is also the sprawling San Luis Valley, a broad swath of agricultural land that is home to the scenic wonders of the Great Sand Dunes and the Sangre de Cristo Mountains. Toward the southern border of the state, towns like San Luis help preserve the Hispanic culture that first took root in the area 300 years ago. The Rio Grande headwaters and the Arkansas River offer some of the finest white-water rafting and kayaking in the state. Heading west, the San Juan Mountains offer a different landscape from their northern counterparts, boasting craggy peaks, roaring streams and incredibly lush flora: a hiker's paradise.

CAÑON CITY & AROUND

Home to the 13 state penitentiaries, Cañon City (population 14,800) is a popular stop for visitors to the Arkansas River, particularly Colorado's top tourist trap, the Royal Gorge. In an effort to keep visitors in the area for an extra day, Cañon City also promotes 'scenic' loop drives to the casino town of Cripple Creek on rough mountain roads that are more tedious than scenic (hint: Cripple Creek and the Florissant Fossil Beds National Monument can both be reached by a paved road from Colorado Springs). One good reason for hanging out in Cañon City is to raft down the Arkansas River, for this is a gateway to whitewater heaven. And if you're interested, there is also (not surprisingly) a prison museum to check out.

Orientation

Most of Cañon City's services are located on Royal Gorge Blvd, as US 50 is called in town, and on Main St. The latter runs parallel to the north side of US 50 from 1st to 15th St, then crosses to continue south of the highway. The Arkansas River lies south of US 50. The turnoff to the privately operated Royal Gorge of the Arkansas River attraction is 8 miles west of town on US 50.

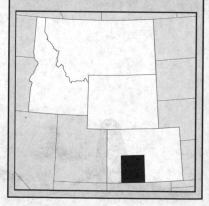

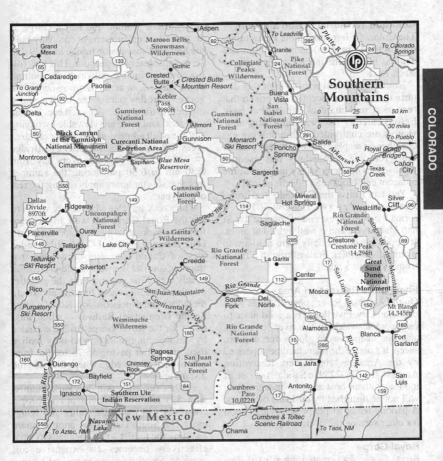

Information

The Cañon City Chamber of Commerce (☎ 719-275-2331) is in the historic Peabody Mansion, 403 Royal Gorge Blvd, and is open weekdays from 8 am to 5 pm. It also operates visitor information booths at either side of town on US 50, from Memorial Day to Labor Day. For information on camping or hiking in the Wet Mountains in the San Isabel National Forest south of Cañon City, stop by the USFS/BLM office (☎ 719-269-8500) east of town at 3170 E Main. Hours are 7:45 am to 4:30 pm weekdays.

The City Market, 1703 Fremont Drive, has an ATM, as does Fremont Bank, across from the City Hall & Museum, on Royal Gorge Blvd and 6th St. The post office is at 1501 Main St. Books, maps and magazines are available at the Book Corral (☎ 719-275-8923), 621 Main St. Sir Thomas More Hospital (☎ 719-269-2000) provides 24-hour emergency care at 1338 Phay Ave, north of US 50 off 15th St. Royal Care Laundry at 735 S 9th St (just south of the 9th St bridge) has coin-op washers and is open daily from 6 am to 10 pm.

Colorado Territorial Prison Museum

The Colorado Territorial State Penitentiary (one of the 13 in town) houses 690 inmates and has been in the incarceration business since 1871.

Not everyone will want to visit this disturbing museum adjacent to the prison that renders a nightmare of life behind bars. Before entering the paid admission area, visitors are confronted with a hulking gas chamber on display in the museum yard. If this gruesome spectacle – last used in 1967 – does not deter you, you can tour the museum cell blocks ($3.50 admission).

You can't miss the Colorado Territorial Prison Museum (☎ 719-269-3015); it forms the entire west end of town at 1st St and Macon Ave and is well lighted at night. It's open in summer daily from 8:30 am to 6 pm and in winter, Friday through Sunday from 10 am to 5 pm.

Five Points Recreation Area

On the Arkansas River about 12 miles west of Cañon City, Five Points is a good place to picnic while watching the river for rafters and the steep canyon slopes for bighorn sheep. It's one of the many facilities operated by the Arkansas Headwaters Recreation Area (☎ 719-539-7289 in Salida), but one of the few without boat access – meaning you will not be disturbed by busloads of rafters. A parking fee of $1 per person is also good for other sites on the river.

Royal Gorge

Royal Gorge was created when hard Precambrian rock underlying a relatively thin veneer of red sandstone resisted erosion from the tremendous glacial meltwater flows over 10,000 years ago. The Arkansas River continues to etch the steep and turbulent stream bed 1100 feet below the bridge. The Santa Fe and the Denver & Rio Grande Western Rail (D&RG) railroads challenged the gorge in the 1870s, anxious to reach the booming mines at Leadville. Soon, however, tourist traffic supplanted mine freight: daylight trains stopped on the narrow shelf to allow passengers to get off and view the chasm.

To further promote the Royal Gorge as an attraction, an amusement company built the 880-foot suspension bridge in 1929 that serves absolutely no purpose. This was followed by an incline railway to the bottom of the canyon, an aerial tramway across the gorge, a trolley across the bridge and a miniature train ride. All of these 'scenic wonders' and more are viewable by paying $12 for adult admission and $9 for children (ages four to 11). The Royal Gorge Bridge (☎ 719-275-7507) is open every day from 8:30 am to 6:30 pm during the summer months; shorter hours apply during the rest of the year.

The savvy traveler who merely wants to see the Royal Gorge can walk to the edge from the parking lot just outside the North Gate entrance on Royal Gorge Rd, 8 miles west of Cañon City. But be warned that trapping tourists is a well-honed profession in this area. First you must run the gauntlet of other attractions that line the approach, including the Buckskin Joe Royal Gorge Scenic (miniature) Railway – often mistaken for the Royal Gorge Bridge entrance by unsuspecting tourists who only realize their error after paying $5.75 for the train ride to the canyon edge where they see the distant bridge.

Farther on, Buckskin Joe Park (admission $7) features Western movie props, complete with daily gunfights and hangings. The South Gate Rd is another snare awaiting the tourist – this one leads to what effectively becomes an expensive toll crossing for visitors too impatient to turn back to US 50. A one-hour horseback ride to the rim of the gorge costs $10 at Royal Gorge Riding Stables (☎ 719-275-4579) on Royal Gorge Rd.

White-Water Rafting

The best way to see the Royal Gorge is on a raft, but the 7 miles of Arkansas River whitewater is not for the timid. During late spring and early summer the Sunshine Falls represent a Class IV-V (very difficult to extremely difficult) level of difficulty. Tour operators typically require rafters to be over 18 years of age during the early season of over 12 when the flow diminishes by midsummer. Easier, yet still exciting, half-day trips on the lower Arkansas from Texas Creek to Parkdale, above the Royal Gorge, offer the potential to see bighorn sheep and are cheaper.

A concentration of rafting guides near the Royal Gorge turnoff, 8 miles west of Cañon City, offer competitive prices and both trips. Unless you enjoy paying for long and uncomfortable bus rides, stick to the nearby river segments mentioned above. (Other rafting trips in the upper Arkansas headwaters are listed under the Buena Vista section later in this chapter.)

Performance Tours (☎ 800-328-7238), at the intersection of US 50 and Royal Gorge Rd, offers a half-day trip under the Royal Gorge Bridge for $45, while the Texas Creek to Parkdale run costs $31 for adults or $26 for children under 12.

Buffalo Joe River Trips (☎ 719-395-8757, 800-356-7984), west of the Royal Gorge Rd at Royal View Campground, offers full-day Class II to V trips for $75 and half-day tours for $45. Similar tours and rates are also offered by Brown's Royal Gorge Rafting (☎ 719-275-7238), 45045 US 50; and American Adventure Expeditions (☎ 719-269-1421, 800-288-0675), on Royal Gorge Rd near US 50. Most guide services operate from May to October.

For a map and information about river access points contact the BLM (☎ 719-269-8500), 3170 E Main St on the east side of town, or the Arkansas Headwaters State Recreation Area (☎ 719-539-7289) in Salida.

Places to Stay

Camping The Wet Mountains in the San Isabel National Forest about 6 miles south of town on Oak Creek Grade Rd (Fremont County Rd 123) offer dispersed camping. *Buffalo Bill's Royal Gorge Campground* (☎ 719-269-3211), near the busy intersection of US 50 and Royal Gorge Rd, is not exactly a wilderness area, but tent sites cost $15 and a coin-op laundry is available. Showers for nonguests cost $3.

Motels The friendly *Sky Valley Motel* (☎ 719-275-2783), 205 Greydene Ave (US 50 frontage), often plays host to international visitors. Clean singles/doubles (no phones) cost $40/48; about half that in winter. Rooms at the older but well-maintained *Holiday Motel* (☎ 719-275-3317), 1502 Main St, cost $44/56 (summer) and are a good value compared to the national chains.

Rooms cost $42/55 in summer ($30/35 in winter) at *El Camino Motel* (☎ 719-275-9125), 2980 E Main St, opposite the Holy Cross Abbey. The rooms are a little frayed around the edges but still comfortable without serious problems. There's a lawn area set back from the highway, with a pool and a funky miniature golf course. Near the prison at 231 Royal Gorge Blvd, the very plain *Parkview Motel* (☎ 719-275-0624) offers basic rooms for $45/55 in summer, $30/35 in winter, and has a coin-op laundry.

Rooms are priced at $65/80 during summer at the *Best Western Royal Gorge* (☎ 719-275-3377), east of the town center at 1925 Fremont Drive. Facilities include a swimming pool, hot tub, playground, trout-fishing pond and laundry. The recently remodeled *Cañon Inn* (☎ 719-275-8676), 3075 E US 50, goes one better, with six hot tubs, a pool and two restaurants. Rooms cost $70/84 in summer, $58/63 in winter.

Hotels Probably the best bet in town, the delightful *St Cloud Hotel* (☎ 719-276-2000), 7th and Main St, was built in 1879 in Silvercliff and was moved to Cañon City in 1886. Until it shut down for a period in the 1980s it was said to be Colorado's longest-running hotel. On a darker note, it once served as the local headquarters for the Ku Klux Klan during the 1920s. The building is listed on the National Register of Historic Places.

While the rooms have been updated, with modern amenities like telephones and televisions, they still have a pleasant antique feel. Best of all, the prices are quite competitive: $55/68 in summer and a bargain rate of $35/45 in winter. However at the time of writing it was due to change ownership, so further renovations and possible price hikes make take place.

Places to Eat

For a simple caffeine and muffin fix stop by the *Paragon Caffe & Booksellers* (☎ 719-275-8575) at 112 S 5th St.

The menu at the unassuming *KJ's Restaurant* (☎ 719-275-5340), 1322 Royal Gorge Blvd, features an unlikely selection of Asian, German and American dishes. The menu makes more sense in light of the owners' background: a Korean-German couple. Asian lunches are $5 to $9, while German entrees are $9 to $12. Next to KJ's you can stock up on fresh Arkansas Valley produce at the *Sunnyside Ranch Market*.

Burritos or chimichangas filled with adobado, spicy chorizo or machaca are delicious Mexican a la carte specialties that cost less than $4 at *Old Mission Deli* (☎ 719-275-6780), 1905 Fremont Drive.

Inside the St Cloud Hotel *Dr B's Bar & Grill* (☎ 719-276-2000) serves up well-prepared lunches and dinners, including some interesting appetizers. In addition to steaks and seafood there are some more offbeat items like the tasty baked vegetable pie.

Merlino's Belvedere (☎ 719-275-5558), 1330 Elm Ave, is probably Cañon City's favorite restaurant. The Italian dinners are reasonably priced and the wine list has some fine selections at fair prices. The restaurant is on the old highway (now Hwy 115), 2 miles southeast of the 9th St Bridge.

Another upscale spot worth trying is *Le Petit Chablis* (☎ 719-269-3333), 512 Royal Gorge Blvd. Locals consider its French cuisine among the best food in town, and well worth the relatively higher prices. It's open Tuesday to Friday from 11:30 am to 1:30 pm and from 5:30 to 8:30 pm (until 9:30 on Friday and Saturday).

Getting There & Away

Bus Greyhound/TNM&O buses running between Pueblo and Grand Junction stop at the Video House (☎ 719-275-0163), 731 Main St. There is one bus daily in either direction: eastbound at 12:45 pm; westbound at 3:50 pm.

Car Cañon City is on US 50, 35 miles west of Pueblo and 48 miles east of Salida.

WESTCLIFFE & SILVER CLIFF

South of the Arkansas River Canyon in the Wet Mountain Valley, Westcliffe and Silver Cliff lie only a mile apart, surrounded by Alpine valley scenery, and within striking distance of the beautiful Sangre de Cristo Mountains. Though there's still a small-town atmosphere, the population has boomed in recent years, and the area is losing is 'undiscovered' status.

In 1870, over 300 German-American farmers and their families arrived from Chicago to build a communal colony at Colfax, about 8 miles south of modern Westcliffe. The Alpine mountain scenery, abundant water and extensive grazing land seemed to assure the colony's success. But issues over land tenure and external opposition from highly individualistic neighbors caused the utopian experiment to flounder. Few of the original group remained in the valley.

By 1880, the high-grade silver ore discovered in 1877 at the Geyser Mine briefly made Silver Cliff Colorado's third-largest city. The rivalry between the nearby towns began in 1885 when Westcliffe was founded at the end of the D&RG narrow gauge line from Cañon City. But the boom waned and Silver Cliff was a near ghost town by 1928 when Westcliffe took over the seat of minuscule Custer County.

Today, the two towns (combined population 900) share a number of services. As a result, the school, post office and chamber of commerce are located between the two towns, which are linked by Hwy 96.

Mountain grasslands in the Wet Mountain Valley extend for about 35 miles between the jagged peaks of the Sangre de Cristo Mountains to the west and the Wet Mountains to the east, capped by the granite summit of Greenhorn Peak (12,347 feet).

Access to USFS lands on either side of the valley is limited to a few routes; otherwise, dire signs threaten trespassers on cattle grazing lands with Old West justice. Nevertheless it's fairly easy to reach the magnificent Sangre de Cristo range, which includes five 14ers in the Crestone Peak group. Other 14ers rise to the south around the prominent Blanca Peak.

Information

At the time of writing, calling the Custer County Chamber of Commerce (☎ 719-783-9163) merely got you a recorded information hotline promoting town attractions and accommodations, but there was talk of an upgrade, so it may be more visitor-friendly by the time you read this. It's at 2 Bassick Place, next to the post office between the two towns.

For information about the San Isabel National Forest and Sangre de Cristo Wilderness, check with USFS ranger stations at Cañon City (☎ 719-269-8500) or La Veta (☎ 719-742-3681). For USGS maps try Valley Ace Hardware in Westcliffe at 211 Main St.

Westcliffe's Colorado Mountain Bank (☎ 719-783-9211), 1000 Main St, has an ATM. The post office is between Westcliffe and Silver Cliff at 4 Bassick Place.

Custer County Medical Clinic (☎ 719-783-2380) in Westcliffe is at 5th and Rosita Sts.

There's a coin laundry on the grounds of Kleine's Trailer Park, 320 Cliff St, on the east side of Silver Cliff.

Silver Cliff Museum

Silver Cliff's former Town Hall & Fire Station, built in 1879, houses a small museum where you can view relics and photographs of the valley's history. The museum is open Memorial Day to Labor Day, Thursday to Sunday, from 1 to 4 pm.

Mountain Biking

Off-road cyclists will find plenty of opportunities in San Isabel National Forest lands on either side of the Wet Mountain Valley. Even the declaration of the Sangre de

Cristo Wilderness in 1993 has not seriously hampered mountain bike riding, though no vehicles of any kind are allowed on wilderness trails. Existing primitive roads, like Hermit and Medano, resemble 'cherry stems' for public access into the wilderness boundary.

The most popular rides use portions of the **Rainbow Trail** (USFS Trail 1336), a 100-mile-long route along the Sangre de Cristo foothills between Salida and Music Pass, about 15 miles south of Westcliffe. The Rainbow Trail is below the wilderness boundary. Convenient access points are from the USFS Alvarado and Lake Creek campgrounds (see Places to Stay).

South of Westcliffe about 20 miles, Medano Pass (10,030 feet) crosses the Sangre de Cristo Wilderness, 9 miles west of Hwy 69 on the signed route. Because of the wilderness status, you may not leave the road to ride on hiking trails. The scenic primitive road continues west 11 miles to Great Sand Dunes National Monument (portions of the trail over sand are difficult).

You can even ride directly from Westcliffe to the Middle Taylor Creek SWA, 8 miles west on Hermit Lake Rd (see Fishing below). If you want an added challenge, the primitive USFS Rd 301 continues along to the 13,000-foot crest of the Sangre de Cristos above Hermit and Horseshoe lakes.

Hiking & Backpacking

Climbers use South Colony Lakes as a base camp, yet even if you don't wish to scale peaks, the 12,000-foot tarn lakes beneath the incredibly rugged Crestone Needle are worthy of a visit. Don't expect solitude, though, as the easy access by a 1- to 2-mile hike along **USFS Trail 1339** attracts anyone with a 4WD. From Westcliffe follow Hwy 69 4 miles south to Custer County Rd 119 (Colony Lane); a sign indicates the road leading to the trailheads for South Colony Lakes, Music Pass and Marble Cave (contact the USFS in Cañon City for spelunking information). As you approach the foothills, a glacial trough extending from the peaks comes into view

COLORADO

along with parallel ridges, called lateral moraines. The 6-mile 4WD road follows South Colony Creek up this trough to the trailhead.

Another hiking option in this area traverses the ridge at Music Pass (11,400 feet) leading to Sand Creek Lakes on the west side of the range. An added attraction of this hike is the presence of bighorn sheep herds near Sand Creek Lakes. The trailhead for **USFS Trail 903** is only about a mile west of Music Pass; the lakes are then within 2 miles of the summit. To reach Music Pass, follow the above directions for South Colony Lakes, but continue south on Custer County Rd 119 (Pass Rd) to USFS Rd 329, a 2-mile 4WD road to the trailhead.

For outstanding views from Comanche and Venable passes on the crest of the Sangre de Cristo Mountains, plus a waterfall, the **Comanche/Venable Loop Trail (USFS Trail 1345)** is hard to beat. The trailhead begins at the Alvarado Campground, also reached by the easy Rainbow Trail. This strenuous route can be done as a 10-mile loop or you can continue west from Comanche Pass along Crestone Creek to Crestone in the San Luis Valley. From Comanche Pass, head north along the crest about a mile to Venable Pass. On the return loop descent, look for Venable Falls about a mile below Venable Lakes. Continue to the intersection with Rainbow Trail and turn right (south) back to the Alvarado Campground.

Fishing

Close to Westcliffe is **Middle Taylor Creek SWA** where restrooms, open camping and picnic tables are close to fishing spots along the stream. Rainbow trout are among the species caught in Middle Taylor Creek. Careful observers may see wildlife like beaver, deer, elk and blue grouse. A 4WD road continues to **Hermit Lake** and **Horseshoe Lake** in USFS lands near the 13,000-foot summits of the Sangre de Cristo Mountains. To reach Middle Taylor Creek from Westcliffe, travel 8 miles to

the west on Custer County Rd 160 (Hermit Lake Rd).

The regularly stocked DeWeese Reservoir, and Grape Creek which flows from it, are included in the **DeWeese SWA**. Anglers can expect good catches of pan-sized rainbow trout. Facilities for camping are available on the south side of the reservoir, 4 miles north of Westcliffe on Custer County Rd 251. To get to the north side go 5 miles north on Hwy 69, then turn right (north) on Copper Gulch Rd 1½ miles until you reach the signed access road. For more information about DeWeese, contact the Department of Wildlife (DOW) office in Pueblo (☎ 719-561-4909).

Horseback Riding

Bear Basin Ranch (☎ 719-783-2519), 11 miles east of Westcliffe, offers two-hour rides for $20 or $50 for a full day on extensive ranch property in the Wet Mountains. All-day trips into the mountains are also available for $65. You can also bunk at the ranch for very little if you bring your own sleeping bag.

Rock Climbing

Among the five jagged 14,000-foot peaks in the Crestone group (Crestone Peak, Crestone Needle, Kit Carson Mountain, Challenger Point and Humboldt Peak), only Humboldt Peak is a nontechnical climb. Gary Ziegler, who owns Bear Basin Ranch (☎ 719-783-2519), is a local authority on the peaks and can guide climbing trips.

Special Events

A rodeo and dance are the featured events at the **Custer County Fair**, held during the last weekend in July. Custer County's population more than doubles during the second weekend of August as jazz artists perform both day and night at **Jazz in the Sangres**. Be sure to reserve a room in advance as this event has steadily grown since it began in 1984. For information about the county fair and jazz festival, you can contact the Custer County Chamber of Commerce (☎ 719-783-9163).

Places to Stay

Camping Kleine's Trailer Park (☎ 719-783-2295), east of Silver Cliff at 320 Cliff St, is mostly geared for RVs (sites cost $10) but does allow tent camping and has showers and adjacent laundry facilities.

Abundant open sites are found at nearby Middle Taylor Creek SWA and DeWeese SWA and on USFS lands. The USFS *Alvarado* campground has 47 sites available for $8. Head south from Westcliffe on Hwy 69 for 3 miles and turn right (west) on Custer County Rd 302 (Schoolfield Rd) for 7 miles to the trailhead. A bit farther out is *Lake Creek*, which has 11 sites for $8 each. Go 15 miles north on Hwy 69 to Hillside (store and post office), turn left on Custer County Rd 198 for 4 miles to campsites and USFS Trail 300 to Rainbow Lake.

B&Bs Purnell's Rainbow Inn B&B (☎ 719-783-2313), 104 Main St, has four modern, comfortable rooms that run $60 for shared bath, $70 for private bath, including a hearty breakfast. In addition to an eight-person hot tub, there's also an ice-cream parlor on site, *Custard's Last Stand*.

Motels At Main and S 6th St (Hwy 69) in Westcliffe, the *Antler Motel* (☎ 719-783-2426) has acceptable singles/doubles for $28/31. Newly remodeled rooms cost $60/65 at the *The Courtyard* (☎ 719-783-9616), 410 Main St, which seems a bit steep when one considers the limited amenities (not even phones!). You will not have any complaints at Silver Cliff's *Yoder's High Country Inn* (☎ 719-783-2656), 700 Ohio St, where rooms cost $33/39, discounted for stays of more than two days. The nicest accommodations are at the *Westcliffe Inn* (☎ 719-783-9275) at the south end of Westcliffe on Hwy 69 at the intersection with Hermit Rd. Rooms cost $40/50, and include use of the indoor hot tub and sauna to soothe trail-sore muscles.

Places to Eat

Westcliffe and Silver Cliff don't offer too many choices. The kitchen at *Susie's Cafe*

& Bar (☎ 719-783-3381), 215 Main St in Westcliffe, is open from 6 am to 9 pm daily, and offers $3 breakfast specials, daily lunch specials and reasonably priced dinners. The menu is pretty much standard American fare, though they veer off on Wednesday for 'Mexican Night.' Across the street, *Shining Mountain Food & Gifts* (☎ 719-783-9143), 212 Main St, is a nonsmoking breakfast and lunch spot that offers soups, sandwiches and a variety of Mexican dishes, with plenty of choices for vegetarians. Breakfasts range from $1 to $2 and lunches anywhere from $1 for a taco to $9 for the three-meat Mountain Club sandwich. The side patio is also a plus.

For home-style cooking go to Silver Cliff, where the *High Country Restaurant* (☎ 719-783-2656), 700 Ohio St, offers a complete lunch and dinner menu in a nonsmoking environment from Tuesday to Saturday. The American fare includes soups and baked goods made daily. Lunches run around $5, while dinners are around $8, more for steaks. In Silvercliff, the *Mining Company Restaurant* (☎ 719-783-9144) on 202 Main St is open daily from 7 am to 9 pm, serving varied fare from $4 to $7.

Getting There & Away

Westcliffe and Silver Cliff lie on Hwy 96, which continues east through the Wet Mountains to Pueblo, 54 miles away. An alternate route from Cañon City, 52 miles away, turns south onto Hwy 69 at the Texas Creek junction with US 50 on the Arkansas River. From the north end of the Wet Mountain Valley to the Huerfano River in the south and on to I-25 at Walsenburg, Hwy 69 offers little traffic through pastoral scenery.

SALIDA

Flanked by the soaring 14ers of the Collegiate Range, Salida (population 5000) enjoys a gorgeous setting and an unusually mild climate, making it one of the more desirable places to live in Colorado. However, as many would-be residents have found out, it's still a small town, with an

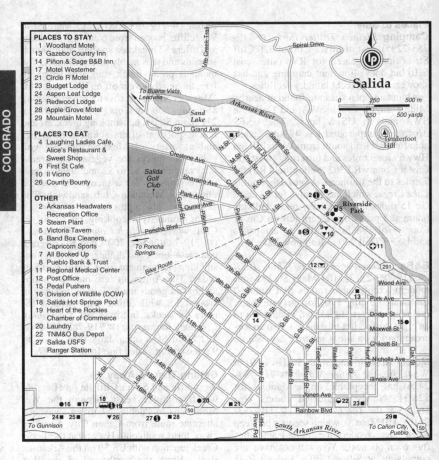

PLACES TO STAY
1 Woodland Motel
13 Gazebo Country Inn
14 Piñon & Sage B&B Inn
17 Motel Westerner
21 Circle R Motel
23 Budget Lodge
24 Aspen Leaf Lodge
25 Redwood Lodge
28 Apple Grove Motel
29 Mountain Motel

PLACES TO EAT
4 Laughing Ladies Cafe,
   Alice's Restaurant &
   Sweet Shop
9 First St Cafe
10 Il Vicino
26 County Bounty

OTHER
2 Arkansas Headwaters
   Recreation Office
3 Steam Plant
5 Victoria Tavern
6 Band Box Cleaners,
   Capricorn Sports
7 All Booked Up
8 Pueblo Bank & Trust
11 Regional Medical Center
12 Post Office
15 Pedal Pushers
16 Division of Wildlife (DOW)
18 Salida Hot Springs Pool
19 Heart of the Rockies
    Chamber of Commerce
20 Laundry
22 TNM&O Bus Depot
27 Salida USFS
    Ranger Station

Salida

0   250   500 m
0   250   500 yards

economy that, unfortunately, leaves little room for newcomers.

Fortunately there's enough space for visitors, who come to enjoy the hiking, rafting, mountain biking and other outdoor activities in town and nearby areas in Chaffee County. When you come back from your outings, there is a fairly good choice of accommodations and several fine restaurants to enjoy.

Salida's position on the lee side of the Continental Divide in the Sawatch Mountains, which include the 14,229-foot Mt Shavano, is responsible for its moderate climate. In fact, the upper Arkansas River valley is a high desert that only receives about 12 inches of annual precipitation with over 300 days of sunshine each year. In the spring, dry Chinook winds sweep down the eastern slopes, removing any vestiges of snow.

History
Before the arrival of Spanish explorers and American expeditions, the valley was inhabited by the Ute tribe. But by 1889 settlers had firmly established themselves, and the Monarch mining district had extracted

$10 million in gold, silver and lead from mineral deposits west of Salida.

Salida became the Chaffee County seat in 1928, wresting that distinction away from rival Buena Vista. Although the rivalry is still apparent in sports and county politics, both communities cooperate in tourist promotion and have joined forces to stop the construction of the proposed Elephant Rock Dam to serve Colorado Springs.

Orientation

US 50 (Rainbow Blvd) is lined with motels and restaurants, while downtown businesses congregate along F St near the river in the historic district. Rainbow Blvd addresses are divided into east and west designations at F St.

Poncha Springs, 5 miles west of Salida at the junction of US 50 and US 285, is used as a mileage reference. Buena Vista is 25 miles north on Hwy 291, a secondary route which passes through Salida's downtown along 1st St and then heads north to link up with US 285.

Good views of the town and valley are available by hiking the spiral trail up 'S' Hill, also called Tenderfoot Hill, reached by crossing the river to Ute Creek Trail north of town.

Information

The Heart of the Rockies Chamber of Commerce (☎ 719-539-2068), 406 W US 50 next to the Hot Springs Pool, is open 9 am to 5 pm daily in summer, weekdays during winter. It provides a free guide to Chaffee County that covers food, lodging and activities in Salida, Buena Vista and Poncha Springs, a walking tour of Salida's historic district, and seasonal 'fun guides' which detail outdoor activities and special events for summer, autumn and winter (spring is apparently too muddy to be really fun).

The Salida USFS Ranger Station (☎ 719-539-3591), 325 W Rainbow Blvd, sells books and topo maps as well as providing information on nearby trails and camping. It's open 8 am to 4:30 pm weekdays.

An ATM is available at Pueblo Bank & Trust (☎ 719-539-6696), 200 F St. The post office is at 310 D St; Salida's zip code is 81201.

Check out the used books and Native American literature at All Booked Up (☎ 719-539-2344), 134 E 1st St.

The Heart of the Rockies Regional Medical Center (☎ 719-539-6661), 448 E 1st St, provides 24-hour emergency care.

The Laundromat at 14th and E St is open daily from 6 am to 10 pm. Band Box Cleaners (☎ 719-539-2426), 119 N F St, has drop-off service. Showers cost $2 at the Salida Hot Springs Pool (☎ 719-539-6738), 410 W Rainbow Blvd.

Hiking

Salida offers hikers convenient access to USFS lands at the Continental Divide intersection of Colorado's two most extensive trails: the **Colorado Trail**, connecting 500 miles of mountain areas between Denver and Durango, and the 100-mile **Rainbow Trail (USFS Trail 1336)** that extends along the east side of the Sangre de Cristo Mountains from the Divide junction south of Marshall Pass to Music Pass. The **South Fooses Creek Trail** is a 6-mile segment of the Colorado Trail that climbs to the Divide beside a trout stream from Chaffee County Rd 225, 13 miles west of Poncha Springs.

A moderate 4-mile hike to Pass Creek Lake (11,600 feet) follows **USFS Trail 1411** from Chaffee County Rds 210 and 212, 2 miles west of Poncha Springs.

Mt Shavano (14,229 feet) is a strenuous 4-mile hike on **USFS Trail 1428**. You can reach the trailhead on foot from the USFS Angel of Shavano Campground (see camping below) by following an easy section of the Colorado Trail north about 2 miles through aspen groves. To bicycle or drive to the trailhead from Poncha Springs head west 2 miles on US 50 and turn right on Chaffee County Rd 250, then turn left on Chaffee County Rd 252 to Blanks Cabin before heading north half a mile to the trailhead.

For further information and descriptions of the trails contact the Salida USFS Ranger Station (see Information above).

COLORADO

Mountain Biking
The most popular ride for experienced cyclists acclimated to high altitudes is the 12-mile Monarch Crest Trail (USFS Trail 531) along the Continental Divide south of Monarch Pass (11,386 feet) to Marshall Pass (10,840 feet). Thunderstorms can be a problem on the exposed crest, but it is easy to turn back during the initial climb if weather, altitude or terrain are too challenging. To get to the trailhead, take US 50 past Monarch Park and turn left on USFS Rd 906.

Cyclists who shuttle to Monarch Pass (see below) can ride the Divide and then choose between three exhilarating descents to Poncha Springs. The easiest route adds 16 miles to the journey and drops from Marshall Pass along old railroad tracks, now the graded Marshall Pass Rd (Chaffee County Rd 200), to US 285 into Poncha Springs. If you want some help getting to the top, High Valley Center (☎ 719-539-6089, 800-871-5145) runs a mountain bike shuttle service to Monarch Pass, 18 miles west of their location at the Conoco gas station, 305 S Main St, Poncha Springs. The ride costs $11 per person. Guided half-day rides with shuttle are offered by American Adventure Expeditions (☎ 719-395-2409) and cost $40.

Another challenging ride climbs about 2000 feet up Methodist Mountain, south of Salida on Chaffee County Rd 107, then Rd 108, to reach the Rainbow Trail (USFS Trail 1336), after which it returns along Bear Creek (Chaffee County Rd 101) and US 50 to complete a 20-mile loop. This route offers 6 miles of single track and another 5 miles of 4WD road. For an extended adventure, the Rainbow Trail continues into the Wet Mountain Valley and the town of Westcliffe, about 75 miles away.

Beginning riders enjoy Garfield Trail, a scenic forest route that follows the gentle gradient of an abandoned railroad spur for an up-and-back ride of under 8 miles. The trail starts in the town of Garfield, just off of Chaffee County Rd 228.

For more information on the area's many bike trails, pick up a free copy of 'Mountain Bike Guide to the 14ers Region' at the Chamber of Commerce or the USFS office. For bike supplies, service and rental visit Pedal Pushers (☎ 719-539-7498), 338 Oak St, which rents front suspension bicycle for $22 per day. Capricorn Sports (☎ 719-539-3971), 123½ N F St, (next to Band Box Cleaners) rents bikes with front suspension for $16 per day.

Downhill Skiing
With over 300 inches of snow each year, the Monarch Ski & Snowboard Area (☎ 719-539-3573, 800-996-7669) offers excellent downhill skiing conditions over 670 acres of terrain with a 1160-foot vertical drop served by four double chairlifts. About two-thirds of the mountain's trails are for intermediate and beginning level skiers, the rest for expert powder hounds. Daily lift tickets are $32 for adults, $18 for children ages seven to 12. For snow conditions, call ☎ 719-228-7943.

Cross-Country Skiing
A portion of the Old Monarch Pass route is groomed by the resort, which offers 2 miles of cross-country skiing. With a vehicle shuttle, you can have more adventurous ski touring by following the old path over the Divide and continuing downhill for 12 miles to the town of Sargents on the western slope.

Floating
In contrast to the daring white-water rapids upstream near Buena Vista or in the Royal Gorge near Cañon City, Salida features rather sedate float trips perfect for families or beginners. For scenic viewing trips, ask to have the raft fitted with oars so you are not bothered by paddling. Many of the area's rafting companies offer trips that involve tedious early morning bus rides to the boat launch sites: try and avoid these unnecessary shuttle excursions unless you're taking overnight trips.

Canyon Marine (☎ 719-539-7476, 800-643-0707), 129 W Rainbow Blvd, also offers part-day 'Salida East' trips for $29 ($23 for kids). Similar scenic trips cost

$28 for adults and $24 for kids at Timberwolf Whitewater Expeditions (☎ 719-539-7508), 4305 E US 50. For a complete list of all outfits permitted to operate on the Arkansas Headwaters, as well as full information on rafting and fishing opportunities, visit the Arkansas Headwaters Recreation Office (☎ 719-539-7289), 307 W Sackett St.

Fishing
During the spring and fall, anglers can expect good fishing for brown and rainbow trout averaging 12 inches on the Arkansas River. Public access is good, as much of the river runs through BLM land. The Department of Wildlife (DOW) also has several fishing easements just upstream from town. Many of the nearby lakes and streams also offer decent cold-water fishing.

For additional information contact the DOW (☎ 719-539-3529), 7405 W Rainbow Blvd. Fishing supplies are available from Salida Sporting Goods (☎ 719-539-6221), 509 E Rainbow Blvd.

Swimming
In 1937 the WPA completed Colorado's largest indoor hot springs pool facility. Water temperatures in three separate sections are maintained at between 92° and 100°F – with lap lanes always available in an 82-foot pool. In addition, private European-style hot baths are offered for $5. The Salida Hot Springs Pool (☎ 719-539-6738), 410 W Rainbow Blvd, is open daily from 1 to 9 pm in the summer, but is closed on Mondays and operates shorter hours on the winter weekdays. Admission costs $5/3 for adults/students.

Golf
The Salida Golf Club (☎ 719-539-1060) at Crestone Ave and Grant St has nine holes amid fragrant Russian olive trees and outstanding mountain views for a very reasonable $11.

Special Events
Salida's annual boat race on the third weekend in June, **FIBArk** (First in Boating

on the Arkansas), features serious kayak and raft races, plus the **Hooligan Race**, an event that sees some rather unique craft (such as a brass bed) take to the waters. The 26-mile race includes lengthy sections of relatively quiet water that test paddling strength. Festivities and live music take place at Riverside Park and the F St bridge.

Late June is also the time for **Salida's Art Walk** through the many galleries and studios in the historic district.

Places to Stay
Camping In the vicinity of Salida, the USFS operates four developed campgrounds (fee charged) and one primitive campground. *O'Haver Lake*, 8 miles southwest of Poncha Springs on US 285 and USFS Rd 243, has 29 sites that cost $9. Seven miles west of Poncha Springs, on your right, is the turnoff to USFS Rd 240 which follows the North Fork of the South Arkansas River 4 miles to *Angel of Shavano*, on the Colorado Trail. It offers 20 sites for $8. Bring your own water and pack out all trash from the primitive *North Fork* campground ($5 fee) at 11,000 feet, another 5 miles up from the beautiful valley. *Garfield*, adjacent to US 50, 12 miles west of Poncha Springs, has 11 sites for $8. Another 2 miles up US 50 brings you to the turnoff to *Monarch Park*, where 36 sites are available for $8.50 each. This campground at 10,500 feet is a good place to get acclimated to the altitude. Reservations (☎ 800-280-2267) can be made for O'Haver Lake, Angel of Shavano and Monarch Park campgrounds.

B&Bs Outdoor enthusiasts should consider staying at the *Piñon & Sage B&B Inn* (☎ 719-539-3227, 800-840-3156), 803 F St, which offers four Southwest-style rooms with shared or private bath in a beautifully restored late-Victorian home. Breakfast is made to order and there's a hot tub on the premises. Rooms start at $55 in summer, $45 in winter. The owners are actively involved in all kinds of outdoor sports, and are happy to give tips on hiking, biking, rafting and other area activities.

The Gazebo Country Inn (☎ 719-539-7806), 507 E 3rd St, is a Victorian house with a white picket fence that offers three rooms with private bath and full breakfast beginning at $65.

The River Run Inn (☎ 719-539-3818), northwest of town at 8495 Chaffee County Rd 160 or 3 miles east of US 285, is listed on the National Register of Historic Places and offers six rooms, two with private bath, for $60 to $70. There is also a small dormitory that has beds for $25.

Motels The *Motel Westerner* (☎ 719-539-2618), 7335 US 50, is not too fancy, but charges only $25/30 for singles/doubles year-round. The *Budget Lodge* (☎ 719-539-6695), 1146 US 50 (Rainbow Blvd), has very basic rooms for $30/35 in summer, $24/28 in winter.

If you don't mind spending a bit more, there are several places that offer quite good value. At the east end of town at 1425 E Rainbow the attractive *Mountain Motel* (☎ 719-539-4420) has older wood-paneled cabin-style rooms with kitchen and sitting area for $45 in summer, as well as newer rooms for $50. Subtract $10 from the rates at other times of the year. Off-the-beaten-track, but only 7 blocks northwest of downtown at 903 W 1st St, the small *Woodland Motel* (☎ 719-539-4980, 800-488-0456) is another good bet, offering immaculate rooms starting at $35/40 in summer. There's a hot tub on the premises.

There's a shaded picnic area with basketball court and horseshoe pit at the older *Apple Grove Motel* (☎ 719-539-4722), 129 W Rainbow Blvd. Rooms with refrigerators and microwave ovens cost $42/52 in summer, $25/35 in the off-season. The *Circle R Motel* (☎ 719-539-6296, 800-755-6296), 304 E Rainbow Blvd, looks pretty well worn, but does have a hot tub and laundry. Rooms run about $40 in summer, $12 less in the off-season.

Well-maintained rooms cost $50/60 at the *Aspen Leaf Lodge* (☎ 719-539-6733, 800-759-0338), 7350 W Hwy 50, which also has a hot tub. A bit more upscale, the *Redwood Lodge* (☎ 719-539-2528,

800-234-1077), 7310 US 50, has a heated pool, two hot tubs, sun decks and a back yard overlooking the mountains. Singles/doubles start at $59/65 in summer (around $20 less in the off-season). Family suites and rooms with enclosed hot tubs are also available.

Hotels & Condominiums *Monarch Mountain Lodge* (☎ 800-332-3668), on US 50, 18 miles west of Salida and 3 miles from the ski resort, has doubles for $79 weekdays ($109 weekends and holidays) during the ski season. Ask about a ski-and-stay package with one night's lodging and a one-day lift pass for about $49 per person ($69 weekends and holidays). *Ski Town Condominiums* (☎ 719-539-3240, 800-678-0341) are next to the Monarch Lodge. High-season rates for a two-bedroom condominium are $90 for up to four people, $10 per additional guest.

Places to Eat
You can get fresh, healthy food, espresso and draft microbrews at the *First St Cafe* (☎ 719-539-4759), 137 E 1st St, Monday to Saturday from 8 am to 8 pm (until 10 pm Friday and Saturday). Housed in a handsome two-story commercial building dating back to 1880, the cafe serves breakfast delights like French toast stuffed with cream cheese and walnuts or a casserole of egg, potatoes and vegetables for about $5. The lunches go for a very reasonable $6.

For an early morning coffee shop, the *County Bounty Restaurant* (☎ 719-539-3546), 413 W Rainbow Blvd, is a surprise, offering homemade granola with a fresh whole-wheat apple muffin for around $3 and an extensive menu that includes about any American-style dish you might ask for.

For dirt-cheap burgers or a cool ice-cream treat from an old-fashioned soda fountain, stop by *Alice's Restaurant & Sweet Shop* (☎ 719-539-9931) at 130 1st St.

For excellent Italian food and a choice of six or seven craft-brewed beers, head to *Il Vicino Wood Oven Pizza & Brewery* (☎ 719-539-5219), 136 E 2nd St. There are

10 types of pizza for around $7 that, along with a salad or the outstanding minestrone soup, should fill two persons.

Definitely worth a visit is the *Laughing Ladies Cafe* (☎ 719-539-6209), 128 W 1st St, which offers a great menu of innovative and diverse dinners and desserts from 5 to 9 pm in a dining room decorated with the work of local artists. It's also open for lunch from 11 am to 3 pm; Sunday brunch runs from 8 am to 2 pm. It's closed Mondays.

Out in Poncha Springs, the historic *Jackson Hotel* (☎ 719-539-4861), 6340 US 285, has played host to the likes of Jesse & Frank James, President Ulysses S Grant, Rudyard Kipling and Susan B Anthony. Its boarding days might be over, but it still lives up to its legacy by serving fine American and Mexican lunches and dinners in an appealing Western setting. The restaurant's owners have done a great job of restoring the place, and the hotel section has been converted into a small museum/antique shop, a nice diversion if you need to wait for a table. Prices range from $7 for burgers and sandwiches to $17 for an 8-oz tenderloin steak. Reservations are recommended.

Entertainment
A good crowd usually shows up for live music at the *Victoria Tavern* (☎ 719-539-4891), 143 N F St, on the corner of Sackett Ave, opposite Riverside Park. With century-old decor, pool tables and numerous fine brews on tap, the 'Vic,' erected as the Park Saloon in 1886, still has a lot of character.

The *Steam Plant*, 200 W Sackett St, features irregular summer performances by visiting dance groups, jazz musicians and other performing artists.

Getting There & Away
Bus Daily TNM&O (☎ 719-539-7474) buses serving Denver and Grand Junction stop at 731 Blake St, near Rainbow Blvd (US 50) on the east end of town. Eastbound buses depart at 11:30 am, westbound at 4:45 pm. The office hours vary, so call ahead. Chaffee Transit (☎ 719-539-3935), 132 W 1st St, provides shuttle service in summer to/from Breckenridge for $25 per person, and winter shuttles to Colorado Springs for $40. Call to check the latest schedules and fares.

Car Located 135 miles west of Denver via US 285, Salida is on the Arkansas River headwaters, 20 miles east of the Continental Divide. Access from Colorado Springs, which is 100 miles east, is via US 50 over Monarch Pass (which, at 11,386 feet, makes for dangerous conditions during winter).

Getting Around
The Ride (☎ 719-539-3797), a limited taxi service within Salida, is available weekdays from 8 am to 4 pm.

BUENA VISTA
Appropriately named but horribly pronounced locally as 'Beyuna Vista,' Buena Vista (population 1800) is a white-water rafting mecca, complete with a city park boat-launching area. To the west, the 'vista' is the lofty Collegiate Peaks area formed (from north to south) by Mts Oxford (14,153 feet), Harvard (14,420 feet), Columbia (14,073 feet), Yale (14,196 feet) and Princeton (14,197). Mountain bicyclists, anglers and rafters overrun the small town during busy summer months when food and lodging become valuable commodities.

Orientation
Cottonwood Creek flows through the center of town and the Arkansas River runs against the cliffs on the eastern side of town. Most travelers pass through on US 24, intersected by E Main St, which leads through downtown to the Arkansas River.

Information
The visitors center (☎ 719-395-6612), in a former church built in 1880 at 343 S US 24, is open weekdays from 9 am to 4 pm and has free copies of the 'Chaffee County Visitors Guide,' seasonal guides detailing outdoor activities, a mountain biking booklet, and a free walking tour guide to historic buildings and sites.

COLORADO

COLORADO

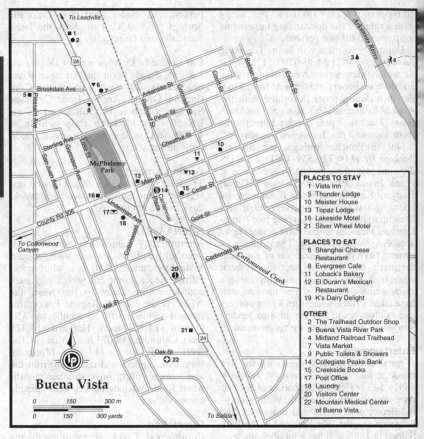

Buena Vista

| 0 | 150 | 300 m |
| 0 | 150 | 300 yards |

To Leadville

To Cottonwood Canyon

To Salida

Arkansas River

McPhelemy Park

Centennial Plaza

Cottonwood Creek

PLACES TO STAY
1 Vista Inn
5 Thunder Lodge
10 Meister House
13 Topaz Lodge
16 Lakeside Motel
21 Silver Wheel Motel

PLACES TO EAT
6 Shanghai Chinese Restaurant
8 Evergreen Cafe
11 Loback's Bakery
12 El Duran's Mexican Restaurant
19 K's Dairy Delight

OTHER
2 The Trailhead Outdoor Shop
3 Buena Vista River Park
4 Midland Railroad Trailhead
7 Vista Market
9 Public Toilets & Showers
14 Collegiate Peaks Bank
15 Creekside Books
17 Post Office
18 Laundry
20 Visitors Center
22 Mountain Medical Center of Buena Vista

The Collegiate Peaks Bank (☎ 719-395-2472), 105 Centennial Plaza, has an ATM. The post office is at 110 Brookdale Ave; the zip code is 81211.

Creekside Books (☎ 719-395-6416), 300 Cedar St, offers a good selection of new books, travel guides and periodicals. Trail guides and maps are available at The Trailhead (☎ 719-395-8001), north of town at 707 US 24.

The Mountain Medical Center of Buena Vista (☎ 719-395-8632) is located west of US 24 at 36 Oak St.

The laundry at 104 Linderman Ave is open daily from 7 am to 10 pm. Public restrooms with coin-operated showers (25¢ per minute) are open daily 24 hours, at the end of E Main beside the Buena Vista Community Center.

White-Water Rafting
Buena Vista is on the map because of the great white-water opportunities on the Arkansas River. The town lies at one of the most exciting portions of the Arkansas Headwaters Recreation Area, a 148-mile-long stretch of state-run recreation facilities and wildlife areas. For maps and complete information on the area, check in with the Arkansas Headwaters Recreation

Office in Salida (☎ 719-539-7289), 307 W Sackett St. Access to boat put-in points usually costs $1 and camping sites are $6, though at the time of writing there were plans to hike these rates.

Upstream from Buena Vista is 'The Numbers,' so named because within 200 yards of the boat launch are six consecutive Class IV and Class V rapids. This stretch demands plenty of respect and should not be attempted without both previous Class IV white-water paddling experience and a knowledgeable guide. To view the awesome spectacle of roaring water coursing down the narrow channel, drive 11 miles north on US 24 and cross the bridge to the Otero pump station, then turn right on Chaffee County Rd 371. Pine Creek Canyon above the bridge contains Class VI – unrunnable – rapids that mark the Arkansas' graduation to a full-fledged river.

Below Buena Vista, Class III-IV (moderately difficult to difficult) rapids churn through the narrow Brown's Canyon – the most popular stretch of the river in the entire state. Full-day trips put in at Buena Vista, while half-day excursions launch at Fisherman's Bridge in Nathrop, 7 miles south of Buena Vista, before charging through the exciting rapids in Brown's Canyon. Most trips end at the Hecla Junction landing reached by Chaffee County Rd 194; the turnoff from US 285 is 2 miles north of the junction with Hwy 291. You can also spend the night in the Brown's Canyon Wilderness Study Area.

Typical rates for full-day Brown's Canyon raft trips, including lunch, run $55 to $59 for adults with around $10 off for children. The recommended minimum age is eight years. Expect to pay the upper amount on weekends and holidays. Most guide companies charge between $28 and $32 for half-day trips. A 5% river user fee is added to all rates. Buffalo Joe River Trips (☎ 719-395-8757, 800-356-7984), 113 N Railroad St, is a company with a good reputation for safe and enjoyable trips. Also try Wilderness Aware (☎ 719-395-2112, 800-462-7238), south of town on Chaffee County Rd 317.

At Johnson Village, where US 24/US 285 crosses the river 2 miles south of Buena Vista, you will find both Good Times Rafting (☎ 719-453-5559, 800-477-0144) and American Adventure Expeditions (☎ 800-288-0675).

At Nathrop, Dvorak's Kayak and Rafting Expeditions (☎ 719-539-6851, 800-824-3795) has also built up a good reputation.

Fishing

With all the rafts in the water, you might wonder if there is any room left for the fish. Yet the Arkansas River has a good supply of fish, mainly wild brown trout. Anglers frequent its banks at the Buena Vista River Park, at the foot of Main St. Other nearby fishing spots include the area near the Midland Tunnels, 4 miles north on Chaffee County Rd 371 and at Ruby Mountain, administered by the Arkansas Headwaters Recreation Area.

Tributary streams to the Arkansas River and mountain lakes are especially popular for fly casting. South of Buena Vista, native cutthroat trout inhabit the headwaters and beaver ponds of Brown's Creek, reached by hiking 5 miles on USFS Trail 1385. Above the Mount Princeton Hot Springs, the Cascades area of Chalk Creek and Chalk Lake are regularly stocked with rainbow trout. West of town, South Cottonwood Creek above Cottonwood Lake is good for brook trout, while nonmotorized boats on the lake capture larger fish. Kokanee salmon inhabit the Clear Creek Reservoir SWA, 13 miles north of Buena Vista on US 24 to the reservoir turnoff. You might also hook into a giant rainbow lunker here.

For more information, a detailed fishing map is offered for sale by the Collegiate Peak Chapter of Trout Unlimited at The Trailhead outdoor shop (☎ 719-395-8001), 707 N US 24.

Mountain Biking

East of Buena Vista, across the pedestrian/bike bridge at the foot of Main St, the Midland Bike Trail follows the gentle grade of the old Colorado Midland Railroad. To avoid the initial 3/4-mile climb up the steep

Whipple Trail to the old depot site, many cyclists begin by shuttling to the end of the 6-mile Midland Trail. At 5 miles east of Johnson Village turn left on USFS Rd 315. The trailhead is about half a mile from the highway. Many other trail options offering challenging climbs are possible from the Midland Trail.

North along the river from Buena Vista Park, the combination of riverside trail and Chaffee County Rd 371 leads to three old railroad tunnels and the Elephant Rock formation just beyond the third tunnel. Midway on the 4-mile trip, you will cross the Arkansas River. For a longer out-and-back ride you can continue another 5 miles north along the river to watch white-water fanatics tackle the near-suicidal Numbers section.

Another appealing – yet more difficult – area to explore on bike is the St Elmo ghost town and, farther up, the remains of the Alpine Tunnel. In 1880 it was the highest (11,524 feet) and costliest railroad tunnel built. To get there, travel south 9 miles on US 285, then turn right (west) on Chaffee County Rd 162 past Mount Princeton Hot Springs to St Elmo, listed on the National Register of Historic Places, about 15 miles from the highway. South from St Elmo, the old railroad grade follows USFS Rd 295 for 8 miles to the Alpine Tunnel, passing Romley and Hancock on the way.

Bike rentals cost $25 with front suspension and repairs are done at the outdoor shop, The Trailhead (☎ 719-395-8001), north of town at 707 US 24.

Hiking & Backpacking
For superior views of Buena Vista with the Collegiate Peaks in the background, head to the Buena Vista River Park at the foot of Main St and cross the pedestrian bridge to climb the cliffside **Whipple Trail** to the old Colorado Midland Railroad depot on the ridgetop.

North of Cottonwood Canyon, the **Collegiate Peaks Wilderness Area** offers Alpine backcountry hiking. After a day or more of acclimation, you can hike to the top of Mt Harvard, Colorado's third-highest peak, or Mt Yale. An easy 4-mile, one-way

hike to Kroenke Lake is a good day trip or the start of a longer backpack trip that includes a scramble up one of the peaks or a crossing of the Continental Divide. From The Trailhead sporting goods store north of town (see Mountain Biking), go west 2 miles on Chaffee County Rd 350, then turn right on Chaffee County Rd 361. After 1 mile, turn left on Chaffee County Rd 365 and continue for 5 miles to the North Cottonwood Creek trailhead for **USFS Trail 1449**. Kroenke Lake is accessed via **Trail 1448**, which branches south from **Trail 1449**.

A free hiking guide describing over 10 other hikes near Buena Vista is available at the visitors center and detailed topo maps and guides are sold at The Trailhead.

Places to Stay
On summer weekends, every room in town is certain to be filled. Prices can fluctuate wildly from the rates that you may be told by the chamber of commerce.

Camping West of town the USFS operates two campgrounds. *Cottonwood Lake* is on South Cottonwood Creek above Cottonwood Lake, about 5 miles down USFS Rd 344 from the Chaffee County Rd 306 turnoff. Campsites cost $9 and are on a first-come, first-served basis. Mountain goats are often spotted on the way to the camp. The large *Collegiate Peaks* campground, on Middle Cottonwood Creek 11 miles west of Buena Vista on Chaffee County Rd 306, offers campsites for $10 and accepts reservations (☎ 800-280-2267).

B&Bs The handsome *Meister House* (☎ 719-395-9220, 800-882-1821) at 414 E Main St was built in the 1890s as a hotel and now offers six rooms that start at $75 in summer, $65 in the off-season. A full breakfast is served in the open courtyard.

Motels & Cabins Cabins on the bank of Cottonwood Creek cost $64 in summer at *Thunder Lodge* (☎ 719-395-2245), 207 Brookdale Ave. In winter, rates start at $50 double occupancy. The *Vista Court Cabins*

& *Lodge* (☎ 719-395-6557), west of downtown at 1004 W Main St, surrounds a large grassy area and patio and represent a good value with cabins for $60 and lodge rooms starting at $50 in summer, $40 and $35 respectively in winter.

The rustic log *Silver Wheel Motel* (☎ 719-395-2955), 520 S US 24, has clean singles/doubles for $51/63, $35/45 in winter. Single/double motel rooms are overpriced at $60/68 in summer at the modest *Topaz Lodge* (☎ 719-395-2427), on the corner of US 24 and E Main St. But rates fall by as much as $20 in winter. Off the busy highway and next to the town park and lake, the *Lakeside Motel* (☎ 719-395-2994) at 112 Lake St, has well-scrubbed doubles available for $50.

For top-end hotel rooms there's the *Vista Inn* (☎ 719-395-8009, 800-809-3495), 733 N US 24. Rooms are nicely furnished and there are three outdoor hot tubs that enjoy great mountain views. Singles/doubles cost $65/80 in summer, $55/65 in winter, and the rate includes a generous Continental breakfast.

Five miles east of town at the mouth of Cottonwood Canyon, *Cottonwood Hot Springs Inn* (☎ 719-395-6434) is a lodging smorgasbord offering tepees for $18 per person, dorm beds for $20, rooms for $52 ($62 on weekends) and cabins with private hot tub for $75. The laid-back atmosphere may not appeal to everyone, but blissful guests can soak in three rock-lined soaking pools.

Places to Eat

Since it opened in 1936, *Loback's Bakery* at 326 E Main St has had tried-and-true formulas for donuts and shepherds bread. The roadside snack bar *K's Dairy Delight* (☎ 719-395-8695) at 223 S US 24 hasn't changed its menu much either since opening next to the shady streamside picnic grounds.

Starting at 6:30 am, the *Evergreen Cafe* (☎ 719-395-8984), 418 N US 24, offers a large breakfast menu, including eggs Benedict. It also serves lunch (mainly burgers and sandwiches) and Italian-style dinners.

The *Shanghai Chinese Restaurant* (☎ 719-395-4950), 527 W Lake St (next to the Vista Super Market on US 24), offers perhaps the best dining bargain in Buena Vista. Lunches cost $4.

El Durán's Mexican Restaurant & Sports Lounge (☎ 719-395-2120), 301 E Main St, offers complete meals, but for under $3 you can get spicy à la carte dishes like a bowl of green chile soup with a tortilla, a burrito or chiles rellenos.

Getting There & Away

Buena Vista is 122 miles west of Pueblo via US 50, Hwy 291 and US 285. It's 83 miles east of Gunnison via US 50 and US 285. Denver is 115 miles northeast by I-70, Hwy 91 and US 24.

AROUND BUENA VISTA
Princeton Hot Springs Area

The turnoff from US 285 to *Mt Princeton Hot Springs Resort* (☎ 719-395-2361), 15870 Chaffee County Rd 162, is 6 miles south of Buena Vista. Choose between outdoor pools and indoor soaking at the century-old bathhouse. Cliffside rooms look out on the Collegiate Peaks and start at $77 for a double. The Princeton Club dining room offers steaks and seafood. If you're not staying you can still access the pools from 9 am to 9 pm (except during the spring run-off when they're closed). Admission is $6 for adults, $3 for children.

The Inn at Chalk Cliffs (☎ 719-395-6068), 16557 Chaffee County Rd 162, is a B&B in a modern home with gorgeous views. Three rooms, all with private bath, start at $75. An added feature are two rock-lined natural hot water soaking pools on the premises. Farther up the road on beautiful Chalk Creek, the *Streamside Bed & Breakfast* (☎ 719-395-2553), 18820 Chaffee County Rd 162, offers doubles with private bath and full breakfast for $71 to $76. This place makes a good base to explore the surrounding San Isabel National Forest.

On your way to the St Elmo ghost town and Alpine Tunnel, you may see bighorn sheep and mountain goat. You definitely should not miss the short trail to **Agnes**

Vaille Falls on your right opposite Chalk Lake. Three USFS campgrounds – *Mt Princeton*, *Chalk Lake* and *Cascade* – are all found within a 1-mile stretch. Each has about 20 campsites that go for $9 each and will most likely require a reservation (☎ 719-800-280-2267) during the popular summer months.

Twin Lakes

Twin Lakes is widely known as the trailhead leading up to 14,433-foot **Mt Elbert**, Colorado's highest peak. It's between Buena Vista and Leadville, 7 miles west of US 24 on Hwy 82 – the white-knuckle route over 12,095-foot Independence Pass (closed in winter) to Aspen. The once natural Twin Lakes now serve as a pumped storage facility, but anglers couldn't care less as long as they continue to catch giant Mackinaw and smaller rainbow trout. During the winter, Twin Lakes is a favorite cross-country ski area for well-informed Coloradans.

Three USFS campgrounds have sites for $9, while those at the large lakeside *White Star* campground cost $10. Reservations (☎ 800-280-2267) are accepted at White Star and *Lakeview*, which offers sites perched on top of a glacial moraine ridgetop overlooking the lakes, only 4 miles west of the junction with US 24. It's also the trailhead for the strenuous 6-mile climb up Mt Elbert; follow the **Colorado Trail** (USFS Trail 1776) for the first 3 miles, then turn left on USFS Trail 1481 to the summit. *Parry Peak* and *Twin Peaks* campgrounds are next to Lake Creek, farther up the valley at 10 and 12 miles respectively west of the junction. For more information contact the Leadville Ranger Station (☎ 719-486-0749).

For unsurpassed German dishes, stop at the *Nordic Inn* (☎ 719-486-1830) in the village of Twin Lakes at 6435 Hwy 82. The historic inn once served as a stagecoach stop and brothel. Rooms in the annex have shared bath and common kitchen, and cost $39/45 a single/double. The main building offers rooms with shared bath for $39/48, rooms with private bath for $55/70. During

the winter, the lodge is open solely on weekends and holidays.

GUNNISON

Gunnison (population 5100) is home to the handsome campus of **Western State College**, opened in 1911. A short excursion through the older residential neighborhoods will reveal numerous Victorians and masonry homes, their lawns and trees watered by the unique Gunnison ditch system. However, most folks blast through on their way to Crested Butte.

The Gunnison Country Chamber of Commerce Visitor's Center (☎ 970-641-1501, 800-323-2453) is on the east side of town at 500 E Tomichi (US 50). Here you can pick up a self-guided historic walking tour booklet, maps of area mountain bike trails, as well as the usual lists of accommodations and activities. The USFS has an office at 216 N Colorado Ave, which is open weekdays from 7:30 am to 4:30 pm.

The Gunnison Bank & Trust at 232 W Tomichi has an ATM. The post office is at 200 N Wisconsin St. The zip code is 81230.

Places to Stay & Eat

A great place to hang your hat and slip off your boots is the *Cattleman Inn* (☎ 970-641-1061, 888-223-3466), 301 W Tomichi, which offers bargain hotel rooms with private bath for $20/25 a single/double. Reservations are recommended in summer and autumn.

Larger, better furnished rooms are available at the friendly *Hylander Inn* (☎ 970-641-0700), though they also cost more: from $38/54 in winter to $52/68 in summer. It's located at 412 W Tomichi, near the visitors center. On the other side of Tomichi Ave, *Bennet's Western Motel* (☎ 970-641-1722) has similar rates.

The main floor restaurant at the Cattleman Inn doubles as the informal board room for locals each morning, while the downstairs *Beef & Barrel* offers reasonably priced home-style dinner specials. The *Sidewalk Cafe* (☎ 970-641-4130), 113 W Tomichi Ave, prepares a vegetarian omelet for $4 and pancakes for $1 each – eat a full stack and get a free breakfast! If you're on your way to Crested Butte and need a caffeine fix, stop by the *Steaming Bean* (☎ 970-641-2408), 120 N Main St (Hwy 135).

Getting There & Away
Air Gunnison County Airport (☎ 970-641-2304) is south of US 50 at 711 Rio Grande Ave. During the ski season Boeing 757 airliners migrate to Gunnison: American offers daily nonstop jets to Dallas-Ft Worth, and Delta flies daily to Atlanta. United Express connects Gunnison with Denver year-round, with some five flights daily. Mountain Air Express also has one daily flight to Denver.

Bus TNM&O buses connecting Pueblo with Grand Junction stop at the Gunnison County Airport Terminal (☎ 970-641-0060), 711 Rio Grande Ave. The eastbound bus departs at 9:30 am, the westbound at 6:45 pm.

Car Gunnison lies on US 50, 65 miles east of Montrose, and 34 miles west of Monarch Pass – the highway to the Divide is a scenic route that follows Tomichi Creek.

Getting Around
To/From the Airport Alpine Express (☎ 970-641-5074, 800-822-4844), at the Gunnison County Airport Terminal, meets all commercial flights in the winter but requires reservations during the summer months. Roundtrip fares to Crested Butte cost $36.

Car At the airport, you can rent from Budget (☎ 970-641-4403), Avis (☎ 970-641-0263) or Hertz (☎ 970-641-2881).

CRESTED BUTTE
On the headwaters to the Gunnison River, the historic mining town of Crested Butte only has 1070 residents, yet its fabulous ski area warrants nonstop jet service from Dallas and Atlanta, GA, to Gunnison County Airport, 28 miles south. A modern ski resort complex, Crested Butte Mountain Resort (CBMR), sits about 2 miles north of the town at the base of the impressive mountain also called Crested Butte. The area is surrounded by forests and rugged mountain peaks in the Elk Mountains, plus three wilderness areas: West Elk, Raggeds and Maroon Bells-Snowmass. The latter area forms a barrier to all but the hearty hiker or mountain bicyclist between Crested Butte and Aspen, only 25 miles to the north as the crow flies.

Visitors will be struck by the stunning beauty of the valley on the approach to Crested Butte from Gunnison. The town also has a laid-back feel that sets it apart from glamour resorts like Aspen and Vail. Whether due to Crested Butte's roots as a coal mining town (as opposed to gold or silver), its sense of community or its relative isolation, the result is a relaxed, friendly atmosphere that makes it easy to while away days and weeks here.

Another good quality of Crested Butte is the progressive approach the ski area has taken toward development. While the CBMR recognizes that further growth in the area is inevitable, it has been working hard to keep new construction confined to areas that are already developed. The goals are to preserve the area's open space and natural beauty, and keep residences and accommodation clustered so that it can be viably served by public transportation. The company is also working with developers to maintain a supply of affordable housing and ensure that the community really benefits from the tourist dollars. Locals are still opposed to the resort's plans to expand its skiable terrain, but most recognize that CBMR is not the kind of steamroller operation that has taken over other ski towns.

History
Utes from the Tabeguache and Uncompahgre bands once hunted in the area during summer months. Following the federal government's removal of the Utes in 1869 to the Los Pinos Indian Agency, a government cow camp was established

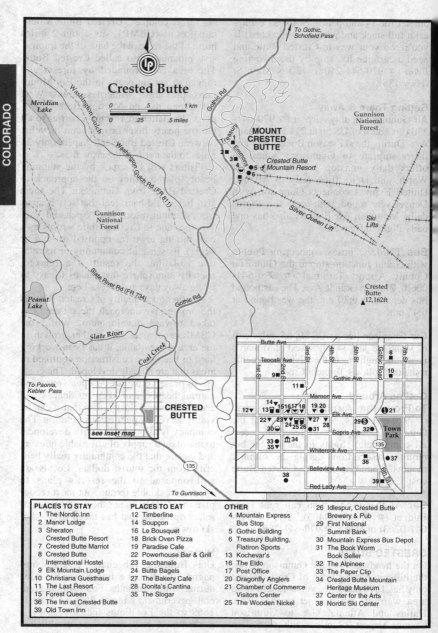

Crested Butte

0   .5   1 km
0   .25   .5 miles

Meridian Lake

Washington Gulch

Washington Gulch Rd (FR 811)

Gunnison National Forest

Gothic Rd

Treasury

Emmons

MOUNT CRESTED BUTTE

Crested Butte Mountain Resort

Silver Queen Lift

Ski Lifts

Crested Butte ▲12,162ft

Slate River Rd (FR 734)

Gothic Rd

Peanut Lake

Slate River

Coal Creek

To Paonia, Kebler Pass

CRESTED BUTTE

see inset map

135

To Gunnison

To Gothic, Schofield Pass

Gunnison National Forest

Inset map

Butte Ave

Teocalli Ave

3rd St   4th St   5th St

Gothic Road

7th St

8

10

9

11

Gothic Ave

Maroon Ave

14   15 16 17 18   19 20   Elk Ave   21

12   13   Town Park

22   23   24 25 26   27   Sopris Ave   29 32

30   31   135

33   34   Whiterock Ave

35

36   37

38   Belleview Ave

39

Red Lady Ave

1st St   2nd St

PLACES TO STAY	PLACES TO EAT	OTHER	
1 The Nordic Inn	12 Timberline	4 Mountain Express Bus Stop	26 Idlespur, Crested Butte Brewery & Pub
2 Manor Lodge	14 Soupçon	5 Gothic Building	29 First National Summit Bank
3 Sheraton Crested Butte Resort	16 Le Bousquet	6 Treasury Building, Flatiron Sports	30 Mountain Express Bus Depot
7 Crested Butte Marriot	18 Brick Oven Pizza	13 Kochevar's	31 The Book Worm Book Seller
8 Crested Butte International Hostel	19 Paradise Cafe	16 The Eldo	32 The Alpineer
9 Elk Mountain Lodge	22 Powerhouse Bar & Grill	17 Post Office	33 The Paper Clip
10 Christiana Guesthaus	24 Butte Bagels	20 Dragonfly Anglers	34 Crested Butte Mountain Heritage Museum
11 The Last Resort	27 The Bakery Cafe	21 Chamber of Commerce Visitors Center	37 Center for the Arts
12 Forest Queen	28 Donita's Cantina	25 The Wooden Nickel	38 Nordic Ski Center
36 The Inn at Crested Butte	35 The Slogar		
39 Old Town Inn			

near Gunnison in 1871. Miners seeking gold and silver began their massive invasion over the hills surrounding Crested Butte in the late 1870s. The town was incorporated in 1880 not as a mining camp but as a supply camp, and in 1881, the D&RG narrow-gauge railroad arrived.

Following the silver collapse in 1893, the coal mines became the focus of attention. Colorado Fuel & Iron recruited immigrant laborers from southern and central Europe, but tragedy struck in 1884 when an explosion at the Jokerville mine killed 58 miners. A plaque at the Crested Butte Cemetery on Gothic Rd memorializes the victims. Coal operations by CF&I ended in 1952, just as tourism was taking hold. The initial rope tow and T-bar were installed on Crested Butte Mountain in 1961, and the first lifts opened in 1963.

Orientation & Information

Most everything in Crested Butte is on Elk Ave, including the Crested Butte-Mount Crested Butte Chamber of Commerce visitors center (☎ 970-349-6438, 800-545-4505), at Hwy 135 and Elk Ave. It's open 9 am to 5 pm daily in summer and winter, but operates only on weekdays during late spring and early autumn. There's a smaller visitors center up the hill at the resort for winter visitors. Both locations offer maps, recreation information and a walking tour guide to the town. The chamber also offers online information on lodging, restaurants and outdoor activities at its website (www.cbinteractive.com).

For a complete seasonal calendar of events, check out the 'Visitors' Guide to Crested Butte & Gunnison County.' Pick up a copy of the *Chronicle & Pilot*, Crested Butte's weekly newspaper (published Friday), which contains a weekly calendar of hikes, presentations and other activities.

The First National Summit Bank (☎ 970-349-6606), with branches at 405 6th St and in Mount Crested Butte's town center, has ATMs. The post office is at 215 Elk Ave, and the zip code is 81224. The Paper Clip (☎ 970-349-7211; fax 970-349-7445), 505 2nd St, has a fax service.

The Book Worm Book Seller (☎ 970-349-6245), 408 3rd St, has a fairly good selection of books about the area. The Laundromat (☎ 970-349-5305) at 608 6th St is open from 7 am to 8 pm.

Things to See

Crested Butte's off-road bike pioneers helped develop the fat-tire mania. In September 1976, the first Pearl Pass Klunker Tour was a response to a challenge from Aspen motorcyclists to ride the 76-mile route over the rocky 12,705-foot pass. Seven of the first 15 participants succeeded. They rode (and carried) 45-pound Schwinn paper-route bikes equipped with coaster brakes – many had high-rise handle bars.

The **Crested Butte Mountain Heritage Museum** (☎ 970-349-1880) is at 200 Sopris Ave, and includes the popular **Mountain Bike Hall of Fame**. Bike displays trace the equipment's evolution and credit the innovators responsible for the sport. Admission is free, but donations are welcome. The museum is open 1 to 6 pm in summer, shorter hours in winter, and closed the rest of the year.

A curious sight is the **two-story outhouse** in the alley behind the Company Store at Elk Ave and 3rd St. Throughout the town is the creative artwork made from chrome car bumpers by Shawn Guerrero and Andy Bamberg.

Skiing

Downhill Skiing Crested Butte Mountain Resort (☎ 970-349-2333, 800-544-8448), formerly Mount Crested Butte, was opened in 1963 with a base elevation of 9375 feet and a healthy average snowfall of 215 inches. Its long-abandoned predecessor, the treacherous Pioneer Ski Area near Cement Creek, had Colorado's first chairlift in 1939.

Crested Butte is a favorite spot for hotdog skiers: experts flock to its lift-accessible 'Extreme Limits' terrain, which make up 550 of the area's 1160 skiable acres. Beginner and intermediate terrain comprise another 485 acres, the remainder being advanced. It only takes one ride on the high-speed quad chairlift Silver Queen to get to the good stuff. Another short excursion on the High Lift and you'll be looking down 2775 feet to the bottom. Thirteen lifts serve the mountain.

Lessons for skiers of all levels and for snowboarding are offered by the Crested Butte Ski School (☎ 970-349-2252, 800-444-9236). Even 'never ever' types are guaranteed to learn to ski in three days for $166. Specialized workshops tackle intermediate and advanced skiing techniques, as well as telemarking. There's also a Children's Ski Center (☎ 970-349-2259). Timed NASTAR races are held daily at 1 pm for $5 and require you to sign up in advance at the ski school desk in the Gothic building. Adult lift tickets cost $47, while children under 12 pay their age in dollars. Lift tickets are free at the start and finish of the season, usually late November to late December 20 and from early to mid-April.

Cross-Country Skiing About 19 miles of machine-set track are available at the Nordic Ski Center (☎ 970-349-1707), Big Mine Park at the south end of 2nd St. They offer rentals and lessons and are open from mid-November to mid-April from 9 am to 5 pm. Trail fees cost $8 for adults and $4 for children. There's also an ice rink at the center.

Equipment Rental At the base of the mountain in the Treasury Building, Flatiron Sports (☎ 970-349-6656) rents a basic adult ski package for $13, not a bad deal considering the equipment is only a year old. New equipment rents for $21, high performance for around $35. Other shops include Crested Butte Sports (☎ 970-349-7516), 35 Emmons Rd, or Gene Taylor's Sports (☎ 970-349-5386), 19 Emmons Rd.

Mountain Biking
Crested Butte has earned a reputation as an Alpine mecca for mountain bikers, and rightfully so. The area is littered with excellent singletrack trails, though elevations of

9000 feet and up mean that those coming from sea level should start off slowly.

The best place to head for maps and information is The Alpineer (☎ 970-349-5210, 800-223-4655), near the intersection of Elk St and Hwy 135. Their book *Crested Butte Bike Trails* is comprehensive and a bargain at $3.50, and the shop also runs a full-time information service specifically to answer questions about biking, hiking and other backcountry activities in the area. Its website (www.alpineer.com) is also worth checking out.

The chamber of commerce also has a map showing trails for biking and hiking, as well as campsites, but it's not detailed enough to use without a supplementary topo map. For a closer look at what the area has to offer, check out Laura Guccione's *Crested Butte and a Bit Beyond*, available at the Alpineer as well as the Book Worm Book Seller.

Recommended rides include the Upper Loop (considered a good 'starter' trail), Strand Hill and 401.

The Alpineer rents standard mountain bikes for $20 per day, while those with front suspension cost $25. You can also get suspension bikes for $22 per day at Flatiron Sports (☎ 970-349-6656), in the Treasury Building at the base of Mount Crested Butte.

Hiking
Trails into the Maroon Bells-Snowmass Wilderness Area from either Schofield Pass or Gothic, both north of the mountain of Crested Butte, offer scenic Alpine hiking. Gothic is the site of the Rocky Mountain Biological Laboratory (RMBL; ☎ 970-349-7231). Check the *Chronicle & Pilot* newspaper's calendar section for hikes led by RMBL naturalists. Consider using Town Taxi (☎ 970-349-5543) to get to the trailhead or to return at the end of your hike.

The chamber of commerce offers a simplified map of trails in the area and describes suggested routes. It's only good for planning – be sure to pick up topo maps or the USFS Gunnison Basin Area Map before heading out. Denis B Hill's *Hiking in Heaven*, available at local bookstores, provides detailed trail descriptions.

Fishing & Wildlife Viewing

On the East River, 13 miles south of Crested Butte, the **Roaring Judy Fish Hatchery** is a wildlife paradise. Bald eagles, which are making a comeback in the area, stalk the easy kokanee salmon pickings at the hatchery during winter months.

Fishing ponds at the hatchery are teaming with trout, and the East River from the hatchery downstream to the **Taylor River** is designated Wild Trout Water. A sizable bighorn sheep population inhabits cliffs in nearby **Taylor Canyon**, and some travelers on Hwy 135 beside the Almont Triangle SWA often see elk.

For information about fishing, hatchery tours or viewing wildlife, contact the Colorado DOW (☎ 970-641-0088), 300 W New York Ave in Gunnison. Gunnison Sporting Goods (☎ 970-641-5022), 133 E Tomichi Ave, sells fishing gear and topo maps. A knowledgeable local fishing guide operates Western Colorado Fly-fishers (☎ 970-349-1228), 307 Elk St in Crested Butte.

White-Water Rafting

Guided trips on the Taylor River booked by Alpine Outside (☎ 970-349-5011), Hwy 135 and Elk Ave, encounter Class III and IV whitewater. Another reputable local outfit is Paddle Trax (☎ 970-349-1100).

Golf

The altitude should add some distance to your drive at Skyland Mountain Golf Resort (☎ 970-349-6131), 2 miles south at 385 Country Club Lane, an 18-hole championship Robert Trent Jones II course. Greens fees cost $55 ($85 on weekends).

Special Events

Blossoms abound by mid-July when 'Beauties' (as local residents are called) hold the **Wildflower Festival** in the 'Wildflower Capital of Colorado' – monarch butterflies also brighten the skies on daily hikes throughout the week. The **Fat Tire Bike Week**, held in June or July, is the sport's oldest festival. At the end of July, **Aerial Weekend** features hot-air balloons, sky-divers, hang gliders and paragliders. In August, 'culcha' creeps in with the **Festival of the Arts** and **Chamber Music Festival**.

Tradition would not allow the **Pearl Pass Tour** to be moved to Fat Tire Bike Week – it remains in September when possible snow flurries add to the challenge of riding to Aspen.

Places to Stay

The story is the same here as at other Colorado ski resorts: prices are steep in summer, soar even higher in winter, and drop to reasonable levels in early fall and late spring when not much is going on. Crested Butte Vacations (☎ 800-544-8448) can help you make reservations and arrange travel-lodging-ski packages that can help ease the fiscal pain.

Camping The Gunnison National Forest's Taylor River Ranger District (☎ 970-641-0471), 216 N Colorado in Gunnison, operates 18 campgrounds north of Gunnison. Most are in Taylor Canyon, southeast of Crested Butte. The closest large campground is *Lake Irwin*, west of town before Kebler Pass at the foot of the Ruby Range, which offers 32 reservable sites (☎ 800-280-2267) for $8 plus the $8.65 reservation fee. Only four sites are available at *Gothic* on a first-come, first-served basis for $5.

The turnoff to *Cement Creek Campground* is south of town about 7 miles – it offers 13 sites for $7.

Hostels Budget travelers are finally getting a break in Crested Butte with the recent opening of the *Crested Butte International Hostel* (☎ 970-349-0588; fax 888-389-0588), 615 Teocalli Ave. Newly built, clean and spacious, the hostel has 52 beds ranging from $17 to $24 (supply your own sheets or rent them from the hostel).

Facilities include a well-equipped kitchen, public laundry, a library and a large common room with a fireplace. Discounts on lift tickets and equipment rentals are available, and HI/AYH members enjoy reduced rates. Reservations are advised (and requires a credit card deposit).

B&Bs *Elk Mountain Lodge* (☎ 970-349-7533), 129 Gothic Ave, is a former boarding house built in 1919. Now it offers 16 rooms with private bath that start at $67 in the summer and $84 in the winter. Rooms on the 3rd floor have dormer windows and are cramped and hot in the summer but they have magnificent views of Crested Butte. *The Last Resort* (☎ 970-349-0445), 213 3rd St at the pedestrian bridge over Coal Creek, features a solarium that heats the energy efficient building. Four spacious rooms with private bath range from $85 to $105 and come with a hearty breakfast. *Christiana Guesthaus* (☎ 970-349-5326), 621 Maroon Ave, offers European-style lodging and breakfasts for $67 in summer, $89 in winter.

Motels & Hotels The ghost of a working girl supposedly visits the former madam's room at the *Forest Queen* (☎ 970-349-5336), 129 Elk Ave. Rooms with shared bath cost $55, those with private bath are $65. Their downstairs bar and restaurant is a comfortable place to meet locals over a pint of microbrew. The modern *Old Town Inn* (☎ 970-349-6184), at Hwy 135 and Belleview Ave, can't boast about its noisy roadside location, but has relatively inexpensive standard motel rooms for $58/73 a single/double during summer, $78/98 in the winter. *The Inn at Crested Butte* (☎ 970-349-1225), 510 Whiterock Ave, offers fairly comfortable doubles from $58 in the summer and $68 in winter.

Up on Mount Crested Butte, the best deal is the *Manor Lodge* (☎ 970-349-5365), at 650 Gothic Rd behind the Sheraton. Rooms are small and basic, offering little more than a place to sleep, but cost only $38 in summer and $60 in winter. Up the next rung on the budget ladder is *The*

Nordic Inn (☎ 970-349-5542), 14 Treasury Rd, which has doubles from $64 in the summer, $98 in winter.

The area's top hotel is the *Crested Butte Marriott* (☎ 970-349-4000), 500 Gothic Rd, right at the base of the mountain next to the Silver Queen high-speed quad. Four-star rooms with all the luxury amenities (including whirlpool baths) start at $88 in summer, $163 in winter. Indoor and outdoor hot tubs, a pool, sauna, gym and business center are among the facilities. A bit less opulent is the newly opened *Sheraton Crested Butte Resort* (☎ 888-222-2469), 6 Emmons Rd, also near the main chairlifts. Doubles start at $70 in summer, $147 in winter.

Long-Term Rentals Crested Butte Mountain Resort (☎ 800-544-8448) has a host of condominiums within walking distance of the chairlifts. Two- and three-bedroom units with kitchens, fireplaces, daily maid service and hot tub access range anywhere from $100 to $500 per night. If there's a group of you, it's worth looking into.

Places to Eat

Locals congregate in the morning at *Butte Bagels*, on Elk near the corner of 2nd St, with indoor and outdoor seating, tasty bagel treats, espresso and smoothies. Another favorite breakfast spot is *The Bakery Cafe* (☎ 970-349-7280), 302 Elk Ave, serving homemade granola with yogurt and lots of goodies. For heartier (but less healthy) American style breakfasts and lunches, try the *Paradise Cafe* (☎ 970-349-6233) at 4th and Elk, which has a nice terrace for warm-weather eating.

For pizza slices around $2 or for delivery of a whole pizza, try *Brick Oven Pizza* (☎ 970-349-5044), 313 3rd St. Even New Yorkers concede it's a pretty good slice. *The Slogar* (☎ 970-349-5765), 517 2nd St, does a good job with the standard meat and potatoes fare, with dinners priced at around $12.

Donita's Cantina (☎ 970-349-6674), 332 Elk St, dishes up pretty good Tex-Mex food, and there's almost no chance you'll complain about either the prices or the portions. The Mexican fare at the *Powerhouse Bar & Grill* (☎ 970-349-5494), 130 Elk Ave, is pricier than Donita's but some prefer it for the lively atmosphere.

For top-end dining, Crested Butte has some good choices. The *Timberline* (☎ 970-349-9831), 21 Elk Ave, has a creative selection Continental and American cuisine, while *Le Bousquet* (☎ 970-349-5808), 201 Elk St, has earned kudos from locals for its excellent French food. In an alleyway behind Kochevar's bar (see below), *Soupçon* (☎ 970-349-5448), offers a selection of fresh fish, plus beef and game dishes that cost between $18 and $25. Dinner seatings at 6 pm and 8 pm require reservations. Finally, *Bacchanale* (☎ 970-349-5257), 208 Elk St, is an upper-end Italian restaurant that offers pasta dishes for around $10 and entrees for $16. Those who have dined there say it's well worth it.

Entertainment
Bars As befits an historic mining town, Crested Butte is loaded with century-old saloons like *Kochevar's* (☎ 970-349-6745), 127 Elk Ave, an 1890s structure built of hand-hewn logs that's listed on the National Register of Historic Places. This is one of the main local watering holes, along with *The Eldo* (☎ 970-349-6125), at 215 Elk Ave, which sometimes has live bands and also sports an outstanding 2nd-story deck that's perfect for late-afternoon beers. The *Idlespur* (☎ 970-349-5026), 226 Elk Ave, is the home of the *Crested Butte Brewery & Pub* and also features live entertainment. Another longstanding saloon is the *Wooden Nickel* (☎ 970-349-6350), 222 Elk Ave, though some locals complain that the owners have tried to cash in on its renown by hiking up the prices.

Theater The *Center for the Arts* (☎ 970-349-7487), south of the Town Park on Hwy 135, offers both summer and winter performances by local groups as well as touring companies.

Getting There & Away
Air Many visitors take advantage of Crested Butte's air link to the outside world via Gunnison County Airport, located 28 miles south. For information on flights, see the Gunnison Getting There & Away section.

Car Crested Butte is 28 miles north of Gunnison on Hwy 135 and about 225 miles from Denver via I-25 and US 50.

Getting Around
To/From the Airport Alpine Express (☎ 970-641-5074, 800-822-4844), Gunnison County Airport Terminal, meets all commercial flights in the winter but requires reservations in summer months. Roundtrip fares to Crested Butte cost $36, unless there is only one of you, in which case you face a minimum run fee of $40 one-way.

Bus The free Mountain Express (☎ 970-349-5616) connects Crested Butte with Mount Crested Butte hourly between 8 am and 10 pm. It carries bikes and skis on exterior racks. The shuttle departs from Old Town Hall, at Elk Ave and 2nd St, and stops at the visitors center before continuing up the hill.

San Luis Valley

The vast intermountain San Luis Valley is dotted with small towns and farming hamlets. Wetland wildlife sanctuaries, the surrounding craggy peaks and the stark beauty of the Great Sand Dunes provide scenic contrast to the wide plains of the valley floor.

On the east side of the valley rise the jagged 14,000-foot peaks of the Sangre de Cristo Mountains, luring hikers and backpackers to its wilderness. Crestone Peak was the last of Colorado's 14ers to be climbed; wilderness hikers often see large herds of Colorado's state animal, the bighorn sheep, on the rough slopes. To the west lie the volcanic San Juan Mountains,

COLORADO

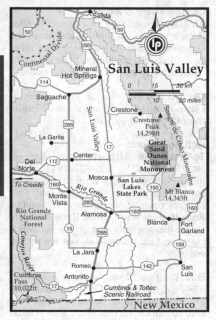

San Luis Valley

which host many outdoor activities. The Rio Grande headwaters flow by the historic mining camp at Creede, now a popular tourist site. In the southern reaches of the valley, a landscape dotted with adobe churches and historic Hispanic villages evokes images of New Mexico.

History

Early Spanish explorers probing the northern Rio Grande for minerals entered the San Luis Valley and encountered nomadic Utes, who had recently acquired horses and were enjoying the relative prosperity that came with their increased mobility and easy hunting of the valley's abundant bison herds. In 1694, during the Spanish reconquest of New Mexico, Governor Diego de Vargas scouted the upper Rio Grande into San Luis Valley but was wary of battling the mounted tribes. The Catholic Church likewise found the conversion of a migratory people a much greater challenge than working with the sedentary pueblo populations to the south. As a result, the San Luis Valley was left to the Utes on the edge of Spain's northernmost frontier.

Mexican land grants attracted the first civilian settlers. West of the Rio Grande, the Mexican government wasted little time settling the Conejos grant in 1833, yet 10 years later the Utes continued to thwart Mexican attempts at settlement. Mexican pioneers met with better fortune east of the Rio Grande on the Sangre de Cristo grant where in 1851 they established San Luis, the oldest permanent settlement in Colorado.

In the 1870s most white Americans merely passed through the San Luis Valley on their way to the San Juan Mountain mining districts. In the area's period as a part of the USA's New Mexico Territory, the federal government awarded much of the extensive Conejos grant to the D&RG railroad. The arrival of steel rails in 1878 attracted homesteaders, and since the rail's arrival, most of the valley has come under the plow.

Each fall, San Luis Valley farmers harvest about $100 million worth of potatoes, temporarily stored in root cellars that range from sod-roofed adobes to cavernous, high-tech, insulated warehouses. Some Anglo farmers are converting to organic techniques that many Hispanics never abandoned. Alternative crops like canola and quinoa, the 'grain of the Andes,' have recently gained a following among the valley's high altitude farmers.

CRESTONE

With a year-round population of just 65, Crestone is surprisingly well known, due mostly to its reputation as a center of spiritual energy. The tangible evidence lies in the unusual variety of religious and spiritual institutions that have set up shop here. These include the Crestone Mountain Zen Center, the Haidakhandi Universal Ashram, the Spiritual Life Institute, the Sri Aurobindo Learning Center and the San Luis Valley Tibetan Project. Some find Crestone's energy to be uplifting, though there are others who sense a darker presence. Either way, there is a unique feel to the place. And there's no question about Crestone's setting: the backdrop of the 14,000-foot peaks of the Sangre de Cristo Mountains is truly stunning.

Along with mystical New Age believers are old-age eccentrics who simply wish to get away from any aspect of urban life and bar its entry to their Shangri-la. Crestone's residents like their environment left unspoiled but don't mind sharing the backcountry trails into the Sangre de Cristo Wilderness with visitors. They just want you to leave when your vacation ends.

Just south of town is the Baca Grande housing estate, which makes for a modern contrast to Crestone's snail-paced lifestyle.

Information

The Crestone-Moffat Business Association (☎ 719-256-4110) has an information board outside town, next to the turnoff for the Baca Grande housing estate. On it is a map and list of lodgings, restaurants and businesses in both Crestone and Baca Grande.

The post office is on Galena St, not far from the town's main intersection.

Baca Grande Ambulance & Fire Department can be contacted in an emergency at ☎ 719-256-4911.

The Alder Terrace Laundromat is on the boardwalk at Galena St and Alder Terrace.

Hiking & Backpacking

Two outstanding trails into the high Sangre de Cristo Wilderness Area begin in Crestone's backyard. Hikers on the **South Crestone Creek Trail** travel about 5 miles to South Crestone Lake, a cirque beneath Mt Adams (13,931 feet). This prime bighorn sheep habitat harbors over 500 sheep that range between Hermit and Music passes. Begin from the top of Galena St above the post office; within a mile you reach USFS Trail 949, following the north side of South Crestone Creek for 1½ miles to a junction. On the right across the creek is USFS Trail 865 to Willow Creek Lakes (and waterfall); to the left

USFS Trail 860 continues to South Colony Lake.

Another option is to go up **North Crestone Creek Trail** to either North Crestone Lake below Fluted Peak (13,554 feet) or to cross the ridge to the east side over either Comanche or Venable passes. From the North Crestone Creek Campground reached by USFS Rd 950 (see below), USFS Trail 744 follows the north side of North Crestone Creek for 1½ miles to a three-way junction: on your right the southernmost trail continues for 3 miles to North Crestone Lake; the middle trail, USFS Trail 746, passes north of Comanche Peak before dropping into the Wet Mountain Valley on USFS Trail 1345; and the northern choice, USFS Trail 747, heads toward Venable Pass (see Westcliffe & Silver Cliff entries earlier in this chapter).

For information about hiking on the west side of the Sangre de Cristo Wilderness Area contact the USFS Saguache Ranger District (☎ 719-655-2547), a quarter mile west of Saguache at 46525 State Hwy 114.

Places to Stay & Eat

Campsites are available for $7 at the USFS *North Crestone Creek Campground*, about 2 miles north of Crestone past the historical Community Center on Alder Terrace Rd. The *Alder Terrace Inn* (☎ 719-256-4975) offers apartment-style single/double rooms with kitchens for $45/50 and is next to the laundry. If no one is there, inquire at the 21st Amendment Liquor store, one block north. In the Baca Grande area, the *Rainbow Bed & Breakfast* (☎ 719-265-4110, 800-530-1992) is a modern home near the mountains with tasteful decor where rooms with shared bath cost $30/40. To get there from Sagauche County T Rd, take the turnoff into the Baca Grande estates for 1 mile, then turn left up a dirt road where you'll see a small sign for the Rainbow: it's up 350 yards on the left.

The *Kitchen Table*, at Alder and Galena Sts, has an interesting menu, including choices like Caribbean chicken dinner ($9) and Cajun blackened tofu ($7.50). It's open Tuesday to Friday from 11 am to 8 pm.

One block away, the *Mountain View Cafe* (☎ 719-256-4009) has a healthy range of breakfast and lunch items (plenty of choice for vegetarians) and at the time of writing was planning to have live music on weekends. It's open Friday to Tuesday.

In the Baca Grande, *Desert Sage* (☎ 719-256-4402) is open daily from 7 am to 2 pm and 5:30 to 8 pm and features outstanding breads and other baked goods. The breakfast burrito for under $5 includes locally grown quinoa. A salad bar is available during lunch for $4 or during dinner for $7. Also try the grilled trout dinner for $11. Friday nights feature fresh seafood specials ranging from $11 to $16.

Getting There & Away

Crestone is on the east side of the San Luis Valley, north of Great Sand Dunes National Monument. From Alamosa, Hwy 17 follows a straight course for 40 miles to Saguache County Rd T, which heads 13 miles east to Crestone.

GREAT SAND DUNES NATIONAL MONUMENT

Colorado's sea of sand is an amazing trick of nature. From the air or nearby mountaintops, the dune field of approximately 55 sq miles stands out starkly from the surrounding terrain. Even more surreal are the fluid shapes and interplay of light on the dunes as you approach by land – particularly when the sun is low on the horizon. Explorers in the dunes lose the perception of depth and scale needed to discern that the tallest dunes rise almost 700 feet. In this beige landscape lacking familiar benchmarks, only other hikers serve as a gauge to judge distance and the size of surrounding dunes.

From high in the San Juan Range to the southwest of the dunes, the blowing wind picks up speed as it flows down the slopes and across the broad San Luis Valley, passing over the Rio Grande. Over thousands of years, the Rio Grande has transported weathered sediments from the San Juan Range into the valley where they accumulate next to sluggish sections of the river.

As the wind passes over these sediments, the smallest particles are carried aloft. Blocked by the Sangre de Cristo Mountains, the wind velocity drops as it courses through the Mosca, Medano and Music mountain passes. The weakened wind cannot carry the sand, and it accumulates in a pocket next to the Sangre de Cristo range to create the Great Sand Dunes.

Orientation

The visitors center is 3 miles north of the park entrance, and access to the dunes is another mile along the road. Most visitors limit their activities to a narrow juncture where the curious Medano Creek (Spanish for 'Dune' Creek) divides the main dune mass from the towering Sangre de Cristo Mountains to the east. The remaining 85% of the monument's area is designated wilderness. From the visitors center, a short trail leads to the Mosca Picnic Area next to Medano Creek, which you must ford to reach the dunes. Across the road from the visitors center, the Mosca Pass Trail enters the Sangre de Cristo Wilderness, and the short Wellington Ditch Trail heads north to campsites and the Little Medano Trail.

North of the visitors center in the piñon pine forest is Pinyon Flats Campground; beyond the campground is the end of the paved road called 'Point of No Return.' From here the Medano Pass Primitive Rd and Little Medano Trail provide access to backcountry campsites that require a permit for overnight wilderness camping.

A privately run store, a campground and lodge at the entrance to the park offers Jeep tours, gas, campsites and cabins for visitors turned away from overflowing park campsites.

Information

Visitors receive a guide and map brochure on entry to the park where an NPS ranger collects an admission fee of $3 per person. Before venturing out to the dunes, stop by the visitors center (☎ 719-378-2312) to check out the exhibits, chat with a ranger or purchase books and maps. Be sure to ask

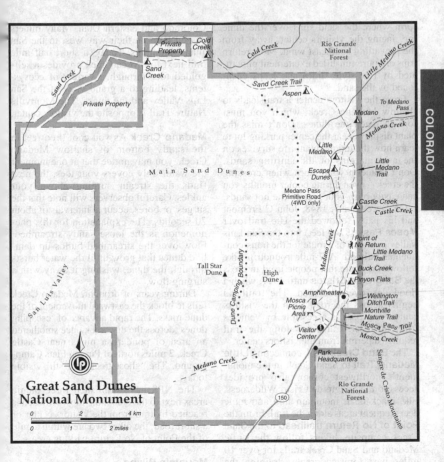

COLORADO

Great Sand Dunes National Monument

0   2   4 km

0   1   2 miles

about scheduled nature walks and nightly programs held at the amphitheater near Pinyon Flats. From Memorial Day to Labor Day the center is open daily from 8 am to 6 pm; otherwise it's open from 8:30 am to 4:30 pm.

Summer weather at the park is moderated by the 8000-foot elevation – the highest temperature recorded was 96° F. Be prepared for summer afternoon thundershowers, and protect your skin from the intense sun and reflection from the sand; sunglasses are imperative. Long sleeves and pants also defend against the voracious

mosquitoes near Medano Creek. Winter snowfall averages 38 inches.

Hiking & Backpacking

American explorer Zebulon Pike may have failed to ascend his namesake peak, but he did surmount a tall dune to spy the Rio Grande in 1807. You too should not miss the opportunity to experience the **dune mass** up close – especially at dawn or dusk when the sun is less brilliant and the dunes take on a variety of colors. To reach the crest of the tallest dunes requires a laborious climb. The steepest dune slopes form where the sand slips over the dune top, facing the visitors center, away from the prevailing southeast wind. Most return trips are pure fun-filled excitement punctuated by free-style slides and leaps cushioned by the sand.

From the visitors center a trail leads to shallow Medano Creek, which you must ford to reach the dunes. Don't miss the plant displays near the center parking lot to learn how the unique plant life survives on the arid margins of the shifting sands. Don't abandon your shoes when crossing the creek – even during cooler months you can easily burn your feet on the hot sands.

On December 3, 1848, John C Frémont and his party followed the Ute trail over **Mosca Pass** (9740 feet) into the San Luis Valley in search of a route for the trans-continental railroad. A 7-mile roundtrip hike follows the route that people used to cross the **Sangre de Cristos** until 1911, when a flood destroyed the road. The trailhead begins across the road from the visitors center. The pass is accessible by vehicles from the east. Camping along the trail requires a permit from the visitors center.

The **Sand Creek Trail**, connecting **Little Medano Trail** to Sand Creek in the monument's northwest corner, also provides access to the Sangre de Cristo Wilderness. Elk, black bear, mountain lion and mule deer frequent areas along the trail. From the **Point of No Return trailhead** to the Sand Creek campsite, hikers follow the Little Medano and Sand Creek trails for over 10 miles past forested creeks draining the Sangre de Cristo. At 9 miles, an open stand of ponderosa pine marks the Cold Creek campsite. Here, the dunes abut a beautiful rugged valley that leads through the Sangre de Cristo Wilderness to Music Pass. At the end of the trail, a thick cottonwood forest follows Sand Creek. Backcountry permits are required for overnight camping.

Montville Nature Trail The Montville Store once stood at the foot of Mosca Pass Trail. It was built in the 1830s by fur trader Antoine Robidoux, who used the pass to transport supplies to his posts in western Colorado and eastern Utah. Many miners passed here on their way west to the San Juan Mountains. Today, a short half-mile trail next to Mosca Creek provides a self-guided tour through a variety of ecosystems, leading to a grand view of the San Luis Valley and the dunes. The Montville Nature Trail is opposite the visitors center.

Medano Creek As you cool tired feet in the sandy bottom of shallow Medano Creek, you may notice that at one moment the water only covers your toes, the next finds the stream surging above your ankles. Careful observers will note that the surges, or bores, occur at intervals of about 20 seconds. The explanation for this phenomenon is the loose sandy streambed. Flow over the streambed builds up dam-like dunes that grow until the water bursts through the dune, washing it away with a surging flow.

During years of drought, Medano Creek fails to block the eastward movement of the dune mass. The rapid advance of 'escaping dunes' across the dry creek once smothered an area of ponderosa pines near Castle Creek, 2 miles north of Pinyon Flats Campground. The 'ghost trees' are still visible today.

The NPS has established three picnic areas next to the creek: the most crowded is reached by trail from the visitors center or a short road; the other two are within a mile of the Point of No Return parking area.

Mountain Biking

Off-road cyclists should plan to slog through some sandy areas before climbing the beautiful narrow valley to **Medano Pass**. The pass is 11 miles from the Point of No Return parking area at the north end of the paved road. Still within the monument boundaries, at 2.6 miles, you'll pass the 'ghost trees' near Castle Creek. At 4 miles is an area of ponderosa pines peeled by Utes who used the bark for food and medicine. Vistas of the dunes disappear 2 miles from the summit, replaced by the sawtooth crags of the Sangre de Cristos. Because this primitive road passes through the Sangre de Cristo Wilderness, vehicles of any type are forbidden to leave the route. A detailed mileage log for the Medano Pass Primitive Rd is available at the visitors center.

For a shorter fat-tire ride, visit the spectacular **Zapata Falls**, south of the monument, which also offer outstanding views of the valley. A consortium of 13 agencies recently opened 4 miles of trail in the **Zapata Falls Special Recreation Area** on the west flank of Blanca Peak.

Bicycle rentals ($15 per day with front suspension), repairs and riding information are available at Kristi Mountain Sports (☎ 719-589-9759) in Alamosa at 7565 US 160, about 1 mile east of the City Market, behind the Conoco gas station.

Organized Tours
Throughout the summer NPS rangers lead interpretive nature walks from the visitors center parking lot. Inquire at the center about specific programs and times.

Great Sand Dunes Tours (☎ 719-378-2222) carries passengers past the dunes and partway up the primitive road to Medano Pass in open-air 4WD vehicles from May to November. The trips take about two hours and leave from the Oasis Store on the monument boundary at 10 am and 2 pm. The cost for the tours is $14 for adults and $8 for children.

Places to Stay
In the peak months of July and August, visitors often fill the 88 sites at *Pinyon Flats Campground*, which are available on a first-come, first-served basis. The campground is open year-round and water is available at all times. Sites cost $10. Backpackers have the option of staying at one of seven designated backcountry campsites requiring hikes ranging from under a mile to Buck Creek, to over 10 miles to Sand Creek. In addition, campers may stay in the main dune mass to the west of the most accessible dunes frequented by day-users. You must obtain a backcountry permit, available free of charge from the visitors center, for overnight wilderness stays.

At the entrance to the monument, the *Oasis Store* (☎ 719-378-2222) offers showers, laundry and barren tent sites for $10. A few primitive cabins cost $30 double occupancy but typically require reservations. Farther uphill from the campground, the *Great Sand Dunes Lodge* (☎ 719-378-2900) is open from April to mid-October and has rooms with balconies offering fine views of the dunes for $79 in summer, $69 in the off-season. There's also a restaurant and an indoor pool.

Getting There & Away
Great Sand Dunes National Monument is northeast of Alamosa. To get there, travel east on US 160 for 14 miles toward prominent Blanca Peak (named for its light-colored granite), turn left (north) on Hwy 150 and follow the road for 19 miles to the visitors center.

AROUND GREAT SAND DUNES NATIONAL MONUMENT
San Luis Lakes State Park
Agricultural development in the fertile San Luis Valley came at the expense of downstream Rio Grande users in New Mexico, Texas and Mexico. In a tardy attempt to meet water obligations to Mexico in accordance with a 1906 treaty, the US Bureau of Reclamation began pumping water from the valley for transfer to the Rio Grande in the 1980s. San Luis Lakes are a part of this conveyance. A small portion of the water pumped by this costly project maintains the Alamosa National Wildlife Refuge and the Blanca Wetlands (see Around Alamosa).

At San Luis Lakes State Park (☎ 719-378-2020), the bleak terrain of sand dunes covered with saltbush and rabbitbrush contrasts with the grassy wetlands – the secondary beneficiary of this governmental largesse. Waterfowl, shorebirds and birdwatchers alike enjoy the newly created wetlands and reservoir, just west of the Great Sand Dunes National Monument. The *Mosca Campground* has a bath house, laundry and drinking fountains, and is a convenient alternative to camping in the monument. Campsites cost $10, plus the

COLORADO

daily vehicle fee of $4. The park is 8 miles west of Hwy 150 on Alamosa County Rd 6N. To get from Alamosa to the park drive 13 miles north on Hwy 17, then turn right (east) on County Rd 6N for 8 miles.

Blanca

Below 14,345-foot Mt Blanca, the small farming town of Blanca (population 297) straddles US 160, 5 miles east of Hwy 150. The Trinchera Irrigation Company and an abandoned two-story adobe building with flying buttresses reinforce the rich impressions of Hispanic heritage in the valley. Travelers to Great Sand Dunes National Monument and nearby wildlife areas may conveniently camp at the *Blanca RV Park*, where shaded tent sites cost $12 and include hot showers.

The *Mt Blanca Game Bird & Trout B&B* (☎ 719-379-3825) is an oasis near the small noncommercial airport 3 miles south of Blanca. Visitors can fish at several stocked ponds on the 9-sq-mile property. Rooms with bath cost $78/88 a single/double. It's located 2½ miles down a small dirt road off of US 160 just east of Blanca.

Blanca is the closest that buses come to Great Sand Dunes National Monument. TNM&O buses running between Denver and Albuquerque can be flagged down near Smith's Store at US 160 and Broadway. Northbound buses roll by around 4:45 pm, southbound at 4 pm. Call the TNM&O terminal at Alamosa (☎ 719-589-4948) for the latest schedule.

Fort Garland

American troops occupied Fort Garland from 1858 to 1883, shortly after the US government fully removed the Utes from the area. At the Fort Garland Museum (☎ 719-379-3512) visitors find a complete restoration of the fort's buildings and exhibits maintained by the Colorado Historical Society. One feature at the fort is a re-creation of the commandant's quarters from the 1866-67 period, when Kit Carson commanded a volunteer regiment here.

Fort Garland Museum is on Hwy 159, next to where it meets up with US 160.

From there it's 10 miles east to the Hwy 150 turnoff to Great Sand Dunes National Monument, 26 miles east to Alamosa or 17 miles south to San Luis via Hwy 159. The museum is open daily between April and October from 9 am to 5 pm; during the winter it's only open Thursday to Saturday from 8 am to 4 pm. Admission is $2.50 for adults, $1.50 for children.

Overnight accommodations are available at *The Lodge* (☎ 719-379-3434), on US 160, a friendly and comfortable place that charges $35/40 a single/double year-round, one of the few places in this part of Colorado that doesn't change rates with each season.

Daily TNM&O buses between Denver and Albuquerque stop at Joey's Navajo Cafe (☎ 719-379-3278); the northbound bus arrives at 4:55 pm, the southbound at 3:50 pm.

ALAMOSA

Located in the center of the San Luis Valley, Alamosa (population 7700) is the largest city in the valley. Alamosa is both an agricultural center and a convenient overnight stop for tourists visiting nearby Great Sand Dunes National Monument or riding the Cumbres & Toltec steam train from Antonito to the south. It's not particularly attractive, but there are pleasant residential areas, shaded trails along the Rio Grande and a few good Mexican restaurants. In addition, Alamosa is home of Adams State College, founded in 1925.

Alamosa was established in 1878 with the arrival of the D&RG Railroad from La Veta Pass to the east. The railroad brought settlers and raised economic expectations for farmers marketing irrigated farm products and for cattle ranchers. In the 1940s and 1950s Fred Harman used local settings for cowboy exploits around his fictional town of Rimrock in *Red Ryder Comics*.

Orientation

Most lodgings are found either along US 160 east of the Rio Grande (in East Alamosa) or west of the central district on US 160/US 285. Numbered streets run

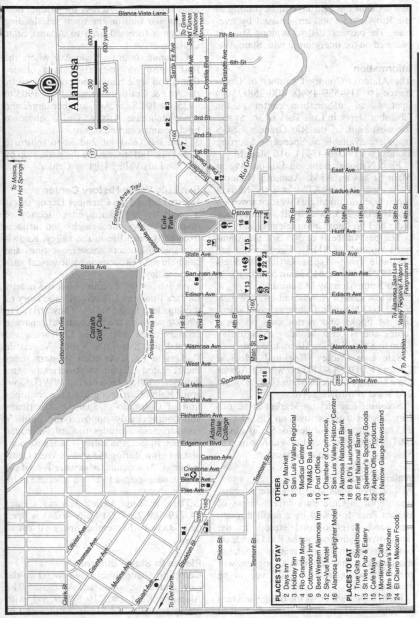

Alamosa

PLACES TO STAY
2 Days Inn
3 Holiday Inn
4 Rio Grande Motel
6 Cottonwood Inn
9 Best Western Alamosa Inn
12 Sky-Vue Motel
16 Alamosa Lamplighter Motel

PLACES TO EAT
7 True Grits Steakhouse
13 St Ives Pub & Eatery
15 Cafe Maya
17 Monterrey Cafe
19 Mrs Rivera's Kitchen
24 El Charro Mexican Foods

OTHER
1 City Market
5 San Luis Valley Regional
   Medical Center
8 TNM&O Bus Depot
10 Post Office
11 Chamber of Commerce,
   San Luis Valley History Center
14 Alamosa National Bank
18 B & D's Laundromat
20 First National Bank
21 Spencer's Sporting Goods
22 Aspen Office Products
23 Narrow Gauge Newsstand

east-west in the grid layout, beginning at the Rio Grande, and are crossed by avenues. The business district is along Main St centered on the intersection with State Ave.

Information
The Alamosa County Chamber of Commerce (☎ 719-589-4840, 800-258-7597) operates an information center at the Chamber Depot in Cole Park at 3rd St and the west bank of the Rio Grande. USGS maps are available at Spencer's Sporting Goods (☎ 719-589-4361), 616 Main St.

First National Bank on Edison Ave at Main St has an ATM. Alamosa National Bank operates an ATM in City Market (open 6 am to midnight) west of town on US 160/US 285, which also has money order and Western Union telegram service.

The post office is at 505 3rd St; Alamosa's zip code is 81101. Fax services are available from Aspen Office Products (☎ 719-589-9084), 610 Main St, from 8:30 am to 5 pm, Monday to Saturday.

Narrow Gauge Newsstand (☎ 719-589-6712), 602 Main St, features a good selection of books and periodicals on local topics and is open Monday to Saturday 8 am to 8 pm, Sunday 10 am to 5 pm.

San Luis Valley Regional Medical Center (☎ 719-589-2511) is west of Adams State College between Main (US 285) and 2nd Sts at 106 Blanca Ave.

Sunshine Laundry on Market St next to City Market west of town on US 160/US 285 has a drop-off service for $5.50 a load. B&D's Laundromat on La Veta Ave next to Safeway has coin-op machines.

Walking Tour
A short river walk starting at the information depot in Cole Park offers views of Blanca Peak followed by a stroll through tree-lined neighborhood streets to the downtown. Paths follow the Rio Grande on both banks from the information depot, but most walkers and certainly all joggers will prefer the wide, well-drained levee on the east side.

From Cole Park cross the bridge and turn left (upstream) along the riverside trail to State Ave Bridge. Across the bridge, note the popular trail on the town side leading through a forested area to Adams State College.

Continue south on State Ave where the first house on your right is a classic Craftsman-style bungalow, popularized by the Arts & Crafts movement from 1905 to 1925. At 101 State Ave, another larger and more elaborate Arts & Crafts home of brick features carved beams.

Turn left (east) at 2nd St to return to Cole Park. Before leaving the park, stop by the San Luis Valley History Center.

San Luis Valley History Center
Located behind the Chamber Depot, this is a small but well-arranged collection of 'then and now' photographs and artifacts from early farm life in the valley. Knowledgeable volunteers answer questions and can help plan excursions to historical sites in the valley.

An interesting exhibit about the nearby La Jara Buddhist Church tells the story of the Japanese in the valley. They arrived in 1908 to work on the railroad, but Japanese farmers came later from California and formed the San Luis Valley Vegetable Packers in 1927. As other Western states incarcerated Japanese-Americans and confiscated their land during WWII, Governor Ralph Carr recognized the contribution of Colorado's Japanese-Americans and courageously opposed the public's anti-Japanese attitudes toward American citizens. In fact, the valley's Japanese population grew during the war as West Coast Japanese-Americans, who were forced off their lands, sought to avoid internment by moving here.

The San Luis Valley History Center (☎ 719-589-9217, 719-589-4624) is open daily June to September from 10 am to 4 pm.

Places to Stay – budget
Camping Campgrounds are found on the east and west sides of Alamosa. The Alamosa *KOA* (☎ 719-589-9757) with grassy tent sites for $16 is 3 miles east of

town on US 160 then north on Juniper Lane. RV sites cost $21 for full hookup.

Motels Among the cheapest rooms in town are at the *Sky-Vue Motel* (☎ 719-589-4945), 250 Broadway, which has basic but clean singles/doubles for $38/46 in summer. On the west side of town at 2051 W Main, the *Rio Grande Motel* (☎ 719-589-9095) has rooms for $37/40 in the off-season, $45/50 in summer.

Places to Stay – middle
In East Alamosa on Sante Fe Ave, rooms cost $54/60 during peak summer season at the modern *Days Inn* (☎ 719-589-9037). The central *Alamosa Lamplighter Motel* (☎ 719-589-6636, 800-359-2138), 425 Main St, is recently remodeled and rooms cost $52/60 in summer, about $15 less in the off-season. The hotel has an annex 5 blocks away with a pool, hot tub and sauna. On the west edge of town the *Super 8 Motel* (☎ 719-589-6447), 2505 W Main St (US 160/US 285), has rooms for $52/65 (peak season), a hot tub, and also provides a Continental breakfast.

Places to Stay – top end
B&Bs An appealing Craftsman-style home and gracious young hosts make the *Cottonwood Inn* (☎ 719-589-3882, 800-955-2623), 123 San Juan Ave, a fine place to stay. Two rooms with shared bath are available for $65, but you can have a private bath for $75 or stay in the spacious Art Deco apartment annex next door for $93 (rates are around 30% lower from November to February).

Motels In summer, rooms cost $61/69 at the *Best Western Alamosa Inn* (☎ 719-589-2567, 800-459-5123), close to the campus at 1919 Main St. It features an indoor pool, restaurant and lounge. In East Alamosa the new *Holiday Inn* (☎ 719-589-5833), 333 Santa Fe Ave (US 160), offers rooms for $84/94 and has a restaurant, indoor pool and sauna. It's not really worth the price, though rates do fall to around $53/63 during the off-season.

Places to Eat
Breakfasts are a bit pricey but quite good at *Cafe Maya* (☎ 719-589-6175), 529 Main St, which also offers some healthy lunch choices. It's open Tuesday to Saturday from 7 am to 4:30 pm, later on Friday and Saturday when it has live music in the evenings.

Mexican restaurants are as numerous as recipes for salsa. Near the campus, *Monterrey Cafe*, 1406 W Main St, is open daily from 7 am and offers huge breakfast burritos smothered with green chile sauce for $4. Their enchilada dinner plate (three enchiladas) is a bargain for under $5. *El Charro Mexican Foods* (☎ 719-589-2262), 421 6th St, offers entrees like chiles rellenos for under $6 or an à la carte potato burrito for under $3. The guacamole tostada for $5 is muy grande – you might consider a half order. *Mrs Rivera's Kitchen* (☎ 719-589-0277), 1019 6th St, has a nice atmosphere, and a slew of tasty entrees for less than $5. For around $6 you can really stuff yourself.

True Grits Steakhouse (☎ 719-589-9954), at Broadway and 1st St, is a sort of shrine to John Wayne that serves all sorts of steak platters: try the petite steak with potato, salad and fresh bread for $7.

Until midnight on Monday to Saturday nights you can select from Colorado microbrews and imported beers with a burger or sandwich at *St Ives Pub & Eatery* (☎ 719-589-0711), on Main between Edison and San Juan Aves.

Getting There & Away
Air The Alamosa San Luis Valley Regional Airport has daily flights on United Express (☎ 719-589-9446) to Denver via Pueblo. The airport is south of the central district on State Ave.

Bus TNM&O buses stop in Alamosa on daily Denver-Albuquerque service at the offices of the local agent, SLV Van Lines (☎ 719-589-4948), on the west side of town south of the railroad tracks at 8480 Stockton St. Northbound buses leave at 4:25 pm, southbound at 4:35 pm. Twin Hearts Express (☎ 505-751-1201) offers

COLORADO

COLORADO

shuttle service to the Cumbres & Toltec Scenic Railroad from the Holiday Inn and Alamosa Inn for under $20 roundtrip.

Car Alamosa is 73 miles west of Walsenburg on US 160, and 23 miles north of Antonito, near the New Mexico border, on US 285, which turns at Alamosa toward Monte Vista, 31 miles west.

Getting Around
L&M Car Rental (☎ 719-589-4651) has its office at the Alamosa San Luis Valley Regional Airport.

AROUND ALAMOSA
Alamosa National Wildlife Refuge
A 2½-mile trail along the Rio Grande and a panoramic overlook on the east side of the refuge give visitors views of the wetland marshes, ponds and river corridor. In the spring and fall look for sandhill cranes and whooping cranes (an endangered species); in the early spring visitors see large concentrations of bald eagles. The USFWS (☎ 719-589-4021) operates a visitors center, open weekdays 7:30 am to 4 pm. To get there from Alamosa, go 3 miles east on US 160 (to just past the Outhouse restaurant), then south on El Rancho Lane.

Blanca Wetlands
The BLM (☎ 719-589-4975) recently restored the wildlife habitat at Blanca Wetlands, east of Alamosa. Activities include **fishing** for bass or trout in newly created ponds and viewing of waterfowl, shorebirds and other species. **Hiking** trails lead throughout the many marshes and ponds, but are closed during the nesting season from February 15 to July 15. Nevertheless, one 'watchable wildlife area' is open all year. To get there from Alamosa, travel 6 miles east on US 160, then 5 miles north on Alamosa County Rd 116S.

SAN LUIS
Tucked into the far southeast margin of the San Luis Valley, the town of San Luis escaped the 'progress' that revoked Hispanic tenure in other parts of the valley

following the incursion of the railroad. The town's population of 900 is today still 95% Hispanic. It's an appealing, friendly place, and slowing down the pace and staying for a few days might allow you to appreciate the sense of community San Luis still conveys.

The character of San Luis is largely the result of isolation. To Spain, the upper Rio Grande was a lost province best left to the mounted nomadic Native American tribes that Spain was unable to dominate. Mexico encouraged civilian settlement and agriculture with the Sangre de Cristo grant in 1843, yet did not establish a plaza at San Luis until 1851.

Under the threat of Ute raids and far from the mercantile and spiritual centers at Taos

---

San Luis People's Ditch & the Commons
Small tracts of rich bottomlands first lured settlers into the San Luis Valley from Taos. In 1852 colonists dug a 4-mile *acequia* (irrigation ditch) from Culebra Creek, called the San Luis People's Ditch, that's still in use. In addition to individual landholdings, in 1863 San Luis set aside about 1½ sq miles as La Vega, a common crop field and pasture used by all the inhabitants. Community members also held common rights to hunt, fish or gather wood in La Sierra, 120 sq miles of privately held lands in the mountains.

But because Americans tend to view land as a commodity, not a cooperative resource, San Luis residents are now struggling to regain a part of La Sierra. During the 1960s, San Luis residents' use of La Sierra and almost 300 acres of La Vega was restricted as a private owner removed their access rights from the deed and erected fences on the land. Violence erupted when San Luis residents initially attempted to defend their rights. The challenge was recently taken to the courts where the people of San Luis and neighboring villages hope to regain rights to La Sierra. ■

and Santa Fe, San Luis developed as a self-sufficient outpost.

The San Luis Visitors Center (☎ 719-672-3321), on Main St opposite the intersection with Hwy 142, is open Thursday to Sunday from 9 am to 1 pm.

San Luis Museum & Cultural Center

This handsome museum and gallery chronicles Hispanic culture in southern Colorado and was recently built to modern solar-heating standards following a plaza design incorporating Old-World architecture. Exhibits on the Penitente Brotherhood are especially intriguing for their insight into this formerly secretive local lay religion. Early isolation from church priests led to religious practices stemming from the Middle Ages. The *morada*, or lodge, where Penitentes met was a place of penitence carried to the extreme of self-flagellation during Lent. In the 1940s such practices were abandoned when the Catholic Church agreed to reverse its policy of banishing the brotherhood, ending the need for secrecy.

The San Luis Museum (☎ 719-672-3611) is open daily from Memorial Day to Labor Day and weekdays the rest of the year. The movie theater in the Cultural Center is open weekends. It's located on Main St, just south of the visitors center.

Stations of the Cross

For many years, San Luis residents re-enacted the capture, trial and crucifixion of Christ during Holy Week beginning on Ash Wednesday in late February or early March. During the Centennial Jubilee of the Sangre de Cristo Parish in 1986, parish members conceived the Stations of the Cross Shrine to formalize this re-enactment. Sculptor Huberto Maestas created 15 dramatic life-size statues stationed along a 1-mile pathway – beginning with Jesus being condemned to death and proceeding to the resurrection. Other volunteers contributed thousands of hours to the shrine.

From the crucifixion on the mesa summit during late afternoon sunsets you can observe the reddish light cast on the Sangre de Cristo Range, including Culebra Peak (14,069 feet), giving the mountains their 'Blood of Christ' name. You can also look out over San Luis and its surrounding fields and pasture. The trailhead to the mesa is located at the junction of Hwys 142 and 159.

Viejo San Acacio

The beautiful Viejo (old) San Acacio is an historic Catholic church where mass is still occasionally held. To get to San Acacio, go 4 miles east of San Luis on Hwy 142, then turn left (south) on Costilla County Rd 15 to the church near Culebra Creek.

Places to Stay & Eat

Fabian's Bed and Breakfast (☎ 719-672-3794), on the south end of town at 125 Main St, has friendly owners and rooms with single/double rooms with shared bath for $65/75. Breakfast is included and is served at the adjacent *Fabian's Cafe* (☎ 719-672-0322). During summer or weekends it's best to make a reservation.

El Convento B&B (☎ 719-672-4223), opposite the church at 512 Church Place, is a unique property owned by the Sangre de Cristo Parish. Originally built as a school in 1905, the substantial adobe building later served as a convent. A recent renovation created four luxurious upstairs rooms, each with private bath, decorated with antiques and handcrafted furniture. Rooms cost $60/70. Downstairs you can purchase local handmade crafts in the Centro Artesano gallery.

For 50 years, Emma Espinosa has cooked Mexican specialties for lunch and dinner at *Emma's Hacienda* (☎ 719-672-9902) on Main St. Walking into Emma's is like arriving at a family reunion: as many as four generations of Espinosas may be working at any one time. Emma's special is red and green enchiladas for $7, or you might try a Pancho Villa Burrito for $5. One major Colorado newspaper voted it the best Mexican restaurant in the state. You may or may not agree, but chances are you won't be disappointed.

COLORADO

Getting There & Away
Limousine Van Twin Hearts Express (☎ 505-751-1201), a bus service that links Alamosa with Albuquerque, will run via San Luis if you book in advance: they might also want you to wait until there are more pick-ups or drop-offs in San Luis. The fare is around $20, less if there are several of you.

Car San Luis is 42 miles from Alamosa. First head 26 miles east on US 160 to Fort Garland, then south on Hwy 159 for 16 miles. From Romeo on US 285 between Antonito and Alamosa, Hwy 142 heads east through Manassa (home of the Jack Dempsey Museum) to San Luis.

ANTONITO & AROUND
Antonito (population 870) is a dusty, run-down place whose only real attraction is the northern terminus of the Cumbres & Toltec Scenic Railroad, a narrow-gauge railway that winds its way through the mountains to Chama, NM. Nearby is a highway that follows the Conejos River into the Rio Grande National Forest where you can camp, fish, observe wildlife or watch the steam train wind its way through Cumbres Pass.

The Cumbres & Toltec Scenic Railroad Depot is a mile south of Antonito at the junction of US 285 (Main St) and Hwy 17. The Antonito Visitors Center (☎ 719-376-2049, 800-835-1098) is on US 285 opposite the railroad depot and is only open in summer.

There is an ATM in Kelloff's Food Market, 512 Main St: the store is open daily from 8 am to 7 pm. The post office is at the corner of Main St and 5th St.

Cumbres & Toltec Scenic Railroad
In 1880 the Denver & Rio Grande (D&RG) Western Rail completed track over Cumbres Pass, linking Chama, NM, with Denver by way of Alamosa. The twisting mountainous terrain could most easily be breached by using narrow-gauge track, 3 feet wide as opposed to the 4-foot, 8-inch standard gauge. Within a few years the line

was extended to Durango, Farmington and the Silverton mining camp, 152 miles away. Railroad buffs encouraged Colorado and New Mexico to buy the scenic Cumbres Pass segment when the Antonito-Farmington line came up for abandonment in 1967. Their efforts led to a compact between Colorado and New Mexico to save the railway as a National Historic Site.

Today, chugging steam engines pull passenger cars up the 10,022-foot Cumbres Pass between Antonito and Chama – the longest and highest narrow-gauge steam line in North America. Along the way, the train follows a precipitous rock ledge 600 feet above the Rio Los Pinos in the Toltec Gorge. At a plodding 12 to 15 mph, the 64-mile ride takes a little over six hours, including water stops and a lunch stop midway at Osier. You can take a roundtrip to Osier, or a trip to the beautiful Cumbres Pass. The through trip to Chama returns by van in a little over an hour. All trips require a full day.

The C&TS can also provide access to the backcountry and prime fishing streams in the USFS lands along the border between Colorado and New Mexico. Backpackers can make reservations for drop-off and later pickup at the water stops. If you wish to camp in Chama, the *Rio Chama RV Campground* (☎ 505-756-2303) offers tent sites only 2 blocks north of the depot.

Trains run daily from Memorial Day to mid-October, during which the Antonito Depot (☎ 719-376-5483) is open from 7:30 am to 6 pm. Dress warmly as the unheated cars, both enclosed and semi-enclosed, can get extremely cold. Beware that steam engine emissions control consists of a wire screen; the only way to avoid the embers and ash is to book a through-trip, which guarantees you a seat in an enclosed car if you wish it.

Adult fares are $34 for the roundtrip from Antonito to Osier, which departs at 10 am and returns at 5 pm. The trip to Cumbres Pass costs $44, leaves at 10 am and returns at 4 pm. The through train trip to Chama costs $52; departure from Antonito is via van at 9:15 am, returning by train at 5 pm. Children 11 years and under pay half fare. Many of the valley's places to stay offer room discounts if they book your trip.

Places to Stay

With lodging or campsites available nearby in the beautiful Conejos River Canyon to the west on Hwy 17 – some camps and cabins are only 5 miles away – there's no reason to stay in glum Antonito. If you do get stuck, you can try the *Park Motel* (☎ 719-376-5582, 888-892-5701), across from the depot at 115 Main St. It's nothing special, but rooms are cheap at $23/33 for singles/doubles. A short walk from the C&TS Depot, the *Narrow Gauge Railroad Inn* (☎ 719-376-5441, 800-323-9469) is a standard motel, with clean rooms for $35/45.

Good Mexican food and standard American dishes are available at the *Dutch Mill Cafe*, 401 Main St, open daily from 6:30 am to 9 pm.

Getting There & Away

Bus TNM&O buses to Albuquerque, NM, or Denver can be flagged down daily in front of the Lee's Texaco Store (☎ 719-376-5949), 217 Main St. Northbound buses come through at 3:40 pm, southbound at 5:05 pm.

Car Antonito 28 miles south of Alamosa on US 285, and 5 miles north of the border with New Mexico. To the west on Hwy 17 is Chama, NM, some 39 miles away over Cumbres Pass.

CONEJOS RIVER

Although a few travelers explore historical sites along the lower Conejos River near Antonito, most visitors prefer the upstream portions of the river to the west of Antonito along Hwy 17. The Conejos is a top fishery, and numerous tributaries and nearby high-elevation lakes also provide good fishing. Bighorn sheep, elk and deer can occasionally be observed near the river or on canyon cliffs. On the steep Hwy 17 ascent toward the Cumbres Pass are superb

vistas of the Conejos River and sheer face of Black Mountain across the valley. The winding tracks pass the picturesque upland meadow, created by fire in 1879, and an historic wooden water tank at Los Pinos. The volcanic character of the San Juan Range is seen in the vivid, ragged rock outcrops encountered soon after crossing Cumbres Pass.

To reach the Conejos River from Antonito, travel directly west on Hwy 17. Or take a short detour to the north along the river, passing the scrawny county seat at Conejos and Colorado's oldest church – the Nuestra Señora de Guadalupe – before rejoining Hwy 17. Another example of early architecture is the adobe San Pedro y San Rafael Church at Paisaje. This handsome building, topped by an octagonal wooden bell tower, can also be reached by Hwy 17 – turn right on Conejos County Rd 1075, 3 miles west of Antonito.

Hiking & Backpacking

The South San Juan Wilderness Area in the Rio Grande National Forest straddles the Continental Divide and is traversed by the Continental Divide National Scenic Trail, which emerges from the backcountry at the Cumbres Pass depot. Unlike many other wilderness areas in Colorado, you will not find roads crisscrossing the South San Juan, nor overused high mountain lakes. Many of the lakes and tributaries to the Conejos River offer good trout fishing.

Trailheads and campsites are located along the river on USFS Rd 250, northwest of Elk Creek. Near Cumbres Pass, USFS Rd 118 leads to Trujillo Meadows Wilderness Area and a USFS campground before reaching a trailhead on the southern boundary of the wilderness. For maps and information contact the Conejos Peak Ranger District (☎ 719-274-8971), 11 miles north of Antonito (3 miles south of La Jara) on US 285.

Fishing

Specially managed 'Wild Trout Waters' are designated by the Colorado Division of Wildlife on the uppermost Lake Fork, plus sections of the Conejos River next to the South San Juan Wilderness and below the Menkhaven Lodge for 4 miles. These streams support self-sustaining native cutthroat trout populations. The DOW manager in Antonito prepares a map and handout on fishing the Conejos River for each season; it's available at the Antonito visitors center and tackle shops. On your way in stop at Cottonwood Meadows Fly Shop (☎ 719-376-5660), 5 miles west of Antonito, for information on fishing conditions and specific regulations for the season. The shop also offers fishing guides for your choice of wading, hiking or horseback trips on the Conejos River and its tributaries from May to November. A one-day trip for one person starts at $200, $225 for two.

Places to Stay & Eat

There's plenty of camping near the river at either USFS campgrounds or privately run sites that often also offer rustic cabins. A few lodges provide very comfortable accommodations. Most places close from late October to April. The following selection is organized by distance from Antonito along Hwy 17.

Only 5 miles from Antonito, Hwy 17 crosses the Conejos River where large cottonwood groves shade nice tent sites at *Mogote Meadow* (☎ 719-376-5774), available with showers for $15. Farther down, *Cottonwood Meadows* (☎ 719-376-5660) offers cabins for $45 double occupancy.

At the 10-mile mark, heavy wool blankets, feather pillows and breakfasts are provided to HI/AYH members at the *Conejos River HI/AYH* (☎ 719-376-2518) for only $9 (nonmembers pay $12). The two dormitories feature the soothing sound of rushing water from the nearby river. The hostel is open from late May to mid-October.

The *USFS Mogote Campground*, 13 miles west of Antonito, has popular sites for $10 next to the river or in an upper area shaded by ponderosa pines. For reservations call ☎ 800-280-2267. A laundry and showers are available 1 mile downstream at *Conejos River Campground*, but the tent sites for $14 are not very appealing. Additional USFS campgrounds upstream on the river include *Aspen* (16 miles) and *Elk Creek* (23 miles), where Hwy 17 leaves the river. Fees at both are $10.

Top-end cabins and B&B accommodations, all with private bath, are available at *Conejos River Guest Ranch* (☎ 719-376-2464), 14 miles west of Antonito. Fully equipped housekeeping cabins cost $85 double occupancy; the comfortably furnished lodge rooms include breakfast and range from $69 to $89 depending on the season.

At 22 miles, *Mrs Rio's Restaurant* (☎ 719-376-5964) is the center of a miniature building boom that detracts from the once pristine landscape. It's open all year daily from 9 am to 9 pm and features Southwestern and Mexican dishes. Behind the restaurant, the *Mountain Home Lodge* (☎ 719-376-2464) is open year-round and has one-bedroom cabins with full kitchens for $70 in summer, $50 in winter. Laundry and showers are available with tent sites for $12 at nearby *Ponderosa Campground*, but the *USFS Elk Creek Campground* is also close by and much prettier.

Rio Grande Headwaters

In the heart of the San Juan Mountains above Creede, far to the west of the San Luis Valley, the Rio Grande begins its 1900-mile journey to the Gulf of Mexico. Most impressions of the Rio Grande come from the final 1800 miles of its path: a deep gorge near Taos, a sere corridor of settlement in New Mexico and an international border renowned for its languid flow that's a foot deep and a mile wide. But the Rio Grande's initial 100 miles – from headwater source to the San Luis Valley floor at Monte Vista – is a turbulent mountain channel of cold, clear water teeming with naturally thriving fish.

COLORADO

MONTE VISTA
Monte Vista (population 4500) is on the west side of the San Luis Valley floor at the intersection of US 160, coming east and following the Rio Grande, and US 285 (Gunbarrel Rd) coming from Saguache in the north. The local economy relies on potatoes, barley for the Coors Brewing Co, and tourists looking for directions and information on the Rio Grande headwaters.

Nearby wildlife areas should appeal to birdwatchers and a few notable lodgings may entice you to spend the night, but most of the tourist flock continues west to roost in the forests along the Rio Grande.

Information
Visitor information is available at the San Luis Valley Information and Education Center (☎ 719-852-0660, 800-835-7254),

Moose Transplants
'Moose droppings' in the Rio Grande headwaters can refer to something other than the 'meadow muffins' that get stuck to your boots if you don't watch where you're walking. Instead, you may have to look up – and you might see a sedated, blindfolded, 1000-pound bull moose suspended from a helicopter sling being whisked to a waiting trailer after being captured with a large net.

From 1991 to 1993 the State Division of Wildlife ferried over 100 moose bulls and cows this way, collecting them from large herds in North Park, UT, and Wyoming and transporting them to a newfound home near Creede.

Over the past 1000 years moose appear to have been expanding their range southward in North America; they probably would have reached the Rio Grande even without intervention from wildlife biologists. Moose are notorious for their wide ranging habitats, and the area's new residents are no exception. Since the initial transplants near North Clear Creek Falls, the moose have been on the move: north over Spring Creek Pass to the Taylor River north of Gunnison; east to the San Luis Valley margins; and south to Durango and Pagosa Springs.

These moose have done well in the semi-arid mountain shrub and oak brush found in the upper Rio Grande. During the spring of 1994, wildlife biologists estimate that the herd naturally expanded up by up to 35 newborn calves; each cow may give birth to one or two calves each year. The USFS wishes to hold the herd to a population of 300 to 350 out of concerns about overgrazing of the riverbank willows.

Although moose are large animals, they are difficult to see. Their nearly black color and stealthy movement hides the moose from casual observance. Furthermore, moose are territorial and spend most of the year alone, but may live in small groups during the winter – particularly during the mating season, or 'rut.' The term rut derives from the Latin *rugire*, meaning 'to roar'; during the fall you might hear bull moose bugle calls echoing through the night.

If you are fortunate enough to encounter a moose, there is little risk to either the animal or yourself as long as you do not approach – cows aggressively defend their young. If you want to get a closer look, use binoculars or a telephoto lens. With a little patience, you'll earn a glimpse of these magnificent creatures. ■

next to the landmark Monte Villa Inn on 1st Ave (US 160). You can pick up fishing and wildlife viewing pamphlets and a 'Monte Vista Downtown District' walking tour booklet. Hours are 8 am to 4:30 pm Monday to Saturday.

The Rio Grande National Forest Headquarters (☎ 719-852-5941), west of town at 1803 W US 160, is the place to get maps and information on public lands in the Rio Grande headwaters. It's open from 8 am to 4:30 pm weekdays.

Birdwatchers and anglers should stop by the Colorado DOW (☎ 719-852-4783) on the east side of town, south of US 160/US 285. Turn right near Haefeli's Honey Farms on to Rio Grande County Rd 1E. Monte Vista Sporting Goods, 831 1st St, has USGS maps for the San Luis Valley and the Rio Grande National Forest.

Near the Monte Villa Inn you will find ATMs at the Bank of Monte Vista, 101 Adams St, and the Rio Grande Savings & Loan, 901 First Ave.

Soap & Suds, 159 Euclid St and US 160/US 285, offers a drop-off service and is convenient to the downtown historic district. The Alta Vista Truck Center 7 miles west of Monte Vista at 895 W US 160 has 24-hour showers and laundry.

Monte Vista National Wildlife Refuge

Six miles south of town on Hwy 15, the Monte Vista National Wildlife Refuge (☎ 719-589-4021) features a 2½-mile self-guided driving loop, the **Avocet Trail**, that provides views of waterfowl that in fall may include a few endangered whooping cranes among the thousands of migrating sandhill cranes.

Since 1975 USFWS biologists have conducted an experiment to place whooping crane eggs in the nests of sandhill cranes at a nesting site in Idaho. The sandhill cranes become foster parents to the light-colored whoopers who accompany their guardians on the journey through the San Luis Valley.

Places to Stay & Eat

The handsome *Monte Villa Inn* (☎ 719-852-5166), located in the center of town at 925 1st Ave, is listed on the National Register of Historic Places. Singles/doubles cost $50/55 year-round. Check out the hotel's dining room, furnished with antiques and heavy chandeliers. The menu includes some fine selections like grilled halibut for $11 and fettuccine for $8.

A bit more outlandish is the *Best Western Movie Manor Motor Inn* (☎ 719-852-5921), 2 miles west of Monte Vista, where you can watch movies on a drive-in screen from the picture window of your motel room (sound is piped into the room). All rooms have screen views and cost $65/69 in summer. Movies are only screened from April to September.

One of the most popular restaurants in the San Luis Valley is the *Restaurante Dos Rios* (☎ 719-892-0969). Provincialism is celebrated at the Dos Rios – the menu displays ads for tractors and irrigation pumps and includes a San Luis Valley baked potato with green chile and cheese for $4. A variety of vegetarian dishes like grilled vegetable fajitas are available, as is a wide selection of salads. The restaurant is open Tuesday to Saturday from 11 am to 9 pm.

LA GARITA

La Garita (Spanish for 'the Overlook') is the scene of outstanding **rock-climbing** opportunities near a historic Hispanic landscape. Here you can find also low adobe root cellars plus a former Hispanic workers union hall, identified by the abbreviation 'SPMDTU,' and an offshoot of the Penitente Brotherhood. A chapel, known as La Capilla de San Juan Bautista, listed on the National Register of Historic Places, and a cemetery stand in stark splendor on a prominent site above the village. The chapel was originally built in 1861, but was rebuilt in 1924 following a fire. Recently renovated, it now houses the **San Juan Art Center**, a cooperative work and display space operated by Artes del Valle (☎ 719-589-4769), an organization that promotes traditional Hispanic folk art. The center is open Memorial Day to Labor Day, weekdays from 10 am to 5 pm and on Saturday from 1 to 5 pm.

Experienced climbers are attracted to the bolted face climbs on the rhyolite rock walls in Penitente Canyon and Rock Canyon. With over 400 routes in the area, there are plenty of opportunities for all levels of experience and skills. Some climbers consider these among the best short climbing routes in Colorado. You can get more information, maps, guidebooks and climbing gear at Casa de Madera (☎ 719-657-2336), 680 Grande Ave in Del Norte, where the owner, Alex Colville, is a climbing guide. The BLM area has several developed fee campgrounds in the area.

La Garita Llamas (☎ 719-754-3345) offers extended pack trips in the remote backcountry of the San Juan Mountains. Unlike horseback trips, llamas carry the gear while you hike unencumbered.

The *La Garita Creek Ranch* (☎ 719-754-2533, 800-838-3833) is southwest of the chapel on Saguache County Rd E-39 at La Garita Creek Ranch. Rooms in the modern lodge with good shared bath facilities cost $69 to $89, and cabins are also available. In summer it operates as a full guest ranch, and most people book week-long stays, which start at $515. Overnight stays are possible, but only if there's a vacancy, and then the rate will be $89 for a room. The ranch offers horseback trail rides: $14 for an hour, $75 for a full day. (See also Del Norte Places to Stay & Eat below.)

To get to La Garita from Monte Vista travel north 20 miles on US 285, turn left (west) at the sign on Saguache County Rd G for 8 miles. Penitente Canyon is southwest from the chapel on County Rd 38.

DEL NORTE

Del Norte (population 1700) is an attractive town beside the Rio Grande del Norte, for which it was named, in the foothills west of the San Luis Valley on US 160. It's one of Colorado's oldest towns, founded in 1860, and by 1873 it was a thriving supply point for mining in the San Juan Mountains. In contrast to the more typical rickety mining camp buildings, wholesale suppliers invested in permanent and substantial structures. Visitors will still find many

sturdy stone buildings in this seat of Rio Grande County. Now Del Norte marks the beginning of 'Gold Medal' fishing on the Rio Grande and is a popular jumping-off point (so to speak) for rock climbers (see La Garita above) and mountain bicyclists.

Information

For visitor information, stop by Casa de Madera (☎ 719-657-2336), 680 Grande Ave (US 160). The USFS Divide District Ranger Station (☎ 719-657-3321) is at 1308 Grande Ave, just past the Skaff's supermarket.

There's an ATM machine in Skaff's Super grocery store at 1215 Grande Ave on the east end of town. It's open 8 am to 7 pm daily. The Los Piños Health Vista Clinic (☎ 719-657-3342) is on the opposite side of Grande Ave.

Rio Grande County Museum & Cultural Center

The Rio Grande County Museum (☎ 719-657-2850), housed in a modern building at Oak and 6th Sts, features Pueblo and Ute rock art, Hispanic history and early photographs of Monte Vista's 'potato row' wagons loaded high with valley spuds at the turn of the century. Special programs include talks and outdoor excursions led by local historians and naturalists. The museum has information for people who want to visit local rock art sites. During the summer the museum is open weekdays from 11 am to 4 pm, and admission is $1.

Fishing

Gold Medal fishing on the Rio Grande begins a mile upstream at the Farmer's Union canal. From here to the Hwy 149 bridge at South Fork is one of Colorado's most productive fisheries, producing 16- to 20-inch trout. The wild strain of rainbows introduced to the river have prospered under the tackle restrictions and possession limits. Current regulations call for catch-and-release on rainbows and limits possession to two brown trout, 16 inches or longer; tackle is restricted to artificial flies or lures. You access the river and signed public property via the bridges on Rio Grande County Rds 17, 18 and 19, plus the Hwy 149 bridge above South Fork.

Mountain Biking

Fat-tire bikes are permitted on all public trails with the exception of designated wilderness areas. A relatively easy ride heads north about 10 miles to La Ventana, a natural arch 'window' in a volcanic dike. Be on the lookout for bighorn sheep, part of a herd of about 100 that inhabits the area around the arch and nearby Eagle Mountain to the east. To get there from Del Norte, cross the river and follow Rio Grande County Rd 22 for 8 miles passing the small airport, turn right on USFS Rd 660 for a quarter of a mile, then turn left and follow the road for about 2 miles to the short trail to the volcanic wall.

Another ride recommended by the USFS follows an old stock driveway along an Alpine ridge on USFS Trail 700 from Grayback Mountain (12,616 feet) east 7 miles to Blowout Pass (12,000 feet). To reach the Grayback Mountain trailhead, you must travel about 20 miles south of Del Norte on USFS Rd 14, then continue another 5 miles on USFS Rd 330.

Places to Stay & Eat

Two motels on the eastern end of Grande Ave (US 160) offer comparable rooms. The *El Rancho* (☎ 719-657-3332), 1160 Grande, has singles/doubles for $30/40, while the *Del Norte Motel & Cafe* (☎ 719-657-3581, 800-372-2331), 1050 Grande Ave, is a bit nicer and charges $31/42 (a few dollars more in summer). The cafe is a pretty good spot for breakfast or lunch.

Stone Quarry Pizza (☎ 719-657-9115), 580 Grande Ave, has a good reputation and features a salad bar and outdoor patio. It's open daily for lunch and dinner in a masonry structure on Grande Ave that is cool on even the warmest summer days. Authentic Mexican specialties like menudo (an offal soup) for $3 are featured at the *La Fuente Supper Club* (☎ 719-657-3492), 540 Grande Ave, but you can also get steaks, jumbo shrimp and vegetable dinners.

SOUTH FORK

Founded around a lumber mill, South Fork (population 390) is not so much a town as a stretch of buildings along US 160, 31 miles west of Monte Vista. However, it also lies at the confluence of the South Fork and the Rio Grande rivers, and is a good base from which to fish the Gold Medal waters of the Rio Grande. During ski season, South Fork provides a lodging alternative to Pagosa Springs for skiers at Wolf Creek (see Pagosa Springs later in this chapter). Exceptional backcountry hiking in the Weminuche Wilderness of the Rio Grande National Forest, Colorado's largest pristine area, is readily accessible from trailheads near South Fork. An abundance of nearby campgrounds also attracts vacationers who want to enjoy a forested mountain setting.

Orientation & Information

At South Fork, US 160 turns south from the Rio Grande toward Wolf Creek Pass 18 miles away, and Hwy 149 continues upstream 21 miles to Creede before crossing the Continental Divide to Lake City.

The Silver Thread Interpretive Center (☎ 719-873-5512, 800-571-0881) is the name of South Fork's visitors center, a reference to the Silver Thread Byway leading to Creede. It has information on outdoor activities and lodging and sells biking and hiking trail maps. Located at the junction of US 160 and Hwy 149, it's open 9 am to 5 pm weekdays and 10 am to 4 pm weekends during summer. In winter it's closed on Sunday.

A post office is just downstream from the river confluence on US 160. Above the confluence, the Rainbow Grocery has an ATM operating during summer months from 7 am to 8 pm and from 7 am to 7:30 pm in the winter.

Fishing

Gold Medal fishing on the Rio Grande surrounds South Fork. Riverbank access from the Hwy 149 bridge or any of the County Rd bridges east of town are typically signed to indicate public right-of-way, but be sure to abide by private property restrictions. Easy Class I float trips allow anglers to fish the entire stretch of river from South Fork to Del Norte. Anglers can fish from a boat over any stretch of the river as long as they do not land their craft on private property or set foot on the river bottom over private property. Starting 4 miles upstream from South Fork, the Coller State Wildlife Area provides access to over 3 miles of the Rio Grande. Overnight camping and snowmobile use are prohibited in the Coller State Wildlife Area.

You can rent rafts at the Spruce Ski Lodge (☎ 719-837-5605).

Wildlife Viewing

The grassy river benches in the Coller State Wildlife Area attract elk, deer and moose during winter months. You can see bighorn sheep throughout the year on the south-facing Palisade cliffs extending from the Coller State Wildlife Area to Wagon Wheel Gap. At the gap, golden eagles soar above the cliff faces and fish the Rio Grande.

The magnificent golden eagle

Hiking & Backpacking

Named for a band of the Ute tribe, the Weminuche Wilderness Area is the most extensive wilderness in Colorado with an area of over 700 sq miles. The Weminuche extends west along the Continental Divide from Wolf Creek Pass to the Animas River near Silverton. By early July you can reach Archuleta Lake (11,800 feet) near the Divide by following **USFS Trail 839** for

about 7 miles from the Big Meadows Reservoir (9200 feet) along Archuleta Creek into the wilderness area. Along the **Continental Divide National Scenic Trail (USFS Trail 813)** you will find many secluded hiking opportunities as the trail passes through 80 miles of the Weminuche Wilderness between Wolf Creek Pass and Stony Pass. One trail of particular interest leads to an undeveloped natural hot spring west of the Divide. To reach Rainbow/Wolf Creek Pass Hot Spring, take **USFS Trail 560** west from the Divide, descending over 6 miles through the Beaver Creek drainage to the West Fork of the Weminuche headwaters of the San Juan River. The spring of over 100°F is to the right on **USFS Trail 561**, about half a mile above the trail junction.

To get to the trailhead at Big Meadows Reservoir, travel south on US 160 for 11 miles to the turnoff on the right (to the west). Proceed to the boat ramp parking area on the north side of the reservoir. You will need maps of both the Rio Grande and San Juan National Forests. Ranger stations for the Rio Grande National Forest are in either Del Norte or Creede; the nearest San Juan National Forest ranger station is in Pagosa Springs (☎ 970-264-2268).

Places to Stay

Camping There are some 300 RV spaces at several private campgrounds within a few miles of South Fork, but not really any appealing tent sites.

Primitive USFS campgrounds cost $10 in the vicinity of South Fork. The closest are at Beaver Creek, about 4 miles south of South Fork. From South Fork go 2 miles southwest on US 160 and turn left across the South Fork of the Rio Grande to USFS Rd 360. Continue 3 miles to *Lower Beaver Creek* and *Upper Beaver Creek* campgrounds; in another 3 miles you reach Beaver Creek Reservoir Wilderness Area and USFS *Cross Creek Campground*. With 56 camping units, the USFS *Big Meadows Campground*, 11 miles south of South Fork near Wolf Creek Pass, is the largest facility in the area and is at the start of several appealing trails. Eight miles upstream from

South Fork on Hwy 149 is the small USFS *Palisade Campground* on the Rio Grande – its 13 sites are nearly always full in summer months.

Motels, B&Bs & Lodges Peak season rates apply during July and August and also during November and December, when the brutal weather makes the nearby Wolf Creek Ski Area an early winter favorite.

One of the first motels to fill up is the *Inn Motel* (☎ 719-873-5514, 800-233-9723), at the junction of US 160 and Hwy 149, where windows open to the river and singles/doubles cost $24/31 in winter and $50 in summer. Also near the highway junction, *Foothills Lodge* (☎ 719-873-5969, 800-510-3897) offers rooms from $40/55 in winter, around $5 less in summer, and has a hot tub. B&B accommodations with shared bath at the *Spruce Ski Lodge* (☎ 719-873-5605, 800-228-5605), about 1 mile east of the visitors center, cost $27/33. Chalet cabins are also available for $40/50 in summer, $5 less in winter.

The *Wolf Creek Ski Lodge* (☎ 719-873-5547, 800-874-0416) on US 160 about half a mile west of the junction, offers quite comfortable rooms for $50/58 in summer, $45/51 in winter.

Places to Eat

The *Electric Blue Moose Cafe* (☎ 719-873-5757), next to the mill on US 160, is highly recommended by locals and offers a mix of Italian, Mexican and American dishes. Next to the Rainbow Grocery, the *Rockaway Cafe* (☎ 719-873-5581) is a quaint place known mainly for its fine steak, but also serves seafood, chicken and large salads.

CREEDE & AROUND

In 1889, late in mining history, Nicholas C Creede discovered a large silver outcropping on Campbell Mountain just north of the present town of Creede. Within a few years Creede was a boomtown of 10,000 often raucous citizens. The D&RG Railroad fueled the tremendous growth by quickly extending the track from Wagon Wheel Gap and bringing trainloads of wild-eyed prospectors to town. By 1893, the appropriately named Mineral County was carved out of adjacent counties, encouraged by Creede's prosperous saloonkeepers who rebelled against Hinsdale County tax collectors.

But the boom turned to bust fairly quickly. In 1892 Creede was leveled by a fire, and in 1893 the nationwide financial panic stung the town with a precipitous drop in the price of silver. By 1900, only a decade after the boom, Creede's population was less than 1900 and dropping fast. The remote region sank into obscurity, except to vacation travelers. Mineral and Hinsdale counties currently vie for the title of least-populated county in the state: each has less than 600 people.

Since 1988, following another silver price drop, all the silver mines of Mineral County have closed, except to visitors who enjoy touring the rugged mining landscape north of town, where tremendous mills cling to spectacular cliffs. Below the vertical-walled mouth of Willow Creek Canyon, narrow Creede Ave is a mix of galleries and shops in historic buildings offering unique gifts. Each summer, visitors crowd the street to attend the renowned Creede Repertory Theatre.

For scenic beauty, the country surrounding Creede is hard to beat. Relatively untrampled trails into the immense surrounding wilderness areas provide appreciative hikers and backpackers with beauty and solitude, as well as access to unique sights like the bizarre volcanic spires and pinnacles of the Wheeler Geologic Area.

Information

At the top of Creede Ave opposite the low-rise Mineral County Courthouse you will find the Creede/Mineral County Chamber of Commerce (☎ 719-658-2374, 800-327-2102), open 8 am to 5 pm Monday to Saturday in summer, 9 am to 5 pm weekdays in winter. Be sure to pick up a walking tour map of historic Creede while at the chamber office. The USFS Divide District Ranger Station (☎ 719-658-2556), 3rd St

Sean·n·stuff

3601 CONWAY
FT. WORTH, TEXAS 76111

TO:

Silver Fox Trailer

1725 E 69th Street

Denver, Colorado 80229

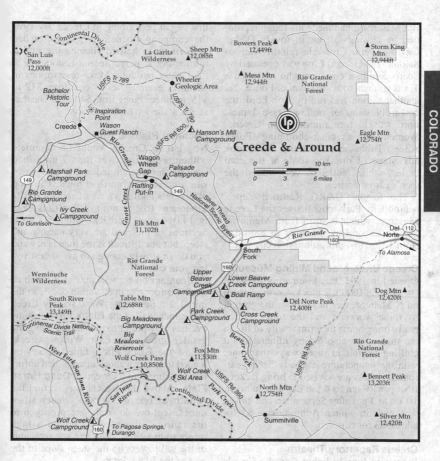

Creede & Around

and Creede Ave, has information on the La Garita and Weminuche wilderness areas. It's open between May and November from 8 am to 12 pm and 12:30 to 4:30 pm. On weekends and in winter try the folks at San Juan Sports on Creede Ave for information on outdoor activities.

The First National Bank, about midway along Creede Ave, has an ATM. The Post Office is on the corner of Wall St and Creede Ave.

Named for Nicholas Creede's prosperous Amethyst Mine, the Amethyst Emporium (☎ 719-658-2430) offers a large selection

of books on the region, including history and nature works in the 'backroom.'

A coin-op laundry is located next to the Last Chance Kitchen, about midway along Creede Ave. Showers are available at the Snowshoe Motel, at the southeast edge of town, for $3.75 including soap and towel.

Creede Museum

Mineral treasures attracted miners by the trainload, but this museum chronicles the more intriguing opportunists and scoundrels who arrived to take advantage of Creede's short-lived prosperity. Former US Marshal

Bat Masterson had made his tough reputation by closing saloons in rowdy Dodge City, KS, yet in Creede he ran the Watrous Saloon. The Orleans Club was operated by Soapy Smith, a con man who imported a Texas gunman to act as Chief of Police. Yet another saloon was run by Bob Ford, the cowardly killer of outlaw Jesse James; Ford was in turn murdered in Creede. Women such as cigar-chomping 'Poker Alice' Tubbs and Calamity Jane took advantage of drunken fools at the card tables, while 'soiled doves' mined the men's carnal desires.

The former D&RG Railroad depot, behind City Park, now houses the Creede Museum, which is open from Memorial Day to Labor Day, Monday to Saturday from 10 am to 4 pm. Admission costs $1.

Creede Underground Mining Museum
Opened in 1992, this fascinating museum (☎ 719-658-0811), 2 blocks north of town on N Main St, was hewn from the ground by mine workers, and the tours, which really bring home the grim reality of life in the mines, are also led by miners. It's a chilling exhibit in more ways than one: with the temperature a steady 51°F year-round, visitors are advised to bring jackets. It's open 10 am to 4 pm daily in summer, 10 am to 3 pm after September, and closed weekends in winter. Admission is $5 for adults, $3 for children.

Creede Repertory Theatre
From mid-June to Labor Day the Creede Repertory Theatre (☎ 719-658-2540) presents talented casts in well-honed productions each night of the week (except some Mondays). Two shows open in June and play alternating nights until July, when two more shows are added to the schedule. A children's program and one-act play are added in August; they are presented as Friday and Saturday matinees, in addition to touring throughout three states. Visitors in late summer can see six plays in four days.

The company has come a long way since 1966, when 12 University of Kansas students first began performing in Creede. By 1993 the company's benefactors and crowded performances helped finance the multi-million-dollar purchase and restoration of the theater building. Make reservations in advance; evening tickets cost from $12 to $15, matinees range from $4 to $8. The theater is at the top of Creede Ave.

Bachelor Historic Tour
No visit to Creede would be complete without bouncing over the 17-mile loop tour of the abandoned mines and town sites immediately north of town. The loop offers outstanding views of the La Garita Mountains (the summit of San Luis Peak is 14,014 feet) and Rio Grande Valley. Sections of the road are very narrow and steep, but not difficult if the road is dry and you drive slowly enough to avoid destroying your car.

Mountain bikers will note that much of the 2000-foot rise in elevation occurs in the initial 2 miles along West Willow Creek that miners called the **Black Pitch** – some cyclists may prefer to tour mines along the gentler grades of East Willow Creek. Below the Black Pitch, failed brakes on loaded teamster wagons often pulled unfortunate animals to their end at **Dead Horse Flats**. Above this treacherous section the **Amethyst**, one of Colorado's richest silver mines, sent ore down the steep canyon to the railroad aboard ore cars on a high rotary tram system. You can see remnants of the tall towers up the steep slope to the east of the Black Pitch.

An excellent illustrated tour booklet prepared by local historians is available for $1 from the Creede Chamber of Commerce, the USFS, the Creede Museum or from a dispenser at the first interpretive stop: West Willow/East Willow Creek junction immediately north of the rock spires that mark the gateway to Willow Creek Canyon.

You can rent a mountain bike for $15 per day at San Juan Sports (☎ 719-658-2359) on Creede Ave, open daily from 9 am to 5:30 pm (10 am to 5 pm in winter). The shop also carries a thorough collection of

USGS topographic maps. Guided mountain bike tours and bike rentals are offered by Mountain Man Rafting & Tours (☎ 719-658-2663).

Wheeler Geologic Area

In 1993, 85 years after it was declared a national monument, the bizarre eroded volcanic forms west of Creede called the Wheeler Geologic Area, was granted wilderness protection when federal lawmakers approved its addition to La Garita Wilderness. The dramatic shapes carved by wind and rain into volcanic tuff framed by evergreen forest attracted early attention, but the remote 11,000-foot setting near the Continental Divide kept all but the hardiest visitors away. By 1950 the monument status was removed.

The USFS East Bellows Trail (Trail 790) is a 17-mile roundtrip hike that climbs nearly 2000 feet from the Hanson's Mill campground to the base of the geologic formations. To get to the trailhead, drive southeast along Hwy 149 for just over 7 miles and turn left on USFS Rd 600 (Pool Table Rd). Continue along this road for 9.5 miles to Hanson's Mill campground. The trail affords some great views and there are lots of places to camp along the way. From Hanson's Mill there is also a 14-mile-long 4WD road that leads to the area.

North Clear Creek Falls

Twenty-five miles west of Creede and only half a mile from signs on Hwy 149, the impressive falls are visible from an overlook on the fenced edge of a deep gorge. From the parking area a short walk over the ridge away from the falls takes you to another viewpoint above the sheer-walled canyon with Bristol Head in the distance. Far below your feet a metal aqueduct carries Clear Creek away from its natural course to the Santa Maria Reservoir as part of a massive effort to regulate the flow of the Rio Grande headwaters.

Hiking & Backpacking

The Upper Rio Grande Walkers (☎ 719-658-2430) describe several of their favorite walks with a map and brochure that also grades each walk's difficulty. All walks are up and back, but the views are so spectacular and different in each direction that you will not mind retracing your steps. The hike through the upland meadow called Phoenix Park is especially appealing, as it begins at the King Solomon Mill at the top of East Willow Creek Canyon and proceeds past waterfalls and beaver ponds. You can pick up maps at the Amethyst Emporium, the last shop on Creede Ave.

Hiking options are nearly limitless within the extensive Weminuche and La Garita wilderness areas on either side of the Rio Grande Valley. Only a few miles above the Equity Mine on the Bachelor Loop north of Creede, you reach both the **Colorado Trail** and the **Continental Divide National Scenic Trail** at the 12,000-foot San Luis Pass. From this boundary of La Garita Wilderness Area you are only 6 miles from the summit of San Luis Peak (14,014 feet). If hiking the Divide beckons you, a good start is to go about 13 miles west from San Luis Pass, following the cliff edge of Snowy Mesa, to the Hwy 149 crossing at Spring Creek Pass (10,901 feet).

A stagecoach line between Del Norte and Silverton operated over Stony Pass from 1874 to 1882. From anywhere along the Continental Divide in this area you will see stunning scenery. Solitude at Stony Pass, however, is frequently interrupted by 4WD vehicles following the 15-mile road from USFS Lost Trail Campground. To avoid such intrusions, hikers will enjoy the relatively easy **West Lost Creek Trail** (USFS Trail 822), which makes a 6-mile (one-way) day hike to the Continental Divide a feasible alternative. From the Lost Trail Campground trailhead take **USFS Trail 821** north about 2 miles to West Lost Trail Creek, which continues northwest for 6 miles to the Divide above Cataract Lake. From high above the embryonic Rio Grande you will have views of the rugged 14,000-foot Handies and Sunshine peaks to the north. To get to the trailhead from

Creede, drive southwest on Hwy 149 for 21 miles, then turn left on USFS Rd 520 and follow this road for 17 miles to the trailhead, passing the Road Canyon and Rio Grande reservoirs on the way.

The Continental Divide National Scenic Trail within the Weminuche Wilderness traverses 80 miles between Stony Pass and Wolf Creek Pass (see South Fork earlier in this chapter). Colorado's largest wilderness naturally presents many additional options beyond the scope of this book. A good source of information if you wish to explore the Continental Divide east of Stony Pass is Dennis Gebhardt's *A Backpacking Guide to the Weminuche Wilderness*.

White-Water Rafting
On the Rio Grande below Wagon Wheel Gap, scenic float trips with a few rapids and quality fishing are the primary attractions of this 20-mile run to South Fork. A good place to put in along Hwy 149 is the Goose Creek Rd Bridge immediately west of the gap. During high water, rafters should beware the closely spaced railroad bridge abutments at Wagon Wheel Gap.

Above Wagon Wheel Gap the Rio Grande meanders through channels clogged with Creede's mining debris after leaving scenic Antelope Park, where recently relocated moose are occasionally visible in the broad meadows. Above Antelope Park, however, the Rio Grande shoots through a narrow canyon in the Weminuche Wilderness, where rafters will find Class III and IV rapids for about 5 miles below the Rio Grande Reservoir. To get to the put-in spot at USFS River Hill Campground, drive 21 miles southwest of Creede on Hwy 149, turn left at USFS Rd 520 and continue almost 4 miles to the camp. The lower portion of the trip to the exit point at Fern Creek Rd Bridge near Freeman's Lodge is a laid-back scenic float.

Rafting tours and equipment rental are available from Mountain Man Rafting & Tours (☎ 719-658-2663) at the intersection of Creede Ave and Hwy 149. Half/full-day trips cost $30/60 ($20/50 for children age 12 and under).

Fishing
On the Rio Grande above Wagon Wheel Gap, anglers will find two choice sections of the river with special regulations for catch-and-release on rainbow trout using either artificial fly or lure, and a two-bag limit on brown trout over 12 inches long. One section between Creede's Willow Creek and Wagon Wheel Gap is mostly private and boat access is necessary. Farther upstream, however, you can fish from public lands on both sides of the river at USFS Marshall Park and Rio Grande campgrounds.

The fishing is good at 11,000 feet at **Ruby Lakes** accessible by USFS Trail 815, a 4-mile hike or horseback ride along Fern Creek. The trailhead is about 1¼ miles along USFS Rd 522, 16 miles southwest of Craig off Hwy 149.

Brown Lakes State Wildlife Area, at 9840 feet, is stocked by the DOW with rainbow and brook trout, but the large browns and native cutthroat are the real attraction. The lakes are surrounded by spruce and fir forests and are located 2 miles west of Hwy 149 and the USFS Silver Thread Campground, 25 miles west of Creede.

Fishing supplies, information and guide services are available in Creede at the Rod & Reel (☎ 719-658-2955), open daily from 7 am to 6 pm. Guided river fishing is offered by Mountain Man Rafting & Tours (☎ 719-658-2663), which charges $195 for a full day for two people.

Special Events
The second weekend in June marks the opening of the Creede Repertory Theater. Although Creede's hard-rock mining days are over, many locals stay in practice – keeping local bars solvent – for the **Days of '92 Mining Competition** leading up to the **Colorado State Mining Championships** during the Fourth of July weekend.

Places to Stay
Camping All of the public forest lands surrounding Creede are open to camping, but 10 USFS campgrounds offering water

and restrooms are in the Divide District above Wagon Wheel Gap. On the banks of the Rio Grande's designated Wild Trout Waters is the popular USFS *Marshall Park Campground*, only 7 miles southwest of Creede, where campsites cost $10. Reservations (☎ 800-280-2267) are required in summer. Nine miles south of Marshall Park, on the Weminuche Wilderness boundary, is the isolated USFS *Ivy Creek Campground* and trailhead. To get there from Marshall Park follow USFS Rd 523 for 4 miles, then turn left on USFS Rd 528 for 3 miles and continue straight on USFS Rd 526. Sites are free.

Plenty of sites are available on the boundary of the Weminuche Wilderness at four campgrounds along USFS Rd 520, 21 miles southwest of Creede on Hwy 149. The largest of the group, *Thirtymile Campground*, offers 33 sites for $9. Near Clear Creek, about 25 miles west of Creede, *South Clear Creek* and *South Clear Creek Falls* are two USFS campgrounds where sites with scenic views cost $9. The secluded canyon sites at *North Clear Creek Campground* are also worth checking out. All three are near North Clear Creek Falls and Brown Lakes wilderness areas. See map for additional campgrounds in the area.

B&Bs Peak season rates are in effect in July and August. Next to the Repertory Theatre, the *Creede Hotel B&B* (☎ 719-658-2608) has four rooms with private baths that cost $59 for a single, $69 for a double. Both the hotel and its excellent restaurant are closed from October to May.

The top-end Old Fire House B&B (☎ 719-658-0212), on Creede Ave, has four fully renovated Victorian rooms and a library lounge. It's also closed from October to May.

Motels On the southeast edge of town, clean singles/doubles at the *Snowshoe Motel* (☎ 719-658-2315) cost $36/49 in summer, $29/36 in winter.

Resorts There are nearly 20 ranches and resorts around Creede ranging from eco-

nomical to extravagant. Following are several of the more accessible places: the Creede/Mineral County Chamber of Commerce (☎ 800-327-2102) can provide more information.

Two miles southeast of Creede, the *Wason Ranch* (☎ 719-658-2413) has two-bedroom cabins equipped with kitchenettes for $54 per day. These are available from May through October. Riverside cottages with three bedrooms and two baths are available year-round and cost $100, with a minimum stay of two days. The ranch also offers fly-fishing lessons, fishing guides and a dory. Families are welcome at the *Antlers Ranch* (☎ 719-658-2423), 5 miles southwest of Creede, which offers motel-style rooms for $50 and cabins starting at $55 on both banks of the Rio Grande. A laundry is also available.

About 8 miles southwest of Creede is the beautiful *Soward Ranch* (☎ 719-658-2295). Open from May to October, it's the only 'centennial' ranch in the area – meaning it's been operated by the same family for more than 100 years. Guests can enjoy fishing from four lakes as well as 4 miles of trout creek on the 1500-acre property. Twelve cabins range in price from $40 to $80 depending on size and amenities. To get there, take Hwy 149 southwest for 7 miles, turn left on Middle Creek Rd, continue for 1 mile and when you get to the fork in the road, bear right, following the signs to the ranch.

Places to Eat

A fine place to start the day is *Journeys* (☎ 719-658-2290), a great little coffee shop that offers the healthiest breakfasts and lunches in Creede, as well as great coffee. There is live music on summer weekends, and the owners can also clue you in on other activities in the area (ask about the Bowling Ball Cannon). The restaurant is on Creede Ave and easy to spot – just look for the bright blue and yellow front. It's open most of the year, except mid-winter.

It can get very busy on theater nights at the *Creede Hotel Restaurant* (☎ 719-658-2680) – don't assume you'll be able to get a plate of fettuccine alfredo or tamari chicken without a reservation. The home-made bread and garden salad are nice accompaniments. If you're visiting in the winter you'll have little choice beyond the *Old Miner's Inn* (☎ 719-658-2767) on Creede Ave, which serves pizza and sand-wiches (but the kitchen closes quite early), or *Mucker's Bucket* (☎ 719-658-9997), on Hwy 149 at the southeast edge of Creede.

A special delight is in store at the *Bristol Inn Restaurant* (☎ 719-658-2455), 18 miles southwest of Creede on Hwy 149, where you can eat Sunday brunch while overlooking Bristol Head from the tall dining-room windows. Each season from Memorial Day to late September the Bristol features a different dinner entree for $10 to $20 that is published on a calendar available at the Creede chamber of commerce. The restaurant is open for dinner Wednesday to Saturday and for brunch on Sunday between mid-May and late September. Reservations are required.

Getting There & Away
Creede is 23 miles west of South Fork on the Silver Thread National Scenic Byway, which follows Hwy 149 for 75 miles between South Fork and Lake City (see Lake City below).

San Juan Mountains

Straddling the Continental Divide and cov-ering an extensive area north of Durango and Pagosa Springs, the San Juan Moun-tains offer scenery that leads admirers to call this range the 'Alps of America.' Vol-canic rock formations distinguish these peaks from other Colorado ranges. Instead of uplifted sedimentary layers forming long parallel ridges, the San Juan Moun-tains are a jumbled mass that displace the Continental Divide west of the Front Range as they project into the southwestern Colorado Plateau. Many regard the lush forests and sharp peaks of this range as the finest scenery the state has to offer.

LAKE CITY
Lake City's 330 residents don't seem to mind its status as the 'flyspeck' seat of Hinsdale County. In 1877 Lake City was known as the 'Metropolis of the Mines' and reached its peak population of 5000, but unlike many mining towns, it attracted optimistic settlers rather than itinerants. The Greek and Gothic Revival architecture and tree-lined streets reflect the settlers' nostalgia for earlier eastern cities.

Orientation
Lake City is on Hwy 149 (Gunnison Ave in town) west of the Continental Divide at Spring Creek Pass and the giant Slumgul-lion earthslide that dammed the Lake Fork of the Gunnison River to form Lake San Cristobal south of town. To the west rises Uncompahgre Peak and four others over 14,000 feet in elevation, creating a barrier between Lake City and Ouray crossed only by the USFS Alpine Byway that requires 4WD vehicles or mountain bikes.

Information
The Lake City Chamber of Commerce (☎ 970-944-2527, 800-569-1874), on Silver St in the center of town, also acts as the USFS and BLM visitors center, selling topo maps and offering free trail information. The *Silver World* began publication in 1875 as 'a miner's paper' and was the first Col-orado newspaper to be published west of the Continental Divide. The First National Bank of Lake City, 3rd and Silver Sts, has an ATM. The post office is at 8th St and Gunnison Ave; the zip code is 81235.

Slumgullion Slide
In 1270 AD a catastrophic earthflow moved almost 5 miles down the mountainside and dammed the Gunnison River to form Lake San Cristobal, Colorado's second-largest lake. A slower but more persistent flow began about 350 years ago and continues at rates of two to 20 feet per year. This active section of the slide, whose name comes from the yellowish mud's resemblance to the watery miner's stew, is either barren or features forests of crooked trees. It's best

Memorial to the Victims of Colorado's Cannibal King

South of town near the junction of Hwy 149 and Lake County Rd 30, a simple plaque in memory of five unfortunate prospectors sits on the spot where they were murdered in 1874.

Ignoring Chief Ouray's warnings about attempting to reach the Breckenridge gold strike in winter weather, six men set out from near present-day Montrose in February, 1874. In April, after severe storms and extreme cold, only one of the men – a fellow named Alferd Packer – emerged near Lake City, without his companions. He told one of the first people he met, Alonso Hartman, of personal hardships and an injury that did not allow him to keep up with the rest of the party. Hartman observed that Packer appeared in remarkably good shape for a man who had endured near starvation. Other parts of his story soon unraveled: his companions were never heard from again. Packer had some of their belongings on his person and Utes found strips of human flesh on Packer's trail.

In June, the five victims were found by a *Harper's Weekly* photographer who noted that one victim had been shot in the back and the others' skulls were crushed. Nearby was a crude cabin where the accused cannibal sat out the storms.

In 1989, Packer's five victims were exhumed for a forensic examination that revealed battered skulls and defensive wounds on their arms and hands. Their remains were reinterred at the site.

Though he protested his innocence, Packer was eventually tried for murder, spent some time in jail and became a vegetarian. He died in 1907 and his grave can be found in Littleton, CO. He has since become somewhat of a legendary figure in the state, inspiring songs, cookbooks, an irreverent 'Alferd Packer Day' at the University of Colorado in Boulder and even a musical! ■

viewed in the morning from Windy Point Overlook, south of town off Hwy 149, at 10,600 feet. Another good view is from the top of Cannibal Plateau Trail (USFS Trail 464), the site where prospector Alferd Packer is said to have had his companions for dinner (see sidebar about Colorado's Cannibal King earlier in this chapter). The trailhead is below Slumgullion Campground, off Cebolla Creek Rd.

Alpine Loop Byway

After 16 miles up Hensen Creek, this unpaved byway becomes a rugged route over Engineer Pass suited only for Jeeps and mountain bikes headed to Ouray. Another part of the 4WD loop heads south along the Lake Fork of the Gunnison River and crosses Cinnamon Pass to Silverton.

Mountain bikes rent for $18 per day ($23 with front suspension) at San Juan Mountain Bikes (☎ 970-944-2274), behind Lake City Market at the north end of town. Cannibal Outdoors (☎ 970-944-2559), 367 S Gunnison Ave, offers trips to Engineer Pass

in an open truck for $39 per person. Rocky Mountain Jeep Rental (☎ 970-944-2262), at the Pleasant View Resort, rents Jeeps for $90 per day.

Hiking & Backpacking

Alpine wildflowers are a prime attraction on the many summer trails in the area. West of Lake City and north of Hensen Creek is the **Big Blue Wilderness Area**, featuring many stunning peaks over 13,000 feet, including two 14ers: Uncompahgre Peak and Wetterhorne Peak. From the Lake City Cemetery it's possible to make an easy two-night loop to Crystal Lake (4 miles) on **USFS Trail 235**, before continuing to Larson Lakes on **USFS Trail 236**, which returns to the cemetery.

The major trailheads into the Big Blue Wilderness follow Hensen Creek west for 5½ miles. Turn right (north) on Nellie Creek Rd (4WD), which travels 5 miles to the trailhead to either Uncompahgre Peak or lengthy **Big Blue Creek Trail**, with good fishing.

Northeast of Lake City, the **Powderhorn Wilderness Area** features the 4-mile-long **BLM Trail 3030** to Powderhorn Lakes, crossing a huge Alpine meadow loaded with wildflowers. This is prime elk habitat. The lakes offer fishing for cutthroat trout. To get to the trailhead, take Hwy 149 north 30 miles, turn right on Indian Creek Rd (Gunnison County Rd 58) and drive for 10 miles to the trailhead sign. To reach the Powderhorn Wilderness from the south, **USFS Trail 461** leads 6 miles to Devils Lake and the Cannibal Plateau. The trailhead is at Brush Creek on USFS Rd 788, 6 miles from the Slumgullion Campground turnoff from Hwy 149.

Day-hikes in the BLM's Alpine Loop Byway south of Lake San Cristobal offer high altitude scenery and peak ascents – but the lower parts of most trails are shared with 4WD vehicles that disperse wildlife and disrupt the solitude.

White-Water Rafting

Local whitewater enthusiasts enjoy the uncrowded Lake Fork of the Gunnison River stretching from High Bridge Creek, 8 miles north of Lake City, for 30 miles to the BLM Redbridge Campground, where the river is stilled as it enters Blue Mesa Reservoir. On the way, the river passes through the spectacular volcanic columns breached by the river to form **The Gate**, a giant notch visible for miles. Above the BLM Gateview Campground, north of Hwy 149 on Lake County Rd 25, the river is mainly a Class II warm-up for the lower stretch of Class III-IV waters that once led into the Gunnison Canyon.

Cannibal Outdoors (☎ 970-944-2559) offers half-day rafting trips that are either scenic floats above the Gate or whitewater thrills below the Gate. Scenic River Tours (☎ 970-944-2306) does similar trips.

Fishing

The Lake City Chamber of Commerce sells booklets with maps of local fishing spots for $1. Popular areas include Lake Fork/ Big Blue Drainages, Cebolla Drainages and Mountain Lakes.

Horseback Riding

Lakeview Guides & Outfitters (☎ 970-944-2401), offers two-hour rides for $27, or longer summer pack trips from their stables at Lake San Cristobal.

Cross-Country Skiing

The Hinsdale Haute Route (☎ 970-944-2269) is a nonprofit organization that maintains four yurts on the Divide between Lake City and Creede. Even novice skiers can enjoy the 2 miles of backcountry travel from Hwy 149 to an overnight stay at the first yurt. The yurts sleep up to eight people and are rented to groups for $100 for the first two nights, and $75 thereafter.

Places to Stay

Camping Two options are available for camping in town. *Lake City Campground* (☎ 970-944-2668) on Bluff St north of 8th St offers grassy tent sites, showers and laundry for $10, RV sites for $14. *Hensen Creek RV Park* (☎ 970-994-2274) has shower facilities and streamside tent sites for $17.

Dispersed camping is available on USFS lands along Hensen Creek immediately east of town. Free BLM riverside campsites are available at *The Gate*, 20 miles north next to Hwy 149, and at *Gateview* and *Redbridge* along Lake County Rd 25, which continues beside the river where Hwy 149 turns east from the river course.

Nine miles southwest of town immediately below Slumgullion Pass (elevation 11,361 feet), the USFS *Slumgullion Campground* offers 21 campsites for $6.

Additional primitive sites are available by continuing east on Cebolla Creek Rd, where rarely used trails enter La Garita Wilderness Area in the Gunnison National Forest's Cebolla Ranger District (☎ 970-641-0471).

B&Bs Open year-round, the restored 1878 *Cinnamon Inn* (☎ 970-944-2641, 800-337-

2335), 426 Gunnison Ave, is filled with watercolor landscapes by Gwendolyn Faber and offers comfortable rooms with shared bath from $75, with private bath from $95.

Motels & Cabins Budget rooms cost $35/45 a single/double at the *Matterhorn Motel* (☎ 970-944-2210, 800-779-8028), on the west side of town on Bluff St. The motel is only open from May to late October. Rooms start at $45 at the *Silver Spur Motel* (☎ 970-944-2231, 800-499-9701), at the corner of 3rd St and Gunnison Ave. Housekeeping cabins on the south edge of town at the *Pleasant View Resort* (☎ 970-944-2262) cost $65. The *Crystal Lodge* (☎ 970-944-2201), 2½ miles south of town on Hwy 149, offers lodge rooms for $55 and cottages for $105 (less in winter). Rooms at the motel-style *Western Belle Lodge and Restaurant* (☎ 970-944-2415), at the north end of town on Hwy 149 N, start at $49 and feature vaulted ceilings and mountain views.

Places to Eat
Lake City Cafe/The Zone (☎ 970-944-2733), 310 Gunnison Ave, offers substantial breakfasts and hearty barbecue entrees, soups and salads for lunch and dinner. A good lunchtime spot is the *Mountain Harvest* (☎ 970-944-2332), next to the Lake City Market at the north end of town. They proudly proclaim 'from meat lovers to tree huggers, we have something for everyone,' and they're pretty much right.

The *Crystal Lodge Restaurant* (☎ 970-944-2201), 2½ miles south on Hwy 149, features impeccable gourmet quality and affordable prices – breakfast and lunch dishes cost about $7, specialty dinners from $11 to $17.

Getting There & Away
Lake City lies on Hwy 149, 47 miles south of the intersection of US 50, which in turn leads west to Gunnison and east to Montrose. From Lake City it's 50 miles south on Hwy 149 to Creede.

OURAY
As the area's favorite son David Lavender wrote of Ouray's spectacular natural setting, 'the best way to see it is to stretch out flat on your back.' Imposing Alpine peaks leave barely a quarter mile of valley floor for Ouray's 800 residents. The biggest attractions here are the Ouray Hot Springs and hiking trails throughout the surrounding mountains.

Founded during the silver boom as Uncompahgre City in 1875, Ouray enjoyed a second spurt of activity following Thomas Walsh's discovery of gold in 1896 – his Camp Bird Mine extracted $27 million in ore.

Ouray is named after the famed chief of the Utes who maintained peace by relinquishing his people's traditional lands to the hordes of miners invading the San Juan Mountains.

The visitor information center (☎ 970-325-4746, 800-228-1876) at the hot springs is open daily in summer (closed Monday and Tuesday in winter) and has information on Jeep tours and hiking in the Mt Sneffels and Uncompahgre wilderness areas, as well as a walking tour map of Ouray's historic buildings. Pick up a copy of the 'Ouray Visitor's Guide' for a schedule of events and suggestions about things to do.

Buckskin Trading Co (☎ 970-324-4044), 636 Main St, has books on local history and guides to hiking, rock climbing and mountain biking in the area.

Ouray Hot Springs
Open year-round, Ouray Hot Springs (☎ 970-325-4638), 1200 Main St, offers a 250-foot-by-150-foot swimming pool at 80° to 85°F, plus a soaking pool at 95°F and a hot pool at 100°F. It's open daily Memorial Day to Labor Day from 10 am to 10 pm, and from noon to 9 pm the rest of the year. Admission is $6.

Hiking & Mountain Biking
Visitors should not miss **Cascade Falls**, a short walk east up 8th Ave. From the USFS

Amphitheatre Campground (see below), the **Cascade Trail** goes to Chief Ouray Mine and upper Cascade Falls, offering incredible views of Ouray during the last half mile as the trail crosses exposed rock faces. The hike takes two to three hours and the Cascade Trail is closed to bikes.

A longer, more strenuous route climbs the **Horsethief Trail** from north of the Hot Springs, across US 550, to the Bridge of the Heavens Overlook Area, offering spectacular views. This area is prime bighorn sheep habitat; a herd of about 50 sheep reside on the upper slopes in summer.

Bicyclists can follow the Uncompahgre River for 10 miles north to Ridgway on the easy Ouray County Rd 17 that traces the abandoned Rio Grande Southern narrow-gauge railroad bed. The route begins as Oak St on the west side of the Uncompahgre River, reached by the 7th Ave Bridge.

For additional hiking and biking suggestions pick up Kevin B Kent's *Ouray Hiking Guide* or Marcus Wilson's *Biking Ouray, A Mountain Biking Guide to Ridgway & Ouray*.

Horseback Riding

The historic Livery Barn (☎ 970-325-4606) at the corner of 8th and Main Sts is a real piece of the past that offers guided day-rides from $17 for one hour to $65 for an all-day trip.

Ice Climbing

The owners of the Ouray Victorian Inn spearheaded the establishment of the **Ouray Ice Park** the world's first dedicated ice-climbing area. By running pipes from mountain streams they have managed to create some 50 routes. Access is free. For information, guide service or instruction, contact the Ouray Victorian Inn (☎ 800-846-8729), 50 3rd Ave. Ice climbers staying at the Inn receive a 15% discount off room rates.

Jeep Tours

Old mine trails connect Silverton, Telluride and Lake City with Ouray on perilous routes amid the 14,000-foot San Juan Mountain summits, aerial ore trams and 19th-century mining ghost towns. The 4WD routes are often snowbound well into June. It's best to leave the driving to someone with experience while you enjoy the scenery. Since 1959, San Juan Scenic Jeep Tours (☎ 970-325-4444, 800-325-4385), 824 Main St, has provided specially modified open-top 4WD tours. The popular half-day trip to Engineer Mountain climbs above 13,000 feet and costs $25 for adults and $13 for children.

Places to Stay & Eat

A glacial headwall forms the backdrop to 30 USFS campsites at the *Amphitheatre Campground* (☎ 800-280-2267 for reservations) over 700 feet above Ouray and about 1 mile from the south end of town on US 550. The steep and narrow campground road limits trailers to only a few sites. Campsites cost $12 plus the reservation fee of $8.65. The surrounding area is popular for cross-country skiing in the winter and also features an overlook of Ouray.

Across the river from town, the *4J+1+1* (☎ 970-325-4418) at 790 Oak St offers shaded tent sites next to the river for $16, with clean showers and a coin-op laundry. It's open mid-May to mid-October.

Discounted ski plans may apply at many of Ouray's hotels. The *Historic Western Hotel* (☎ 970-325-4645), 210 7th Ave, has restored Victorian-style rooms from $45 and looks to be an interesting place to spend a night or two. The family-run *Ouray Cottage Motel* (☎ 970-325-4370) at the corner of 4th and Main Sts, has knotty-pine doubles for $55 in summer. A nice feature is the telescope pointed toward the nearby cliffs frequented by bighorn sheep. The handsomely restored *St Elmo Hotel* (☎ 970-325-4951), 426 Main St, opened in 1898 and offers nine B&B rooms with private baths and period furnishings starting at $92 in summer, less the rest of the year.

The Groundskeeper Coffee House (☎ 970-325-0550), 524 Main St, has local topo maps laminated in the table tops for study while you sip an espresso over breakfast. Next door the *Mountain Garden Restaurant* offers home-style breakfasts, include a few healthy alternatives. It's also open for dinner part of the year.

In 1886 the *Bon Ton Restaurant* (☎ 970-325-4951), below the St Elmo Hotel at 426 Main St, was considered the best establishment in Ouray, and still is one of the top spots. Prices range from $12 to $21.

Getting There & Away

Bus TNM&O buses pass through Ouray northbound for Montrose (10:40 am) and southbound for Durango (6:55 am). There's no established stop: just make sure you're on Hwy 550 at the right time and flag the bus down in a place where it has room to pull over.

Car Ouray is on Hwy 550, 34 miles south of Montrose and 80 miles north of Durango.

TELLURIDE

With 300 inches of snow annually, a 3000-foot vertical drop to the ski lifts in town, a dramatic box canyon setting and a rich mining history, Telluride (population 1500) is one of Colorado's most popular ski towns. Ever since Telluride was designated a National Historic Landmark in 1964 – well before skiing arrived – conscientious citizens have strictly followed preservation guidelines. Many newer buildings follow Victorian designs so closely that it is sometimes difficult to tell the modern from historic construction.

The hip youths and artists who flocked to Telluride in the 1960s and 1970s are now established voices in the town's affairs, seeking to prevent resort success from destroying the quality of life that makes the town a real joy to visit. Cars are discouraged from continuing past the 'intercept parking' lot near the visitors center at the entrance to the town. From there, most elect to walk, but free buses operate on a loop along Pacific and Colorado Aves, or you might borrow one of the bikes from a fleet of 'Earth Cruisers' provided by the town. The pink and yellow single-speed bikes may be picked up and left at any of the three bike parking areas enclosed by cement barriers along Colorado Ave.

History

The first mining claim in Telluride was laid in 1875, but until the Utes lost their claim to the lowlands in 1880, miners were forced to approach the area from the east over high mountain passes. In spite of its isolation, the town attracted over 600 immigrant silver and gold miners. In 1890, after the Rio Grande Southern narrow-gauge railroad arrived, Telluride's population jumped to about 5000.

Repeal of the Sherman Silver Purchase Act by Congress in 1893 crippled the area's silver mining, and gold mining declined after a 1901 fire destroyed not only the Smuggler Union Mine but also sparked miners' demands for reasonable wages and eight-hour workdays.

Before the arrival of developer Joseph Zoline from Beverly Hills in 1968, most of the stools in the Sheridan Bar were still occupied by Telluride's nearly 400 mine workers. The Coonskin Ski Area opened in February 1973 and the mining era ended with the closure of the Idarado in 1978. A new era of national tourist access began in 1985 when Telluride's mesa-top commercial airport, the highest in the nation at 9086 feet, inaugurated scheduled flights.

Edward Abbey included a short and entertaining story 'Telluride Blues – A Hatchet Job' in his book *The Journey Home: Some Words in Defense of the American West*. Renowned historian David Lavender was born in Telluride – his talents are appropriately applied in the short book *The Telluride Story*.

Orientation

Colorado Ave, also known as Main St, is where you'll find most of the restaurants, bars and shops. The town's small size means you can get everywhere on foot, so you can leave you car at the intercept parking lot at the south end of Mahoney Drive (near the visitors center) or wherever you're staying.

COLORADO

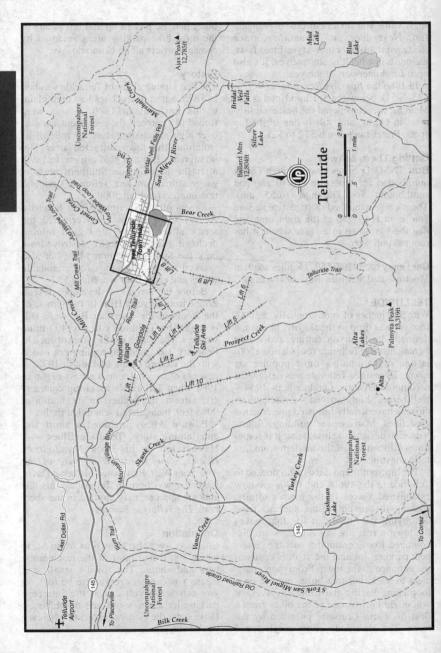

From town you can reach the ski mountain via two lifts and the gondola. The latter also links Telluride with Mountain Village, the true base for the Telluride Ski Area. Located 7 miles from town along Hwy 145, Mountain Village is a 20-minute drive, but only 12 minutes away by gondola, which is free for foot passengers.

Ajax Peak, a glacial headwall, rises behind the town to form the end of the U-shaped valley that contains Telluride. To the right (south) of Ajax Peak, Colorado's highest waterfall, Bridal Veil Falls, cascades 365 feet; a switchback trail leads to a restored Victorian powerhouse atop the falls. To the south, Mt Wilson reaches 14,246 feet among a group of rugged peaks that form the Lizard Head Wilderness Area.

Information

Telluride Visitor Services (☎ 970-728-3041) operates a 24-hour visitor information center at 666 W Colorado Ave (above Rose Victorian Food Mart), at the west entrance to town, complete with restrooms and ATM. The center is staffed on winter weekdays from 9 am to 5 pm and daily during the summer until 7 pm. In the same building is Telluride Central Reservations (☎ 888-355-8743), which handles accommodations and festival tickets. Online information about lodging, restaurants, skiing and other activities can be found at www.telluridemm.com.

Telluride Ski & Golf Company (☎ 970-728-7533, 800-801-4832) can answer questions about the ski area. For a snow report call ☎ 970-728-7425.

A historical walking tour is published in the 'Telluride Visitor's Guide.' The *Telluride Daily Planet* is a free daily newspaper that lists special events, restaurant deals and nightly entertainment.

The Bank of Telluride (☎ 970-728-2000), 238 E Colorado Ave, offers ATMs at the bank and at the visitors center. Unfortunately, the San Miguel Valley Bank burned down shortly after Butch Cassidy and 'The Wild Bunch' robbed it in 1889.

The post office is at 101 E Colorado Ave and the zip code is 81435. Mail Boxes Etc (☎ 970-728-8111; fax 970-728-8128), 398 W Colorado Ave, offers both fax and postal services.

Bookworks (☎ 970-728-0700), 191 S Pine St, is the town's biggest bookstore, with more than 10,000 titles. Between the Covers (☎ 970-728-4504), 224 W Colorado Ave, offers a good selection of regional history and local maps and guides plus espresso drinks.

Telluride Sports (☎ 970-728-4477), 150 W Colorado Ave, has topo and USFS maps, sporting supplies and information.

Telluride Medical Center (☎ 970-728-3848) is at 500 W Pacific Ave.

The Washateria, 197 W Columbia Ave, is a coin-op laundry. Showers are available at the Town Park swimming pool for a $1.50 fee in quarters. During the Bluegrass Festival, you can harmonize in the showers at Telluride High School for $2.

Downhill Skiing

The Telluride ski area's Oak St (Lift 8) and Coonskin (Lift 7) chairlifts, only 2 blocks from Colorado Ave, are at the 8700-foot base of the imposing Front Face. From Plunge Summit at 11,890 feet, it's over 3100 feet back to town on mostly advanced and expert terrain. The Front Face is one of three distinct areas served by a total of 12 lifts that require almost no waiting in line. Over the ridgetop of the Front Face is Mountain Village where the Gorrono Basin caters to intermediate skiers and the broad slopes of Sunshine Mountain are ideal for beginners. Rookies should take the free mountain tour from experienced hosts – it's offered daily at 10 am and meets at the top of lifts 3 and 7.

The sprawling Mountain Village development provides ski facilities, housing and a golf course. All lodgings offer ski-in, ski-out convenience and there are short lift lines to beginner and intermediate slopes on even the most crowded days. If the advanced intermediate Telluride Trail back to town is too daunting, or your legs are simply worn out, take the gondola.

The ski area opens for Thanksgiving and closes in early April, operating daily from

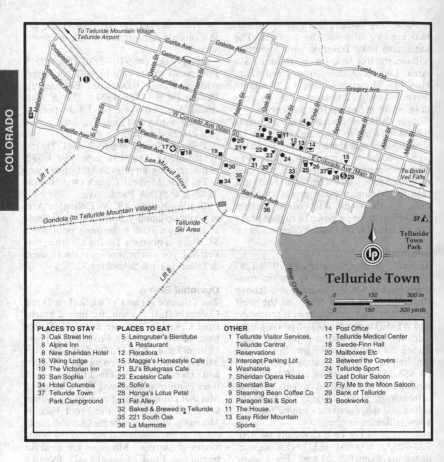

PLACES TO STAY
3 Oak Street Inn
6 Alpine Inn
8 New Sheridan Hotel
16 Viking Lodge
19 The Victorian Inn
30 San Sophia
34 Hotel Columbia
37 Telluride Town
    Park Campground

PLACES TO EAT
5 Leimgruber's Bierstube
   & Restaurant
15 Floradora
15 Maggie's Homestyle Cafe
21 BJ's Bluegrass Cafe
23 Excelsior Cafe
26 Sofio's
28 Honga's Lotus Petal
31 Fat Alley
32 Baked & Brewed in Telluride
35 221 South Oak
36 La Marmotte

OTHER
1 Telluride Visitor Services,
   Telluride Central
   Reservations
2 Intercept Parking Lot
4 Washateria
7 Sheridan Opera House
8 Sheridan Bar
9 Steaming Bean Coffee Co
10 Paragon Ski & Sport
11 The House
13 Easy Rider Mountain
    Sports
14 Post Office
17 Telluride Medical Center
18 Swede-Finn Hall
20 Mailboxes Etc
22 Between the Covers
24 Telluride Sport
25 Last Dollar Saloon
27 Fly Me to the Moon Saloon
29 Bank of Telluride
33 Bookworks

9 am to 4 pm. Daily adult lift tickets cost $49 and children's tickets run $26 from mid-December to mid-April – before mid-December, tickets cost $32 and $17.

Telluride Ski School (☎ 970-728-7518) offers full-day ski/snowboard clinics for $80/85 as well as advanced 'adventure clinics,' private instruction and children's programs.

Cross-Country Skiing
Public trails in Town Park facilitate Nordic skiing along the San Miguel River and the Telluride Valley floor west of town.

Instruction and rentals are available from the Nordic Center in Town Park. Lessons start daily under the tent at 11 am and cost $30 for 1½ hours. A rental and lesson package costs $38.

Access to trails above Lift 10 in the Telluride Ski Area costs $13.

Experienced skiers will appreciate San Juan Hut Systems' (☎ 970-728-6935) five crude huts linking Telluride with Ouray, separated by backcountry USFS roads and trails 5 to 7 miles in length. Ski between huts or establish a base camp to stage day trips into the Mt Sneffels Wilderness Area.

You can rent the huts – each provided with eight bunks and cooking facilities – for $22 per person at 117 N Willow St.

Mountain Biking

An easy smooth gravel **River Trail** connects Town Park with the Coonskin ski lift area and continues to Hwy 145 for a total trail distance of about 2 miles. If you want a bit more of a workout, continue up **Mill Creek Trail**, west of the Texaco near where the River Trail ends – after the initial climb the trail follows the contour and ends at the Jud Wiebe Trail (hikers only) where cyclists turn back.

At the east end of Pine St, **Bear Creek** is an up-and-back ride that climbs 1000 feet in a little over 2 miles to reach a tiered waterfall.

From Ophir, site of a former railroad loop 7 miles south on Hwy 145, you can follow the **Old Railroad Grade** along the South Fork of the San Miguel River downhill for 8 miles to Ilium where the **Ilium Trail** returns to the junction of Hwy 145 into Telluride. At Ophir, take the USFS Rd 625 to the historic power plant site at Ames, turn left and cross a bridge before continuing on switchbacks to another bridge above the falls that lead to the old railroad grade.

Consider the beauty of taking a week-long backcountry bike tour without a load of camping gear, guides or support vehicles. Riding in its purest form is offered by San Juan Hut Systems (☎ 970-728-6935), 117 N Willow St, where you pick up the keys to huts, stocked with food and sleeping bags, about 35 miles apart over a 205-mile route from Telluride to Moab, UT. For around $400, riders get route descriptions and maps to the huts, plus three meals a day for seven days of remote Colorado Plateau cycling.

Easy Rider Mountain Sports (☎ 970-728-4734), 101 W Colorado Ave, is the town's main cycling shop, and has rentals, repairs and, of course, sales. Standard/front suspension mountain bikes rent for $19/24 per day. Rates at Telluride Sports (☎ 970-828-7547), at 150 W Colorado Ave, are

$20/26. You can also try Paragon Ski & Sport (☎ 970-728-4525), with stores at 217 W Colorado Ave in Telluride and the Granita complex in Mountain Village. The complete guide to mountain biking around Telluride is Dave Rich's *Tellurides*, available at the above shops.

Telluride is the site of many bike races (see Special Events below).

Hiking & Backpacking

The **Jud Wiebe Trail**, a 2.7-mile loop from town, offers views after a 1300-foot climb and is the only trail near town dedicated to foot travel. Take Oak St north to Tomboy Rd and continue to the gated road on your left to reach the signed trailhead. The return portion of the loop ends at the north end of Aspen St.

The **Bear Creek** trail is a little over 2 miles, but ascends 1040 feet to a beautiful cascading waterfall. From this trail you can access the strenuous **Wasatch Trail**, a 12-mile loop that heads west across the mountains to **Bridal Veil Falls**. The Bear Creek trailhead is at the south end of Pine St, across the San Miguel River.

It's a little over 2 miles to Bridal Veil Falls on the switchback road that gets heavy Jeep traffic to Silverton by midday. Backpackers will find plenty of solitude amid the 14,000-foot summits in nearby Lizard Head and Mt Sneffels wilderness areas.

Telluride Sports (see Mountain Biking above) has topo maps and USFS Uncompahgre Forest maps. If you are traveling through Montrose, stop by the Montrose Public Lands Office (☎ 970-240-5300), 2505 S Townsend Ave, to pick up maps and information.

Fishing

Although the San Miguel River is no Gold Medal fishery, it does offer some excellent dry fly-fishing for rainbow and brown trout from mid-June to December. A DOW fishing easement is less than a mile south of Placerville. Telluride Sports has all the gear you will need and houses Telluride Fly-fishers, which offers guides and instruction.

Special Events

Something is going on just about every weekend in Telluride – from the laid-back **Steps to Awareness Festival** in May, or intimate gourmet experiences with noted sommeliers at June's **Wine Festival**, to events that fill the streets with crowds and attract headline performers and noted filmmakers.

Four days of outdoor adventure and environmental films and filmmakers are featured at **Mountainfilm** over Memorial Day weekend.

The **Telluride Bluegrass Festival** is a major week-long event attracting 10,000 visitors: it drives some locals crazy but it's one of the best music festivals held in the US. It's staged at the Town Park in late June and kicks off with three days of group jam sessions, amateur competitions and classes, followed by four days of performances that showcase over 20 nationally known artists. Four-day tickets cost about $130 and are available from Planet Bluegrass (☎ 970-449-6007, 800-624-2422). Four-day passes including one week's camping range from $150 to $170.

For one weekend in August, the **Telluride Jazz Celebration** at Town Park becomes the focus for jazz in America. Tickets cost about $100 and are available from Telluride Central Reservations (☎ 800-525-3455). In late August, fungiphiles sprout up at the **Telluride Mushroom Festival** featuring a Main St Mushroom Parade, plus a cooking and tasting party at Elks Park.

Most of the world's premier film events are held in towns that don't have a drive-in; nevertheless, the **Telluride Film Festival** over Labor Day weekend offers free open-air films along with many national and international premieres.

Blues musicians take the stage while microbrews dominate the stands during the **Brews & Blues Festival** in mid-September.

Places to Stay

Insufficient and overpriced accommodation is Telluride's Achilles' heel, the result of a 10-year love affair with building condominiums at the expense of hotels and motels. Aside from the campgrounds, there really are no cheap places to stay. Ways to cut costs include booking package deals and taking the risk of arriving without a reservation, which allows you to take advantage of often lower walk-in rates. Telluride Central Reservations (☎ 888-355-8743) can provide information on lower-rate periods and ski-free packages: the latter are valid only during the beginning and end of the season (when snow conditions aren't great), and usually include two lift tickets and other coupons in the cost of a double room.

Most of the rates quoted below reflect average winter and summer prices. If you arrive in the off-season (late spring and early fall) you may enjoy considerably lower tariffs.

Camping Right in Telluride Town Park, the *Telluride Town Park Campground* (☎ 970-728-9645) offers 42 campsites, usually hot showers and swimming and tennis from mid-May to October. Developed campsites cost $11 and five primitive sites cost $9, all on a first-come, first-served basis. Campsites usually fill up by Friday during summer and are totally booked out by ticket holders during the week of the Telluride Bluegrass Festival.

Two campgrounds in the Uncompahgre National Forest (☎ 970-327-4261) are within 15 miles of Telluride on Hwy 145 and are also fee sites: *Sunshine* offers 15 first-come, first-served campsites for $8; facilities at *Matterhorn* include showers and electrical hookups for some of the 26 campsites, which cost $10 or $14.

Free dispersed USFS sites with a pit toilet are available at Ilium, 6 miles west of town on the South Fork of the San Miguel River and at Alta Lakes, 13 miles southwest of town, reached by USFS Rd 632.

B&Bs Built in 1903, the *Alpine Inn* (☎ 970-728-6282, 800-707-3344), 440 W Colorado Ave, is a restored home with a large enclosed breakfast area that looks out on the ski slopes. Two rooms with shared bath cost $75 each during summer and up to $130 during regular winter season – six other rooms with private bath typically start at $145 during the winter. On the opposite side of the street, the *Johnstone Inn* (☎ 970-728-3315, 800-752-1901), 403 W Colorado Ave, is another nicely redone Victorian home, and charges $140 for doubles with private bath during most of the winter. Rates fall to $80 during summer and $70 during the off-season.

Hotels The *Oak Street Inn* (☎ 970-728-3383), 134 N Oak St, continues to offer the least expensive rooms in town. Spartan rooms with shared bath cost $42/58 a single/double throughout the year, except for holidays and festivals. The *Victorian Inn* (☎ 970-728-6601) at 401 W Pacific Ave hardly looks Victorian, and is really just an overpriced motel. However it is conveniently close to the Oak St lift and gondola. Doubles with shared bath are around $101 in winter, those with private bath $113; rooms with private baths run $113 to $155 during peak season.

The *New Sheridan Hotel* (☎ 970-728-4351), 231 W Colorado Ave, replaced the original 1881 hotel in 1895 and has continued to provide lodging ever since. The days when these rooms with shared bath were the cheapest ski accommodations around are long gone – regular winter rates are now $90 for a room with a shared bath, $155 for one with a private bath.

If you're going to shell out this kind of cash, you might want to consider the *Hotel Columbia* (☎ 970-728-0660, 800-201-9505), located 300 W San Juan Ave, right across the street from the gondola. Each of the hotel's 21 rooms has a balcony, fireplace, mountain views and the service is said to be excellent. A rooftop hot tub and a library are other nice details. Doubles range from $150 to $215 in winter, $165 in summer. Nearby, the *The San Sophia* (☎ 970-728-3001 800-537-4781), 330 W Pacific Ave, is another high-end option. Doubles, including breakfast and après-ski snacks, start at $180 in winter, $135 in summer.

Condominiums If there are several of you, renting a condominium may be a more affordable and comfortable way to go. With hundreds of units to choose from, the best way to pursue this option is through one of the management companies. Telluride Resort Accommodations (☎ 970-728-6621, 800-538-7754) is the largest, handling lodgings in town and in Mountain Village. Hotel-type rooms in Telluride's lower-end condos, such as the *Schroedl Fall Line* or *Viking Lodge*, range from $140 to $170 during the regular ski season and usually include two bedrooms, a kitchen and a living room. Units closer to the bottom of the slopes will naturally cost more.

Places to Eat

Restaurants in Telluride generally offer small portions at high prices, but the food is usually quite good.

One affordable standout is the popular *Baked & Brewed in Telluride* (☎ 970-728-4775), 127 S Fir St, which offers baked goods, pizza, delicious daily specials, home-brewed beer and a nice porch to catch the morning rays while enjoying breakfast. It's open from 5:30 am to 10 pm. Another budget option is *Fat Alley* (☎ 970-728-3985), 122 South Oak St, which has Southern-style barbecue and some good veggie choices. It's one of the only spots in town where you can get lunch for around $6. Serving up $5 lunches, as well as cheap breakfasts is *Maggie's Homestyle Cafe* (☎ 970-728-3334), 217 E Colorado Ave.

If you're just looking for a caffeine fix, walk no farther than *The Steaming Bean Coffee Co* (☎ 970-728-0220), 221 W Colorado Ave, which has fine brewed coffee, espresso and specialty coffee drinks. If the music is obnoxious, take advantage of the benches in front of the shop.

Floradora (☎ 970-728-3888), 103 W Colorado Ave, has been around since 1974. Some locals avoid it, possibly because it's popular with visitors, but the food is good and prices are pretty reasonable. The menu was recently revised, with input from culinary institute members, and

COLORADO

features American and Mexican fare with a slightly international twist.

Another place that gets mixed reviews is the *Excelsior Cafe* (☎ 970-728-4250), 200 W Colorado Ave. Some like the pricey breakfasts and Italian lunches and dinners, others complain about meager portions.

Honga's Lotus Petal (☎ 970-728-5134), 138 E Colorado Ave, has become a favorite for its well-prepared Asian dishes, and unlike some of Telluride's other 'better' restaurants, you won't walk away hungry from a meal here. It's open nightly from 6 to 10 pm.

Sofio's (☎ 970-728-4882), 110 W Colorado Ave, is recommended for breakfasts, Mexican specialties, smoothies, fresh-squeezed orange juice and espresso drinks. Lunches and dinners range from $6 to $12. *BJ's Bluegrass Cafe* (☎ 970-728-5335), set back at 300 W Colorado Ave, offers fairly good individual pizzas, Mexican dishes, sandwiches and live bluegrass music on weekends. Prices are higher than the food warrants, but a good band helps to make up for it.

Nearer the top-end is *Leimgruber's Bierstube & Restaurant* (☎ 970-728-4663), 573 W Pacific, where Paulaner beer is on draft and meat-lovers can stuff themselves on German fare and wild American game. Located in a handsomely restored home, *221 South Oak* (☎ 970-728-9507) is also a good place to splurge on lunch or dinner. The menu changes daily to feature fresh ingredients and a selection of salads. Reservations are recommended, and the restaurant is usually closed in early fall and late spring.

The seasonal *La Marmotte* (☎ 970-728-6232), in the historic masonry ice house at 150 W San Juan Ave, offers a nice selection of hors d'oeuvres for $8 to $16 as well as gourmet French dinner entrees priced at $20 to $27.

Entertainment
Most of the historic *Sheridan Bar* (☎ 970-728-3911), 231 W Colorado Ave, survived the waning mining fortunes while the Sheridan Hotel was busy selling off chan-

deliers and finely-carved furnishings to help pay the heating bills. Now over-dressed visitors occupy stools and chat about upcoming film releases next to the occasional old-timer who hasn't been driven out by escalating property values.

Two watering holes popular with locals are *The Last Dollar Saloon* (☎ 970-728-4800), 100 E Colorado Ave, where on cold nights you can sip whiskey in front of the fireplace, and *Swede-Finn Hall* (☎ 970-728-2085) 427 W Pacific, which has billiards and a fine beer selection.

For live music, the best place in town is the *Fly Me to the Moon Saloon* (☎ 970-728-6666), 132 E Colorado. Local and national acts come through here, and it's also one of the few late-night spots in town. Another one is *The House* (☎ 970-728-6207), 131 N Fir St, a sometimes rowdy place that caters more to a college crowd.

Mainstream first releases plus special showings of ski and art films are featured at the *Nuggett Theater* (☎ 970-728-3030), 207 W Colorado Ave.

The Telluride Repertory Company presents live theater productions at the *Sheridan Opera House* (☎ 970-728-6363), built in 1914. Movies are also screened here.

Getting There & Away
Air Commuter aircraft serve the mesa-top Telluride Airport (☎ 970-728-4868), flanked by 14,000-foot peaks, 5 miles east of town. The airport has limited instrument approach capability, so if weather is poor flights may be diverted to Montrose, 65 miles north.

United Express offers daily service to Denver year-round, while America West Express has flights to Phoenix, AZ. During ski season Montrose Regional Airport (☎ 970-249-3203) has direct flights to and from Chicago and Denver (on United), Houston and Newark, NJ (Continental), and Phoenix (America West).

Montrose Airport Shuttle Shuttles between the Montrose airport and Telluride cost $25 if a minimum of three people are traveling. Contact Telluride Transit (☎ 970-

728-6000, 800-800-6228), Skip's Telluride Taxi & Shuttle Service (☎ 970-728-6667) or Mountain Limo (☎ 970-728-9606).

Car Telluride is 65 miles southeast of Montrose, and is reached by taking Hwy 550 to Ridgeway, where you turn right (west) on Hwy 62 until it terminates at Hwy 145. From here head left (south) and continue until Hwy 145 turns right toward Cortez. Bypass the turn and continue straight for 3 miles into Telluride town.

Getting Around
To/From the Airport Shuttles from the Telluride airport to town or Mountain Village cost $7. See the Montrose Airport Shuttle section above for names and numbers of transport companies.

Car Thrifty (☎ 970-728-3266), 129 W San Juan, offers free shuttle service from Telluride airport if you've reserved a car with them. Hertz (☎ 970-728-3161) and Budget (☎ 970-728-4642) both have locations at the airport. Telluride Outside (☎ 970-728-3895, 800-831-6230) has 4WD vehicles and will pick you up at either Montrose or Telluride airports.

SILVERTON
An historic mining town in the San Juan Mountains, Silverton (population 540) is a throwback to another era – the entire town was designated a National Historic Landmark in 1966. Silver and gold miners invaded the area after the Brunot Agreement removed the Ute bands in 1873. Mining activity peaked in the early 1900s, but since 1991, when the Sunnyside mine closed, the economy has been dependent on the seasonal tourist train from Durango.

Jokes about Silverton having the busiest train depot in Colorado are sadly becoming true with Amtrak's recent cutbacks elsewhere in the state. For a few hours each day between early May and mid-October, train passengers fill the streets and gift shops, then clear out after the last gun duel has been staged and the last train leaves town. (See Durango for more on this scenic

steam train ride.) Winter tourism is picking up a bit, but from November to March there are still so few people in Silverton that one local joked 'you could shoot a shotgun down Greene St' (and not hit anyone).

Between Silverton and Ouray, US 50 is known as the 'Million Dollar Highway' because the roadbed fill contains valuable ore. The route passes many old mine headframes and some extraordinary Alpine scenery. However, it is a dangerous road in rain and snow, so take extra care, and obey the posted speed limits, which are as low as 25 mph in some sections – notably where the road snakes between steep mountain walls and sheer 1000-foot cliffs.

A visitors center (☎ 970-387-5654, 800-752-4494), south of town at the junction of Greene St and US 550, is open daily from 9 am to 5 pm (hours are shorter in winter). You can also get information after hours at the nearby Greene St Grocery (☎ 970-387-5652), 717 Greene St, or the TNT Market (☎ 970-387-5341) at 959 Greene St.

San Juan County Museum
The old county jail, at the corner of Greene and 15th Sts by the turgid waters of Cement Creek, still has bars on the upper floor cells and now houses the county museum (☎ 970-387-5838) featuring displays on mining and the railroad. The museum is the starting point for a walking tour of the historic district and offers a free map and guide. It's open daily Memorial Day to mid-October from 9 am to 5 pm. Admission costs $2.

Jeep Tours
Old mine roads lead to remote workings above timberline in many directions around Silverton. A difficult route over Bear Pass leads to Telluride, while the Alpine Loop Byway, an assemblage of rugged 4WD routes, leads to either Ouray or Lake City. Information about the Alpine Loop Byway is available from the BLM (☎ 970-641-0471) in Gunnison, or you can get maps from the visitors center. San Juan Backcountry (☎ 970-387-5565), located

COLORADO

at Greene and 11th Sts, offers half-day trips to Cinnamon Pass on the Alpine Loop for $40.

Places to Stay & Eat

Two miles west of town on US 550, USFS Rd 585 leads about 4 miles to the *South Mineral Campground*, with 26 USFS campsites available for $8 on a first-come, first-served basis.

At the south end of town the *Triangle Motel* (☎ 970-387-5780), 864 Greene St, offers comfortable singles/doubles for $40/60 in summer, $25/35 in winter. Nearby the *Prospector Motel* (☎ 970-387-5466), 1015 Greene St, is an OK value at $38/57. It's open from early March to late November.

One of the most interesting and enjoyable places to stay in town is the Victorian *Teller House Hotel* (☎ 970-387-5423, 800-342-4338), 1250 Greene St, where in summer rooms with shared bath cost $48, $68 with private bath. Rates are lower the rest of the year. The place gives one a real feel for what a late-19th-century boarding house was like, though the current version is no doubt less crowded and more fragrant! Check out the caricatures of locals penciled on the walls near the front desk: they're as old as the hotel itself.

Antique furnishings are featured in the imposing 1882 *Grand Imperial Hotel* (☎ 970-387-5527, 800-341-3340), open year-round at 1219 Greene St. Rooms range from $59 to $79, but fall to half that price between November and April. The Imperial's *Gold King* dining room is worth a visit. Fully restored, the top-end 1902 *Wyman Hotel* (☎ 970-387-5372, 800-609-7845), 1371 Greene St, has beautiful singles/doubles for $70/80. Rates include a full breakfast, afternoon tea and homemade cookies. It's open most of the year but closes in November and from mid-February to April – call ahead to check.

At 5 am, locals begin dropping in at the *Lunch Box* (☎ 970-387-5658), 1124 Greene St, to eat standard American breakfasts. The interesting *Brown Bear* (☎ 970-387-5630), 1129 Greene St, is one of the few places in town that's guaranteed open for lunch and dinner year-round, a good thing as the food is tasty and the staff friendly.

Eclectic items hang from the ceiling at the *Handlebars* (☎ 970-387-5395), 117 E 13th St (but the breaded and fried Rocky Mountain oysters no longer hang from the bull). The restaurant is open during the rail season and offers nightly entertainment.

Getting There & Away

Bus TNM&O buses stop in front of the Lunch Box at 1124 Greene St.

Train Purchase one-way tickets to Durango or Weminuche Wilderness trailheads on the Durango & Silverton Narrow Gauge Railroad (as available) from the 1882 Silverton Depot (☎ 970-387-5416), open from early May to mid-October. A bus operated by Durango Transport (☎ 800-626-2066) leaves for Durango several times daily and allows passengers to board the train back to Silverton for the cost of a roundtrip fare (see Durango).

DURANGO

On the Animas River, Durango (population 13,900) is a year-round destination for travelers, many of whom flock to ride the steam-driven Durango & Silverton Narrow Gauge Railroad – an especially scenic trip during the colorful fall season. Outdoor enthusiasts enjoy mountain biking and rafting during the summer and skiing during the winter months.

Durango was the brainchild of General William Jackson Palmer, founder of the Denver & Rio Grande Railroad that reached the Animas River in 1881 as it progressed toward the mining camp at Silverton to the north.

Durango overshadowed a small town immediately north called Animas City, founded in 1876 to serve the miners. According to legend, the Río de las Animas Perdidas (River of Lost Souls) refers to the Utes killed by Spanish troops. Earlier inhabitants of the area included Ancestral Puebloans – the Falls Creek Caves north of

COLORADO

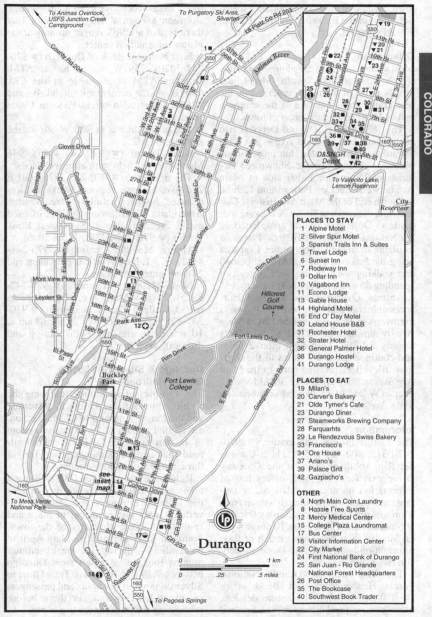

PLACES TO STAY
1 Alpine Motel
2 Silver Spur Motel
3 Spanish Trails Inn & Suites
5 Travel Lodge
6 Sunset Inn
7 Rodeway Inn
9 Dollar Inn
10 Vagabond Inn
11 Econo Lodge
13 Gable House
14 Highland Motel
16 End O' Day Motel
30 Leland House B&B
31 Rochester Hotel
32 Strater Hotel
33 Francisco's
36 General Palmer Hotel
38 Durango Hostel
41 Durango Lodge

PLACES TO EAT
19 Milan's
20 Carver's Bakery
21 Olde Tymer's Cafe
23 Durango Diner
27 Steamworks Brewing Company
28 Farquarhts
29 Le Rendezvous Swiss Bakery
33 Francisco's
34 Ore House
37 Ariano's
39 Palace Grill
42 Gazpacho's

OTHER
4 North Main Coin Laundry
8 Hassle Free Sports
12 Mercy Medical Center
15 College Plaza Laundromat
17 Bus Center
18 Visitor Information Center
22 City Market
24 First National Bank of Durango
25 San Juan - Rio Grande
   National Forest Headquarters
26 Post Office
35 The Bookcase
40 Southwest Book Trader

Durango

0   .5   1 km

0   .25   .5 miles

town are among the most important excavation sites for the Basketmaker II (1 to about 500 AD) period.

Orientation

Most visitor facilities are along Main Ave, which runs north to south. Motels are mostly north of the town center, while the restaurants and shops are at the southern end of Main Ave, in the heart of town.

The 1882 D&RG Railroad Depot is also at the south end of Main Ave – just head toward the steam whistles, burning coal and billowing clouds of smoke. Showpiece Victorian buildings line either side of Main Ave between Buckley Park around 12th St, the north end of the Main Ave Historic District, and the depot at 5th St. A walking tour guide to Durango's central area, listed on the National Register of Historic Places, is available from the visitors center. Consider using the bus (see Getting Around below) and walking through this area instead of spending $5 or $6 to park near the depot.

Animas Overlook has a wheelchair-accessible trail and bathrooms on the mesa northwest of Durango, reached from Main Ave by turning west on 25th St to La Plata County Rd 204. Turn right after 2 miles and continue another 3 miles to the overlook. Bicyclists traveling north of the Main Ave Animas River Bridge should switch over to W 2nd Ave rather than continue on Main Ave.

Information

The visitor information center (☎ 970-247-0312, 800-525-8855), 111 S Camino del Rio, south of town at the Gateway Drive exit from US 550, offers lots of information on accommodations, restaurants and outdoor activities. It's open from 8 am to 7 pm Monday to Saturday (closing at 5 pm in winter) and from 10 am to 4 pm on Sunday. You can access much of their information by visiting the Durango website (www.durango.org).

The San Juan-Rio Grande National Forest Headquarters and BLM office (☎ 970-247-4874), 701 Camino del Rio, offers camping and hiking information and

forest maps weekdays from 8 am to 5 pm. Between Memorial Day and Labor Day there is also a USFS ranger on duty at the visitor information center.

First National Bank of Durango (☎ 970-247-3020), 259 W 9th St, has an ATM. Another ATM is available at the City Market, on the corner of Railroad Ave and 9th St, which also offers Western Union service.

The post office is at 222 W 8th St; the zip code 81302.

Klatt Travel (☎ 970-247-4455), 946 Main Ave, can help with air travel needs.

The Bookcase (☎ 970-247-3776), 601 E 2nd Ave, has new regional works and lots of used books, including rare Western Americana. Overflowing shelves of used books are available at Southwest Book Trader (☎ 970-247-8479), 175 E 5th St.

Mercy Medical Center (☎ 970-247-4311), 375 E Park Ave, has outpatient and 24-hour emergency care.

North Main Coin Laundry (☎ 970-247-9915), 2980 N Main Ave, offers showers for $3. College Plaza Laundromat (☎ 970-247-8255), 509 E 8th Ave, is open 8 am to 10 pm daily and has both coin-op and drop-off services.

Durango & Silverton Narrow Gauge Railroad

The 45 miles of spur track following the scenic Animas River Gorge to Silverton, and the longer Antonito to Chama section, are all that remain of the extensive system of the narrow-gauge D&RG Western Railroad that carried passengers and freight through the Colorado Mountains.

Riding the steam-driven D&SNGR (or a bike) is the only appropriate way to visit the isolated mining community of Silverton – cars just seem out of place and spoil the historic character of the town. Trains to Silverton run from late April to November – during the peak summer months four trains depart from Durango between 7:30 and 10:10 am. Travel time to Silverton is about 3¼ hours and passengers spend at least two hours there before reboarding the train for the trip home.

The historic train has a 1st-class parlor car, enclosed coaches and open gondola cars for the cinders and ash crowd. Some passengers may elect to layover in Silverton and experience the peace and quiet after the last train departs. The train also stops at Elk Park on the Colorado Trail near Molas Pass.

Touring bicyclists might consider purchasing a one-way ticket (available on a limited basis) and paying to check the bicycle as baggage to Silverton. Because the trains rarely have unoccupied seats, layovers and flag stops require prior arrangement with the Durango ticket office.

The D&SNGR ticket office (☎ 970-247-2733, 888-872-4607), 479 Main Ave, urges passengers to purchase tickets four to six weeks prior to their trip. Roundtrip fares are $49 for adults, $25 for children under 12, $85 for the 1st-class parlor car. Other trains that only go 26 miles to a turnaround at Cascade Canyon operate during summer evenings (subject to change), as well as in the late spring and winter (come well dressed!) when trains do not serve Silverton. These trips include a stop for passengers to wander next to the river for an hour and cost $42.

With prior arrangements, the train will drop-off at Cascade Canyon, which offers backcountry access on USFS Trails 675 and 504 to Columbine Pass in the Weminuche Wilderness Area.

Tours of the Durango railyard are available May through October for $5.

Road & Mountain Biking

An easy road ride circles for either 15 or 30 miles around the Animas Valley, north of Durango's 32nd St. On the east side of the Animas River, take La Plata County Rd 250 for 15 miles north to Baker's Bridge – site of the cliff-jumping scene in the film *Butch Cassidy and the Sundance Kid*. Return by crossing the bridge, proceeding around the KOA camp to follow the Hwy 550 shoulder south to Hermosa, then turn right onto La Plata County Rd 203. This takes you by Trimbles Hot Springs and

back to town. The 15-mile route also starts on County Rd 250, but turns left earlier at County Rd 252 (Trimble Lane), crosses Hwy 550 and turns left again on County Rd 203.

Off-road riders can set off for the Animas Overlook, about 5 miles from the corner of 25th St and Main Ave. The 3-mile, 1550-foot descent from the overlook to Junction Creek Rd is featured in the Iron Horse Bicycle Classic competition. A 5-mile loop climbs to the mesa top of Animas City Mountain from the trailhead at the north end of W 4th Ave. Near the Purgatory Ski Area there are a number of trail options, including the 8-mile Worlds Cross-Country Course that you can access via their chairlifts ($6).

Find out about other rides by purchasing the informative booklet *Bicycle Routes on Public Lands of Southwest Colorado* for $7 from the USFS office in Durango. Hassle Free Sports (☎ 970-259-3874, 800-835-3800), 2615 Main Ave, offers bike repairs and rentals for $25 per day (with front shock). For guided tours with sag support on road or dirt, contact Southwest Adventures (☎ 970-259-0370), 12th St and Camino del Rio, which offers rentals, both guided and unguided tours and drop-off services to area trailheads.

White-Water Rafting & Kayaking

The upper Animas River between Silverton and Tacoma provides 28 miles of challenging Class IV-V whitewater for fit athletic types, but one unrunnable section of the Animas Gorge requires a portage. A 4-mile run between 39th St and Camino del Rio is rated Class III and served as the site for the National Kayaking Competition in 1990. In addition, easy sections suited for family float trips begin near town.

Kayakers flock to Whitewater Park, a quarter-mile stretch of river north of the visitors center that features a permanent world-class slalom course. From the park you can watch the paddlers practice or compete in river races.

Rivers West (☎ 970-259-5077), 520 Main Ave opposite the train depot, offers a one-hour introduction to rafting on the Animas River for $12 and two-hour trips for $19. More adventurous rafters can combine a shuttle trip to Silverton on the D&SNGR train with a trip on the upper Animas. This package trip costs $175 for one day, or $325 for a two-day trip. Mountain Waters Rafting (☎ 970-259-4191, 800-748-2507), 108 W College Ave, and Durango Rivertrippers (☎ 970-259-0289, 800-292-2885), 720 Main Ave, offer similar trips.

Horseback Riding & Pack Trips

Rapp Guides & Packers (☎ 970-247-8923), 47 Electra Lake Rd, offers a variety of backcountry pack trips in the San Juan Mountains including a three-day stay at a Needleton base camp reached by the D&SNGR. Most visitors choose far shorter rides, such as one- and two-hour trips from their Haviland Lake Corral, north of Durango. Rapp Guides also offers winter sleigh rides. Over the Hill Outfitters (☎ 970-247-9289) runs full-day rides ($85 including lunch) from their stables near the Ponderosa KOA, 12 miles north of town.

Other Activities

If you're into swimming, Trimble Hot Springs (☎ 970-247-0111), 6 miles north of Durango on the west side of US 550, offers three outdoor pools, including an Olympic-size swimming pool maintained at 85°F year-round. The facilities include private tubs, women's fitness studio and massage. Admission costs $7 for adults, $5 for children age 12 and under. The center is open 8 am to 11 pm in summer, 9 am to 10 pm in winter.

Play golf at Durango's 18-hole Hillcrest Golf Course (☎ 970-247-1499), 2300 Rim Drive, on the Fort Lewis College Mesa overlooking town. Green fees are $17.

Special Events

The seasonal *Durango Magazine* lists a complete calendar of events.

The **Iron Horse Bicycle Classic** (☎ 970-259-4621) in late May deserves the classic title – this 47-mile road race to Silverton, first run in 1972, pits human power against the steam train. The event has grown to include three days of bicycle rides and races with plenty of off-road activities.

In addition to hosting national whitewater competitive events each year, Durango sponsors **Animas River Days** over three days in late June.

Places to Stay

Rates are depressingly high during the peak summer season, and all of Durango's 40-plus motels can be booked up. If you need assistance finding a vacancy, contact Durango Central Reservations (☎ 970-247-8900, 800-979-9742) Monday to Saturday from 8 am to 5 pm. The visitors center (☎ 800-525-8855) can also provide information and phone numbers for lodgings. Rates peak in summer, ease off in fall and spring, and usually fall by around 50% in winter.

Places to Stay – budget

Camping USFS campsites can be reserved (☎ 800-280-2267) for a fee of $8.65 plus an $8 nightly campsite charge at *Haviland Lake*, 18 miles north of Durango. Other campgrounds in the San Juan National Forest (☎ 970-247-4874) are on a first-come, first-served basis and include the large *Junction Creek* ($8 fee), only 3 miles west of the corner of Main Ave and 25th St; *Purgatory* ($8 fee), next to US 550 opposite the Purgatory Ski Area turnoff; and *Sig Creek* ($6 fee), on USFS Rd 578, 7 miles west of the resort.

Eight miles north of Durango on the valley plain, the private *Hermosa Meadows Camper Park* (☎ 970-247-3055, 800-748-2853) offers 90 shaded tent sites with laundry and showers next to the Animas River for $15. You can fish or launch your kayak from the campground or rent a bike to ride into Durango or nearby Trimble Hot Springs. *Durango East KOA* (☎ 970-247-0783) is 5 miles east of Durango at 30090 US 160, while *Ponderosa KOA* (☎ 970-247-4499), is 10 miles north of town on La Plata Country Rd 250. Both of the campgrounds have stores, restaurants and wooded and open sites for $18.

Hostels The rather unkempt *Durango Hostel* (☎ 970-247-9905), 543 E 2nd Ave, offers the bare necessities for $12 a night. It has had a reputation for being a bit seedy, but at the time of writing the owners appeared to be trying to improve things.

Motels One of the best values in town is the low-key *End O' Day Motel* (☎ 970-247-1722), 350 E 8th Ave, where singles/doubles are $34/42 in summer, one of the lowest motel prices in town. Rooms are small but comfortable and the hotel has a tree-covered ridge as its backyard. Nearby at 474 College Ave, the *Highland Motel* (☎ 970-247-0452) has very basic rooms, but seems clean and well maintained. In summer rooms cost $35/40, those with kitchenettes, $50.

At the northern tip of town, the *Silver Spur Motel* (☎ 970-247-5552, 800-748-1715), 3416 Main Ave, usually keeps its summer rates capped at $40/44, and even has a pool in the back.

Places to Stay – middle
Motels Durango has dozens of places that are remarkably similar and all charge $60 to $70 for a double in summer, around $35 in winter. The less-expensive places are mostly located at the northern end of Main Ave.

The attractive and well laid-out *Sunset Inn* (☎ 970-247-2653, 800-414-5984), 2855 Main Ave, has a hot tub and pool and is a relatively good value at $58/68 during the summer peak. A bit farther north, the *Spanish Trails Inn and Suites* (☎ 970-247-4173) also has a pool, guest laundry and lots of rooms, most of which cost $59 during summer. *The Vagabond Inn* (☎ 970-259-5901), 2180 Main Ave, has some rooms in a renovated roadhouse that are pretty interesting, though perhaps not fascinating enough to warrant the $88 peak summer rate. But rooms in the adjacent motel unit are $68, and facilities include a pool, hot tub and guest laundry.

If you want to be right downtown, the *Durango Lodge* (☎ 970-247-0955), 150 5th St, is near the railroad depot and offers a pleasant stay. Rooms are pricey during summer, starting at $77, but that's what you pay for location, a pool and hot tub.

Here are some other mid-range offerings in Durango (rates quoted are for double occupancy during peak season):

Alpine Motel
    3515 N Main Ave (☎ 970-247-4042,
    800-818-4042), $68
Dollar Inn
    2391 Main Ave (☎ 970-247-0593,
    800-727-3746), $60 to $78
Econo Lodge
    2002 Main Ave (☎ 970-247-4242),
    $60 to $84, hot tub, pool
Rodeway Inn
    2701 Main Ave (☎ 970-259-2540),
    $60 to $90, hot tub, pool, laundry
Travelodge
    2970 Main Ave (☎ 970-247-1741),
    $60 to $90

Places to Stay – top end
B&Bs The *Gable House* (☎ 970-247-4982), 805 E 5th Ave, is housed in a former Victorian hospital and offers rooms with shared bath for between $75 and $85. The *Leland House B&B* (☎ 970-385-1920, 800-664-1920), near the town center at 721 E 2nd Ave, has rooms from $95 in summer.

Hotels Durango has several intriguing Victorian hotels to choose from: prices are high but not much more than a Holiday Inn or high-end Best Western, and the surroundings are far more interesting.

The 1898 *General Palmer Hotel* (☎ 970-247-4747, 800-523-3358), 567 Main Ave, is an elegant Victorian hotel that's been restored to near perfection. Rooms start at $145 in summer, $95 in winter. Along similar lines, the *Strater Hotel* (☎ 970-247-4431, 800-247-4431), 699 Main Ave, was built in 1887 and has elaborately furnished rooms from $120. Film buffs may prefer the *Rochester Hotel* (☎ 970-385-1920, 800-664-1920), 726 E 2nd Ave, which has 15 rooms decorated in themes of Western

COLORADO

movies filmed in and around Durango. Rates start at $125 in summer, $85 in winter.

Places to Eat

As with accommodations, there's a lot to choose from in Durango, although prices aren't quite as steep when it comes to eating.

Among the most popular breakfast and lunch places is *Carver's Bakery* (☎ 970-259-2545), 1022 Main Ave, where you can get everything from fresh muffins and espresso to hearty omelets with home fries, veggie burgers and spinach lasagna. *Le Rendezvous Swiss Bakery* (☎ 970-385-5685), 750 Main Ave, also draws a good crowd and offers a slightly more refined menu and atmosphere. For cheap and hearty American breakfasts, head for the *Durango Diner* (☎ 970-247-9889), 957 Main Ave, where biscuits and gravy with roasted green chiles can be had for around $3.

Though it can get crowded and smoky, the historic-looking *Olde Tymer's Cafe* (☎ 970-259-2990), 1000 Main Ave, has good lunches for around $6, outdoor patio seating and is frequented by locals as well as tourists. Both food and beer are quite good at *Steamworks Brewing Company* (☎ 970-259-9200), 801 E 2nd Ave, a relatively new place that has quickly built up a strong following.

Francisco's (☎ 970-247-4098), 601 Main Ave, features New Mexico-style lunch and dinner dishes in a large and busy restaurant. If you like it spicier, try *Gazpacho* (☎ 970-259-9494), 431 E 2nd Ave, which serves good northern Mexican and New Mexican dishes; combination plates, including a whole section of vegetarian options, start at $7.

The Italian dishes at *Farquarhts* (☎ 970-247-5440), 725 Main Ave, are not all that exciting, but you do get a lot of food for your money. Northern Italian dinner specialties are featured at *Ariano's* (☎ 970-247-8146), 150 E College Drive St; pasta dishes start at around $10. Another upscale Italian place that gets good reviews is *Milan's* (☎ 970-382-8865), 1150B Main Ave.

The *Ore House* (☎ 970-247-5707), 147 E College Ave, does a fine job with steak and seafood. Among the most respected top-end places in town is the *Palace Grill* (☎ 970-247-2018), in the former Palace Hotel next to the train depot: it's known for its excellent aged beef, game and fresh fish dishes.

Entertainment

Farquarht's offers live rock music and dancing on weekends and some weeknights as well. *Lady Falconburgh's Barley Exchange* (☎ 970-382-9664) has a selection of more than 100 beers, and hops on weekends.

The *Diamond Circle Melodrama* (☎ 970-247-3400), in the Strater Hotel, offers nightly summer theater performances starting at 8 pm for $14.

Getting There & Away

Air Durango-La Plata County Airport (☎ 970-247-8143) is 18 miles southeast of Durango via US 160 and Hwy 172. American Airlines offers daily jet service to Dallas during the winter ski season. Otherwise, you are on commuter turbo-prop equipment. United Express has daily flights to Denver, while America West and Mesa Airlines have daily flights to Phoenix, AZ, and Albuquerque, NM, respectively.

Bus Greyhound/TNM&O buses provide daily service on US 550 north to Montrose, Delta and Grand Junction and south to Albuquerque. The Bus Center (☎ 970-259-2755), 275 E 8th Ave, offers lockers and the ticket agent is available from 7:30 am to 12 pm and 3:30 to 5 pm weekdays, plus Saturday morning. The agent also opens the office to meet buses Sunday and holidays. Daily northbound departures are at 7 am, southbound at 9:50 am.

Car Durango lies at the junction of US 160 and US 550. It's 42 miles east of Cortez via US 160, 49 miles west of Pagosa Springs and 190 miles north of Albuquerque via US 550 (NM Hwy 44) and I-25.

Getting Around

To/From the Airport Durango Transportation (☎ 970-259-4818) is open 24 hours and has frequent airport shuttles from 4:45 am to 6:30 pm. The one-way fare is $15 and you must book a seat at least two hours in advance.

Bus The Durango Lift (☎ 970-259-5438) runs a trolley bus service along Main Ave from 6:30 am to 10 pm every 15 minutes (from 7 am to 7 pm every 30 minutes in winter): the fare is 25¢. There is also a bus service that makes an hourly clockwise circuit of town – south on Main Ave and north via the Fort Lewis College for a 50¢ fare.

Car At Durango-La Plata County Airport you can rent cars from Budget (☎ 970-259-1841), Avis (☎ 970-247-9761), National (☎ 970-259-0068), Dollar (☎ 970-259-3012) and Hertz (☎ 970-247-5288).

AROUND DURANGO

Purgatory Ski Area

It figures that the Purgatory Ski Area (☎ 970 247-8900, 800-979-9742), 25 miles north of Durango on US 550, would have excellent ski conditions – averaging 250 inches of snow annually and plenty of bright sunny days – it was founded by a USFS weather expert in 1967. One high-speed quad and four triple and four double chairlifts provide access to 75 runs with a maximum vertical drop of 2000 feet. Half the trails are rated intermediate, with the remainder divided between beginner and expert slopes. Daily lift tickets run $40 for adults, $18 for kids age six to 12.

Facilities include a cross-country ski center, a ski school for the disabled and a snowboard park. The resort also has accommodations and restaurants at the base.

Places to Stay The resort's restaurants and *Purgatory Village Hotel* (☎ 800-693-0175) are at the base of the lifts. Regular winter room rates are $110 for a double and condominiums begin at $220 for a one-bedroom unit for four people. The nearby *Best Western Lodge at Purgatory*

(☎ 970-247-9669) offers rooms at $100 during the regular winter season, and for $130 during holidays.

Southern Ute Indian Reservation

Unlike their neighbors at the Ute Mountain Indian Reservation, the Southern Utes – primarily composed of the Muache and Capote bands – live on a checkerboard reservation resulting from their sale of individually owned allotments to Hispanic and Anglo farmers and ranchers. The town of Ignacio, home of the tribal headquarters on the Los Pinos River 25 miles southeast of Durango, is not on Ute land. To get there, continue east for 10 miles on Hwy 172 from the Durango-La Plata County Airport, or exit US 160 at Bayfield and travel south on 'Buck Hwy,' La Plata County Rd 521.

This tri-ethnic community with chile ristras and adobe buildings is reminiscent of New Mexican villages. The Southern Utes are proud of their integration and some claim that it has fostered a better business sense than that found on cooperative reservations. On the east bank of the Los Pinos, the Ouray Memorial Cemetery features the gravesites of Chiefs Ouray and Buckskin Charley – prominently located at the center of the Catholic and Protestant sections.

Southern Ute Culture Center Find out about traditional Ute life from the attractive museum displays of artifacts, clothing and ceremonies. Photographs document the Los Pinos Agency, established in 1869 after the Ute chiefs traveled with Kit Carson to Washington, DC, and signed the Treaty of 1868 that relinquished their traditional homeland to the incoming miners.

The Culture Center Museum (☎ 970-563-9583) is open during summer months from 9 am to 6 pm and 10 am to 3 pm on weekends. It's closed Sunday from October 1 to May 15. Admission costs $1.

Sky Ute Lodge & Casino The *Sky Ute Lodge & Casino* (☎ 970-563-3000, 800-876-7017) is a Ute-owned facility that includes a modern motel and restaurant that caters to guests of the casino, open 20 hours daily from 8 am to 4 am, 24 hours on weekends. Rooms at the lodge are a pretty good value at $70 in summer, $50 in winter. The *Pinos Nuche Restaurant* reflects the ethnic diversity of the area – it offers a flaky fry bread in the Ute taco, standard American fare, plus pasta dishes and Southwest specialties. An ATM is located in the lobby.

CHIMNEY ROCK ARCHAEOLOGICAL AREA

Here, stunning rock spires house Ancestral Puebloan (Anasazi) ruins overlooking the Piedras River, 42 miles east of Durango on US 160. Recent research suggests that the site was a Chacoan outlier that furnished timber to the distant communities to the south. Another recent discovery suggests the twin pinnacles were used to observe lunar astronomical events. By 1125 AD the site, like others in the Southwest, was abandoned as a consequence of drought.

Guided tours are the only way to visit the hundreds of structures – including the Great Kiva – that once housed between 1200 and 2000 inhabitants. A fire lookout tower offers views of the excavated Chacoan sites perched high on the rock formation. Two-hour walking tours are scheduled from May 15 to September 30 daily at 9:30 am and 10:30 am and 1 pm and 2 pm. The entrance station is 2 miles south of US 160 on Hwy 151. Admission is $4 for adults and $2 for children. For more information call Chimney Rock (☎ 970-883-5359) or the San Juan National Forest Pagosa Ranger District (☎ 970-264-2268).

PAGOSA SPRINGS

West of Durango, on US 160 at the junction with US 84 to Espanola, NM, the open ponderosa pine forests give way to the gaudy tourist billboards and traffic of Pagosa Springs. Pagosa is a Ute term for 'boiling water' and refers to the town's main draw: hot springs that provide heat

for many of the town's 1600 residents. The steam rises from many spots along the San Juan River as it flows past volcanic rock formations in the center of town.

The Pagosa Springs Area Chamber of Commerce (☎ 970-264-2360, 800-252-2204) operates a large visitors center located across the bridge from US 160 and offers a seasonal *Pagosa Country Magazine* describing local attractions and activities, including fishing, hiking and mountain biking. More information about what to do in the San Juan National Forest is available from the USFS Pagosa Ranger Station (☎ 970-264-2268) at the corner of 2nd and Pagosa Sts.

Wolf Creek Ski Area

Downhill Skiing With an annual snowfall of 435 inches, Wolf Creek (☎ 970-264-5639), 25 miles north of Pagosa Springs, boasts having 'the most snow in Colorado.' Two triple chairs, two double chairs and a high-speed poma lift carry you up 1425 feet to the 11,775-foot summit and advanced trails – comprising 35% of the area. Intermediate and beginning terrain respectively comprise 45% and 20%. In addition, a snowcat brings skiers to the expert and isolated Water Fall area.

Adult lift tickets cost $34 and children's passes are $22. Food and drinks are available at the base of the slope. For a taped snow and road condition report, call ☎ 800-264-5639.

Cross-Country Skiing Many backcountry and groomed trails are available and lead into quiet, pristine forest. Contact the Pagosa Ranger Station for details.

Places to Stay & Eat

You may find it worth stopping over to soak in the hot springs at *The Spring Inn* (☎ 970-264-4168, 800-225-0934), where multiple pools overlook the San Juan River within view of US 160. Visitors may use the facilities during the day, but guests at the inn have exclusive use of the incredible soaking pool at the river's edge during the evening and early morning hours.

During the peak summer season, rooms cost up to $90, but fall as low as $54 in winter. A 'Ski and Soak' package that includes lodging and Wolf Creek lift tickets cost $60.

For a more economical stay try the *San Juan Motel* (☎ 970-264-2262), 191 E Pagosa St, where newly redone singles/doubles cost $58/63 during summer peak. Older rooms are available for $42/47 and there are also cabins for $62, as well as a campground where tent sites cost $14, RV hookups $21. If you're skiing Wolf Creek, you might also want to consider staying in South Fork, 18 miles northeast of the ski

area along US 160 (see the South Fork entry earlier in this chapter).

For breakfast or lunch, try the *East 356 Bistro* (☎ 970-264-3356), 356 E Pagosa St, diagonally across from the San Juan Motel. The food is excellent and healthy, and there's a decent veggie selection. Breakfast runs from $3 to $5, while lunches cost around $7. *Amore's House of Pasta* (☎ 970-264-2822), 121 E Pagosa St, serves pasta dinners from $6. The *Elkhorn Cafe* (☎ 970-264-2146), 438 Pagosa St, is a town stalwart, offering simple American and Mexican lunches for under $5 and dinners for $5 to $7.

Western Colorado

Western Colorado's arid landscape of flat-topped mesas and multihued, deeply incised canyons is part of an extensive plateau country. Native Americans refer to this land of multicolored canyon walls as 'the land of frozen rainbows.'

Generally less frequented by visitors, western Colorado nonetheless has plenty of stunning scenery to offer. Best known are probably the fascinating ruins of the cliff dwellings at Mesa Verde National Park. Near Grand Junction, the scenic Colorado National Monument exemplifies the 'frozen rainbows' that are found along the Colorado Plateau, as does Dinosaur National Monument in the northwest corner of the state. Other highlights include the Alpine meadows, forests and streams hidden away atop the 10,000-foot Grand Mesa, the shadowy lure of the plunging Black Canyon of the Gunnison River and the little-traveled roads and trails of the Dolores River Canyon.

Already well known to pre-Columbian peoples, western Colorado's plateau land represented an obstacle for European and American explorers. Spanish explorer Juan de Oñate first named Río Colorado (literally, River Red) in 1605. In 1776, an expedition led by Spanish Father Francisco Atanasio Domínguez and Father Silvestre Vélez Escalante grappled with the forbidding terrain along the Dolores River in their fruitless search for a path to Monterey, California, and possible mission sites. This plateau country remained uncharted terrain for Americans until 1869, when Major John Wesley Powell made the first of his two epic voyages down the Green and Colorado rivers to christen the 'Colorado Plateau.'

The Colorado Plateau's uppermost formations consist largely of flat, windblown sand deposits that erode in vertical cliffs, while the underlying layers of shale form a sloping gradient around the base of most mesas. Such formations extend from the Green River in Wyoming south into New Mexico and Arizona. In southern Colorado, the San Juan Mountains mark a volcanic intrusion into plateau country (this spectacular range is covered in the Southern Mountains chapter).

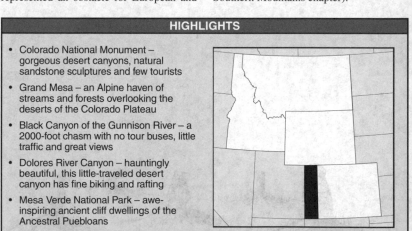

HIGHLIGHTS

- Colorado National Monument – gorgeous desert canyons, natural sandstone sculptures and few tourists

- Grand Mesa – an Alpine haven of streams and forests overlooking the deserts of the Colorado Plateau

- Black Canyon of the Gunnison River – a 2000-foot chasm with no tour buses, little traffic and great views

- Dolores River Canyon – hauntingly beautiful, this little-traveled desert canyon has fine biking and rafting

- Mesa Verde National Park – awe-inspiring ancient cliff dwellings of the Ancestral Puebloans

COLORADO

Northern Plateau

Northwestern Colorado is the state's 'empty' quarter, a thinly populated region of high desert that in remote times was dinosaur country. These days the region's wilderness areas are largely the province of hunters, and in autumn the area is overrun with camouflage-clad outdoorsmen. The Northern Plateau includes some beautiful scenery, though not as spectacular as that farther to the south.

CRAIG

Lying on the north bank on the Yampa River between the towns of Meeker and Steamboat Springs, Craig (population 8500) is more of a pit stop than a destination, unless you're a hunter and it's autumn. US 40 runs through the middle of town, where it's known as Victory Way, and this is where you'll find most services.

Craig's Moffat County visitors center (☎ 970-824-3046), 360 E Victory Way, is open weekdays 8 am to 5 pm. The BLM's Little Snake Resource Area Office (☎ 970-824-4441) is at 1280 Industrial Ave. It's a little hard to find because Industrial Ave is a discontinuous street; from W Victory Way take Mack Lane south beyond 4th St.

First Security Bank has an ATM at 250 W Victory Way. The post office is at 556 Pershing St; Craig's zip code is 81625.

If you need a break from the road and end up staying in Craig, you can check out the **Museum of Northwest Colorado**, 590 Yampa Ave, which has good displays on local history, a small display of fossils and an exhibit on the Denver Northwestern & Pacific Railroad.

Places to Stay & Eat

Accommodations are reasonably priced but prices may rise during hunting season, mid-September to late November. One of the best bargains is *Trav O Tel Motel* (☎ 970-824-8171), at 224 E Victory Way, which has small but efficiently designed rooms starting at $25/single. Farther east at

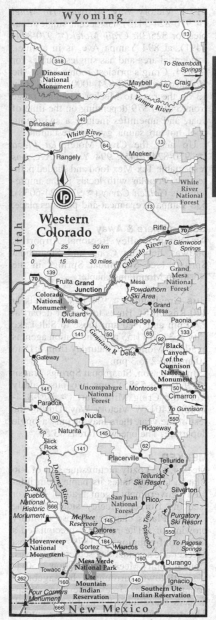

517 E Victory Way, *Westward Ho Motel* (☎ 970-824-3413) has decent singles/doubles for $25/38. *Craig Motel* (☎ 970-824-4491), at 894 Yampa Ave, is in a quiet, residential area and has singles/doubles for $29/34. Craig's priciest rooms are at the *Holiday Inn* (☎ 970-824-4000), 300 S Hwy 13 on the road to Meeker. Doubles range from $49 to $79 depending on the time of year, and amenities include a swimming pool, hot tub, sauna, gym and restaurant.

Up near the Craig Motel, *La Plaza* (☎ 970-824-7345), 994 Yampa Ave, has respectable Tex-Mex food and shaded patio seating. Popular with locals is the unpretentious *Golden Cavvy* (☎ 970-824-6038), 538 Yampa Ave, a meat-and-potatoes place.

Getting There & Away

Air Yampa Valley Regional Airport is midway between Craig and Steamboat Springs (see Steamboat Springs in the Northern Mountains chapter).

Bus Greyhound (☎ 970-824-5161) is at 470 Russell St. Buses to Denver depart at 2:40 pm and 1:20 am; those to Salt Lake City at 3 and 11:55 pm. The station agent is available Monday to Saturday from 8:15 to 10 am and 2 to 3 pm.

In ski season, Steamboat Springs Transit (☎ 970-879-5585) runs two buses daily from the Craig Mini Mart (☎ 970-824-7740), 2401 W Victory Way. During the rest of the year, there may be only a single departure. The one-way fare is $3.50.

MEEKER

Meeker, the cozily picturesque seat of Rio Blanco County, takes its name from infamous government agent Nathan Meeker (see the Horace Greeley sidebar in the Eastern Plains chapter), whose arbitrary plowing of a Ute racetrack precipitated a fatal confrontation in 1879 which cost Meeker and several other settlers their lives. Contemporary Meeker (population 2150) is a small town surrounded by sagebrush country where Greek-American sheepherders graze huge flocks for their wool. The tiny but well-preserved downtown

Ike's

Barring the blizzard of the century, no one approaching Craig on US 40 from Steamboat Springs can miss the rolling hillsides covered by something that, according to local Yellow Pages, is Ike's Automatic Transmission Shop. In fact, Ike's is a sprawling junkyard which may hold more wrecks than there are licensed vehicles in Moffat County. According to local legend, the sight so aggravated Lady Bird Johnson that it prompted her to launch her famous nationwide beautification program during her husband Lyndon's presidency. Ike's is not really photogenic, but it is unforgettable. ∎

includes several buildings of historical and architectural interest, most notably St James Episcopal Church (1889), 368 4th St, and the brick Meeker Hotel (1896), 560 Main St. There's no pressing reason to visit Meeker, but you can get information here on the nearby White River National Forest. If you're passing through it makes for a pleasant enough overnight stop.

Information

The Meeker Chamber of Commerce (☎ 970-878-5510) maintains an information office at 710 W Market St, though it keeps irregular hours. The White River National Forest's Blanco Ranger District Office (☎ 970-878-4039) is at 317 E Market St. The BLM's White River Resource Area Office (☎ 970-878-3601) is southwest of town at 73544 Hwy 64.

The First National Bank of the Rockies is at 504 Main St. The post office is at 365 6th St; Meeker's zip code is 81641.

Pioneers Hospital of Rio Blanco County (☎ 970-878-5047) is at 345 Cleveland.

The Meeker Laundry (☎ 970-878-9987) is at 225 8th St.

Places to Stay & Eat

Meeker is gets booked up with hunters from late September to mid-November; it would be wise to phone ahead if you're planning a stay around this time.

Meeker Town Park, at the foot of 4th St, has $5 campsites but no showers; there's a 15-day limit and gear must be packed up daily by 9 am. For a shower try the Rustic Lodge (see below), which charges $3 per person. *Stagecoach Campground* (☎ 970-878-4334), which is 2 miles south of Meeker at the junction of Hwy 13 and Hwy 64, is a shady riverside facility with $16 tent sites, $25 for sites with full hookups.

The congenial *Valley Motel* (☎ 970-878-3656), 723 Market St, has singles/doubles for $30/35 ($10 higher in hunting season) and a hot tub. *Meeker Hotel* (☎ 970-878-5255), 560 Main St, is a historic building with restored 19th-century rooms. Singles with shared bath are $35, doubles with private bath are $45; suites start around $100. Rates are a bit higher on weekends and during hunting season. At the east end of town, *Rustic Lodge* (☎ 970-878-3136), 173 1st St, has two-person cabins for $40, $5 each additional person. There is also a house unit with three bedrooms, each priced at $30. All cabins have kitchenettes, and there's a hot tub and a restaurant with bar on the premises.

Meeker Cafe, next to the Meeker Hotel has reasonably priced burgers, sandwiches and other lunch items. Dinners are a bit pricier at $8 to $15, but portions are large. *The Bakery & Cafe* (☎ 970-878-5500), 265 6th St, opens for breakfast at 6 am and also serves lunch and gourmet coffees.

Getting There & Away
On the north bank of the White River near the junction of Hwy 13 and Hwy 64, Meeker is 45 miles south of Craig and 42 miles north of Rifle, which is just off I-70. Rangely is 78 miles west via Hwy 64.

AROUND MEEKER
Flattops Scenic Byway
This graveled road (Rio Blanco County Rd 8) east of Meeker is a more scenic alternative route to Steamboat Springs

than US 40 via Craig. It intersects Hwy 131 near Yampa (snow closes the route in winter), and also provides access to the Rio Blanco National Forest's Flat Tops Wilderness, a 367-sq-mile roadless area with countless Alpine lakes favored by hikers and anglers. The scenic and popular Trapper's Lake has five developed campgrounds; camping permits are $10. You can also access several nice hikes from here. The USFS ranger station in Meeker has information and maps for the area. The 'Flat Tops Trail Scenic Byway' brochure has a map showing points of interest along the route, which has 17 accessible campgrounds ranging from $3 to $10.

Ute Indian Monument
This monument at the Thornburg Battle Ground, 20 miles northeast of Meeker via Rio Blanco County Rd 15, marks the place where the Ute resistance attacked US Army Major Thomas Thornburgh's 5th Cavalry, while it was en route to support Nathan Meeker. Thornburg died in the battle, which lasted from September 29 to October 6, 1879. The site is also accessible from Moffat County Rd 45, off Hwy 13 about 5 miles south of Hamilton.

DINOSAUR NATIONAL MONUMENT
Although dinosaurs once inhabited much of the earth, in only a few places have the proper geological and climatic conditions combined to preserve their skeletons as fossils. Paleontologist Earl Douglass of Pittsburgh's Carnegie Museum discovered this dinosaur fossil bed, one of the largest in North America, in 1909. Six years later, President Woodrow Wilson acknowledged the scientific importance of the area by declaring it a national monument.

Today visitors can view Dinosaur Quarry, now completely enclosed within a building to protect the fossils from weathering, in which over 1600 bones have been exposed. Apart from dinosaur bones, the monument's starkly eroded canyons provide the visitor with scenic drives, hiking, camping, backpacking and river-running.

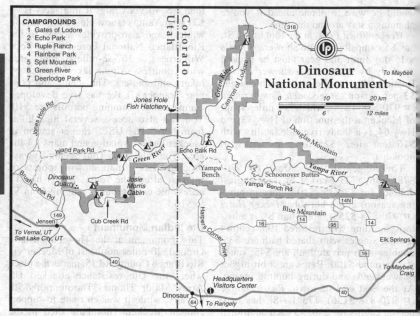

CAMPGROUNDS
1 Gates of Lodore
2 Echo Park
3 Ruple Ranch
4 Rainbow Park
5 Split Mountain
6 Green River
7 Deerlodge Park

Orientation

Dinosaur National Monument straddles the Utah-Colorado state line. Monument headquarters and most of the land is within Colorado, but the quarry (the only place to see fossils *in situ*) is in Utah.

Information

At the town of Dinosaur, a Colorado welcome center offers maps and brochures for the entire state.

Information is available from Dinosaur National Monument Headquarters visitors center (☎ 970-374-3000), which has an audio-visual program, exhibits and a bookstore. It's open 8 am to 4:30 pm weekdays year-round, plus weekends in summer; closed New Year's Day, Thanksgiving and Christmas Day. There's also a visitors center at Dinosaur Quarry.

Entrance to the monument's headquarters visitors center is free, but entrance to all other parts of the monument (including Dinosaur Quarry) is $10 per private vehicle,

$2 for cyclists or bus passengers. Golden Eagle/Access cards are accepted.

Summer daytime temperatures average upwards of 80°F – carry drinking water if hiking. Winter snows may eliminate access to some of the areas described below, though the quarry road is usually open.

Dinosaur Quarry

The Jurassic strata containing the fossils give a glimpse of how paleontologists transform solid rock into the beautiful skeletons seen in museums, and how they develop scientifically reliable interpretations of life in the remote past. Ranger-led walks, talks and tours explain the site; information can also be gleaned from brochures, audio-visual programs and exhibits. There is a gift and bookshop.

Dinosaur Quarry (☎ 435-789-2115) is open daily from 8 am to 7 pm Memorial Day to Labor Day; the rest of the year hours are 8 am to 4:30 pm; closed New Year's Day, Thanksgiving and Christmas Day.

During the busy summer season, park in the lower lot and either walk about a half-mile to the quarry or wait for the free shuttle bus. Disabled visitors can drive all the way to the small parking lot at the quarry, as can the general public during off-peak hours.

Car Tours & Hiking Trails

There are several drives with scenic overlooks and interpretive signs, leading to a number of trailheads for short nature walks or access to the backcountry.

East of Dinosaur Quarry, paved **Cub Creek Rd** winds for 10 miles, ending at **Josie Morris' Cabin**. Josie Morris was a tough woman who lived here some 50 years – legend has it that Butch Cassidy was among her many suitors. On the way to the cabin are a couple of nature trails (each about 2 miles) with Native American petroglyphs. Split Mountain and Green River campgrounds are nearby (see Places to Stay below).

Paved **Harpers Corner Drive** leaves US 40 at park headquarters and heads north 31 miles into the heart of the backcountry, crossing the Utah-Colorado state line a couple of times. This scenic and popular drive has several turnouts with vistas and interpretive signs, picnic areas and trailheads, but no campgrounds. Trails include the very short Plug Hat Butte Nature Trail 4 miles from headquarters, the 4-mile Ruple Point Trail 25 miles from headquarters and the mile-long Harpers Corner Trail at road's end. Both the Ruple Point and Harpers Corner trails lead to dramatic views of the Green River canyon. (Trail distances noted here are outbound only – double the figure for the roundtrip)

Unpaved **Echo Park Rd** leaves Harpers Corner Drive about 25 miles north of headquarters. Vehicles with high clearance or 4WD are recommended for this 13-mile drive, which descends sharply to Echo Park at the confluence of the Yampa and Green rivers. The steep road can get very slick after rain. There is a primitive campground in a splendid setting at Echo Park, and hiking is ideal despite the lack of maintained trails. The road is impassable to large motor homes or trailers, though ordinary cars can make it in dry weather – ask at headquarters first. People with trucks or 4WDs can also explore the rough, 38-mile-long **Yampa Bench Rd**, which leaves Echo Park Rd about 8 miles from Harpers Corner Drive. This road affords views of the Yampa River before coming out on US 40 at Elk Springs, about 34 miles east of headquarters.

A few miles south of Dinosaur Quarry, Hwy 149 meets the paved Brush Creek Rd, which soon connects with paved but narrow **Jones Hole Rd**. This road goes 48 miles around the west and north sides of the monument to Jones Hole Fish Hatchery (☎ 970-789-4481), open daily 7 am to 3:30 pm. From the fish hatchery, the **Jones Hole Trail** descends 4 miles to the Green River, passing Native American petroglyphs and crossing Ely Creek, where backcountry camping is allowed (with permit).

The unpaved **Island Park Rd** leaves from about 15 miles along the Jones Hole Rd and descends 12 miles to Rainbow Park and another 5 miles to Ruple Ranch. Both are on the Green River and have primitive campgrounds. Road condition warnings for Echo Park Rd also apply here.

The 12-mile **Gulch Rd** west of Elk Springs leads to Deerlodge Park on the Yampa River at the east end of the monument. Hwy 318 leads from Maybell to the scenic **Gates of Lodore** on the Green River at the northeast end of the monument. Both places have campgrounds and ranger stations open in summer.

Backpacking

Most hikers take one of the trails described above, but a few prefer even more remote areas. There are designated backcountry campsites only on the Jones Hole Trail; otherwise wilderness camping is allowed anywhere at least one-quarter mile from an established road or trail. Backpackers must register with a ranger at one of the visitors centers or ranger stations, where you can receive free permits and review the best routes with a ranger.

COLORADO

Fishing

Fishing is permitted only with the appropriate state permits, available from sports stores or tackle shops in Dinosaur or Vernal, UT. Check with park rangers about limits and the best places.

White-Water Rafting

The Yampa River is the only major Colorado River tributary not severely impounded by dams. Both the Yampa and Green rivers offer excellent river-running opportunities, with plenty of exciting rapids and whitewater amid splendid scenery. From mid-May to early September, trips range from one to five days. Adrift Adventures (☎ 800-824-0150) offers one-day trips; Adventure Bound (☎ 970-241-5633, 800-423-4668), 2392 H Rd in Grand Junction, is a popular rafting outfitter and guide service. Contact monument headquarters for a complete list of concessionaires.

Experienced rafters wishing to raft independently need a permit from the River Ranger Office (☎ 970-374-2468), open weekdays 8 am to noon. Permits are limited and most are issued many months in advance (especially for multiple-day trips), so plan well ahead.

Places to Stay

The monument's main campground is *Green River*, 5 miles east of Dinosaur Quarry along Cub Creek Rd, with 88 sites. Open May to September, it has bathrooms and drinking water but no showers or hookups. Sites are $5 to $10 per night; the campground may fill on summer weekends (no reservations), but rarely fills midweek.

For camping during winter when Green River is closed, try nearby *Split Mountain*, which lacks water but is free (closed in summer). Free camping is also permitted at *Rainbow Park*, *Deerlodge Park*, *Gates of Lodore* and *Echo Park*. Only the latter two have drinking water and all are closed in winter. Call the visitors centers to check on opening dates and availability.

There are no lodges in the monument but Vernal has a good selection of motels and restaurants, and the town of Dinosaur also has a couple of motels and restaurants.

Getting There & Away

Dinosaur National Monument is 88 miles west of Craig via US 40 and 120 miles east of Salt Lake City, UT, by I-80 and US 40. Dinosaur Quarry is 7 miles north of Jensen, UT, on Cub Creek Rd (Utah Hwy 149). Monument headquarters is just off US 40 on Harpers Corner Drive, about 4 miles east of the town of Dinosaur.

RANGELY

Rangely is an isolated coal and oil town on Hwy 64, about 56 miles west of Meeker and about 90 miles north of Fruita and Grand Junction via Hwy 139. Visitors to nearby Dinosaur National Monument may wish to detour through Rangely due to access to the very fine rock art sites along Hwy 139 just south of town.

The surprisingly good **Rangely Museum** (☎ 970-675-2612), 434 W Main St, is open 10 am to noon, 1 to 5 pm Monday to Saturday, and 1 to 5 pm Sunday. There are several notable pre-Columbian rock art sites on nearby BLM lands; look for self-guided tour brochures along Hwy 64 East and West, the Dragon Trail south of Rangely and Cañon Pintado.

Places to Stay & Eat

Shady *Rangely Camper Park*, a municipal site just north of Main St (Hwy 64) at the east end of town, is a real bargain at $5 without hookups but with hot showers (sites with electrical hookups are $10).

The *4 Queens Motel* (☎ 970-675-5035), 206 E Main St, charges $44 for a double, which includes free swimming passes to the town recreation center. *Escalante Trail Motel* (☎ 970-675-8461), 117 S Grand Ave, has singles/doubles for $36/40 and gives a $5 coupon for the Subway restaurant in front of the motel if reservations are made in advance.

The *Cowboy Corral* (☎ 970-675-8986), 202 W Main, is exactly the kind of steakhouse its name implies. *Magalinos* (☎ 970-675-2321), at 124 Main St, has good-value lunches and dinners; *Max's Pizza* (☎ 970-675-2670), at 855 E Main St, is a local favorite.

CAÑON PINTADO HISTORIC DISTRICT

Most of the several rock art sites in the area just south of Rangely along Hwy 139, observed by the Domínguez-Escalante Expedition of 1776, date from the Fremont cultures that inhabited the area from about 600 to 1300 AD, although the later Utes also made their contributions. Like the Ancestral Puebloans farther south, the Fremont peoples cultivated maize, beans and squash in the well-watered valleys but also hunted and gathered in the higher, drier areas.

Look for green and white BLM rods which indicate the sites along Hwy 139. The nearest site to Rangely, 1.3 miles south of the junction with Hwy 64, is a panel about 50 yards west of the highway showing several abstract and anthropomorphic shapes. At the 4.1-mile point west of the highway is a conspicuous Fremont ruin that may have served as a watchtower.

At the 10.5-mile point on the east side of the highway, **East Fourmile Canyon** requires a short hike along the nearby cliff face on the north side of the canyon, crossing a fairly deep arroyo past a crumbling pioneer cabin and then on toward the east. This is probably the best concentration of Cañon Pintado sites; note the polychrome concentric circles (the BLM claim description of these as 'stunning' is an exaggeration, but they're worth seeing).

At 14.2 miles, the **Philadelphia Draw** site is accessible by a dirt road leading about a mile to the east; look to your left after crossing the second cattle guard. The artwork is easy to find, but it's faint in the morning sun; watch for rattlesnakes under the overhang. At 15.4 miles on the west side of the highway, the conspicuous **White Birds** site also displays what appear to be multicolored chiles.

One-half mile south, across from a picnic site and toilet constructed by the BLM, the main **Cañon Pintado** site includes an image of Kokopelli, a flute-playing figure common in the Ancestral Puebloan art of the Southwest; the BLM has reinforced the spalling sandstone with a cable and bolts. This site was specifically described in the journals of the Escalante Expedition.

Readers especially interested in the rock art of this area should look for FA Barnes's exhaustively titled *Canyon Country Prehistoric Rock Art: An Illustrated Guide to Viewing, Understanding, and Appreciating the Rock Art of the Prehistoric Indian Cultures of Utah, the Great Basin and the General Four Corners Region* (Treasure Chest Publications, 1982). Another worthwhile source, with a more manageable title, is Sally J Cole's *Legacy on Stone: Rock Art of the Colorado Plateau and Four Corners Region* (Johnson Books, 1990).

Central Plateau

Stretching south from the Colorado River to the San Juan Mountains is the platcau country of Grand Mesa and the lower Gunnison River. This area is home to some excellent geological formations and scenery. Two NPS units, the Colorado National Monument near Grand Junction and the Black Canyon of the Gunnison east of Delta and Montrose, are largely underappreciated and offer great opportunities for tranquil nature exploration, even during the summer peak.

The region also contains productive farmlands along the Colorado and Gunnison rivers and rugged volcanic uplands on the Grand Mesa and Uncompahgre Plateau.

GRAND JUNCTION

In the midst of one of Colorado's most productive agricultural zones, Grand Junction (population 34,500) is western Colorado's main urban center. The city is quite spread out, sprawling east and west across the Grand Valley. Planners have partially turned downtown Main St into a pleasant pedestrian mall by reducing roads, planting trees, providing benches and placing sculptures

COLORADO

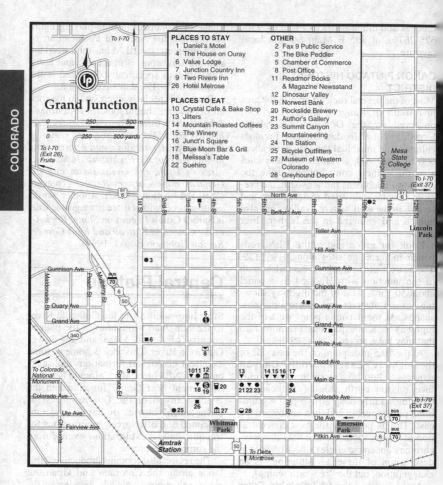

Grand Junction

PLACES TO STAY
1 Daniel's Motel
4 The House on Ouray
6 Value Lodge
7 Junction Country Inn
9 Two Rivers Inn
26 Hotel Melrose

PLACES TO EAT
10 Crystal Cafe & Bake Shop
13 Jitters
14 Mountain Roasted Coffees
15 The Winery
16 Junct'n Square
17 Blue Moon Bar & Grill
18 Melissa's Table
22 Suehiro

OTHER
2 Fax 9 Public Service
3 The Bike Peddler
5 Chamber of Commerce
8 Post Office
11 Readmor Books
    & Magazine Newsstand
12 Dinosaur Valley
19 Norwest Bank
20 Rockslide Brewery
21 Author's Gallery
23 Summit Canyon
    Mountaineering
24 The Station
25 Bicycle Outfitters
27 Museum of Western
    Colorado
28 Greyhound Depot

at regular intervals throughout. This has helped the city retain something of a small-town atmosphere.

The city of Grand Junction has become the administrative and commercial center of Mesa County and is home to Mesa State College. Though a nice enough place in its own right, the town mainly functions for travelers is as a base for exploring the nearby scenic wonders of the Colorado National Monument and the Grand Mesa.

History
Paleo-Indians lived in the Grand Valley and surrounding areas 10,000 or more years ago. At the time of European contact, the Utes occupied most of the region. Guided by the Utes, the first European visitors to the area were members of the Domínguez-Escalante Expedition. Explorers such as Kit Carson and John C Frémont paved the way for settlers and, by the 1880s, a trickle became a flood.

Pressured by the settlers, the US government ignored treaties that acknowledged the Utes' rights to the land, removing them to reservations in southern Colorado and eastern Utah. By the late 19th century, farmers had begun to exploit water from the river for their crops and orchards. Grand Valley has remained one of Colorado's most productive agricultural regions, but in recent years the tourist industry has gained strength due to the striking surrounding countryside.

Orientation

The I-70 Business Loop enters town from the west at I-70 exit 26 (River Rd) and proceeds downtown via 1st St and Ute and Pitkin Aves, eventually rejoining the interstate at the suburb of Clifton (exit 37). US 6 (North Ave) parallels the I-70 Business Loop through town, while US 50 (5th St) diverges south toward Delta and Montrose.

Downtown Grand Junction is a compact, pedestrian-friendly grid bounded by 1st St on the west, North Ave (the US 6 Bypass) on the north, 12th St on the east and Pitkin Ave (eastbound I-70 Business Loop) on the south. Hwy 340, the western extension of Grand Ave, crosses the Colorado River via a bridge and leads to Monument Rd, the eastern approach to Colorado National Monument. Hwy 340 then continues northwest, paralleling I-70, toward the town of Fruita and the western entrance to the monument.

Information

Tourist Offices Grand Junction has a large Visitor & Convention Bureau Information Center (☎ 970-244-1480, 800-962-2547) at the junction of I-70 and Horizon Drive. It's open daily 8:30 am to 5 pm (until 8 pm in summer) and has loads of information and maps on the city, surrounding scenic areas and other parts of western and southern Colorado.

A somewhat more limited selection of information is available at the downtown Grand Junction Area Chamber of Commerce (☎ 970-242-3214), 360 Grand Ave, and at the Amtrak station.

The USFS Grand Junction Ranger District Office (☎ 970-242-8211), 764 Horizon Drive, is open from 8 am to 5 pm Monday to Friday. Staff at he BLM Grand Junction Area Office (☎ 970-244-3000), opposite Walker Field Airport at 2815 H Rd, are helpful and it has a good book selection. Hours are 7:30 am to 4:30 pm weekdays.

Money Norwest Bank has a downtown ATM at 359 Main St.

Post & Communications The main post office is at 241 N 4th St. Grand Junction sprawls enough to have several zip codes; the main post office zip is 81501. Fax-9 Public Service (☎ 970-243-8279; fax 970-243-3498), 1015 North Ave, offers 24-hour fax service.

Bookstores Readmor Books & Magazine Newsstand (☎ 970-242-7229), 344 Main St, has a good selection of fiction, nonfiction, newspapers, magazines and USGS maps. The Author's Gallery (☎ 970-241-3696),

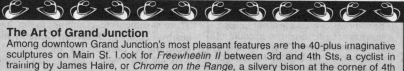

The Art of Grand Junction

Among downtown Grand Junction's most pleasant features are the 40-plus imaginative sculptures on Main St. Look for *Freewheelin II* between 3rd and 4th Sts, a cyclist in training by James Haire, or *Chrome on the Range*, a silvery bison at the corner of 4th and Main Sts. Art on the Corner (☎ 970-245-2926) can provide more information on the works on display, some of which are for sale.

In addition, the **Western Colorado Center for the Arts** (☎ 970-243-7337), 1803 N 7th St, is a modern facility emphasizing the work of local artists. It's open 10 am to 5 pm Tuesday to Saturday. ∎

537 Main St, has an extensive collection of used books (35,000 volumes at last count) and a pleasant atmosphere for browsing and hanging out.

Medical Services St Mary's Hospital (☎ 970-244-2273) is at 2635 N 7th St at the intersection with Patterson Ave.

Historic District

Downtown Grand Junction's well-restored historical buildings infuse the city with a early 20th-century ambiance in and around Main St. Notable examples include the Wayne Aspinall Federal Building (1915), at the corner of 4th St and Rood Ave, the Neoclassical Mesa County Courthouse (1922) which is at the corner of 6th and Main Sts, and the Avalon Theater (1923) on Main and 7th Sts. For a detailed guide to these and other buildings, pick up the 'Grand Junction Downtown Walking Tour' pamphlet at the visitors center or chamber of commerce. Both offices also have walking tour brochures for historic homes along 7th St.

Museum of Western Colorado

This small but well-arranged museum (☎ 970-242-0971), 248 S 4th St, changes exhibits regularly; special exhibits have included an intriguing history of the press in Grand Junction and an elaborate display on Colorado baseball and its significance in community development. The major permanent exhibit is a timeline of world and local events. Admission is $2/1 adults/children two to 17.

The paleontology division of the museum runs **Dinosaur Valley** (☎ 970-243-3466) at 362 Main St. The center features a display of dinosaur parallel tracks – a series of fossilized footprints – which some researchers interpret as evidence that dinosaurs traveled in herds and thus had a social structure. This exhibit, plus the active paleontology laboratory, will appeal mostly to adults, but children will enjoy the mobile mechanical models of *Triceratops*, *Stegosaurus* and standard species. Admission is $4/3.50/2.50 adults/seniors/children.

Hours for both museums are 10 am to 4 pm Tuesday to Saturday (open Monday in summer).

Rock Climbing

There's some fine climbing to be had nearby, notably in **Unaweep Canyon** and **Monument Canyon** in the Colorado National Monument. Climbers can consult KC Baum's *Grand Junction Rock: Rock Climbs of Unaweep Canyon & Adjacent Areas*, available at Summit Canyon Mountaineering (☎ 970-243-2847), 549 Main St. Climbers can also stop by Summit Canyon for climbing equipment, topographic maps and tips on where to go.

The Price of Celebrity

Grand Junction's most famous citizen is writer Dalton Trumbo (1905-1976), who authored the scripts of major Hollywood epics like *Exodus*, *Hawaii* and *Papillon*, as well as the caustically antiwar *Johnny Got His Gun*. The controversial Trumbo was also a member of the so-called 'Hollywood Ten' group of leftist screenwriters who refused to testify before the inquisition of the US House of Representatives' Un-American Activities Committee in the late 1940s. After serving time in prison for contempt of Congress, Trumbo was blacklisted by the film industry. Working anonymously after his release, he was unable to claim public credit for his screenplay *The Brave One* – written under the pseudonym 'Robert Rich' – which won an Academy Award in 1956.

In Grand Junction, however, Trumbo is best known for his early novel *Eclipse*, a transparently fictionalized account of local life which, even 70 years later, is so sensitive a topic that the Museum of Western Colorado cannot present a Trumbo retrospective without risking the loss of funding from the descendants of families he caricatured. Trumbo's personal papers reside at the University of Colorado in Boulder – a safe distance from Grand Junction. ■

COLORADO

Mountain Biking
Some of Colorado's finest mountain biking areas can be found around Grand Junction. Major trails include the 142-mile Grand Junction to Montrose **Tabeguache Trail** (pronounced 'tab-a-watch'), and the 128-mile **Kokopelli Trail**, which stretches from nearby Fruita to Moab, UT. While doing the full length of these trails would require extensive preparation, both offer plenty of loops and other shorter ride possibilities. There are also numerous trails north of the town of Fruita 13 miles west of Grand Junction, which is rapidly becoming one of Colorado's top mountain biking destinations.

Most of these trails have been built and are maintained by the Colorado Plateau Mountain Bike Trail Association (COPMOBA), a nonprofit group of cyclists, bike shops and federal and state land offices that promotes environmentally responsible mountain biking. The group publishes maps of the above trails, including 'Tips & Loops' with options for shorter rides. The maps are available at the visitors center, the Chamber of Commerce and at bike shops in town. For more information, write COPMOBA, PO Box 4602, Grand Junction, CO 81506.

Grand Junction bike shops can provide detailed information on bike routes and how to access them. One of the best places to check is The Bike Peddler (☎ 970-243-5602) at 710 N 1st St, which also has great rates for repairs and tune-ups. Tompkin's Cycle Center (☎ 970-241-0141), 301 Main St, is another good option. Bicycle Outfitters (☎ 970-245-2699), 248 Ute Ave, offers rental discounts to guests staying at the Hotel Melrose. In Fruita, the bike shop to visit is Over the Edge Sports (☎ 970-858-7220), 202 E Aspen Ave. In addition to renting good quality mountain bikes, the shop is known for its friendly and knowledgeable staff.

White-Water Rafting
Adventure Bound (☎ 970-2455428, 800-423-4668), at 2392 H Rd, runs some intriguing single- and multiple-day river trips throughout western Colorado and Utah, including the Yampa and Green rivers in Dinosaur National Monument and the Westwater Canyon on the Colorado River. Rates average around $100 per day and include food, all federal land access fees and ground transport.

Horseback Riding
Mt Garfield Stables (☎ 970-464-0246) is located north of town near its namesake mountain, which towers over the airport and I-70. Rides in the scenic areas around Mt Garfield and the Bookcliffs start at $15 per hour ($12 for guests at the Melrose Hotel). The stables offer free pick-up from your hotel with minimum two-hour ride. This operation has gotten good reviews from visitors and enjoys a good deal of repeat business.

Golf
A short distance from downtown, Lincoln Park Golf Course (☎ 970-242-6394) is a nine-hole public facility with green fees of only $9 ($11 on weekends). Tiara Rado Golf Course (☎ 970-245-8085), west of town at the base of Colorado National Monument, reached via Hwy 340 to 2063 S Broadway, is an 18-hole public course with greens fees ranging from $15 to $18.

Special Events
The **Colorado Stampede Rodeo** happens in June, **Dinosaur Days** take place in July and the **Mesa County Fair** in August. In late September, Grand Junction celebrates local wineries with the three-day **Colorado Mountain Winefest**, featuring a bicycle tour of the Palisades wineries (see Around Grand Junction below).

Places to Stay
Grand Junction has abundant accommodations that are generally good value. Downtown is the most interesting area, but most of the newer places are along Horizon Drive (I-70 exit 31) near the airport. Summer is peak season, but seasonal price differences are only about 10%.

Camping There's plenty of good camping on surrounding NPS and BLM lands. Within city limits, try the *KOA Campground of Grand Junction* (☎ 970-434-6644), 3238 E I-70 Business Loop near Patterson Rd, reached by I-70 exit 37. Rates are $19 for tents, $21 for water and power, $23 for full hookups.

Hostels The nicely appointed *Hotel Melrose* (☎ 970-242-9636, 800-430-4555), 337 Colorado Ave, is housed in a restored 1908 building and offers dormitory beds (four to a room) for $12 (though open to everyone, HI/AYH members get first priority when space is limited). The hotel offers free airport pick-up for hostelers staying at least two nights, and also provides guests with discounts for bike and car rentals and horseback riding. It's conveniently located just several blocks away from downtown and the Amtrak and Greyhound stations. The Melrose also has some very nice hotel rooms (see below) and the friendly owners are happy to provide tips on sights and activities in the area. Reservations are advised year-round.

B&Bs The late 19th-century *Junction Country Inn* (☎ 970-241-2817), 861 Grand Ave, has rooms ranging from $35 (shared bath) to $79 (suite). Rooms at *The House on Ouray* (☎ 970-245-8452), a restored Victorian at 760 Ouray Ave, are all named for influential Colorado women. Singles/doubles range from $55/65 to $65/75.

Motels One of the cheapest spots near downtown is *Daniel's Motel* (☎ 970-243-1084), 333 North Ave, which has basic but adequate doubles for $35. Closer to Main St is *Value Lodge* (☎ 970-242-0651), 104 White Ave; singles/doubles are $34/37 and it has a swimming pool. The consistent (if unexciting) *Motel 6* (☎ 970-243-2628), out near the airport at 776 Horizon Drive, has singles/doubles for $30/35.

In the downtown area, *Two Rivers Inn* (☎ 970-245-8585) at 1st and Main Sts has fairly nice rooms, a pool, hot tub and discount breakfasts; singles/doubles go for $44/48. The owner can be a bit surly and the traffic noise from 1st St can be a little loud, but it's not a bad place to stay.

One of the better deals along Horizon Drive near the airport, the *Best Western Horizon Inn* (☎ 970-245-1410, 800-544-3782), 754 Horizon Drive, has singles/doubles for $45/50, a swimming pool, hot tub and complimentary Continental breakfast. *Budget Host* (☎ 970-243-6050), at 721 Horizon Drive, offers similar rates, a swimming pool and laundry facilities, though it's not as nice as the Best Western. Right at I-70 and Horizon Drive, the *Howard Johnson* motel (☎ 970-243-5150 is friendly and clean, with an outdoor pool and rooms from $50.

Hotels The *Hotel Melrose* (see Hostels above) has nicely furnished rooms in early 20th-century style with shared bath for $22 to $28; rooms with private bath are $34 to $59 – pretty much the best deal in town. Rates vary with the season, peaking in summer. The hotel offers free airport service for guests staying in private rooms, regardless of length of stay.

The *Grand Junction Hilton* (☎ 970-241-8888, 800-445-8667), 743 Horizon Drive, is considered the fanciest spot in town, with base rates staring at $89. The *Holiday Inn* (☎ 970-243-6790, 800-465-4229), 755 Horizon Drive, is a bit less upscale but still boasts both indoor and outdoor pools. Rates start at $74.

Places to Eat
Try the attractive *Crystal Cafe & Bake Shop* (☎ 970-242-8843), 314 Main St, for excellent breakfasts, lunches and baked goods. *Jitters* (☎ 970-245-5194), at 504 Main St, features '50s-style soda fountain decor and serves good breakfasts, sandwiches, espresso and Italian sodas. Another place for caffeine addicts is *Mountain Roasted Coffees* (☎ 970-242-5282), 620 Main St.

Junct'n Square (☎ 970-243-9750), at 119 N 7th St, specializes in pizza and is a good lunch choice. The *Rockslide Brewery* (☎ 970-245-2111) has decent lunches and dinners, though locals like it more for the beer. The *Blue Moon Bar & Grill* (☎ 970-242-5406), 120 N 7th St, is a lively spot with good salads and some interesting sandwiches and entrees (try the tuna steak sandwich).

Suehiro (☎ 970-245-9548), 541 Main St, is one of the few Japanese restaurants in western Colorado: the sushi is said to be good, though Grand Junction is admittedly a bit far from the ocean. *The Winery* (☎ 970-242-4100), at 642 Main St, downtown's most upscale restaurant, is a steak and seafood venue open for dinner only. Though only recently opened, *Melissa's Table* (☎ 970-245-8222), 319 Main St, is already quite popular for its gourmet menu.

For the best Southwest-Mexican food in town, head to *WW Peppers* (☎ 970-249-9251), 753 Horizon Court just off Horizon Drive.

Entertainment
Western Colorado doesn't generally have much in the way of nightlife, but Grand Junction does okay. The *Blue Moon Bar & Grill* (see Places to Eat above) often has good bands on the weekends, as does *The Station* (☎ 970-241-4613), at the corner of 7th and Main Sts. The *Poor House* (☎ 970-257-0475), at 715 Horizon Drive, is a rowdy college hangout that also offers live music several nights a week.

Getting There & Away
Air Walker Field, Grand Junction's commercial airport, is 6 miles northeast of downtown and just north of I-70, most easily reached by exit 31 (Horizon Drive).

America West has three to four flights daily to Phoenix, AZ, while Skywest (Delta Connection) has up to seven flights daily to Salt Lake City, UT. United has six to eight flights a day to Denver. Be warned that schedules are frequently subject to change and flights are often canceled if demand is slack.

Bus From the Greyhound depot (☎ 970-242-6012), at 830 S 5th St, there are five buses per day to Denver, three to Las Vegas, NV, and one to Salt Lake City. TNM&O

runs a daily bus to Montrose and Durango with connections to Albuquerque, NM, and one to Salida and Pueblo, with connections to Dallas.

Train Amtrak's passenger depot (☎ 970-241-2733) is at 339 S 1st St next to the old depot; there's a small information booth here as well. Amtrak's daily *California Zephyr* between Chicago and Oakland, CA, stops at 11:50 am eastbound, 5:20 pm westbound.

Car Grand Junction is 248 miles west of Denver via I-70 and 30 miles east of the Utah state line along the same interstate.

Getting Around
Enterprise Rent A Car (☎ 970-242-8103), with a convenient downtown location at 406 S 5th St two blocks from the Hotel Melrose, rents to drivers under 25 (though you still must be at least 21 and hold a major credit card). Hotel Melrose guests also get a discount here. Hertz (☎ 970-243-0747), Avis (☎ 970-244-9170), National (☎ 970-243-6626) and Budget (☎ 970-244-9155) have locations at Walker Field Airport. Thrifty Rent A Car (☎ 970-243-7556) is at 750¼ Horizon Drive.

AROUND GRAND JUNCTION
Dinosaur Hill
In 1900 paleontologist Elmer Riggs discovered the enormous and previously unknown *Brachiosaurus altithorax* near Grand Junction. He soon followed up with a nearly intact *Apatosaurus excelsus* (brontosaurus) at this site south of the Colorado River near Fruita. The site, which includes Riggs's original quarry and several fossil remnants in place, is now commemorated with a small reserve and interpretive trail. To get there, take Hwy 340 (I-70 exit 19) south from Fruita; the road continues south to Colorado National Monument.

Little Bookcliffs Wild Horse Range
Managed by the BLM, this 47-sq-mile unit is one of only three reserves in the entire country that is dedicated to protecting the

descendants of early Spanish horses. About 80 mustangs roam the area, reached by driving north from Grand Junction on 25 Rd. It is also accessible from the ghost town of Cameo (I-70 exit 46, then 10 miles north) or from DeBeque (I-70 exit 62). Hiking, horseback riding and mountain biking are permitted in the area, but most trails are fairly challenging. Camping is also allowed. Contact the BLM Grand Junction Resource Area Office (☎ 970-244-3000) for information and maps.

Wineries
Colorado is less than famous for its wines, but the Grand Valley, particularly nearby Palisade (I-70 exit 32), is home to a cluster of wineries producing both whites (mostly Chardonnay) and reds (Merlot and Pinot Noir) that are worth checking out. The dry climate, with a combination of warm days and cool nights, is in many ways ideal for grapes but occasional bitterly cold winters threaten the vines.

Plum Creek Cellars (☎ 970-464-7586), at 3708 G Rd in Palisade is open daily from 10 am to 5 pm. Carlson Vineyards (☎ 970-464-5554), 461 35 Rd, is open daily from 11 am to 6 pm, and Colorado Cellars Winery (☎ 970-464-7921), at 3553 E Rd, is open weekdays from 9 am to 4 pm, noon to 4 pm Saturday. Grande River Vineyards (☎ 970-464-5867), 3708 G Rd No 2, is open daily 10 am to 6 pm.

GRAND MESA
Towering above the Grand Valley, this 'island in the sky' is a lava-capped plateau rising more than 11,000 feet at its highest point. Its broad summit offers a delightful respite from the Grand Valley's summer heat, beautiful Alpine scenery and an interesting four-hour loop drive from Grand Junction via I-70, Hwy 65 and US 50 (with plenty of opportunities for side trips and stopovers). The highway passes through a number of distinct environments as it climbs the 6000-foot mesa, ranging from canyons of sage, piñon pines and junipers through areas of scrub oak and montane forests of Engelmann spruce

and Douglas fir to sub-Alpine forests and meadows.

There are several visitors centers on and around the mesa: The Grand Mesa Byway Welcome Center (☎ 970-856-3100) is on Hwy 65 in Cedaredge on the southern side of the mesa. Atop the mesa near Cobbet Lake, the Grand Mesa visitors center is at the intersection of Hwy 65 and USFS Rd 121. Land's End visitors center is at the southwest end of Land's End Rd, which leads to Hwy 50 and Grand Junction. All the centers generally operate from late May to mid-October. The USFS also has a ranger station (☎ 970-487-3534) at 218 High St in Collbran on the north side of the mesa.

Maps of trails and campsites and information on accommodations are also available from the visitors center in Grand Junction. 'The Grand Mesa Scenic Byway' is an annual publication that includes maps, important phone numbers, lodging, restaurant and historical information for the area.

Powderhorn Ski Area
Barely half an hour east of Grand Junction, on the northern slopes of Grand Mesa, is the convenient ski center (☎ 970-268-5700, 800-241-6997). Though not the most challenging terrain in the state, it often has excellent quality powder. Mostly intermediate runs traverse the 1650-foot vertical drop. Rentals and lessons are offered.

Crag Crest National Recreation Trail
Starting about half a mile west of Carp Lake on Hwy 65, this 10-mile loop follows the crest of the mesa before returning via a lower section past a series of attractive lakes; there's also an eastern trailhead from USFS Rd 121, a lateral off Hwy 65 just south of Carp Lake. The trail offers views of the Grand Valley and Uncompahgre Plateau to the west, Battlement Mesa to the north, the Elk Mountains to the east and the San Juan Mountains to the south.

Places to Stay
There are 12 USFS *campgrounds* in the Grand Mesa National Forest, most of which

levy fees of $7 to $9. There are also *lodges* at Alexander Lake (☎ 970-856-6700), Grand Mesa (☎ 970-856-3250) and Powderhorn (☎ 970-268-5700). Rates generally range from $35 to $50 for motel or lodge rooms to $65 and $70 for cabins equipped with kitchens. Some lodges close for the winter, so call ahead to check.

COLORADO NATIONAL MONUMENT

From the Uncompahgre Uplift of the Colorado Plateau, 2000 feet above the Grand Valley of the Colorado River, half a dozen or more accessible colorful sandstone canyons precipitously descend to the flatlands. Once dinosaur country, this 32-sq-mile scenic wonder is one of the most rewarding side trips possible from an interstate highway, well worth a detour by car but even better for backcountry exploration. Open all year, it's an exceptional area for hiking, camping and road biking.

History

The US government created the monument after sustained lobbying by the citizens of Grand Junction and at the urging of John Otto, one of the oddest champions

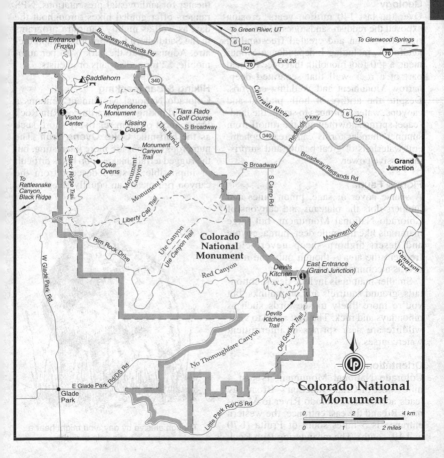

Colorado National Monument

imaginable of a national park. The socialist Otto once assaulted Colorado Governor James Peabody with a sharpened candlestick in Peabody's office, and after his release from prison lived as a hermit in the canyon country west of Grand Junction.

He built trails throughout the area to make it more accessible to the public; finally, his efforts paid off. After the monument was established, Otto served as park caretaker until 1927 for a token wage. He eventually found his way west to California, where he died in the city of Yreka.

Geology
Over the last 140 million years, erosion exposed the reddish sandstones of the Morrison formation and created freestanding landforms, including Independence Monument, a 450-foot monolith that once formed part of a rock wall that separated deep, narrow Monument and Wedding canyons. Despite the aridity of both plateau and canyons, water continues to sculpt the landscape; spring snowmelt and the runoff from summer thunderstorms can create ephemeral waterfalls of great beauty and surprising erosive power.

Flora & Fauna
A sparse cover of sage, piñon pines and junipers dots the plateaus and canyons of Colorado National Monument, but large mammals like the mule deer, puma, coyote and desert bighorn sheep nevertheless frequent the area – though only the mule deer is a common sight.

Smaller mammals include desert cottontails, ground squirrels and chipmunks, but you're more likely to see birds such as piñon jays and rock. The best spots to view wildlife are near springs or intermittent watercourses.

Orientation
Colorado National Monument is just 4 miles west of Grand Junction – Broadway leads across the Colorado River to Monument Rd and the east entrance; the western entrance is 5 miles south of Fruita (I-70 exit 19, south). The meandering Rim Rock Drive, which links the two entrances, is a popular drive with many exceptional overlooks, and an even better bicycle route. The best way to see the monument is on foot through the canyons.

Information
The Colorado National Monument visitors center (☎ 970-858-3617), on the plateau at the north end of the park, is open daily 9 am to 5 pm (8 am to 7 pm Memorial Day to Labor Day). There are brochures, including the standard NPS map of the monument, a selection of books and maps and a theater for audiovisual presentations. NPS rangers offer guided hikes throughout the day, as well as nightly campfire programs in the Saddlehorn Campground Amphitheatre. Admission to the park is $4 per automobile, $2 for pedestrians or cyclists.

Hiking & Backpacking
Colorado National Monument contains a variety of hiking trails starting on Rim Rock Drive, most of them relatively short, such as the half-mile **Coke Ovens Trail**. The numerous canyons are more interesting, but the rugged terrain makes loop hikes difficult or impossible; a steep descent from the canyon rim means an equally steep ascent

Though elusive by day, you might hear a coyote's eerie yelp at night.

on the return. One alternative is to use either a car or bicycle shuttle, since some trailheads outside the park are reached most easily from Hwy 340, the Broadway/Redlands Rd between Fruita and Grand Junction.

Perhaps the most rewarding trail is the 6-mile **Monument Canyon Trail**, leading from Rim Rock Drive down to Hwy 340 past many of the park's most interesting natural features, including the Coke Ovens, the Kissing Couple and Independence Monument. Another possibility is the less precipitous **Liberty Cap Trail**, which links up with the much steeper **Ute Canyon Trail** to form a lengthy 14-mile loop. The Ute Canyon Trail is more of an undeveloped cross-country route, though never difficult to follow because its narrow walls restrict off-trail roaming. Some hikers may prefer to begin with the steep descent into Ute Canyon, returning up the Liberty Cap Trail.

The backcountry of Colorado National Monument is open for backpacking, but requires carrying water and camping at least a quarter-mile from any road and 100 yards off all trails. Backcountry permits are also required, and can be obtained free of charge at the Saddlehorn visitors center.

Hikers should watch out for thunderstorms that can cause flash floods in the monument's normally dry watercourses; be aware of weather reports and stick to high ground accordingly. There are rattlesnakes in the area but hikers are unlikely to encounter them. In hot weather, carry plenty of water to avoid heat exhaustion.

Road Biking

Rim Rock Drive is a popular ride for cyclists, usually done in a loop via Hwy 340. The eastern approach from Grand Junction is shorter but steeper; the western approach from Fruita involves a continued climb even after reaching the visitors center. On the western approach, take special caution for automobile traffic through the tunnels.

Be aware that mountain bikes are strictly prohibited on all park trails.

Rock Climbing

Features like Independence Monument and The Island, both along Monument Canyon Trail, are challenges to rock climbers – not least because their sedimentary rock is more fragile than the more stable granite faces found elsewhere in the state. (For information on maps, local tips and equipment, see Rock Climbing in the Grand Junction section above.)

Places to Stay

Saddlehorn Campground near the visitors center has the only formal sites within the park proper; for \$10, you get spectacular views of the canyons and the Grand Valley below. Backcountry camping (defined as being at least a quarter-mile off the road and 100 yards from any trail) is free.

DELTA

Once known as Uncompahgre (after the Utes it displaced), this gateway to the north rim of the Black Canyon of the Gunnison is a small but attractive crossroads town (population 4200). Its downtown historic district is graced by a series of interesting murals along Main St and its cross streets depicting Delta's history, society and environment. The murals are a good reason to stop here for lunch and an afternoon stroll.

The Delta Chamber of Commerce (☎ 970-874-8616), 301 Main St, is open weekdays 9 am to 5 pm and has information on sights in and around town. The USFS Grand Mesa, Uncompahgre and Gunnison National Forest Headquarters (☎ 970-874-6600) is south of town at 2250 US 50.

Norwest Bank has an ATM at 500 Palmer St. The post office is at 360 Meeker St; the zip code is 81416.

Places to Stay

Delta has several convenient campgrounds/-RV parks. The shady *Flying A Campground* (☎ 970-874-9659), 676 N US 50, charges \$11 to \$13 for tent sites, \$16 for full hookups. Across the highway at 677 N US 50, the *Riverwood Inn* (☎ 970-874-5787) is equally shady and slightly cheaper.

At the *South Gate Inn* (☎ 970-874-9726, 800-621-2271), at 2124 S Main St, rates start at $30 and include pool and hot tub access. The *El-D-Rado Motel* (☎ 970-874-4493), 702 Main St, has $30/35 singles/doubles (but no pool or hot tub). The *Flying A Motel* (☎ 970-874-9659) at 676 N US 50, has clean singles/doubles for $37/41. Going slightly upmarket, the *Sundance Best Western* (☎ 970-874-9781), 903 Main St, has rooms ranging from $40 to $49.

Places to Eat
The Eatery (☎ 970-874-9634), 305 Main St, is a pleasant soup and sandwich place. *Leon's Mexican Restaurant* (☎ 970-874-0309), at 420 Main St, has decent, moderately priced food. *Daveto's* (☎ 970-874-8277), 520 Main St, is the choice for Italian food.

Getting There & Away
Bus TNM&O/Greyhound (☎ 970-874-9455) buses depart from the depot at 270 E Hwy 92 (1st St) once daily for Montrose, Durango, and Albuquerque, N.M., and Montrose, Salida and Pueblo. There are also two buses daily to Grand Junction, where you can connect with buses to Denver, Salt Lake City, UT, and points beyond.

Car At the confluence of the Gunnison and Uncompahgre rivers, Delta is 40 miles southeast of Grand Junction and 21 miles northwest of Montrose via US 50.

PAONIA
For its size, Paonia (population 1600) offers a surprising combination of natural beauty, working-class society and liberal culture. Surrounded by the North Fork Valley's charming countryside of farms and wildlands, it also has a bundle of late 19th-century buildings in superb condition and is the home of *High Country News*, one of the country's most outspoken environmental publications. The casual visitor hardly notices that coal mining is still a significant local industry.

Information
The main street is north-south Grand Ave; most services are located along this strip, though some restaurants and lodging can be found along Hwy 133. Just to keep things confusing, most locals refer to Grand Ave as 'Main St,' not to be confused with Main Ave, which lies one block west of Grand Ave.

The chamber of commerce (☎ 970-527-3886), in the DE Frey office at 124 Grand Ave, is usually open weekdays 9 am to 3 pm, though hours vary as the office is a volunteer operation. The USFS Paonia Ranger Station (☎ 970-527-4131) is on Rio Grande Ave eight blocks east of Grand Ave along 3rd St, then one long block north (left).

Paonia State Bank is at 128 Grand Ave. The post office is at 125 Grand Ave; the zip code is 81428.

The Clock Laundromat is on 3rd St just east of Grand Ave.

Historic District & Murals
Grand Ave in downtown Paonia features interesting early 20th-century buildings, most notably Curtis Co Hardware (1902) and the United Mine Workers Building (1903). Away from Grand Ave there is an excellent selection of Victorian houses, as well as landmarks like the turreted Queen Anne-style Christian Church at the corner of E 3rd St and Box Elder Ave.

An excellent mural of Paonia's history adorns the wall in the mini-park just north of the Paradise Theatre on Grand Ave. An even more imposing five-wall mural at the corner of 3rd St and Grand Ave depicts five successive nightly camps of the Domínguez-Escalante Expedition in August 1776.

Farmers Market
From July to mid-October, Tuesdays and Fridays 9 am to 4 pm, North Fork Valley farmers bring fresh and organic produce to the Paonia Farmers Market in the mini-park north of the Paradise Theatre.

High Country News Tour
Available by subscription only, the West's crusading, environmentally oriented news-

paper started nearly 30 years ago in Lander, WY, under the auspices of rancher-conservationist Tom Bell. The publication moved to Paonia after it was purchased by Ed and Betsy Marston. (Bell is now 'Publisher Emeritus.') Deadlines permitting, the staff welcomes visitors for office tours (☎ 970-527-4898) at 119 Grand Ave, a retrofitted former feed and auto parts store that won a US Department of Energy award for its energy efficiency.

Subscriptions to *High Country News*, which appears biweekly (one issue only in January and July), are $28 a year for individuals. Write: PO Box 1090, Paonia, CO 81428, or phone (☎ 800-905-1155).

West Elk Wilderness

Readily accessible from Paonia via a 4WD road that parallels Minnesota Creek, Gunnison National Forest's expansive West Elk Wilderness is a 900-square-mile roadless area with a dense 200-mile trail network capped by the 13,035-foot West Elk Peak. There are other points of access along Hwy 133 east of Paonia and from Crawford south of Paonia. Pamphlets with details about the area's various recreational

People-Powered Radio

Anyone traveling in the area should tune into Paonia's lively community-based NPR affiliate, KVNF-FM (90.9), which recalls the free-form radio of the 1960s in its mix of music, news and opinion. Besides *Morning Edition*, *All Things Considered* and other news features, it carries an eclectic mix of local programs featuring bluegrass, new releases, blues, Latin and rock music.

KVNF-FM is also heard in other nearby communities including Delta/Cedaredge (89.9), Montrose (89.1), Ouray (90.1), Lake City (88.7), Ridgway (88.9), Hotchkiss (98.3) and Grand Junction (99.1). It makes for a good traveling companion as you drive through the area's beautiful scenery. ∎

activity opportunities are available at the Paonia and Delta USFS offices.

Special Events

On the 4th of July, **Paonia Cherry Days**, celebrating the season's first fruit to reach the market, also features a rodeo. The **Delta County Fair & Rodeo** takes place in August at nearby Hotchkiss.

Places to Stay & Eat

The lack of accommodations helps keep outsiders from overrunning Paonia, but also means that reservations are necessary if you're going there in autumn, when hunters book up all the rooms.

Rates at the friendly family-run *Rocky Mountain Inn* (☎ 970-527-3070), at 3rd and Niagara Sts, start at $39 for doubles. The *Redwood Arms Motel* (☎ 970-527-4148), about a mile west of town at 1478 Hwy 133, has singles/doubles for $40/50.

A restored hotel that first opened in 1906, the *Bross Hotel Bed & Breakfast* (☎ 970-527-6776), 312 Onarga St one block east of Grand Ave, now has 10 early 20th-century rooms ranging from $60 to $85. Modern amenities include hot tub, phones and fax service.

The Diner (☎ 970-527-4774), 203 Grand Ave, is a conventional American restaurant open for breakfast, lunch and dinner Monday to Saturday; breakfast and lunch only on Sunday. *Linda's 3rd St Bistro* (☎ 970-527-6146) is only open Thursday to Saturday, but locals say Linda's Mexican food is definitely worth trying. Next door, *Moonrise Espresso Co* (☎ 970-527-5551) has tasty baked goods and all sorts of coffees. It's open 7 am to 2 pm weekdays; 8 am to noon Saturday. *The Casa* (☎ 970-527-4343), 312 Grand Ave, is Paonia's most upscale restaurant, serving Italian, Mexican and vegetarian dishes pricier than anyplace else in town but also better – well worth it for a splurge.

Getting There & Away

At the base of the West Elk Mountains, on the east bank of the North Fork of the

Gunnison River, Paonia is 29 miles east of Delta via Hwys 92 and then 133, and 72 miles south of Glenwood Springs by Hwy 133.

MONTROSE

Montrose (population 11,000) is an agricultural center and wholesale supply point for Telluride, 65 miles to the south. The Ute Museum in town and the Black Canyon of the Gunnison National Monument to the east on Hwy 50, typically visited as a day trip, are the only real attractions for visitors.

Recent improvements at Montrose Regional Airport make it a viable alternative when adverse weather shuts down the airfield at Telluride.

Information

The Montrose Chamber of Commerce (☎ 970-249-5000, 800-923-5515) is located at 1519 E Main St (Hwy 50), east of the Red Barn restaurant. Among other pamphlets, it offers a visitor's guide listing accommodations, restaurants and things to see and do in the area. Hours are 9 am to 5 pm weekdays. There's also a smaller visitors center (☎ 970-249-1726) open 9 am to 4 pm Monday to Saturday at the Ute Indian Museum (see below).

The Montrose Public Lands Office (☎ 970-240-5300) combines the offices of the BLM, NPS and USFS. It's located toward the south edge of town at 2505 S Townsend Ave (Hwy 550, within city limits). The office offers maps and access information for surrounding public lands and is open weekdays 7:30 am to 4:30 pm. For information on viewing wildlife, stop by the Colorado DOW (☎ 970-249-3431), 2300 S Townsend Ave.

Bank One has a 24-hour ATM machine at 401 E Main St, not far from the intersection with Townsend Ave. The post office is at 321 S 1st St; the zip code is 81401.

Ute Indian Museum

Near the US 550 bridge over the Uncompahgre River south of town, the Ute Indian Museum (☎ 970-249-3098), 17253 Chipeta Rd, was the homestead site of Chief Ouray

and his wife Chipeta. Gallery exhibits of photos, artifacts and clothing highlight and explain Ute ceremonies and the sad chronology of the occupation of their Colorado lands.

Chipeta died in Utah in 1924 and her remains were returned to the homestead in 1925 at the request of Montrose citizens who gathered almost 5000 people into a mile-long procession to the crypt.

The museum is open May 15 to September 30, 10 am to 5 pm Monday to Saturday, 1 to 5 pm Sunday. Admission is $2.50/1.50 adults/children.

Places to Stay & Eat

Near the Chamber of Commerce, the *Log Cabin Motel* (☎ 970-249-7610), at 1034 E Main St, is a cozy little place with singles/doubles for $32/38 (rates are slightly higher in summer, lower in winter). In the same area, the basic but clean *Trapper Motel* (☎ 970-249-3426, 800-858-5911), 1225 E Main St, has singles/doubles from $38/43. At 10 N Townsend Ave near the intersection with Main St, the *Mesa Hotel* (☎ 970-249-3773) looks interesting but is actually a bit grotty and geared more toward long-term residents. Rooms with kitchenettes cost $38.

At 320 Main St, *Stockmen's Cafe & Bar* (☎ 970-249-9946) is a local fixture serving typical western American and Mexican fare, including hefty breakfasts. Just down the street at the corner of Main and Cascade Sts, *Daily Bread Bakery* (☎ 970-249-8444) serves tasty breakfasts and lunches as well as fined baked goodies 6 am to 4 pm Monday to Saturday.

Getting There & Away

Air Passengers to/from Telluride are the primary customers at the Montrose Regional Airport (☎ 970-249-8455), north of town on US 50. United Express runs flights to Denver, while America West has direct flights to Phoenix, AZ. During ski season there are direct flights to and from Chicago and Denver (United), Houston, TX, and Newark, NJ, (Continental), and Phoenix (America West).

Telluride Shuttle Shuttles to Telluride cost $25 with a four-person minimum. Contact Telluride Transit (☎ 970-249-6993) or Skip's Telluride Taxi & Shuttle Service (☎ 970-240-4348).

Bus TNM&O buses stop at the depot (☎ 970-249-6673), 132 N 1st St in the old Coors building, opposite a mural of fighting cocks. Two northbound buses serve Grand Junction, while one southbound bus travels to Durango and an eastbound bus serves Pueblo.

Getting Around
At the airport you will find Budget (☎ 970-249-6083) and Hertz (☎ 970-249-9447).

BLACK CANYON OF THE GUNNISON NATIONAL MONUMENT
Black Canyon's dark narrow gash above the Gunnison River is not the most photogenic spot in Colorado – shadows are everywhere, hence the name – but the almost 2000-foot-deep chasm evokes a sense of awe and vertigo for some visitors as they look over the edge. In some places, Black Canyon is narrower than it is deep. As an NPS ranger commented, 'Black Canyon is like most national parks were 20 years ago' – no tour buses, little traffic and outstanding views.

Orientation & Information
Except as a vista from the South Rim, the remote North Rim has little to offer. From Montrose, it's 8 miles to the Hwy 347 turnoff, then 7 miles to the visitors center on the South Rim. At the junction, Black Canyon Corner (☎ 970-249-5113) offers a good selection of topo maps of the region.

The visitors center (☎ 970-249-1915) is at Gunnison Point, the second viewpoint, and offers detailed displays on the canyon's geology and wildlife.

Admission costs $7 per vehicle or $4 for bikes and is good for seven days. Visitors receive a map and brochure describing the monument (also available in German).

NPS rangers provide information and free permits for camping and technical

climbing in Black Canyon. In winter the visitors center is closed but South Rim Rd is plowed to Gunnison Point for cross-country skiers. There is no phone at the North Rim Ranger Station, which offers climbing information and a nearby campground. In the winter, the North Rim Rd from Crawford is closed.

South Rim Rd
The 6-mile-long plateau-top road takes you to the edge of the canyon and to 11 overlooks, some reached by short trails of up to 1½ miles roundtrip. Many of the canyon walls have a fin-like appearance resulting from the differing erosion rates of the rocks. The light igneous rocks known as pegmatite dikes, molten intrusions into the rock mass, are more resistant to erosion than the darker metamorphosed gneiss.

At the narrowest part of Black Canyon, **Chasm View** is only 1100 feet across yet 1800 feet deep. Rock climbers are frequently seen on the opposing North Wall, among the most popular and challenging climbs in the park. Colorado's highest cliff face is the 2300-foot **Painted Wall** – just straying from the fenced overlook represents a Class III scramble that most will find scary.

An ideal way to see the canyon is by cycling along the smooth pavement with a 2000-foot drop by your side – you definitely get a better feel for the place than if you're trapped in a car.

Hiking
The **Rim Rock Trail** connects Tomichi Point with the visitors center only a quarter-mile away. From the visitors center, the easy 1½-mile loop **Oak Flat Trail**, on the plateau through gambel oak, Douglas fir and aspen, offers good views of Black Canyon. Plan to take the **Warner Point Nature Trail**, a 1½-mile roundtrip at the end of South Rim Rd, before watching the sunset from either High Point or Sunset View overlooks. Rangers can provide information and a backcountry permit if you want to descend one of the South Rim's three unmarked routes on talus to

the infrequently visited riverside camp-sites. From the remote North Rim, the **SOB Trail** heads to the river.

Fishing

From the upstream boundary of the Monu-ment to the confluence with the North Fork is some of the best fishing in Colorado for large numbers of 16- to 25-inch rainbow and brown trout. Whoppers over five pounds are not uncommon in this 26-mile stretch of Gold Medal water.

Within the monument itself, the so-called trails into the canyon are just steep rock chutes that entail a strenuous day of work to complete the roundtrip, difficult if you're laden with fishing gear. Four longer and less strenuous trails reach the lower gorge below the monument from Peach Valley Rd east of Olathe.

Places to Stay

Near the entrance station, *South Rim Campground* has over 100 campsites on a first-come, first-served basis and drinking water hauled in by tank truck. Camping is $8 in summer, free in winter. You can camp near the river at the *East Portal Camp-ground*, a part of the Curecanti National Recreation Area, for the same fees. The *North Rim Campground*, accessed by a dirt road beyond the North Rim Ranger Sta-tion, also costs $8 per night; closed in winter.

CURECANTI NATIONAL RECREATION AREA

The Gunnison River, once free-flowing through the canyons, is now plugged by three dams to create Curecanti. A more apt and official title is the Wayne N Aspinal Storage Unit, named for a US Represen-tative (1948-73) who never met a water project he did not like. Many RVs are strangely attracted to the bleak and windy shores of chilly Blue Mesa Reservoir which the NRA surrounds.

Stunning landforms that survived immer-sion are the unsinkable Curecanti Needle and Dillon Pinnacles, a volcanic breccia capped by welded tuff.

The Elk Creek visitors center (☎ 970-641-2337, ext 205), on US 50 6 miles west of the junction with Hwy 149 to Lake City, offers topo maps and exhibits describing the area's cultural and natural history. It's open daily 8 am to 4.30 pm (until 6 pm in summer). There are also information cen-ters at Cimarron and Lake Fork, which only operate from late May to late September.

Places to Stay Curecanti has 10 camp-sites, most of which charge fees of $8 or $9 in summer, sometimes less in spring and summer. Some, such as *Elk Creek* and *Lake Fork*, are developed, with showers and flush toilets, while others are more basic. For hikers there are also small camp-grounds at the end of the Curecanti Creek Trail (2 miles) and Hermit's Rest Trail (3 miles). The latter descends 1800 feet, so be prepared for a steep climb back out.

Southern Plateau

The southwest section of this region is also know as the 'Four Corners' area, in refer-ence the point where the borders of Colo-rado, New Mexico, Arizona and Utah meet. This is the only place in the country where four state borders intersect. Here the mountains and mesas give way to desert, a stark contrast with the rest of Colorado.

The prime attractions in this area are the many ruins of the pre-Colombian peoples known formally as the Ancestral Puebloans. These early inhabitants built elaborate primordial cities at Mesa Verde – first on the mesatops, later high above the canyon floors in the recesses of cliff faces. Together the Mesa Verde National Park and Ute Mountain Tribal Park protect the archaeological remains at hundreds of these prehistoric communities, while pro-viding access to a few of the most spectac-ular sites for nearly a million visitors each year. Encircling the southern national park boundaries is the 195-sq-mile Ute Moun-tain Tribal Park. No road access exists between the two parks.

Nearby towns such as Cortez and Mancos offer places to stay and further information about the Ancestral Puebloans and their legacy. A bit farther north is the sleepy Dolores River Canyon, which offers untrammeled access to desert backcountry hiking, biking and river-rafting.

Four Corners Monument

Navajo sand painter Lyn Elwood, a resident of Shiprock, New Mexico, works in Arizona, parks her truck in Colorado and eats lunch in Utah – all at what is the closest thing to a tourist trap in the Colorado Plateau, the Four Corners Monument. It's actually entertaining to watch the antics of tourist as they pose on all fours on this inlaid concrete monument to political geography – where the borders of four states meet. Then it's your turn!

In addition, Native Americans operate 40 licensed stalls – *ramadas* – that encircle the monument, selling food and handicrafts. Four Corners Monument is 38 miles south of Cortez on US 160; the turnoff is on your right soon after crossing the San Juan River. It's open daily from 7 am to 7 pm; admission is $1.

DOLORES

Dolores (population 1000), enjoys a scenic location in the narrow Dolores River Canyon 11 miles north of Cortez on Hwy 145. Housed in a replica of the town's old railroad depot, the Dolores visitors center (☎ 970-882-4018, 800-807-4712), at 421 Railroad Ave (Hwy 145), has information on lodging and outdoor activities in the area. It's open from May to October 9 am to 5 pm Monday to Saturday, 10 am to 4 pm Sunday. Adjacent to the visitors center is the **Galloping Goose Museum**, which has displays and one example of the rather odd-looking gasoline-powered vehicles used by the Rio Grande Southern Railroad to continue rail service into the San Juan Mountains during the economic troubles of the 1930s.

You can find out about nearby camping and hiking opportunities in the San Juan National Forest at the USFS Dolores Ranger Station (☎ 970-882-7296) at the corner of 6th St and Central Ave. It's open 8 am to 5 pm weekdays year-round. To get cleaned up after your outings, the Dolores Laundry & Public Showers, 302 Railroad Ave, offers a shower and towel for about $3.

The first weekend of June is **River Raft Days**, a playful event that Dolores residents have informally staged on the Dolores River for years in just about anything that would float. Now it also features a strenuous competitive paddle race attracting teams in three classes that put in 9 miles upstream from town. To register for the 'fun float' contact the Dolores Chamber of Commerce (☎ 970-882-4018).

Places to Stay & Eat

The *Dolores River RV Park* (☎ 970-882-7761), located about 1½ miles east of town at 18680 Hwy 145, has pleasantly located tent sites for $11. RV hookups are $18.

At the east end of town, the *Outpost Motel* (☎ 970-882-7271, 800-382-4892) has small but clean singles/doubles for $39/49, as well as cabins for $89. Most of the motel rooms have kitchenettes and the courtyard features a pleasant little wooden deck overlooking the Dolores River. *Dolores Mountain Inn* (☎ 970-882-7203, 800-842-8113), 701 Railroad Ave (Hwy 145), has immaculate modern rooms for $54/58 ($40/45 in winter). The motel's genial owner also offers bike rentals, shuttle service and guided tours.

Near the visitors center and listed on the National Register of Historic Places, the three-story *Rio Grande Southern Hotel* (☎ 970-882-7527), 101 S 1st St, dates from 1893 and has B&B singles/doubles with shared bath for $35/50; rooms with private bath are $49/65. The restaurant has good breakfasts, including tasty omelets and homefries for $5, as well as inexpensive lunch specials. The hotel is closed from late November to early March.

The Outpost Motel, Dolores Mountain Inn and Rio Grande Southern participate in a 'Half Price Ski Telluride' program, offering savings for winter visitors who

The Sorrows of the Dolores

The loneliest area of Colorado may be the Dolores River Canyon. In 1776 Father Escalante gave the river its Spanish name, Río de Nuestra Señora de los Dolores (River of Our Lady of Sorrows); much later Alfred Castner King provided a poetic interpretation of the 'river of sorrow.' After losing his sight, King published the poem 'Dolores' in a 1907 collection of his work on the San Juan Mountains titled *The Passing of the Storm*. The following lines from 'Dolores' reflect the feeling of solitude that the starkly beautiful red rock landscape evokes:

…Long ago, ere the foot of the white man	Gone, gone are this people forever,
Had left its first print on the sod,	Not a vestige nor remnant remains
A people, both free and contented,	To gather the maize in its season
Her mesas and cañon-ways trod.	And join in the harvest refrains;
Then Dolores, the river of sorrow,	But the river still mourns for her people
Was a river of laughter and glee…	With weird and disconsolate flow,
As she playfully dashed through the cañons	Dolores, the river of sorrow,
In her turbulent rush to the sea….	Dolores – the river of woe.

King's reference to the 'weird flow' rings true in many ways. Paradox Valley is so named because the river cuts across the narrow part of the valley through notches in the rimrock cliffs, rather than flowing along the valley length. The stunning palisade formation at Gateway Palisades marks the entrance to Unaweep Canyon which slices through the Uncompahgre Plateau. 'Unaweep' is a Ute term meaning 'the canyon with two mouths,' a reference to its curious drainage divided between East Creek, which flows to the Gunnison River, and the West Creek mouth. An 1889 attempt to engineer an elaborate 'hanging flume' on the walls of the Dolores Canyon to deliver water to its intended target, the Lone Tree Placer mine, failed through miscalculation.

Another well-regarded author, David Lavender, chronicled his early experiences in the Dolores River Canyon during the 1930s. In a folksy first-person manner, Lavender captures the life of the rancher in this remote corner of Colorado in his 1943 book *One Man's West* (University of Nebraska Press, 1977). Lavender witnessed the boom-and-bust that uranium mining brought to the region, leaving the land as forsaken as before mining arrived. Later editions of the book note the sudden attention that atomic weapons brought to the haunting canyonlands of the Dolores River during WWII. ■

stay in Dolores before heading to Telluride 68 miles to the northeast.

Get started with a good espresso at the *German Stone Oven Bakery Cafe* (☎ 970-882-7033), 811 Railroad Ave. The owners serve delicious Belgian waffles or German pancake breakfasts for under $5. An extensive *Bierliste* is offered by the *Old Germany Restaurant* (☎ 970-882-7549), at 200 S 8th St, which has tasty German entrees like pork tenderloin with potato dumplings, soup, salad and dessert for $16.

DOLORES RIVER CANYON

This area used to be bustling with uranium mine activity, reflected by the good condi-tion of Hwy 141 through Unaweep Canyon, widened in the 1950s by the US Atomic Energy Commission to provide access to the now abandoned mines and mills. The wildflower meadows in the deep canyon are silent now that traditional ranch operations have resumed as the economic mainstay. Most recently, rafting and mountain biking have boosted the local economy.

Stark sandstone formations, mesas covered with dark patches of piñon-juniper and sagebrush valleys, whose primary inhabitants are prairie dogs and ever-watchful raptors, are reminiscent of Utah's canyon lands. The Dolores and San Miguel rivers beckon some travelers, while the

'Uranium Road' may intrigue others. A great sandstone formation, the **Palisade**, looms as you follow the winding road down to the isolated Dolores River Canyon and the small community at Gateway.

Hwy 141 is designated as part of the Unaweep/Tabeguache Scenic & Historic Byway. Tabeguache Utes inhabited the Uncompahgre Plateau until they were removed to Utah in 1881. (Tabeguache means 'place where the snow melts first.') The **Tabeguache Trail** follows the Uncompahgre Plateau through the Uncompahgre National Forest.

Orientation & Information

To travel between Cortez and Grand Junction, you can either combine the winding, twisting, narrow Hwys 145 and 62 through the scenic San Juan Mountains over Lizard Head Pass and Dallas Divide with US 50, or take the winding, twisting, narrow Hwy 141. Fewer travelers choose the latter route, which stretches 159 miles along the Dolores River Canyon between Dove Creek, 35 miles north of Cortez, and the US 50 turnoff to Unaweep Canyon, 9 miles south of Grand Junction.

A brochure describing the sights along these routes is available at the Colorado Welcome Center in either Cortez or Fruita. The Nucla-Naturita Chamber of Commerce (☎ 970-865-2350), 217 W Main St (Hwy 141) in Naturita, or the Dove Creek Chamber of Commerce (☎ 970-677-2245), 128 Hwy 666, also offer this and other information.

Dove Creek

Located on US 666 35 miles north of Cortez and 2 miles south of Hwy 141, Dove Creek (population 710) claims to be the 'Pinto Bean Capital of the World.' Recently nonirrigated growers have rediscovered the beans grown by the Anasazi (Ancestral Puebloans) and found that they are sweeter, prettier and – most importantly – cause less flatulence than the high-carbohydrate pinto bean. Anasazi beans are marketed by Adobe Milling (☎ 970-677-2620, 800-542-3623) which offers gourmet beans and recipes to visitors. Unfortunately, the nearest restaurants serving 'gourmet' beans are in Mesa Verde and Durango, but you can sample a bowl of old-fashioned gas-inducing pinto beans at the *Blue Mountain Cafe* (☎ 970-677-2261), US 666 at the north end of town. Rooms at the *Country Inn Motel* (☎ 970-677-2234) start at $34, $28 in winter.

Naturita

Compared to the surrounding area, Naturita (population 490), situated along Hwy 141 and the San Miguel River 59 miles north of Dove Creek, is a thriving metropolis. The yellow carnotite ore (containing uranium) brought a burst of activity to a region that has since reverted to a largely uninhabited state.

Overlooking the valley, the *Bunkhouse Motel* (☎ 970-865-2893), 118 Hwy 97, offers singles/doubles for $30/35. Rooms start at $38 at the *Ray Motel* (☎ 970-865-2235), at 123 Main St (Hwy 141). Across the street, the *Yellow Rock* (☎ 970-865-2599) serves hamburger steak dinners for about $5.

Bedrock

An 18-mile side trip on Hwy 90 follows a still-used stock driveway into Paradox Valley to the Dolores River crossing and the solitary Bedrock Store (☎ 970-859-7395). Built in 1876, the store's two-story masonry construction makes a visit to the refrigerated cold case a real treat on a hot day. Historic displays of old merchandise make this one of the most unique stops in the state.

At the west end of the valley, the La Sal Mountains rise like a forested island amid a desert. From the Hwy 90 turnoff to Paradox, it's 14 miles to Buckeye Reservoir in the Manti-La Sal National Forest in Utah.

White-Water Rafting

Although the McPhee Reservoir interrupts the Dolores River, the 150-mile stretch from below the dam to the Utah state line offers springtime runs that are unequaled for their combination of the beauty and solitude of canyon country with occasional technical whitewater challenges. The terrain along the river changes from ponderosa pines to piñon-juniper and red rock. You can even continue all the way to the Colorado River above Cataract Canyon through Canyonlands National Park.

From the USFS Bradfield Campground & Launch Site (see Around Cortez – Places to Stay later), it's a 49-mile trip with some Class IV rapids to Slick Rock.

From Slick Rock to the historic Bedrock Store in the Paradox Valley it's another 48 miles on Class II-III waters. The 48-mile trip from Bedrock to Gateway passes the historic hanging flume cantilevered from the shear walls of the Dolores Canyon and includes a few stretches of Class IV whitewater. By early June, the entire excursion may take 10 days due to low water.

If planning your own trip, be sure to purchase Ralph DeVries' and Stephen Maurer's *Dolores River Guide*. Alternatively, a couple of commercial river guides offer package trips into this desert wilderness. Wilderness Aware (☎ 800-462-7238) offers three-, six- and 10-day trips that explore the cultural and natural history along the river for $325 to $900. Also try Rocky Mountain Adventures (☎ 800-858-6808), which has a good reputation and international rafting experience; they offer three- and six-day trips for $300 and $600.

Mountain Biking
A 26-mile trail along the red-rock Dolores River Canyon from Dove Creek to near Slick Rock offers an easy ride and swimming opportunities during the first 11 miles to the Pyramid. The remainder is a more challenging ride involving a potentially dangerous river ford followed by steep climbs. Stop by the Dove Creek Chamber of Commerce (☎ 970-677-2245) for information on river conditions and a map and description of the route. One-way riders on this trail can arrange for a shuttle with Slick Rock Shuttle Service (☎ 970-677-2772).

The 142-mile **Tabeguache Trail**, comprising single-track trails and Divide Rd

across the Uncompahgre Plateau, connects Montrose and Grand Junction; the trail is marked by brown fiberglass posts every half-mile. For a map and trail log contact the Colorado Plateau Mountain Bike Trail Association (☎ 970-241-9561), PO Box 4602, Grand Junction, CO 81502. Forest maps and camping information for the Dolores Canyon area are available from the USFS Dolores Ranger Station (☎ 970-882-7298) in Dolores, while maps and information for the Tabeguache are available at the USFS offices in Montrose (☎ 970-240-5300) and in Grand Junction (☎ 970-242-8211).

MANCOS
The historic homes and landmark buildings in Mancos (population 1000), between Cortez and Durango, make for a worthwhile afternoon stop or a pleasant place to stay while visiting Mesa Verde National Park, only 8 miles west.

Historic displays and a walking tour map are available at the visitors center (☎ 970-533-7434), at the corner of Main St and Railroad Ave (US 160). It also has information on outdoor activities in the area and local ranches that offer horseback rides and Western-style overnight trips.

Places to Stay & Eat
At the east end of Grand Ave, the Mancos River runs beside the town's wooded *Boyle Park*. Tent campsites and restrooms are free; a small donation goes to help fund park upkeep. Please register with the park host in the trailer at the park entrance.

The best bet in town is *Old Mancos Inn* (☎ 970-533-9019), 200 W Grand Ave. The hotel's friendly owners, Dean and Greg, have worked hard to renovate the place and provide very pleasant rooms for reasonable prices. Four rooms with shared bath cost $25 year-round; rooms with private bath are $45. An outside deck and a hot tub add yet more value. This is also one of the few truly gay-friendly hotels in Colorado.

Comfortable singles/doubles cost $35/45 ($25/30 in winter) at *Enchanted Mesa Motel* (☎ 970-533-7729), 862 W Grand

Ave. The *Mesa Verde Motel* (☎ 970-533-7741), 191 Railroad Ave, isn't as cozy but does have a hot tub. Singles/doubles are usually around $40/47.

How about spending the night in a former fire lookout tower? Standing 55 feet above a meadow 14 miles north of Mancos at 9800 feet elevation, the *Jersey Jim Lookout* is on the National Register and is complete with its Osborne fire-finder and topographic map. The tower accommodates up to four adults (bring your own bedding) and must be reserved long in advance: the reservation office opens March 1 and the entire season is usually booked out within two or three days. To make reservations call ☎ 970-533-7060. The nightly fee is $45, with a two-night maximum; children under eight are not admitted.

For breakfast or lunch the *Dusty Rose Cafe* (☎ 970-533-9042), 200 W Grand Ave, offers tasty dishes with fresh ingredients at reasonable prices. An upscale steak and seafood dinner choice is *Millwood Junction* (☎ 970-533-7338), at the corner of Main St and Railroad Ave. Folks from miles around come to Mancos on Friday night for the $14 seafood buffet.

CORTEX

Cortez (population 8700), is the main lodging spot for visitors to Mesa Verde National Park and other nearby Ancestral Puebloan ruins. It's not much more than a place to stay, but people are friendly and there are some reasonably priced motels and a few nice restaurants. Those seeking a more relaxed environment can try Mancos, 17 miles east, or Dolores, 11 miles north.

US 160 becomes Main St as it runs east-west through the middle of town, then Broadway, where it turns south and joins up with Hwy 666. Main St is where you'll find nearly all the lodging and restaurants, though there are a few motels on Broadway.

The Colorado Welcome Center (☎ 970-565-4048), 928 E Main St, is housed in an adobe-style building at the City Park. It has maps, brochures, some excellent pamphlets and maps on local activities such as fishing

and mountain biking, plus materials to help you plan a vacation throughout the state. A self-guided downtown walking tour brochure, 'Crossroads Culture Walk,' is also available here. Hours are from 8 am to 5 pm (6 pm in summer). The Cortez Chamber of Commerce (☎ 970-565-3414) is also housed in the building.

First National Bank (☎ 970-565-3781), at 140 W Main St, has an ATM. The City Market, on the northeast corner of E Main and Harrison Sts, has a Valley National Bank ATM and offers Western Union service. The post office is at 35 S Beech St; the zip code is 81321.

Quality Book Store (☎ 970-565-9125), 34 W Main St, sells travel books and maps and offers a good selection on local history and Native American cultures.

Southwest Memorial Hospital (☎ 970-565-6666), at 1311 N Mildred Rd, has a 24-hour emergency room.

A laundry is at the corner of E Main St and Mildred Rd opposite the City Park and Colorado Welcome Center. M&M Truckstop (☎ 970-565 6511), south of town at 7006 US 160/666, offers showers for $5 plus a $5 key deposit.

Colorado University Center Museum
Throughout the year this museum (☎ 970-565-1151), 25 N Market St, hosts exhibits on the Ancestral Puebloans as well as visiting art displays in its gallery.

The **Cultural Park** is an outdoor space where Ute, Navajo and Hopi tribal members share their cultures with visitors through dance, crafts demonstrations, or food prepared in *hornos* (traditional clay ovens). Weaving demonstrations and Ute Mountain art are also displayed and visitors can check out a Navajo hogan and Ute tepee.

Summer evening programs feature Native American dances four nights a week at 7:30 pm, followed at 8:30 by cultural programs such as Native American storytellers or occasionally Mexican dances or cowboy poet gatherings. At the time of writing Native Americans dances were held in the city park Friday and Saturday nights (they may shift back to the museum). The CU Center Museum is open Monday to Saturday; summer hours are from 10 am to 9 pm, 10 am to 5 pm in winter.

Places to Stay

Camping Sadly, the only campground in town not right next to a highway or dedicated to RVs is the *Cortez-Mesa Verde KOA* (☎ 970-565-9301), at the east end of town at 27432 E Hwy 160 (there's a big sign to point the way). Tent sites are a pricey $18, full RV hookups $24. It's open mid-May to mid-September.

B&Bs *A Bed & Breakfast on Maple St* (☎ 970-565-3906), 102 S Maple St, is as unpretentious as its name suggests. A real home-style place, it has four rooms with private bath ranging from $59 to $99. There is also an outdoor hot tub and backyard barbecue grill available to guests. It's open year-round.

Kelly Place (☎ 970-565-3125), at 14663 Montezuma County Rd G (McElmo Canyon) 15 miles west of Cortez, is a unique adobe-style guest lodge on a 100-acre archaeological and horticultural preserve founded by the late botanist George Kelly, author of many outstanding guides to Rocky Mountain plants. Tastefully appointed singles/doubles cost $59/69 and include private bath and breakfast. Cabins with kitchenettes are available for $89. Horseback rides, cultural tours and archaeological programs are also on offer.

Motels There is a good selection of locally run motels in Cortez, freeing you from having to patronize the ubiquitous national chains. After Memorial Day and before Labor Day it's not a good idea to arrive without a room reservation – walk-in rates rise to whatever the market will bear.

Summer or winter the basic but clean *Ute Mountain Motel* (☎ 970-565-8507), 531 S Broadway, has three budget singles for $20. Normal summer rates for singles/doubles are still comparatively cheap at $35/44, dropping to $20/28 in winter. Another economy choice is the *Aneth Lodge* (☎ 970-

565-3453), at 645 E Main St, where high-season rates for fairly large, comfortable rooms are $36/49.

Taking a slight step up in quality, the *Budget Host Inn* (formerly Bel Rau Lodge, ☎ 970-565-3738), 2040 E Main St, has a pool, hot tub and spacious, spotless rooms for $45 in summer; singles/doubles are as low as $28/32 in winter. On the west side of town, the *Sand Canyon Inn* (☎ 970-565-8562, 800-257-3699) is another pleasant spot with a pool, sundeck, laundry. Peak summer rates for singles/doubles are $45/52; expect to pay around $10 less any other time.

Still farther west the friendly owners of the *Arrow Motor Inn* (☎ 970-565-7778 800-727-7692), at 440 S Broadway, offer recently renovated rooms for $49/56 in summer. Facilities include a pool, hot tub and laundry. *The Tomahawk Lodge* (☎ 970-565-8521, 800-972-6232), 728 S Broadway, also has a pool, newly redone rooms, 24-hour coffee and tea and singles/doubles for $35/47 (summer rates).

Also in this area is the *Anasazi Motor Inn* (☎ 970-565-3773), at 640 S Broadway. It's not bad but rooms are overpriced at $55/69 for singles/doubles; even winter rates are fairly steep.

Cortez has also attracted members of the various motel chains, along with their inflated prices, including two Best Westerns, a Comfort Inn, a Super 8 and a Holiday Inn Express. All cost more than they're worth but if you're stuck, consult the 800-number appendix in the back of this book for relevant phone numbers.

Places to Eat

You can start the day with fresh pastries at the *Belgian Quality Bakery* (☎ 970-565-3753), 44 W Main St, or an espresso and light breakfast next door at the Quality Book Store's *Earth Song Haven* (☎ 970-565-9125), which also serves tasty lunches featuring fresh ingredients.

Good $5 lunch specials are available weekdays at the *Main Street Brewery & Restaurant* (☎ 970-544-9112), 21 E Main St. The dinner menu gets more interesting with a mix of Southwestern, Mexican and Italian dishes, resulting in some unusual items like the 'Bratwurst Burrito.' There are nightly specials and entrees range from $7 to $13. Their house-brewed beer is excellent, reason enough in itself to stop by.

Locals nominate *Francisca's* (☎ 970-565-4093), 125 E Main St, as the best Mexican food in town, and good taste comes at a pretty good price: lunches and dinners range from $4 to $10. It's open Tuesday to Saturday. For standard American family fare, there's *Homesteaders* (☎ 970-565-6253), 45 E Main St, open all day for barbecue dinners and fresh-baked pies and breads.

At the upper end, *Nero's Italian Restaurant* (☎ 970-565-7366), 303 W Main St, is another local favorite, winning high marks for the presentation of entrees and its excellent soups. Prices range from $9 to $12 for pasta dishes, $10 to $18 for meat entrees. The *Dry Dock Lounge & Restaurant* (☎ 970-564-9404), 220 W Main St, also occupies the higher-end bracket, dishing up steak and seafood platters with a Southwestern flair. Both restaurants have patio dining areas, a nice feature during the warmer months.

Shopping

Native American handicrafts are available at the numerous 'trading posts' that line the highway to Mesa Verde National Park. You will find everything from rubber tomahawks and cheap imported rugs to distinctive handcrafted pottery, jewelry and costly Navajo rugs. Comparison shopping will help identify quality differences and is itself an educational exercise. Prices tend to be competitive – don't be fooled by the '50% off sale' signs. Bead and turquoise jewelry making is a cottage industry practiced by many tribal members soon after leaving the cradle – jewelry offers the best bargains and most opportunities to buy directly from the artisan.

The Notah Dineh Trading Company (☎ 970-565-9607), 345 W Main St, features an outstanding collection of museum-quality goods in the front showroom, a cash/pawn window in the back and a museum downstairs that displays items that are not for sale. To buy directly from Native American artisans and merchants, head south to Towoac or the numerous stalls at Four Corners where you are certain to find plenty of inexpensive, authentic gifts for your friends back home.

Getting There & Away

Air Cortez Municipal Airport is served by United Express, which offers daily turbo-prop flights to Denver and Farmington, NM. Most Denver flights are routed through Farmington, though there is usually one direct flight a day. The airport is 2 miles south of town off US 160/666.

Car In the extreme southwest corner of the state, Cortez is easier to reach from either Phoenix, AZ, or Albuquerque, NM, than from Denver, 379 miles away by the shortest route. East of Cortez, US 160 passes Mesa Verde National Park on the way to Durango, the largest city in the region, 45 miles away. To the northwest, Hwy 145 follows the beautiful Dolores River through the San Juan Mountains on an old Rio Grande Southern narrow-gauge route over Lizard Head Pass to Telluride, 77 miles distant.

Getting Around

U-Save Auto Rental (☎ 970-565-9168) operates out of the Cortez Airport. Quality Rental (☎ 970-565-2106) is located in town at 410 W Main St.

AROUND CORTEZ
Anasazi Heritage Center

One of the largest archaeological projects in the Four Corners region was undertaken along the Dolores River between 1978 and 1981, prior to the filling of the McPhee Reservoir. The Anasazi Heritage Center (☎ 970-882-4811), 27501 Hwy 184, 10 miles north of Cortez or 3 miles west of Dolores, offers modern displays of Ancestral Puebloan artifacts found during this project and other archaeological work in the area. Hands-on exhibits include weaving, corn-grinding, tree-ring analysis and an introduction to how archaeologists examine potsherds.

Between 1 and 1300 AD, Ancestral Puebloans inhabited the hilly sites of the Escalante and Domínguez ruins overlooking the Montezuma Valley. A short interpretive nature trail leads to the hilltop Escalante ruin which was discovered in 1776 by Father Francisco Atanasio Escalante and Father Silvestre Vélez Domínguez. Archaeologists believe the Escalante site was linked with the Chaco Culture, an Ancestral Puebloan society that existed nearly 200 miles south in New Mexico.

The BLM operates the museum and the nonprofit museum shop offers a wide variety of books, maps and nature guides ranging from professional reports to introductory materials suited for the general public. It's open daily 9 am to 5 pm (until 4 pm in winter). Admission is $3.

Crow Canyon Archaeology Center

The Crow Canyon Archaeological Center (☎ 970-565-8975, 800-422-8975), 23390 Montezuma County Rd K, offers an educational day-long program that visits the Sand Creek Ancestral Puebloan excavation site west of Cortez. Programs teach the significance of found artifacts and are offered from June to mid-September, Wednesdays and Thursdays. This is an excellent way to learn about Ancestral Puebloan culture first-hand. The fee is $45/25 adults/children under 18.

An adult research program costs $850 and includes Southwestern meals and log cabin lodging for a week. Classroom time culminates with visits to the dig site and active participation in excavation. Reservations are required for both programs.

Lowry Pueblo Ruins National Historic Landmark

The ruins at Lowry Pueblo, north of Cortez and 9 miles west of Hwy 666 at Pleasant View, underwent heavy stabilization in 1994 to give visitors an opportunity to explore this Ancestral Puebloan site and even enter a central *kiva* (a usually round,

ceremonial structure constructed partially underground). Near the pueblo, constructed between 1060 and 1170 AD, is one of the largest Great Kivas in the Four Corners region. When researchers from Chicago's Field Institute first excavated the site during the 1930s, they discovered an elaborate painting in the central kiva, which was removed for display at the Anasazi Heritage Center in 1987.

Note the distinctive Chaco-style masonry using narrow slabs and small dark stones to create a banding effect on the south wall. This and other evidence support the theory that Lowry Pueblo was a Chaco Culture outpost housing about 100 occupants who were part of the greater network of civilization centered in Chaco Canyon in New Mexico. Self-guided walking tour brochures are available at the site. Picnicking is permitted but overnight camping is not allowed. For further information contact the BLM San Juan Resource Area (☎ 970-247-4082) located in Durango.

Fishing

The 11-mile stretch of the lower Dolores River below McPhee Dam to the Bradfield Bridge is a state-designated quality water stream where a catch-and-release program is in effect. To reach the area, turn east off US 666 onto Montezuma County Rd DD 1 mile north of Pleasant View. Follow the signs for 6 miles to the Bradfield Bridge and USFS campground; from the bridge, the Lone Dome Rd follows the east bank of the river to the dam.

If trolling is your preference, McPhee Reservoir offers both warm- and cold-water species in the recently flooded Dolores River Canyon. Perhaps to make amends for drowning Ancestral Puebloan ruins, burial sites and untold artifacts, the reservoir is kept well-stocked for the visiting angler. McPhee Marina (☎ 970-882-2257, 800-882-2038) offers tackle and half-day boat rentals from $65.

Pick up the 'Guide to Fishing in Mesa Verde Country' at the Colorado Welcome Center for additional information.

Road & Mountain Biking

The Four Corners area offers some outstanding mountain bike trails among piñon-juniper woodland and over 'slickrock' mesa trails. The dispersed ruins at Hovenweep National Monument (see below) are ideal riding destinations. In fact, the roads are often better suited for bikes than cars. Check in at the ranger station for directions and to get suggestions for sites to visit within 10 miles. Remember that archaeological sites hold invaluable clues to the American heritage and must not be disturbed in any manner.

A good ride begins at the Sand Canyon archaeological site west of Cortez and follows a downhill trail west for 18 miles to Cannonball Mesa near the state line. If you're looking for a shorter ride, at the 8-mile mark the Burro Point overlook of Yellow Jacket and Burro Canyons is a good place to turn back. To get to Sand Canyon, take US 666 north from Cortez, turn left (west) on Montezuma County Rd P and continue 7 miles before making a left (south) turn.

Fat-tire enthusiasts should not miss the 26-mile trail from Dove Creek to Slick Rock along the Dolores River (see Dolores River Canyon below).

Pick up a copy of 'Mountain and Road Bike Routes' for the Cortez-Dolores-Mancos area, available at the Colorado Welcome Center in Cortez and at local chambers of commerce. It provides maps and profiles for 11 road and mountain bike routes. The booklet 'Bicycle Routes on Public Lands of Southwest Colorado' also describes area rides in good detail. It's available for $7 from the USFS Dolores Ranger Station (☎ 970-882-7296), 100 N 6th St in Dolores. Contact the Colorado Plateau Mountain Bike Trail Association (☎ 970-241-9561) for even more routes and information.

In Cortez, Kokopelli Bike & Board (☎ 970-565-4408), at 30 W Main St, rents mountain bikes for $20 per day, including helmet, air pump, water bottle and tools. They can also provide information about trails in the area.

Places to Stay

A few walk-in tent sites are available for $8 at the USFS *McPhee Campground* (☎ 970-882-9905, 800-280-2267), but most of the 70 reservable campsites are set up for RVs and cost $10, plus $2 for showers. The sites look out over the Montezuma Valley and are convenient to McPhee Recreation Area and reservoir fishing 14 miles north of Cortez on Hwy 184.

Below McPhee Dam to the reservoir, the USFS operates three campgrounds on a first-come, first-served basis: *Bradfield*, *Cabin Canyon* and *Ferris Canyon*. Tent sites are $8 at each. To reach them from US 666, travel 1 mile north of Pleasant View (20 miles north of Cortez), turn east on Montezuma County Rd DD and follow the signs for 6 miles to the bridge. The Bradfield site is a half-mile downstream from the bridge; the other two are within 6 miles to your right (south) on USFS Rd 504. For more camping locations in the San Juan National Forest contact the USFS Dolores Ranger Station (☎ 970-882-7296).

MESA VERDE NATIONAL PARK

Among national parks, Mesa Verde is unique for its focus on preserving cultural relics so that future generations may continue to interpret the puzzling history of its settlement and then abandonment by early inhabitants.

The people of Mesa Verde have been commonly referred to as Anasazi, a term archeologists borrowed from a Navajo word thought to mean 'the Ancient Ones.' However, Native American tribes in Arizona and New Mexico who count the Puebloans among their ancestors recently pointed out that since the latter were not related to the Navajo, using the name 'Anasazi' is inappropriate. The National Park Service has changed its literature to reflect this situation; whether other government and private organizations follow suit is yet to be seen.

History

A US Army lieutenant recorded the spectacular cliff dwellings in the canyons of

COLORADO

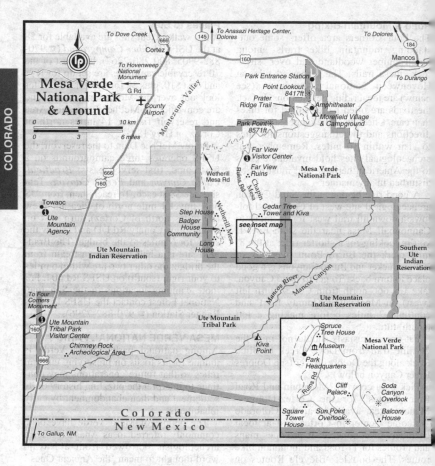

Mesa Verde in 1849-50. The large number of sites on Ute tribal land, and their relative inaccessibility, protected the majority of these antiquities from pot-hunters.

The first scientific investigation of the ruins in 1874 failed to identify Cliff Palace, the largest cliff dwelling in North America. Discovery of the 'magnificent city' occurred only when local cowboys Richard Wetherill and Charlie Mason were searching for stray cattle after a December 1888 snowfall. It's likely that Wetherill had learned about Cliff Palace from Acowitz, a Ute tribal member. The cow-

boys exploited their 'discovery' for the next 18 years by guiding both amateur and trained archaeologists to the ruins, particularly to collect the distinctive black-on-white pottery.

Disturbances by casual collectors and the large-scale 'mining' of artifacts by professionals prompted calls to protect the ruins. The shipping of artifacts overseas motivated Virginia McClurg of Colorado Springs to embark on a long campaign to preserve the ruins and their contents. Along with other members of the Colorado Federation of Women's Clubs, she met with

Ancestral Puebloan Settlement

Why the Ancestral Puebloans entered Mesa Verde is a subject of speculation. Habitations in Mesa Verde evolved greatly between 450 AD, when the earliest simple structures were constructed, and 1300 AD when the great cities were mysteriously left behind.

The earliest period of settlement, the so-called Modified Basket Maker phase that extended to about 750 AD, found the Ancestral Puebloans dispersed across the mesatops in small clusters of permanent pithouse dwellings – semisubterranean structures with posts supporting low-profile roofs.

During the Developmental Pueblo Period, up to 1100 AD, Ancestral Puebloans built surface houses with simple shared walls – like row-house apartments – forming small hamlets surrounded by fields of maize, beans and squash.

The following Classic Pueblo phase, to 1300 AD, saw the Mesa Verde Ancestral Puebloans elaborate on the earlier structures using masonry building materials. Their efforts housed a peak population of perhaps several thousand in pueblo villages, the precursors to cities. Greater clusters of people created opportunities for united accomplishments and perhaps a rudimentary division of labor, social organization, political control and even organized raids on neighboring villages. During this period the Ancestral Puebloans developed subsurface roundrooms, or kivas – for decades believed by archaeologists to be only for ceremonial use, but more recently seen to have more basic functions as well. At this time the Ancestral Puebloans also developed hydraulic schemes to irrigate crops and provide water for villages.

There is mounting evidence of regular communication between Mesa Verdeans and Chaco Canyon peoples in northwestern New Mexico during this period. Some researchers suggest that the political, economic and social influences extended from even farther afield in Mesoamerica (present-day Mexico and Central America).

The Puebloans suddenly moved to the alcoves of the cliff faces around 1200 AD. Community size depended on available cliff space, so while small cavities may have contained only a few compartments, there were many larger communities with over 200 compartments, including elaborate blocks or rooms, cantilevered balconies, sunken roundrooms and even tower structures – many connected with internal passageways.

Ancestral Puebloans inhabited the cliff dwellings for less than a century before disappearing in accord with a regional demographic collapse that is the greatest unexplained event of the era. Death, disease, invasion, internal warfare, resource depletion and climatic change are among the hardships that these peoples faced. Tree-ring chronologies offer proof of a widespread drought from 1276 to 1299 AD, yet this explanation fails to account for the earlier population decline at Chaco Canyon or Mesa Verde's survival of earlier droughts. Population movements did occur and it is probable that many Ancestral Puebloans migrated south to the Pueblos of present-day New Mexico and Arizona.

Although archaeologists adopted the Navajo term Anasazi during the 1930s to refer to these early inhabitants of the American Southwest, they have often mistaken it to mean 'ancient people.' Instead, and much to the chagrin of modern Pueblo peoples of Ancestral Puebloan heritage, it literally means 'enemy ancestors' in the Navajo tongue.

Period	*Chronology*
Hunter-Gatherer	5500 BC
I Basketmaker	1 AD-450 AD
II Modified Basketmaker	450-750
III Developmental Pueblo	around 750 to 1100
IV Classic Pueblo	around 1100 to 1300

Ute chieftains in 1903 near present-day Towaoc. As a result, the Ute tribe graciously consented to release interest in the canyons containing the cliff houses.

McClurg's efforts led Congress to protect artifacts on federal land with passage of the Antiquities Act and to establish Mesa Verde National Park in 1906. Part of the enabling legislation mandated that, unlike other national parks, the backcountry would be closed to public access.

Responsible Tourism

Preserving the Ancestral Puebloan ruins while accommodating ever-increasing numbers of visitors continues to challenge the National Park Service. The NPS strictly enforces the Antiquities Act, which prohibits removal or destruction of any such items and also prohibits public access to many of the approximately 4,000 known ruins.

Opportunities for trail hikes are extremely limited. Only a handful of stabilized ruins can withstand the trampling and climbing of throngs of visitors. Consider Mesa Verde to be a gigantic outdoor museum: stay on the path or behind the obvious barricades unless guided by an NPS ranger.

Increased visitation and NPS restrictions conspire against casual tourists trying to enjoy the park on a brief visit of only a few hours. Windshield tourists expecting a passive scenic excursion will be disappointed. If you only have time for a short visit, visit the Chapin Mesa Museum and try a walk through the crowded Spruce Tree House ruins where you can climb down a wooden ladder into the cool chamber of a kiva. However, Mesa Verde rewards travelers who set aside a day or more to take the ranger-led tours of Cliff Palace and Balcony House, explore Wetherill Mesa, linger in the museum or participate in a campfire program.

If possible, avoid peak-season crowds from mid-July to September, when the weather may be uncomfortably hot. Late May or mid-September, when most schools are in session, is an ideal time to take advantage of all services but the Wetherill Mesa interpretive tours.

Orientation

Ancestral Puebloan ruins are found throughout the canyons and mesatops of Mesa Verde, a high plateau south of Cortez and Mancos. The North Rim summit at Park Point (8571 feet) towers more than 2000 feet above the Montezuma Valley. From Park Point the mesa gently slopes southward to 6000-foot elevation above the Mancos River in the Ute Mountain Tribal Park. The mesatop is dissected by parallel canyons, typically 500 feet below the rim that carry the drainage southward. Mesa Verde National Park occupies 81 square miles of the northernmost portion of the mesa and contains the largest and most frequented cliff dwellings and surface ruins.

The park entrance is off US 160 midway between Cortez and Mancos. From the entrance it's about 21 miles to Park Headquarters, Chapin Mesa Museum and Spruce Tree House. Along the way are Morefield Campground (4 miles), the panoramic viewpoint at Park Point (8 miles) and the Far View visitors center opposite the Far View Lodge and Restaurant (about 11 miles). Towed vehicles are not allowed beyond Morefield Campground.

Chapin Mesa contains the largest concentration of ruins in the area. South from Park Headquarters, Ruins Rd consists of two one-way circuits. Turn left about one-quarter mile from the start of Ruins Rd to visit Cliff Palace and Balcony House on the east loop. Take the west loop by continuing straight to mesatop ruins and many fine cliff dwelling vantages. Taking the west loop first allows you to roughly follow the Ancestral Puebloan chronology in proper sequence.

At Wetherill Mesa, the second-largest concentration of ruins, visitors may enter stabilized surface ruins and two cliff dwellings. From the junction with the main road at Far View visitors center, the 12-mile mountainous Wetherill Mesa Rd snakes along the North Rim, acting as a natural barrier to tourbuses and indifferent travelers. The road is open only from the second week in June to Labor Day.

Information

Tourist Offices Far View visitors center (☎ 970-529-4543) is open 8 am to 5 pm, late spring through early autumn. More comprehensive information is available at the Chapin Mesa Museum, but visitors must first stop at Far View to obtain the required tickets ($1.35) for tours of Cliff Palace or Balcony House. Modestly priced guides to individual sites are available in French, German and Spanish versions at either center.

Park Headquarters (☎ 970-529-4461) is open weekdays during park hours. For additional information write Mesa Verde National Park, CO 81330. The Chapin Mesa Museum (☎ 970-529-4475) is open daily from 8 am to 5 pm (6:30 pm in summer) and provides information on weekends when Park Headquarters is closed.

Fees The park entry fee is $10 per each vehicle passenger, $5 for bicyclists, hikers and motorcyclists, and is valid for seven days. The combined brochure and map handed to each visitor is also available in French, Spanish and German. Park roads are open 8 am to sunset, except Wetherill Mesa Rd, which closes at 4:30 pm. Winter vehicle travel on Ruins Rd is subject to weather conditions. You may snowshoe or cross-country ski on the roadway when conditions permit.

Post The post office is at Park Headquarters on Chapin Mesa; the zip code is 81330.

Bookstores The Mesa Verde Museum Association (☎ 970-529-4445), located in the Chapin Mesa Museum, has an excellent selection of materials on the Ancestral Puebloan and modern tribes in the American Southwest.

Laundry & Showers From May to mid-October Morefield Village, near the Morefield Campground turnoff, has 10¢ showers and $1 per load washers. It's open 24 hours.

Ancestral Puebloan Ruins

Chapin Mesa There is no other place where so many remnants of Ancestral Puebloan settlement are clustered together, providing an opportunity to see and compare examples of all phases of construction – from pithouse to pueblo villages to the elaborate multiroom cities tucked into cliff recesses. Pamphlets describing most excavated sites are available at either Far View visitors center or Chapin Mesa Museum.

On the upper portion of Chapin Mesa are the **Far View Ruins**, perhaps the most densely settled area in Mesa Verde after 1100 AD. The large walled pueblo ruins at Far View House enclose a central kiva and planned room layout that originally was two stories high. To the north is a small row of rooms and attached circular tower that likely extended just above the adjacent 'pygmy forest' of piñon pine and juniper trees. This tower is one of 57 found throughout Mesa Verde that the Ancestral Puebloans may have built as watchtowers, religious structures or astronomical observatories for agricultural schedules. They also built a system to divert streamwater to fields and into nearby Mummy Lake Reservoir – a masonry ditch also led toward Spruce Tree House.

Near Park Headquarters, an easy walk without ladders or steps leads to **Spruce Tree House**. This sheltered alcove, over 200 feet wide and almost 90 feet deep, contains about 114 rooms and eight kivas and once housed about 100 people. One kiva has a reconstructed roof and ladder for entry. During the winter when many portions of the park are closed, access to this ruin is by ranger-led tours only. Spruce Tree House is open daily 9 am to 5 pm.

South from Park Headquarters, the 6-mile Ruins Rd circuit connects 10 excavated mesatop ruins, three accessible cliff dwellings and many vantages of inaccessible cliff dwellings from the mesa rim. It is open 8 am to sunset. Perhaps the most photographed ruin in the park is the secluded four-story **Square Tower House** on the west loop of Ruins Rd. Among the excellent late afternoon views of many cliff dwellings from **Sun Point** is the vista of Cliff Palace, sighted by Richard Wetherill in 1888. The mesatop ruins on the west loop of Ruins Rd also feature the astronomically aligned **Sun Temple**.

On the east loop of Ruins Rd, you must have a ticket to take part in the one-hour guided tours of either **Cliff Palace** or **Balcony House**, open daily 9 am to 5 pm (closed in winter).

Foot access to Cliff Palace, the largest ruin in the park, resembles the approach taken by the Ancestral Puebloans – visitors must climb a stone stairway and four 10-foot ladders. This grand representative of engineering achievement, with 217 rooms and 23 kivas, provided shelter for as many as 250 people. However, the inhabitants were without running water – springs across the canyon below Sun Temple were the most likely water sources. Use of small 'chinking' stones between the large blocks is strikingly similar to Ancestral Puebloan construction employed at distant Chaco Canyon.

The residents of Balcony House had outstanding views of Soda Canyon, 600 feet below the sandstone overhang that served as the ceiling for 35 to 40 rooms. Panoramic views, however, were apparently secondary to either concerns for security (entry was via a narrow tunnel) or the attraction of two reliable springs. Today, visitors enter the obviously stabilized ruins by a 32-foot ladder to see the cantilevered balcony and enjoy clambering throughout the tunnel and ruins.

Wetherill Mesa The less frequented western portion of the park offers a comprehensive display of Ancestral Puebloan relics. From the second week in June to Labor Day, the winding Wetherill Mesa Rd is open daily 8 am to 4:30 pm. The **Badger House Community** consists of a short trail between four excavated surface ruin sites depicting various phases of Ancestral Puebloan development. For a complete chronological circuit, continue

on the trail to **Long House**, the second largest cliff dwelling in Mesa Verde (for this you'll first need a ticket $1.35 purchased at the Far View visitors center). The nearby **Step House**, initially occupied by Modified Basketmaker peoples residing in pithouses, later became the site of a Classic Pueblo period masonry complex of rooms and kivas. Stairways and indentations in the rocks provided access to the partially irrigated crops in the terraces on the mesatop.

Park Point
The fire lookout at Park Point (8571 feet) is the highest elevation in the park and accordingly offers panoramic views. To the north are the 14,000-foot peaks of the San Juan Mountains; in the northeast can be seen the 12,000-foot crests of the La Plata Mountains; to the southwest, beyond the southward sloping Mesa Verde plateau, is the distant volcanic plug of Shiprock; and to the west is the prone human-like profile of Sleeping Ute Mountain.

Look for mule deer and wild turkeys in the dense growth of serviceberry and gambel oak next to the road. The sturdy hardwood from the gambel oak provided the Ancestral Puebloans with handy digging tools and fuel. Near the lookout are yucca plants, indicative of the semiarid climate, with edible fruits that resemble and taste like cucumber.

Hiking
Backcountry access to the ruins is specifically forbidden within Mesa Verde National Park. However, there are several marked trails open to hikers.

From Park Headquarters and adjacent Chapin Mesa Museum, two trail loops, each under 3 miles in length, are accessed from the short path to Spruce Tree House. All hikers must first register at Park Headquarters. While you're there, pick up pamphlets for the **Petroglyph Point Trail** and the self-guided tour of Spruce Tree House.

From the museum overlook of Spruce Tree House, follow the path to the canyon floor. Return via **Petroglyph Point Trail** to view the petroglyphs etched into the naturally varnished rock surface and interpret the uses of native plants. After climbing about 300 feet back to the rim, either return directly to Park Headquarters or continue to the left on another loop, the **Spruce Canyon Trail**.

From the amphitheater parking area near Morefield Campground, a spur trail climbs to **Point Lookout** about 2 miles away, where you may witness a fabulous sunset over Sleeping Ute Mountain (elevation 9884 feet). The 8-mile **Prater Ridge Trail** loop starts at the Hopi group area in Morefield Campground. Neither trail requires a permit.

Road Biking
Finding convenient parking at the many stops along Ruins Rd is not a problem for those on bikes. Only the hardiest cyclists, however, will want to enter the park by bike and immediately face the grueling 4-mile ascent to Morefield Campground, followed by a narrow tunnel, to reach the North Rim. An easier option is to unlimber your muscles and mount up at Morefield, Far View visitors center or Park Headquarters.

If you choose to cycle, note that the NPS prohibits bicyclists from Wetherill Mesa Rd, and throughout the park secure bicycle parking is rare. Ride *only* on paved roadways.

Organized Tours
ARA Mesa Verde (☎ 970-529-4421), the park concessionaire, offers two guided tours daily May to mid-October.

Introductory three-hour tours of excavated pit homes, views of cliff dwellings and a tour through Spruce Tree House depart from Morefield Campground at 9 am and from Far View Lodge at 9:30 am. Tickets are $16/8 adults/children.

A full-day tour ($21/8 adults/children) includes the morning tour sites and then goes on to examine later architecture and social developments, also taking in the Cliff Palace. For further information contact ARA Mesa Verde at PO Box 277, Mancos, CO 81328.

Places to Stay
Although there are plenty of mid-range places to stay in nearby Cortez and Mancos, within the national park the visitor must choose between two extremes: camping or staying at a high-end lodge. An overnight stay in the park allows convenient access to the many ruins during the best viewing hours, participation in evening programs and the sheer pleasure of watching the sunset over Ute Mountain from the quiet of the mesatop.

With 450 campsites only 4 miles from the park entrance *Morefield Campground*, open May to mid-October, has plenty of capacity for the peak season. Grassy tent sites at Navajo Loop are conveniently near Morefield Village (with a general store, gas station, restaurant, showers and laundry) and cost $10. Full hookups are available for $17. Contact ARA Mesa Verde (☎ 970-529-4421) for information or to reserve group campsites.

The *Far View Lodge* (☎ 970-529-4421), 15 miles from the park entrance perched on the mesatop, has rooms with Southwestern furnishings, private balconies and outstanding views. Rooms are available mid-April to the third week in October; the off-peak rate is $73; Memorial Day to Labor Day it's $93. Compared to top-end lodging in Cortez, the Far View Lodge is a good value and offers a memorable visit.

Places to Eat
Knife Edge Cafe in Morefield Village offers breakfast 7:30 to 10 am and dinner 5 to 8 pm. The *Far View Terrace*, immediately south of the visitors center, serves reasonably priced meals 6:30 am to 9 pm (closed during winter months). Near the Chapin Mesa Museum, the *Spruce Tree Terrace* serves sandwiches, salads and the like 8 am to 5 pm daily.

The *Metate Room* (☎ 970-529-4421) at the Far View Lodge is the nearest restaurant to Dove Creek serving gourmet Anasazi beans (a variegated pinto bean). Open nightly 5:30 to 9:30 pm, the Metate Room also serves steak, seafood, game specialties and good Mexican dishes for $12 to $20.

Entertainment

Free evening campfire programs are held June to Labor Day nightly at the *Morefield Campground Amphitheater*. For information contact the NPS at the Far View visitors center, or call ☎ 970-529-4461 or 970-529-4475.

HOVENWEEP NATIONAL MONUMENT

Hovenweep, meaning 'deserted valley' in the Ute language, is a remote area of former Ancestral Puebloan settlements straddling the Colorado/Utah border, 42 miles west of Cortez via McElmo Canyon Rd from US 160. This was once home to a large population before drought forced people out in the late 1200s. Six sets of unique tower ruins are found here, but only the impressive ruins in the Square Tower area are readily accessible.

Three easy- to moderate-loop hiking trails (none longer than 2 miles) leave from near the ranger station and pass a number of buildings in the Square Tower area. The trails give both distant and close-up views of the ancient ruins whose fragile unstable walls are easily damaged – please stay on the trail and don't climb on the ruins. Visitors are reminded that all wildlife is protected – including rattlesnakes – but you are more likely to see the iridescent collared lizard scampering near the trail. Brochures are available for the self-guided tours and also describe plant life along the trails.

The Hovenweep National Park Service Ranger Station (☎ 970-749-0510) is open 8 am to 5:30 pm daily. Rangers answer questions and sell maps and interpretive booklets. The monument is administered by Mesa Verde National Park (☎ 970-529-4461) which has further information.

Biting gnats are a problem mid-May to July. Wear long sleeves and pants.

Places to Stay

The NPS campground is about a mile from the ranger station and is open year-round on a first-come, first-served basis. The 31 sites rarely fill, but are busiest in summer. There are toilets and picnic facilities; the fee is $10. Spring water is available when weather permits, usually from April to October only.

Getting There & Away

From US 160/US 666 south of Cortez, turn at the sign for the Cortez airport onto Montezuma County Rd G, which follows McElmo Canyon east through red-rock country north of Sleeping Ute Mountain and Ute tribal lands. At the Utah border you cross onto the Navajo Reservation and can expect sheep, goats or even a cattle drive on the road. A signed road to the monument turns right (north) from McElmo Creek.

A couple of miles farther west past Hovenweep is Battle Rock, the site of a fabled fierce battle between Navajo and Utes.

UTE MOUNTAIN INDIAN RESERVATION

The Weminuche band of Utes objected to the dispersed allotments offered by the US government and left their Mouache and Capote cousins in the Southern Ute Reservation to establish a tribal camp in the shadow of Sleeping Ute Mountain in 1895. Towaoc (population 700), 12 miles south of Cortez, is the tribal center for the Ute Mountain Ute Reservation. The formerly nomadic peoples retain a more communal lifestyle than their dispersed Navajo and Southern Ute neighbors. Nevertheless, intermarriage is not uncommon, as the Bear Dance in early June attracts single members from other tribes to participate in the ritual of seeking a mate following hibernation.

Dramatic changes have followed the opening of the popular **Ute Mountain Casino** (☎ 970-565-8800, 800-258-8007), 11 miles south of Cortez on US 160/US 666. Since Congress enacted the Indian Gaming Regulatory Act in 1988, casinos have brought jobs and money to the tribal governments; this is the first federal economic program to do so. The casino is open 20 hours daily, 8 to 4 am and attracts a steady stream of 'donors' among Cortez residents and visiting tourists.

Traditional Ute handicrafts focused on beadwork, baskets and leatherwork articles used in a nomadic existence. Since 1970, Ute Mountain Pottery (☎ 970-565-8548), on US 160/US 666, has welcomed visitors to watch Ute artists produce reasonably priced original designs. Visitors are also welcome at the Ute Mountain Tribal Center (☎ 970-565-3751), 3 miles west of US 160/US 666, where you can arrange to visit the Ancestral Puebloan cliff dwellings in Ute Mountain Tribal Park.

Ute Mountain Tribal Park

In Ute Mountain Tribal Park, spectacular cliff dwellings and other unstabilized ruins exist in a secluded and undeveloped setting. Organized backcountry tours are the subject of some controversy among preservationists who wish to see NPS access restrictions extended to all cultural artifacts in the region.

A Ute Mountain Tribal Park guide must accompany all nontribal members who want to enter this portion of the Ute Mountain Reservation.

Tribal members lead full-day tours of surface ruins, cliff dwellings and Ute pictographs. Visitors should be prepared to drive 80 miles on unpaved roads and hike

about 3 miles. Tour rates are on a sliding scale: parties of less than 10 pay $25 per person, those over 10 pay $15/person. Nonmotorists may travel with the tour guide for an additional $5. Half-day tours are also available for $15/person. Tours leave daily at 8:30 am from the Ute Mountain Park Tribal Park visitors center, 20 miles south of Cortez at the junction of US 160 and US 666. The impressive spire of Chimney Rock provides a nearby landmark.

Mountain-bike tours, overnight backpack hikes and photographic tours can also be arranged. Information and reservations are obtained at the visitors center (☎ 970-565-9653, 800-847-5485).

Places to Stay

Sleeping Ute RV Park & Campground (☎ 970-565-8800, 800-889-5072) is open year-round with an indoor pool, laundry, showers and game room behind the Ute Mountain Casino. Sites with full hookups are $12. *Ute Mountain Tribal Park*, the park's no-frills campsite along the Mancos River, costs $10 per vehicle and requires advance reservations and joining a tour. Food and drinking water are not available in the park.

Eastern Plains

Most visitors blast through the Eastern Plains on their way to the Rocky Mountains, and with good reason. While making your way slowly across the plains offers a nice view of a slice of small-town Americana, few spots are genuinely worth a special trip. A good case might be made for visiting the displays of nature and wildlife at Pawnee National Grassland or rock art on the canyon walls beside the Purgatoire River in the Comanche National Grassland. Keen history buffs may also enjoy tracing the path of pioneer travelers along the Santa Fe Trail, including a stop at Bent's Old Fort National Historic Site. Perhaps the best thing about this scenically tame part of the state is its people: in the Eastern Plains you'll find some of the friendliest folks in Colorado.

Before the arrival of European settlers in the 1820s, the eastern Plains were home to several tribes: the Apache, Pawnee and Comanche in the south and the Cheyenne and Arapaho in the north. Though the Apache successfully kept the Spanish from moving northward, by the late 1860s Native American buffalo hunts had been replaced by ranchers' cattle roundups and farming.

GREELEY

Greeley (population 69,000), the largest city in the Eastern Plains, was founded as a cooperative agricultural colony along the railroad. Horace Greeley used his *New York Tribune* in the 1870s to exhort settlers to 'go west' to his agrarian utopia headed up by Nathan Meeker on the plains, midway between Denver and Cheyenne, WY. Greeley's economic foundation is the rich irrigated farmland near the confluence of the Cache la Poudre and South Platte rivers, plus Colorado's biggest cattle operations.

Since the initial arrival of educated colonists, the performing arts have been popular in Greeley. The University of Northern Colorado (UNC) campus is renowned for its jazz and summer theater programs. The elaborate Union Colony Civic Center also hosts a series of plays in addition to providing performance space for Greeley's Philharmonic Orchestra and Chamber Orchestra.

Orientation

US 85 and US 34 both have bypass routes that skirt the central city, as well as business routes that go through the heart of it. Most restaurants and lodgings are on either 8th Ave (Business US 85) parallel with the railroad, or the intersecting 10th St (Business US 34). The avenues in town run

---

HIGHLIGHTS

- Greeley – Horace Greeley's utopian experiment is now home to farmers, ranchers and symphony musicians

- Pawnee National Grassland – 193,000 acres of stark, tall-grass prairie, home to raptors and the stunning Pawnee Buttes

- Bent's Old Fort National Historic Site – an impressive restoration that recreates life on the Santa Fe Trail in the 1840s

COLORADO

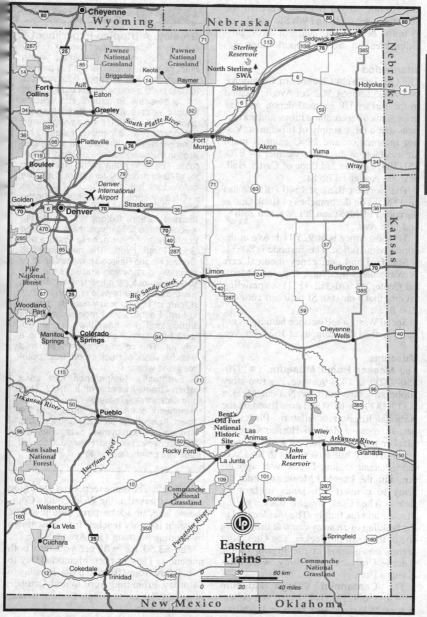

Eastern Plains

north-south, streets run east-west. In the downtown area, 8th and 9th Sts are closed to traffic between 8th and 9th Aves, providing pleasant strolling opportunities.

Information

The Greeley/Weld Chamber of Commerce (☎ 970-352-3566), 902 7th Ave, is located in the former UP railroad depot, and has maps, lists of accommodations and restaurants and a large supply of brochures. Visitor information and UNC campus maps are available at the visitors center (☎ 970-351-2097) on the 3rd floor of Carter Hall, near 8th Ave and 17th St.

The Norwest Bank at 1540 8th Ave has an ATM, as do the branches of Bank One at the corner of 7th St and 9th Ave, and 26th St and 11th Ave.

The post office is at 925 11th Ave at the corner with 10th St. The zip code is 80631.

Standard and emergency medical care is available at the North Colorado Medical Center (☎ 970-352-4121), a sprawling facility that's on 16th St between 16th and 21st Aves.

Speed Wash, a self-service laundry, is not far from the UNC campus at 1624 8th Ave.

Museums

The **Meeker Home Museum**, (☎ 970-350-9221), at 1324 9th Ave, is a two-story adobe structure built by Nathan Meeker (1817-1879) in 1870 and now listed on the National Register of Historic Places. In part to repay a debt to Horace Greeley, Meeker took a position as a government agent to the White River Utes in the Colorado Plateau region. Feuds over agriculture with the Utes led Meeker to order the army to convert Ute lands to farming fields. The Utes fought back, killing Meeker and his family. The incident led to the building of an army camp at the present site of the town of Meeker. The Utes, after laying down arms at the urging of the Apache-Ute mediator Ouray, were relocated to Utah.

The **Centennial Village Museum** (☎ 970-350-9220), 1475 A St, is a collection of 28 historic structures and exhibits,

Greeley: A Utopian Experiment

New York Tribune editor Horace Greeley coined the phrase, 'Go west, young man, go west!' in the 1870s. His promotion was a pragmatic appeal for workers to help build a cooperative colony based on large-scale irrigation. His articles sought settlers who 'practiced temperance,' had $1000 in savings and belonged to an organized religion. He misrepresented the site as a forested area in the shadows of the Rocky Mountains – causing many of the first arrivals in 1870 to promptly turn back. Still, the colony took hold.

Greeley chose Nathan Meeker to be his western representative. Meeker then located Union Colony in the fertile wedge immediately upstream from the confluence of the Cache la Poudre and South Platte rivers. The newly opened Denver Pacific Railroad provided another compelling attraction and sold the land to the colony for the townsite which was platted with streets wide enough to allow a team of horses and wagon to make a U-turn. Each colonist received a 5-acre agricultural plot near town, or an 80-acre tract farther away, in addition to a city lot. The colonists soon prospered with harvests of truck crops, fruit, potatoes and wheat.

Eventually, temperance lost favor when Greeley went 'wet' in 1977. Now the wide streets leave plenty of room for a network of bike lanes throughout the town. Agricultural products and services still lead all employment categories, but Eastman Kodak and Hewlett Packard operate plants nearby. ■

including a Cheyenne teepee, an 1860s log cabin that served as the Weld County Courthouse and an adobe farm building. The museum is easily reached from downtown by heading north on 11th Ave to A St.

The $3.50 fee will get you into both museums. They're open Memorial Day to Labor Day from 10 am to 5 pm Tuesday to Saturday. From mid-April to mid-October, hours are 10 am to 3 pm. Both museums close in winter.

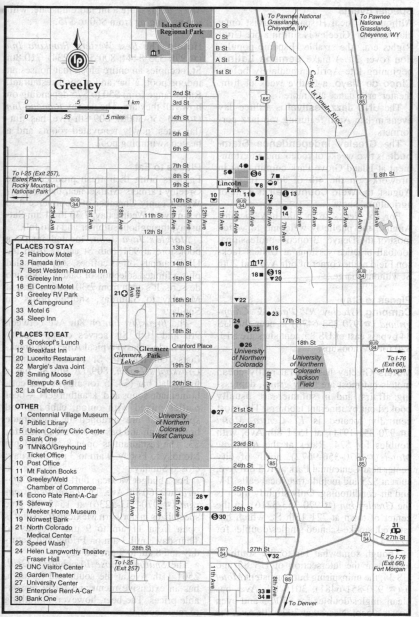

Greeley

0   .5   1 km
0   .25   .5 miles

PLACES TO STAY
2 Rainbow Motel
3 Ramada Inn
7 Best Western Ramkota Inn
16 Greeley Inn
18 El Centro Motel
31 Greeley RV Park
     & Campground
33 Motel 6
34 Sleep Inn

PLACES TO EAT
8 Groskopf's Lunch
12 Breakfast Inn
20 Lucerito Restaurant
22 Margie's Java Joint
28 Smiling Moose
     Brewpub & Grill
32 La Cafeteria

OTHER
1 Centennial Village Museum
4 Public Library
5 Union Colony Civic Center
6 Bank One
9 TMN&O/Greyhound
     Ticket Office
10 Post Office
11 Mt Falcon Books
13 Greeley/Weld
     Chamber of Commerce
14 Econo Rate Rent-A-Car
15 Safeway
17 Meeker Home Museum
19 Norwest Bank
21 North Colorado
     Medical Center
23 Speed Wash
24 Helen Langworthy Theater,
     Fraser Hall
25 UNC Visitor Center
26 Garden Theater
27 University Center
29 Enterprise Rent-A-Car
30 Bank One

COLORADO

Special Events
Although a local Hispanic activist once claimed that 'Greeley is still in a pre-Civil Rights era,' the sizable Hispanic population (over 20%) make **Semana Latina**, beginning late April immediately before **Cinco de Mayo**, a festive week of film, theater, arts, dance and more.

The **UNC Jazz Festival** is a three-day event in late April featuring top jazz performers.

The **Greeley Independence Stampede** is two weeks of rodeo and entertainment at Island Grove Park culminating in fireworks on the 4th of July. In early August, the **Weld County Fair** is a major agricultural show.

For six weeks from mid-July to mid-August, the public is welcome to watch most of the Denver Broncos' professional football practice sessions at UNC's Jackson Field at the corner of 6th Ave and 20th St without charge.

Places to Stay
Camping *Greeley RV Park & Campground* (☎ 970-353-6476) is near the US 34 bypass east of US 85; tent sites are $13, $20 for RV hookups.

Motels Greeley has several really cheap motels but most are fairly grimy, depressing affairs, and in summer are usually booked out by itinerant laborers. The most centrally located is *El Centro Motel* (☎ 970-351-1911), at 1521 8th Ave, with doubles for $24. Rates at the *Rainbow Motel* (☎ 970-356-9672), north of city center near Centennial Park at 105 8th Ave, start at $25 and include free local calls, TV and air-conditioning. Only slightly nicer is the *Greeley Inn* (☎ 970-353-3216), in the center of town at 721 13th St, which has tattered, smoke-scented singles/doubles for $27/34.

Though somewhat far to the south of town near the intersection of US 85 and US 34, the uninspiring but consistent *Motel 6* (☎ 970-351-6481), 3015 8th Ave, has clean singles/doubles for $30/35 and even boasts a pool. Nearby at 3025 8th Ave, the *Sleep Inn* is quite a bit more upscale, with rooms ranging from $60 to $75.

Hotels The *Best Western Ramkota Inn* (☎ 970-353-8444, 800-528-1234), 710 8th St, occupies an entire block that houses an indoor pool, a bar and a good restaurant. Rates range from $50 to $75 depending on how full they are. The nearby *Ramada Inn* (☎ 970-356-3000), 609 8th Ave, has similar rates, newly renovated rooms and a heated swimming pool.

Places to Eat
Farmers bring their fresh produce to the Greeley Farmers' Market near the Greeley/Weld County Chamber of Commerce 4 to 6 pm every Wednesday, 7:30 to 11 am Saturday, throughout summer and into fall.

Margie's Java Joint, located inside a bookstore at 931 16th St across from the UNC campus, offers coffees, soup and salad plus a limited selection of baked goods and desserts. It's open from 7:30 am to midnight Monday to Saturday, shorter hours on Sunday.

The *Breakfast Inn* on 8th Ave between 9th and 10th Sts serves cheap, hearty (and fairly greasy) typical American breakfasts. On the 9th St pedestrian mall, *Groskopf's Lunch*, 809-1A 9th St, has a fine salad bar ($4.75 for all you can eat), homemade soups and 'krautburgers' – beef patties mixed with onion, cabbage and spices that are wrapped in homemade bread dough and baked. Not a bad deal for $3. The restaurant is open 8 am to 3 pm Monday to Friday, 9 am to 3 pm Saturday; closed Sunday.

For a budget Mexican buffet try *La Cafeteria* at 2760 8th Ave. The *Lucerito Restaurant* (☎ 970-353-5236) at 1542 8th Ave specializes in northern Mexican food and is open from 11 am to 9 pm Tuesday to Thursday, until 3 am on Friday and Saturday and 8 am to 9 pm Sunday.

The *Smiling Moose Brewpub & Grill*, 2501 11th Ave at the south end of town, has an extensive menu and fairly reasonable prices. The beer, however, is nothing to rave about.

Entertainment

Check the *Union Colony Civic Center* (☎ 970-356-5000), 701 10th Ave, for performances in the new theater hall.

The *UNC College of Performing & Visual Arts* (☎ 970-351-2200) offers more than 250 public events annually, including recitals, concerts and exhibits. Most are free of charge. Summer *symphonic concerts* are held Tuesday evenings in July at the outdoor Garden Theater near 10th Ave and Cranford Place.

Another popular attraction is UNC's *Little Theater of the Rockies*, started in 1934 as the first summer stock program in Colorado. From mid-June to late July, plays and musical are staged Thursday through Saturday at the Helen Langworthy Theater in Fraser Hall at the corner 17th St and 10th Ave. Admission ranges from $10 to $15.

Getting There & Away

Bus Three northbound buses and three southbound TNM&O/Greyhound buses running between Denver and Cheyenne, WY, stop in front of the TNM&O ticket office (☎ 970-353-5050) inside the Arix Building, 800 8th Ave. The office is open Monday to Friday 7:30 am to 4 pm, Saturday 7:30 am to 1 pm. It's best to buy tickets at the office, as they cost more when bought directly from the driver.

Shuttle Rocky Mountain Shuttle (☎ 970-356-3366) provides eight daily shuttles to/from your door and Denver International Airport for $22, $40 for two. Bikes cost an extra $5.

Car Greeley is 50 miles east of Estes Park via US 34 and just over 50 miles north of Denver via US 85. From Fort Morgan, drive west on I-76 for 21 miles, then head northwest on US 34 for 40 miles.

Getting Around

Bus Buses operate between established bus stops throughout Greeley, Monday to Saturday during commute hours. Adult fare is 75¢. Check the telephone book for a map of the 10 routes. Bus schedules are available at

the public library at the corner of 7th St and 9th Ave, at the Safeway at 11th Ave and 12th St or by calling ☎ 970-350-9287.

Car Econo Rate Rent-A-Car (☎ 970-351-6969) is at 1030 7th Ave. You can also try Enterprise Rent-A-Car (☎ 970-356-3008) at 2541 11th Ave.

Taxi Shamrock Yellow Cab (☎ 970-352-3000) serves Greeley.

PAWNEE NATIONAL GRASSLAND

Stretching across the plains northeast of Greeley, 193,000 acres of stark, tall-grass prairie have been spared the plow. Amid the solitude of this far-reaching preserve – a raptor nesting site – are the scenic Pawnee Buttes. This area is best known among birdwatchers, who flock here in the spring and early summer to observe the wide variety of raptors and other feathered creatures.

The Pawnee National Grassland had its origin in the repurchase of 'sub-marginal lands' by the US government in the 1930s, and became protected in the 1960s. Agricultural ghost towns, like Keota, and abandoned farmsteads dot the landscape. As you travel the grassland, note that wind is harnessed both by Chicago Aeromotors (to pump water for cattle) and slowed by 'living fences' of trees planted to control erosion and blowing snow.

Orientation

The grassland is divided into two extensive tracts: in the west is the Crow Valley Area and the hamlet of Briggsdale; to the east is the Pawnee Area and a store at Raymer. The highlight for most visitors is the panoramic view of Pawnee Buttes, north of the map speck called Keota. A checkerboard pattern of public and private ownership in the area requires care to avoid trespassing.

Access to the area is via Hwy 14 which forms the start of the 'Pawnee Pioneer Trails,' a route of paved and gravel roads that weaves in and around the grassland before heading east to Sterling.

COLORADO

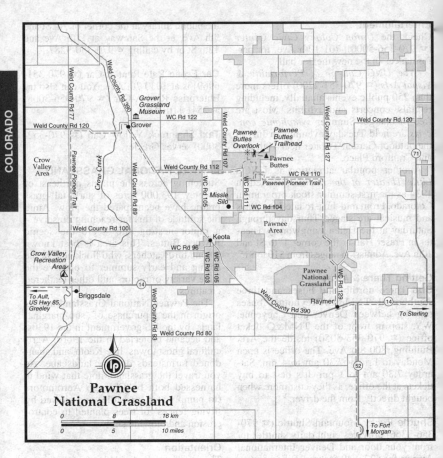

Weld County Rd 390

Weld County Rd 77

Weld County Rd 120

Grover Grassland Museum

Grover

WC Rd 122

Weld County Rd 107

Pawnee Buttes Overlook

Pawnee Buttes Trailhead

Pawnee Buttes

Weld County Rd 127

Weld County Rd 120

71

Crow Valley Area

Pawnee Pioneer Trail

Crow Creek

Weld County Rd 89

Weld County Rd 112

WC Rd 105

WC Rd 111

WC Rd 104

WC Rd 110

Pawnee Pioneer Trail

Pawnee Area

Missle Silo

Weld County Rd 100

Keota

Crow Valley Recreation Area

WC Rd 96

WC Rd 103

WC Rd 105

14

Pawnee Area

Pawnee National Grassland

WC Rd 129

Raymer

14

To Sterling

To Ault, US Hwy 85, Greeley

Briggsdale

Weld County Rd 93

Weld County Rd 80

Weld County Rd 390

52

Pawnee National Grassland

0   8   16 km
0   5   10 miles

52

To Fort Morgan

Information

It's strongly recommended to first stop at the USFS Pawnee National Grassland Ranger Station (☎ 970-353-5004), which is actually 34 miles southeast of the grassland at 660 East O St in northern Greeley, a block east of the intersection with US 85. (If you're coming from Greeley city center, note that East O St and West O St are cut off from each other: the best way is to approach via Hwy 85 and take the O St exit.) The station is open 8 am to 4:30 pm Monday to Friday. A detailed USFS map of the grassland is available for $4; birding tour

guides, larger scale maps to the Pawnee Buttes and other information are also on offer. You'll need the maps to make your way around the confusing warren of roads crisscrossing the grasslands.

To request materials by mail, send a check or money order to USDA Forest Service at District Ranger, 660 O St, Greeley, CO 80631. You can also purchase the grassland map from the friendly owners of the Pawnee Station Restaurant in New Raymer on Hwy 14 or at the Briggsdale market, provided either place is open; both tend to keep erratic hours.

Grover Grassland Museum

The 110-year-old wooden depot housing the museum (☎ 970-895-2349) on the east end of the small town of Grover, once on the now defunct Chicago, Burlington & Quincy railroad, is listed on the National Register of Historic Places. Opening hours are not set, so it's best to call ahead and schedule a visit.

Pawnee Buttes

Standing 300 feet above the plains, the Pawnee Buttes are a stunning variation in an otherwise level landscape. Sudden afternoon downpours carved the vertical cliffs of the buttes and bluffs, wearing away the soft sandstone and undercutting the cap rock (don't stand too close to the edge!). Note the formation of new steep-sided buttes north of the overlook, which one day may also become an isolated butte.

Once your ears become accustomed to the silence of the prairie, listen for wildlife. The cliff faces of the bluff provide nesting habitat for many bird species, including the ferruginous hawk and the prairie falcon. The chestnut-collared longspur, mountain plover, American avocet and burrowing owl also call this treeless land home. The overlook cliffs are closed to visitors from March to July to protect nesting activity. Binoculars and a telephoto lens are the only ways to get close-up views of nest areas.

From the bluff you might also observe an unsuspecting coyote stalking small game or playing. Spring hikes have the added reward of abundant fields of wildflowers

Blue grama is one of the grasses that make up the Pawnee Grassland.

among the grasses. Yucca and prickly pear cactus dot the land – often invading once overgrazed areas. Climbing the crumbling cliffs is not recommended and would disturb endangered bird species.

The limited number of signs directing visitors over the gravel roads to Pawnee Buttes make it essential that you carefully study the map to avoid getting lost; it's 11 miles from Keota to Pawnee Buttes. Take water and a hat. An easy 1½-mile trail leads to the base of the Buttes from the signs near the overlook entrance gate. Mountain bikes are not permitted on the trail.

Missile Silo

An active Minuteman III silo is located near the route to Pawnee Buttes. From Keota drive north 3 miles on Weld County Rd 105, then right onto Weld County Rd 104 and go a little over 2 miles: Silo 08 is on the left. It is one of over 200 Minuteman silos dispersed a minimum of 4.2 miles apart in an extensive field over a large area of southeastern Wyoming, southwestern Nebraska and a small part of northeast Colorado. There may be no one around but don't try hopping the barbed-wire fence for a closer look – you will likely soon have company in the form of US Air Force military police.

Birdwatching

A self-guided birdwatching tour route and map are available in a color brochure at the USFS office in Greeley. Bird lists are also available. If you did not pick up these materials before entering the Grassland, try the USFS Briggsdale Work Center (☎ 970-656-3532), just north to the Crow Valley Recreation Area, where the tour begins. During wet weather, travel on the unpaved roads by passenger automobile is not recommended. The best time for birdwatching is February to July, after which activity dies down. Remember to be very careful as you observe: birds are particularly vulnerable to any human interference and just strolling up for a closer look can cause adults to flee, leaving their chicks exposed to the environment and predators.

Road Biking

The 36-mile birdwatching tour described above can be enjoyed via bicycle. You may want to modify the counterclockwise circuit to return on Weld County Rd 96 rather than Hwy 14. Be prepared for possible afternoon cloudbursts in summer months.

Places to Stay & Eat

The only developed campground in the entire grassland area is the USFS *Crow Valley Recreation Area*, with shaded $8 sites. The campground entrance is immediately north of Hwy 14 on Weld County Rd 77, a half-mile from Briggsdale.

In the friendly, tiny town of Grover, *The Plover Inn* (☎ 970-895-2275), 223 Chatoga St, is a B&B that mostly caters to birders. It has four suites that can accommodate a total of 16 people. Rates range from $60 to $90 for two people. Northwest of Grover near the intersection of Weld County Rds 130 and 59 is *West Pawnee Ranch* (☎ 970-895-2482), a working ranch that has three guest rooms: two with private bath for $50 and $55, and a two-room 'Prairie House' which can house two couples or a family for $90.

Grover has two small cafes, one of which also has a small grocery store. If you're planning to camp or picnic it's probably best to do your shopping in Greeley or some other larger town. You may also be able to pick up snack items at the Briggsdale Market.

Getting There & Away

To get to the grasslands from the USFS Ranger Station in Greeley, head north 10 miles on US 85 to Ault and the Hwy 14 intersection. Turn right toward Briggsdale, 24 miles away. From Briggsdale it's another 22 miles to Grover and then another 20 miles or so to the Pawnee Buttes.

FORT MORGAN

Fort Morgan (population 10,000) is about 80 miles northeast of Denver on I-76, about 40 miles west of Sterling. Though not really a destination in itself, there are some nice diversions if you decide to stay overnight here, including the **Fort Morgan Museum**, which, along with Western history displays, has exhibits on the town's most famous native, WWII-era Big Band leader Glenn Miller. The pleasant **Riverside Park**, a 240-acre wildlife preservation area along the South Platte River, encompasses wetlands, swimming pools, sports fields and a nature trail where you may see deer, turkeys, eagles, herons and foxes.

For more information on the town, stop by the Fort Morgan Chamber of Commerce (☎ 970-867-6702) at 300 Main St.

Places to Stay & Eat

Fort Morgan's handsome *Riverside Park* has a number of free wooded tent sites and restrooms in an area beyond the popular picnic grounds near the east parking lot. Parking for RVs is available near the children's playground. Showers are available during summer months at the park's swimming pools.

Singles/doubles go for $29/35 at the small and basic *Fort Morgan Motel* (☎ 970-867-8264), 525 W Platte Ave. Similar rates are available at *The Deluxe Motel* (☎ 970-867-2459), 817 E Platte Ave. The *Central Motel* (☎ 970-867-2401), at 201 W Platte Ave, has quiet and clean singles/doubles with microwave ovens and refrigerators for $37/43. The *Best Western Park Terrace* (☎ 970-867-8256), at 725 Main St, has a swimming pool, hot tub and restaurant; rates are $48/55.

Breakfast is served all day at *Memories Restaurant* (☎ 970-867-8205) in the Best Western at 725 Main St. It's a popular spot serving fresh fruit pies and Mexican and standard American entrees daily 5:30 am to 9 pm.

Carnivorous Americana reigns at *Country Steakout* (☎ 970-867-7887), a lunch and dinner restaurant east of Main St at 19592 E 8th Ave. The Steakout is the best restaurant in town, renowned for quality steaks; seafood and spaghetti are also on the menu.

Getting There & Away

Amtrak's *California Zephyr,* which serves Chicago-San Francisco (Emeryville) via

Denver, stops daily at the depot on Ensign St south of Railroad Ave. The eastbound train departs at 9:50 pm, westbound 6:42 am.

Greyhound buses stop in front of Pets Are People Too (☎ 970-867-8072 for bus schedule information), 835 E Platte Ave. There are three buses daily to Denver and two daily to Omaha, NE.

STERLING
Sterling's main claim to fame is its collection of imaginative (and sometimes bizarre) tree carvings of animals, people and surreal characters from fables, which can be seen from sidewalks around town. Sterling (population 10,500) is also home to the **Overland Trail Museum**, where excellent exhibits bring to life the hardships and experiences of early pioneers and the region's history. The museum is located on US 6 just a mile east of town on the south bank of the South Platte River. A park near the museum is a convenient rest stop for weary travelers contemplating the 125 mile journey southwest to Denver.

Detailed information on Sterling is available at the Logan County Chamber of Commerce (☎ 970-522-5070, 800-544-8609), located in the restored Union Pacific depot at Front and Main Sts.

Places to Stay & Eat
The city-owned Pioneer Park, on the western edge of town next to Hwy 14, offers free camping and restrooms.

Small singles/doubles at the *Crest Motel* (☎ 970-522-3753), 516 S Division St at the corner of 3rd St, are a good value for $25/28. Basic, clean singles/doubles are available for $29/34 at the *Colonial Motel* (☎ 970-522-3382), 915 S Division St. Another centrally located place is the *Oakwood Inn* (☎ 970-522-1416), 810 S Division, which has well-kept singles/doubles equipped with refrigerators and microwave ovens for $30/35. More upscale, with prices to match, is the *Best Western Sundowner* (☎ 970-522-6265) located next to the Overland Trail Museum immediately after crossing the South Platte River from I-76 (exit 48). Singles/

doubles go for $70/79; most rooms have a private balcony or porch, and the facilities include a heated pool, hot tub, fitness center, laundry and picnic area.

TJ Bummers (☎ 970-522-8397), at 203 Broadway, is a pleasant surprise: breakfast, lunch and dinner are served 5:30 am to 9 pm daily in smoke-free surroundings. The 'Hobo Dinner,' a foil-baked stew, costs $5 and a full rack of baby back ribs with side dishes is $11. *Delgado's Dugout* (☎ 970-522-0175) serves inexpensive Mexican lunches and dinners every day except Monday in the basement of the former First Baptist Church at 116 Beech St. *Fergie's West Inn Pub*, 324 W Main St between 3rd and 4th Aves, offers a selection of beers and deli sandwiches.

Getting There & Away
Greyhound buses stop at the Days Inn Motel (bus office ☎ 970-522-5522), 12881 Hwy 61, an inconvenient freeway location about 2 miles south of Sterling. There are three buses a day to Denver, two daily to Omaha, NE.

JULESBURG
In the extreme northeastern corner of Colorado on the South Platte River, Julesburg was once known as the 'Wickedest City in the West,' an end-of-the-line outpost packed with brothels and bars. Today its main feature for visitors is the Colorado Welcome Center (☎ 970-474-2054), at the junction of I-76 and US 385 (I-76 exit 180), open 8 am to 5 pm daily. Julesburg proper is about 3 miles beyond the Welcome Center across the river and a modern rail overpass – this is where road-weary travelers will find a place to spend the night. Free primitive camping on the south bank of the South Platte River is available at Lions Park, immediately south of Julesburg on US 385. The two-story *Grand Motel* (☎ 970-474-3302), 220 Pine across Third St from the courthouse, has a coin laundry on the premises and clean singles/doubles with phone and cable TV for $25/34. Another budget option is the *Holiday Motel* (☎ 970-474-3371), on the western edge of town at

the junction of US 138 and 385; singles/doubles are $26/32. A little more expensive is the *Platte Valley Inn* (☎ 970-474-3336, 800-562-5166), next to the freeway exit, where singles/doubles cost $43/46.

I-70 CORRIDOR
Between Denver and the Kansas border, I-70 runs through some of the state's blandest landscape. The only reason to stop in this area is if you're in danger of falling asleep at the wheel.

Some travelers bound for Denver have found themselves too frazzled by the endless drive through the plains of Kansas and have sought shelter in the motels of **Limon**, 86 miles east of the Colorado capital. Most of the accommodation in this little agricultural town is located in the downtown area accessed by exit 361. At the *KOA* (☎ 719-775-2151), adjacent to I-70 exit 361, grassy tent sites cost $15, but you must endure the freeway noise. The three-story *Midwest Country Inn* (☎ 719-775-2373), 795 Main St, is a comfortable place: rooms have attractive quilt bedspreads and some antique furnishings and cost $34/40 singles/doubles. The nearby *Safari Motel* (☎ 719-775-2363), 637 Main St, has a swimming pool, coin laundry and singles/doubles for $30/40 (higher in summer). Near exit 361 is the *Preferred Motor Inn* (☎ 719-775-2385) with swimming pool and hot tub; singles doubles are $36/42.

Just 12 miles from the Kansas border, 163 miles east of Denver, the town of **Burlington**, boasts several motels and a Colorado Welcome Center (☎ 719-346-5554) located at the I-70 exit, along with its Thursday cattle auctions. If you're in town for any length of time, venture north of the railroad tracks off 15th St to the 1905 Kit Carson County Carousel, which sports 46 hand-carved animals.

RV sites are available for $10 at *Campland* (☎ 719-346-8763), on the east side of town at the corner of 4th St and Senter Ave. The lowest rates in town are at the *Kit Carson Motel* (☎ 719-346-8513), 700 Rose Ave, with $25/29 singles/doubles. The brick

Western Motor Inn (☎ 719-346-5371), at the corner of Rose Ave and Lincoln St, has clean, quiet singles/doubles for $28/31. An enclosed pool and children's play area are added amenities at *Sloan's Motel* (☎ 719-346-5333 800-362-0464), 1901 Rose Ave; singles/doubles go for $34/38.

US 50 Corridor

Between 1822 and 1872, caravans of goods followed the Mountain Route of the Santa Fe Trail along the Arkansas River between St Louis and Santa Fe. At Bent's Fort, the traders left the comfort of the river valley and its resources to angle across the barren plains toward Raton Pass and Santa Fe. Today, US 50 follows the Arkansas River and US 350 roughly follows the Santa Fe Trail, linking La Junta and Trinidad. The agricultural economy relies on grain farming, much of which is fed to cattle grazed on the poorer lands; summer hail and wind can wreck a crop.

LA JUNTA
La Junta (mispronounced 'La Hunt-ah') is Spanish for 'The Junction,' namely th eonce here between the main line and Denver branch of the Santa Fe railroad. For the few travelers who roam the Eastern Plains, it's still a junction of sorts, lying between Bent's Old Fort National Historic Site to the northeast and the Comanche National Grassland to the south. La Junta (population 8000), while not stunning, offers a pleasant snapshot of small-town American life yet to be overrun by freeways, shopping malls and tourist kitsch. Ranchers from the Rocky Mountains to the far corners of the eastern plains come to La Junta's livestock auctions to market their range-fed animals, lending the town a distinctive Western flair.

Orientation
Through traffic on US 50 follows east-west 1st St through town, south of the Arkansas River and the railroad. Colorado

COLORADO

COLORADO

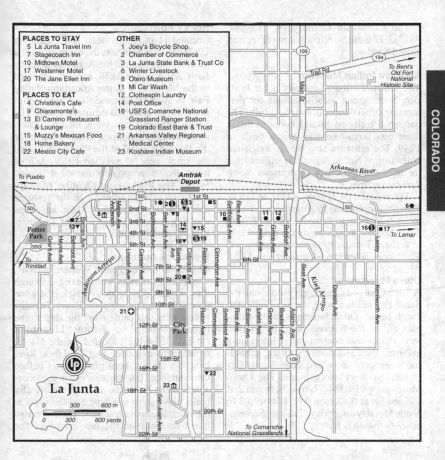

PLACES TO STAY
5 La Junta Travel Inn
7 Stagecoach Inn
10 Midtown Motel
17 Westerner Motel
20 The Jane Ellen Inn

PLACES TO EAT
4 Christina's Cafe
9 Chiaramonte's
13 El Camino Restaurant & Lounge
15 Muzzy's Mexican Food
18 Home Bakery
22 Mexico City Cafe

OTHER
1 Joey's Bicycle Shop
2 Chamber of Commerce
3 La Junta State Bank & Trust Co
6 Winter Livestock
8 Otero Museum
11 Mi Car Wash
12 Clothespin Laundry
14 Post Office
16 USFS Comanche National Grassland Ranger Station
19 Colorado East Bank & Trust
21 Arkansas Valley Regional Medical Center
23 Koshare Indian Museum

Ave is the main business artery, extending south from the rail depot at 1st St. On the east side of town, Hwy 109 crosses the Arkansas River, going north to connect with Hwy 194 leading to Bent's Old Fort, 6 miles away.

Information

The La Junta Chamber of Commerce (☎ 719-384-7411), at 110 Santa Fe Ave on US 50 opposite the Amtrak Depot, has useful maps and information and is open from 9 am to 5 pm Monday to Friday. The USFS Comanche National Grassland Ranger Station (☎ 719-384-2181), 1420 E 3rd St, has detailed information on the grasslands (see Comanche National Grassland below).

ATMs are located at the Colorado East Bank & Trust, at 405 Colorado Ave, and La Junta State Bank & Trust Co near the corner of Colorado Ave and 1st St.

The Spanish-style post office, which is on the National Register of Historic Places, is at the corner of 4th St and Colorado Ave.

The Arkansas Valley Regional Medical Center (☎ 719-384-5412) is at 1100 Carson Ave at the corner of 10th St.

The Clothespin Laundry (☎ 719-384-9812), 717 E 3rd St, offers a drop-off service; closed Sunday.

Koshare Indian Museum

The Koshare tribe is actually a La Junta Boy Scout group locally famous for performing tribal dances in June and July. The dancers literally go through hoops of fire in their own kiva-like auditorium built in 1949. The museum also has an extensive collection of Native American artifacts that includes examples from most major North American tribes.

The museum (☎ 719-384-4411), at 115 W 18th St, is open June to August from 10 am to 5 pm Monday to Saturday, from 12:30 to 5 pm Sunday. Winter hours are from 12:30 to 4:30 pm Tuesday to Sunday. Admission is $2. Dances, when staged, usually cost $5.

Otero Museum

A 1865 Concord stagecoach used along the Santa Fe Trail is among the exhibits in the coach house. Other buildings in the complex are on the National Register of Historic Places and contain many interesting exhibits, such as a doctor's office, schoolroom, grocery store and completely furnished two-story adobe home. The Otero Museum (☎ 719-384-7406) is between 2nd and 3rd Sts at Anderson Ave. It's open 1 to 5 pm Monday to Friday, June to September. Admission is free.

Rocky Ford

Located 11 miles northeast of La Junta on US 50, Rocky Ford was the name given to a safe crossing point in the Arkansas River by Kit Carson. Since 1878, revelers attracted to the Melon Pile at the **Arkansas Valley Fair** in August, Colorado's oldest continuous fair, have stuffed themselves on Rocky Ford's delicious honeydew melons, watermelons and cantaloupes. When residents of the 'Melon Capital of the World' dedicated the small general aviation field south of town, they appropriately named it 'Melon Field.' The Rocky Ford Chamber of Commerce (☎ 719-254-7483), in the restored Santa Fe Depot at 105 N Main, has maps showing over 30 produce farms and markets open to the public.

Livestock Auctions

Check out this authentic Western activity, which few tourists know exists, though they would likely pay to watch if it were on display at a theme park. Every Tuesday auctioneers sell cattle from the ring to the highest bidders at **Winter Livestock** (☎ 719-384-4491), located on the US 50 frontage road just east of La Junta. Ring handlers merely herd placid cows before the audience, but must sidestep the occasional mean bull. The atmosphere literally reeks of Western ranching and the dress is bib overalls, boots and hats. There are also horse auctions on the last Friday of the

Before the railroads ruled, the bumpy ride of horse-drawn stagecoaches brought many out West.

month. The nearby **La Junta Livestock** (☎ 719-384-7781) holds cattle auctions every Wednesday.

Road & Mountain Biking

You can ride to Rocky Ford on the paved country backroads from La Junta. A 32-mile counterclockwise loop crosses the Arkansas River to N La Junta on Hwy 109, then turns left (west) on Hwy 266 to Rocky Ford. Return by traveling south on Hwy 71 to Hawley where a left turn (east) on Hwy 10 heads back to La Junta. The wide-open spaces of the Comanche National Grassland (see below) invite fat-tire enthusiasts to explore the unexpected greenness of its canyons, follow an old stage route or just cruise the gravel roads across the plains.

Joey's Bicycle Shop (☎ 719-384-6575), 112 W 1st St (US 50), has supplies (take extra tire tubes) and local riding experience to share with visitors. They also rent mountain bikes for $12/15 standard/suspension and are open Tuesday to Saturday.

Places to Stay

Grassy tent and RV sites are available for $16/19 at the *KOA* (☎ 719-384-9580), 2 miles west of town on US 50. A bit farther out, there are free shaded sites with restrooms but no drinking water at the *Holbrook Reservoir SWA*. To get there from La Junta, go 5 miles northwest on US 50 to Swink, turn right onto Otero County Rd 24.5 and go north for 3 miles, then right onto Otero County Rd FF.

The *La Junta Travel Inn* (☎ 719-384-2504) has the cheapest singles/doubles in town at $27/29, but is across from the noisy railyards on busy US 50 at 110 E 1st St. Popular cowboy poet Baxter Black once slept at the immaculate *Midtown Motel* (☎ 719-384-7741), 215 E 3rd St, the only motel in town that's away from US 50 traffic noise. Singles/doubles are a good value at $28/36. The *Westerner Motel* (☎ 719-384-2591), near the USFS office on the east side of town at 1502 E 3rd St, has comfortable rooms for $30/34. Old toy collectors will want to check out the collection in the front office. On the west side of town

at the intersection of US 50 and US 350, the 1960s cinderblock *Stagecoach Inn* (☎ 719-384-5476) has amiable staff, a swimming pool and clean rooms for $36/45.

The Jane Ellen Inn (☎ 719-384-8445, 800-743-2108), 722 Colorado Ave, is an attractive B&B with three rooms (two with shared bath) from $50.

Places to Eat

Christina's Cafe (☎ 719-384-7508) at 116 Colorado Ave has friendly service, breakfast specials from $3 and overflowing dinner plates that include a potato, salad and roll for $6. The *Home Bakery* (☎ 719-384-2922), 418 Colorado Ave, also serves breakfast and is open at 6 am.

A testament to its large Hispanic population, La Junta has quite a few Mexican restaurants. Though the name may not sound authentic, the menu is quite traditional at *Muzzy's Mexican Food*, 315 Colorado Ave, where à la carte tacos and enchiladas are $1.50 and combination platters are $4 to $5. *El Camino Restaurant & Lounge* (☎ 719-384-2871), offers good Mexican dishes for lunch and dinner at 816 W 3rd St; closed Sundays and Mondays. The *Mexico City Cafe* (☎ 719-384-9518), in a residential neighborhood at 1617 Raton Ave, is a popular spot with combo plates for $4 to $5, though it caters to a more mainstream American palate.

Among the best alternatives to Mexican food is *Chiaramonte's* (☎ 719-384-8909), 208 Santa Fe Ave, featuring steaks and a surprisingly extensive seafood dinner menu. Most dinners are priced above $10, but the lunch menu has sandwiches, soups and salads for less than $5.

Getting There & Away

Train The Amtrak *Southwest Chief* serves Chicago and Los Angeles daily and stops at the Amtrak Depot (☎ 719-384-2275) on 1st St (US 50) at the corner of Colorado Ave. A ticket agent is on duty at minimum from 7:30 to 10:30 am and from 6:30 to 9:30 pm. The westbound train is scheduled to arrive at 9:35 am, while the eastbound train arrives at 8:56 pm.

COLORADO

Bus TNM&O buses stop at the Mi Car Wash (☎ 719-384-9288), at 619 E 3rd St, Tickets are available for the four daily westbound buses to Pueblo and beyond, or the four eastbound buses to either Wichita, KS, or Dallas.

Car La Junta is 50 miles west of Lamar and 64 miles east of Pueblo on US 50 along the Arkansas River, and 81 miles northeast of Trinidad along the old Santa Fe Trail route followed by US 350, which enters town on 5th St.

BENT'S OLD FORT NATIONAL HISTORIC SITE

An impressive restoration and preservation effort went into the site surrounding this port, a hub of commerce on the Santa Fe Trail from 1833 to 1849. Parking is relegated to an area some distance from the fort so visitors can appreciate the historic authenticity of approaching on foot. Upon entering the front gate, the pioneer trader was greeted, as are visitors today, by a bustle of commotion within the compound. It is all the more impressive to consider that this fort was reconstructed in 1976 from little more than a foundation and a few drawings.

At the fort you can view a 20-minute film, take a 45-minute tour with a ranger or simply walk through the rooms on your own. Demonstrations of frontier skills like blacksmithing, carpentry or the preparation of hides are presented during summer months.

Bent's Old Fort (☎ 719-383-5010, TTY 719-383-5032) is on Hwy 194 8 miles east of La Junta or 13 miles west from Las Animas. From Memorial Day to Labor Day it's open from 8 am to 5:30 pm, 9 am to 4 pm the rest of the year. Admission is $2 for adults; from November to February, admission is free.

COMANCHE NATIONAL GRASSLAND

Southeastern Colorado suffered greatly from the drought and economic depression of the 1930s. The Dust Bowl disaster of the 1930s, an environmental collapse caused by poor soil management, led the federal government to purchase land and protect it from plowing and overgrazing. Since 1954, the Comanche National Grassland has been managed by the USFS. It currently consists of two extensive management units: the Timpas Unit south of La Junta, which includes readily accessible portions of the Santa Fe Trail and the many scenic, historic and archaeological sites along the Purgatoire River; and the Carrizo Unit, an even larger but more isolated area located near Springfield south of Lamar. Information and trail descriptions are available from the USFS Comanche National Grassland Ranger Station (☎ 719-384-2181), 1420 E 3rd St in La Junta.

Vogel Canyon

This small tributary to the Purgatoire River is an ideal picnic area. Four short hiking and mountain bike trails wind down to the canyon bottom, an oasis of lush vegetation and springs, and back up to the juniper trees and shortgrass prairie of the mesatop. Between 300 and 800 years ago, Native Americans lived near the springs in the canyon and etched petroglyphs on the canyon walls. A few recent vandals have added their work as well. To reach Vogel Canyon from La Junta, travel south on Hwy 109 for 13 miles. At the Vogel Canyon sign turn right (west) for a mile, then left (south) for 2 miles to the parking area. If you attempt to bike the trails, note that the initial drop into the canyon is a steep, technical challenge.

Picket Wire Canyon

Due to Anglos' inability to pronounce 'Purgatoire,' the canyon's name eventually degraded to 'Picket Wire.' In stark contrast to the shortgrass prairie, buckhorn cholla and sparse juniper woodland of the plains surrounding Picket Wire Canyon, the Purgatoire River cuts an oasis corridor along its path. Access to Picket Wire Canyon is not easy, but few other places in this region offer so much to the hiker or cyclist. The suggested 11-mile roundtrip trek to the Dinosaur Tracks is best accomplished on a mountain bike. There are four other hikes ranging from 2 to 18 miles.

The **Dinosaur Tracks**, found in the limestone rock about 5 miles from the trailhead, comprise the largest track site in North America. Parallel tracks left by the *Apatosaurus* (also known as Brontosaurus) indicate that these huge herbivores lived in herds – as the stump-like footprints of old and young all head in the same direction. Also present are the three-toed prints of the flesh-eating *Allosaurus*, which was possibly stalking the herd.

Nearby are the ruins of **Dolores Mission & Cemetery**, built between 1871 and 1889, when Mexican pioneers established the first modern settlement in the canyon.

To reach the Picket Wire Canyon trailhead from La Junta, travel south on Hwy 109 for 13 miles. At the Vogel Canyon sign turn right (west) on Otero County Rd 802 and continue for 8 miles. Turn left (south) on Otero County Rd 25 and continue for 6 miles before turning left (east), where a corral and bulletin board mark the very poor USFS Rd 500. Passenger cars should park here. Bicyclists or high-clearance vehicles may continue three-quarters of a mile east to a wire gate (please keep closed) and another 2 miles to the locked pipe gate at the trailhead. If you have a high-clearance 4WD vehicle you can participate in all-day jeep tours led by the USFS, which run from April to July and September to October. The tours cost $10 and are very popular; the Comanche National Grassland Ranger Station starts taking reservations in January.

SANTA FE TRAIL

In 1821, Mexico achieved independence from Spain, opening up trade opportunities between the new country and the USA. The conduit for this commerce became the Santa Fe Trail, linking St Louis, MO, with Mexico's northern center at Santa Fe in what is now New Mexico. At the outset in 1822, the Santa Fe Trail was a pack trail following a path where animals would find grass. Later the freight capacity of the trail was increased with the development of

wagon routes over the difficult terrain at Raton Pass and Apache Cañon in New Mexico.

You can visit three historically significant Santa Fe Trail sites within 27 miles of La Junta along Hwy 350. No services or drinking water presently exist along the 80-mile La Junta-Trinidad route, so gas up and bring supplies.

At 13 miles, turn right (north) on Hwy 71 for a half-mile to the **Sierra Vista Overlook**, where the first views of the Rocky Mountains represented a major milestone in the journey across the plains from the east. From the bluff you can share the same distant view and see the fenced corridor marking the trail for hikers wishing to follow a 3-mile segment to the **Timpas Creek Picnic Area**. Timpas Creek was the first source of water for Santa Fe Trail travelers after leaving the Arkansas River. From 1861 to 1871 the Metcalf Ranch, previously located here, served as a stagecoach station.

Timpas Creek Picnic Area is located 16 miles southeast of La Junta on the right (west) side of the highway: take Otero County Rd 16.5 across the railroad tracks and turn right to the parking lot.

You can see wagon ruts at the **Iron Spring** water stop on the Santa Fe Trail. This site was also a stagecoach station from 1861 to 1871. At 27 miles southwest of La Junta on US 350, turn left (south) onto Otero County Rd 9 and proceed 1 mile.

LAMAR

If your mind is numb from hours of driving through Kansas wheatfields, Lamar, 32 miles west of the Kansas border, might make for a good overnight stop. If you stop early, or just want to stroll around after lunch, check out the **wooden windmills**, said to be among the finest examples to be found in the entire state. One is across from the railroad depot and the other is in the front yard of the Colorado Windmill Society's president at 900 S Main St.

You can also pick up information for your Colorado vacation at the Colorado Welcome Center (☎ 719-336-3483), located in a fully restored railroad depot at Main and Beech Sts. It's open daily 8 am to 5 pm.

Places to Stay & Eat

The *Mike Higbee State Wildlife Area*, 4 miles east of Lamar on US 50, offers free unimproved campsites along the Arkansas River. Free overnight camping is also allowed at the *Lamar Roadside Park* located at the Prowers County Fairgrounds at the south entrance to town.

The cheapest rooms in town are at *Stockmens Motor Inn* (☎ 719-336-2271), at the corner of Olive and Main Sts, with $18/25 singles/doubles. Women might feel more comfortable with one of the other budget choices, however. The conveniently located *Motel 7* (☎ 719-336-7746), at 113 N Main St, is a friendly place with clean singles/doubles for $28/35, including Continental breakfast. Try to avoid the rooms near noisy US 50. Singles/doubles for $31/37 at the *Blue Spruce Motel* (☎ 719-336-7454) are set back from 1801 S Main St and have soundproof brick walls, plus Willow Creek Park is just around the corner. There's also a *Motel 6* (☎ 719-336-7471) not too far away at 1201 N Main. At the time of writing it hadn't yet opened, but you can likely expect the same clean if drab rooms and single/double rates of $30/35.

The top spot in town is the *Cow Palace Inn* (☎ 719-336-7753, 800-678-0344), at

1301 N Main. Rooms cost $75/80, and facilities include an indoor heated pool, hot tub, lounge and restaurant.

Cheap and hearty breakfast specials start from around $3 at the *Main Cafe* (☎ 719-336-5736), at 114 S Main, open daily 6:30 am to 9 pm. Reasonably priced sandwiches, burgers, Mexican dishes and steaks are found on the lunch and dinner menus. The *Hickory House* (☎ 719-336-5018), at 1115 N Main, is the top-end steakhouse featuring baby back ribs in barbecue sauce.

Getting There & Away

United Express has flights to Denver from Lamar Municipal Field 4 miles southwest of town.

The TNM&O/Greyhound Bus Station (☎ 719-336-5291) is near the courthouse at 401 S Main. There are four buses daily to Denver, three daily to Amarillo and Dallas, and one eastbound serving Wichita, KS. Some departure times are in the middle of the night, so it's wise to call ahead.

The Amtrak *Southwest Chief*, serving Los Angeles and Chicago, stops daily at the depot (☎ 719-336-3483) on US 50 and Beech St, which also houses the Colorado Welcome Center. Westbound trains leave at 8:18 am, eastbound 9:45 pm.

Lamar is situated 50 miles east of La Junta and 32 miles west of the Kansas border on US 50.

Wyoming

LEE FOSTER

Facts about Wyoming

From the Black Hills and Devils Tower to the geysers and fumaroles of Yellowstone National Park and the granite summits of the Teton and Wind River mountains, Wyoming is a state of physical contrasts, where broad arid basins and sagebrush plains yield to forested mountains.

Over 150 million years ago this landscape was a tropical marshland ruled by dinosaurs. Subsequent volcanoes and glaciation shaped and molded the topography, and now a rich fossil record and great deposits of coil and oil are the legacy of those past epochs. Today's tall forests and open plains are remarkable wildlife habitat. Pronghorn antelope herds cross the high desert, and moose, elk and bear roam the mountain country. Trout are in every stream, and beautiful birds nest in all types of habitat.

Such remarkable physical diversity provides one of America's best arenas for outdoor activity, from fishing and boating to hiking, camping, climbing and skiing.

Wyoming also has a colorful history of pioneer migration and settlement, overlaying the enduring presence of the Shoshone and Arapaho people, who today live on the Wind River Indian Reservation. The Wild West legacy is indelibly imprinted on the culture. Almost every town has a rodeo, and the era of mountain men and Indians is reenacted in pageants statewide. Each summer, 3 million visitors come to see Yellowstone and Grand Teton national parks, more than six times the total population of Wyoming! And every winter, skiers flock to world-famous Jackson Hole.

INFORMATION
State Tourist Offices

The Wyoming Division of Tourism, which operates under the Wyoming Department of Commerce, shares a building with the Frank Norris Jr Wyoming Information Center (☎ 307-777-7777, 800-225-5996; fax 307-777-6904), Etchepare Circle off College Drive (I-25 exit 7), Cheyenne, WY 82002. It's open 8 am to 5 pm daily. Other Wyoming Information Centers are at various gateways: I-80 in Pine Bluffs; I-80 in Evanston; I-80 9 miles east of Laramie; I-90 in Sundance; I-90 in Sheridan; and US 26/US 89/US 191 in Jackson. Ask for the very helpful seasonal 'Wyoming Vacation Guide' and a state highway map. For online info, check out the state website (www.state.wy.us).

To check on road conditions across the state, call ☎ 307-733-9966.

Useful Organizations

The Wyoming Department of Commerce, Division of State Parks & Historic Sites (☎ 307-777-6323; fax 307-777-6472), is at 122 W 25th St, Herschler Building, 1st Floor E, Cheyenne, WY 82002. Ask for their 'Wyoming State Parks & Historic Sites' brochure. You can also visit their website (commerce.state.wy.us/sphs). The Wyoming Department of Commerce, Wyoming State Board of Outfitters and Professional Guides (☎ 307-777-5323, 800-264-0981; fax 307-777-6715), are at 1750 Westland Rd, Cheyenne, WY 82002.

WYOMING

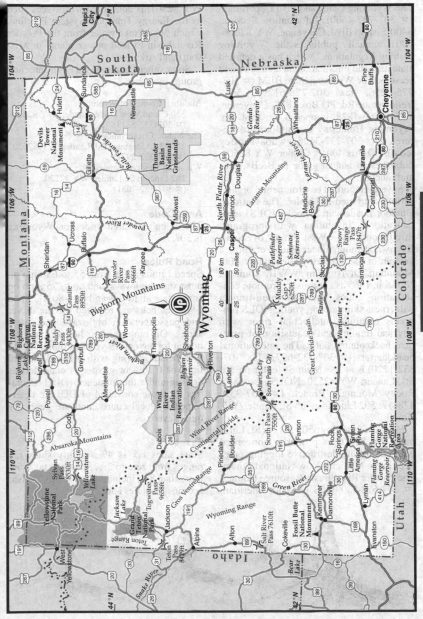

The Wyoming Game and Fish Department (☎ 307-777-4600), Information Section, 5400 Bishop Blvd, Cheyenne, WY 82006-0001, annually publishes the 'Wyoming Fishing Regulations,' which has a detailed state map and information on area laws and seasons. The Wyoming State BLM (☎ 307-775-6256; fax 307-775-6129), 5353 Yellowstone Rd, PO Box 1828, Cheyenne, WY 82003-1828, is open 9 am to 4 pm. Wyoming Homestay & Outdoor Adventures (☎ 307-237-3526; whoa@coffey.com), PO Box 40048, Casper, WY 82604, publishes an annual guide to B&Bs, inns and ranches.

Several important environmental organizations are based in Lander. The National Outdoor Leadership School (NOLS) is an educational institution with programs throughout the West and overseas. Renowned mountaineer Paul Petzoldt, a veteran of the US Army's legendary 10th Mountain Division in WWII, founded NOLS in 1965 as a means to promote conservation ethics and minimum-impact wilderness skills among youth. NOLS programs combine intellectual rigor with physical training and acquisition of practical backcountry skills. The international headquarters (☎ 307-332-6973; fax 307-332-1220) is at 288 Main St (enter on 3rd St), Lander, WY 82520. NOLS also has a Rocky Mountain Branch (☎ 307-332-4784) at 502 Lincoln at 5th St, Lander, WY 82520.

Friends of the Bow, 505 S 12th St, Laramie, WY 82070, is primarily concerned with controlling destructive logging practices in the Medicine Bow National Forest. The Powder River Basin Resource Council (☎ 307-672-5809), 23 N Scott, Sheridan, WY 82801, is concerned with issues such as the Energy Transport System Pipeline, which would take water from the Powder River basin to feed power plants in Missouri and Arkansas.

Some other Lander-based environmental groups include:

Audubon Council of Wyoming
    350 Grand View Drive, Lander, WY 82520
    (☎ 307-332-5213)
The Nature Conservancy
    258 Main St, suite 200, Lander, WY 82520
    (☎ 307-332-2971)
Wyoming Outdoor Council
    262 Lincoln St, Lander, WY 82520
    (☎ 307-332-7031)

Area Code

The telephone area code for Wyoming is 307.

Road Rules

Speed Limits range from 55 to 65 mph on most state highways, and up to 75 mph on some state highways and on I-80, I-25 and I-90. Seatbelts are required for the driver and passengers on highways and interstates. On motorcycles, helmets are required for anyone 19 years or older.

A person driving with a blood alcohol limit of 0.10% or greater is classified as driving under the influence (DUI). Penalties for those convicted of DUI are determined by local courts, and are generally quite severe.

Taxes

State sales tax is 4%; county sales tax ranges from zero to 2%. State bed tax is no more than 8%, including the 1% to 2% bed tax most counties add.

Southern Wyoming

Southern Wyoming has historically been a transit zone rather than a destination in its own right. Major emigrant routes including the Oregon, Mormon Pioneer, Overland and Pony Express trails, as well as the transcontinental telegraph, Overland Stage and Union Pacific Railroad (UP) passed through. Today I-80 traverses this region between the Wyoming-Nebraska and Wyoming-Utah state lines. During the 1970s energy crisis, plentiful coal and oil shale brought a boom and counties in southwestern Wyoming built elaborate public facilities, such as community recreation centers, which they now struggle to keep open in the face of declining budgets. Southeastern Wyoming, with its reliance on the federal and state government, is more stable economically than southwestern Wyoming's boom-and-bust country along I-80. The region is politically conservative, with Mormon areas such as Bridger Valley looking strongly toward Utah for cultural and spiritual guidance.

Southeastern Wyoming

The grasslands of the Front Range south of the North Platte River give way to three mountain ranges: Laramie, Medicine Bow and the Sierra Madre, along the crest of which runs the Continental Divide. Medicine Bow National Forest covers parts of these mountains.

CHEYENNE
At the western edge of the Great Plains, Cheyenne (population 52,000; elevation 6062 feet) is Wyoming's state capital, the state's largest city and the seat of Laramie County. Historically a cattle town and famous for Cheyenne Frontier Days cele-

brations, its economy is supported mainly by the state government and a large air force base. More than a third of all jobs are in the public sector; the largest private employers are medical services and the UP. Cheyenne retains an historic downtown and various worthwhile cultural attractions, museums and parks. For visitors arriving from the east and south, Cheyenne is the gateway to most Wyoming destinations.

History
Cheyenne owes its development to the US military and the UP. In 1865, surveying possible railroad routes through the Laramie Mountains under orders from President Abraham Lincoln, General Grenville Dodge

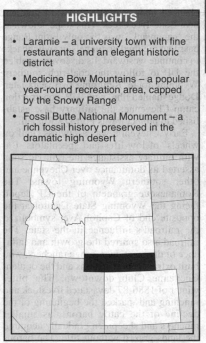

HIGHLIGHTS
• Laramie – a university town with fine restaurants and an elegant historic district
• Medicine Bow Mountains – a popular year-round recreation area, capped by the Snowy Range
• Fossil Butte National Monument – a rich fossil history preserved in the dramatic high desert

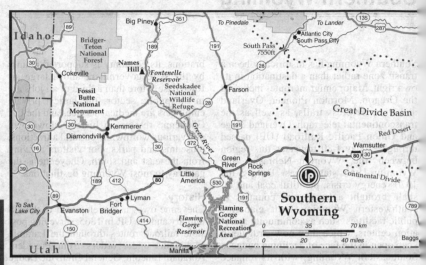

chanced upon a gentle eastward gradient near Lone Tree Creek. This slope, known as the 'gangplank,' was the only Front Range pass that required no tunnels or switchbacks to continue westward. Its discovery enabled the UP to follow the coal-rich southern Wyoming route. Returning two years later, Dodge named the new UP construction camp Cheyenne; the military base established to protect it was Fort DA Russell.

Early Cheyenne was a lawless 'hell on wheels' of low-lifes and speculators. But with military assistance the railroad soon asserted its dominance over Cheyenne and other southern Wyoming towns. The Romanesque grandeur of the UP depot, facing the Wyoming State Capitol at the opposite end of Capitol Ave, symbolized the railroad's influence in the state. The railroad also spurred the growth and influence of the great open-range ranchers, who built extravagant mansions and the opulent Cheyenne Club downtown. The bitter winter of 1886-87 devastated livestock and ranching and marked the beginning of the decline of the cattle barons, as smaller ranchers and sheepmen gradually acquired the lands grazed without title. The barons did not retreat without a fight, hiring brutal

'stock detectives' and private armies to drive away their competitors.

During the 20th century, Cheyenne grew through state government and the military. Fort DA Russell, renamed Fort Warren (now FE Warren Air Force Base), grew enormously after WWII with construction of nuclear missile sites nearby.

Orientation

Lincolnway (US 30, I-80 Business), which replaces 16th St, is the main east-west road. The railroad tracks run along the south side of Lincolnway, and downtown is north of the tracks. The main north-south roads are Central Ave (southbound) and Warren Ave (northbound); at various points these roads also form parts of US 87 Business, US 85, I-180, I-25 Business and Greeley Hwy. Central Ave divides east-west street addresses. (Downtown streets do not run directly north-south, but rather northwest to southeast.) Many grocery stores and fast-food restaurants are along Dell Range Rd north of the airport.

Information

Tourist Offices The Cheyenne Area Convention & Visitors Bureau (☎ 307-778-

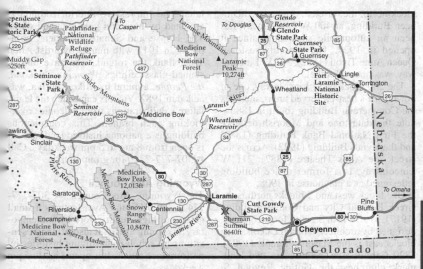

3133, 800-426-5009; info@cheyenne.org), 309 W Lincolnway, is open 8 am to 6 pm daily Memorial Day to Labor Day, and 8 am to 5 pm weekdays the rest of the year. The Greater Cheyenne Chamber of Commerce (☎ 307-638-3388), 301 W Lincolnway, has limited information.

Money Downtown banks with ATMs include: Community First National Bank, at 1800 Carey Ave; Norwest Bank, at 1700 Capitol Ave; First Bank, at 2020 Carey Ave; and American National Bank, at 1912 Capitol Ave.

Post & Communications The post office is located in the Joseph C O'Mahoney Federal Center, at 2120 Capitol Ave between 21st and 22nd Sts; the zip code is 82001. For fax services, try Kinko's Copies (☎ 307-635-3441; fax 307-635-6744), at 1419 Albany Ave.

Travel Agencies Capitol Tours & Travel (☎ 307-632-7878) is at 121 E 18th St. The American Express representative is Travel Management Agency Inc (☎ 307-634-8202, 800-548-2731), 1400 Dell Range Blvd in Frontier Mall.

Road Conditions Call ☎ 307-635-9966 for Cheyenne area road and travel information.

Medical Services United Medical Center (☎ 307-634-2273) is at 300 E 23rd St.

Laundry & Showers Easy Way Laundry (☎ 307-638-2177) is at 900 W Lincolnway. Lady Saver Coin Laundry (☎ 307-632-2292), 117 W 5th St, is open 7 am to 11 pm daily. Go to the Cheyenne Municipal Pool (☎ 307-637-6455), adjacent to Lions Park off Kennedy Rd at Carey Ave, for showers; call for hours.

Walking Tour
To get a feel for Cheyenne, begin a walking tour at the Plains Hotel (1911) on the corner of Lincolnway and Central Ave. One block west, at 1518 Capitol Ave, the Phoenix Block (1882) has housed a hotel, stores and offices. The sandstone blocks of the imposing Romanesque UP depot (1886), 121 W 15th St, though presently in disrepair, still suggest the power of 'Uncle Pete.' Two blocks west is the Hofmann Building (1880), 316 W 15th St; note the cast-iron facade of this former saloon. One

block north, the turreted, ornamented Din-neen Building, at 400 W Lincolnway, has been an automobile showroom since it opened in 1927. The superbly restored Queen Anne Tivoli (1892), 301 W Lincoln-way, was once a brothel.

The 200 block of W Lincolnway, one of downtown's best-preserved areas, includes the Commercial Building (built in 1883 – note the datestone and Moorish details), the First National Bank Building (1882) and the Hynds Building (1922). Across the street, the Atlas Theatre (1887), 211 W Lincolnway, is a former office building redesigned as a playhouse in 1908.

One block west and 3 blocks north is the Greek Revival City and County Building (1917), 319 W 19th St, with Ionic columns, designed by architect William Dubois. Two blocks east is the Masonic Temple (1901), 1820 Capitol Ave. Nearby are two land-mark churches: the Gothic Revival St Mark's Episcopal Church (1893), 1908 Central Ave, and the First United Methodist Church (1894), 18th St and Central Ave, a red sandstone combination of Romanesque and Gothic Revival styles. Wild Bill Hickok was married here in 1876.

The Rainsford District, east of Warren Ave, is a woodsy residential area with his-toric houses like the Queen Anne Lane House (1881), 1721 Warren Ave, and the Corson House (1884), 209 E 18th St. Sev-eral interesting Queen Anne houses are another block east of 18th St on Evans Ave. The Whipple House (1883), an Italianate Victorian, 300 E 17th St, belonged to Cheyenne cattle baron Ithamar Whipple, a founder of the Wyoming Stock Growers Association (WSGA). One block west, merchant Erasmus Nagle built both the Romanesque Nagle-Warren Mansion (1888), 222 E 17th St, and the earlier Nagle House (1880), 216 E 17th St.

Wyoming State Capitol
The gold-leaf dome of the Wyoming State Capitol, on 24th St at Capitol Ave, tops an imposing sandstone building quarried from Rawlins and Fort Collins, CO. First occu-pied in 1888, it was expanded two years

later. The impressive interior rotunda is crowned by blue and green stained glass. The House and Senate chambers, com-pleted in 1917 with murals by artist Allen True, flank the rotunda and have unique stained-glass ceilings. *Wyoming, the Land, the People*, a mural by Mike Kopriva, was added in 1982. Visitors can watch the legis-lature's deliberations from balconies over-looking each branch. This conspicuous building is a national historic landmark. It is open from 8 am to 5 pm weekdays. Call ☎ 307-777-7220 for group tours.

Wyoming Arts Council
The Wyoming Arts Council (☎ 307-777-7742), 2320 Capitol Ave, features a small gallery of high-quality work by contempo-rary Wyoming artists. It also offers presen-tations by scholars and living histories by performance artists. It is open 8 am to 5 pm weekdays.

Supreme Court & State Library
Completed in 1937, the Neoclassical Supreme Court & State Library (☎ 307-777-7281), 2301 Capitol Ave, consists of Indiana limestone, with an interior of Ten-nessee marble.

Wyoming State Museum
The Wyoming State Museum (☎ 307-777-7022 weekdays, 307-777-7024 weekends) occupies most of the ground floor of the Barrett State Office Building, 2301 Central Ave. This respectable but unexceptional museum's best attractions are the fre-quently changing traveling exhibitions from other institutions, such as the Smith-sonian and the Library of Congress. The museum sends some of its best displays to other museums around the state. It is open 8:30 am to 5 pm weekdays year-round, and 9 am to 4 pm Saturday and 1 to 4 pm Sunday Memorial Day to Labor Day. It is also open from noon to 4 pm Saturday, but closed Sunday, during winter.

Historic Governors' Mansion
In a pleasant residential neighborhood, the Historic Governors' Mansion (☎ 307-777-

Cheyenne still 'plays' Wild West with rodeos and other cowboy feats.

7878), 300 E 21st St at House Ave, is a three-story brick Georgian Revival building (1904) with Corinthian columns. Intended as a comfortable residence for the state's highest official, it was far more modest than the homes of Cheyenne's cattle barons. The last governor to occupy the mansion was Ed Herschler, Wyoming's only three-term executive. The mansion became a museum in 1977. Open from 9 am to 5 pm Tuesday to Saturday, admission is free.

Old West Museum

The Old West Museum (☎ 307-778-7290), 4501 N Carey Ave, at Frontier Park (I-25 exit 12, Central Ave to Kennedy Rd), is a record of early Cheyenne, the Cheyenne Frontier Days and its rodeos since 1897. It has a rotating exhibition displaying 40 horse carriages of the 125 that it owns. It is open 9 am to 5 pm weekdays and 10 am to 5 pm weekends with extended summer hours. Admission is $3 for adults, $2 for seniors and teens; children under 13 are admitted free.

Cheyenne Botanic Gardens

The Cheyenne Botanic Gardens (☎ 307-637-6458), 710 S Lions Park Drive in Lions Park, boasts three solar-heated greenhouses harboring tropical and subtropical plants. Volunteers grow seasonal vegetables for low-income nutrition programs. The gardens' practices integrate pest management, avoiding chemical pesticides, and feature a garden of drought-tolerant plants suited to Wyoming's high desert. The gardens are open during daylight. The conservatory is open 8:30 am to 4:30 pm weekdays and 11 am to 3:30 pm weekends.

Warren Heritage Museum

The Francis E Warren Air Force Base, the US Air Force's 'longest continuously active base,' claims to be 'home to the most powerful missile wing in the free world.' Former Cheyenne Mayor Worth Story once proclaimed that his city was 'proud to be the nation's number-one target for enemy missiles.' Established in 1867 to protect laborers on the Transcontinental Railroad, the base grew dramatically during WWI and, in 1930, was renamed for former Senator and Governor FE Warren. The US Air Force acquired the base after WWII and it became the Strategic Air Command's first all-missile base in 1958. It retains many red-brick Colonial Revival buildings from its early days, one of which now houses the Warren Heritage Museum (☎ 307-773-2980), which has exhibits on local and regional military history. It is open 8 am to 4 pm weekdays. Enter the base via Gate 1 (I-25 exit 11, Randall Ave); look for the three conspicuous (and presumably disarmed) Atlas missiles.

Organized Tours

The Cheyenne Street Trolley runs two-hour tours of downtown, the FE Warren Air Force Base and the Old West Museum mid-May to mid-September. Tours depart from the corner of Lincolnway and Capitol Ave 10 am and 1:30 pm Monday to Saturday and 1:30 pm Sunday. The fare is $8/4 for adults/children (two to 12). Buy

WYOMING

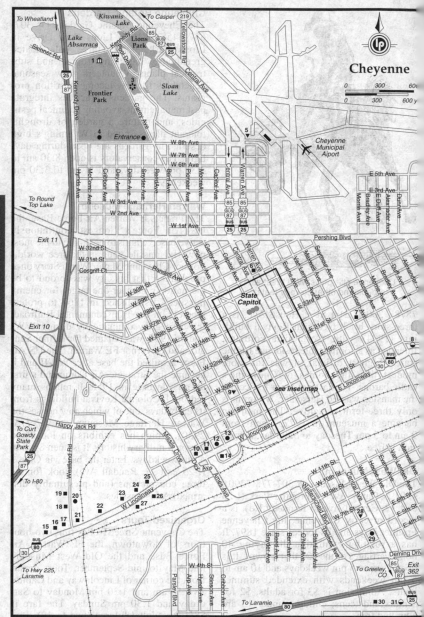

Cheyenne

To Wheatland
Lake
Absarraca
Skinner Rd
Kiwanis
Lake
Kennedy Rd
To Casper
219
Lions
Park
85
BUS
87
BUS
25
Yellowstone Rd
Central Ave
Cheyenne
Municipal
Aiport

1
2
Kennedy Drive
3
Sloan
Lake
Frontier
Park
4
Entrance
Carey Ave
5

W 8th Ave
W 7th Ave
W 6th Ave

E 5th Ave
E 4th Ave
E 3rd Ave

25
87

To Round
Top Lake
Hynds Ave
McConn Ave
Gribbon Ave
Dey Ave
Dillon Ave
Snyder Ave
Reed Ave
Pioneer Ave
Morrie Ave
Bent Ave
Capitol Ave
Central Ave
Warren Ave

W 3rd Ave
W 2nd Ave

W 1st Ave

85
87
BUS
25

85
87
BUS
25

Alexander Ave
Bradley Ave
Morrie Ave
Dunn Ave

Pershing Blvd

Exit 11

W 32nd St
W 31st St
Cosgrif Ct
Randall Ave
W 30th St
W 29th St
W 28th St
W 27th St
W 26th St
W 25th St
W 24th St

Thomes Ave
Carey Ave
Pioneer Ave
Capitol Ave
Warren Ave

6

State
Capitol

Seymour Ave
Maxwell Ave
Van Lennen Ave
Evans Ave

E 23rd St

E 21st St

7

Bradley Ave
Morrie Ave
parkland

8
BUS
80

Exit 10

W 22nd St
W 20th St
W 18th St

Ames Ave
Dey Ave
O'Neil Ave

9

see inset map

E 19th St

E 17th St
E Lincolnway

Happy Jack Rd
To Curt
Gowdy
State
Park
25
87
To I-80

Missile Drive
Westland Rd

W Lincolnway

W 11th St
W 10th St
W 9th St
W 8th St
W 7th St

Walterscheid Blvd
House Ave
Thomes Ave

Maxwell Ave
Van Lennen Ave
Evans Ave
Warren Ave
Hope Ave
Central Ave

E 6th St
E 5th St
E 4th St

12
13
10
11
14

To Hwy 225,
Laramie

25
23
24
19
20
18
21
22
15
16
17

W Lincolnway
26
27

Dey Ave
Ames Ave

28

29

80
30

To Greeley
CO

85
87

Exit
362

BUS
25

W 4th Ave

Parsley Blvd
Gribbon Ave
Alp Ave
Stinson Ave
Hynds Ave

Reed Ave
Bent Ave
O'Neil Ave
Starhard Ave
Snyder Ave

Deming Driv

To Laramie

80

30
31

WYOMING

PLACES TO STAY
6 Avenue Rose B&B
7 Porch Swing B&B
10 Guest Ranch Motel
11 Sands Motel
14 Ranger Motel
15 Econo Lodge
16 La Quinta Inn
17 Days Inn
18 Motel 6
19 Luxury Inn
21 Super 8 Motel
22 Lincoln Court
23 Best Western
    Hitching Post Inn
24 Atlas Motel
25 Frontier Motel
26 Wyoming Motel
27 Stage Coach Motel
30 Holiday Inn
44 Rainsford Inn B&B
54 Plains Hotel

PLACES TO EAT
5 Cloud Nine
9 Dynasty Cafe
28 Los Amigos Mexican
    Restaurant
41 Twin Dragon
48 Lexie's
56 Medicine Bow Brewing
    Company of Cheyenne

OTHER
1 Old West Museum
2 Cheyenne Municipal Pool
3 Cheyenne Botanic
   Gardens
4 Frontier Park Ticket Office
8 CTP Transfer Station
12 Easy Way Laundry
13 Enterprise Rent-a-Car
20 Wyoming State Board
    of Outfitters &
    Professional Guides
29 Lady Easy
    Coin Laundry
31 Greyhound, TNM&O,
    Powder River Coach
    USA Bus Depot
32 Wyoming Arts Council
33 Supreme Court
    & State Library
34 Wyoming State Museum
35 United Medical Center
36 Post Office
37 Historic Governors' Mansion
38 First Bank
39 American National Bank
40 Community First
    National Bank
42 The Java Joint
43 Capitol Tours & Travel
45 Manitou Gallery
46 Cheyenne Gunslingers
    Sody Saloon
47 Norwest Bank
49 Cheyenne Area
    Convention
    & Visitors Bureau
50 Chamber of Commerce
51 Atlas Theatre
52 The Wrangler
53 Gallery West
55 Lincoln Movie Palace
56 Below the Bow
    Comedy Club

tickets at the Cheyenne Area Convention & Visitors Bureau (see Information above).

Cheyenne Frontier Days

When Cheyenne 'realized it was through living the real thing' as historian Earl Pomeroy wrote, 'it turned to playing the Wild West.' So began Cheyenne Frontier Days in 1897. Novelist Frank Norris wrote:

The Frontier has become conscious of itself . . . and this self-consciousness is a sign, surer than all others, of the decadence of a type, the passing of an epoch.

Wyoming's biggest special event has daily rodeos, concerts, parades, dances, air shows, free pancake breakfasts, chili cook-offs and just about everything else. Cheyenne's Frontier Park, 4501 N Carey Ave, is the center of activities; some events take place at other locations around town. Upcoming dates are July 23 to August 1, 1999, and July 21 to July 30, 2000.

Rodeo tickets cost $8 to $18; concert tickets cost $11 to $17. For ticket information, contact Cheyenne Frontier Days Tickets (☎ 307-778-7222, 800-227-6336; fax 307-778-7229; cfdrodeo@wyoming .com), PO Box 2477, Dept CACVB, Cheyenne, WY 82003-2477, or go to the ticket office, 8th Ave at Frontier Park, during the rodeo. For online information, check out the event website at (www.cfdrodeo.com).

Places to Stay

It is hard to escape the continual noise from the railroad tracks anywhere along Lincolnway. Reservations are essential during Cheyenne Frontier Days when everything within a 50-mile radius of Cheyenne is full; rates can double even as far away as Laramie or Greeley, CO.

Camping Cheyenne's best RV park is *AB Camping* (☎ 307-634-7035), 1503 W College Drive (I-25 exit 7). Near a busy road, it is well landscaped and comfortable. Tent sites cost $10; sites with full hookups $19. It is open March to October. The *Cheyenne KOA Kampground* (☎ 307-638-8840, 800-562-1507), 8000 I-80 E Service Rd at

Campstool Rd (I-80 exit 367), is open April to October. Tent sites cost $20; sites with full hookups $27.

The unappealing and shadeless *Restway Travel Park* (☎ 307-634-3811, 800-443-2751), 4212 Whitney Rd at the east end of US 30 is a last-ditch choice. Tent sites cost $15; sites with full hookups are $16. The *Greenway Trailer Park* (☎ 307-634-6696), 3829 Greenway St, has sites with full hookups ($13) but no tent sites.

B&Bs Three B&Bs are within walking distance of downtown. *The Porch Swing B&B* (☎ 307-778-7182; fax 307-635-6744), 712 E 20th St, has singles ranging from $43 to $53, and doubles ranging from $49 to $59. Rooms at the *Rainsford Inn B&B* (☎ 307-638-2337; fax 307-634-4506), 219 E 18th St, range from $75 to $95. Both are non-smoking. The comparable *Avenue Rose B&B* (☎ 307-635-2400), 100 E 27th St, only has rooms with shared bathrooms.

Accommodations in north Cheyenne include the *Howdy Pardner B&B* (☎ 307-634-6493), 1920 Tranquility Rd, Cheyenne, WY 82009 ($45/60 a single/double), and *The Storyteller Pueblo* (☎ 307-634-7036, 307-778-8509), at 5201 Ogden Rd, Cheyenne, WY 82009 ($50), which features Native American art.

Motels Along W Lincolnway (I-25 exit 9) are the *Atlas Motel* (☎ 307-632-9214), 1524 W Lincolnway (singles/doubles $26/30); the German-run *Wyoming Motel* (☎ 307-632-8104), 1401 W Lincolnway, which occasionally has rooms for $20; the *Frontier Motel* (☎ 307-634-7961), 1400 W Lincolnway ($30); the friendly *Guest Ranch Motel* (☎ 307-634-2137, also rings to Sands Motel), 1100 W Lincolnway; and the *Ranger Motel* (☎ 307-634-7995), 909 W Lincolnway ($22/27). North of W Lincolnway are *Motel 6* (☎ 307-635-6806), 1735 Westland Rd ($32/37), and *Luxury Inn* (☎ 307-638-2550), 1805 Westland Rd ($25/30).

Singles/doubles cost $32/38 at the *Quality Inn* (☎ 307-632-8901, 800-876-8901), 5401 Walker Rd (I-25 exit 12).

Several budget places are situated along E Lincolnway. The *Home Ranch Motel* (☎ 307-634-3575), 2414 E Lincolnway, is probably the best ($28/30). Otherwise try the *Cheyenne Motel* (☎ 307-632-5505, also rings Firebird Motel), 1905 E Lincolnway, or the adjacent *Firebird Motel* ($30/35).

I-25 exit 9 has several good if unexciting mid-range places, including the *Econo Lodge* (☎ 307-632-7556), 2512 W Lincolnway ($35), and *Super 8 Motel* (☎ 307-635-8741), 1900 W Lincolnway ($44). Others are the *Lincoln Court* (☎ 307-638-3302), 1702 W Lincolnway ($36/40), *Stage Coach Motel* (☎ 307-634-4495), 1515 W Lincolnway ($30/33), and *Sands Motel* (☎ 307-634-7771), 1022 W Lincolnway $35/41.

W Lincolnway (I-25 exit 9) is also home to some pricier spots. Singles/doubles cost $49/59 at *La Quinta Inn* (☎ 307-632-7117), 2410 W Lincolnway, and $55/60 at the *Days Inn* (☎ 307-778-8877), 2360 W Lincolnway. Rooms at the *Best Western Hitching Post Inn* (☎ 307-638-3301, 800-221-0125; fax 307-778-7194), 1700 W Lincolnway, start at $68; they have three restaurants, a fitness center, pool and Jacuzzi.

Hotels Rooms start at $34 at downtown's *Plains Hotel* (☎ 307-638-3311), 1600 Central Ave at Lincolnway; check the banquet room for signed endorsements from presidents and other politicians who ate here long ago. The isolated *Little America Hotel & Resort* (☎ 307-775-8400, 800-445-6945), 2800 W Lincolnway west of I-25, starts at $69/79. The *Marriott Fairfield Inn* (☎ 307-637-4070), 1415 Stillwater Ave near Frontier Mall, is north of the airport ($60). The *Holiday Inn* (☎ 307-638-4466), 204 W Fox Farm Rd at the junction of I-80 and US 85, costs $69/79.

Places to Eat

Cheyenne has a decent selection of restaurants. *The Java Joint* (☎ 307-638-7332), 1720 Capitol Ave, offers breakfast (good pastries, muffins and espresso) and light lunches in pleasant surroundings. Non-smoking *Lexie's* (☎ 307-638-8712), 216 E 17th St, has an appealing menu of reason-ably priced sandwiches, hamburgers and Italian and Mexican dishes. It's open for all meals, and has a pleasant deck. *Medicine Bow Brewing Co of Cheyenne* (☎ 307-778-2739), 115 E 17th St, serves average pub food with a good selection of beers. *Cheyenne Gunslingers Sody Saloon* (☎ 307-635-1028), 218 W 17th St, is an old-fashioned soda fountain.

Los Amigos Mexican Restaurant (☎ 307-638-8591), 620 Central Ave, is south of the railroad tracks. *Dynasty Cafe* (☎ 307-632-4888), 600 W 19th St at O'Neil Ave, offers a menu of Chinese and Vietnamese food. *Twin Dragon* (☎ 307-637-6622), 1809 Carey Ave, specializes in Mandarin and Szechuan cuisine, with a good selection of seafood. Both have inexpensive lunches, and Dynasty Cafe serves a buffet.

Locals agree that *Cloud Nine* (☎ 307-635-1525), 300 E 8th Ave at Cheyenne Municipal Airport terminal, serves the best beef in town. North of the airport, *Avanti Restaurant* (☎ 307-634-3432), 4620 Grandview at Dell Range Rd, serves Italian cuisine.

Entertainment

The *Cheyenne Little Theatre* (☎ 307-638-6543) offers musicals and melodramas at 2706 E Pershing Blvd and at the downtown Atlas Theatre (☎ 307-635-0199), 211 W Lincolnway. The *Medicine Bow Brewing Co of Cheyenne* has live music; downstairs is the *Below the Bow Comedy Club*.

Shopping

One of Wyoming's biggest Western wear shops is The Wrangler (☎ 307-634-3048), 1518 Capitol Ave. Gallery West (☎ 307-632-1258), 1601 Capitol Ave in the Majestic Building, sells Western art, as does Manitou Gallery (☎ 307-635-0019), 1715 Carey Ave.

Getting There & Away

Air Cheyenne Municipal Airport (☎ 307-634-7071), 200 E 8th Ave, has daily United Express flights to Denver. However, it can be cheaper to fly into Denver International Airport (DIA) and rent a car there or take the DIA Shuttle (see below).

WYOMING

DIA Shuttle Laramie-based Cowboy Coach (☎ 307-742-7006) runs shuttles between DIA and Cheyenne. The shuttle picks up at the Best Western Hitching Post Inn, 1700 W Lincolnway, at 7:25 and 10:25 am, 2:25 and 5:25 pm. The one-way/roundtrip fare is $28/45.

Bus All bus lines use the depot at 120 N Greeley Hwy (US 85 at I-80 exit 362). Greyhound Bus Lines (☎ 307-634-7744) has two daily northbound departures to Billings, MT (1:20 am and 12:15 pm), six runs a day southbound to Denver (1:40, 7:15, 11:30, 11:35 am, 2:15 and 5:10 pm), three eastbound to Chicago (4:35 am, 5:55 and 8:35 pm) and three westbound to San Francisco (8:05 am, 12:05 and 11:10 pm).

Daily TNM&O buses (☎ 307-634-7744) go to Denver thrice daily via Fort Collins and Greeley, CO, with connections southbound to Dallas and El Paso, TX, as well as eastbound to Chicago.

Daily Powder River Coach USA (☎ 307-635-1327, 307-634-7744) buses go to Denver (1:40, 11:30 am, 5:10 pm) three times a day; the fare is $24/48 one-way/roundtrip. Daily buses also follow two routes to Billings, MT (1:20 am and 12:15 pm). One route goes through the Bighorn Basin and the other route, which requires a change of bus in Douglas, goes via Gillette, Buffalo and Sheridan. The one-way/roundtrip fare on both routes is $68/136.

Car Cheyenne is northeast of the junction of east-west I-80 and north-south I-25. North-south US 85 passes through Cheyenne, leading south to Greeley and north to Torrington, Lusk, Newcastle and the Black Hills. Cheyenne is 100 miles north of Denver and 50 miles east of Laramie.

Getting Around
Bus The Cheyenne Transit Program (CTP; ☎ 307-637-6253), 2022 Capitol Ave, operates buses 6:30 am to 5 pm weekdays. The fare is $1/50¢ for adults/children; transfers are free. CTP Dial-A-Ride service operates Saturday; call 8 am to 3 pm weekdays to make a reservation. The Dial-A-Ride fare

is $2. Buses on all routes depart hourly 15 minutes after the hour from the CTP Transfer Station on E Lincolnway at Morris Ave, 1½ miles east of downtown. Passengers can flag a bus down anywhere along its route. Schedules and routes may vary during Cheyenne Frontier Days.

The seven color-coded CTP routes are: Yellow, to northern Cheyenne, downtown and the airport; Orange, to FE Warren Air Force Base; Pink, to Western Hills, downtown and the airport; Red, to Laramie County Community College, the bus depot and Fox Farm Rd; Blue, to eastern Cheyenne; Purple, to downtown; and Green, to Buffalo Ridge.

Car At the airport, you'll find Avis (☎ 307-632-9371), Dollar (☎ 307-632-2422) and Hertz (☎ 307-634-2131). Other rental firms include Enterprise Rent-a-Car (☎ 307-632-1907), 800 W Lincolnway; Rent-A-Wreck (☎ 307-638-0713), 416 E Lincolnway; and Affordable Rent-A-Car (☎ 307-634-5666, 800-711-1564), 701 E Lincolnway.

Taxi You can call AA Taxi (☎ 307-634-6020), A-1 Veterans Cab (☎ 307-634-4444) or Checker/Yellow Cab Co (☎ 307-635-5555) for a taxi.

AROUND CHEYENNE
Happy Jack Rd (Hwy 210) leads west from Cheyenne toward Vedawoo Glen into the Medicine Bow National Forest (see Around Laramie later in this chapter). This lovely rural area has nice B&Bs and guest ranches: *Windy Hills Guest House* (☎ 307-632-6423; fax 307-637-2824), 393 Happy Jack Rd; the highly regarded 120-acre *A Drummond's Ranch* (☎/fax 307-634-6042), 399 Happy Jack Rd; and *Bit-O-WYO Ranch B&B* (☎ 307-638-8340), 470 Happy Jack Rd.

Terry Bison Ranch is a guest ranch (☎ 307-634-4171), 51 I-25 Service Rd East (I-25 exit 2), 7 miles south of Cheyenne and 2 miles north of the Wyoming-Colorado state line, and a self-conscious tourist attraction. It has guest cabins, an RV park and other amusements, including horseback rides, the twice-weekly Hell on Wheels Rodeo and the wryly entertaining Terry Bison Trailblazers, who perform droll versions of country music standards like 'Tumbling Tumbleweeds' and 'Ghost Riders in the Sky.' It is open late-May to mid-September.

Curt Gowdy State Park

Curt Gowdy State Park (☎ 307-632-7946), 1351 Hynds Lodge Rd off Happy Jack Rd (Hwy 210), 24 miles west of Cheyenne (I-25 exit 10B) and 23 miles east of Laramie, is named for a Wyoming-born sportscaster. Historically, bison roamed these plains and Native Americans (Shoshone, Crow, Pawnee and Comanche) camped here during the hunt. Today its two reservoirs, Granite Springs and Crystal Lake, offer boating, summer fishing and winter ice fishing (for rainbow, brown and lake trout, and Kokanee salmon), waterskiing, hiking and camping, but no swimming. Migratory water fowl, including trumpeter swans, visit the area April to May. The day-use fee is $3 ($2 for Wyoming residents). The campground ($4) has separate areas for backpackers and for those traveling with horses. (Also see Around Laramie for other nearby activities.)

Daellenbach Manufacturing Company

An offbeat sight is the 18-acre 'estate' of Francis Daellenbach, who turned a surplus Atlas missile silo into a subterranean home and small factory for precision machine parts. It operated as an ICBM missile site with nuclear warheads from 1960 to 1964. In 1964 Daellenbach paid $3000 for the site, whose development cost the US Air Force $1.5 million. Daellenbach, who has no telephone, willingly shows visitors around the site and his house. To reach this unusual homestead, take I-25 exit 47 (Bear Creek Rd East) north of Cheyenne. Follow it 4½ miles to the turnoff at the end of the pavement.

LARAMIE

Laramie (population 28,000) is on the high-altitude Laramie Plains: the city sits at an altitude of 7165 feet. It lies between the Medicine Bow Mountains to the west and the Laramie Mountains to the east, surrounded by the inviting and accessible Medicine Bow National Forest. Many towns along the I-80 corridor are only for passing through, but Laramie is a place to stop, stay and appreciate. Laramie owes its prosperity and stability to the stately campus of the University of Wyoming (UW), which employs 5500 residents. Laramie is also Wyoming's cultural capital with an abundance of museums and a thriving historic downtown. The city of Laramie, interestingly, is the seat of Albany County, while the state capital, Cheyenne, is the seat of Laramie County.

History

Prior to the arrival of settlers, several Native American nations (Shoshone, Crow, Arapaho, Cheyenne and (Sioux) Oglala and Brulé) contended for Laramie Plains resources. By the early 19th century, trappers like French-Canadian Jacques LaRamie sought beaver in the area. The obscure LaRamie died at the hands of the Shoshone, but somehow left an improbable legacy in the place names of a city, county, river, mountain range and conspicuous 10,274-foot peak.

Decades after the fur trade declined, the US Army built Fort Sanders to protect westward emigrants on southern Wyoming's new Overland Trail, but the 1868 arrival of the UP was the event that spurred Laramie's growth. In the early years, though, the UP brought a host of troublemakers and speculators who gave the town an unsavory reputation it undoubtedly deserved. Among the town's more infamous visitors were Jack McCall, arrested here after shooting Wild Bill Hickok in Deadwood, SD, in 1876, and Jesse James, a robbery suspect who was released before authorities realized his identity.

The new territorial prison quickly filled with those gamblers and gunfighters who had not been lynched in the streets. Eventually a more genteel Laramie attracted individuals like humorist and newspaper

WYOMING

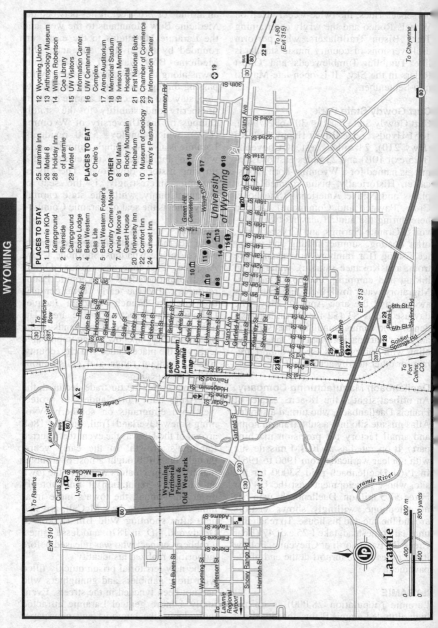

PLACES TO STAY

1 Laramie KOA
    Kampground
2 Riverside
    Campground
3 Econo Lodge
5 Best Western Foster's
    Country Corner Motel
7 Annie Moore's
    Guest House
20 University Inn
22 Comfort Inn
24 Sunset Inn
25 Laramie Inn
26 Motel 8
28 Holiday Inn
    of Laramie
29 Motel 6

PLACES TO EAT

6 Chelo's

OTHER

8 Old Main
9 Rocky Mountain
    Herbarium
10 Museum of Geology
11 Prexy's Pasture
12 Wyoming Union
13 Anthropology Museum
14 William Robertson
    Coe Library
15 UW Visitors
    Information Center
16 UW Centennial
    Complex
17 Arena-Auditorium
18 Memorial Stadium
19 Ivinson Memorial
    Hospital
21 First National Bank
23 Chamber of Commerce
27 Information Center

University of Wyoming

Wyoming Territorial
Prison & Old West Park

Laramie

editor Bill Nye. Laramie also saw the first women in Wyoming to perform jury duty. Landing UW was a major coup that helped transform it into the 'Gem of the Plains.'

Orientation

Most of Laramie is northeast of I-80 and east of the Laramie River. The main north-south road is 3rd St. Grand Ave is the main east-west road. US 30/US 287 and I-80 Business follow 3rd St through most of Laramie. They diverge at Grand Ave; US 30 and I-80 follow Grand Ave east, and US 287 continues south along 3rd St. Ivinson St divides north-south street addresses. Laramie's historic downtown is bounded by 1st and 5th Sts and Sheridan and Clark Sts. Grocery stores and fast-food restaurants are along Grand Ave east of 30th St.

Information

Tourist Offices The Laramie Area Chamber of Commerce (☎ 307-745-7339, 800-445-5303) as well as the Albany County Tourism Board (☎ 307-745-4195; actb@lariat.org) are at 800 S 3rd St. They are open 8 am to 5 pm weekdays. An information center in an old yellow UP caboose at 3rd St and Boswell Drive (I-80 exit 313) is open 8 am to 5 pm weekends during summer. The UW Visitors Information Center (☎ 307-766-4075, 800-342-5996), 1406 Ivinson Ave, is open 8 am to 5 pm weekdays and 8 am to noon Saturday. Their informative campus brochure details a walking tour. The Laramie Area Events Hot Line (☎ 307-721-7345) is a joint venture with the Laramie Area Chamber of Commerce, Albany County Tourism Board (covering Laramie, Rock River and Centennial) and the UW.

The USFS Medicine Bow-Routt National Forest & Thunder Basin Grassland Forest Headquarters Laramie Ranger Station (☎ 307-745-8971, 307-745-2300), 2468 Jackson St at the junction of Hwy 230 and Hwy 130, offers abundant information on recreational possibilities in the Medicine Bow and Laramie mountains. It is open 7:30 am to 5 pm weekdays year-round and 7:30 to 11:30 am Saturday during summer.

Money ATMs are at 1st Interstate Bank, 221 Ivinson Ave; Community First National Bank, at S 3rd St and Garfield; First Bank, 568 N 3rd St; and First National Bank, 2020 Grand Ave at 20th St.

Post & Communications The post office is at 152 N 5th St; the zip code is 82070. Lincoln Printing (☎ 307-742-2022; fax 307-721-8130), 370 N 3rd St, provides fax services.

Bookstores Befitting a university town, Laramie boasts some of Wyoming's best bookstores. At 105 Ivinson Ave, Personally Recommended Books/The Second Story (☎ 307-745-4423) is quite a delightful place; its spacious general display area, which includes a small cafe, is surrounded by smaller rooms stocked with specialty books. The Chickering Bookstore (☎ 307-742-8609), 203 S 2nd St, also has a good selection, while High Country Books (☎ 307-742-5640), 306 S 2nd St, has a large stock of used books and is an excellent place for browsing.

Newspapers The Fort Collins weekly *Scene* publicizes events in northern Colorado and southern Wyoming and is widely distributed in Laramie.

Road & Weather Conditions Call ☎ 307-742-8981 for road conditions, and ☎ 307-742-3441 for weather conditions.

Medical Services Ivinson Memorial Hospital (☎ 307-742-2141) is at 255 N 30th St.

Laundry The Spic & Span Laundromat (☎ 307-745-3939), at 272 N 4th St, is open 7:30 am to 9 pm daily.

Historic Downtown District

Laramie has one of the most interesting historic districts in the state, with Victorian architecture dating from the 1860s. The UP depot, 1st and Kearney St, was restored by the Laramie Plains Museum and is now rented out for private functions. The Jensen Building (1890), 313 S 2nd St, and the

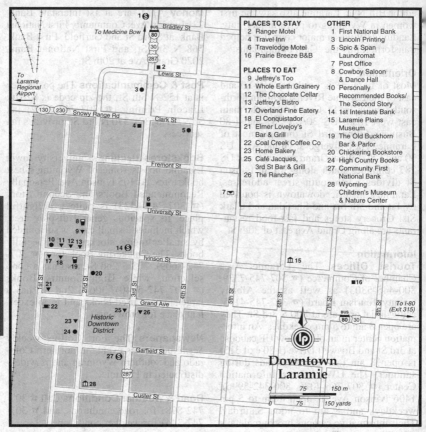

WYOMING

PLACES TO STAY
2   Ranger Motel
4   Travel Inn
6   Travelodge Motel
16 Prairie Breeze B&B

PLACES TO EAT
9   Jeffrey's Too
11 Whole Earth Grainery
12 The Chocolate Cellar
13 Jeffrey's Bistro
17 Overland Fine Eatery
21 Elmer Lovejoy's
    Bar & Grill
22 Coal Creek Coffee Co
23 Home Bakery
25 Café Jacques,
    3rd St Bar & Grill
26 The Rancher

OTHER
1   First National Bank
3   Lincoln Printing
5   Spic & Span
    Laundromat
7   Post Office
8   Cowboy Saloon
    & Dance Hall
10 Personally
    Recommended Books/
    The Second Story
14 1st Interstate Bank
15 Laramie Plains
    Museum
19 The Old Buckhorn
    Bar & Parlor
20 Chickering Bookstore
24 High Country Books
27 Community First
    National Bank
28 Wyoming
    Children's Museum
    & Nature Center

Downtown
Laramie

nearby building at 305 2nd St both have elaborate, ornate cornices. The brickwork at 220 S 2nd St and the adjoining buildings as far as Grand Ave all date to the 1880s. In the 1870s, Edward Ivinson built the former First National Bank, 206 2nd St, and the nicely painted Midwest Building, 202 S 2nd St. The building at 201 S 2nd St was a bank that failed during the Great Depression; now a clothing store, the changing rooms were originally bank vaults.

The superb MCB Gallery, 204 Ivinson Ave, was named after Melville C Brown, a judge and Laramie's first mayor. A block north, the Elks Building (1910), 103 S 2nd

St, displays a Neoclassical style. According to some accounts, the 3rd floor at 123 Ivinson Ave was removed when it shook in strong westerly winds. Across the street, the former Kuster Hotel (1869), 108 Ivinson Ave, is the city's oldest stone building. The former Phillips Hotel (1890), 107½ Ivinson Ave (with its original entrance at 117½ S 1st St), was once a dance hall (note the folding seats for wallflowers) and later a brothel. The former Johnson Hotel (1900), at Grand Ave, was one of the city's social centers.

The Albany County Historic Preservation Board produces a brochure of historic residential architecture west of the railroad tracks and west and south of the university.

University of Wyoming

Wyoming's only four-year institution of higher education is a federal land-grant university which began instruction in 1887, five years before statehood. From its original 17-acre site and single building, it has now expanded to an inviting, tree-shaded campus of dignified Gothic sandstone buildings. Most points of interest to visitors are between 9th and 15th Sts.

Among campus landmarks are **Old Main**, the present administration building, near 9th St and Ivinson Ave, which, when built in 1887, was the entire campus. The meadow of **Prexy's Pasture**, criss-crossed by paved walkways, is still the focus of the campus' historic core. At its southeast edge, north of the 13th St entrance, is the **Wyoming Union**, a favorite student meeting place with a cafeteria, the university bookstore, amusements and souvenirs. South of the Union is the **William Robertson Coe Library**. The UW Fine Arts Center (☎ 307-766-6666, 307-766-3327 ticket office) is home to theater, dance, art and music, and hosts concerts and exhibits in its galleries. The UW Planetarium (☎ 307-766-6150) is also of interest.

UW Museums The **Anthropology Museum** (☎ 307-766-5136 anthropology department), in the Anthropology Building on Ivinson Ave at 14th St, displays materials dating from the earliest human habitation of Wyoming to the present, plus artifacts from other parts of North America, Asia and even Easter Island. It is open 8 am to 5 pm daily.

The **Museum of Geology** (☎ 307-766-4218), in the east wing of the SH Knight Geology Building near the northwest corner of Prexy's Pasture, preserves more than 120,000 catalogued specimens of rocks, minerals and fossils. It attracts the public for its impressive fossil specimens. Unique specimens include *Apatosaurus*, the herbivorous dinosaur that is commonly, but mistakenly, called brontosaurus (the

reconstructed *Apatosaurus* skeleton is one of only five in the USA and the only one west of the Mississippi); *Archiceratops*, one of few on display in the entire world; and the Fossil Butte garfish, the world's largest complete freshwater fossil fish. The museum is open 8 am to 5 pm weekdays and 10 am to 3 pm weekends; admission is free.

Other museums include the **Rocky Mountain Herbarium**, in the Aven Nelson Building near 9th St, with its collection of more than half a million dried plant specimens, and an entomology museum. Call ☎ 307-766-4075 for more information on UW museums.

UW Centennial Complex The strikingly modern Centennial Complex (☎ 307-766-4114), 2111 Willett Drive (22nd St entrance off Grand Ave), contains the American Heritage Center and the University Art Museum (☎ 307-766-6622). Built for the centennial of Wyoming statehood and officially opened in 1993, permanent exhibits include paintings by Alfred Jacob Miller and material on popular icons like early cowboy star Hopalong Cassidy. The information desk is open from 8 am to 5 pm weekdays, from 11 am to 5 pm Saturday and 7:30 am to 4:30 pm weekdays during summer. A downstairs restaurant serves lunch.

The **American Heritage Center** is a major research facility with exhibits on Western history, performing arts, politics, mining, water resources, business history, music and aviation. The **University Art Museum** houses a diverse collection of European, Asian, African, American and Native American art, along with 20th-century photography. It is open 9:30 am to 4:30 pm Tuesday to Friday, 11 am to 5 pm Saturday, and 10 am to 3 pm Sunday. Admission is $3.50 for adults, $1.50 for seniors and children.

Laramie Plains Museum

Built by banker Edward Ivinson in 1892 and occupying a full block, the Laramie Plains Museum (☎ 307-742-4448), 603

Ivinson Ave, is really a memorial to the influential Ivinson family. Born in the Virgin Islands and educated in England, Ivinson came to Wyoming in 1868. He became a merchant and timber broker to the railroad and later worked in the banking industry. After Ivinson's death the mansion became an Episcopal girls' boarding school, which closed in 1958. It remained vacant until its acquisition and restoration in 1973, and is now on the National Register of Historic Places. It is open for guided tours only 9 am to 7 pm Monday to Saturday and 1 to 4 pm Sunday during summer; 10 am to 3 pm weekdays and 1 to 3 pm Saturday during spring and fall; and 1 to 3 pm Monday to Saturday during winter. Admission is $4/3/2 for adults/seniors (60+)/students; it's free for children under six.

Wyoming Children's Museum & Nature Center

The Wyoming Children's Museum & Nature Center (☎ 307-745-6332), 412 S 2nd St, is a participatory museum that engages children in topics like wildlife and habitat, the Oregon Trail, and the arts and humanities. It is open 9 am to 1 pm Tuesday, 1 to 5 pm Wednesday to Thursday and 10 am to 4 pm Saturday. Admission is $2/1 for adults/children.

Wyoming Territorial Prison & Old West Park

Wyoming Territorial Prison & Old West Park (☎ 307-745-6161, 800-845-2287), 975 Snowy Range Rd (I-80 exit 311), is a curious restoration of an early prison with a theme park atmosphere. The **National US Marshals' Museum** is open daily 10 am to 6 pm mid-May to September. Admission is $6.50/6/3.25 for adults/seniors (60+)/children (six to 12). Family admission is $18. Admission is free to the **Wyoming Frontier Town**, open daily 11 am to 5 pm June to August. The **Horse Barn Dinner Theatre** is held 6 pm Thursday to Saturday June to August, Wednesday to Saturday during July and Friday and Saturday during September. Admission is $23/22/17 for

adults/seniors (60+)/children (six to 12). Reservations are required. The Mountain Man Rendezvous is a popular July special event.

Special Events

The **Laramie River Night Rodeo** starts in June, and **Laramie Jubilee Days** take place in July.

Places to Stay

Laramie has good, moderately priced accommodations. Reservations are recommended and rates are higher during Cheyenne Frontier Days (see Cheyenne).

Camping The depressing *Riverside Campground* (☎ 307-721-7405), on Curtis St east of I-80 exit 310, charges $7 for bleak tent sites. The *Laramie KOA Kampground* (☎ 307-742-6553, 800-562-4153), at 1271 W Baker St (I-80 exit 310), is a slight improvement. Tent sites cost $14, and sites with full hookups cost $20.

B&Bs Two B&Bs are within walking distance of downtown and the UW campus. The friendly *Annie Moore's Guest House* (☎ 307-721-4177, 800-552-8992), 819 University Ave, is a 1910 Victorian built by rancher Sayer Hansen. Singles/doubles, all with shared bathroom and no TV, start at $45/55. Another Victorian, the *Prairie Breeze B&B* (☎ 307-745-5482, 800-840-2170; fax 307-745-5341), 718 Ivinson Ave, is nearby.

Motels The best deal is *Motel 6* (☎ 307-742-2307), 621 Plaza Lane (I-80 exit 313), where singles/doubles cost $26/31. At the sprawling *Motel 8* (☎ 307-745-4856, 888-745-4800), 501 Boswell Drive (I-80 exit 313), large, comfortable doubles range from $36 to $46. Doubles start at $36 at the *Travel Inn* (☎ 307-745-4853, 800-227-5430), 262 N 3rd, and *Ranger Motel* (☎ 307-742-6677), 453 N 3rd St.

Moving more toward the middle price range, the *Best Western Foster's Country Corner Motel* (☎ 307-742-8371, 800-526-5145), 1561 Snowy Range Rd (I-80 exit

311), has singles/doubles for $46/52. The *Laramie Inn* (☎ 307-742-3721, 800-642-4212), 421 Boswell Drive (I-80 exit 313), costs $48/58. It has two restaurants, one serving burgers and the other Italian food. Nearby is the attractive *Sunset Inn* (☎ 307-742-3741, 800-308-3744), 1104 S 3rd, with a pool and hot tub ($40/46). Singles/doubles cost $49/59 at the following: *Travelodge Motel* (☎ 307-742-6671, 800-942-6671), 165 N 3rd St; *Best Western Gas Lite* (☎ 307-742-6616, 800-942-6610), 960 N 3rd; *University Inn* (☎ 307-721-8855, 800-869-9466), 1720 Grand Ave; and *Econo Lodge* (☎ 307-745-8900, 800-303-6851), 1370 McCue St (I-80 exit 310).

Singles/doubles at the *Comfort Inn* (☎ 307-721-8856, 800-228-5150), at 3420 Grand Ave (I-80 exit 316), start at $54/59. Rooms at the *Holiday Inn of Laramie* (☎ 307-742-6611, 800-526-5245), 2313 Soldier Springs Rd (I-80 exit 311), $59 a single or double.

Places to Eat
Laramie has some of Wyoming's better restaurants. *Jeffrey's Bistro* (☎ 307-742-7046), 123 Ivinson Ave at 2nd Ave, offers a varied menu of salads, sandwiches, dinners and large dessert portions amid pleasant decor and good music with friendly service. It isn't cheap, but it's still a good value. Next door, *Jeffrey's Too* (☎ 307-742-0744), 116 S 2nd St, has delectable breads, pastries and espresso. Open at 7 am and continuing through dinner, it is cheaper than the bistro. In most parts of Wyoming *Café Jacques* (☎ 307-742-5522), 216 E Grand Ave, would be the best in town, but it falls short of Jeffrey's Bistro. Adjoining it, under the same management, is the *3rd St Bar & Grill*.

The *Overland Fine Eatery* (☎ 307-721-2800), 100 Ivinson Ave, has tasty breakfasts and also serves lunch and dinner. *Coal Creek Coffee Co* (☎ 307-745-7737), 110 E Grand Ave, has light meals, espresso and Italian sodas. The *Home Bakery* (☎ 307-742-2721), 304 S 2nd St, makes appealing baked goods, though some are a bit sugary. The pleasant and casual *Elmer*

Lovejoy's Bar & Grill (☎ 307-745-0141), 101 Grand Ave, has microbrews on tap. *El Conquistador* (☎ 307-742-2377), 110 Ivinson Ave, has a good Mexican menu, but most locals swear by *Chelo's* (☎ 307-745-5139), 357 W University Ave, west of the railroad tracks. Beef eaters can try *The Rancher* (☎ 307-742-3141), 309 S 3rd St.

For domestic and imported food, including cheeses, coffees, teas, grains and dried fruits, check out the *Whole Earth Grainery* (☎ 307-745-4268, 800-368-4268), 111 Ivinson Ave. *The Chocolate Cellar* (☎ 742-9278), at 115 Ivinson Ave, has imported chocolates, jellybeans and candies.

Entertainment
The Old Buckhorn Bar & Parlor (☎ 307-742-3554), 114 Ivinson St, is a downtown favorite with university students, while the *Cowboy Saloon & Dance Hall* (☎ 307-721-3165), 108 S 2nd St, attracts country music fans and line dancers.

Getting There & Away
Air Laramie Regional Airport (☎ 307-742-4164), 555 General Brees Rd, is off Hwy 230 4 miles west of I-80 exit 311. Daily United Express (☎ 307-742-5296) flights serve Denver, CO, though, as with Cheyenne, it may cost less to fly into Denver International Airport (DIA) and rent a car there or take the DIA Shuttle (see below).

DIA Shuttle Laramie-based Cowboy Coach (☎ 307-742-7006) runs shuttles between DIA and Laramie. The shuttle picks up at the Holiday Inn of Laramie, 2313 Soldier Springs Rd (I-80 exit 311) at 6:30, 9:30 am, 1:30 and 4:30 pm. The one-way/roundtrip fare is $33/45.

Bus All bus lines share the depot at Tumbleweed Express, a gas station at 4700 Bluebird Lane off Grand Ave (I-80 exit 316) at the east end of Laramie. Greyhound Bus Lines (☎ 307-742-5188) is open 7 am to 7 pm. Eastbound buses stop at 2:20 am and 10:35 am, 3:10 and 7:30 pm; westbound buses at 12:55, 1:10 am and 10:55 am, 12:55 and 8:55 pm.

Powder River Coach USA departs for Denver at 2:45 and 10:15 am; the one-way/roundtrip fare is $31/62. Greyhound Bus Lines also departs at 3:35 pm for Cheyenne, with connections on Powder River Coach USA to Denver.

Car Laramie is along the north side of I-80, 50 miles west of Cheyenne and 99 miles east of Rawlins. US 287 leads 121 miles south to Denver via Ft Collins, CO. Hwy 130 (Snowy Range Scenic Byway) leads west across the Snowy Range to Saratoga in the Platte Valley. Hwy 230 heads southwest to Walden, CO.

Getting Around
Car Avis (☎ 307-745-7156) and Dollar (☎ 307-742-8805) both have locations at the airport. Enterprise (☎ 307-721-9876) is at 2208 E Grand Ave.

Taxi Call Laramie Cab (☎ 307-745-8294) for a taxi.

AROUND LARAMIE
Laramie Plains
West of Laramie and east of Sheep Mountain, dozens of lakes and reservoirs dot the Laramie Plains, interspersed by roads, ranches and national wildlife refuges at Bamforth, Mortenson Lake and Hutton

Puma, mountain lion, panther or cougar?
– All of the above.

Lake. The area boasts excellent fishing and wildlife viewing. On Hwy 130, 11 miles west of Laramie, are **trail ruts** from the Overland Trail, the major pioneer route across the Laramie Plains from 1862 to 1868.

Sheep Mountain Game Refuge
The USFS-managed Sheep Mountain Game Refuge encompasses the prominent Sheep Mountain south of Hwy 130 between Laramie and Centennial. There is no motor vehicle access but the roadside wildlife viewing is excellent. Keep a lookout for pronghorn antelope, golden eagle, elk, mule deer and mountain lion.

Pole Mountain Area
I-80 crosses Sherman Summit (8640 feet) between Laramie and Cheyenne, about 12 miles southeast of Laramie. The Summit Information Center (☎ 307-721-8040), 150 Happy Jack Rd (I-80 exit 323), is open 9 am to 7 pm daily May to October. Adjacent to the building and picnic area is the **Abraham Lincoln Memorial**, a 12½-foot bust of President Lincoln, for whom US 30 (Lincoln Hwy) was named to commemorate his support for the Transcontinental Railroad.

Ames Monument
East of Laramie, about 2 miles south of I-80 exit 329, is a 65-foot limestone pyramid that once marked the highest point on the Transcontinental Railroad. Erected in 1881-82, Ames Monument has seemed out of place since the railroad tracks were relocated a few miles southeast to the now non-existent town of Sherman. The monument was a collaboration between famed architect Henry Hobson Richardson and sculptor August Saint-Gaudens, in honor of railroad speculators Oakes and Oliver Ames, who were both implicated in the Credit Mobilier bribery scandal during the construction of the UP.

Vedauwoo Glen
Free-standing granite formations tower above the high plains and the surrounding

The Creation of the Cowboy

Owen Wister's *The Virginian*, the most popular book in America when published in 1902, invented and established the Western hero. Wister created the archetype for all later cowboys from Hopalong Cassidy to Roy Rogers and John Wayne. A Harvard-educated Philadelphia aristocrat, Wister was a college chum and lifelong friend of Teddy Roosevelt, with whom he shared a romanticized passion for the West. At a time when the West was an alien place to most Americans, Wister captured the character of the cowboy, creating a myth that has lived on in the popular imagination. ■

juniper-dotted slopes of picturesque Vedauwoo Glen. Three unique and easily accessible rock formations (Vedauwoo Rocks, Devil's Playground and Turtle Rock), formed during the Ice Age, are along the Middle Crow Creek. The area attracts picnickers, photographers, campers and rock climbers. The name Vedauwoo means 'earthborn spirits,' and Native Americans believe the rock formations were created by playful humans and animals. The site is in the Sherman Mountains 13 miles southeast of Laramie (I-80 exit 329) on USFS Rd 700. (The scenic USFS Rd 700 is unpaved north of the recreation area, and connects to Happy Jack Rd.) Camping costs $5.

MEDICINE BOW

Medicine Bow (population 389; elevation 6642 feet), once a thriving town, has remained an icon for the Wild West. On the south side of US 30 is the **Medicine Bow Museum** in the former UP depot adjacent to the **Owen Wister Cabin**, moved from Jackson in 1976. Bypassed by I-80 to its south and deserted by more than half its population after the energy bust of the early 1980s, Medicine Bow sits quietly on US 30/Hwy 287, the once-busy Lincoln Hwy. Most visitors stop to admire the *Virginian Hotel* (☎ 307-379-2377), built nine years after the publication of Owen Wister's famous novel *The Virginian*. The hotel with a bar and restaurant has the ambiance of a bygone era; try a night in the Owen Wister Suite. Camping is free in the city park. Medicine Bow is 55 miles northwest of Laramie, 36 miles east of Walcott and 91 miles south of Casper.

COMO BLUFF NATIONAL NATURAL LANDMARK

In 1877 the first major discovery of large dinosaur fossils was made at Como Bluff. This dinosaur fossil bed is considered one the world's best and has provided excellent specimens for numerous natural history museums. To reach the quarries from US 30/US 287, 12 miles east of Medicine Bow, turn north onto Marshall Rd (Albany County Rd 610) and continue 5 miles north to the site, which is marked by the large piles of tailings rather than fossils. Extensive prairie dog colonies line the roads. Nearby is **Fossil Cabin**, built entirely of dinosaur bones.

Medicine Bow Mountains & Sierra Madre

The 11,000-foot summits of the Snowy Range cap the rugged Medicine Bow Mountains west of Laramie and south of I-80. Southwest are the Sierra Madre and the Continental Divide. The Medicine Bow National Forest extends across both mountain ranges. Between them is the North Platte River valley where the hot-springs resort of Saratoga is the main settlement. The twin towns of Riverside and Encampment are the gateways to the Sierra Madre. The **Snowy Range Scenic Byway** (Hwy 130), built in the 1930s by the Civilian Conservation Corps, traverses the Snowy Range at Snowy Range Pass (10,847 feet) between Centennial and Saratoga. The

79-mile byway, the only paved road across the Medicine Bow Mountains, provides easy access to this popular recreational area with lovely scenic overlooks, trails, fishing areas and campgrounds. The byway is usually open Memorial Day to October, and is a delightful alternative to traveling I-80 between Laramie and Walcott, east of Rawlins.

CENTENNIAL

Centennial (population 100; elevation 8076 feet), site of an 1875 gold rush, is a pleasant town in the prairie grassland at the eastern base of the Medicine Bow Mountains, on Hwy 130 28 miles west of Laramie. Rail enthusiasts will enjoy the **Nici Self Museum** (☎ 307-742-7158), open 11 am to 4 pm weekends July 4 to Labor Day or by appointment.

Rooms at *The Old Corral B&B* (☎ 307-745-5918, 800-678-2024), with a popular restaurant, cost $40/50. The comparable *Friendly Motel* (☎ 307-742-6033), which also issues fishing licenses, and *Brooklyn Lodge B&B* (☎ 307-742-6916) are nearby. The *Trading Post Restaurant & Saloon* (☎ 307-721-5074) serves steaks and seafood, and has live music on weekends.

MEDICINE BOW MOUNTAINS

The Medicine Bow Mountains extend 90 miles between Elk Mountain (Hwy 72 at I-80) to the north and Colorado's Cameron Pass to the south. These impressive mountains formed over 70 million years ago. From open tundra above the treeline (at 11,000 feet) streams descend through aspen forests to semi-arid prairies at 5500 feet. The mountains have been inhabited for 12,000 years, since Native Americans began coming here in summer to hunt and to cut mountain mahogany for making bows. The name Medicine Bow derives from their annual bow-making gatherings and ceremonial powwows to cure diseases. Regions of the mountains and recreational activities are generally divided into two distinct areas: the eastern (or lower) area below treeline; and the central and western (or upper) area above treeline.

Information

Maps, along with trail, fishing and campground information, are available from two USFS Medicine Bow-Routt National Forest locations on Hwy 130. The Centennial Visitors center, on Hwy 130 5 miles west of Centennial, is open 9 am to 4:30 pm daily year-round. Ask here about campground site availability. The Brush Creek Information Center (☎ 307-326-5562), in a log cabin on Hwy 130 several miles west of the Snowy Range Pass at the western edge of the forest, is open Memorial Day to Labor Day. Medicine Bow National Forest maps cost $3. (Also see Laramie, Saratoga and Encampment & Riverside for the nearest USFS offices.)

Snowy Range

Above treeline rises the Snowy Range of the Medicine Bow Mountains. The stacked Snowy Range resulted from glaciation which spread over Libby Flats, the expansive meadows southeast of the range. The oldest rock in the range is dated at 2.5 billion years, and above Mirror and Belamy lakes is a striking 1000-foot Precambrian quartzite cliff. Access to the Snowy Range is along Hwy 130 west of the Snowy Range Pass. The entire area is subject to windy, cold and very changeable weather.

The area is popular for **hiking**; the USFS *Snowy Range Trails* brochure helps to plan hikes. From the Libby Flats Observation Lookout on Hwy 130, 13 miles west of Centennial, superb views extend south into Colorado and west toward the Continental Divide. The **Libby Flats Wildflower Trail** introduces the flora – Alpine phlox, bluebell, cinquefoil, rose clover and yarrow – that gives the Alpine tundra its summer color.

The rocky **Medicine Bow Peak Trail** leads to the summit (12,013 feet) of the Snowy Range's highest peak. From the Lake Marie trailhead (10,600 feet) hike 3.6 miles one-way (about two to 2½ hours) to the top. Retrace your steps from the summit, or descend along the **Lake Trail** past Lookout Lake to the Mirror Lake Picnic Area, and walk back along the road to the Lake Marie trailhead. From Lewis

Lake trailhead, beyond Sugarloaf Campground northeast of the Lake Marie trailhead, a steeper route to the summit skirts behind Sugarloaf Mountain (11,398 feet). The **North Gap** and **Lost Lake** trails also begin at the Lewis Lake trailhead. The 3½-mile **Lost Lake Trail** heads northeast to Brooklyn Lake.

The 2.1-mile **Tipple Trail** runs between Miner's Cabin at Medicine Bow Peak Overlook and a trailhead near Lake Marie. Nearby a 0.2-mile trail goes to 50-foot Lake Marie Falls. At Silver Lake, 2 miles west of Lake Marie, a 1.6-mile trail loops the lake and the longer **Meadow Falls Trail** heads south.

Southwestern Medicine Bow Mountains

Two wilderness areas, Savage Run and Platte River, on the southwestern side of the Medicine Bow Mountains, are reached from Hwy 230 southeast of Riverside. The 23-sq-mile **Savage Run Wilderness Area** with three trailheads is off USFS Rd 500. The adjacent 36-sq-mile **Platte River Wilderness Area**, with four trailheads, is off USFS Rd 492 22 miles south of Riverside and about 3 miles north of the Wyoming-Colorado state line. This little-used area offers fishing, boating, hiking, wildlife viewing and camping. Bighorn sheep, elk, mule deer and black bear frequent both areas.

Kennaday Peak Lookout

East of Saratoga is Kennaday Peak (10,808 feet), the last functioning fire lookout in the Brush Creek Ranger District. Originally sited here in the 1930s, it was rebuilt in 1964 to include a ground-level visitors center, which is usually open 8 am to 5 pm Friday to Tuesday. From Hwy 130, take USFS Rd 100 (North Brush Creek Rd) north 6 miles from the Brush Creek Visitors center, and follow USFS Rd 215 another 6 miles to the summit.

Skiing & Snowboarding

The Snowy Range Ski and Recreation Area (☎ 307-745-5750, 800-462-7669), at 6416

Mountain Mist Court, is on Hwy 130, 5 miles west of Centennial or 32 miles west of Laramie, and east of the Snowy Range Pass. Downhill skiers and snowboarders enjoy its maximum 990-foot vertical drop. Base elevation is 9000 feet. The 25 runs include six beginner, 11 intermediate, and eight advanced; the longest is 1.8 miles. Daily lift tickets cost $27/14/14 for adults/seniors (60+)/children (six to 12). Easily accessible USFS trails provide good cross-country skiing. A cafeteria and lounge serve food, and instruction and rentals are available. It is open from 9 am to 4 pm daily Thanksgiving to Easter.

Mountain Biking

Popular mountain biking trails are well east of the Snowy Range Pass. The popular 6-mile loop on the **Libby Creek Trail** begins at the Green Rock trailhead, south of Hwy 130, and can be combined with a big descent down the **Barber Lake Trail** to the Libby Creek Recreation Area. North of Hwy 130 near Brooklyn Lake, the **North Fork Trail** descends to USFS Rd 101 and North Fork Campground. Three other rides loop around the Little Laramie trailhead. Another is near the Corner Mountain trailhead farther east on Hwy 130. Pick up the USFS 'Mountain Bikers' handout for a map and route details.

Places to Stay

The closest USFS campgrounds to the Snowy Range Pass, *Sugarloaf* and *Nash Fork*, are east of the pass off Hwy 130. The picturesque *Silver Lake Campground* is on Hwy 130, 2 miles west of the Lake Marie trailhead. Other pleasant campgrounds are near Corner Mountain and Barber Lake Rd.

Snowy Mountain Lodge (☎ 307-742-7669), PO Box 151, Centennial, WY 82055, is 2 miles from the ski area. Beds in the bunkhouse cost $15; two- to four-person cabins range from $35 to $80.

ENCAMPMENT & RIVERSIDE

Encampment (population 500; elevation 7323 feet) is an architecturally charming

WYOMING

mountain community and gateway to the copper country ghost towns of the Sierra Madre. Once a rendezvous site for Native Americans and trappers, its townsite was platted in 1897, the same year that miner Ed Haggarty struck copper along the nearby Continental Divide. By 1902, an aerial tram ran 16 miles from the Ferris-Haggarty mine to the smelter at Encampment. By 1908, the smelter was out of business. Now, beef and tourism are Encampment's economic mainstays while its timber industry is in decline. The hamlet of Riverside (population 85; elevation 7137 feet) lies 1 mile away.

Orientation & Information
Hwy 70 makes 90° turns through Encampment; first as McCaffery St, then as 6th St and then as MacFarland St. Riverside and Encampment share a joint information center in a tiny log building on Hwy 70, one-quarter mile south of Hwy 230. It is open only during summer; ask for the 'Historic Houses of Grand Encampment' brochure. The USFS Medicine Bow-Routt National Forest & Thunder Basin National Grassland Brush Creek-Hayden Resource Center (☎ 307-327-5481), 204 W 9th St at Freeman, is open from 7:30 am to 4:30 pm weekdays. The post office is at 6th and MacFarland Sts.

Grand Encampment Museum
The Grand Encampment Museum (☎ 307-327-5308), on Barrett St near 6th St, concentrates an excellent collection of furnished historic buildings transported from their original sites. Its main building is jammed with regional artifacts and a small research library. Several towers from the aerial tram, complete with cables and ore buckets, stand nearby along with a USFS fire lookout tower from the Snowy Range. The outbuildings include several provocative false-fronts and are open only for 1½-hour guided tours. The museum is open 1 to 5 pm Sunday to Tuesday and 10 am to 5 pm Wednesday Memorial Day to Labor Day, and weekends September and October. Admission is free.

Places to Stay & Eat
Encampment *Grandview Park*, adjacent to the museum, allows free camping in a very small signed area along 6th St. Camping (three-day maximum) is also free at the *Encampment City Trailer Park*, which is behind the Sage Brush Senior Center. Donations are welcome.

Doubles at the treeless *Vachers Bighorn Lodge* (☎ 307-327-5110), 508 McCaffery St, cost about $25; it has a hot tub. *Grand & Sierra B&B Lodge* (☎ 307-327-5200), 1016 Lomax St, PO Box 312, Encampment, WY 82325, is a modern log house; singles/doubles cost $60/70 or $40/50 with shared bathroom. When it's time to eat, *Betty's Grand Encampment Cafe* offers a unique dining experience.

Riverside The shady and pleasant *Lazy Acres Campground & Motel* (☎ 307-327-5968) is along the Encampment River. Tent sites cost $7/9 singles/doubles; sites with full hookups $10/12. Motel rooms cost $23. Showers cost $2.50 for nonguests.

Getting There & Away
Encampment is on Hwy 70, 19 miles south of Saratoga and 1 mile southwest of Riverside, which is on Hwy 230 east of the junction with Hwy 70.

SIERRA MADRE
The Continental Divide follows the crest of the Sierra Madre west of Encampment, as does the **Continental Divide National Scenic Trail** (see Encampment & Riverside for the nearest USFS office). Small lakes, creeks and rivers are on both the east and west sides of the range. Hwy 70 (Battle Hwy) traverses the range heading west where it eventually intersects Hwy 789 at Baggs on the west side. Historic sites are along this stretch of Hwy 70, and from Battle Pass (11,004 feet) the views are splendid. Hwy 70, open Memorial Day to October, is a beautiful fall drive to view aspens changing color.

Two wilderness areas offer extensive trails and campgrounds: **Encampment River Wilderness Area**, in a narrow canyon directly south of Encampment, with several access points; and **Huston Park Wilderness**, about 10 miles west of Encampment along the Continental Divide, just south of Hwy 70.

SARATOGA & AROUND

The pleasant hot-springs resort of Saratoga (population 1969; elevation 6786 feet) sits in a sagebrush plain along the North Platte River at the western base of the Medicine Bow Mountains. A timber town now in transition, Louisiana Pacific's noisy sawmill operates all night and some houses boast 'this family lives on timber dollars.' But as the timber industry and the town's population decline, Saratoga's long-standing tourism grows. Its mineral baths, claimed to be 'beneficial to rheumatism, eczema, paralysis, stomach trouble, kidney disease, "nerves" and all forms of blood and skin disease,' draw visitors from around the state. Motels are reasonable, restaurants are decent and downtown has nice Western shops. The North Platte River offers fly-fishing and floating and also serves as a gateway for excursions into the Medicine Bow Mountains and Sierra Madre.

History

Saratoga's hot springs were a favorite retreat for Native Americans until the arrival of settlers. William Cadwall built a rustic bathhouse here in 1878, when it was known as Warm Springs. The current name was adopted in admiration and imitation of New York State's fashionable Saratoga Springs resort. Construction of the Wolf Hotel (on the National Register of Historic Places) in 1893 was a step in this direction. Saratoga relied, however, on mining and timber for most of the 20th century.

Orientation & Information

Hwy 130 is 1st St in town, the main north-south road. Many businesses are on Bridge Ave, which divides north-south street addresses. The Saratoga/Platte Valley Chamber of Commerce (☎ 307-326-8855; fax 307-326-5703) is at 115 Bridge St, PO Box Saratoga, WY 82331-1095 (Bridge Ave becomes Bridge St west of downtown). The USFS Medicine Bow-Routt National Forest Brush Creek-Hayden Ranger Station (☎ 307-326-5258), is on the east side of S Hwy 130 about one-quarter mile south of the Hacienda Motel. It is open 7:30 am to 4:30 pm weekdays. The kiosk outside usually has useful information. ATMs are at Community First National Bank, at 302 N 1st St, and Rawlins National Bank, at 209 S 1st St. The post office is at 105 W Main Ave. Perue Printing & Office Products (☎ 307-326-5037), 101 E Main Ave, provides fax services.

Municipal Pool & Hot Springs

On the banks of the North Platte River at the east end of Walnut Ave, this former state park reverted to local control in 1982. Its famous **Hobo Pool**, with temperatures ranging from 117° to 128°F, is open 24 hours daily year-round. Admission is free. The municipal pool, which is not a mineral spring, is open 11 am to 4 pm and 6 to 9 pm daily Memorial Day to Labor Day. Admission is nominal.

Saratoga Museum

The Saratoga Museum (☎ 307-326-5511), 104 Constitution Ave in the former UP depot (1915), features railroad memorabilia and Native American artifacts. On the attractively landscaped grounds are a bandshell, a UP boxcar and caboose in mint condition, a vintage sheepherder's wagon with wooden wheels and canvas roof and an older log cabin. It's open 1 to 5 pm daily Memorial Day to Labor Day, and admission is free.

Activities

To arrange **floating** and **fishing** trips, contact Hack's Tackle & Outfitters (☎ 307-326-9823), 407 N 1st St just before the bridge, Platte Valley Anglers (☎ 307-326-5750) at 112 S 1st St, or Great Rocky Mountain Outfitters (☎ 307-326-8750), 216 E Walnut Ave. Two nearby **rock climbing** sites, southeast of Hwy 130/230 junction, are Baggett Rocks and Bennett Peak (8312 feet).

Places to Stay

Camping *Deer Haven RV Park* (☎ 307-326-8746), 706 N 1st St, is north of the North Platte River bridge. Grassy tent sites cost $5; sites with full hookups are $10. The shaded but forlorn *Saratoga RV Park* (☎ 307-326-8807), 116 W Farm Ave, is closer to town and has showers. Tent sites cost $8; sites with full hookups $12. The *Saratoga Lake Campground* is at the north end of town 1 mile east of Hwy 130. The *Riverside RV Park*, east of the river at E River St and E Pic Pike Rd, has cramped, shadeless sites with full hookups ($10). The best sites ($18) are at the *Saratoga Inn & RV Park* (see below), including access to resort facilities.

Motels The *Silver Moon Motel* (☎ 307-326-5974), at 412 E Bridge Ave, costs $35/43, while the comparably priced *Sage & Sand Motel* (☎ 307-326-8339), 304 S 1st St, has some kitchenettes. The *Wolf Hotel* (☎ 307-326-5525), 101 E Bridge Ave, is a good value. Rooms start at $40, and the restaurant and bar are highly regarded. The tidy, riverside *Riviera Lodge* (☎ 307-326-5651), 104 E Saratoga Ave, is comparable. The *Hacienda Motel* (☎ 307-326-5751), on Hwy 130 south of the airport, is slightly more. The *Saratoga Inn* (☎ 307-326-5261), east of the river on E Pic Pike Rd, is a modest resort with a pool, spa, tennis courts, golf course and private fishing. Rates start at $50.

Places to Eat

Mom's Kitchen (☎ 307-326-5136), 402 S 1st St, is a breakfast favorite. Moderately priced lunches and dinners are worth a try at *Stumpy's Eatery* (☎ 307-326-8132), 218 N 1st St. Popular and delicious *Bubba's Bar-B-Que* (☎ 307-326-5427), 119 N River St, is part of well-regarded chain. *Lollypops* (☎ 326-5020), 107 E Bridge Ave, serves espresso and sandwiches with a good variety of homemade ice creams. The

Wolf Hotel and the *Saratoga Inn* both offer more elaborate meals.

Entertainment

At the *Rustic Bar* (☎ 307-326-5965), 124 E Bridge Ave, you can catch some live C&W music on weekends.

Getting There & Away

Saratoga is on Hwy 130, 20 miles south of I-80 and 79 miles west of Laramie. It is 18 miles north of Riverside and Encampment and 45 miles from the Wyoming-Colorado state line via Hwy 230.

Great Divide Basin

The Continental Divide crosses I-80 twice between Rawlins and Rock Springs, forming a basin 90 miles long. The color of the soil lends it the name Red Desert. Interestingly, all precipitation in the basin stays there – water neither flows east to the Atlantic Ocean nor west to the Pacific. The region, which appears desolate at first glance, is actually rich in natural beauty and wildlife.

RAWLINS

Rawlins (population 9380; elevation 6755 feet) is the only sizable town along I-80 between Laramie and Rock Springs. Like most southern Wyoming towns, it owes its origin to the railroad and its economy to minerals – particularly the coal that gives Carbon County its name. (The nearest large mine is at Hanna, 40 miles east of Rawlins.) The area around Rawlins is also one of the world's finest for jade. Rawlins' most impressive landmark and its major attraction is the Wyoming Frontier Prison. The town seems somewhat indifferent to tourism.

History

Named for General John A Rawlins, who helped survey the UP route through the area, Rawlins grew quickly, suffering the

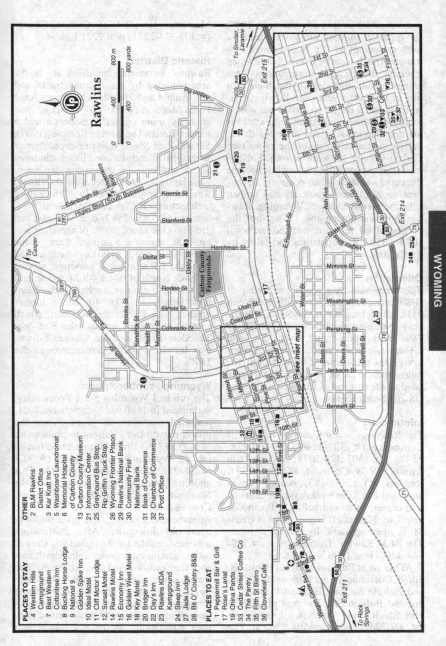

Rawlins

800 m
800 yards
400
0
0   400

To Sinclair,
Laramie

To Casper

To Rock
Springs

Higley Blvd (South Bypass)

Inverness Blvd

Edinburgh Blvd

Kooniz St

Stanford St

Harshman St

Delta St

Daley St

Rodeo St

Illinois St

Colorado St

Utah St

Koorniz St

Monroe St

Washington St

Pershing St

Jackson St

Bennett St

Carbon County
Fairgrounds

Airport Rd

E Railroad Ave

Water St

State St

see inset map

PLACES TO STAY
4   Western Hills
    Campground
7   Best Western
8   Cottontree Inn
8   Bucking Horse Lodge
9   National 9
9   Golden Spike Inn
10 Ideal Motel
11 Cliff Motor Lodge
12 Sunset Motel
14 Rawlins Motel
15 Economy Inn
16 Golden West Motel
18 Key Motel
20 Bridger Inn
22 Day's Inn
23 Rawlins KOA
    Kampground
24 Sleep Inn
27 Jade Lodge
28 Bit O' Country B&B

PLACES TO EAT
1   Peppermill Bar & Grill
17 Rose's Lariat
19 China Panda
33 Cedar Street Coffee Co
34 The Pantry
35 Fifth St Bistro
36 Cloverleaf Cafe

OTHER
2   BLM Rawlins
    District Office
3   Kar Kraft Inc
5   Washboard Laundromat
6   Memorial Hospital
    of Carbon County
13 Information Center
21 Carbon County Museum
25 Greyhound Bus Stop,
    Rip Griffin Truck Stop
26 Wyoming Frontier Prison
29 Rawlins National Bank
30 Community First
    National Bank
31 Bank of Commerce
32 Chamber of Commerce
37 Post Office

usual disorder in its early years. In 1878, for instance, railroad employees foiled a robbery attempt by Big Nose George Parrott and Dutch Charlie Burris, but lawmen tracking the escaped desperadoes were ambushed and shot dead. After their capture in Montana a year later, Rawlins vigilantes lynched Burris on arrival but waited to dispatch the brutal Parrot until after his murder conviction. Even after his death, Parrott continued to make the news (see Carbon County Museum below). Following incorporation in 1886, Rawlins became the county seat, with an economy dependent on wool, beef, minerals and timber. Like the rest of southern Wyoming, Rawlins boomed during the 1970s, but the decline of oil prices devastated the town and by 1990 its population had fallen by nearly 20%.

Orientation
The main east-west roads are Cedar St (I-80 exit 215) and Spruce St (I-80 exit 211), which together are also US 30 Business. North-south 3rd St (US 287/Hwy 789) links Spruce and Cedar Sts, and divides east-west street addresses. Downtown is the grid enclosed by Walnut St, the railroad tracks, 10th St and 3rd St. Higley Blvd, at the east end of Cedar St, is also the US 287 South Bypass.

Information
The Rawlins/Carbon County Chamber of Commerce (☎ 307-324-4111, 800-228-3547; fax 307-324-5078; rcccoc@trib .com), 519 W Cedar St, PO Box 1331, Rawlins, WY 82301-1331, is open 9 am to noon and 1 to 5 pm weekdays. An information center, in an old yellow UP caboose near City Market off Higley Blvd at Cedar St, is open sporadically during summer. The BLM Rawlins District office (☎ 307-328-4200) is at 1300 N 3rd St.

ATMs are at Rawlins National Bank, 220 5th St, Community First National Bank, 4th and Buffalo Sts, and Bank of Commerce, 3rd and Buffalo Sts. The post office is at 106 5th St. The Washboard Laundromat (☎ 307-324-2434) is at 504 23rd St. The

Memorial Hospital of Carbon County (☎ 307-324-2221) is at 2221 Elm St.

Historic District
Rawlins' interesting buildings are in the area bounded by the railroad tracks and 6th, Walnut and 2nd Sts. The Queen Anne Ferris Mansion (1903), 607 W Maple, was an early mine owner's residence and a former B&B. The Shrine Temple (1909), 5th and Pine Sts, is well preserved despite several filled and stuccoed lower windows. South and east of the prison are many Neoclassical, Art Deco and Gothic Revival examples of early 20th-century architecture. The France Memorial Presbyterian Church (1882) is at W Cedar and 3rd Sts. One block south of the church is Front St; across the railroad tracks is the former UP depot (1901), which closed when the UP terminated passenger service in 1983. North of it, on 4th St, are several interesting buildings, including the Rainbow Hotel, 114-116 4th St, a former brothel. The former Ferris Hotel, which saw distinguished guests like President Theodore Roosevelt and Thomas Edison, was Rawlin's social center through the 1970s.

Wyoming Frontier Prison
The original Wyoming State Penitentiary, authorized in 1886 and completed in 1901, operated for over 80 years. When the prison moved to its current location south of I-80 in 1981, the old prison was turned into the Wyoming Frontier Prison (☎ 307-324-4422), 500 W Walnut St at 5th St. This ghoulishly fascinating museum is on the National Register of Historic Places. Crowned by turrets on its distinctive Romanesque exterior, the grim building overlooks downtown. After confronting unheated cellblocks, the forbidding shower room, maximum security cells, death row and the gallows and gas chamber, one leaves with a sense of unease. In the cafeteria, all prisoners ate facing the same direction. Its walls are covered by now-peeling murals painted by one-armed prisoner Art Orcutt. In 1988 a low-budget

horror film *Prison* was filmed here. Unlike the sanitized Wyoming Territorial Prison in Laramie, this is the real thing.

Administered by the Old Pen Joint Powers Board, it is open 8 am to 7 pm during summer. Admission is free. Worthwhile half-hour guided tours operate 8:30 am to 6:30 pm daily Memorial Day to Labor Day; tours are by reservation only the rest of the year. The tour costs $3.50 for adults, $3 for seniors (55 and up) and children (six to 14); it's free for children under six. For an even creepier experience, try the night tours on summer weekends.

Carbon County Museum
The Carbon County Museum (☎ 307-328-2740), 904 W Walnut St, holds such grisly artifacts as Big Nose George Parrott's death mask and a pair of shoes made from his skin by physician (and future Wyoming governor) John Osborne. Osborne, who later became a US Congressman and then a State Department official under President Woodrow Wilson, gave Big Nose George a post-mortem lobotomy but found nothing abnormal about his brain. The museum also contains noteworthy exhibits on Native American pottery and basketry, sheepwagons and historic photographs. It is open 1 to 4 pm weekdays during May, 10 am to 5 pm daily and 7 to 9 pm weekdays June to August, and 10 am to 5 pm weekdays during September. Admission is free.

Places to Stay
Rawlins has abundant, reasonably priced lodgings along Cedar and Spruce Sts; the latter tend to be comparatively cheaper. Rates drop slightly during winter.

Camping Both campgrounds are barren and shadeless and often windy and dusty, but have showers and laundry. Tent sites cost $12 and sites with full hookups cost $18 at *Western Hills Campground* (☎ 307-324-2592, 307-328-2082), 2500 Wagon Circle Rd. The *Rawlins KOA Kampground* (☎ 307-328-2021, 800-562-7559), Hwy 71 and Washington St along the interstate

(I-80 exit 214), is open mid-June to October. Tent sites cost $18; sites with full hookups are $27.

B&Bs The only B&B around is *Bit O' Country B&B* (☎ 307-328-2111, 888-328-2111), 221 E Spruce St.

Motels Ranging from $20 to $30 are: *Jade Lodge* (☎ 307-324-2791), 415 W Spruce St; *Economy Inn* (☎ 307-324-4561), 713 W Spruce St; the quieter *Golden West Motel* (☎ 307-324-4452), 822 W Pine St, one block south of W Spruce St; the attractive *Rawlins Motel* (☎ 307-324-3456), 905 W Spruce St; and *Ideal Motel* (☎ 307-324-3451), 1507 W Spruce St.

Doubles start at $34 at the attractive *Sunset Motel* (☎ 307-324-3448, 800-336-6752), 1302 W Spruce; *Cliff Motor Lodge* (☎ 307-324-2905), at 1500 W Spruce; *National 9 Golden Spike Inn* (☎ 307-328-1600), 1617 W Spruce; and *Bucking Horse Lodge* (☎ 307-324-3471), 1720 W Spruce St, some equipped with kitchenettes. Similarly priced are the tidy *Key Motel* (☎ 307-324-2728), 1806 E Cedar St, and *Bridger Inn* (☎ 307-328-1401), 1904 E Cedar St.

Of the more expensive places, the best is the comparatively new *Sleep Inn* (☎ 307-328-1732), 1400 Higley Blvd (I-80 exit 214), which also has fax and laundry. Doubles start at $53. The *Day's Inn* (☎ 307-324-6615), 2222 E Cedar St (singles/doubles $40/50), and *Best Western Cottontree Inn* (☎ 307-324-2737, 800-662-6886), 23rd and W Spruce Sts ($74), are overpriced and need remodeling.

Places to Eat
In a cheerfully renovated building, the *Fifth St Bistro* (☎ 307-324-7246), 112 5th St, serves espresso, bagels, muffins, croissants, homemade bread, sandwiches and Italian sodas. For coffee and ice cream, go to *Cedar Street Coffee Co* (☎ 307-324-5233), 509 W Cedar St. The Mexican food at *Rose's Lariat* (☎ 307-324-5261), 410 E Cedar St, is authentic and appealing, and the staff very friendly. Despite 25 successful years, it's almost a hole in the wall with only one booth

WYOMING

and a dozen counter seats, plus a single table outside during summer. Downtown, *Cloverleaf Cafe* (☎ 307-324-9841), at 113 4th St, serves Navajo tacos. *Peppermill Bar & Grill* (☎ 307-324-8100), 1602 Inverness Blvd, has standard American fare, and *China Panda* (☎ 307-324-2198), 1810 E Cedar St, serves Chinese. *The Pantry* (☎ 307-324-7860), 221 W Cedar St, offers the most diverse menu in town as well as the best atmosphere in the Victorian Italianate Blake House (1881).

Getting There & Away

Bus Greyhound Bus Lines (☎ 307-328-2103), 1400 S Higley Blvd, is at the Rip Griffin Truck Stop (I-80 exit 214). Daily eastbound buses stop at 12:35 am and 5:40 pm; westbound buses stop at 2:40 am and 2:45 pm.

Car Rawlins is along the north side of I-80, 94 miles west of Laramie and 106 miles east of Rock Springs. US 287/Hwy 789 leads northwest to Muddy Gap Junction (46 miles). US 287/Hwy 789 then leads west to Lander (82 miles), and Hwy 220 leads northeast to Casper (73 miles).

Getting Around

Kar Kraft Inc (☎ 307-324-6352), at 1111 E Daley, rents cars locally.

AROUND RAWLINS
Sinclair

Six miles east of Rawlins, Sinclair's company-town architecture, dating from 1923, evokes the Mediterranean rather than the high desert. When the Lincoln Hwy passed through this refinery town it was called Parco after its founder, the Producers & Refiners Corporation. It adopted the name Sinclair on being sold to oil magnate and convicted felon Harry Sinclair's company in 1934. The vacant Parco/Sinclair Hotel and other buildings are on the National Register of Historic Places, but the malodorous Sinclair Refinery still dominates the town. An old UP caboose decorates the shaded city park. At *Su Casa* (☎ 307-328-1745) the Mexican dishes, including seafood, draw crowds.

Seminoe State Park

Seminoe State Park (☎ 307-320-3013) is set along the northwest shores of Seminoe Reservoir on the North Platte River, 34 miles north of Sinclair. The park's name comes from a 19th-century French trapper, Basil Cimineau Lajeunesse. The sagebrush prairie, surrounded by white sand dunes, is an ideal habitat for thousands of pronghorn antelope and sage grouse. The nearby Seminoe Mountains and the surrounding landscape offer excellent hiking, boating, canoeing and water skiing. The **Miracle Mile** of the North Platte River, below the Seminoe Dam and 12 miles north of the campground, is renowned for its trout and walleye fishing. Get fishing licenses and supplies from the Seminoe Boat Club (☎ 307-325-3043), 10 miles southeast of the park, or at Miracle Mile Ranch (☎ 307-320-6710) near the fishing area. Take Seminoe Rd (Carbon County Rd 351; I-80 exit 219) to the campground ($4) along the northwest shore of the reservoir. Admission is free.

Sinclair to Alcova
Back Country Byway

From Seminoe State Park (see above) continue north on unpaved Carbon County Rd 351 to Leo Junction. Then take Carbon County Rd 291, which turns into Natrona County Rd 407, to Alcova on Hwy 220. Natrona County Rd 407 also offers access to the Pathfinder Reservoir. High clearance or 4WD vehicles are recommended for this scenic drive.

ROCK SPRINGS

Rock Springs (population 22,500; elevation 6271 feet), founded in 1868, owes its existence, and its gritty character, to the UP and the coal-mining industry. The railroad brought German, Chinese, Danish, Scottish, Finnish, Italian and Slovene laborers to work in the mines. In 1875 the miners went on strike over wages, only to be replaced by Chinese miners who were willing to work for lower wages. By 1885, widespread resentment towards them culminated in the massacre of 28 Chinese and the burning of Rock Springs' Chinatown,

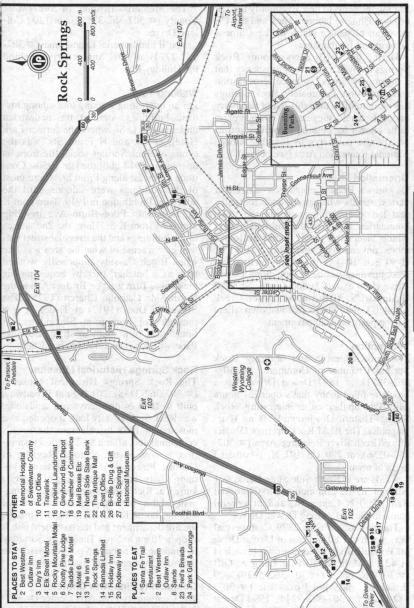

Rock Springs

0   400   800 m
0   400   800 yards

To Airport,
Rawlins

To Farson,
Pinedale

To Green
River

WYOMING

see inset map

Western
Wyoming
College

PLACES TO STAY
2   Best Western
    Outlaw Inn
3   Day's Inn
4   Elk Street Motel
5   Rocky Mountain Motel
7   Knotty Pine Lodge
12 Saddle Lite Motel
13 Motel 6
13 The Inn at
    Rock Springs
14 Ramada Limited
15 Holiday Inn
20 Rodeway Inn

PLACES TO EAT
1   Santa Fe Trail
    Restaurant
2   Outlaw Inn
8   Sands
23 Fred's Breads
24 Park Grill & Lounge

OTHER
9   Memorial Hospital
    of Sweetwater County
10 Post Office
11 Travelink
16 Imperial Laundromat
17 Greyhound Bus Depot
18 Chamber of Commerce
19 Mail Boxes Etc
21 North Side State Bank
22 The Antique Mall
25 Post Office
26 Bi-Rite Drug & Gift
27 Rock Springs
    Historical Museum

forcing residents to flee. Eventually the UP brought Chinese laborers back and the US government paid a claim to the Chinese government for damages.

During the 1970s energy boom, Rock Springs enjoyed a notorious prosperity that also brought drugs, violence, prostitution and corruption. Fortunately, Rock Springs has more to offer than this list of unsavory incidents would suggest; the town prefers to be known for cultural resources and as one of the gateways to Flaming Gorge National Recreation Area (see below).

Orientation
Downtown Rock Springs is a warren of narrow streets which were once footpaths that led to coal mines within the town boundaries. South of the railroad tracks, which bisect the town, streets follow a more conventional pattern. Elk St/US 191 (I-80 exit 104) is the main north-south road, but most businesses are along Dewar Drive (I-80 exit 102) and Center St (I-80 Business/US 30 Business). Bitter Creek parallels Center St except downtown where it disappears beneath pavement.

Information
The knowledgeable and obliging Rock Springs Chamber of Commerce (☎ 307-362-3771), at 1897 Dewar Drive, has a brochure-filled lobby that's open 24 hours daily. Pick up their rather interesting 'Rock Springs Historic Downtown Walking Tour' pamphlet. The BLM Rock Springs District office/Green River Resource Area (☎ 307-352-0256), at 280 US 191 N, is situated north of town.

ATMs are at North Side State Bank, 601 N Front St, the Community First National Bank, 200 N Center St, and at several banks in the malls along Dewar Drive.

The post office is at 2829 Commercial Way, north of I-80 and east of Dewar Drive off Foothill Blvd; the downtown branch is at 422 S Main St. Bi-Rite Drug & Gift (☎ 307-362-6601; fax 307-362-5229), 409 Broadway, and Mail Boxes Etc (☎ 307-382-8228; fax 307-382-8244), 1993 Dewar Drive, suite 1, provide fax services.

The Memorial Hospital of Sweetwater County (☎ 307-362-3711) is at 1200 College Drive.

You'll find Imperial Laundromat (☎ 307-382-2774) at 1669 Sunset Drive, behind the Holiday Inn.

Walking Tour
For an interesting walking tour among historic buildings, start at the pedestrian underpass at C St, where the former Park Hotel, at Elk and N Front Sts, was the center of Rock Springs social life from its opening in 1914 until the late 1950s. Continue northeast along Front St, where most of the buildings were saloons until the advent of Prohibition in 1919. Turn onto K St, then onto Pilot Butte Ave trending northeast from K St. Here, the 2nd stories of the buildings and the irregular street pattern give a sense of what the area was like when Butch Cassidy supposedly worked here as a butcher, thereby acquiring his nickname. Turn west on Bridger Ave to the North Side Catholic Church (1925). The Slovenski Dom (1913) at Tisdel St is a reminder of immigrant Slovenians. At Soulsby St turn south to shady Bunning Park, which has an attractive bandshell.

Rock Springs Historical Museum
The Rock Springs Historical Museum (☎ 307-362-3138), 201 B St at Broadway, built in 1894 of distinctive red sandstone, was Rock Springs' city hall. It opened as a museum in 1988 to celebrate the town's centennial and, after a $1.7 million restoration, is now on the National Register of Historic Places. It is southwestern Wyoming's only remaining building of the style known as Richardson Romanesque. Permanent exhibits include presentations on coal mining, home life in early Rock Springs, the fire department and the basement jail. It is open 10 am to 5 pm Tuesday to Saturday in summer and noon to 5 pm Wednesday to Saturday in winter. Admission is free.

Community Fine Arts Center
The Community Fine Arts Center (☎ 307-362-6212), 400 C St in the library building,

has permanent exhibits by local and state artists and a major mural of the 1885 massacre. The center hosts special exhibitions and events as diverse as cowboy poetry readings, ballet and children's theater. The gallery is open noon to 5 pm Monday and Thursday, 10 am to noon and 1 to 5 pm Tuesday, Wednesday and Friday, 6 to 9 pm Monday, Wednesday and Thursday, and noon to 5 pm Saturday.

Special Events

In mid-May, Rock Springs hosts the **All Girl Rodeo**, one of few in Wyoming. The three-day **Desert Balloon Extravaganza** takes place the second week of July at Paul J Wataha Park near the Sweetwater County Fairgrounds, on the northern outskirts of town. The **Great Wyoming Polka & Heritage Festival** takes place in late August.

Places to Stay

The bleak and treeless *Rock Springs KOA Kampground* (☎ 307-362-3063), 86 Foothill Blvd (I-80 exit 99), is 5 miles west of town and 1 mile north. Tent sites cost $16; sites with full hookups are $22.

Rock Springs has reasonably priced motels with minimal seasonal rate variation. Most accommodations cluster around Dewar Drive and Elk St, but the cheapest are around 9th St east of Elk St and north of downtown. Singles/doubles cost $17/22 at the *Saddle Lite Motel* (☎ 307-362-1846), 1411 9th St. Starting at $26 are the *Knotty Pine Lodge* (☎ 307-362-4515), 1234 9th St, and friendly *Elk Street Motel* (☎ 307-362-3705), 1100 Elk St. The *Rocky Mountain Motel* (☎ 307-362-3443), 1204 9th St, and *Motel 6* (☎ 307-362-1850), 2615 Commercial St off Foothill Blvd, cost $30/35.

Mid-range places include: *Rodeway Inn* (☎ 307-362-6673), 1004 Dewar Drive ($42/46); *Day's Inn* (☎ 307-362-5646), 1545 Elk St ($49/53); and *Ramada Limited* (☎ 307-362-1770, 888-307-7890), 2717 Dewar Drive ($55/65). The best hotels are: *The Inn at Rock Springs* (☎ 307-362-9600, 800-442-9692 in Wyoming), 2518 Foothill Blvd ($58/64); *Best Western Outlaw Inn*

(☎ 307-362-6623), 1630 Elk St ($70/77); and *Holiday Inn* (☎ 307-382-9200), 1675 Sunset Drive ($75).

Places to Eat

The best bakery, *Fred's Breads* (☎ 307-362-9212), 601 Broadway, also serves light breakfasts and sandwiches. The *Best Western Outlaw Inn* serves inexpensive lunch specials in its cafe. *Sands* (☎ 307-362-5633), 1549 9th St, serves Cantonese, Szechuan and Mandarin dishes. The popular and often crowded *Santa Fe Trail Restaurant* (☎ 307-362-5427), 1635 Elk St, serves rather bland Tex-Mex and southwestern food, but its ingredients are fresh. Specials are Navajo tacos (chili con carne on a fried tortilla with onion and other toppings) and fry bread. The *Park Grill & Lounge* (☎ 307-362-3701), 19 Elk St in the once elegant Park Hotel, has an appealing Italian menu with daily lunch specials. Half-orders of pasta are a good value.

Getting There & Away

Air Rock Springs is connected with Denver by United Express (☎ 307-382-5887) out of the Rock Springs/Sweetwater County Airport (☎ 307-382-4580), 382 Hwy 370 (I-80 exit 111), 7 miles east of Rock Springs.

Bus Greyhound (☎ 307-362-2931), 1655 Sunset Drive (next to Burger King), is open 9 am to noon and 1 to 5 pm weekdays, and 10 am to noon and 1 to 5 pm Saturday. Daily buses go westbound to Salt Lake City, UT (4:20, 6, 10:05 am, 5:35, 7 and 8:15 pm), eastbound to Cheyenne (12:20, 3:05, 10:30 and 11:05 pm), and to Denver (8 am and 3:30 pm).

Car Rock Springs sprawls along the north and south sides of I-80, 101 miles west of Rawlins and 7 miles east of Green River. US 191 leads north to Farson, Pinedale and Jackson, or south to Flaming Gorge National Recreation Area. Hwy 430 leads south to the Wyoming-Colorado state line and Dinosaur National Monument (see the Western Colorado chapter).

WYOMING

Getting Around
Bus Star Transit (☎ 307-382-7827), 1130 Billie Drive, operates Rock Springs' public transportation.

Car Both Avis (☎ 307-362-5599) and Hertz (☎ 307-382-3262) have locations at the airport. Wayne's Car Rental (☎ 307-362-6970) is at 1539 Foothill Blvd.

Taxi Call City Cab (☎ 307-382-1100) if you need a taxi.

AROUND ROCK SPRINGS
Aspen Mountain
Aspen Mountain (8680 feet) offers picnic sites and panoramic views. Take Hwy 430 southeast of Rock Springs to Aspen Mountain Rd (Sweetwater County Rd 4-27), and follow it to the summit.

Reliance Historic Coal Tipple
The massive Reliance Historic Coal Tipple sorted and graded coal and loaded it onto railcars. Completed in 1936 but now obsolete, the structure is open for a self-guided tour of the area's mining history. Take US 191 (I-80 exit 104) 3 miles north of Rock Springs to Reliance Rd (Sweetwater County Rd 4-42), and head east 2 miles.

Greater Sand Dunes Area
An historically important backcountry route crosses the fascinating high desert north of Rock Springs. Take US 191 10 miles north and follow Tri-Territory Rd (Sweetwater County Rd 4-17) east, named for the site marking the boundary of the Louisiana Purchase, Mexican Cession and the Northwest Territories. Go past Boar's

Tusk, a volcanic monolith, and stop to see the White Mountain (7702 feet) **petroglyphs** on a south-facing brown sandstone cliff. These Native American drawings date from the late 17th to early 19th centuries. Cross the vast **Killpecker Dune Field**, one of North America's largest dunes. Blowing sand covers snowbanks here, creating unusual eolian ice cells. Continue through the Jack Morrow Hills to Hwy 28 east of Farson. (Stop at the Farson Mercantile, 'Home of the Big Cone' for ice cream.) The area is teeming with wildlife; an elk herd roams the dunes area and its birthing area is near the Steamboat Mountain (8683 feet) rim. Camping is allowed throughout this BLM land, but there are no facilities; bring water, a map and compass. A high-clearance 4WD vehicle is also necessary.

Southwestern Wyoming

The Green River, which flows north to south through badlands and arid mountains, is the focus of recreation in southwestern Wyoming. This sparsely populated and desolate region teems with wildlife and has a rich fossil history.

FLAMING GORGE NATIONAL RECREATION AREA
Flaming Gorge was named by John Wesley Powell for the fiery red sandstones he saw during his first descent of the Green and Colorado rivers in 1869. Between 1957 and 1964, the Bureau of Reclamation built Flaming Gorge Dam, which backed up the Green River for over 90 miles to form the Flaming Gorge Reservoir with a 375-mile shoreline. The Flaming Gorge NRA (elevation 6040 feet), which was established in 1968 and administered by the USFS Ashley National Forest, is almost equally divided between Wyoming and Utah. But the better scenery, campgrounds, visitors centers and recreational opportunities are found on the Utah side.

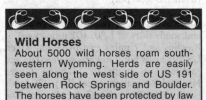

Wild Horses
About 5000 wild horses roam southwestern Wyoming. Herds are easily seen along the west side of US 191 between Rock Springs and Boulder. The horses have been protected by law since 1971 under BLM authority. ∎

Its prime attractions are boating and year-round fishing. The reservoir is stocked with half a million fish annually, and various fishing records have been set here. Visitors come for picnicking, hiking, backpacking and camping in the summer, and cross-country skiing, snowshoeing and snow camping in the winter. Large mammals like moose, elk, pronghorn antelope and mule deer are common; bighorn sheep, black bear and mountain lion are occasionally seen.

Orientation

Flaming Gorge NRA is south of Rock Springs via US 191 (east side) and south of Green River via Hwy 530 (west side). South of the Wyoming-Utah border Hwy 530 becomes Utah Hwy 44, which intersects US 191 at Greendale Junction. Six miles north on US 191 is the Flaming Gorge Dam.

Information

Write in advance to District Ranger, Flaming Gorge NRA, USDA Forest Service, Box 278, Manila, UT 84046, for information. The Flaming Gorge NRA Headquarters (☎ 801-784-3445), at the junction of Hwy 43 and Hwy 44, Manila, UT, is open 8 am to 4:30 pm weekdays year-round and also weekends during summer. USFS offices with additional information are:

Ashley National Forest Flaming Gorge Information – see Green River later in this chapter

Flaming Gorge District
  PO Box 157, Dutch John, UT 84023
  (☎ 801-885-3204)

Vernal Ranger District
  355 N Vernal Ave, Vernal UT 84078
  (☎ 801-789-1181)

The Flaming Gorge Area Chamber of Commerce (☎ 801-784-3445), PO Box 122, Manila, UT 84046, is also helpful.

The NRA's south entrance is at Greendale Junction. A $2 user pass, available at the USFS offices above or at the Rock Springs and Green River chambers of commerce, is required. Visitors receive a free copy of the 'Flaming Gorge Dam and Reservoir' brochure with a useful map and information. The year-round NRA receives most visitors May to October. Most services close during winter, but a few stay open and snowplows maintain roads.

The NRA has two visitors centers. Flaming Gorge Dam visitors center (☎ 801-885-3135), on US 191 at the dam, is open 8 am to 8 pm Thursday to Saturday, and 8 am to 7 pm Sunday to Wednesday during summer, and 9 am to 5 pm daily the rest of the year. The Red Canyon visitors center (☎ 801-889-3713), 4 miles west of Greendale Junction and 2 miles north of Utah Hwy 44, is open 9:30 am to 5 pm daily mid-May to October. The Red Canyon visitors center has impressive views. Both visitors centers have exhibits and a bookstore, and offer ranger-led activities. The Flaming Gorge Natural History Association (☎ 801-885-3305; fax 801-781-5251), PO Box 188, Dutch John, UT 84023, sells books and maps via mail.

Scenic Loop Tour

I-80 travelers can take a 100-mile drive around Flaming Gorge, stopping at scenic overlooks. The drive takes four to five hours beginning and ending in either Rock Springs or Green River.

Flaming Gorge Dam

Free guided tours depart from the Red Canyon visitors center between 9 am and 5 pm during summer. An elevator within the dam drops 42 stories (502 feet) to the base of the structure. A walkway goes along the top of the dam.

Swett Ranch

This ranch, 1½ miles off US 191 half a mile north of Greendale Junction and 5 miles south of the dam, dates from 1909 and offers a look at homesteading history. It is open 9 am to 5 pm Thursday to Monday Memorial Day to Labor Day.

Sheep Creek Canyon Geological Area

The 13-mile Sheep Creek Canyon Geological Loop leaves Utah Hwy 44 about 15 miles west of Greendale Junction and returns to Hwy 44 about 7 miles farther north. Brochures, available at the visitors centers, and roadside signs interpret the area's geology. The loop has dramatic scenery and picnic areas but no campgrounds. Snow closes the loop during winter.

Spirit Lake Rd

Two miles along the Sheep Creek Canyon Geological Loop, unpaved USFS Rd 221 branches west and leads about 20 miles to Spirit Lake, which has free camping but no potable water: 4WD vehicles are recommended. Near the beginning of USFS Rd 221, a sign for **Ute Mountain Fire Lookout Tower** points up USFS Rd 005, a steep 2-mile dirt road leading to Utah's first and only remaining fire tower (8834 feet). From the top are great views and signs explaining what life was like for 1930s fire lookouts. A couple of miles past the Ute Tower turn, USFS Rd 096 leads about 2 miles to Browne Lake and another free campground without potable water.

Hiking

Elk sometimes visit the gently rolling terrain of the 5-mile **Canyon Rim Trail**, which begins at Red Canyon visitors center and ends at the Greendale overlook, 1 mile west of Greendale Junction off Utah Hwy 44. The **Leidy Peak Trail** climbs nearly 4000 feet in 8 miles from the southeast shore of Browne Lake (see Spirit Lake Rd above) to the 12,028-foot summit, the NRA's highest. The **Little Hole National Recreation Trail** follows the true left bank of the Green River below the dam.

Fishing

The reservoir offers world-class fishing year-round. Catches have included record-breaking Kokanee salmon and small-mouthed bass as well as lake, brown and rainbow trout. Day/season permits, available from ranger stations, marinas or lodges, cost $5/40. Fly-fishing is excellent on Green River and some of its tributaries. These rivers are carefully managed with occasional closures and catch-and-release regulations designed to maintain the high quality of fishing. Guides are available,

although many charge $100 a day; ask at marinas (see Boating below) or lodges (see Places to Stay & Eat below).

Boating

The lake has nine boat launches, two marinas in Utah and another marina in Wyoming. All marinas offer boat and fishing gear rentals, gas, camping, a store and guided fishing trips. Seven miles east of Manila, UT, on the Lucerne Peninsula, Lucerne Valley Marina (☎ 801-784-3483, 888-820-9225; fax 801-784-3433) has the longest season, with limited boat rentals beginning in March and ending in November. They also have the only houseboat rentals. Cedar Springs Marina (☎/fax 801-889-3795), off US 191, 2 miles south of the dam, is open April to October. Wyoming's Buckboard Marina (☎ 307-875-6927, 800-824-8155) is east of Hwy 530, 25 miles south of Green River. Fishing boat rentals start at $40/65 for half/full day; ski boat rentals cost $95/170; and pontoon boat rentals range from $70 to $85 for a half day and $120 to $140 for a full day. Some also offer hourly rentals.

Rafting

The 7-mile Class I-II stretch of the Green River below the dam is a popular half-day run. The put-in is just below the dam and the take-out is at Little Hole, although bigger rapids are downstream of Little Hole. River raft, canoe and kayak rentals are available from Flaming Gorge Lodge (see Places to Stay below), Flaming Gorge Flying Service (☎ 801-885-3338, 801-885-3370), at the Dutch John airport, and Flaming Gorge Recreation Service (☎ 801-885-3191; fax 801-885-3350), US 191 at South Blvd, Dutch John, UT. Rentals start at $20 for inflatable kayaks and range from $30 to $70 for rafts depending on the size. Shuttles are easily arranged and will cost about $25.

Winter Activities

Winter brings solitude and calm. Routes for **cross-country skiing** are marked along Canyon Rim Trail and around Swett Ranch, and there are plenty of unmarked possibilities for more adventurous skiers. For **ice fishing** visit Browne and Spirit lakes.

Places to Stay & Eat

There are more than two dozen campgrounds ($10 to $24) in and around Flaming Gorge, most of them operated by private concessionaires and not the USFS. Campgrounds are concentrated at the southern end of the NRA with clusters of campgrounds near the dam, Red Canyon and Sheep Creek Bay. Others are more remote, like *Antelope Flat Campground*, 5 miles west of Dutch John on the reservoir's east side. Some free lakeside campgrounds are accessible only by boat. Most campgrounds are open May to October.

The Flaming Gorge Corporation (☎ 801-784-3483, 888-820-9225; fax 801-784-3433), PO Box 10, Manila, UT 84046, operates five campgrounds: *Firehole Campground* ($11), on US 191, 23 miles south of Rock Springs, with showers; *Red Canyon Campground* ($11), with an Alpine setting ideal for wildlife viewing, hiking, fishing or horseback riding; *Lucerne Campground* ($12), near Lucerne Marina, shaded and on the lake with nearby fishing; *Stateline Cove* ($5), near Lucerne Campground, with fishing and swimming; and the shaded *Buckboard Campground* ($11), on Hwy 530, 20 miles south of Green River.

The year-round *Flaming Gorge Lodge* (☎ 801-889-3773; fax 801-889-3788), off US 191, 4 miles south of the dam, has motel rooms (starting at $59) and one- and two-bedroom condominiums with kitchens (starting at $95). Open April to October, *Red Canyon Lodge* (☎ 801-889-3759), near Red Canyon visitors center, has rustic one-bedroom ($36) and two-bedroom ($46) cabins with shared bathrooms; cabins with private bathrooms cost $10 more. Deluxe two-bedroom cabins with a kitchenette start at $100. The lodge is next to Green Lake with a restaurant, private fishing area, tackle store and boat rentals. Basic no-frills accommodations and restaurants are also available in Manila and Dutch John.

Getting There & Away

Three roads lead from Wyoming to the Flaming Gorge NRA: US 191 goes south from Rock Springs to Dutch John (62 miles); Hwy 530 goes south from Green River to Manila (48 miles); and Hwy 414 goes southeast from Mountain View in the Bridger Valley to Manila (55 miles). From Vernal, UT, US 191 goes north 36 miles to Greendale Junction.

GREEN RIVER

This working-class railroad town (population 14,000; elevation 6100 feet) was the starting point for John Wesley Powell's epic descent of the Colorado River in 1869. Today it is one of the gateways to the Flaming Gorge National Recreation Area. Founded in 1868 and the seat of Sweetwater County, Green River sits at the base of sandstone Castle Rock, the prominent landmark above town. The Green River Parks & Recreation Department (☎ 307-875-5000 ext 151), 50 E 2nd St N, is developing the ambitious **Green River Greenbelt** project, which will link Flaming Gorge NRA to Seedskadee National Wildlife Refuge.

Orientation

Downtown Green River is south of I-80 and north of the Green River itself. The railroad tracks separate downtown from the river; a pedestrian overpass and two other streets provide river access. Flaming Gorge Way (I-80 Business/US 30 Business) is the main road through downtown (from I-80 exit 89 or 91); its eastern end intersects Uinta Drive (Hwy 530), the main north-south road. North-south downtown street addresses are divided by Flaming Gorge Way; east-west streets are divided by Center St. Newer businesses and residential areas are along Uinta Drive south of the river.

Information

The Green River Chamber of Commerce (☎ 307-875-5711) shares its location with the USFS Ashley National Forest Flaming Gorge Information (☎ 307-875-2871), 1450 Uinta Drive, and both are open 8 am

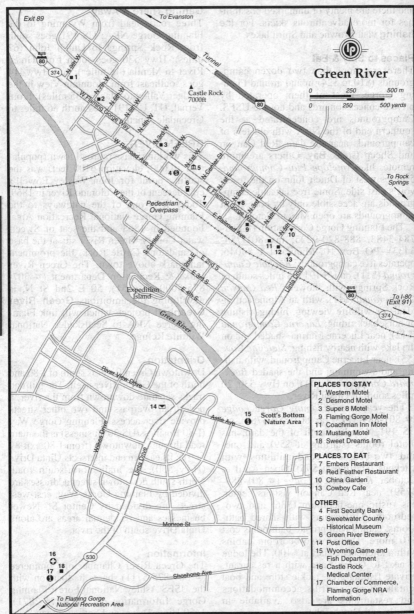

Green River

0   250   500 m
0   250   500 yards

Exit 89

To Evanston

Tunnel

▲ Castle Rock
7000ft

To Rock
Springs

To I-80
(Exit 91)

Pedestrian
Overpass

Expedition
Island

Green River

River View Drive

Scott's Bottom
Nature Area

Astle Ave

Wilkes Drive

Uinta Drive

Monroe St

Shoshone Ave

To Flaming Gorge
National Recreation Area

PLACES TO STAY
1   Western Motel
2   Desmond Motel
3   Super 8 Motel
9   Flaming Gorge Motel
11 Coachman Inn Motel
12 Mustang Motel
18 Sweet Dreams Inn

PLACES TO EAT
7   Embers Restaurant
8   Red Feather Restaurant
10 China Garden
13 Cowboy Cafe

OTHER
4   First Security Bank
5   Sweetwater County
    Historical Museum
6   Green River Brewery
14 Post Office
15 Wyoming Game and
    Fish Department
16 Castle Rock
    Medical Center
17 Chamber of Commerce,
    Flaming Gorge NRA
    Information

to 5 pm weekdays and 8 am to 4:30 pm weekends. The Wyoming Game and Fish Department Green River District office is at 351 Astle Ave.

There is an ATM is at First Security Bank, 125 W Flaming Gorge Way at N 1st St W. The post office, 350 Uinta Drive at River View Drive, is south of the river. The Castle Rock Medical Center (☎ 307-875-6010) is at 1400 Uinta Drive.

Historic Buildings

The Green River Historic Preservation Commission publishes the detailed *Self-Guided Tour of Historic Green River*, but many of the buildings it describes have been either razed or altered beyond recognition. Highlights include the woodframe St John's Episcopal Church (1892), W 2nd St N, and the gabled Third School/Masonic Building (1891), Flaming Gorge Way at N 1st St E. The best view of the UP depot (1910) is from the pedestrian overpass to Expedition Island. Three blocks of Railroad Ave, N 2nd E to N 1st St W, have vintage buildings, including the restored Green River Brewery (1901), 50 W Railroad Ave, an eccentric building now on the National Register of Historic Places.

Sweetwater County Historical Museum

The interesting Sweetwater County Historical Museum (☎ 307-872-6435), 80 W Flaming Gorge Way, features a valuable display of 'ledger art.' These are paintings and drawings with indigenous themes created by 19th-century Plains Indians using imported materials like pencils and crayons on paper from accounting ledgers. It's open from 9 am to 5 pm weekdays year-round and also from 1 to 5 pm Saturday July to August; admission is free.

Expedition Island

Expedition Island, at the foot of S 2nd St E, south of the railroad tracks, is where Powell's 10-man crew launched their four wooden boats into the river in 1869. Markers around the island commemorate Powell's achievements and those of moun-

tain men, early tourists and the first commercial outfitters.

Scott's Bottom Nature Area

This 15-acre riparian habitat along the Green River has an easy walking trail for viewing local flora and fauna. Call Peak Environmental Management (☎ 307-875-2893) to arrange a guided tour. From Uinta Rd south of the railroad tracks, turn east on Astle Ave and then follow Service Rd to the nature area.

Places to Stay

Tex's Travel Camp (☎ 307-875-2630) is on Hwy 374 west of town (I-80 exit 85 or 89); follow the signs. Sites start at $16; the few tent sites have some grass. They have a store, laundry and showers. Motels are less abundant and more expensive than in nearby Rock Spring, and trains rumble through town, only a block from Flaming Gorge Way, all night.

Rooms start at under $30 at: the *Mustang Motel* (☎ 307-875-2468), 550 E Flaming Gorge Way; *Desmond Motel* (☎ 307-875-3701), 140 N 7th St W; and the friendly, but faded *Flaming Gorge Motel* (☎ 307-875-4190), 316 E Flaming Gorge Way. The *Coachman Inn Motel* (☎ 307-875-3681), 470 E Flaming Gorge Way, and *Western Motel* (☎ 307-875-2840), 890 W Flaming Gorge Way, are comparably priced (singles/doubles $38/42). The *Super 8 Motel* (☎ 307-875-9330), 280 W Flaming Gorge Way, costs $40/45. The two top-end places are *Oak Tree Inn* (I-80 exit 91), the town's newest property, and *Sweet Dreams Inn* (☎ 307-875-7554), at 1420 Uinta Drive, which is farthest from the railroad tracks and so may be the best place for a good night's sleep.

Places to Eat

The *Embers Restaurant* (☎ 307-875-9983), 95 E Railroad Ave, is a popular breakfast spot and steakhouse. The *Cowboy Cafe*, 580 E Flaming Gorge Way, is open 24 hours. The *Red Feather Restaurant* (☎ 307-875-6625), 211 E Flaming Gorge Way, has a varied and fairly sophisticated menu. For ethnic food, try *China Garden* (☎ 307-874-3259), 190 N 5th St East, or *Trudel's Gasthaus* (☎ 307-875-8040), 520 Wilkes Drive, which specializes in Mexican food and serves the occasional German dish.

Getting There & Away
Green River is along the south side of I-80, 7 miles west of Rock Springs and 86 miles east of Evanston.

SEEDSKADEE NATIONAL WILDLIFE REFUGE
Mountain men like Jedediah Smith and Joseph LaBarge once trapped beavers in this prime riparian habitat 25 miles north of the town of Green River (I-80 exit 83), east of Hwy 372 along the Green River itself. It takes its name from a Shoshone word meaning 'Prairie Chicken River.' In addition to over 200 species of birds, the refuge contains a wealth of decaying historic sites, including Oregon Trail crossings. A 4WD vehicle is recommended. For guided fishing and float trips, contact Green River Fly-fishing Outfitters (☎ 307-875-2358), 218 Uinta Drive, Green River.

A USFWS-administered information center is off Hwy 372 just north of its junction with Hwy 28. Contact the Refuge Manager (☎ 307-875-2187), PO Box 700, Green River, WY 82935, for more information. The nearest campground is the BLM *Fontenelle Creek Campground* ($5) by Fontenelle Dam; three campgrounds below the dam are free. (Also see Names Hill later in this chapter.)

LITTLE AMERICA
In the high desert along I-80 between Green River and Bridger Valley is Little America (I-80 exit 68).The world's largest truck stop appears like a mirage with a 150-room motel and pool, many two-bedroom suites, several 24-hour coffee shops, a convenience shop and delicatessen, gift shops, a bar and even its own post office with its own zip code, 82929. Little America was the inspiration of sheepherder SM Covey, who, after suffering a night in a winter storm, envi-

sioned a shelter in the area. In 1930, Covey recalled photographs of Admiral Byrd's 'Little America' base in Antarctica and applied that name to the artificial oasis he built in the middle of nowhere. The original Little America, a modest landmark with a diner called the Palm Room, burned to the ground in 1948, but was rebuilt into this extravagant facility visited by more than a million people annually. It has also expanded into a chain, with Little Americas in Cheyenne, Salt Lake City, UT, San Diego, CA, Flagstaff, AZ, and Idaho's Sun Valley Resort. Singles/doubles at Little America (☎ 307-875-2400, 800-634-2401) start at $53/59. Showers are free with a full tank of gas, although only truckers usually take advantage of this service.

BRIDGER VALLEY & AROUND
Lyman (population 1896) is a Mormon farming community 5 miles east of Fort Bridger (population 150). The area's largest single employer is the trona (soda ash) mining industry, which provides raw material for products like glass, pulp and paper, baking soda and pharmaceuticals. Tourists flock to this unassuming valley to visit the Fort Bridger State Historic Site & Museum.

Information
The helpful Greater Bridger Valley Chamber of Commerce (☎ 307-787-6738), 100 E Sage St at S Main St (in Lyman Town Complex), PO Box 1506, Lyman, WY 82937, is open from 11 am to 4 pm Monday to Thursday. The USFS Wasatch-Cache National Forest Mountain View Ranger District (☎ 307-782-6555), 321 Hwy 414 E, Mountain View, is open 8 am to 4:30 pm weekdays.

Fort Bridger State Historic Site
This site (☎ 307-782-3842) on I-80 Business (I-80 exit 34), PO Box 35, Fort Bridger, WY 82933 is a 1987 reconstruction of Jim Bridger's Bridger Trading Post. Built in 1846, the original trading post became a US military outpost in 1858 and

Passion for Pelts

Beaver pelts were the center of the Wyoming fur industry from 1820 to 1840. Individuals as well as companies trapped beaver whose pelts were sent as far as St Louis and New York City to make men's hats. During this heyday, trappers, Native Americans and traders frequently came together for rendezvous where 'beaver pelts were gold.' By the 1840s, the beaver population had declined and the hats had gone out of fashion. The out-of-work trappers then became guides, scouts or businessmen at trading posts along the emigrant trails. ■

was crucial to the Pony Express and Overland Trail. The restored Commanding Officer's quarters (1883) contains period furniture in excellent condition. The museum features exhibits on Native Americans, mountain men, the post sutler or merchant and local military history.

The site is open 8 am to sunset daily year-round. The museum is open 9 am to 4:30 pm daily mid-April to mid-October (with slightly extended hours June to Labor Day). Admission is $1; children get in free. One-hour ($2) and two-hour ($3) guided tours are scheduled 9 am to 4 pm daily; tours cost $1 for children 11 and under.

Other Sights

The **Trona Mining Museum of Bridger Valley** (☎ 307-787-6916) in the Lyman Town Complex (see Information above) has a scale model of a trona processing plant. It's open noon to 4 pm Tuesday to Friday; admission is free.

Built by Moses Byrne in 1869, the **Piedmont Charcoal Kilns** provided fuel for the pioneer smelters of the Utah Valley. Three full kilns and a fragment of another remain. Take Hwy 410 south from Mountain View to Robertson, and continue west on Uinta County Rd 204 to the site. Alternatively, follow the unpaved Piedmont Rd (Uinta County Rd 173) south 7 miles from I-80 exit 23B.

Mountain Man Rendezvous

The Fort Bridger State Historic Site is the venue for the annual Fort Bridger Mountain Man Rendezvous on Labor Day weekend. This hugely popular event includes primitive firearms shoots, knife and tomahawk throwing and Native American dancing (the latter sponsored by the Wyoming Arts Council). Contact the Fort Bridger Rendezvous Association (☎ 307-782-3842), PO Box 198, Fort Bridger, WY 82933, for information.

Places to Stay & Eat

Reservations for hotel rooms and campsites are essential during the Fort Bridger Rendezvous.

Fort Bridger Singles/doubles cost $30/35 at the *Wagon Wheel Motel* (☎ 307-782-6361), Fort Bridger. Uninspiring sites at its adjacent RV Park cost $15. Try the homemade pies at their *Wagon Wheel Cafe*, 270 N Main. The *Fort Bridger RV Camp* (☎ 307-782-3150, 800-578-6535) is nearby; it has laundry and showers.

Lyman The *Lyman/Fort Bridger KOA Kampground* (☎ 307-786-2188, 800-562-2762), on Hwy 413 (I-80 exit 41) in Lyman, is open mid-May to September. Its shadeless but grassy tent sites cost $15; sites with full hookups are $19. They have a pool. The *Valley West Motel* (☎ 307-787-3700, 800-884-7910), 110 E Clark, Lyman, costs $35/37; some rooms have kitchenettes.

Getting There & Away

Bus Greyhound buses stop in Lyman daily, heading east at 1:55 and 9:10 pm and west at 5:55 am and 6:10 pm.

Car The Bridger Valley sprawls south of I-80 between exits 34 and 41. It is 44 miles west of Green River and 33 miles east of Evanston. Hwy 414 leads southeast 61 miles to Manila, UT.

UINTA MOUNTAINS

The Uinta Mountains in northeastern Utah are unusual in that they run east-west; all

WYOMING

other major mountain ranges in the lower 48 states run north-south. Several peaks rise to over 13,000 feet, including Kings Peak (13,528 feet), Utah's highest peak. The central summits are all within the 800-sq-mile High Uintas Wilderness Area. The Uintas span two national forests: the Wasatch-Cache in the west, and the Ashley in the east. There is no national park here, no visitors center, scenic overlooks, restaurants or motels. Of the hundreds of high country lakes, over 600 are stocked annually (some by air) with trout and whitefish. Alpine wildlife is plentiful.

Access to the northern side of the Uinta Mountains is from Wyoming via Hwy 150 from Evanston, and Hwys 414 and 410 from the Bridger Valley (or via Hwy 43 from Manila, UT). Mirror Lake Hwy (Hwy 150) leads south from Evanston over Bald Mountain Pass (10, 678 feet) to Kamas, UT. Thirty miles south of Evanston off Hwy 150, the Lilly Lake Nordic Ski Association, with the cooperation of the USFS and the Evanston Parks & Recreation District, maintains 340 acres of groomed cross-country skiing trails (closed to snowmobiles). Hwy 410 offers access to Kings Peak. Popular with hikers and backpackers, the shortest route to the summit requires a 32-mile roundtrip hike with over 4000 feet of elevation gain. Park at the Henry's Fork trailhead (9400 feet).

EVANSTON

Only 5 miles east of the Wyoming-Utah state line, Evanston (population 12,059; elevation 6748 feet) is the Uinta County seat and the westernmost town along I-80 in Wyoming. Established on the Transcontinental Railroad in 1868, it has experienced several boom-and-bust cycles, most recently during the 1970s energy boom. With a rejuvenated and pleasant downtown, good access to the nearby Uinta Mountains and abundant and affordable motels, Evanston has begun to benefit from tourism.

Orientation

Downtown Evanston is north of I-80. Its main roads are Bear River Drive (I-80 exit 6), Front St (I-80 exit 5), and Harrison Drive (I-80 exit 3), which replaces 11th St between Front and Lombard Sts. At Evanston's west end, Harrison Drive is called W Lincoln Hwy.

Information

The Evanston Chamber of Commerce (☎ 307-789-2757, 800-328-9708), 36 10th St at Front St facing Depot Square, shares a building with the Uinta County Museum (see below). It is open 9 am to 5 pm weekdays year-round, 10 am to 4 pm weekends during summer. Ask for the informative brochure 'Evanston, Wyoming: A Walking Tour.' The Bear River Travel Information Center (☎ 307-789-6540), 601 Bear River Drive (I-80 exit 6), has a good selection of state maps and brochures. It is open 8 am to 5 pm daily. The USFS Wasatch-Cache National Forest (☎ 307-789-3194), Hwy 150 S, suite A, is open from 8 am to 4 pm weekdays.

ATMs are at First Security Bank, 724 Front St, First National Bank, 1001 Main St, and Community First National Bank, 849 Front St.

The post office is on Harrison Drive between Front and Main Sts. Mail Boxes Etc (☎ 307-789-8284), 1101 Main St, provides fax services.

The IHC Evanston Regional Hospital (☎ 307-789-3636, 800-244-3537 in Wyoming) is at 190 Arrowhead Drive. Follow Yellow Creek Rd south from 6th and Lombard Sts, and turn west on Arrowhead Drive.

Historic Buildings

Among Evanston's restored buildings is the brick UP depot (1900) at the east end of 10th St. The Beeman Cashin Implement Depot (1883) to its west is a restored frame building that was moved here in 1984 and is now used for social functions. Alongside it, the Joss House, 920 Front St, is a replica of the Chinese temple that served Evanston's once populous Chinatown. The original burned to the ground in 1922. Along Center St are the frame-structure United Presbyterian Church

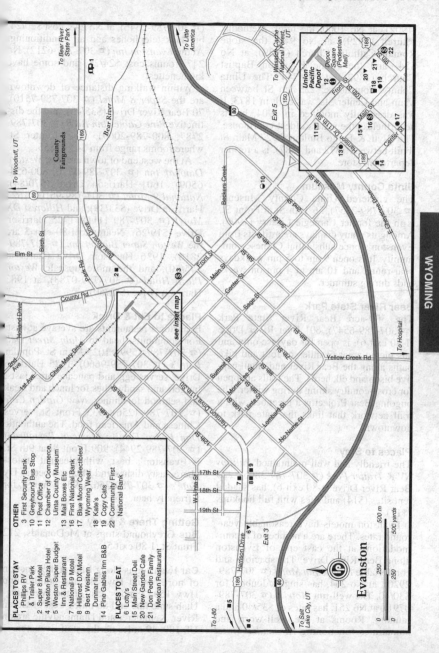

WYOMING

Evanston

PLACES TO STAY
1 Phillips RV
  & Trailer Park
2 Super 8 Motel
4 Weston Plaza Hotel
5 Weston Super Budget
  Inn & Restaurant
7 National 9 Motel
8 Hillcrest DX Motel
9 Best Western
  Dunmar Inn
14 Pine Gables Inn B&B

PLACES TO EAT
6 Lotty's
15 Main Street Deli
20 New Garden Cafe
21 Don Pedro Family
  Mexican Restaurant

OTHER
3 First Security Bank
10 Greyhound Bus Stop
11 Post Office
12 Chamber of Commerce,
  Uinta County Museum
13 Mail Boxes Etc
16 First National Bank
17 Blue Moon Collectibles/
  Wyoming Wear
18 Kate's
19 Copy Cats
22 Community First
  National Bank

(1902), at No 1000, the brick Methodist Church (1929), at No 949, the stone Roman Catholic Church (1939), at No 824, and the frame Evanston Baptist Church (1892), at No 744. The Uinta County Courthouse, 225 9th St between Main and Center Sts, was built in 1873. It was drastically modified in 1904, but is nevertheless the state's oldest courthouse. The Blyth & Fargo Building, 927 Main St (built between 1872 and 1887), is a former department store.

Uinta County Museum

The cluttered Uinta County Museum (☎ 307-789-2757), 36 10th St at Front St, is in the former Carnegie Library (1906). Among its many displays are artifacts from Evanston's once substantial Chinese community. It is open 9 am to 5 pm weekdays year-round and 10 am to 4 pm on weekends during summer.

Bear River State Park

The 300-acre Bear River State Park (☎ 307-789-6547), 601 Bear River Drive (I-80 exit 6), is open for day use only and has picnic areas, 3 miles of foot and bike paths along the Bear River and small captive bison and elk herds. The trails are open for cross-country skiing during winter. The ongoing Bear Project is a greenbelt with a trail network that links the state park to downtown.

Places to Stay

The friendly and well-maintained *Phillips RV & Trailer Park* (☎ 307-789-3805), 225 Bear River Drive (I-80 exit 6), has shaded tent sites ($14) and sites with full hookups ($17).

Evanston motels have reasonable year-round rates. There are a number of accommodations at the east end of Evanston along Bear River Drive. The spacious and comfortable *Prairie Inn Motel* (☎ 307-789-2920), at No 264, has singles/doubles for $30/40. The well-run *Motel 6* (☎ 307-789-0791), at No 261, has rates of $35/40 and a laundry. Rooms at the well-worn and sometimes functioning *Alexander Motel*

(☎ 307-789-2346), at No 248, cost $20/24, but lack telephones and air conditioning. At the *Evanston Inn* (☎ 307-789-6212), No 247, rooms cost $24/28, and some have kitchenettes.

Within walking distance of downtown are the *Super 8 Motel* (☎ 307-789-7510), 70 Bear River Drive ($35/43), and the distinctive *Pine Gables Inn B&B* (☎ 307-789-2787, 800-789-2069), 1049 Center St, where rooms range from $45 to $55.

At the west end of town are *Best Western Dunmar Inn* (☎ 307-789-3770, 800-654-6509), 1601 Harrison Drive ($70/84); *National 9 Motel* (☎ 307-789-9610), 1624 Harrison Drive ($33/39); and *Hillcrest DX Motel* (☎ 307-789-1111), 1725 Harrison Drive ($19/26). Nearer to I-80 exit 3 are the *Weston Super Budget Inn* (☎ 307-789-2810), 1936 Harrison Drive (starts at $45/50), and the more upscale *Weston Plaza Hotel* (☎ 307-789-0783), at 1983 Harrison Drive ($55/60).

Places to Eat & Drink

Evanston's restaurants are average at best. For doughnuts, head to *Main Street Deli* (☎ 307-789-1599), 1025 Main St. Popular *Lotty's* (☎ 307-789-9660), 1925 Harrison Drive, serves egg and pancake breakfasts, burgers and sandwiches for lunch and steak and seafood for dinner. *New Garden Cafe* (☎ 307-789-1256), 933 Front St, serves Chinese and American food. The authentic *Don Pedro Family Mexican Restaurant* (☎ 307-789-2944), 909 Front St at 9th St, is Evanston's best, with pleasant atmosphere, tasty dishes and Mexican beers. Try *Kate's* (☎ 307-789-7662), 936 Main St, for a friendly beer.

Getting There & Away

Bus Greyhound stops at McDonalds, 212 Front St (I-80 exit 5).

Car Evanston is along I-80, at the junction of northbound Hwy 89 and southbound Hwy 150, 3 miles east of the Wyoming-Utah state line and 86 miles west of Green River. Kemmerer and Diamondville are on US 189, 49 miles northeast of Evanston.

Getting Around

Call F&M Taxi Service (☎ 307-799-7306) for a taxi.

KEMMERER & DIAMONDVILLE

Kemmerer (population 3126; elevation 6927 feet), the seat of Lincoln County, north of I-80 on the Hams Fork River, is a high-desert coal town named for coal magnate MS Kemmerer. It is better known as the home of James Cash Penney, whose modest retail outlet here was the springboard to the phenomenally successful nationwide department store chain. Recent cutbacks in the mining industry, still the area's biggest employer, have brought serious unemployment and economic difficulties.

Neighboring Diamondville was named for the superior quality of its coal, which resembles black diamonds. Diamondville (population 864) has many historic buildings, although most are dilapidated. The imposing two-story Mountain Trading Company, at Diamondville Ave and Brilliant St, was once the company store and later served as storage for the local wool clip. North of it, the Smoke House, on Diamondville Ave, was an early saloon. Mine management officials lived along Paper Collar Row, now set off by the small, attractive Miner's Memorial Park.

Orientation

US 30/US 189 run contiguously through Kemmerer and Diamondville along Pine Ave, Coral St and Central Ave. Kemmerer has confusing street numbers; numbers on each block of Pine Ave rise from north to south, but numbers within those blocks rise from south to north. The Hams Fork River flows along the eastern edge of town.

Information

The Kemmerer-Diamondville Chamber of Commerce, in the center of Kemmerer's Herschler Triangle Park, is open 8 am to 5 pm weekdays, 9 am to 6 pm Saturday and noon to 4 pm Sunday. Ask for the 'Kemmerer-Diamondville Area Visitor Guide & Map' and the 'A Walk Through Diamondville's Historical Past' brochure.

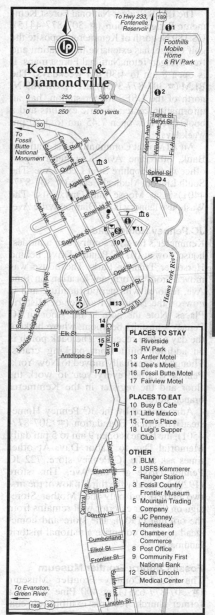

Kemmerer & Diamondville

0   250   500 m
0   250   500 yards

To Hwy 233, Fontenelle Reservoir

Foothills Mobile Home & RV Park

To Fossil Butte National Monument

Hams Fork River

To Evanston, Green River

PLACES TO STAY
4 Riverside RV Park
13 Antler Motel
14 Dee's Motel
16 Fossil Butte Motel
17 Fairview Motel

PLACES TO EAT
10 Busy B Cafe
11 Little Mexico
15 Tom's Place
18 Luigi's Supper Club

OTHER
1 BLM
2 USFS Kemmerer Ranger Station
3 Fossil Country Frontier Museum
5 Mountain Trading Company
6 JC Penney Homestead
7 Chamber of Commerce
8 Post Office
9 Community First National Bank
12 South Lincoln Medical Center

WYOMING

The USFS Bridger National Forest Kemmerer Ranger Station (☎ 307-877-4415), US 189 N, north of Kemmerer opposite the golf course, has extensive information and free Bridger-Teton National Forest maps. It is open 8 am to 4:30 pm weekdays. The BLM (☎ 307-877-3933), at 312 US 189 N, north of the USFS ranger station, has an information center, historic exhibits and a bookstore. It is open 7:45 am to 4:30 pm weekdays.

An ATM is at Community First National Bank, 801 Pine Ave. Kemmerer's post office is on Sapphire St at Cedar Ave. The South Lincoln Medical Center (☎ 307-877-4401) is at Moose and Onyx Sts. The Washouse laundry is off Diamondville Ave.

JC Penney Homestead

Kemmerer's favorite son lived in a modest house, now at 107 JC Penney Drive, behind Herschler Triangle Park. The house was moved from its original location on Pine Ave, restored with period furniture and is now on the National Register of Historic Places. Note the hole in the floor of JC Penney's upstairs bedroom, where he kept the day's store receipts. The back porch is an addition built from packing crates. Though he eventually moved to New York, Penney returned every year to work the floor and the register in the Kemmerer branch store.

Administered by the JC Penney Homestead Historical Foundation (☎ 307-877-4501), the home is open 9 am to 5 pm daily Memorial Day to Labor Day. At other times ask at the JC Penney store, 722 JC Penney Drive at Pine Ave. This store (1929) is actually the third in town; the first two burned and only the 'Mother Store' sign on the rear exterior wall remains from the original (1902). The store and homestead together comprise a national historic landmark.

Fossil Country Frontier Museum

The Fossil Country Frontier Museum (☎ 307-877-6551), at 400 Pine Ave in a former church, features exhibits on coal mining. In 1923, 99 local miners died in the second-largest mining disaster in Wyoming's history. Other exhibits include dinosaurs, moonshining and Native American artifacts. It is open from 10 am to 4 pm Monday to Saturday.

Places to Stay

None of the campgrounds in town allow tent camping or have toilets. The two defect-riddled RV parks are grim: *Foothills Mobile Home & RV Park* (☎ 307-877-6634), US 189 N near the USFS office; and *Riverside RV Park* (☎ 307-877-3416), 11 Willow Ave ($12).

Kemmerer's motels are plain but generally clean and friendly. Try the *Antler Motel* (☎ 307-877-4461), 419 Coral St (singles/doubles $20/24); *Fossil Butte Motel* (☎ 307-877-3996; fax 307-877-3242), 1424 Central Ave ($26/31); or *Dee's Motel* (☎ 307-877-6226), 1325 Central Ave ($25/30). In Diamondville, the superior *Fairview Motel* (☎ /fax 307-877-3938), 61 US 30, costs $28/32.

Places to Eat

The *Busy B Cafe* (☎ 307-877-6820), 919 Pine Ave, serves standard American breakfasts. *Little Mexico*, 817 S Main, is a nice cafe. *Tom's Place* (☎ 307-877-9412), 1433 Central Ave, is passable. In Diamondville, *Luigi's Supper Club* (☎ 307-877-6221), 807 Susie Ave, serves Italian meals.

Getting There & Away

Kemmerer and Diamondville are at the junction of US 30 and US 189, 46 miles northwest of Little America, 49 miles northeast of Evanston, 11 miles east of Fossil Butte National Monument, and 68 miles south of Big Piney.

FOSSIL BUTTE NATIONAL MONUMENT

Fossil Butte is the site of the smallest of three great lakes which existed in Eocene times, 50 million years ago, when large parts of present-day Wyoming, Utah and Colorado were rich subtropical lowlands.

After existing for 2 to 3 million years, Fossil Lake gradually disappeared. The imprint of its unusual flora and fauna is preserved in the deep sediments exposed today. Around the former shoreline of the 50-mile-long, 20-mile-wide lake, turtles, alligators and crocodiles lounged among palms, figs and cypress. Fish fossils are the most abundant, and so well preserved that paleontologists are able to use them to study their physiology.

The national monument, established in 1972, encompasses 8200 acres of high desert supporting pronghorn antelope, badgers, coyotes, white-tailed jackrabbits, cottontails, least chipmunks and Richardson's ground squirrels. In wetter areas like Cundeck Ridge and Fossil Butte itself, extensive stands of aspen, willow and cottonwood shelter moose, mule deer, marmots, porcupines, red foxes and golden-mantled ground squirrels.

Information

The Fossil Butte visitors center (☎ 307-877-4455) is open 8 am to 7 pm daily June to August, 8 am to 4:30 pm the rest of the year. Its intriguing museum displays over 75 fossil specimens and has interpretive information on Fossil Lake. The bookstore sells field guides and extensive titles about geology and fossils. Admission to the monument is free. During summer there is an evening campfire program at the Chicken Creek Picnic Area. Camping is not allowed within the monument but is possible on surrounding undeveloped BLM land. (See Kemmerer & Diamondville earlier in this chapter, or Cokeville below for the nearest places to stay.)

Activities

A 4-mile scenic route makes for pleasurable **driving**, with views of Fossil Butte, Wasatch Badlands and wildlife. Two **hiking** trails offer a look at the area's ecosystems and its geological, cultural and natural history. The 1½-mile Fossil Lake Trail begins 2½ miles north of the visitors center and passes through a spring-fed aspen grove. Rangers guide weekend hikes on this trail during summer. The 2½-mile self-guiding Historic Quarry Trail, at the eastern end of the monument, climbs 600 feet to the now abandoned fossil quarry site and loops back past the base of Fossil Butte. The trail's right fork is steeper and less direct.

Several private landowners nearby permit **fossil hunting** (June to Labor Day) and help prepare fossils for display. Reservations are required. Ulrich's Fossil Gallery (☎ 307-877-6466), outside the monument entrance, is a reputable fossil preparer. Fossil hunting is *not* allowed within the national monument.

Getting There & Away

Fossil Butte National Monument is north of US 30, 11 miles west of Kemmerer via US 30 and 14 miles east of the US 30 junction with Hwy 89. Take Fossil Butte Rd (Lincoln County Rd 300) north of US 30 a short distance to Chicken Creek Rd.

COKEVILLE

From Kemmerer two routes lead north, ultimately to Jackson. One follows US 30 and US 89 passing through Cokeville and the Star Valley (see the Greater Yellowstone chapter); the other follows US 189 through Big Piney. Founded in 1874, Cokeville (population 493; elevation 6191 feet), 44 miles northwest of Kemmerer, takes its name from its coal-mining past. The **Pine Creek Ski Area** (☎ 307-279-3201), off Hwy 232 6 miles east of town, offers downhill skiing in winter and fishing during summer. Its maximum vertical drop is 1200 feet to a base elevation of 7500 feet. The Cokeville visitors center (☎ 307-279-3200), 10558 US 30 at Hwy 231, displays fossil dinosaur tracks and a 1935 Chevrolet fire engine in mint condition. It is open 8 am to 5 pm Tuesday to Saturday Memorial Day to Labor Day.

Camping is free (there's a two-day maximum) in *Cokeville Park* on E Main St (Hwy 231) at Park St near the railroad tracks. The *Hideout Motel* (☎ 307-279-

3281) and the *Valley Hi Motel* (☎ 307-279-3251), both on US 30, have singles/doubles starting at $28/35.

NAMES HILL

Alternatively, US 189 from Kemmerer leads north to the southern side of the Wind River Range (see the Wind River Country chapter) and Jackson. About 40 miles northeast of Kemmerer at the north end of Fontenelle Reservoir is Names Hills, on the west side of US 189 south of LaBarge Creek Rd. Westbound emigrants on the Oregon Trail carved their names and messages in its pliant limestone, and crossed the Green River nearby on a Mormon ferry. Two sets of Shoshone petroglyphs also adorn the rock face. A 1990 survey catalogued over 2000 inscriptions, the earliest of which was dated 1827. An 1844 inscription attributed to Jim Bridger is dubiously authentic, since Bridger himself was illiterate. Take a look at the undated carving by JW Daugherty of Pennsylvania, whose block letters with serifs are among the most artistic.

Prairie Wyoming

The vast prairie of Northeastern Wyoming is bounded by the southern Laramie Mountains, the western Bighorn Mountains and the Black Hills along the Wyoming-South Dakota state line. The picturesque valleys of the North Platte, Belle Fourche and Powder rivers course through arid sage-covered landscape. The appeal of Prairie Wyoming is often subtle, yet driving between popular destinations like Devils Tower National Monument and the Cloud Peak Wilderness Area presents continual opportunity for visiting historic sites and viewing wildlife. The region's stark beauty is accentuated by herds of pronghorn antelope and white-tailed deer that surely outnumber the friendly people who live here.

modest revival and only 30 minutes away, Casper Mountain offers outdoor fun.

History

Before the coming of the Europeans, the Shoshone and Lakota frequented the North Platte River valley. From the 1840s, Oregon-bound travelers crossed the river on Mormon ferries here en route to South Pass. The first permanent settlement was Louis Guinard's trading post, which became the US Army's Platte Bridge Station. Lakota and Cheyenne resistance to the invasion of their lands led in July 1865 to a major confrontation between Native American forces under Red Cloud and the US Cavalry at Platte Bridge. This led to the

North Platte River Valley

The North Platte River flows eastward from Casper, where Oregon Trail pioneers, who had followed this river valley across eastern Wyoming, set out through central Wyoming. Towns and historic sites cluster along the river, while sheep and cattle graze the surrounding grasslands. Thick coal seams and oil fields underlay all.

CASPER

The 1941 WPA Guide's description of Casper (population 49,000; elevation 5338 feet) as an 'industrialized cow-town' still fits Wyoming's most centrally located and second-largest city. The Natrona County seat is a mercantile powerhouse whose primary products, cattle, sheep, coal and oil, make it an economic rival to Cheyenne. Casper has surprising cultural resources too, including the Nicolaysen Art Museum, the Casper College museums and performing arts centers. Downtown Casper is enjoying a

HIGHLIGHTS

- Devils Tower National Monument – a monolithic volcanic rock formation sacred to Native Americans
- Fort Laramie National Historic Site – a well-preserved and restored Oregon Trail site with a frontier atmosphere
- Sundance – a quaint town nestled beneath the Bearlodge Mountains in the Black Hills

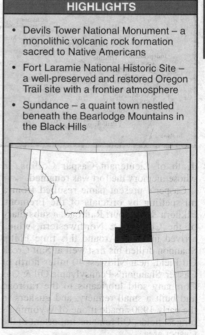

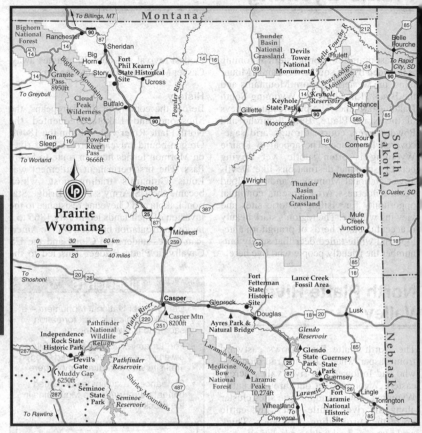

Prairie Wyoming

0   30   60 km
0   20   40 miles

death of Lieutenant Caspar Collins, in whose memory the fort was renamed.

Casper's present name resulted from a misspelling by officials of the Fremont, Elkhorn & Missouri Railroad, a subsidiary of the Chicago & Northwestern, which arrived in 1888. Around this time Philip Shannon drilled his first well at Salt Creek Oil Field, near Midwest 40 miles north of Casper. Shannon's Pennsylvania Oil & Gas Company sold lubricants to the railroad and built a small refinery, and gushers in the early 1900s made it one of Wyoming's biggest fields. Oil remains important in the Casper area.

Orientation

Most of Casper is south of the North Platte River and I-25. Downtown Casper is bounded roughly by I-25 on the north, Beverly St on the east, Poplar St (Hwy 252) on the west and 15th St on the south. It is a relatively regular grid with a few diagonal roads: Yellowstone Hwy; Midwest Ave; Collins Drive; and CY Ave (Hwy 220). Exits to downtown are E Yellowstone Hwy (I-25 exit 185 and 186), Center St (I-25 exit 188A) and Poplar St (I-25 exit 188B). CY Ave, which begins at 9th and Ash Sts and leads southwest, is most easily reached via Poplar St (Hwy 252) from I-25

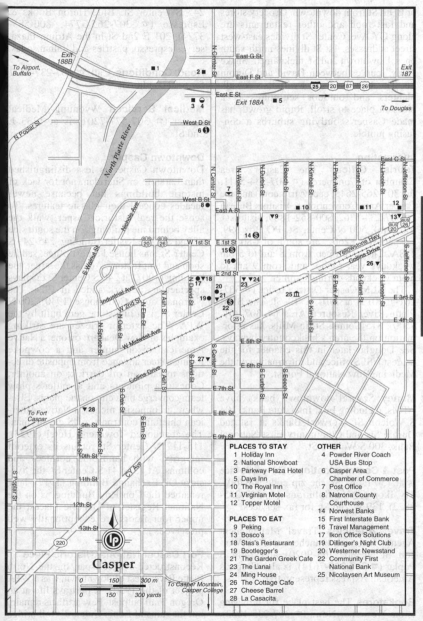

Casper

PLACES TO STAY
1. Holiday Inn
2. National Showboat
3. Parkway Plaza Hotel
5. Days Inn
10. The Royal Inn
11. Virginian Motel
12. Topper Motel

PLACES TO EAT
9. Peking
13. Bosco's
18. Stas's Restaurant
19. Bootlegger's
21. The Garden Greek Cafe
23. The Lanai
24. Ming House
26. The Cottage Cafe
27. Cheese Barrel
28. La Casacita

OTHER
4. Powder River Coach USA Bus Stop
6. Casper Area Chamber of Commerce
7. Post Office
8. Natrona County Courthouse
14. Norwest Banks
15. First Interstate Bank
16. Travel Management
17. Ikon Office Solutions
19. Dillinger's Night Club
20. Westerner Newsstand
22. Community First National Bank
25. Nicolaysen Art Museum

Map scale: 0 – 150 – 300 m / 0 – 150 – 300 yards

or E 9th St from downtown. Grocery stores and fast food and other restaurants are along CY Ave. Center St divides east-west street addresses; 1st St divides north-south ones. Downtown 2nd St, nicknamed 'Snake Alley,' curves between David and Durbin Sts. This tree-lined street with its sidewalk planters and outdoor sculptures is a pleasant place to stroll. Rapid growth has made Casper's outlying suburbs a confusing jumble.

Information
Tourist Offices The Casper Area Chamber of Commerce (☎ 307-234-5311; fax 307-265-2643; cacc@trib.com) and the Casper Area Convention & Visitors Bureau (☎ 307-234-5362, 800-852-1889; visitors@trib.com), 500 N Center St, PO Box 399, Casper, WY 82602, are south of I-80 exit 188A. They are open from 8 am to 5 pm weekdays year-round, and from 9 am to 6 pm weekends during summer.

The BLM Casper District office (☎ 307-261-7600) is at 1701 E 'E' St. The BLM Platte River Resource Area (☎ 307-261-7500), 815 Connie St, in Mills, has information on the area's backcountry byways. See Douglas later in this chapter for the nearest USFS office and information on the Medicine Bow National Forest.

Money Several downtown banks have ATMs, including First Interstate Bank, 104 S Wolcott St, Norwest Banks at 1st and Durbin Sts and Community First National Bank, 300 S Wolcott St.

Post & Communications The post office is at 150 E 'B' St; the zip code is 82601. Try Ikon Office Solutions (☎ 307-235-8822), 139 W 2nd St, for fax services.

Travel Agencies Travel Management Agency Inc, with branches at 150 S Wolcott St (☎ 307-265-9020) and 1744 S Poplar (☎ 307-265-7614), is also Casper's American Express representative.

Bookstores The best place for browsing is the Westerner News (☎ 307-235-1022), 245 S Center St. Blue Heron Books & Espresso (☎ 307-265-3774, 800-585-3774), 201 E 2nd St in the Atrium Plaza, serves espresso, pastries and Italian sodas.

Road Conditions Call ☎ 307-237-8411 for road conditions.

Medical Services Wyoming Medical Center (☎ 307-577-7201) is at 1233 E 2nd St.

Downtown Casper
Downtown Casper is less distinguished than Laramie or Sheridan, not for lack of historic buildings but because newer facades conceal their classic features. To sense the real historic Casper, walk the alley behind the buildings on the south side of 2nd St. The Kistler Building, 245-249 S Center St, has housed a post office, saddle shop and tent factory. Across the street, the building (1907) at 240 S Center St displays spectacular tilework added in 1924. The Natrona County Courthouse (1940), 200 N Center St, is a limestone gem built by the WPA. The exterior friezes are striking examples of New Deal art: on one, a Native American bison hunter and a cowpoke roping a steer advance from opposite directions toward an oil derrick; on another, Conestoga pioneers and a settler's plow team converge on a city on the plains. Elsewhere, in opposite niches, a Native American chieftain confronts a US cavalryman. The abandoned Townsend Hotel (1923), 115-117 N Center St, retains its exterior integrity, with handsome cornices and columns. At 137-141 S Center St, the five-story Oil Exchange Building (1917), later renamed the Con Roy Building, is on the National Register of Historic Places; the upper four floors are exceptionally well preserved.

Fort Caspar National Historic Place
Reconstructed Fort Caspar, on the North Platte River west of downtown, was a WPA project of the 1930s. It portrays life at an Oregon Trail outpost. Few artifacts remain, but the ruins of Louis Guinard's toll bridge

Oglala Lakota Chief Red Cloud won a battle but lost the war against the white man.

are worth a look. The sutler's store has a good selection of Western books.

Other structures include the blacksmith's shop, a corral, the Overland Stage station, the commissary storehouse, the Guinard trading post and a carriage shed. The outpost was abandoned in 1867 with the construction of Fort Fetterman (see Fort Fetterman State Historic Site below). The **Fort Caspar Museum** (☎ 307-235-8462), 4001 Fort Caspar Rd, has interesting photo panels of African American cowboys (one in four cowboys was African American). It is open 8 am to 7 pm Monday to Saturday and noon to 7 pm Sunday mid-May to mid-September, and 8 am to 5 pm weekdays and 1 to 4 pm Sunday during winter. Admission is free. To reach the site, take I-80 exit 188B to Wyoming Blvd or head west on W 13th St from downtown.

Nicolaysen Art Museum & Discovery Center
The Nicolaysen Art Museum & Discovery Center (☎ 307-235-5247), 400 E Collins

Drive, is a former power plant. This 1920s brick building once housed three diesel generators on concrete slabs beneath its 30-foot ceilings. It later served as a lumberyard, then sat vacant for several years before being refurbished into its present form in 1990 at a cost of $2.6 million. It is open 10 am to 5 pm, Tuesday to Sunday, and 5 to 8 pm Thursday, Memorial to Labor Day. Admission is $2/1 for adults/children.

Casper College Museums
Casper College, primarily a junior college with a few four-year programs, is one of Casper's top cultural resources. Its **Tate Mineralogical Museum** (☎ 307-268-2514, 307-268-2447 tour information), 125 College Drive (off S Poplar St), has both permanent and special exhibitions of fossils (including a preparation lab open to the public), Wyoming jade, meteorites and minerals. Open 9 am to 5 pm weekdays and 10 am to 3 pm Saturday, admission is free. The **Werner Wildlife Museum** (☎ 307-268-2108), 405 E 15th St, is essentially an homage to taxidermy.

Fishing & Boating
Wyoming Choice River Runners (☎ 307-234-3870), 513 N Lennox, offers float and fishing trips on the sedate North Platte River and nearby reservoirs, and rents gear.

Special Events
July's **Casper Classic Bicycle Race**, a grueling ride up Casper Mountain, attracts bicyclists from all over. The **Central Wyoming Fair & Rodeo** is in early August at the Central Wyoming Fairgrounds, at Wyoming Blvd and Fort Caspar Rd.

Places to Stay
Casper has a large choice of accommodations off I-25 at E Yellowstone Hwy, Center St and Poplar St. Seasonal rate changes are negligible.

Camping Open late February to December, the *Casper KOA Kampground* (☎ 307-237-5155, 800-423-5155), 2800

WYOMING

E Yellowstone Hwy (I-25 exit 185) is a shadeless, unappealing area close to I-25. Sites cost $14/19 (tent/full hookup). *Fort Caspar Campground* (☎ 307-234-3260), 4205 Fort Caspar Rd (I-25 exit 188B) beyond the Fort Caspar Museum, offers little shade but good river access. Tent sites cost $11, sites with full hookups cost $16. It is open year-round and has laundry and showers. The comparably priced *Antelope Campground* (☎ 307-577-1664), 1101 Prairie Lane, Bar Nunn (I-25 exit 191) off Salt Creek Hwy, has a pool, hot tub, laundry and showers.

B&Bs *Durbin Street Inn B&B* (☎ 307-577-5774; fax 307-266-5441; dfrigon@trib .com), 843 S Durbin St, is within walking distance of downtown. Rooms start at $60; those with shared bathroom start at $45. Nearby, the *Antique B&B* (☎ 307-265-2304), 939 S Wolcott St, costs $65.

Motels Downtown, *The Royal Inn* (☎ 307-234-3501, 800-967-6925), 440 E 'A' St, is one of the best budget deals in Wyoming, with clean, spacious singles for $23 (these are relatively few and upstairs). Other downtown options are the *Virginian Motel* (☎ 307-266-3959), 830 E 'A' St at Jefferson St ($24), and the similarly priced *Topper Motel* (☎ 307-237-8407, 888-262-8677), 728 E 'A' St.

At $29 are the *Ranch House Motel* (☎ 307-266-4044), 1130 E 'F' St, and *National 9 Showboat* (☎ 307-235-2711), 100 W 'F' St. Singles/doubles cost $28/33 at *Motel 6* (☎ 307-234-3903), 1150 Wilkins Circle near I-25 exit 188A.

Along Yellowstone Hwy are the *Colonial House Motel* (☎ 307-577-1263), 1914 E Yellowstone (less than $20); *Yellowstone Motel* (☎ 307-234-9174), 1610 E Yellowstone ($30); *Sage & Sand Motel* (☎ 307-237-2088), 901 W Yellowstone ($27); and *Bel Air Motel* (☎ 307-472-1930), 5400 W Yellowstone ($22). West of downtown are the *Westridge Motel* (☎ 307-234-8911, 800-356-6268), 955 CY Ave ($29), and *Commercial Inn* (☎ 307-235-6688), 5755 CY Ave ($32).

Casper's pleasant *Super 8 Motel* (☎ 307-266-3480, 888-266-0497), 3838 CY Ave, is the best one in Wyoming. Singles/doubles cost $40/45. The *Kelly Inn* (☎ 307-266-2400, 800-635-3559), 821 N Poplar St, has a whirlpool and sauna; doubles range from $41 to $47. Doubles at the *1st Interstate Inn* (☎ 307-234-9125), I-25 at Wyoming Blvd, cost $43. Singles/doubles cost $43/47 at the *Days Inn* (☎ 307-234-1159), 301 E 'E' St. Rooms start at $50 at the *Parkway Motel* (☎ 307-234-2162), 5102 W Yellowstone, and the *Best Western Casper* (☎ 307-234-3541, 800-675-4242), 2325 E Yellowstone Hwy.

Hotels Singles/doubles cost $50/65 at the *Hampton Inn* (☎ 307-235-6668), 400 W 'F' St (I-25 exit 188B). The *Parkway Plaza Hotel & Convention Centre* (☎ 307-235-1777, 800-270-7829,), 123 W 'E' St (I-25 exit 188A), has a pool and restaurants ($55/60). The *Casper Hilton Inn* (☎ 307-266-6000), 800 N Poplar, has a pool and Jacuzzi. Rooms range from $58 to $70. Rooms start at $75 at the *Holiday Inn* (☎ 307-235-2531), 300 W 'F' St.

Places to Eat
Casper has several decent restaurants. For breakfast and lunch, try *The Garden Creek Cafe* (☎ 307-265-9018), 251 S Center St. This simple, charming place serves high-quality food. Lunches include homemade soups and deli or grilled sandwiches, with good vegetarian selections. *The Cottage Cafe* (☎ 307-234-1157), 116 S Lincoln St, is a cute and popular spot. The *Cheese Barrel* (☎ 307-235-5202), is at 544 S Center St. Bagel lovers head to *Chesapeake Bagel Bakery* (☎ 307-237-3036), 2711 CY Ave.

La Casacita (☎ 307-234-7633), 633 W Collins Drive, is a popular Tex-Mex restaurant. For Chinese food, try *Peking Chinese Restaurant* (☎ 307-266-2207), 333 E 'A' St, or *Ming House Restaurant* (☎ 307-265-1838), 233 E 2nd St. The *Lanai* (☎ 307-237-7516), 201 E 2nd St in the upper level of the gallery, does not claim to be authentically Polynesian, but has good sandwiches and tasty 'Island Lunches' like Hawaiian chicken salad. *Bosco's Italian Restaurant* (☎ 307-265-9658), 847 E 'A' St, is also good; reservations are recommended. Except for its gyro sandwiches, Greek food is limited to Friday nights at *Stas's Restaurant* (☎ 307-237-3557), 129 W 2nd St; check out the specials. *Bootlegger's* (☎ 307-473-2668), 256 S Center St, is a slightly pricey restaurant serving steaks, seafood, pasta, calzone and pizza. Its adjacent brewery offers malts and serves excellent burgers, sandwiches and salads. The *Casper KOA Kampground* (see Places to Stay above) has a buffalo barbecue and ice cream social nightly during summer.

Entertainment
Dillingers Night Club (☎ 307-265-5873), 256 S Center St upstairs from Bootlegger's, has live music nightly. The *Casper Events Center* (☎ 307-577-3030), 1 Events Drive, north of I-25 via Poplar St, is the venue for many concerts. The *Casper Planetarium* (☎ 307-577-0310), 904 N Poplar St, runs family-oriented programs during summer. Admission is $2/5 for adults/families.

Getting There & Away
Air Casper is served by SkyWest/The Delta Connection and United Express out of the Natrona County International Airport (☎ 307-472-6688), about 6 miles west of downtown off US 20/US 26. Note the Richard Jacobi *Casper Centennial Mural* inside the terminal.

SkyWest/The Delta Connection flies daily to Salt Lake City, UT, while United Express offers daily service to Denver.

Bus Powder River Coach USA (☎ 307-265-2353, 307-266-1904) is at 123 W 'E' St in the Parkway Plaza Hotel, Room 1159. It is open 6 to 10:30 am and 11:30 am to 5 pm weekdays, 6 to 10 am and 3:30 to 4:30 pm Saturday, and 6 to 7:30 am and 3:30 to 4:30 pm Sunday. Daily buses depart Casper at 7 am and 7:55 pm for Douglas and Cheyenne; the 7:55 pm bus continues to Denver (tickets must be purchased and baggage checked by 5 pm). Daily buses depart Casper at 7:15 am for Cody, and another for Billings, MT, via the Bighorn Basin (Shoshoni, Thermopolis, Worland and Greybull). Another daily bus departs Casper at 4:30 pm for Billings via Buffalo and Sheridan.

Car Casper is along the south side of I-25 178 miles northwest of Cheyenne and 112 miles south of Buffalo. US 20/US 26 leads west to Shoshoni (94 miles). Hwy 220 leads southwest to Muddy Gap Junction (73 miles) where it meets US 287/Hwy 789, which leads west to Lander (82 miles) or south to Rawlins (46 miles).

Getting Around
Car Avis (☎ 307-237-2634, Budget (☎ 307-266-1122), and Hertz (☎ 307-265-1355) are at the airport. Others include Budget (☎ 307-266-2251), 3333 CY Ave, and Enterprise Rent-A-Car (☎ 307-234-8122), 535 N Beverly. Try Aries Car Rentals (☎ 307-234-3501), 440 E 'A' St, or Around Town Rent-A-Car (☎ 307-265-5667), 804 N Poplar St, for cheaper rates.

Taxi Call A1 Cab (☎ 307-472-1213), RC Cab (☎ 307-235-5203), Rapid Cab (☎ 307-235-1903) or Tom's Taxi (☎ 307-237-8178, 800-484-6676 ext 8208).

CASPER MOUNTAIN
Casper Mountain (8200 feet), the prominent peak to the south of Casper, offers ample recreation. Head south from Casper on Casper Mountain Rd (Hwy 251) or take Hwy 258 (I-25 exit 185) from the east to Casper Mountain Rd, which becomes Circle Drive (Natrona County Rd 505), a decent gravel road. It traverses Casper Mountain, descending the drainage of Big Red Creek and eventually coming out on Hwy 487. Hwy 487 continues south to Medicine Bow or west to Hwy 220, which permits either a return trip to Casper or a visit to Oregon Trail sites (see Around Casper below). Camping is possible at several areas and costs about $5.

Hogadon Basin Ski Area

The modest Hogadon Basin Ski Area (☎ 307-235-8499) offers downhill and cross-country skiing. The 600-foot vertical drop to the base elevation of 7500 feet is suitable for beginner and intermediate downhill skiers. The area also boasts 15 miles of groomed cross-country trails and 60 miles of snowmobile trails. Full-day lift tickets cost $20/17/14 for adults/teens/children; half-day tickets (9 am to 12:30 pm or 12:30 to 4 pm) cost $15 for all ages. The ski season is Thanksgiving to April; call ☎ 307-235-8369 for a snow and ski report. For rentals, try Mountaineer's Mercantile (☎ 307-577-6004), 8455 Casper Mountain Rd, Mountain Sports Ski Rental (☎ 307-266-6904), 8700 S Hogadon Rd, or Hogadon Ski Rentals (☎ 307-265-0399), 9752 N Hogadon Rd.

Crimson Dawn Museum

Crimson Dawn Park Museum (☎ 307-235-1303, 307-235-9325), 1620 Crimson Dawn Rd, is the bequest of longtime Casper Mountain resident Neal Forsling, a painter and storyteller who spent nearly 50 years on the mountain with her husband, her daughters and the mystical creatures who populate her stories and paintings. Open 11 am to 7 pm Saturday to Thursday mid-June to mid-October, admission is by donation. Nearby is the USFS *Tower Hill Campground* on East End Rd.

Muddy Mountain

Popular with hikers, Muddy Mountain (7941 feet), is just southeast of Casper Mountain. Gravel roads link Muddy Mountain to Casper Mountain and Hwy 487. The BLM *Rim Campground* (8200 feet; $4) has no potable water.

AROUND CASPER
Pathfinder & Alcova Reservoirs

South of Hwy 220 southwest of Casper are the Pathfinder and Alcova reservoirs, formed by dams on the North Platte River. The **Pathfinder National Wildlife Refuge** encompasses the Pathfinder Reservoir's shoreline. It is noted for its exceptional bird life, walleye and trout. Two primitive campgrounds are at the reservoir's north end. Alcova Reservoir is east of Pathfinder with a marina, nature trails and several campgrounds. Above where the North Platte River enters Alcova Reservoir is Fremont Canyon, a popular **rock climbing** area with climbs up to 5.13, many with roofs. The **Sinclair to Alcova Back Country Byway** heads south from Alcova Reservoir (see Around Rawlins in the Southern Wyoming chapter).

Oregon Trail Sites

Several Oregon Trail sites are along Hwy 220 between Casper and Muddy Gap at the junction of Hwy 287. Enterprising Mormon stonecutters charged $1 to $5 to inscribe passing emigrants' names on the surface of Independence Rock, a 200-foot high dome of exfoliating granite. This 'Great Register of the Desert' was a far more difficult medium than the limestone and sandstone of other Oregon Trail sites like Names Hill and Register Cliff. Exposed above the surrounding sediments of the Sweetwater River valley, it is on Hwy 220 about 50 miles southwest of Casper. **Independence Rock State Historic Site** is also a national historic landmark.

A few miles west of Independence Rock and north of Hwy 220 is the paved BLM overlook of **Devil's Gate**, a narrow notch in the Rattlesnake Mountains carved by the Sweetwater River. Nearby is **Martin's Cove**, a national historic place and visitors center. Farther west along the river is the granite **Split Rock**, north of US 287/Hwy 789 west of Muddy Gap.

DOUGLAS

Douglas (population 5100; elevation 4815 feet), founded when the Fremont, Elkhorn & Missouri Valley Railroad extended through central Wyoming in 1886, provided access to the region's early mining and ranching zones. It was named for Illinois Senator Stephen Douglas (best known as Abraham Lincoln's debate opponent) and became known as the 'Gateway City' for the railroad. Douglas is the seat of Converse County, of which the major industries are sheep and cattle ranching, coal and uranium mining and oil.

Orientation

Most of Douglas, including the downtown, is east of the North Platte River. The main north-south street is 4th St. Center and Richards Sts are the main east-west streets. Grocery stores and fast-food restaurants are on Richards St at the south end of town.

Information

The informative Douglas Area Chamber of Commerce (☎ 307-358-2950), 121 Brownfield Rd, in the Railroad Interpretive Center (see below), is open 9 am to 4 pm weekdays. The USFS Medicine Bow-Routt National Forest and USFS Thunder Basin National Grassland Douglas Ranger Station (☎ 307-358-4690), 2250 Richards St east of town, is open 7:30 am to 4:30 pm. In a unique program, visitors accompany USFS personnel on their regular rounds. These are not tours but rather an opportunity to learn about activities like forest management and timber sales, grazing allotments and archaeological surveys.

Community First National Bank has an ATM at 240 S 4th St. The post office is at

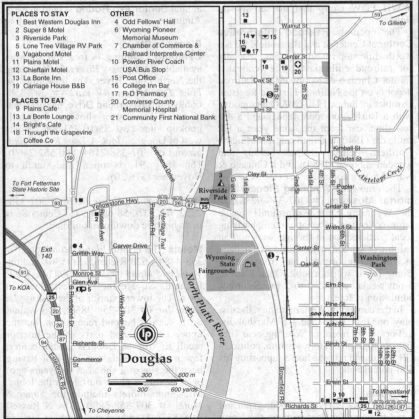

PLACES TO STAY
1 Best Western Douglas Inn
2 Super 8 Motel
3 Riverside Park
5 Lone Tree Village RV Park
8 Vagabond Motel
11 Plains Motel
12 Chieftain Motel
13 La Bonte Inn
19 Carriage House B&B

PLACES TO EAT
9 Plains Cafe
13 La Bonte Lounge
14 Bright's Cafe
18 Through the Grapevine
    Coffee Co

OTHER
4 Odd Fellows' Hall
6 Wyoming Pioneer
   Memorial Museum
7 Chamber of Commerce &
   Railroad Interpretive Center
10 Powder River Coach
    USA Bus Stop
15 Post Office
16 College Inn Bar
17 R-D Pharmacy
20 Converse County
    Memorial Hospital
21 Community First National Bank

Douglas

129 N 3rd St. Try the R-D Pharmacy for books at 206 E Center St. Converse County Memorial Hospital (☎ 307-358-2122) is at 111 S 5th St. Do your laundry at Sudsy Duds at Richards and Harrison Sts.

Things to See
The original business district and most **historic buildings** are on N 2nd St. On the National Register of Historic Places are the original **Douglas City Hall** (1915), 130 S 3rd St, and the College Inn Bar, a prefab built in Chicago in 1906 and assembled here on the original site of Pringle's Saloon (1886). The intriguing Odd Fellows' Hall, on S Riverbend Drive, served as part of a WWII POW camp that housed mostly Italians.

The open-air **Railroad Interpretive Center** at Center St and Brownfield Rd is a worthwhile stop for anyone, but especially for railroad enthusiasts. The renovated former Chicago & Northwestern Railroad depot is on the National Historic Register. Exhibits include a 1940 CB&Q locomotive with a Burlington route tender and a 48-seat diner car from the same year; a UP cattle car (1940) and mail car; a Burlington Northern deluxe sleeper (1950) and wooden caboose (1884); and a Chicago & Northwestern commuter car (1915).

The renowned **Wyoming Pioneer Memorial Museum** (☎ 307-358-9288), in the Wyoming State Fairgrounds, has a large collection of weapons emphasizing local participation in foreign wars and an exhibit of barbed wire dating as far back as 1868. The original bar from the La Bonte Inn is worth a look. Open 8 am to 5 pm weekdays and 1 to 5 pm Saturday, admission is free.

In the context of Western history, the display on Tom Horn and US Marshal Joe LeFors is of interest. Note the near life-size photograph of Horn's patron, politician CB Irwin, and pity the horse supporting his 500-pound bulk.

Activities
Riverside Park is a popular fishing spot and a put-in point for float trips on the North

Platte River. Along the river's west bank is a pleasant bicycle path.

Special Events
Since 1905, Douglas has hosted the annual **Wyoming State Fair**. With agricultural and livestock displays, rodeos, a carnival, live entertainment and more, the fair runs one week in mid-August. Admission is $2 per day (children under nine free); special concerts require separate admission.

In June, Douglas celebrates **Jackalope Days**, claiming the fictitious jackrabbit with antlers as its own. The Wyoming State **High School Rodeo Finals** take place in late June at the fairgrounds, while the annual **Senior Pro Rodeo** is held in early August.

Places to Stay
Camping Camping is free and showers available at the grassy *Riverside Park* along the North Platte River. The less-attractive *Lone Tree Village RV Park* (☎ 307-358-6669), off S Riverbend Drive, has grass but no trees, laundry or showers. Tent/full-hookup sites cost $5/10. About 2 miles west of Douglas, *Jack-A-Lope KOA Kampground* (☎ 307-358-2164, 800-562-2469), 168 Hwy 91, is open mid-March to November ($16/20).

B&Bs *Carriage House B&B* (☎ 307-358-2752, fax 307-358-6954), 413 Center St, is in an historic downtown building.

Motels The erratic *Plains Motel* (☎ 307-358-4484), 628 Richards St ($30), and the *Vagabond Motel* (☎ 307-358-9414), 430 E Richards St, are the cheapest places in town. The lower exterior of the historic *La Bonte Inn* (☎ 307-358-9856), 206 Walnut St, is scarred beyond recognition, but the upper exterior and parts of the interior recall its role as Douglas' social center: few modern motels can boast of having been the site of a shootout (50 years ago) or of having a ghost buffalo in the lobby. Mid-range motels include the *Super 8 Motel* (☎ 307-358-6800), 314 N Russell Ave ($37/44) and the comparable *Chieftain*

A Well-Known Son of a Gun

Tom Horn (1860-1903) was 'probably the best tracker, most experienced man-hunter and one of the deadliest killers in the West,' according to Western author/historian Lauran Paine. Horn left his home in Missouri at age 15 and drifted west to settle among the Apache Indians of the Arizona Territory. He stayed for 10 years, serving as a US Army scout during the Apache wars, and was instrumental in arranging the great warrior chief Geronimo's surrender. Later Horn worked as a Pinkerton agent and deputy US marshal out of Denver. His dispassionate ability to hunt and shoot men made him a feared legend as a stock detective for the cattle outfits of the unfenced range. Always on the side of the cattle barons and against the 'sodbusters,' Horn served the powerful Wyoming Stock Growers Association in the bloody Johnson County War. With the eruption of the Spanish-American War in 1898, Horn, along with other Wild West types, joined Teddy Roosevelt's 'rough-riders' in Cuba. After the war, Horn headed back to Wyoming, but the Wild West was dying as industry and farming took over. He worked as an executioner for the cattlemen in their last efforts to stave off the inevitable, but in 1903 Horn's life ended when he was hung from the gallows for the murder of Willie Nickell, a sheepherder's son. ■

Motel (☎ 307-358-2673), 815 E Richards. The only top-end hotel is the *Best Western Douglas Inn* (☎ 307-358-9790), 1450 Riverbend Drive (I-25 exit 140); rooms cost $69/77.

Places to Eat

Restaurants are uninspiring here, but try *Through the Grapevine Coffee Co*, 301 Center St, to start your day. Early risers can go to *Bright's Cafe* (☎ 307-358-3509), 108 N 3rd St, which opens at 5:30 am. Built with doors and other materials scavenged from older buildings, the *Plains Cafe* across the street from the Plains

Motel is open 24 hours. The best values may be the *La Bonte Lounge* (☎ 307-358-5210) or the restaurant in the Best Western Douglas Inn.

Getting There & Away

Bus Powder River Coach USA (☎ 307-358-4484 Plains Motel) stops at the Plains Cafe (☎ 307-358-4489), 628 Richards St. Daily buses depart Douglas for Billings, MT, via Gillette (3:50 am and 2:35 pm); Billings via Casper and the Bighorn Basin (5:05 am); and Cheyenne and Denver, CO (8:20 am and 9:40 pm).

Car Douglas is on the north side of I-25 46 miles east of Casper and 60 miles north of Wheatland. Hwy 59 leads 115 miles north to Gillette.

AROUND DOUGLAS
Fort Fetterman State Historic Site

Founded in 1867 as part of the campaign against the northern Plains Indians, this Bozeman Trail and Oregon Trail outpost was to be a supply point for other posts along the route. It soon found itself isolated on the frontier after the Fort Laramie Treaty of 1868 eliminated forts Reno, Phil Kearny and CF Smith. It was named for Captain William J Fetterman, who died in a foolish battle near Fort Phil Kearny in 1866. It suffered from supply shortages and bitter winters, and desertions were frequent. In the 1870s, Fetterman became the organizing site for military campaigns along the Powder River, but the US Army abandoned it in 1882 after the end of Native American resistance. It survived briefly as Fetterman City, a frontier town without boundaries, but the railroad's choice of Douglas as a rail access point meant the town's end.

Only two original buildings remain from the original fort: the restored officers' quarters, which serves as a museum and visitor's center, and the ordnance warehouse. The nearby Hog Ranch, once notorious for prostitution and gambling, was where Sheriff Malcolm Campbell arrested the Colorado cannibal Alferd Packer in 1883.

WYOMING

In mid-June, **Fort Fetterman Days** include living history programs.

The buildings at the Fort Fetterman State Historic Site (☎ 307-358-2864, 307-684-7629), off Hwy 93, 7 miles northwest of Douglas, are open 9 am to 5 pm daily Memorial Day to Labor Day. The grounds are open sunrise to sunset, but the site is closed in winter. Admission is free.

Ayres Park & Natural Bridge
Converse County's Ayres Park & Natural Bridge lie beneath striking red sandstone cliffs. The natural bridge, about 50 feet high with a 90-foot span at its base, is purported to be the only natural bridge in the US with a stream below. (However, it is not even the only one in the state.) Here the sandstone eroded, allowing La Prele Creek to flow through the rock. The park, which is ideal for a picnic, is open 8 am to 8 pm. Camping is free (three-night maximum) with written permission from the caretaker who lives near the entrance. Take I-25 exit 151, 6 miles west of Douglas, and go south 5 miles on Natural Bridge Rd.

WHEATLAND & AROUND
The Platte County seat of Wheatland is not typically a destination. It is, however, a very useful stop for area information. The Platte County Visitor's center & Chamber of Commerce (☎ 307-322-2322; fax 307-322-3419) at I-25 exit 78 is open 8 am to 4 pm weekdays.

In the Medicine Bow National Forest northwest of Wheatland is **Laramie Peak** (10,274 feet). Visible for nearly 100 miles from the east, this Oregon Trail landmark let westbound pioneers know when they had reached the Rocky Mountains. Today Laramie Peak is popular for hiking, camping, fishing, snowmobiling and cross-country skiing. **Sybille Wildlife Preserve**, 6 miles south of Wheatland and a few miles west of I-25, is a good place to look for bighorn sheep.

GUERNSEY & AROUND
Guernsey (population 1155; elevation 4354 feet) is east of the scenic North Platte River

along US 26. The post office is at 101 S Wyoming Ave. The Guernsey Visitor's Center Museum is also on S Wyoming Ave.

Oregon Trail Sites
Two major Oregon Trail sites are along the North Platte River near Guernsey. **The Oregon Trail Ruts National Historic Landmark**, where pioneer wagons wore six-foot-deep ruts through the soft sandstone, is south of Guernsey 0.4 miles west of S Wyoming Ave. Continue 1.8 miles southeast to **Register Cliff**, where pioneers carved their names (1829 to 1847) into the limestone. Call ☎ 307-836-2334 for more information on self-guided tours of these sites.

Guernsey State Park
Guernsey State Park (☎ 307-836-2334), just northwest of Guernsey, takes its name from mining entrepreneur Charles Guernsey, who abducted a group of Denver-bound US senators by sidetracking their train in order to show them his dam site and, astonishingly, succeeded in persuading them of its desirability. Completed in 1927, nearly 20 years after his audacious ploy, the park has several historic buildings and houses the excellent Guernsey State Park Museum/visitors center, built by the Civilian Conservation Corps in the 1930s. Open Memorial to Labor Day, the park offers boating on Guernsey Reservoir, picnicking and hiking. The day-use fee is $3 ($2 for Wyoming residents). Camping costs $4. The park has two entrances: the South Entrance is on Hwy 317 off US 26 just west of Guernsey; the North Entrance is on Hwy 270 5 miles north of Guernsey.

Places to Stay
The pleasant, grassy *Larson Park*, on S Wyoming Ave, has tent and hookup sites ($5/8) and showers ($2). The popular *Bunkhouse Motel* (☎ 307-836-2356), 350 W Whalen St, has rooms for about $30.

FORT LARAMIE
The town of Fort Laramie (population 243) is on US 26 21 miles northwest of Torring-

ton and 13 miles east of Guernsey (28 miles from I-25 exit 92). Tourist information is in a log building on US 26. Camping (three-day maximum) is free at the municipal campground (☎ 307-837-2711), S Laramie Ave south of US 26 and the railroad tracks. The *Chuckwagon RV Park* is near US 26 and the railroad tracks. Modestly priced motels and restaurants are also in town.

FORT LARAMIE NATIONAL HISTORIC SITE

Founded as a frontier trading post by fur trader William Sublette in 1834, sold to the American Fur Company in 1836 and acquired by the US Army in 1849, this Oregon Trail landmark is the most worthwhile historic site in eastern Wyoming. The well-restored buildings are filled with period artifacts behind Plexiglas barriers. The NPS conducts interpretive programs, including park tours, living history presentations and historic weapons demonstrations. On the north side of the park, directly behind Old Bedlam, is an attractive, shady picnic area.

History

Even before 1849, Fort Laramie (originally known as Fort William, then Fort John) played a critical role in the opening of the frontier to emigrants, who streamed across the plains en route to Oregon and California. After acquiring the post, the army immediately began construction of more substantial buildings than the cabins and adobes of what was the last major opportunity for transcontinental emigrants to obtain supplies, repair their wagons and change horses or oxen.

Fort Laramie was a rendezvous point for the Lakota as well, but this changed as increasing numbers of emigrants violated Native American lands. Outright warfare developed in the 1860s and 1870s, as the US broke a series of treaties that guaranteed the northern Plains Indians their hunting grounds north of the North Platte River and, later, the Black Hills of northeastern Wyoming and South Dakota. In both cases, the invasive miners provoked the Native American response. In the case of Red Cloud's War, in 1866-68, the army built several posts along the Bozeman Trail to facilitate the passage of miners and the cattle herds that provisioned them, in deliberate violation of previous territorial agreements.

Fort Laramie was the base for the US Army's Great Sioux Campaign of 1876, ordered by President Ulysses S Grant. This campaign, which included the battles of Rosebud Creek (June 17) and the Little Bighorn (June 24), ultimately broke Sioux resistance. Fort Laramie continued as an army center while the Northern Plains Indians were gradually forced onto reservations.

By 1890, having outlived its usefulness, the fort was abandoned and most of the buildings sold at auction. For a time, settlers inhabited the buildings but the state acquired the property in 1936 and transferred it to the NPS two years later.

Orientation & Information

The fort proper lies within a bend of the Laramie River, a tributary of the North Platte, and the remaining buildings encompass a broad parade ground. The fort was built without walls or blockhouses because the Native American challenge was slight in the immediate area.

The grounds are open 8 am to dusk daily. The museum and information center (☎ 307-837-2221) is open daily 8 am to 6 pm, inside which the Fort Laramie Historical Association (☎ 800-321-5456) runs a bookstore. A library containing 25,000 computerized records of travelers who passed through Fort Laramie in the 19th century is on the 2nd floor of the Cavalry Barracks. It is open 9 am to 4:30 pm weekdays, except Wednesday mornings. Admission to the site is $2 (16 and under are free) and includes a brochure depicting the fort as it was in 1888, with current buildings indicated by number. For a brochure, write to Superintendent's Office, Fort Laramie State Historic Park, PO Box 86, Fort Laramie, WY 82212.

WYOMING

Walking Tour
The best starting point for a self-guided walking tour is the visitors center, formerly the Commissary Storehouse (1884). Directly to the south is the still-functioning and very warm Old Bakery (1876). At the southwest corner of the parade ground, the New Guardhouse (1876) was for disciplining rowdy soldiers; directly behind it, the General Sink or latrine drained raw sewage into the river. A short distance upstream, the Old Guardhouse (1866) held serious prisoners in a solitary confinement dungeon without furniture, heat or light. At the parade ground's west end, the Captain's Quarters (1870) was a duplex for junior officers and their families. On its north side is Old Bedlam (1849), Wyoming's oldest surviving military building. It was here, in 1866, that Portugee Phillips broke into the bachelor officers' Christmas celebrations with news of the Fetterman massacre near Fort Phil Kearny, after a breakneck four-day ride. At the east end of the parade ground, the Post Surgeon's Quarters (1875) is a duplex officers' quarters with Victorian furnishings. Immediately to its east are the relatively modest Lieutenant Colonel's Quarters (1884) and the Post Trader's Store (1849, but restored to appear as in 1876). Duck into its Enlisted Men's Bar (an 1883 addition) for ice-cold root-beer, cider or sarsaparilla. Continue east to the sprawling Cavalry Barracks (1874), which served as a store, saloon and dance hall after the fort closed in 1890. On the slope to its north are ruins of the Hospital (1873).

Getting There & Away
From the town of Fort Laramie, the site is 3 miles southwest on Hwy 160.

LUSK & AROUND
Signed **Wildlife Viewing Tours**, north of Lusk (population 1500) off US 85, offer good opportunities to spot pronghorn antelope, white-tailed deer, hawks and eagles. Other **scenic drives** are along the old Cheyenne-Deadwood stage trail through Hat Creek north of Lusk, or by the Rawhide Buttes southwest of Lusk.

The Niobrara Chamber of Commerce (☎ 307-334-2950, 800-223-5875) is at 322 S Main St. In the same building is the **Stagecoach Museum & Bookstore** (☎ 307-334-3444), open from 10 am to 4 pm weekdays; admission is $2.

Places to Stay & Eat
Sites cost $11 at *BJ's Campground* (☎ 307-334-2314), 902 S Maple St, three blocks east of US 85. Singles/doubles start at $38/40 at the *Best Western Pioneer Court* (☎ 307-334-2640), 731 S Main St. The *Covered Wagon Motel* (☎ 307-334-2836), 730 S Main St, is a nicer option at $58/71.

Just north of Mule Creek Junction on the west side of US 85 (mile marker 198.35), 50 miles north of Lusk, is the *Sage & Cactus Village* (☎ 307-663-7653, 307-663-7610, fax 307-663-7699). On bluffs overlooking the Cheyenne River, this circle of tepees offers a unique family-oriented experience; call for rates.

LANCE CREEK NATIONAL NATURAL LANDMARK
At **Lance Creek Fossil Area** innumerable dinosaur, mammal and plant fossils, including 51 species never before identified, were discovered. The site, which covers 558 sq miles, is east of Hwy 272 just north of Hwy 270, northwest of Lusk. From Lusk take either US 85/US 18 north or US 20/US 18 west to Hwy 270.

Black Hills

In remote northeastern Wyoming, the Black Hills span the Wyoming-South Dakota state line. Named for the ponderosa pine forests that blanket these beautiful limestone and red sandstone hills, the Black Hills have one of America's most distinctive natural attractions, the famous Devils Tower National Monument.

NEWCASTLE
The pleasant, isolated town of Newcastle (population 3000; elevation 4334 feet), at

the junction of US 16 and US 85, is the southern gateway to the Black Hills National Forest and a great place to get information. The Newcastle Chamber of Commerce (☎ 307-746-2739, 800-835-0157), PO Box 68, Newcastle, WY 82701, is on US 16 west of US 85. The BLM Newcastle Resource Area (☎ 307-746-4453), 1101 Washington Blvd (US 16), is open 7:45 am to 4:30 pm weekdays. The USDA Service Center (☎ 307-746-2783), 1225 Washington Blvd (US 16), houses the offices of the USFS Rocky Mountain Region, the USFS Black Hills National Forest and the USFS Elk Mountain Ranger District. They have detailed trail guides for hikes in the Black Hills and South Dakota and sell the useful national forest ($4), Thunder Basin National Grassland and Trails Illustrated 'Black Hills Southeast South Dakota' ($9) topographic maps.

From Newcastle, US 16 leads east toward Rapid City, SD, and popular South Dakota attractions like Wind Cave National Park and the Jewel Cave and Mount Rushmore national monuments. US 85 leads northeast through the oak-carpeted Salt Creek Valley toward Sturgis, SD. At Four Corners, 18 miles north on US 85, Hwy 585 heads north 28 miles to Sundance.

SUNDANCE

Nestled in the Black Hills, Sundance (population 1139; elevation 4750 feet) is known for its rich history, ranching tradition, wildlife and natural beauty. Sundance Mountain (see below) gives its name to the town, the Crook County seat. Founded in 1879 and incorporated in 1887, the town is probably more famous for giving Butch Cassidy's companion Harry Longabaugh his nickname, the Sundance Kid, after the Pennsylvania teenager spent 18 months in the town's jail for horse theft. (He was in fact pardoned for his crimes on February 4, 1889, the day before his sentence was due to be completed.) It is the self-proclaimed white-tailed deer capital, and these abundant animals share the plains with prong-horn antelope and the occasional buffalo.

The town's pleasant atmosphere and its convenient location along I-90 make it a good base for exploring Devils Tower National Monument, the Bearlodge Mountains and the Black Hills of South Dakota.

Orientation

Cleveland Ave (US 14), which divides north-south street addresses, is the main east-west road. Main St parallels it one block north. The main north-south road is S 6th St (Hwy 585).

Information

Contact the Sundance Area Chamber of Commerce (☎ 307-283-1000) at PO Box 1004, Sundance, WY 82729. A tourist information building is at the I-90 exit 189 rest area. It is open 8 am to 7 pm daily during summer, 8 am to 5 pm in October; closed the rest of the year. The USFS Black Hills National Forest Bear Lodge Ranger District (☎ 307-283-1361), US 14 E, PO Box 680, Sundance, WY 82729, has knowledgeable staff, mammal and bird lists and copious information on the area's mountain biking, trails and camping (see Bearlodge Mountains & Black Hills later in this chapter).

The post office is at 2nd and Main Sts. Call ☎ 307-682-9966 for road and weather conditions. Crook County Memorial Hospital (☎ 307-283-3501) is at 713 Oak St.

Crook County Museum & Art Gallery

Harry Longabaugh's court records are the pride of the Crook County Museum (☎ 307-283-3666), in the Crook County courthouse basement on Cleveland between 3rd and 4th Sts. Other exhibits include a diorama of the Vore Buffalo Jump (see Around Sundance below), Native American artifacts, recreations of pioneer rooms and a country store and Western memorabilia. Perhaps the most interesting is a tribute to Bob Brislawn, a packer and teamster for the USGS Topographic Survey who also identified and bred Spanish mustangs from genetically distinctive feral horses, descendants of those brought by the Spaniards to 16th-century Mexico. It also houses a gallery featuring works by local artists. They are open 8 am to 8 pm weekdays, 9 am to 4 pm Saturday, June to August, and 8 am to 5 pm weekdays the rest of the year (except when it is closed January to February). Admission is free.

Sundance Mountain

Sundance Mountain (5829 feet) is the prominent peak south of Sundance. It was called the 'Temple of the Sioux' by Plains Indians who held one of their most significant ceremonies here, the sacred and secretive Sun Dance. For a personalized guided tour to the top by foot, bike, horseback or vehicle, call ☎ 307-283-2193.

Places to Stay

Open year-round, *Mountain View Campground* (☎ 307-283-2270, 800-792-8439), on Government Valley Rd 1 mile east of town, has little shade but is well maintained, with a pool and laundry. Tent/full-hookup sites cost $13/18. (See Bearlodge Mountains & Black Hills later in this chapter for nearby USFS campgrounds.)

Motel rates may drop by up to 30% in winter. Plain, boxy *Deane's Pineview Motel* (☎ 307-283-2262), 117 N 8th St, has rooms for about $30; some have kitchenettes. Singles/doubles cost $36/38 at the *Arrowhead Motel* (☎ 307-283-3307, 800-456-6016), 214 Cleveland Ave. Next door, the *Bear Lodge Motel* (☎ 307-283-1611, 800-341-8000), 218 Cleveland Ave, costs $40/46.

A newer Sundance property is the refreshing *Sundance Inn* (☎ 307-283-1100, fax 307-283-1104), US 14 E (I-90 exit 189); rooms starts at $54. The *Best Western Inn at Sundance* (☎ 307-283-2800, 800-238-0965) 121 S 6th St (I-90 exit 187), starts at $68/75. Both have a pool, hot tub and laundry.

Places to Eat

Sundance's restaurants are friendly and inexpensive, if unexciting. The *Log Cabin Cafe* (☎ 307-283-3393), US 14 E, is a good choice for all meals. The *Aro Family Restaurant* (☎ 307-283-2000), 205 Cleveland Ave, serves steak and seafood. *Higbee's Cafe* (☎ 307-283-2165), 101 N 3rd St, serves American food. *Flo's Place* (☎ 307-283-2205), 226 S Hwy 585, serves sandwiches, pizza and soft ice cream. On a hot summer day, dip into *The Country Cottage & Yogurt Garden* (☎ 307-283-2450), 423 Cleveland Ave, for sundaes or frozen yogurt.

Getting There & Away

Bus Powder River Coach USA stops at the Bear Lodge Motel, 218 Cleveland Ave. Daily buses depart for Rapid City, SD, at 9:25 am and Gillette at 6:10 pm.

Car Sundance is along the north side of I-90 18 miles west of the Wyoming-South Dakota state line and 33 miles east of Moorcroft. Devils Tower, on Hwy 24, is 27 miles northwest of Sundance via US 14. Hwy 585 leads south to Four Corners (28 miles), where it meets US 85. US 85 continues south to Newcastle (18 miles).

AROUND SUNDANCE

Keyhole State Park

Keyhole State Park (☎ 307-756-3596), built under a compact with South Dakota, is along the Keyhole Reservoir on the Belle Fourche River. It is on US 14 5 miles north of Moorcroft, which is 33 miles west of Sundance and 26 miles east of Gillette. It offers fishing for walleye, northern pike and small-mouth bass. The area sports more than 225 bird species and is a winter migratory stop for bald eagles. Ice fishing and snowmobiling are popular winter activities. The day-use fee is $3 ($2 for Wyoming residents). Camping in the barren and desolate landscape costs $4.

Vore Buffalo Jump

Vore Buffalo Jump is one of the most important archaeological sites in North America. Over a 350-year period pre-Columbian peoples drove more than 20,000 bison into this sinkhole, which filled slowly with sediment, thus preserving bones and stone artifacts that offer insight into early Plains cultures, as well as data on climatic and environmental changes. The University of Wyoming is collaborating with the private Vore Buffalo Jump Foundation (☎ 307-283-1192) in Sundance to excavate the site and develop a visitors center. Visitors may see ongoing excavation during early summer. The site is northeast of Sundance, near the Wyoming-South Dakota state line. Take I-90 exit 199, then go 3 miles east on US 14.

BEARLODGE MOUNTAINS & BLACK HILLS

The Bearlodge Mountains north of Sundance are bounded by US 14, Hwy 24, Hwy 11 and I-90, while the Black Hills extend from South Dakota into northeastern Wyoming. The area offers plentiful year-round recreational opportunities, but the USFS occasionally closes some USFS roads to protect big game like elk and wild turkeys from poaching where road density is high.

Geology

Volcanic intrusives or laccoliths are characteristic of the northern Black Hills. The most well-known of these igneous rocks are Devils Tower (see Devils Tower National Monument below), Inyan Kara Mountain (see below) and Bear Butte near Sturgis, SD.

Flora & Fauna

Ponderosa pine, aspen and oak forests blanket the hills. The region has a substantial white-tailed deer population, and about 1500 Rocky Mountain elk wander the Black Hills in two herds, one of which is in the dense pine forests along the Wyoming-South Dakota state line. Pronghorn antelope roam the grassland around Newcastle, while mule deer are found in rugged ravines and foothills. Bison roam in South Dakota just beyond the Wyoming-South Dakota state line. Bighorn sheep, introduced in 1959, are occasionally spotted around Inyan Kara, as are mountain goat. More than 111 species of birds, including bald eagle and game birds like the Merriam's wild turkey, frequent the area.

Warren Peak Lookout

Take US 14 west from Sundance to Warren Peak Rd (USFS Rd 838), and continue to Warren Peak Lookout (☎ 307-283-1525). From this forest fire lookout tower (6656 feet) four states, Devils Tower and the Bighorn Mountains are visible. The drive takes 30 minutes. While USFS Rd 838 is not paved beyond the lookout, the well-graded road continues through aspen groves, known locally as 'The Emerald Forest,' toward Cook Lake. It is also possible to head west on the scenic USFS Rd 847 and down Lytle Creek Valley (on County Rd 196) to Devils Tower.

Cook Lake Recreation Area

North of Cook Lake, cliff swallows build nests in the limestone bluffs that tower above the pine and aspens in picturesque Beaver Creek Valley. Keep an eye out for wildlife when you hike, fish or birdwatch around the lake, including beaver dams along a 2-mile section of the perennial creek in the aspen forest below. Popular loop trails include a walk around Cook Lake and the Cliff Swallow Trail, which begins from the northwest end of the Cook Lake campground. Take USFS Rd 838 north from US 14 west of Sundance or south from Hwy 24 east of Alva. Alternatively, from north of Devils Tower on Hwy 24 head east on Black Tail Creek County Rd 209 to USFS Rd 838. From Hwy 111 head west on Farrall Rd.

Inyan Kara Mountain

West of Hwy 585, a short drive south of Sundance is the 6368-foot Inyan Kara (pronounced 'inyan kaga' by Native Americans). One of three Black Hills igneous intrusives, Inyan Kara was a landmark for westward settlers and an important Lakota and Cheyenne ceremonial site.

Ghost Towns

The northern Black Hills have several ghost towns, including former mining and lumber camps, a mill and a ranch. The USFS provides a list of these long-gone settlements (see Sundance earlier in this chapter).

Hiking & Horseback Riding

The **Bearlodge Trails** lead through the Bearlodge Mountains. The 50-mile **Sundance Trail System** starts from the USFS Sundance Campground and the 6-mile **Carson Draw Trails** starts from the USFS Reuter Campground. Both trail systems can also be reached by USFS roads. Corrals are at the USFS Sundance Campground. **Beaver Creek Trail**, east of Four Corners at the junction of US 85 and Hwy 585, is excellent.

Mountain Biking

The USFS developed the **Bearlodge Fat Tire Trails** with designated sport, advanced and expert trails. Check out the challenging 'South Fork Tent' and the 'Edge.' Routes are off USFS Rds 838, 884 and 899 south of Warren Peak Lookout. Pick up a topographic route map from the USFS in Sundance (see Sundance earlier in this chapter). If you are here in June, do not miss the **Bearlodge Fat Tire Challenge**.

Cross-Country Skiing

Two prime areas are the 6 miles of weekly groomed **Carson Draw Trails** that begin from the USFS Sundance Campground and the 11 miles along the **Beaver Creek Trail** on the Wyoming-South Dakota state line.

Places to Stay

A few minutes' drive from Sundance are two USFS campgrounds: *Sundance Campground* ($10), off Government Valley Rd, 3 miles north of Sundance, is open April to November; en route to Warren Peak Lookout, the USFS *Reuter Campground* ($8), off USFS Rd 838, is open year-round.

The USFS *Cook Lake Campground* (ranges from $6 to $10) is along the southeast shore of Cook Lake, off USFS Rd 843. Some sites are a short distance northwest of the lake. Reservations are possible at the above campgrounds.

Camping is free at the USFS *Bearlodge Campground* on Hwy 24 between the towns of Alva and Aladdin. The remote and high (6500 feet) USFS *Beaver Creek Campground* ($8) is a few miles east of the

US 85/Hwy 585 junction at Four Corners, 28 miles southeast of Sundance.

DEVILS TOWER NATIONAL MONUMENT

'The heart of everything that is,' said Sioux leader Arvol Looking Horse, describing Devils Tower. The tower retains strong cultural and religious significance today for 23 Native American tribes, including the Sioux, Cheyenne, Arapaho, Kiowa and Crow. The volcanic mass rises dramatically above the Belle Fourche Valley and surrounding Black Hills. The monument, which covers only about 2 sq miles, offers hiking, wildlife viewing, bird watching, picnicking and camping. It is a must-see for those traveling between the Black Hills and western Wyoming's national parks.

History

Long before trappers and settlers reached Wyoming, Plains Indians worshiped at the landmark they called Mateo Tepee or Bear Lodge. One legend says a grizzly bear menaced several girls playing in the area. Taking refuge on a rock, the girls pleaded to be saved. The rock rose to carry them out of the bear's reach; the columns of Devils Tower are scratches left by the bear's claws.

Explorers probably first saw the tower in 1855. Colonel Richard Dodge of the USGS applied the English name 'Devils Tower' in 1875 as a translation of an alternative Native American usage. The government took control of the Black Hills in violation of the Fort Laramie treaties of 1851 and 1868, which had guaranteed the region to the Lakota and other tribes. Their action was spurred by the discovery of gold in 1875 in present-day South Dakota and the subsequent invasion of miners. The government consistently reduced reservation lands by allowing non-Native Americans access to the region for ranching and recreation as well as mining. This precipitated an all-out war that, despite victories like that over Custer at the Little Bighorn, eventually cost the Native Americans their territory. Devils Tower was and is one of the most revered and sacred sites within the Black Hills and its loss after the Northern Plains wars of the 1870s was a shock to the culture and religion of the Sioux, Cheyenne, Arapaho, Kiowa, Crow and Eastern Shoshone.

Some settlers applied to homestead the territory encompassing the tower, but creation of a forest reserve kept the land in the public domain. Wyoming politicians argued to establish a national park, but nothing happened until passage of the Antiquities Act of June 1906. President Theodore Roosevelt declared it a national monument on September 24, 1906.

William Rogers and Willard Ripley, two local ranchers, made the tower's first ascent on July 4, 1893, via a wooden ladder that remains partially intact on the southeast face. The first technical ascent was led by Fritz Wiessner on June 28, 1937. George Hopkins, a stunt parachutist, brought national notoriety in 1941 when he landed on the summit and, unable to descend, was rescued by climbers.

The NPS and the Civilian Conservation Corps developed the monument between WWI and WWII as tourism gradually increased. Devils Tower was also featured in Steven Spielberg's 1977 science-fiction movie *Close Encounters of the Third Kind*.

Devils Tower's most recent history is entangled in debate and litigation. Native Americans' recent proposal to change the towers' official name back to Bear Lodge has met with strong local opposition. Native Americans who revere the site and journey here during the summer solstice also want its formal recognition as a sacred site. Acknowledging the tower as a valuable cultural resource, the NPS adopted a Climbing Management Plan in March 1995 that includes a voluntary June climbing ban. Climbers who want unrestricted access filed suit claiming the use of public land for religious purposes violates the constitutional separation of church and state. Native Americans counter that the government is not supporting any one religion, but instead is supporting their freedom of religious expression. The pending outcome has wide-ranging implications for other national parks and monuments around the country.

Geology

The tower consists of igneous rock formed over 60 million years ago, when molten magma pushed toward the surface of the sedimentary rocks above it, but cooled before it could break through and spread as lava. As it cooled, the magma formed a block of porphyritic crystalline rock that divided into the distinctive columns that form its exterior. Erosion of the surrounding sedimentary rock gradually exposed the tower. As this process continued, some of the weaker exterior columns tumbled to form talus slopes. The monolithic formation (5117 feet) rises 867 feet from its base and 1267 feet above the Belle Fourche River. Its base diameter is 1000 feet; the surface area of the tower's summit is about 1½ acres.

Flora & Fauna

Devils Tower is surrounded by the distinct ponderosa pine forests of the Black Hills, vast grassland of the Great Plains, cactus-covered badlands and the Red Beds formations carved by the Belle Fourche River. These dramatically different environments support a variety of wildlife, including 90 species of birds (prairie falcons nest on the tower's crags and ledges), prairie

The venomous rattlesnake is one good reason to watch where you walk in the Prairies.

WYOMING

rattlesnakes, black-tailed prairie dogs, wild turkeys and white-tailed deer.

Information

The visitors center (☎ 307-467-5283), 3 miles beyond the entrance station (☎ 307-467-5377), is open mid-spring to fall. Hours are 7:30 am to 9 pm daily June to September; otherwise 8 am to 4:45 pm. Informative exhibits and information on activities and wildlife are available. The Devils Tower Natural History Association (☎ 307-467-5283), PO Box 37, Devils Tower, WY 82714, operates the adjacent well-stocked bookstore. The entrance permit, valid for seven days, costs $8 per vehicle and $3 per pedestrian, cyclist, or motorcyclist.

The post office is outside the entrance station. The NPS does not maintain a medical or rescue team at Devils Tower. The nearest trauma facilities are in Gillette (see Gillette – Information later in this chapter) and Spearfish, SD.

Prairie Dog Town

The black-tailed prairie dog *(Cynomys ludovicianus)*, a member of the squirrel family, inhabits semi-arid zones in clusters of burrows known as prairie dog towns. The road to the monument passes one such area just west of the entrance station. Hundreds of these sociable critters emerge from their burrows, defend their territories by verbally warning off challengers, communicate by kisses, barks and calls and retreat when danger nears (eg, a hawk). Take caution, as prairie dogs bite, carry fleas and can transmit diseases such as rabies and bubonic plague, and rattlesnakes sometimes shelter in their burrows.

Prairie dogs thrive in protected areas like this and in remote prairies like the Thunder Basin National Grassland, but are detested by ranchers. They dig up pasture land and consume edible grasses, and their holes can cause injury to livestock. Pest control efforts have reduced their overall numbers: government agencies poison them at the behest of the livestock industry and the

The prairie dog is a social creature that lives in burrow colonies.

Colorado Plateau town of Nucla holds a needlessly cruel annual prairie dog shoot.

Hiking

Each of the monument's four trails offers a unique perspective on the tower and area. The paved 1¼-mile **Tower Trail**, which begins at the visitors center, is the not-to-be-missed classic walk around the tower's base. Circle the tower clockwise and do not disturb any prayer bundles you see. The seldom-used 3-mile **Red Beds Trail**, which also begins at the visitors center, goes around the periphery of the tower, offering pleasant views of the Black Hills, the Belle Fourche Valley and some interesting limestone caves; the **South Side Trail** connects it to the Belle Fourche Campground. The 1½-mile **Valley View Trail** begins at the campground's amphitheater and skirts the southeast side of Prairie Dog Town. The 1½-mile **Joyner Ridge Trail** loops to and from West Rd north of the tower. Watch for rattlesnakes and poison ivy.

Horseback Riding

Riding is allowed within the monument, but start from the Devils Tower KOA Kampground.

Rock Climbing

Devils Tower is listed as one of North America's Top 10 Classic climbs and attracts up to 3500 climbers annually. The 190-plus technical routes, most of which are crack and multipitched face climbs, range from 5.6 to 5.13. Today's climbers prefer short, highly technical routes that fall short of the summit. The NPS requires anyone going above the talus slope at the tower's base to register at the visitors center during summer (during winter, register at the administration building) before and after their climb. Overnight camping on the tower is not allowed. Other than the obvious dangers, Devils Tower's unique hazards include everything from spiny plants to poisonous snakes, wasps and falcons. Some routes may be closed mid-March to mid-summer to protect nesting falcons. Consider the voluntary June climbing ban initiated by the NPS when planning your climb.

For instruction and guided climbs, contact Tower Guides Climbing School (☎/fax 307-467-5659, May to September), PO Box 24, Devils Tower, WY 82714, and (☎ 303-245-6992, October to April) PO Box 3231, Grand Junction, CO 81502; or Sylvan Rocks Climbing School & Guide Service (☎ 605-574-2425), PO Box 600, Hill City, SD 57745.

Places to Stay & Eat

Camping is permitted in Keyhole State Park (see Around Sundance earlier in this chapter), Bearlodge Mountains and Black Hills (see above), and in Sundance (see Sundance earlier in this chapter). The nearest motels are in Hulett, Sundance and Moorcroft.

The NPS *Belle Fourche Campground* is open April to late October. Sites cost $12 and fill up early. Evening campfire programs are held in the amphitheater. Open year-round, *Fort Devils Tower* (☎ 307-467-5655), 601 Hwy 24, has tent sites ($10) and sites with full hookups ($14). Showers cost $3 for non-campers. *Devils Tower KOA Kampground* (☎ 307-467-5395), near

the entrance station, charges $16/21 for tent/full-hookup sites. It is open mid-May to mid-September and has a pool and cafe. *Devils Tower Trading Post* (☎ 307-467-5295) sells some groceries. On Hwy 24 10 miles north of Devils Tower is Hulett, the nearest town with meager motels and restaurants.

Getting There & Away

Devils Tower is on Hwy 24 6 miles north of Devils Tower Junction at US 14, which is 26 miles northeast of Moorcroft (I-90 exit 154), 22 miles northwest of Sundance (I-90 exit 185), and 125 miles west of Mount Rushmore National Monument.

Powder River Country

The Powder River and its numerous forks and tributaries flow northeast through the sagebrush prairies north of Casper, between the snow-capped Bighorn Mountains to the west and the Thunder Basin Grassland and the Black Hills to the east. Historically, the Bozeman Trail and the Deadwood Stage from Cheyenne passed through this area, igniting conflicts between white migrants and Native Americans, who viewed these incursions as threats to their territory. Today the region depends largely on coal and uranium for its livelihood. At the eastern foot of the Bighorn Mountains abutting the Great Plains, the pleasant agricultural and ranching towns of Buffalo and Sheridan welcome visitors.

GILLETTE & AROUND

In 1974, a *New York Times* reporter described the mineral boomtown of Gillette as

... a raw jumble of rutted streets and sprawling junkyards, red mud and dust, dirty trucks and crowded bars, faded billboards and sagging utility lines, and block after block of house trailers squatting in the dirt like a nest of giant grubs. ...

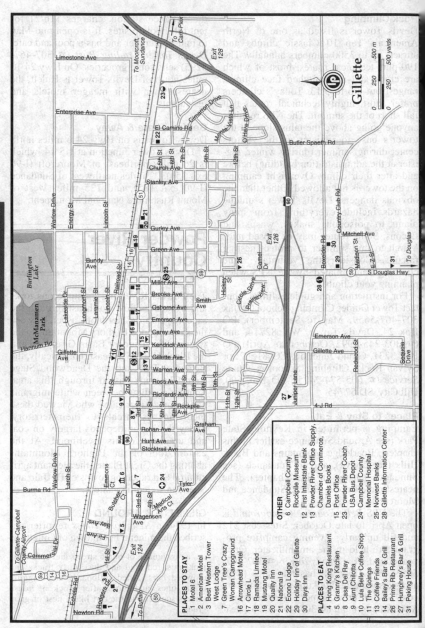

Gillette

making it all the more startling that Gillette (population 21,000; elevation 4538 feet) received a Lady Bird Johnson Roadside Beautification Award in 1992. An onslaught of shopping malls and fast-food franchises, the consequence of Gillette's coal-fueled prosperity, is overwhelming the area. Gillette, Wyoming's fourth-largest city and the seat of Campbell County, is economically the region's most important city, and has a local campus of Northern Wyoming Community College. Many businesses have fled downtown for the malls (though some older buildings have been reincarnated as offices), and the scale of downtown's newer buildings, like City Hall and the multistory First Interstate Bank, seems exaggerated for this small town.

History

Once called Donkey Town for nearby Donkey Creek, then Rocky Pile for a local landmark, Gillette acquired its permanent name from Weston Gillette, a surveyor and civil engineer who helped bring the CB&Q Railroad in 1891. Local ranchers made Gillette the largest shipping point on the CB&Q Railroad, with stockyards holding up to 40,000 sheep and 12,000 cattle. Coal, however, is the fuel that runs the economy; it is so abundant that the 1930s WPA guide describes 'more than 30 burning coal mines, apparently ignited by lightning, by campers' fires or by spontaneous combustion.' The massive Wyodak Mine, east of town, contains a 65-foot seam worked since 1922, when it may have been the world's largest strip mine. Petroleum and uranium are also found, but the area's relatively clean-burning, low-sulfur coal remains in high demand, and 30% of the population works in mining.

Orientation

Downtown Gillette is north of I-90 and south of US 14/US 16 (2nd St), the main east-west road; 2nd St turns into Hwy 51 east of Hwy 59. Douglas Hwy (Hwy 59), the main north-south road, bisects Gillette. Many motels and restaurants are along 2nd St, but the newer ones are along Douglas Hwy (I-90 exit 126).

Information

The Gillette Convention & Visitors Bureau (☎ 307-686-0040, 800-544-6136; gillettecvb@wyoming.com), 1810 S Douglas Hwy, shares a log building with the Gillette Information Center (adjacent to the Flying J Travel Plaza, I-90 exit 126). They are open 8 am to 5 pm weekdays, 8 am to 6 pm Saturday, and noon to 5 pm Sunday. Their extensive information includes details about coal-mine and wildlife viewing tours. The Campbell County Chamber of Commerce (☎ 307-682-3673), 314 S Gillette Ave, is open 9 am to 4:30 pm weekdays. The BLM Survey Project office (☎ 307-686-6750) is at 1901 Energy Court, Suite 160.

First Interstate Bank has an ATM at 222 S Gillette Ave. Norwest Banks is at 500 S Douglas Hwy. The post office is downtown at 311 Kendrick St; the zip code is 82716. For fax services, try Powder River Office Supply (☎ 307-682-4522, fax 307-682-0531), 310 S Gillette Ave, or Mail Boxes Etc (☎ 307-687-0353, fax 307-687-7111), 2610 S Douglas Hwy. Daniels Books (☎ 307-682-8266) is at 320 S Gillette Ave. Campbell County Memorial Hospital (☎ 307-682-8811) is at 501 S Burma Rd.

Campbell County Rockpile Museum

This popular museum (☎ 307-682-5723), 900 W 2nd St, built alongside Gillette's most unmistakable natural feature, displays Native American and pioneer artifacts, including a sheepwagon, a chuckwagon and an ornate horse-drawn hearse. It is open 9 am to 8 pm Monday to Saturday and 12:30 pm to 6:30 pm Sunday June to August, and 9 am to 5 pm Monday to Saturday the rest of the year. Admission is free.

Coal Mines & Power Plants

Sixteen mines around Gillette produce 90% of Wyoming's coal. Several mines and related industries are open for tours, usually 8 am to 3 pm daily during summer and by

WYOMING

appointment. Contact the Gillette Convention & Visitors Bureau for details. Views of the area's largest strip mine, which produces 2.7 million tons of coal annually, are possible from the **Wyodak Overlook** east of Gillette off US 14/US 16 (I-90 exit 132). Half of this output fuels the 330-megawatt **Wyodak Power Plant** (☎ 307-686-1248), 5 miles east of Gillette. Tours are available 9 am to 3 pm weekdays.

Durham Buffalo Ranch
South of Gillette on Hwy 59 is Durham Buffalo Ranch (☎ 307-939-1271), one of the country's largest buffalo ranches. Tours are by appointment only.

Special Events
Mid-June's **Cowboy Days** and July's **National High School Rodeo Finals** (one of Wyoming's biggest events) draw enthusiastic crowds.

Places to Stay
Gillette has abundant lodgings at reasonable, sometimes rock-bottom, prices. Rates may drop slightly after October 1.

Camping *Green Tree's Crazy Woman Campground* (☎ 307-682-3665), 1001 W 2nd St, is central and well-shaded, with showers and a hot tub. Tent sites cost $12; sites with full hookups cost $20. *High Plains Campground* (☎ 307-687-7339), 160 S Garner Lake Rd (I-90 exit 129), is barren and less appealing; tent sites cost $11. Both have laundry.

Motels & Hotels The friendly, Pakistani-run *Arrowhead Motel* (☎ 307-686-0909), 202 S Emerson Ave at 2nd St, has quiet and comfortable rooms for $29. The *Mustang Motel* (☎ 307-682-4784), 922 E 3rd St, is comparable. Near I-90 exit 124, singles/doubles cost $30/35 at the *Motel 6* (☎ 307-686-8600), 2105 Rodgers Drive, and *American Motel* (☎ 307-686-1989, 800-785-1989), 2011 Rodgers Drive. Rooms at the *Circle L* (☎ 307-682-9375), 401 E 2nd at Osborne Ave; *Ramada Limited* (☎ 307-682-9341, 800-272-6232), 608 E 2nd near

Miller Ave; *National 9* (☎ 307-682-5111), 1020 Hwy 51 E; and *Econo Lodge* (☎ 307-682-4757), 409 Butler Spaeth Rd at Hwy 51 E, cost about $35/40. Nearby is the *Quality Inn* (☎ 307-682-2616, 800-228-5151), 1002 E 2nd St ($40/50).

The *Best Western Tower West Lodge* (☎ 307-686-2210, 800-762-7375), 109 N US 14/US 16 (I-90 exit 124), costs $52/57. Off Hwy 59 (I-90 exit 126) are *Days Inn* (☎ 307-682-3999, 800-329-7466), 910 E Boxelder Rd ($50); and *Holiday Inn of Gillette* (☎ 307-686-3000, 800-686-3368), 2009 S Douglas Hwy ($65).

Places to Eat
Lula Belle Coffee Shop (☎ 307-682-9798), 101 N Gillette Ave, is Gillette's most popular breakfast spot, specializing in colossal breakfast rolls encased in a sugary glaze. *Coffee Friends* (☎ 307-686-6119), 320 S Gillette Ave, serves espresso, gourmet coffees, bagels, sandwiches and Italian sodas. *Granny's Kitchen* (☎ 307-687-1200), 1310 W US 14/US 16, is at 2nd St and Fir Ave.

Bailey's Bar & Grill (☎ 307-686-7678), 301 S Gillette Ave, has turned an old post office into a stylish restaurant with appealing sandwiches and dinner entrees. Two other popular places for drinks and food are *Humphrey's Bar & Grill* (☎ 307-682-0100), 408 W Juniper Lane, a sports bar, and *The Goings* (☎ 307-682-6805), 113 S Gillette Ave. The *Prime Rib Restaurant* (☎ 307-682-2944), 1205 S Douglas Hwy, is the premier steak house.

For Chinese, try the inexpensive lunch and dinner specials at *Peking House* (☎ 307-682-7868), 2701 S Douglas Hwy, or the *Hong Kong Restaurant* (☎ 307-682-5829), 1612 W 2nd St. *Casa del Rey* (☎ 307-682-4738), 409 W 2nd St, and *Las Margaritas* (☎ 307-682-6545), 2107 S Douglas Hwy, serve Mexican lunches and dinners. *Aunt Chilotta* (☎ 307-682-0610), 400 W 2nd Ave, is a step above the usual Mexican fast food.

Entertainment
The *Cam-Plex* (☎ 800-358-1897, 307-682-8802 ticket office), 1635 Reata Drive at

Garner Lake (I-90 exit 129) and Boxelder Rds, is a sprawling complex covering over 1½ sq miles. The Cam-Plex Heritage Center includes a fine arts theater for live performances, films and lectures. Its art gallery is open 8 am to 5 pm weekdays and during events. The Cam-Plex Morningside Park is home to rodeo and horse racing at Energy Downs.

Getting There & Away
Air Gillette is connected with Denver, CO, by United Express (☎ 307-687-1088) out of the Gillette-Campbell County Airport (☎ 307-686-1042) 2000 Airport Rd, off US 14/US 16 5 miles north of Gillette. Some flights continue to/from Sheridan.

Bus The Powder River Coach USA (☎ 307-682-0960, 307-682-1888) bus depot is at 1700 E US 14/US 16 (I-90 exit 128). Daily buses go to Sheridan and Billings, MT (8 am and 7:30 pm); Casper, Cheyenne and Denver (6:15 am and 7:30 pm); and Rapid City, SD (8:20 am).

Car Gillette is along the north side of I-90 68 miles east of Buffalo and 63 miles west of Sundance. Hwy 59 leads south to Douglas (115 miles) via Wright (37 miles). US 14/US 16 leads 26 miles east to Moorcroft and north and west to Sheridan, although I-90 is a more direct route.

Getting Around
Car Avis (☎ 307-682-8588) and Hertz (☎ 307-686-0550) are at the airport. Also try A&A Auto Rental (☎ 307-686-8250), 1200 E 2nd St, or Enterprise Rent-A-Car (☎ 307-686-5655), at the Holiday Inn of Gillette.

Taxi For a lift call Yellow Checker Cab (☎ 307-686-4090).

THUNDER BASIN NATIONAL GRASSLAND
South of Gillette sprawls the enormous Thunder Basin National Grassland. Hwy 59, between Douglas and Gillette, is the main north-south road through the region. No services or campgrounds exist, although camping is permitted. Detailed information is available from the USFS in Douglas (see Douglas earlier in this chapter).

KAYCEE & AROUND
Kaycee (population 316; elevation 4660 feet) sits along the Powder River; about 30 miles west, a red sandstone escarpment called the 'red wall' runs north-south for about 20 miles. Few routes penetrated these cliffs, and a narrow defile leading into a hidden valley became known as the Hole in the Wall. This was made famous as an outlaw hideout by Robert LeRoy Parker (Butch Cassidy), Kid Curry and other members of the Wild Bunch during the late 1890s.

East of Kaycee, the **Pumpkin Buttes**, named for their orange color, dominate the landscape, rising some 1000 feet above the surrounding prairie. These flat-topped buttes were used by Native Americans as lookouts and also by travelers on the Bozeman Trail as landmarks.

Today Kaycee is a small agricultural and ranching area with some oil production and mining. The Kaycee Area Chamber of Commerce (307-738-2444) is at 414 Park Ave, PO Box 147, Kaycee, WY 82639.

The legendary and dapper Butch Cassidy – an outlaw and a gentleman.

The **Hoofprints of the Past Museum** (☎ 307-738-2381), 344 Nolan Ave, recalls Kaycee's wild history. The museum is open 9 am to 7 pm Monday to Saturday and 1 to 5 pm Sunday Memorial Day to Labor Day, and 9 am to 5 pm Monday to Saturday and 1 to 5 pm Sunday Labor Day to November. Admission is free.

The Middle Fork of the Powder River, west of Kaycee, is known for **trout fishing**. In the Middle Fork canyon are the **Outlaw Caves**; take Hwy 190 (Barnum Rd) 16 miles west of Kaycee at I-25/US 87 to Barnum. Continue south on Arminto Rd to the Outlaw Cave Trail and free BLM *Outlaw Cave Campground* (no potable water). North of Barnum, along Beaver Creek, is the site of the historic **Dull Knife Battle**. Hole-in-the-Wall Country Tours (☎ 307-738-2243), at the Texaco station, runs five- to seven-hour tours of the area, where a lot of roads are suitable only for 4WD.

Back Country Byway

The 103-mile long BLM South Bighorn/Red Wall National Back Country Byway traverses the southern Bighorn Mountains southwest of Kaycee and northwest of Casper off US 20/US 26. Passing geological formations, historic ranches and interesting wildlife habitats, the byway leaves US 20/US 26 15 miles northwest of Casper at USFS Rd 125, heads north to Bucknum, continuing on USFS Rd 110 past Buffalo Creek to Centennial Sheep Monument, before turning south sharply, passing two free BLM campgrounds, and returning to US 20/US 26 at Waltman via USFS Rds 109, 105 and 104. East of Waltman and south of US 20/US 26 is **Hell's Half Acre** (☎ 307-472-0018), unusual caves, spires and geological formations where Native Americans trapped buffalo. Wildlife in the area include mule deer, mountain lion, white-tailed deer, pronghorn antelope, wild turkey and raptors. High-clearance vehicles are recommended.

Places to Stay & Eat

Kaycee has a few very basic motels and restaurants. Camping is free in *Kaycee City*

Park. For the most authentic old West experience, stay at the *Willow Creek Ranch at the Hole-in-the-Wall* (☎ 307-738-2294), PO Box 10, Kaycee, WY 82639, the historic site of the Hole-in-the-Wall gang's hideout. This working sheep and cattle ranch, 35 miles southwest of Kaycee, offers varied 'rawhide' activities.

Getting There & Away

Kaycee is on I-25 45 miles south of Buffalo. Hwy 387 links Wright, at the edge of the Thunder Basin National Grassland, with Kaycee.

MIDWEST & AROUND

Teapot Dome is a distinctive sandstone butte resembling a teapot (the spout and handle, however, broke off in a 1962 storm), near the town of Midwest, near the junction of Hwy 259 and Hwy 387, 6 miles east of I-25/US 87 and 39 miles north of Casper. Built in the 1920s, the Midwest Museum, 525½ Peake St, focuses on the area's oil fields and chronicles the Teapot Dome scandal.

BUFFALO

Settlers founded the Johnson County seat of Buffalo (population 3900; elevation 4654 feet) after the US Army forced the Lakota Sioux onto reservations in the Black Hills. This town literally bears the

Teapot Dome Scandal
In 1921 Albert B Fall, Secretary of the Interior during the administration of President Warren G Harding, leased the Teapot Dome Naval Petroleum Reserve, the world's largest light oil field, to the Sinclair Crude Oil Purchasing Company. Fall did this without competitive bidding and received in return interest-free 'loans,' effectively bribes. In the resulting national scandal, Fall went to prison and Sinclair was convicted of a felony. The US Supreme Court restored the Teapot Dome oil fields to the US government in 1927. ∎

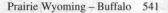

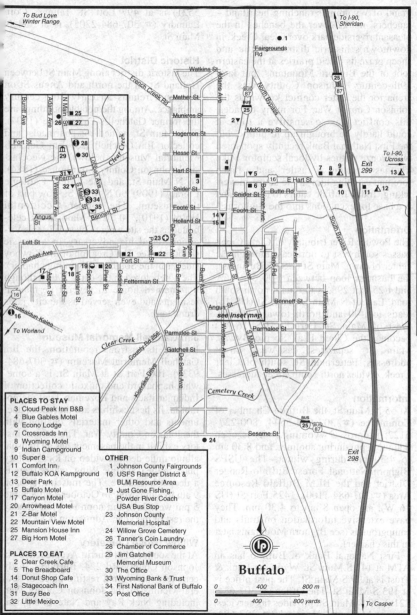

PLACES TO STAY
3   Cloud Peak Inn B&B
4   Blue Gables Motel
7   Econo Lodge
7   Crossroads Inn
8   Wyoming Motel
9   Indian Campground
10 Super 8
11 Comfort Inn
12 Buffalo KOA Kampground
13 Deer Park
15 Buffalo Motel
17 Canyon Motel
20 Arrowhead Motel
21 Z-Bar Motel
22 Mountain View Motel
25 Mansion House Inn
27 Big Horn Motel

PLACES TO EAT
2   Clear Creek Cafe
5   The Breadboard
6   Donut Shop Cafe
18 Stagecoach Inn
31 Busy Bee
32 Little Mexico

OTHER
1   Johnson County Fairgrounds
16 USFS Ranger District &
    BLM Resource Area
19 Just Gone Fishing,
    Powder River Coach
    USA Bus Stop
23 Johnson County
    Memorial Hospital
24 Willow Grove Cemetery
26 Tanner's Coin Laundry
28 Chamber of Commerce
29 Jim Gatchell
    Memorial Museum
30 The Office
33 Wyoming Bank & Trust
34 First National Bank of Buffalo
35 Post Office

Buffalo

0   400   800 m
0   400   800 yards

brand of Wyoming's ranching heartland – ranchers' marks cover the benches in the pleasant riverside park over Clear Creek, in downtown's historic district. Cattle and sheep graze its placid prairies at the eastern foot of the Bighorn Mountains, but late-19th-century Johnson County was the arena for the bitter conflict known as the Johnson County War. For many decades, this conflict was so sensitive a topic it could hardly be brought up in public, but the First National Bank recently sponsored two bronze statues by local sculptor Mike Thomas depicting a 'rustler' and a ranch foreman catching him in the act of maver-icking. Today Buffalo caters to tourism and is a base for excursions into the Bighorns.

Orientation

The Powder River tributary of Clear Creek passes southwest to northeast through the center of town. Main St (US 87 Business), the business loop between I-90 exit 56A and I-25 exit 298, is the main north-south road. East of N Main St, Hart St (US 16) leads to I-90 and north toward Ucross. West of Main St, Fort St (US 16 W) becomes the Cloud Peak Scenic Byway. Main St separates east-west street addresses; Fetterman St, south of Clear Creek, divides north-south street addresses.

Information

At 55 N Main St, the Buffalo Chamber of Commerce (☎ 307-684-5544, 800-227-5122; nadgross@wyoming.com) is open 8 am to 6 pm during summer, and 8:30 am to 4:30 pm during winter. The USFS Bighorn National Forest Buffalo Ranger District and the BLM Buffalo Resource Area (☎ 307-684-1100), 1425 Fort St (US 16 W), are open 8 am to 4:30 pm. They have extensive information on trails and campgrounds (see Bighorn Mountains later in this chapter).

First National Bank of Buffalo has an ATM at 141 S Main St. Wyoming Bank & Trust is at 99 S Main St. The post office is at 193 S Main St. The Office (☎ 307-684-2215), 33 N Main St, provides fax services. County Memorial Hospital (☎ 307-684-

5521) is at 497 Lott St. Tanners Coin Laundry (☎ 307-684-2205), is at 334 N Main St.

Historic District

The historic district along Main St between Holland St on the north and Angus St on the south retains an early 20th-century ambiance. Among the notable buildings are the former Gatchell's Drug Store (1904), 76 S Main St, named for pharmacist and collector Jim Gatchell (see Jim Gatchell Memorial Museum below), the Neoclassical Johnson County Courthouse (1884), 76 N Main St, and the former Carnegie Library (1909), 90 N Main St, now part of the museum. The former **Occidental Hotel** (1910), 10-30 N Main St, is celebrated as the site where Owen Wister's Virginian faced his adversary in a classic shoot-out (see The Creation of the Cowboy sidebar in the Southern Wyoming chapter). The hotel closed in the early 1980s, though it remained home to several permanent residents and even served as the city jail's drunk tank.

Jim Gatchell Memorial Museum

Despite its lustrous reputation, the Jim Gatchell Memorial Museum (☎ 307-684-9331), 100 Fort St at Main St, is a somewhat haphazard and quixotic collection of Indian artifacts and Bozeman Trail memorabilia. Its best exhibits are dioramas, documents and other materials dealing with the Johnson County War. The natural history exhibit in the basement has an unusual albino mule deer. A video on local history plays in the Carnegie Wing, where there is a decent bookstore. The museum is open 9 am to 8 pm, May to October, and 8 am to 5 pm weekdays and noon to 4 pm Sunday the rest of the year. Admission is $2.

Willow Grove Cemetery

At the south end of Burritt Ave, reached via Johnson County Rd 224, Buffalo's shady cemetery is the final resting place of several victims of the Johnson County War, including Nick Ray and Nate Champion, along with more recent celebrities such as

Johnson County War

Also called the Powder River War, this was one of many similar conflicts throughout the West, all related to the end of the open-range tradition. After the Native Americans and the bison had been driven from the plains, cattle barons freely grazed their animals on the vast prairie. But the ever-increasing smaller ranchers and settlers challenged their political and economic supremacy. The Wyoming Stock Growers Association (WSGA), run by absentees like Thomas Sturgis of New York, saw the little guys as cattle thieves who acquired their herds by rustling (changing of brands) or by mavericking (unauthorized branding of newborn calves belonging to the large companies). The WSGA used its influence to pass legislation preventing branding except at the annual WSGA roundup, in effect creating a government-sanctioned monopoly.

During the bitter winter of 1886-87, 3 million cattle starved and many cattle companies went bankrupt. Fewer cattle meant unemployment, so more cowboys engaged in mavericking and rustling. The companies hired cold-blooded stock detectives like Tom Horn (see A Well-Known Gun sidebar earlier in this chapter) to enforce their hegemony. Judges were in the pockets of the WSGA, but juries were often sympathetic to accused rustlers – all 13 prosecutions brought in Johnson County in 1889 failed to obtain convictions. Consequently, the WSGA often took matters into its own hands. In 1892, stock growers Frank Walcott and William Irvine hired a group of Texan gunslingers, including the infamous Frank Canton, to teach the Johnson County 'rustlers' a lesson.

Arriving by special train in Casper and carrying a hit list of their opponents, the Texans ambushed the Kaycee Ranch, 50 miles south of Buffalo. Nick Ray and Nate Champion, two notorious rustlers, were there. Ray was killed, but Champion's determined resistance enabled news to get to other settlers. Champion died at the ranch, but the settlers rallied to surround the Texans at the TA Ranch, just south of Buffalo. The 6th US Cavalry intervened, ostensibly to arrest the mercenaries, and moved them to Fort Fetterman and Cheyenne, where Johnson County was responsible for their upkeep. Unable to pay the costs of lengthy incarceration and an expensive trial, the county declined to prosecute and all the accused went free. ■

TJ Gatchell and Vera Keyes (designer of Wyoming's state flag). Perhaps the most notable is Joe LeFors, the US Marshal who apprehended Tom Horn and was one of the trackers of Butch Cassidy and the Sundance Kid.

Clear Creek Trail System

From its beginning on South Bypass, south of E Hart St, the partially paved Centennial Trail, a segment of the trail system, runs west presently 11.2 miles to a picnic area at Mosier Gulch on US 16. The trails are closed to horses or motorized vehicles. Pick up 'The Clear Creek Trail System' brochure and map of this pleasant route through town.

Fort McKinney

Along Clear Creek, west of Buffalo via US 16, the current **Veterans' Home of Wyoming** (☎ 307-684-5111) still retains some original buildings (1878) from its days as a US Army outpost. Call before visiting.

WYOMING

Horseback Riding
Sweetgrass Ranch (☎ 307-752-2106), 39 Maverick Trail, offers daily rides in the Bighorn foothills.

Special Events
Powder River Days fill the first weekend in July. The **Johnson County Fair & Rodeo**, held at the fairgrounds, lasts nearly a week in early August. August's other notable event is the **Basque Festival**, which honors descendants of sheepherders who began to arrive in the early 20th century.

Places to Stay
Camping Three campgrounds are near I-25 exit 299 and I-90 exit 58. *Indian Campground* (☎ 307-684-9601), 660 E Hart St, is shady and well-maintained. Tent/full-hookup sites cost $14/18. At the *Buffalo KOA Kampground* (☎ 307-684-5423, 800-562-5403), 87 US 16 E, sites cost $18/24. *Deer Park* (☎ 307-684-5722, 800-222-9960), 146 US 16 E, has sites for $16/21. Two miles west of Main St, beyond the Veterans' Home, the *Big Horn Mountains Campground* (☎ 307-684-2307, 800-648-7628), 8935 US 16 W, is friendly and comfortable, but lacking shade and hard to find, especially after dark. Sites cost $13/16. Each campground has a pool and showers; it is usually open April to October. Mountain View Motel (see below) also has a few grassy tent sites.

B&Bs Two B&Bs, both with Jacuzzi, are within walking distance of downtown. The friendly *Mansion House Inn* (☎ 307-684-2218), 313 N Main, an attractively decorated 1906 Queen Anne home, has singles/doubles starting at $34/39. The *Cloud Peak Inn B&B* (☎ 307-684-5794, 800-715-5794), 590 N Burritt Ave, has rooms ranging from $40/50 to $60/70.

Motels Most motels are on E Hart St (US 16) and Fort St (US 16 W); the latter area is generally cheaper. Summer rates may be up to 50% more than winter rates. Singles/doubles in rustic cabins cost $35/38 at the *Mountain View Motel* (☎ 307-684-2881),

585 Fort St. The friendly and professional *Z-Bar Motel* (☎ 307-684-5535, 800-341-8000 reservations), 626 Fort St, is well-maintained and shady. Their cabins cost $36/40. Nearby is the *Arrowhead Motel* (☎ 307-684-9453, 800-824-1719), 749 Fort St ($32/34). The tidy, yet barren, *Canyon Motel* (☎ 307-684-2957, 800-231-0742), 997 Fort St, costs $30/34.

Nearest to downtown is the *Big Horn Motel* (☎ 307-684-7822, 800-936-7822), 209 N Main. More worn are the *Buffalo Motel* (☎ 307-684-5230), 370 N Main St ($34/38), and the cabins at the *Blue Gables Motel* (☎ 307-684-2574, 800-684-2574), 662 N Main St ($30/34).

The *Econo Lodge* (☎ 307-684-2219), 333 E Hart St, has single/doubles for $39/44. Rooms at the *Wyoming Motel* (☎ 307-684-5505, 800-666-5505), 610 E Hart St, start at $41. They have some kitchenettes, a spa, and laundry. The *Super 8* (☎ 307-684-2531), 655 E Hart St, starts at $40. At I-25 is the *Comfort Inn* (☎ 307-684-9564), 65 US 16 E ($50/55). Across the street is the *Crossroads Inn* (☎ 307-684-2256, 800-852-2302), 75 N Bypass ($54/59). They have a restaurant and pool.

Lodges West of Buffalo off US 16, within 20 miles of town, are a few good lodges. Most offer horseback riding (about $16/hour, $45/half-day and $75/day) and pack trips ($140/day) in the surrounding area and Cloud Peak Wilderness Area. They are the *South Fork Inn* (☎ 307-684-9609), PO Box 204, Buffalo, WY 82834; *Bear Track Lodge* (☎ 307-684-2528), 8885 US 16 W, Buffalo, WY 82834; and *The Pines Lodge* (☎ 307-684-5204, 307-680-8545, 307-351-1010), PO Box 100, Buffalo, WY 82834.

Places to Eat
Buffalo restaurants are unexceptional. In the same location since 1928, the *Busy Bee* (☎ 307- 684-7544), 2 N Main St alongside Clear Creek, often fills for breakfast and lunch, and also serves dinner. The *Donut Shop Cafe* (☎ 307-684-5446), 386 N Main St, is another busy breakfast venue. *The Breadboard* (☎ 307-684-2318), 190 E Hart

St, is a decent sandwich shop. *Little Mexico* (☎ 307-684-7396), 4 S Main St, has decent Mexican food (starting at $5). The *Stagecoach Inn* (☎ 307-684-2507, 845 Fort St), serves hearty buffet meals ($6). The *Clear Creek Cafe* (☎ 307-684-7755), 820 N Main St, has an extensive menu of reasonably-priced lunches (mostly sandwiches and omelets) and dinners (veal, steaks and seafood under $15).

Getting There & Away
Bus Powder River Coach USA stops at Just Gone Fishing, 777 Fort St at Spruce St. Northbound buses to Sheridan and Billings, MT, depart at 9:05 am and 8:35 pm; southbound buses to Casper and Cheyenne leave at 4 am and 5:30 pm.

Car Buffalo is at the junction of I-90 and I-25 31 miles south of Sheridan, 66 miles west of Gillette, and 109 miles north of Casper. US 16 leads west across the Bighorn Mountains via Powder River Pass (9666 feet) to the Bighorn Basin town of Worland.

Getting Around
Buffalo Area Transport System (BATS; ☎ 307-684-9551) primarily serves the community's seniors, but call if you need a ride.

AROUND BUFFALO
Bud Love Winter Range
A scenic loop drive through the Bud Love Winter Range, northwest of Buffalo, is recommended for late-afternoon roadside wildlife viewing. Mule deer, white-tailed deer, wild turkey and pronghorn antelope are common, and elk frequent the range during winter. From downtown Buffalo, follow DeSmet St north from Fort St out of town on Johnson County Rd 91.5 (French Creek Rd), take the left fork and continue 10 miles through the range. Go right at the next fork onto Rock Creek Rd, and return to Buffalo.

Fort Phil Kearny State Historical Site
Even as the US government talked peace with the Plains Indians at the end of the Civil War, it was building army posts

north of the North Platte River to protect Montana-bound gold seekers. At the confluence of Big and Little Piney creeks, midway between Sheridan and Buffalo, the Bozeman Trail outpost of Fort Phil Kearny survived only two years, from 1866 to 1868, in the face of Sioux, Cheyenne and Arapaho forces united to defend their Northern Plains hunting grounds.

After the UP reached Idaho in 1868 and miners could bypass the Bozeman Trail, the US Army abandoned Fort Phil Kearny (in part to keep the Native Americans away from the railroad tracks) and the Cheyenne burned it to the ground. What remains at this site is a partial reconstruction of some buildings, archaeological excavations, a visitors center, memorials to Native Americans and nearby battlefields, including the Wagon Box and Fetterman Fight sites. A memorial also stands to Manuel Felipe Cardoso, better known as John 'Portugee' Phillips, who made a four-day ride to Fort Laramie with news of Captain William J Fetterman's massive defeat by Native Americans in December 1866.

The **Bozeman Trail Days**, with its rich history program and chuckwagon meals, is held Friday to Sunday the third weekend in June. Contact the Bozeman Trail Association, PO Box 5013, Sheridan, WY 82801 for information.

The visitors center, museum (☎ 307-684-7629, 307-684-7687) and grounds are open 8 am to 6 pm daily mid-May to September. The grounds are also open noon to 4 pm October to mid-May. Admission is $1. Take I-90 north of Buffalo 17 miles to US 87 (I-90 exit 44) and continue 3 miles northwest on Hwy 193 to the site.

Dry Creek Petrified Tree
A self-guided walking tour explores the Dry Creek Petrified Tree area, which was a large marsh 60 million years ago. Follow I-90 7 miles southeast of Buffalo to I-90 exit 65 and go 5 miles north to the site.

STORY & BIG HORN
The quaint communities of Story and Big Horn are in the Bighorn foothills between

Buffalo and Sheridan. Both offer quiet alternatives to the region's larger towns, with easy access to less-frequented Big Horn National Forest trailheads. The area's B&Bs afford opportunities for fishing, hiking, wildlife viewing, and horseback riding.

Things to See
Scotsmen William and Malcolm Moncreiffe originally settled the Quarter Circle A Ranch on Little Goose Creek in 1892. They sold it to Illinois-born New Yorker Bradford Brinton in 1923. Brinton raised horses and collected Western art. His 20-room house now displays over 600 paintings, sketches and sculptures by Charles M Russell, Frederick Remington, John J Audubon and others. The **Bradford Brinton Memorial Museum & Historic Ranch** (☎ 307-672-3173), 239 Brinton Rd off Hwy 335 2 miles southwest of Big Horn, is open 9:30 am to 5 pm daily mid-May to Labor Day. The **Big Horn Equestrian Center**, one of the country's oldest polo clubs, holds matches Sunday afternoon May to September.

Places to Stay & Eat
In Story are the *Piney Creek B&B* (☎ 307-683-2911), 11 Skylark Lane, 2½ miles west of the Hwy 193/Hwy 194 junction, and the rustic *Ponderosa Pines* (☎ 307-751-4210), 179 N Piney. In Big Horn, the B&Bs have mountain views: *Blue Barn B&B* (☎ 307-672-2381), a converted dairy barn, and the pleasant *Spahn's Big Horn Mountain B&B* (☎ 307-674-8150), with log cabins.

In Story, *The Waldorf A'Story Deli* (☎ 307-683-2400), 19 N Piney Rd, at the Piney Creek Grocery, has gourmet food, home-style soups, sandwiches as well as desserts.

Getting There & Away
Big Horn is 6 miles north of Story and 5 miles south of Sheridan. Take US 87, which parallels I-90 to its west (or Meade Creek Rd (I-90 exit 33) to US 87) to Hwy 335 and head southwest.

SHERIDAN
The region's most interesting town is Sheridan (population 14,000; elevation 3915 feet), the seat of Sheridan County, where both coal and cattle contribute to the economy and sometimes come into conflict. At the eastern foot of the Bighorn Mountains in the Big Goose Valley, Sheridan's wealth of historic buildings makes it an interesting visit. Early in the 20th century, coal supplanted beef as the mainstay of the local economy. All-night coal trains rumble on the Burlington Northern Railroad's tracks, yet Sheridan is not a gritty mining town and local merchants and officials are doing a remarkable job of restoring the downtown to its former glory. The ranching sector remains significant, often in surprising ways. Some of the earliest settlers were gentlemen horse breeders from Britain.

History
The Plains Indians kept settlers out of the northern Bighorns until 1877. Colonization proceeded slowly until John Loucks purchased the isolated Mandel post office in 1882 and named the new settlement after his Civil War commander, General Philip Sheridan. Sheridan and the surrounding area seceded from Johnson County, to the south, to form a separate county in 1888. The turning point in its history, however, was the arrival of the railroad, which spurred development of local coal fields. These attracted Eastern European immigrants, who left an enduring cultural mark on the town; even today, there is an autumn polka festival. In the late 1930s residents upset with politics in Cheyenne called for northern Wyoming to secede and form the new state of Absaroka. State government's attention to the locals' grievances smoothed over the problem, although not before Sheridan's street commissioner declared himself governor of Absaroka and even selected a staff.

Orientation
US 87 and US 14 combine just west of I-90 exit 25 with I-90 Business as Coffeen Ave.

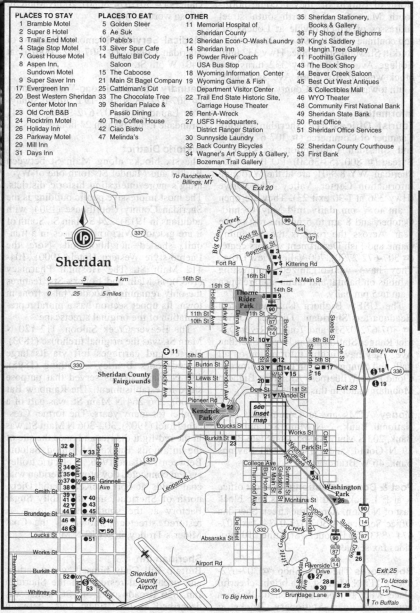

PLACES TO STAY
1 Bramble Motel
2 Super 8 Hotel
3 Trail's End Motel
4 Stage Stop Motel
7 Guest House Motel
8 Aspen Inn,
  Sundown Motel
9 Super Saver Inn
17 Evergreen Inn
20 Best Western Sheridan
   Center Motor Inn
23 Old Croft B&B
24 Rocktrim Motel
26 Holiday Inn
28 Parkway Motel
29 Mill Inn
31 Days Inn

PLACES TO EAT
5 Golden Steer
6 Ae Suk
10 Pablo's
13 Silver Spur Cafe
14 Buffalo Bill Cody
   Saloon
15 The Caboose
21 Main St Bagel Company
25 Cattleman's Cut
33 The Chocolate Tree
39 Sheridan Palace &
   Passio Dining
40 The Coffee House
42 Ciao Bistro
47 Melinda's

OTHER
11 Memorial Hospital of
   Sheridan County
12 Sheridan Econ-O-Wash Laundry
14 Sheridan Inn
16 Powder River Coach
   USA Bus Stop
18 Wyoming Information Center
19 Wyoming Game & Fish
   Department Visitor Center
22 Trail End State Historic Site,
   Carriage House Theater
26 Rent-A-Wreck
27 USFS Headquarters,
   District Ranger Station
30 Sunnyside Laundry
32 Back Country Bicycles
34 Wagner's Art Supply & Gallery,
   Bozeman Trail Gallery

35 Sheridan Stationery,
   Books & Gallery
36 Fly Shop of the Bighorns
37 King's Saddlery
38 Hangin Tree Gallery
41 Foothills Gallery
43 The Book Shop
44 Beaver Creek Saloon
45 Best Out West Antiques
   & Collectibles Mall
46 WYO Theater
48 Community First National Bank
49 Sheridan State Bank
50 Post Office
51 Sheridan Office Services
52 Sheridan County Courthouse
53 First Bank

WYOMING

Sheridan

To Ranchester,
Billings, MT

Exit 20

Big Goose Creek

Kool St

Seymour St

Fort Rd

Kittering Rd

N Main St

16th St

16th St

15th St

14th St

Thorne
Rider
Park

Holloway Ave

Parker Ave

Diana Ave

11th St

11th Ave

10th St

Broadway

Skeels St

Joe St

8th St

8th St

Valley View Dr

Sheridan County
Fairgrounds

Kentucky Ave

Highland Ave

5th St

Burton St

Lewis St

Clarendon Ave

Brooks St

Gould St

5th St

Sheridan Ave

Exit 23

Pioneer Rd

Dow St

1st St

Mandel St

Kendrick
Park

see
inset
map

Loucks St

Burkitt St

Works St

Park St

Carlin St

College Ave

Coffeen Ave

Wyoming Ave

Leopard St

Thurmond Ave

S Main Ave

Big Horn Ave

Sumner Ave

Gladstone St

Washington
Park

Montana St

Little Goose Creek

Absaraka Ave

De Smet

Avoca Ave

Sugarland Drive

Airport Rd

Sheridan
County
Airport

Colleen Ave

Riverside
Drive

S Sheridan
Ave

Exit 25
To Ucross

To Big Horn

To Buffalo

32

Alger St

Brooks St

N Main St

Geudt St

Broadway

33

34
35
37
38

36

Grinnell
Ave

Smith St

39
41
42
44

40

45

Brundage St

46

47

48

49

50

Loucks St

51

Works St

Burkitt St

52

53

Whitney St

Thurmond Ave

S Main St

Colleen Ave

North of Burkitt St, they become north-south Main St, the north-south street addresses of which divide at Loucks St, and continue north to I-90 exit 20. South of Burkitt St, Main St becomes Hwy 332 until College Ave, where Hwy 332 turns one block west to Big Horn Ave and heads south toward Sheridan County Airport.

Information
Tourist Offices The Sheridan County Chamber of Commerce (☎ 307-672-2485) and Sheridan Convention & Visitor's Bureau (☎ 800-453-3650), PO Box 7155, Sheridan, WY 82801, are at the Wyoming Information Center, Valley View Drive (Hwy 336 at I-90 exit 23). They are open 8 am to 7 pm daily mid-May to mid-October, and 8 am to 5 pm the rest of the year. Across the road is the Wyoming Game and Fish Department visitors center (☎ 307-672-2790), 700 Valley View Drive. They have well-organized, interesting exhibits on habitat and fauna and are open 8 am to 5 pm daily.

The USFS Bighorn National Forest Headquarters/Sheridan District Office (☎ 307-672-0751) and Tongue River District Ranger Station are at 1969 S Sheridan Ave. They have useful information on all trails and campgrounds in the Bighorns and Cloud Peak Wilderness Area (see Bighorn Mountains later in this chapter).

Money ATMs are at Community First National Bank, 2 N Main St, and First Bank, 203 S Main St, Sheridan State Bank, 29 N Gould, and First Federal Savings Bank, 46 W Brundage.

Post & Communications The post office is at E Loucks and Gould Sts, one block east of N Main. Across the street, Sheridan Office Service (☎ 307-672-0724, fax 307-674-7333), 50 E Loucks St, Suite 210, provides fax services.

Bookstores The Book Shop (☎ 307-672-6505), 117 N Main St, is a bright, cheerful place with a good selection of Western books. Sheridan Stationery, Books &

Gallery (☎ 307-674-8080), 206 N Main St, is also worth a visit.

Medical Services Memorial Hospital of Sheridan County (☎ 307-672-1000) is at 1401 W 5th St.

Laundry Sheridan Econo-Wash Laundry (☎ 307-672-7899) is at 19 E 5th St. Sunnyside Laundry (☎ 307-672-9222), at 747 Brundage Lane, is open 24 hours.

Historic District
The six blocks along Main St between Burkitt and Mandel Sts form one of Wyoming's more interesting historic districts. The most impressive public building is the Sheridan County Courthouse (1904, with additions in 1913), 224 S Main St. South of it are gracious Victorian houses in a tranquil, shaded neighborhood. Note the Pueblo-style Western Hotel (1900), 104-112 Main St. The Hospital Pharmacy (1883), at Main and Loucks Sts, features the only remaining wooden false front in town. Its upper section has a mural representation of the original streetscape.

The Beaver Creek Saloon, 112-120 N Main St, was the original firehouse (1893). Horses and carriages left via its large arched doors. Bentley's Clothing (1895), 180 N Main St, has served that purpose since its establishment. The Rainbow Bar (1906), 256-264 N Main St, was part of a brothel for many years. The former Crescent Hotel (1908), 302-306 N Main St, was in the red-light district and once the site of the infamous Bucket of Blood Saloon. Between 1910 and 1926, an electric trolley system connected downtown Sheridan with coal fields at Fort McKenzie and Dietz, north of Sheridan, and the Holly Sugar Factory at the south end of town. A restored streetcar, known as the Coal Miner's Trolley, is at 612 N Main St.

Sheridan Inn
Buffalo Bill Cody himself was a partner and occasional resident of the Sheridan Inn, 856 Broadway at 5th St, which was described as the 'finest hotel between

Chicago and San Francisco in its heyday.' This elaborately gabled structure, based on a Scottish hunting lodge by architect Thomas Kimball, and built in 1893 for $25,000, attracted people from throughout the region to its enormous ballroom, restaurant and saloon (the oak-mahogany bar was custom made in England). It was the first building in town with running water, electric lights and telephone; 66 guest rooms graced the 2nd and 3rd floors. Famous guests included presidents Theodore Roosevelt and William Howard Taft, artist Charles M Russell, novelists Ernest Hemingway and Mary Roberts Rinehart and humorist Will Rogers. The hotel closed in 1965 and narrowly averted the wrecker's ball in 1967, when a last-minute savior purchased it. It sat empty for several years, but is gradually being restored under the auspices of the Sheridan Heritage Center. The Sheridan Inn (☎ 307-674-5440), a national historic landmark, is now a bar, restaurant and museum. A few sections are open for self-guided tours ($1); call for times.

Trail End State Historic Site
The Trail End State Historic Site (☎ 307-674-4589, 307-672-1729), 400 Clarendon Ave, is locally known as the Kendrick Mansion. Designed by architect Glenn Charles McAllister of Billings, MT, this lavish three-story Flemish Revival residence was built between 1908 and 1913 by owner John Kendrick, a cattle baron who served Wyoming briefly as governor and nearly 30 years as US senator. Ironically, the family spent little time there after Kendrick became governor in 1914. Instead it became one of Wyoming's most opulent summer homes. Exterior building materials include Wyoming granite, Indiana limestone and Kansas brick. The interior displays exquisite oak and mahogany woodwork, an Italian marble fireplace and early luxuries like an elevator and a built-in vacuum system. Its most dazzling feature may be the spacious 3rd-floor ballroom, with a maple dance floor and an orchestra loft. Eula Kendrick, nearly 20 years her husband's junior, lived here after his death

in 1933 until her own in 1961. For some years it stood neglected until its acquisition by the Sheridan County Historical Society and eventual transfer to the state. The grounds are landscaped with indigenous plants and trees. It is open 9 am to 6 pm daily, June to August, and 1 to 4 pm the rest of the year. Admission is free, and picnicking is allowed on the lovely grounds.

Special Events
The Sheridan County Fairgrounds, at the west end of 5th St, is the venue for most special events: mid-June's **North American Cowboy Roundup**; July's **WYO Rodeo**, a key stop on the professional rodeo circuit; and August's **Sheridan County Rodeo**.

Places to Stay
Most places to stay are along Main St north of 5th St and along Coffeen Ave. Rates drop up to 30% during winter.

Camping Camping is free at *Washington Park* on Coffeen Ave near the south end of town (one-night maximum), but the street noise is considerable. *Sheridan/Big Horn Mountains KOA Kampground* (☎ 307-674-8766, 800-562-7621), 63 Decker Rd, is north of town (I-90 exit 20). Tent/full-hookup sites cost $16/20. Open May to October, it has a pool, hot tub and laundry and holds a nightly barbecue.

B&Bs Downtown, the *Old Croff House B&B* (☎ 307-672-0898), 508 W Works, is open June to September. Twin-bed rooms range from $65 to $75; the suite costs $90. The 550-acre *Ranch Willow B&B* (☎ 307-674-1510, 800-354-2830), 501 US 14 (I-90 exit 25), is 4½ miles east of I-90.

Motels & Hotels Rates for most budget motels range from $25 to $30. The *Guest House Motel* (☎ 307-674-7496, 800-226-9405), 2007 N Main St, is the best budget choice. Others on N Main St include the *Bramble Motel* (☎ 307-674-4902), 2366 N Main St; *Stage Stop Motel* (☎ 307-672-3459), 2167 N Main; *Super Saver Inn*

(☎ 307-672-0471), 1789 N Main; and *Aspen Inn* (☎ 307-672-9064), 1744 N Main. Along Coffeen Ave, try *Rocktrim Motel* (☎ 307-672-2464), 449 Coffeen Ave (I-90 exit 25) or *Parkway Motel* (☎ 307-674-7259), 2112 Coffeen Ave.

Rooms at the *Trail's End Motel* (☎ 307-672-2477), 2125 N Main St, start at $32. Singles/doubles at the *Evergreen Inn* (☎ 307-672-9757, 800-771-4761) 580 E 5th St, cost $35/37. The *Mill Inn* (☎ 307-672-6401), 2161 Coffeen Ave, which is in fact a former flour mill, and *Sundown Motel* (☎ 307-672-2439), 1704 N Main, have comparable rates.

Downtown, the *Best Western Sheridan Center Motor Inn* (☎ 307-674-7421), 612 N Main St, has a restaurant and coffee shop. Singles/doubles cost $60/62. Rooms start at $65 at the *Super 8 Motel* (☎ 307-672-9725), 2435 N Main (I-90 exit 20). The *Days Inn* (☎ 307-672-2888, 800-329-7466), 1104 Brundage Lane, has rooms for $73/$78 and a pool. The *Holiday Inn Holidome* (☎ 307-672-8931), 1809 Sugarland Drive, starts at $86.

Places to Eat

Ciao Bistro (☎ 307-672-2838), 120 N Main St, is the best restaurant in Wyoming outside Jackson Hole. People drive hours for this tiny, casual yet sophisticated bistro's superb dishes and fine California wines. Imaginative salads, sandwiches and pasta are reasonably priced. Lunch (under $7.25) is first-come, first-served, although waiting is not unusual; for dinner (up to $13), reservations are necessary.

The Coffee House (☎ 307-674-8619), 123 N Main St, serves espresso, pastries and sandwiches. Nearby is *Melinda's* (☎ 307-674-9188), 57 N Main St. The *Main St Bagel Company* is at Main and Dow Sts. The *Silver Spur Cafe* (☎ 307-672-2749), 832 N Main St, offers conventional Western breakfasts and lunches. *The Chocolate Tree* (☎ 307-672-6160), 5 E Alger St, serves deli sandwiches, burgers and desserts.

Sheridan Palace & Passio Dining (☎ 307-672-2391), 138 N Main, serves Mediterranean and American dishes including gyros and pita bread sandwiches. *Pablo's Restaurant & Cantina* (☎ 307-672-0737), 1274 N Main St, has so-so Mexican food. *Ae Suk* (☎ 307-672-0357), 2004 N Main St, is Sheridan's sole Chinese restaurant. Beefeaters can try *Cattleman's Cut Steak House* (☎ 307-672-2811), 927 Coffeen Ave, or the *Golden Steer* (☎ 307-674-9334), 2071 N Main St.

For some atmosphere, try *The Caboose* (☎ 307-674-0700), 841 Broadway in the old brick railroad depot across from the Sheridan Inn. The *Buffalo Bill Cody Saloon* (☎ 307-674-5440, 307-674-5049) in the Sheridan Inn is a nostalgic choice for lunch, dinner or just drinks.

Entertainment

The restored *WYO Theater* (☎ 307-672-9084), 38 N Main St, presents a variety of year-round live performances and concerts. The restored *Beaver Creek Saloon* (☎ 307-674-8181), 112 N Main St, is probably the best downtown bar; take a look at the old photographs.

Shopping

For Western wear, King's Saddlery (☎ 307-672-2702, 800-443-8919), 184 N Main St, is unsurpassed. A free museum at the rear of the store has an astonishing collection of cowboy memorabilia, including carriages and 500-plus saddles. Best Out West Antiques & Collectibles Mall (☎ 307-674-5003), 109 N Main St, includes both the Lannan and the Medicine Wheel (☎ 307-672-0124) galleries. Other downtown galleries are the Foothills Gallery (☎ 307-672-2068), 134 N Main St; Hangin Tree Gallery (☎ 307-674-9869), 142 N Main St; Wagner's Art Supply & Gallery (☎ and fax 307-672-2454), 214 N Main St (original art and jewelry); and Bozeman Trail Gallery (☎ 307-672-3928), 214 N Main St (19th- and 20th-century Western art and Indian beadwork).

Getting There & Away

Air The Sheridan County Airport (☎ 307-674-4222) is at the south end of town via

Big Horn Ave (Hwy 332). Daily United Express (☎ 307-674-8455) flights link Sheridan with Denver, CO; some flights continue on to Gillette.

Bus Powder River Coach USA (☎ 307-674-6188) stops at the Evergreen Inn, 580 E 5th St. Buses depart twice daily northbound to Billings, MT (10 am and 9:30 pm) and southbound to Cheyenne (and Denver) via Buffalo, Gillette, Casper and Douglas (3:25 am and 4:55 pm).

Car Sheridan is along the west side of I-90 31 miles north of Buffalo and about 25 miles south of the Wyoming-Montana state line. US 14 leads east to Gillette via Ucross, although I-90 is a more direct route. US 14 leads west from Ranchester, 15 miles north of Sheridan, across the Bighorn Mountains via Granite Pass (8950 feet) and to the Bighorn Basin town of Greybull.

Getting Around

Car Avis (☎ 307-672-2226) and Enterprise (☎ 307-672-6910) are at the airport. Try Rent-A-Wreck (☎ 307-674-0707), 1809 Sugarland Drive, for cheaper rates.

Taxi Call Sheridan Transportation Taxi (☎ 307-674-6814) for a taxi.

AROUND SHERIDAN

The North Tongue River, north of Sheridan, is popular for trout **fishing**. For gear, including a wide selection of specialty flies, visit Fly Shop of the Bighorns (☎ 307-672-5866), 227 N Main St, Sheridan. The battle of the Tongue River was fought between the US Army and the Arapaho at **Connor Battlefield State Historic Site**. The site, near Ranchester north of Sheridan, today offers fishing and camping. **Mountain biking** is a major attraction and Sheridan has several good bicycle shops. Visit Back Country Bicycles (☎ 307-672-2453), 334 N Main St, for sales, rentals, repairs and information. **Hang gliders** like nearby Sand Turn, west of Dayton off US 14, on the west face of the Bighorns, for its excellent air currents.

BIGHORN MOUNTAINS

The Bighorn Mountains rise dramatically between the western Bighorn River and the eastern Powder River because of thrust faults on their east and west flanks. Broad plateaus span the 30-mile breadth and 80-mile length of the range, where large natural mountain meadows of grass and wildflowers are interspersed with lodgepole pine and spruce and fir forests. All this open country, much within the Bighorn National Forest, means easy wildlife viewing. Bighorn sheep, for which the mountains were named, were reintroduced to the region in 1987 and today are found in Shell Canyon. Grizzly bears are not found this far east, but black bear are. Elk are permanent residents.

The Bighorn Mountains are a jewel that should not be missed by those traveling to or from Yellowstone and Grand Teton national parks. The three scenic east-west roads across the mountains are US 16 (Cloud Peak Skyway) between Buffalo and Worland via Powder River Pass (9666 feet); US 14 (Bighorn Scenic Byway) between Ranchester, north of Sheridan, and Greybull via Granite Pass (8950 feet) and US 14 Alternate (Medicine Wheel Passage) between Burgess Junction and Lovell via Baldy Pass (9430 feet). Along these roads are numerous trailheads, picnic areas, scenic overlooks and dozens of inviting USFS and BLM campgrounds. Pick up the free USFS 'Bighorn Bits and Pieces,' a concise and informative guide to trails and campgrounds in the Bighorn National Forest available from USFS offices in Buffalo, Sheridan, Greybull and Worland. A few private lodges offer basic accommodations, campsites and services. (See Bighorn Mountains in the Bighorn Country chapter.)

Scenic Drives

Three short scenic drives are in the Bighorns west of Buffalo and east of Powder River Pass off US 16. The 10-mile Pole Creek Rd (USFS Rd 31) leaves US 16 20 miles west of Buffalo and rejoins it below the Powder River Pass; look for mule deer.

Nearby is **Sheep Mountain Lookout**. Continue 2 miles west on US 16 to Sheep Mountain Rd (USFS Rd 28), and follow this road 5 miles to its end; the Powder River Pass and Cloud Peak can be seen from the lookout. To reach stunning **Crazy Woman Canyon**, head west 25 miles on US 16 from Buffalo, look for the well-signed Crazy Woman Canyon Rd, then turn east and follow the road down the scenic canyon to Hwy 196. Continue north on Hwy 196 10 miles to Buffalo.

Cloud Peak Wilderness Area

The 295-sq-mile Cloud Peak Wilderness Area, with more than 250 lakes and 150 miles of maintained trails, stretches along the backbone of the Bighorn Mountains between US 14 and US 16. The area is named for glacially formed, often obscured **Cloud Peak** (13,175 feet), the highest summit in the Bighorns. The ultimate **Solitude Loop**, a 53-mile trail, circles the Cloud Peak Wilderness Area. All visitors to the wilderness area, including day-use and overnight visitors, must register at nearby USFS offices (see Buffalo and Sheridan earlier in this chapter).

Trailheads on its four sides access the wilderness area. The main trailheads from the east side, each with campgrounds, are Hunter Corral, 13 miles west of Buffalo via US 16 and then 3 miles west on USFS Rd 19 and USFS Rd 394; Circle Park, 15 miles southwest of Buffalo via US 16 and USFS Rd 20; and Elgin Park.

From the south, **Mistymoon Trail** is the most direct route to Cloud Peak's summit. From US 16 near the head of Tensleep Canyon, west of Powder River Pass, turn north onto USFS Hwy 27 and continue 7½ miles to its end at West Tensleep Lake (9100 feet) and the Mistymoon trailhead. The backpack takes three days with two nights, usually camping at Mistymoon Lake both nights. The non-technical route follows the southwest ridge to the summit. Snow and ice remain until mid-summer. Wilderness rock climbing is possible near Cloud Peak and adjacent Black Tooth Mountain. Contact the USFS in Buffalo for climbing information (see Buffalo earlier in this chapter).

From the west side of the range, the main trailhead is for **Shell Creek Trail**. Two miles east of Shell Falls (see Shell Canyon in the Bighorn Country chapter) on US 14, turn southeast on USFS Hwy 17 and USFS Rd 271 to Adelaide Lake and the trailhead.

From the north side, follow Hwy 335 from Sheridan and Big Horn to USFS Rd 26 and USFS Rd 293 to Cross Creek Campground and Coffeen Park trailhead. An alternative route is the Twin Lakes trailhead, 12 miles farther west from the Coffeen Park turnoff via USFS Rd 26 and USFS Rd 285.

Skiing

High Park Ski Area, on US 16 45 miles west of Buffalo, offers downhill skiing with a base elevation of 8200 feet and a maximum vertical drop of 600 feet. Cross-country skiing areas off US 16 are Pole Creek (22 miles west of Buffalo) and Willow Park (46 miles west of Buffalo, west of Powder River Pass).

Bighorn Country

Bighorn Country encompasses the watersheds of the Shoshone and Bighorn rivers, north of the Owl Creek, east of the Absaroka and west of the Bighorn mountains. South of the Wyoming-Montana state line, this region is bordered by Yellowstone National Park to the west and the Wind River Country to the south. South of Thermopolis the Bighorn River emerges from the Wind River Canyon and flows north across the barren Bighorn Basin, where dinosaurs trod, hot springs still hint at the volcanism that once engulfed the region and traditional ranching has metamorphosed into a symbol for tourism.

HIGHLIGHTS

- Bighorn Mountains – scenic highways traverse meadow-carpeted plateaus and access the dazzling Cloud Peak Wilderness Area

- Medicine Wheel National Historic Landmark – a sacred site atop the Bighorn Mountains with Bighorn Basin views and superb camping nearby

- Cody – the heart of the Bighorn Basin, where Wild West legends live on

Bighorn Basin

Cody's Wild West bluster contrasts with the sleepy ranch and farm towns that hug the main rivers of the Bighorn Basin. Cool canyons descend from the mountains surrounding this basin, which is a storehouse of prehistoric dinosaur and animal remains that date back to the Paleocene and Cretaceous epochs.

CODY

Cody (population 7897; elevation 5095 feet), south of the Shoshone River and east of Rattlesnake and Cedar mountains, rivals Jackson as Wyoming's premier tourist town, at least during summer. Rather than erecting new pseudo-Western facades, local businesses have retained or restored their original storefronts, giving Cody a veneer of greater authenticity. Its tourist pitch, however, is still palpable: all day, a 1950s vintage car sporting longhorns cruises Sheridan Ave to publicize the Cody Nite Rodeo (see later in this section). Cody's major tourist attraction is the Buffalo Bill Historical Center. In addition to tourism, Cody's economy includes oil, timber, small industry, farming and ranching.

History

The town of Cody is inextricably linked to the self-promoting vanity of William (Buffalo Bill) Cody, who more than willingly loaned his surname to a town founded by real estate speculator George Beck in 1901. Beck and his backers exploited Cody's fame as a Pony Express rider and Wild West showman to promote settlement, attract the CB&Q Railroad and lobby for a massive dam on the Shoshone River. The town's ultimate strength turned out to be its proximity to Yellowstone National Park. Buffalo Bill himself built the landmark

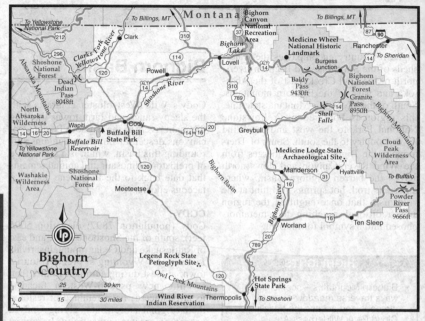

Montana

To Yellowstone National Park

212

296

Clark

310

114

Powell

120

ALT 14

Shoshone River

Dead Indian Pass 8048ft

Absaroka Mountains

Shoshone National Forest

North Absaroka Wilderness

Wapiti

14 16 20

To Yellowstone National Park

Buffalo Bill Reservoir

Buffalo Bill State Park

Cody

Shoshone National Forest

Washakie Wilderness Area

120

Meeteetse

Bighorn Country

0   25   50 km

0   15   30 miles

Legend Rock State Petroglyph Site

Owl Creek Mountains

120

Wind River Indian Reservation

To Billings, MT

Bighorn Canyon National Recreation Area

37

Bighorn Lake

Lovell

ALT 14

310

789

20

14 16

Greybull

Bighorn River

Bighorn Basin

Manderson

31

Hyattville

16

Worland

20

789

Hot Springs State Park

Thermopolis

To Shoshoni

To Billings, MT

87   90

Medicine Wheel National Historic Landmark

Ranchester

14   To Sheridan

Burgess Junction

Baldy Pass 9430ft

Bighorn National Forest

Granite Pass 8950ft

14

Shell Falls

Bighorn Mountains

Cloud Peak Wilderness Area

To Buffalo

Powder River Pass 9666ft

Medicine Lodge State Archaeological Site

16

Ten Sleep

WYOMING

Irma Hotel, named for his daughter, to take advantage of this closeness. Its imported French cherrywood bar cost more ($100,000) than the hotel itself ($80,000). By 1910, Cody became the seat of newly constituted Park County. The discovery of oil in the Elk Basin north of Cody spurred further growth. Journalist Caroline Lockhart, a resourceful Eastern transplant, published and edited the *Cody Enterprise*. She also penned several novels, including *Lady Doc*, which made her no friends among Cody's self-appointed elite.

Orientation
Cody's principal commercial area is eastwest Sheridan Ave (US 14/US 16/US 20), which turns south at 8th St and then west at Yellowstone Ave. Five blocks north of Sheridan Ave, 16th St divides into US 14 Alternate. South of Sheridan Ave, 17th St divides into US 14/US 16/US 20 and Hwy 120.

Information
Tourist Offices The Cody Country Chamber of Commerce (☎ 307-587-2777, 307-587-2297), 836 Sheridan Ave, PO Box 2777, Cody, WY 82414, is in the Stock Center, a lodgepole-pine cabin built in 1927. They sell a $1 pamphlet with B&W photos of important landmarks. Call Cody Area Central Reservations (☎ 888-468-6996) for area hotel and motel reservations.

The USFS Shoshone National Forest Wapiti Ranger District (☎ 307-527-6921), 203A Yellowstone Ave, east of the junction with South Fork Rd, is open 8 am to 4:30 pm weekdays. The BLM Cody Resource Area office (☎ 307-587-2216), 1002 Blackburn St, is east of downtown. The Wyoming Game and Fish Department (☎ 307-527-7125) is at 2820 Hwy 120.

Money ATMs can be found at Key Bank, 1130 Sheridan Ave; at the Shoshone First Bank at 1401 Sheridan Ave; and Western

Bank, 627 Yellowstone Ave. Two grocery stores also have ATMs: Albertsons, 17th St at Stampede Ave, and Buttery Fresh Foods, 16th St at Rumsey Ave.

Post & Communications The post office is at 1301 Stampede Ave; the zip code is 82414. Mail Boxes Etc, 1108 14th St, provides fax services.

Travel Agencies Big Horn Travel (☎ 307-587-5503, 800-735-8361) is at 1817 17th St.

Bookstores Cody Newsstand (☎ 307-587-2843), at 1121 13th St, has a broad selection of newspapers, magazines and Western books. Nearby is the Book Source, 1027 14th St. Find used books at the quirky Wyoming Well Book Exchange (☎ 307-587-4249), 1902 E Sheridan Ave.

Medical Services West Park Hospital (☎ 307-527-7501, 800-654-9447) is at 707 Sheridan Ave.

Laundry The surprisingly pleasant Skippy's Laundromat (☎ 307-527-6001), 728 Yellowstone Ave, is open 8 am to 9:30 pm daily.

Buffalo Bill Historical Center

The Buffalo Bill Historical Center (☎ 307-587-4771; bbhc@wave.park.wy.us), 720 Sheridan Ave, sometimes called (with considerable hyperbole) the 'Smithsonian of the West,' consists of four museums (see below) and the Harold McCracken Research Library. In total, it is an homage to male Anglo-Saxon Western myths, which Buffalo Bill's promotion of the Wild West molded into the enduring image of the region. The center hosts special events and offers daily Western film programs. It has an excellent gift shop of Western and Native American crafts and a superb bookstore with many recent titles. Tickets are valid for two consecutive days and cost $8 for adults, $6.50 for seniors, (age 62+), $4 for children age 13 to 21 and $2 for children age six to 12. Admission is free for children under six.

Buffalo Bill Museum The Historical Center's original collection began in 1927 as a record of the life of William F Cody and presents a wealth of fascinating, if uncritical, information about his Wild West shows.

Plains Indian Museum This large museum includes a substantial exhibit entitled 'The People Today,' which suggests that Native Americans have adapted to modern life without forfeiting their distinctive identities, although most items date from the late 19th and early 20th centuries, and accounts of urban Native Americans and life on the reservation are conspicuously absent. One interesting display details the co-opting of Native Americans and their symbols, such as Indian silhouettes on vehicle license plates and state highway markers, tribal names used as brands and the naming of collegiate and professional athletic teams. Another excellent exhibit covers tepees and the symbolism of their designs and Native American religion, including the Ghost Dance and the Native American Church. The 19th-century 'winter count' calendars, showing key events spiraling outward from a given base year, are fascinating documents.

Whitney Gallery of Western Art This major collection of Western artists like George Catlin, Alfred Jacob Miller, Alfred Bierstadt, CM Russell, Frederic Remington and Nathaniel Wyeth, with portraits of well-known Indian leaders of the 19th century, provides visual insight into the complexity of the Western experience.

Cody Firearms Museum The most interesting exhibit in this inventory of guns is the re-creation of a stage stop between Cody and Meeteetse.

Old Trail Town Museum of the West

Old Trail Town Museum of the West (☎ 307-587-5302), 1831 Demaris St off Yellowstone Ave, is a peculiar collection of log cabins and false-front wooden buildings, including a trading post, stage stop

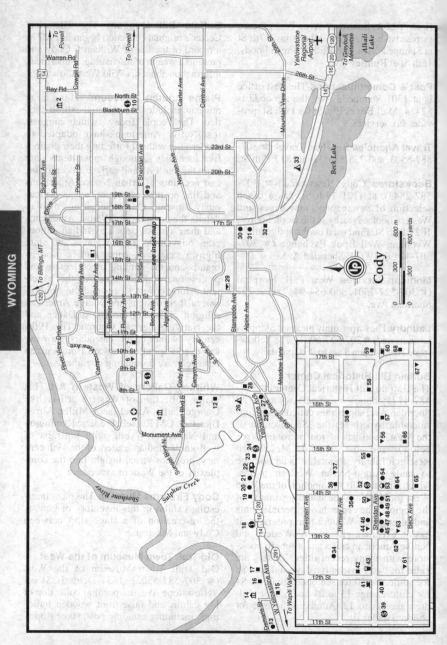

WYOMING

and saloon. Many buildings were relocated here from the old stage road between Fort Washakie and Red Lodge, MT. Antique horse-drawn vehicles line the boardwalk along 'Main Street.' Trail Town features the gravesite of legendary 19th-century mountain man and trapper John 'Jeremiah' Johnson. Displaced from post-mortem luxury near Beverly Hills, CA Johnson now suffers tourist-trap indignity in a town named for the flamboyant Western show-biz contemporary he detested. Open 8 am to 8 pm daily, mid-May to mid-September, admission is $3; free for children under 12.

Cody Nite Rodeo

Cody's highly popular Nite Rodeo (☎ 307-587-5155), 421 W Yellowstone Ave, PO Box 1327, Cody, WY 82414, takes place at 8:30 pm nightly, June to August, at the rodeo grounds at Stampede Park. Tickets cost $9/4 for adults/children (seven-12) for grandstand seating and $11/6 for Buzzard's Roost seating, closer to the chutes and action. Admission is free for children under seven.

Special Events

Cody hosts a variety of special events: in February, the Buffalo Bill Birthday Ball; in April, the Cowboy Poetry & Range Ballads; June, the Frontier Festival and Plains Indian Powwow; July the Cody Stampede; and August, the Buffalo Bill Festival.

Places to Stay

Summer rates can be up to 50% higher than during other seasons; many places close during winter. Reservations are recommended during summer, but campgrounds usually have sites available.

Camping *Gateway Campground* (☎ 307-587-2561), 203 Yellowstone Ave, has shady tent sites ($12) and shadeless sites with full hookups ($17). *Camp Cody Trailer Park* (☎ 307-587-9730), 415 Yellowstone Ave, is less attractive ($18). A popular choice of cyclists, *Ponderosa Campground* (☎ 307-587-9203), 1815 Yellowstone Ave at 8th St, has somewhat noisy tent sites ($15), sites with full hookups ($23), laundry and showers. *Cody KOA Kampground* (☎ 307-587-2369, 800-562-8507), on US 14/US 16/US 20 east of the junction with Hwy 120, charges $18/25 for tent/full-hookup sites. Near the airport, the treeless *Absaroka Bay Campground*, 2001 17th St, has sites for $15. 7 K's Motel & RV Park (see below) also has a few tent sites.

B&Bs The least expensive is *Casual Cove B&B* (☎ 307-587-3622), 1431 Salisbury Ave, which starts at $65. In a former church is *Parson's Pillow B&B* (☎ 307-587-2382, 800-377-2348), 1202 14th St ($85). *Windchimes Cottage* (☎ 307-527-5310, 800-241-5310), 1501 Beck Ave, ranges from $75 to $80. Home of journalist Caroline Lockhart, *The Lockhart Inn B&B* (☎ 307-587-6074, 800-587-8644), 109 W Yellowstone Ave, ranges from $75 to $95, but is close to a busy road. *Cody Guest Houses* (☎ 307-587-6000, 800-587-6560), 1401 Rumsey Ave, rents rooms in a Victorian house, lodges and cottages.

Motels Several properties start between $45 and $50: the friendly *Uptown Motel* (☎ 307-587-4245), 1562 Sheridan Ave; *Mountaineer Court* (☎ 307-587-2221), 1015 Sheridan Ave; *Big Bear Motel* (☎ 307-587-3117), 139 W Yellowstone Ave; *7 K's Motel & RV Park* (☎ 307-587-5890, 800-223-9204), 232 W Yellowstone Ave; and *Rainbow Park Motel* (☎ 307-587-6251, 800-341-8000 reservations), 1136 17th St. The fully non-smoking *Carriage House* (☎ 307-587-2572, 800-531-2572), 1816 8th St, has log cabins on attractive grounds ($55). Slightly more expensive are the *Holiday Motel* (☎ 307-587-4258, 800-341-8000 reservations), 1807 Sheridan Ave; *Gateway Motel* (☎ 307-587-2561), 203 Yellowstone Ave, with cabins and motel rooms; and *Skyline Motor Inn* (☎ 307-587-4201, 800-843-8809), 1919 17th St.

Most of the chain properties fall in the top-end category, at least in terms of price. *Best Western Sunrise Motor Inn* (☎ 307-587-5566), 1407 8th St ($85), and *Best Western Sunset Inn* (☎ 307-587-4265, 800-624-2727), 1601 8th St ($99), are near the Buffalo Bill Historical Center. The homey *Buffalo Bill Village* (☎ 307-587-5544, 800-527-5544), 1701 Sheridan Ave, has rooms ranging from $65 to $100. *Western Six Gun Motel* (☎ 307-587-4835, 800-231-6486), 433 Yellowstone Ave, starts at $65.

Hotels The remodeled *Pawnee Hotel* (☎ 307-587-2239), 1032 12th St, is friendly and has a nice garden, with singles/doubles for $32/36. Rooms with shared bathroom start at $28.

The historic *Irma Hotel* (☎ 307-587-4221, 800-745-4762), 1192 Sheridan Ave, a sculpted bison head above its entrance, has rooms in the original hotel ($95) and annex ($65). The *Holiday Inn* (☎ 307-587-5555, 800-527-5544), 1701 Sheridan Ave, has a good location.

Places to Eat
Patsy Ann's Pastry & Ladle (☎ 307-527-6297), 1243 Beck Ave, has bread, pastries and soups. *Peter's Cafe Bakery* (☎ 307-527-5040), at 1191 Sheridan Ave, serves espresso and specializes in buffalo burgers. *Paul & Beth's Cody Coffee Company & Eatery*, 1136 17th St, is another choice.

Colter's Hell

Only a roadside sign marks Colter's Hell, a thermal area along the south bank of the Shoshone River just west of Cody's Stampede Park. Trapper John Colter came upon this area when reconnoitering the upper reaches of the Yellowstone in 1807. The name Colter's Hell was, and often still is, mistakenly applied to present-day Yellowstone National Park. ■

Buffalo Bill Cody – a self-made icon
of the Old West.

The Ice Cream Parlor, 1320 Sheridan Ave, serves soup and sandwiches.

Jeremiah's *Proud Cut Saloon* (☎ 307-527-6905), 1227 Sheridan Ave, is big on beef, but the service can be sluggish. The *Silver Dollar Bar & Grill* (☎ 307-587-3554), at 1313 Sheridan Ave, deals mostly in burgers. *Pizza on the Run* (☎ 307-587-5550), 1108 13th St, has so-so fast food. *Granny's Fine Food* (☎ 307-587-4829), 1550 Sheridan Ave, is your basic family restaurant.

Hong Kong Chinese Restaurant (☎ 307-527-6420), 1201 17th St, serves Cantonese and Mandarin food. *La Comida* (☎ 307-587-9556), 1385 Sheridan Ave, has an appealing but expensive menu and pleasant outdoor seating. *Maxwell's Fine Food & Spirits* (☎ 307-527-7749), 937 Sheridan Ave, has an excellent selection of salads, reasonably priced sandwiches and a variety of dinners. In a class by itself is *Franca's Italian Dining* (☎ 307-587-5354), at 1421

Rumsey Ave, open Wednesday to Sunday for dinner only (with reservations). Fixed multicourse dinners range from $15 to $26; pasta entrees are $13.

Whole Foods Trading Company (☎ 307-587-3213), 1239 Rumsey Ave, sells natural and camping foods.

Entertainment
Angie's (☎ 307-587-3554), 1313 Sheridan Ave, has comedy and live music.

Shopping
A motherlode of Western wear and art galleries lines Sheridan Ave. The Harry Jackson Art Museum (☎ 307-587-5508), 602 Blackburn St, is open for tours ($3) 10 am to 7 pm weekdays.

Getting There & Away
Air SkyWest/The Delta Connection connects Cody with Salt Lake City, UT, with daily flights out of Yellowstone Regional Airport (☎ 307-587-5096), 3001 Duggleby Drive, 1 mile east of Cody at the junction of US 14/US 16/US 20 and Hwy 120.

Bus Powder River Coach USA (☎ 307-754-3914) buses stop at Daylight Donuts, 1452 Sheridan Ave at 14th St. Buses depart Cody at 10:45 am for Billings, MT, and at 1:30 pm for Casper.

Car Cody is at the junction of US 14/US 16/US 20 and Hwy 120. US 14/US 16/US 20 leads east to Greybull (47 miles) and west to Yellowstone National Park's East Entrance (51 miles). US 14 Alternate leads northeast to Lovell (47 miles) via Powell. Hwy 120 leads north to Hwy 296 and Yellowstone's Northeast Entrance (about 70 miles) and south to Thermopolis (85 miles).

Getting Around
Car Avis (☎ 307-587-5792) and Hertz (☎ 307-587-2914) are at the airport. Others include Budget (☎ 307-587-6066), 3227 Duggleby Drive; Rent-A-Wreck of Cody (☎ 307-527-5549, 800-452-0396), 2515 Greybull Hwy; and Thrifty (☎ 307-587-8855), 3001 Duggleby Drive.

Taxi Phidippides (☎ 307-527-6789) offers airport and taxi service from Cody throughout the Bighorn Basin, and to Yellowstone National Park and Billings; ask at the airport gift shop.

Try Yellowstone Expedition Services (☎ 307-587-5452) for airport shuttles, trips within Cody ($3) and tours.

AROUND CODY
Heart Mountain Relocation Center
During WWII, more than 110,000 Japanese Americans were incarcerated due to the unfounded, racist fear that they threatened national security. At the base of Heart Mountain (8123 feet), the prominent peak north of Cody, was the desolate Heart Mountain Relocation Center where 10,700 people were detained during 1942-45. Only a few buildings, which are on the National Register of Historic Places, remain of what was then Wyoming's third-largest city. The Heart Mountain Wyoming Foundation (☎ 307-754-3471), PO Box 547, Powell, WY 82435-0527, promotes truth and understanding about the internment. From US 14 Alternate 10 miles northeast of Cody, turn west onto Park County Rd R19 and continue half a mile to the memorial. Some buildings are visible from US 14 Alternate.

Worland Caves
The limestone Worland Caves at Spirit Mountain (also known as Cedar Mountain) are west of Cody just south of US 14/US 16/US 20; turn onto a dirt road about half a mile west of the South Fork Rd (Hwy 291) junction. The area is administered by the BLM, having lost its prior status as Shoshone National Monument. Contact the BLM Cody Resource Area office (see Cody above) for permits to explore the caves and maps.

South Fork Shoshone River
Hwy 291 heads southwest from US 14/US 16/US 20 just beyond the USFS office at the west end of Cody and follows South Fork Rd (Hwy 291) along the river. The waterless but free USFS *Deer Creek Camp-ground* is 47 miles southwest of Cody on USFS Rd 479. Trailheads lead west into the Teton Wilderness Area and southeastern Yellowstone National Park.

Buffalo Bill State Park
Buffalo Bill State Park (☎ 307-587-9227), 6 miles west of Cody along US 14/US 16/US 20, centers on the Buffalo Bill Reservoir and Dam. Having acquired water rights to irrigate nearly 266 sq miles in the Bighorn Basin, but lacking the capital to develop adequate storage, Buffalo Bill and his associates got the US Bureau of Reclamation to build the 328-foot Shoshone Dam. Begun in 1905, it was the world's highest dam at its completion in 1910. Renamed Buffalo Bill Dam by President Truman in 1946, it is on the National Register of Historic Places and is a national civil engineering landmark. The dam provides drinking water for Cody, hydroelectricity for the Western Area Power Administration and boating and fishing on the reservoir.

The Buffalo Bill Dam visitors center (☎ 307-527-6076) is open 8 am to 9 pm daily, May to September. The day-use fee is $3 ($2 for Wyoming residents). Along the banks of the reservoir are the shadeless and windy North Shore Bay (☎ 307-527-6274) and North Fork (☎ 307-527-6057) campgrounds ($4). Several nearby ranches offer horseback riding and pack and fishing trips.

Rafting
White-water rafting is popular on the **North Fork Shoshone River**. Elk, Bighorn sheep and moose are often seen from the river. The rafting season is mid-May to mid-September in the Red Rock and Lower canyons and Memorial Day to late July for the North Fork. Rafting Red Rock Canyon (6 miles) takes two hours and costs $18/15 adults/children; kayaking is possible. A three-hour, 13-mile trip along the geologically interesting Lower Canyon downstream of Red Rock Canyon costs $24/20. Half-day North Fork trips cost $45.

To book a rafting trip, contact Red Canyon River Trips (☎ 307-587-6988), River Runners (☎ 307-527-7238, 800-535-7238), 1491 Sheridan Ave, Cody, or Wyoming River Trips (☎ 307-587-6661, 800-586-6661), 1701 Sheridan Ave and 233 Yellowstone Ave, Cody; from October to March write Wyoming Rivertrips, PO Box 1541B, Cody, WY 82414.

Fishing
North Fork Anglers (☎ 307-527-7274), 1438 Sheridan Ave, Cody, sells gear and runs fly-fishing excursions into the nearby backcountry. Other local outfitters include Yellowstone Troutfitters (☎ 307-587-8240), 239A Yellowstone Ave, Cody, and Aune's Absaroka Angler (☎ 307-587-5105), 754 Yellowstone Ave.

Mountain Biking
Olde Faithful Bicycles (☎ 307-527-5110, 800-775-6023), 1362 Sheridan Ave, Cody, rents mountain bikes and offers guided mountain bike tours.

Rock Climbing
Two popular rock-climbing areas are in the granite Shoshone Canyon along US 14/US 16/US 20 about 3 miles west of Cody. The **Boulder Garden** has bouldering, top roping and bolted leads. Cross the old bridge to the true left (north) bank of the Shoshone River and follow the dirt road to the Boulder Garden. Farther west, **The Island** has clean rock and crack climbing. Park before the first of three tunnels by the power lines on US 14/US 16/US 20. Walk through the first two tunnels: the climbing area is along the highway before the third tunnel. Ask at Cody Rock Gym (☎ 307-587-5222), 1314 Sheridan Ave, or next door at Foote's Mountaineering, 1306 Sheridan Ave, for details.

POWELL
John Wesley Powell, the Colorado River explorer and visionary who headed the Bureau of Reclamation's Shoshone irrigation project, is the namesake of this agricultural community. The area grows beans, barley and sugar beets. Powell (population 5292; elevation 4365 feet) is not a destina-

tion itself, but has motels, free camping and a useful USFS office.

Orientation & Information
Coulter Ave (US 14 Alternate), the main east-west road, parallels the Garland Irrigation Canal. The business district is north of Coulter Ave. Absaroka St divides east-west street addresses, and 1st St divides north-south ones.

The Powell Valley Chamber of Commerce (☎ 307-754-3494, 800-325-4278), 111 S Day St at Coulter Ave, PO Box 814, Powell, WY 82435, is open 8:30 am to 4:30 pm weekdays. The USFS Shoshone National Forest Clarks Fork Ranger District (☎ 307-754-7207), 1002 Rd 11 (at the Park County Rd R11 turnoff), 1½ miles southwest of Powell off US 14 Alternate, is open 8 am to 4:30 pm weekdays. They administer land along the Beartooth Scenic Byway and Chief Joseph Scenic Hwy (see Absaroka Mountains later in this chapter).

ATMs are at Key Bank, 105 E 2nd St; First National Bank, at First and Clark Sts; and Blair's Market, 331 W Coulter Ave. The post office is at 270 N Bent St near Third St.

Homesteader Museum
The Homesteader Museum (☎ 307-754-9481), 133 S Clark St at 1st St, displays artifacts from Powell's pioneer era. It is open 1 to 5 pm Tuesday to Friday May to September, and 10 am to noon and 1 to 5 pm Friday and Saturday the rest of the year. Admission is free.

Places to Stay & Eat
Proximity to Cody inflates Powell's rates. The *Homesteader Park*, off US 14 Alternate at the east end of town, near Park County Rd R8, allows free camping (48-hour maximum). The *Park County Fairgrounds* (☎ 307-754-5421), 549 E 6th St, offers RV sites starting at $10 from April to September.

Singles/doubles cost $45/55 at the *Best Choice Motel* (☎ 307-754-2243, 800-308-8447), 337 E Second St at Day St. *The Lamplighter Inn* (☎ 307-754-2226), 234 E

First St at Clark St, costs slightly more. Motels on Second St between Gilbert and Ingalls Sts are *Park Motel* (☎ 307-754-2233), at 737 E 2nd St ($45/55); *Super 8 Motel* (☎ 307-754-7231), 845 E Coulter Ave ($50/60); and *Best Western King's Inn* (☎ 307-754-5117), 777 E 2nd St ($63/71).

Burgers and fast food are the norm in these parts. The limited choices include *Hansel & Gretel's* (☎ 307-754-2191), 13 S Bent St, for lunches; *Pizza on the Run* (☎ 307-754-5720), 215 E 1st St; and the *Best Western King's Inn* coffee shop and dining room.

Getting There & Away
Bus Powder River Coach USA (☎ 307-754-3914) stops at Accents & Accessories, a wooden storefront at 127 N Bent St near Second St. Buses go to Cody (12:40 and 3:05 pm), Billings, MT (11:30 am), and Cheyenne via Casper (1:55 pm).

Car Powell is along US 14 Alternate 24 miles northeast of Cody and 26 miles west of Lovell.

LOVELL
Lovell (population 2131; elevation 3814 feet), or the 'Rose City' as it calls itself, is the gateway to the Bighorn Canyon National Recreation Area at the western base of the Bighorn Mountains. This Mormon agricultural settlement with a significant Hispanic population produces sugar beets and is home to several major mining concerns.

Orientation & Information
Lovell has numbered east-west streets and named north-south avenues. East-west Main St (US 14 Alternate/US 310/Hwy 789) replaces 4th St. The Chamber of Commerce & Information Center (☎ 307-548-7552), 287 E Main St, PO Box 295, Lovell, WY 82431, is open 8:30 am to 12:15 pm and 1 to 5 pm daily. At the east end of town, the USFS Bighorn National Forest Medicine Wheel Ranger District (☎ 307-548-6541), 604 E Main St, is open 8 am to noon and 1 to 5 pm weekdays. Nearby is the

Bighorn Canyon National Recreation Area visitors center (see below).

An ATM is at First National Bank of Powell, 284 E Main St. The post office is at 167 E 3rd St. The North Big Horn Hospital (☎ 307-548-2771), 1115 Lane 12, is at the south end of town. Mustang Laundry is at 340 Montana Ave between 3rd and Main Sts.

Places to Stay
Camping and showers are free at shady *Lovell Camper Park* (72-hour maximum), on Quebec Ave between 1st and 2nd Sts. The shadeless but pleasant *Camp Big Horn RV Park* (☎ 307-548-2725), 595 E Main St, is behind the Super 8 Motel; pay for tent sites ($7) and sites with full hookups ($12) at the motel's front desk.

The *Western Motel* (☎ 307-548-6613), 180 W Main St between Jersey and Kansas Aves, has rooms for $32, while the dreary *Uptown Motel* (☎ 307-548-2741), at 43 E Main St, charges $25/30 for singles/doubles. The *Cattlemen Motel* (☎ 307-548-2296), at 470 Montana Ave, and the *Horseshoe Bend Motel* (☎ 307-548-2221), 375 E Main St, both cost around $34/37. The *Super 8 Motel* (☎ 307-548-2725), 595 E Main St, costs $40/44.

Places to Eat
The *Rose Bowl Cafe* (☎ 307-548-7121), 483 Shoshone Ave at Park Ave, is popular for breakfast. *Pizza on the Run* (☎ 307-548-2206), at Park and Shoshone Aves, has reasonable takeout; *Hot Stuff Pizza* (☎ 307-548-2888), 127 E 3rd St near Montana Ave, is an alternative. *The Big Horn Restaurant* (☎ 307-548-6811), 605 E Main St, is large but mediocre.

Getting There & Away
Bus Powder River Coach USA (☎ 307-548-7231) stops at Rexall Drug, 164 E Main St. Buses depart daily for Greybull-Thermopolis-Casper (2:50 pm) and for Billings, MT (11:50 am).

Car Lovell is on US 14 Alternate and US 310/Hwy 789 26 miles east of Powell, 50 miles northeast of Cody, and 100 miles west of Sheridan. US 310/Hwy 789 leads south to Greybull (32 miles); US 310 goes north to Billings (90 miles). US 14 Alternate, the **Medicine Wheel Passage**, heads east to Burgess Junction.

BIGHORN CANYON NATIONAL RECREATION AREA

The Bighorn River carved a canyon 2500 feet deep and 50 miles long through the desert, and Montana's Yellowtail Dam created Bighorn Lake, the centerpiece of this area. The Bighorn Canyon NRA encompasses the river, lake and surrounding land. This narrow corridor straddles the Wyoming-Montana state line northeast of Lovell, between the Pryor Mountains to the west and the Bighorn Mountains to the east. The NRA covers 188 sq miles, although 88 sq miles are to revert to the adjacent Crow Indian Reservation in Montana.

Bighorn Canyon environments range from desert shrubland inhabited by feral horses, snakes and rodents to juniper woodlands with large mammals like coyotes, deer and bighorn sheep. Canyonside pine and fir forests house mountain lion, bear, elk and mule deer, while short-grass prairie once fed grazing bison. The area hosts large numbers of raptors.

At the south end of the NRA, 6 miles east of Lovell, the **Yellowtail Wildlife Habitat Management Area** is a wetlands managed jointly by the NPS and the Wyoming Game and Fish Department. Besides cottonwood riparian and permanent and seasonal pool environments, it also contains cultivated lands that support wildlife.

History

Inhabited more than 10,000 years ago, Bighorn Canyon was controlled by the Crow when trappers first saw it in the early 19th century. In 1864, the US Army built Fort CF Smith on the east side of the canyon to protect miners traveling on the Bozeman Trail, but pulled out in 1868 following the Fort Laramie Treaty. Still, whites continued to chip away at Indian territory, and

open-range cattle ranching became a way of life, complemented by early dude ranches.

Water management in the area began with the Crow, who had 54 sq miles under irrigation by 1904, but really got going in 1966 with the completion of the 525-foot Yellowtail Dam near Fort Smith, MT. This was the centerpiece of the Bureau of Reclamation/US Army Corps of Engineers scheme, combining flood control, navigation, hydroelectricity and irrigation, that created Bighorn Lake. In recent years, however, the water flow into the reservoir has fallen dramatically because of dry conditions. Many other factors may be involved, but if this continues, the recreational attributes of the NRA will, quite literally, evaporate.

Orientation

Bighorn Canyon NRA is divided into the South and North districts. The South District is accessible only from Wyoming, the North District from Hardin, MT. (See the Montana Plains chapter in the Montana section for information on the North District.) Hwy 37, the only road through the South District, is 3 miles east of Lovell off US 14 Alternate. Six miles from the entrance is a junction to Horseshoe Bend,

The mule deer is also called the blacktail deer.

which has a marina and campground. Hwy 37 enters Montana about 4 miles beyond the junction and continues to Barry's Landing, another reservoir access point, where it dead-ends.

Information
The Bighorn Canyon NRA visitors center (☎ 307-548-2251), 20 E US 14 Alternate, is at the east end of Lovell just northeast of the US 310/Hwy 789 junction. It features interesting displays on the area's ecology, geology, archaeology and Native Americans, and its solar design provides 70% of its heat even during harsh winters. Open 8:15 am to 5 pm daily, it also sells books and maps.

The NPS ranger stations at Layout Creek and Horseshoe Bend also offer information. The NPS also distributes the 'Canyon Echoes' newsletter, published annually by the Bighorn Canyon Natural History Association, PO Box 396, Lovell, WY 82431. Free permits, required for overnight backcountry trips, are available from the visitors center or ranger stations. The day-use fee is $5, but camping is free.

Pryor Mountain Wild Horse Range
Feral mustangs, descendants of the original Spanish breeds brought to Mexico in the 16th century, roam the BLM-managed 38,013-acre Pryor Mountain Wild Horse Range, established in 1968. The range overlaps the NRA from Horseshoe Bend north to Layout Creek. Sightings are common along the west side of Hwy 37 between Devil Canyon Overlook and Mustang Flat. The animals have multiplied so prolifically that the BLM runs a wild horse and burro adoption program offering selected animals to the public.

Devil Canyon Overlook
About 3 miles north of the Wyoming-Montana state line, reached by a short, paved lateral off the main highway, the Devil Canyon Overlook peeks 1000 feet into Bighorn Canyon for impressive views of its Paleozoic sediments and sightings of the resident raptors.

Hillsboro
The homestead of GW Barry was once a post office and dude ranch; several buildings remain standing. It is 1 mile east of Hwy 37, about 2 miles north of the Layout Creek Ranger Station and accessible by foot only.

Lockhart Ranch
Where Hwy 37 descends to Barry's Landing, a dirt road (passable for cars but not for RVs) heads about 2½ miles north toward journalist Caroline Lockhart's L Slash Heart Ranch, a 7050-acre retreat she acquired in 1926 for $2250. After her death in 1962 at the age of 91, some of her ashes were scattered around the ranch.

Visiting the ranch requires a short hike down the slope from the ranch gate, which prevents vehicles from entering the grounds. The main house, the sod-roofed storage cabins, a storage shed cooled by a subterranean spring, the stables and garage and a chicken coop remain. Though the exteriors are in good repair, the interiors are deteriorating. A steel-girder bridge crosses the creek, and a picnic table sits in the shade near the main house. North of the Lockhart Ranch is the boundary of the Crow Indian Reservation.

Boating
The Horseshoe Bend Marina (☎ 307-548-7230, 307-548-7858) is open 8 am to 10 pm daily, Memorial to Labor Day, but weekend boat tours may start in mid-April. Boat rentals (pedal, fishing and pontoon) range from $3/hour to $36/hour. One-hour reservoir boat tours start at $12/9 for adults/children. Boat charters to Devil Canyon ($40 minimum) and Barry's Landing ($72 minimum) also depart from Horseshoe Bend Marina. Late-season boat tours may depart from Barry's Landing when the reservoir's water levels are low.

Fishing
The Montana and Wyoming Game and Fish departments stock Bighorn Lake with brown and lake trout, as well as ling and perch, but the most popular game fish is

walleye. The appropriate state fishing license is obligatory.

Caving

Bighorn Caverns, on the east side of the NRA, is a favorite destination for spelunkers, but access is by permit only (see Information above). Parties must be three to six persons and at least one person must have previously done the trip. No more than two groups may visit the caverns at once. Camping is not permitted. Spelunkers in need of experienced partners should contact Jim Thomas (☎ 307-548-2771, 307-548-6372) at Lovell's North Bighorn Country Hospital. The John Blue Canyon Rd (BLM Rd 1122) to Bighorn Caverns is a 4WD route. For a map of the caverns, contact Bighorn Press (☎ 206-546-8025), 18002 1st Ave N, Seattle, WA 98177.

Places to Stay & Eat

Campgrounds are at the barren *Horseshoe Bend* and the shadier *Barry's Landing*. A boat-in or hike-in campground at *Medicine Creek*, 1½ miles north of Barry's Landing, lacks drinking water. The *Horseshoe Bend Marina* has a small cafe and grocery store.

CROOKED CREEK NATIONAL NATURAL LANDMARK

Near the Bighorn Canyon NRA entrance is the Crooked Creek Natural Area, where fossils from the Cretaceous Period, 150 million years ago, were found. This is one of only two North American sites with skeletons of carnivorous land vertebrates. From Hwy 37, turn west onto Bighorn Country Rd 17 and then north on Crooked Creek Rd to the site.

GREYBULL

Greybull (population 1790) is primarily a crossroads. US 16/US 20 runs north-south through town as 6th St. US 14 heads east as Greybull Ave toward Shell Canyon and the Bighorn Mountains. The Greybull Area Chamber of Commerce (☎ 307-765-2100), 333 Greybull Ave, is open 10:30 to 11:30 am and 3 to 4 pm Monday to Saturday. The adjacent **Greybull Museum**

(☎ 307-765-2444), 325 Greybull Ave, has a unique collection of ammonites and dinosaur fossils worth a look. It is open 10 am to 8 pm weekdays and 10 am to 6 pm Saturday June to September; hours vary the rest of the year. Admission is free. The USFS Bighorn National Forest Paintrock Ranger District (☎ 307-765-4435) is at 1220 N 8th St.

Greybull KOA Kampground (☎ 307-765-2555, 800-562-7508), at 2nd St and 3rd Ave N, along the Bighorn River, has laundry, showers and a pool. Tent sites cost $17; sites with full hookups are $22. Singles/doubles cost $30/40 at the *Yellowstone Motel* (☎ 307-765-4456), 247 Greybull Ave, and $32/36 at the *K-Bar Motel* (☎ 307-765-4426, 800-690-4426), 300 Greybull Ave.

The Powder River Coach USA bus depot is in front of the chamber of commerce. Daily buses depart for Billings, MT, via Lovell at 11:05 am, and leave for Worland-Thermopolis-Shoshoni-Casper-Douglas-Cheyenne at 3:35 pm. Greybull is on US 14 32 miles south of Lovell, 37 miles north of Worland, 52 miles east of Cody and 97 miles west of Sheridan.

WORLAND

Worland (population 5740), an oil-rich agricultural area along the Bighorn River, is a major crossroads with a few basic motels and restaurants. US 16/US 20 enters from the north on 10th St; at Big Horn Ave, US 16 turns east onto Bighorn Ave toward Tensleep Canyon and the Bighorn Mountains, while US 20 turns west. The Worland Chamber of Commerce (☎ 307-347-3226) is located at 120 N 10th St, half a block north of Big Horn Ave. The USFS Bighorn National Forest Tensleep Ranger District (☎ 307-347-8291) is at 2009 Big Horn Ave. The BLM Worland District office (☎ 307-347-9871) and Bighorn Basin Resource Area (☎ 307-347-5100) are both at 101 S 23rd St.

Getting There & Away

Air Worland is served by United Express, which flies daily to Denver, CO, out of the

Worland Municipal Airport, south of town via 15th St.

Bus Powder River Coach USA (☎ 307-347-8175) departs for Billings, MT, via Greybull and Lovell at 10:25 am and for Thermopolis-Shoshoni-Casper-Douglas at 4:20 pm.

Car Worland is on US 20/Hwy 789 at the junction of US 16 33 miles north of Thermopolis, 37 miles south of Greybull, and 95 miles west of Buffalo.

THERMOPOLIS
The resort town of Thermopolis (population 3247; elevation 4326 feet) has the world's largest mineral hot springs. Dr Julius Schuelke first coined the name in the late 1890s, combining the Latin *thermae* (hot springs) with the Greek *polis* (city). The town is north of the Owl Creek Mountains and straddles the Bighorn River, which emerges from the Wind River Canyon south of town.

History
The Shoshone and Arapaho ceded the hot springs and their surroundings to the US government in 1896, severing it from the northeast corner of the Wind River Indian Reservation in exchange for about $60,000 in cattle and food supplies. Shoshone Chief Washakie stipulated that the healing waters remain free of charge, and in 1899 the state legislature honored the chief's provision by establishing Hot Springs State Park (see below). In its early years, the remote hot springs area was frequented by outlaws from the Hole-in-the-Wall Gang, but it was the 1913 arrival of the CB&Q Railroad from Billings that put Thermopolis on the map. Thanks to medical institutions like the Gottsche Rehabilitation Center, and the healing waters, tourism has steadily flourished.

Washakie's grant of the *Bah Guewana* (smoking waters) is celebrated in Thermopolis' **Gift of the Waters Pageant**, which was begun in 1925 and is held annually the first weekend in August. A substantial number of Native Americans participate in the event.

Orientation
The main streets are north-south 6th St (US 20) and east-west Broadway (Hwy 120) on the west bank of the river. Hot Springs State Park is along the east bank, reached by bridges on Broadway and Park St.

Information
The Thermopolis Hot Springs Chamber of Commerce (☎ 307-864-3192, 800-786-6772; hotspot@wyoming.com) is at 700 Broadway. ATMs are at Don's IGA, 225 S 4th St, and 1st State Bank, 435 Arapahoe St and 5th St at Warren St. The post office is at 440 Arapahoe St. Business with Pleasure (☎ 307-864-2385), 535 Broadway, provides fax services. The Hot Springs County Memorial Hospital (☎ 307-864-3121) is at 150 E Arapahoe St. For laundry, you can go to either the Scrub Board Laundromat (☎ 307-864-2101), 210 4th St, or the Wishy-Washy Washateria (☎ 307-864-5332), 630 Shoshoni St.

Hot Springs Historical Museum & Cultural Center
The Hot Springs Historical Museum & Cultural Center (☎ 307-864-5183), 700 Broadway, has a spacious museum and a large open-air section on local farm economy and Thermopolis' role as a transportation hub, with a CB&Q caboose. Inside the museum is the original cherrywood bar from the Hole in the Wall Saloon, once frequented by Butch Cassidy and the Sundance Kid. Open 8 am to 5 pm, Monday to Saturday, admission is $2/1.50/1 for adults/seniors/children (6-17) and $5 for families.

Hot Springs State Park
Along the east bank of the Bighorn River, Hot Springs State Park is Wyoming's first and most popular state park. The 3000 gallons of water that surge from **Big Horn Spring** every minute average 127°F, making it one of the world's largest mineral springs. Visitors can relax for free in the comfortable 104°F waters of the nearby

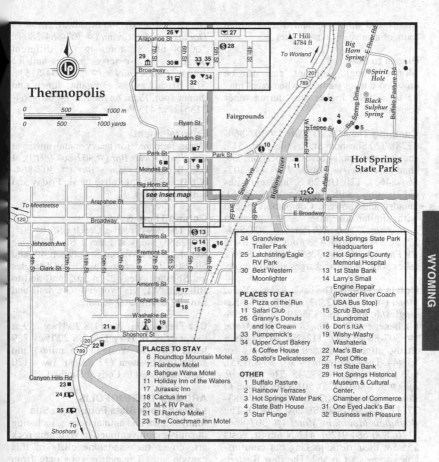

Thermopolis

0   500   1000 m
0   500   1000 yards

Fairgrounds

Hot Springs
State Park

see inset map

To Meeteetse

To Shoshoni

PLACES TO STAY
6 Roundtop Mountain Motel
7 Rainbow Motel
9 Bahgue Wana Motel
11 Holiday Inn of the Waters
17 Jurassic Inn
18 Cactus Inn
20 M-K RV Park
21 El Rancho Motel
23 The Coachman Inn Motel

24 Grandview
Trailer Park
25 Latchstring/Eagle
RV Park
30 Best Western
Moonlighter

PLACES TO EAT
8 Pizza on the Run
11 Safari Club
26 Granny's Donuts
and Ice Cream
33 Pumpernick's
34 Upper Crust Bakery
& Coffee House
35 Spatol's Delicatessen

OTHER
1 Buffalo Pasture
2 Rainbow Terraces
3 Hot Springs Water Park
4 State Bath House
5 Star Plunge

10 Hot Springs State Park
Headquarters
12 Hot Springs County
Memorial Hospital
13 1st State Bank
14 Larry's Small
Engine Repair
(Powder River Coach
USA Bus Stop)
15 Scrub Board
Laundromat
16 Don's IGA
19 Wishy-Washy
Washateria
22 Mac's Bar
27 Post Office
28 1st State Bank
29 Hot Springs Historical
Museum & Cultural
Center,
Chamber of Commerce
31 One Eyed Jack's Bar
32 Business with Pleasure

State Bath House (☎ 307-876-3765);
towels and bathing suits are available for
a nominal rental fee. It is open 8 am to
5:30 pm, Monday to Saturday, and from
noon to 5:30 pm Sunday.

Other sights are the **Rainbow Terraces**,
formed by lime and gypsum secreted from
the mineral waters and encircled by a
boardwalk; the nearby **Swinging Bridge**
over the Bighorn River; the gurgling **Black
Sulphur Spring**; and the 1000-acre **Buffalo Pasture**, where about a dozen bison
roam. The park's expansive lawns and its
massive shade trees make for a delightful

picnic spot. Within the park, the private
Hot Springs Water Park (☎ 307-864-9250)
has a pool, spa and water slide. The private
Star Plunge (☎ 307-864-3771) also has
water slides.

The park headquarters (☎ 307-864-
2176), located at 220 Park St, are open
7:30 am to 4 pm weekdays. The park is
open 6 am to 10 pm daily. Camping is not
permitted.

Wyoming Dinosaur Center
The Wyoming Dinosaur Center (☎ 307-
864-2997, 800-455-3466) has a museum of

fossils and dinosaurs and offers guided tours of nearby excavation sites.

Places to Stay

Motels, though abundant, can still be crowded during summer, when rates may be up to 30% higher than during other seasons.

Camping The *M-K RV Park* (☎ 307-864-2778), 720 Shoshoni St, has sites from $13, showers and a noisy roadside location. The shady *Grandview Trailer Park* (☎ 307-864-3463), 120 US 20 S, has tent sites ($13), sites with full hookups ($16), laundry and showers. Comparably priced with similar amenities is the pleasant *Latchstring/Eagle RV Park* (☎ 307-864-5262), 204 US 20 S. The *Fountain of Youth RV Park* (☎ 307-864-3265), 250 N US 20 2 miles north of town, charges slightly more.

Hotels & Motels The basic *Bahgue Wana Motel* (☎ 307-864-2303), 401 Park St, has singles/doubles for $35/40; some have kitchenettes. *The Coachman Inn Motel* (☎ 307-864-3141), 112 US 20 S, has a shady, attractive garden and rooms for $33/44. The *Cactus Inn* (☎ 307-864-3155), 605 S 6th St, costs $32/45. The *Jurassic Inn* (☎ 307-864-2325), 501 S 6th St, and *El Rancho Motel* (☎ 307-864-2341, 800-283-2777), 924 Shoshoni St, cost $40/50. The *Roundtop Mountain Motel* (☎ 307-864-3126, 800-584-9126), 412 N 6th St, costs $55/58; their rustic-looking but comfortable cabins start at $62. The *Best Western Moonlighter* (☎ 307-864-2321), 600 Broadway, starts at $58. The *Holiday Inn of the Waters* (☎ 307-864-3131), 115 E Park St, starts at $95 and prominently displays the owner's photographs and big game trophies from around the world in its *Safari Club* restaurant.

Places to Eat

The Upper Crust Bakery & Coffee House (☎ 307-864-3665), 517 Broadway, serves espresso, pasta lunches and homemade desserts. For moderately priced hot and cold sandwiches, try *Spatol's Delicatessen*

(☎ 307-864-3960), 500 Broadway. *Granny's Donuts and Ice Cream* (☎ 307-864-2809), 200 N 6th St, touts its '13 different burgers' and also serves pastries and ice cream. *Pumpernick's* (☎ 307-864-5151), 512 Broadway, is a popular lunch and dinner spot. *Pizza on the Run* (☎ 307-864-3135) is at 415 Park St.

Entertainment

Come prepared for heavy metal music at *One Eyed Jack's Bar* (☎ 307-864-9919), at 633 Broadway. *Mac's Bar* (☎ 307-864-3763), US 20 S, has live music Friday and Saturday nights.

Getting There & Away

Bus The Powder River Coach USA (☎ 307-864-2858) stops at Larry's Small Engine Repair, at 421 Warren St between 4th and 5th Sts. Buses go to Casper and Douglas via Shoshoni (leaving at 5:05 pm) and to Billings, MT, via Worland, Greybull and Lovell (leaving at 9:40 am).

Car Thermopolis is on US 20/Hwy 789 at the junction of Hwy 120. US 20/Hwy 789 leads north to Worland (35 miles) and south to Shoshoni (32 miles). Hwy 120 leads northwest to Cody (85 miles).

AROUND THERMOPOLIS
Legend Rock State Petroglyph Site

Many human and animal figures, including the only rabbit yet found in Wyoming rock art, cover the sandstone cliffs in this canyon site. The petroglyphs date from 2000 years to just 100 years ago. Arrange site visitation and pick up the gate key at the Hot Springs State Park headquarters (see Thermopolis earlier in this chapter), or at the State Bath House when the state park is closed. The turnoff to the site is on Hwy 120 21 miles northwest of Thermopolis, 31 miles southeast of Meeteetse; look for the sign to Hamilton Dome at Upper Cottonwood Creek Rd and head west 5¼ miles. Then go 2¼ miles on the unpaved BLM Rd 1305, just past the second cattle guard, to the site turnoff at BLM Rd 2861.

The endangered black-footed ferret makes its home in Meeteetse and likes to snack on prairie dogs.

Wind River Canyon

See Wind River Canyon in the Wind River Country chapter for full details.

MEETEETSE

Facing the plains from the eastern escarpment of the Carter Mountains, Meeteetse (population 386; elevation 6000 feet) is an appealing village along the Greybull River. Remarkably for its size, it has three excellent museums and the surrounding countryside is home to the black-footed ferret, one of the world's most endangered mammals. Built in 1899, the Meeteetse Mercantile, 1946 State St, is the town's most conspicuous landmark and still serves as the general store.

Information

Drop by the Meeteetse Tourist Information (☎ 307-868-2423), 1033 Park Ave, PO Box 509, Meeteetse, WY 82433, or the kiosk at Riverside Park, near the bridge on the east bank of the river. The USFS Shoshone National Forest Meeteetse Ranger Station (☎ 307-868-2536) is at 2044 State St; enter from Mondell Ave. The post office is at 1022 Park Ave. The Key Bank is next door

at 1026 Park Ave and there is laundry on Park Ave at Franklin St.

Things to See & Do

Of Meeteetse's three museums, the most noteworthy is the **Charles J Belden Museum**, at State St (Hwy 120) and Park Ave (Hwy 290), focusing on B&W prints by one of the West's best photographers. Born in 1887 in San Francisco and educated at MIT, Belden married into a local ranching family and practiced his craft throughout the region with large-format cameras (many of his photographs of farm and ranch life adorn the pages of the classic WPA guide to Wyoming). The museum is open 9 am to 5 pm daily, May to September.

The **Meeteetse Hall Museum** (☎ 307-868-2423), 942 Mondell Ave, pays homage to cowboy culture. It is open 10 am to 5 pm Monday to Saturday and 1 to 4 pm Sunday during summer. The **Meeteetse Museum & Archives**, 1033 Park Ave, in the Hogg, Cheeseman & McDonald's Bank, is open 8:30 am to 4 pm Monday to Saturday; note the interesting diagonal entryway of this handsome brick building.

Places to Stay & Eat
The *Vision Quest Motel* (☎ 307-868-2512), 2207 State St, and the *Oasis Motel* (☎ 307-868-2551), 1702 State St, are budget motels starting at $25; the latter also has a few campsites. The spacious *Broken Spoke Cafe* (☎ 307-868-2362), 1943 State St, serves breakfasts (omelets, biscuits and gravy), lunches (burgers) and dinners (steak). Its biggest attraction may be its nickel cup of coffee. Nearby are *Outlaw Pizza* (☎ 307-868-2585), 1936 State St, and *Elk Horn Bar* (☎ 307-868-9245), 1916 State St.

Getting There & Away
Meeteetse is on Hwy 120 31 miles southeast of Cody and 52 miles northwest of Thermopolis.

Bighorn Mountains

The Bighorn Mountains, marking the eastern extent of the Bighorn Basin, are crossed by three scenic east-west roads: US 14 is the **Bighorn Scenic Byway** from Greybull to Ranchester, north of Sheridan, via Granite Pass (8950 feet); US 14 Alternate is the **Medicine Wheel Passage** between Lovell and Burgess Junction via Baldy Pass (9430 feet); and US 16 is the **Cloud Peak Skyway** between Worland and Buffalo via Powder River Pass (9666 feet). Burgess Junction is the junction of US 14 and US 14 Alternate, midway between Lovell and Ranchester. The Burgess Junction visitors center has information, an interpretive trail and exhibits and sells books and maps. A few private lodges near Burgess Junction offer basic accommodation, campsites and services (also see Bighorn Mountains in the Prairie Wyoming chapter).

MEDICINE WHEEL NATIONAL HISTORIC LANDMARK
At nearly 10,000 feet, on the western slope of Medicine Mountain, is the Medicine Wheel, a circular arrangement of irregularly shaped flat stones with 28 spokes radiating from its center. The Medicine Wheel is profoundly sacred to the Northern Cheyenne, Crow, Shoshone, Sioux and other Native American tribes that frequent the site and revere the Bighorn Mountains. Among the famous Native Americans who have worshipped here are Washakie of the Shoshone, Red Plume of the Crow and perhaps Chief Joseph of the Nez Percé. It was constructed sometime between 1200 AD and 1700 AD, but who made it and what it means are matters of some speculation. It may represent a likeness of the Sun Dance Lodge of Crow legend. The sunrise of the summer solstice aligns with the Medicine Wheel and Duncum Mountain to the east, suggesting astronomical significance.

Circle the Medicine Wheel clockwise, staying on the marked path. Respect it as you would any place of worship, and do not touch the religious offerings and flags left at the site. (A fence actually surrounds the Medicine Wheel, to protect it from vandals.) USFS rangers are at the parking lot and the site 7 am to 7 pm daily, June to October. The site is closed for a few days around the summer solstice, and may be closed for brief periods of time without notice for Native American ceremonies. The north-facing trail can be snow-covered into June, and weather is changeable and often cold and windy.

From Lovell follow US 14 Alternate about 27 miles east, or from Burgess Junction follow US 14 Alternate west about 30 miles to the USFS Hwy 12 turnoff. Drive with caution as US 14 Alternate between Big Horn Lake and Baldy Pass is a 10% grade over 10 miles with 3600 feet elevation change. (RVs and vehicles with trailers are not recommended.) Follow the unpaved USFS Hwy 12 north about 1½ miles to the parking lot. All visitors must then walk on the road the last 1½ miles to the site.

Places to Stay
Camp near the Medicine Wheel at any of the three campgrounds along US 14 Alternate east of Big Horn Lake and west of Baldy Pass. The BLM *Five Spring Falls*

Campground ($6) is on the north side of
US 14 Alternate at the base of the 10%
grade, about 12 miles (by road) from the
site. It is possible to hike from this campground to the Medicine Wheel. Follow the
steep trail from the campground to USFS
Hwy 12 west of Medicine Mountain. One
mile east of the USFS Hwy 12 turn-off is
the USFS *Porcupine Campground*, north
of US 14 Alternate. USFS *Bald Mountain
Campground* is an eighth of a mile farther
east, south of US 14 Alternate. Both are
scenic campgrounds set in pine forest.

SHELL CANYON

US 14 rises from the Bighorn Basin town
of Greybull into Shell Canyon, where colorful layers of sedimentary rock and
dinosaur fossils are found. Several guest
ranches are east of Shell (population 50).
The *Shell Campground* is at the west end
of town.

The **Shell Falls Interpretive Site**, on
US 14 east of Shell, has an information
center, bookstore, short trails and overlooks of the 120-foot **Shell Falls**, which
pours 3600 gallons of water per second
over Precambrian granite and Domolite
erratics. The canyon and falls take their
name from some of the earliest fossils of
hard-shelled creatures found in the remaining sandstones and limestones that capped
most of the Bighorn Mountains hundreds
of millions of years ago. Copman's Tomb
is the distinctive peak rising to the north
above Shell and Cedar canyons.

East of upper Shell Canyon below
Granite Pass is Antelope Butte (☎ 307-
655-9530, fax 307-655-9529), a popular
downhill skiing area with a base elevation
of 8200 feet, 18 runs and a maximum
1000-foot vertical drop. Full-day lift
tickets cost $20/18/12 for adults/seniors/
children (under 16); half-day tickets cost
$16/14/10. Several trailheads lead into the
Bighorns. Nearby USFS campgrounds
include *Paintrock Rd*, east of US 14.

US 14 continues across Granite Pass to
Burgess Junction; from there you can drive
east to Ranchester or loop back to Lovell in
the Bighorn Basin via US 14 Alternate.

RED GULCH & ALKALI NATIONAL BACK COUNTRY BYWAY

This 32-mile unpaved road is usually passable May to mid-October and is suitable
for 2WD vehicles with high clearance, but
passage is not advised in wet conditions.
The byway traverses Potato Ridge, connecting US 14 a few miles west of Shell to
Hwy 31 just north of Hyattville. The drive
takes two to three hours. This is a scenic
alternative route between Shell Canyon
and Hyattville (see below).

HYATTVILLE & AROUND

Few travelers make their way to the quiet
and remote community of Hyattville (population 100; elevation 4685 feet) at the
western foothills of the Bighorn Mountains. The *Paintrock Inn* offers family
dining, but bringing your own food, supplies and camping gear is recommended.

Medicine Lodge State Archaeological Site

Medicine Lodge is a major archaeological
area containing petroglyphs and pictographs on red sandstone cliffs, and a rich
habitation site occupied for more than
10,000 years. The area is a transition zone,
or ecotone, between the plains and the
mountains, which provided prehistoric
peoples with access to a variety of food
resources.

Medicine Lodge is 6 miles northeast of
Hyattville. Before town, turn north and go
one mile on the paved Alkali Rd. Then turn
east onto Cold Springs Rd and continue
3 miles. A sign at the junction of Bighorn
County Rd 52 directs you onto an unpaved
road which leads 2 miles to the site.

Jointly administered by the Wyoming
State Park & Historic Sites (☎ 307-469-
2234), BLM and Wyoming Game and Fish
Department, the site has an interesting visitors center, a free campground (maximum
14 days) and a small shop. Fishing is
pleasant in the adjacent stream.

Paintrock Canyon

This narrow, red-shale canyon east of
Hyattville is accessible by foot. Take Hwy

31 to its end; a trail follows Paint Rock Creek up the canyon and into the Cloud Peak Wilderness Area.

Getting There & Away
Hyattville is on Hwy 31, which can be reached from Worland to the south or Greybull to the north by turning east off US 16/US 20 at Manderson. From US 16 in Tensleep there are two alternative routes to Hyattville: Tensleep Rd/Hyattville Rd (Washakie County Rd 54) or Lower Nowood Rd (Washakie County Rd 47).

TENSLEEP CANYON
Steep red and white limestone cliffs carved by glaciers and the creek enclose this dramatic canyon on US 16 east of Worland and west of the Powder River Pass.

Absaroka Mountains

At the western extent of the Bighorn Basin are the Absaroka Mountains, an eroded volcanic range named by the Crow Indians. The enormous Shoshone National Forest, part of the Yellowstone Timberland Reserve, the country's first, established by President Benjamin Harrison in 1891, covers the mountains, and the Shoshone River cuts a dramatic course through them along the Wapiti Valley, providing access to Yellowstone National Park's East Entrance.

For information on access to the Absarokas from Montana, see the Yellowstone Country chapter in the Montana section.

WAPITI VALLEY
The North Fork (Shoshone River) Scenic Byway (US 14/US 16/US 20) leads west from Cody to the East Entrance of Yellowstone National Park, passing through the 53-mile long Wapiti Valley. The valley's name comes from the Algonquin Indian word *wapiti*, which means 'pale white' and was used to differentiate the lighter-colored elk from darker-colored moose. Hemmed in by the rugged Absaroka Mountains and the Shoshone National

Forest, the North Fork wends its way through a picturesque canyon. The North Absaroka Wilderness Area to the north and the Washakie Wilderness Area to the south are home to bear, deer, elk, moose, bighorn sheep and a few buffalo. An extensive network of trails leads through the wilderness areas along (rainbow and cutthroat) trout streams, past hidden lakes and into Yellowstone National Park.

The valley's scenery and dramatic rock formations make the **Shoshone Canyon** much more than just a beautiful place to picnic en route to or from Yellowstone National Park. One of Wapiti Valley's most scenic areas is **Holy City**, a cluster of eerie volcanic landforms north of the Shoshone River, just west of the Wapiti Wayside Exhibit.

Information
The Wapiti Valley Information Center, 29 miles west of Cody next to the Wapiti Wayside Exhibit, offers detailed information on the valley's frequent grizzly bear sightings. It's open 8 am to 8 pm weekdays, and 8:30 am to noon and 12:30 to 5 pm weekends, Memorial to Labor Day. Built in 1903, the adjacent Wapiti Ranger Station is the nation's oldest existing ranger station and a national historic landmark, with tours 9 am to 4 pm weekdays. Lodges East of Yellowstone Valley, PO Box 21, Wapiti, WY 82450, provides information on family-owned, member dude ranches and lodges in the Wapiti Valley.

Hiking & Horseback Riding
Washakie Wilderness Area Two main trailheads with corrals are near the USFS Elk Fork and Eagle Creek campgrounds. The **Elk Fork Trail** follows the Elk Fork and then Rampart Creek up steadily to Overlook Mountain (11,869 feet).

At the USFS Blackwater Pond Picnic Area, USFS Rd 435 heads south and crosses the Shoshone River over a bridge. It climbs a short distance past the Blackwater Creek Ranch, following Blackwater Creek, to a trailhead. After about 1 mile, the trail divides. The **Memorial Trail** climbs south and east to Clayton Mountain and a monument to smokejumpers who died in the Blackwater Fire of 1937. The **Natural Bridge Trail** continues south, climbing steadily through dense forest before emerging onto the meadows of Sheep Mesa, beneath Fortress Mountain (12,085 feet).

From Eagle Creek, the trail crosses a pass beneath Eagle Peak (11,358 feet) and descends to the Thorofare Trail in Yellowstone; it leads across Two Ocean Plateau north to the east shore of Yellowstone Lake or south to the Teton Wilderness Area.

North Absaroka Wilderness Area A trail follows Clearwater Creek for views of Sleeping Giant Mountain. The main trailhead is at Pahaska Tepee. Here the **Pahaska-Sunlight Trail** heads north, branching northeast to the Sunlight Basin, west to Yellowstone's Pelican Valley, or continuing north to Yellowstone's Lamar Valley.

Skiing
The **Sleeping Giant Ski Resort**, south of US 14/US 16/US 20, has a base elevation of 7000 feet with a maximum vertical drop 500 feet.

Places to Stay
Camping Nine USFS campgrounds ($9) are in the Wapiti Valley (5900 feet to 6700 feet) along US 14/US 16/US 20 28.6 miles to 48.6 miles west of Cody. *Wapiti*, *Elk Fork*, *Clearwater* and *Newton Creek* campgrounds are furthest from the road in cottonwood and/or pine forest. All campgrounds are along the river offering easy access to trout fishing. Day use costs $3. Most campgrounds are open mid-May to September, but can be closed or open only to hard-shell camping at any time because of grizzly bear activity.

Lodges The Wapiti Valley's dude ranches and lodges make a great base for exploring Yellowstone National Park or Cody, and most offer fishing, hiking, rock climbing, guided horseback rides (one hour starts at

$16, two hours at $24, half-day at $40, and full-day at $80) and overnight horse-packing trips (starting at $125).

South of US 14/US 16/US 20 is *Blackwater Creek Ranch* (☎ 307-587-5201). From east to west, all along the north side of US 14/US 16/US 20 are *Absaroka Mountain Lodge* (☎ 307-587-3963); the *Elephant Head Lodge* (☎ 307-587-3980), named for a nearby rock formation, with cabins starting at $62; *Shoshone Lodge* (☎ 307-587-4044); and *Pahaska Tepee* (☎ 307-527-7701, 800-628-7791, fax 307-527-4019), Buffalo Bill's former hunting lodge on the National Register of Historic Places with doubles starting at $96. Many offer weekly rates.

CLARKS FORK CANYON
The Clarks Fork of the Yellowstone River, Wyoming's only National Wild and Scenic River, runs along much of the **Chief Joseph Scenic Hwy** (Hwy 296) and US 212 linking Cody (via Hwy 120 north) with Yellowstone National Park's Northeast Entrance (62 miles away). The 1200-foot gorge of the Clarks Fork separates the 50 million year old volcanic rock of the Absaroka Mountains from the 2 billion-year-old granite of the Beartooth Plateau.

Take Hwy 120 16 miles north of Cody to the start of Hwy 296. It heads northwest, climbing to Dead Indian Pass (8048 feet). Indians used to wait here and kill game that migrated through the pass between summer pastures in the mountains and winter ranges in the plains. At the western base of the Dead Indian Pass is the USFS *Dead Indian Campgrounds*. Nearby Hwy 296 crosses Sunlight Creek. Here USFS Rd 101 heads southwest into the breathtakingly beautiful Sunlight Basin. Hwy 296 continues northwest to the junction of US 212. Along this stretch of Hwy 296 are a few guest ranches and other USFS campgrounds, including *Hunter Peak* and the lovely forested *Lake Creek*. Two main trailheads from Hwy 296, Dead Indian and Sunlight Creek, lead southwest into the North Absaroka Wilderness Area. A trail also follows much of Clarks Fork north of

WYOMING

Hwy 296. Two USFS ranger stations, Sunlight and Crandall, along Hwy 296, as well as the USFS office in Powell (see earlier in this chapter), have information on area trails and campgrounds.

Near the junction of Hwy 296 and US 212 is a popular rock climbing area. US 212 west of this junction dips into Montana toward Yellowstone with huge Absaroka views. Several more USFS campgrounds are en route to the entrance, the best of which are *Crazy Creek* and *Fox Creek*, both still in Wyoming.

BEARTOOTH RANGE
US 212 east of the junction with Hwy 296 enters the Beartooth Mountains and is known as the **Beartooth Scenic Byway**.

It leads northeast toward Billings, MT, via Red Lodge, MT. The section of US 212 in Wyoming crosses Beartooth Pass just south of the Wyoming-Montana state line. North of US 212 is the Absaroka-Beartooth Wilderness Area. Look for mountain goats on crags and in Alpine plateaus when hiking or driving in this area.

Easily accessible USFS campgrounds along US 212 are *Lily Lake*, *Beartooth Lake* and *Island Lake*. The hiking is excellent: two trails worth investigating are the **Beartooth Loop National Recreation Trail** that begins east of the pass and heads south, looping back to US 212 west of the pass; and **Beartooth High Lakes**, which begins west of the pass, heading north from US 212.

Wind River Country

Dominating this region are Wyoming's highest mountains, the glaciated Wind River Range, which mark the Continental Divide. The cultural legacy, past and present, of the Native Americans – Shoshone, Gros Ventre, Bannock, Sheepeater and Crow – who traveled the range when European trappers and explorers like Benjamin Bonneville and John C Frémont arrived in the early 19th century, is almost as dominant. The most notable feature of the area besides the mountains themselves is the Wind River Indian Reservation, home to the Shoshone and Arapaho.

In the latter half of the 19th century the Oregon Trail and its Lander Cutoff brought more travelers to the region. Much of the area remained under Native American control, but increasing numbers of emigrants stayed in the region and took up cattle ranching. With the arrival of the railroad, the Lander-Riverton area was settled and placed under irrigated agriculture. Later on, timber and minerals became important products and economic mainstays. With the boom and bust of these industries, however, tourism has become more important, growing rapidly by taking advantage of the region's spectacular natural assets. But even though tourism has a long history in the area – the first 'dude,' Scottish nobleman William Stewart, paid William Sublette to take him to the Green River Rendezvous of the 1830s – small communities like Dubois and Pinedale are ambivalent about their increasing popularity.

HIGHLIGHTS

- Wind River Range – Wyoming's highest mountain range, with superb trails along the Continental Divide
- Sinks Canyon State Park – ranked one of America's top 50 state parks
- Dubois – a rustic town with one of the densest populations of bighorn sheep nearby

RIVERTON

Riverton (population 9202; elevation 4956 feet) was carved out of the Wind River Indian Reservation after the promise of irrigation water persuaded the Shoshone and Arapaho to surrender part of their lands in 1906. The town, northeast of the confluence of the Wind and Little Wind rivers, has a long-standing rivalry with its neighbor Lander, whose 'old money' inhabitants look down on Riverton's 'nouveau riche.'

Irrigated agriculture is a major industry, with malt barley (purchased by the Coors Brewery in Colorado), hay, corn and sugar beets the main crops. Over most of the 20th century, Riverton farmers have expanded onto reservation lands, which presently may be leased but not sold to non-Native Americans. Issues of water and land continue to be significant and sensitive. Transport of trona employs a number of people.

Orientation

Newer businesses, motels and fast-food restaurants are along north-south Federal Blvd (US 26/Hwy 789). East-west Main St

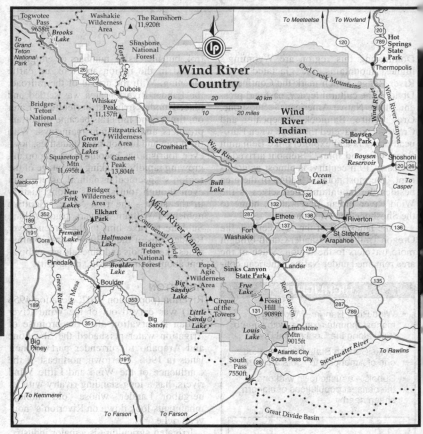

Wind River Country

Togwotee Pass 9658ft
Brooks Lake
To Grand Teton National Park
Washakie Wilderness Area
The Ramshorn 11,920ft
Horse Creek
Shoshone National Forest
Owl Creek Mountains
To Meeteetse
To Worland
Hot Springs State Park
Thermopolis
Wind River Canyon
Wind River
Bridger-Teton National Forest
Dubois
Whiskey Peak 11,157ft
Fitzpatrick Wilderness Area
Green River Lakes
Squaretop Mtn 11,695ft
Gannett Peak 13,804ft
Crowheart
Wind River
Wind River Indian Reservation
Boysen State Park
Boysen Reservoir
Shoshoni
To Jackson
New Fork Lakes
Bridger Wilderness Area
Elkhart Park
Bull Lake
Ocean Lake
To Casper
Fremont Lake
Halfmoon Lake
Wind River Range
Continental Divide
Bridger-Teton National Forest
Ethete
Fort Washakie
St Stephens
Arapahoe
Riverton
Cora
Pinedale
Boulder Lake
Boulder
The Mesa
Popo Agie Wilderness Area
Sinks Canyon State Park
Lander
Big Sandy Lake
Frye Lake
Red Canyon
Green River
Big Sandy
Cirque of the Towers
Little Sandy Lake
Fossil Hill 9089ft
Louis Lake
Limestone Mtn 9015ft
Sweetwater River
To Rawlins
Big Piney
To Kemmerer
Atlantic City
South Pass City
South Pass 7550ft
Great Divide Basin
To Farson
To Farson

0   20   40 km
0   10   20 miles

WYOMING

(US 26), which begins at Federal Blvd, is the main road, and divides north-south addresses. 1st St divides east-west ones.

Information

The Riverton Chamber of Commerce (☎ 307-856-4801, 800-325-2732; fax 307-856-4802), 101 S 1st St, in the former railroad depot, is open 8 am to 5 pm weekdays. For regional information contact the Wind River Visitors Council (☎ 800-645-6233), PO Box 1449, Riverton, WY 82501.

First Interstate Bank has an ATM at E Main St and Broadway Ave. Key Bank has one at S 2nd St E and E Main St. The post office is at 501 E Main St (zip code 82501). (It has an exceptional mural titled *Lambing Time* by George van der Sluis on an inside wall. Some old-timers recall a second mural depicting cattle that may have been obliterated by a remodeling job.) The Print Shop (☎ 307-856-3503; fax 307-856-1108), 706 W Main St, and Artcraft Printers (☎ 307-856-3684), 612 E Main St, have fax services.

Books & Briar (☎ 307-856-1797), 313 E Main St, carries a large selection of books on Wyoming and Native American history. They also have magazines and topographic maps.

JAMES BLANK

KIMBERLEY O'NEIL

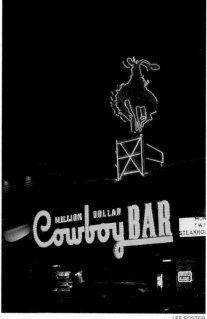

LEE FOSTER

Wyoming

Top: Stagecoach pulls into Jackson
Bottom Left: Beguiling Devils Tower

Bottom Right: Whoop it up at the Cowboy Bar

JOHN MOCK

RAY HILLSTROM

LEE FOSTER

TONY WHEELER

Wyoming

Top Left: Spirit catcher, Medicine Bow National Monument
Bottom: Tidy arrangement of hay bales, along US 16

Top Right: Ghostly stage express stop
Middle Right: Moose, Yellowstone National Park

Columbia-Riverton Memorial Hospital (☎ 307-856-4161, 800-967-1646 in Wyoming) is northwest of downtown. Take 8th St north or N Federal Blvd 3½ miles west to 2100 W Sunset Drive.

The Driftwood Laundry (☎ 307-856-4811), 611 W Main St, is in the same building as the Driftwood Motel.

Riverton Museum

The Riverton Museum (☎ 307-856-2665), 700 E Park Ave, in a remodeled church, is developing interpretive exhibits on Native American lands and water with displays of a frontier school, general store and well-preserved horse carriages. In the basement is the stuffed Desert Dunn, one of Wyoming's most famous bucking horses. Open 10 am to 4 pm Tuesday to Saturday; admission is free.

Central Wyoming College Arts Center

The college's Arts Center (☎ 307-856-9291, 800-735-8418), 2660 W Park Ave,

off US 26 west of town, has a series of exhibitions, plays, dances and concerts.

Special Events

Riverton's major spring event is **Native American Week & Central Wyoming College Powwow**. The week-long **1838 Mountain Man Rendezvous** (☎ 307-856-7306), held in early July on the Little Wind River at the east end of Monroe Ave, includes a rodeo. Late July brings the **Hot Air Balloon Rally**, one of the state's most colorful events. The **Fremont County Fair & Rodeo** is held over five days in early August. In October, there is a **Cowboy Poetry Gathering**.

Places to Stay

Beside the river, *Fort Rendezvous Campground* (☎ 307-856-1144), 10368 Hwy 789 north of town, has sites with full hookups ($12), some with shade.

Most motels are on or near Federal Blvd; others are on W Main St. Seasonal rates

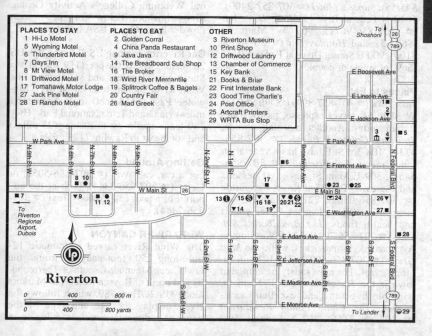

PLACES TO STAY
1 Hi-Lo Motel
5 Wyoming Motel
6 Thunderbird Motel
7 Days Inn
8 Mt View Motel
11 Driftwood Motel
17 Tomahawk Motor Lodge
27 Jack Pine Motel
28 El Rancho Motel

PLACES TO EAT
2 Golden Corral
4 China Panda Restaurant
9 Java Java
14 The Breadboard Sub Shop
16 The Broker
18 Wind River Mercantile
19 Splitrock Coffee & Bagels
20 Country Fair
26 Mad Greek

OTHER
3 Riverton Museum
10 Print Shop
12 Driftwood Laundry
13 Chamber of Commerce
15 Key Bank
21 Books & Briar
22 First Interstate Bank
23 Good Time Charlie's
24 Post Office
25 Artcraft Printers
29 WRTA Bus Stop

Riverton

vary little. Budget places, starting around $25, are the *Mt View Motel* (☎ 307-856-2418), 720 W Main St; *Wyoming Motel* (☎ 307-856-6549), 319 N Federal Blvd; and *Jack Pine Motel* (☎ 307-856-9251), 120 S Federal Blvd. *Tomahawk Motor Lodge* (☎ 307-856-9205, 800-637-7378), 208 E Main St, costs $37/42 for singles/doubles.

Mid-range motels are the *El Rancho Motel* (☎ 307-856-7455, 800-650-7455), 221 S Federal Blvd ($32/40); *Driftwood Motel* (☎ 307-856-4811, 800-821-2914), 611 W Main St ($36/45); *Hi-Lo Motel* (☎ 307-856-9223, 800-492-9223), 414 N Federal Blvd (starts at $38/44); and the *Paintbrush Motel* (☎ 307-856-9238, 800-204-9238), 1550 N Federal Blvd, north of the railroad tracks, three-fourths of a mile north of Sunset Drive ($38/55). The *Thunderbird Motel* (☎ 307-856-9201), 302 E Fremont Ave, costs $40/50.

Top-end places are the *Sundowner Station Motel* (☎ 307-856-6503, 800-874-1116), 1616 N Federal Blvd (starts at $45/55); *Super 8 Motel* (☎ 307-857-2400), 1040 N Federal Blvd ($45/50); *Days Inn* (☎ 307-856-9677), 909 W Main St ($60/65); and *Holiday Inn* (☎ 307-856-8100), 900 E Sunset Drive at Federal Blvd ($69 for single or double).

Places to Eat

Java Java (☎ 307-857-3999), S 8th St W at W Main St, serves espresso, pastries and Italian sodas. Another morning choice, *Splitrock Coffee & Bagels* (☎ 307-856-4334), 108 3rd St E, also has a vegetarian lunch menu. *Country Fair* (☎ 307-856-5451), 309 E Main St, has good desserts and espresso. The *Wind River Mercantile* (☎ 307-856-0862), 221 E Main St, has inexpensive deli sandwiches, frozen yogurt and health foods. The *Breadboard Sub Shop* (☎ 307-856-7044), 124 E Washington Ave, has good sandwiches, while the *Mad Greek* (☎ 307-856-5007), 719 E Main St, offers gyros. The most satisfying choice in town is the *The Broker*, 203 E Main St, with plush booths and excellent sandwiches. The *China Panda Restaurant* (☎ 307-856-7666), 302 N Federal Ave,

serves Chinese cuisine. The *Golden Corral* (☎ 307-856-1152), 400 N Federal Blvd, and the *Trailhead Family Restaurant* (☎ 307-856-7990), 831 N Federal Blvd (near the Holiday Inn), are unexceptional.

Entertainment

Good Time Charlie's (☎ 307-856-4285), 502 E Main St, has live country-rock music.

Getting There & Away

Air United Express (☎ 307-856-1307) operates daily flights to and from Denver. Riverton Regional Airport, 4700 Airport Rd, is about 3 miles west and north of Riverton off US 26.

Bus The Wind River Transportation Authority (WRTA; ☎ 307-856-7118) runs bus service between Riverton, Lander and the Wind River Indian Reservation. WRTA stops on Federal Blvd at Monroe Ave (look for the marked telephone pole next to the Maverick gas station) and in front of Central Wyoming College's Activity Center. (See Shoshoni below for the nearest Powder River Coach USA bus stop.)

Car Riverton is along US 26/Hwy 789. US 26 leads east to Casper (119 miles) via Shoshoni (22 miles) and west across the Wind River Indian Reservation over Togwotee Pass (9658 feet) to Jackson (168 miles) via Grand Teton National Park. Hwy 789 leads southwest to Lander (25 miles) and southeast to Rawlins (123 miles).

Getting Around

For a car, call Avis (☎ 307-856-5052) or Hertz (☎ 307-856-2344), both at the airport. For a taxi, call Cowboy Taxi (☎ 307-856-7444).

WIND RIVER CANYON

The Wind River carved a dramatic 12-mile-long 2500-foot canyon through the Owl Creek Mountains, south of Thermopolis and north of Boysen Reservoir. Markers along US 20/Hwy 789, which follows the river, display the age and type of the exposed sedimentary rock, ranging from

WYOMING

Precambrian rocks (2.9 billion years old) to relatively youthful Triassic (a mere 200 million years old).

Boysen State Park

Boysen Dam tames the Wind River creating Boysen Reservoir, the centerpiece of largely barren Boysen State Park. A marina is at its northern end with some surprisingly attractive campsites not far off US 20/Hwy 789. The *Lower Wind River Campground* near the tunnel is the best.

Rafting

The Wind River below the dam has Class III-IV rapids, and some tamer sections. Half/full-day rafting trips start at $20/60. To book a trip, contact Wind River Canyon Whitewater, Inc (☎ 307-864-9343, 307-486-2253 winter), 210 US 20 S, Suite 5, Thermopolis, WY 82443, and PO Box 592, Crowheart, WY 82512, during winter. The season is April to October; reservations are necessary April to May.

SHOSHONI

Shoshoni (population 497) looks like a ghost town. Gunshops and junkshops peddling rusty lawnmowers line 2nd St, while plastic sheeting covers the windows of Idaho St's abandoned brick buildings; only the air-conditioned *Yellowstone Drug Company* (great malts and shakes, mediocre short orders) and the adjacent bar survive. A block south of 2nd St, at the foot of Wyoming St, is the restored 1907 city jail. Contact the Shoshoni Chamber of Commerce (☎ 307-876-2561) at PO Box 324, Shoshoni, WY 82649. Over Memorial Day weekend Shoshoni hosts the Wyoming State Fiddle Championships.

If you are stuck here, *Desert Inn Motel* (☎ 307-876-2273), 605 W 2nd St, has cheap rooms, as does the *Shoshoni Motel* (☎ 307-876-2216), 503 W 2nd. The only restaurants are *Dodie's Diner*, 502 E 2nd St, and the *Wrangler Cafe*, 605 W 2nd St.

Getting There & Away

Bus Powder River Coach USA (☎ 307-876-2561) buses stop at Trail Town Supply, 107 W 2nd St, which is next to the Conoco gas station. Buses go to Casper-Douglas (6 am) and Billings, MT, via the Bighorn Basin (9 am). Contact WRTA (☎ 307-332-7118) for buses to Riverton and other Wind River Country destinations.

Car Shoshoni is at the junction of US 20/Hwy 789 and US 26 near Boysen Reservoir, 15 miles northeast of Riverton and 32 miles south of Thermopolis.

LANDER

Cheerful Lander (population 7266; elevation 5357 feet) straddles the Middle Fork of the Popo Agie ('popo azhey') River, a southern tributary of the Wind River. At the foot of the Wind River Range, Lander is a base for many outdoor activities. The presence of the National Outdoor Leadership School (NOLS) lends a college-town atmosphere, and along Main St are mini-parks and inviting wooden benches at regular intervals. Off Main St, broad tree-lined streets with gracious older houses offer pleasant strolling to attractive parks.

History

Though its namesake was Colonel Frederick W Lander, surveyor of the Lander Cutoff to the Oregon Trail in 1857-58, the town of Lander owes its existence to the Wind River Indian Reservation. In 1869, at the request of Chief Washakie, the US Army established Camp Augur to protect Shoshone lands from settlers. Ironically, the camp attracted even more miners and settlers to the area. Then, after the Bannock tribe voluntarily moved to Idaho in 1872, the US government carved half a million additional acres from the remaining Shoshone Reservation to encourage more settlement in the Popo Agie Valley. Lander then became the seat of Fremont County, which comprised almost one-quarter of the state's territory, and nearly became the state capital in 1904. In 1884 Wyoming's first oil well was drilled about 8 miles east of town, and the railroad arrived in 1906 (and stopped coming in 1972).

Orientation

Main St (US 287) is west of the river; newer suburbs are east. Main St divides north-south street addresses; the river divides east-west ones. From Main St, S Fifth St leads to westbound Fremont St, Sinks Canyon Rd (Hwy 131) and Sinks Canyon State Park (see later in this chapter).

Information

Tourist Offices The Lander Area Chamber of Commerce (☎ 307-332-3892, 800-433-0662; landerchamber@rmisp.com), 160 N First St (in the former railroad depot), is open 9 am to 8 pm weekdays early June to mid-August, and 9 am to 8 pm the rest of the year. The USFS Shoshone National Forest Washakie District Ranger Station (☎ 307-332-5460), 333 Hwy 789 S east of Buena Vista Drive, has useful information on the Popo Agie Wilderness Area and other nearby hiking and camping areas. It is open 9 am to 5 pm Monday to Thursday, and 9 am to 8 pm Friday to Sunday. Other useful offices are the BLM Lander Resource Area (☎ 307-332-8400), 1335 Main St, and the Wyoming Game and Fish District (☎ 307-332-2688), 260 Buena Vista Drive.

Useful Organizations Lander is home to several important environmental organizations and NOLS (see Useful Organizations in the Facts about Wyoming chapter). Check the NOLS' bulletin board for anyone seeking rides or partners for climbing, hiking and other activities.

Money ATMs are at Key Bank, 303 Main St, Central Bank & Trust, Third and Main Sts, and First Bank at Fifth and Main Sts.

Post & Communications The post office is at 230 Grand View Drive; the zip code is 82520. Reed's Moghaun Office Supplies (☎ 307-332-7850), at Fifth and Main Sts next to Cabin Fever Books, provides fax services.

Bookstores The Booke Shoppe (☎ 307-332-6221), at 160 N Second St, carries a good selection of field guides and hiking maps and has a large, shady garden for reading. Cabin Fever Books (☎ 307-332-9580), 163 S Fifth St, has a good selection of used books, a friendly atmosphere and an old-fashioned cooler with ice-cream bars.

Medical Services To reach Lander Valley Medical Center (☎ 307-332-4420, 307-856-1420), 1320 Bishop Randall Drive, head east across the river to Buena Vista Drive and go south past the golf course.

Laundry & Showers American Dry Cleaners (☎ 307-332-5454) is at 494 Main St. Showers cost $1.75 at the Lander Community Swimming Pool (☎ 307-332-2272), 450 S Ninth St at Dabch Ave; call for hours.

Historic Buildings

On First St just north of Main St, along the Popo Agie River, is the former Chicago & Northwestern Railroad depot (1908); Lander was the end of the line, 'where the rails meet the trails.' Lander's most imposing historic landmark, the Lander Mill (1888), 129 Main St, is still a livestock feed dealer; its exterior is little changed. On the north side of Main St, at the back of the lot between 144 and 166, is a log cabin dating from around 1876. Centennial Park, just down the block, is a pleasant spot to relax. The ground floor of the Odd Fellows Hall (1886), 202 Main St, is now the Stockgrowers Bar; the building is largely unchanged. The former Fremont Lumber Company (1887), 159 N Second St, once a newspaper office, has been restored.

Pioneer Museum

Lander's sprawling Pioneer Museum (☎ 307-332-4137), 630 Lincoln St, depicts pioneer life in the area, with a notable display of farm machinery and transportation; note the vintage circus wagon. Also interesting is the collection of motor vehicle license plates, which inexplicably fails to mention that Wyoming's depiction of a cowboy on a bucking horse started a

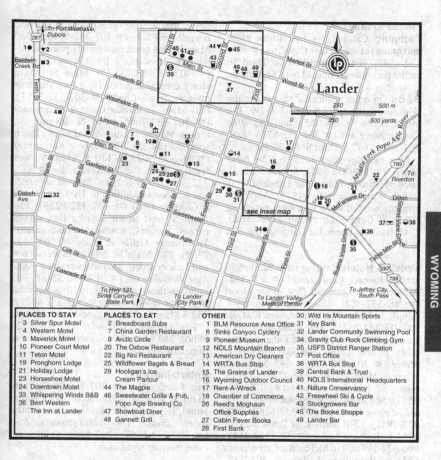

PLACES TO STAY	PLACES TO EAT	OTHER	30 Wild Iris Mountain Sports
3 Silver Spur Motel	2 Breadboard Subs	1 BLM Resource Area Office	31 Key Bank
4 Western Motel	7 China Garden Restaurant	6 Sinks Canyon Cyclery	32 Lander Community Swimming Pool
5 Maverick Motel	8 Arctic Circle	9 Pioneer Museum	34 Gravity Club Rock Climbing Gym
10 Pioneer Court Motel	20 The Oxbow Restaurant	12 NOLS Mountain Branch	35 USFS District Ranger Station
Teton Motel	22 Big Noi Restaurant	13 American Dry Cleaners	37 Post Office
19 Pronghorn Lodge	25 Wildflower Bagels & Bread	14 WRTA Bus Stop	38 WRTA Bus Stop
21 Holiday Lodge	29 Hooligan's Ice	15 The Grains of Lander	39 Central Bank & Trust
23 Horseshoe Motel	Cream Parlour	16 Wyoming Outdoor Council	40 NOLS International Headquarters
24 Downtown Motel	44 The Magpie	17 Rent-A-Wreck	41 Nature Conservancy
33 Whispering Winds B&B	46 Sweetwater Grille & Pub,	18 Chamber of Commerce	42 Freewheel Ski & Cycle
36 Best Western	Popo Agie Brewing Co	26 Reed's Moghaun	43 Stockgrowers Bar
The Inn at Lander	47 Showboat Diner	Office Supplies	45 The Booke Shoppe
	48 Gannett Grill	27 Cabin Fever Books	49 Lander Bar
		28 First Bank	

nationwide trend of using state symbols on license plates. It is open 10 am to 5 pm weekdays, 1 to 4 pm weekends, during the summer, and 1 to 5 pm Wednesday to Friday and 1 to 4 pm Saturday the rest of the year; admission is free.

Rock Climbing

Wild Iris Mountain Sports (☎ 307-332-4541), 325 Main St, is the place to ask about rock climbing. The Gravity Club Rock Climbing Gym (☎ 307-332-6339), 221 S Second St, offers showers for climbers camping in the area. (See Around Lander.)

Mountain Biking

Lander is a popular area for mountain biking. Freewheel Ski & Cycle (☎ 307-332-6616, 800-490-6616 in Wyoming), 258 Main St, and Sinks Canyon Cyclery (☎ 307-332-2237, 800-824-8318), 738 Main St, repair and rent mountain bikes.

Special Events

The annual **International Climbers' Festival** (☎ 307-332-4541), PO Box 1304, Lander, WY 82520, which is held the second week in July, attracts climbers from around the world.

WYOMING

Places to Stay

Camping Camping is free (three-night maximum) at the *Lander City Park* (☎ 307-332-4647), 405 Fremont St, near Third St, on the park's south side, May to September.

B&Bs On quiet residential streets are the *Whispering Winds B&B* (☎ 307-332-9735), 695 Canyon St ($44/55), and the *Blue Spruce Inn B&B* (☎ 307-332-8253, 888-503-3311), 677 S Third St ($65/75).

Five minutes from town is *The Bunk House* (☎ 307-332-5624, 800-582-5262), 2024 Mortimore Lane at the Lander Llama Ranch, which sleeps five ($75). About 10 minutes west of town in a rural setting is *Piece of Cake B&B* (☎ 307-332-7608), 2343 Baldwin Creek Rd (ranges from $75 to $115).

Motels & Hotels Ranging from $25 to $35 are the *Pioneer Court Motel* (☎ 307-332-2653), 181 N Sixth St; *Downtown Motel* (☎ 307-332-3171, 800-900-3171 in Wyoming), 569 Main St; and *Maverick Motel* (☎ 307-332-2821), 808 Main St, with a steak and seafood restaurant. Other comparably priced motels include *Horseshoe Motel* (☎ 307-332-4915), 685 Main St; *Western Motel* (☎ 307-332-4270), 151 N Ninth St; and *Teton Motel* (☎ 307-332-3582), 586 Main St. Singles/doubles at the *Silver Spur Motel* (☎ 307-332-5189, 800-922-7831), 1240 Main St at Tenth St, cost $35/38. *Holiday Lodge* (☎ 307-332-2511, 800-624-1974), 210 McFarlane Drive, costs $35/40. *Pronghorn Lodge* (☎ 307-332-3940), 150 E Main St, costs $39/42; some rooms have kitchenettes. Rooms at *Best Western The Inn at Lander* (☎ 307-332-2847), 260 Grand View Drive, start at $70.

Places to Eat

The Magpie (☎ 307-332-5565), 159 N Second St, has good pastries (the blueberry coffeecake is sublime) and is the best spot in town for espresso or a light lunch. The *Wildflower Bagels & Bread* (☎ 307-332-9728), 545 Main St at Fifth St, specializes in baked goods. The popular *Showboat Diner* (☎ 307-332-2710), 173 Main St, has basic, inexpensive breakfasts and lunches. *Breadboard Subs* (☎ 307-332-6090), 1350 Main St, has good, moderately priced sandwiches. *Hooligan's Ice Cream Parlour* (☎ 307-332-5050), 351 Main St, has a shady creekside patio. Try a fruit shake or malt at *Arctic Circle* (☎ 307-332-3957), 620 Main St. *China Garden Restaurant* (☎ 307-332-7666), 140 N Seventh St, serves Mandarin cuisine and offers lunch specials ($4.25). *The Oxbow Restaurant* (☎ 307-332-0233), 170 E Main St, has family dining. *Big Noi Restaurant* (☎ 307-332-3102), 280 N Hwy 789, serves steak and seafood in addition to Thai cuisine.

Gannett Grill (☎ 307-332-8228), 126 Main St next to the Lander Bar, serves pizzas, burgers, sandwiches and salads. *Sweetwater Grille & Pub* (☎ 307-332-7388), 148 Main St, has an espresso bar and Lander's only microbrewery: the *Popo Agie Brewing Co* (☎ 307-332-3248). Ten miles northeast of Lander, in Hudson, is the popular *Club El Toro* (☎ 307-332-4627), 132 S Main St, featuring steak and seafood.

The Grains of Lander (☎ 307-332-5966), 388 Main St, sells a good selection of health foods.

Entertainment

The *Lander Bar* (☎ 307-332-7009), 126 Main St at First St, in the former Lander Hotel, is good for a casual, if not exactly quiet, drink. The *Stockgrowers Bar* (☎ 307-332-5357), 202 Main St, has an even rowdier reputation.

Getting There & Away

Bus The Wind River Transportation Authority (WRTA; ☎ 307-856-7118) provides both regularly scheduled weekday and on-demand service between Lander and Fort Washakie, Ethete, Arapahoe, Riverton, Dubois and Rock Springs. WRTA also serves Riverton Regional Airport ($13). WRTA's Lander stops are in the used car lot at Lincoln and Fourth Sts and at the Alco Discount Store, 275 Grand View Drive. (See Shoshoni earlier in this chapter for the nearest Powder River Coach USA bus stop.)

Car Lander is at the junction of US 287 and Hwy 789, 9 miles northwest of the junction of US 287/Hwy 789 and Hwy 28. US 287 leads northwest through the Wind River Indian Reservation over Togwotee Pass (9658 feet) to Grand Teton National Park. Hwy 789 leads northeast to Riverton (24 miles) and southeast to Rawlins (128 miles). Rock Springs is 126 miles southwest of Lander via Hwy 28 and US 191.

Getting Around
Car Try Rent-A-Wreck (☎ 307-332-9965, 888-332-9965), 323 N Second St at the corner of Washakie St, or Fremont Motor Company (☎ 307-332-4355, 888-584-2445), 961 S Hwy 789, for local rentals.

AROUND LANDER
Sinks Canyon State Park
National Geographic Traveler called Sinks Canyon State Park one of America's top 50 state parks. The Middle Fork of the Popo Agie River flows through the narrow canyon, disappearing into the soluble Madison limestone, called the **Sinks**, and emerging with increased volume and higher temperature over a quarter of a mile downstream in a trout-filled pool called the **Rise**. Despite considerable research, details of the river's course are inconclusive. USGS testing in 1983 demonstrated that red dyes poured into the water above the Sinks took over two hours to reach the Rise. Scientists hypothesized that the water passes through a large underground aquifer that slows its advance, or that the convoluted subterranean passages have the same effect. It could even be a combination of the two. In any event, the sudden disappearance of the copious flow intrigues a steady stream of visitors.

The surrounding habitat supports deer, moose, elk, muskrat, marmot, mink and bighorn sheep. The latter were transplanted from the Whiskey Basin near Dubois in 1987 as part of a program to reestablish the species in the historic range. Fishing is not permitted in the Rise.

Sinks Canyon State Park Headquarters (☎ 307-332-6333) is at 3079 Sinks Canyon Rd. The Sinks Canyon visitors center (☎ 307-332-3077) has worthwhile geology, hydroelectricity and Native American exhibits. It also offers information on easily accessible rock art sites and occasional caving tours of Wind River Grotto ($10). Day use is free.

Friends of Sinks Canyon (☎ 307-332-6181), PO Box 1425, Lander, WY 82520, monitors possible threats to the park's integrity, like the proposed project to widen and pave upper Hwy 131 to the Popo Agie Falls trailhead, about 1½ miles west of the park.

The two park campgrounds, *Sawmill* north of the visitors center and *Popo Agie* south of it, cost $4 and fill up early. Both campgrounds are along the Popo Agie River in open forest but close to the road and dusty. Other USFS campgrounds are nearby (see The Loop below). The park is on Sinks Canyon Rd (Hwy 131) 6 miles south of Lander and is also accessible from Hwy 28, just north of South Pass City, via Louis Lake Rd (USFS Rd 300), an unpaved 27-mile route to the south entrance.

The Loop
'The Loop' refers to Sinks Canyon Rd (Hwy 131), which leads southwest from Lander through Sinks Canyon State Park past Frye Lake to where it meets Louis Lake Rd (USFS Rd 300). The Loop continues southeast on Louis Lake Rd past Fiddlers and Louis lakes, through Grannier Meadows, to Hwy 28. The area offers rock climbing, mountain biking, hiking, backpacking, fishing and boating.

Four USFS campgrounds ($6) are along the Loop. *Sinks Canyon Campground*, 10 miles south of Lander, is open May to October. The other three are open July to mid-September: *Worthen Meadows*, 16 miles from Lander to Frye Lake plus 2½ miles on USFS Rd 302 to the reservoir; *Fiddlers*, 23.5 miles from Lander; and *Louis Lake*, 28 miles from Lander. *The Resort at Louis Lake* (☎ 307-332-5549, 888-422-2246), on USFS Rd 300 10 miles northwest of Hwy 28, has rustic log cabins starting at $60. They rent mountain bikes,

WYOMING

boats, camping gear, skis and snow-mobiles, and outfit pack trips.

Popo Agie Wilderness Area

South of Sinks Canyon State Park, at the southeast end of Shoshone National Forest, is the readily accessible 158-sq-mile Popo Agie Wilderness Area. **Popo Agie Falls Trail** offers an easy morning's hike to several waterfalls and attractive swimming pools. Both the Popo Agie Trail and the **Stough Creek Lakes Trail**, at the end of USFS Rd 302, lead into the high country on the east side of the Continental Divide, with opportunities for loop trips to the area's many lakes or for extended backpacking trips toward Boulder or Pinedale.

Rock Climbing

Lander has several world-class rock climbing areas: Sinks Canyon State Park, Fossil Hill and Wild Iris. **Sinks Canyon State Park**, 6 miles southwest of Lander, has routes on sandstone, dolomite and granite ranging from 5.4 to 5.13, with more than 150 5.9 to 5.13+ routes. The rock's southern exposure makes it a good early- or late-season climbing area. To reach **Fossil Hill** from Sinks Canyon State Park, take the dirt road south to the top of the switchbacks, follow the left fork then park in the aspen grove. About 20 routes ranging from 5.10 to 5.13 are on the nearby west-facing dolomite cliffs. **Wild Iris** is 29 miles south of Lander off Hwy 28. At the top of the hill on Hwy 28, turn west on Limestone Mountain Rd (USFS Rd 326) and continue 1.3 miles to the fork. Take the right fork 0.4 miles and park before the quarry. Over 150 routes on this dolomite rock range from 5.7 to 5.14, many offering short, steep or overhanging climbs. Climbing is also possible at **Baldwin Creek**, but a 4WD is necessary to reach the overhanging limestone climbing area at the end of Baldwin Creek Rd, a few miles west of Lander.

Camping is free on USFS land: many climbers use sites (with no facilities) about 2 miles beyond Sinks Canyon State Park. Alternative campgrounds are in the park and along the Loop Rd (see above). Climbers are asked not to camp at Wild Iris; try the nearby BLM campgrounds (see Atlantic City & South Pass City below).

RED CANYON NATIONAL NATURAL LANDMARK

The verdant valley of the Little Popo Agie River contrasts dramatically with the nearly crimson sandstone, created by oxidized iron, of Red Canyon. About 200 million years old, the red rocks lined the margins of an ancient sea. The canyon is 15 miles southeast of Lander on US 287; Fremont County Rd 235 (Red Canyon Rd) makes a scenic loop by vehicle or mountain bike.

ATLANTIC CITY & SOUTH PASS CITY

Atlantic City

Enigmatically named Atlantic City may have acquired its moniker through former residents of its New Jersey namesake or from its location on the east side of the Continental Divide. Founded in 1868 by miners from South Pass, it once boasted both an opera house and the first brewery in the territory. By the 1950s it was nearly a ghost town, but enjoyed a minor revival a decade later when US Steel developed an open-pit mine at Iron Mountain along Hwy 28. The mine closed in the 1980s, but the town retains a handful of historic buildings in its scenic Rock Creek surroundings. **St Andrew's Episcopal Church** (1911) has a woodstove dated 1883. The **Gratrix Cabin**, dating from the 1860s, was the residence of a justice of the peace who claimed to have lived in three counties (Carter, Sweetwater and Fremont), two territories (Dakota and Wyoming) and one state (Wyoming) without ever moving.

South Pass City State Historical Site

North of the strategic South Pass (see below), South Pass City served passing emigrants and, in the late 1860s, boomed with gold strikes at the Carissa Lode, Atlantic City and Miners Delight. Like many early mining camps, South Pass City experienced a brief period of lawlessness, with Native American raids and general disorder. At the same time, South Pass City claimed its place in history by championing the cause of women's suffrage, thanks to local legislator William Bright's sponsorship of a bill to grant women the right to vote. The town languished after the mining boom went bust in 1873, but the state acquired the site in 1966 and restored 27 of the original log, frame and stone buildings.

Among the intriguing structures are the Smith-Sherlock Store (1896), the nicely outfitted Blacksmith Shop (1915), the South Pass Hotel (1868) and the ore-crushing Franklin Mine Stamp Mill (1869), moved here for protection from vandals. The Variety Theater, built on the foundations of an 1860s store, hosts special events like plays, films and musicals. The visitors center, a former dance hall (1890), offers video presentations and a bookstore, while the Smith Store (1874) contains interpretive exhibits on South Pass City.

Frequently during summer, archaeologists excavate sites around the park and willingly entertain questions. South Pass City is, according to The World Monument Fund (of New York), one of the 100 most endangered historic sites in the world. But the BLM, which owns the site, has not tried to place it on the National Register of Historic Places. The site (☎ 307-332-3684) is open 9 am to 6 pm daily, May 15 to September 30. Admission is $1; free for children under 18.

Activities
Trails for **cross-country skiing** start at the Old Rock Shop on Hwy 28, 35 miles south of Lander. An access trail follows Willow Creek north of Hwy 28 while four loops wind through aspens. Other activities include **fly-fishing** in nearby Sweetwater River and **mountain biking** on the extensive network of backcountry roads.

Places to Stay & Eat
Open June to October, two pleasant BLM campgrounds ($6) in mixed forest are about 2 miles north of Atlantic City and 2 miles off Hwy 28: *Atlantic City*, where many Wild Iris climbers camp, is in an aspen grove on Fremont County Rd 237

and *Big Atlantic Gulch* is half a mile to the east on BLM Rd 2324.

In Atlantic City, *Atlantic City Mercantile* (☎ 307-332-5143, 888-257-0215), in the former Giessler Store & Post Office (1893), has a steak house and saloon, along with sites with full hookups ($15) and cabins (starting at $56). Next door, the *Sagebrush Saloon & Cafe* (☎ 307-332-7404) serves quiche, an unexpected entree in this area. Rooms start at $80 at *Miner's Delight Old West B&B* (☎ 307-332-3513, 888-292-0248), the former Carpenter Hotel (1904).

Getting There & Away
Atlantic City and South Pass City are along unpaved Fremont County Rd 237, off Hwy 28 about 35 miles south of Lander. Atlantic City is 3 miles south of Hwy 28 and 4 miles north of South Pass City. The paved Fremont County Rd 479 connects Hwy 28 directly to South Pass City, which is 2 miles to the east.

SOUTH PASS NATIONAL HISTORIC LANDMARK
South Pass (7550 feet) is on Hwy 28 10 miles southwest of South Pass City. Between 1843 and 1912, nearly half a million emigrants, miners and trappers crossed South Pass, the gentlest route across the Continental Divide. Farther west is the

Continental Divide Snowmobile Trail
Crossing the divide five times, the Continental Divide Snowmobile Trail consists of 360 miles of continuous, groomed trails at 9000 feet, from Lander and Pinedale via Dubois and Togwotee Pass to Grand Teton and Yellowstone national parks and West Yellowstone, MT. The trip is usually done in two to four days, December to April, with overnight stops in Pinedale and Dubois. Snowmobilers must register ($15) at state park offices, snowmobile dealers or service stations. Maps are available from USFS or BLM offices. ■

Parting of the Ways, where the Oregon and Mormon Pioneer trails split: the Oregon Trail headed west to Oregon and California, and the Mormon Pioneer Trail turned southwest to Utah.

Wind River Indian Reservation

Home to over 2500 Eastern Shoshone and more than 5000 Arapaho, the 3594-sq-mile Wind River Indian Reservation is Wyoming's only Indian reservation. Under the US Constitution the reservation is an autonomous political entity, operating its own tax and court systems, game and fish department, public transportation and monitoring water quality. Oil, gas and grazing royalties finance many of these services. The reservation is not so picturesque as the postcard photographs of events like pow-wows would suggest, but a visit can offer an interesting glimpse into Native American life. Nearby communities like Lander and Riverton have minimal contact with the reservation. Despite high infant mortality and substance abuse problems, the reservation is a positive symbol of cultural identity. Cultural centers promote the study of Native American languages and participation in traditional religious events like sun dances.

History

The Wind River Indian Reservation reveals the complexity of the relationships of Native Americans to non-Native Americans, and the relationships between groups of Native Americans with distinct interests. Ironically, the Shoshone, who were once allied with the US government, now share the same reduced territory with the defeated Arapaho. The Shoshone had always been friendly to settlers and the first Treaty of Fort Bridger in 1863 granted the Shoshone a large area consisting of parts of present-day Colorado, Utah, Idaho, Montana and Wyoming. After the treaty proved impossible to enforce, the famed Shoshone Chief Washakie obtained, by the second Treaty of Fort Bridger in 1868, an area stretching from the Popo Agie Valley (comprising the core of the current reservation) to South Pass.

But gold strikes at South Pass chipped away at the reservation's south margin. For a cash indemnity and the promise of government protection, Chief Washakie accepted the further reduction of the reservation. After the end of the Plains Indians wars of the 1870s, the US government asked the Shoshone to share temporarily the reservation with their traditional adversaries, the Arapaho. Chief Washakie reluctantly agreed, and the arrangement soon became permanent. Today the Arapaho outnumber the Shoshone by more than two to one.

In 1906, the Riverton Project usurped even more land from the reservation, forming a prosperous white enclave surrounded by reservation lands. In 1989, however, US Supreme Court rulings upheld Native American water rights, placing the Shoshone and Arapaho in a much stronger position with Riverton farmers.

Much of the enmity between the Shoshone and Arapaho dissipated during the 20th century, but the two peoples retain distinct identities and intermarriage is uncommon. Missionary activity may have contributed to this: Jesuits evangelized the Arapaho in the late 19th century, while Episcopalians converted the Shoshone. Between 1910 and 1917, the Episcopalians also constructed St Michael's Mission at Ethete.

Orientation

The reservation consists of several small towns, the most important of which are the administrative center of Fort Washakie, primarily a Shoshone town, and the Arapaho settlements of Ethete and St Stephens.

Information

The Shoshone Tribal Cultural Center (☎ 307-332-9106), 15 North Fork Rd, Fort Washakie, occupies the former Bureau of

Little is known about Sacagawea, the Shoshone guide of Lewis and Clark.

valid here; reservation licenses for Wyoming residents/nonresidents are daily $7/10, weekly $25/35 and annual $35/60. Even hikers on the reservation must have a license.

Washakie Cemetery
The great Shoshone Chief Washakie's remains rest in this fenced cemetery on the north side of North Fork Rd, west of US 287. The headstone on his grave reads 1804-1900, but Washakie ('Always loyal to the government and his white brothers') may well have been over 100 years old when his remarkable life ended.

Sacagawea Cemetery
West of US 287 and Fort Washakie via South Fork Rd and Dushell Lane, this Shoshone graveyard purportedly holds Sacagawea, Lewis and Clark's famous Shoshone guide. Episcopal missionary John Roberts claimed Sacagawea died on the reservation in 1884, but an alternative account is that she died in South Dakota in 1812.

Arapaho Cultural Museum
Part of the historic St Michael's Mission complex at Ethete, the Arapaho Cultural Museum (☎ 307-332-2660) has a collection of fine artifacts, plus a superb collection of photographs of reservation residents. Unfortunately, the building is inadequate and exhibits unexplained. The museum is open 10 am to 6 pm Monday to Saturday May to October. Visitors, however, may have to locate the Episcopal vicar (a Shoshone) to gain admission. The rest of the year, call for an appointment.

St Stephens Mission
Founded as a Jesuit mission in 1884, St Stephens is in the village of Arapahoe, a few miles southwest of Riverton. The mission church is embellished with geometric Arapaho designs.

Crowheart Butte
This landmark mountain, north of US 26/US 287 about 35 miles southeast of Dubois, is the site of Chief Washakie's 1866 victory over the Crow in a dispute

Indian Affairs (BIA) building (on the National Register of Historic Places), and has self-guiding tour maps and historic and cultural exhibits. It is open 9 am to 4 pm weekdays. The North American Indian Heritage Center in St Stephens is open 9 am to 5 pm weekdays, April to December. Check the weekly *Wind River News*, which is published in Lander, for reservation news. State sales tax is not collected on the reservation.

Contact the Shoshone-Arapaho Tribal Fish and Game Department (☎ 307-332-7207), PO Box 217, Fort Washakie, WY 82514, for their brochure listing outfitters and mapping the reservation's excellent fisheries. Wyoming fishing licenses are not

WYOMING

over Wind River hunting grounds. In celebration he displayed the heart of a fallen Crow warrior on his lance. Most of the battle was fought near Black Mountain, to the north, but Crowheart Butte is now considered a sacred site with access prohibited to non-Native Americans.

Special Events

Dates for the numerous annual reservation events vary from year to year, so confirm them with the Shoshone and Arapaho cultural centers (see above). Non-Native Americans are welcome at religious ceremonies, but cameras, video cameras and tape recorders are not.

Since **Powwows** are more social than religious gatherings, cameras are generally allowed, but ask permission. Likewise, etiquette requires standing for the grand entry, including the presentation of flags and opening prayer, and rising during the singing of an honor song, dropping of a feather or men's traditional dancing. Follow the lead of Native Americans. Alcohol and drugs are prohibited. Important events include:

United Tribes Powwow
　　Central Wyoming College, Riverton (May)
Big Wind Powwow
　　Crowheart (June)
Yellow Calf Memorial Powwow
　　Ethete (June)
Arapaho Community Powwow
　　Arapahoe (June)
Shoshone Treaty Day Celebration
　　Fort Washakie (June)
Shoshone Indian Days
　　Fort Washakie (June)
Shoshone Stampede Rodeo
　　Fort Washakie (June)
Northern Arapaho Powwow
　　Arapahoe (July)
Eastern Shoshone Sundance Ceremony
　　Fort Washakie (July)
Sosonreh Heritage Circle
　　Fort Washakie (July)
Shoshone Tribal Fair
　　Fort Washakie (August)
Ethete Powwow
　　Ethete (August)
Labor Day Powwow
　　Ethete (September)

Places to Stay & Eat

Two campgrounds are usually open May to October. *Rocky Acres Campground* (☎ 307-332-6953), 5700 US 287 4½ miles northwest of Lander, charges $9/12 for tent/full-hookup sites and has laundry and showers. The friendly *Ray Lake Campground* (☎ 307-332-9333), 39 Ray Lake Rd off US 287 8 miles north of Lander, costs $7/13.

German-owned *El Ranchito* (☎ 307-332-2060), next to the Hines General Store in Fort Washakie, has a Shoshone cook who prepares Mexican food, including, of course, Indian tacos. Friday afternoons they have a cookout of ribs, baked beans and potato salad.

Red Rock Lodge (☎ 307-455-2944, 307-455-3272), on US 26/US 287 near Crowheart about 25 miles east of Dubois, has double rooms for $25 and RV sites for $15; tepees and tent sites cost $5, including showers. It also has a bar and restaurant.

Shopping

The Singing Horse Gallery (☎ 307-856-6688) in the North American Indian Heritage Center sells Shoshone and Arapaho crafts, including war charms, feather ornaments, collector dolls and rawhide items like parfleches, shields and warbonnet cases.

Shoshone Tribe Arts & Crafts, at the Texaco station in Fort Washakie, open daily 8 am to 5 pm, sells mostly jewelry. Warm Valley Arts & Crafts (☎ 307-332-7330), on North Fork Rd in Fort Washakie, has a selection of crafts.

Getting There & Away

Bus The Wind River Transportation Authority (WRTA; ☎ 307-856-7118) provides regular weekday and on-demand bus service between Fort Washakie, Ethete, Kinnear, Lander, Hudson, Arapahoe and Riverton. Regular stops include the Hines General Store in Fort Washakie, the stoplight intersection in Ethete and Z's Country Corner in Kinnear. You can also flag down buses en route. The fares are 75¢ for 15 miles; seniors pay only 25¢ for unlimited mileage. Children under five ride free. WRTA goes to the Rock Springs/ Sweetwater County Airport for $45 as needed; reservations are required.

The nearest Powder River Coach USA (☎ 307-332-3102) bus stop is in Shoshoni (see Shoshoni earlier in this chapter).

Car Fort Washakie is along US 287 about 15 miles northwest of Lander. Ethete is about 5 miles east of Fort Washakie at Ethete Rd and Hwy 132. St Stephens is on Rendezvous Rd (Hwy 138) 3 miles southwest of Riverton. US 26 and US 287 join south of the Wind River, about 16 miles north of Fort Washakie, and run together to Grand Teton National Park via Dubois.

Upper Wind River Valley

The Wind River headwaters descend from the eastern slopes of Togwotee Pass. South of the river the glacially carved granite Wind River Mountains carry the Continental Divide for over 100 miles. To the north of Wind River are the forested volcanic Absaroka Mountains. The enormous Shoshone National Forest covers parts of both mountain ranges. The name 'Wind' comes from the warm winter chinook winds that limit snow accumulation. Dubois is the only town in the upper valley, east of which is the semi-arid Dubois badlands comprised of red sandstone. Hiking, climbing, fishing, horseback riding and snowmobiling are the most popular activities. Several guest ranches are in the area. The short summer season lasts August to September.

FITZPATRICK WILDERNESS AREA
Access to the 311-sq-mile Fitzpatrick Wilderness Area is southeast of Dubois, south of US 26/US 287. At the end of USFS Rd 257 (Trail Lake Rd) at the head of the Torrey Valley, 8 miles south of US 26/US 287, the **Glacier Trail** begins. The

two-hour hike to Lake Louise begins here, as does one of two equally popular trails for **Gannett Peak** (13,804 feet), Wyoming's highest. This approach to Gannett Peak is drier, hotter, longer and tougher than the approach from Elkhart Park (see Around Pinedale later in this chapter), but the summit day is easier. The longer **Dinwoody Trail** joins the Glacier Trail approach to Gannett Peak. Llamas and horses frequently pack gear for extended backcountry trips; numerous outfitters are in Dubois.

The largest glaciers in the lower 48 states descend from the Winds. Many technical summits range up to 5.10; snow and ice routes lead to Gannett's summit. For instruction and guided climbs in the Wind River Range, contact Exum Mountain Guides (☎ 307-733-2297; fax 307-733-9613), PO Box 56, Moose, WY 83012.

DUBOIS & AROUND
Picturesque Dubois (population 895; elevation 6917 feet), originally settled by Scottish and Slavic immigrants, is a small farming and ranching community between the Wind River Indian Reservation and Grand Teton National Park. An old beaver trapping area, Dubois for years supplied railroad ties for the CB&Q Railroad, though nowadays tourism is replacing the waning timber economy and trophy heads and stuffed big game animals serve only as reminders of a fading way of life. Locals will snicker at anyone using the standard Gallic pronunciation of Dubois; locals say 'dew-boys.'

Orientation & Information
US 26/US 287, the main road, enters Dubois from the southeast as S 1st St, then turns sharply west to become Ramshorn St which runs east-west through town. Horse Creek Rd (USFS Rd 285), which goes north from Dubois just west of the creek, is the dividing line for east-west street addresses. The Wind River flows south of US 26/US 287.

The Dubois Chamber of Commerce (☎ 307-455-2556, 800-645-6233), 616 W

Ramshorn St, PO Box 632, Dubois, WY 82513, is open 9 am to 4 pm weekdays, and 10 am to 3 pm Saturday. The USFS Shoshone National Forest Wind River Ranger Station (☎ 307-455-2466), 1403 W Ramshorn St, about 1 mile west of downtown, has a series of handouts on campgrounds and hiking trails.

The post office is at 804 W Ramshorn St. Weber Office Supply (☎ 307-455-3150), 103 S 1st St, provides fax services. Two Ocean Books (☎ 307-455-3554), 128 E Ramshorn St, has a small but excellent selection of Western writers and natural history. A laundry is at 410 W Ramshorn St.

National Bighorn Sheep Interpretive Center

The National Bighorn Sheep Interpretive Center (☎ 307-455-3429, 888-209-2795), 907 W Ramshorn St, is dedicated to the conservation of the Rocky Mountain bighorn sheep and its habitat. It offers a series of videos along with exhibits on other threatened species and environments, and is open 9 am to 8 pm daily, Memorial to Labor Day, and 9 am to 4 pm Thursday to Monday the rest of the year. Admission is $2/75¢ for adults/children, $5 for families.

Whiskey Basin Wildlife Habitat Area

Whiskey Basin has one of America's densest concentrations of bighorn sheep, with Torrey Valley, beneath Whiskey Peak (11,157 feet), being the winter range for 900 bighorn sheep as well as other mammals and waterfowl. Turn onto Fish Hatchery Rd off US 26/US 287 4½ miles east of Dubois and turn immediately left onto USFS Rd 257 (Trail Lake Rd); look for the sign to Whiskey Basin Wildlife Habitat Area. The 8-mile Trail Lake Rd along Torrey Creek passes Julia, Torrey, Ring and Trail lakes. Roadside wildlife viewing is excellent; bring binoculars. The National Bighorn Sheep Interpretive Center offers five-hour weekend tours ($30) from mid-November to April. Two brochures describe the route in detail: 'Self-Guided Wildlife Tour of the Whiskey Basin Wildlife Habitat Area' by the National Bighorn

Sheep Interpretive Association and one for the 'Audubon Camp in the West,' a camp jointly run by the Audubon Society and Wyoming Game and Fish Department.

Wind River Historical Center (Dubois Museum)

This well-organized museum (☎ 307-455-2284), 909 W Ramshorn St, displays unique facets of life in the Dubois region, including a fine diorama of hunting drives, the history of the now-vanished Sheepeater branch of the Shoshone, tie-hack camps (including WWII German POWs), a relief map of the Dubois area and full mounts of bighorn sheep. The museum also contains a collection of early outbuildings from around the area, including a homestead cabin, a two-seater outhouse and the classic Swan's Service Station. Open 10 am to 5 pm, mid-May to mid-September.

Tie-Hack Country

Pick up the 'A Self-Guided Tour of Tie-Hack Country' handout at the Wind River Historical Center, which details flumes, headgates and other area logging industry remnants. Many sites are south of US 26/US 287, along Union Pass and Sheridan Creek Rds. From Union Pass, six mountain ranges are visible.

Near the **Tie Hack Memorial Wayside**, 17 miles west of Dubois, the Wyoming Tie & Timber Company hired ax-wielding Scandinavian immigrants to spend their winters hacking out railroad ties, which were then floated down the Wind River during spring runoff to Riverton for the use of the Chicago & Northwestern Railroad. Between 1914 and 1946, the hacks cut over 400,000 ties annually.

Fishing

For fishing gear, maps and information, contact the Wind River Fly Shop (☎ 307-455-2140), 211 W Ramshorn St, Whiskey Mountain Tackle (☎ 307-455-2587), 102 W Ramshorn St, or Welty's General Store (☎ 307-455-2377), 113 W Ramshorn St. The **Dubois Fish Hatchery**, 5 miles east of Dubois on Fish Hatchery Rd, produces nearly 7 million eggs annually of rainbow, cutthroat, brown, brook, golden and grayling trout. Most are shipped elsewhere, but about a million find their way into local streams.

Places to Stay

Dubois gets crowded and expensive during summer, so reservations are recommended. The river-front *Circle Up Camper Court* (☎ 307-455-2238), 225 W Welty St, has shady tent sites ($14) and barren sites with hookups ($19). They also have coin-operated showers, six-person tepees ($15) and four-person cabins ($20) without bedding.

The friendly and tranquil *Red Rock Ranch Motel* (☎ 307-455-2337), 5810 US 26 2 miles east of town, has kitchenette singles/double with no TV or telephone for $35/40. *Motel 8* (☎ 307-455-3694), 1414 Warm Springs Drive, at the west end of town, costs $40/45. Rooms at the *Rendez-vous Motel* (☎ 307-455-2844), 1342 W Ramshorn St, start at $39. *Twin Pines Motel* (☎ 307-455-2600; twinpines@wyoming.com), 218 W Ramshorn St, starts at $40/50. Comparably priced motels include the *Trail's End Motel* (☎ 307-455-2540), 511 W Ramshorn St; *Wind River Motel* (☎ 307-455-2611), 519 W Ramshorn St; and *Pinnacle Buttes Lodge & Campground* (☎ 307-455-2506; fax 307-455-3874), 3577 US 26.

Rooms at the *Black Bear Country Inn* (☎ 307-455-2344, 800-873-2327), 505 W Ramshorn St, cost $42/48. Slightly more is the *Super 8 Motel* (☎ 307-455-3694), 1414 Warm Springs Drive ($46/61). Next to Horse Creek is the pleasant and attractive *Stagecoach Motor Inn* (☎ 307-455-2303, 800-455-5090; fax 307-455-3903), 103 E Ramshorn St ($46/58), with a pool and nightly outdoor cookout during summer. The *Branding Iron Motel* (☎ 307-455-2893, 800-341-8000 reservations; brandingiron@wyoming.com), 401 W Ramshorn St, costs $48/59. The Western-style *Chinook Winds Mountain Lodge* (☎ 307-455-2987, 800-863-0354; chinook@wyoming.com), 640 S 1st St, ranges from $50 to $80.

Places to Eat

The *Daylight Donuts & Village Cafe* (☎ 307-455-2122), 515 W Ramshorn St, is a daybreak coffee shop that at nightfall transforms into a passable steakhouse. *Wild West Deli* (☎ 307-455-3354), 206 W Ramshorn St, offers appealing sandwiches and salads, but closes by 6 pm. *The Hang-Out* (☎ 307-455-3800), 8 Stalnaker St, has bagels, espresso, soups, submarine sandwiches and salads.

For Dubois cowboy grub, try the family-oriented *Cowboy Cafe* (☎ 307-455-2595), 115 E Ramshorn St; *Rustic Pine Steak House* (☎ 307-455-2772), 119 E Ramshorn St; or the *Ramshorn Inn* (☎ 307-455-2400), 202 E Ramshorn St. *Lake's Lodge* (☎ 307-455-2171), 10 miles south of town on Union Pass Rd, has more variety. The *Outlaw Saloon* (☎ 307-455-2387), 204 W Ramshorn St, is another good option worth investigating.

The popular *Old Yellowstone Garage* (☎ 307-455-3666), 116 E Ramshorn, a place to splurge, attracts diners from as far away as Jackson with its varied menu, featuring superb pizza and pasta, espresso bar and ample outdoor seating.

Getting There & Away

Dubois is on US 26/US 287 78 miles west of Riverton, 75 miles northwest of Lander and 55 miles east of Moran Junction via Togwotee Pass. The Wyoming Centennial Scenic Byway follows US 191 and US 287 between Dubois and Pinedale via Grand Teton National Park.

DUBOIS TO TOGWOTEE PASS

The dramatic Pinnacle Buttes loom over the grizzly bear habitat of the upper Wind River valley northwest of Dubois. (See the Greater Yellowstone chapter for Togwotee Pass and destinations west.)

Horse Creek Rd (USFS Rd 285) leads 12 miles north of Dubois to the **Ramshorn Basin**, above which towers The Ramshorn (11,920 feet). Here trails begin that cross passes such as Shoshone Pass into the 1100-sq-mile **Washakie Wilderness Area**. From Ramshorn Basin, USFS Rd

285 continues as Wiggins Fork Rd for 17 miles to the Frontier Creek trailhead; 4WD is recommended. The USFS campgrounds ($6) in the area are *Horse Creek* (7500 feet) in Ramshorn Basin and *Double Cabin* (8053 feet), at the Frontier Creek trailhead.

The scenic **Brooks Lake Recreation Area**, 5 miles north of US 26/US 287 on Brooks Lake Rd (USFS Rd 515), is popular for fishing and camping. From the northwest shore of Brooks Lake meanders the very pleasant **Jade Lakes Trail**, while the **Yellowstone Trail** leads north into the Teton Wilderness Area. Other trails circle Pinnacles Buttes via Kissinger Lakes east of Brook Lake. Kissinger Lakes are also accessible via Long Creek Rd (USFS Rd 659) north of US 26/US 287. The USFS campgrounds ($9) are *Falls* (8000 feet), on US 26 23 miles west of Dubois, and *Pinnacles* and *Brooks Lake*, on opposite sides of Brooks Lake (9200 feet).

Nearby year-round *Brooks Lake Lodge* (☎ 307-455-2121), 458 Brooks Lake Rd, on the National Register of Historic Places, features fishing and horseback riding during summer and cross-country skiing and hearty midday meals during winter.

Wind River Mountains – Southwest Side

The steep southwest side of the Wind River Mountains contrasts dramatically with the gentle forested slopes on the northeast. Dozens of creeks and rivers flow through the Bridger-Teton National Forest where a multitude of lakes offer great fishing. North of Pinedale is Fremont Lake, the largest; southeast are Half Moon and Boulder lakes; and northwest are Willow, New Fork and Green River lakes. Many trails follow the creeks and rivers that feed these lakes into the 669-sq-mile **Bridger Wilderness Area**, where meadows, high plateaus and secluded valleys are teeming with wildlife. Pinedale, which is north of a

vast sage-covered plateau called The Mesa, is the base for excursions into the Winds.

PINEDALE
Beneath the southwest slope of the Wind River Range, along Pine Creek, a tributary of the Green River, the Sublette County seat of Pinedale (population 1330; elevation 7175 feet) is a place to enjoy year-round outdoor activities. Pinedale, a friendly beef and timber town extends an amiable if sometimes ambivalent welcome to visitors.

Orientation
Pine Creek flows south through town. US 191, the main road, runs east-west through town where it is known as Pine St. Tyler Ave divides east-west street addresses. East of Bridger Ave US 191 turns south and Fremont Lake Rd (also called Skyline Drive) turns north.

Information
The Pinedale Area Chamber of Commerce (☎ 307-367-2242), 32 E Pine St, PO Box 176, Pinedale, WY 82941, between Tyler Ave and Fremont Ave, is open 9 am to 5 pm weekdays during summer. The USFS Bridger-Teton National Forest Pinedale Ranger Station (☎ 307-367-4326), 210 W Pine St, is open 8 am to 4:30 pm weekdays. The BLM Pinedale Resource Area office (☎ 307-367-4358), 432 E Mill St off Pine St, is at the east end of town. They have extensive campground and trail information available on the Wind River Range and the area north of Rock Springs. The Wyoming Game and Fish Department's regional office (☎ 307-367-4352), at 117 S Sublette Ave, publishes a free pocket guide to the fishing lakes of the Bridger Wilderness Area.

First National Bank of Pinedale is at 61 E Pine St. The post office is at 413 W Pine St. Moosely Books (☎ 307-367-6622), 7 W Pine St, has great Western books in a pleasant setting. Pinedale Medical Clinic (☎ 307-367-4133) is at 619 E Hennick St, just off Fremont Lake Rd and north of the Museum of the Mountain Man. Do laundry at Highlander Center, 313 W Pine St.

Museum of the Mountain Man

Financed by the successful Green River Rendezvous (see below), the 15,000-sq-foot Museum of the Mountain Man (☎ 307-367-4102), 700 E Hennick Rd, off Fremont Lake Rd half a mile northeast of town, may be the finest museum of its kind, with critical interpretations of early European exploration of the West, the fur trade and pioneer settlement in western Wyoming. It is open 10 am to 6 pm daily, May to September. Admission is $4/3/2 for adults/seniors/children (six-12).

Green River Rendezvous

The Green River Rendezvous, one of Wyoming's biggest special events, is a reenactment of the arrival of traders and settlers in the upper Green River area, their interactions with the Native Americans and the establishment of the fur trade. The rendezvous first took place in 1936, and some of the original participants still attend. It is clearly a commercial event though the entire populace eagerly collaborates, even to the point of making their own buckskin clothing. Local native John Barlow, a lyricist for the Grateful Dead, serves as the event's narrator. The rendezvous is much more than a pageant: it includes lectures and living history presentations at the Museum of the Mountain Man, live entertainment at Town Square, the Pelt & Plew Special (an inexpensive buffalo feed) and rodeos. The rendezvous takes place the second weekend of July.

Places to Stay

Northbound travelers may find that Pinedale is where rates rise due to proximity to Jackson and the Greater Yellowstone area; even mediocre motels are not very cheap, especially during summer. Reservations are recommended during the Green River Rendezvous (see above).

Camping The uninspiring and shadeless but friendly *Pinedale Campground* (☎ 307-367-4555), 204 Jackson Ave south of Pine St, is the only campground. Grassy tent sites cost $11; sites with full hookups cost $18. Showers for nonguests cost $4.

B&Bs The *Window on the Winds B&B* (☎ 307-367-2600, 888-367-1345; fax 307-367-2395), 10151 US 191, 1 mile west of Pinedale, is a modern house; rooms range from $45 to $75. At the *Branding Iron Bunkhouse B&B* (☎ 307-367-2146), 146 Ehman Lane, 2 miles northwest of town, singles/doubles cost $45/55. *The Chambers House B&B* (☎ 307-367-2168, 800-567-2168), 111 W Magnolia St, has rooms ranging from $50 to $80. The attractive *Pole Creek Ranch B&B* (☎ 307-367-4433) is at 244 Fayette Pole Creek Rd.

Motels Most places are east of Pine Creek. Rates at attractive creekside *Rivera Lodge* (☎ 307-367-2424), 442 W Marilyn St, start at $48. The rooms are clean but small and have no telephone; some have kitchenettes. The well-maintained *Log Cabin Motel* (☎ 307-367-4579), 49 E Magnolia St, starts at $45. Comparably priced are the shabby *Camp O' the Pines Motel* (☎ 307-367-4536), 38 N Fremont Ave, with some kitchenettes, and the *Half Moon Lodge Motel* (☎ 307-367-2851), 46 N Sublette Ave. Rooms at the *Sun Dance Motel* (☎ 307-367-4336, 800-833-9178), 148 E Pine St, cost $59/64. The undistinguished *ZZZZ Inn* (☎ 307-367-2121), 327 S Pine St, is overpriced at $65. The *Wagon Wheel Motel* (☎ 307-367-2871), 407 S Pine St, costs $45/55.

At the west end of town is the old and worn *Pine Creek Inn* (☎ 307-367-2191), 650 W Pine St, overpriced at $46/52. The newer *Best Western Pinedale Inn* (☎ 307-367-6869), 850 W Pine St, is the fanciest place in town.

Places to Eat

Food tastes in Pinedale are evolving beyond traditional cowboy cuisine. *Sue's Breadbox* (☎ 307-367-2150), 423 W Pine St, has sourdough rolls, good blueberry muffins and cinnamon rolls, as does *Fife's Sourdough House* (☎ 307-367-2698), 119 S Fremont St. *Grinders* (☎ 307-367-4769),

807 W Pine St, has takeout sandwiches. *Sweet Tooth Saloon*, 44 W Pine St, part of Moose Creek Trading Company, has excellent sandwiches on homemade bread, with sidewalk seating and occasional live music during summer. *McGregor's Pub* (☎ 307-367-4443), 21 N Franklin Ave, has a diverse and appealing menu and a shady patio. The *Fremont Peak Restaurant* (☎ 307-367-2259), 20 W Pine St, has very good German food and desserts. *Wrangler Cafe* (☎ 307-367-4233), 905 W Pine St, is a traditional Pinedale eatery, as is the *Patio Grill & Dining Room* (☎ 307-367-4611), 35 W Pine St. *Faler's Thriftway* (☎ 307-367-2131), 341 E Pine St, is a general store with a deli.

Entertainment
Pinedale has several bar/restaurants that offer live music: *Calamity Jane's* (☎ 307-367-2469), also modestly known as the *World Famous Corral Bar*, 30 W Pine St; *The Cowboy Bar* (☎ 307-367-4520), 104 W Pine St; and the *Stockman's Steak Pub* (☎ 307-367-4563), 117 W Pine St.

Getting There & Away
Pinedale is on US 191, which leads northwest to Jackson (77 miles) and south to Rock Springs (106 miles). The Wyoming Centennial Scenic Byway follows US 191 and US 287 between Pinedale and Dubois via Grand Teton National Park.

Getting Around
Sublette Stage (☎ 307-367-6633), 36 E North St, is a taxi company that also provides transport to the nearest airports as well as nearby trailheads.

AROUND PINEDALE
Fremont Lake
Four miles north of Pinedale via Fremont Lake Rd (also called Skyline Drive) is the south shore of Fremont Lake, the largest on the southwestern side of the Wind River Range. The glacially formed lake (7400 feet), named for General John C Frémont, has a 22-mile shoreline and is 600 feet deep. The sandy beach at its south end is good for swimming. Fishing for grayling, brook and golden trout is popular.

The USFS *Fremont Lake Campground* ($6) is midway up the lake's eastern shore. At the south end, the *Lakeside Lodge Resort* (☎ 307-367-2221), Fremont Lake, PO Box 1819, Pinedale, WY 82941, has a good restaurant, an RV Park ($16), cabins (singles/doubles $45/55) and motel rooms ($50/55). Its marina rents canoes, pontoons, and fishing boats. It is open May 15 to September. Other lodges off Fremont Lake Rd are *Ponderosa Lodge* and *White Pine Lodge*.

White Pine Ski Area
The White Pine Ski Area (8480 feet) along Fremont Lake Rd has a small downhill area (one run with a 900-foot vertical drop) and extensive, groomed cross-country trails. The USFS 'Skyline Drive Nordic Touring Trails' brochure details several loop routes, also popular for hiking and mountain biking, around Fortification Mountain, Lower Sweeney Lake and Elkhart Park (see below).

Elkhart Park
At the end of the scenic 15-mile Skyline Drive is Elkhart Park (9480 feet), a popular Wind River trailhead. Volunteer-staffed Elkhart Park visitors center is open 9 am to 6 pm daily, June 1 to Labor Day. Nearby is the USFS *Trails End Campground* (9100 feet, $5). The best day hike is the 4-mile **Pole Creek Trail** through spruce and pine forest to **Photographer's Point** (10,340 feet), for a spectacular view of the Continental Divide and Gannett Peak. The trail continues north from Photographer's Point toward Jackson, Fremont and Gannett peaks. This approach to Gannett Peak is higher, shorter and easier, but the summit day harder, than the Glacier Trail approach from Dubois (see Fitzpatrick Wilderness Area earlier in this chapter).

Fishing
Fishing sites are almost unlimited around Pinedale, from the Green and New Fork rivers of the lowlands to expansive Fremont Lake in the foothills and hundreds of

smaller lakes in the high country. Ice fishing is popular. Randall's Fishing Guide Service (☎ 307-367-4857), 118 S Maybell Ave, Pinedale, specializes in fly-fishing trips.

Mountain Biking

The Mesa, with 780 sq miles of public land, offers varied desert terrain for mountain biking and is the site of the annual **Fat Tire Challenge Mountain Bike Race** in August. Coast to Coast (☎ 307-367-2116), 641 W Pine St, Pinedale, sells bicycles and does repairs. Wyoming Rivers & Trails (☎ 307-537-5666), on Hwy 353 north of Boulder, runs half-day and multiple-day mountain bike trips. (See Elkhart Park above.)

Hiking & Backpacking

The major trailheads for backpacking into the Winds are Green River Lakes (see below), New Fork Lakes, Willow Creek Guard Station and Spring Creek Park, northwest of Pinedale; Elkhart Park (see above); and Boulder Lake, Scab Creek and Big Sandy, southeast of Pinedale.

In Pinedale, the Great Outdoor Shop (☎ 307-367-2440), 332 W Pine St, and Wind River Sporting Goods (☎ 307-367-2419), 234 E Pine St, sell gear and maps. Several outfitters arrange backcountry trips, many with pack animals, including Wind River Hiking Consultants (☎ 307-367-2560), PO Box 1557, Pinedale, WY 82941.

GREEN RIVER LAKES

The upper Green River was once a prime area for tie hacks. Railroad ties were cut in winter and floated during the spring runoff down to the town of Green River, 130 miles south. Today the Green River Lakes are the westernmost trailhead for the Wind River Range, and are reached by driving 6 miles west of Pinedale on US 191 and then 40 miles north on Hwy 352; only the first 25 miles of this route are paved. En route to the lakes, watch for **Kendall Dace** on USFS Rd 10091, beyond Hwy 352, along the Green River. Here a two-inch-long species of freshwater fish live their entire

lives in the 84.4°F Kendall Warm Springs, the only place they are found on the planet. Breeding males are purple; females green.

When hiking around the lower of the two Green River Lakes, take the warm south-facing slope on the north side in the morning; return via the shady north-facing slope in the afternoon. **Square Top Mountain** (11,695 feet) is a massive, and often photographed, landmark butte.

A good day hike to **Clear Creek Natural Bridge**, where the creek has cut a channel through weak limestone, is the easy two-hour walk from the **Highline Trail** at the north end of Green River Lakes, through a burned lodgepole forest. About 1 mile before you reach the natural bridge, a log bridge crosses the creek to a spur trail to **Slide Lake**, which features a natural water slide. The **Lakeside Trail** returns to the USFS *Green River Lakes Campground* (8000 feet, $6) on the west side of the lake, which has few spots with panoramas of the Winds. The Highline Trail is also the starting point for traversing the 100-mile crest of the Wind River Range to Little Sandy Lake.

BOULDER & AROUND

Boulder (population 75; elevation 7016 feet) is not much more than the junction of US 191 and Hwy 353 southeast of Pinedale. Singles/doubles at the *Boulder Inn Motel* (☎ 307-537-5480) cost $55/65. The adjacent *Basecamp Restaurant* is open for breakfast, lunch and dinner, with deli sandwiches, beef dinners and occasional live country music. No campgrounds are in this desolate town. Boulder Lake Rd heads north off Hwy 353 (Big Sandy-Elkhorn Rd, USFS Rd 215).

Big Sandy Trailhead

Camping is free at the USFS *Big Sandy Campground* (9100 feet), the trailhead for **Cirque of the Towers**, a highly regarded wilderness climbing area. A semicircle of over 15 granite peaks, with names like Lizard Head, Wolf's Head, Warbonnet, Warrior, Watchtower and Overhanging Tower, has fine routes ranging from 5.7 to

5.12. Several trails from the Big Sandy trailhead lead to passes that cross into the Popo Agie Wilderness Area. From Boulder, follow Hwy 353 (Big Sandy-Elkhorn Rd) east to the small settlement of Big Sandy, and continue on USFS Rd 215 to the Big Sandy trailhead. Alternatively, from Hwy 28 southwest of South Pass, take Farson-Little Sandy Rd (USFS Rd 101) north to the Big Sandy-Elkhorn Rd.

Greater Yellowstone

The Greater Yellowstone ecosystem, a 43,750-sq-mile area in Wyoming, Montana and Idaho, comprises Yellowstone and Grand Teton national parks, seven national forests in the three states and three national wildlife refuges. Environmentalists and conservationists consider this area an intact natural ecosystem, the largest in the lower 48 states, with rivers, forests, prairies and wildlife that ought to be managed as a sustainable unity. During the 1990s a 12% annual growth rate has pressured the ecosystem's finite resources. Yellowstone National Park is the area's main attraction, and the area's history is largely the history of the park and its development. This chapter covers most of the ecosystem within northwest Wyoming.

HIGHLIGHTS

- Yellowstone National Park – the world's first national park and home to North America's most spectacular wildlife, a wonderland of geysers, hot springs, forested mountains, Alpine lakes and waterfalls

- Old Faithful geyser – Yellowstone's star attraction

- Grand Teton National Park – the jagged granite spires tower over world-renowned ski resorts

Yellowstone National Park

Yellowstone National Park, established on March 1, 1872, is the world's first national park. The park was created primarily to preserve the area's unique geological features: the geothermal phenomena, the Grand Canyon of the Yellowstone, the fossil forests and Yellowstone Lake. But Yellowstone is also home to the largest concentration of wildlife in the lower 48 states, and its abundant Alpine lakes, rivers and waterfalls are world-renowned. Five distinct regions comprise the 3472-sq-mile park (starting clockwise from the north): Mammoth, Roosevelt, Canyon, Lake and Geyser countries. In 1912 *National Geographic* published its first article about Yellowstone, recommending that visitors allow 5½ days to visit the park. The same holds true today, although it is easy to spend more time. This cornucopia of natural features attracts up to 30,000 visitors daily, and 3 million visitors each year. Unfortunately, the park's great appeal threatens to destroy the very features that draw such numbers.

History
Hunter-gatherers occupied the Yellowstone plateau for more than 8500 years after the region's last glaciers melted. In 1807, when John Colter was the first white man to visit the area, the only inhabitants were Tukudikas or Sheepeaters, a Shoshone-Bannock people who hunted bighorn sheep. The Crow and Blackfeet also visited the area. Other Native American tribes occasionally passed through Yellowstone country even

extraordinary geothermal features, at first dismissed as tall tales, brought increased scientific interest. This led to a series of expeditions, culminating in the US Geological and Geographical Survey (USGS), headed by FV Hayden, in 1871. Hayden's scientific work was fairly pedestrian, but two members of his party, landscape painter Thomas Moran and photographer William Henry Jackson, produced works of art that excited interest in the area and, with lobbying from the Northern Pacific Railroad, led to the designation in 1872 of Yellowstone as a national park – in large part because the US Congress could not imagine any other use for this remote area.

At first, the US Congress failed to fund direct protective activities. The US Army managed the park from 1886 until the creation of the NPS in 1916 (the NPS ranger's uniform owes its distinctive doughboy hat to the US Army's tenure in the park). Under the US Army, the park's features were largely maintained in their existing state, but with the changeover to the newly formed NPS, policies of predator eradication, habitat destruction in the name of development and uncontrolled hunting outside park boundaries led to the creation of an artificial and ultimately unsustainable ecology.

The NPS now admits that efforts to exterminate predators were mistaken. The intensive development of a small area (about 1%) of the park for tourism, however, continues to raise controversy. The park's 270 miles of roads are crowded, and the more than 2000 buildings, 2184 hotel rooms and cabins and 15 restaurants are seen by some as an artificial distraction from the park's natural splendor. The NPS sees it as meeting public demand. Historian Daniel Boorstin offered a singular explanation for the conundrum of Yellowstone's popularity; according to Boorstin, the park's tourist appeal is

after its declaration as a national park. One of the most extraordinary historic episodes was the 1877 flight of the Nez Percé, led by Chief Joseph, who fled their ancestral lands in Oregon to avoid persecution by the US Army. In crossing Yellowstone, the Nez Percé briefly seized several tourists before continuing north up the Clarks Fork River toward Canada. They were eventually captured in Montana.

Mountain men in search of furs came after Colter, but the fur trade soon declined. Next came miners, inspired by gold strikes in Montana, but the results were disappointing. Then reports of Yellowstone's

due to the fact that its natural phenomena – its geysers and paint pots which erupt and boil on schedule – come closest to the artificiality of 'regular' tourist performances.

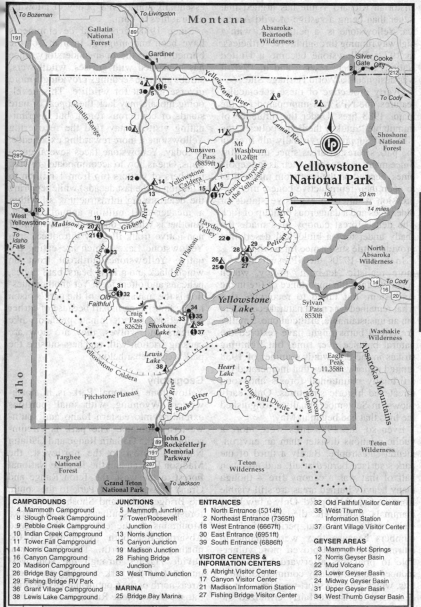

WYOMING

CAMPGROUNDS
4. Mammoth Campground
8. Slough Creek Campground
9. Pebble Creek Campground
10. Indian Creek Campground
11. Tower Fall Campground
14. Norris Campground
16. Canyon Campground
20. Madison Campground
26. Bridge Bay Campground
29. Fishing Bridge RV Park
36. Grant Village Campground
38. Lewis Lake Campground

JUNCTIONS
5. Mammoth Junction
7. Tower/Roosevelt Junction
13. Norris Junction
19. Madison Junction
28. Fishing Bridge Junction
33. West Thumb Junction

MARINA
25. Bridge Bay Marina

ENTRANCES
1. North Entrance (5314ft)
2. Northeast Entrance (7365ft)
18. West Entrance (6667ft)
30. East Entrance (6951ft)
39. South Entrance (6886ft)

VISITOR CENTERS & INFORMATION CENTERS
6. Albright Visitor Center
17. Canyon Visitor Center
21. Madison Information Station
27. Fishing Bridge Visitor Center

32. Old Faithful Visitor Center
35. West Thumb Information Station
37. Grant Village Visitor Center

GEYSER AREAS
3. Mammoth Hot Springs
12. Norris Geyser Basin
22. Mud Volcano
23. Lower Geyser Basin
24. Midway Geyser Basin
31. Upper Geyser Basin
34. West Thumb Geyser Basin

Historian Richard White has argued that rather than being a vestige of wild America, Yellowstone is 'a petting zoo with a highway running through it.' Nevertheless, in 1972, Yellowstone became a United Nations biosphere reserve and in 1978 it was designated a World Heritage Site.

Overly protective of these spectacular features, the NPS was unprepared for the major 1988 fires. Under the influence of immutable 'Smokey the Bear' policies, the NPS had suppressed virtually all fires in the park's forested areas since the 1940s. Since many tree species, such as lodgepole pines, depend on the heat from minor fires to open their reproductive cones, fire suppression resulted in extensive stands of older trees and a dangerous buildup of fuel. The dense forest canopy also made the shady understory a biological desert that provided little sustenance for wildlife.

In the mid-1970s, the NPS switched to a more realistic 'let-burn' policy, which acknowledged the importance of fire in the ecosystem, but failed to recognize that what remained was not a natural ecosystem but an unsustainable, artificial one. Smaller prescribed burns might have restored the natural balance over time, but lightning strikes in the dry, windy summer of 1988 ignited major wildfires that incinerated the artificially maintained forests and soon threatened historic structures. Only early snows, in September, finally extinguished the fires that had begun in May.

Even so, the 1988 fires were more a public relations disaster than an environmental catastrophe. Barely a third of the park's surface burned at all, and not even half of that was a canopy fire – though many heavily burned areas are still visible from the Grand Loop Rd. Only a few large mammals, mostly elk, died. Small mammals, on the other hand, perished in large numbers because they were unable to outrun the fires and proved more vulnerable to predators afterward because of reduced shelter. Nearby commercial interests, which suffered short-term losses from decreased tourism, unfairly criticized the essentially sound NPS policy of allowing natural fires to burn.

Since 1988, ecological developments have been encouraging. In many of the burned areas, the open understory since has flourished with grasses, wildflowers, shrubs and tree seedlings providing a more diverse habitat for wildlife. This developing mosaic may lack the appeal of pure stands of coniferous forest, but discriminating visitors may find the recovering Yellowstone a more rewarding experience.

Today, Yellowstone faces several questions. One is how to accommodate growing numbers of visitors (up from 1 million to 3 million in the last decade) while repairing the deteriorating infrastructure, all within a meager $20 million annual budget. Another is what to do about an invasion of non-native trout, illegally introduced into Yellowstone Lake, which are eating the native Yellowstone cutthroat trout on which black and grizzly bears, bald eagles, pelicans and otters feed. Yet another question is the management of the park's bison herds: flourishing in part because of earlier NPS efforts to exterminate predators like cougars and wolves, they are now are causing friction with ranchers outside the park (see sidebar below).

Geography

Yellowstone National Park is in northwestern Wyoming, with small portions extending into eastern Idaho and southwestern Montana. The park is circumscribed by the Gallatin Range and Gallatin National Forest to the northwest, the Madison Plateau and the Targhee National Forest to the west, the Teton Range and Grand Teton National Park to the south, the Bridger-Teton and Shoshone national forests to the southeast, the Absaroka Mountains to the east and the rugged Absaroka-Beartooth Mountains to the northeast and north. The Continental Divide zigzags through the southwest quadrant of the park, trending east-west. Areas north of the Continental Divide drain into the Yellowstone River, areas south into

Slaughtering a National Symbol

Revered by Native Americans and a national symbol, the Yellowstone bison are the country's last wild herd. Despite protection within Yellowstone National Park, the herd's existence is threatened. As of December 1997 bison numbers were a dangerously low 2000, down from 4300 a few years before. Harsh winters cause bison to forage outside the park and many stray north toward Gardiner, MT. During the 1996-97 winter ranchers around Gardiner slaughtered over 1000 to prevent the spread of brucellosis (*Brucellosis abortus*), a bacteria that causes domestic cows to abort their calves. Brucellosis spreads from the park's abundant elk population to the bison, which are themselves unaffected by the bacteria. Whether or not brucellosis can actually spread from bison to cattle is unknown as scientific studies have yet to be conducted. But public outrage soared upon viewing footage of the 1996-97 bison slaughter, filmed by the Missoula, MT-based group Cold Mountain, Cold Rivers.

No policy to halt continuing bison slaughter has been implemented, but a long-term management plan is being studied that would allow bison to stray outside the park into designated safe foraging areas, limit the maximum number of bison inside the park and/ or vaccinate bison against brucellosis. Yellowstone's chief bison specialist does not believe brucellosis can be eradicated, however, because of the park's high elk concentration. Snowmobiling in the park also affects winter bison movement and is being studied as part of the problem. To lend support, contact the National Parks and Conservation Association (☎ 800-628-7275), which launched the 'Bison Belong' campaign calling for an end to the bison slaughter. ■

the Snake River. The lowest point is near the North Entrance (5314 feet); the highest point is Eagle Peak (11,358 feet) on the eastern boundary. Yellowstone's large Central Plateau (mostly above 7000 feet) is in one of the world's largest volcanic calderas, bisected by the Yellowstone River.

Geology

Volcanic activity characterizes Yellowstone National Park: catastrophic eruptions occurred here about 2 million, 1.2 million and most recently about 590,000 years ago. The last eruption emptied an underground magma chamber, spewing 240-cubic miles of debris. The resulting collapse of this chamber created the 28- by 47-mile-wide **Yellowstone caldera** in the central and southern portions of the park. Lava eventually filled the caldera. Other lava flows created numerous lakes and the 20-mile-long **Grand Canyon of the Yellowstone**. The canyon was later blocked three times by glaciers. Each time melting glaciers created outburst floods that deepened the canyon, which reached its present form

only about 10,000 years ago. The Yellowstone River now flows through this canyon, which ranges from 800 to 1200 feet in depth and 1500 to 4000 feet in width. Its yellowish volcanic rock walls are comprised mainly of rhyolite. **Yellowstone Lake** is one of North America's highest freshwater lakes at over 7000 feet. It is also one of the world's largest Alpine lakes at 136 sq miles and covers part of the Yellowstone caldera. It has 110 miles of shoreline and its greatest depth is 390 feet. Volcanic activity also created unique fossil forests, some as old as 50 million years, in the northern portion of the park.

The park has some 10,000 geothermal features, including 200 to 250 active geysers, more than all other geothermal areas on the planet combined. Heat from the earth's molten rock (magma), which is closer to the surface here than anywhere else on earth – just 3 to 5 miles underground – fuels these geothermal features. The role of this and similar hot spots in mountain building, the theory of plate tectonics and the extinction of the dinosaurs is the subject of considerable research and speculation.

The bulging of twin magma chambers on the rim of the Yellowstone caldera indicate possible future eruptions, and geologists say another eruption of the magnitude that created the Yellowstone caldera is plausible – but not for another 10,000 years or so.

Climate

Yellowstone has a humid continental climate with often unpredictable and extreme weather conditions. Wind, rain and lightning storms are common and can occur at any time of the year: the park has had huge snowstorms on July 4, and has recorded a January temperature of 50°F. Visitors need to check current weather conditions and be prepared for any type of weather at any time of year. Most visitors come during summer, when daylight remains until about 9:30 pm, allowing ample time for later afternoon and evening excursions. Yellowstone has much to offer during any season.

Temperature Average high temperatures in April and May range from 40° to 50°F, with low temperatures ranging from 0° to –20°F. During late May and June high temperatures are from 60° to 70°F. During summer high temperatures at lower elevations are usually around 70°F, and occasionally reach 80°F, with low temperatures ranging from 40° to 30°F. Temperatures are 10° to 20°F cooler at high elevations. The average monthly temperature, however, is 50°F.

Average high temperatures during fall are 40° to 60°F, with low temperatures ranging from 20° to 0°F. Winter high temperatures average 0°F, but occasionally rise to 20°F, with low temperatures ranging from 0°F to subzero. Occasionally, a warm chinook wind raises winter high temperatures to 40°F, melting the snowpack. More often, the wind-chill factor intensifies because of cold winter winds.

Precipitation The annual rainfall varies with the park's topography, ranging from 10 inches in the north to about 80 inches in the southwest. Snow lingers into April and May. June is usually rainy. July and August are drier, but afternoon thunderstorms with lightning are not uncommon. During fall and winter snowstorms occur with increasing frequency. The average winter snowfall is 150 inches, with 200 to 400 inches at the higher elevations.

Flora

Yellowstone's wide variety of habitats supports a diversity of plants. Aquatic grasses and plants thrive in the marshes, rivers and lakes. Surprisingly, a large community of algae along with plants like the yellow monkey flower *(Mimulus guttastus)* flourish in and around geothermal features. The sparsely vegetated northern desert (around Mammoth Hot Springs) supports grasses, sagebrush and Rocky Mountain juniper. Lower-elevation mixed sagebrush and grasslands (for example, the Hayden and Pelican valleys) are filled with wildflowers, grasses and shrubs and have relatively warm, dry weather. Douglas fir, quaking aspen, shrubs and berry bushes blanket the mixed forests from 6000 to 7000 feet between Mammoth Hot Springs and Tower/Roosevelt Junction. Lodgepole pine *(Pinus contorta)* forests, which range from 7600 to 8400 feet (eg, along Yellowstone Lake), cover 60% of the park's broad plateaus and comprise 80% of the park's forests. At elevations over 8400 feet (at the base of Mt Washburn and along Yellowstone Lake) the forests are predominantly Engelmann spruce *(Picea engelmannii)* and sub-Alpine fir *(Abies lasiocarpa)*, mixed with lodgepole pine that shade the spruce and fir. Above treeline, over 10,000 feet (Mt Washburn's summit), is Alpine tundra that supports lichen, sedges, grasses and flowers like Alpine buttercup and phlox.

Fauna

Yellowstone contains seven species of native ungulates (hoofed mammals): Yellowstone bison (buffaloes; *Bison bison)*, Rocky Mountain elk *(Cervus elaphus nel-*

soni), moose *(Alces alces shirasi)*, Rocky Mountain bighorn sheep *(Ovis canadiensis)*, mule deer *(Odocoileus hemionus)*, pronghorn antelope *(Antilocarpa americana)* and mountain goat *(Oreamnos americanus)*. Black bear *(Ursus americanus)* and about 200 endangered grizzly bear *(Ursus arctos horribilis)* also call Yellowstone home. Other notable species are red fox *(Vulpes vulpes)*, the threatened gray wolf *(Canis lupus)*, coyote *(Canis latrans)* and mountain lion *(Felis concolor missoulensis)*.

The spectacular Rocky Mountain trumpeter swan *(Cygnus buccinator)*, the most notable of Yellowstone birdlife, is hardy enough to winter here, but its numbers are declining. It has proved difficult to wean them from winter feeding, and Canadian trumpeter populations have crowded them out. Other large birds include osprey, great blue heron, sand hill crane, golden eagle, the endangered bald eagle, Canada geese and white pelicans. Smaller birds like ouzels (dippers), magpies and yellow-headed blackbirds abound.

In marshland and aquatic areas look for bald eagle, beaver and moose, and trout in fast-moving streams. Moose favor flat meadows near streams with protective cover like pine forest and willow shrubs. Such areas include Canyon Country and the Lewis River south of Lewis Lake. Bison, elk, and mule deer frequent geothermal areas. Bison are found in three main areas of the park: Lamar Valley, Pelican Valley at the north end of Yellowstone Lake and the corridor over Mary Mountain between Hayden Valley and Lower Geyser Basin along the Firehole River. August is rutting season. The northern desert teems with bighorn sheep, elk, mule deer and pronghorn antelope. The sagebrush and grasslands support pronghorn antelope, elk, bison, badger, Uinta ground squirrel, pika and yellow-bellied marmot *(Marmota flaviventris)*. Coyote, elk, mule deer and bobcat roam in mixed forests. Elk roam along the edge of forests; the largest herd is west of Madison Campground. In lodgepole forest look for bear, squirrel, snow-

The red fox can be identified by its reddish-yellow fur and bushy tail.

shoe hare and porcupine. The latter two also inhabit the spruce and fir forests. Grizzly bear habitat is open meadows and grasslands near whitebark and lodgepole pines. Stay alert throughout the park and recognize when you are in bear habitat. Yellow-bellied marmot and bighorn sheep live in the Alpine tundra.

Orientation

Yellowstone National Park has five entrance stations. The historic arched North Entrance (5314 feet) on US 89 near Gardiner, MT, is the only one open year-round. The other four are typically open early May to late October: the Northeast Entrance (7365 feet) on US 212 near Cooke City, MT; the East Entrance (6951 feet) on US 14/US 16/US 20 at the head of the Wapiti Valley; the South Entrance (6886 feet) on US 89/US 191/US 287 north of Grand Teton National Park; and the West Entrance (6667 feet) on US 191 near West Yellowstone, MT. Roads named for each entrance lead from it to the main road through the park, the Grand Loop Rd (see Grand Loop Rd later in this chapter).

Maps USGS topographic maps are readily available, but hikers may prefer either the Trails Illustrated 1:168,500 *Yellowstone*

WYOMING

National Park or from Earthwalk Press (☎ 800-828-6277) the 1:106,250 *Hiking Map & Guide: Yellowstone National Park*, both with 80-foot contour intervals. Both maps indicate areas burned in the 1988 fires, but Earthwalk Press' map divides these areas into canopy and mixed burns. The Trails Illustrated map is available in English, German, French, Spanish and Japanese. Other Trails Illustrated maps, at 1:83,333, cover Mammoth Hot Springs, Old Faithful, the Tower/Canyon area and Yellowstone Lake. American Adventures Association, 1865 S Main St, Salt Lake City, UT 84115, publishes easy-to-read 1:125,000 trail maps of north and south Yellowstone.

Information

Entrance Permit & Fees The park is open year-round, although some roads and entrances close during the winter (see Road & Weather Conditions below). Reservations are not necessary for entry, but a park entrance permit is. Permits, available at all five park entrance stations (credit cards accepted) and valid for seven days for both Yellowstone and Grand Teton national parks, cost $20 per private (noncommercial) vehicle, $15 per person for individuals entering by motorcycle or snowmobile and $10 per person for individuals entering by bicycle, skis or on foot. Keep the entrance fee receipt to reenter the park or to enter the other park. An annual area pass for Yellowstone and Grand Teton national parks costs $40.

Tourist Offices Write to the National Park Service, Visitor Services Office, PO Box 168, Yellowstone National Park, WY 82190 for a park information packet. The Yellowstone National Park headquarters (☎ 307-344-7381 office and 24-hour recorded information, TTY 307-344-2386; www.nps.gov/yell), at Fort Yellowstone, Mammoth Hot Springs, is open 8 am to 4:30 pm daily.

AmFac Parks & Resorts (☎ 307-344-7311, TTY ☎ 307-344-5395), Reservations Dept, PO Box 165, Yellowstone National Park, WY 82190-0165, is the concessionaire for park activities, as well as camping and accommodations.

Yellowstone's visitors centers and information stations are usually open 9 am to 5 pm daily, with extended hours from 8 am to 7 pm during summer. Most are closed or are only open for shortened hours Labor to Memorial Day; the Albright visitors center is open year-round and the Old Faithful visitors center is open during winter. Check the park newspaper for a listing of current hours of operation. The visitors centers and information stations are:

Albright Visitors Center
    Mammoth Country (☎ 307-344-2263)
Canyon Visitors Center
    Canyon Country (☎ 307-242-2550)
Fishing Bridge Visitors Center
    Lake Country (☎ 307-242-2450)
Grant Village Visitors Center
    Lake Country (☎ 307-242-2650)
Old Faithful Visitors Center
    Geyser Country (☎ 307-545-2750)
Madison Information Station
    Geyser Country
West Thumb Information Station
    Lake Country

Any daily ranger-led activities are posted on their bulletin boards. Visitors with disabilities can pick up a park brochure describing accessible facilities and attractions, or contact the Special Populations Coordinator (☎ 307-344-2019).

The West Yellowstone Chamber of Commerce & Visitors Center in Montana also has a helpful national park counter where you can purchase your entrance permit. Credit cards, however, are not accepted there.

Money ATMs are at the Canyon Lodge, Lake Yellowstone Hotel and Old Faithful Inn. The front desks of all park accommodations exchange foreign currency 8 am to 5 pm weekdays.

Post The only year-round post office is at Mammoth Hot Springs (zip code 82190). Seasonal post offices are at Canyon, Lake and Grant villages and Old Faithful.

Bookstores The Yellowstone Association for Natural Science, History and Education, Inc (☎ 307-344-2293, 307-344- 2296 memberships), PO Box 117, Yellowstone National Park, WY 82190, is a nonprofit organization supporting educational, historic and scientific programs in the park. Memberships start at $25/year. They operate bookstores, usually open 9 am to 5 pm, at the park's visitors centers, information stations and Norris Geyser Basin which sell books, pamphlets and maps. They also publish various informative pamphlets with maps on the park's main attractions. The pamphlets cost 25¢ and are available at visitors centers, bookstores and in weatherproof boxes (with a slot for donations) at the sites.

Road & Weather Conditions Call ☎ 307-344-2114 or the park headquarters to check road and weather conditions prior to your visit, as road construction, rock or mud slides and snow can close park entrances and roads at any time.

Park entrances and roads are generally closed to motor vehicles during the winter (mid-November to mid-March). However, the North Entrance is open year-round, as is the Grand Loop Rd between Mammoth and Tower/Roosevelt junctions and the Northeast Entrance Rd between Tower/Roosevelt Junction and Cooke City, MT. (US 212, however, closes mid-October to Memorial Day between Cooke City and Red Lodge, MT.)

Park entrances and roads are generally open to motor vehicles May 1 and close the first Sunday in November. The first roads to open, in mid-April, are the West Entrance Rd and these sections of the Grand Loop Rd: Mammoth Hot Springs to Norris Junction, Norris Junction to Madison Junction and Madison Junction to Old Faithful. The South and East entrances, the Grand Loop Rd over Craig Pass (8262 feet) between West Thumb Junction and Old Faithful and the East Entrance Rd typically open in early May. The Grand Loop Rd between Tower and Canyon junctions over Dunraven Pass (8859 feet) usually opens by Memorial Day.

Publications *Yellowstone Journal*, PO Box 950, Gardiner, MT 59030, is a tourism-oriented independent monthly that provides extensive information. An annual subscription costs $9. *Inside Greater Yellowstone*, a publication of the Greater Yellowstone Coalition in Bozeman, MT, is an advocate of the region's environmental protection and restoration.

Visitors receive a free copy of the park's newspaper, 'Yellowstone Today,' and 'Discover Yellowstone,' a brochure with a useful orientation map and schedule of the ranger-led activities, special events, exhibits and educational activities. The brochure is available in German, French, Spanish and Japanese.

Yellowstone Net News (www.yellowstone .net) is an online newspaper rated among the world's top 25 websites, definitely a good way to survey the scene from your desk or laptop.

Medical Services Yellowstone Park Medical Services operates three clinics: Mammoth Hot Springs Clinic (☎ 307-344-7965), Old Faithful Clinic (☎ 307-545-7325) and Lake Hospital (☎ 307-242-7241), near the Lake Yellowstone Hotel, which offers 24-hour services. All are open 8:30 am to 5 pm daily during summer; Mammoth Hot Springs Clinic is open year-round. NPS emergency medical technicians and medics (☎ 307-344-2132) are on call 24 hours a day year-round

Laundry & Showers Canyon Village, Fishing Bridge RV Park and Grant Village have laundry and showers; Old Faithful Lodge has showers only; and Lake Lodge has laundry only. Showers cost $3.50. All facilities close during winter.

Dangers & Annoyances Most problems in Yellowstone stem from inappropriate visitor behavior around wildlife. All of Yellowstone's animals are wild and potentially dangerous. Do not harass, feed or approach wildlife. Stay at least 100 yards away from bears and at least 25 yards away from other wildlife; it is illegal to approach

WARNING

MANY VISITORS HAVE BEEN GORED BY BUFFALO

BUFFALO CAN WEIGH 2000 POUNDS AND CAN SPRINT AT 30 MPH, THREE TIMES FASTER THAN YOU CAN RUN

THESE ANIMALS MAY APPEAR TAME BUT ARE WILD, UNPREDICTABLE, AND DANGEROUS

DO NOT APPROACH BUFFALO

In other words, use a telephoto when taking snaps of buffalo.

any closer. Recognize bear habitat (see Fauna earlier in this chapter) and exercise extreme caution around bears – grizzlies maul a few visitors annually. Keep campsites spotless. Lock all foods out of sight inside your vehicle or in bearproof containers. Otherwise, hang food out of the bears' reach. Do not hike alone or after dusk, stay on designated trails and make noise to alert bears to your presence. Bison, which can weigh 2000 pounds and sprint at 30 mph, actually injure (gore) more visitors than bears do.

Stay on existing boardwalks and maintain a safe distance from all geothermal features. Visitors who approach too closely risk serious injury and death. Thin crusts can break, giving way to water near or exceeding boiling. Watch children closely and keep pets, where permitted, on a short leash.

Burned in the 1988 fires, many dead trees – called 'snags' – still stand. Snags can fall down at any time, especially when

it is windy. Do not lean against or shove any damaged trees, and watch and listen for falling trees in campgrounds and when hiking through burned areas.

Safe driving can reduce aggravation and accidents. Slowing down to look at wildlife increases the risk of causing an accident, and is the usual cause of traffic jams. If you want to look, pull completely off the road before stopping. If you cannot safely get off the pavement, do not stop, park or leave your vehicle unattended in the middle of the road. The park's speed limit is generally 45 mph, but often actual driving speed is much slower.

Grand Loop Rd Scenic Drive

Conceived by Lt Daniel C Kingman in 1886 and named by writer Harry W Frantz in 1923, the 142-mile Grand Loop Rd follows a figure-8 pattern as it passes most of the park's major attractions. The 12-mile Norris/Canyon Rd links Norris and Canyon junctions, dividing the Grand Loop Rd into two shorter loops: the 96-mile Lower (South) Loop and the 70-mile Upper (North) Loop.

A clockwise drive from the North Entrance begins at Mammoth Hot Springs (6239 feet). Head east to Tower/Roosevelt Junction then south and cross the Dunraven Pass (8859 feet) to Canyon Junction. The Dunraven Pass offers awesome views of the Absaroka and Teton mountains and the Grand Canyon of the Yellowstone. Continue south along the Yellowstone River through Hayden Valley to Fishing Bridge Junction (7792 feet), then skirt Yellowstone Lake to West Thumb Junction. Then head west and cross Craig Pass (8262 feet) to Old Faithful. Turning north, follow the Firehole River to Madison Junction (6806 feet). The road goes northeast through the Gibbon River Canyon to Norris Junction, where it turns north to Mammoth Hot Springs. (See Organized Tours below for Grand Loop Rd sightseeing tours.)

Activities

The following paragraphs provide introductory information, including permit

Driving Distances in Yellowstone National Park

From	To	Distance
North Entrance	Mammoth Junction	5 miles
Mammoth Junction	Norris Junction	21 miles
Norris Junction	Madison Junction	14 miles
Mammoth Junction	Tower/Roosevelt Junction	18 miles
Tower/Roosevelt Junction	Northeast Entrance	29 miles
Tower/Roosevelt Junction	Canyon Junction	19 miles
Canyon Junction	Norris Junction	12 miles
Canyon Junction	Fishing Bridge Junction	17 miles
Fishing Bridge Junction	East Entrance	27 miles
Fishing Bridge Junction	Grant Village	21 miles
Grant Village	South Entrance	22 miles
Grant Village	Old Faithful	17 miles
Old Faithful	Madison Junction	16 miles
Madison Junction	West Entrance	14 miles

details and regulations, for activities that are possible in the various geographic sections of Yellowstone National Park. See the geographic sections for more detailed activities information.

Backpacking Backpackers, as well as those traveling by canoe and on horseback, can explore Yellowstone's backcountry from over 85 trailheads that give access to 1200 miles of trails. The 150-mile Howard Eaton Trail, named for a famous Bighorn Mountain guide and dude rancher, is the park's longest trail. A free backcountry use permit, available at visitors centers and ranger stations, is required for overnight trips. Backcountry camping is only allowed in some 300 designated sites. The backcountry use permit is site specific and details where you have permission to camp. About 60% of backcountry sites can be reserved in advance by mail; a $15 reservation fee applies regardless of the number of nights. Backcountry use permits are issued no more than 48 hours in advance on a first-come, first-served walk-in basis for the remaining 40% of backcountry sites. Before setting out, read 'Beyond Road's End,' an informative pamphlet describing Yellowstone's backcountry regulations and guidelines. At higher elevations, trails often remain snow-covered until late July. Many of the park's rivers and streams do not have bridges and must be forded.

Horsepacking Horsepacking parties must also obtain a backcountry use permit (see Backpacking above) for overnight trips. For day trips a day horse use permit, also available at most ranger stations, is required. The 'Horsepacking in Yellowstone' pamphlet details regulations.

Fishing Seven known fish species swim Yellowstone's waters: cutthroat, rainbow, brown, brook and lake trout, Arctic grayling and mountain whitefish. The useful pamphlet 'Fishing Regulations' details the park's complex rules, including allowable fishing sites, tackle and bait restrictions, species size and possession limits and its nontoxic fishing program. The fishing season is usually from the Saturday of Memorial Day weekend to the first Sunday in November, except for streams flowing into Yellowstone Lake and some tributaries of the Yellowstone River, which open July 15. The Yellowstone River through Hayden Valley and some other rivers are closed to fishing; others may close during the season due to bear activity.

A fishing permit is required for anyone age 16 and older. It costs $10 for 10 days or

$20 for the entire season; non-fee permits are required for those ages 12 to 15. Fishing permits are available from ranger stations, visitors centers and general stores. A boat permit (see Boating below) is required for float tubes, which are allowed only on the Lewis River between Lewis and Shoshone lakes. These permits are available from the South Entrance, Lewis Lake Campground, Grant Village Backcountry Office, Bridge Bay Marina and Lake Ranger Station.

Boating Boating is permitted May 1 to November 1, although some areas may close during the season. Motorized vessels are only allowed on Lewis Lake and parts of Yellowstone Lake. (Unpredictable weather and high wind on Yellowstone Lake's open water can capsize a small vessel: be cautious and recognize that hypothermia occurs quickly in the lake's average 45°F waters.) Sylvan, Eleanor and Twin lakes and Beach Springs Lagoon are closed to boating. All streams in the park and the Yellowstone River are also closed to boating, except on the Lewis River between Lewis and Shoshone lakes where hand-propelled vessels are allowed. Launching is permitted only at these designated sites: Bridge Bay, Grant Village (opens mid-June) and Lewis Lake. Hand-carried vessels may launch at Sedge Bay. Read the 'Briefed Boating Regulations' pamphlet for more information.

A boating permit is required for all vessels. Permits for motorized vessels cost $10/week or $20/year and are available from the Canyon visitors center, Bridge Bay Marina, the Grant Village visitors center, Lewis Lake Campground and the South Entrance. Permits for nonmotorized vessels cost $10/year or $5/week and are available from the Albright visitors center, the Northeast Entrance and Bechler Ranger Station.

Road & Mountain Biking Cycling is possible late April to October when the park's roads, which range from 5300 feet to 8860 feet, are usually snow-free. Cyclists are permitted to ride on public roads and a few designated service roads, but are not allowed to ride on trails or off-road in backcountry areas. Most roads are narrow and do not have shoulders: watch for careless drivers and wide RVs. Snowbanks cover many roadsides through June, making cycling more dangerous.

The 'Bicycling in Yellowstone National Park' brochure has a map showing suggested routes, such as the 3-mile mountain bike ride from the trailhead at the end of Chittenden Rd to Mt Washburn's summit (10,243 feet). Bicycle repairs, parts and rentals are not available within the park. It is typically 20 to 30 miles between most facilities and services.

Backroads (☎ 510-527-1555, 800-462-2848; fax 510-527-1444), 801 Cedar St, Berkeley, CA 94710-1800, markets six-day cycling adventures in Yellowstone; another trip also includes cycling in Grand Teton National Park (see below) and rafting the Snake River.

Skiing & Snowmobiling Most park trails are not groomed, but unplowed roads and trails are open to cross-country skiing. Some roads are groomed for snowmobiles and other oversnow vehicles. A backcountry use permit (see Backpacking above) is required for overnight trips. Such trips require extra caution as streams and geothermal areas can be obscured by snow: carry a map and compass when you venture off designated trails or roads.

More than a dozen outfitters offer ski trips and another 20 outfitters either rent snowmobiles or offer guided snowmobile trips. Most are based in Moran, Cody, Jackson or Tetonia, ID, and Bozeman or West Yellowstone, MT. Check in West Yellowstone for snowcoach trips.

Organized Tours
Guided eight- to 10-hour bus tours of Yellowstone National Park operate during summer on the Grand Loop Rd. AmFac Parks & Resorts (☎ 307-344-7311) runs three daily tours: **Grand Loop** from Gardiner, MT ($29/14 adults/children aged 12

LEE FOSTER

JOHN MOCK

JOHN ELK

JOHN ELK

Yellowstone National Park

Top Left: Grand Canyon of the Yellowstone, Canyon Country

Bottom: The otherworldly Morning Glory pool, Geyser Country

Top Right: Old Faithful in winter, Geyser Country
Middle Right: Grand Prismatic Spring, Geyser Country

JOHN ELK

JOHN ELK

Grand Teton National Park

to 16) or Mammoth Hot Springs ($28/13) late May to early September; **Upper Loop** from Lake Yellowstone Hotel and Fishing Bridge RV Park ($24/12) or Canyon Lodge ($20/10) mid-June to late September; and **Lower Loop** ($26/13) from Old Faithful Inn, Grant Village, Lake Yellowstone Hotel, Fishing Bridge RV Park and Canyon Lodge, late May to early September.

Other outfitters offer similar tours: the Lower Loop is $33/23 adults/children, the Upper Loop is $33/23 and combination Grand Loop and Grand Teton National Park is $46/32. To book a bus tour, contact:

Buffalo Lines
    429 Yellowstone Ave, West Yellowstone, MT (☎ 406-646-9564, 800-426-7669)
Gray Line of Yellowstone
    1580 W Martin Lane, PO Box 411, Jackson, WY 83001 (☎ 307-733-4325, 800-443-6133; fax 307-733-2689)
    PO Box 994, West Yellowstone, MT 59758 (☎ 406-646-9374, 800-523-3102, 800-733-2304 in winter)
Greyhound Bus Lines
    Bozeman, MT (☎ 406-587-3110)
    Livingston, MT (☎ 406-222-2231)
    Idaho Falls, ID (☎ 208-522-0912)
    West Yellowstone, MT (☎ 406-646-7666)

Powder River Tours (☎ 307-527-6316) offers Yellowstone Tours (East Entrance) via the Wapiti Valley June to September. One daily bus departs Cody at 7:30 am, stops at Pahaska Tepee (8:30 am), continues into Yellowstone National Park to Lake Hotel (10 am), Old Faithful (arrives 11:30 am, departs 1:30 pm), Canyon Lodge (3:30 pm), Lake Hotel (5 pm) and returns to Pahaska Tepee (6 pm) and Cody (7 pm).

MAMMOTH COUNTRY

Mammoth Country is known for its geothermal areas, Mammoth Hot Springs and Norris Geyser Basin, its fossil forests and its numerous lakes and creeks, towered over by the peaks of the Gallatin Range to the northwest.

Orientation

Mammoth Country is in Yellowstone's northwest corner. The North Entrance Rd meets the Grand Loop Rd at Mammoth Junction, just beyond Mammoth Hot Springs; the Grand Loop Rd leads east to Tower/Roosevelt Junction and south to Norris Junction. From Norris Junction, the Norris/Canyon Rd goes east to Canyon Junction, and the Grand Loop Rd continues southwest through the Gibbon Canyon to Madison Junction. The North Entrance is the nearest.

Fort Yellowstone

Mammoth Hot Springs was known as Fort Yellowstone from 1886 to 1918, when the US Army managed the park. The **Mammoth Visitors Center Museum** (☎ 307-344-2263), adjacent to the Horace M Albright visitors center, was once the Bachelor Officers' Quarters. The museum

Million-Dollar Microbes

In 1966 now-retired microbiologist Dr Thomas D Brock discovered *Thermus aquaticus*, or 'Taq,' the hot-water microbe that creates an enzyme commonly used in DNA fingerprinting. The discovery of this microbe in the hot springs at Yellowstone National Park began an ongoing debate about bioprospecting and the commercial use of national park resources. The NPS has customarily issued free permits for scientific research teams (30 currently have permits), but microbes harvested for free have generated millions of dollars of revenue for the biotechnology industry. The Taq enzyme alone generates over $100 million a year. Until recently, no legal mechanism existed for the NPS or the park to receive royalty payments for such scientific discoveries, but in August 1997 a California-based biotechnology firm made the first royalty agreement with the park for harvesting microbes. Experts acknowledge that as much as 99% of Yellowstone's microbes have yet to be discovered. ■

features 19th-century paintings by Thomas Moran and photographs by William Henry Jackson, both of whom accompanied the 1871 Hayden expedition, and exhibits from the park's prehistory to the present.

Mammoth Hot Springs
The imposing Lower and Upper terraces of Mammoth Hot Springs are the product of dissolved subterranean limestone deposited when the waters of the springs cooled on contact with the atmosphere. The terraces owe their colors to bacteria and algae that flourish in the still warm, but not super-heated, surface waters. Rangers lead hikes around the terraces and give history and wildlife talks.

Lower Terraces Boardwalks wend their way around these terraces, and connect to the Upper Terrace Loop. One of the park's more curious sights is the Rocky Mountain elk that lounge on expanding Opal Terrace. Ornate travertine formations characterize colorful **Minerva Spring**, which has been called the park's 'most beautiful spring.' Nearby is the hot spring cone called **Liberty Cap**, named for caps worn by colonial patriots during the late 18th century.

Upper Terrace Loop A one-way road loops counterclockwise around the Upper Terrace; no vehicles longer than 25 feet are permitted. From the **Overlook** are impressive views of the Lower Terraces and Fort Yellowstone. A short boardwalk goes to **Canary Spring**, yellowed by sulfur-depositing bacteria. All other features are visible from the road.

Blacktail Plateau Drive
The Blacktail Plateau is south of Grand Loop Rd between Mammoth and Tower/Roosevelt junctions. An unpaved road offers stunning views of the area.

Obsidian Cliff
Eight miles north of Norris is a black glassy cliff formed by lava flows. Native Americans used this rock to make arrowheads, which were traded across North America.

Roaring Mountain
In the 1800s this hillside's rock fissures 'roared.' This curious spot, 3 miles north of Norris (east of the road), now just hisses and rumbles.

Norris
Named for Philetus W Norris, one of the park's five superintendents during US Army administration, Norris was a former US Army outpost. The historic log Norris Soldier Station at Norris Campground, built in 1908, houses the **Museum of the National Park Ranger** (☎ 307-344-7353), usually open 9 am to 6 pm. Exhibits detail the evolution of the ranger's profession since its military origins. The Gibbon River flows through meadows in front of the museum, making it a pleasant place to relax and look for wildlife.

Norris Geyser Basin
North and west of Norris Junction, the Norris Geyser Basin is North America's most volatile and oldest known continuously active geothermal area, having been active for more than 115,000 years. It is also the site of Yellowstone's hottest recorded temperatures, as three intersecting faults underlain by magma are within 2 miles of the surface here. Its geothermal features change seasonally: clear pools transform into spouting geysers or mud pots and vice versa. Barely 1000 feet below the surface, scientific instruments have recorded temperatures as high as 459°F.

Norris Geyser Basin has two distinct areas: Porcelain Basin and Back Basin. Overlooking Porcelain Basin is the **Norris Museum** (☎ 307-344-2812), which became the park's first in 1930. It is open 9 am to 5 pm mid-May to early June, 8 am to 8 pm during summer and 9 am to 5 pm through September. About three-quarters of a mile of boardwalks loop through the open **Porcelain Basin**, the park's hottest exposed basin, past the Crackling Lake and Whirligig geysers. About 1½ miles of boardwalks wend through forested **Back Basin**. Here the world's tallest active geyser, **Steamboat Geyser**, whose infrequent eruptions reach up to 300 feet, drains into Cistern Spring. Dramatic **Echinus Geyser**, the largest acidic geyser, erupts regularly (every 35 to 75 minutes) with eruptions reaching up to 60 feet and sometimes continuing for more than an hour. Rangers lead walks of Norris Geyser Basin that depart the Norris Museum at 9:30, 10:30 am, 1:30 and 3:30 pm.

Hiking & Backpacking

The **Beaver Ponds Trail**, a 5-mile loop with gentle climbs and considerable wildlife, begins near Liberty Cap at Mammoth Hot Springs, ascends north through the fir and spruce forests along Clematis Creek and in 2½ miles reaches beaver ponds in meadows, where beavers are usually active in the morning and evening.

West of Mammoth is Sepulcher Mountain (9652 feet). The loop-hike via **Howard Eaton Trail** climbs 3400 feet to its summit and returns via Snow Pass.

The **Wraith Falls Trail** begins at the pullout east of Lava Creek Picnic Area, east of Mammoth Junction on the Grand Loop Rd, then follows Lupine Creek to the base of 79-foot Wraith Falls, a 1-mile hike.

A hike to the summit of Bunsen Peak (8564 feet), south of Mammoth, offers outstanding panoramas of the Gallatin Mountains, Blacktail Plateau, Swan Lake Flats and the Yellowstone River valley. From Mammoth, go 5 miles south on Grand Loop Rd and turn east onto Old Bunsen Peak Rd to the trailhead. (The road is closed to vehicles, but open to cyclists.) The **Bunsen Peak Trail** climbs 1300 feet over 2 miles on the Old Bunsen Peak Rd to the top. Return by the same route. If not closed because of grizzly bear activity, you can also return via the **Osprey Falls Trail**, which drops 500 feet into the unique rock formations of Sheepwater Canyon, then follows Gardiner River to the base of the 150-foot Osprey Falls.

An appealing longer hike is the 12½-mile **Blacktail Deer Creek Trail**, 7 miles east of Mammoth. It descends 1100 feet from the trailhead north into the Black Canyon of the Yellowstone. After crossing

the river, it continues downstream (northwest) to Gardiner, MT, necessitating a vehicle shuttle.

Three longer east-west backpacking routes begin west of Mammoth and lead to US 191 in Montana: the **Bighorn Pass Trail** begins from Indian Creek Campground, while the **Fawn Pass Trail** and **Sportsmen Lake Trail** to its north both begin west of Mammoth. The **Mount Holmes Trail** (10,336 feet) begins south of Indian Creek and heads west to the summit.

Two short trails are near Norris. A 2-mile trail connects Norris Geyser Basin to Norris Campground. A 1-mile trail through open forest leads to **Artist Paint Pot**, another geothermal area; the trailhead is 4½ miles south of Norris Junction on the Grand Loop Rd.

Horseback Riding

Mammoth Corrals, near the Lower Terraces, offers one-hour guided horseback rides ($19) departing at 8, 9:30, 11 am, 1:30, 3, 4:30 and 7 pm daily, mid-May to late September.

ROOSEVELT COUNTRY

President Theodore Roosevelt visited this area in 1903 and established the rustic Roosevelt Lodge near Tower/Roosevelt Junction in 1906. Visitors wanting a real Wild West experience can still find it here. Fossil forests, the commanding Lamar River Valley and its tributary trout streams and the craggy peaks of the Absaroka Mountains are the highlights of this, the most remote, scenic and undeveloped region in the park.

Orientation

Roosevelt Country is in the park's northeast corner. The Northeast Entrance Rd, which passes through the Lamar Valley, meets the Grand Loop Rd at Tower/Roosevelt Junction, which then leads west to Mammoth Hot Springs and south to Tower Falls and Canyon Junction. The Northeast Entrance is the nearest. The Tower Ranger Station is west of Tower/Roosevelt Junction. The Lamar Ranger

WYOMING

Return of the Wolf

Gray wolves *(Canis lupus)*, the ultimate symbol of wilderness, have been a barometer of the NPS wildlife management policy in Yellowstone National Park. At first strongly protected, they were then deliberately eradicated, then reintroduced under considerable controversy and, at the time of this writing, are threatened with a court-ordered eviction.

The gray wolf flourished in the late 19th century when livestock replaced bison herds in the Great Plains ecology, thereby increasing the wolves' food supply. Wolves continued to inhabit the Greater Yellowstone region after the creation of the national park in 1872 and the institution of US Army administration. The US Army protected the park's fauna, including predators like the wolf and puma. The creation of the NPS in 1916 paradoxically led to the wolf's extinction within a few years under misguided predator control policies intended to protect game like elk. The last gray wolf den was destroyed near Tower Falls in 1923. Under these policies armed NPS rangers eradicated wolf and puma, thereby allowing game populations to increase to unsustainable levels. The size of elk herds was controlled only by starvation or by farcical (if not tragic) approaches like the slaughter at Gardiner, MT, where hunters waited just outside the park boundary to blast away as the unwary animals left protected territory.

Recognizing the need for a natural sustainable control regime, the NPS made plans to introduce Canadian wolves. Ranchers in the surrounding region were predictably suspicious of reintroduction, claiming that the carnivore would reduce game populations and that adequate compensation for livestock killed by wolves was unlikely. They also argued that the wolf had already returned to the park, though some reported sightings may have been mistaken. The gray wolf, 26 to 34 inches high at the shoulder, 5 to 6 feet long (from nose to tail) and 70 to 120 lbs, is much more imposing than the smaller coyote, but inexperienced viewers could easily confuse the two from a distance.

The USFWS, NPS and USFS proposed a compromise, revising the wolves' status from 'endangered' to 'threatened,' thereby giving ranchers the right to shoot any wolves attacking their livestock. In February 1995, they introduced 14 wolves in acclimation pens in the Lamar Valley. As of August 1997, 24 wolf packs totaling 180 animals were resident in Yellowstone National Park, north-central Idaho, and western Montana. The organization Defenders of Wildlife has reimbursed ranchers for livestock depredation. As of August 1997, 44 sheep and 37 cattle have been lost to wolves, and more than $30,000 compensation has been paid. Biologists expect the gray wolf population to stabilize by 2001, and to remove the gray wolf from the list of threatened species.

In December 1997, however, a federal judge in Wyoming ordered the 'removal' of the reintroduced wolves and their offspring. Curiously, both livestock and conservation groups brought suit against the reintroduction. The Wyoming Farm Bureau Federation opposed it as a threat to ranching, and the Audubon Society and the Sierra Club Legal Defense Fund opposed it because of the change in the wolves' status. Based principally on arguments put forward by these two conservation groups, the judge found the entire reintroduction illegal, and so ordered the wolves' removal. His ruling is under appeal, but this legal sophistry threatens to undo a conservation success. ■

Station is at Buffalo Ranch, on the North-east Entrance Rd.

Petrified Forest

Here volcanic ash fossilized a redwood tree 50 million years ago; the remaining stump of rock is 20 feet high (it was once taller, but vandals reduced its size). The turnoff is west of Tower/Roosevelt Junction.

Calcite Springs Overlook

About 1½ miles south of Tower/Roosevelt Junction, the Calcite Springs Overlook offers northern views of the Grand Canyon of the Yellowstone.

Tower Falls

South of Tower/Roosevelt Junction, Tower Creek drops over the 132-foot Tower Falls before joining the Yellowstone River. From a scenic overlook of the falls 100 yards from the store, a trail descends 200 feet on switchbacks over half a mile to the base of the falls.

Lamar Valley

Elk and bison make the broad Lamar Valley, covered by mixed sage and grass-lands, surrounded by rolling hills and guarded by granite bluffs to the west, their winter range. Established in 1907, **The Yellowstone Institute** (☎ 307-344-2294), PO Box 117, Yellowstone National Park, WY 82190, is a nonprofit educational field program offering two- to five-day outdoor courses in the humanities and cultural and natural history. The historic **Buffalo Ranch** is the institute's headquarters, where most courses are held from late May to late September, with some in January and February. Academic credit is available. Courses start at $45 per day, excluding food and accommodations. Buffalo Ranch's log sleeping cabins start at $12; use of their central kitchen costs extra.

Hiking & Backpacking

The 4-mile **Lost Lake Loop** trail begins behind Roosevelt Lodge, passing Lost Lake en route to the petrified tree from where it descends to the Tower Ranger Station.

From the stagecoach road near Tower/Roosevelt Junction, the **Garnet Hill Trail** is an easy two- to three-hour loop north of the Grand Loop Rd, with a possible extension up Hellroaring Creek. The trailhead can also be reached from the Gravel Pit parking area 3½ miles west of Tower/Roosevelt Junction.

The **Yellowstone River Picnic Area Trail** leads south 2 miles to The Narrows, an area offering spectacular views of the northernmost portion of the Grand Canyon of the Yellowstone. The trailhead is on the Northeast Entrance Rd 1½ miles east of Tower/Roosevelt Junction. Cross to the south side of the river and follow the trail south past interesting features like Over-hanging Cliff and the Basalt Columns. Retrace your steps, or continue east to a petrified forest at Specimen Ridge, making a full-day trip. Alternatively, the **Fossil Forest Trail** leads to Specimen Ridge along an unmaintained route; this trailhead is 4 miles east of Tower/Roosevelt Junction on the Northeast Entrance Rd.

The **Slough Creek Trail**, which begins 0.4 mile before the Slough Creek Camp ground, is a pleasant hike along a popular fishing stream. It is possible to head east up Elk Tongue Creek, cross Bliss Pass and descend along Pebble Creek to the Pebble Creek Campground. Fording Pebble Creek can be tricky early in the season.

A trailhead from a pullout on the North-east Entrance Rd 1½ miles south of the Pebble Creek Campground leads 0.6 miles through fir forest to **Trout Lake**.

An extensive trail network branches off the upper Lamar Valley. The **Lamar River Trail** leaves the Northeast Entrance Rd along Soda Butte Creek, above its conflu-ence with the Lamar River. Other trails off this one lead east to Cache Creek and west to traverse Specimen Ridge and rejoin the trail from The Narrows. The main trail con-tinues south along the Lamar River, ulti-mately leading toward the Wapiti Valley.

Horseback Riding

Roosevelt Corrals at Roosevelt Lodge are open mid-June to early September. One-hour guided horseback rides depart at 9:30,

10:30 and 11 am ($19), two-hour rides at 1:30 and 2 pm ($29).

Stagecoach Rides
Roosevelt Lodge offers stagecoach rides 10:30, 11:30 am, 1:30, 2:30, and 3:30 pm daily, mid-June to early September ($6/5 for adults/children). Their Old West Cookout via horseback (the one-hour ride departs at 5:15 pm, the two-hour ride at 4:30 pm) or horse-drawn wagon (5:30 pm) takes place nightly mid-June to mid-September (starts at $28/17 for adults/children).

CANYON COUNTRY
A series of scenic overlooks and a network of trails along the canyon rims and into the canyon highlight the beauty of the Grand Canyon of the Yellowstone. The park's most impressive panoramas extend north from Canyon Junction to Tower/Roosevelt Junction. Mud Volcano is Canyon Country's primary geothermal area.

Orientation
Canyon Country is in the central part of the park. From Canyon Junction, the Grand Loop Rd leads north over Dunraven Pass to Tower Falls and Tower/Roosevelt Junction and south through Hayden Valley to Fishing Bridge Junction and Yellowstone Lake. Canyon Village and Canyon Ranger Station are east of Canyon Junction along North Rim Drive. The Norris/Canyon Rd goes west from Canyon Junction over the Central Plateau to Norris Junction.

Grand Canyon of the Yellowstone
The Yellowstone River flows north from Yellowstone Lake through Hayden Valley, tumbling over Upper Falls (109 feet) and Lower Falls (308 feet) before dropping into the Grand Canyon of the Yellowstone. Rangers lead excursions and hikes, departing from the Canyon visitors center, along the canyon rims. Bring binoculars and look for osprey that nest in the canyon during late spring and stay until September.

North Rim Three scenic overlooks are along the 2½-mile North Rim Drive (one-

The Name Yellowstone
Heated water reacting with volcanic rock in the Grand Canyon of the Yellowstone produced the beautifully colored canyon walls. The name Yellowstone, however, did not originate from this canyon, but from the yellow-colored riverbanks near the confluence of the Yellowstone and Missouri rivers in Montana. It was here that in 1797-98 British fur trader David Thompson used the term 'yellow stone' to describe the area near the Mandan villages of the upper Missouri. ■

way beyond Canyon Village): **Inspiration**, **Grandview** and **Lookout** points. From Glacial Boulder near the Inspiration Point parking lot, the **Cascade Overlook Trail** goes northeast to the **Silver Cord Cascade Overlook**. Lookout Point offers the best views of the Lower Falls, and an adjacent three-eighths-mile trail drops 500 feet to **Red Rock** for even closer views. A lush three-quarter-mile trail begins at the southernmost parking lot beyond Lookout Point and descends 600 feet to the Brink of the Lower Falls. The **North Rim Trail** links Inspiration Point to the Chittenden Bridge on South Rim Drive. From Inspiration Point the walk is 2½ miles to the **Upper Falls Overlook** and three-quarters of a mile farther to the bridge. Upper Falls Overlook is also accessible by road: the turnoff is south of Canyon Junction and Cascade Creek on the Grand Loop Rd.

South Rim South Rim Drive leads to the canyon's most spectacular overlook, at **Artist Point**, passing the **Upper Falls Viewpoint** en route. **Uncle Tom's Trail**, which begins near the Upper Falls Viewpoint, is a steep route that descends 500 feet to the base of the Lower Falls. The 3¼-mile **South Rim Trail** follows the canyon rim from Chittenden Bridge to **Point Sublime** via Artist Point, just beyond the half-way point.

Two trails meander through meadows and forests past several small lakes southeast of the South Rim. The **Clear Lake Trail** begins at the parking lot near Upper Falls Viewpoint and skirts Clear Lake before joining the **Ribbon Lake Trail**, which leads to Ribbon Lake and the Silver Cord Cascade. To avoid retracing your steps several variations are possible, including returning along the South Rim Trail.

Washburn Hot Springs Overlook
South of Dunraven Pass, the Washburn Hot Springs overlook is one of the best places to view the **Yellowstone caldera**.

Hayden Valley
The Yellowstone River is broad and shallow as it meanders through the vast grasslands of Hayden Valley. This old lake bed was formed during the last ice age when a glacial outburst flooded the Hayden Valley. The former lake bed's silt and clay soil supports the rich shrubs and grasses favored by bison, but are impermeable to most trees. Trout swim the waters where aquatic vegetation thrive, and geese, white pelicans, osprey and bald eagles fly overhead. This picturesque, treeless valley is excellent for birdwatching and roadside wildlife viewing, but is closed to fishing except for two short catch-and-release stretches. Rangers lead excursions in the valley, departing from the Canyon visitors center.

Mud Volcano
The Mud Volcano area, 10 miles south of Canyon Junction and 6 miles north of Fishing Bridge Junction, contains an assortment of mud pots and other gurgling features that emit a sulfurous odor. A 1-mile boardwalk loop passes Mud Cauldron (whose bubbles are from escaping gases rather than boiling water), Mud Geyser, Sour Lake (whose foul water is a function of sulfuric acid produced by bacteria), Mud Volcano and the consistently violent Dragon's Mouth. During a series of earthquakes in 1979, the mud pots developed enough heat and gases literally to cook lodgepoles and grasses on some hillsides. Mud Volcano, however, has not erupted since it was first seen by the 1871 USGS expedition. Across the road, Sulfur Cauldron has a 1.2 pH level, roughly the equivalent of battery acid. Grizzly bear and bison frequent the area, especially during spring. Rangers lead excursions to Mud Volcano, departing from the Fishing Bridge Visitors center.

Hiking & Backpacking
The descent to **Seven Mile Hole Trail**, on the north side of the Grand Canyon of the Yellowstone, begins off North Rim Drive at Glacial Boulder just before Inspiration Point. The trail follows the canyon rim, offering spectacular views for a few miles before plunging into the canyon. Steep sections of the trail are slippery even when they are dry.

Two trails lead to the summit of **Mt Washburn** (10,243 feet), northeast of Dunraven Pass. One trailhead is at the parking lot at the end of the unpaved Chittenden Rd, which leaves the Grand Loop Rd north of the pass. Whitebark pine and fir give away quickly to Alpine tundra as the trail ascends more than 1000 feet over 2.8 miles to the summit. Return the same way or traverse the peak by descending 3.2 miles to the Dunraven Pass Picnic Area, necessitating a vehicle shuttle. At Mt Washburn's summit are a fire lookout (closed to the public) and a shelter with a telescope. The summit view includes three mountain ranges: Beartooth, Absaroka and Teton. Bighorn sheep roam the hillsides, as do marmot. Allow three to five hours roundtrip. Mt Washburn can also be approached from the east via the longer Seven Mile Hole Trail.

The easy **Cascade Lake Trail** begins from the picnic area of the same name on the Grand Loop Rd 1½ miles north of Canyon Junction. Follow the right fork 2½ miles from the trailhead, which leads steeply through meadows and whitebark pines to **Observation Peak** (9397 feet). The trail continues past Cascade Lake, where it joins the **Grebe Lake Trail**, which passes Grebe and Wolf lakes; these are also accessible from trailheads on the Norris/Canyon Rd.

The **Mary Mountain Trail** traverses the Central Plateau east-west connecting Hayden Valley to Lower Geyser Basin. The trailhead is located north of Alum Creek. The **Plateau Trail** traverses the Central Plateau north-south, from the trailhead on Canyon/Norris Rd west of Canyon Junction, and joins the Mary Mountain Trail at Mary Lake.

Horseback Riding
Canyon Corrals are along the west side of the Grand Loop Rd south of Canyon Junction. One-hour guided horseback rides depart at 8, 8:30, 10 am, 1, 1:30, 2:30, 3, 4, 4:30, 6:30, and 7 pm, mid-June to mid-September ($19); a two-hour ride departs at 9:30 am ($29).

LAKE COUNTRY
Yellowstone Lake (7733 feet), the centerpiece of Lake Country, is one of the world's largest Alpine lakes and home to the country's largest inland population of cutthroat trout. The Upper Yellowstone River flows north from the lake through the Hayden Valley to the Grand Canyon of the Yellowstone. In the mountains south of Yellowstone Lake, the mighty Snake River begins its long journey through Wyoming and Idaho to Oregon and the Columbia River. The often snowcapped Absaroka Mountains rise dramatically east and southeast of the lake.

Orientation
Lake Country is in the southeast corner of the park. A 22-mile section of the Grand Loop Rd hugs Yellowstone Lake's north and west shoreline between Fishing Bridge Junction at its north end and West Thumb Junction at its west. Fishing Bridge is immediately east of Fishing Bridge Junction along the East Entrance Rd. Lake Village and Bridge Bay are off the Grand Loop Rd just south of Fishing Bridge Junction along Bridge Bay itself. Grant Village, which hugs the south shore of the lake's West Thumb Bay, is off South Entrance Rd

2 miles south of the West Thumb Junction. The South and East entrances are the nearest. The Snake River Ranger Station is adjacent to the South Entrance; another ranger station is at Bridge Bay.

Yellowstone Lake
Yellowstone Lake has excellent fishing and boating and is a prime bird and wildlife habitat. Lake Village's **Lake Yellowstone Hotel**, built in 1890, is on the National Register of Historic Places. Gull Point Drive is a scenic picnic and popular fishing area. Rangers lead excursions along Yellowstone Lake's shoreline, departing from the Fishing Bridge visitors center.

Fishing Bridge
Fishing Bridge spans the Yellowstone River near its outlet at the northern end of Yellowstone Lake. In 1973 the bridge was closed to fishing and remains so. Visitors now enjoy watching spawning cutthroat trout from the bridge and at Le Hardy Rapids 3 miles north of the bridge.

Bridge Bay Marina
Bridge Bay Marina offers dock rentals and hourly outboard/rowboat rentals mid-June to mid-September. Daily one-hour **sightseeing cruises** of northern Yellowstone Lake operate early June to late September. Cruises depart from Bridge Bay Marina at 9:30, 11 am, 1:30, 3, 4:30, 6:30, and 7:30 pm; tickets cost $7.50/4 for adults/children (two to 11).

AmFac Parks & Resorts' guided **fishing trips** on Yellowstone Lake depart from Bridge Bay Marina mid-June to mid-September. Hourly rates start at $45 with a two-hour minimum. The marina area itself is closed to fishing.

West Thumb Geyser Basin
West Thumb is a small volcanic caldera created about 150,000 years ago inside the much larger Yellowstone caldera. Waters from Yellowstone Lake filled it creating West Thumb Bay, a circular inlet on the lake's western end. West Thumb Geyser Basin, near the West Thumb Junction, has

a half-mile shoreline boardwalk loop with a shorter inner loop that passes more than a dozen geothermal features. At **Fishing Cone**, along the lakeshore, anglers literally used to cook their catch, although not, as fabled, by swinging their rod directly from the lake into the cone's boiling water. **Abyss Pool** is one of the deepest springs in the park, while the **Thumb Paint Pots**, after years of relative inactivity, have given indications of recovering the energy that once flung boiling mud 25 feet into the air. Rangers lead excursions to West Thumb Geyser Basin, departing from the Grant Village visitors center.

Grant Village
Lakeside Grant Village has a boat launch. Nearby are five spawning streams for cutthroat trout, which often close during late spring and early summer because of bear activity.

Hiking & Backpacking
A section of the 150-mile **Howard Eaton Trail** follows the Yellowstone River north from the parking lot east of Fishing Bridge. The **Pelican Creek Trail**, which starts at Pelican Creek Bridge 1 mile east of the Fishing Bridge visitors center, is an easy 1-mile loop through lodgepole forest and across wetlands. **Storm Point** juts into the northern end of the lake. The 2-mile walk around the point begins near Indian Pond; here you can look for bison, moose, marmots and waterfowl. For the best views in the area, hike the 3-mile round-trip **Elephant Back Mountain Trail**. The 800-foot climb begins from the trailhead 1 mile south of Fishing Bridge Junction. The 3-mile **Natural Bridge Trail** starts at the Bridge Bay Marina parking lot; a bicycle path also leads to this feature carved by Bridge Creek. A few miles west of Yellowstone Lake and north of the East Entrance Rd is the **Avalanche Peak Trail**. This steep, unmarked trail climbs over 2000 feet to Avalanche Peak (10,565 feet) affording excellent lake views.

A 2-mile round-trip walk climbs 400 feet through meadows to the **Yellowstone Lake Overlook** with outstanding views of the lake and the Absaroka Mountains. The trailhead, south of West Thumb Junction near the entrance to West Thumb Geyser Basin, heads west off the South Entrance Rd. At the pullout just west of West Thumb Junction is the trailhead for the **Duck Lake Trail**. The half-mile walk to Duck Lake demonstrates the effects of the 1988 fires and offers views of Yellowstone Lake.

South of Grant Village, marshy meadows surround Riddle Lake, a favorite of moose. The trailhead is on the South Entrance Rd 3 miles south of Grant Village, just south of the Continental Divide sign. The 5-mile roundtrip trail traverses the Continental Divide and drops down to the lake.

Kayaking
OARS (☎ 209-736-4677, 800-328-0290, 800-346-6277; fax 209-736-2902), PO Box 67, Angels Camp, CA 95222-9901, offers three-day kayaking trips of Yellowstone Lake's southeast arm, which is in a 'no motor zone,' excellent for wildlife viewing.

GEYSER COUNTRY
Geyser Country has the most geothermal features in the park, concentrated in Upper Geyser, Black Sand, Biscuit, Midway Geyser and Lower Geyser basins. The Firehole River and its tributaries flow through the area, containing 21 of the park's 110 waterfalls. Anticipated eruption times of several geysers are posted at the Old Faithful visitors center, Old Faithful Lodge and Old Faithful Inn. The Firehole and Madison rivers offer superb fishing, and the meadows along them support large wildlife populations.

Orientation
Geyser Country is in the park's southwest corner. From West Thumb Junction, the Grand Loop Rd goes west over Craig Pass (8262 feet) to the Old Faithful area (18 miles), crossing the Continental Divide twice en route. It then continues along the Firehole River to Madison Junction from

Geothermal Features

Each of the park's 10,000 geothermal features behaves and appears in a unique way. A **geyser** is a hot spring that erupts periodically when ground-water becomes superheated at depth, but cannot evaporate because of the weight of overlying water. Eventually the boiling water and steam work their way through channels in the bedrock to the surface and expel the water and steam into the air, relieving the pressure and starting the cycle anew. A **hot spring** differs from a geyser because its water circulates rapidly underground, enabling the rising hot water to dissipate heat and the cooled water to remain underground. A **mud pot**, a hot spring with less water, forms when sulfuric acid decomposes rock, turning it into clay, which then mixes with hot water to making bubbling mud. A hot spring that lacks liquid water is a **fumarole**, which expels only steam from its vent. ∎

where it heads northeast along the Gibbon River. The West Entrance Rd meets the Grand Loop Rd at Madison Junction. The West and South entrances are the nearest.

Upper Geyser Basin

Upper Geyser Basin contains 180 of the park's 200 to 250 geysers, the most famous being **Old Faithful**. Boardwalks, footpaths, and a cycling path along the Firehole River link the five distinct geyser groups, the farthest of which is only 1½ miles from Old Faithful. Rangers lead interpretive walks in Upper Geyser Basin.

Geyser Hill Group Erupting every 79 minutes or so to visitors' delight, **Old Faithful** spews over 8000 gallons of water 100 to 180 feet into the air. Consistent seepage from neighboring **Giantess Geyser** (known for infrequent, but violent eruptions) and **Vault Geyser** have created deposits of sinter (geyserite) terraces that look like scaled relief maps, while **Aurum**

Geyser resembles a human ear in outline. A short trail goes up to Observation Point on Geyser Hill, looping back to the boardwalks.

Castle-Grand Group Next is **Grand Geyser**, one of the world's tallest predictable geysers, which erupts in bursts. Across the river is **Castle Geyser**, which erupts every 10 to 12 hours. It is the park's largest cone-shaped geyser and perhaps its oldest.

Giant-Grotto Group The boardwalks pass **Beauty Pool** en route to **Giant Geyser**, which produces stupendous eruptions more than 250 feet into the air, but may be dormant for years. Nearby **Grotto Geyser** has smaller but extended eruptions, lasting up to 10 hours.

Daisy Group The predictable **Daisy Geyser** erupts every 90 to 115 minutes, except when nearby **Splendid Geyser** erupts.

Morning Glory-Riverside Group The picturesque **Riverside Geyser** puts on an amazing show: 20-minute eruptions occur about every seven hours. Another visitor favorite, well worth the walk, is beautiful **Morning Glory Pool**.

Old Faithful Inn

Seattle architect Robert C Reamer designed Old Faithful Inn, a national historic landmark. Its construction with native logs began in 1903 and was completed in 1904. Later additions came in 1913 and 1928. The log rafters of its lobby rise nearly 90 feet, while the main fireplace chimney contains over 500 tons of rock. Historic Inn tours depart from the fireplace at 9:30, 11 am, 2 and 3:30 pm. The observation deck upstairs provides views of the Old Faithful geyser. It is a worthwhile visit, even for nonguests.

Black Sand Basin & Biscuit Basin

Black Sand Basin, 1 mile northwest of Old Faithful, and Biscuit Basin, 2 miles farther north, are two interesting roadside thermal areas. The black sand at the former is derived from volcanic glass (obsidian). The latter is best known for biscuit-like deposits surrounding **Sapphire Pool**, which were destroyed during eruptions after a 1959 earthquake. Trails, each half a mile long, link Upper Geyser Basin's Daisy Group to both basins; cycling is allowed on the trail to Biscuit Basin.

Midway Geyser Basin
Two miles south of the south entrance to Firehole Lake Drive (see below) is Midway Geyser Basin. The algae-created indigo waters of the 370-foot wide **Grand Prismatic Spring**, the park's largest hot spring, and now-dormant **Excelsior Geyser**, which used to release more water (4000 gallons of water per minute) than any other geyser in the park, are its key geothermal features.

Firehole Lake Drive
Firehole Lake Drive is a one-way road starting 2 miles north of Midway Geyser Basin and about 1 mile south of the Fountain Paint Pot parking lot. It passes several large geysers, including **Great Fountain Geyser**, which soars up to 200 feet at intervals of eight to 12 hours, and **Firehole Lake**, a large hot spring with an average temperature of 158°F. Nearby Hot Lake collects the runoff from Firehole Lake.

Lower Geyser Basin
Roughly midway between Madison Junction and Old Faithful, **Fountain Paint Pot** offers a popular half-mile loop boardwalk through the hot springs and mud pots, which vary in color depending on the presence of bacteria and algae as well as the composition of the surrounding rock. The grassy basin supports the park's largest bison herd.

Firehole Canyon Drive
The one-way Firehole Canyon Drive leaves the Grand Loop Rd south of Madison Junction. Dark rhyolite cliffs tower above the **Firehole Swimming Area**, one of the few locations in the park open for swimming.

Hiking & Backpacking
Two trailheads lead to 200-foot Fairy Falls, northwest of Midway Geyser Basin, and the popular **Fairy Creek Trail**. First is the Steel Bridge trailhead, 1 mile south of Midway Geyser Basin, which leads 2.6 miles one-way through burned lodgepole pine forest to the falls. Alternatively, follow Fountain Flat Drive, which leaves the Grand Loop Rd at Lower Geyser Basin, to the barricade. Continue walking on the road to its end and then head west to the falls. Retrace your steps from here or continue to Imperial Geyser. Beyond Imperial Geyser, the Fairy Creek Trail heads southwest to meet the Little Firehole River where it turns sharply east and heads to Biscuit Basin on the Grand Loop Rd. A vehicle shuttle is necessary unless you walk north on another trail along the west side of the Grand Loop Rd back to either trailhead. It is about 10 miles between Imperial Geyser and Biscuit Basin.

The **Mystic Falls Trail** begins at the west end of Biscuit Basin near Avoca Spring and parallels the Little Firehole River. Switchbacks lead to the top of the 70-foot falls, where you can continue to the **Little Firehole Meadows Trail**. To return to Biscuit Basin, take the right fork and descend to an overlook of Upper Geyser Basin; bring binoculars. The loop is about 2½ miles.

The trailhead to **Lone Star Geyser** is on the Grand Loop Rd 3½ miles east of Old Faithful near the Kepler Cascades pullout. The trail follows the Firehole River 2½ miles to the 9-foot high cone-shaped Lone Star Geyser, which erupts every three hours. Bicycles are permitted to the geyser but not beyond.

The **DeLacy Creek Trail** leads to Shoshone Lake, the park's largest backcountry lake. The trailhead is on the Grand Loop Rd, east of Craig Pass near the DeLacy Creek Picnic Area about 9 miles west of West Thumb Junction. The trail is 3 miles one-way to the lake. Alternatively, longer trails lead from Lone Star Geyser to Shoshone Geyser Basin at the west end of the lake where routes circle the lake.

From the trailhead north of Lewis Lake, about 5 miles south of Grant Village, a 7-mile loop follows the **Lewis River Channel** between Lewis and Shoshone lakes. It also links up with the DeLacy Creek and Shoshone Lake trails.

Fishing

The Firehole (between Biscuit and Midway Geyser basins), Madison and Gibbon (downstream from Gibbon Falls) rivers are open only for fly-fishing.

PLACES TO STAY

NPS and private campgrounds, cabins, lodges and hotels are in the park, but during summer high demand for all types of accommodations makes it difficult to find any place to stay without a reservation.

Camping inside the park is only permitted in 12 designated campgrounds (see Places to Stay – budget below), and is limited to 14 days from June 15 to Labor Day, and 30 days the rest of the year. Check-out time is 10 am, and quiet hours are 8 pm to 8 am. Each campground usually holds a nightly campfire program in its amphitheater; days, times and topics are prominently posted. (See Backpacking earlier in this chapter for regulations on backcountry camping.) Late June to mid-August, it is best to have a reservation or to secure a campsite early in the morning as all campgrounds are typically full by 11 am. Sign boards at park entrances list campground availability; 'full' does not necessarily mean 'full,' go to the campground and ask about availability. If, however, you arrive late in the day without a reservation, you are unlikely to find a campsite inside the park. Some campsites ($4) are reserved for backpackers and cyclists (without vehicles) at all campgrounds except Slough Creek and Canyon. Alternative campgrounds outside the park also fill up early each day; those nearest to the park fill up first and require driving many miles.

Most hotels and cabins are open mid-May to early October, but dates can vary depending on weather. AmFac Parks & Resorts (see Information earlier in this section) operates the park's nine accommodations, all of which accept reservations: Mammoth Hot Springs Hotel & Cabins, in Mammoth Country; Roosevelt Lodge Cabins in Roosevelt Country; Canyon Lodge & Cabins, in Canyon Country; Lake Lodge Cabins, Lake Yellowstone Hotel & Cabins and Grant Village, in Lake Country; Old Faithful Lodge Cabins, Old Faithful Snow Lodge & Cabins and Old Faithful Inn, in Geyser Country.

Of the cabin options, the rustic Lake Lodge is the most peaceful: grab a rocking chair on the porch and soak up the scenery. A stay at the Roosevelt Lodge offers the most authentic Western experience. The Lake Yellowstone Hotel is indeed a grand reminder of a bygone era, but its cabins are tiny boxes, like most others in the park, scattered in a shadeless area near the less-than-picturesque parking lot.

The grand properties of the park are the Mammoth Hot Springs Hotel, Lake Yellowstone Hotel and Old Faithful Inn. Not all rooms are equal, however, and the best, of course, are the most expensive. The other accommodations are less distinctive and more modern. The clusters of condo-like boxes called 'lodges' (eg, Lodge A, Lodge B) at Grant Village have been dismissed by author Alston Chase as 'an inner-city project in the heart of primitive America, a wilderness ghetto' the architecture of which is 'a curious mixture of Cape Cod and Star Wars.'

Places to Stay – budget

Camping AmFac Parks & Resorts (see Information earlier in this section) operates the only five campgrounds that accept reservations. When you have a choice of campgrounds, its setting and proximity to activities can help you select which ones you might enjoy most.

Canyon Campground (7734 feet) – With 271 sites, Canyon offers the most tent-only sites and is also the most densely forested. Its high elevation makes it colder than many other campgrounds. Canyon Country, near Canyon Village and the center of the park; open early June to mid-September. ($15/23 tents/RVs)

Fishing Bridge RV Park (7792 feet) – Only hard-shelled RVs (341 sites) are allowed to camp here because of heavy bear activity. Lake Country, along the north shore of Yellowstone Lake 1 mile east of Fishing Bridge Junction; open mid-May to late September. ($25)

Bridge Bay Campground (7735 feet) – This is largely an open, shadeless and grassy area surrounded by forest, with 429 sites. Its more desirable and remote tent-only loops (E, F) have a few more trees and offer lovely lake views. Adjacent to the Bridge Bay Marina, it appeals largely to those interested in fishing and boating. Lake Country, along the northwest shore of Yellowstone Lake 3 miles southwest of Lake Village; open late May to late September. ($15/23)

Grant Village Campground (7770 feet) – This forested campground (425 sites) is the only one on Yellowstone Lake and has a nearby boat launch. Lake Country, along the west shore of Yellowstone Lake 22 miles north of the South Entrance; open late May to late September. ($15/23)

Madison Campground (6806 feet) – In a sunny, open forest in a broad meadow, Madison has 280 sites. Bison herds and the park's largest elk herd frequent the meadows to its west. Above the banks of the Madison River, it is a good base for fly-fishing. Tent-only sites are ideally placed along the river. Geyser Country, west of at Madison Junction along the Madison River 14 miles east of the West Entrance, 16 miles north of Old Faithful; open early May to early November. ($15/23)

The NPS operates seven campgrounds on a first-come, first-served basis:

Mammoth Campground (6239 feet) – The least attractive campground in the park, Mammoth is a barren, dusty sagebrush-covered area with sparse shade. In a hairpin bend in the road below Mammoth Hot Springs, its 85 sites get a lot of road noise. But its relatively low elevation makes it the warmest campground and a good choice for late-season visits. Mammoth Country, near the North Entrance, Mammoth Hot Springs; open early May to mid-October. ($12/23 tents/RVs)

Indian Creek Campground (about 7300 feet) – Surrounded by moose territory, this sparse and somewhat desolate campground with 75

sites is in open forest on a low rise. Generators are not allowed. Mammoth Country, 8 miles south of Mammoth Junction; open early June to mid-September. ($10/23)

Norris Campground (7484 feet) – Scenic Norris Campground, with 116 sites, is in open forest on an idyllic, sunny hill overlooking the Gibbon River and bordering meadows. It offers nearby fishing and wildlife viewing opportunities. Mammoth Country, along Gibbon River north of Norris Junction; open mid-May to late September. ($12/23)

Tower Fall Campground (6650 feet) – High above Tower Creek, this campground's 32 sites are in an open pine forest, at the edge of burned forest. Generators are not allowed. Roosevelt Country, 3 miles southeast of Tower/Roosevelt Junction; open mid-May to late September. ($10/23)

Slough Creek Campground (about 6400 feet) – The remote Slough Creek Campground (29 sites), 2.2 miles up an unpaved road, is in grizzly habitat along a peaceful fishing stream adjacent to meadows. It has a couple of walk-in sites and offers easy access to the Slough Creek Trail. Generators are not allowed. Roosevelt Country, 10 miles northeast of Tower/Roosevelt Junction; open late May to early November. ($10/23)

Pebble Creek Campground (about 6800 feet) – Surrounded on three sides by the distinctive rock faces and rugged cliffs of the Absaroka Mountains, remote Pebble Creek Campground (36 sites) has the most dramatic physical setting of the park's campgrounds. It is along the banks of a creek in an open forest in grizzly habitat. Generators are not allowed. Roosevelt Country, near the Northeast Entrance at the lower end of Icebox Canyon; open mid-June to late September. ($10/23)

Lewis Lake Campground (7779 feet) – On a forested rise above the lake, this campground has 85 sites. The boat launch provides easy access to Lewis Lake and the Lewis River for boating and fishing. Snow often remains here through June because of its high elevation and shaded location, so it may not be the best early-season campground. It has a few walk-in and tent-only sites. Generators are not allowed. Geyser Country, about 10 miles north of the South Entrance at the south end of Lewis Lake; open mid-June to early November. ($10/23)

WYOMING

Cabins Cabins with shared bathroom are the park's least expensive places: *Old Faithful Lodge Cabins* ($25), *Mammoth Hot Springs Hotel & Cabins* ($38) and the rustic *Roosevelt Lodge Cabins* (range from $27 to $45).

Hotels Rooms with shared bathroom ($47) are at the *Mammoth Hot Springs Hotel & Cabins*, *Old Faithful Inn* and *Old Faithful Snow Lodge & Cabins*.

Places to Stay – middle
Cabins The most affordable cabins with bathroom are at the centrally located *Old Faithful Lodge Cabins* ($41), *Lake Lodge Cabins* ($45) and *Canyon Lodge & Cabins* ($49). Cabins with bathroom cost $69 at *Mammoth Hot Springs Hotel & Cabins*, *Roosevelt Lodge Cabins*, *Lake Yellowstone Hotel & Cabins* and *Old Faithful Snow Lodge & Cabins*.

Hotels *Old Faithful Snow Lodge & Cabins* has the least expensive rooms in this category ($56). Rooms at *Mammoth Hot Springs Hotel & Cabins* cost $70; those at *Grant Village* and *Old Faithful Inn* are $74.

Places to Stay – top end
Cabins Deluxe cabins with bathroom cost $90 at *Canyon Lodge & Cabins*, *Lake Lodge Cabins* and *Old Faithful Snow Lodge & Cabins*.

Hotels Top-end rooms cost $90 at *Lake Yellowstone Hotel & Cabins*, a yellow monstrosity, *Grant Village* and *Old Faithful Inn*. *Canyon Lodge & Cabins* rooms cost $97. Premium category rooms range from $121 to $131 at *Lake Yellowstone Hotel & Cabins* and from $98 to $221 at *Old Faithful Inn*. Suites (bedroom and parlor) are available at *Mammoth Hot Springs Hotel & Cabins* ($236), *Old Faithful Inn* ($305) and *Lake Yellowstone Hotel & Cabins* ($357).

PLACES TO EAT
Snack bars, delis and grocery stores are in several locations in the park. Moderately priced cafeteria-style meals are served at *Canyon Lodge Cafeteria*, *Lake Lodge Cafeteria* and *Old Faithful Lodge Cafeteria*. Other possibilities are the *Grant Village Lake House Restaurant* and *Old Faithful Snow Lodge Restaurant*. The *Roosevelt Lodge Dining Room* requires reservations.

More elaborate meals are served at *Mammoth Hot Springs Hotel Dining Room* (☎ 307-344-5314), *Canyon Lodge Dining Room* (☎ 307-242-3999), *Lake Yellowstone Hotel Dining Room* (☎ 307-242-3899), *Grant Village Restaurant* (☎ 307-242-3499) and *Old Faithful Inn Dining Room* (☎ 307-545-4999). Lunches are reasonably priced, but can be crowded. Dinners are more expensive and require reservations. Call ☎ 307-344-7901 for dining information and reservations at any of the above restaurants.

GETTING THERE & AWAY
Air
Year-round airports nearest to Yellowstone National Park are in Jackson (56 miles), Cody (52 miles), Bozeman, MT (65 miles; see Yellowstone Country in the Montana section), Billings, MT (129 miles; see The Southeast Corner in the Montana section) and Idaho Falls, ID (107 miles; see Eastern Idaho in the Snake River Plain chapter of the Idaho section). The airport in West Yellowstone, MT, is usually open June to early September. It can be more affordable to fly into Salt Lake City, UT (390 miles), or Denver, CO (563 miles), and rent a car there.

Bus
No public transport exists to or within Yellowstone National Park. During the summer, commercial buses to the park operate from Jackson and Cody. Buses operate to West Yellowstone, MT, and Gardiner, MT, from Bozeman, MT, year-round. Greyhound Bus Lines operates daily buses between Idaho Falls, ID, and Bozeman via West Yellowstone during summer. Gray Line of Yellowstone takes passengers on its daily tour buses from

West Yellowstone and Jackson to Old Faithful during summer (see Organized Tours earlier in this chapter).

John D Rockefeller Jr Memorial Parkway

Managed by the NPS through Grand Teton National Park, the John D Rockefeller Jr Memorial Parkway is a 7½-mile corridor linking Yellowstone and Grand Teton national parks. The US Congress recognized Rockefeller's contribution in creating the Grand Teton National Park by designating this 24,000-acre parkway in his honor in 1972. Activities focus around historic Flagg Ranch, which became a US Cavalry post in 1872 and later a private guest ranch in 1910.

The parkway reflects the geologic contrast between Yellowstone and Grand Teton national parks, as the jagged granite Tetons give way to rounded hills capped by younger sedimentary rock. Volcanic cliffs along the Snake River and outcrops on Huckleberry Mountain west and east of Flagg Ranch respectively mark the outer reaches of volcanic Yellowstone.

Orientation & Information
North-south US 89/US 191/US 287 is the main road through the parkway. The turn-off to Flagg Ranch Rd is 2 miles south of the South Entrance to Yellowstone National Park and 15 miles north of Colter Bay Village. The turnoff to Grassy Lake Rd, which leads west to Ashton, ID, is immediately to the right off Flagg Ranch Rd. To reach Flagg Ranch Resort continue straight for half a mile.

Contact Flagg Ranch Resort (☎ 307-543-2861, 800-443-2311; fax 307-543-2356; info@flaggranch.com), PO Box 187, Moran, WY 83013, the NPS concessionaire, to book parkway accommodations and activities. The NPS-run Rockefeller Parkway Visitor Information Station, near

the Grassy Lake Rd turnoff, is open 9 am to 6 pm daily June to August.

Activities
Flagg Ranch Rafting offers three-hour **floating** trips (10 am, 1, 4 and 5 pm) mid-June to early September ($30/22 for adults/children); one-hour trips cost $20/15. A **hiking** trail runs beside the volcanic walls of the Flagg Canyon of the Snake River. To book a two- to four-day float trip on the Snake River between Flagg Ranch Resort and Jackson Lake, contact OARS (☎ 209-736-4677, 800-328-0290, 800-346-6277; fax 209-736-2902), PO Box 67, Angels Camp, CA 95222-9901. During winter, Flagg Ranch Resort rents snowmobiles (starting at $127/day), cross-country skis ($8/12 half/full day) and snowshoes ($6/10).

The east-west Grassy Lake Rd links US 89/US 191/US 287 to US 20 at Ashton, ID, offering an infrequently used 'back way' into the national parks. Numerous lakes and streams in the Jedediah Smith and Winegar Hole wilderness areas, with endless **hiking**, **fishing** and **camping** options, are south and north of Grassy Lake Rd respectively. Grassy Lake Rd is also a good route for **mountain biking**.

Places to Stay & Eat
When other campgrounds in the national parks are full, try the less-known and free USFS *Sheffield Creek Campground* on the east side of US 89/US 191/US 287 just south of Flagg Ranch Rd. *Flagg Ranch Village* is open mid-May to mid-October and mid-December to late February. *Flagg Ranch Campground* has tent and full-hookup sites ($17/25) and a nightly campfire program in their amphitheater Sunday, Tuesday, Thursday and Saturday. Times and topics are posted. Along the banks of the Snake River is their *motel*, where rooms range from $64 to $91. *Cabins* cost from $77 to $120. Rates escalate weekly during peak seasons. Its *restaurant* serves breakfast and dinner during summer and all meals during winter. Shuttles go to Jackson and the Jackson Hole Airport.

WYOMING

Grand Teton National Park

The jagged granite spires of the Teton Mountains are the centerpiece of spectacular Grand Teton National Park. Twelve glacier-carved summits rise above 12,000 feet, crowned by the Grand Teton (13,770 feet). This 40-mile-long range towers above Jackson Hole, where lakes and streams, including the nascent Snake River, mirror the soaring peaks.

History
At least 12,000 years ago people hunted and gathered in Jackson Hole and the Tetons. When Europeans first reached the area in the early 19th century Blackfeet, Crow, Shoshone and Gros Ventre tribes all frequented the valley. The Shoshonean Snake Indians referred to the high peaks as *teewinot* (many pinnacles). John Colter, having split off from the Lewis and Clark Expedition, traveled here in 1807-08. Trappers like Colter and Davey Jackson made their living in the Tetons, but it was raffish French-speaking trappers who dubbed the three most prominent peaks *Les Trois Tetons* for their ostensible resemblance to female breasts. Jackson, in partnership with Jedediah Smith and William Sublette, acquired the Mountain Fur Company in 1826. A cousin of President Andrew Jackson, Davey Jackson claimed the low-lying Snake River drainage as his informal trapping territory, and so lent his name to the expansive valley. Not until the 1880s did permanent settlers inhabit the area, and by the early 20th century dude ranching was proving more profitable than cattle ranching.

Still, transformation of the Tetons into a national park was no foregone conclusion, as commercial ranching and hunting interests resisted attempts to transfer USFS and private lands to the NPS. At its creation in 1929, Grand Teton National Park included only the main part of the Teton Range and the lakes immediately below. Distressed at Jackson Hole's commercial development, John D Rockefeller Jr purchased over 55 sq miles of land to donate to the park.

After President Franklin D Roosevelt declared Jackson Hole a national monument in 1943, Rockefeller's bequest came under NPS jurisdiction. In 1950, legislation conferred national park status and expanded the boundaries to include most of Jackson Hole, but elk hunting and an airport remain islands of private interest within the park. The Grand Teton Lodge Company, founded by Rockefeller, is the park's major concessionaire. Today, this is the only national park with a commercial airport, and the only one outside Alaska that permits hunting.

Geography & Geology
Grand Teton National Park lies south of Yellowstone National Park between the Targhee and Bridger-Teton national forests to the west and east respectively. The steep eastern side of the Teton Range overlooks the Snake River and Jackson Hole, while the gentler west side slopes away toward Idaho's Teton Valley. Much of the national park lies within the valley of Jackson Hole (see Jackson Hole later in this chapter), where Jackson Lake, a natural body of water raised an additional 65 feet by a dam, catches the Snake River as it flows south from its source in Yellowstone National Park.

The fault-block Teton Mountains, which still support a dozen relict glaciers, are the youngest range of the Rocky Mountains. Between 5 million and 9 million years ago, sedimentary rocks west of the north-south Teton Fault rose along a 40-mile front, building a new mountain range 10 to 15 miles wide, 7000 feet above the subsiding land to the east. At the highest elevations, the relatively soft sandstone, shales and other sediments eroded, leaving resistant granite exposed to the elements. Freezing ice wedged and shattered this crystalline rock along its weakest joints, creating impressive pinnacles; then slow-moving Alpine glaciers ground other areas into

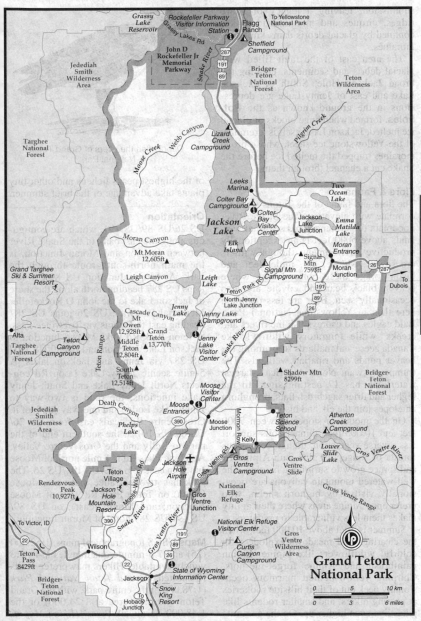

WYOMING

To Yellowstone National Park

Grassy Lake Reservoir

Rockefeller Parkway Visitor Information Station

Flagg Ranch

Sheffield Campground

Jedediah Smith Wilderness Area

Grassy Lakes Rd

John D Rockefeller Jr Memorial Parkway

Snake River

Bridger-Teton National Forest

Teton Wilderness Area

Targhee National Forest

Moose Creek

Webb Canyon

Lizard Creek Campground

Pilgrim Creek

Leeks Marina

Two Ocean Lake

Colter Bay Campground

Jackson Lake

Colter Bay Visitor Center

Jackson Lake Junction

Emma Matilda Lake

Moran Canyon

Elk Island

Moran Entrance

Mt Moran 12,605ft

Signal Mtn Campground

Signal Mtn 7593ft

Moran Junction

To Dubois

Leigh Canyon

Grand Targhee Ski & Summer Resort

Leigh Lake

Teton Park Rd

North Jenny Lake Junction

Cascade Canyon

Jenny Lake

Jenny Lake Campground

Mt Owen 12,928ft

Alta

Targhee National Forest

Teton Canyon Campground

Grand Teton 13,770ft

Middle Teton 12,804ft

Jenny Lake Visitor Center

Teton Range

South Teton 12,514ft

Snake River

Shadow Mtn 8299ft

Bridger-Teton National Forest

Death Canyon

Moose Visitor Center

Jedediah Smith Wilderness Area

Moose Entrance

Phelps Lake

Moose Junction

Teton Science School

Mormon Row

Atherton Creek Campground

Lower Slide Lake

Gros Ventre River

Kelly

Gros Ventre Rd

Jackson Hole Airport

Gros Ventre Campground

Gros Ventre Slide

Gross Ventre River

Rendezvous Peak 10,927ft

Jackson Hole Mountain Resort

Teton Village

Moose-Wilson Rd

National Elk Refuge

Gros Ventre Range

Gros Ventre Junction

To Victor, ID

Snake River

Gros Ventre River

National Elk Refuge Visitor Center

Gros Ventre Wilderness Area

Wilson

Curtis Canyon Campground

Teton Pass 8429ft

Jackson

State of Wyoming Information Center

Bridger-Teton National Forest

Snow King Resort

To Hoback Junction

Grand Teton National Park

0   5   10 km

0   3   6 miles

LP

submission, leaving a legacy of sharp ridges, cirques and mountainside lakes confined by glacial debris dams known as moraines.

The area east of the fault filled with glacial debris and sediments, creating the broad Jackson Hole. South of Jackson Lake and east of Jenny Lake are depressions in the ground known as the **Potholes**, formed when huge blocks of glacial ice melted. Jackson Lake itself is a remnant of the Yellowstone ice sheet, whose broad moraines trapped the melted ice before the Snake cut a channel through them.

Flora & Fauna

The flora and fauna of the Tetons strongly correlate with elevation. The Snake River floodplain of permanent and seasonal wetlands above 6000 feet is an exceptionally productive environment, though winters are severe. Moose, elk, mule deer and bison forage these bottomlands, where beaver, black bear and coyote are also occasionally seen. Bear are less common here than in Yellowstone National Park. Bald eagles and ospreys fish the rivers and creeks, while migratory wildfowl like Canada geese and mallards stop among the beaver ponds and riparian wetlands. The trumpeter swan, North America's largest waterfowl, has 17 nesting sites. In the higher and drier sagebrush flats, pronghorn antelopes join the elk and bison.

On the mountain slopes between 7000 feet and 10,000 feet, thinner soils support less diverse vegetation, though coniferous forests of lodgepole pine, sub-Alpine fir and spruce grow to surprising heights. The well-watered mountain canyons are occasionally visited by bighorn sheep, who prefer open Alpine areas where their agility makes them less vulnerable to predators.

Summer is brief above 10,000 feet, when the clearings and meadows explode with colorful wildflowers like lupine, Indian paintbrush and Alpine forget-me-nots. Chirping yellow-bellied marmots occasionally peek out of their hillside rookeries at passing hikers, and smaller rodents like pikas live even higher up. On the summits

Osprey fish the rivers of Grand Teton National Park.

of the highest peaks lichens and other tiny plants take advantage of the brief summer.

Orientation

US 26/US 89/US 191, which are contiguous along the east bank of the Snake River between Jackson and Moran Junction, is the main north-south route through the park. At Moran Junction US 89/US 191 joins US 287 heading north along the shore of Jackson Lake to the John D Rockefeller Memorial Parkway; US 26 joins US 287 heading east to Dubois via Togwotee Pass.

Teton Park Rd links Moose Junction to Jackson Lake Junction and US 89/US 191/US 287 via Jenny and Jackson lakes. A 5-mile scenic Jenny Lake Loop Rd connects North Jenny Lake and South Jenny Lake junctions; the road is two-way to Jenny Lake Lodge and one-way south of it. Gros Ventre Rd heads east from US 26/US 89/US 191 at the southern end of the park to Kelly and the Gros Ventre Valley. Antelope Flats Rd is 1 mile north of Moose Junction east of US 89/US 191/US 26. The park has two entrance stations: Moose (south) on Teton Park Rd west of Moose Junction; and Moran (east), on US 89/US 191/US 287 north of Moran Junction.

Maps USGS topographical maps, 1:62,500 ($5) and 7.5-minute quadrangles ($4), are widely available. Hikers may prefer Trails Illustrated' *Grand Teton National Park* (1:78,000 of the entire park, with the Grand Teton climbing area at 1:24,000) or the 1:48,000 Earthwalk Press' *Hiking Map &*

WYOMING

Guide: Grand Teton National Park, which covers only the southwest portion of the park but includes most of the key hiking areas.

Information
Entrance Permit & Fees The park is open year-round, although some roads and entrances close during winter. Visitors must purchase a park entrance permit, which is valid for seven days for entry into both Grand Teton and Yellowstone national parks. Reservations are not necessary to enter the park.

The entrance fee is $20 per private (non-commercial) vehicle, $15 per person for individuals entering by motorcycle or snowmobile and $10 per person for individuals entering by bicycle, skis or on foot. The fee for commercial vehicles (such as tour buses) is $30 (one to six seats), $45 (seven to 25 seats), or $100 (26 or more seats). An annual area pass for Yellowstone and Grand Teton national parks costs $40. Keep the entrance fee receipt to reenter a park or to enter the other park.

Visitors receive a free copy of the park newspaper *Teewinot* and a brochure containing a good orientation map, available in German, French, Spanish, Hebrew and Japanese.

Tourist Offices Grand Teton National Park (☎ 307-739-3399; fax 307-739-3438, TTY 307-739-3400) headquarters, PO Box 170, Moose, WY 83012, shares the building with the Moose visitors center.

Visitors centers, which sell books and maps, are:

Moose Visitors Center
    Teton Park Rd, a half-mile west of Moose
    Junction (☎ 307-739-3399 information,
    307-739-3309 backcountry hiking or
    climbing permits)
Jenny Lake Visitors Center
    Teton Park Rd, about 8 miles north of
    Moose Junction
Colter Bay Visitors Center
    US 89/US 191/US 287, 6 miles north of
    Jackson Lake Lodge (☎ 307-739-3594,
    TTY 307-739-3544)

The Colter Bay visitors center is open 8 am to 5 pm mid-May to September, with extended summer hours to 8 pm. The Jenny Lake visitors center is open 8 am to 7 pm June to August. Moose is open 8 am to 5 pm year-round with extended summer hours to 7 pm. The **Indian Arts Museum**, at the Colter Bay visitors center, has an appealing selection of artifacts, some for sale. The park newspaper details the extensive ranger-led activities, including walks and hikes, coffees and talks, lake cruises, Indian Arts Museum tours, wildlife viewing outings and campfire programs. Activities are also posted at the visitors centers.

Concessionaires Three park concessionaires operate various accommodations, restaurants, marinas and activities:

Grand Teton Lodge Company
    PO Box 240, Moran, WY 83013
    (☎ 307-543-2811 information)
    Headquarters, Jackson Lake Lodge
    (☎ 307-543-2855)
    Colter Bay Village, Jackson Lake Lodge
    and activities reservations
    (☎ 307-543-3100, 800-628-9988)
    Jenny Lake Lodge reservations
    (☎ 307-733-4647)
Signal Mountain Lodge
    PO Box 50, Moran, WY 83013
    (☎ 307-543-2831; fax 307-543-2569)
Dornan's in Moose
    PO Box 39, Moose, WY 83012
    (☎ 307-733-2522; fax 307-733-3544;
    dornans@sisna.com)

Money ATMs are at Dornan's and Jackson Lake Lodge.

Post Post offices are at Colter Bay (zip code 83001), Kelly (83011), Moose (83012) and Moran (83013).

Bookstores Contact the Grand Teton Natural History Association (☎ 307-739-3403), PO Box 170, Moose Village, WY 83012, for a catalog of books and maps about the park.

Medical Services Grand Teton Medical Clinic (☎ 307-543-2514 during summer,

WYOMING

WYOMING

307-733-8002 the rest of the year), opposite Jackson Lake Lodge, is open 10 am to 6 pm daily during summer.

Laundry & Showers Showers cost $2 at Colter Bay Village, which also has laundry.

Dangers & Annoyances Black bears and, to a much lesser extent, grizzly bears are present in Grand Teton National Park (for cautionary advice see Yellowstone National Park).

Areas east of US 26/US 89/US 191, west of US 26/US 89/US 191 along the Snake River between Moose and Moran junctions and the John D Rockefeller Jr Memorial Parkway are open to elk hunting mid-October to early December. The NPS 'Elk Ecology & Management' pamphlet has more details and a map. Exercise caution when venturing into these areas during hunting season.

Teton Science School
The highly regarded Teton Science School (☎ 307-733-4765; fax 307-739-9388; tss@ wyoming.com), PO Box 68, Kelly, WY 83011, offers one- to four-day natural history seminars for children and adults. Fees start at $50/day; academic credit is available. Topics include Alpine ecology, geology and glaciology, hydrology, entomology and flora and fauna.

Historic Buildings
Half a mile north of Moose Village, a paved road leads to a short trail and William Menor's homestead cabin on the Snake River's west bank, where until 1927 **Menor's Ferry** operated across the river. Laurence Rockefeller paid to restore the boat in 1949. The nearby **Chapel of the Transfiguration**, built in 1924, has a superb view of the Tetons through the altar window.

East of Blacktail Butte, an unpaved road connects Antelope Flats Rd on the north with Gros Ventre Rd to the south, passing **Mormon Row**, a series of barns and cabins built by early Mormon settlers. The backdrop of the Tetons makes this exceptionally popular with photographers.

Rancher Pierce Cunningham, an early major supporter of Grand Teton National Park, lived at **Cunningham Cabin**, 6 miles south of Moran Junction; a short trail elucidates local homesteading.

Signal Mountain Summit Rd
This 5-mile paved road east of Teton Park Rd goes to Signal Mountain's summit and a panoramic view. Be aware that the road is not suitable for RVs or vehicles with trailers. A 6-mile roundtrip hiking trail also leads to the summit from Signal Mountain Campground.

Hiking & Backpacking
The park has 200 miles of hiking trails, but higher elevations often remain snow-covered until late July. Obtain the NPS brochure 'Day Hikes' or 'Backcountry Camping' to plan your walk. A free backcountry use permit, available at the Moose Village or Colter Bay visitors centers or Jenny Lake Ranger Station, is required for overnight trips. Backcountry reservations can be made in advance by mail January to mid-May; write park headquarters (see Information above).

The north-south **Teton Crest Trail**, which runs just west of the main summits, can be accessed from the east by several steep canyons. The main trailheads, south to north, are Granite Canyon, south of the Moose visitors center on the Moose-Wilson Rd; Death Canyon, south of the Moose visitors center at the end of an unpaved road off the Moose-Wilson Rd; Taggart Lake, north of the Moose visitors center on Teton Park Rd; Lupine Meadows, south of Jenny Lake at the end of an unpaved road off Teton Park Rd; Jenny Lake, off Teton Park Rd; and String Lake/Leigh Lake on Jenny Lake Loop Rd.

Day Hikes Hikes around Jenny Lake, Hidden Falls and Inspiration Point start from String Lake trailhead. Walk along the northwest shore of lovely Jenny Lake to Hidden Falls. Inspiration Point, a steep half-mile farther, is the start of the popular and more level Cascade Canyon Trail.

Continue back around the south shore of Jenny Lake to the Jenny Lake trailhead. One of the most popular Teton day hikes, many people take the shuttle boat across Jenny Lake (see Boating below). String Lake is the most popular picnic area, with dramatic views of the north face of Teewinot Mountain and Grand Teton from the sandy beaches along the east side.

Bradley and Taggart lakes have a self-guiding trail, less heavily used than Jenny Lake, offering several easy loop options ranging from 3 to 5 miles total. A classic 10-mile round-trip hike to Surprise and Amphitheater lakes begins at Lupine Meadows trailhead. The strenuous trail climbs 3000 feet to the lakes, high on Disappointment Peak with Grand Teton in the background.

Two Ocean and Emma Matilda lakes are east of Jackson Lake. Turn north onto Pacific Creek Rd about 1 mile west of Moran Junction and drive 4 miles to the parking area. A mostly flat 6-mile hike starting from the east end circles Two Ocean Lake with fine Teton views. It is a 13-mile loop to circle both lakes via panoramic Grand View Point.

Backpacking From Granite Creek trailhead, a one-night 19-mile loop on the Valley Trail goes up Open Canyon and down Granite Canyon. A two- to three-night 26-mile loop goes through Granite Canyon and Death Canyon via the Teton Crest Trail. A 38-mile trip up Granite Canyon, along the Teton Crest Trail and down Paintbrush Canyon to the String Lake trailhead takes four nights. The classic 20-mile Cascade-Paintbrush loop, one of the most popular, can be done as an overnight trip or a long day hike, starting from the String Lake trailhead.

Climbing & Mountaineering
The Tetons are a favorite destination for rock climbers and mountaineers. Excellent short routes abound, as well as the classic longer summits like Grand Teton, Mt Moran and Mt Owen. The Jenny Lake Ranger Station (☎ 307-739-3343), open

8 am to 6 pm June to September, is ground zero for climbing information. All climbers staying overnight need a backcountry use permit (see Hiking & Backpacking above) and must register at the Jenny Lake Ranger Station during summer or at the Moose visitors center the rest of the year. Call ☎ 307-739-3604 for recorded climbing information. The American Alpine Club's Climbers Ranch (☎ 307-733-7271), on Teton Park Rd just south of the Teton Glacier turnout, operates an inexpensive summer dormitory with cooking facilities and showers for climbers.

For instruction and guided climbs, contact Exum Mountain Guides (☎ 307-733-2297; fax 307-733-9613; exum@wyoming .com), PO Box 56, Moose, WY 83012, or Jackson Hole Mountain Guides (☎ 307-733-4979, 800-239-7642), 165 N Glenwood St, PO Box 7477, Jackson, WY 83002. Exum runs climbing schools at Hidden Falls on Jenny Lake's west shore and at the upper cliffs at the Jackson Hole Mountain Resort, accessed by the aerial tram, and has a base camp at Grand Teton's Lower Saddle (11,600 feet). Exum is the only guide service permitted to guide all routes in the Teton Range year-round.

Biking
Mountain Bike Outfitters (☎ 307-733-3314), at Dornan's Market in Moose Village, rents bikes and provides a map of Jackson area cycling routes. Among the recommended rides from Moose Junction are the wide-shouldered Teton Park Rd north to Jackson Lake Junction, the Teton Village Rd south to Teton Village and the Mormon Row/Kelly Loop via Antelope Flats Rd and the Gros Ventre Junction.

Boating & Floating
All private craft must obtain a permit, which costs $10 for motorized and $5 for non-motorized craft (rafts, canoes or kayaks) and are issued at the Moose and Colter Bay visitors centers. Motorized craft (maximum 7½ horsepower) are allowed only on Jackson, Jenny and Phelps lakes. Lakes permitting hand-propelled nonmotorized craft are

WYOMING

Jackson, Two Ocean, Emma Matilda, Bearpaw, Leigh, String, Jenny, Bradley, Taggart and Phelps. Sailboats are only permitted on Jackson Lake.

The park has three marinas. Signal Mountain Marina rents canoes/rowboats ($8/hour, $60/day), motorboats ($16/105), and pontoons ($45/180). Their scenic float trips cost $32/16 for adults/children; half-day guided fishing trips start at $160. Colter Bay Marina, operated by Grand Teton Lodge Company, handles fishing gear and licenses and motorboat, rowboat and canoe rentals. They also arrange lake cruises. Leek's Marina (☎ 307-543-2494), north of Colter Bay Junction, has a gas dock and overnight buoys.

Teton Boating Company (☎ 307-733-2703) runs shuttles and cruises and rents fishing boats. Shuttles cross Jenny Lake between the east shore boat dock near the Jenny Lake visitors center and the west shore boat dock, offering quick (12-minute) access to Inspiration Point and the Cascade Canyon Trail. The one-way shuttle fare is $3.25/2 for adults/children (seven to 12); roundtrip is $4/2.25. Shuttles run every 20 minutes 8 am to 6 pm, but expect long waits for return shuttles 4 to 6 pm. Scenic Jenny Lake cruises (10, 11 am, 1 and 2 pm) cost $7.50/4.50 for adults/children (seven to 12). Fishing boat rentals cost $10/hour plus $7 for each additional hour, or $45/day.

Several outfitters run leisurely Snake River **float trips** ($30/20 for adults/children). Two launch sites, north of the Snake River Overlook (2½ hours) and south of Teton Point Turnout (1½ hours), are north of Moose Junction on US 26/US 89/US 191. To book a float trip, contact Barker-Ewing Float Trips (☎ 307-733-1800), Moose; Grand Teton Lodge Company (see Information above); Fort Jackson River Trips (☎ 307-733-2583, 800-735-8430), 135 N Cache Drive, Jackson; National Park Float Trips (☎ 307-733-6445, 307-733-5500), Moose; or Solitude Float Trips (☎ 307-733-2871).

For unique and organized one- to five-day **kayaking trips** on Jackson Lake with island camping, contact OARS (☎ 209-

736-4677, 800-328-0290, 800-346-6277; fax 209-736-2902), PO Box 67, Angels Camp, CA 95222-9901.

Fishing
Whitefish and cutthroat, lake and brown trout abound in park rivers and lakes. Fishing is subject to NPS and Wyoming state regulations, available at visitors centers. Licenses are issued at Moose Village store, Signal Mountain Lodge and Colter Bay Marina. Grand Teton Lodge Company offers guided Jackson Lake fly-fishing trips.

Horseback Riding
Jackson Lake Lodge Corral and Colter Bay Village Corral offer guided horseback rides for $16/hour or $38/half-day; breakfast and evening rides, either on horseback or by wagon, are also available. Contact the activities desk at Jackson Lake Lodge and the activities booth near the General Store at Colter Bay Village.

Birding
The NPS distributes the useful, one-page 'Bird-Finding Guide' with descriptions of prime migratory bird habitat. Good sites are Oxbow Bend 1 mile east of Jackson Lake Junction, Blacktail Ponds north of Moose Junction and lakeshore sites like Willow Flats, one half-mile north of Jackson Lake Junction.

Organized Tours
Grand Teton Lodge Company operates narrated bus tours ($18/10 for adults/children ages three to 11) Monday, Wednesday and Friday; tours of both national parks cost $53/30.

Places to Stay
NPS campgrounds and privately run cabins, lodges and motels are in Grand Teton National Park. Most campgrounds and accommodations are open early May to early October, depending on weather.

Camping Camping inside the park is permitted in designated campgrounds only and is limited to 14 days (seven days at

Jenny Lake). Campgrounds usually hold a nightly campfire program in their amphitheater. Days, times and topics are prominently posted. The NPS (☎ 307-739-3603 for recorded information) operates the park's only five campgrounds on a first-come, first-served basis. Demand for campsites is high early July to Labor Day, and most campgrounds fill by 11 am. (Jenny Lake fills first and much earlier; Gros Ventre fills last.) If campsites are full, try alternative private and USFS campgrounds outside the park; those nearest the park fill first.

When you have a choice of campgrounds (ranging from 6600 feet to 6900 feet), its setting and proximity to activities can help you select the one you might enjoy most.

Lizard Creek Campground – On a forested peninsula along the north shore of Jackson Lake, Lizard Creek Campground has 60 sites, several walk-in sites. US 89/US 191/US 287, about 8 miles north of Colter Bay Junction. ($12)

Colter Bay Campground – The expansive, wooded Colter Bay Campground has 310 large, private sites near the east shore of Jackson Lake, with tent-only sites reserved for backpackers and cyclists ($2), and a separate RV park. US 89/US 191/US 287, 3 miles north of Jackson Lake Junction. ($12/27 tent/RV)

Signal Mountain Campground – Sparse lodgepole pines dot Signal Mountain Campground (86 sites) along the southwest shore of Jackson Lake. Some sites farther away from the lake offer more privacy. Teton Park Rd, 5 miles south of Jackson Lake Junction. ($12)

Jenny Lake Campground – The very congenial and popular tent-only Jenny Lake Campground (49 sites) is convenient to many trailheads, and has sites reserved for cyclists ($2). Teton Park Rd, about 8 miles north of Moose Junction. ($12)

Gros Ventre Campground – Sprawling Gros Ventre Campground, surrounded by sagebrush and shaded by cottonwoods near the Gros Ventre River, has 360 sites, more than 100 of them for tents only. It is closer to the Teton Science School (see above) and the Gros Ventre Mountains than most of the park's lakes, rivers and trails. Gros Ventre Rd, 4½ miles northeast of US 26/US 89/US 191/US 287 at Gros Ventre Junction. ($12)

Lodges & Cabins The Grand Teton Lodge Company operates Colter Bay Village, Jackson Lake Lodge and Jenny Lake Lodge. Signal Mountain Lodge operates a property of the same name. Dornan's in Moose operates the Spur Ranch Log Cabins. Contact the appropriate park concessionaire (see Information earlier in this section) for reservations.

Colter Bay Village (☎ 307-543-2828), half a mile west of Colter Bay Junction, offers two types of accommodations: tent village ($26 excluding showers) and cabins (semi-private bathroom $30; one room with private bathroom $60 to $85; and two-room, four-person cabins $87 to $109). The tent village is comprised of tent cabins, simple log and canvas structures with two bunk beds (without bedding), a wood-burning stove, table and benches and an outdoor barbecue. The *Jackson Lake Lodge*, 1 mile north of Jackson Lake Junction, offers motel rooms (standard rooms $99, lake-view rooms $175) and cottages ($113 to $125). Singles/doubles at the exclusive *Jenny Lake Lodge*, off Teton Park Rd, cost $275/300; suites range from $485 to $505. Rates include some meals, bicycle rentals and guided horseback riding.

The lakeside *Signal Mountain Lodge*, on Teton Park Rd 2 miles southwest of Jackson Lake Junction, has three types of accommodations: cabins (one-room cabins start at $75, two rooms at $99), motel rooms (standard rooms range from $95 to $135; lake-front rooms start at $152) and apartments/bungalows (ranging from $125 to $165).

The nonsmoking *Spur Ranch Log Cabins*, at Dornan's in Moose, is open year-round. One-bedroom, four-person cabins range from $125 to $150 June to September; $100 to $125 during October, mid-December to March and during May; and $75 to $100 November to mid December

WYOMING

and during April. Rates for two-bedroom, six-person cabins are up to $50 more.

Places to Eat

The Restaurant at Leek's Marina (☎ 307-733-5470), north of Colter Bay Village, open for lunch and dinner, serves sandwiches, soups, salads, burgers and pizza. Colter Bay Village's *John Colter Chuckwagon* is open 7:30 am to 9 pm daily for moderately priced breakfast, lunch and dinner buffets in a relaxed atmosphere. Nearby, the *John Colter Cafe Court Pizza & Deli* serves sandwiches, salads, pizza, and rotisserie chicken and is a good place for a quick meal or to get food to go for a day trip. A snack bar is adjacent to the grocery store.

Jackson Lake Lodge's *Mural Room*, featuring 'Rocky Mountain cuisine,' serves breakfast, lunch and dinner; dinner reservations are recommended. The more casual *Pioneer Grill* at Jackson Lake Lodge, open 6 am to 10:30 pm daily, also offers box lunches and fills thermos bottles for day trips. Signal Mountain Lodge's *Aspens* has a coffee shop, lounge and dining room specializing in American and seafood dishes. The upscale *Jenny Lake Lodge Dining Room* requires dinner reservations; for men, jackets are preferred. They serve a special buffet on Sunday evenings.

Dornan's *Original Moose Chuckwagon* (☎ 307-733-2415) in Moose Village is an open-air restaurant with Teton views; some tables are inside tepees. They serve pancake and egg breakfasts ($6.25), sandwiches and salads for lunch and steak and prime rib dinners (all you can eat for $12). Pizza, pasta and subs are served from noon to 8 pm in the lounge at *Dornan's Pizza & Pasta Company*. A deli counter is in the nearby grocery store, where espressos are also available.

Getting There & Away

Three roads lead to the park: US 26/US 89/US 191 from Jackson to the south; US 26/US 287 from Dubois to the east; and US 89/US 191/US 287 from Yellowstone National Park to the north.

Jackson Hole

Early European visitors used the term 'hole' to describe an open valley surrounded by mountains. Jackson Hole is such a place, bounded by the Gros Ventre and Teton ranges to the east and west respectively, and the Yellowstone lava flows and the Hoback and Wyoming ranges to the north and south. The communities of Jackson, Teton Village and Wilson and much of the Grand Teton National Park lie within this broad valley.

Jackson Hole and the Tetons are home to three resorts: the world-class Jackson Hole Mountain, Snow King and Grand Targhee Ski & Summer resorts (the latter in Alta, WY, on the west side of the Teton Range; see the Eastern Idaho section in the Snake River Plain chapter). Moose, elk and bison roam the valley floor against the backdrop of the snowcapped Tetons, making Jackson Hole one of Wyoming's most breathtaking destinations. But recreation is the driving force of its popularity, making it Wyoming's most expensive destination. Downhill skiing is the featured activity, but summer visitors find no shortage of things to do: from hiking and biking to rafting and horseback riding.

JACKSON

Jackson (population 4700; elevation 6234 feet), the commercial heart of the area, can cause sensory overload. 'Real' Wyomingites disparage it as a tourist enclave where celebrities frequent fancy restaurants, rapacious realtors push overpriced condominiums and fatuous vacationers swarm shopping malls. Bogus false-front arcades, more befitting Disney's Frontierland, overwhelm its once picturesque center. Jackson has nearly 2200 motel rooms, the worst traffic in Wyoming and a crime problem of primarily ski and bicycle theft. But it also supports a vigorous cultural life of live theater, concerts, cinemas, museums and bookstores.

Orientation

US 89/US 26/US 191, the main road through town, follows east-west Broadway into downtown, where it turns north onto Cache Drive. Broadway divides north-south street addresses; Cache Drive east-west ones. The pedestrian-oriented downtown centers around the traditional Town Square, at Broadway and Cache Drive.

Information

Tourist Offices The Wyoming Information Center, 532 N Cache Drive, operated by the chamber of commerce, is open 8 am to 8 pm daily during summer, and 8 am to 5 pm weekdays and 10 am to 2 pm weekends during winter. The staff is helpful and well-informed and offers a wide variety of brochures and pamphlets, many with discount coupons. The Jackson Hole Chamber of Commerce (☎ 307-733-3316, 307-733-7606; jhchamber@sisna.com), 555 E Broadway, is open 8 am to 5 pm weekdays.

The Jackson Hole Visitors Council, PO Box 982, Jackson Hole, WY 83001, operates Jackson Hole Central Reservations (☎ 307-733-4005, 800-443-6931; fax 307-733-1286; jhcr@sisna.com), a reservation service for all lodging, skiing and transportation open 8 am to 6 pm weekdays and 8 am to 4 pm weekends. They also sell a Ski Three Multi Area Lift Voucher ($220 for five vouchers) good at any of the three area resorts. Ask for their 'Jackson Hole Wyoming Spring, Summer, Fall' and/or 'Jackson Hole Wyoming Winter Vacation Planner' brochures. The Jackson Hole website (www.jacksonhole.com) has information on town and ski resort accommodations, restaurants, activities and more.

The USFS Bridger-Teton National Forest headquarters (☎ 307-739-5500) and Jackson Ranger District (☎ 307-739-5400), 340 N Cache Drive, open 8 am to 4:30 pm Monday to Saturday, have maps of surrounding national forests and wilderness areas.

Useful Organizations The Jackson Hole Alliance for Responsible Planning (☎ 307-733-9417), 40 E Simpson St, PO Box 2728, Jackson, WY 83001, lobbies for protection of biodiversity in the Greater Yellowstone Ecosystem.

Money ATMs are at The Bank of Jackson Hole, with locations at 990 W Broadway and at the corner of Broadway and Cache Drive; Community First National Bank, 120 W Pearl Ave; and Jackson State Bank, 112 Center St, 50 Buffalo Way, and also inside Albertson's Supermarket, 520 W Broadway.

Post & Communications The post office is at 220 W Pearl Ave (zip code 83001). Mail Boxes Etc (☎ 307-733-9250; fax 307-733-9032), 970 W Broadway, provides fax services.

Travel Agencies Jackson Hole Travel Service (☎ 307-733-2310, 800-228-4915; fax 307-733- 2390), 565 N Cache Drive, is the American Express representative. Après Vous Travel (☎ 307- 733-0353, 800-322-5766; fax 307-733-3487), 270 W Pearl Ave, is not particularly friendly but conveniently located.

Bookstores Teton Bookshop (☎ 307-733-9220), 25 S Glenwood St, has a fine selection of Western and general interest books. Valley Bookstore's (☎ 307-733-4533, 800-647-4111), 125 N Cache Drive, is even larger.

Publications Jackson's two free daily newspapers are the *Jackson Hole Daily* and the *Daily Guide*. The free *Jackson Hole Weekend Guide* appears Friday and lists local entertainment possibilities, as does *Stepping Out*.

Medical Services St John's Hospital (☎ 307-733-3636), 625 E Broadway, is the major medical facility. Several emergency clinics include InstaCare of Jackson (☎ 307-733-7003), 545 W Broadway, and Emerg-A-Care (☎ 307-733-8002), 970 W Broadway.

Laundry Go to the Soap Opera Laundromat (☎ 307-733-5584), 835 W Broadway,

Jackson

0   125   250 m

0   125   250 yards

To Jackson Hole Airport,
Grand Teton National Park

National
Elk Refuge

Perry St

Mercill Ave

Millward St   Glenwood St   191

89   26

Gill Ave

Teton Ave

Jean St   Moran St   Gros Ventre St   Moose St

Miller
Park

Jackson St

Center St   Willow St   Deloney Ave

Town
Square   E Broadway

W Broadway

Cache Drive

Glissold St   Jackson St   King St   Vine St

Pearl Ave

Simpson Ave

Hansen Ave

Cache Creek

Kelly Ave

Snow King Ave   Karns Ave   Snow
King
Resort

Teton
County
Fairgrounds

Snow King Ave

To Hoback
Junction

Flat Creek Drive

WYOMING

or Ryan Cleaners (☎ 307-733-2938) is at
545 N Cache Drive.

Things to See

The immediate downtown area retains a
handful of worthy historic landmarks. The
Jackson Hole Museum (see below) was
originally Deloney's General Merchandise
(1906). West and one block north of the
museum, St John's Episcopal Church
(1911 to 1915) is a dignified log building
with a unique stockade-type bell tower.
The log building at 132 N Cache Drive was
the Teater Studio, where local artist Archie
Teater painted landscapes and historic

scenes, some of which still adorn the walls
of 15 Deloney Ave at N Cache Drive.

Jackson's **Town Square**, once a rubbish
dump for local merchants, became a landmark after a 1932 federal beautification
program honoring George Washington's
200th birthday. A popular reenactment of
a **Town Square Shootout** occurs at
6:30 pm nightly Memorial to Labor Day.
At its southeast corner, the early 1900s
Wort Winter Cabin is a shoot-out prop that
once belonged to the family that built the
Wort Hotel. The Van Vleck Cabin (1910),
135 E Broadway, belonged to a local pioneer family. The Miller House (1921), 211

PLACES TO STAY

3 Wagon Wheel Motel & Campground
7 Cache Creek Motel
12 Inn on the Creek
13 Stagecoach Motel
14 The Alpine House
15 Trapper Inn
17 Teton Inn
18 The Bunkhouse, Anvil Motel, El Rancho Motel
20 Rusty Parrot Lodge
21 Prospector Motel
29 The Parkway
30 Four Winds Motel
38 HC Richards B&B
39 Sundance Inn
40 Wort Hotel
46 Golden Eagle Motor Inn
58 Hitching Post Lodge
62 Rawhide Motel
63 Pony Express Motel
81 Buckrail Lodge
82 Twin Trees B&B

PLACES TO EAT

22 The Blue Lion Restaurant
25 Sugarfoot Cafe
28 The Bunnery
42 Million Dollar Cowboy Bar
45 Jedediah's
50 Mountain High Pizza Pie
57 Snake River Grill
59 Bubba's Bar-B-Que
61 Market Place Deli
64 Pearl Street Bagels
67 Anthony's Italian Restaurant

68 Lejay's Sportsmen's Cafe
69 Shades Cafe
70 Hot or Not Deli
71 Sweetwater Restaurant
72 Mama Inez

OTHER

1 Wyoming Balloon Company
2 Ryan Cleaners
4 Dave Hansen Whitewater
5 Wyoming Information Center
6 Jackson Hole Travel Service
8 Eagle Rent-A-Car
9 Lewis & Clark River Expeditions
10 Jackson Hole Historical Society & Museum
11 USFS Bridger-Teton National Forest Headquarters & Jackson Ranger District
16 Thrifty
19 Snake River Kayak & Canoe School
23 Teton Cyclery
24 Jackson Hole Mountain Guides
26 Teton Mountaineering
27 Dirty Jack's Wild West Theatre
31 Jackson Hole Playhouse
32 Jackson Hole Museum
33 Skinny Skis
34 Valley Bookstore
35 Jackson State Bank
36 St John's Hospital

37 Salt Lake City Airport Shuttle (in Daylight Donuts)
41 Jackson Hole Whitewater
43 Wyoming Studios
44 Wyoming Outfitters
47 Chamber of Commerce, Jackson Hole Land Trust
48 Lone Eagle, Gart Sports
49 Hoback Sports
51 Sands Whitewater River Trips
52 Stone's Boots
53 Barker-Ewing Jackson Hole River Trips, Lone Eagle Whitewater, Grand Teton Main Stage Theatre
54 The Bank of Jackson Hole
55 The Rancher, Mad River Boat Trips, Inc
56 Jack Dennis Outdoor Shop
60 The Board Room of Jackson Hole Professional Snowboard Shop
65 Teton Bookshop
66 Budget
73 Après Vous Travel
74 Post Office
75 Community First National Bank
76 Mountain Property Management
77 Jackson State Bank, Albertsons
78 Snake River Brewing Co
79 Jackson Hole Alliance for Responsible Planning
80 Teton Mountain Bike Tours

E Broadway, belonged to usurious banker Robert Miller.

The **Jackson Hole Museum** (☎ 307-733-2414), 105 N Glenwood St, presents local history from the hunter-gatherer epoch to the present. Open 9:30 am to 6 pm Monday to Saturday and 10 am to 5 pm Sunday Memorial Day to October 1, admission is $3/2/1/6 for adults/seniors/students/families. The museum director conducts one-hour Jackson walking tours at 10 am Tuesday, Thursday and Saturday. The tour costs $2/1/5 for adults/seniors/families.

The **Jackson Hole Historical Society & Museum** (☎ 307-733-9605), 105 Mer-

cill Ave, a museum and research facility, focuses on Plains Indians, early Jackson Hole settlement and the creation of Grand Teton National Park. Its research collection includes photographs, a library, documentary archives, oral histories and newspapers. Open 8 am to 5 pm weekdays, admission is free.

The **National Museum of Wildlife Art** (☎ 307-733-5771), 2820 Rungius Rd, 3 miles north of Jackson, displays paintings and sculptures by George Catlin, Albert Bierstadt, Karl Bodmer and Carl Rungius. An historic photographic exhibit covers cowboy culture. On permanent display is the recreation of John Clymer's Teton Village studio. The 51,000-sq-foot facility, built of Arizona sandstone, blends into the landscape of Rising Sage Hillside overlooking the National Elk Refuge. It is open from 10 am to 6 pm Monday to Saturday and 1 to 6 pm Sunday Memorial Day to September 30, and 10 am to 5 pm Tuesday to Saturday and 1 to 5 pm Sunday October to Memorial Day. Admission is $3 for adults with discounts for seniors/students.

Over 8000 Rocky Mountain elk winter at the USFWS-administered, 39-sq-mile **National Elk Refuge** (☎ 307-733-9212), northeast of Jackson via Elk Refuge Rd, an extension of E Broadway. It was established in 1912 after Jackson Hole development disrupted seasonal elk migration routes. When snow covers the native grasses, the elk are fed pelleted alfalfa hay. The refuge offers winter sleigh rides (☎ 307-733-0277), departing from the National Museum of Wildlife Art. Also in the refuge is the **Jackson National Fish Hatchery** (☎ 307-733-2510), 1500 Fish Hatchery Rd, reached from US 89 N.

Activities
People looking for **climbing** partners can check out the bulletin board at Teton Mountaineering (☎ 307-733-3595), 170 N Cache Drive. Teton Rock Gym (☎ 307-733-0707), at 1116 Maple Way, offers sport climbs of all levels and difficulty ($10/day).

The Jackson Hole Land Trust (☎ 307-733-4707), 555 E Broadway, a private organization that owns 11 sq miles in Jackson Hole, protects vital habitats by purchasing key properties or persuading ranchers to grant conservation easements in exchange for tax advantages. They offer some **hiking**, **horseback riding** and **mountain biking** on their property.

The Jackson Hole Golf & Tennis Club (☎ 307-733-3111), 5000 Spring Gulch Rd, is 8 miles north of Jackson and 1 mile west of US 89 at Gros Ventre Junction. Green fees at their 18-hole **golf** course start at $80 depending on the time of year. Hourly **tennis** fees are $13.

Special Events
Jackson Hole hosts many events: check local listings to see what's happening. The **Elk Antler Auction** takes place every spring at Town Square. The **Teton County Fair** (☎ 733-0658) takes place in late July at the Teton County Fairgrounds, Snow King Ave and Flat Creek Rd. The **Jackson Hole Rodeo** (☎ 307-733-2805) takes place at the fairgrounds at 8 pm Wednesday and Saturday Memorial Day to Labor Day. The **Jackson Hole Fall Arts Festival** lasts nearly three weeks in mid-September.

Places to Stay
Summer and winter high seasons rates are at least 30% higher than – and sometimes double – the low-season prices quoted here. Reservations are essential during peak times.

Places to Stay – budget
Camping The cramped *Wagon Wheel Campground* (☎ 307-733-4588), 435 N Cache Drive, attracts climbers and backpackers, but management is indifferent. Tent/full-hookup sites cost $11/27. The *Virginian RV Park* (☎ 307-733-7189), 750 W Broadway, has RV-only sites starting at $34. The pleasant *Jackson South/Hoback Junction KOA Kampground* (☎ 307-733-7078, 800-562-1878), off US 26/US 89/US 191, 12 miles south of Jackson, has grassy tent sites ($23) and sites with full hookups ($32).

Hostels *The Bunkhouse* (☎ 307-733-3668 c/o Anvil and El Rancho motels; fax 307-733-3957), 215 N Cache Drive, has $18 beds with a modicum of privacy in modest basement cubicles with kitchen access. Nonguests can shower for $5.

Motels In Jackson 'budget' means rates starting under $70 for a double, and often ranging over $100. Within walking distance of downtown are the friendly *Teton Inn* (☎ 307-733-3883, 800-851-0070; fax 307-733-3133), 165 W Gill Ave, the best of the lot ($40); *Virginian Lodge* (☎ 307-733-2792, 800-262-4999; fax 307-733-

0281; virginian@wyoming.com), 750 W Broadway ($44); *Rawhide Motel* (☎ 307-733-1216, 800-835-2999; fax 307-733-1216), 75 S Millward St ($58); *Sundance Inn* (☎ 307-733-3444, 888-478-6326; fax 307-733-3440), 135 W Broadway ($59); *El Rancho Motel* (☎ 307-733-3668, 800-234-4507; fax 307-733-3957), 215 N Cache Drive ($65); and *Pony Express Motel* (☎ 307-733-3835, 800-526-2658), 50 S Millward St ($66). The pleasant *Stagecoach Motel* (☎ 307-733-3451) is at 291 N Glenwood St.

North of town, convenient to the National Elk Refuge, are the *Elk Refuge Inn* (☎ 307-733-3582, 800-544-3582), 1755 N US 89 ($56) and *Flat Creek Motel* (☎ 307-733-5276, 800-438-9338; fax 307-733-0374), 1935 N US 89 ($60).

South of downtown along US 89 are the *Days Inn of Jackson Hole* (☎ 307-733-0033; fax 307-733-0044), 350 S US 89 ($69); the popular *Motel 6* (☎ 307-733-1620; fax 307-734-9175), 600 S US 89 (singles/doubles $52/58); and *Super 8 Motel* (☎ 307-733-6833; fax 307-739-1828), 750 S US 89 ($64/74).

Places to Stay – middle

Motels Moderately priced motels start between $70 and $100; all are downtown.

Starting under $80 are the *Buckrail Lodge* (☎ 307-733-2079), 110 E Karns Ave ($70); *Wagon Wheel Motel* (☎ 307-733-2357), 435 N Cache Drive (singles/doubles $76/81); *Hitching Post Lodge* (☎ 307-733-2606, 800-821-8351; fax 307-733-8221), 460 E Broadway ($78); *The Parkway* (☎ 307-733-3143, 800-247-8390; fax 307-733-0995), 125 N Jackson St ($79); and *Best Western The Lodge at Jackson Hole* (☎ 307-739-9703, 800-458-3866; fax 307-739-9168), 80 Scott Lane ($79).

Others starting under $90 include the *Prospector Motel* (☎ 307-733-4858, 800-851-0070; fax 307-733-3133), 155 N Jackson St (singles/doubles $80/90); the friendly *Anvil Motel* (☎ 307-733-3368, 800-234-4507; fax 307-733-3957), 215 N Cache Drive ($85); *Trapper Inn* (☎ 307-733-2648, 800 341 8000 reservations; fax

307-739-9351), 235 N Cache Drive ($88); *Cache Creek Motel* (☎ 307-733-7781, 800-843-4788; fax 307-733-4652), 390 N Glenwood St ($88); *Four Winds Motel* (☎ 307-733-2474, 800-228-6461), 150 N Millward St ($89); and *Golden Eagle Motor Inn* (☎ 307-733-2042), 325 E Broadway (singles/doubles $89/98).

Places to Stay – top end

B&Bs Several B&Bs are within walking distance of downtown: *HC Richards B&B* (☎ 307- 733-6704; fax 307-733-0930), 160 W Deloney Ave ($90); nonsmoking *The Alpine House* (☎ 307-739-1570, 800-753-1421), 285 N Glenwood St ($115), run by former US Olympic athletes Hans and Nancy Johnstone; *Twin Trees B&B* (☎ 307-739-9737, 800-728-7337), 575 S Willow St at Snow King Ave ($115); and *Nowlin Creek Inn* (☎ 307-733-0882, 800-533-0882), 660 E Broadway (ranges from $125 to 155). Contact the Jackson Hole B&B Association (☎ 307-734-1999), 1225 N Green Lane, Wilson, WY 83014, for more information.

Lodges & Hotels The *Rusty Parrot Lodge* (☎ 307-733-2000, 800-458-2004; fax 307-733-5566), 175 N Jackson Ave, starts at $100. The venerable *Wort Hotel* (☎ 307-733-2190, 800-322-2727; fax 307-733-2190), 50 N Glenwood St, occupying almost an entire block, starts at $115. The lavishly decorated *Inn on the Creek* (☎ 307-739-1565, 800-669-9534; fax 307-734-9116), 295 N Millward St, has a wonderful setting in which to indulge yourself; rooms start at $149.

Long-Term Rentals See Teton Village – Places to Stay later in this chapter for reputable property management firms.

Places to Eat

Jackson has the most sophisticated grub in Wyoming. Plenty of places are unconscionably expensive and pretentious, but many offer good values, especially (but not exclusively) the lunch specials. The Jackson Hole Restaurant Association publishes

WYOMING

an annual 'Jackson Hole Dining Guide' that includes menus.

Bubba's Bar-B-Que (☎ 307-733-2288), 515 W Broadway, lively and spacious but often crowded, serves an unexpected combination of delicious ribs and vegetarian dishes. *The Bunnery* (☎ 307-733-5474, 800-349-0492), 130 N Cache Drive, has a varied breakfast and lunch menu, with a good selection of breads, muffins and pastries to go. *Jedediah's* (☎ 307-733-5671), 135 E Broadway, popular for breakfast, also serves lunch and dinner. Eggs and biscuits and gravy are their specialties; prices are very reasonable. *Pearl Street Bagels* (☎ 307-739-1218), 145 W Pearl Ave, serves espresso, bagels and sandwiches. The *Market Place Deli* (☎ 307-733-5387), 245 W Pearl Ave, has good takeout items. The *Hot or Not Deli* (☎ 307-733-3354), 75 E Pearl Ave, is the best deli in town and serves tasty ice cream. The *Snake River Grill* (☎ 307-733-0557), 84 E Broadway, comes highly recommended for luncheon salads, sandwiches, specials and pizzas, plus more elaborate dinners. *Mama Inez* (☎ 307-733-9166), 380 W Pearl Ave, serves tasty Mexican food.

The *Sweetwater Restaurant* (☎ 307-733-3553), 85 S King St, serves good, reasonably priced lunch and dinner, but is often very crowded, so go early or late. The *Shades Cafe* (☎ 307-733-2015), 82 S King St, is a good and moderately priced alternative for breakfast, sandwiches and gourmet burritos. Another good spot is the *Sugarfoot Cafe* (☎ 307-733-9148), 145 N Glenwood St. *Mountain High Pizza Pie* (☎ 307-733-3646), 120 W Broadway, offers Italian fast food, while *Anthony's Italian Restaurant* (☎ 307-733-3717), 50 S Glenwood St, is a more upscale Italian restaurant open for dinner only. *The Blue Lion Restaurant* (☎ 307-733-3912), 160 N Millward St, is a French restaurant serving excellent seafood and wild game.

The *Lame Duck* (☎ 307-733-4311), 680 E Broadway, a popular Mandarin Chinese restaurant, also serves Southeast Asian dishes as well as sushi. Moderately priced *Chinatown* (☎ 307-733-8856), 850 W Broadway, prepares various Cantonese, Hunan, Szechuan and Peking dishes. Beefeaters can try *Lejay's Sportsmen's Cafe* (☎ 307-733-3110), 72 S Glenwood St, open 24 hours, or the *Gun Barrel Steakhouse* (☎ 307-733-3287), 862 W Broadway, serving Jackson's best steak.

Entertainment

Theater Jackson's theater companies stage Broadway-style musical comedies at the *Jackson Hole Playhouse* (☎ 307-733-6994), 145 W Deloney Ave, and at the *Grand Teton Main Stage Theatre* (☎ 307-733-3670), Broadway and Cache Drive. Meanwhile, *Dirty Jack's Wild West Theatre* (☎ 307-733-4775), 140 N Cache Drive, offers plays on Western caricatures.

Bars Jackson's nightlife landmark is the venerable *Million Dollar Cowboy Bar* (☎ 307-733-2207), 25 N Cache Drive. *The Rancher* (☎ 307-733-3886), 20 E Broadway, is another local favorite. *Snake River Brewing Co* (☎ 307-739-2337), 265 S Millward St, also serves pizza and pasta. The *Virginian Saloon* (☎ 307-739-9891), 750 W Broadway, has big-screen TV and a daily happy hour 5 to 7 pm.

Shopping

Western wear outlets include Corral West Ranchwear (☎ 307-733-0247), 840 W Broadway; Wyoming Outfitters (☎ 307-733-3877), 165 Center St; Stone's Boots (☎ 307-733-3392), 80 W Broadway at Glenwood St; and Wyoming Studios (☎ 307-733-4875), 230 Spruce Drive.

Jackson has about 40 commercial art galleries, a few of which handle local work. Others are chains with branches around the country. The Jackson Hole Gallery Association (☎ 307-739-8911), PO Box 1093, Jackson, WY 83001, publishes a widely available free brochure, called the 'Art Gallery Guide.'

Getting There & Away

Air The Jackson Hole Airport (☎ 307-733-5454), 1250 E Airport Rd, west of US 26/US 89/US 191, is 7 miles north of Jackson,

within Grand Teton National Park. Some
airlines reduce or suspend services outside
the peak summer and winter seasons.

Delta Air Lines (☎ 307-733-7920) and
SkyWest/The Delta Connection fly daily
between Jackson Hole and Salt Lake City,
UT, but note that it may be more affordable
to fly into Salt Lake City and rent a car
there. Daily United/United Express flights
link Jackson Hole and Denver, CO, while
weekend American Airlines flights connect
Jackson Hole with Chicago.

Salt Lake City Airport Shuttle Jackson
Hole Express (☎ 307-733-1719, 800-652-
9510; fax 307-739-3053) runs shuttles
between Salt Lake City Terminal 1 (departs
5 pm) and Daylight Donuts, 20 N Jackson
St, Jackson (departs 6 am). The fare is
$40/65 one-way/roundtrip and takes about
5½ hours. The shuttle operates once daily
mid-December to mid-April and Wednesday to Saturday the rest of the year.

Bus Idaho Falls-based CART operates an
as-needed service between Jackson and
Idaho Falls, ID, via Idaho's Teton Valley.

Car Jackson is along US 26/US 89/US
191, south of Grand Teton National Park.
US 26/US 89/US 191 leads north to Moran
Junction (31 miles) where US 89/US 191
continues to Yellowstone's South Entrance
(57 miles). US 26 leads north and east over
Togwotee Pass (9658 feet) to Riverton
(168 miles) via Dubois and the Wind River
Indian Reservation, and south to Alpine
(35 miles) at the Wyoming-Idaho state line.
US 89 leads north through Grand Teton
and Yellowstone national parks to Gardiner, MT, and southwest to Salt Lake City
(270 miles), the nearest metropolitan area.
US 191 leads south to Hoback Junction (12
miles) and Rock Springs (178 miles).

Getting Around
Bus The Southern Teton Area Rapid
Transit (START; ☎ 307-733-4521) runs
three color-coded routes between Jackson
and Teton Village. START operates 7 am to
8 pm weekdays, April to November every

two to three hours, and December to March
every 20 minutes. The fare is $1 around
Jackson and $2 one-way between Jackson
and Teton Village.

Car Alamo (☎ 307-733-0671), Avis (☎ 307-
733-3422), Budget (☎ 307-733-2206, 800-
533-6100) and Hertz (☎ 307-733-2272) are
at the airport. In town are Budget (☎ 307-
733-6868, 800-722-2002), 75 S Glenwood
St; Eagle Rent-A-Car (☎ 307-739-9999,
800-582-2128), 375 N Cache Drive;
National (☎ 307-733-0735), 345 W Broadway; Rent-A-Wreck (☎ 307-733-5014),
1050 US 89 S; and Thrifty (☎ 307-739-
9300), 220 N Millward St.

Taxi Call All-Star Taxi (☎ 307-733-2888,
800-378-2944), AllTrans Inc (☎ 307-733-
3135) or Buckboard Cab (☎ 307-733-1112).
A trip between the airport and downtown
costs $12.

SNOW KING RESORT
The year-round, 400-acre Snow King Resort
(☎ 307-733-5200, 800-522-5464), 400 E
Snow King Ave, on Jackson's southern
edge at a base elevation of 6237 feet, offers
downhill skiing, ice skating in an indoor
rink, horseback riding and mountain
biking, as well as restaurants and accommodations.

Three lifts serve various **downhill ski**
runs with a maximum vertical drop of 1571
feet (15% beginner, 25% intermediate,
60% advanced). Full-day lift tickets cost
$28/18 for adults/children (under 14), half-
day tickets (after 1 pm) are $20/12. Hourly
skiing costs $7. The ski season is Thanks-
giving to March. Night skiing is popular.
This north-facing slope catches less snow
than other resorts, but is well-suited for
children and families.

During summer, the **scenic rides** on the
Snow King Chair Lift offer views of five
mountain ranges; tickets cost $7/6/5 for
adults/seniors (60+)/children (six to 12). A
ticket with lunch at Panorama House, the
restaurant at the top, costs $10. When you
hike to the summit, a chairlift ride down
only costs $1. The lift operates 9 am to

6 pm daily, mid-May to early September, with extended summer hours.

The meandering 2500-foot **Alpine Slide of Jackson Hole** (☎ 307-733-7680) located behind the resort is open late May to mid-September. **Horseback rides** depart from nearby Snow King Stables (☎ 307-733-5781).

The resort offers hotel rooms (ranging from $180 to $190), suites ($210 to $360), and condominiums ($230 to $430). Its popular *Shady Lady Saloon* features live jazz.

JACKSON HOLE MOUNTAIN RESORT

Jackson Hole Mountain Resort draws skiers from around the world with its awesome 4139-foot vertical drop, long runs and deep powder. From the 6311-foot base at Teton Village (see below) to the summit of Rendezvous Mountain (10,450 feet), the greatest continuous vertical rise in the United States makes this one of the country's top ski destinations. The resort is active year-round with hiking, mountain biking and horseback riding once the snow has melted.

Information

Jackson Hole Mountain Resort (☎ 307-733-2292 information, 800-443-6931, 307-733-2291 or 888-333-7766 24-hour ski and snow conditions; info@jacksonhole.com) is at Teton Village, WY 83025. The Jackson Hole Guest Service Center (☎ 307-739-2753) is in the Clock Tower building. The resort office (☎ 307-733-4005) is at 140 E Broadway, Jackson.

Jackson Hole Aerial Tram

The Jackson Hole Aerial Tram (☎ 307-739-2753) rises over 2.4 miles to the top of Rendezvous Mountain, offering great views of Jackson Hole and providing quick access to Grand Teton National Park highcountry trails. It is open 9 am to 5 pm late May to late September, and often to 7 pm when demand is high. The tram costs $15/13/6 for adults/seniors/children (six to 17). Hikers who take the Granite Canyon Trail to Rendezvous Mountain can ride the tram free to Teton Village. Tram arrivals

can either hike down Granite Canyon Trail or choose from a series of shorter trails: the half-mile **Summit Nature Loop**; the **Cody Bowl Trail** (3 miles); and **Rock Springs Bowl** (4.2 miles). Hiking boot rentals cost $5; sack lunches $7.

Skiing

Revered by experts and enthusiasts the world over, the resort's 2500 acres of ski terrain are blessed by 380-plus annual inches of snow. The runs (10% beginner, 40% intermediate, 50% advanced) are served by nine lifts, an aerial tram and the Bridger gondola. Full-day lift tickets cost $48 for adults and $36 for seniors and children under 15, half-day tickets (after 12:30 pm) are $36/18. The ski season is usually Thanksgiving to early April. Former Olympic skier Pepi Stiegler operates the Jackson Hole Ski School (☎ 307-739-2663; lessons@jacksonhole.com). The Jackson Hole Nordic Center (☎ 307-739-2629) offers 22 miles of groomed track and wide skating lanes with rentals and instruction. High Mountain Helicopter Skiing (☎ 307-733-3274) delivers skiers to the fluffy powder in the surrounding mountains. The 'Jackson Hole Mountain Map & Skiers Guide' diagrams Teton Village.

There are several Teton Village shops that rent or sell downhill gear: Jack Dennis Outdoor Shop (☎ 307-733-6838), Jackson Hole Sports (☎ 307-739-2623), Teton Village Sports (☎ 307-733-2181) and Wildernest Sports (☎ 307-733-4297). For Nordic, look in Jackson: Skinny Skis (☎ 307-733-6094), 65 W Deloney Ave; Teton Mountaineering (☎ 307-733-3595), 170 N Cache Drive; and Jack Dennis Outdoor Shop (☎ 307-733-3270), 50 E Broadway. The Board Room of Jackson Hole Professional Snowboard Shop (☎ 307-733-8327), 245 W Pearl Ave, Jackson, is a nonskiers' alternative.

Places to Stay & Eat

On the mountain there are three restaurants: *Corbet's Cabin* at the top of the tram, *Casper Restaurant* at the base of the Casper lift and *Shades of Thunder* for quick lunches or snacks at the base of the Thunder lift. (For accommodations, see Teton Village below and Jackson above.)

Getting There & Away
Jackson Hole Mountain Resort and Teton Village are west of Hwy 390 (also called Teton Village Rd and Moose-Wilson Rd), 6 miles west of Jackson via Hwy 22 and then 6 miles north of Wilson on Hwy 390, 1 mile south of the Grand Teton National Park boundary and 20 miles from the Jackson Hole Airport.

TETON VILLAGE & AROUND
Teton Village is a Bavarian-style development of hotels, restaurants and shops at the base of Rendezvous Mountain and Jackson Hole Mountain Resort. Teton Village hotels, restaurants and a Jackson State Bank (with ATM) are clustered in a semi-circle along W McCollister Drive. On Hwy 390 south of Teton Village are the Teton Pines Country Club and Jackson Hole Racquet Club. Jackson Hole Trail Rides (☎ 307-733-6992, 307-733-5047) has guided **horseback rides** ($18/hour, $45 half-day, $75 full-day); call for scheduled departure times. Teton Village hosts the **Grand Teton Music Festival** (☎ 307-733-1933, 800-959-4863) in Walk Festival Hall July to August.

Places to Stay
Camping The *Teton Village KOA Kampground* (☎ 307-733-5354, 800-562-9043), 2780 N Moose-Wilson Rd, is on Hwy 390 south of Teton Village and 1½ miles north of Hwy 22. Tent/full-hookup sites are $24/32.

B&Bs South of Teton Village west of Hwy 390 are the *Wildflower Inn B&B* (☎ 307-733-4710; fax 307-739-0914), Shooting Star Lane, PO Box 11000, Jackson, WY 83002 (ranging from $140 to $225), and the comparably priced nearby *Painted Porch B&B* (☎ 307-733-1981), PO Box 6955, Jackson, WY 83002.

Hotels Seasonal rates vary widely and frequently. Some hotels also charge a 'resort fee.' *The Hostel X* (☎ 307-733-3415) has basic rooms for a bargain $40. Starting at $90 are the rooms at the *Crystal Springs Inn* (☎ 307-733-4423), above Teton Village Sports, and *The Village Center Inn* (☎ 307-733-3155, 800-735-8342; fax 307-733-3183). Starting at $150 are *The Alpenhof Lodge* (☎ 307-733-3242, 800-732-3244; fax 307-739-1516; alpenhof@sisna.com), *Sojourner Inn* (☎ 307-733-3657, 800-445-4655) and *Best Western The Inn at Jackson Hole* (☎ 307-733-2311, 800-842-7666; fax 307-733-0844).

Resorts The Teton Pines Country Club & Resort (☎ 307-733-1005, 800-238-2223) has luxurious suites and a championship 18-hole golf course; green fees cost $95 mid-June to mid-September. They also operate Teton Pines Nordic Center. Jackson Hole Racquet Club Resort (☎ 307-733-3990, 800-443-8616) offers condominiums and workout facilities with easy access to the country club.

Long-Term Rentals Reputable property management firms for condominiums, townhouses and homes throughout Jackson Hole are:

Alpine Vacation Rentals
   3200 McCollister Drive, PO Box 387, Teton Village, WY 83025 (☎ 307-734-1161, 800-876-3968; fax 307-734-0206; avr@alpinevacation.com)
Jackson Hole Property Management
   PO Box 568, Teton Village, WY 83025 (☎ 307-733-7945, 800-443-8613; fax 307-733-0244)
Mountain Property Management
   175 S King, PO Box 2228, Jackson, WY 83001 (☎ 307-733-1684, 800-992-9948; fax 307-739-1686)
Teton Village Property Management
   PO Box 249, Teton Village, WY 83025 (☎ 307-733-4610, 800-443-6840; fax 307-733-3183; tvpm@sisna.com)

Places to Eat
Teton Village The well-established *Mangy Moose Saloon* (☎ 307-733-4913) is a steak and seafood restaurant (entrees start at $10) and spirited nightspot with live music.

Downstairs is *The Rocky Mountain Oyster* (☎ 307-733-5525) serving moderately priced breakfasts, burgers, pizza, soups and sandwiches. The *Alpenhof Dining Room* (☎ 307-733-3462) has a cosmopolitan dinner menu; reservations are advised. Entrees range from $16 to $25; try the caribou roulade: sausage stuffed with goat cheese and venison. A good value with an attractive outdoor summer deck, the *Alpenhof Bistro & Dietrich's Bar* (☎ 307-733-3242) serves wild game ($13) as well as seafood and prime rib.

South of Teton Village *Vista Grande* (☎ 307-733-6964), on Hwy 390 south of the Teton Village KOA Kampground, is the area's best Mexican restaurant, with entrees under $12. *Calico Italian Restaurant* (☎ 307-733-2460), north of Vista Grande, is popular. *Stiegler's Restaurant & Bar* (☎ 307-733-1071), 4040 W Lake Creek Drive at the Jackson Hole Racquet Club, is an Austrian alternative with a menu in German, French and English. *The Grille at the Pines*, at Teton Pines Country Club, has a varied menu including fresh seafood; reservations are recommended.

WILSON

The small community of Wilson is on Hwy 22 west of Jackson, at the junction of Hwy 390 leading north to Teton Village. The **Snake River Institute** (☎ 307-733-2214), 5450 W Hwy 22, presents an exceptional series of free or moderately priced lectures, field trips and tours from its Hardeman Barns location. The **Chambers Memorial to Homesteaders Museum** (☎ 307-733-3075, 307-733-2146), 980 Wenzel Lane, displays household, shop and farm implements along with buggies, buckboards, old skis and snowshoes. Open by appointment only, admission is free.

One of Jackson Hole's better restaurants, *Nora's Fish Creek Inn* (☎ 307-733-8288), 5600 W Hwy 22, pulls 'em in for breakfast and serves great prime rib. The *Stagecoach Bar* (☎ 307-733-4407), 5755 W Hwy 22, is a wildly popular venue: Thursday is disco

night and every Sunday the legendary Stagecoach Band performs.

AROUND JACKSON HOLE
Mountain Biking

Some of the more popular mountain bike rides include Cache Creek, southeast of Jackson into the Gros Ventre; Game Creek, along USFS Rd 30455 east off US 26/US 89/US 191 south of Jackson; Spring Gulch Rd, west of and parallel to US 26/US 89/US 191 between Hwy 22 and Gros Ventre Junction; and Shadow Mountain, along USFS Rd 30340 northeast of Antelope Flats at eastern edge of Grand Teton National Park. Hardcore riders can try Old Pass Rd, the old way to Teton Pass, south of the current Hwy 22. South of US 189/US 191, south of Hoback Junction near Bondurant is Monument Ridge: a ride up Cliff Creek to the ridgetop offers superb views of the Gros Ventre and Wind River mountains.

Hoback Sports (☎ 307-733-5335), 40 S Millward St, Jackson, rents, sells and repairs mountain bikes and has a good map of area bike trails; consider a tandem rental. Teton Cyclery (☎ 307-733-4386), 175 N Glenwood St, Jackson, is an excellent bike shop with friendly, knowledgeable service. Teton Mountain Bike Tours (☎ 307-733-0712, 800-733-0788), 433 S Cache Drive, Jackson, rents bikes (delivering them free to your hotel) and runs several half-day (ranging from $40 to $60) and full-day (starting at $70) tours. The Jackson Hole Adventure Cycling Association (☎ 406-721-1776), PO Box 8308, Missoula, MT 59807, sells a map ($5) describing 20 Jackson Hole rides.

Horseback Riding

Bar-T-5 Corral (☎ 307-733-5386, 800-772-5386), 790 Cache Creek Drive, offers one-hour ($15) and two-hour ($25) guided rides in Cache Creek, east of Jackson. A-OK Corral (☎ 307-733-6556), on US 26/189/US 191 just north of Hoback Junction, offers guided hourly rides ($14) and full-day excursions. Both offer evening excursions and cookouts.

Rafting & Floating

White-water rafting is popular through the Class III Snake River canyon, south of Jackson along US 89/US 26 between Hoback Junction and Alpine. Ospreys and eagles nest in trees along the river, and wildlife viewing is possible. Half-day rafting trips put in at West Table Creek; they take out at Sheep Gulch (8 miles). Full-day trips put in at Pritchard Creek (upstream of West Table Creek), take a break at Pine Creek campsite and take out at Sheep Gulch (16 miles). Half-day trips start at $30/20 for adults/children, full-day trips at $55/45 and overnight trips at $110/80. The rafting season is May to Labor Day. It can get crowded on the river during July and August. Costs typically include transportation to and from Jackson.

Half-day scenic float trips (starting at $25/20) on a 13-mile section of the swift-flowing Snake River do not go through any white-water rapids. Float trips put in south of Grand Teton National Park and take out north of Hoback Junction. Passing through Jackson Hole wetlands offers opportunities for birdwatching and wildlife viewing along the way.

To book a Jackson-based rafting or floating trip, contact:

Jackson Hole Whitewater
    PO Box 3695, Jackson, WY 83001
    650 W Broadway (☎ 307-733-1007,
    800-648-2602; fax 307-733-6908)
Barker-Ewing Jackson Hole River Trips
    PO Box 3032, Jackson, WY 83001
    45 W Broadway (☎ 307-733-1000,
    800-448-4202)
Dave Hansen Whitewater
    455 N Cache Drive
    800 W Broadway (☎ 307-733-6925)
Lewis & Clark River Expeditions
    PO Box 720, Jackson, WY 83001
    335 N Cache Drive (☎ 307-733-4022,
    800-824-5375; fax 307-733-0345)
Lone Eagle Whitewater
    Pink Garter Plaza, Town Square
    (☎ 800-321-3800)
    Gart Sports, 455 W Broadway
    (☎ 307-733-1090, 800-321-3800)
Sands Wildwater River Trips
    PO Box 696B, Wilson, WY 83014

    110 W Broadway (☎ 800-358-8184
    reservations)
    1450 US 89 S across from High School Rd,
    Jackson (☎ 307-733-4410, 800-358-8184;
    fax 307-734-9064)
Mad River Boat Trips Inc
    PO Box 10940, Jackson Hole, WY 83002
    Chet's Way, 60 E Broadway
    (☎ 800-458-7238)
    1255 S US 89 (☎ 307-733-6203,
    800-458-7238; fax 307-733-7626;
    info@mad-river.com)

Canoeing & Kayaking

Jackson Hole Kayak School (☎ 307-733-2471), 1035 W Broadway, Jackson, and Snake River Kayak & Canoe School (☎ 307-733-3127, 800-529-2501), 155 W Gill Ave, Jackson, offer instruction. For kayak and canoe rentals, try Leisure Sports (☎ 307-733-3040), 1075 US 89 S, and Lone Eagle Expeditions (☎ 307-733-1090, 800-321-3800), south of Jackson, Star Route 45-C, Jackson, WY 83001.

Hot Air Ballooning

Rainbow Balloon Flights (☎ 307-733-0470, 800-378-0470) and Wyoming Balloon Company (☎ 307-739-0900), 450 E Sagebrush, offer hour-long flights over the Tetons for $185/125 for adults/children (six to 12). The season is early June to mid-September, weather permitting.

GROS VENTRE MOUNTAINS

The Gros Ventre Mountains ('big belly' in French) east of Jackson Hole are bounded on three sides by rivers: the Snake to the west, Hoback to the south and Gros Ventre to the north. The Continental Divide forms its eastern boundary and the upper Gros Ventre Valley accesses the Wind River Mountains east of the Continental Divide. The most impressive views of the Gros Ventre are from Hoback Canyon (along US 189/US 191), looking at its rocky south face. A vast slide in 1925 dammed the Gros Ventre River, causing a huge flood. Today the forested north-facing slopes above Gros Ventre River (along Gros Ventre Rd east of Kelly) are called the **Gros Ventre Slide Geological Area**; a half-mile interpretive trail offers views. The resulting Upper Slide and Lower Slide lakes attract anglers. The Gros Ventre Wilderness Area and part of the Bridger-Teton National Forest cover its slopes.

Hiking

The Gros Ventre offer superb day hikes with big views and wildlife. **Sheep Mountain** (10,755 feet), also called Sleeping Indian, is the most prominent peak east of Jackson Hole, and sizable bighorn sheep herds wander its rocky slopes. Access to the trailhead for Sheep Mountain is via Flat Creek Rd from the south or Gros Ventre Rd to the north; 4WD is necessary. East of Snow King Mountain and southwest of Sheep Mountain is **Jackson Peak** (10,741 feet), another great hike. Head up from either Elk Refuge Rd, which becomes USFS Rd 30440 (take the right fork from the north) or the longer route via USFS Rd 30450 (Cache Creek Rd) from the south. **Goodwin Lake** is 2½ miles beyond the northern trailhead (at 8000 feet). From Hoback Canyon, other routes into the Gros Ventre Wilderness Area begin along USFS Rd 30500 and Granite Creek.

Places to Stay

USFS campgrounds along Gros Ventre Rd (beyond the Antelope Flats Rd turnoff and north of Kelly) are *Atherton Creek*, 5.5 miles; *Red Hills*, 10 miles; and *Crystal Creek*, 10.4 miles. *Curtis Canyon Campground* is off USFS Rd 30440, off Elk Refuge Rd east of Jackson. *Granite Creek Campground* is off USFS Rd 30500 north of Hoback Canyon.

MORAN JUNCTION TO TOGWOTEE PASS

US 26/US 287 climbs east from Grand Teton National Park's Moran Junction through the forested slopes of the Bridger-Teton National Forest to Togwotee Pass (9658 feet). The pass, named for a Shoshone guide who led the US Army Corps of Engineers here in 1873, is on the Continental Divide. North of US 26/US 287 is the 914-sq-mile Teton Wilderness Area,

and to the south is the more-distant Gros Ventre Wilderness Area. In 1987, the highest elevation tornado ever recorded leveled a 20-mile-long by 2-mile-wide swath of trees in the Teton Wilderness Area; one year later, more than a third of the wilderness burned in the Yellowstone fires.

The USFS Bridger-Teton National Forest (Buffalo Ranger District) Blackrock Ranger Station (☎ 307-543-2386, 307-739-5600), on US 26/US 287 8 miles east of Moran Junction, is open 8 am to 4:30 pm. The paved Buffalo Valley Rd (USFS Rd 30050), which heads northeast from US 26/US 287 east of Moran Junction, leads to part of the **Turpin Meadow Recreation Area**. Turpin Meadows are the grassy sage-covered meadows west of Togwotee Pass. The unpaved Four-Mile Meadow Rd links Buffalo Valley Rd with US 26/US 287 to its south. The Teton views from the **Togwotee Overlook** along US 26/US 287 are memorable.

Biking

US 26/US 287 is a popular touring route for cyclists heading east into the Wind River Country. The climb from Moran Junction is long, so most cyclists camp at the free cyclists-only USFS *Blackrock Bike Campground*, 3 miles east of the Blackrock Ranger Station below Turpin Meadows, before crossing the pass.

The area south of US 26/US 287 has great mountain biking. The most popular ride begins on the south side of Togwotee Pass, goes to Lily Lake and makes a big descent on USFS Rd 30160 to the Blackrock Ranger Station, with impressive Teton and Absaroka mountain views.

Places to Stay

The USFS campgrounds along US 26/US 287 are nice. *Hatchet Campground* ($5) is a quarter-mile west of the Blackrock Ranger Station. Just a half-mile north of Buffalo Valley Rd is the free *Box Creek Campground*, with corrals, but no potable water. *Turpin Meadows Campground* ($5), on USFS Rd 30050 4 miles north of US 26/87, is near several trailheads. *Grand Teton*

Park KOA Kampground (☎ 307-733-1980, 307-543-2483, 800-562-3948), on US 26/ US 287 6 miles east of Moran Junction, has tent and full-hookup sites ($20/29), showers and laundry. *Turpin Meadow Ranch*(☎ 307-543-2496, 800-743-2496), Buffalo Valley Rd, PO Box 379, Moran, WY 83013, is a center for all things Western: horseback riding, covered wagon outings, dancing, fishing and cookouts.

Star Valley

Star Valley, a geographically isolated Mormon enclave in western Wyoming, is physically close to Idaho but linked economically to Jackson Hole 40 miles away, where many of its residents work. US 89, the main route from Jackson to Salt Lake City, UT, parallels the Salt River through this north-south valley, which exits via the 7% grade of Salt River Pass (7630 feet) at the valley's southern end. Pelicans are abundant along the river, and fishing is good. Star Valley's neat communities, from north to south, are Alpine, Freedom, Thayne, Afton and Smoot. The Wyoming-Idaho border and Caribou National Forest are west of the Star Valley, with the Salt River Range, the Bridger-Teton National Forest and Greys River to the east.

ALPINE
Alpine, at the junction of US 26 and US 89, is a sprawling crossroads near the confluence of the Salt, Snake and Greys rivers, just before they empty into Idaho's Palisades Reservoir. Alpine's motels and restaurants are unappealing, but its natural setting is attractive, folks are friendly and rates are reasonable.

Campers should head to the USFS campgrounds off US 26 along the Palisades Dam (see Snake River Plain chapter in the Idaho section). The Bavarian-style *Alpen Haus* (☎ 307-654-7545, 800-343-6755), on US 26 at US 89, has standard rooms starting at $42 and deluxe rooms at $66. East of the Alpen Haus, the *Nordic Inn* (☎ 307-

654-7556) has distinctive rooms that are a good value starting at $65; reservations are advisable. Across from the Nordic Inn, the *Best Western Flying Saddle Lodge* (☎ 307-654-7561) ranges from $48 to $75. The *Lakeside Motel & Restaurant* (☎ 307-654-7506), south of the river, has basic rooms starting at $40.

The valley's two best restaurants are *Bertrand's* German-Saxon cuisine in the Alpen Haus and *Brenthoven's Restaurant* in the Nordic Inn. *Bette's Home Cookin* is popular.

FREEDOM
Freedom, between Etna and Thayne, is on Hwy 34 1 mile west of US 89, along the river. Here **Freedom Arms** claims to produce 'the world's finest handgun' and gladly gives factory tours. Many of Freedom's original Mormon settlers came here to avoid persecution for polygamy. Hwy 34 continues west in Idaho on the **Bear Lake-Caribou National Scenic Byway** (see Snake River Plain chapter in the Idaho section).

THAYNE
Thayne, 15 miles south of Alpine, is known for the **Star Valley Cheese Co**, which produces its main product by the ton. Sample bags are available. Its cafe serves reasonably priced American breakfasts and lunches beneath big game trophies like Yukon caribou, African sable, kudu, waterbuck, moose and even Cape buffalo. Beware the sugary homemade pies.

AFTON & AROUND
The main landmark of Afton (population 1510) is the **Elkhorn Arch**, which stretches across Washington St (US 89). Made from 3011 sets of Rocky Mountain elk antlers, the arch spans 75 feet and weighs over 15 tons.

Orientation & Information
Going north-south, US 89 is called Washington St in Afton, with numbered avenues running perpendicular to it. Eastbound 2nd Ave leads a short distance into the Salt Range.

The Afton Area Chamber of Commerce, on Washington St at 2nd Ave, is open 9 am to 5 pm daily, Memorial to Labor Day. Staffed by volunteers whose practical knowledge is limited, it has an abundance of brochures and pamphlets. The Star Valley Chamber of Commerce (☎ 307-886-9831, 800-426-8833) is at 416 Washington St, PO Box 1097, Afton, WY 83110. A better source of information is the USFS Bridger-Teton National Forest Greys River Ranger Station (☎ 307-886-3166), 125 Washington St, which also sells books and maps of the Caribou, Targhee and Bridger-Teton national forests. It is open 7:30 am to 4:30 pm weekdays and 9 am to 5 pm, Memorial to Labor Day.

An ATM is at First Security Bank, 485 Washington St. The post office is at 31 W 4th Ave. PrintStar Printing (☎ 307-886-9331; fax 307-886-9370) provides fax services. The Star Valley Hospital (☎ 307-886-3841, 800-479-5494) is at 110 Hospital Lane, just south of the Lincoln County Fairgrounds.

Things to See & Do
Afton's bright **CallAir Aviation Museum**, at the airport south of town, is a 15,000-sq-foot hangar commemorating the area's remarkable aviation history, which began with the manufacture of ski planes for use in areas of heavy snowfall. Exhibits include antique airplanes, historic photographs and videos and the current products of Afton-based Aviat, Inc. It is open 9 am to 6 pm Monday to Saturday. The **Aviat Light Aircraft Manufacturers** (☎ 208-886-3151), 672 Washington St, produce stunt planes and small aircraft for farm, ranch and wildlife management purposes. They offer tours 11:30 am and 3 pm daily. Afton's June **Aviation Days** attract classic airplanes, hot air balloons and military displays.

The **Gardiner Mill**, on 2nd Ave east of US 89, dates from the late 19th century, and includes a millstone from 1889.

Swift Creek Recreation Area
Periodic Spring is the only cold-water geyser in North America and the largest of the world's three intermitting springs. Indians called it 'the spring that breathes.' The spring now supplies Afton's water. Along Swift Creek, the spring starts and stops every 12 to 20 minutes, peaking during late summer and fall. A three-quarter-mile trail leads to the spring. Follow 2nd Ave, which becomes USFS Rd 10211 5 miles east from Afton.

Places to Stay
The USFS *Swift Creek Campground* ($5), 1½ miles east of town on Swift Creek Rd (via 2nd Ave), is a nice forested site on the creek. Rooms at the *Corral Motel* (☎ 307-886-5424), 161 Washington St, and the friendly *Lazy B Motel* (☎ 307-886-3187), 219 Washington St, start at $34. The *Best Western Hi Country Inn* (☎ 307-886-3856), 689 S Washington St, starts at $45. About a half-mile south of town, the *Mountain Inn Motel* has a spa and tennis courts.

Places to Eat
Valley Vineyard (☎ 307-886-9215), 967 Washington St, serves deli food. The *Homestead Coffee Shop & Fine Dining* (☎ 307-886-5558), on US 89 just south of town, serves wild game, including bison, elk, venison and even rattlesnake, along with standards like beef and homemade pies. The *Elkhorn Restaurant* (☎ 307-886-3080), 465 Washington St, has a conventional American menu, as does the *Golden Spur Cafe* (☎ 307-886-9890), 486 Washington St. *Colter's Lodge* (☎ 307-886-9891), 355 Washington St, has more varied fare; try their Timberline steak.

GREYS RIVER LOOP RD
The Greys River Loop Rd is a two-lane graded but rugged route that heads east off US 89 about 10 miles south of Smoot and south of the Salt River Pass, which marked the Lander Cutoff of the Oregon Trail. The road enters Bridger-Teton National Forest, crossing the Salt River Range, and follows the Greys River north to rejoin US 89 in Alpine. This narrow road is great for **mountain biking** and passable for most

cars, but is not suitable for RVs or vehicles with trailers. North of the LaBarge Creek Rd junction, at **Triple Divide**, the drainages of the Colorado, Snake and the Great Basin river systems flow their separate ways. Nearby LaBarge Creek Rd goes southeast and parallels LaBarge Creek, home to genetically pure Colorado River cutthroat trout. Several USFS campgrounds ($5) are along the Greys River Loop Rd: *Bridge*, 3 miles east of Alpine; *Lynx*, 10 miles farther; *Murphy Creek*; *Moose Flat*; and *Forest Park*, near the winter elk feeding ground.

Montana

MICHAEL CLARK

Facts about Montana

Although its name means 'mountain' in Spanish, Montana is best described by its nicknames. Historically (and now officially) the 'Treasure State,' Montana owes its foundation to gold and copper mining interests and, more recently – in the 1920s – the discovery of oil. Dubbed 'Big Sky Country' after AB Guthrie Jr's novel *The Big Sky* (1947), Montana's ever-changing and infinitely vast sky is indeed what dominates any view. The sky is also important for the precipitation it brings (or doesn't bring) in this land of ranchers, farmers and outdoor types. And since the publication of Montana's definitive literary anthology *The Last Best Place* (1988), which, perhaps not coincidentally, came out during a real estate boom fueled by out-of-state buyers, Montana has come to represent in popular imagination a place that remains the way the 'Old West' once was.

Artists, authors, real estate developers, students and movie stars have found Montana increasingly attractive for its space, recreational opportunities and 'live and let live' ethic. Some Montanans are happy about this influx of new blood – they consider it rich in opportunities and feel that new cultures and philosophies are needed in such a homogeneous society. Others, however, feel that the traditional Montana lifestyle may be threatened by too much influence from the outside. Montana-bred coalitions, such as the Freemen and the Constitutionalists, are examples of a vigilant opposition to what is perceived as ever-increasing government regulation and the 'liberal' ways of others in American society.

Montana's beauty lies in its landscape. With only six people per square mile and three of those six living in urban centers, there is plenty of wild territory to explore. The remote badlands of Makoshika State Park offer a delicate yet harsh landscape that few people take time to visit. On the other side of the Rockies, and Montana's tourist spectrum, Glacier National Park and Flathead Lake offer classic Alpine beauty and well-trodden trails.

Famous, trout-filled rivers flow from Yellowstone National Park towards Bozeman (Montana's fastest-growing town) through mountain ranges – Gallatin, Madison, Absaroka – that are wonderful for backcountry exploration. Slightly east, the high Alpine tundra atop the Beartooth Plateau is unique in its geology and its accessibility to motorists – via the highest road in the USA. And then there's the state's history that's intertwined – from the wide-open prairies, irrigated by the Missouri River and explored by Lewis and Clark, to Old West mining towns like Helena, Butte and Bannock, to battlefields where historic skirmishes such as the battles of the Little Bighorn, Big Hole and Rosebud took place. Home to the University of Montana and an energetic student population, Missoula is arguably Montana's most enjoyable town and is a good starting point for most itineraries.

INFORMATION
State Tourist Offices

Montana's statewide tourist board is Travel Montana (☎ 406-444-2654, 800-847-4868 outside Montana), 1424 9th Ave, PO Box 200533, Helena, MT 59620. Its free publications, available at chambers of commerce, tourist information centers and large hotels throughout the state, include a state road map and the 'Montana Vacation Guide,' which has colorful photos and area attractions listed for even the smallest towns. For online information check out their website (www.travel.mt.gov/). Also free, but usually only available by contacting Travel Montana, are the 'Montana Travel Planner,' which has details on accommodations, campgrounds and outfitters, and the 'Montana Winter Guide' with cross-country and downhill skiing, winter touring and accommodation information.

Travel Montana divides the state into six 'tourist zones' and publishes detailed guides for each one, available from Travel Montana or the chamber of commerce/visitors information center of the largest city within each zone: Kalispell or Missoula for 'Glacier Country;' Butte, Helena or Dillon for 'Gold West Country;' Great Falls for 'Russell Country;' Bozeman, Gardiner or West Yellowstone for 'Yellowstone Country;' Fort Peck or Malta for 'Missouri River Country;' and Billings or Miles City for 'Custer Country.'

For information on road conditions throughout the state, call ☎ 800-332-6171.

Useful Organizations

Most environmental and conservation organizations belong to the Montana Environmental Information Center (☎ 406-443-2520), PO Box 1184, Helena, MT 59624. Their web page (www.ixi.net/meic) has links to such groups as: the Greater Yellowstone Coalition (☎ 406-586-1593), which monitors environmental issues in the Wyoming, Montana and Idaho areas around the Park; the Clark Fork-Pend Oreille Coalition (☎ 406-542-0539), PO Box 7593, Missoula, MT 59807, which has won several victories against mining companies over proposals to establish mines along the Blackfoot, Landers Fork and Clark Fork rivers; and Alliance for the Wild Rockies (☎ 406-721-5420), 415 N Higgins Ave, Missoula, MT 59802, which has a far-reaching and very active political agenda.

Buffalo Nations (☎ 406-848-9867), PO Box 242, Gardiner, MT 59030 and (☎ 406-646-0070), PO Box 957, West Yellowstone, MT 59758, is a volunteer organization committed to stopping the slaughter of Yellowstone bison that wander out of national park boundaries onto private land in search of food during winter. Volunteers haze the bison back onto National Park Service (NPS) land and help local ranchers repair damaged fences. Volunteer, and get a free winter 'vacation' in West Yellowstone!

The Northern Rockies Natural History Association (☎ 406-586-1155), PO Box 42, Bozeman, MT 59771 (www.beyond yellowstone.com), publishes state-specific books about Montana's national parks and wilderness areas. For fishing permits and information, contact the Department of Fish, Wildlife & Parks (DFWP; ☎ 406-444-3750), 1420 E 6th Ave, Helena, MT 59620.

Pride, the national gay and lesbian organization, has offices in Helena (☎ 406-442-9322, 800-610-9322 within Montana), PO Box 755, Helena, MT 59624, and Bozeman (☎ 406-388-1481), PO Box 7380, Bozeman, MT 59771. More state-specific (but geared mostly towards men) is Gay Montana, part of the national Lambda Organization. Its headquarters (☎ 406-994-4636) are in the Strand Union Building of Missouri State University in Bozeman.

Area Code

Montana's telephone area code is 406.

Road Rules

After years of having no speed limit, in 1997 Montana established a somewhat ambiguous daytime automobile speed limit of 'reasonable and prudent.' This is subject to interpretation by highway patrol officers, but is defined as 'a rate of speed no greater than is reasonable and proper under the

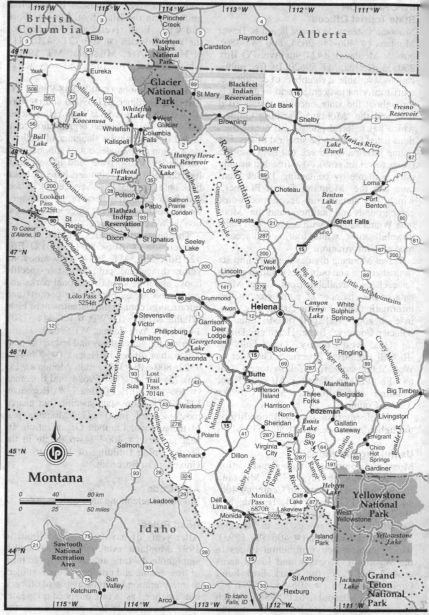

MONTANA

Montana

0   40   80 km
0   25   50 miles

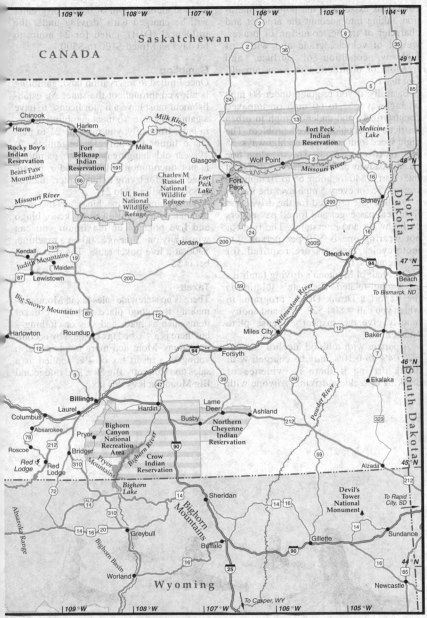

conditions existing at the point of operation, taking into account the amount and character of traffic, condition of brakes, weight of vehicle, grade and width of highway, condition of surface, and freedom of obstruction to view ahead.' Got that?

Basically, if you're going under 80 mph on highways, 55 to 60 mph on unpaved country roads, and under 30 mph in urban districts, you shouldn't have a problem. The night speed limit is 65 mph on highways, 55 mph on two-lane roads. The speeding fine on any roadway during the day is $70. Night fines start at $40 for going 66 to 70 mph and increase $5 for every 5 mph over the limit.

Seatbelts are required for the driver and front-seat passenger and for all passengers on highways and interstates. The fine for not wearing one is $20 per person. On motorcycles, helmets are required for anyone under 18.

Over half of Montana's driving fatalities are alcohol-related. The state's solution is the Report a Drunk Driver program, in which you call ☎ 800-525-5555 and anonymously give the suspect's license plate number.

A person with a blood alcohol content of 0.04% to 0.10% *may* be charged with drunk driving if there is evidence of drinking or reckless driving. Anyone with a blood alcohol level of 0.10% or greater will be charged with 'driving under the influence' (DUI), jailed for 24 hours to 60 days and fined $100 to $500.

Gambling

Once limited to reservation land, gambling is allowed throughout the state. An establishment must have a liquor license to have a gaming license, so most gambling occurs in bars. Ironically, you must be 21 to purchase liquor but only 18 to gamble, so 19-year-olds hanging out in bars gambling is not uncommon! Minors under 18 are fined $100 for trying to buy liquor; the fine is $50 if you're 18 to 21.

Video gambling machines are the most popular options, followed by keno, bingo and live poker. The maximum you can win at any one time is $800 on a machine, $300 at a live poker table. The maximum bet is $5.

Taxes

There is no statewide sales tax in Montana – making it a good place to buy big-ticket items such as bikes and skis or clothing – but there is a 4% bed tax charged by accommodations. More and more towns are also voting in a resort tax of 4%, applied as a sales tax. Currently Big Sky, Red Lodge and Big Mountain levy this tax.

Gold Country

Southwestern Montana is where much of the state's modern history began. When gold was discovered in Bannack's Grasshopper Creek in 1863, just as rushes in California, Nevada and Colorado were ending, thousands of people flocked to this previously undeveloped land. Aware of the millions of dollars in gold flowing from Bannack, the chief justice of Idaho Territory (of which Montana was a part) successfully lobbied to make Montana a separate state. To encourage white settlement of the area, the government drove Native Americans off their homelands and forced them onto reservations.

Miners moved from one big strike to the next, establishing rough-and-tumble towns in Alder Creek (Virginia City) and Last Chance Gulch (Helena). With the land cleared of Indian settlements, ranchers and cattlemen poured into the Bitterroot, Big Hole, Beaverhead and Deer Lodge valleys with herds earmarked for use at mining camps. Businessmen who recognized that exploiting miners was generally more profitable than exploiting mineral deposits set up service and trade towns such as Missoula, Dillon and Deer Lodge. In the 1870s and 1880s, as the advent of electricity created an enormous demand for copper wire, Marcus Daly struck the world's largest and purest vein of copper, thrusting Butte into the limelight as one of the richest towns in the USA.

Towns that endured the boom-and-bust cycle became the urban centers of this area, while mining camps and ghost towns scattered around the mountains are some of the most fascinating attractions.

MISSOULA
Home to the University of Montana (U of M), Missoula (population 51,204) is the state's cultural hub. There are films and lectures, theater performances and concerts (from the Missoula Symphony Orchestra to contemporary rock, reggae and funk groups) year-round, plus a plethora of bars that support a thriving local music scene. Montana's largest concentration of cafes perpetuates the city's energy, serving up a variety of food and drink that is more 'California' than Montana. The museums around town are adequate, but most people head outdoors on their day off: the

---

HIGHLIGHTS

- Big Hole Valley – this vast and lonely high-altitude valley is about as off the beaten track as you can get and still find some good bars and accommodations

- Gates of the Mountain Wilderness – where bald eagles nest in a remarkable limestone canyon that once played visual tricks on Lewis and Clark

- Helena – Montana's capital is historically rich and replete with interesting things to see and do

- Missoula – with its outdoorsy student population, vibrant arts scene and rousing nightlife

MONTANA

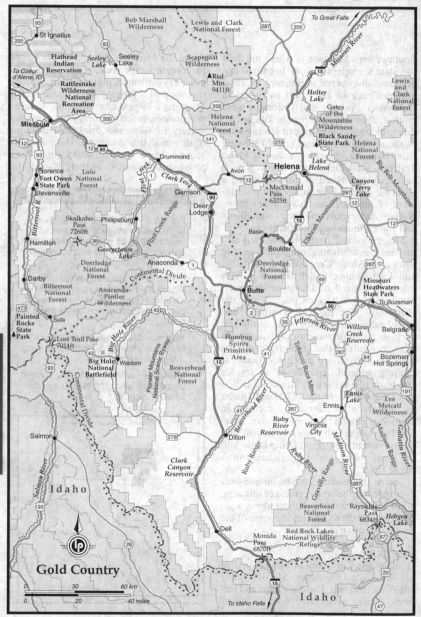

Gold Country

Rattlesnake and Blue Mountain wilderness areas are spittin' distance from town, the Bitterroot Range spans its western edge, and the Clark Fork River courses right through it all. The only bummer here is winter's poor air quality, exacerbated by a nasty inversion layer that can darken the sky for weeks at a time.

While downtown Missoula is dominated by students who are drawn to U of M's creative writing department (the second oldest in the USA, after Harvard) or forestry department, the greater Missoula area still survives on timber and agriculture. Head out to the Historical Fort Missoula and you'll pass fields of cattle and hay bales, and smell the pulp of the Stone Container Corporation mill. New housing developments are quickly encroaching on this space, however, and locals joke about Missoula becoming the next Los Angeles. Politics revolve around land-use issues, and most folks – the outdoorsy intellectuals that talk of trailheads and road-less

wilderness areas, as well as the 'old guard' that fights for personal property protection measures – contend that protection and conservation are key.

History
The Salish, Blackfeet and Flathead Indians were the first inhabitants of Missoula, which takes its name from the Salish word *Im-i-sul-a*, meaning 'by the chilling waters.' The Salish regularly passed through Hellgate Canyon (the gap between Mt Jumbo and Mt Sentinel) on their way to hunt buffalo; the Blackfeet would trap them in the narrow gorge and attack them from above. Lewis and Clark traveled through this same gorge in 1804, as did trappers and hunters in the 1820s.

In the 1840s Jesuit missionaries established St Mary's Mission 30 miles south and planted the area's first crops. The Mullan Rd, a major trade and travel artery that connects Fort Benton to Walla Walla, Washington, ran through Hellgate Canyon. Frank

---

How Montana Took a Bite out of Idaho

When Abraham Lincoln sent surveyors west to define the border between newly formed Montana and the already existing Idaho Territory, the Continental Divide was the proposed demarcation. The surveyors traveled through rough mining camps like Helena and Bannack and participated in the local activities – gambling and 'entertainment' – as all good travelers do. But, by the time they reached the Deer Lodge Valley, they found themselves short on cash. Little did they suspect they had already crossed the Continental Divide. Whether the surveyors sold their maps and equipment to fund the rest of their trip, or lost them in a drunken gambling match is unclear, but the result was long-lasting: following an old trail through Missoula's Hellgate Canyon, the surveyors came upon the massive and rugged Bitterroot Range and, mistaking it for the Continental Divide, declared the Bitterroots Montana's western border. Thus, Montana received its western third and Idaho ended up disfigured and bottom-heavy.

Without this error, Montana would be an entirely different state – square, average size, flat and primarily prairie land, much more like the Dakotas than its Rocky Mountain neighbors. It would also lack some of its main tourist destinations (notably Flathead Lake, the Bob Marshall Wilderness and Glacier National Park), its cultural hub of Missoula and prime timberlands in the Bitterroot Valley and northwest corner. ∎

To US 93, Airport

PLACES TO STAY
3 Travelodge
4 Uptown Motel
18 Royal Motel
19 City Center Motel
20 Ponderosa Motel
21 Downtown Motel
23 Creekside Inn
24 Campus Inn
41 Best Western
    Executive Motor Inn
42 Holiday Inn Parkside
45 Village Red Lion Inn
46 Goldsmith's B&B
49 Holiday Inn
    Express Riverside
53 Birchwood Hostel

PLACES TO EAT
1 The Depot
6 Worden's
10 Black Dog Cafe
12 Zimorino's
22 Broadway Market
25 The Shack
28 Mammyth
    Bakery Cafe
31 Butterfly Herbs
40 Hob Nob
47 Goldsmith's
50 Bernice's Bakery
51 Crystal Theater/
    The Bridge
52 Second Thought

BARS
2 Iron Horse
   Brewpub
5 The Old Post
7 Charlie B's
26 Reds
27 The Ritz
29 Rhino
30 Jay's Upstairs
35 Top Hat
37 Stockman's Club

OTHER
8 Missoula County
   Courthouse
9 Horizon Books
11 Garden City
    News
13 The Trail Head
14 Adventure Cycling
15 Missoula Museum
    of the Arts
16 USFS Northern
    Region Headquarters
17 Hellgate Station
    Post Office
32 Grizzly Hackle
33 Carousel
34 Monte Dolack
    Gallery
36 Art Fusion
38 Pipestone
    Mountaineering
39 Wilma Theater
43 Front St Theater
44 Missoula Public
    Library
48 Chamber of
    Commerce

Clark Fork River

Missoula

MONTANA

Worden and CP Higgins constructed the Missoula Mills near the Mullan Rd, attracting a steady flow of people stopping en route to and from the goldfields. In 1883 rail lines for the Northern Pacific Railroad were laid through the town, and in 1895 the university was established, cementing Missoula's regional importance.

Orientation

Missoula sits in the cradle of five valleys where the Bitterroot River, the Blackfoot River and Rattlesnake Creek converge with the Clark Fork of the Columbia River. I-90 runs past the north side of downtown Missoula. US 93 becomes US 12 coming into town, passes the airport, then turns into W Broadway. Orange St and Van Buren St are the main freeway exits in town, the latter leading straight to the university.

The Clark Fork River divides the town north-south, with the university to the south. It's a nice 20-minute walk from the university to downtown, and both are within a half-mile of most accommodations. A good way to explore is to park near the university, walk through the campus, turn west (left) onto the riverside path, and cross over the Higgins St bridge into downtown. Downtown, Higgins Ave is the main street going north-south, with Front St and Broadway the east-west arteries.

Information

Tourist Offices The chamber of commerce (☎ 406-543-6623, 800-526-3465), one block south of the I-90 Van Buren St exit at 825 E Front St, distributes free maps of Missoula. These are also available at Adventure Cycling (☎ 406-721-8791) at 150 E Pine St.

Money The First Interstate and Security Federal Savings banks are on Higgins Ave north of the bridge; ATMs are also in the Safeway, Buttrey and Albertsons supermarkets on W Broadway and on Brooks St.

Post There's a post office branch downtown at 200 E Broadway; Missoula's zip code is 59801.

Bookstores The University Bookstore (☎ 406-243-4921) in the U of M student center, and Horizon Books, next to the Black Dog Cafe at 138 W Broadway, have regional guides and contemporary Montana literature, while Garden City News, downtown at 329 N Higgins Ave, carries out-of-state newspapers and is open until 10 pm.

Newspapers Pick up a free copy of the *Independent* (issued every Thursday) at a cafe or bookstore to find out about current happenings, or look in the Entertainment section of Friday's *Missoulian*.

Medical Services Missoula's Community Medical Center (☎ 406-728-4100) is on Fort Rd, just west of Reserve St.

Laundry Sparkle Laundry, on the corner of Higgins and 6th Sts, is open from 8 am to 10 pm weekdays, 9 am to 11 pm weekends.

Museums & Galleries

The Missoula Museum of the Arts, housed in the city's original Carnegie library building at 335 N Pattee St, hosts contemporary exhibits and installations by U of M art students. Hours are from noon to 5 pm Monday to Saturday; $2 (free on Tuesdays). Murals by artist Edgar Samuel Paxon decorate the ceilings of the Neoclassical Missoula County Courthouse, at 220 Broadway, and can be viewed weekdays from 8 am to 5 pm.

Front and Higgins Sts are home to most of Missoula's galleries. Particularly outstanding are Art Fusion, 111 N Higgins, with ceramics, jewelry and sculpture by regional artists, and the Monte Dolack Gallery, 139 W Front, which has the biggest collection of Dolack art (colorful prints of his fish and wildlife paintings) in his native state.

Missoula's Carousel

Missoulians talk passionately about their beautiful attraction, the first hand-carved carousel to be made in the USA in the last 60 years. Located in Caras Park near the river, it took five years to build and was completed in 1995. Local organizations and businesses sponsored the project and the creation of the individual horses, which were carved primarily by local volunteers. A ride on the carousel costs just 50¢, though watching it spin is as much fun as hopping aboard. It's open daily from 11 am to 5:30 pm, longer in summer.

University of Montana

Since its inception in 1893, U of M has grown from a refurbished schoolhouse on 40 acres of land with 50 enrolled students to a 640-acre campus with a student body of 10,600. Among its illustrious creative writing department grads are Dorothy Johnson, Wallace Stegner, Ivan Doig, and William Kittredge, who coedited with Annick Smith *The Last Best Place*, a well-known anthology of Montana literature.

The best way to enter the campus is from the south end of Van Buren St where there is a pay parking lot. Walk south towards the clock tower and you'll hit the main quad (bordered by the tower, the student center and main library) at the center of the campus.

MONTANA

The 84-year-old 'M' on Mt Sentinel has metamorphosed over the years, from whitewashed rocks to wood to shale to the current concrete. The view from here is spectacular – join the sunset-seeking pilgrims on the switchback climb starting from the east edge of campus, near the football stadium.

Historical Museum at Fort Missoula

Housed in what used to be the core of Fort Missoula, three blocks west of Reserve St on South Ave (take bus No 1 or No 9), this museum's indoor galleries house forestry, transportation and military memorabilia, plus various exhibits on Missoula's development. Outside are original and relocated historical structures – a fire lookout, schoolhouse, church, and depot – with reconstructed scenes and period decorations. It's open from Memorial Day to Labor Day, from Tuesday to Saturday 10 am to 5 pm, Sunday noon to 5 pm; and the rest of the year from Tuesday to Sunday noon to 5 pm; closed Monday; $3.

Smokejumper Visitors Center

This visitors center (☎ 406-329-4934), located 7 miles west of downtown on W Broadway (take bus No 10), is a bustling home base and training center for the heroic men and women who parachute into forests to combat raging wildfires. The history and act of smokejumping is quite fascinating and well chronicled in the center's exhibits. There's also a reconstructed lookout tower and free tours (on the hour from 10 am to 4 pm) given by smokejumpers who give first-hand accounts of their adventures. It's open daily from Memorial Day to Labor Day, 9 am to 5 pm.

Fort Missoula

Fort Missoula was built in 1877 to provide fearful settlers a sense of protection from the neighboring Flathead Indians. The fort itself never saw any conflict between the settlers and Indians.

The quirkiest period in the fort's history (and the most indicative of Missoula's future) came in the 1890s with the formation of the 25th Infantry Bicycle Corps, Lieutenant James Moss' brainchild to test the feasibility of bicycles in the military. According to Moss, bicycles were less expensive than horses and didn't require nearly as much care. Besides frequent dispatch trips down the Bitterroot Valley and into Yellowstone Park, the corps made a 1900-mile trip from Missoula to St Louis, Missouri, only to return by train as the bicycle idea never took.

During WWI Fort Missoula was used as a training center, and in 1933 it became the Northwest Regional Headquarters for the Civilian Conservation Corps (CCC). Then, in 1941, the fort was turned over to the Department of Naturalization and Immigration for use as a detention center for Italian merchant seamen seized on Italian ships in US harbors. Some of Missoula's older population remembers the 'invasion' of young Italians who stole the hearts of the women in town. After the bombing of Pearl Harbor, Japanese-Americans were also interned here. At the end of WWII the fort served as a prison for court-martialed military personnel until it was decommissioned in 1947. The museum opened in 1975. ■

Rocky Mountain Elk Foundation & Wildlife Visitors Center

The RMEF, 2291 W Broadway (take bus No 2 or 10), is the fastest-growing conservation organization in the country, and home to a large collection of stuffed North American big-game animals and related paintings and sculptures. Somewhat ironically, most RMEF members are avid hunters, so their interest in conserving animals is primarily for recreational purposes. It's open daily 8 am to 6 pm; free.

Rattlesnake National Recreation Area & Wilderness

Six miles north of Missoula, in the Lolo Forest, the Rattlesnake NRA consists of 95 sq miles of the upper Rattlesnake Valley drainage divided into a national recreation area and wilderness. Most people use the Rattlesnake for day hikes and bike trips within a 3-mile 'South Zone' radius of the main entrance. Getting to the more remote areas requires at least 11 miles of hiking (one-way), but it's well worth it for the number of small lakes in the area. Camping is allowed only beyond the South Zone. Bicycles are allowed on most trails that border the wilderness area.

There are maps posted at the entrance, located 6 miles north of town via Van Buren St (which becomes Rattlesnake Drive). Anyone venturing beyond the South Zone should pick up a map at the Missoula Ranger District Office at Fort Missoula or at the USFS headquarters (☎ 406-329-3511) downtown at the corner of Pine and Pattee Sts.

Bus No 5 gets you to within 2 miles of the entrance, but you must walk or hitch (especially easy on weekends) from there.

Blue Mountain Recreation Area

Blue Mountain, 2 miles west of Missoula, is geared more toward families and weekend recreationalists. Trails range from a quarter-mile to 11 miles, and many of them are open to motorcycles and all-terrain vehicles. At the base of the mountain in the Maclay Flat is a paved, wheelchair-accessible trail lined with informative panels that makes a 1¾-mile loop through open meadows. At the top of Blue Mountain (accessible by USFS Rd 365) is a 'working' fire lookout staffed July and August from 9 am to 6 pm. Only three people are allowed in the lookout at a time. For maps and information, call or visit the Missoula Ranger District Office or USFS headquarters.

Activities

Outdoors stores are Missoula's best resources for trip information. The Trail Head (☎ 406-543-6966), on the corner of Higgins and Pine Sts, is all-purpose and rents skis, rafts, canoes, kayaks, backpacks, stoves and sleeping bags. Pipestone Mountaineering (☎ 406-721-1670), 101 S Higgins Ave, has climbing information, guides and equipment. Anglers should stop by Grizzly Hackle (☎ 406-721-8996), 215 W Front St, for guided trips on the various rivers, fishing information and gear. Wild Rockies Tours (☎ 406-728-0566) is a reputable guide company that leads one-day canoe, mountain bike and hiking trips for around $55 per person.

Hiking Grab a copy of the free 'Trails Missoula' guide (available at the chamber of commerce, outdoors stores and the hostel) for hikes in the Missoula area. One of the nicest, most accessible jaunts is along the riverside path on the south side of the Clark Fork; start at McCormick Park (west of the Orange St bridge) and head east past the university and back into Hellgate Canyon. Adventurous types can ascend the steep Mt Sentinel Trail (about a mile past the university) up the back of Mt Sentinel and come out on the mountain's summit above the university. Another popular trek is up to the 'M' on Mt Sentinel; the trail starts near the university football stadium, from the east edge of campus.

Skiing The challenging **Snowbowl Ski Area** (☎ 406-549-9777), 17 miles north of Missoula, is mostly for advanced skiers. It has a vertical drop of 2600 feet (the biggest in Montana) and 1200 acres serviced by two chairlifts, a rope-tow and a

T-bar. Adult tickets cost $35, $22 with a valid student ID, $12 for children. Take West Broadway to Reserve St and turn north. Snowbowl Rd is on the west side of Reserve St where the pavement ends. There's a free shuttle on weekends and holidays that leaves from the Buttrey's supermarket on Broadway, east of Van Buren St; call the mountain for departure times.

Located 7 miles east of Missoula, **Marshall Mountain** (☎ 406-258-6000) is more family and beginner oriented. There's one chairlift, a T-bar and a rope-tow servicing 1500 vertical feet. Full-day tickets cost $17, $15 with a valid student ID; two-hour and four-hour tickets cost $6 and $12, respectively. A child's ticket costs $8; kids under five ski free. Night skiing costs $8 and includes a free beer at the lively bar at the base of the mountain.

There are extensive backcountry possibilities in the Rattlesnake Recreation Area and from the top of Marshall Mountain; contact the Trail Head for information and ski rentals. Also, if you don't mind the 1½-hour drive, the Bitterroot Valley (later in this section) has two excellent ski areas.

Rafting The stretch of the Clark Fork River that goes through Alberton Gorge, 35 miles west of Missoula, is considered the area's best river rafting with Class III and IV rapids. Pangaea Expeditions (☎ 406-721-7719) offers full ($55) and half-day ($45) trips through the gorge, as well as overnight trips ($150) down the Blackfoot River and two-hour trips ($25) through Hellgate Canyon.

Special Events
On Wednesdays in the summer from 11:30 am to 1 pm at the north end of the Higgins Ave bridge, **Out to Lunch in Caras Park** is a citywide picnic with live entertainment and local restaurants selling food. The **Missoula Farmer's Market**, held Tuesday evenings and Saturday mornings between Higgins and Pattee Sts, has live music and more than 90 vendors offering fruit, vegetables, flowers, baked goods and crafts. The first week of April brings wildlife biolo-

gists, filmmakers and environmentalists together for the widely acclaimed **International Wildlife Film Festival**, begun in 1977. Participants include the BBC and National Geographic.

Places to Stay
Accommodations fill up quickly in late August and early September when students head back to school, and in May during graduation celebrations. Most lodging is on Broadway between Van Buren and Orange Sts, walking distance to the campus and downtown.

Camping Three miles west of downtown, the *Missoula/El-Mar KOA* (☎ 406-549-0881), 3695 Tina Ave (it's well signed off W Broadway), is a little urban, but has nice views of the Bitterroot Range to the west. Facilities include a pool, hot tub, grocery store, laundry and petting zoo. Tent/RV sites are $15/22. From W Broadway (US 93) turn south on Reserve St, and Tina Ave is the first street on the right.

Hostels The superbly located *Birchwood Hostel* (☎ 406-728-9799), 600 S Orange St, has two single-sex dorms, one coed dorm and a family room that sleeps four (reserve in advance). Bathrooms are clean, the kitchen is fully stocked and rental bikes are available for a small fee. Cost is $9 for HI/AYH members, $11 for nonmembers. Lockout is from 9 am to 5 pm and the curfew – negotiable if the hostel is not too full – is midnight. Call before 9 am or after 5 pm for reservations.

B&Bs *Goldsmith's B&B* (☎ 406-721-6732), 809 E Front St, has a great porch overlooking the river, rooms with hand-tiled bathrooms and hardwood floors and a sunny reading room with a TV and fireplace. There's also a small refrigerator and microwave for guest use. Breakfast is served at Goldsmith's Restaurant next door. Rooms cost $65/75 to $95/105.

Hotels & Motels The best budget motels are the *Downtown Motel* (☎ 406-549-5191),

502 E Broadway, the *City Center Motel* (☎ 406-543-3193), at 338 E Broadway. and the *Ponderosa Motel* (☎ 406-543-3102), 800 E Broadway, which offer dated, no-frills rooms for around $40. The *Royal Motel* (☎ 406-542-2184), one block north of Broadway at 388 Washington St, and the *Uptown Motel* (☎ 406-549-5141), near the courthouse at 329 Woody St, have quieter locations and more modern rooms for about $48; the Uptown Motel also has one three-bed room that sleeps six for $70.

In the mid-range, your best bet is the new *Holiday Inn Express Riverside* (☎ 406-549-7600), 1021 E Broadway, with $65 rooms, free breakfast and guest laundry. On Broadway, the *Campus Inn* (☎ 406-549-5134, 800-232-8013), with a Jacuzzi and Continental breakfast, and the *Creekside Inn* (☎ 406-549-2387, 800-551-2387), with an outdoor pool, have comparable rooms for $65. There's also the *Travelodge* (☎ 406-728-4500; 800-578-7878) at 420 W Broadway, and *Best Western Executive Motor Inn* (☎ 406-543-7221) in the heart of downtown at 201 E Main St.

Missoula's upscale accommodations cater to conference groups and business travelers, offer numerous weekend and winter packages and have fitness rooms, spas and indoor pools. The *Village Red Lion Inn* (☎ 406-728-3110, 800-547-8010), 100 Madison St, two blocks south of E Broadway, is a good choice for its riverside location and popular lounge (featuring live music most nights). Rooms cost $94 to $115. Rooms at the *Holiday Inn Parkside* (☎ 406-721-8550, 800-399-0408), two blocks south of E Broadway at 200 S Pattee St, look onto an indoor courtyard and cost $85 to $105.

Places to Eat
There are supermarkets on the east and west ends of Broadway, across from the hostel on Orange Ave and near the fast-food restaurants south of town along Brooks St and Stephens Ave. The *Good Food Store* (☎ 406-728-5823), 920 Kensington St, one block west of Brooks St, has a great selection of organic produce, bulk foods and healthcare products. *Butterfly Herbs*, 232 N Higgins Ave, makes teas that are famous throughout the state.

Missoula's best values are student-oriented cafes and delis where you order at the counter. Among the better options are *Food For Thought*, across from the university at the corner of Arthur and Daly Sts. Creative breakfasts, sandwiches and salads cost around $5, pasta and stir-frys (served after 4 pm) are $8. *Second Thought*, 529 S Higgins, is their smaller version with a condensed menu. The *Mammyth Bakery Cafe*, 131 W Main, has similar fare and hot lunch specials served buffet-style. Especially good are the stacked muffuletta sandwiches or the various other deli offerings at *Worden's*, on the corner of Higgins and Spruce Sts, or the bread and the breakfast pastries from minuscule *Bernice's Bakery*, south of the river at 190 S 3rd St. There are good eats in several bars too (see Entertainment below) if you don't mind the cigarette smoke.

Hob Nob, a cozy restaurant tucked in the back of the Union Club on Main St, is worth seeking out. Sandwiches served with their signature sweet potato fries are $5, daily specials are $10 to $13 and live jazz bands play Thursday through Saturday nights. Above the Crystal Theater at 515 S

A Taste of Italy
The *Broadway Market*, on the corner of E Broadway and Madison, is a rich little piece of Missoula history and one of the only places to find authentic Italian gorgonzola, *bresaola, pan dolce* and home-made pesto in Montana. Owner Alfredo Cipolata, originally from Venice, Italy, came to the USA for the world's fair and was detained in the Fort Missoula internment camp during WWII. He married a local woman in 1943, opened this market, and has been in business ever since. If you speak Italian, stop by and say 'buongiorno.' The market is open without fail Monday to Saturday from 8 am to 7 pm. ∎

Higgins, *The Bridge* has wood-fired pizzas, fresh fish and good Caesar salads, while *Zimorino's*, 424 N Higgins Ave, is the place for traditional pizzas and Italian fare. Good choices for breakfast are *Goldsmith's*, 809 E Front St, which has a deck overlooking the river, and *The Shack*, 222 W Main, which has weekend brunch specials. The *Black Dog Cafe*, 138 W Broadway, is a completely vegetarian restaurant with a hip atmosphere and excellent homemade salad dressings; closed Monday night and Sunday.

Housed in an old railroad building at the corner of Railroad and Ryman Sts, *The Depot* is Missoula's finest dinner spot, specializing in prime rib and seafood. Their indoor-outdoor deck is more casual, and has a great microbrew selection and appetizers, hot sandwiches and excellent Caesar salads for under $10.

Entertainment
Call the chamber of commerce (☎ 406-543-6623), pick up a copy of the *Independent* or look in the Entertainment section of Friday's *Missoulian* for what's going on around town.

The *Wilma Theater* (☎ 406-543-4166), on the north side of the Higgins Ave bridge at 131 S Higgins, and the *Crystal Theater* over on the south side of the bridge, show foreign and alternative films, as well as the occasional Hollywood blockbuster. The Wilma is also home to the noteworthy Missoula Symphony Orchestra and Chorale whose season runs from October to May.

The *Front St Theater* (☎ 406-728-1911), 221 E Front St, Missoula's main live performance venue, is home to the Montana Repertory Theater group, which is part of the U of M drama department, and the Montana Players Inc. The *Missoula Children's Theater (MCT)*, 200 N Adams, boasts the largest touring children's theater in the USA.

Bars Missoula's compact downtown lends itself to bar-hopping, and there are some real gems to explore. The *Iron Horse Brewpub*, housed in the old railroad depot at the north end of Higgins Ave, has an outdoor beergarden and homemade Bavarian-style beer. A few blocks down Higgins, *Charlie B's* is a Missoula institution that attracts all ages and types with pool, Bud on tap and righteous Creole grub (shrimp po'boys, gumbo, jambalaya) served until 2 am. On Ryman St you'll find *The Ritz*, *Reds* and the *Rhino*, all frequented by raucous U of M students; the *Rhino* has an amazing beer selection. Rodeo riders, fans and ranchers hang out at the *Stockman's Club* at 125 W Front, whose original neon sign reveals its late 1940s vintage.

For live music (usually folk, rock, reggae or a combination thereof) head to the *Top Hat*, 134 W Front, *Jay's Upstairs*, 119 W Main, or Missoula's best jazz spot, *The Old Post*, 103 W Spruce, which also serves Southwest-style food until midnight.

Getting There & Away
Air The new Missoula County international airport (☎ 406-728-4381) is 5 miles west of Missoula on US 12 W; take W Broadway until it becomes US 12. Delta, Horizon Air and Northwest Airlines are the main carriers, flying to Kalispell, Seattle, WA, Salt Lake City, UT, and Minneapolis, MN.

Bus All bus lines arrive and depart from the slightly run-down Greyhound bus depot, 1 mile west of town at 1660 W Broadway. There is one daily bus to Great Falls ($14), one to Kalispell via Polson and Whitefish ($22), one to Helena ($12), and three to Billings ($22) via Butte ($18) and Bozeman ($18). A Greyhound bus departs once daily for long-distance trips to San Francisco ($132), Seattle ($85) and Minneapolis ($98). Call the depot (☎ 406-549-2339) for current schedules.

Getting Around
To/From the Airport There is an airport shuttle that you can call from the white courtesy phone (in the baggage claim area) that charges $11 per person. But Yellow Cab (☎ 406-543-6644) only charges $10 for one person plus $1 for each additional person.

Bus The free Emerald Line Trolley makes a full loop of downtown every 20 minutes, weekdays until 4 pm. Mountain Line Buses (☎ 406-721-3333) connect downtown to greater Missoula, Monday to Saturday until 6 pm. Individual rides are 85¢, an unlimited day-pass is $1.75. Schedules are available at the chamber of commerce, the Trail Head outdoors store, the hostel and the bus depot.

Car Hertz, Avis, Budget and National have counters in the airport. Less expensive options are Rent-a-Wreck (☎ 406-721-3838), Thrifty Car Rental (☎ 406-542-1540), Ugly Duckling (☎ 406-542-8459), and (usually the cheapest) Enterprise Rent-a-Car (☎ 406-721-1888), which all have pickup services.

BITTERROOT VALLEY

If you're en route to Idaho, on a day trip from Missoula or bound for the backcountry, the Bitterroot Valley is an excellent travel corridor. Flanked by the Sapphire Range in the east and the rugged Bitterroot Range in the west, US 93 follows the course of the Bitterroot River for 60 miles, past ranches, timber mills, log home manufacturers and antique stores. Hamilton, the valley's largest town, is about halfway down the valley and makes a good base to explore from. North of Hamilton the valley is wide and the river's habitat supports migratory bird populations and large herds of elk and deer. South, between Hamilton and the Idaho border, the valley narrows to become a canyon and US 93 hugs the river between steep red walls. Here, there's good fishing as well as access to the wilderness areas of Selway-Bitterroot, Frank Church River of No Return and Anaconda-Pintler.

Residents outside the valley say you'll find a mixed bag of nuts in the Bitterroot, from Freemen and Constitutionalists to business folk that commute to Missoula. A recent influx of newcomers accounts for the Buddhist meditation groups and holistic healing centers springing up in the area, which was traditionally considered one of the most conservative in Montana.

The valley is named after the elusive bitterroot plant, characterized by its showy pink or whitish flowers and a white, forked root. It only grows on dry hillsides and flowers on average just six weeks of the year. The Salish Indians used the plant's bitter root to flavor stews and sauces. Luckily, early settlers referred to the plant by its Salish name instead of its Latin name, otherwise we would be driving through the 'Lewisia Rediviva Valley.' Somehow 'Bitterroot' just seems more Montana.

History

This fertile valley is the traditional homeland of the Bitterroot Salish Indians. Their interest in the 'magical' powers of the black-robed clergy brought Father Pierre De Smet to the area and helped establish St

'Black Robes' Bring Powerful Medicine

Christianized Iroquois who came from the northeast with trappers and traders brought stories of great men in black robes who wielded powerful medicine and had strong connections to the heaven land beyond. Interested in obtaining some of this power to help them with their farming and their battles, the Bitterroot Salish sent a messenger to St Louis to ask the Catholic Church to send a 'Black Robe' (priest) to the West. But the church declined the request: the journey from St Louis was long and hard, and the West was considered dangerous and full of savages. Refusing to give up, the Salish (also known as the Flathead Indians) made three more separate entreaties until the church sent Father Pierre De Smet in 1841.

When Father De Smet expressed his desire to share his medicine with (or, convert) the Blackfeet – the Flatheads' most feared and hated enemy – the Flathead people became suspicious and angry with him. Two seasons of drought followed, and the relationship between the tribe and the missionaries rapidly deteriorated. Many Indians continued to worship as Catholics, but in the past 20 years or so, there has been a strong revival of traditional ceremonies as well. ■

MONTANA

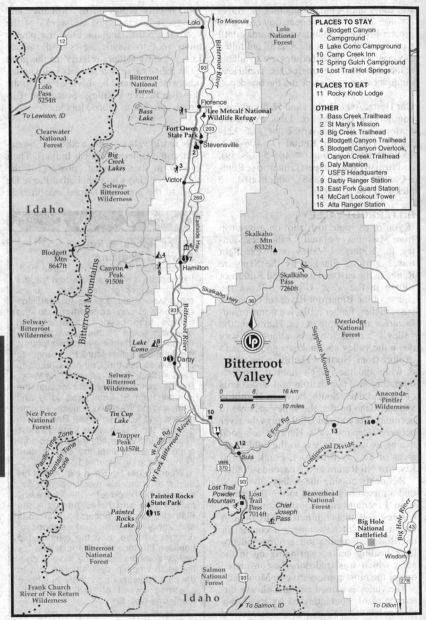

Mary's Mission near Stevensville in 1841. In 1850, John Owen, a trader with the US Army, bought the mission property and turned it into a trading post which thrived for 22 years as a farm, ranch, gristmill and general center of activity.

Under the Hellgate Treaty of 1855, the US government was supposed to survey the Bitterroot Valley to determine if it was a better site for the Salish than the proposed Flathead Reservation in the Mission and Jocko valleys. By the time the survey started, the valley had so many white settlements (mostly of people who had failed in the goldfields but decided to stay), that the government succumbed to economic pressure and decided (without ever completing the survey) that the Salish needed to move. Half the tribe moved immediately, under a war chief named Arlee, but the other half remained with their tribal chief Victor, and his son Charlo, until they were escorted out by the army in 1891.

Marcus Daly came to the Bitterroot Valley in 1889 to diversify his copper holdings and acquire the timber needed for his giant smelter in Anaconda. He built the first of the valley's lumber mills, established Hamilton as the county seat and set up a 2000-acre horse ranch. He bought riverfront land along the Bitterroot, heavily forested acreage in the Sapphire and Bitterroot mountains and 50 acres for his family and beloved racehorses – a total of 31 sq miles.

Daly also tried to buy neighboring Grantsdale from its founder Henry Grant, but Grant's asking price sent Daly into an outrage. 'Go to hell!,' he told Grant, 'I'll see grass growing in the streets of Grantsdale before I pay that kind of money.' So Daly built his lumber mill near present-day Hamilton and hired Grant as his foreman. Hamilton grew to be the Bitterroot's center of trade and services (and grass did end up growing in the streets of Grantsdale). Daly's holdings eventually dwindled and the valley incorporated sugar beet crops – to supply Missoula's sugar mill – into its timber-based economy.

Orientation & Information

Stevensville (population 1965), Hamilton (population 4059) and Darby (population 851) are the valley's main towns, each with gas stations, a bank, post office, laundromat and a Bitterroot National Forest ranger station on its main street. The Forest Supervisor's Office (☎ 406-363-7117), in Hamilton at 1801 N 1st St, has the widest selection of maps and literature for surrounding wilderness areas. The Bitterroot Chamber of Commerce (☎ 406-363-2400), 105 E Main St, on the corner with US 93 in Hamilton, has information about attractions, restaurants and lodging, and gives out free tourist maps. Chapter One Bookstore, 252 Main St in Hamilton, has regional guides and information on happenings in the valley.

A scenic, less-traveled alternative to US 93 is the East Side Hwy (Hwy 269), which starts in Florence and passes through Stevensville, Corvallis and a few tiny agricultural towns before it reconnects with US 93 in Hamilton.

St Mary's Mission

Established in 1841 by Father Pierre De Smet, St Mary's Mission occupies a picturesque piece of land on the western edge of Stevensville. Most of its original structures are still intact, and its graveyard has stones and old wooden crosses that date back to the 1800s. The mission thrived for nine years, establishing the area's first crops and mills and acting as its social hub. When the Salish were moved to the Flathead Reservation in 1891, St Mary's ceased being a mission, but the church remained active until 1954.

Guides give tours ($3/1 adults/children) of the buildings from Memorial Day to Labor Day, 10 am to 5 pm, with the last tour departing at 4:15 pm. A small museum gift shop (same hours as the tours) has a good selection of local history books. The grounds are always open.

Lee Metcalf National Wildlife Refuge

Established in 1963 with funds from duckstamp sales (both stamps and a license are

MONTANA

legally required for duck-hunting), the 2800-acre Lee Metcalf National Wildlife Refuge supports pileated woodpeckers, ospreys, heron, geese and other waterfowl, otter, muskrat, beaver and white-tailed deer. Footpaths meander through an open pine stand to the Bitterroot River, and a hiking trail with viewing blinds (camouflaged enclosures for birdwatching) provides close-up views of waterfowl. Exciting battles occur during peak migration periods (fall and early spring), when the ospreys return to their nests and have to evacuate the geese who have occupied the nests in their absence. The refuge is 4 miles north of Stevensville, well marked from town (turn east at the ranger station on Main St) and from US 93 (turn east at Florence and continue south for 6 miles).

On the road that connects US 93 and Stevensville, is Fort Owen State Park where archeologists from U of M have reconstructed the homestead, barracks and well-

house of Fort Owen. The entrance is on private property, making access a bit problematic unless someone from U of M is on duty (usually in summer from 9 am to 5 pm).

The Marcus Daly Mansion

Built in 1890 to serve as the summer home of copper king Marcus Daly and his wife Margaret, this palatial spread has 24 bedrooms and 15 bathrooms and has sheltered, among others, Theodore Roosevelt, Will Rogers and artist Charles Russell. The exquisitely manicured grounds include a tennis court, swimming pool, carriage house and three-quarter size playhouse, and the house itself has such modern marvels as electricity, elevators and a 4th-floor ballroom.

The mansion (☎ 406-363-6004) is 2 miles north of Hamilton on Hwy 269; turn east on A St from US 93. Volunteers dressed in period clothing lead tours from May 1 to September 30, Tuesday to Sun-

Paramilitary Groups

Montanans have long felt a great attachment to their land and to their rights of steward-ship. The vast expanse of the area enabled early settlers to acquire large acreage, and their exploitation of natural resources through mining, logging and raising livestock led to increasing industrial development.

As the state grew, ranchers developed an unwritten code of conduct – in essence: 'Do your own thing, as long as you don't hurt anybody,' and 'Don't mess with someone else's water or land.' But, the decline of the mining industry and the growth of tourism are changing the face of Montana.

In 1972, a new state constitution was drafted that reflected contemporary environmental concerns. Meanwhile, increased federal oversight in the form of clean water and wetlands preservation acts, the Brady Law (which imposes a waiting period for gun purchases) and the growing authority of the Bureau of Land Management have threatened the locals' long-cherished autonomy.

To protect themselves from what they feel is the usurpation of their rights 'by the tyranny of a runaway, out-of-control government' (in the words of the Militia of Montana), some angry citizens have formed paramilitary groups. Made up of primarily white, right-wing conservatives from the Bitterroot Valley, the groups claim legitimacy through their interpretation of the US Constitution's Second Amendment – namely, their right to form militias and bear arms. But some also believe in 'Christian Identity,' a doctrine developed by a former Ku Klux Klansman, that claims (among other things) that present-day Jews are 'the race of Cain' and that 'racial purity' is God's plan. Some groups have set up 'common law' courts that deny government authority, evade taxes and even issue their own checks.

Many militia members also belong to the Patriots, a decentralized movement that includes Christian Identity churches, Aryan Nation members, pro-gun groups and consti-

day from 11 am to 4 pm. Admission is $5/3 adults/children. There is wheelchair access to the 1st floor only. The grounds are open from 10 am to 5 pm and admission is free.

Darby

In 1888 a small post office was founded at the present site of Darby. When the surrounding community grew large enough to require a name, local settlers, feeling very patriotic, chose the name 'Harrison' after President Benjamin Harrison. The federal government soon informed them that a Harrison, Montana, already existed and that they would have to choose another name for their town. After several failed attempts at gathering a second town meeting, Mr Darby, the postmaster, signed his name to the town deed and sent it back to Washington, DC.

Since the owner of Darby Lumber Company retired and sold the business in 1994, art galleries, antique stores and cafes have settled in Darby's old wooden buildings,

and turned the three-block town into somewhat of a tourist attraction. Midway through town on the east side of Main St is Darby's original town square, with the public library (located in the old firehouse) on the north side and Darby's Pioneer Memorial Museum (housed in an old chicken coop) on the east side. The Darby Historical Ranger Station, on the north end of town where Main St is again called US 93, was built by the Civilian Conservation Corps (CCC) in 1937-39 and now houses displays of old ranger and firefighter equipment; it's open daily from 9 am to 5 pm.

Activities

Stop by a ranger station in Stevensville, Hamilton or Darby for maps and current trail information. Pipestone Mountaineering (☎ 406-363-3855), 315 W Main St in Hamilton, rents equipment, sells topo maps and is open weekends.

tutionalists, and taps into an anti-Semitic and bigoted vein not unique to Montana. (In fact, in 1997, the Southern Poverty Law Center identified 523 anti-government Patriot organizations, including 221 militia groups, across the US.) Some Patriot groups only adhere to the Bill of Rights, denying the freedoms for African-Americans and women that were recognized in later amendments, while others are known for their tactics of intimidation and violence toward law enforcement officials.

On March 25, 1996, a militia group associated with the Patriot movement known as the Freemen began an 81-day standoff with the FBI at their ranch in Jordan, MT. The group holed up on the estate when the FBI arrested two of their leaders for fraud and tax evasion. This standoff, along with the bombing of the Alfred P Murrah Federal Building in Oklahoma City, OK, the previous year, helped to bring nationwide attention to the militia movement. Timothy McVeigh, who was convicted of the bombing, had ties to a religious militant organization and had apparently acted in retaliation for the deaths caused by earlier FBI standoffs in Waco, TX, and Ruby Ridge, ID.

To some extent, the Oklahoma City bombing discredited the militia movement – the American public was horrified by this act of homegrown terrorism. And these groups remain on the fringes of society. Their anger toward the government notwithstanding, they now rely more on the media than violence as a tool to achieve their aims. When actor Steven Seagal was filming *The Patriot* in Ennis, for example, he received threats from persons identifying themselves as militia members. The Militia of Montana quickly denied involvement and offered to act as movie consultants to present a fair portrayal of their kind. John Trochmann, head of the group, seized this opportunity to publicize one of his group's positions (fear of a United Nations-led conspiracy to form a New World Order), stating: 'I hope he (Seagal) will come to the rescue of America, to stop the encroachment of global government.' ■

– Joslyn Leve

MONTANA

Lake Como, 4 miles west of US 93, north of Darby, is a good family destination. The day-use area at the east end of the reservoir has a swimming beach, boat launch and picnic area. The **Lake Como National Recreation Loop Trail** extends around the reservoir for a level 7 miles, crossing the **Rock Creek Trail** which heads west into the Selway-Bitterroot Wilderness Area. Another good spot is the remote Painted Rocks State Park whose lake has a boat launch, handicap-access fishing dock, potable water and campground. At the north end of the lake is the Alta Ranger Station, one of the first USFS ranger stations in the USA, built in 1899, and the wheelchair-accessible **Alta Pine Interpretive Trail**. To reach the park, turn southwest off US 93, 4 miles south of Darby on West Fork Rd and continue 24 miles.

Hiking There are 29 drainages that cut east-west through the Bitterroot Range, creating dramatic canyons and epic hiking possibilities. Trailheads are well signed off US 93, usually 2 to 8 miles west via maintained roads. Popular day hikes include the non-technical but steep trail to the lookout tower atop St Mary's Peak (near Stevensville), the easy 1½-mile jaunt to the Blodgett Canyon Overlook (near Hamilton) and the 7-mile trip to Bass Lake at the south side of St Joseph's Peak (near Stevensville).

With more effort you can get to the top of stately Trapper Peak or into the Selway-Bitterroot Wilderness Area along the Big Creek and Storm Creek trails (both near Darby). For multiple-day adventures, follow the West Fork of the Bitterroot River (southwest of Darby via West Fork Rd) to the little-used but very beautiful Frank Church River of No Return Wilderness that extends into central Idaho; stop at the Darby or West Fork ranger station for maps and information (open in summer).

Fishing Most fishing access points (well signed off US 93) are in the north end of the valley between Victor and Hamilton, or south of Darby. There are also good, less-frequented spots along the East Fork of the Bitterroot, off the East Fork Rd which meets US 93 at Sula. For lake fishing, head to Lake Como (well signed off US 93, about 8 miles north of Darby) or hike up to any of the small lakes off the Bass Creek, Big Creek or Canyon Creek trails.

For fishing information, licenses and equipment stop in at the Fishaus (☎ 406-363-6158), 702 N First St (US 93), which is one block north of Main St, in Hamilton; for hiking information, head to a ranger station.

Skiing One of Montana's best ski deals is the $17 lift ticket at Lost Trail Powder Mountain (☎ 406-821-3508), 13 miles south of Sula on US 93. The place is small (a 2400-foot vertical drop covered by two chairlifts and two surface lifts) but gets an average of 300 inches of light, dusty powder per year. You also have the thrill of carving turns across the Continental Divide and the Montana-Idaho border.

Cross-country skiers should turn east on Hwy 43 (towards Wisdom), before reaching Lost Trail, to access a vast network of trails at Chief Joseph Pass. The Darby and Sula ranger stations have trail maps, as do sports stores in Missoula and Hamilton. Another good cross-country destination is the unplowed Skalkaho Hwy (Hwy 38), which turns east 3 miles south of Hamilton and heads into the Sapphire Mountains.

Places to Stay
Camping For an atypical camping experience, inquire about renting the East Fork Guard Station Cabin or McCart Lookout Tower; reservations (☎ 406-363-3131) are usually required well in advance.

There are undeveloped (no water, no toilets, no fee) spots where you can pitch a tent at most trailheads and fishing access points. Lake Como, Painted Rocks State Park and the Blodgett Canyon trailhead each has a campground with toilets, potable water, fire rings and $7 to $11 sites. The largest concentration of USFS campgrounds are south of Darby on US 93, and on Spring Gulch, West Fork and East Fork Rds. Most have toilets, water, fire rings and cost $6 to $9. The *Sula Store & Camp-ground* (☎ 406-821-3364) charges $4 per person to camp on a large lawn behind the store and has cabins with two bunk beds and a kitchen for $19.

Motels Darby has a few good small motels on its Main St (US 93), including the *Log Cabin Motel* (☎ 406-821-3282), with $35 cabins and $45 rooms; *Bud & Shirley's* (☎ 406-821-3401), with a popular restaurant and rooms for $45/51; and the *Wilderness Motel* (☎ 406-821-3405), at the south end of town, with rooms for $33/44, tent/RV sites for $4/12, and a hostel-style bunkhouse with showers and kitchen facilities for $15 per person.

Hamilton is the best place to find chain accommodations. *Comfort Inn* (☎ 406-363-6600), *Super 8* (☎ 406-363-2940), and the *Best Western Hamilton Inn* (☎ 406-363-2142) are all on US 93 and range in price from $40 to $75.

Resorts On a 120-acre working ranch, the *Camp Creek Inn* (☎ 406-821 3508), north of Sula at 7674 US 93, has rooms with quilt-covered wooden beds and antique farm furniture for $48 to $72, including breakfast. In winter they have ski packages with Lost Trail Powder Mountain.

Lost Trail Hot Springs (☎ 406-821-3574, 800-825-3574), 6 miles north of the US 93/Hwy 43 junction, is a quiet backcountry resort with a big pine lodge, bar and restaurant, log cabins ($58), a few motel rooms ($48) and a basketball court. The pool and hot tub (open from 8 am to 10 pm daily, to 6 pm on Tuesday) are naturally heated and untreated and can be visited even if you aren't staying at the resort ($4 for non-guests).

Places to Eat
There are supermarkets on US 93 in Hamilton and Darby and a slew of fastfood restaurants near Hamilton.

In downtown Hamilton, *Wild Oats*, 217 Main St (upstairs), serves breakfast and lunch for under $6 and has good vegetarian options. *Nap's*, on Second St two blocks

north of Main St, is the place for huge $5 burgers. *La Trattoria*, 315 Third St, is where locals go for a nice Italian meal.

A good choice for families, *Trapper's*, 516 Main St in Darby, has a huge menu for breakfast, lunch and dinner. Also on Main St, the *Darmont Hotel* is Darby's original drinking establishment and a colorful spot for burgers, steaks, pizza and fried shrimp; the kitchen is open until 11 pm.

The *Rocky Knob Lodge* (☎ 406-821-3520), 12 miles south of Darby on US 93, is famous for its hickory-smoked spare ribs, trout, and roasted chicken. Dinner is $9 to $16, lunch, around $7.

Entertainment
Hamilton is home to the Riverstreet Theater, which hosts folk music and dance performances, and two live theater companies – Shantilly Theater Group and Hamilton Players – that perform in a restored schoolhouse. Tickets and information are available at Chapter One Bookstore, 252 Main St.

People venture great distances for the English pints and pub atmosphere of *The Hamilton*, half a block west of US 93 in the small town of Victor. The owner wears a kilt, pulls a perfect Guinness and makes excellent fish and chips. For a totally different scene, make the rounds in Darby. The *Lone Wolf*, *Valley Bar* and the *Darmont Hotel* (also known as *The Sawmill*), all on Main St, are classic western bars with tin ceilings, pool tables and live music most weekends. The Darmont has a great collection of old saws hanging (yikes!) from the ceiling.

THE BIG HOLE VALLEY
The Big Hole River originates east of the Continental Divide in the Bitterroot Range of the Rocky Mountains (the border between Montana and Idaho) and flows north through a wide valley. Then it turns east and south to meet the Jefferson River and eventually becomes part of the Missouri. North of the river's headwaters, the Big Hole creates a valley between the Rockies and Pioneer Mountains whose elevation is above 6000

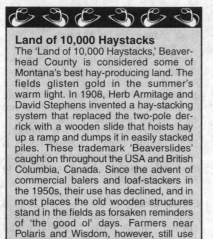

Land of 10,000 Haystacks

The 'Land of 10,000 Haystacks,' Beaverhead County is considered some of Montana's best hay-producing land. The fields glisten gold in the summer's warm light. In 1908, Herb Armitage and David Stephens invented a hay-stacking system that replaced the two-pole derrick with a wooden slide that hoists hay up a ramp and dumps it in easily stacked piles. These trademark 'Beaverslides' caught on throughout the USA and British Columbia, Canada. Since the advent of commercial balers and loaf-stackers in the 1950s, their use has declined, and in most places the old wooden structures stand in the fields as forsaken reminders of 'the good ol' days. Farmers near Polaris and Wisdom, however, still use the slides at peak haying-time. ■

feet. Montanans like to say that the Big Hole is 'uphill from everywhere.'

Outside Alaska, the Big Hole River is the last stream-dwelling in the USA for the endangered Arctic grayling (recognizable by their gray spotted bellies, these fish must be released immediately after being caught). The best fishing in the area is on the stretch of the Big Hole River between the Wise and the Beaverhead rivers, north of Dillon off I-15. Trout also live in the Big Hole: rainbows dominate the Wise River area, while browns are more common in the lower stretches.

Most activity in the area centers around Dillon (see Dillon later in this chapter), but the small towns and wide-open spaces along Hwy 43 and County Rd 278 – where one person acts as the gas station attendant, bartender and undertaker – are where you really get the flavor of this sparsely populated and infrequently visited place.

History

Because of its elevation, the valley only sees summer from about mid-July to September and thus remained a wilderness long after surrounding valleys were settled. Flathead

Indians, who called the area the 'Land of the Big Snows,' came up from the Bitterroot Valley to gather camas bulbs, and trappers, who used the term 'hole' to describe high mountain valleys, came through hunting buffalo, elk, deer and antelope. But settlement didn't come until ranchers discovered the valley's rich grass supply in the 1890s. Since then, the Big Hole has been serious ranch country with most ranches holding 2000 to 5000 acres. In the past 10 years, however, parcels have been divided into smaller holdings and recreation has become an important soft industry.

The Battle of the Big Hole From 1863 to 1877 settlers poured into the area and put pressure on the government to 'contain' the Nez Percé on the reservation established for them. General George Custer's defeat in the Battle of the Little Bighorn in 1876 prompted further demands that the government demonstrate control over the native population. (See The Battle of the Little Bighorn sidebar in the Montana Plains chapter.) So in 1877, the US Army began intensive measures to get all the Nez Percé who were still resisting to move to the reservation in northern Idaho and keep them there. The government officials who negotiated this arrangement made it very clear that the only alternative was war – a war the Indians knew they could not win.

Then three young braves went on a raid that left several whites dead (the first known case of Nez Percé spilling white blood) and war became inevitable. Thunder Comes Rolling over the Mountains (better known as Chief Joseph) realized that the only hope of survival for his people lay in heading across Montana towards Canada, where Chief Sitting Bull and his people had found refuge. Outgunned, outnumbered and outflanked, the 800 or so Nez Percé fought off or eluded the relentless armies that doggedly pursued them over 1800 miles of mountainous terrain. At first, the tribe hoped it would be permitted to peacefully go on its way, but the Battle of the Big Hole changed that.

Believing that General Howard's army was several days away and, more importantly, unaware that a second military force – 162 men under Colonel John Gibbon's 7th Cavalry – had joined the chase, Chief Looking Glass chose to set up camp beside the Big Hole River to rest and prepare for the next leg of their journey. Gibbon's scouts spotted the Nez Percé the following afternoon (August 8), and the next morning before dawn, the soldiers and 34 volunteers situated themselves across the river on 'Battle Hill,' 200 yards west of the camp. As dawn broke, a Nez Percé accidentally stumbled onto the concealed soldiers and the skirmish began with a chaotic volley of gun and cannon fire.

The battle lasted two days, until both sides had suffered so many casualties that caring for the dead and injured took precedence over continuing battle. If any victory was won, it was by the Nez Percé, who cut off one group of soldiers and captured and disassembled the army's howitzer. Both sides, however, felt defeated: Gibbon was wounded and his command out of action; and the Nez Percé had lost 90 members of their tribe, most of them women, children and elders.

Big Hole Battlefield National Monument

Just west of Wisdom, in the heart of the Big Hole Valley, the Big Hole Battlefield marks the site where the Nez Percé suffered the greatest loss of life during their extraordinary 1800-mile journey towards Canada, before finally meeting defeat at the Bear's Paw Battlefield. Because of its semi-remote location, Big Hole Battlefield National Monument (☎ 406-689-3155) is much less visited than Montana's other battlefield sites. The visitors center, which has informational brochures, a small museum, a video presentation and a selection of books, is open from 8 am to 6 pm daily. From the visitors center, a road leads to the battlefield itself, half a mile away. Four different trails lead to key battle sites with wooden markers shaped like hats (blue for soldiers, beige for volunteers) and feathers marking where people fell.

Jackson Hot Springs

Halfway between Bannack and Wisdom, Jackson Hot Springs (☎ 406-834-3151) was discovered in 1806 by Lewis and Clark, who used its 104°F pool to boil meat and 'restore' themselves. Nowadays it's a good

The Bannack Boom

On July 28, 1862, John White discovered sizable deposits of placer gold in Grasshopper Creek. Within months, hundreds of hopeful miners arrived, and by 1863 Bannack had a population of over 3000. The majority of newcomers dreamed of striking it rich in the goldfields, yet many chose (often because of frustration or starvation) to take up more stable occupations as saloon keepers, blacksmiths, bakers, butchers, grocers, postmen and so on, which resulted in Bannack's evolution from mining camp to town.

In 1863, President Abraham Lincoln appointed Sidney Edgerton as Chief Justice of Idaho Territory. After coming west and seeing Bannack's prosperity, Edgerton successfully lobbied the US Congress for a division of Idaho Territory. He returned to Bannack as governor of the newly formed Montana Territory, proclaimed Bannack the capital and directed elections. The first Territorial Legislature met in Bannack on December 12, 1864.

Bannack's boom was short. Less than a year after its birth, Bannack lost its legislature and 70% of its population to Virginia City. A small mining community stayed on, however, and when new technology enabled miners to dig deeper into the earth, Bannack's economy was revitalized: In 1895, Bannack paid $35,000 for the world's first electric dredge, which brought in $38,000 worth of gold in the first week of operation. Bannack became a state park in 1954, but people continued to live and mine here up into the 1970s. ∎

The Vigilantes

A rough, self-seeking man in a town of rough, self-seeking men, Henry Plummer stands out as the man who made Bannack famous. Educated in the east, charismatic and poised, Plummer came to Bannack in 1863 and was elected sheriff one year later. Within eight months of public 'service,' Plummer and his gang of road agents, the 'Innocents,' had killed 102 people. Mainly they were after gold (supposedly they acquired $6 million worth in all), but they readily killed anyone deemed inadequately cooperative. Their favorite route was the stage between Bannack and Virginia City. One agent in Virginia City owned a business right next to the stage loading dock, where he would watch goods being loaded and then mark the stage with the gang's code numbers if it was worth robbing.

When the citizens of Bannack and Virginia City caught on that it was the sheriff who was responsible for most of the killing and robbery in the area, they were at first cowed; people cleared the streets when Plummer came riding into town and went silent when he walked in a room. But a group of citizens, most of them Freemasons sworn to secrecy under oath, formed a vigilance group, the infamous 'Vigilantes.' In a two-day swoop, the Vigilantes hunted down and hung – from gallows that Plummer himself had built – 28 of the Innocents, including Plummer, whom they surprised during Sunday dinner at his in-laws' house. Most of the Innocents were buried in Virginia City, but Plummer's grave was laid separate from the rest of the cemetery. It has been dug up so many times now that nothing is left.

Even after the Innocents were gone, the Vigilantes continued their righteous yet bloody activities. Rarely asking questions, let alone trying offenders in a courtroom, they killed so many law-breakers that even innocent men began to fear for their lives. Thomas Dimsdale published his *Vigilantes of Montana* as a newspaper series in 1865 and as a book one year later; this firsthand account is considered fundamental reading on the subject. RE Mather in *Vigilante Victims* (Historical West Publishing Company, San Jose, 1991) and FE Boswell in *Hanging the Sheriff* (Northern Utah Press, Salt Lake City, 1987) argue that Plummer and others were unjustly hung without trial. ■

place to stop for a drink and some local atmosphere or to stay a few days and experience the valley's solitude. The large knotty pine lodge has a cozy dining room, TV area and a bar where live bands perform on weekend nights. Cabins are $60, economy cabins with shared bath are $30. A plunge in the pool is $5.

Wisdom

At the junction of Hwy 43 and County Rd 278, Wisdom (population 200) consists of two bars, two restaurants, a motel and a gas station. Despite its proximity to Butte (74 miles) and Dillon (64 miles), the town's unpaved streets, dilapidated wooden buildings and sagebrush-covered surroundings make you feel that you've stepped back in time about a hundred years. It's the hub for local cattle ranchers and a good place to stop for a few minutes, even if only to poke your head

in the bar and inquire how the fishing is (always a good question, even if you don't fish). *Fetty's Cafe* serves heaping open-faced sandwiches and good burgers, and the *Big Hole Crossing* has steak, chicken and fish and a decent gift shop. If the gas station appears closed, ask for help at the bar across the street next to Fetty's. The *Nez Percé Motel* (☎ 406-689-3254), on the east side of the Hwy 43 junction, charges $33/40 for nice rooms with a bath and TV.

Bannack Historic State Park

Bannack was the site of Montana's first gold strike, gold rush, school, frame house, Freemason lodge and territorial legislature. Today it stands out as the Grand Ghoul of ghost towns, preserved in its natural state as if the gold-seekers will return at any moment. State park rangers lead informative and entertaining tours of the town and the old mine, or you can wander around on your own or with the self-guided tour map (free at the entrance). The visitors center (☎ 406-834-3413) at the park's entrance has a good selection of Western books and videos pertaining to Bannack's history and it's a good place to spend a few minutes before exploring the park. Adjacent to the park on the bank of Grasshopper Creek is a campground with toilets, potable water, picnic tables and fire rings where rangers give campfire talks. Sites cost $7 per night.

Bannack Days, held the third weekend in July, attempts to reenact Bannack's gold rush period with costumed performers, live music, arts and crafts booths, parades and wagon rides. The park, 25 miles west of Dillon on County Rd 278 and another 4 miles south from its unmarked turnoff, is open year-round during daylight hours; $3 per vehicle.

Pioneer Mountains National Scenic Byway

The 35-mile, windy, rollercoaster road between the towns of Wise River and Polaris cuts right through the middle of the Pioneer Range alongside the Wise River. This is a scenic alternative to I-15 (which runs parallel on the east side of the Pioneers) that takes about an hour longer to drive, without any stops. The northern part of the road is surrounded by jagged granite peaks and thick pine forests, while the southern part gives way to a wide, grass-covered valley that opens into the Big Hole Valley between Big Hole Pass (7360 feet) and Badger Pass (6760 feet). In winter the road is plowed from the south to Elkhorn Hot Springs and from the north to Crystal Park, but there is no through access.

Crystal Park About 2 miles south of Wise River, what looks like an abandoned battlefield is actually a 68-million-year-old granodiorite intrusion – rich with quartz amethyst crystals – that has been worked over by recreational diggers. Most crystals are six-sided, pointed at both ends and clear or brown in color, though some unusual ones show up from time to time. The best

bet is to find a relatively deep hole and dig in sideways beneath the sand-like granodiorite; crumbly reddish-brown zones mark traces of veins that might contain crystal pockets. It's helpful to have a shovel, some sort of prying tool (a crowbar works well) and a screen to sift dirt. Elkhorn Hot Springs (see below) rents equipment for a small fee, but just digging with a stick will usually yield at least a few pieces.

Elkhorn Hot Springs At rustic Elkhorn Hot Springs (☎ 406-834-3434), 13 miles north of County Rd 278, nine log cabins (each with its own outhouse), a two-story lodge, two concrete pools (one hot, one extra-hot) and a shower house line both sides of the narrow canyon that shelters the hot springs. Established in 1924, Elkhorn used to be *the* place for local ranchers to soak their weary bones and drown their sorrows on a Saturday night. The clientele is still local, interspersed with out-of-state snowmobilers during the winter. Pool-use costs $4 per day.

Hiking From the Pioneer Mountains National Scenic Byway, hikers can access several well-maintained, well-marked trails leading to high mountain lakes and peaks. Topographical maps and information are available in Wisdom, Wise River and Dillon. The **Pioneer Loop National Recreation Trail** extends 35 miles along the backbone of the West Pioneer mountains, passing several lakes. To reach the trailhead, 16 miles north of Elkhorn Hot Springs take USFS Rd 90 west. This trail gives access to the **Sandy Lake/Lily Lake Trail**, which begins on the west side of the ridge, 9 miles east of Wisdom, making a point-to-point hike possible with two cars. One mile south of Elkhorn Hot Springs, the **Blue Creek Trail** is an easy 7-mile hike through lodgepole pine forests and small meadows.

Skiing Winter sports attract as much tourist traffic to the Wise River area as do summer events. **Maverick Mountain**, 7 miles south of Elkhorn Hot Springs, is a small, steep mountain with one chairlift and one T-bar to service its 2120-foot vertical drop. Elkhorn Hot Springs is a hub of snowmobile activity but also has a good network of cross-country trails that lead into the Pioneer Mountains and cross over to the Crystal Park area. You can rent equipment in Dillon at Backcountry Bike & Boards (☎ 406-683-9696), 35 E Bannack, or at Elkhorn Hot Springs (though their selection is limited).

Places to Stay & Eat Camping is available at seven public campgrounds (well marked off the road), each of which has pit toilets, fire rings, picnic tables and $6 sites. The *Grasshopper Inn* (☎ 406-834-3456), about 4 miles north of Polaris, is a full-service lodge whose restaurant and bar act as the area's main watering hole and weekend entertainment venue; single/double rooms cost $35/45. The richly carved mahogany back bar sailed around Cape Horn from England to San Francisco, made its way by wagon to Bannack and then Dillon and finally found a home at the Grasshopper. Elkhorn Hot Springs has rooms or cabins for $25/45 including use of the pools. Meals in the lodge cost between $3 and $7 and are served from 6 am to 9:30 pm daily.

DILLON

Dillon (population 4382) came into existence when a local rancher refused to give up his land for the right-of-way of the Utah & Northern Railroad, and entrepreneurs with businesses at the railroad terminus pooled their money and bought him out. Then they sold a strip of land to the railroad, town lots at private auctions, and when the gold rush in nearby Bannack died out, secured Dillon's place as the Beaverhead County seat.

Primarily a ranchers' town, Dillon has feed, fertilizer and lumber companies at its edges and some terrific old bars with tin ceilings, high facades and ornate back bars. Western Montana College, which educates about 80% of the state's teachers, is also important to Dillon's economy though it

doesn't have much of a student scene since the campus is small and many students commute from outlying communities. There are many chain motels off I-15 near Dillon, making it a good overnight stop.

Orientation & Information

Dillon lies just east of I-15, 65 miles south of Butte. Hwy 41 heads northeast from I-15 at the south edge of town and zigzags through Dillon along Atlantic, Helena and Montana Sts. The Beaverhead River is 1 mile northwest of downtown.

The Chamber of Commerce and Visitor's Center (☎ 406-683-5511) is in the old UP railroad depot at S Montana St between Sebree and Glendale Sts and has a good walking tour map of the town. The USFS Headquarters for the Beaverhead National Forest (☎ 406-683-3900) is at 420 Barrett St. Banks with ATMs are located on Idaho and Montana Sts. Clean Critter Laundry, at 230 N Montana St, is open daily from 9 am to 9 pm. The Bookstore (☎ 406-683-6807), 26 N Idaho St, has new and used paperbacks, plus a good Western Americana selection.

Things to See & Do

You can pick up discounted outdoorwear at the Patagonia Outlet (☎ 406-683-2580), 34 N Idaho. The Beaverhead County Museum, housed in the old railroad depot at 15 S Montana St, has a wealth of mining articles found at Bannack and a one-of-a-kind fireplace made of local rock, petrified wood and geodes. It's open from 10 am to 8 pm weekdays, 1 to 5 pm weekends, June to August (10 am to 5 pm weekdays the rest of the year) and is free.

At the confluence of Blacktail Deer Creek and the Red Rock and Beaverhead rivers, Dillon is also a good place for **fishing**. Cornell Park, a quarter mile past the KOA (see below) on Park St offers easy access to the Beaverhead River and has picnic tables. A good map of local fishing spots is available at Fishing Headquarters (☎ 406-683-6660), 610 N Montana, whose owner leads guided float and walk-in trips on the Beaverhead and Jefferson rivers for $150 per person.

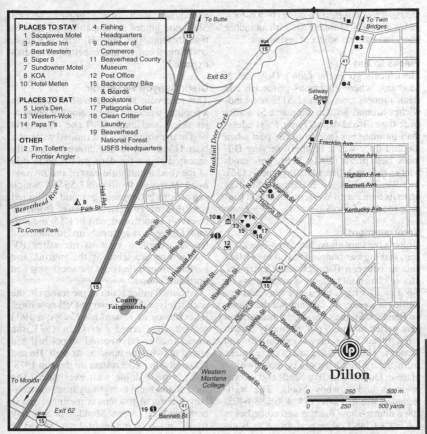

PLACES TO STAY
1 Sacajawea Motel
3 Paradise Inn Best Western
6 Super 8
7 Sundowner Motel
8 KOA
10 Hotel Metlen

PLACES TO EAT
1 Lion's Den
13 Western-Wok
14 Papa T's

OTHER
2 Tim Tollett's Frontier Angler
4 Fishing Headquarters
9 Chamber of Commerce
11 Beaverhead County Museum
12 Post Office
15 Backcountry Bike & Boards
16 Bookstore
17 Patagonia Outlet
18 Clean Critter Laundry
19 Beaverhead National Forest USFS Headquarters

Dillon

MONTANA

Store hours are 7 am to 8 pm daily. Tim Tollett's Frontier Angler (☎ 406-683-5276), 680 N Montana, is another reputable fishing shop that also rents rafts and offers a shuttle service to people with their own gear.

Montana High Country Tours (☎ 406-683-4920), 1036 E Reeder St, leads riding tours into the Beaverhead National Forest for $350 the first two days plus $150 each additional day.

Places to Stay

Dillon's *KOA* (☎ 406-683-2749) is in a nice, if unshaded, location beside the river at 735 Park St. Tent/RV sites cost $17/25.

The cheapest, dingiest and loudest place in town is Dillon's once grand *Hotel Metlen* (☎ 406-683-2335), across the tracks from the railroad depot at 5 S Railroad Ave. Rooms cost $15. The *Sundowner Motel* (☎ 406-683-2375, 800-524-9746), 500 N Montana St at Franklin Ave, has singles/doubles for $31/34. An excellent value is the *Sacajawea Motel* (☎ 406-683-2381), 775 N Montana St, which charges $20/27 for a basic room (no phone) and $31 for a room with a kitchenette.

Chain-owned options include the *Super 8* (☎ 406-683-4280, 800-800-8000) at 550 N Montana St, which charges $45/60, and the *Paradise Inn Best Western* (☎ 406-683-4214) at 650 N Montana St, with an indoor pool, Jacuzzi and adjacent restaurant.

Places to Eat
Most locals go to the *Lion's Den*, 725 N Montana, where enormous prime rib and steak dinners cost around $11, hot sandwiches around $6. On Montana St across from the railroad depot, *Papa T's* is a less-than-intimate bar (not so in the past when the 2nd floor was a brothel), serving Dillon's best pizza ($9 to $15), deli sandwiches ($5) and 'heart-healthy' meals ($6). The *Western-Wok*, 17 E Bannack St, lives up to its name with Western decor and Chinese food for $6 to $9.

Entertainment
Dillon's bars are all within a two-block circuit, making bar-hopping easy. On N Montana St between Bannack and Center Sts, *Moose's* has pool tables and microbrews on tap, *Papa T's* has a big dance floor and live music on weekends, and around the corner on Bannack St, the *Office* has a full bar and gets started around 5 pm. Formerly a gathering place for railroad executives and tycoons, *Hotel Metlen*, across the tracks from the railroad depot, is the rowdiest place in Dillon, with live bands and crowds in jeans and cowboy boots. The well-regarded *Wapiti Players* (☎ 406-683-6402) stage dinner-show dramas and comedies at the Elk's Club Lodge; performances begin with a 6:30 pm cocktail hour and cost $15. The *Depot Players* stage their vaudeville shows in the old railroad depot. Inquire at the chamber of commerce for details.

DILLON TO THE IDAHO BORDER
Following the Beaverhead River from its junction with the Jefferson River, the Lewis and Clark Expedition camped for several days at what they dubbed 'Camp Fortunate,' now Clark Canyon Reservoir (see below). Just as the explorers made ready to move on, they encountered a party of Shoshone (including Sacagawea's brother, whom she had not seen in five years), who were very generous. Besides equipping the

expedition with strong horses, several Shoshone guides accompanied the expedition through the high Bitterroot Range, enabling them to make better time than expected.

Clark Canyon Reservoir
This reservoir, 18 miles south of Dillon, is a popular weekend destination for boaters, jet skiers and anglers. 'Lake' fishing is best at the south end, but limited without a boat. Good river fishing, however, is easily accessed above the dam, on the north side of the road a half mile east of the *Beaverhead Marina* (☎ 406-683-5556), which sells fishing licenses, gas and a limited selection of groceries. Across from the reservoir's north end, east of I-15, the *Buffalo Lodge* serves lunch and dinner and has an excellent view of the water. RV spaces are available at the marina and barren campgrounds dot the southwest and northeast shores.

About 20 miles south of the reservoir, the once lively railroad town of Dell now owes its existence to *Yesterday's Calf-A*, a 1903 schoolhouse turned eatery. In 1973, the owner tried to buy the old school bell and ended up with the building as well. He and his family opened a restaurant there in 1978, and it's been doing well ever since. The food is good and everything from the hamburger buns to the lemon meringue pie is homemade. It's open Monday to Saturday from 7 am to 10 pm (until 9 pm October to May) and Sunday from 7 am to 8 pm.

Italian Peaks
On the other side of I-15, west of Dell, Big Sheep Creek Rd parallels the interstate then heads southwest for 19 miles to Nichola Creek Rd in the foothills of the Italian Peaks area. This high, arid region is home to mountain goats, elk and the endangered gray wolf. The **Continental Divide National Scenic Trail** stretches for 50 miles along the Montana-Idaho border here and crosses the highest point on Montana's portion of the Divide – the 11,141-foot Eighteenmile Peak. Multiple-day backpacking trips are the norm since the area is

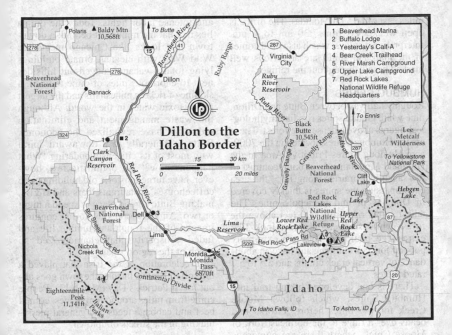

Dillon to the Idaho Border

1 Beaverhead Marina
2 Buffalo Lodge
3 Yesterday's Calf-A
4 Bear Creek Trailhead
5 River Marsh Campground
6 Upper Lake Campground
7 Red Rock Lakes
  National Wildlife Refuge
  Headquarters

so remote and a day or so is required to reach the elevations where you can see down into both states. The best access is via the Bear Creek trailhead; at Nichola Creek Rd turn west and go another 7 miles to Bear Creek Rd. The trailhead is 1½ miles farther, but can only be reached by car when the roads are in good condition. Maps are available at the Beaverhead National Forest office (☎ 406-683-3900) in Dillon.

Red Rock Lakes National Wildlife Refuge

Between I-15 and US 20 (a popular route to West Yellowstone), in the shadow of the Centennial Mountains, which create the Montana-Idaho border and over which runs the Continental Divide, lies Red Rock Lakes National Wildlife Refuge. This is an important nesting site for the rare trumpeter swan, sandhill crane, Barrow's goldeneye and great blue heron. The 50-sq-mile refuge was established in 1935 to protect the trumpeter swan, whose

population – due to the popularity of plumes in women's fashions – had fallen to just 73. Even today, only about 110 exist in the surrounding valley.

With its grasslands, marshes and lakes connected by navigable streams, the refuge is a good spot for canoeing. You can canoe Lower Red Rock Lake in the fall, and Upper Red Rock Lake and Red Rock Creek from July 15 until the first freeze. Fishing access is available on Odell, Elk Springs and Red Rock Creeks, and at the east end of the refuge, off Culver Rd, on Widgeon and Culver Ponds.

Two campgrounds, *River Marsh* on the east end of Lower Red Rock Lake, and *Upper Lake* on the south shore of Upper Red Rock Lake, are free. Both are equipped with fire grates and toilets, but tables and water are available at Upper Lake only.

A map and guide is available at the refuge headquarters (☎ 406-276-3536) in the small settlement of Lakeview, 28 miles west of Hwy 87 (at Henry's Lake) and 28

MONTANA

miles east of I-15 (at Monida). The office is open weekdays from 7:30 am to 4 pm. Interpretive displays, which also hold copies of the map and guide, are at various well marked points throughout the refuge.

HUMBUG SPIRES

Roughly halfway between Butte and Dillon, nine white granite spires rise like mythological figures above a dense pine forest. These are the Humbug Spires, located in the 7000-acre Humbug Spires Primitive Area in the Highland Mountains. In striking contrast to the sagebrush prairies along I-15, the area encompassing the spires is thickly covered in Douglas fir and lodgepole pine. The tallest spires rise up to 600 feet above the forest while smaller ones just look like extra-large boulders. They are extremely popular for rock climbing and have an abundance of vertical crack climbs and 5.5 to 5.7 rated routes.

There is one developed hiking trail into Humbug Spires, which follows Moose Creek for 1½ miles before it forks and heads over a ridge to the northeast fork of Moose Creek, where there are numerous game trails that branch off in all directions. These trails are popular for backpacking and require a map and compass to navigate. The main trail takes you another 1½ miles to an abandoned miner's cabin and a magnificent outcropping called the Wedge – this is a good day-hike destination. The trailhead parking lot is 3 miles east of I-15 at the Moose Creek interchange up an improved dirt road; there's a registration box, maps and an outhouse at the parking lot.

The best place to find out about climbs in the spires is at Pipestone Mountaineering (☎ 406-782-4994) at 829 S Montana St in Butte, or Sagebrush Outdoor Gear (☎ 406-683-2329) in Dillon.

BUTTE

In the late 1800s and early 1900s, mines around Butte (population 35,000) produced record amounts of silver and copper. Such intense mining created a dramatic existence for the locals, marked by erratic employment spurts, mining magnate rivalries

and intense labor fights. Today the drama lies in what the mines left behind: a downtown that looks like Chicago meets the Wild West with elegant, ornate buildings lying totally vacant, gouged-out hillsides next to enormous piles of mine tailings, a skyline of rickety mineshafts and the largest pit of toxic water in the world. Although the waste management and elimination industries have revitalized the economy, Butte is generally in a downward spiral with most of its citizens wondering 'What happens now?' An optimistic few, however, have turned historic old buildings into coffeehouses, restaurants, bars and B&Bs, making Butte a good place to spend a night or two. An afternoon's exploring conjures images of the rough-and-tumble life and faded prosperity that characterized so much of the region's past.

In celebration of the Irish that played a big roll in Butte's history, the town goes all-out for St Patrick's Day (March 17). People come from miles around for parades, corned beef and cabbage feeds and general merry-making in the streets of uptown.

History

Until the 1920s, Butte was the only town of any size between Minneapolis and Seattle, and it was home to some of the richest, most powerful men in the country. In 1864 GO Humphrey and William Allison arrived from Virginia City's gold camp and found placer deposits in Silverbow Creek. Ten years later, William L Farlin laid claim to several outcrops of quartz, which turned out to be rich with silver. In 1878, two years after the town incorporated, the Utah & Northern Railroad linked Butte to the Union Pacific's main line; the rush turned into a boom. By 1885, Butte had a population of 14,000.

The 1870s to the 1880s was Montana's most intense period of mining. The enormous demand for copper wire created the wealth and fame of both Marcus Daly, who struck the world's largest and purest vein of copper, and William Andrews Clark. By the turn of the century both were equally powerful figures. These two 'Copper Kings'

Greater Butte

PLACES TO STAY
7 Butte KOA
8 War Bonnet Inn
9 Day's Inn
10 Comfort Inn
12 Super 8
13 Butte Plaza Inn

PLACES TO EAT
5 Joe's Pasty Shop

OTHER
1 Montana Tech
    World Museum of Mining
2 Berkeley Pit Overlook
3 Greyhound Depot
4 Civic Center
6 Chamber of Commerce
11 Suds & Fun Laundromat

MONTANA

were both business and political rivals who changed the course and character of Montana politics for many years. (For more on the Copper Kings see the sidebar below.)

Accounts of Butte's early days are bittersweet. When smoke rose from the mine stacks, all of Butte was employed, well paid and eager to spend. When no smoke bloomed from the stacks – either due to a labor strike or panic on the market – the entire town fell into a slump. Even during such periods of inactivity, Butte's air remained so thick with rank gas and acidic smoke that plants could

only survive indoors and streetlights had to be left on during the day.

Neighbors bonded together in times of disaster or unemployment, but divisions among workers were pronounced: Irish, Welsh and Cornish miners enjoyed privileged status (Irish mine operators wrote their help wanted ads in Gaelic so only fellow Irish could apply), while Italian, German and Finnish miners, if only because they lacked strength in numbers, generally worked the night shift or held more dangerous positions. Chinese settlers, with whom the white settlers refused to work in the mines, were given the lowest paying jobs, usually cooking, doing laundry or dumping garbage.

Unlike the decline of so many other mining communities, Butte's was not due to the total depletion of its mineral resources – the copper veins could have produced ore for an estimated 200 years to come. It was more a case of big business (the mining companies) and big labor (the unions), in their efforts to do each other in, unwittingly contributing to their own demise. The drastic drop in copper prices during the Great Depression didn't exactly help the situation.

In 1980, Atlantic-Richfield bought the Anaconda Company, which at one time practically ran the state and was known in Butte simply as 'The Company.' Two years later, the last pump shut down – the first time in a century that Butte's mines were totally silent. Citizens seriously questioned Butte's chances of survival, but chain-owned businesses, notably restaurants and automotive stores, revitalized the economy. Nonetheless, Butte, once Montana's largest city, currently ranks fifth and is slipping.

Orientation

I-90 and I-15 run through Butte together, cutting the city into 'uptown' (on the hill to the north), and 'the flats' (along Harrison Ave south of I-90/I-15). Uptown, where the mining took place, remains the heart of Butte where the historic district and most tourist sights are. Granite, Broadway and Park Sts are the main east-west thoroughfares; Excelsior Ave, Montana St, Main St and Utah Ave run north-south, connecting uptown to the flats. The flats is essentially post-1960s Butte, consisting of motels, fast-food chains and the Butte Plaza Mall.

Information

You can get good maps and regional information from Butte's tourist information center and chamber of commerce (☎ 406-723-3177, 800-735-6814), at 1000 George St, north of I-15/I-90. The Old No 1 Trolley Tour covers all of Butte's major sights in 1½ hours for $4. Tours leave from the chamber of commerce at 10:30 am, 1:10, 3:30 and 7 pm between Memorial Day and Labor

The Copper Kings

Full of corrupt politics, scandalous characters and multi-million-dollar mud-slinging battles, the 'Copper King' era is one of Montana's most colorful periods. At the center of the controversy, echoes of which linger to this day, were two remarkable men: Marcus Daly and WA Clark.

Daly came to Butte in 1876. At age 15, he had left Ireland to escape the potato famine and landed in New York with 'nothing in his pocket save his…Irish smile.' He found his way west to San Francisco where he heard about people making fortunes in mining. Working the Comstock Lode in Nevada, Daly emerged as a shrewd judge of silver properties and it was in this capacity that he came to Butte on behalf of some Salt Lake City bankers. Daly soon deserted his bank connections and sank a shaft of his own on a claim previously considered valueless. The bankers laughed at him when he began to strike copper instead of silver, and Daly himself was disappointed, but the last laugh was his. A copper revolution occurred in the 1880s as electric lighting systems and motors became commercially available products. Suddenly, Daly found himself sitting on an enormous fortune. Butte emerged as the world's copper capital, and Marcus Daly owned it.

William A Clark came to Bannack eager to make his fortune in gold. Originally from Pennsylvania, he was a well-educated man who arrived in Montana's wilderness with three books: one on geology, one on law and *Poems by Burns* for 'recreational' reading. To start, he acquired working capital by transporting mail from Missoula to Walla Walla, Washington. In 1872 he began buying mining properties in Butte, and by 1900, Clark was, among other things, a stockholder in the Butte Electric Light Company, president of the

MONTANA

Day; arrive 15 minutes early to ensure getting a space on the trolley.

ATMs are downtown along Harrison Ave at Montana Bank, First Citizens Bank and inside Albertson's supermarket. There is also an ATM uptown at the First Bank of Butte, on the corner of Park and Main Sts. The post office is at 49 W Park St.

Books & Books (☎ 406-782-9520), 206 W Park St, has a wide variety of books about Butte plus a good selection of national newspapers. For rare Western Americana titles, try Second Edition Used Books (☎ 406-723-5108) at 129 W Broadway.

St James Community Hospital (☎ 406-782-8361), 400 S Clark St, has a 24-hour emergency room.

Next to the Town Pump gas station at the corner of Dewey Blvd and Harrison Ave, Suds & Fun Laundromat (☎ 406-494-7004) is open 24 hours and has a TV and study area.

Butte's Historic District
Uptown Butte is one of the USA's largest historic districts. Concentrated along Park, Broadway and Granite Sts, the city's old buildings – massive works of brick, stone, tile and glass – clearly recall Butte's opulent era. Detailed self-guided tour maps are available at the chamber of commerce and at the Arts Chateau.

Arts Chateau Built in 1898 to resemble a French chateau, the Arts Chateau (☎ 406-723-7600), 321 Broadway, serves as a heritage museum and arts center – the only publicly owned facility of its kind in Montana. Art galleries with rotating exhibits are on the 1st floor, while the upper two floors house period furniture and clothing. On Wednesdays, marionette shows are performed in the 3rd-floor ballroom. The chateau is open 11 am to 4 pm Tuesday to Saturday, with extended hours in summer. Admission is $5.

Copper King Mansion In what must surely disgust Marcus Daly's ghost, William Andrew Clark's former residence is billed as the Copper King Mansion (☎ 406-782-7580), 219 W Granite St. Built in

Colorado Smelting and Mining Company, president of the Rocky Mountain Telephone Company and owner of the Butte *Miner*.

Clark had always dreamed of a political career and, at a time when politics and business went hand in glove, believed that his industrial clout would gain him a seat in the US Congress. In 1888, he won the Democratic nomination and confidently made ready to go to Washington, DC only to discover, to his utter disbelief, that he had been defeated by a young, unknown Republican. Upon investigation, Clark learned that his opponent was supported by Daly and that Daly had somehow persuaded Anaconda and Butte (Democratic strongholds) to go Republican. Clark took Daly to court, claiming that votes had been sold.

Over the next 12 years, a bizarre and treacherous battle ensued. The bitter personal enmity between the two men was played out on the grandest scale, permeating all political activity and dividing society. Both men owned newspapers, each of which dutifully spread the message of its owner, and both men were quite prepared to use the enormous leverage they enjoyed as employers for political ends.

Their next big engagement was sparked by the issue of which city would become the capital when Montana gained statehood. 'Capital fights' were common in the West, but few were marked by the rancor or expense of Montana's. Clark won that round of the battle (he backed Helena against Daly's choice of Anaconda), but what he really wanted was to get to the Senate, and Daly wanted just as badly to keep him from getting there. When Clark finally did get elected senator in 1900, he was quickly forced to resign as a result of bribery charges leveled by Daly from what turned out to be his deathbed in New York. ■

MONTANA

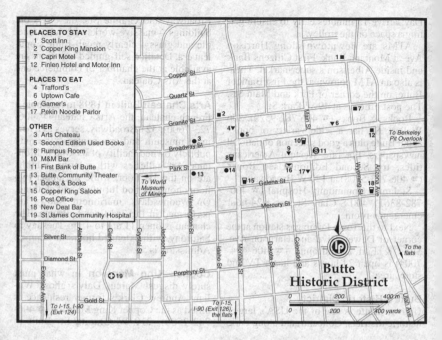

PLACES TO STAY
1 Scott Inn
2 Copper King Mansion
7 Capri Motel
12 Finlen Hotel and Motor Inn

PLACES TO EAT
4 Trafford's
6 Uptown Cafe
9 Gamer's
17 Pekin Noodle Parlor

OTHER
3 Arts Chateau
5 Second Edition Used Books
8 Rumpus Room
10 M&M Bar
11 First Bank of Butte
13 Butte Community Theater
14 Books & Books
15 Copper King Saloon
16 Post Office
18 New Deal Bar
19 St James Community Hospital

Butte
Historic District

MONTANA

1888, the 35-room estate boasts priceless crystal and Wedgwood china collections, Asian and Egyptian rugs and colorful comb-textured walls. Although restored in somewhat garish fashion by the owner (who operates it as a B&B, see below), the mansion's elegance still shines. One-hour tours depart between 9 am to 5 pm daily from May to September, only on weekends in April and October; it's closed the rest of the year.

Berkeley Pit
Once the largest truck-operated, open-pit copper mine in the USA, the Berkeley Pit, north of I-15/I-90 off Continental Drive, is now the country's deepest and most toxic body of water. From 1955 to 1980, the mine yielded 290 million tons of copper ore, but when the pumps shut down in 1980, water from the old mining shafts in the surrounding mountains collected in the pit to form an 800-foot-deep pool, now a high-priority Superfund toxic clean-up site.

On the east side of Continental Drive is a gift shop and, through a short tunnel next to the store, a viewing platform.

Mineral Museum
In the Main Hall of the Montana College of Mineral Science and Technology (Montana Tech), the Mineral Museum (☎ 406-496-4414) houses an outstanding collection of rare gems and minerals. Adjacent to the museum's main room is a working seismology center staffed by Montana Tech students. Visitors are welcome from 9 am to 6 pm daily from June to September, and from 9 am to 4 pm daily the rest of the year, plus 1 pm to 5 pm on weekends in May, September and October. Admission is free.

World Museum of Mining
Opened in 1965 on the site of the Orphan Girl, an inactive silver and zinc mine, this museum (☎ 406-723-7211), located behind the Montana Tech campus at the western end of Park St, is worth at least an hour of

exploration. Indoor and outdoor exhibits chronicle every aspect of Butte's mining culture, and there's a replica of an 1899 Butte mining camp – Hell Roarin' Gulch. It is open from 9 am to 9 pm daily between Memorial Day and Labor Day, from 10 am to 5 pm Tuesday to Sunday in October, November and April. Admission is $3.

Our Lady of the Rockies

High on a hill, 17 miles east of Butte, stands the 90-foot-tall steel statue of Our Lady of the Rockies – the second tallest statue in the USA (the Statue of Liberty is the first). The statue was built by a man who prayed (with apparent success) to the Virgin Mary for his wife's recovery from an operation. Construction coincided with a major layoff in the mines, so dispirited out-of-work miners put their energy into the project and increased the statue's original height from 5 to 90 feet. To the dismay of many, however, the city pays thousands of dollars to illuminate the statue at night. You can see the statue from just about anywhere in town but to go there you must join the tour (☎ 406-782-1221), which leaves from the Butte Plaza Mall at 3100 Harrison Ave, takes three hours and costs $10.

Places to Stay

Camping The *Butte KOA* (☎ 406-782-0663), one block north and one block east of I-90 exit 126, charges $16/22 for tent/RV sites. Facilities include a playground, swimming pool, store and deli and laundry room.

B&Bs It's worth paying a little extra to stay in one of Butte's B&Bs, both uptown within walking distance of most sights. The *Copper King Mansion* (☎ 406-782-7580), in William A Clark's former mansion at 219 W Granite St near Idaho St, has five richly decorated rooms for $55 to $95. The *Scott Inn* (☎ 406-723-7030), 15 W Copper, has a friendly owner from California who adores Butte's history. Modern rooms in the historical old house are $65 to $85.

Motels Good options uptown include the budget *Capri Motel* (☎ 406-723-4391), at 220 N Wyoming St, with single/double rooms for $28/32 and the *Finlen Hotel and Motor Inn* (☎ 406-723-5461), 100 E Broadway at Arizona Ave, whose rooms cost $50/55.

Chain accommodations, where the going rate for a standard room is around $55, are near the I-90/I-15 on Harrison Ave. These include *Days Inn* (☎ 406-494-7000), *Super 8* (☎ 406-494-6000, 800-800-8000) and *Comfort Inn* (☎ 406-494-8850). For $20 more you get a swimming pool, fitness center and Continental breakfast at Best Western's *Butte Plaza Inn* (☎ 406-494-3500, 800-543-5814), the *Copper King Inn* (☎ 406-494-6666, 800-332-8600) and *War Bonnet Inn* (☎ 406-494-7800, 800-443-1806).

Places to Eat

Butte's culinary specialty is the pasty, a compact yet hearty pie native to Cornwall, England, that resembles a turnover or calzone and is filled with meat, onions and potatoes or turnips. Arguments about who makes the best pasty are not to be taken lightly; some good choices are *Gamer's*, 15 W Park St (see below), *Joe's Pasty Shop*, 1641 Grande Ave near the Civic Center, and the *Trafford's*, 7 S Montana St.

At one time, Butte's restaurants were worth a detour in themselves. The onslaught of chain-owned fast-food joints put an end to that in the 1980s. There are still, however, a few 'institutions' left. Dingy in an old-style charming sort of way, *Gamer's* is where locals meet for breakfast and lunch. You serve your own coffee and make your own change. Nearly a century old, the *Pekin Noodle Parlor*, on Main St between Park and Galena Sts, has greasy Chinese food, individual 'dining cabins' and Pepto-Bismol pink walls – in other words, it's a must! Its hours are 5 pm to midnight, to 3 am Friday and Saturday.

For fancier fare head to the *Uptown Cafe* (☎ 406-723-4735), 47 E Broadway, whose four-course menu changes daily and features seasonal specialties. Dinner costs around $15, lunch around $8.

MONTANA

Entertainment

Butte's bars deserve museum status. Though lacking the crowded, vigorous atmosphere of yore, they still have a gritty and authentic feel. Highlights are the *M&M Bar* at 9 N Main St, the *New Deal Bar* at 333 S Arizona St, the *Rumpus Room* at 71 E Park St and the *Copper King Saloon* at 1000 S Montana St.

Founded in 1976, the *Butte Community Theater* stages light comedies and musicals for three consecutive weekends in October at various venues. Call ☎ 406-782-9523 for more information. Under the direction of Leopold Medina, the accomplished *Butte Symphony Orchestra* (☎ 406-723-5590) performs a full schedule, featuring regional artists from October to April. Tickets are available at the door for $8.

Getting There & Away

Butte sits just west of the Continental Divide at the foot of the Rocky Mountains, and astride I-90 and I-15. It's 65 miles from Helena, 82 miles from Bozeman, 64 miles from Dillon and 120 miles from Missoula. Butte is a good place to fill up, as it generally has the cheapest gas prices in Montana.

Greyhound and Intermountain Bus lines have daily service to Dillon ($11 one-way), Missoula ($21 one-way), Helena ($11 one-way), Bozeman ($14 one-way) and Billings ($31 one-way). Both use Butte's Greyhound depot (☎ 406-723-3287) at 101 E Front St.

Getting Around

City Taxi (☎ 406-723-6511), 3 S Main St, is Butte's one and only taxi service.

BUTTE TO MISSOULA

The 120-mile stretch between Butte and Missoula encompasses the rugged Flint Creek Range and is extremely scenic, whether you take I-90 or the Pintler Scenic Hwy. Anaconda, whose history is significantly intertwined with Butte's, is accessible via both routes. Those with excess time in Butte or Missoula or with a passion for picturesque roads might consider driving the loop as a day trip.

Anaconda

Marcus Daly's original company town, Anaconda (population 10,300) was named after the serpent that allegedly strangles any competition that gets in its way. This metaphor was right on target in the late 1880s when the Anaconda Company was the world's largest producer of copper. This town's abundant water and timber and its proximity to Butte made an ideal location for Marcus Daly to build his own smelter, eliminating the need to send the copper to Wales.

The first plant was built in 1883 1 mile west of Anaconda, but by 1887 the mine's output had so increased that more facilities were needed. Construction of the present plant began in 1902, and 17 years and 2,466,392 bricks later, the stack blew its first puff of smoke. Decreasing demand and increasing foreign competition in recent decades led to a slow death, and in 1980 the parent company, Atlantic-Richfield, shut down the operation.

Driving by on Hwy 1 or I-90 to ogle the giant smelter without actually stopping in Anaconda is not a bad call, though golfers may want to check out the 18-hole Old Works Golf Course designed by Jack Nicklaus (☎ 406-563-5989) that's built on the old smelter works site just south of town. Besides being a decent course, it is the only one in the world where black mine tailings are used for sandtraps.

Orientation & Information Hwy 1 runs west through Anaconda as Park St, the main thoroughfare. Commercial St parallels Park St, and Main St crosses the two of them midway through town. Anaconda's visitors center (☎ 406-563-2400) is housed in the old railroad depot on Cherry St, between Park and Commercial Sts. It's open 8 am to 6 pm weekdays, and 9 am to 5 pm weekends. The main post office is at 218 Main St. Both Bank of Montana and Norwest Bank, on Park St, have ATMs.

Butte to Missoula

1 Grant-Kohrs Ranch
2 Deer Lodge National
   Forest Ranger Station
3 Jericho Bay Campground
4 Piney Point Campground
5 Sandy Beach Campground
6 Denton's Point
7 Georgetown Lake Lodge
8 Racetrack Campground
9 Indian Creek Campground

MONTANA

Things to See & Do The bus tour that leaves from the visitors center at 10 am and 2 pm from Monday to Saturday is well worth the $3 price and may be all the sightseeing one needs. If time and interest permit, several sights deserve further exploration.

Housed in Anaconda's 1894 city hall at the corner of Commercial and Cedar Sts, the Copper Village Arts Center has several good gift shops and a contemporary gallery space, open from 10 am to 5 pm Tuesday to Saturday. The Hearst Free Library, 401 Main St, was a gift to Anaconda in 1898 from Phoebe Apperson Hearst. Anyone curious about Art Deco architecture need go no farther than the Washoe Theater, 305 Main St, whose pounded metal decorations are, amazingly enough, not made from copper. Musical and alternative films are shown here nightly. Sitting at the south end of Main St, Anaconda's crowning architectural achievement is the Deer Lodge County Courthouse, built in 1898.

Mount Haggin sits at 10,665 feet, just south of town. Though not a destination wilderness area, it does offer a day's worth of mountain biking or cross-country skiing. Sven's, on the corner of 3rd and Hickory, has maps, current trail information and rental equipment.

Places to Stay Anaconda's motels are a good value. Downtown, the *Marcus Daly Motel* (☎ 406-563-3411, 800-535-6528 in Montana), 119 W Park St, charges $40/48 for single/double rooms. The *Trade Wind Motel* (☎ 406-563-3428, 800-248-3428), 1600 E Commercial St, charges $30/37. For local color and potential Saturday night entertainment, try the $25 rooms at *Copper Town Inn* (☎ 406-563-2372), above the Copper Town Bar at 23 Main St. The *Vagabond Lodge Motel* (☎ 406-563-5251, 800-231-2660), at the east end of town at 1421 E Park St, has a quiet location and nice rooms for $35/44.

Pintler Scenic Hwy
Much of the Pintler Scenic Hwy (Hwy 1) travels along Flint Creek, where Indians once collected flint to make tools and weapons. Today the route acts as primary access to **Georgetown Lake**, a popular weekend destination for area residents who come to snowmobile in the winter and fish for kokanee salmon and trophy-sized bull trout the rest of the year. The main turnoff is at Denton's Point Rd, where *Georgetown Lake Lodge* (☎ 406-563-7020), a woodsy log-cabin lodge with a large deck overlooks the lake. It has a restaurant and lounge, store, laundry room and very nice rooms for $62 between Memorial Day and Labor Day, $35 the rest of the year. The adjacent campground (☎ 406-563-6030), owned by the same family, charges $9/16 for tent/RV sites. Campgrounds on the lake's west side are more remote and tend to have more

shade; recommended are the *Piney Point*, *Sandy Beach* and *Jericho Bay* campgrounds, all of which have toilets, potable water and a boat launch, and cost around $4 per night. On the south side of the lake is a trailhead that leads into the **Anaconda-Pintler Wilderness**, which spans south over 248 sq miles including 30 miles of the Continental Divide.

North of the lake are some terrific old mining towns. In the last five years **Philipsburg** has transformed into a bang-up tourist town with fresh coats of paint on the old buildings, a place to mine sapphires and even an espresso bar! As such, it loses much of its authenticity but its museum (☎ 406-859-3020) at 155 S Sansome – with a small but excellent collection of artifacts and photographs from the National Ghost Town Hall of Fame – is worth visiting (it's free).

Truer to its original form, **Granite** is 4 miles southeast of Philipsburg up a steep and winding dirt road. Known as the 'Silver Queen,' Granite's mines produced $45 million worth of silver over an 11-year period. At its peak, Granite had a grand hotel, 18 saloons, several fraternal organizations and an aerial tramway that transported raw ore from the mines to the stamp mills where the rock was broken down and the silver was separated. Most of the town burned down over the years, but there are still plenty of old structures left to see. Surrounding land is privately owned (rumor has it that mining will resume here one day) but visitors are welcome to poke around; a box of information sheets is at the site.

Deer Lodge Valley
A bit faster than the Pintler Scenic Hwy, I-90 follows the Clark Fork River through the Deer Lodge Valley with the Continental Divide rising in the east, the Flint Creek Range capped by Montana's own Pike's Peak (9335 feet) in the west. This area, once called 'Oregon country' in reference to the destination of many of its passers-through, was a major thoroughfare for Indians, trappers and traders traveling the Clark Fork River. Its abundant water and

Salmon-fishing is one of the attractions of Montana's lakes and rivers.

vegetation offered welcome relief from the dusty prairies, so much so that many who came with intentions of continuing west ended up staying.

Grant-Kohrs Ranch Montana's foremost cattle ranch from the 1860s to the early 1900s is now preserved as a National Historic Site (☎ 406-846-3388). John Grant, seeing that the valley was a natural stopping point for people coming over the Continental Divide and noticing the emaciated state of cattle on the trail, came up with a scheme in which he would trade one of his fat, healthy cows fed on rich Montana grass for two of these bony, sickly cows, which the Grants would then fatten up and either keep or trade again for better quality stock. The Grants amassed an enormous cattle holding and in 1862, just in time to capitalize on traffic bound for Bannack, built a base ranch in the Deer Lodge Valley. German-born Conrad Kohrs, among the disillusioned gold-seekers who left Bannack, ended up buying Grant's ranch and expanded it to become one of the country's largest ranches. At its peak the ranch extended into four states and encompassed over a million acres. You can visit the working stables, ranch-hands barracks, carriage house, barn and 23-room house, in which the Kohrs lived, daily from 9 am to 5:30 pm between June 1 and Labor Day (until 4:30 pm the rest of the year) for $2.

Deer Lodge As the nearest town to the Grant-Kohrs Ranch, Deer Lodge (population 3782) experienced substantial growth with the arrival of the Northern Pacific Railroad in 1883 and the Milwaukee Railroad in 1905. Named after a salt lick Native Americans called 'Lodge of the White Tail Deer,' the town has remained primarily a center for surrounding agricultural communities and the site of several state correctional facilities and sanitariums. Established in 1871 and active until 1979, the Montana Territorial Prison is now the **Old Montana Prison Complex** (☎ 406-846-3111), home to interesting historical exhibits and the Towne Ford Museum's collection of antique cars, open 8 am to

9 pm daily. Admission to the complex, which includes the car museum, the prison itself, a 'Frontier Montana' history exhibit and antique doll collection, is $8. Convicts quarried stone and built the complex which contains cellblocks, a recreation area, theater and a maximum security ward. To alleviate overcrowding, the prison allowed inmates to live on ranches, farms and government job sites. Convicts contributed substantially to Deer Lodge's labor pool during the World Wars and played a major role in New Deal-era projects.

The *Old Prison Players* stage off-Broadway musicals in the old prison recreation center. Performances, amateur but still entertaining, run Wednesday to Saturday nights at 8 pm and cost $6. Tickets and schedules are available inside the Old Montana Prison Complex.

Places to Stay The best campgrounds and lodging in the area are in or near Deer Lodge. The no-fee USFS *Racetrack Campground*, 11 miles southwest of town on I-90, then 8 miles west on Racetrack Rd (USFS Rd 169), has 13 spaces, potable water and pit toilets. A fun option for those who plan ahead is the Deer Lodge Ranger District's rental cabin at Darby Lake in the Flint Creek Range, which sleeps six people and costs $21 per night; information is available at the Deerlodge National Forest Ranger Station (☎ 406-846-1770) at 91 N Frontage Rd, near the Grant-Kohrs Ranch.

The *Deer Lodge KOA* (☎ 406-846-1629), north of town at 413 Park St, charges $16/24 for tent/RV sites and has a swimming pool and playground. In the town itself are the *Western Big Sky Inn* (☎ 406-846-2590), 210 Main St, which charges $36/42 for single/ double rooms, and *Scharf's Motor Inn* (☎ 406-846-2810), 819 Main St, which charges $36/44 for a view of the old prison. One block off Main St the *Downtowner Motel* (☎ 406-846-1021), 500 4th St, has quiet rooms for $33/42. There is a *Super 8* (☎ 406-846-2370, 800-800-8000) right off I-90 at 1150 Main St, with a pool and rooms for $38/45.

The Flint Creek Range has good, though not stellar, hiking trails; much of the land in the valley is still privately owned, so access is extremely limited. Good starting points are the USFS Racetrack Campground and Indian Creek Campground.

HELENA

A prosperous yet small-scale city, Helena (population 27,982) offers more things to do than any other urban center in Montana. As the state capital it enjoys a stable economy and hustle and bustle pace set by well-dressed businessfolk and politicians, sort of a novelty for Montana. Its sights are free, and between them are galleries, nice stores, elegant homes and late 19th-century buildings that now house unlikely businesses like Chinese acupuncture and holistic healing centers. There are also several good day trips that take you out into the surrounding mountain and lake country, scattered with old mining camps and 'Lewis and Clark Were Here' markers.

History

In 1863 John Cowan, DJ Miller, Reginald Stanley and John Crab (subsequently known as the Four Georgians) left the goldfields of Virginia City to explore a new strike on Kootenai Creek. After they met discouraged miners coming from that direction and decided to turn back towards the Marias, they found a small amount of gold at Prickly Pear Creek. They continued on to the Marias but, not finding enough 'color' to sustain them through winter, decided to return to Georgia. Crossing again over Prickly Pear Creek, one of the four joked 'OK boys, this is the last chance,' and thrust his pan into the creek. Enough gold came up that soon the word was out that Last Chance Gulch was paying off. Just as the placer gold was petering out and Helena appeared fated to become another boom and bust town, rich quartz lodes (which require long-range programs, skilled workers and heavy investment for extraction) were discovered.

When Montana became a state in 1889, the two favorite capital city candidates were Anaconda, owned by Marcus Daly, and Helena, backed by Daly's rival WA Clark. The battle between cities became a fight for political supremacy between the two men. Helena won by a slim majority, but a new twist to the story surfaced in 1989, when the house where the votes were counted was gutted for renovation. Adjacent to the ballot-counting room, a secret room was discovered, along with documents thought to be phony tally sheets giving Helena twice the amount of votes actually cast for the town. All is speculation, but Anaconda's citizens like to claim that the capital should have been theirs.

Orientation

Helena, surrounded by the Helena National Forest, is shadowed by the Continental Divide to the west and the Big Belt Mountains to the east. US 12, which jogs through town as Euclid, Lyndale, Montana and Eleventh Aves, goes west to I-90 and Missoula, and south (with US 287) to Townsend, where it turns east and crosses the rest of the state. I-15 skirts the east side of town, intersected by US 12.

The two main exits off of I-15 are (southbound) Cedar St which turns into N Main St then into Last Chance Gulch, and (northbound) Eleventh Ave which branches west at the intersection of I-15 and US 12, heads a few blocks north of the capitol complex and continues to Last Chance Gulch. There is absolutely no grid, so be armed with a map.

Information

The chamber of commerce (☎ 406-442-4120, 800-743-5362) is downtown at 225 Cruse Ave, open 9 am to 5 pm weekdays. In summer, head to the Visitor's Center (☎ 406-447-1540), 2003 Cedar St, 1 mile north of downtown, just east of I-15, open 9 am to 7 pm daily.

The Helena National Forest Office (☎ 406-449-5201), across from the Helena Regional Airport at 2880 Skyway Drive, has topographical maps and recreation information, while the Montana Fish, Wildlife & Parks department (☎ 406-444-2535),

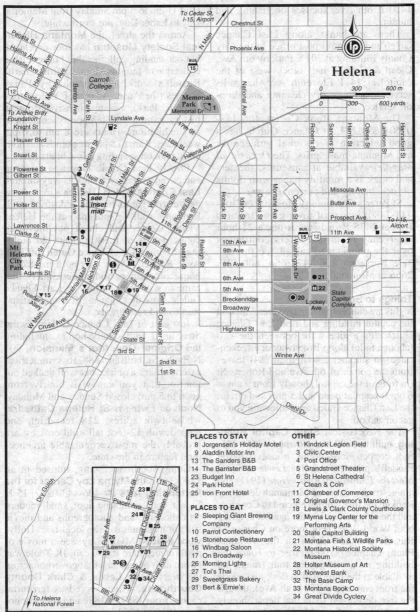

Helena

0   300   600 m
0   300   600 yards

PLACES TO STAY
8   Jorgensen's Holiday Motel
9   Aladdin Motor Inn
13 The Sanders B&B
14 The Barrister B&B
23 Budget Inn
24 Park Hotel
25 Iron Front Hotel

PLACES TO EAT
2   Sleeping Giant Brewing Company
10 Parrot Confectionery
15 Stonehouse Restaurant
16 Windbag Saloon
17 On Broadway
26 Morning Lights
27 Toi's Thai
29 Sweetgrass Bakery
31 Bert & Ernie's

OTHER
1   Kindrick Legion Field
3   Civic Center
4   Post Office
5   Grandstreet Theater
6   St Helena Cathedral
7   Clean & Coin
11 Chamber of Commerce
12 Original Governor's Mansion
18 Lewis & Clark County Courthouse
19 Myrna Loy Center for the Performing Arts
20 State Capitol Building
21 Montana Fish & Wildlife Parks
22 Montana Historical Society Museum
28 Holter Museum of Art
30 Norwest Bank
32 The Base Camp
33 Montana Book Co
34 Great Divide Cyclery

MONTANA

1420 E 6th Ave, focuses on fishing and hunting.

There are banks along Last Chance Gulch and a central post office in the City County Building at 301 S Park by 6th Ave. Clean & Coin, a half block west of the capitol at 1411 Eleventh Ave, has self-service machines, dry cleaning and drop-off service.

The Montana Book Co (☎ 406-443-0260), 331 N Last Chance Gulch, has a good selection of regional guidebooks and Montana-made gifts. The *Occasional Magpie*, available at museums, theaters and cafes, is a monthly paper with tidbits of local history and current events.

St Peter's Community Hospital (☎ 406-444-2480) is east of town going towards I-15 at 2475 Broadway. It has a 24-hour emergency room and offers continuous over-the-phone medical advice through Tele Nurse (☎ 406-447-2666, 800-557-2666 in Montana).

Things to See

Sights are concentrated in two areas: around the capitol building and near Last Chance Gulch. It's a nice walk between the two (about a mile) along Broadway or Brecken-ridge. In summer a tour train ($4) leaves from the corner of 6th Ave and Roberts St (in front of the capitol) hourly from 9 am to 6 pm (except at noon and 5 pm) and circles the Last Chance Gulch area, allowing you to get on and off.

The Neoclassical **State Capitol Building**, built in 1899 and crowned with a 165-foot copper-faced dome, houses Charlie Russell's priceless painting *Lewis & Clark Meet the Flathead at Ross's Hole* (1911) and a noteworthy statue of Montanan Jeannette Rankin, the first woman elected to Congress and the only person to vote against entering both World Wars. (For more on Charles M Russell see the sidebar in the Montana Plains chapter.) You're free to roam the building on a self-guided tour (maps are available at the information desk just inside the front entrance at 1301 6th Ave), though the free docent-led tours that depart hourly from 10 am to 4 pm Monday to Saturday

(and 11 am to 3 pm Sunday from Memorial Day to Labor Day) are worthwhile.

Across the street, the **Montana Historical Society Museum** has four unrelated, but outstanding galleries that house a large collection of famous Montana artist Charlie Russell's work, photographs by F Jay Haynes (the Ansel Adams of Yellowstone National Park), a comprehensive Montana history exhibit and temporary contemporary exhibitions. Hours are 8 am to 6 pm weekdays, 9 am to 5 pm weekends and holidays; plan on spending a few hours here.

Prickly Pear Creek, long ago dried up and paved over, now winds its way through **Last Chance Gulch** (Helena's main business district) as an historic pedestrian mall. Pick up a walking tour map at the Helena Visitor Center and check out the often comic details of these elegant old buildings. South of Last Chance Gulch (off Park Ave), Reeder's Alley was built in 1870 to house old miners and muleskinners that came to seek their fortune in Last Chance Gulch. Now they house gift shops, artists' studios and restaurants.

Just east of Last Chance Gulch, Ewing St is lined with stately homes, including the **Original Governor's Mansion**, 304 N Ewing St, built in 1888. Its symmetrical exterior hides a quirky but well decked out interior that you can visit hourly from noon to 5 pm; closed Sunday and Monday. North on Ewing is **St Helena Cathedral** whose twin spires, 218 feet high and topped with 12-foot-tall gold crosses, are probably the most recognizable architectural feature in the state.

Going south on Ewing, housed in an 1890s jail is the **Myrna Loy Center for the Performing Arts** (☎ 406-443-0287),15 N Ewing. It has a mosaic floor, small modern art collection, and photographs and movie stills of its namesake, the local-born Hollywood actress, Myrna Loy; see a movie or performance here if you can. JK Toole was sworn in as Montana's first governor across the street in the **Lewis & Clark County Courthouse**, which served as territorial capitol from 1887 to 1888 and state capitol from 1889 to 1902.

The **Holter Museum of Art**, 12 E Lawrence St, displays changing exhibits of contemporary painting, photography, ceramics, sculpture and weaving and has an interesting gift shop. Hours are 11:30 am to 5:30 pm Tuesday to Friday, noon to 5 pm weekends.

One of the foremost schools of pottery in USA, the **Archie Bray Foundation** (☎ 406-443-3502), 4 miles west of downtown at 2915 Country Club Ave (take Euclid to Joslyn and turn right), is a magical place where pottery is scattered irreverently across the landscape, and artists in residence are busy sculpting, throwing and firing their latest works. A self-guided tour (available from the small visitor center) leads you around the old brickworks grounds (once owned by Bray's father) past site-specific sculptures and beehive-like kilns. Hours are 10 am to 5 pm Monday to Saturday.

Activities

The Base Camp (☎ 406-443-5360), 333 N Last Chance Gulch, rents tents, backpacks, skis, canoes and kayaks, has topo maps and a helpful, knowledgeable staff.

Mount Helena City Park has six **hiking** and **mountain biking** trails that wind around the base and to the summit of 5460-foot-high Mount Helena, an epic spot from which to take in views of the town and the Big Belt Mountains (ask someone to point out the 'Sleeping Giant' mountain). The trails begin at the Adams St parking lot, four blocks west of Benton Ave. A large, detailed map gives a description of each trail. From the southwest side of the park, the Mount Helena Ridge National Recreation Trail gives access to hundreds of miles of trails in the Helena National Forest, including the 7-mile ramble to Park City, an abandoned mining town; pick up a map ($4) at The Base Camp for this terrain. The Great Divide Cyclery (☎ 406-443-5188), 336 N Jackson St, rents mountain bikes for $10 a day and is a good source for local trail tips.

The best trout **fishing** near Helena is at Holter, Hauser and Canyon Ferry Lakes (see Around Helena later in this section). Trophy-sized brown trout, weighing in at over 15 pounds, make regular appearances in the Missouri River below Hauser Dam. In the fall, anglers come to fish for kokanee salmon. The best access sites are along Prickly Pear and Wolf Creeks, 20 to 35 miles north of Helena west of I-15.

The Great Divide Ski Area (☎ 406-449-3746), 20 miles northwest of Helena in Marysville (see Around Helena later in this section), has decent downhill **skiing** with 55 runs (roughly half of them expert) on 70 acres. Lifts operate daily (except Tuesday) and Thursday to Saturday nights. The Continental Divide National Scenic Trail at MacDonald Pass, 20 miles west of Helena on US 12, is a good cross-country spot as is Stemple Pass, 30 miles northwest of Helena on Hwy 279.

Special Events

The **Montana Traditional Jazz Festival**, held the last week of June, draws praise even from hardcore jazz aficionados. Dixieland and Big Band artists come from all over the northwest and daytime performances are free (tickets to evening shows cost $10 to $15). In February, the longest **dogsled race** in the lower 48 states begins downtown and continues for 500 grueling miles.

Pop and Big Band groups play outdoor summer concerts on Thursday evenings in Memorial Park, north of Lyndale Ave where Last Chance Gulch becomes N Main St; the music usually starts at 8 pm.

Places to Stay

Camping Helena has two campgrounds, neither of which inspires wilderness dreams. The *Branding Iron Campground & RV Park* (☎ 406-443-5998), 1803 Cedar St, just west of I-15 exit 193, has a lounge with a full bar and video poker machines; its tent/RV sites cost $12/21. Better suited for families, the *Helena KOA* (☎ 406-458-5110), 3 miles north of downtown on Montana Ave, has a swimming pool, hot tub, playground, volleyball and basketball courts and a general store;

tent/RV sites go for $16/22. Campers who don't mind a little extra driving can head to one of the nearby lakes for more serene settings (see Around Helena later in this chapter).

B&Bs Helena's B&Bs are well worth the splurge. If you stay in one B&B in Montana, try *The Sanders* (☎ 406-442-3309), at 328 N Ewing and 7th Ave. The house was built in 1875, and has elegant decor, friendly staff and excellent food; rooms are $65 to $105. One block north at 416 N Ewing, across from the cathedral, *The Barrister* (☎ 406-443-7330) is an 1874 Victorian originally built as priests' quarters. Rooms cost $85 to $115; children under 10 are not allowed.

Motels Prices go up and rooms fill quickly on weekdays at these places. On the east edge of town near the I-15/US 12 interchange is a concentration of chain motels, each with discount packages, Continental breakfast, pool, Jacuzzi and fitness center; rooms are $60 to $75. The best are the *Shilo Inn* (☎ 406-442-0320, 800-222-2244), *Best Western Colonial Inn* (☎ 406-443-2100), and *Holiday Inn Express* (☎ 406-449-4000). A bit cheaper (but with similar facilities) are the family owned *Aladdin Inn* (☎ with politicians, *Jorgensen's Holiday Motel* (☎ 406-442-1770, 800-272-1770), 1714 Eleventh Ave, both with $55 to $65 rooms. The conveniently located, *Budget Inn* (☎ 406-442-0600), 524 N Last Chance Gulch, has $45 to $50 rooms.

Hotels Rooms in the 100-year-old *Park Hotel* (☎ 406-442-0960), 432 N Last Chance Gulch, are a bit run down but considering the great location (the infamous Unabomber Ted Kaczynski must have liked it – he stayed here over 20 times), are a bargain for $20/24 single/double; use the bathroom down the hall and pay $4 less. Across the street in a similar building, the *Iron Front Hotel* (☎ 406-443-2400), 415 N Last Chance Gulch, has two rooms that rent nightly (the rest rent weekly or monthly) for $21 without bath. And then there's the always reliable if predictable *Motel 6* (☎ 406-442-9990), 800 N Oregon St, two blocks south of the I-15 Eleventh Ave exit, with a small indoor pool and single/double rooms for $31/42.

Places to Eat

Helena has a wide selection of restaurants, from fast-food chains along Eleventh Ave to more elaborate dining downtown. Many restaurants cater to the working crowd and offer good lunches for under $10. Supermarkets are along Eleventh Ave, east of downtown.

Making chocolates and ice cream since 1935, the *Parrot Confectioners*, 42 Last Chance Gulch, still has its original green booths and chrome stools along its soda fountain. The *Sweetgrass Bakery* at 322 Fuller Ave is an essential stop for fresh bread and cinnamon rolls; *Morning Lights*, 400 Fuller, has good coffee and late-night entertainment.

Tiny *Toi's Thai* (☎ 406-443-6656), 423 N Last Chance Gulch, has first-rate Thai food (probably Montana's best) for around $12. Reservations are required (a few hours before you want to eat is usually OK). The lively *Windbag Saloon*, 19 S Last Chance Gulch, is Helena's most popular gathering place for microbrewed beers, burgers and pasta ($6 to $11); desserts are on the rich, exotic side. *Bert & Ernie's*, on the corner of Last Chance Gulch and Lawrence St, has big salads, sandwiches and the award-winning Cajun fowl burger for under $10.

For fancier dining try the *Stonehouse Restaurant*, in an elegant old house at the end of Reeder's Alley, whose seasonal menu includes salmon and venison, or *On Broadway*, 106 Broadway, which has an excellent wine list, seafood, house-made pasta and casual atmosphere.

Entertainment

Helena's active theater scene revolves around the *Myrna Loy Center for the Performing Arts* (☎ 406-443-0287), 15 N Ewing St, which shows US and foreign films nightly and hosts local and national performers. Other performance venues include the *Grandstreet Theater* (☎ 406-443-3311), at the corner of Park Ave and Lawrence St, which produces off-Broadway comedies and musicals, and the Moorish-style Civic Center at 340 Neill Ave (at Park Ave), home to the *Helena Symphony* (☎ 406-442-1860). Pick up a copy of the *Lively Times* at cafes, the visitors center or the Myrna Loy Center for current performance listings.

The bars on Last Chance Gulch were the only watering holes in town until the terrific *Sleeping Giant Brewing Company* (called the 'Brewhouse') installed itself near the Civic Center. Now this is the place to be, especially from 3 to 6 pm when three half-pints of beer cost $3 and appetizers are $1 off; lunch and dinner are under $10.

Spectator Sports

The Helena Brewers (☎ 406-449-7616), a Pioneer League baseball team, plays its home games at Kindrick Legion Field, just north of Lyndale Ave on Main St. They always draw a crowd and everyone seems to have a rip-roarin' good time. The season runs from mid-June to early September. Tickets are available at the ballpark for around $5.

Getting There & Away

Air Helena Regional Airport (☎ 406-442-2821) is at 2850 Skyway Drive, 2 miles north of downtown Helena and a half mile east of I-15. Airport hours are from 5 am to midnight. Delta has three flights daily to Salt Lake City via Great Falls, and Horizon Air has three flights to Spokane, WA, via Billings.

Bus Rimrock Stages service Helena's bus depot (☎ 406-442-5860), 7 miles east of town on US 12. Daily buses go to Great Falls ($13), Butte ($10), Missoula ($17), Billings ($31) and Bozeman ($14). Taxi fare from the depot to downtown is $6.

Getting Around

Car National Car Rental (☎ 406-442-8620) and Hertz (☎ 406-449-4167) are both at

Helena Regional Airport and provide pick-up and drop-off service for renters within the city limits.

Taxi Old Trapper Taxi (☎ 406-449-5525) is Helena's 24-hour taxi service.

AROUND HELENA
Gates of the Mountains Wilderness

Despite its location less than 20 miles from Helena, this is the least-used wilderness area in Montana. Its name comes from Gates of the Mountains Canyon, the area's most impressive feature, which Lewis and Clark thought was a dead end until they rounded a certain bend in the river to discover the canyon 'open like a gateway to reveal a continuation.' Cut through more than 1000 feet of rock, the towering limestone canyon walls are pierced by caves, laden with marine fossils and decorated with Kelsia moss, which is actually a very rare type of rose that grows in pink and purple clusters close to the waterline.

The best way to see the canyon is by the tour boat (☎ 406-458-5241) that departs from the south shore of Holter Lake, 18 miles north of Helena on I-15. Mule deer, mountain goats, osprey and bald eagles are frequently spotted on these trips, and the captain gives a good historical narration. Boats stop at the Merriwether Picnic Area (where Lewis and Clark camped); you can disembark and catch a later boat back to the dock. Hiking trails from the picnic area lead to Vista Point, Colter Campground and Mann Gulch where 13 crosses mark the graves of smokejumpers (firefighters who parachute into the heart of forest fires) who died there in 1949. The owner of the tour boat company also leads all-day guided hikes into the fire site. The boat departs at 11 am and 2 pm weekdays, with an additional boat at noon on weekends. In July and August trips are added at 1 and 3 pm weekdays, 4 pm Saturday, and hourly between 10 am and 5 pm Sunday. Brochures are available from the Helena Chamber of Commerce.

The rest of the 44-sq-mile Gates of the Mountains Wilderness Area is relatively

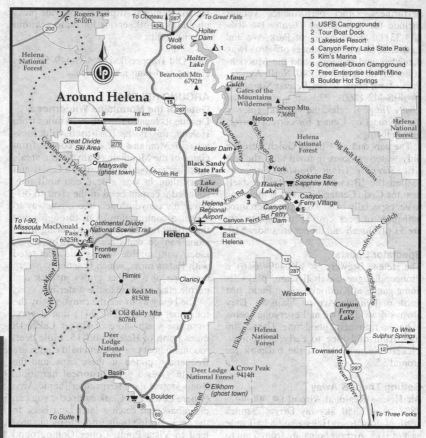

Around Helena

1 USFS Campgrounds
2 Tour Boat Dock
3 Lakeside Resort
4 Canyon Ferry Lake State Park
5 Kim's Marina
6 Cromwell-Dixon Campground
7 Free Enterprise Health Mine
8 Boulder Hot Springs

unused but offers excellent hiking and backpacking. Some trail suggestions are the dramatic but easy **Refrigerator Canyon Trail**, the lush but longer **Hanging Valley Trail** and the easy-to-access **River Trail**; pick up a map ($4) at the Helena National Forest Office or The Base Camp in Helena.

Holter, Hauser & Canyon Ferry Lakes
These 'lakes' are really Missouri River reservoirs dammed by concrete gravity structures that generate electricity for the greater Helena area. They give Helena resi-

dents a chance to go boating, fishing and camping within 20 miles of home. Holter Lake, the northernmost reservoir (43 miles north of Helena via I-15/ US 287) is the most scenic and bordered by Gates of the Mountains Wilderness Area. Three USFS campgrounds on the lake's eastern shore, accessible off I-15 via Beartooth Rd, are nestled between the lake and the rugged cliffs of the Beartooth Wildlife Management Area, home to mountain goats, bighorn sheep and waterfowl. The campgrounds have pit toilets, potable water and fire rings. Tent sites cost from $4 to $7. The

Helena National Forest Office (☎ 406-449-5201) can provide information.

Just 15 miles northeast of Helena, Hauser Lake gets much more traffic than Holter Lake does. Samuel Hauser, seventh governor of Montana Territory, worked a gravel bar on the lake's west shore for gold but found a huge sapphire strike instead. Visitors who want to spend $25 to pick through a pile of gravel can buy buckets of sapphire concentrate from the **Spokane Bar Sapphire Mine** (☎ 406-227-8989). To get there, follow York Rd east to milestone 8 and then turn right on Castles Rd. **Black Sandy State Park**, 7 miles north of Helena on I-15, then 4 miles east on Lincoln Rd and 3 miles north on Hauser Dam Rd, has interpretive displays that describe the history of the Dam. Its campground has a boat ramp, flush toilets and $8 sites. The *Lakeside Resort* (☎ 406-227-6076 or 406-227-6413) on the lake's north shore, 12 miles from Helena on the south side of York Rd, has a popular summertime restaurant and bar, a swimming beach, boat rentals and campsites for $12/20 tent/RV.

With over 75 miles of shoreline, three full-service marinas and four campgrounds, Canyon Ferry Lake is where most of the action is. A visitors center at Canyon Ferry Village (☎ 406-228 9347), 10 miles east of Helena on Canyon Ferry Rd, provides information on the history of Canyon Ferry Dam and the geology of the surrounding area. Four state park campgrounds are clustered around the narrow northern end of the lake, where the reservoir begins to flow into a steep canyon. All have boat ramps, pit toilets and $6 to $11 sites.

Kim's Marina (☎ 406-475-3723), 2½ miles past the Canyon Ferry Dam on the lake's east shore, rents all types of watercraft and has tent/RV sites for $12/18, as well as a few log cabins for $38 a night.

Rogers Pass

Most Montanans know Rogers Pass, about 40 miles north of Helena on Hwy 200, for the afternoon of January 20, 1954, when it set a record for the lowest temperature ever recorded in the state (–70°F). Birders, however, know it as a fantastic locale on a migratory corridor used by bald and golden eagles and a variety of hawks each November, and tundra swans and snow geese in the spring. For further information contact the Montana Audubon Society (☎ 406-443-3949), PO Box 595, Helena, MT 59624.

MacDonald Pass

This pass crosses the Continental Divide about 15 miles west of Helena, giving access to the **Continental Divide National Scenic Trail** and (in winter) a great network of cross-country ski trails. There's a signed pull-out off US 12 where the trails begin. About half a mile away, the USFS *Cromwell-Dixon Campground* has $6 campsites, potable water and pit toilets.

On the eastern side of the pass (well signed off US 12), **Frontier Town** is an odd fulfillment of John R Quigley's lifetime dream: he began this full-size replica of a frontier town (complete with a blacksmith's shop, general store, chapel and brewery) in the 1940s and kept working on it until his death in 1979. The best reasons to go are the glass chapel overlooking the valley (still used for many weddings) and the pine-log dining room, with tree-stump seats and a panoramic view, where you can get a truly Western-size dinner for around $10. The restaurant is open Wednesday to Saturday from 5 to 9 pm and Sunday from 4 to 8 pm.

Ghost Towns

The town of **Marysville**, 20 miles northwest of Helena on Hwy 279, was the country's leading gold producer in the 1890s, but as the mine reached poorer ore quality, Marysville's boom turned to bust and miners were forced to seek their fortunes elsewhere. Today, Marysville is a picturesque jumble of old wooden structures, rusty mining equipment and underground tunnels where Chinese miners drove away evil spirits with food offerings (small white mice dipped in honey) and incantations.

Southeast of Helena, between US 12 and I-15, rise the rugged limestone peaks of the Elkhorn Mountains. The abandoned town of **Elkhorn**, 11 miles north of Hwy 69 on USFS Rd 258, is an archetypal ghost town. Scenes from the movie *The Real West* were filmed here, making good use of the well-preserved cemetery, two-story Fraternity Hall and old signs that still line the dusty wooden sidewalks. A $14-million silver strike and minor discoveries of gold and lead gave Elkhorn its economic lifeblood, but in 1888 production began to slow and a serious diphtheria epidemic the next year put the town permanently out of operation.

'Health Mines'

Forty-five miles south of Helena, signs lining I-15 advertise 'health mines,' old uranium mines whose radioactive radon emissions are touted by some (namely the folks who own them) as a cure for bursitis, arthritis, emphysema, multiple sclerosis and just about any other ailment. The tourist business generated by these mines is the mainstay of **Basin**, an old silver-mining camp whose main street is lined with photogenic old buildings dating back to the early 1900s. The oldest mine around is the Free Enterprise Health Mine, situated at the top of a hill 2 miles northwest of Boulder, and still owned by the family who 'discovered' radon's beneficial effects when a guest from Los Angeles who was inflicted with bursitis miraculously healed two days

after visiting the mine. It is open from 8 am to 6 pm daily between March and November. Be aware that this is *not* a standard treatment in the USA, and people are advised to consult a physician before and after (to ensure that the radon hasn't done any harm) trying this. Most people will want to avoid this.

Originally a stagecoach stop between Fort Benton and Helena, **Boulder** (population 1589) became a town after Boulder Hot Springs (see below) started attracting wealthy guests to its spa facilities in the 1880s and the state built the Montana Home for the Feeble Minded (now the Montana Development Center) in 1892. The town acts as trade center for the Boulder River Valley and visitor central for health-mine enthusiasts. Lined with brick storefronts and crowned with the gargoyle-studded 1889 Jefferson County Courthouse, Boulder's main street offers several reasonably priced motels, two restaurants and a bowling alley.

Three miles south of Boulder on Hwy 69, **Boulder Hot Springs** (☎ 406-225-4339) is one of Montana's oldest tourist facilities, with a grand old lodge and 104°F soaking pools. Though only hinting at its former elegance, the resort is in a peaceful spot beside the Boulder Mountains where the owners hold self-help classes and retreats. Lovely single/double guest rooms cost $40/65, including breakfast and a geothermal plunge; just a soak is $5.

Glacier Country

Montana's northwest corner contains some of its most visited tourist attractions. Glacier National Park encompasses the northernmost section of Montana's portion of the Rocky Mountains, bordered by the Bob Marshall Wilderness Complex which extends south through the Rockies almost to Helena. These are the best destinations for hiking, backpacking, camping or back-country skiing in the state.

From west of the Rockies to where Montana meets Idaho is a growing tourist region centered around Whitefish and Flathead Lake. In contrast, the farthest northwest corner remains some of the least-visited land in Montana.

HIGHLIGHTS

- Chinese Wall – this 13-mile-long, 1000-foot-high cliff is the backbone of the Bob Marshall Wilderness Complex

- Going-to-the-Sun Rd – Glacier National Park's only thoroughfare is heavily traveled but still striking for its proximity to glacial features and Alpine scenery

- Flathead Lake – whose stunningly blue waters are surrounded by woodsy camp-like resorts and cherry orchards

Any portion of the area offers a scenic drive. US 2 affords the most direct route from Seattle to Glacier National Park and is paralleled by train tracks which once helped drive the area's economy and now provide a novel mode of transportation.

THE MISSION VALLEY

Named for the Jesuit mission in St Ignatius, the Mission Valley has good wildlife viewing areas, has been richly influence by Native American culture and has a string of funky antique stores along US 93. The knife-like ridges of the Mission Mountains, which look much higher than they are because they rise straight up from the valley floor, make a scenic backdrop to the valley's farms, ranches and small reservation towns. Most land here is part of the Flathead Indian Reservation, but the only time people make a distinction between towns that are on the 'res' and those that aren't is when they go to buy cigarettes – tobacco isn't taxed on reservation land.

The Mission Mountains Tribal Wilderness, on the west side of the range, was the first tribal land to be put aside by an Indian nation as a wilderness preserve. The area is famous for its bear population which hangs out around McDonald Peak from mid-July to October, feasting on huckleberries and ladybugs.

Orientation & Information

Most communities in the valley are scattered along US 93, with the exception of Charlo and Moiese, which are on Hwy 212. St Ignatius (population 913), Ronan (population 1877), and Pablo (population 300) are the largest towns in the valley, each with a gas station, post office and laundry; Ronan also has a bank.

Coming from the south, the best place to stop for information is Doug Allard's Trading Post (☎ 406-745-2951), on US 93 in St Ignatius. From the north, stop at The People's Center (☎ 406-675-0160), 2 miles

Glacier Country

MONTANA

north of Pablo on US 93, or the Mission Valley Visitors Center (☎ 406-676-8300), on US 93 in Ronan, housed in a 100-year-old log cabin.

St Ignatius Mission

Built in 1854 by Jesuit Missionaries, this was Montana's second mission and a teaching center for the Pend d'Oreille and Kootenai tribes. Within 35 years a boys school, sawmill, flour mill, printing press and hospital grew up around the mission, with much help from the Sisters of Providence, the first women of European descent to cross the Rocky Mountains. The

mission church is decorated with colorful murals painted by the mission cook, Brother Joseph Carignano, depicting New Testament scenes. Next door is an excellent, if small, museum with memorabilia from the mission's past. The church and museum, which are east of Hwy 93 in town, are open daily 9 am to 5 pm. Mass is held Sundays at 9 am.

National Bison Range

Started in 1908 with the progeny of Montana's few surviving buffalo, the National Bison Range is the closest thing to an overland safari Montana has to offer. Pronghorn, elk, mountain goats and big-horn sheep share the 129-sq-mile range, which encompasses the thick-forested Red Sleep Mountain, wetlands and prairie grasslands.

There are two driving tours: a 19-mile, two-hour journey to the top of Red Sleep Mountain and a 3-mile, 20-minute jaunt that keeps to the lowlands. There is also a picnic area, short interpretive hike and excellent visitors center inside the entrance, which is about 20 miles from St Ignatius via Hwys 200 and 212, or 16 miles from Ronan on Hwy 212. Roads are open dawn to dusk and the visitors center (☎ 406-644-2211) is open daily from 8 am to 8 pm, to 4:30 pm in the winter. A 10-mile and a 2-mile drive stay open most of the winter.

Ninepipe & Pablo Reservoirs

Both designated National Wildlife Refuges, Ninepipe Reservoir, 5 miles south of Ronan, and Pablo Reservoir, 3 miles northwest of Ronan, cover 4500 acres of water, marsh and upland grasses – prime waterfowl habitat. The most numerous nesting birds are Canada geese, mallards, pintails, American widgeons, shovelers, ruddy ducks, gadwalls and mergansers. Fall is the prime migrating season when they number over 80,000 (they've actually been known to pass the 200,000 mark).

After turning west off US 93 onto Hwy 212 towards Ninepipe, there are marked trailheads where you can park and set out on foot. Dawn and dusk are the best viewing times. Ninepipe has good fishing for yellow perch and largemouth bass, Pablo is prime for rainbow trout. No boats or flotation devices are allowed and a joint state-tribal permit (available at Doug Allard's Trading Post in St Ignatius) is required. Camping is not an option at either one, though picnicking is.

The People's Center (Sqelixw/Aqtsmakni*K')

The Mission Valley's new pride and joy is The People's Center (a mile north of Pablo on US 93) translated as 'Sqelixw' in Salish and 'Aqtsmakni*K' in Kootenai, both

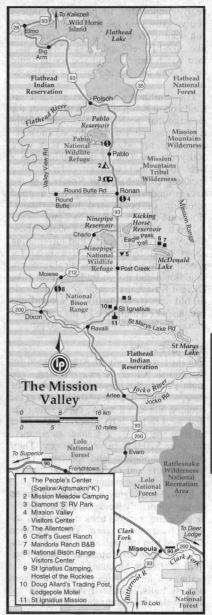

The Mission Valley

0   8   16 km

0   5   10 miles

1 The People's Center (Sqelixw/Aqtsmakni*K')
2 Mission Meadow Camping
3 Diamond 'S' RV Park
4 Mission Valley Visitors Center
5 The Allentown
6 Cheff's Guest Ranch
7 Mandorla Ranch B&B
8 National Bison Range Visitors Center
9 St Ignatius Camping, Hostel of the Rockies
10 Doug Allard's Trading Post, Lodgepole Motel
11 St Ignatius Mission

MONTANA

nearly impossible to pronounce unless you've grown up speaking the dialect. If you want to have a go at it, try something like 'ske-LEE-ef' and 'ackt-s-MUK-nik,' then watch those around you try to figure out if you're choking or just trying to sneeze.

The building's architecture and its hands-on museum are meant to convey the message that the Native American culture is very much alive with traditions and ceremonies as important today as they were 500 years ago. One of the highlights is a free audio tour with an elder's voice speaking either Salish or Kootenai in the background. The gift shop has a good selection of books and local artwork. Hours are daily from 9 am to 9 pm.

Nearby is Salish Kootenai College whose library is a great place to find information about local tribes and often used for genealogical and anthropological research. Traditional and not-so-traditional art (like Dwight Billedeaux's eagle sculpture made of old car parts) is found around the campus. For a tour, stop by the admissions office weekdays from 8 am to 4:30 pm.

Special Events
The little community of Arlee (named for the Salish Chief Arlee, meaning 'red night') hosts the biggest **powwow** in the state, which is also one of the biggest in the country. For a full week, culminating the first weekend in July, dancers come from all over the USA and Canada to compete for over $20,000 in prize money. Their families, supporters and spectators bring jewelry, arts and crafts and food carts to round out the entertainment.

Evaro hosts highly comical **mule races** during 4th of July weekend. Events include an endurance run, flat track racing and a 26-mile cross-country race. Those of open mind and iron stomach might want to investigate the **Mission Mountain Testicle Festival** (a 'Rocky Mountain oyster' fry) that features a local delicacy harvested from hapless bulls. The festivities around the feed, welcome even to those who opt for a

Architectural Symbolism
Dominating the Sqelixw /Aqtsmakni*K' is a rotunda, symbolizing a drum – the heartbeat of the people. It is made of three kinds of stone to represent the three major cultures on the reservation: granite from the Bitterroot, the traditional homeland of the Salish; flagstones from the Perma area, home of the Pend d'Oreille; and gray argillite from the northern part of the reservation where the Kootenai people live. The rotunda's skylight ceiling is made of patterned glass with triangles of blue (representing the water and mountains), green (vegetation), red (Native Americans) and white (the wisdom of the people). ■

less adventurous lunch, include a wine-tasting and live bands. The whole affair takes place in early June at the Branding Iron Bar & Grill (☎ 406-644-9430) in Charlo, west of US 93 on Hwy 212.

Places to Stay
There are some good nontraditional places to stay in the valley; for chain motels, head north to Polson or south to Missoula.

Camping There's free camping behind the senior citizens center in Charlo, near the Bison Range; toilets and a sink are the only facilities. Just north of St Ignatius at the corner of US 93 and Airport Rd, *St Ignatius Camping* (☎ 406-745-3959) has $8 tent spots, $15 RV spots, and beds in a bunkhouse for $9 per person, laundry facilities and a fully heated communal bath house. It also has a funky hostel (see Hostels below). A mile north of Ronan, the *Diamond 'S' RV Park* (☎ 406-676-3641) has $12 tent spaces, $24 RV spots on a large working ranch, with friendly owners, a store and laundry; open April 1 to mid-November. For year-round deluxe camping head 2 miles farther north to *Mission Meadow Camping* (☎ 406-676-5182), a big operation with $11 tent spots, $20 RV spots, an indoor heated pool, hot tub, store and laundry.

Hostels The 16-bed bunkhouse at *Hostel of the Rockies* (☎ 406-745-3959), at the same location as St Ignatius Camping (see Camping above), is what the owner calls an 'earthship,' a partially subterranean structure made of tires, cans and concrete. Bed space, $10 per person, is reserved until 7 pm for people who arrive by bicycle. After that it's first-come, first-served. There's no curfew or lockout, and check-in is from 7 am to 9 am, and between 5 and 10 pm. There are no kitchen facilities.

B&Bs & Motels On US 93 in St Ignatius, the *Lodgepole Motel* (☎ 406-745-9192), part of Doug Allard's Trading Post, has standard rooms for $38/47 single/double. The log cabin style *Mission Inn* (☎ 406-745-3312, 406-745-2050) has two rooms with shared bath for $40 each and a two-room suite with a private bath for $75, including breakfast. They also have a guest house on Ramshead Ranch, 9 miles east of town, that they rent on a weekly basis (call for prices).

The *Mandorla Ranch B&B* (☎ 406-745-4500, 800-852-6668), 4 miles south of Ronan at 6873 Allard Rd, off Eagle Pass Trail, is the valley's most established B&B, with five rooms for $90 to $105. At the end of Eagle Pass Trail, *Cheff's Guest Ranch* (☎ 406-644-2557) has swimming, horseback riding and pack trips into the Bob Marshall and Mission Mountain wilderness areas. Occasionally (and you're in luck if it's the occasion) they rent rooms by the night for around $60; otherwise it costs about $1400 per week.

Places to Eat
Restaurants in the valley are pretty spread out and not too exciting. If the weather is right, picnicking at Ninepipe or Pablo Reservoir, or St Mary's Lake is the way to go. *Rod's IGA*, the big supermarket in Ronan, has a full deli and bakery. The *Allentown*, on US 93 between Ronan and

St Ignatius, has the best variety of food (dinner only) in the valley, with prices starting at $8. In St Ignatius, the *Old Timer Cafe* serves good, standard food Monday

The Flathead Indian Reservation

The Flathead Indian Reservation is the only reservation in Montana west of the Continental Divide. The Salish and Kootenai tribes (known jointly as the Flathead Indians) came from a northwest coastal culture, yet had more in common with the Plains Indians east of the Continental Divide. There are various explanations for the origin of the name 'Flathead' (including the theory that the tribes once practiced a ritual in which they would flatten their infants' heads). Whatever the case, the name stuck and is now used to refer to any of the tribes – Salish, Kootenai and Pend d'Oreille living on the reservation.

The present-day boundaries of the reservation were established by the 1855 Hellgate Treaty. When asked to move out of the Bitterroot Valley to the reservation, the Salish Chief Victor refused to move his people. His son, Charlo, also refused to leave. Then, in 1872 the Salish war chief, Arlee, signed an agreement to move 'his' half of the people north to the reservation and thus became the official chief in the eyes of the federal government. Charlo stayed behind with tribal members who allied with him until 1891, when he moved to the Flathead Reservation requesting only 'enough ground for my grave.'

In 1887 the Allotment Act (reinforced in 1910 by the Dawes Act) divided the reservation land into 80- and 160-acre parcels and assigned a family to each plot. Not only did this destroy the Indian communal way of life, it gave the government 'surplus land' – land that was not claimed by a family. The government opened those plots of land to homesteaders who started pouring in to the valley. Today, less than 20% of the 20,000 people living on the Flathead Reservation are actual tribal members. ■

MONTANA

to Saturday from 6:30 am to 9 pm, Sunday from 8 am to 2 pm.

FLATHEAD LAKE

With 128 miles of wooded shoreline, picturesque bays and inlets and a large population of trout and landlocked salmon, Flathead Lake is one of Montana's most popular destinations. It is also the largest body of fresh water west of the Mississippi. It started forming about 10,000 years ago when moraines built up around the edge of lingering glacial ice. As the ice melted, the bed filled with water to form the lake.

It's a good day-trip from Missoula, Kalispell/Whitefish, or Glacier National Park, and an excellent place to spend a few days camping and swimming. You can easily drive around the lake in four hours, but should plan for stops along the way.

At the south end of the lake, **Polson** (population 4316) is the area's service center, with a western-style main street and the biggest concentration of motels, restaurants and gas stations. Its funky Miracle of America Museum, 2 miles south of town on US 93, is definitely worth a stop, exhibiting of all kinds of Americana, from dollhouses to guns used in the Vietnam War. Also worth a visit is Kerr Dam (8 miles southwest of town via 7th Ave), which is built 54 feet higher than Niagara Falls.

At the lake's opposite end, **Bigfork** is a quaint tourist village with artsy shops, good restaurants, an excellent live performance theater and red geraniums hung along Electric Ave, its main drag. Between the two you've got campgrounds, summer camp style resorts, and, on the lake's east side, cherry orchards that produce fat, mahogany-red cherries. On **Wild Horse Island**, where wild horses thought to be descendants of Pend d'Oreille and Flathead horses roam, and **Painted Rock**, a large outcropping with ancient pictographs on it, are good destinations for boaters and kayakers. If you don't want to risk running in to Flathead Nessie, a distant cousin to the Loch Ness Monster who has been lurking in the lake since the 1930s, opt for

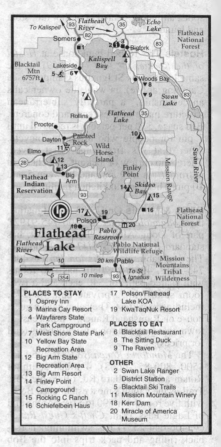

PLACES TO STAY
1 Osprey Inn
3 Marina Cay Resort
4 Wayfarers State
    Park Campground
7 West Shore State Park
10 Yellow Bay State
    Recreation Area
12 Big Arm State
    Recreation Area
13 Big Arm Resort
14 Finley Point
    Campground
15 Rocking C Ranch
16 Schiefelbein Haus

17 Polson/Flathead
    Lake KOA
19 KwaTaqNuk Resort

PLACES TO EAT
6 Blacktail Restaurant
8 The Sitting Duck
9 The Raven

OTHER
2 Swan Lake Ranger
    District Station
5 Blacktail Ski Trails
11 Mission Mountain Winery
18 Kerr Dam
20 Miracle of America
    Museum

a lake cruise on the *Port Polson Princess* pleasure cruiser which leaves from the KwaTaqNuk Resort in Polson, or the *Far West* which leaves from Somers at the lake's north end.

Orientation & Information

In Polson, the Polson Chamber of Commerce (☎ 406-883-5969), part of Sailmaker Realty at 302 Main St, and the KwaTaqNuk Resort (☎ 406-883-3636) on US 93, have the most information about the lake area. On the north end, the Bigfork Chamber of Commerce (☎ 406-837-5888), in the south end of the Lakehill Shopping

Center on Hwy 35, has information about restaurants and lodging. For maps and campground information, stop by the Swan Lake Ranger District Station (☎ 406-837-5081), west of Bigfork on Ranger Station Drive. Each town has a post office, laundry, supermarket and gas stations, as does the small community of Lakeside on the west shore.

Activities
The cheapest place to rent rowboats, powerboats, water skiing and fishing equipment is the Big Arm Resort (☎ 406-849-5622), about 11 miles north of Polson on US 93. All-day **fishing** trips, available through Eagle Fishing Charters, cost around $150 per person. Near Bigfork, the Marina Cay Resort (☎ 406-837-5861) rents ski boats and **waverunners**, and gives **parasailing** flights. On the west shore in Lakeside, Whitecap Sailing (☎ 406-844-3021) has **canoe** and **sailboat** rentals and fishing charters.

For **windsurfing**, inquire at Flathead Surf & Ski at KwaTaqNuk Resort (☎ 406-883-3900, 800-358-8046), and for **kayak** rentals head to Bear Dance outdoor gear and clothing company (☎ 406-883-1700), both in Polson. Glacier Raft Company (☎ 406-883-5838, 800-654-4359) runs two **rafting** trips daily down the smooth-flowing lower Flathead River. Their office is across from the Cherry Hill Motel in Polson.

Bigfork's par-72 **golf** course, the Eagle Bend Golf Club (☎ 406-837-7300), 2 miles northwest of town off Hwy 35, was home to the 1994 USGA Amateur Public Links Championship and is rated as the number one course in Montana; call three days in advance for a tee time. The Polson Country Club (☎ 406-883-2440) has an 18-hole course right by the lake; call two days in advance for a tee time.

The best **hiking** and only **skiing** around the lake is on the west shore near Lakeside. Blacktail Ski Trails is a vast cross-country network that will soon be connected to a downhill resort. In summer, the trails offer well-marked terrain and a good view of the lake. To get there, take

Giant versus Geologist
According to legend, Paul Bunyan, the folkloric giant lumberjack, had such an affinity for Polson that during one hard year he decided to help the economy by moving the outlet of the lake from Elmo to Polson. The story goes, he dug a channel out of the lake, past the west side of town, diverting the path of the water from its natural glacial outlet (the Big Draw) to the Flathead River.

According to geologists, however, it was a glacial moraine that blocked the old valley of Flathead River near Elmo and forced it to find its present course. ■

the road that branches west, past the Blacktail Restaurant, off US 93 and continue 6½ miles to the lower Blacktail trailhead parking lot; the upper parking lot is 1½ miles farther. There are large posted trail maps at both parking lots. The Wild Bill Trail, accessible from the upper lot is a favorite day-hike.

Places to Stay – camping
East Side The lake's best camping is on its east side. A quarter mile south of Bigfork, the *Wayfarers State Park Campground* has shady sites for $7; *Finley Point Campground*, on a picturesque promontory among fir and pine trees, has $12 sites and $3 day-use facilities; prettiest of all is the *Yellow Bay State Recreation Area* with $7 sites, pit toilets, fire rings and a swimming beach. Next door is U of M's biological research station which studies the life of lakes, ponds and streams; tours are available in the summer, weekdays from 8 am to 5 pm.

West Side Choose from *West Shore State Park*, with $6 sites, a day-use picnic area and boat launch (the campsites away from the lake are peaceful and uncrowded, those on the lake are a bit hectic); or *Big Arm State Recreation Area*, arguably the most crowded campground and day-use area on the lake, with $7 sites and a $3 day-use fee.

MONTANA

Polson Deluxe campgrounds here include the *Polson/Flathead Lake KOA* (☎ 406-883-2151), 1 mile north of Polson on a hill above US 93, with $16 tent sites, $19 RV sites, a heated swimming pool, sauna, laundry facilities and store, and the *Rocking C Ranch* (☎ 406-887-2537), 7 miles northeast of Polson on Hwy 35, with mini-golf, a casino and lounge, restaurant and live music on the weekends; tent sites are $12, RV spots $16.

Places to Stay – motels & resorts
Polson Polson has the most choices, the nicest being the *KwaTaqNuk Resort* (☎ 406-883-3636, 800-882-6363), owned by the Confederated Salish and Kootenai Tribes and operated by Best Western. There's indoor and outdoor pools, a hot tub, sauna and lakeside restaurant and bar; rooms cost $90 to $105 from June to September, and $55 to $75 the rest of the year. Smaller motels include the *Cherry Hill Motel* (☎ 406-883-2737), on a small hill across from the lake, with rooms for $52/62 single/double; the *Port Polson Inn* (☎ 406-883-5385, 800-654-0682) with lake-front rooms for $62, non-view rooms for $45 and kitchenette suites starting at $75. Northeast of Polson on Hwy 35, the *Schiefelbein Haus* (☎ 406-887-2431) is a well-kept motel with friendly owners and nice rooms for $55 year-round (no lake access, though Finley Point is nearby).

Mission Mountain Winery
Operating since 1985 on the southwest shore of Flathead Lake, Mission Mountain Winery is Montana's only commercial winery. It produces six wines – four white, one red and one blush – using mostly Washington grapes, though the winery's own grapes are used for the pinot noir. Tours are available on request and tastings are provided daily from 10 am to 5 pm. ∎

Lakeside All the accommodations in Lakeside, on the west shore, are on US 93, within a mile of restaurants and stores, and have lake access. The *Sunrise Vista Inn* (☎ 406-844-3864) has a nice lawn overlooking the lake and $60 rooms. Rooms at the *Bayshore Resort Motel* (☎ 406-844-3131, 800-844-3132) have small kitchens and cost $68. Next door, the *Lakeside Resort Motel* (☎ 406-844-3570, 800-348-4822) has log cabins and smallish rooms for $57 to $95, depending on the view.

Bigfork The *Harbor* (☎ 406-837-5550), 425 Grand Ave, is the only lodging in the heart of Bigfork. Rooms are above a lively restaurant/bar and cost $73/89 for a single/double. To check in or inquire about rooms talk to the bartender. *Marina Cay* (☎ 406-837-5861, 800-433-6516) is Bigfork's all-purpose, year-round lakeside resort that has everything from convention facilities to fishing charters. Most accommodations, from hotel suites to family condos, are on the lake and cost $65/80 single/double to $165 for a unit that sleeps four. The resort is half a mile from the village, where the Bigfork Village Loop connects with Hwy 35 N.

Somers One of the best values is the *Osprey Inn* (☎ 406-857-2042, 800-258-2042), on the north end of the lake near the water. This beautiful B&B has a hot tub, dock and view of Mission Mountains. The hosts encourage birdwatching, use of their canoe and rowing shell and often make a campfire at night. Reservations are recommended and a two-night minimum stay is required in July and August.

Places to Eat
When in Polson, stop by *Price's Good Food*, 3 blocks east of Main St on US 93, for straightforward breakfast or lunch under $6. The *Watusi Cafe*, 318 Main St, has interesting salads and sandwiches and a host of vegetarian options for around $7. At 501 Main St, *Terrapin Station* is the place to go for coffee, $6 pasta dinners and live music. The *Rancho Deluxe*, west of

downtown at 604 6th St W, is where locals go for steaks and prime rib ($11 to $16).

The *Blacktail Restaurant & Lounge* is a good stop in Lakeside for breakfast, lunch and dinner under $10.

Bigfork is the lake's uncontested fancy dining destination. There's excellent, reasonably priced cuisine and an elegant atmosphere at *Showthyme*. Locals go to *Sabo's*, one block east of Electric Ave, for microbrews, pizza, salads and grilled sandwiches under $10, and to *Brookie's Cookies*, on south end of Electric Ave, to satisfy a sweet tooth. South of Bigfork, near Woods Bay, *The Sitting Duck* has one of the best views of the lake and good food for around $10.

Entertainment
South of Woods Bay, *The Raven* is the lake's best pub, with a deck overlooking the lake, live music and a great beer and wine selection. It also serves appetizers, sandwiches and burgers. Farther south, the beer garden at the *Schiefelbein Haus* is both oddly decorated and situated, but a fun place to swill away the afternoon.

Friday and Saturday nights swing dancing at the rustic *Bigfork Inn*, at the corner of Electric and Grand Aves, attracts folks from all over the valley. The scene at *Sabo's*, 1 block off Electric Ave midway through town, is a bit more rockin.' They've got Ping-Pong and pool tables, live bands (on the rooftop deck in summer) and microbrews. The *Bigfork Summer Playhouse* (☎ 406-837-4886), on Electric Ave, performs Broadway musicals or off-Broadway comedies with actors from all over the Northwest. Performances are Monday to Saturday nights, with matinees on weekends. Prices start at $12/10 for adults/children under 12 and increase by $2 increments after June 12 and July 3 until Labor Day weekend.

The *Port Polson Players* perform new renditions of old, often obscure classics and dramatic comedies. Performances are held in the Mission Valley Performing Arts Center (the former Polson Golf Course clubhouse), a half-mile east of downtown off US 93. Tickets are $10/9 for adults/students and seniors, and the box office (☎ 406-883-9212) is open Wednesday to Sunday from noon to 8:30 pm.

WHITEFISH & KALISPELL
Once a major hub for the Great Northern Railroad, Whitefish (population 5793) has an Old West ambiance, lively bars, covered sidewalks and good gift shops. It sits in the shadow of Big Mountain, one of Montana's premiere year-round resorts (known mostly for downhill skiing), and is spittin' distance from Whitefish Lake. Kalispell (population 15,678), 13 miles south, is Flathead Valley's commercial center. It's not a particularly charming city but home to several worthwhile sights and the valley's concentration of budget lodging and fast food. Glacier National Park is about an hour's drive northeast from either city.

History
The little settlements at Demersville, a steamboat landing on the Flathead River, 4½ miles southeast, and Ashley, half a mile west, were moved here piece by piece and became Kalispell. The name, given to the town by local businessman Charles Conrad, is a Blackfeet word that means 'grassy land above the lake.'

Born in Virginia, Charles Conrad fought in the Civil War on the Confederate side, but became disillusioned with the politics of the 'states' so he traveled to Fort Benton. There he married a Blackfeet woman, and together they moved west to Kalispell with the IG Baker Company to settle and (profit from) the Great Northern Railroad route. Under her guidance, Conrad acted as representative to the Blackfeet Nation in several land negotiations and was a staunch defender of Native American land rights.

Orientation & Information
US 93 connects the two cities, and continues northwest from Whitefish up to Eureka, and south from Kalispell down to Flathead Lake. US 2 runs east-west through Kalispell.

The Whitefish chamber of commerce (☎ 406-862-3501) in the Burlington Northern Railroad Depot at the north end of Central Ave, has the best selection of brochures and makes local lodging arrangements.

Bookworks, in downtown Whitefish at the corner of Central and 1st St, has guidebooks and a good selection of maps. Information on the surrounding Flathead National Forest is available from the Tally Lake Ranger Station (☎ 406-862-2508), 1 mile west of Whitefish on US 93 W.

In Kalispell, the Kalispell Area Chamber of Commerce (☎ 406-752-6166) has its office in an old railroad administration building on the corner of Center and Main Sts. Flathead National Forest Headquarters (☎ 406-758-5204), south of downtown and half a block east of Hwy 93 at 1935 3rd Ave E, has maps, trail guides and information on the flora and fauna of the Bob Marshall Wilderness and Glacier National Park.

Both towns have banks, post offices and medical services. To wash your duds in Whitefish, head to Martins Cleaners & Laundromat, on the corner of 3rd St and Baker Ave (open from 7 am to 10 pm). In

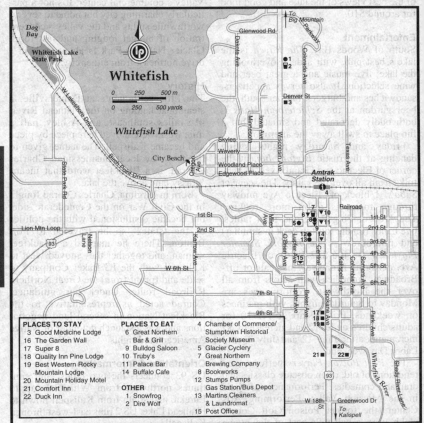

PLACES TO STAY
3   Good Medicine Lodge
16 The Garden Wall
17 Super 8
18 Quality Inn Pine Lodge
19 Best Western Rocky
    Mountain Lodge
20 Mountain Holiday Motel
21 Comfort Inn
22 Duck Inn

PLACES TO EAT
6   Great Northern
    Bar & Grill
9   Bulldog Saloon
10 Truby's
11 Palace Bar
14 Buffalo Cafe

OTHER
1   Snowfrog
2   Dire Wolf
4   Chamber of Commerce/
    Stumptown Historical
    Society Museum
5   Glacier Cyclery
7   Great Northern
    Brewing Company
8   Bookworks
12 Stumps Pumps
    Gas Station/Bus Depot
13 Martins Cleaners
    & Laundromat
15 Post Office

Kalispell, try Sanitone next to Fred Meyer Supermarket at the corner of E Montana and 3rd Ave E.

Big Mountain

The area's biggest attraction is undoubtedly Big Mountain, which has 3000 acres of skiable terrain, a 2300-foot vertical drop and nine chairlifts. In the summer the resort is a quiet, self-contained recreation area catering to families. There are daily guided nature hikes, fly-fishing lessons, horseback riding, mountain-bike trails and tennis courts. A **gondola** to the top of the mountain offers incredible views of Flathead Valley and the peaks of Glacier National Park. At the summit is a cafeteria, bar and a nature center that has hands-on displays and binoculars to use.

Whitefish

In Downtown Whitefish, stop in at the **Stumptown Historical Society Museum**, housed in the old Great Northern Railroad Depot next to the chamber of commerce, to see photographs of Hell Roaring Ski Course where the Big Mountain ski area was born. The sexy architecture of the new **Great Northern Brewing Company** on Central Ave might catch your eye (it's visible from the railroad depot) – go have a look: the free tasting room is open daily and has a great view.

Kalispell

It's definitely worth a trip to Kalispell to visit the **Conrad Mansion**, the completely restored Norman-style home of businessman extraordinaire Charles Conrad. The mansion (☎ 406-755-2166), on Woodland Ave between 3rd and 4th Sts E, was built in 1895 by the architect of St Mary's Lodge in Glacier National Park and retains most of its original furnishings and decorations, including Tiffany glass windows, drinking fountains, an intercom system and elevator. One-hour tours, given 9 am to 8 pm daily from May 15 to October 15, cost $5.

Housed in Kalispell's late-19th-century Carnegie Library building on the corner of 2nd Ave E and 3rd St, the **Hockaday**

Center for the Arts is the Flathead Valley's most important art museum. It focuses on contemporary work mostly by Montana artists and has a terrific gift shop. Hours are Tuesday to Friday 10 am to 5 pm, Saturday 10 am to 3 pm. Admission is free. People gather on weekends at the **Kalispell Open Market**, at the Kalispell Fairgrounds, west of town at the corner of W Idaho St and Meridian Rd (entrance and main parking lot are on Meridian), to sift, sort, sell, barter and buy new and used 'stuff.'

Activities

Sportsman Ski Haus, on US 93 in Whitefish, and also at the junction of US 2 and US 93 in Kalispell, is the best all-purpose gear store around. Both locations offer a vast selection of equipment and maps, and good rental rates.

Skiing Lift tickets at Big Mountain cost $32 adult, $25 student/senior, $18 for ages seven to 12 (kids under six ski free); night skiing is available mid-December through March for $12. The mountain's Platter Puppies program (a combination ski school and day-care center) is rated one of the best in the country. Snowfrog (☎ 406-862-7547), on the way to Big Mountain at 903 Wisconsin Ave in Whitefish, is run by friendly folks and has cheapest ski rentals in town. (For information on getting to the mountain from Whitefish, see Getting Around later in this section.)

A ski shuttle from Kalispell stops at the Best Western Outlaw Inn, Diamond Lil and Aero Inn (all south of town on US 93) for $5 roundtrip.

Cross-country skiers can get maps and equipment at Sportsman Ski Haus (see above) and head to Glacier National Park, Round Meadow or (for tame, groomed trails) the Whitefish Lake Golf Course.

Hiking There are two routes up to Big Mountain, 3.8 miles and 5.6 miles long, which wind through wildflowers, beargrass and, in July, huckleberries. You can ride the gondola to the summit ($9) and hike down, or hike up and ride down for free.

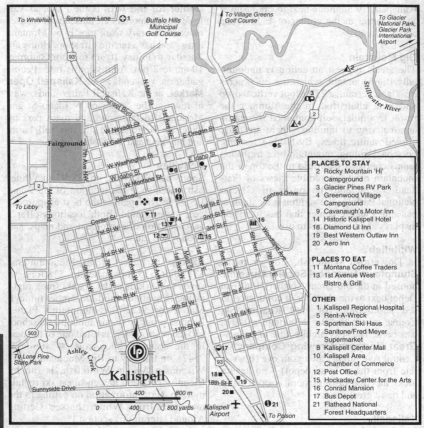

To Whitefish   Sunnyview Lane   ⊕1   Buffalo Hills
                                         Municipal
                                         Golf Course

To Village Greens
Golf Course

To Glacier
National Park,
Glacier Park
International
Airport

93

Sunset Blvd

Stillwater River

3

4

2

N Main St

N Nevada St

Fairgrounds

W California St

E Oregon St

5

2

7th Ave NW

7th Ave NE

1st Ave NE

W Washington St

E Idaho St

6   7

W Idaho St

W Montana St

10

To Libby

Railroad

Meridian Rd

8   9

i

To Libby

Center St

11

1st St E

1st St W

13 14

2nd St E

Conrad Drive

12

3rd St E

15

16

Woodland Ave

503

3rd St W

6th Ave E

7th Ave E

Ashley Creek

7th St W

9th St W

9th St E

To Lone Pine
State Park

11th St W

11th St E

13th St E

LP

93

17

Kalispell

18   19

18th St E

Sunnyside Drive

20

0   400   800 m

0   400   800 yards

Kalispell
Airport

21

To Polson

PLACES TO STAY
2   Rocky Mountain 'Hi'
    Campground
3   Glacier Pines RV Park
4   Greenwood Village
    Campground
9   Cavanaugh's Motor Inn
14 Historic Kalispell Hotel
18 Diamond Lil Inn
19 Best Western Outlaw Inn
20 Aero Inn

PLACES TO EAT
11 Montana Coffee Traders
13 1st Avenue West
    Bistro & Grill

OTHER
1   Kalispell Regional Hospital
5   Rent-A-Wreck
6   Sportman Ski Haus
7   Sanitone/Fred Meyer
    Supermarket
8   Kalispell Center Mall
10 Kalispell Area
    Chamber of Commerce
12 Post Office
15 Hockaday Center for the Arts
16 Conrad Mansion
17 Bus Depot
21 Flathead National
    Forest Headquarters

Far more options are available at Jewel Basin in the Swan Valley (see Bob Marshall Country later in this chapter).

Mountain Biking There are over 20 miles of single track from the top of Big Mountain. A $14 day-pass gives you unlimited rides to the top; bike rentals are available at the base. More committed cyclists will want to explore the Tally Lake area, 16 miles west of town, and Haskill Basin, 6 miles east of town. The Glacier Cyclery (☎ 406-862-6446), west of Baker Ave at 336 2nd St in Whitefish, has maps and guided rides and rents bikes for $15/20 for a half-day/full-day.

Other Activities To find Whitefish Lake's **swimming** beach, take Baker Ave across the railroad bridge and keep to the left along Edgewood Place until it ends at the lake. For more serenity (but no lifeguard or snack stand) head to the lake's northern end via Wisconsin Ave which turns into (at the Big Mountain turnoff) East Lakeshore Drive; there are several roads – Lakewood Court, Rest Haven Drive, Eagle Point – that turn off to the lake.

Most of Kalispell's outdoor activities, with the exception of golf, revolve around Flathead Lake. The small community of Somers, 8 miles south of Kalispell on US 93, acts as the primary access point to the lake, at Kalispell Bay.

There are three excellent choices for **golf** enthusiasts: the 36-hole Whitefish Lake Golf Club (☎ 406-862-4000), 3 miles west of town on US 93; the 27-hole Buffalo Hills Municipal Golf Course (☎ 406-756-4545), north of downtown Kalispell (via N Main St) on the hill where Charles Conrad used to keep his private buffalo herd; and the Village Greens (☎ 406-752-4666), an 18-hole course that is part of a new 'adult living' development and usually less crowded than the others. From Kalispell, turn left (north) off Hwy 2 onto 7th Ave NE, which becomes Whitefish Stage Rd, go 2 miles and turn right on W Evergreen. For a tee time at any of them, call after 7 am, two days in advance.

Air Big Sky Balloon Adventures (☎ 406-862-3432) offer **hot-air balloon rides** that depart from Whitefish and soar above the Flathead Valley from where you can see the peaks of Glacier National Park and the Bob Marshall Wilderness. Flights last two and a half hours, cost $130 per person and include champagne.

Special Events
The **Flathead Music Festival** takes place near the end of July and features big-name musical performers (everything from bluegrass to classical) in an outdoor amphitheater on Big Mountain.

Kalispell's Fairgrounds host the **Huckleberry Festival** the second week in August and the **Northwest Montana Fair and Rodeo** one week later. From mid-April to mid-October, the **Kalispell Farmers' Market** sets up produce, baked goods and crafts booths in the Kalispell Center Mall on Saturday mornings and Tuesday evenings.

Entertainment
Along Central Ave in Whitefish you'll find some classic old watering holes, including the *Palace Bar*, *Bulldog Saloon* and the *Great Northern Bar and Grill*, loved for its collection of old signs, pool and Ping-Pong tables and 4 to 6 pm happy hour. The *Dire Wolf*, north of town on Wisconsin Ave, is a popular post-ski stop; it's got live bands on weekends and is a 100% nonsmoking establishment. For live theater, head to Bigfork (see Flathead Lake above).

Places to Stay
The lodges and condos at the base of Big Mountain are good choices for families (children under 12 stay free) and those who want easy access to outdoor activities. For information and reservations contact the mountain's central reservation service (☎ 406-862-1960, 800-858-5439).

Camping The *Whitefish Lake State Park* campground, on the southwest edge of the lake, has pit toilets, fire rings, potable water and $6 sites; for reservations call ☎ 406-862-3991. The *Diamond K RV Park & Chuckwagon* (☎ 406-862-4242), 4 miles south of Whitefish on US 93, caters to RVs ($19 per rig) but has 15 tent sites ($12), a store, laundry and hot showers; its barbecues attract loads of people not staying at the campground.

Kalispell is an RV mecca. On US 2 from Kalispell east are the *Greenwood Village Campground* (☎ 406-257-7719), with $20 sites and the option of hooking up to cable TV for an extra $2; the *Glacier Pines RV Park* (☎ 800-533-4029) with $19 sites; and the *Rocky Mountain 'Hi' Campground* (☎ 406-755-9573), with $18 sites, a large playground and canoe launch and great view of the Swan Range.

B&Bs Whitefish's B&Bs are a good value when compared to similarly priced motels. A few blocks from downtown at 504 Spokane Ave, *The Garden Wall* (☎ 406-862-3440) is a picture of elegance and grace with rooms for $70 to $105. More casual and outdoorsy, the *Good Medicine Lodge* (☎ 406-862-5488), north of town at 537 Wisconsin Ave, has a hot tub and easy access to Big Mountain; rooms cost $65 to $120.

Motels & Hotels During peak season (Memorial Day to Labor Day and Christmas to Easter) – especially in Whitefish – reservations are necessary and prices go up about 20%. Hotels in Whitefish usually fill up more quickly than those in Kalispell. Chain accommodations are much nicer in Whitefish than in Kalispell.

South of Whitefish on US 93 you'll find the *Best Western Rocky Mountain Lodge* (☎ 406-862-2569), *Quality Inn Pine Lodge* (☎ 406-862-7600) and *Comfort Inn* (☎ 406-862-4020), each with a pool, Jacuzzi, fitness center and offering Continental breakfast. Prices are $95 to $110 in peak season, and around $50 in the off-season. With a Jacuzzi only, *Super 8* (☎ 406-862-8255) charges $80 and $41, respectively.

Near these, but off the highway, the *Duck Inn* (☎ 406-862-3825) charges $60 to $85 year-round; rooms are quiet and each has a deck, fireplace, view and access to a TV room and Jacuzzi. Nearby, the *Mountain Holiday Motel* (☎ 406-862-2548) has a pool, sauna and $45 to $60 rooms year-round (kids under 12 stay free).

Kalispell's chain and budget motels are on US 93 south of town and US 2 east of town. The best deal downtown is the *Historic Kalispell Hotel* (☎ 406-755-8100, 800-858-7422), 100 Main St, which has $65 rooms, a fitness room and Continental breakfast. Part of the Kalispell Center Mall downtown, *Cavanaugh's Motor Inn* (☎ 406-752-6660, 800-843-4667) is a hub of activity and a stopping point for tour groups; they have a pool, atrium, restaurant and $100 rooms.

Places to Eat

If you can stand the smoke, the bars on Central Ave in Whitefish serve good, cheap food until 10 pm. Also on Central is *Truby's*, a local favorite for wood-fired pizza, salads and pasta. The *Buffalo Cafe*, on 3rd St between Central and Spokane Aves, is one of those great breakfast spots that you hear about all over the state; most things are under $6. *Jimmy Lee's*, a half

mile south of town on US 93, has decent Chinese food for around $10 per person. For a fancier meal, the *Whitefish Lake Restaurant* (☎ 406-862-5285) at the Whitefish Lake Golf Club has a nice menu, a rustic setting and unbeatable view; reservations are recommended. On Big Mountain, the *Hellroaring Saloon & Eatery* is in the original 1940s lodge crammed with ski memorabilia. The bar lives up to its name on winter weekends.

The one place you shouldn't miss in Kalispell is *Montana Coffee Traders*, across from the mall at 328 W Center St, which has an in-house bakery, fresh soups and hearty sandwiches. Kalispell's upper-end dining venue is the *1st Avenue West Bistro & Grill* (☎ 406-755-4441), at the corner of 1st Ave W and 2nd St W, with a great wine list, fresh seafood and live jazz.

Getting There & Away

Air Glacier Park International Airport (☎ 406-257-5994) is halfway between Whitefish and Kalispell on US 2. Delta Airlines (☎ 800-221-1212), Horizon Air (☎ 800-547-9308) and United Express (☎ 800-241-6522) make frequent connections to Missoula, Salt Lake City, and to Spokane and Seattle, WA. Airport services include a coffee shop, gift store and car rental agencies (see Getting Around below).

Bus Intermountain Transport (☎ 406-755-4011) connects Whitefish to Missoula ($18), via Kalispell. Buses stop at the Stumps Pumps gas station at 403 2nd St in Whitefish, and the depot at 15 13th St E in Kalispell.

Train From Whitefish, Amtrak (☎ 406-862-2268) has an eastbound train to Chicago (via Glacier National Park) that's scheduled to depart at 7:35 am, and a nightly westbound train to Portland, OR, and Seattle (7:57 pm departure). The ticket office and depot are appropriately housed in the railroad depot at the north end of Central Ave.

Getting Around

To/From the Airport The Airport Shuttle Service (☎ 406-752-2842) charges $15 per person for trips between the airport and Whitefish or Kalispell.

Bus The Whitefish Area Rapid Transit (WART; ☎ 406-862-3501) runs between downtown Whitefish and Big Mountain and costs $2 per person each way. The shuttle leaves from the Whitefish Lake Lodge at 8:30 am, and from the corner of 1st St and Baker Ave, and the corner of 3rd St and Central Ave after that. The shuttle leaves the mountain at 5 pm.

Car Avis (☎ 406-257-2727), Budget (☎ 406-755-7500), Hertz (☎ 406-257-1266) and National (☎ 406-257-7144) all have booths at Glacier Park International Airport. For cheaper rates, try the Duck Inn (see Places to Stay above) or Rent-A-Wreck (☎ 406-755-4555, 800-654-4642), 2622 Hwy 2 E; both can arrange airport shuttle service, and the Duck Inn rents vehicles to its guests.

COLUMBIA FALLS

Columbia Falls (population 3922) is a mere shadow of the bustling industrial town it was in the 1940s. CF Aluminum Company, Plum Creek Timber and FH Stoltze Land & Lumber are the major employers, whose plants and mills give Columbia Falls its distinct (fresh-cut wood and processed pulp) smell. However, over the past five years or so, each company has reduced its work force by at least 25%, with the timber companies making the most drastic cuts.

Roughly half-way between Whitefish and Glacier National Park, the town acts as a pit stop and resting place for travelers. There are a few chain-owned budget motels, a bank, sports stores, a big supermarket and plenty of fast-food restaurants along US 2, the town's main thoroughfare.

Places to Stay

The fishing access site on the Flathead River, which is a half mile east of town, has no developed campsites or facilities but

you can set up a tent as long as you take it down by 9 am.

At the junction of US 2 and US 206, *Glacier Mountain Shadows Resort* (☎ 406-892-7686, 800-766-1137) has a pool, volleyball court, restaurant, store and laundry. Tent sites are $10, RV spots $16 for two people ($2 each additional person) and motel rooms are $58/73 single/double in summer, around $45 the rest of the year.

Nestled up to the base of Columbia Mountain, 1 mile southeast of town on Jensen Rd, is *Columbia Mountain Cabins* (☎ 406-892-4565). Five fully equipped cabins that sleep four to six people rent for $65 per night, with reduced rates for stays of three nights or longer. The bathroom and shower facilities are 100 feet from the cabins across a small creek.

The *Glacier Inn Motel* (☎ 406-892-4341) is on the east edge of town, south of US 2. Rooms cost $50/54 for a single/double from Memorial Day to Labor Day, $35/40 the rest of the year.

The *Old River Bridge Inn* (☎ 406-892-2182), 2 miles north of town on US 2, is Columbia Falls' weekend entertainment center with a restaurant, bar and casino. All rooms have double beds and cost $30 per person in summer, $25 per person the rest of the year. Rooms are far enough from the action to remain quiet.

Moving considerably more upscale, *The Inn at Meadow Lake* (☎ 406-892-7601) at the Meadow Lake Golf Course, has deluxe rooms, condos and townhouses alongside the fairway. In winter the golf course becomes a cross-country ski center and daily shuttles transport people to Big Mountain. Rooms start at $109, condos and townhouses at $129.

The *Bad Rock Country B&B* (☎ 406-892-2829, 800-422-3666) has rooms and log cabins with fireplaces, a 5 pm social hour and rooms for $110 to $155 in summer, $98 to $136 the rest of the year. No pets or children under 10. Take Hwy 206 south of the US 2/Hwy 206 intersection. After 2 ½ miles, turn right at Badrock Rd and continue for three-quarters of a mile.

Places to Eat

Leon and Evelyn Syth have owned and operated the *Pines Cafe* on US 2 at the Nucleus Ave junction for 22 years and have not moved an inch towards modernizing their menu. The big draw (besides the huge mounted fish on the wall, which is decorated according to the season) is Leon's barbecued ribs and chicken, cooked outside on a kettledrum barbecue, available after 3 pm. It's open daily from 6 am to 8 pm.

The *Glacier Cafe*, on the south side of US 2, a quarter mile east of Nucleus Ave, gets most of the local business for breakfast and lunch; closed Sunday. The *Old River Bridge Inn* (see Places to Stay above) is popular for steak and prime rib.

For more elaborate dining, there's *Tracy's* (☎ 406-892-7601), at Meadow Lake Golf Club, with a big menu including pastas and fresh game (elk, pheasant, duck). Reservations are recommended and casual dress is acceptable.

NORTHWEST CORNER

Between US 93 and the Montana-Idaho border is territory that even most Montanans haven't explored. The area is similar to the Pacific Northwest in climate, vegetation and its reliance on the timber industry, and has more interaction with Canada and Idaho (in terms of commerce and tourism) than it does with the rest of the state. The waterways are perhaps the main link between the northwest corner and rest of Montana. The Clark Fork and Kootenai rivers, which drain the Cabinet, Purcell, Salish and Whitefish ranges, receive water from most of the state west of the Continental Divide.

Hwy 200, US 2 and US 93 are the travel arteries through here, each one as scenic as the others. US 93 gets the least use from American visitors but offers access to rugged and wonderful hiking destinations near Eureka, undeniably the most charming town in the region. Lake Koocanusa, formed by the Libby Dam on the Kootenai River, snakes its way up to Canada and offers a plethora of fishing and camping spots.

History

David Thompson, who was the area's first documented explorer, navigated the Kootenai River in 1808 and then sent explorer and furrier Finan McDonald to set up a fur-trading post near the site of present-day Libby. Other than the trappers and traders who frequented the post, the area remained unsettled until placer gold and silver were found in local creeks in 1869. But the mining population was just a drop in the bucket compared to the influx of settlers brought by the Great Northern Railroad in 1893. With the iron horse's arrival, Montana's northwest corner became prime timber country and Libby became an important lumber town.

Growing environmental concerns have made a slight dent in the industry's activity, and negotiations between timber companies and environmentalists are becoming more frequent and less futile.

Mining will never compete with the timber industry in these parts, but some does occur on a small scale and rumor has it that prospectors have their eyes on the rich silver and copper deposits beneath the Cabinet Mountain Wilderness.

Eureka

At the northeast end of Lake Koocanusa, 8 miles from the Canadian border and 50 miles north of Whitefish by US 93, Eureka (population 1108) is a funky little town that acts as social and commercial hub of the Tobacco Valley. It's both a lumber and a tourist town. It is also increasingly important for its Christmas tree farms, adding an interesting twist to its economy, which relies both on nurturing trees and cutting them down. There's also a lot of good hiking in the surrounding forest, representing a third tree-based asset to the local economy. Locals up here are exceptionally friendly and the drive between Eureka and Whitefish along US 93 makes an excellent day trip.

Downtown you'll find an array of nice gift shops (the local pottery is especially good) and, on the south edge of town, the rustic **Historical Village Museum** where several of the town's original buildings are open for exploration.

Orientation & Information US 93 goes north to Canada, south to Whitefish and runs through town as Dewey Ave, where you'll find a grocery store, a bank with an ATM and most businesses. The Ranger Station (☎ 406-296-2536) is on the north end of town where Hwy 37 turns west off US 93 towards Lake Koocanusa.

Hiking The Whitefish Range, east of Eureka, has seen less logging than other ranges in the area and thus offers some of the best hiking. The 3-mile **North Fork Deep Creek Trail** is an easy climb to a ridge overlooking the Williams Creek drainage that can be done in a few hours. The trailhead is 6 miles east of US 93 on Deep Creek Rd 368 (turn left at the trailhead sign just before the Deep Creek Bridge).

Even easier is the 1½-mile **Bluebird Basin Trail** which leads to Paradise and Bluebird lakes. It starts at the same trailhead as the **Wolverine/Therriault Trail** which has multiple-day and loop options that pass by backcountry campgrounds. Reach the trailhead by turning east off of

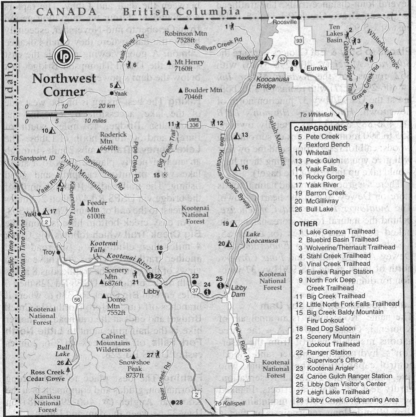

CAMPGROUNDS
5 Pete Creek
7 Rexford Bench
10 Whitetail
13 Peck Gulch
14 Yaak Falls
16 Rocky Gorge
17 Yaak River
19 Barron Creek
20 McGillivray
26 Bull Lake

OTHER
1 Lake Geneva Trailhead
2 Bluebird Basin Trailhead
3 Wolverine/Therriault Trailhead
4 Stahl Creek Trailhead
6 Vinal Creek Trailhead
8 Eureka Ranger Station
9 North Fork Deep
   Creek Trailhead
11 Big Creek Trailhead
12 Little North Fork Falls Trailhead
15 Big Creek Baldy Mountain
   Fire Lookout
18 Red Dog Saloon
21 Scenery Mountain
   Lookout Trailhead
22 Ranger Station
   Supervisor's Office
23 Kootenai Angler
24 Canoe Gulch Ranger Station
25 Libby Dam Visitor's Center
27 Leigh Lake Trailhead
28 Libby Creek Goldpanning Area

MONTANA

US 93 onto Grave Creek Rd 114 and continuing 14 miles to Forest Rd 319; turn left and continue another 14 miles to the trailhead at road's end. At the end of Stahl Creek Rd 7021, also off Grave Creek Rd 114 (10 miles from US 93), the **Stahl Creek Trail** climbs 3 miles to Stahl Peak Lookout from where you have terrific views into Glacier National Park.

A popular backpacking and backcountry ski destination is **Ten Lakes Basin**, a pocket of dazzling glacial lakes on the east side of the Whitefish Range's westernmost ridge. You can access the basin on a vigorous day hike along the **Gibralter Ridge Trail** which connects to several long-distance trails. The trailhead is also on Grave Creek Rd 114, 5 miles east of US 93.

Places to Stay & Eat Choices here are the *Silverado Motel* (☎ 406-296-3166) with $52 rooms, or the *Ksanka Motor Inn* (☎ 406-296-3127) with rooms for $36; both are at the US 93/Hwy 37 junction north of downtown. *Huckleberry Hannah's B&B* (☎ 406-889-3381), has friendly owners, $55 to $90 rooms and acres of surrounding woods; call for reservations and the owners will give you directions (writing them here would take up the rest of the page!).

There's a grocery store and natural foods store on Dewey Ave in the heart of town. The *Sunflower Bakery and Coffeehouse*, behind the natural foods store, has terrific baked goods and lunches for under $5. Locals also like *Sophie's Emporium*, 205 Dewey Ave, for lunch and *Four Corners*, north of town at the US 93/Hwy 37 junction for dinner.

Lake Koocanusa & Libby Dam

The name 'Koocanusa' is an amalgam of Kootenai, Canada and USA – the three nations meant to benefit from the reservoir's hydroelectric power and flood-control capabilities. The Kootenai, who live south on the Flathead Reservation, hardly feel any practical effects. Flanked by the Salish and Purcell mountains, the slim 90-mile-long reservoir is in fact a beautiful site despite its controversial birth: shackling the river to feed the Columbia River farther south depleted wildlife habitat, flooded productive land and altered the river's natural flow. Hwy 37 skirts the reservoir's east side for about 65 miles between US 93 and US 2.

Built in 1972, Libby Dam is a straight-axis, concrete gravity dam 17 miles east of Libby off Hwy 37. Free guided tours are offered from the visitors center (☎ 406-293-5577) on the west side of the dam, hourly from 10 am to 4 pm daily, Memorial Day to Labor Day; the center is open daily from 9:30 am to 6 pm.

There are numerous **bald eagle nests** between the dam and Libby. The raptors are abundant during the migration period from October to mid-November, especially below the dam where they catch kokanee salmon. A good viewing point is the east side of the David Thompson Bridge, just below the dam's powerhouse.

Hiking The best hiking is on the west side of the lake, accessible by crossing the Koocanusa Bridge, 15 miles south of Eureka and 50 miles north of Libby. The **Lake Geneva Trail** climbs 2 miles through an area of newly planted trees to a small lake with primitive camping and good fishing. The trailhead is 10 miles north of the bridge via USFS Rd 470 then 2½ miles northeast to the end of Young Creek Rd 303.

An easy creek-bottom hike is along the **Big Creek Trail** which follows Big Creek 4 miles then climbs to a fire road (and another trailhead) where you have good views of the water. The trailhead is 8 miles south of the bridge on USFS Rd 228 then 6 miles east on Big Creek Rd 336 to where it branches off (just before North Big Creek Bridge) and ends at the trailhead. A shorter hike is the half-mile jaunt to **Little North Fork Falls**, off Big Creek Rd 336, 2 miles east of USFS Rd 228.

Fishing The best place to find fishing information, guides and equipment is at the Kootenai Angler (☎ 406-293-7578) on Hwy 37 between the dam and Libby.

Places to Stay The biggest campgrounds on the lake are along Hwy 37: *Rexford Bench* has 106 sites, showers and a boat launch and takes reservations (☎ 800-280-2267); *Peck Gulch* has 75 sites and lake access; *Rocky Gorge* has 120 sites (most of them paved) but gets the least amount of traffic.

The west side of the reservoir is more primitive. USFS Rd 228 (the Lake Koocanusa Scenic Byway) starts on the west side of the Koocanusa Bridge (15 miles south of Eureka on Hwy 37) and heads south to where it meets Hwy 37 at the Libby Dam. The *Barron Creek* and *McGillivray* campgrounds are on the southern portion of the road and get relatively little use.

To the west of the lake, in the Kootenai National Forest are five different fire lookout towers equipped with cots and/or bunk beds which sleep four to eight people and cost $25 per night. Popular is the *Big Creek Baldy Mountain Fire Lookout*, 23 miles north of Libby off Pipe Creek Rd, while others are more remote and require a hike or a ski to reach the door. Information is available from the Libby Ranger Station Supervisor's Office (see Orientation & Information below).

Libby

Under the J Niel Lumber Company's direction, Libby (population 2701) thrived and promised a limitless future in the timber industry – the deep, dense and massive forest seemed as though it would never run out of trees. Or so everyone thought. Since then other companies have bought and sold the mill, continually exploiting the forests. The present-day owner is Stinson Lumber Company, employing almost 60% of the town's population. With logging on the decline, Libby's new economic 'hope' is mining – the town's original industry – extracting silver, lead and gold from the Cabinet and Purcell mountains.

A bumper sticker that reads 'This family is supported by the timber industry' declares the town's political and environmental leanings. A more lighthearted view

of logging permeates the town (and region) during **Libby Logger Days**, held the second week of July, when professional loggers compete for prizes with chain saws, cross-cut saws, axes and sheer strength.

Orientation & Information Libby sits at the junction of US 2 and Hwy 37, 89 miles from Kalispell, 190 miles from Missoula and 31 miles from the Idaho border. The Ranger Station Supervisor's Office (☎ 406-293-6211) is about 1 mile west of town on the north side of US 2. You can pick up information and maps which cover the surrounding Kootenai National Forest and get details on camping, hiking and fishing conditions. The smaller Canoe Gulch Ranger Station (☎ 406-293-7773) is 13 miles east of Libby on Hwy 37.

Downtown on US 2 are the post office and a bank with an ATM. A&J Suds & Scrub, also on Hwy 37, is open Monday to Saturday 7 am to 9 pm, Sunday 10 am to 4 pm.

Things to See & Do In Libby proper there's the **Heritage Museum** with a collection of musical instruments, logging equipment and mining tools (open from Memorial Day to Labor Day, daily from 10 am to 6 pm; free) and **Montana City Old Town**, where reconstructed stores, a church and schoolhouse imitate Montana's Old West character; its Opera House Theater stages nightly vaudeville acts during summer months.

Three miles north of Libby on Hwy 37, **Wildlife Recapture and Raft Rental** (☎ 406-293-7878) leads wildlife photo safaris and guided raft trips on the Kootenai River for around $125 per person.

Eight miles northwest of Libby on the north side of US 2, the Kootenai River drops 200 feet with a powerful, breathtaking roar at **Kootenai Falls** – the largest undammed falls in the Northern Rockies and one of the largest in the USA.

If you go south from Libby on US 2 and turn west down Bear Creek Rd for 18 miles, the USFS allows recreational gold panning along a quarter-mile stretch of Libby Creek. Old pie tins, hats and

Frisbees work well as gold pans if you happened to leave yours at home. There is usually a ranger at the parking lot during summer months.

Places to Stay & Eat Free camping is available in *Firemen's Park*, behind the visitors center. *Cabinet Mountain Conoco* (☎ 406-293-4942), 2 miles west of downtown on US 2, has a store, laundry room, five tent sites for $11 per night and 20 RV spaces for $21 per night.

The *Pioneer Junction Motel* (☎ 406-293-3781) and the *Evergreen Motel* (☎ 406-293-4178) have similar rooms for around $30. The *Venture Motor Inn* (☎ 406-293-7711, 800-221-0166), US 2 W, has a fitness center, pool, hot tub and restaurant; rooms start at $60.

Libby's best food is served at its bars. The favorites of the old guard are the 'buckburgers' ($1 each) at the *Pastime Saloon*, 216 Mineral Ave, an institution since 1916. The *Red Dog Saloon*, 8 miles north of Libby on Pipe Creek Rd, has vegetarian options and a good selection of microbrews. There's a *Rosauer's* supermarket on US 2 and, across the street, the *Caboose Restaurant & Lounge* which serves full dinners. The *Libby Cafe*, near City Hall at 411 Mineral St, is a good choice for breakfast.

Getting There & Away Libby's link to the outside world is Amtrak (☎ 800-872-7245). The eastbound train comes by at 4:30 am and the westbound at 11:30 pm; a one-way ticket to Seattle costs $94, to Whitefish $25. Libby's train depot is downtown at E 1st and Main Sts.

Bull River Valley
Northwest of Libby, Bull Lake Rd (Hwy 56) heads south from US 2 into the Bull River Valley and the heart of the Cabinet Mountains. After 22 miles it passes **Bull Lake**, known for rainbow, golden, bull and brown trout and mountain whitefish. The campground on the southern edge has pit toilets, a picnic area, fire rings and potable water; sites cost $9 per night.

South of the lake, USFS Rd 398 heads west to the valley's main attraction – the **Ross Creek Cedar Grove**. A short self-guided nature trail leads through the 100-acre preserve of towering western red cedars that average 175 feet in height, eight feet in diameter and date back 500 years.

Troy & Yaak River Valley
Sixteen miles northwest of Libby and 14 miles from the Idaho border on US 2, Troy (population 1031) is at the southern foot of the Yaak River Valley, the lowest point in Montana at 1892 feet. Immortalized by author Rick Bass in *Winter Notes* and *The Book of Yaak*, the lonely and beautiful valley is one of the most important biological corridors between the Canadian Rockies and the Cabinet Mountain Wilderness Area. Unfortunately, much of the land is owned by lumber companies who are fighting hard for their right to cut, and the Asarco Corporation which recently began silver-mining operations in the surrounding Purcell and Cabinet mountains. The environmental and political battles against Asarco, led by the Pend-Oreille Coalition (based in Missoula) are particularly fierce.

Troy is the area's service center and has a bank, supermarket and gas station. From Troy the Kilbrennan Lake Rd heads north to where it joins the Yaak River Rd and continues north to the most remote settlement in Montana's northwest – the 'town' of Yaak, consisting of the Dirty Shame Saloon and the Yaak Mercantile.

A good way to explore the old-growth larch and red cedar forests around Yaak is by foot or skis along the **Vinal Creek Trail**. From town, take USFS Rd 68 3 miles north, then follow USFS Rd 746 along the Yaak River for 5 miles to the trailhead near Vinal Creek (look for the bridge). This is prime deer and elk winter habitat.

Places to Stay USFS campgrounds around Troy have pit toilets, potable water, fire rings and picnic areas and charge $6 to $9 per night. The easiest to find is the *Yaak River Campground*, 7 miles northwest on

US 2, which has 43 sites. Smaller and more remote are those on Yaak River Rd which begins at US 2, 10 miles northwest of Troy. *Yaak Falls Campground* has seven sites, *Whitetail* has 12 sites and the *Pete Creek Campground* with 13 sites is northeast of Yaak along USFS Rd 92.

On US 2 in Troy, the *Holiday Motel* (☎ 406-295-4117) has rooms for $30/32 single/double (check in at the BP gas station next door), and the *Ranch Motel* (☎ 406-295-4332) has $33 rooms. The IGA Supermarket is open daily from 8 am until 9 pm, and the *Silver Spur* is a good spot for a meal.

Cabinet Mountains Wilderness
Southwest of Libby, bordered by US 2 and Hwy 56, the Cabinet Mountains Wilderness encompasses 148 sq miles of deep canyons, small lakes, waterfalls and snow-capped peaks in the Kootenai National Forest. Six miles northwest of Libby, Cedar Creek Rd (USFS Rd 402) ends at the **Scenery Mountain Lookout Trail**, which travels 2½ miles to a lookout tower atop Scenery Mountain (6876 feet). A series of trails leads from the lookout tower into the surrounding wilderness.

The steep **Leigh Lake Trail**, at the end of USFS Rd 4786 (take Bear Creek Rd to access road), offers good views of Mt Snowy, the forest's highest peak at 8712 feet, and is a good point from which to explore the wilderness area.

Information and maps are available from the Libby and Canoe Gulch ranger stations (see Libby above).

Bob Marshall Country

The Bob Marshall Wilderness Complex, affectionately called 'the Bob,' runs roughly from the southern boundary of Glacier National Park in the north, to Rogers Pass (on Hwy 200) in the south. Within the complex are three designated wilderness areas that are separate only because they were designated at different times. These are (unbroken from north to south): the Great Bear Wilderness, the Bob Marshall Wilderness and the Scapegoat Wilderness. National Forest lands surround most of the complex, offering developed campgrounds, road access to trailheads and quieter country when the Bob gets loaded with hunters in autumn.

The sheer enormity of this wilderness is one of its biggest attractions. The core lands (not including the surrounding 1563 sq miles of National Forest) encompass 2344 sq miles, 3200 miles of trails and sections that are more than 40 miles from the nearest road. The chances of finding total solitude here are very good, and the diversity of geology, plants and wildlife is incredibly rich.

None of the Bob's peaks reach above 10,000 feet (the highest is Red Mountain at 9411 feet), but the relief is such that they appear much higher than they are. The Swan Range in the west dominates the Seeley-Swan Valley 9000 feet below. The Rocky Mountain Front in the east rises straight up out of the plains in a limestone wall that is often likened to the top half of the Grand Canyon. Between these two gateway ranges lies the Continental Divide Range, which contains the Bob's most famous feature – the 13-mile-long Chinese Wall whose eastern side is a sheer 1000-foot cliff.

These ranges run northwest-southeast and are separated from each other by the large river valleys of the Two Medicine, Sun, Dearborn, and South and Middle Forks of the Flathead which start here. It is these waterways, plus Birch and Badger creeks, that act as main navigation and penetration routes into the Bob.

In the Bob and its surrounding national forests live mountain goats, bighorn sheep, grizzly bears, bald and golden eagles and elk herds that are more populous than they were 100 years ago.

One of the most important wildlife features of this area is the Sun River Game Preserve, set aside in 1912, which protects the Sun River elk herd on the Rocky Mountain Front between Choteau and Augusta.

Bob: the Man, the Myth, the Legend

The most important passion of life is the overpowering desire to escape periodically from the strangling clutch of mechanistic civilization. To us the enjoyment of solitude, complete independence, and the beauty of undefiled panoramas is absolutely essential to happiness. . . a person might die spiritually if he could not sometimes forsake all contact with his gregarious fellowmen, and the machines which they have created, and retreat to an environment where there was no remote trace of humanity.
— Bob Marshall, from *Impressions from the Wilderness* (The Living Wilderness Journal, autumn 1937) written in Montana and Idaho's Selway-Bitterroot Wilderness.

It is very fitting that one of the USA's most-beloved wilderness areas is named after one of its most renowned preservationists – Bob Marshall, who inspired friends, students and government officials with his love for the wild. Born in New York in 1901, Marshall grew up in an urban environment but constantly dreamed of adventures. In his early teens he began to explore the Adirondacks, and by age 21 he had published a book chronicling his climbs to 42 of the region's 46 peaks over 4000 feet (he eventually climbed all 46).

After receiving his master's in forestry from Harvard and his PhD from Johns Hopkins University, Bob wrote books on forest preservation including *The People's Forest* (Harrison Smith & Robert Haas, New York, 1933), in which he writes:

Under their present management, the American forests are drifting into constantly expanding ruin . . . The time has come when we must discard the unsocial view that our woods are the lumberman's and substitute the broader ideal that every acre of the woodland in the country is rightly a part of the people's forest.

These principles were the foundation for *A National Plan for American Forestry*, a collaborative report written by Marshall and his fellow foresters, which set the groundwork for the wilderness preservation movement in Washington, DC, and led to the organization of the Wilderness Society. Bob Marshall died at the young age of 39 when he suffered a heart attack while traveling by train from Washington, DC, to New York. ■

Orientation & Access

You can access the Bob from the Seeley-Swan Valley in the west, Hungry Horse Reservoir in the north, the Rocky Mountain Front in the east and off Hwy 200 in the south. The easiest (and thus, most popular) access routes are from the Benchmark and Gibson Reservoir trailheads in the Rocky Mountain Front. Roads to these trailheads are plowed and well-marked and take you right up to beautiful terrain that is representative of what's in the backcountry. Trails from this side ascend gradually and are close to the Chinese Wall and other well-known features of the area.

Other good access points are the Holland Lake and Pyramid Pass trailheads on the Seeley-Swan side. Trails in this range generally start very steeply, reaching a pass and the wilderness boundary after about 7 miles. It takes another 10 miles or so to really get into the heart of the Bob. There are good day-hikes from all sides.

No permits are necessary to travel in the Bob, though fishing and hunting licenses are required. Group size is limited to 15 people and you may camp in one location for 14 days, after which you must move at least 5 miles to another campsite.

Information

For an extended backcountry trip it's best to consult maps well in advance. The USGS 'Bob Marshall, Great Bear, and Scapegoat Wilderness Complex' map is the best topo-trail map and shows access roads from the west (Seeley-Swan) and north (Hungry Horse); the 'Lewis and Clark National Forest – Rocky Mountain Division' map shows trailheads and access roads on the east (Rocky Mountain Front) side a little better. Both maps are available ($4 each) by mail from the USGS or the ranger stations listed below, or can be bought at most book, sporting goods and hardware stores in the region. The ranger stations that tend to the Bob include:

Augusta Information Station
    405 Manix St, Augusta (☎ 406-562-3247)
Flathead National Forest Headquarters
    1935 3rd Ave E, Kalispell (☎ 406-758-5204)
Hungry Horse Ranger Station
    on Hwy 2 in Hungry Horse
    (☎ 406-387-3000)
Lewis & Clark National Forest
    Supervisors Office
    1101 15th St N, No 401, Great Falls (☎ 406-791-7700)
Seeley Lake Ranger Station
    3 miles north of Seeley Lake on Hwy 83
    (☎ 406-677-2233)
Spotted Bear Ranger District
    55 miles south of Hungry Horse
    (☎ 406-758-5376); open in summer only
Swan Lake Ranger District
    in Bigfork (☎ 406-837-7500)
Rocky Mountain Ranger District
    1102 Main Ave NW, Choteau
    (☎ 406-466-5341)

Outfitters

Because of its size, many people choose to explore the Bob on horseback. You can hire an outfitter to pack-in your gear, allowing the luxury of setting up a well-stocked base camp; the outfitter can then pick you up at an agreed-upon location several days or weeks later, or simply let you pack yourself out. You can also hire an outfitter to act as cook, trip-planner and guide for multiple-day trips, or sign up for a trip that the outfitter has pre-arranged. Prices vary according to the level of service and length of trip desired.

There are many outfitters, especially around Choteau, Augusta and Seeley Lake. Cheff's Guest Ranch (☎ 406-644-2557), based in the Mission Valley, has an excellent reputation and has been leading Bob Marshall trips for over 50 years. Prices are about $185 per person, per day, with a week costing $1295. Salmon Forks Outfitters (☎ 406-892-5468), also has

highly qualified guides and specializes in fall and winter hunting trips. The Great Northern Llama Co (☎ 406-755-9044, 800-755-4652) uses llamas in place of horses and has good rates for pack-in/pack-out services.

THE ROCKY MOUNTAIN FRONT

This eastern boundary of the Bob – called the Front Range or Front – is where the prairie meets the Rocky Mountains in one 100-mile-long, 1000-foot-high swoop. Many experienced outdoors folks consider this their favorite part of the Bob (if not their favorite chunk of wilderness in the USA). Sitting east of the Continental Divide, the Front's climate is dry, windy and colder than the terrain to the west. In early spring when areas west of the Divide are still under snow the Front Range is often covered with wildflowers. Vegetation on the mountain sides is relatively sparse which makes for great views of the reefs, mesas and peaks which lie between the Front Range and the Continental Divide.

Blackfeet Indian Reservation

The Blackfeet Reservation sits in the short-grass prairies to the east of Glacier. The Blackfeet Nation includes the Northern Piegan, Southern Piegan (Blackfeet) and Blood tribes that came south from the Alberta area in the 1700s. Originally an agrarian people, the Blackfeet took quickly to horses and guns, which helped them tremendously on buffalo hunts, and they developed a reputation as the fiercest warriors in the West. By the 1800s, when trappers and explorers arrived, the Blackfeet controlled the northern plains and the western mountain passes in present-day Glacier Park. Today, the Blackfeet control their destiny through oil drilling, ranching, farming and manufacturing pencils. Information about the reservation is available from the Blackfeet Planning Department (☎ 406-338-7406), PO Box D, Browning, MT 59417.

The **Museum of the Plains Indians** (☎ 406-338-2230), 18 miles east of Glacier Park in Browning (at the intersection of

MONTANA

US 2 and US 89), is one of Montana's better Native American museums. A highlight of the museum is *Winds of Change*, a multimedia presentation, narrated by Vincent Price, about the evolution of Indian cultures on the northern plains. It's open daily from 9 am to 5 pm from June to September; and 10 am to 4:30 pm weekdays the rest of the year; admission is free.

During July, **North American Indian Days** takes place on the Tribal Fairgrounds adjacent to the museum. The four-day program, which includes dancing, games, parades and many encampments, is one of the largest gatherings of US and Canadian tribes in the Northwest.

Badger-Two Medicine

The northern section of the Front, from US 2 to where Birch Creek crosses US 89, is drained by the Two Medicine River and Badger Creek. It's an important biological corridor between Glacier National Park, the Bob and the Blackfeet Indian Reservation which lies directly east. Peaks here are less rugged or dramatic than in the other part of the Front Range, but as a result, they see less traffic from people and pack animals. Most trails into the area start at Swift Reservoir, 18 miles west of US 89; the turnoff is at a well-marked rest area half a mile north of Dupuyer. Walling Reef is the awesome escarpment on the south side of the reservoir. Two recommended climbs in the area are Family Peak and Morningstar Mountain.

Teton River Drainage

South of Badger-Two Medicine is the Teton River Drainage whose two main access routes are along the North, West and South Forks of the Teton River. The road that leads to these trailheads turns west off US 89 about two and half miles north of Choteau and is marked by 'Ski Area' and 'Eureka Recreation Area' signs. About 16 miles from the highway, the road splits north and south. The North Fork Rd leads to the Teton Pass Ski Area, a friendly little mountain with three lifts and $20 tickets. This road is plowed all winter, making it

the best access for ski touring in the Bob. Three miles past the ski area, at road's end, is the West Fork Ranger Station and a USFS campground. Popular destinations from this trailhead are Teton Pass and Mount Patrick Gass from where you have a spectacular view of the Continental Divide Range.

The South Fork Rd passes a USFS campground and ends at a trailhead that is very popular for accessing the Chinese Wall via Headquarters Pass. There's also a great day-hike from here to the beautiful Alpine Our Lake near Rocky Mountain Peak, the highest peak in the Front Range.

Choteau

Choteau (population 1791) is essentially a farm town with one main street – called Main St, of course – and a three-story sandstone courthouse on the south end of town where US 89 splits to go southeast to Great Falls and southwest as US 287 to Helena. There is a ranger station on the north end across from the lovely *Best Western Stage Stop Inn* (☎ 406-466-5900), which has a pool and $55 rooms. *Rex's Food Farm* on First Ave NE, which crosses Main St at the only stoplight in town, is the best place to stock up on groceries and supplies before heading into the Bob and has an ATM. It's open Monday to Saturday 7 am to 9 pm, Sunday until 5 pm.

Choteau is also home to the **Old Trail Museum**, 823 N Main, famous for its involvement (along with the Museum of the Rockies in Bozeman and the Nature Conservancy) in paleontological digs that have discovered Maiasaur nests and eggs on nearby Egg Mountain. It's open daily from 10 am to 5 pm (often closed from noon to 1 pm for lunch), from May to September.

Augusta

South of Choteau on US 287, Augusta (population 300) is a picturesque Western town with raised sidewalks along its one main street and a disproportionate number of bars. Latigo and Lace, one of the only stores in town, has local handcrafted goods of exceptional quality. Most traffic coming through Augusta is from the roads that lead through town to the Gibson Reservoir and Benchmark trailhead, main access points to Sun River Country (see below). The Augusta Information Station, 1 block west of Main St on Manix St, has good maps and guidebooks to the Bob.

The *Bunkhouse Inn* (☎ 406-562-3387), 122 Main St, has rooms for $35 to $55 with shared bath and a light breakfast.

Sun River Country

The North and South Forks of the Sun River are some of the most heavily used access routes into the Bob, and with good reason: there are large elk and bighorn sheep herds in the area; access is easy via the roads from Augusta and trailheads here put you within 5 miles of the Continental Divide.

The North Fork is dammed by Gibson Dam to form the **Gibson Reservoir**, a 5-mile-long body of water with a USFS campground on its east end and a hiking trail along its north side. The road from Augusta to the reservoir is well-marked starting from near the Augusta Information Station on Manix St.

Trails through Deep Creek Canyon, Hannan Gulch and Mortimer Gulch head north from the east end of the reservoir to intersect trails that head west into the heart of the Sun River Game Preserve. Another popular route is from the west end of the reservoir along the South Fork trail to Prairie Reef. A 6-mile uphill climb to the top of Prairie Reef is rewarded with awesome views of the Chinese Wall.

Augusta's Main St turns into the road ('Benchmark Road') that goes through Ford and Wood Creek Canyons, past the Nilan Reservoir and ends at the **Benchmark Trailhead** where there are two USFS campgrounds. This trailhead is heavily used by outfitters and thus has plenty of horse and hunting traffic. The big attraction is the excellent access to the Chinese Wall along the west branch of the Sun River's South Fork and over White River Pass. Renshaw Mountain, a good climb with excellent views from its peak, is also accessed from here.

SWAN VALLEY

Swan River flows north from the Mission Mountains into Flathead Lake, and the Clearwater River flows south from the Missions to the Blackfoot River. They meet here in the Swan Valley and together form 10 lakes, strung like a chain of emeralds between the Mission Range in the west and Swan Range in the east.

Accessing the Bob from the Swan Range is a bit problematic since trails are steep and require several days' journey to reach the center. Road access to the trailheads is easy, however, and the valley is a scenic destination in itself. Hwy 83, which runs

1 Holland Lake Campground
2 Holland Lake Lodge
3 Glacier Lake Trailhead
4 Lake Alva Campground
5 Morrell Falls National
   Recreation Trailhead
6 Pyramid Pass Trailhead
7 Tamaracks Resort
8 Wapati Resort
9 Seeley Lake Ranger Station
10 Seeley Lake Campground
11 River Point Campground
12 Big Larch Campground
13 Double Arrow Lodge

Swan Valley

MONTANA

the length of the valley, makes a good route between Missoula and Flathead Lake/ Glacier National Park.

Swan Lake, the northernmost and largest lake in the valley, has a National Wildlife Refuge on its southern end that encompasses marsh and wetlands, and is home to blue heron, osprey, bald eagles, bear, deer, elk and moose. Take Hwy 83 south from Bigfork and turn west on Porcupine Creek Rd.

Mission Mountains Wilderness
This 115-sq-mile wilderness area occupies the rugged east side of the Mission Range from roughly 8 miles north of Seeley Lake to 13 miles south of Swan Lake. Its 45 miles of trails cover very challenging terrain where thin, gravely soil and dense brush make cross-country travel pretty tough. Elevations range from 4500 to 9000 feet, with the average somewhere around 7000 feet. This area tends to attract experienced hikers and climbers more than the weekend-warrior types, perhaps because wildlife is abundant and grizzly bear sightings are frequent here.

On the west side of the range is the rugged Mission Mountains Tribal Wilderness (☎ 406-675-2700 for general information), the first land to be set aside by an Indian nation as a wilderness preserve. A permit is required to enter the area ($7 for three days, $11 for the season, for nonresidents of the Flathead Indian Reservation) and can be bought at sporting goods and grocery stores in the area.

Major access points into the Mission Mountains Wilderness from the Seeley-Swan Valley are along trails that parallel creeks – Glacier Creek, Piper Creek, Fatty Creek and Beaver Creek. The most accessible is the **Glacier Lake Trailhead** near Condon. Day-hikers should head to Jim Lakes Basin, east of Hwy 83 at the end of Cold Creek Rd. Maps, books and current trail, road and wildlife information are available from the Swan Lake Ranger Station (☎ 406-837-5081) in Bigfork and the Seeley Lake Ranger Station (☎ 406-677-2233), 3 miles north of Seeley Lake on the

west side of Hwy 83. (The Seeley Ranger Station also has information about the Mission Mountain and Bob Marshall wilderness areas.) And be sure to check with rangers about bear activity before venturing into the backcountry.

Seeley Lake
The valley's hub is the one-block town of Seeley Lake, 27 miles north of the Hwy 83/ Hwy 200 junction. Here you'll find the valley's only concentration of motels, a post office, gas station, visitors information center (in a small log cabin on the west side of Hwy 83) and *The Washouse*, which has public showers and a coin-op laundry.

At the north end of town, Morrell Creek Rd heads east 9 miles to where it splits to go north (left) toward the **Morrell Falls National Recreation Trail** trailhead and south (right) to the **Pyramid Pass** trailhead. Morrell Falls is a popular day-hike destination, 2½ miles from the trailhead. The Pyramid Pass trail is popular with pack outfitters and thus sees much horse traffic; it's 4 miles from the trailhead to the pass and Bob Marshall Wilderness boundary, another 23 miles to the South Fork of the Flathead River. There are cross-country ski trails that branch off Morrell Creek Rd about 5 miles before it splits; trail maps and equipment rentals are available at the Tamaracks Resort and Double Arrow Resort.

Places to Stay The USFS campgrounds around the Seeley Lake cost $8 (or $9 for a riverside site) and can be reserved by calling ☎ 800-280-2267. There is a nonrefundable $8.65 reservation fee, however, in addition to the regular fee. Right between Hwy 83 and Seeley Lake, *Big Larch* fills up quickly with the weekend party types and large groups. A bit more remote are the *River Point Campground*, 2½ miles northwest of Seeley Lake on Boy Scout Rd, and the *Seeley Lake Campground*, 1 mile farther north on the same road, which has a boat launch and swimming beach.

Two miles south of Seeley Lake on the east side of Hwy 83, *Double Arrow Resort*

(☎ 406-677-2777, 800-468-0777) is the valley's premiere resort with a big lodge, log cabins ($65 to $115), an 18-hole golf course, spa, pool and good dining room.

One mile north of Seeley Lake, the *Wapati Resort and Elkhorn Motel & Cafe* (☎ 406-677-2775, 800-867-5678) has quiet lakeside cabins for $90 and motel rooms for $45; the cafe is open daily from 7 am to 10 pm. One mile farther north, the *Tamaracks Resort* (☎ 406-677-2433, 800-477 7216) is a mellow cluster of old cabins, RV and tent spots that caters to outdoors types. It has two docks and rent boats, canoes, cross-country skis, snowmobiles and ice skates. Cabins sleep two to 10 people and range from $58 to $110.

The *Duck Inn Motel* (☎ 406-677-2335, 800-237-9978) has charmless but adequate rooms with TVs, phones and showers for $35/40 a single/double. Across the highway, the *Seeley Lake Resort & RV Park* (☎ 406-677-2939) caters to families with well-equipped rooms on the lake for $40/55 single/double and RV hookups for $10.

Places to Eat The only supermarket in the valley is *Ward's Food Farm*, on Hwy 83 at the south end of town; it's open from 7 am to 9 pm (until 7 pm on Sunday). The two most popular grub stations in Seeley Lake are *Pop's Drive In*, on the east side of Hwy 83, for burgers, shakes and fries, and the *Filling Station* for family-style breakfasts, sandwiches and dinners. For fine dining and Sunday brunch the *Seasons Restaurant* (☎ 406-677-2777) in the Double Arrow Resort has a country-club atmosphere and fittingly expensive food.

Holland Lake

Another favorite trailhead is at Holland Lake, 3 miles east of Hwy 83 via Holland Lake Rd. From the east end of the lake, trails follow Holland Creek through one of the only breaks in the massive west face of the Swan Range. A good day-hike is the 7-mile **Upper Holland Lake-Sapphire Lake** loop. Trails from the loop head north past Pendant Lake or the Necklace Lakes to give access to Holland Peak, the second-

highest peak in the Bob and arguably the most spectacular in the Swan Range, the east side of which holds active glaciers. Big Salmon Creek starts on this peak and flows into Big Salmon Lake, 8 miles east, and the South Fork of the Flathead, another 4 miles away.

Another access route to the South Fork of the Flathead is from Upper Holland Lake over Gordon Pass and along Gordon, Bartlett, Burnt or Holbrook creeks.

There's a nice USFS campground on the west end of Holland Lake. A mile farther, at the trailhead and road's end is the 70-year-old *Holland Lake Lodge* (☎ 406-754-2282, 800-648-8859), a rustic mountain retreat that epitomizes 'cozy,' complete with a sauna, game room, lounge, restaurant and equipment rentals. Rooms and cabins cost $55 to $110, tent sites are $8 and RV hookups $12.

Jewel Basin

About 32 miles east of Kalispell at the north end of the Swan Range, the Jewel Basin has 24 sq miles of designated hiking-only area enveloping 27 lakes and 35 miles of trails in the Flathead National Forest. The area is mostly used for day-hikes, but the upper lakes in the basin's interior are perfectly suited for camping. Jewel Basin's increasing popularity is evident in some of the easily reached areas, where a solitary weekend hike can become an unintended social event filled with 'Excuse me, Hi, Pardon me, Hi again' exchanges along the trail. Crowds aside, the trails comprise a fun network that leads you to peaks, ridges and lakes, and are numerous enough that you can make a loop out of almost any trip. Trail No 7 leads 1 mile past Birch Lake to the more isolated Squaw and Crater lakes. Trails to ridgetops provide views beyond the basin to the Hungry Horse Reservoir and Flathead Lake.

To reach Jewel Basin take Echo Lake Rd (at the only blinking light on Hwy 83) to Foothills Rd, which leads to the Jewel Basin parking lot. Altogether, the route between Hwy 83 and Jewel Basin is roughly 10 miles, the last six of which are

MONTANA

on a well-maintained dirt road. The main parking lot is on Jewel Basin's west side. The road ascends most of the elevation gain (the parking lot sits at 5500 feet), but a 1000-foot vertical climb to the basin still awaits at the lot. Four trails make the climb from the parking lot.

Access is also possible from USFS roads branching off the main road along the west side of Hungry Horse Reservoir.

HUNGRY HORSE RESERVOIR

Hungry Horse gets its name from two husky freight horses, Tex and Jerry, who were working in the rugged wilderness of the Flathead River's South Fork area. Apparently they wandered away from their sleigh during the severe winter of 1900-1901 and were not found for over a month. By the time they were recovered, they were so hungry and weak that they had to be fed for four days until they could make it back to civilization.

The Hungry Horse Reservoir is 34 miles long, 3½ miles wide at its widest point and 500 feet deep, covering a total of 37 sq miles. Its shoreline zigzags wildly to meet the drainage of the surrounding Flathead National Forest, creating a plethora of fingers, inlets and bays. Elk, deer and bear are common in the area, though intense logging has forced them farther into the wilderness over the past 15 years. Stumps throughout the reservoir are hazardous to boaters and swimmers, so recreation is pretty much limited to fishing.

As you can imagine, this is not the most scenic access to the Bob. It's convenient, however, for people going to and from Glacier Park. There are roads down both sides of the reservoir which meet at the Spotted Bear Ranger Station (open summer only) and USFS campground. The east side road, which starts a mile east of the town of Hungry Horse (look for the 'Martin City' signs on US 2), is the better of the two. The West Side Rd starts at the Hungry Horse Dam Visitor's Center, 3 miles south of US 2, and is windy and has potholes galore. From the ranger station there's a good nontechnical (but very steep) climb up to

Spotted Bear Mountain, and numerous trails that head south along the South Fork of the Flathead River into the very heart of the Bob; the Picture Ridge trail is highly recommended.

To circle the reservoir, allow six hours and have a full tank of gas.

HWY 200

Heading into the Scapegoat Wilderness portion of the Bob from the south, off Hwy 200, is a good option for anyone with time constraints. There are plenty of good dayhike destinations and trailheads are easy to get to because of the many logging roads in the area. Even if you don't venture into the backcountry, Hwy 200 through the Blackfoot Valley is a scenic route between Missoula and Great Falls or Helena. Lincoln, the only real town along the highway, used to bill itself as a 'Gateway to the Wilderness' but is now better known as home of Theodore Kaczynski, the infamous Unabomber. Most residents appreciate it if you are more interested in the nearby mountains than in seeing where Kaczynski did his errands. The one-street town has a supermarket (open daily until 9 pm) with an ATM, gas station and a handful of restaurants.

The best wilderness access from Hwy 200 is 6 miles east of Lincoln, up the Landers Fork of the Blackfoot River via USFS Rd 330 (well-marked opposite USFS Aspen Grove Campground). The road goes 8 miles north to popular Copper Creek Campground and on another mile and a half to the Indian Meadows trailhead. **Heart Lake**, 5 miles from the trailhead in the Helena National Forest, is the starting point for several trails that head north into the Bob. There are numerous lakes – including Webb, Parker and Meadow – that are a bit too far for a day-hike but make good one or two night wilderness destinations. The most direct access into the Bob from Heart Lake is via Bighorn Creek.

The Garnet Range

Roughly 35 miles from Missoula on the southeast side of Hwy 200 is a large pullout and parking lot with an outhouse and large posted map. As the map shows, a road leads from the parking lot through the heavily forested Garnet Range shared by the BLM and the University of Montana Department of Forestry. The main road is improved gravel and is passable by most cars when conditions are good; several steep sections can be difficult with rain, snow or ice. View points along the road offer excellent northward vistas of the Swan Range and occasionally the peaks in Glacier National Park. Hiking trails from the road are well-marked, the most popular being the half-mile climb up to Garnet Ghost Town, a gold and barite (used for making paint) mining town inhabited from 1895 to 1910.

In fall the road is used by hunters, so be sure to wear bright orange. In winter the road is used by snowmobilers and gives access to a good network of maintained cross-country ski trails.

You can actually drive over the range and come out on I-90 near the small town of Drummond, but it's not recommended since the road is extremely rough and twisty from the Garnet Ghost Town trail to the interstate, and there are many logging roads that cross it and not many signs.

Glacier National Park

Small in size but rich in scenery and biological diversity, Glacier National Park (or simply 'Glacier') is Montana's most revered tourist attraction. Naturally it draws large crowds in July and August when visitors centers and peripheral attractions are more crowded than anyone except business owners would like, but the majority of Glacier's visitors stick close to roads, developed areas and short hiking trails. Head into the backcountry, to the northwest corner or up into Waterton, the park's Canadian extension, and you'll have the place to yourself (in a relative sense).

Even those who don't have the time or desire to explore the remote reaches will likely be satisfied with a drive over Going-to-the-Sun Rd from where you can see tremendous examples of glacial activity and, often, mountain goats and bighorn sheep. In winter, when Going-to-the-Sun Rd is closed but surrounding access roads lead to snowshoe and cross-country ski trails, the park is left to the wildlife and hearty souls who enjoy the great outdoors.

History

The two most influential figures in the park's history are James Willard Shultz and George Bird Grinnell. Shultz lived for months at a time among the Blackfeet people whom he considered his relatives and closest friends, and was among the men who first laid eyes on much of Glacier's interior. He introduced the area to Dr Grinnell, editor of the popular *Forest & Stream* magazine, and together with their Blackfeet friends, they explored the area and named many of its mountains, rivers and lakes. Grinnell dubbed the area the 'Crown of the Continent' and lobbied Congress for 10 years until, in 1910, President Taft signed the bill creating Glacier National Park.

In his lobbying efforts, Grinnell had much contact with the Canadian government who, in 1895, had designated the northern extension of Glacier as Kootenay Lakes Forest Park. After Glacier National Park was officially dedicated, Canada expanded Kootenay Lake Park and boosted its status to create Waterton Lakes National Park. The two national governments, along with Rotary International, declared the two parks an International Peace Park to signify harmonious relations between the two countries (preserving the parks' unique biological corridor was a backseat issue at that point).

As the parks' surroundings continued to develop, the biological riches preserved within became more and more valuable and were increasingly studied. In 1995 Waterton/Glacier International Peace Park was designated a World Heritage Site for its vast cross section of plant and animal

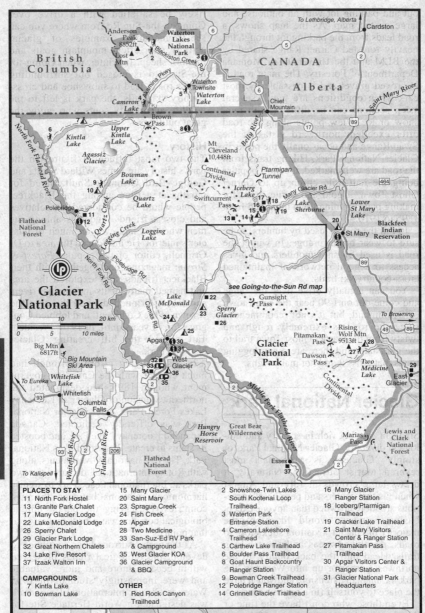

MONTANA

species. Basically the equivalent of a Nobel Prize, this designation is given to sites of 'outstanding universal value to all the citizens of the world, not just the countries in which they may be located' and must be ratified by 147 nations.

Tourism is now an integral part of Glacier's economy, but visitors did not come regularly to the park until around 1912 when the Great Northern Railroad's James J Hill instigated an intense building phase to promote his Empire Builder line. Railway employees built grand hotels and a network of tent camps and mountain chalets each a day's horseback ride from each other. Visitors would come for several weeks at a time, touring each day by horse or foot, and stay in these elegant but rustic and rather isolated accommodations.

WWII forced the closure of almost all hotel services in the park and many buildings fell into disrepair and were eventually demolished. Several grand old lodges – Glacier Park Inn, Lake McDonald Lodge, Sperry Chalet and Two Medicine Chalet are protected under the National Historic Preservation Act as designated National Landmarks (Sperry and Granite Park Chalets, once used as overnight huts by backcountry travelers, are being refurbished and will reopen to backcountry guests in the near future).

The popularity of motorized transport came quickly, and in 1921 federal funds were appropriated to connect the east and west sides of Glacier National Park by building the Going-to-the-Sun Rd. Continually repaired, improved and expanded, the road is the primary travel artery and arguably the park's highlight.

Geography & Geology
When the Rockies were being formed about 100 million year ago, a 30-mile-wide, 2-mile-thick slab (called the Lewis Overthrust) of ancient Precambrian rock shifted up and moved from west to east about 50 miles. This shift left 2-billion-year-old rock sitting atop 100-million-year-old rock in the area that is now Glacier National Park.

From Vision Quests to Railroads
Blackfeet Indians dominated the area that is now Glacier National Park and journeyed from the western mountains to hunt buffalo on the eastern plains. Crow, Sioux and Assiniboine visited the mountains on vision quests to worship and experience the spirits of creation, weather and knowledge who lived there.

European explorers, looking for a route to the Pacific Ocean, traveled through the area in the 1880s. Rumors about a low pass over the Continental Divide kept the explorers searching around the area for many years until 1889, when John F Stevens, employed by the Great Northern Railroad, found Marias Pass, the lowest pass between Mexico and Canada, whose easy grade made an easy crossing. In 1891 the iron horse finally rolled across the southern part of Glacier National Park. ■

From 2 million to 12,000 years ago, repeated episodes of ice created huge valley glaciers (like those in the Himalayas) that covered much of the park's surface. These gargantuan rivers of ice flowed like spike-covered conveyor belts through the previously V-shaped valleys, carving them into wide U-shaped valleys with steep, scoured cliffs forming their sides. Somewhat resembling an elongated half pipe, good examples of this feature are visible from the Going-to-the-Sun Rd, looking west toward the upper end of St Mary Lake and looking southwest from near Haystack Creek towards the west end of Lake McDonald.

Cirques and hanging valleys are other distinct glacial features which make Glacier such a spectacular place to explore. At the head of U-shaped valleys are giant cirques, resembling massive amphitheaters, that are often filled with lakes (called tarns) and act as camping destinations where many hiking trails end and climbing begins, especially in the Many Glacier and Belly River areas. Home to most of the park's waterfalls, including Birdwoman Falls on the

MONTANA

Going-to-the-Sun Rd, hanging valleys are produced when main-valley glaciers cut down into their canyons more rapidly than smaller glaciers from tributary valleys.

Perhaps the park's most identifiable glacial feature, familiar to those who have seen pictures of Switzerland's famous Matterhorn (or have been to Disneyland and seen the replica), are glacial horns – sheer mountain peaks eroded on three or four sides. These are not to be confused with thin-walled arêtes (like the one the Going-to-the-Sun Rd crosses, west of Logan Pass) formed by glaciers cutting away at the walls of adjoining cirques leaving a near-vertical, razor-thin ridge.

The glaciers that carved the park's landscape melted approximately 10,000 years ago, allowing humans to appear on the scene. Between about 9000 and 5000 years ago, the glaciers which once measured 3000 feet thick disappeared for the most part. The 'Little Ice Age,' a period of global cooling in the 1700s, rebuilt many of the area's glaciers and by the mid-1800s the glaciers were the largest they had ever been since the Pleistocene era. Over the past 100 years, however, the glaciers have been rapidly retreating. Highway-like glaciers no longer exist in the park, but travelers who have never seen a glacier before will find the park's 50 or so small Alpine gla-ciers impressive.

Flora & Fauna

When the Lewis Overthrust shifted, it brought Pacific Northwest species to within 30 miles of the plains, a phenomena that hasn't occurred anywhere else in the world. On the west side of the park are mini temperate rainforests typical of the Pacific Northwest; a good example is reached by the Trail of the Cedars, off Going-to-the-Sun Rd near Lake McDonald. On the east side of the park, especially around the border town of East Glacier, you'll find sage and jackrabbits that belong to a prairie landscape and climate. In between are flora and fauna more typical of the Rockies including boreal species and Alpine species that cover over a third of the park.

Because all of these micro-ecosystems are concentrated in a relatively small area, there has been a good deal of crossbreeding that has produced a wealth of unique species. Besides the 1200 plant species known to exist in the park, others that are not yet classified are continually discovered and researched.

To the casual observer, Glacier's variation in landscape largely correlates with its altitude. Forests flourish on valley floors, while mountain ridges above 6000 feet resemble Arctic tundra. As a rule, the farther up the side of the mountain you go, the tougher it is for plants to grow and large animals to survive.

Wildflowers begin to appear at lower elevations around mid-May (depending on snowmelt) and can last into August at high elevations. Some of the most prolific wildflowers are bright pink fireweed, purple harebells, broad-leafed cow's parsnip, spiky-stocked devil's club and the ever-present beargrass – fist-size bunches of white flowers clustered at the end of large stocks that look like giant cotton swabs (despite its name, bears don't have much interest in the plant, though moose and elk like to munch the stocks). In the fall, espe-

Elk can be seen in various areas throughout Glacier Country.

cially on the east side around Two Medicine Lake, green forests are sprinkled with the bright gold of Western larch, one of the world's few deciduous conifers that are common in the Swiss Alps.

Canada is much less developed and populated than the USA and as a result has a larger predator population. Because Glacier and Waterton are protected as a contiguous biological corridor, Glacier has a link to that relatively undeveloped land. Glacier is the only place in the lower 48 states where wolves, mountain lions and grizzlies have maintained continuous existence.

There's also an abundance of elk, moose whitetail and mule deer throughout the park and, at higher elevations, mountain goats, bighorn sheep, marmots and pikas (small members of the rabbit family who scurry about on the rocky slopes making bird calls to confuse hikers). Unfortunately, one of the best places to see mountain goats is in the parking lot of the Logan Pass visitors center, where the animals come to lick sodium-rich antifreeze off the ground.

Orientation
Glacier's 1562 sq miles are delineated by the North Fork of the Flathead River in the west, US 2 in the south, US 89 and the Blackfeet Reservation in the east and the Canadian border in the north. Waterton Lakes National Park extends north from Glacier's northern border into the Canadian province of Alberta.

Glacier is divided into five regions, each revolving around a ranger station. The Polebridge area encompasses the park's northwest corner. The southwest corner is referred to as Lake McDonald and includes the area around Lake McDonald, the park's west entrance and Apgar Village. Two Medicine, in the southeast corner, is 12 miles northwest of East Glacier and US 89, and envelops the Two Medicine Valley and its lakes. North of East Glacier on US 89, St Mary is the eastern end of the Going-to-the-Sun Rd and border community for the Blackfeet Reservation. Many Glacier, in the northeast corner, is 13 miles west of US 89, by Swiftcurrent Lake. Hiking trails connect

---

Please Don't Feed the Bears
Back in 1915, only five years after the opening of Glacier National Park, James Shultz wrote that bears within the park were already becoming tame and were breaking into meat-houses of different camps. Things have not changed much in the past 80 years, except that the grizzlies and black bears have since also acquired an appetite for peanut butter, tuna fish and potato chips. All food and anything with a strong odor (toothpaste, deodorant, hair products) must be stored in a vehicle or tied up in a bag (backpacks or stuff-sacks work well) with a 25-foot rope on a bear-pole (provided at all park campsites). Hikers should make enough noise on the trail, especially at blind corners and in heavily berried areas, to alert animals of their approach (so as not to alarm them and provoke aggressive defensive behavior). Any bear sightings or encounters should be immediately reported to a park ranger. (For general bear information, see the Facts about the Rocky Mountains chapter.) ∎

---

all of these regions, but the Going-to-the-Sun Rd, a 50-mile scenic road which connects West Glacier to St Mary, is the only paved road that directly cuts across the park.

Information
Tourist Offices There are visitors centers and ranger stations at Apgar, Logan Pass and St Mary; Many Glacier and Polebridge only have ranger stations.

It's worthwhile to write (Glacier National Park, West Glacier, MT 59936), call (☎ 406-888-7800) or go online (www.nps.gov/glac/) before your trip to receive the free 'Glacier National Park Trip Planner,' which has maps and information on camping, accommodations, activities and seasonal programs in the park. Upon entering the park you'll receive the quarterly *Waterton – Glacier Guide* newspaper which details opening hours and activities for that particular season.

MONTANA

Park headquarters (☎ 406-888-7800, TTY 406-888-7806), in West Glacier between US 2 and the Apgar Ranger Station, takes care of administrative chores and provides visitor information year-round. A recording of current park events (☎ 406-888-5551) tells of ranger-led hikes, programs and special events going on in the park and mentions any unique conditions (storm threats, fire danger) that visitors should be aware of.

The Glacier Natural History Association (☎ 406-888-5756), in West Glacier's Belton railroad station, sells field-guides, books and maps for the park. It's open weekdays from 8 am to 5 pm. Central Reservations (☎ 406-226-5551) makes reservations at any of the park's lodges or motels.

The Glacier Institute (☎ 406-756-1211; www.nps.gov/glac/inst.htm), PO Box 7457, Kalispell, MT 59904, offers afternoon to week-long field classes that range from Blackfeet History to Insect Ecology to the Art of Fly-Fishing.

Entrance Fees A seven-day pass for anyone arriving by car, motorcycle or RV is $10. Those coming on foot or by bicycle pay $5. Remember that this fee does not include entrance to Waterton Lakes National Park. A one-year Glacier National Park Pass costs $20.

Backcountry Permits Day hikers do not need permits, but backpackers staying overnight in the park do. Permits are available at the Apgar and St Mary's visitors centers, and the Many Glacier Ranger Station. Being in the backcountry without one may result in a $200 fine. Despite all of the rigmarole involved in getting one, permits help to insure safety for backpackers, decrease the overuse of campgrounds and make backcountry rangers' jobs much easier.

Permits cost $4 per person per day. Half are available on a first-come, first-served basis on the day of or day before departure. The other half are available starting May 1 for the entire season. Reservations cost $20 for up to six people and can be made in advance by calling ☎ 406-888-7800, or by writing to 'Glacier National Park – Backcountry Permits,' West Glacier, MT 59936. At least half of the backcountry campsites will be available for reservation two days to 24 hours before departure on a first-come, first-served basis from a park visitors center.

Money The nearest banks to Glacier are in Columbia Falls and Browning. Most merchants in Waterton Lakes National Park accept US currency, though Canadian currency is not widely accepted in Glacier National Park. There are ATMs at Lake McDonald, Many Glacier and Glacier Park Lodges.

Post There are post offices in West Glacier (zip code 59936) and East Glacier (zip code 59434), and substations where you can post mail and buy stamps in Polebridge, Lake McDonald and in the grocery store at St Mary's Lodge.

Books An excellent historical account of life in the Glacier area is James Willard Shultz's *Blackfeet Tales of Glacier National Park* (Harvard Press, 1916). The Glacier Natural History Association in East Glacier publishes many useful books and natural history guides, including *Place Names of Glacier/Waterton National Parks* (Glacier Natural History Association, 1985) by Jack Holterman, which tells how and why mountains and rivers were named things like 'Gunsight' and 'Two Medicine.' Vicky Spring's *Exploring Waterton and Glacier National Parks* (The Mountaineers, 1985) is an excellent guide to the park's natural features, hiking trails and accommodations.

Medical Services For all emergencies within the park contact a ranger by calling park headquarters (☎ 406-888-7800) or dial 911. The best hospital in the area is Kalispell Regional Hospital (☎ 406-752-5111), 310 Sunnyview Lane, or, in Canada, Cardston Municipal Hospital (☎ 403-653-4411) in Cardston, Alberta.

MONTANA

Laundry & Showers Coin-operated laundry facilities and hot showers are available at the KOA and the Glacier Campground & BBQ in West Glacier and at the Y Lazy R RV Park & Campground in East Glacier.

Pets Dogs and cats are not allowed in the hotels in the park, or on any park trails.

Going-to-the-Sun Rd

In 1927, the various access roads on both sides of Glacier National Park were connected by the Going-to-the-Sun Rd, which crosses the Continental Divide at Logan Pass. As proof of American engineering ability (still new on the international scene when the road was built), the engineers spurned the multiple switchbacks of typical Alpine roads and found a route which required only two major turns.

Beginning at Apgar at the park's west entrance, the road skirts Lake McDonald's east shore from where you have excellent views of Stanton Mountain at the northeast end of the lake. Glacier Park 'cover shots' are often taken along this part of the road. Starting at the lake's northeast end, the road parallels the clear-flowing McDonald Creek through a narrow valley with steep-sided mountains on both sides. An excellent chance to experience the park's Pacific Northwest climate is along the **Trail of the Cedars**, a half-mile wheelchair accessible loop that begins from the well-marked Avalanche Creek parking lot. Avalanche Lake, which is 2 miles from the trailhead, is a good half-day hike destination.

North of Avalanche Creek, the road begins to approach the **Garden Wall** whose 9000-foot spine runs from Logan Pass north to Swiftcurrent Pass along the Continental Divide. This granite arête is the main dividing line between the west and east sides of the park. As the road ascends the Garden Wall it offers fantastic views of McDonald Creek and the park's westernmost clump of glacial peaks which lie northwest of the road. A parking lot at the road's major hairpin turn (called the Loop) has interpretive panels that show the peaks' names.

Between the Loop and Logan Pass, Going-to-the-Sun Rd traverses the Garden Wall passing the Weeping Wall and Bird Woman Falls, which flow constantly from May to November.

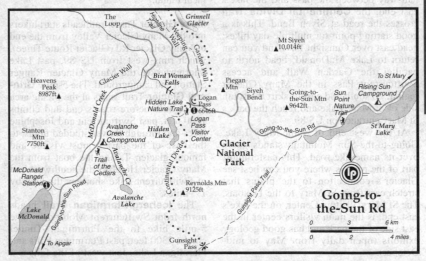

MONTANA

Going-to-the-Sun Rd

At **Logan Pass** there's an excellent visitors center with natural history displays, ranger talks and a good bookstore; open daily from mid-June to October. A popular trail from the upper level of the visitors center leads along the 1½-mile boardwalk to the **Hidden Lake Overlook**; the trail crosses the Continental Divide, passes hanging gardens and climbs (about 500 feet) to a basin lake at the foot of Mt Reynolds.

Another good hike from Logan Pass is along the **Highline Trail**, which starts across the road from the visitors center and travels north 7½ miles along the Garden Wall to the Granite Park Chalet. Wildflowers are abundant June to mid-August, and in September mountain goats and bighorn sheep are common. A 1-mile spur trail from the trail's north end climbs steeply to the top of the Garden Wall, where the Grinnell and Salamander glaciers are visible. The Loop Trail continues 4 miles past the chalet and meets Going-to-the-Sun Rd at the Loop parking lot, so a point-to-point hike is possible with two cars or the willingness to hitchhike.

East of Logan Pass the road skirts the south side of Piegan Mountain and follows Reynolds Creek to St Mary Lake. About half-way between the pass and the lake's east end, the **Continental Divide Trail** crosses the road at Siyeh Bend. This is a good starting point for multiple-day hikes: head east over Gunsight Pass and you can return to Lake McDonald; head north to parallel the Garden Wall and access Swiftcurrent Pass in the Many Glacier region; go south and east to skirt the south side of St Mary Lake and reach the park's St Mary entrance on US 89.

At the west end of Saint Mary Lake, Going-to-the-Sun Mountain stands guard over its namesake road. This easternmost part of the road is where you can best see Glacier's connection to the plains that stretch east from St Mary to the Dakotas. The St Mary Visitors Center, on the lake's east end, is the main visitors center in the east side of the park and has good geology exhibits (open daily from May to mid-October).

Without stopping, the drive from Apgar to St Mary takes about an hour and a half. Most people, however, take at least three hours to complete the picturesque trip. To make a loop trip, drive one-way on Going-to-the-Sun Rd then back along US 2 on the park's southern border.

From mid-October to mid-June, the road is closed from the Loop to St Mary. This is a good time to walk, run, bike or ski (depending on conditions) along the road.

Hiking

Visitors centers give out excellent hiking maps (divided into Lake McDonald, Logan Pass/St Mary, Many Glacier and Two Medicine areas) that have a map on one side and a spreadsheet – which tells the length, elevation gain, special features and trailhead locations – on the other. Each one covers 12 to 15 hikes.

Glacier Wilderness Guides and Montana Raft Co (☎ 406-387-5555; www.gorp.com/glacierwg/default.htm) is the only hiking and backpacking guide service licensed to operate in the park. Day-hikes cost $50 per person with a four-person minimum, four to six day trips cost $380 to $570 per person; it's an additional $10 for equipment rental.

Many Glacier Three trailheads start hikers into the Many Glacier Valley from the end of Many Glacier Rd (Glacier Route Three), which runs west from US 89, past Lake Sherburne, to the Many Glacier Ranger Station and campground. The 5-mile **Grinnell Glacier Trail** starts at the picnic area half a mile before road's end and climbs 1600 feet, past Swiftcurrent and Josephine lakes and through flower-studded fields, to the base of the park's most visible and famous glacier. Taking the boat from the Many Glacier Hotel to the southwest end of Swiftcurrent Lake shortens the hike by 1½ miles.

The **Iceberg/Ptarmigan Trail** heads north from Swiftcurrent Motor Inn. The 5-mile hike to the Ptarmigan Tunnel climbs 2300 feet, past Ptarmigan Falls and Ptarmigan Lake. Just west of the falls is a spur trail that heads south 2 miles to Iceberg Lake, an icy-blue cirque lake at the base of a sheer 3000-foot cliff; a flotilla of icebergs usually remains in the lake into July and August.

The 183-foot-long Ptarmigan Tunnel is the park's only tunnel constructed for hikers. Passing solo through it without encountering anyone (or anything) else on the way is supposedly a harbinger of good luck.

The 6-mile **Cracker Lake Trail**, a 1400-foot climb, offers some of the most accessible, dramatic scenery in the park. It starts in open grasslands (at the south end of the Many Glacier Hotel parking area), then follows Cracker Creek through its canyon, where 4100-foot cliffs rise up on both sides and ends at Cracker Lake in a cirque capped by 10,014-foot Mt Siyeh. There is quite a bit of horse traffic along the first few miles of this trail.

Two Medicine Valley Most trails in the Two Medicine Valley begin at the north end of Two Medicine Campground, or a half mile south at the east end of Two Medicine Lake, just past the boat dock. Taking the boat across the lake shaves almost 3 miles off any trail that passes the west end of the lake.

The **No Name Lake/Upper Two Medicine Lake Trail** rambles along the north shore of Two Medicine Lake and splits at mile 3½ to head either northwest another 1½ miles to No Name Lake and on through Bighorn Basin to Dawson Pass (3 miles beyond the split), or southwest to Upper Two Medicine Lake (1½ miles past the split) which rests in a cirque below Lone Walker Mountain. **Twin Falls**, a quarter-mile spur from the Upper Two Medicine Lake Trail, should not be missed.

The 7-mile **Pitamakan Pass Trail** heads northeast from Two Medicine Campground, around the east side of Rising Wolf Mountain and then west along the Dry Fork (which is very wet in the spring) of the Two Medicine River. Pitamakan Pass and Dawson Pass can be combined to make a 16.9-mile loop, a favorite route for backpackers with only a few days to spend in the backcountry.

Pitamakan Pass is named after a female Blackfeet chief who was so strong and brave in battle, often stealing more horses and counting more *coups* than anyone else in the war party, that she earned the title of the man's name 'Pi'tamakan.'

Polebridge Glacier's northwest corner is the least visited part of the park. Most trails up here follow a creek through a thick pine forest to a southwest-northeast trending lake, much like Lake McDonald which is the southernmost and largest on this side of the park. Dutch Creek, Logging Creek and Quartz Creek are all trails of this sort and can be reached off Polebridge Rd (Glacier Route Seven).

The most variety for hiking (and skiing) is found near **Bowman Lake**, accessible by car from the Polebridge Ranger Station. At the lake's south end is a campground, small ranger station and trails that extend in all directions. The Bowman Creek trail skirts the lake's northwest shore and continues to Brown Pass, surrounded by spectacular peaks and glaciers. Here the Boulder Pass Trail heads west to Upper Kintla and Kintla lakes (near the Agassiz Glacier, one of the biggest in the park) and east to the Goat Haunt backcountry ranger station and Waterton Lake (a popular route into Canada).

Waterton North of the Canadian border, the approaches to spectacular hikes are much shorter since roads penetrate quite far into the 'backcountry.' South of Waterton Park's entrance station (at the junction of Canadian Hwys 5 and 6), the Akamina Pkwy heads south and west, past Waterton Townsite, Upper Waterton, Middle Waterton and Waterton lakes. From the Townsite, where the park's headquarters and services are, the **Carthew Creek Trail** heads west along the base of Buchanan Ridge and ends at Cameron Lake (at the end of the Akamina Pkwy); this is a great overnight point-to-point hike for parties with two cars. Also starting at the Townsite is the primary route into Glacier National Park, along the west side of Waterton Lake. The **Cameron Lakeshore Trail**, at the end of the parkway is an easy yet scenic day-hike.

In the north part of Waterton, at the end of Blackiston Creek Rd, the **Red Rock Canyon Trail** is a great day-hike through a steep-walled canyon. Popular with backpackers is the **Snowshoe-Twin Lakes-South Kootenai Pass Loop**, which circles Anderson Peak and Lost Mountain.

Rafting

Glacier Raft Co (☎ 406-888-5454, 800-235-6781) is the oldest and arguably most reputable raft company in the area. Trips down the North Fork and Middle Fork of the Flathead River cost $28 for a half-day, $95 for a full-day including lunch. They also rent cabins and offer good rafting and accommodations packages.

Also reputable are Great Northern Whitewater (☎ 406-387-5340, 800-735-7897) and Glacier Wilderness Guides and Montana Raft Co (☎ 406-387-5555), which run similar trips and have competitive prices.

Road Biking

Glacier keeps its hiking trails off-limits to cyclists, so there is no mountain biking allowed. The closest thing to it is riding along the Polebridge Rd (Glacier Route Seven), which goes from the Fish Creek Campground near Apgar to the Polebridge Ranger Station and on to Bowman Lake or up to the Canadian Border along the North Fork of the Flathead River. This road is mostly dirt, gets relatively light traffic and is surrounded by thick forests.

Good road biking near the park is along its eastern boundary on Hwys 49 and 89, which parallel the Continental Divide for 31 miles between East Glacier and St Mary. From East Glacier the 8-mile side trip to Two Medicine Lake (the cutoff is 4 miles north of East Glacier) is beautiful, but very steep in some parts.

During peak season (from Memorial Day to Labor Day, unless otherwise posted)

cyclists are prohibited from riding on the Going-to-the-Sun Rd from 11 am to 4 pm. There are bike campsites ($3) at all campgrounds except Bowman and Kintla lakes in the northwest corner. Spaces are reserved for cyclists until 9 pm. Bike rentals are available in Apgar and at Scenic View Bicycle Rentals (☎ 406-226-9238) in East Glacier.

Fishing

No permit is required to fish Glacier's lakes and rivers. The North Fork and Middle Fork of the Flathead River are subject to Montana state fishing regulations (and thus require a fishing license) outside the park, but not within it. Fishing regulations and area restrictions are available at visitors centers. Favorite fishing spots among park rangers are Lake McDonald, Glenns Lake, Bowman Lake and Kennedy Creek. Cutthroat trout dominate Glacier's waters, but brook trout, whitefish, kokanee salmon and Arctic grayling also live in the park.

Boat rentals are available at Lake McDonald, the Apgar Village Inn, Many Glacier Hotel and at Two Medicine Lake.

Horseback Riding

Riders may bring their own horses into the park, but no stable rentals are available. A free brochure, available at visitors centers, explains the restrictions and regulations concerning horseback riding in the park.

Guided trips, lasting from one hour to all day, are available at Glacier Park Lodge, Lake McDonald Lodge, Many Glacier Hotel, St Mary's Lodge and West Glacier (see Places to Stay below).

Winter Activities

Winter weather on the western side of the Continental Divide is generally snowy and overcast, while the eastern side of the divide tends to be windy and sunny. Going-to-the-Sun Rd from West Glacier to the head of Lake McDonald is plowed all winter, as are US 89 and US 2, which allow some access to Glacier's southern boundary, St Mary Valley and Many Glacier Valley. Roads into the eastern interior may be open depending on conditions.

All of Glacier's trails and roads are open for **snowshoeing** and cross-country or backcountry **skiing** (snowmobiles are prohibited). The NPS 'Glacier Cross-Country Skiing' and 'Glacier Backcountry Winter Camping' brochures, available year-round from park headquarters and seasonally from ranger stations and visitors centers, outline trails in the Apgar, Marias Pass (on US 2), St Mary, Two Medicine Valley and Polebridge areas.

Guided cross-country trips and a network of groomed trails are available at the Izaak Walton Inn (☎ 406-888-5700) in Essex (on US 2). The North Fork Hostel (☎ 406-888-5241, 800-775-2938) in Polebridge is open year-round and has cross-country ski and snowshoe rentals (free for guests).

The Apgar Visitors Center is open on weekends and has current road, weather and camping conditions for the entire park. East Glacier, West Glacier and Essex have accommodations during the winter months when all hotels inside the park are closed.

Ranger-Led Activities

Rangers lead a variety of summer activities, including morning strolls, day-hikes, junior ranger programs and campfire talks. Schedules and activities vary from year to year, but always center around the Apgar Visitors Center, Logan Pass Visitors Center, St Mary's Lodge, Many Glacier Campground and Goat Haunt Ranger Station. Current schedules and topics are listed in the 'Nature with a Naturalist' insert in the *Waterton/Glacier Guide* newspaper given to people upon entering the park and available at park ranger stations.

Organized Tours

Glacier Park Inc's fleet of red 'jammer' buses (named for the days when the coaches did not have automatic transmission and drivers ground and jammed the gears) are vintage 15-passenger motor coaches with rollback canvas tops that make half-day ($30 per person) and full-day ($55) tours throughout the park and (from East Glacier and St Mary) to the Museum of the Plains Indians in Browning ($20). Buses stop at all major turnouts, points of interest, visitors centers and Apgar Village Inn, Lake McDonald Lodge, Rising Sun Motor Inn, Swiftcurrent Motor Inn, Many Glacier Hotel, St Mary's Lodge and Glacier Park Lodge. Information is available at hotel information desks, or by calling ☎ 406-226-9311, ext 609, May 15 through September; ☎ 602-207-6000 the rest of the year.

Sun Tours (☎ 406-226-9220) gives a Historical Perspectives tour led by Blackfeet tribal members that focuses on the Native American interpretation of the park's history. Tours leave from East Glacier and St Mary in the morning, travel over Going-to-the-Sun Rd and return by the same route in approximately six hours.

Places to Stay

Campgrounds and lodges within the park are generally open from early May to mid-October. East Glacier and West Glacier offer year-round accommodations and overflow space when the park fills up – a frequent occurrence in summer. To be near nightlife, stay in Kalispell or Whitefish.

Places to Stay – budget

Camping – Glacier National Park The NPS (☎ 406-888-7800 for campsite availability information) maintains 10 campgrounds. Sites fill up by mid-morning, particularly in July and August. Tent sites for people in cars and RV sites cost $10 per night and fees for campers without cars are $3. Campfires are allowed in designated fireplaces, though are generally discouraged and often prohibited when fire conditions are hazardous. Because sites fill up quickly, many campers end up staying at private campgrounds just outside the entrance in West Glacier.

Year-round primitive camping is available at Apgar, Avalanche and St Mary and no fees are collected after October 1. Rising Sun Outdoor Adventures (☎ 406-892-2602 in the summer, ☎ 406-862-2423 the rest of the year), 15 miles from the West Glacier entrance in Columbia

MONTANA

Glacier Park Chalets

Built during the railroad phase in the 1910s, two of Glacier's high-mountains chalets are slated to reopen by 2000. When the chalets first opened, they were part of a grand circuit that park visitors made from one lodge to another, built one day's ride (by horse) apart. Compared to Glacier Park and McDonald lodges, the chalets were rustic and gave guests the sense of 'roughing it.'

After WWII, the chalets were opened to guests for overnight stays in the backcountry. People could hike up to the chalet with a day-pack and have meals and bedding provided for them for one night. Granite Park Chalet is accessible via the Highline Trail, 7 miles from Logan Pass, or from the steeper and shorter loop trail off Going-to-the-Sun Rd at the Heaven's Peak lookout. Sperry Chalet, at the southern foot of Gunsight Mountain and the Sperry Glacier, is reached from the Sperry Chalet Trail which starts from Lake McDonald Lodge, or the Gunsight Trail from the south end of St Mary Lake.

Eventually the chalets fell into disrepair and were finally closed in the early 1980s. They still make good hiking destinations (they're both boarded up, but fun to inspect from the outside), though now you must hike back down from them or be prepared with your own camping gear. When the chalets (both on the National Register) reopen, they will provide the same services that they did after WWII: bunks, bedding and meals. ■

Heights, rents tents, backpacks, stoves and any other equipment you would need for a couple days of backcountry hiking and camping; reservations are advised since their stock is limited.

Often dictated by what's available, some favorite campground choices are: touristy *Apgar Campground*, on the southwest end of Lake McDonald near Apgar Village, convenient for campfire programs and ranger-led activities; lakeside *Sprague Creek Campground*, 1 mile south of Lake McDonald Lodge; unprotected *Rising Sun Campground*, 10 miles west of St Mary on the north shore of St Mary Lake, popular with travelers approaching the park from the east; and the *Many Glacier Campground*, surrounded by peaks and popular with hikers.

Twelve miles north of East Glacier, *Two Medicine Lake Campground*, at the southern foot of Rising Wolf Mountain, is busy in the daytime due to boat tours on the lake and the historic Two Medicine Camp Store, but relatively uncrowded at night.

Built by the Great Northern Railroad in 1911 to accommodate saddle horse travelers, the Two Medicine Camp originally consisted of a large dormitory, dining hall and five cabins. When Going-to-the-Sun Rd increased auto traffic through the park, Two Medicine was sold to the government and taken over by the Civilian Conservation Corps. Franklin D Roosevelt was inducted into the Blackfeet Tribe at Two Medicine in 1934 and afterwards held one of his famous fireside chats in front of its grand hearth. The Two Medicine chalets have since been destroyed, leaving only (what is now) the camp store.

In the park's northwest corner are its two most remote campgrounds: *Kintla Lake Campground* and *Bowman Lake Campground*, both north of the Polebridge entrance and accessible via dirt roads. These campgrounds do not reserve spaces for hikers or cyclists.

Camping & Cabins – West Glacier Campgrounds and cabins in West Glacier are generally open from May 1 to September 30. San-Suz-Ed and Great Northern Chalets are open year-round.

Three miles west of the park entrance and a half mile north of US 2, the *Lake Five Resort* (☎ 406-387-5601) has a summer-camp atmosphere. Cabins with four beds, a bathroom and kitchenette cost $92 per night, tent sites are $14 and RV sites are $18. Families return annually and often stay for at least a week, so reservations are highly recommended.

Next to the Lake Five turnoff, 2½ miles west of the park on US 2, is the *San-Suz-Ed RV Park & Campground* (☎ 406-387-5280) with tent sites ($15) and RV sites ($22) that are protected from US 2 by a thick stand of pine and fir trees; shower and laundry facilities are exceptionally clean.

The *West Glacier KOA* (☎ 406-387-5341), 2½ miles west of the park entrance and 1 mile south of US 2, has 42 tent sites ($18) and 106 RV sites ($26), cabins ($30), a store, laundry facilities, horseshoe court, breakfast barbecue and nightly slide shows. Very similar is the *Glacier Campground & BBQ* (☎ 406-387-5689) on the south side of US 2, 1 mile west of the park's entrance, which has $15 tent sites and $18 RV sites.

Glacier Raft Co (☎ 406-888-5454, 800 235-6781) rents nice pine cabins for $65 to $95.

Camping – East Glacier The *Firebrand Campground & Y Lazy R RV Park* (☎ 406-226-5573) is in a shadeless grass field 2 blocks south of US 2 on Lindhe Ave. It has 10 tent sites ($11) and 30 RV sites ($13), clean restrooms and showers and laundry facilities. All sites have unobstructed views of the surrounding peaks. It's open June 1 to September 15.

The *Sears Motel* (see below) has five tent sites ($10) and 12 RV sites ($14) behind the motel on a scenic but barren piece of land.

Hostels The HI/AYH hostel *Brownie's* (☎ 406-226-4426), on the 2nd story of Brownie's Grocery & Deli on the east side of Hwy 49, is usually packed with young travelers and is consequently a great place to find hiking or backpacking partners. Accommodations are in crowded eight-bed, single-sex dorm rooms ($12), or, if you call early enough, private rooms with double beds ($20). The common room and kitchen are both clean and well-stocked. The hostel is locked from 9:30 am to 5 pm, except when the weather is bad; no curfew. Sleeping bags are not allowed; sheets,

blankets and pillows are provided free of charge. It's open May to mid-September.

Also in East Glacier, the *Backpacker's Inn* (☎ 406-226-9392), behind Serrano's Mexican Restaurant, 1 block south of US 2, offers a quiet alternative to Brownie's. There are three dorm rooms (two single-sex and one coed), each with three bunk beds. Rooms tend to be on the chilly side and a large shady yard acts as the hostel's only common area, so think twice before staying here when the weather is bad. Beds cost $10 per person, $12 if you don't have your own sleeping bag. The hostel is locked from 10 am to 5 pm; the restaurant is open 5 pm to 9 pm and handles check-in; there are no kitchen facilities.

Ultra-rustic and charming, the *Northfork Hostel* (☎ 406-888-5241) in Polebridge has tent sites ($8 per person), small and large cabins ($25/40) and beds ($12) year-round. All guests have use of the kitchen facilities and reading area plus free use of mountain bikes, cross-country skis and snowshoes.

Places to Stay – middle
Motels – West Glacier The *Vista Motel* (☎ 406-888-5311, 800-831-7101), on a hillside above US 2, 2 miles west of the park entrance, has 26 rooms for $46/55 single/double and an outdoor pool.

The *Glacier Highland Resort Motel* (☎ 406-888-5427, 800-766-0811) is at the turnoff to the park's west entrance on US 2, across from the train station. Above the rest of the complex are 33 motel units and a hot tub, looking out towards the mountain peaks. Rooms cost $62/70 single/double May 15 to September 15 and $55/60 the rest of the year.

The closest motel to the park entrance is the *River Bend Motel* (☎ 406-888-5662), on the north side of the railroad tracks and US 2. It has rooms, a bit on the shabby side, for around $55.

Motels – East Glacier All rooms and cottages in East Glacier are within a half mile of the junction of US 2 and Hwy 49. Most places are open from May to October and charge around $20 extra (per room) in July and August; prices below are for July and August unless otherwise noted.

The *East Glacier Motel* (☎ 406-226-5593), on the west side of Hwy 49, has cute cottages with double beds that cost $65 in July and August; $35 in May, June, September and October. Motel units with kitchenettes cost $47 and $70 respectively.

On Hwy 49, *Jacobsen's Scenic View Cottages* (☎ 406-226-4422) are protected from the highway by cottonwood trees. Cottages with a queen-size bed cost $58, a double bed and single bed are $65 and $45 respectively. The *Mountain Pine Motel* (☎ 406-226-4403), on the west side of Hwy 49, has rooms and a few free-standing cabins for around $50.

The *Sears Motel* (☎ 406-226-4432), on the west side of Hwy 49, is the only motel in town with cable TV; rooms cost $48/53 single/double. The *Whistling Swan Motel* (☎ 406-226-4412) on US 2 has small rooms for $46.

One block south of US 2, *Porter's Alpine Motel* (☎ 406-226-4402) has rooms (which share a covered entry) for $66, and one cabin for $125.

Places to Stay – top end

Glacier National Park In the early 1910s James Hill's Great Northern Railroad built a series of grand hotels to entice wealthy travelers to visit Glacier National Park. Guests would arrive by train at the Belton station in West Glacier or the Glacier National Park station at East Glacier and then be transported by 'jammer' bus or horse-drawn carriage to their lodge of choice. Guests often stayed for several weeks at a time, journeying from one lodge to the next – about one day's ride by horse. Glacier's historic lodges are now operated by Glacier Park Inc (see Organized Tours above) and cost $55 to $105 per room. Most have a restaurant or coffee shop, laundry facilities, showers and general store.

Outside the park boundaries in East Glacier, the *Glacier Park Lodge* (☎ 406-226-9311) is the flagship of Glacier's grand hotels. Perhaps more than any other, this lodge testifies to the grand visions of the Great Northern Railroad. Sixty Douglas fir timbers (estimated to be 500 to 800 years old) support interior balconies surrounding the lobby and a 65-foot ceiling with two skylights and two massive iron chandeliers. Blackfeet Indians called the lodge 'Oom-Coo-La-Mush-Taw,' or 'Big Tree Lodge.' The lobby and annex don't appear to have changed much since 1913; the rooms, however, with elegant baths, telephones and TVs, are a different story. In keeping with modern amenities, the lodge has added an outdoor pool and pitch-and-putt and nine-hole golf courses.

The *Apgar Village Inn* (☎ 406-888-5632) sits at the southern end of Lake McDonald in the midst of the heavily trafficked and well-equipped Apgar Village (it has a store, two restaurants, gift shop and horse, boat and bike rentals). On the Going-to-the-Sun Rd, *Lake McDonald Lodge* (☎ 406-888-5431) has a cozy hunting-lodge atmosphere and a beautiful location on Lake McDonald; many of the hotel's 100 rooms look out to the lake.

In the heart of the park on the north shore of Swiftcurrent Lake, surrounded by dramatic peaks, the *Many Glacier Hotel* (☎ 406-732-4411 or 602-207-6000) looks like a Swiss Alpine chalet. With 208 rooms, Many Glacier is the largest hotel inside the park. Its remote location has made Many Glacier a bit precarious at times: in the spring of 1964 a major flood trapped the general manager, chef and 75 employees in the hotel for 10 days without electricity or heat.

Blackfeet Indians call the lake and river that pass in front of the *Swiftcurrent Motor Inn* (☎ 406-732-5531 or 602-207-6000) 'Ixikuoyi-Yetahtai' which means 'swift-flowing stream.' Once employee dormitories for the Great Northern Railroad and a teepee camp for people wanting a sense of being 'out West,' the inn now acts primarily as an overflow space for the Many Glacier Hotel (guests have access to all of the hotel's facilities) and lodging for hikers who want to explore the Many Glacier region.

MONTANA

The *Rising Sun Motor Inn* (☎ 406-732-5532) on the upper north shore of St Mary Lake, 6 miles from St Mary Village, was constructed in 1940 as a resting point for motorists making the (at that time) grueling Going-to-the-Sun Rd drive.

For anyone venturing across the border into Waterton Lakes National Park in Alberta, the seven-story *Prince of Wales Hotel* (☎ 403-859-2231), sits on a bluff overlooking icy-blue Waterton Lake. The hotel has 81 rooms, a restaurant, lounge, tea room, gift shop, boat tours of Waterton Lake and a nearby golf course. This much-photographed place is worth a look, even if you're not planning to stay.

Essex The *Izaak Walton Inn* (☎ 406-888-5700), halfway between East Glacier and West Glacier and a half mile north of US 2, is a popular cross-country ski destination. Decorated with old railroad memorabilia, including four cabooses that have been converted into charming rooms, the inn is worth a stop for travelers skirting the park's southern border. Amenities include a good but overpriced restaurant, rustic bar and access to hiking and cross-country ski trails. Rooms cost $78 to $140, and ski packages that include meals and equipment start at $685 per week.

West Glacier The *Great Northern Chalets* (☎ 406-387-5340, 800-735-7897), 1½ miles west of the park entrance on the north side of US 2, are West Glacier's most deluxe accommodations but their highway-side setting is a drawback. Each chalet has a TV/VCR, stocked kitchenette and fireplace, and costs between $95 and $165 a night, including the use of a lap pool and hot tub. The owners also operate fly-fishing, white-water rafting and helicopter tours through Great Northern Whitewater.

Places to Eat
Unlike the accommodations around the park, most restaurants are open year-round. In summer, there are grocery stores with an array of camping supplies in Apgar, Lake

McDonald Lodge, Rising Sun and at the Swiftcurrent Motor Inn.

In East Glacier *Serrano's* serves up good Mexican food for under $10 and has a rousing bar scene on weekends. *Brownie's Grocery & Deli* has a well-rounded grocery supply and makes all its own breads, cookies, pastries and bagels – and always has a pot of strong coffee on the stove.

Your best bet in West Glacier is to head to Hungry Horse, Columbia Falls or (better yet) Whitefish.

The dining room in Waterton's Prince of Wales Hotel is perfect for a nice meal and has a great view.

Getting There & Away
Air The closest airport to Glacier National Park is the Glacier International Airport near Kalispell, 20 miles southeast of the park's west entrance. Delta, Horizon Air and United Express fly into this airport. (See Whitefish & Kalispell – Getting There & Away), but more airlines service the airport in Great Falls, 158 miles from East Glacier. Travelers flying to Canada land at either Lethbridge, Alberta, 80 miles northeast of the Waterton Lakes entrance, or Calgary, 165 miles to the north.

Train Amtrak's *Empire Builder* follows the southern border of Glacier National Park with stops at East Glacier (Glacier Park Station) and West Glacier (Belton Station). Eastbound trains stop at East Glacier in the morning (around 9 am) and westbound trains stop in the evening (around 7 pm). Riding time between East Glacier and West Glacier is approximately 30 minutes. Tickets are available at East Glacier's station from 6 am to 11:30 am and 6 to 7:30 pm. Travelers boarding the train in West Glacier must buy tickets onboard. A one-way ticket from either station to Havre is $36, to Seattle is $114 and to Minneapolis, MN, is $167.

Getting Around
The speed limit is 45 mph on all Glacier National Park roads unless otherwise posted. Vehicle restrictions are imposed on

MONTANA

the Going-to-the-Sun Rd only. Vehicles or combinations wider than 8 feet or longer than 21 feet, are prohibited between Avalanche Creek Campground and the Sun Point picnic area. Trailers may be parked temporarily at campgrounds, or at Sun Point on the east side of the park.

Bus The NPS runs a shuttle bus service on Going-to-the-Sun Rd to cope with traffic and increasingly strict size restrictions for recreational vehicles (hopefully Glacier will eventually limit all transportation to shuttle service). Glacier Park Inc (see Organized Tours above) operates a variety of shuttle services through the park,

including its Hikers Express, which leaves from Many Glacier Hotel in the morning and drops passengers off at three trailheads: Siyeh Bend, Logan Pass and The Loop (for $16, $17 and $20 respectively, per person each way; park entrance fees are not included).

Car In West Glacier rental cars are available from the Glacier Highland Resort (☎ 406-888-5427, 800-766-0811). In East Glacier the Glacier Park Trading Co (☎ 406-226-4433) handles Avis car rentals, and Sears Motel (☎ 406-226-4432) has a private fleet of cars. All car-rental companies offer vans and 4WD vehicles.

Yellowstone Country

'Yellowstone Country' refers to the part of Montana directly north and west of Yellowstone National Park. This chapter covers the three rivers that feed into the park, including the Yellowstone River, running through the Paradise Valley, and the Madison and Gallatin rivers – both tributaries of the Missouri River. The college town of Bozeman is also covered here. The Madison, Gallatin and Paradise valleys are current hotbeds of develop-

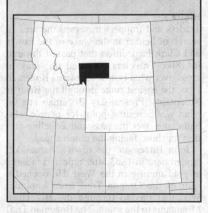

ment, fueled by media coverage and an influx of artists, authors and filmmakers. Big Sky's recent ranking as one of the 'Top 10 Ski Resorts in the USA' by a popular ski magazine has helped stoke the fire. With Yellowstone as a magnet, these valleys (which run north-south between I-90 and Yellowstone) have always been heavily traveled. But while they are mainly viewed as routes to Yellowstone National Park, each of these valleys is a destination in itself, especially if you plan on hiking, fishing or skiing.

Only 50 miles long and easily admired from the road (though a hike will reveal more beauty), Paradise Valley is well-suited to day trips from Bozeman, Livingston or the Mammoth Hot Springs area of Yellowstone National Park.

The Absaroka-Beartooth Wilderness and Red Lodge areas are harder to get to (Billings is the largest gateway town) and thus less traveled than the three 'big-name' valleys that link Yellowstone with Bozeman. The rugged, high-Alpine scenery of the Beartooth Plateau is unlike anything else you'll see in the state.

BOZEMAN

Developed as a rest area for weary travelers, Bozeman (population 28,500) continues to be a place where people stay longer than they had planned. Each fall a new contingent of college students comes to study at Montana State University (MSU), and many of them stay well beyond the four-year mark. Skiers arrive here in the winter and find that they are still here in the summer three years later and have metamorphosed into anglers and mountain bikers.

Some Montanans have mixed feelings about the number of tourists who have come to Bozeman, fallen in love with the land and now own 20 acres down the Madison River. Californians fed up with traffic and Coloradans fed up with Californians have

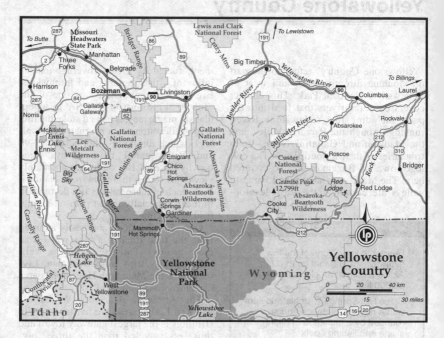

relocated to Bozeman. Its inflated reputation often leads people to believe that Bozeman is one of Montana's major towns, but Bozeman's importance and popularity are relatively new. Montanans, while in accord that Bozeman is a fun place to go, are often shocked to learn that 'Bozeman' is synonymous with 'Montana' for many people.

Bozeman's ambiance is equally influenced by its student population, 'small-town' agricultural roots and natural setting at the foot of the Bridger Mountains and Gallatin Valley. As the commercial center of a rich agricultural community, Bozeman is the business and recreational meeting point for farmers and ranchers. The university breeds a sizable backpack-wearing, espresso-drinking crowd.

With these two populations feeding its commercial and retail market, Bozeman enjoys a solid economy that fosters enthusiasm in the community. Music and the arts flourish, the Museum of the Rockies is touted by scientists and tourists alike, high-end boutiques and gift shops fill century-old buildings along Main St and you can bet that one out of every three people you encounter has been hiking, bike riding or skiing earlier in the day.

History

Traders and trappers traversed the area in search of beaver in the wake of the Lewis and Clark Expedition that passed through in 1806. Travelers funneled this way to cross over what is now known as Bozeman Pass, the easiest route through the Bridger Mountains. Present-day Bozeman sits on what was a resting point for people who had come over the pass and a fueling station for those facing the climb ahead.

John Bozeman, the town's namesake, landed here in 1863 after repeated failures at gold mining in the West. He opened a spur of the Oregon Trail from Laramie, WY, that passed through the Big Horn Mountains to the south. The Bozeman Trail was initially very successful, but after the Sioux – in an attempt to prevent settlement on their land – raided several wagon trains, the trail was deemed too dangerous for travel. Determined to remain in the West, Bozeman transferred his travel and business skills to a more stable clientele, becoming the head supplier for Fort Ellis, a protective fort 3 miles east of town.

In 1883, the same year that the town incorporated, the Northern Pacific Railroad connected Bozeman to both coasts. Trade and commerce quickly expanded, and travelers recognized Bozeman as a launching point for trips to Yellowstone National Park. The founding of Montana State University in 1893 sealed the community's success. Just over 100 years later, after a quiet, constant existence, Bozeman is the fastest-growing city in Montana.

Orientation

Bozeman sits at an elevation of 4754 feet, halfway between the western foot of the Bridger Range and the Gallatin River. I-90 follows the old Northern Pacific route through the mountains via Bozeman Pass, then heads west past the northeast edge of downtown and away toward Three Forks and Butte. Hwy 10 parallels I-90 northwest of town between Bozeman and Three Forks. There are two freeway exits for Bozeman off I-90. The Main St exit is best for people coming from the east; it runs west toward downtown. The 7th Ave exit puts you on 7th Ave, which heads south to meet Main St at a major intersection 2 blocks east of downtown.

Downtown Bozeman is easily navigable. Main St is the primary artery, with Mendenhall St running parallel 1 block north and Babcock St 1 block south. Grand Ave runs from north to south, perpendicular to Main St, and is the dividing line between named (Bozeman, Black, Tracy, Willson) and numbered avenues. West of town, Main St drops south before becoming Huffine Lane, the road that

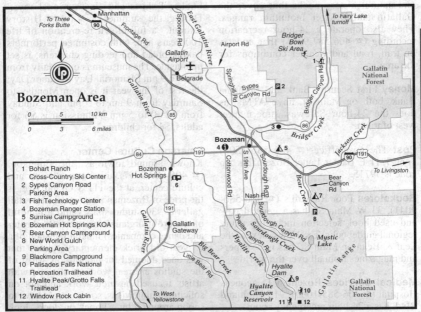

Bozeman Area

0   5   10 km
0   3   6 miles

1 Bohart Ranch
   Cross-Country Ski Center
2 Sypes Canyon Road
   Parking Area
3 Fish Technology Center
4 Bozeman Ranger Station
5 Sunrise Campground
6 Bozeman Hot Springs KOA
7 Bear Canyon Campground
8 New World Gulch
   Parking Area
9 Blackmore Campground
10 Palisades Falls National
   Recreation Trailhead
11 Hyalite Peak/Grotto Falls
   Trailhead
12 Window Rock Cabin

leads to US 191 S, toward Big Sky and West Yellowstone.

The MSU campus is 10 blocks south of Main St between 3rd and 11th Aves. Tree-lined streets and 100-year-old homes characterize the blocks between downtown and the university. A good way to explore the town is to park downtown and walk over to the campus through the residential areas or vice versa.

Information
Tourist Offices Bozeman's chamber of commerce (☎ 406-586-5421, 800-228-4224) puts out an outstanding, free annual visitors guide, available at most places to stay and in their gas-station-turned-office at 1205 E Main St, 1 mile east of downtown. The Visitors Information Center (open summer only), at 1001 N 7th Ave, is convenient for people coming off I-90 from the west.

The USFS Bozeman Ranger Station (☎ 406-587-6920), 3710 Fallon St, 4 miles west of downtown off US 191, has maps and natural history books that cover the Gallatin and Bridger mountain ranges. They also operate a 24-hour recreation recording (☎ 406-587-9784) that updates on trail, road and weather conditions for the area.

Money First Security Bank and Montana Bank, both on Main St, have ATMs, as does the 24-hour Safeway supermarket west of town.

Post The post office (☎ 406-586-1508) is at 5711 E Baxter Lane; Bozeman's zip code is 59715.

Bookstores Poor Richard's (☎ 406-586-9041), 33 W Main St, has a general new and used book selection including many regional guidebooks. The News, next to the Leaf & Bean on Main St, has newspapers and magazines from all over the world.

Medical Services Bozeman Deaconess Hospital (☎ 406-585-1000), 915 Highland Blvd, has a 24-hour emergency room.

Laundry East Main Laundry, on the east edge of town at 536 E Main St, has a drop-off service that costs roughly $2 per load and is open until 7:30 pm.

Museum of the Rockies
Montana State University's Museum of the Rockies (☎ 406-994-3466), at the corner of S 7th Ave and Kagy Blvd, is the largest and most entertaining museum in Montana. Visitors journey through a chronological procession of exhibits, from dinosaurs to early Native American art and artifacts to full-scale replicas of modern Montana buildings. The Taylor Planetarium, one of the few facilities in the world that can simulate the three-dimensional effects of flight through space, has popular shows in the afternoon. Even better is the 'Tour of the Night Sky' (from a Native American perspective) on Friday and Saturday nights. Besides being a great visual show, the program presents Native American stories, myths and legends about the universe.

The museum store is a good place to buy books, T-shirts and 'instructional toys.' During the summer a 'Living History Exhibit,' a full-blown re-creation of life 100 years ago, with costumed performers baking bread and feeding chickens, is set up outside. The museum is open daily from 9 am to 9 pm Memorial Day to Labor Day; the rest of the year it is open Monday to Saturday from 9 am to 5 pm and Sunday from 12:30 to 5 pm. Admission is $6 for adults, $4 for children.

Emerson Cultural Center
Known around town as 'the Emerson' (☎ 406-587-9797), this nonprofit arts and culture center, at the 111 S Grand Ave, is the pride of Bozeman's art scene. Ten retail galleries, 30 studio spaces and a handful of nonprofit organizations (mostly theater and dance companies) inhabit the shell of a 75-year-old brick elementary school that was once doomed for demolition. Most of the studios are real working studios, with artists focused on their work and not on soliciting public visits, so you might have to snoop around a bit – knock on doors, look

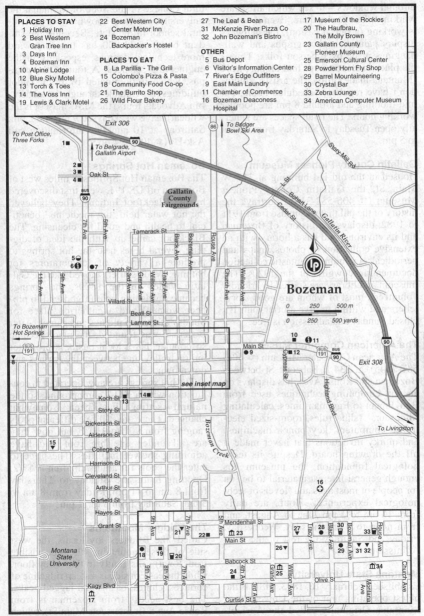

PLACES TO STAY
1 Holiday Inn
2 Best Western
   Gran Tree Inn
3 Days Inn
4 Bozeman Inn
10 Alpine Lodge
12 Blue Sky Motel
13 Torch & Toes
14 The Voss Inn
19 Lewis & Clark Motel
22 Best Western City
   Center Motor Inn
24 Bozeman
   Backpacker's Hostel

PLACES TO EAT
8 La Parrilla - The Grill
15 Colombo's Pizza & Pasta
18 Community Food Co-op
21 The Burrito Shop
26 Wild Flour Bakery

27 The Leaf & Bean
31 McKenzie River Pizza Co
32 John Bozeman's Bistro

OTHER
5 Bus Depot
6 Visitor's Information Center
7 River's Edge Outfitters
9 East Main Laundry
11 Chamber of Commerce
16 Bozeman Deaconess
   Hospital

17 Museum of the Rockies
20 The Haufbrau,
   The Molly Brown
23 Gallatin County
   Pioneer Museum
25 Emerson Cultural Center
28 Powder Horn Fly Shop
29 Barrel Mountaineering
30 Crystal Bar
33 Zebra Lounge
34 American Computer Museum

Bozeman

0   250   500 m
0   250   500 yards

MONTANA

through windows – to see which artists are working when you're there. Even if no one is working (a rare occasion), the hallways display paintings, photographs and wallhangings made by Emerson folks. This is the place in Bozeman to find unique, truly 'Montana-made' gifts. The artists' studios don't have regularly scheduled hours, but mid-morning and around 8 pm are popular working hours. The retail spaces are generally open Tuesday to Saturday from 10 am to 5 pm.

Gallatin County Pioneer Museum

Housed in the old jail building at 317 W Main St, the Gallatin County Pioneer Museum (☎ 406-582-3195) portrays the history of the jail that was in use from 1911 to 1982, displays the history of Bozeman and its environs, and has a library with an extensive collection of photos, maps and periodicals, including a fantastic collection documenting cowgirls of the 1920s. The museum and library are staffed by friendly volunteers, most of whom are good storytellers and willing to give a brief tour. It's closed Sunday and admission is free.

The American Computer Museum

The American Computer Museum (☎ 406 587-7545), at 234 E Babcock St between Bozeman and Rouse Aves, has displays on ancient computing techniques used from Babylonian to Egyptian times, calculating 'dinosaurs' (slide rules, room-sized electronic computers, key punch machines) and quirky inventions that never made it off the drawing board. Despite its technological foundation, the museum has enough general-interest material to be fun for people of most ages and 'levels of technological experience.' Hours are daily from 10 am to 4 pm June to August, and from noon to 4 pm Tuesday, Wednesday, Friday and Saturday the rest of the year. Admission is $2.

Montana State University

Established February 16, 1893, MSU is the oldest operating unit of the University of Montana. Originally called the Agricultural College of the State of Montana, the university was long known as *the* agricultural school in the state. Recently the student body of 11,000 has turned toward more technical degrees, especially in the engineering sciences. A tour of the campus, which is dominated by brick Tudor buildings, is available through the studentrun Advocats tours (the MSU mascot is the wildcat) leave weekdays at 9 am and 2 pm, Saturday at 10 am. For information call Ask-Us (☎ 406-994-4636).

Bozeman Hot Springs

The Bozeman Hot Springs, 8 miles west of Bozeman off US 191, were first discovered by the Blackfoot Indians. They believed the hot water held 'big medicine,' beneficial to health and good for cleansing. The Blackfoot came up with the idea of digging several holes near the hot springs to produce a variety of temperatures for bathing. When settlers moved into the Gallatin Valley in the 1800s, the springs became a washing hole (a godsend to pioneer women) and a gathering place for Sunday afternoon picnics and games. After Bozeman was founded, the place became so popular that a local business promoter built a trolley line between the springs and downtown.

The hot springs are now operated in conjunction with a KOA campground, so the natural setting has been somewhat changed. There are still five different pools ranging from 90° to 110°F, but now they are all under one big roof and have adjoining shower facilities. The price to enter the pools for adults/children is $3/2. Opening hours are Sunday to Thursday from 8 am to 11 pm, Friday from 8 am to 5 pm, Saturday from 5 to 11 pm.

The Bridger Mountains

Called 'the Bridgers' by locals, the west side of these mountains (the side visible from town) rolls gently to the valley floor, while the eastern side is a steep ridgeline of cornices, chutes, basins and jagged peaks. The best access from Bozeman is from Rouse Ave S (it intersects Main St), which heads north and under the I-90 overpass before veering into Bridger Canyon Rd; signs for Bridger Bowl Ski Area line the route. Before the road crosses to the east side of the range, there's a picnic spot and trailhead for the 'M,' the MSU symbol visible from miles around. This is a popular sunset destination. Across the road, **Bozeman's Fish Technology Center** works on fish research and management programs, such as the recovery of Arctic grayling from the Big Hole River and restoration of the greenback cutthroat in Colorado. A self-guided tour takes you through the hatching grounds and laboratories, open daily from 8 am to 4:30 pm.

Bridger Canyon Rd continues east and then north, flanked by cattle and horse ranches and the occasional B&B. About 14 miles past the 'M,' Bridger Bowl offers downhill skiing (see below) and a great place to watch the golden and bald eagle migration in early November. When the birds come through (usually the first week in November), the mountain often opens one of its chairlifts to get to the top and see the birds up close; hiking up is another viable option. Just south of Bridger Bowl, the little cabin of Bohart Ranch cross-country ski center is a good mountain biking departure point and has an 18-hole 'folf' (Frisbee golf) course; bring your own disc.

About 6 miles past Bridger Bowl the road enters National Forest land and hiking opportunities abound. An excellent destination is **Fairy Lake**, 9 miles west of the main road (it's well signed), where there is a campground, picnic area and trailheads at the foot of an awe-inspiring ridge. A steep 3-mile hike takes you to the top of Sacajawea Peak, the highest in the range (9665 feet).

Hyalite Canyon & Reservoir

South of Bozeman via 19th Ave and Hyalite Canyon Rd, the Hyalite area is named for the mineral hyalite, a colorless, often translucent opal that laces many of the canyon's ridge lines. Hanging valleys and waterfalls are characteristic of the area. Surrounded by the Hyalite Peaks at the south end of Hyalite Canyon, 200-acre Hyalite Reservoir provides Bozeman with drinking water and recreationalists with campgrounds, hiking, cross-country ski trails and wheelchair-accessible fishing piers.

The area's best hiking is from roads that extend south of the reservoir. Along West Fork Rd is the **Hyalite Peak/Grotto Falls trailhead**, the departure point (at 7000 feet) for a 7-mile climb up to Hyalite Peak (10,299 feet); from the peak, the **Gallatin Divide Devil's Backbone Trail** extends 40 miles along a jagged ridge of the Gallatin Range. East Fork Rd ends 4 miles south of the reservoir at the easy, half-mile **Palisades Falls National Recreation Trail**, which leads to cascading Palisades Falls.

The summer hiking trails at Hyalite Canyon Recreation Area double as cross-country ski trails in the winter. From Blackmore Campground, accessible from the parking lot along the top of Hyalite Dam, are a moderate 4-mile loop and a 14-mile ski-mountaineering loop. The area is also considered one of the best ice-climbing spots in the USA. Stop by Barrel Mountaineering, downtown on Main St, for guides and equipment.

The *Window Rock Cabin*, 1 mile south of the reservoir, is a small field station built in the 1940s that sleeps six people (wheelchair accessible). It's equipped with wood stoves, tables and chairs, an ax, shovel, bucket and cleaning supplies and costs $20 per night. Campgrounds on the north and east sides of the reservoir have wheelchair-accessible pit toilets, fire rings and picnic areas, and cost $9 per night. To get information on campgrounds and cabins, or to make cabin reservations (done on a first-come, first-served basis), contact the Bozeman Ranger Station (☎ 406-587-6920).

Hiking & Climbing

The two main hiking areas around Bozeman are the Bridger Mountains, northeast of town, and Hyalite Canyon to the south. The Bridgers are attractive in that you can drive into some pretty spectacular scenery

MONTANA

and be on a peak or ridge in a few steep miles. Hyalite offers the same rugged beauty, but only after a few miles of hiking along a creek through a forested canyon. For detailed trail and topo maps, stop by the Bozeman Ranger Station (☎ 406-587-6920) or any of the outdoors stores on Main St.

Ron Brunckhorst, arguably Montana's best climber, lives in Bozeman and runs a very reputable guide service called Reach Your Peak (☎ 406-587-1708) that runs rock and ice climbing, mountaineering and backcountry ski tours. Prices are about $130 per person per day.

Skiing
Downhill Bridger Bowl Ski Area (☎ 406-587-2111, 406-586-2389 for 24-hour ski and road conditions) is 16 miles northeast of Bozeman via Bridger Canyon Rd (take Rouse Ave S from downtown). It is an intimate mountain with a vertical drop of 2000 feet and an annual snowfall of over 350 inches. Six lifts cover enough terrain that you can ski all day without getting bored, yet it's much more laid back and inexpensive than Big Sky (see Big Sky later in this chapter). The Ridge and Fingers offer extreme skiing for those who want to climb 400 feet above chairlift-served terrain and use avalanche transceivers and a snow shovel. There is no resort on the hill, but food and ski and snowboard rentals and lessons are available at the Roundhouse at the base of the mountain. The season lasts roughly from mid-November to mid-April, with the best conditions usually in February and March.

Cross-Country There are numerous cross-country trails around Bozeman, some better than others depending on how the snow is falling. Bangtail (☎ 406-587-4905), 500 W Main St, is a ski and bike shop with a hard-skiing staff that usually knows where the conditions are good. They rent cross-country and telemark skis by the day ($15) or week ($74).

Operated from a humble log cabin half a mile from Bridger Bowl, Bohart Ranch Cross-Country Ski Center (☎ 406-586-9070) is a day-use area with 18 miles of groomed tracks, a rental and repair shop and reportedly high-quality instructors. Full-moon skiing and giant bonfires are extremely popular when the weather is right. A day pass costs $9.

There are also several trails that climb to Mystic Lake in the Hyalite area, south of Bozeman in the Gallatin Range. This area is popular for snow-camping and ice-fishing as well. A 5½-mile ski-mountaineering route begins at the New World Gulch Parking Area, accessible via Bear Canyon Rd. To reach it, take I-90 4½ miles west to the Bear Canyon Rd exit and head south past the Bear Canyon Campground; it's just beyond there.

Pack Trips
Outback Llamas (☎ 406-587-7964), 2045 Trailcrest Drive, Bozeman, MT 59718, offers day-hikes for $50. The price includes llama, lunch and a naturalist guide; credit cards aren't accepted.

Rafting
Montana Whitewater (☎ 800-799-4465), 12 miles south of Bozeman on US 191, runs trips on the Gallatin and Yellowstone rivers. It costs $20 for a half-day, $65 for a full-day.

Fishing
Bozeman's prime fishing spots are south of town on the Gallatin River, and southeast, below Livingston, in the Paradise Valley (on the Yellowstone River). Rivers Edge Outfitters (☎ 406-586-5373) offers guided fishing trips for $210 per day, rents equipment by the day or week and has a full schedule of classes teaching dry-land fly-fishing, fly-tying and rod building. The staff is knowledgeable and helpful with tackle suggestions, and hands out a free map of area streams. They are located south of I-90 at 2012 N 7th Ave.

Downtown in the Powder Horn Fly Shop, on the corner of Black Ave and Main St, the Bear Creek Anglers (☎ 406-763-4201) is the oldest outfitter in town and only hires guides who grew up around the area. Trips start at $180 for a half-day.

Places to Stay

Bozeman's B&Bs are reasonably priced, while larger chains offer reduced rates during the off-season (usually from October to May). Independently owned accommodations east of downtown along Main St are more than adequate for people who spend more time outdoors than in their room.

Camping There are numerous public campgrounds in Gallatin Canyon and the Bridger Mountains, areas that are between 22 and 48 miles from Bozeman. The three campgrounds at *Hyalite Canyon Recreation Area* are 11 to 18 miles from Bozeman on Hyalite Canyon Rd, and have wheelchair-accessible facilities. Except for Spanish Creek and Spire Rock in Gallatin Canyon, and Battle Ridge and Fairy Lake in the Bridgers, the public camping fee is $7 per unit per night; the others are free. A full list of public campgrounds is available at the Bozeman Ranger Station.

Bozeman Hot Springs KOA (☎ 406-587-3030), 8 miles west of Bozeman off I-90, is the only campground in the area open year-round. They have the rights to the adjacent Bozeman Hot Springs pools, so guests get $1 off admission to the pools. One of the 50 tent sites costs $18, while an RV site costs $27.

Bear Canyon Campground (☎ 406-587-1575) is 3 miles east of Bozeman, off I-90 exit 313, in a wide-open spot with fantastic views of the Bridger Mountains. It has a heated pool, laundry facilities and store. Tent sites cost $10, RV hookups cost $13; if you pay in advance for six nights, the seventh night is free. They are open May 1 to October 31.

The *Sunrise Campground* (☎ 406-587-4797), 31842 Frontage Rd, is about 2 miles east of Bozeman off I-90 exit 309. Easy access to Bozeman is the selling point of this clean and lively site. Tent sites cost $10, and RV hookups cost $15. It's open April 15 to November 15.

Hostels The *Bozeman Backpackers Hostel* (☎ 406-586-4659) is centrally located 2 blocks south of Main St at 405 W Olive St, between 4th and 5th Aves. This is an independent hostel that serves as a hub for young travelers interested in outdoor activities, so it's a good place to meet potential hiking or skiing partners, and to find rides into the mountains. Bunks cost $12 per night, per person. The facilities are clean and include a full kitchen, laundry and a parking lot. There is no curfew or lock-out. They also offer a hostel-to-hostel shuttle to Cooke City ($25), over the Beartooth Pass Hwy (see Red Lodge later in this chapter).

Motels & Hotels The *Lewis & Clark Motel* (☎ 406-586-3341, 800-332-7666), 824 W Main St, is a glitzy affair that looks like it belongs on the Reno strip (it's not quite large enough to be Las Vegas material). They have three stories of rooms with sliding glass doors overlooking a busy intersection. Positive aspects are the pool, sauna, Jacuzzi and sundeck. June to September prices are $55/68 a single/double. During the rest of the year, rates drop to $34/49.

Three blocks closer to downtown at 507 W Main St, the *Best Western City Center Motor Inn* (☎ 406-587-3158) has a small indoor pool and Jacuzzi, and an in-house lounge and supper club. From Memorial Day to Labor Day the rates are $60/75 ($90 for a triple). The rest of the year they drop to $45/60.

Half a mile east of downtown at 1010 E Main St, the *Blue Sky Motel* (☎ 406-587-2311, 800-845-9032) has clean rooms for $60/62 year-round. Across the street at 1017 E Main, the *Alpine Lodge* (☎ 888-922-5746) has newly remodeled rooms for $52; suites that have a kitchen and sleep six cost $68.

On N 7th Ave, near I-90, are chain hotels that offer pools, spas, restaurants and light breakfasts. These include *Holiday Inn* (☎ 406-587-4561), *Best Western GranTree Inn* (☎ 406-587-5261), *Days Inn* (☎ 406-587-5251) and the *Bozeman Inn*

MONTANA

(☎ 406-587-3176), 1235 N 7th Ave. Rates for all of these are around $85 May to September, $55 the rest of the year.

B&Bs There are literally dozens of B&Bs in the greater Bozeman area. Many of them are 10 to 20 miles out of town on Bridger Canyon Rd, or on US 191 near Gallatin Gateway. For a full listing, ask for an accommodations list from the chamber of commerce. The two below are in central Bozeman.

Torch & Toes (☎ 406-586-7285, 800-446-2138), 309 S 3rd Ave, is in an elegant 1906 brick house with lace curtains, leaded-glass windows, period furniture, a hand-crank Victrola and a hot tub. It has three rooms, all with a private bath, costing $80 per night. Behind the main house is a carriage house that sleeps six and has a kitchenette for $90 per night.

The Voss Inn Bed and Breakfast (☎ 406-587-0982), 319 S Willson Ave, housed in a 100-year-old mansion, offers six large bedrooms, each with a private bath for $75 to $90.

Places to Eat

Every town should have a market like Bozeman's Community Food Co-Op, 908 W Main St. The store has a fantastic deli, salad bar, juice bar, bakery and a wide selection of bulk food items. You can eat at the small tables inside or out on the grass. Hours are daily from 8 am to 10 pm.

The large student population demands to be fed and coffee'd quickly, cheaply and in a lively atmosphere. The Leaf & Bean, 35 W Main St, is Bozeman's primary caffeine merchant. A wide range of ages and dress-types gather here to read, work, hang out or enjoy occasional live music; they're open 7 am to 10 pm daily. Wild Flour Bakery, 1 block south of Main St at 19 S Willson Ave, has whole-grain breads and pastries and soups and pizzas for lunch.

Right across from MSU at the corner of 10th and College Aves, Colombo's Pizza & Pasta is a student hangout where everything – sauce, dough, even sausage – is made from scratch. Lunch specials include an all-you-can-eat soup and salad bar ($5).

For a more upscale atmosphere with wine and microbrews, try McKenzie River Pizza Co, 232 E Main St. Their ingredients are fresh and unusual and prices are quite good.

Spanish Peaks Brewery, west of downtown at 120 N 19th Ave, is a lively microbrewery with an adjoining first-rate 'Italian caffe.' The house specialty is brick-oven pizza ($9 to $13), and they also have a wide selection of pastas ($10 to $16) and a few seafood entrees ($12).

Bozeman's Mexican food scene is dominated by 'wraps,' which are far from authentic, but tasty, big and cheap. A California-expat runs The Burrito Shop, at 203 N 7th Ave, and serves such items as chorizo and eggs ($4) and a black-bean veggie burrito for under $5. La Parillia – The Grill, 1533 W Babcock, serves Thai, Cajun and Mexican wraps ($5 to $7) in a colorful atmosphere; their deck is great in warm weather.

Climbing higher up the culinary ladder, John Bozeman's Bistro – usually just called 'The Bistro' – (☎ 406-587-4100), 242 E Main St, is an old Bozeman standby with a wide-ranging menu that includes everything from filet mignon to salmon to jambalaya. Dinner will run about $15, lunch around $6. The weekend breakfast menu attracts people from all over the Gallatin Valley.

Entertainment

Pick up the free monthly papers the Tributary and the BoZone for the latest entertainment calendars. They're available at most cafes, bookstores and markets.

Bars The Haufbrau, 22 S 8th Ave, evinces its history as a student hangout with wooden MSU class shields hanging on the walls and ceilings. Live music on weekends, and occasionally on weeknights, ensures a crowded bar and spilled beer. Microbrewed and regular beers on tap cost $1.25 per glass, $6 per pitcher. Behind the Haufbrau, The Molly Brown is big, noisy and stocked with eight pool tables and 20 beers on tap.

Downtown at 123 E Main St, the *Crystal Bar* is a relic with an old neon sign and long wooden bar. Students and local ranchers share the floor, making it an entertaining place to soak up some local color. The rooftop deck is a great place to relax on summer afternoons.

Spanish Peaks Brewery (see Places to Eat above) is a bright place made famous by Black Dog Ale and Spanish Peaks Porter. This is where those beers originate and where you can sample some of the brewmaster's experiments, like Spring Rye Ale and Sweetwater Wheat, which are not sold commercially.

Music The *Zebra Lounge*, half a block north of Main on Rouse Ave S, hosts rock, funk, soul and reggae shows.

The *Bozeman Symphony* (☎ 406-585-9774) is comprised of students and community members from throughout the Gallatin Valley, and it is often joined by the Bozeman Symphonic Choir. Monthly performances take place at the Willson School Auditorium, 2 blocks south of Main St on Willson Ave, from February to May. The *Intermountain Opera Association* (☎ 406-585-2889) performs opera classics twice a year (usually in the spring) also in the Willson School Auditorium.

Performing Arts Lively Arts (☎ 406-994-5828) is the main booking agency for Bozeman entertainment. They produce and sponsor a variety of shows – children's theater, string quartets, stand-up comedians – at venues throughout Bozeman.

MSU Plays, reportedly an exceptional group, performs alternative or little-known contemporary plays. All performances are held in the beautiful Strand Union Theater on the MSU campus. Scheduling varies, so call ☎ 406-994-3904 for performance information.

The *Vigilante Theater Company* (☎ 406-586-3897) is a comedy-based community theater company that performs original works. Parodies are especially popular.

Currently their performances are held at the Emerson Cultural Center.

The *Montana Ballet Company* (☎ 406-587-7192) performs twice a year: the second weekend in August (the title changes each year) as well as the first weekend in December for the traditional Nutcracker. Performances are held in the Willson School Auditorium.

Getting There & Away

Air The modern and ever-expanding Gallatin airport (☎ 406-388-6632) is 8 miles northwest of Bozeman, near the town of Belgrade. The airport is serviced by Delta and Skywest; both can be reached at the airport desk (☎ 406-388-4021). Horizon and Northwest also share an airport counter (☎ 406-388-4202). Delta and Skywest are routed through Salt Lake City on their way to southwestern destinations. Horizon and Northwest fly to/from Washington, Oregon and Alaska.

Bus The Greyhound bus depot (☎ 406-587-3110), 625 N 7th St, is half a mile from downtown. Greyhound and Rimrock Trailways service all Montana towns along I-90 and also go west through Idaho to Seattle, and east through South Dakota to Minneapolis.

Karst Stages (☎ 406-586-8567) runs one morning and one evening bus to Big Sky for around $15 and to West Yellowstone for around $20. Service is not available from November to June.

Train Though too expensive to be classified as 'public transportation,' Montana Rockies Rail Tours (☎ 800-519-7245) runs trips between Bozeman and Sandpoint, ID, along the original route of the Northern Transcontinental Railroad, completed in 1883. The trip includes bus transfers between Spokane, WA, and Sandpoint, meals and accommodation on the *Montana Daylight* in 'Explorer,' 'BigSky' or 'Gold Nugget' class for $400/600/1050 respectively. Longer trips go through Livingston, the Paradise Valley and Yellowstone National Park.

Getting Around

To/From the Airport Hotels that offer free airport shuttles include the Best Western GranTree and Holiday Inn. If the shuttles are already at the airport, they will often let you catch a ride to their location (roughly 2 miles north of downtown) for a couple of bucks. A taxi from the airport will cost about $10 to $12.

Car The car rental agencies in the Gallatin airport are Budget (☎ 406-388-4091), Avis (☎ 406-388-6414), Hertz (☎ 406-388-6939) and National (☎ 406-388-6694).

In downtown Bozeman, Rent-a-Wreck (☎ 406-587-4551, 800-344-4551), 5 E Mendenhall St, has slightly lower prices than the others and will arrange for airport pick-up service. All car-rental agencies have rugged 4WD vehicles available, as well as ski racks.

Taxi City Taxi, Bozeman's one taxi service, is available by calling ☎ 406-586-2341.

Ski Shuttles The Bridger Bowl Ski Bus (☎ 406-586-8567) runs weekends and holidays from various locations in Bozeman. The bus to Bridger leaves around 8 am and returns from Bridger 30 minutes after the lifts close. Driving time is about 25 minutes, and tickets cost $3 one-way, $5 roundtrip.

THE MISSOURI HEADWATERS

The Madison, Jefferson and Gallatin rivers converge here to form the headwaters of the Missouri-Mississippi River drainage (the largest in North America), 2464 miles above its mouth. Before Lewis and Clark arrived in 1805, explorers looking for the headwaters could practically smell the saltwater from here, believing the mighty river was part of a northwest passage leading to the Pacific Ocean and the exotic 'Orient' beyond. Competition to control such a route began in 1541 when Spanish explorer Francisco Vásquez de Coronado first heard of a 'mighty river to the north,' and ended in an American victory when Napoleon sold the Louisiana Territory in 1803.

Lewis and Clark arrived at the confluence July 25, 1805, and after several days' exploration determined that neither of the rivers was the Missouri itself, and that each was a separate fork. Lewis wrote, 'Both Captain Clark and myself corresponded in opinion with respect to the impropriety of calling either of these streams the Missouri and accordingly agreed to name them after the President of the US and Secretaries of the Treasury and State' – hence the names Jefferson, Madison and Gallatin.

In 1810, the Missouri Fur Company established a trading post but abandoned it the same year after Blackfeet and grizzlies killed eight men. The 1860s' gold boom brought visions to some entrepreneurs of a town at the confluence if ferry service could be extended up from Fort Benton. The town was laid out, but the commercial activity never materialized. In 1865 they tried again with a second Gallatin City, which had brief prosperity as a ferry link to Virginia City, Bannack and Last Chance Gulch (Helena). When the railroad came in 1883 and bypassed the town by 2 miles (instead opting for Three Forks), Gallatin City was finished.

Missouri Headwaters State Park

Four miles northeast of I-90, on the road between Three Forks and Trident, Missouri Headwaters State Park gives you an up-close-and-personal view of the convergence of the Gallatin, Madison and Jefferson rivers. The park stretches for 1½ miles, with information areas, maps and interpretive panels at both ends of the park. At the north end there's a boat dock, a grassy picnic area and a lovely swimming spot on the Gallatin River. The south end has a shadeless campground ($5 per night) with pit toilets, picnic tables and fire rings. Some of the original buildings of Gallatin City stand near the visitor information area. A trail runs the length of the park between the campground and the north-end interpretive area. If you choose not to do the trail on foot, there are parking areas at several points along the route.

MONTANA

Three Forks

Four miles south of the Missouri headwaters, just off I-90, Three Forks (population 1200) is the town that Gallatin City would have become had the Milwaukee Railroad chosen a route 2 miles north. Today, however, Three Forks is just another once-upon-a-time railroad town that relies on local ranchers and passing tourists for its livelihood. The one exceptional highlight in Three Forks, worth pulling off the highway to see, is the **Sacajawea Inn** (☎ 406-285-6515), 5 N Main St, which was moved to its present location from Gallatin City in 1908. Completely finished in 1910, the inn has an Arts & Crafts-style interior, mahogany floors, high wood-trimmed ceilings and a large porch with wooden rocking chairs. Rooms are $45 to $75, including a light breakfast, and the dining room has meals for under $10.

Also on Main St is the **Three Forks Heritage Museum**, housed in an old bank building (open Monday to Saturday from 9 to 11 am, 1 to 5 pm and 7 to 9 pm, Sunday from 1 to 7 pm), and the **Three Forks Saddlery**, which makes custom saddles and has one of Montana's most complete selections of Western clothes and tack. The third weekend in July, Three Forks hosts the big WRA Rodeo, which attracts participants and fans from all over the Western USA.

Lewis & Clark Caverns State Park

Before these awesome caverns were designated a state park in 1930, a local miner named Dan Morrison led tours down into 'Morrison's limestone caves.' His tours directly defied a government ordinance declaring that trespassing was prohibited on railroad-owned land, but there was enough public interest and enough profit – each tour cost $1 – that he took the risk. Tours took 12 hours, were illuminated only by candlelight and involved a significant amount of climbing, sliding and rappelling. When Morrison died in the 1920s after a successful 30-year run at giving tours, the government reversed its decision and dedicated the area as a park.

1 Potosi Campground,
    Potosi Peak Trailhead
2 Bear Claw Bar
    & Supper Club
3 Valley Garden Campground
4 T Lazy B Ranch
5 Diamond J Ranch
6 Varney Bridge Campground
7 Papoose Creek Trailhead

Missouri
Headwaters
& North
Madison
Valley

Amazingly enough, nothing yet bore the title 'Lewis and Clark,' so the caverns took their names.

The famous explorers didn't actually discover the caverns, even though they passed by them while traveling the Jefferson in 1805. Another 81 years passed until two local ranchers investigated a cloud of steam rising from 'Cave Mountain' and found the caves.

The formations within the caves are absolutely spectacular. Besides the stalagmites, stalactites and columns typically found in limestone caves, two erratic growths – helectites and globulites (cave popcorn) – bending upwards in gravity-defying formations are present.

The caverns are on Hwy 2 (which forks off of US 287), 17 miles west of Three Forks. A deluxe visitors center (☎ 406-287-3541), gift shop and café are at the cave's entrance, 3 miles inside the park from the highway. Two-hour tours (which can get chilly even in midsummer) leave every 20 to 30 minutes from the visitors center from 9 am to 7 pm June 15 to Labor Day, 9 am to 5 pm the rest of the year; the park is usually closed from November to April. Tickets for adults/children cost $6/3.50. Between the highway and visitors center is a campground, several picnic areas and a viewpoint that overlooks the Jefferson.

Madison Buffalo Jump

Northern Shoshoni Indians used the semi-circular limestone bluffs near the Madison River as a *pishkun*, or buffalo jump, for 2000 years, ending this practice about 200 years ago. This particular pishkun has a great deal of archaeological value due to the wealth of bison bones, tepee rings and ceremonial pipes found in the vicinity.

To reach the displays, picnic sites and toilets near the jump, take the Logan exit off I-90 (23 miles west of Bozeman) and go 5½ miles south on Buffalo Jump Rd.

MADISON VALLEY

The Madison Valley is known for two things: fishing and mining. Most of the Madison River from Ennis south to West

Buffalo Jumps

Buffalo jumps, or *pishkun*, were used by many Indian tribes as mass hunting tools. In the fall, when bison cows were fat, tribes journeyed to their pishkun site, where they camped and performed sacred dances and rituals to ensure a successful task. The site had to be a flat, wide expanse with a long, sheer cliff of at least 30 feet on one side.

Runners, chosen for their speed and agility, purified themselves in the sweat lodge to rid themselves of human odor, then put on buffalo, antelope or wolf skins. In disguise they lured a bison herd into a roundup area that led to a drive lane marked by large decorated cairns called 'dead men.' The head runner, dressed in a full buffalo robe with head and horns still attached (imagine the weight of this!), would then catch the attention of the lead bison and begin to run towards the cliff. The trick was to run at a pace fast enough that the bison had too much momentum when they reached the cliff's edge, but slow enough that they wouldn't get spooked and escape the herd.

Other people hiding behind the dead men kept the bison within the drive lanes – by spooking or swatting them – and when the herd reached the cliff the head runner jumped out of the way, usually into a hole that had been dug by the cliff's edge. The bison that survived the fall were killed by hunters waiting near the bottom of the fall. ■

Yellowstone is considered 'blue ribbon' fishing, attracting people from all over the world. Steven Segal recently bought 29,000 acres near Ennis, the valley's hub, and filmed *The Patriot* using the town as its main set. Hardly visible to passers-through, mining in the Madison Valley began with gold finds around Pony in the 1860s, and continues today with the world's largest talc-producing district in the Gravelly Range.

Not as rugged as the Gallatin Valley or as varied in scenery as the Paradise Valley, the

Madison offers a route to Yellowstone that has wide-open, prairie-like scenery and excellent fishing opportunities. Blessed with crystal-clear riffles and pools, the Madison is primarily a brown and rainbow trout river, though whitefish and Arctic grayling live here as well. The Madison's best fishing is between Ennis and Quake Lake, accessible from six fishing access sites along US 287. Fly shops, which sell licenses and are the best sources of fishing information, are concentrated in Ennis and West Yellowstone.

Pony

If you're looking to see a real outpost of a mining town (one of Montana's best examples, since it has not yet fallen to commercial tourism) head 6 miles west of US 287 to the town of Pony (population 81), where glorious old brick buildings – the bank, public school, Masons Hall – stand among unpaved streets at the foot of the Tobacco Root Mountains. The only businesses in town are the post office and the Pony Bar which has a good photo collection on the wall.

One time larger than Butte, Pony was Montana's largest gold mining town in the 1880s. When copper and lead came into demand during the World Wars, its mines shut down for lack of interest and laborers. A large mining company tried to reopen the mines in the late 1980s, but environmentalists managed to stop them on account of the poisonous tailings that would have ended up in the creek.

There's a maintained dirt road at the entrance to Pony that leads 6 miles to Potosi Campground from where you can access the Potosi Peak and Louise Lake National Recreation Trails, good day-hikes into the high, lake-studded plateau of the Tobacco Roots.

Ennis

In a state where every other town claims to be *the* fishing capital, Ennis (population 1100 people, 110,000 fish) could very well be the real thing. Set on the west bank of the Madison River, at the junction of US 287 and Hwy 287, Ennis is flanked by the Madison Range to the east, the Tobacco Root Mountains and Gravelly Ranges to the north and west. But the town's focus is undeniably the river. Since the filming of *A River Runs Through It*, the Madison has become the armchair angler's dream and Ennis has become the natural hub for anglers who don't have their own vacation homes; you will see more out-of-state license plates in Ennis than in any other town its size.

Still charming in a 'Western outdoorsman' way, Ennis has a one-street downtown lined with fly shops, Western-wear stores, real estate offices and a movie theater that acts as the hub of activity on Friday and Saturday nights. It's worth a stroll along Main St to see Jim Dolan's sculptures of cowboys and fishermen. The Blue Heron, 129 Main St, has an exceptional collection of antique fishing rods and reels, used cowboy boots and hats, sculpted silver cowboy spurs and local guidebooks. The store is open daily from 9 am to 5 pm April to December. One of the town's most attractive features is the number of guest ranches nearby, many of which sprang up in the 1930s.

Information The chamber of commerce (☎ 406-682-4388) is at the east end of Main St; it is open weekdays from 9 am to 5 pm. A few doors down is a bank and ATM. Local fly shops on Main St are good resources for fishing information.

Just west of town on Hwy 287 is the main post office and Laundry Village, which has coin-op machines, dry-cleaning services and public showers. The laundry's hours are Monday to Saturday from 8 am to 9 pm, Sunday from 9 am to 9 pm.

Fishing Few people come to Ennis without casting a line at some point in their stay. The Madison River from Hebgen Lake north to Varney Bridge (11 miles south of Ennis) is open to fishing year-round. Ennis' three fly shops all have good reputations. Since the same pool of guides is used by all three, it doesn't really matter which shop

The Politics of Fishing

In conducting the state's most definitive study on catch-and-release fishing, Dick Vincent did more for Montana's fishing populace than even Robert Redford and Brad Pitt. Catch-and-release fishing, which allows anglers to fish for sport rather than for dinner, dictates that all fish caught have to be returned to the river so that their stock won't be depleted. Using Ennis as his base, Vincent proved that a fishery could be sustained at the same level if catch-and-release fishing were practiced than if no fishing were allowed and hatchery fish were introduced. This refuted the 'no fishing' laws that Montana had imposed on some fished-out rivers, notably the upper Madison and Gallatin. As a result, the Department of Fish, Wildlife & Parks eliminated state hatcheries and now uses the excess money to buy private land and signs for fishing-access sites, thereby decreasing fishing traffic. National hatcheries, like the one just east of Ennis, still operate to produce lake stock. ∎

you go to – just make sure you get a guide with at least four years of experience. The Tackle Shop (☎ 406-682-4263; fax 406-682-4106), 127 Main St, offers guided trips for $250 per day for two people, including lunch; the shop is open daily from 7 am to 9 pm. Madison River Fishing Company (☎ 406-682-4293, 800-227-7127; fax 406-682-4744), 109 Main St, has the same rates but also offers half-day packages for $150. RJ Cain & Company (☎ 406-682-7451), 1½ miles south of town on US 287, generally caters to out-of-state anglers who stay in the Rainbow Valley and El Western motels.

Places to Stay USFS campgrounds, which are coupled with fishing access sites, are plentiful around Ennis; all have fire rings, picnic tables and pit toilets, and cost $5 to $7 per night. Half a mile east of town on the Madison River's east bank, surrounded by cottonwoods, is the *Ennis Fishing Access Campground*. The *Valley Garden Campground* is 2½ miles northeast of town, reached by turning east on Jeffers Rd from US 287, a mile east of Ennis. The *Varney Bridge Campground* is 12 miles south of town off Hwy 287.

Ennis' motels are expensive and tend to fill up quickly in summer. The two

'budget' motels are a few doors away from each other on the south end of US 287. The *Riverside Motel* (☎ 406-682-4240, 800-535-4139) has a range of rooms starting at $38. The *Silvertip Lodge* (☎ 406-682-4384), run by super-skiers Dick and Kate Barr, has cozy rooms with small refrigerators and coffee makers for $39.

Just north of town on US 287, the *Sportsman's Lodge* (☎ 406-682-4242) is very woodsy and has a lively lounge and restaurant; wood cabins cost $45, motel rooms $55.

A mile south of town on US 287, *El Western* (☎ 406-682-4217) rarely has a vacancy due to anglers who come for weeks at a time; rooms cost $65 and log cabin cottages with full kitchens are $90 to $130. Next door, the *Rainbow Valley Motel* (☎ 406-682-4264, 800-452-8254) is the same type of operation but with a common lounge area for guests and an indoor pool; singles/doubles cost $45/60 or $50/70 with a kitchen.

In the Madison Range's foothills, within 20 miles of Ennis, there are some notable guest ranches. Ten miles east of Ennis up Jack Creek Rd, the *Diamond J Ranch* (☎ 406-682-4867), PO Box 577, Ennis, MT 59729, is the Madison Valley's most complete family dude ranch. A one-week minimum stay is required ($750), and it includes all of the horseback riding, fishing, swimming, tennis and skeet shooting one can handle. Three meals a day are provided in the camp-style dining room. Most of their clients return year after year.

Two miles closer to Ennis on Jack Creek Rd, the *T Lazy B Ranch* (☎ 406-682-7288) is an altogether different experience. This mellow ranch, built in the 1930s, is first and foremost a 'fly-fisherman's ranch,' though non-anglers are also welcome. Owner Bob Walker is a fly-fishing guide who takes guests out on the Madison or points independent guests toward where the fish are biting. Horseback riding is also available. Jack Creek runs through the grounds, separating the lodge and family-style dining room from the three cabins that share a central bathhouse. Meal times depend on guests' fishing schedules. Prices start at $160 per person ; the ranch is open late May to early October.

Places to Eat Largely supported by tourist dollars, Ennis' restaurants are surprisingly pricey for a town this size. The *Economy IGA Food Market* on Main St is the place in the valley to do marketing and has a great deli. It's open until 9 pm.

Good casual choices include the *Ennis Cafe* and *Madison River Bakery and Pizza*, both on Main St. For fine dining, try the highly touted *Continental Divide* (☎ 406-682-7600), 315 E Main St. The *Bear Claw Bar and Supper Club* (☎ 406-682-4619), 7 miles north of Ennis on US 287 in McAllister, has good, moderately priced meals; steaks, chicken and seafood dinners cost $6 to $12.

Bear Trap Canyon
At the heart of the first BLM Wilderness Area in the USA, Bear Trap Canyon offers 9 miles of scenic hiking and fishing along a steep-sided gorge. The Madison exits Ennis Lake through Madison Dam at the southern end of Bear Trap, 7 miles south of the trailhead; since you can't hike on the dam, this must be an out and back hike.

The area can get crowded on weekends, but the sweeping, unobstructed view from the river up to the Spanish Peaks of the Madison Range – a mile higher in the east – is worth the detour at any time.

To reach the trailhead parking lot, head east on N Ennis Lake Rd from US 287 at McAllister, over a bridge and south following the signs marked 'Trail Creek/Barn Creek Trail.'

Virginia City
At the southern foot of the Tobacco Root Mountains and northern end of the Gravelly Range, Virginia City is on Hwy 287, 13 miles from Ennis. The town was born when Bill Fairweather and his companions struck gold in Alder Gulch in 1863. Returning to Bannack for supplies, the men tried to conceal their excitement, but fellow miners could 'see the gold in their eyes.' A party from Bannack followed Fairweather back to Alder Gulch and soon the word was out. Within one year 35,000 people came to the gulch, leaving Bannack a ghost town. What remains of Virginia City (population 150) are old buildings, most from the late 19th century, that have been considerably spruced up and now house museums, shops, art galleries and inns. Virginia City has been central to all of Norman Fox's novels, including *Gunsmoke* and *Roughshod*, and its cemetery and main street have been featured in many Hollywood Westerns. Still, beneath its touristy veneer, Virginia City is a functioning community, the seat of Madison County and a popular snowmobile destination. Allow at least one full day.

Things to See Virginia City is one big historical site: every building has its own story, told by a National Register of Historic Places placard on its exterior. Most structures are made of stone quarried from hills to the northeast.

The **Virginia City/Madison County Historic Museum** has two floors of local memorabilia, including Calamity Jane's front door knob; admission is $1. The **Thompson-Hickman Memorial Museum** displays real local color – including George

'Clubfoot' Lane's foot and a cannon once used during Fourth of July festivities (the cause of some serious controversy when it blew up several houses).

Atop the hill on the north side of town is **Boot Hill Cemetery**, where Henry Plummer's notorious road agents are buried (Plummer himself was laid to rest in the town of Bannack).

At the far west side of town, the Virginia City Short-Line Train makes the 25-minute, 1½-mile trip to **Nevada City** for $4. Nevada City is Virginia City's historical sister, site of the first vigilante execution and filming location of nine movies, including *Little Big Man*, *Missouri Breaks* and *Return to Lonesome Dove*. Here you'll find an outstanding train museum and a music hall with dozens of old music machines still in operation. The Nevada City Museum is basically an uninhabited version of Virginia City with a $5 admission fee.

Places to Stay Because most people just visit for the day, Virginia City's accommodations are surprisingly cheap.

The nearest campground is the *Alder KOA*, 4 miles west on Hwy 287. Decorated with 1950s furniture that looks as if it has never been used, the *Virginia Terrace Motel* (☎ 406-843-5368) on the north end of town has large, clean rooms for $35. Central to Virginia City activity is the *Fairweather Inn* (☎ 406-843-5377, 800-648-7588). Rooms with shared bath cost $37; with private bath, $45. The *Virginia City Country Inn* (☎ 406-843-5515), 1 block south of Main St, is an 1879 Victorian B&B with rooms from $45 to $65. Two blocks east, at 306 E Idaho St, the *Stonehouse Inn* (☎ 406-843-5504), the first house in Virginia City to have electricity, has $65 rooms. Owned by the Fairweather Inn, the *Nevada City Hotel* in Nevada City has 'Old West' rooms for $60 and restored 1860s cabins for $45; all have private baths.

Entertainment Virginia City's garish stage shows are integral to its existence. The *Brewery Follies* (☎ 406-843-5218) is a slightly off-color song-and-dance comedy staged in the old Gilbert Brewery; tickets cost $8. The *Virginia City Opera House* stages three 19th-century melodramas each year; tickets cost $10 (call ☎ 406-843-5314 for ticket reservations). Reservations are recommended for all shows.

Ennis to West Yellowstone

South of Ennis the Madison River drops out of view as it forms the bottom of a narrow canyon bordered by 100-foot cliffs. You can reach the river from two camping and fishing access sites in the West Madison Recreation Area, well signed off the highway. The dramatic peaks of the Madison Range, part of the Lee Metcalf Wilderness, are visible in the east. The one trail into the Lee Metcalf from this side (others are from the Gallatin Valley on the range's east side) is up Papoose Creek, about halfway between Ennis and the US 287/Hwy 87 junction.

Just north of the US 287/Hwy 87 junction is a turnoff to Cliff and Wade lakes. Popular with West Yellowstone residents for weekend camping trips, the lakes are side by side, 6 miles off US 287 in a wide, unshaded part of the Madison Valley.

Quake & Hebgen Lakes Just before midnight on August 17, 1959, an earthquake measuring 7.1 on the Richter scale shook the earth, drastically changing the landscape of the upper Madison River Canyon. Two large fault blocks in the Hebgen Lake area tilted and dropped. The lake's north shore dropped 18 feet, and parts of US 287 dropped into the water, taking several lodges along with it. A massive landslide buried two campsites and blocked the Madison River, forming Quake Lake in the process. The same quake caused major changes in the thermal features of Yellowstone National Park, especially around the Mud Volcano area.

Across from the landslide area, the Madison River Canyon Earthquake Area Visitor Center (☎ 406-646-7369) has a working seismograph, photographs from the quake and a half-mile interpretive trail that leads to a vista point of the area; the center is open daily from 9 am to 6 pm Memorial Day to Labor Day. The best before/after pictures of the landslide area are at the Slide Inn Motel and store, 3 miles west of the visitors center on US 287.

Hebgen Lake, connected to Quake Lake by a scenic stretch of river, has a dam that amazingly withstood the earthquake's rocking activity. Between the visitors center and the dam, **Beaver Creek Rd** turns north off the highway. The road follows Beaver Creek, through an area notorious for grizzly sightings, 3 miles to the Avalanche Lake/Blue Danube Lake trailhead. Both lakes make excellent day-hike destinations. The West Fork Beaver Creek Trail also departs from here and links to other trails in the Taylor-Hilgard Unit of the Madison Range, the jagged peaks that are visible to the north. One-eighth of a mile past the trailhead parking lot a side road branches off to the right and leads 200 yards to the USFS Beaver Creek cabin which you can rent year-round ($28 per night). It has bunk beds to sleep six, a cookstove and utensils, firewood and an ax; contact the Ranger Station in West Yellowstone for reservations.

The Cabin Creek area, on US 287 a mile past Beaver Creek Rd, has a USFS campground, a trailhead with more good day-hike possibilities and a 'scarp area' that offers a good view of the land shift that occurred during the earthquake. Across US 287, the *Campfire Lodge Resort* (☎ 406-646-7258) is a good place for breakfast and rents cabins for $45 to $70.

Targhee Pass Instead of taking US 287 along Quake and Hebgen lakes, it's possible to reach West Yellowstone via US 87, which turns south of US 287 just west of Quake Lake. This route skirts the southwest base of the Lions Head area of the Madison Range then intersects with Hwy 20, which goes east over Targhee Pass to West Yellowstone. This route gives access to some wild and beautiful backcountry that often gets overlooked by people making a beeline for Yellowstone.

There are three scenic, remote USFS campgrounds with pit toilets, potable water and fire rings on the south side of Hebgen Lake (opposite the Quake Lake area). Reach these by turning north on Denny Creek Rd (USFS Rd 176), just east of the Super 8 Motel on Hwy 20 (about halfway between Targhee Pass and West Yellowstone); there is a big power transmitter and wooden 'Gallatin National Forest Recreation Area' sign at the turnoff.

There are some good hikes in the area and two Continental Divide National Scenic Trail access points. The Mile Creek trail, well signed off Hwy 87, 9 miles south of US 287, heads back along Mile Creek through a narrow valley with 9000-foot peaks on its east side and then hits a series of switchbacks that will take your breath away and not return it until you've reached the divide half a mile later. Better suited to day-hikes, the **Targhee Creek Trail** starts 1 mile off Hwy 20 and passes through fir and pine forests with occasional views of the surrounding peaks; the Divide is 6 miles from the trailhead.

WEST YELLOWSTONE

If not a particularly attractive town, West Yellowstone is well equipped to lodge, feed and briefly entertain visitors headed to Yellowstone National Park, a quarter mile from the town center. Perhaps the most redeeming factor of West Yellowstone is the ease with which things are accomplished since businesses are all in a compact grid, about a mile square. Also within a bike ride, ski or long run from town, wilderness abounds that is not part of the park and thus free and often uncrowded in the height of tourist season. The town thrives during the high seasons (June to September and mid-December to mid-March) and resembles a ghost town in between. With a drastic rise in snowmobile popularity, winter business is becoming as profitable as traditional summer tourism, so the year-round population is increasing steadily, as is the brown haze which settles on the town shortly after December 1, when the park opens for snowmobiling.

MONTANA

History

In 1908, the town of Riverside opened its post office at the end of the Union Pacific Railroad track. One year later, Dick Murray opened Murray's Yellowstone Hotel (still standing as the Madison Motel), and Sam and Ida Eagle opened a general store on Yellowstone Ave that is still in operation (as Eagle's Store) and thus Yellowstone (renamed the same year) began as a town welcoming travelers. The Union Pacific Complex, consisting of the depot, a dining hall (or 'beanery') and lodge, was the hub of activity and the community's major employer. Each afternoon,

a line of 'beanery queens,' dressed in formal servants' attire, would meet arriving trains and escorted travelers to the dining hall for a welcome dinner and park orientation.

Yellowstone National Park's popularity brought enough visitors to support service businesses besides those of Union Pacific, and with the growth of automobile travel, independent operations grew to overshadow the railroad's. In 1920 the community changed its name from simply Yellowstone to West Yellowstone in order to define itself geographically and avoid confusion between the town and the park.

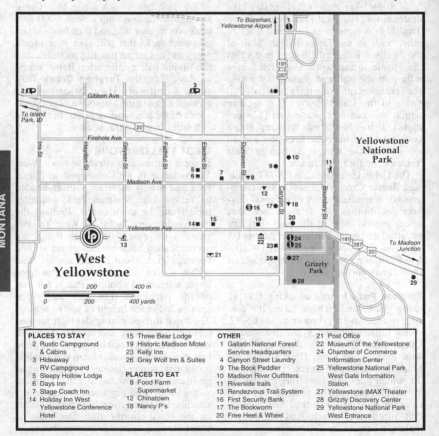

MONTANA

PLACES TO STAY
2 Rustic Campground
   & Cabins
3 Hideaway
   RV Campground
5 Sleepy Hollow Lodge
6 Days Inn
7 Stage Coach Inn
14 Holiday Inn West
   Yellowstone Conference
   Hotel

15 Three Bear Lodge
19 Historic Madison Motel
23 Kelly Inn
26 Gray Wolf Inn & Suites

PLACES TO EAT
8 Food Farm
   Supermarket
12 Chinatown
18 Nancy P's

OTHER
1 Gallatin National Forest
   Service Headquarters
4 Canyon Street Laundry
9 The Book Peddler
10 Madison River Outfitters
11 Riverside trails
13 Rendezvous Trail System
16 First Security Bank
17 The Bookworm
20 Free Heel & Wheel

21 Post Office
22 Museum of the Yellowstone
24 Chamber of Commerce
   Information Center
25 Yellowstone National Park
   West Gate Information
   Station
27 Yellowstone IMAX Theater
28 Grizzly Discovery Center
29 Yellowstone National Park
   West Entrance

Orientation & Information

West Yellowstone is arranged in a grid. US 191 and US 287 meet 8 miles north and run through town as Canyon St (West Yellowstone's main drag) then turn east at Yellowstone Ave to enter the park. US 20 heads west towards Idaho as Firehole Ave.

West Yellowstone's Chamber of Commerce Information Center (☎ 406-646-7701) is in Grizzly Park on Canyon St, one block south of Yellowstone Ave. One building south, the Yellowstone National Park West Entrance Information Station (☎ 406-646-7332) has information specifically concerning the park, including campground availability. The Gallatin National Forest Service Headquarters (☎ 406-646-7369) is on Canyon St, 2 blocks north of Firehole Ave.

There's a First Security Bank at 23 Dunraven St, half a block north of Yellowstone Ave, and an ATM in the lobby of the Stagecoach Inn. The spiffy new West Yellowstone Post Office is on Electric St, 1 block south of Yellowstone Ave. The zip code is 59758. The Canyon Street Laundry (☎ 406-646-9733), 312 Canyon St, has coin-operated machines, drop-off service and public showers.

There are two noteworthy bookstores in town, both with Yellowstone Park books galore: the Book Peddler (☎ 406-646-9358) at 106 Canyon St and the Bookworm (☎ 406-646-9736), 14 Canyon St, which has a good used book selection.

Grizzly Park

Opened in August 1993, Grizzly Park (in the southeast corner of town off Yellowstone Ave and Canyon St) is home to the **Grizzly Discovery Center**, where five bears (Kodiak and grizzly) and nine gray wolves are kept in a pseudo-natural setting for people to view. Why keep live animals in captivity a quarter mile from one of the largest natural habitats in the lower 48 states? The concept is to educate travelers about the nature of bears, how and why you should minimize contact with them and how to react to their behavior should you stumble across one. Most of the bears here have been tagged as 'problem bears' – repeat offenders of garbage bin raids or harmful people encounters. Opponents of the center feel that it is unjust to hold these bears in captivity; proponents feel that the bears are better off under the center's protection, and are ultimately saving the lives of other bears and people.

The center is open daily from 9 am to dusk. Bear-related movies show every 25 minutes in the center's theater. Tickets, good for reentry the entire day, cost $7 for adults, $5 for seniors and children.

Next door, the **Yellowstone IMAX Theater** may be the only way for summer travelers to see Yellowstone in the winter or without crowds – all on a screen six stories high. Showings run on the hour from 9 am to 9 pm May to September, and from 1 to 9 pm October to April. Admission for adults/children is $9/5.

Museum of the Yellowstone

Housed in the old UP railroad depot built in 1909, this museum (☎ 406-646-7814) at 124 Yellowstone Ave, thoroughly covers all aspects of West Yellowstone's and Yellowstone National Park's existence. Highlights include drawings and sculptures by Donald Clarke (a Blackfeet Indian from East Glacier), three full-sized bison (part of the last plains herd) and Old Snaggletooth, Yellowstone National Park's infamous garbage-munching bear that used to entertain visitors at the West Yellowstone dump until poachers shot him in 1970. Videos are shown on request in the museum theater.

Hours are 8 am to 9 pm; admission for adults is $5, for students and seniors $3.

Activities

With most people heading straight for the park, there are plenty of uncrowded trails in the surrounding Gallatin National Forest west and south of town. Free Heel and Wheel (☎ 406-646-7744) is the place to stop for maps, equipment and friendly advice on hiking, mountain bike and cross-country ski trails. The shop holds free group activities (trail runs, mountain bike

MONTANA

rides, etc) five days a week, usually in the morning or afternoon; stop by for the week's schedule. The park is closed to vehicles from mid-October to December and mid-April to mid-May, but open to bikes or skis (depending on the weather).

The Rendezvous Trail System is the training ground for US Olympic cross-country ski teams. The trails begin just off Yellowstone Ave at Geyser St and offer 15 miles of traditional **cross-country skiing** and **skate-skiing**. Less developed and more scenic are the Riverside Trails, which start on the east side of Boundary St between Madison and Firehole Aves. The main trail cuts through 1½ miles of fir and pine and comes out near the Madison River, where there are old NPS roads and other trails that meander along the river through prime wildlife viewing areas. Both of these trail systems offer great **mountain biking** and **trail running** when the snow melts. Free Heel and Wheel rents bikes and skis and has trail maps.

The headwaters of three great **fishing** rivers, the Missouri, Yellowstone and Snake, lie within Yellowstone National Park, supporting abundant populations of trout. Follow the riverside trails to the Madison where there are abundant access points. Madison River Outfitters (☎ 406-646-9644; fax 406-646-9630), 117 Canyon St, rents fishing equipment and offers one-day float and walk trips for $135 per person. Extended three- to six-day packages start at $900 per person. The store also has a wide selection of camping gear, outdoor clothes and guidebooks, and is open daily 9 am to 8 pm.

Organized Tours

Gray Line (☎ 406-646-9374) sends tour buses into Yellowstone National Park from West Yellowstone in the summer. The 'Lower Loop Adventure' (daily) heads through Firehole Canyon en route to Old Faithful. The 'Upper Loop Adventure' (running Monday, Tuesday, Thursday and Saturday) heads through the northern part of the park, past Mammoth Hot Springs

and over Dunraven Pass. Both full-day tours begin and end at the Stagecoach Inn in West Yellowstone and cost $36/23 for adults/children.

In winter Yellowstone Alpine Guides (☎ 406-646-9591) offers all day snow-coach tours to Old Faithful ($79 per person) and the Grand Canyon of the Yellowstone ($89). They provide a picnic lunch and stop at the more famous geyser basins for short walking tours. They also have a daily tour that integrates cross-country skiing into the Old Faithful tour.

Places to Stay

Considering the number of motel signs, the lack of variety in accommodations is surprising. Motel room quality and price are nearly interchangeable; variables are location (the ones closest to Canyon St being most convenient) and amenities such as a pool or hot tub. High season runs from June to September and mid-December to mid-March. During the off-season the few places that remain open, including the Stagecoach Inn, Days Inn and Kelly Inn, offer super low rates. Reservations fill up two to six months in advance for high-season periods.

Camping Camping near town is allowed only in developed campgrounds, most of which are primarily RV parks. The nicest tent campgrounds around are on Hebgen Lake (see Quake & Hebgen Lakes earlier in this section). Clustered on US 20 at the west end of town, most campgrounds are open May to mid-October, and charge around $12/25 for tent/full-hookup sites.

The *Hideaway RV Campground* (☎ 406-646-9049), 2 blocks west of Canyon St at the corner of Gibbon Ave and Electric St, is one of the smaller, quieter options. *Rustic Campground & Cabins* (☎ 406-646-7387), 624 US 20 at the corner of Gibbon Ave, 6 blocks west of Canyon St, has four RV sites for every tent and five cabins with two bunk beds (cabins cost $40 per night). The *Madison Arm Resort & Marina* (☎ 406-646-9328), 3 miles north of town and 5 miles west of US 191/ US 287, would be a nice destination even if it wasn't so close to Yellowstone. The campground is well-suited to tenters and there's a marina with swimming beach and boat rentals. Lack of shade is the main drawback.

The *Yellowstone Park KOA* (☎ 406-646-7606), 6 miles west of town on US 20, is a huge facility with a pool, hot tub, game room and nightly barbecue. The passing traffic on US 20 can be annoying.

Hostels The *Historic Madison Motel* (see below) has hostel rooms on its 2nd floor, each with three beds and a sink; beds cost $15 for HI/AYH members, $18 for nonmembers. There is no curfew and no kitchen.

Motels & Hotels The *Historic Madison Motel* (☎ 406-646-7745, 800-838-7745), 139 Yellowstone Ave, was built in 1909 as Murray's Yellowstone Hotel, the town's first year-round motel. The motel is now open from Memorial Day to mid-October and has rooms for $35 to $42 with private bath, $30 without. In back, the Madison's modern motel rooms run $42 to $75.

The *Three Bear Lodge* (☎ 406-646-7353, 800-646-7353), 217 Yellowstone Ave, is decked out in pine logs from the lobby to the hot-tub room and motel corridors. Rooms start at $71. The nearby *Midtown Motel* on Dunraven Ave is owned by the Three Bear Lodge and shares its pool and hot tub. Rooms are $58 to $78. Check-in and reservations for both are handled at the lodge.

A real gem, the *Sleepy Hollow Lodge* (☎ 406-646-7707), 124 Electric St, has small log cabins with kitchens for around $65.

Next door, the *Days Inn* (☎ 406 646-7656, 800-548-9551) at 118 Electric St, has a heated indoor pool, hot tub, sauna and free coffee and pastries in the morning. Rooms cost $68 to $100 year-round.

A long-time hub of West Yellowstone activity, the *Stage Coach Inn* (☎ 406-646-7381, 800-842-2882), 209 Madison Ave, has a comfortable reading area, hot tub

and good restaurant. Rooms (some with refrigerators) start at $32 in the off-season, $75 in high-season.

The *Holiday Inn West Yellowstone Conference Hotel* (☎ 406-646-7365), on the corner of Electric and Yellowstone Aves, has rooms with refrigerator, microwave and private Jacuzzi. Prices start at $134 for a room with two queen-size beds; low-season rates are about $20 cheaper.

The two new-kids-in-town are the *Kelly Inn* (☎ 406-646-4544, 800-259-4672) and *Gray Wolf Inn & Suites* (☎ 406-646-0000, 800-852-8602), next to each other on Canyon St across from Grizzly Park. Both have a pool, spa, free Continental breakfast and rooms in the $55 to $95 range.

Places to Eat
The *Food Farm Super Market*, at the corner of Madison Ave and Dunraven St, is open daily from 7 am to 9 pm year-round.

The place to go for coffee, pastries, pizzas and fresh bread is *Nancy P's* on Canyon St between Madison and Yellowstone Aves, but seating is limited and they close at 5 pm.

The *Barrel Bar* in the Stagecoach Inn makes the best pizza in town after 5 pm. The adjacent restaurant has excellent breakfast ($5), lunch and dinner ($6 to $12) though the coffee-shop atmosphere doesn't quite live up to the food. The *Firehole Grill* on US 20 at Faithful St does great barbecue and is a lively place to be on weekend nights.

For surprisingly good Chinese food under $10 head to *Chinatown* on Madison Ave between Canyon and Dunraven Sts; they'll make anything spicy if you ask.

GALLATIN VALLEY
From its headwaters in the northwest corner of Yellowstone National Park, the Gallatin River flows up the valley to meet the Madison and Jefferson Rivers and their master, the Missouri River, at Three Forks. The river cuts through a narrow, rugged gorge between the Madison and Gallatin ranges. US 191 follows the river's edge the entire length of the valley beginning just

MONTANA

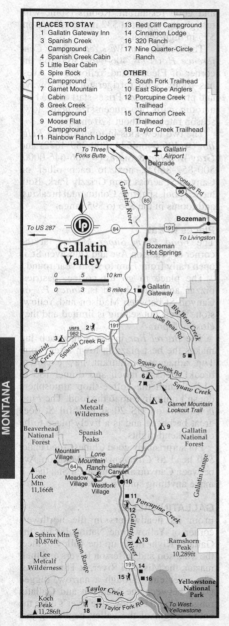

PLACES TO STAY
1 Gallatin Gateway Inn
3 Spanish Creek Campground
4 Spanish Creek Cabin
5 Little Bear Cabin
6 Spire Rock Campground
7 Garnet Mountain Cabin
8 Greek Creek Campground
9 Moose Flat Campground
11 Rainbow Ranch Lodge
13 Red Cliff Campground
14 Cinnamon Lodge
16 320 Ranch
17 Nine Quarter-Circle Ranch

OTHER
2 South Fork Trailhead
10 East Slope Anglers
12 Porcupine Creek Trailhead
15 Cinnamon Creek Trailhead
18 Taylor Creek Trailhead

To Three Forks Butte
Gallatin Airport
Belgrade
Frontage Rd
Gallatin River
85
90
Bozeman
To US 287
84
191
To Livingston
Gallatin Valley
Bozeman Hot Springs
0   5   10 km
0   3   6 miles
1 Gallatin Gateway
Big Bear Creek
Little Bear Rd
USFS 982
2
191
3
Spanish Creek
Spanish Creek Rd
5
Squaw Creek Rd
4
6
7
Squaw Creek
8 Garnet Mountain Lookout Trail
Lee Metcalf Wilderness
9 Gallatin National Forest
Beaverhead National Forest
Spanish Peaks
Mountain Village
Lone Mountain Ranch
64
Meadow Village
Gallatin Canyon
10
Westfork Village
Lone Mtn 11,166ft
11
Porcupine Creek
12
Gallatin Range
Sphinx Mtn 10,876ft
Madison Range
Gallatin River
13
Ramshorn Peak 10,289ft
Lee Metcalf Wilderness
191
14
15
16
Yellowstone National Park
Koch Peak 11,286ft
Taylor Creek
17 Taylor Fork Rd
18
To West Yellowstone

MONTANA

west of Bozeman, crossing briefly into Yellowstone National Park and continuing to West Yellowstone. In the valley's northern end, beautiful roadcuts show swirling bands of pink and black gneiss, Precambrian basement rock that dates back 2½ billion years. North of the turnoff to Big Sky (see Big Sky later in this section) the cliffs rise so steeply and so close that they appear to be teetering over the highway; south of the turnoff, massive white ledges of the Madison Range give the highway a little more room. The major resort of Big Sky, the biggest draw in the region, is to the west of the valley. Yellowstone-bound travelers have funneled south through this corridor since the arrival of the railroad in 1906.

Due to its narrow configuration, development in the valley itself is limited to occasional tourist services – guest ranches, lodges, outfitters – spread out every 10 miles or so. The exception is around the Big Sky turnoff 36 miles south of Bozeman where you'll find an increasing number of gas stations, accommodations, outfitters, banks and bookstores. October to mid-December and April to mid-June are the only 'off' seasons here and the winter often brings more visitors than the summer.

Gallatin Gateway

Lurking behind a dense stand of oak and aspen at the valley's north end (13 miles south of Bozeman), the *Gallatin Gateway Inn* (☎ 406-763-4672) was built by the Milwaukee Railroad in 1927 to act as the terminus for the Yellowstone line, and thus became a gateway to the park. Its cream-colored stucco walls and red-tile roof stand out strikingly against the green mountain backdrop. The inn has a pool, hot tub, casting pond and fleet of mountain bikes for guest use. Gourmet food and a beautifully appointed dining room attract both tourists and locals, mostly for 'special occasion' meals. Single/double rooms are $75/80 and about $15 cheaper in low season. The bar has live music on weekends and is a favorite watering hole for Bozeman's outdoorsy thirty-something crowd.

Spirit Maiden Speaks

The Gallatin Valley was originally claimed by the Blackfeet, but Bannack, Crow, Sioux and Shoshone passed through on hunting parties. The valley was recognized by ancient tradition as a place where even hostile tribes would camp side by side. Legend says that during the war between the Sioux and the Nez Percé, a flame appeared on Mount Bridger, and Manna Sette (Spirit Maiden) said to all:

Behold this beautiful valley of flowers. Great Spirit has made it for his children. It is like a beautiful maiden, encircled by a white necklace of white-topped mountains. It is carpeted with flowers, and watered by sparkling streams. This is the home of the red man. He comes here to rest. In this valley of flowers there must be no war, all must be peace, rest and love. ∎

Lee Metcalf Wilderness Complex

The Lee Metcalf Wilderness Complex covers 389 sq miles of Gallatin and Beaverhead National Forest land west of US 191. The premier hiking and backcountry ski destination here – and one of the best known in the state because of Bozeman's Spanish Peaks Brewery – is the **Spanish Peaks**, named for a group of Spaniards who took refuge in the area after having a close encounter with a band of Crow Indians. On a clear day you can see the distinct cluster of glacial valleys, ridges and peaks (25 of which are over 10,000 feet) rising sharply out of the general profile of the Gallatin Range, all the way from Bozeman. When you get closer to the peaks, these tight, jagged thrusts of Precambrian basement rock become even more alluring.

Access trails are well-marked from the west side of US 191. The Taylor Fork Road, 56 miles south of Bozeman, heads west 8 miles to a junction then south 2 miles to the Taylor Creek Trail. Another recommended access point is USFS Spanish Creek Camp-

ground at the end of USFS Rd 982, about 22 miles south of Bozeman.

Hiking & Mountain Biking

Hiking trails – all open to mountain biking – head into the mountains along numerous creek drainages from both sides of the Gallatin River. Maps of the area are available at the Bozeman Ranger Station. In the southern half of the valley, after the highway enters Yellowstone National Park (marked by roadside signs), there is a trailhead about every 2 miles. Well maintained and marked with distance indicators, these are recommended for people who have no intention of buying a map.

A great destination on the eastern side of the valley is the Gallatin Petrified Forest. Access is actually easier from Tom Miner Basin on the eastern side of the mountains (off US 89), but the **Porcupine Creek Trail**, about 4 miles south of the Big Sky turnoff, makes a 22-mile loop to the forest; Portal Creek (4 miles from the trailhead) is a good day-hike destination on this same trail. The 1½-mile climb to the top of the **Storm Castle Trail** offers great views; the last quarter mile, across loose scree, is especially strenuous and tricky at points. A favorite hike/post-hike combo is to hike up to the fire lookout at the top of the **Cinnamon Creek Trail**, then have lunch or dinner at the Cinnamon Lodge, near the trailhead on US 191.

Fishing

The Gallatin is touted as one of the country's best and most famous trout rivers. The upper river is fast-moving with many rapids, so the best fishing is a bit farther north, between the narrowest part of Gallatin Canyon and Gallatin Gateway. Float fishing is prohibited the entire length of the river, but the shallow water makes for easy access. There are fishing access sites at Greek Creek, Moose Flat and Red Cliff campgrounds, but local anglers swear that anywhere you cast a line is bound to be good.

East Slope Anglers (☎ 406-995-4369), 100 yards south of the Big Sky turnoff, has a store full of equipment for rent or sale, and offers guided fly-fishing trips with instruction (if needed).

Places to Stay

Camping & Cabins Numerous public campgrounds snuggle up to the base of the Gallatin Range on the east side of US 191. *Spire Rock Campground*, 26 miles south of Bozeman, then 2 miles east on Squaw Creek Rd No 132, is a no-fee USFS campground beautifully slotted between Storm Castle and Garnet mountains at the edge of Squaw Creek. *Greek Creek Campground*, 5 miles farther south, doubles as a fishing access site. The *Red Cliff Campground*, 48 miles south of Bozeman, has 68 sites ($7 per vehicle), which means there's almost always space available.

The USFS *Little Bear Cabin*, 13 miles southeast of Gallatin Gateway off Little Bear Rd, is reached by a 10-mile hike. *Spanish Creek Cabin* sits 7½ miles west of US 191 via Spanish Creek Rd. From the trailhead it is a 3½-mile hike or ski to the cabin; unfortunately, roaring snowmobiles also use the trail. There is one bunk bed and two single beds. East of US 191, the *Garnet Mountain Cabin*, an old fire lookout tower with fantastic views into the Lee Metcalf Wilderness and Spanish Peaks area, is at the end of the popular 10-mile Garnet Mountain Lookout Trail. Because of avalanche danger, the cabin is accessible during summer only. Cabins cost $26 per night and are equipped with wood stoves, firewood, cooking supplies and blankets. Contact the Bozeman Ranger Station (☎ 406-587-6920) for information and reservations.

Lodges & Guest Ranches Quite a number of rustic ranches and picturesque lodges lace the Gallatin Valley around Big Sky. All of them provide easy access to Big Sky, but also act as destinations in and of themselves.

The *Rainbow Ranch Lodge* (☎ 406-995-4132), 5 miles south of the Big Sky turnoff, has 12 rooms ($65 to $98) with views of either the mountains or the river, five acres of Gallatin River frontage, an outdoor Jacuzzi and a great fireplace. Its restaurant

is a favorite splurge for valley locals. The Big Sky Shuttle stops right at the lodge.

The *Cinnamon Lodge* (☎ 406-995-4253) is right on the Gallatin River about 10 miles south of the Big Sky turnoff. They get a very mixed clientele, from seniors in RVs to families overloaded with sports equipment to groups of serious hunters and fly fishermen. Accommodations include furnished log cabins with baths and kitchens ($118), and a few basic motel rooms ($45). Its restaurant, which is a very Western-feeling bar and cafe, serves excellent Mexican food from 7 am to 9 pm.

The *Nine Quarter-Circle Ranch* (☎ 406-995-4276), 20 miles south of Big Sky, is an authentic dude ranch. The same family has owned the ranch for 40 years and meals, pack trips and nightly entertainment are all done family-style (everyone gets involved) in a very casual atmosphere. Weekly rates starting at $700 include accommodations, meals and activities.

The *320 Ranch* (☎ 406-995-4283, 800-243-0320), 12 miles south of Big Sky, has cozy log cabins, with or without cooking units, starting at $68. There is enough going on at the ranch – trail rides, fly fishing, sleigh-ride dinners – that you might just want to skip Big Sky altogether. They have a fishing shop, restaurant and saloon on the premises.

BIG SKY

Big Sky, 48 miles south of Bozeman off US 191, is Montana's largest destination resort, and the realization of newscaster Chet Huntley's dreams. In 1969, Huntley and a group of large investors (Conoco, Burlington Northern, Montana Power, Chrysler Corporation and Northwest Orient Airlines) bought the Crail Ranch property and built the area's first ski hill in the shadow of Lone Mountain, the awe-inspiring peak that stands conspicuously above the resort. After Huntley's death in 1974, Boyne USA Resorts took over and has poured millions of dollars into further development of the resort.

Now you can take a tram to the top of 11,166-foot Lone Mountain and ski 6 miles to its base. From a mountainside cluster of services the resort has grown into four separate communities that spread from the base of Lone Mountain all the way down to US 191 in the Gallatin Valley. It's conceivable that the entire Gallatin Valley from Bozeman to West Yellowstone will someday be referred to as 'Big Sky.'

Orientation & Information

The four 'communities' at Big Sky are named according to their geographical location: Mountain Village, Meadow Village, Westfork Village and Gallatin Canyon. All four are connected by a free shuttle service in summer and winter. The lodge and mall at the base of the ski lifts in Mountain Village are the center of winter activity. Meadow Village and Westfork Village, 6 and 8 miles down the mountain, get the bulk of summer traffic since they're convenient for exploring the Gallatin River and Yellowstone National Park. These two also have services – post office, bars, the Country Store, Gallatin Gourmet, Rocco's – that are the most used by locals and are thus open year-round.

To receive brochures and information about Big Sky, contact Big Sky Ski & Summer Resort (☎ 800-548-4486), PO Box 160001, Big Sky, MT 59716. The 'Big Sky Guide' is a complete service directory, published annually, and the *Lone Peak Lookout* is the community's year-round weekly newspaper. Both are available at most hotels and real estate offices, or at the publishing office (☎ 406-995-4133) in the Meadow Village Center.

Skiing

Big Sky is comprised of Andesite Mountain (elevation 8800 feet) and also Lone Mountain (elevation 11,166 feet), with a 3030-foot vertical drop and 2100 acres of skiable terrain, a 15-passenger tram, two gondolas, five high-speed detachable quads and four chairlifts. The north side of Lone Mountain has some fantastic double-diamond chutes and bowls, accessible by the tram and limited to expert skiers only. Andesite Mountain caters

more to inter-mediates, and beginners will find plenty of easy terrain off the Explorer lift (next to the main parking lot) and Gondola I.

Lifts operate 9 am to 4 pm, and night skiing (4 to 9 pm) is usually an option on weekends from December to March. Full-day/half-day ticket prices are $42/36; children under 10 ski free (but 11-year-olds are considered adults!). There are multiple rental shops between the Big Sky turnoff and the lifts. Mad Wolf Ski and Sport Shop (☎ 406-995-4369), 100 yards south of the Big Sky turnoff on US 191, tends to have the best prices. For snow conditions, call ☎ 406-995-2526.

Down near Westfork Village, the Lone Mountain Ranch (☎ 406-995-4670, 800-514-4644) has 65 km of groomed cross-country trails and a full-service lodge. This is a great, relatively undiscovered spot. Day-passes cost $10.

Other Activities

In summer Lone Mountain is great for both **hiking** and **mountain biking**. For a trail map, stop by the activities desk in Huntley Lodge in Big Sky. A gondola shuttles people and bikes to the top of the mountain 9 am to 6 pm daily for $12 (unlimited use). Buy tickets at Big Mountain Sports in the Mountain Mall at the base of the mountain. A good hike for serious hikers is from the summit of the gondola (elevation 10,000 feet) up to the peak of Lone Mountain. Less ambitious is the climb down from the gondola to the base of the mountain. Walking Stick Tours (☎ 406-995-4265) has several organized hikes per day from points around the valley but focuses on the Big Sky area. The average cost is $25 per person.

Adventures Big Sky (☎ 406-995-2324), on US 191 at the Big Sky turnoff, has **white-water rafting** trips ($37/68 for a half/full day) and **kayak trips** ($41), and also rents mountain bikes ($18/25 a half/full day).

Horseback riding can be arranged through the activities desk at the Huntley Lodge and Big Sky Stables; cost is about

$25 per hour, $60 for a half-day and $110 for a full day including lunch. A reputable private operation is the 320 Ranch (☎ 406-995-4283, 800-243-0320), 12 miles south of Big Sky off US 191. Horse rentals cost $17 per hour. The ranch also offers a number of special packages such as breakfast trail rides, dinner chuckwagons and overnight pack trips.

Places to Stay
The free Big Sky ski shuttle stops at all accommodations, including those down in the valley on US 191. Information on renting condominiums, cabins and houses in Big Sky is available from Big Sky Chalet Property Management (☎ 406-995-2665, 800-845-4428), PO Box 1032, Bozeman, MT 59715. Stay at the Mountain Village and you can walk to the lifts; stay at Westfork or Meadow Village and you can walk to nearby shops, restaurants and bars.

The *Golden Eagle Lodge* (☎ 406-995-4800, 800-548-4488), in the Meadow Village, has rooms for $45/65 year-round, with good ski packages (like $98 per night for a room and lift ticket). It's close to Meadow Village's shops and home to Rocco's, a good restaurant and bar. They also have houses and condos for rent (three night minimum). Plush rooms at the *River Rock Lodge* (☎ 406-995-2295, 800-995-9966), in Westfork Village, include down comforters and a fireplace. Rooms start at $120 ($95 on the rare off-season occasion).

The main accommodations at the base of the mountain (closed in fall and spring) are the *Huntley Lodge & Shoshone Condominium Hotel* (☎ 406-995-4211, 800-548-4486), with beautifully appointed hotel rooms for $96/106. Also near the lifts is the *Shoshone*, with a variety of condo-style lofts and suites (with kitchenettes) that sleep four to 10 people for $87 to $241 per night. Between the lodge and hotel there are 294 units, three indoor and outdoor pools, a health club, sauna, Jacuzzi and tennis courts, plus a slew of retail shops, restaurants and lounges.

Places to Eat
Big Sky's eating scene is more international and of a higher quality than in many parts of Montana. The *Country Store* in Meadow Village has a full selection of groceries, beer and wine and a deli. For bulk and organic food, stop by *The Hungry Moose*, between Meadow and Westfork villages. The *Gallatin Gourmet*, in Meadow Village, is easily the best place to go for a casual lunch or dinner. They have excellent baked goods, beer on tap, sandwiches and specials for under $7. Also good for pastries and coffee is *Blue Moon Bakery* in Westfork Village.

For a fun bar atmosphere, darts, pool and good pizza, head to *Uncle Milnkies* in Westfork Village. *Rocco's*, in the Golden Eagle Lodge near Meadow Village, has inexpensive Mexican and Italian food, a friendly atmosphere and good margaritas. For a really nice meal, people claim *The First Place*, on the golf course (also near Meadow Village) has the best food and best prices around. Down in the valley just south of the Big Sky turnoff, the restaurants at *Buck's T-4* and the *Rainbow Ranch Lodge* (see Places to Stay – Gallatin Valley earlier in this chapter) were both written up in a popular ski magazine as among the best 'après-ski meals' in the USA.

LIVINGSTON
In the late 1880s the Northern Pacific Railroad laid tracks across the Yellowstone River and began building Livingston, incorporating the nearby settlement of Clark City. Livingston became a major stopping point and locomotive repair site, making Paradise Valley the earliest travel corridor to Yellowstone National Park and Livingston the primary jumping-off point.

Essentially what Bozeman was 10 years ago, Livingston (population 7500) still has – a rough-and-tumble, small-town feel. The saloons that legendary sharp-shooting frontierswoman Calamity Jane and Kitty O'Leary frequented during Livingston's railroad days remain relatively unchanged and the town's farm supply and hardware stores still cater to local ranchers. In the past decade, however, artist Russell Chatham moved his gallery into town, while the book *Kayaking the Full Moon* immortalized Livingston as *the* place from which to start a journey down the Yellowstone River and Bozeman has grown large enough to need 'overflow' space. This influx of outside activity has brought a few excellent restaurants, some upscale boutiques and art galleries to town. The beauty of all this is that these businesses have taken up residency in Livingston's picturesque old buildings and have only added to the town's appeal.

The bit of sprawl that is beginning to build around the edges is limited to the area around the I-90/US 191 interchange.

Orientation

Livingston sits at the north end of Paradise Valley, flanked by the Bridger, Gallatin and Absaroka ranges, where I-90 meets the Yellowstone River. US 89 heads north to Great Falls (170 miles away) and south to Gardiner and Yellowstone National Park (53 miles away); Bozeman is 35 miles east. Gallatin and Park Sts are the main thoroughfares running east to west, while Main

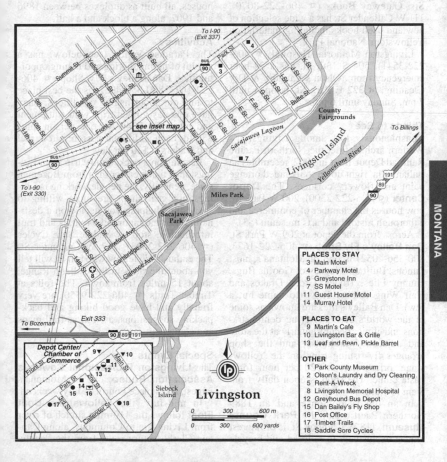

Livingston

0   300   600 m
0   300   600 yards

PLACES TO STAY
3 Main Motel
4 Parkway Motel
6 Greystone Inn
7 SS Motel
11 Guest House Motel
14 Murray Hotel

PLACES TO EAT
9 Martin's Cafe
10 Livingston Bar & Grille
13 Leaf and Bean, Pickle Barrel

OTHER
1 Park County Museum
2 Olson's Laundry and Dry Cleaning
5 Rent-A-Wreck
8 Livingston Memorial Hospital
12 Greyhound Bus Depot
15 Dan Bailey's Fly Shop
16 Post Office
17 Timber Trails
18 Saddle Sore Cycles

MONTANA

St runs north to south and separates numbered streets (to the west) from lettered streets.

Information

Livingston's chamber of commerce (☎ 406-222-0850) is in the old Livingston Depot's baggage room at 212 W Park St. The USFS Mill Creek Station (☎ 406-333-4314), 1 mile south of town on US 89, has information on fishing, hiking, camping and USFS rental cabins.

The main post office (☎ 406-222-0912) is on 2nd St between Park and Callender Sts. Gateway Books (☎ 406-222-8070), 111 W Callender St, has a wide selection of new and used books including material on Yellowstone National Park.

Livingston Memorial Hospital (☎ 406-222-3541), 504 S 13th St, has a 24-hour emergency room. Olson's Laundry & Dry Cleaning, at 322 E Park St, is open until 7 pm, Sunday until 6 pm.

Things to See

Conspicuously lost among Livingston's Western architecture, the Northern Pacific Railroad Depot, built in 1902, resembles an Italian villa, right down to its faded orange paint and flowery cornices. The **Depot Center** (☎ 406-222-2300), 200 W Park St, now houses the chamber of commerce and a thorough history and arts museum ($3).

Across from the depot at 209 W Park St, **Dan Bailey's Fly Shop** (☎ 406-222-1673, 800-356-4052) is one of Montana's most famous. Built on a legacy of Goofus Bugs, Humpy Flies, Trudes, Green Drakes and Hair Wing Rubber Legs (to name but a few), Dan Bailey's flies are known as some of the world's best. Fly-tying demonstrations and clinics occur regularly at the store and adjacent warehouse, and the shop arranges fly-fishing trips on the Yellowstone; prices start at $20 per hour for a basic clinic. The shop is open daily from 8 am to 7 pm.

In an old schoolhouse and an 1889 Northern Pacific car, the **Park County Museum**, 118 W Chinook St, is of interest almost exclusively to railroad and bicycle enthusiasts; it is open daily from noon to 5 pm June to Memorial Day.

Four small, one-story houses on B St, between Clark and Geyser Sts, are all that remain of Livingston's once-thriving **red-light district**. Livingston was an end-of-the-track location and a place where the section crews picked up their paychecks – need more be said? Though technically illegal, Livingston's prostitution achieved a certain 'illegitimate respectability' – partially due to the amount of money the well-dressed, well-fed women pumped into the economy – and grew to encompass nine houses, all built as duplexes between 1896 and 1907, along a block and a half.

Activities

The Paradise Valley (see below) has a wealth of hiking, biking and fishing opportunities. Dan Bailey's Fly Shop (☎ 406-222-1673, 800-356-4052) is the best place to find out about fishing conditions. They have one-day guided trips with equipment and lunch for $240 for one person, plus $35 for each additional person; a rod, reel and waders is $20 per day.

Leaving on a backcountry trip from Livingston is much easier than from Bozeman since, generally, the people working in Livingston's gear shops are more willing to spend time helping you decide on a destination. For mountain bike rentals and trail information, stop by Saddle Sore Cycles (☎ 406-222-2628), 117 W Callender St. The enthusiastic fellow who runs it will tell you about the rides in the Gallatin Range, about 15 miles from town. The folks at Timber Trails (☎ 406-222-9550) are very friendly and have good hiking and backpacking suggestions, as well as trail maps and equipment.

Special Events

The **Livingston Professional Cowboys Association Rodeo**, one of Montana's largest, takes place Fourth of July weekend.

In mid-July, the **Yellowstone Boat Float** follows the 110-mile stretch of river from Livingston to Columbus, along Captain Clark's return route from the Pacific.

Martha Jane Cannary picked up a rifle and became Calamity Jane.

Anything that faintly resembles a boat is allowed to participate, as long as its passengers are willing to get wet and wild. More conventional is the **Park County Fair**, held the second week of August.

Places to Stay

Livingston has a wide range of accommodations, from seedy downtown motels to cushy B&Bs. Rates increase by about 20% from Memorial Day to Thanksgiving weekend. The *Main Motel* (☎ 406-222-8103), 130 North F St, has the cheapest rooms in town at $20/25 single/double, but reeks of smoke and does not take credit cards.

The *Parkway Motel* (☎ 406-222-3840), 1124 W Park St, has double rooms for $32 in winter, $56 in summer, while the large *Guest House Motel* (☎ 406-222-1460), 105 W Park St, has a restaurant, lounge and rooms for $41/45 single/double. The *SS*

Motel (☎ 406-222-0591), on S Main St south of Sacajawea Lagoon, has a small pool and rooms for $35/40.

The *Murray Hotel* (☎ 406-222-1350), 201 W Park St, is a piece of Livingston history, and quite a bargain with rooms starting at $40.

You can stay where Arnold Schwarzenegger did, at the *Greystone Inn B&B* (☎ 406-222-8319 or 406-222-8350), 122 S Yellowstone St, which charges $40 to $75 for elegant rooms and a big 'country-style' breakfast.

Places to Eat

There's a large *Buttrey's* supermarket west of town; take Park St west towards the I-90/US 191 junction.

The best place in town for coffee and pastries is the *Leaf & Bean*, in the Park Place Bldg on Park St between Main and 2nd Ave. The *Pickle Barrel*, in the same building, has good soup and huge hot and cold sandwiches for under $7 and is open until 9 pm. Across the street, *Martins Cafe* is popular with ranchers for its straightforward diner food. For good food, a first-rate wine list, reasonable prices and plush atmosphere, try Russell Chatham's *Livingston Bar and Grille* (☎ 406-222-7909), 130 N Main St, which has a back bar that came from San Francisco by wagon train around 1910 and got considerable use by Calamity Jane.

Getting There & Away

Greyhound (☎ 406-222-1460) leaves from 107 W Park St, next to the Guest House Motel; buses take I-90 to Billings, Butte, Helena and Missoula.

Getting Around

Cars and 4WD vehicles are available from Rent-A-Wreck (☎ 406-222-0071, 800-255-0071) at the corner of Park and 6th Sts.

PARADISE VALLEY

When Livingston developed as a railroad town in the 1880s, the Paradise Valley – named by early settlers who were impressed with the valley's relatively warm climate and

MONTANA

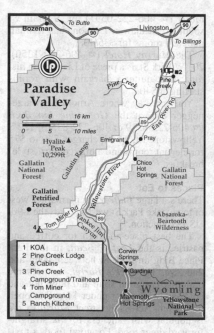

Paradise
Valley

1	KOA
2	Pine Creek Lodge & Cabins
3	Pine Creek Campground/Trailhead
4	Tom Miner Campground
5	Ranch Kitchen

awe-inspiring scenery – became the first travel corridor to Yellowstone National Park. Gardiner, 50 miles south of Livingston and just north of the Mammoth Hot Springs entrance to Yellowstone, is still one of the park's most popular entry points.

US 89 follows the Yellowstone River through this broad valley, flanked by the Gallatin Range to the west and the Absaroka Range to the east. The East River Rd offers a parallel alternative to US 89 and gets a bit less traffic, though it is narrower and rough in parts.

Fishing access sites (there are 16 of them between Livingston and Gardiner) put you right down at river's edge, and Forest Service access roads connect the valley floor to hiking, mountain biking and ski trails in the Absaroka-Beartooth Wilderness just east of East River Rd. Fishing is good from late June through October and floaters (in rafts, kayaks and canoes) take to the river from late June through August.

The massive slabs of uplifted rock that form narrow canyons on the valley's northern and southern ends include pale gray Madison limestone and travertine limestone (quarried near Gardiner for decorative use).

Pine Creek

Twelve miles south of Livingston, where Pine Creek flows east into the Absaroka Range past impressive Mt Delano and Elephant Head Mountain, is the small town that shares its name. There's a beautifully situated *KOA* between US 89 and the East River Rd that charges $18 for tents, $24 for RVs. On the East River Rd, the *Pine Creek Lodge & Cabins* (☎ 406-222-3628) has nice cabins for $52 and a restaurant open from 7 am to 9 pm daily. The deck, cozy bar and really good food attract customers from all around the area.

South about 2 miles, Lucckock Park Rd goes 3 miles east to the USFS *Pine Creek Campground*, which has $7 sites and pit toilets. A quarter of a mile beyond the campground is the Pine Creek Trail trailhead. An easy 1-mile hike takes you to Pine Creek Falls, a double cascade that is well known among ice climbers. From here, the trail switchbacks up another 4 miles to pristine Pine Lakes where you have great views of the surrounding peaks.

Chico Hot Springs

At the mouth of Emigrant Canyon, 22 miles south of Livingston and 30 miles from Yellowstone National Park, Chico Hot Springs (☎ 406-333-4933) is a piece of Montana history that has done well in keeping up with the times. Established in 1900, the resort captured nearby hot springs in a large concrete pool and built an elegant lodge and stables around them. It became a luxurious getaway for local cattle barons and a side trip for Yellowstone National Park visitors. The place is unpretentiously elegant and has been restored with great attention to rustic detail, worth a visit just to poke around. Accommodations come in a variety of sizes and prices (rooms in the main lodge with shared bath are $69, chalets that sleep up to 12 with a kitchen start at $149) but are very reasonable for what you get. A plunge in the pool for nonguests costs $3.

Chico's 'activity center' offers horseback riding, raft trips down the Yellowstone and dogsled treks (in winter), and rents mountain bikes and cross-country skis.

The *Chico Inn Restaurant* is known throughout Montana and northern Wyoming; dinner will cost around $30 per person, including wine.

Tom Miner Basin

Tom Miner Rd heads west of US 89, 17 miles north of Gardiner and 35 miles south of Livingston, into one of the prettiest pockets of land in the area. Following Tom Miner Creek up towards its origin in a high basin of the Absarokas, the washboard road ends 12 miles west of the highway at USFS *Tom Miner Campground*, which has pit toilets and $7 sites. There are several trails that start at the campground, including a 3-mile loop through the **Gallatin Petrified Forest**, where remnants of wood and fossils between 35 million and 55 million years old stand upright among the Absaroka's volcanic rocks. Some of the logs are remains of trees buried where they grew, but most are deposits of a great mud flow activated when volcanoes erupted in the area about 50 million years ago.

Tom Miner Rd to Gardiner

South of the Tom Miner turnoff, US 89 winds through Yankee Jim Canyon, a narrow gorge cut through folded bands of extremely old rock (mostly gneiss) which look like marble cake. The Yankee Jim river access and picnic point is a good place to watch people float the river. Just south is the *Ranch Kitchen*, which has great food, a nice general store and coffee bar/bookstore. It's run by the Church Universal and Triumphant, which basically means that all the produce is organic, books are of the spiritual/self-help kind and they don't serve alcohol.

GARDINER

A quintessential gateway town founded and fed on tourism, Gardiner is the only entrance to Yellowstone National Park open to automobile traffic year-round. Park St is the dividing line between Park County and Yellowstone National Park, and Mammoth Hot Springs is 5 miles south. The only real points of interest here, aside from the abundant food and lodging, are the Roosevelt Arch, dedicated by Teddy Roosevelt himself in 1903, and Kellem's Montana Saddlery, at the corner of 2nd and Main Sts, which produces beautiful custom-made saddles. The town is friendly though, and makes a good base from which to explore the northern reaches of the park.

Orientation

Gardiner is 53 miles south of Livingston via US 89, which is known as Scott St where it parallels the Yellowstone River and 2nd St where it turns south to cross the river. Note that most locals still simply say 'highway 89,' as street names are a recent phenomenon in town.

The Yellowstone River, which flows east to west through town, divides Gardiner into two distinct sections: the older grid to the south, bordering the national park, and the newer strip along Scott St, where most tourist services now operate. A short distance east of the bridge is the confluence of the Yellowstone and Gardiner rivers.

Information

The chamber of commerce (☎ 406-848-7971) is at the corner of Main and 3rd Sts. It's open Monday to Friday from 9 am to 5 pm, noon to 5 pm in winter, and occasionally on Saturdays. There's an unattended information kiosk at the corner of 3rd and Park Sts.

The USFS Gallatin National Forest's Gardiner District Office (☎ 406-848-7375) is on Scott St, just west of Yellowstone St and north of the river. First National Park Bank on Scott St has an ATM. The post office is on Main St between 2nd and 3rd Sts (zip code 59030). The nearest medical

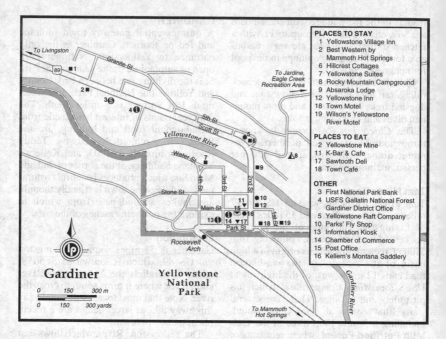

Gardiner

Yellowstone National Park

0   150   300 m
0   150   300 yards

To Livingston

Granite St

To Jardine,
Eagle Creek
Recreation Area

5th St
Scott St
Yellowstone River
Water St
Stone St
Main St
Park St
Roosevelt
Arch

Gardiner River

To Mammoth
Hot Springs

PLACES TO STAY
1   Yellowstone Village Inn
2   Best Western by
    Mammoth Hot Springs
6   Hillcrest Cottages
7   Yellowstone Suites
8   Rocky Mountain Campground
9   Absaroka Lodge
12 Yellowstone Inn
18 Town Motel
19 Wilson's Yellowstone
    River Motel

PLACES TO EAT
2   Yellowstone Mine
11 K-Bar & Cafe
17 Sawtooth Deli
18 Town Cafe

OTHER
3   First National Park Bank
4   USFS Gallatin National Forest
    Gardiner District Office
5   Yellowstone Raft Company
10 Parks' Fly Shop
13 Information Kiosk
14 Chamber of Commerce
15 Post Office
16 Kellem's Montana Saddlery

facility is the Mammoth Clinic (☎ 307-344-7965) at Mammoth Hot Springs in Yellowstone National Park, open 8:30 am to noon and 2 to 5 pm.

Activities
On the Yellowstone River **river rafting** trips often run through Yankee Jim Canyon, one of Montana's more famous white-water spots. The Yellowstone Raft Company (☎ 406-848-7777), at 406 Scott St, runs half-day trips for $30, full-day for $65 including lunch. They also have **kayaking** lessons on the river for $65. Headwaters Angler (☎ 406-848-7110), in the Yellowstone Outpost mall near the west end of Scott St, does similar floats.

Several outfitters run **fishing** trips and **horseback riding** into Yellowstone and other nearby mountain areas, including Wilderness Connection (☎ 406-848-7287), Hell's A-Roarin' Outfitters (☎ 406-848-7578) and North Yellowstone Outfitters (☎ 406-848-7651). Rides start at around

$10 per hour, $50 per half day and $90 per full day. Parks' Fly Shop (☎ 406-848-7314), on 2nd St between Stone and Main Sts, publishes an angler's map of Yellowstone National Park and surrounding areas, including the Gallatin and Missouri rivers to the west. Prices are around $100 per person (including lunch and equipment), less with three or more people.

Places to Stay
Accommodations are abundant, but summer prices are often double what they are the rest of the year. Reservations are advisable because of Gardiner's proximity to Yellowstone National Park.

Camping The woodsy USFS *Eagle Creek Recreation Area*, 2 miles northeast of Gardiner on Jardine Rd, has water and pit toilets but no hook-ups. Sights are $6 per vehicle.

Friendly *Rocky Mountain Campground* (☎ 406-848-7251), overlooking the river

MONTANA

from Jardine Rd, has a store and excellent panoramas of Yellowstone but very little shade. Tent sites cost $16, sites with water and electricity cost $20 and those with full hookups are $22. A two-person tent cabin is available for $22; another four-person cabin costs $24.

B&Bs The *Yellowstone Inn* (☎ 406-848-7000), at the corner of Main and 2nd Sts, is a picturesque Victorian where rooms with shared bath cost $59 and rooms with private bath start at $98; off-season rates are 10% to 20% lower. *Yellowstone Suites* (☎ 406-848-7937), 506 4th St, is a stone house of similar price and vintage.

Motels & Hotels The newly remodeled *Town Motel* (☎ 406-848-7322), on Park St between 1st and 2nd Sts, charges $52/60 a single/double in summer. Rates at *Wilson's Yellowstone River Motel* (☎ 406-848-7303), on Park St east of 1st St, start at $50 a double; it is open mid-April to the end of October.

North of the river at 200 Scott St, *Hillcrest Cottages* (☎ 406-848-7353) has cottages with kitchenettes for $60 a double, $80 for up to six people. The *Yellowstone Village Inn* (☎ 800-228-8158), at the west end of Scott St, has doubles for $80.

The *Best Western by Mammoth Hot Springs* (☎ 406-848-7311), on Scott St between Hellroaring and Travertine Sts, is top end, with doubles starting at $90. Modern but surprisingly unobtrusive, the *Absaroka Lodge* (☎ 406-848-7414, 800-755-7414) overlooks the river just north of the Yellowstone Bridge, and all rooms have good views of the north entrance of Yellowstone National Park. Summer rates start at around $90 and go to $100 for rooms with two queen-size beds and a kitchenette.

Places to Eat
The *Town Cafe*, next to the Town Motel on Park St, is a good family-style spot with breakfast, lunch and dinner year-round; their upstairs dining room (open in summer for dinner) has an excellent view into the

park. Also open year-round is the *K-Bar & Cafe*, at the corner of 2nd and Main Sts, with pizza and daily lunch specials, in addition to steak and seafood dinners. The *Yellowstone Mine*, in the Best Western on Scott St, is not as popular with locals, but serves good food and is open until 10 pm.

In summer, try the *Sawtooth Deli*, 220 W Park St, which serves hot and cold subs and a nice selection of salads.

LIVINGSTON TO BILLINGS
I-90 leaves its mountain setting behind at Livingston as it heads towards the open ranges and prairies of eastern Montana. But south of the highway lies some of the most dramatic and accessible parts of the Absaroka and Beartooth ranges, most of which are part of the Absaroka-Beartooth Wilderness. A scenic alternative to I-90 between Livingston and Big Timber is Swingley Rd, which turns into W Boulder Rd and meets Boulder River Rd, 16 miles south of Big Timber (see Boulder River

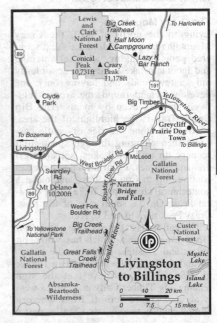

Livingston to Billings

MONTANA

The Mountains' Crazy Name

There are several stories of how the Crazy Mountains got their name. The Indians called them the Mad Mountains, and believed that they should only be admired from afar. The Anglo variation, 'Crazy Mountains,' comes either from a direct translation of the Indian name, inspired by the powerful winds that come howling and shrieking down the steep canyons, or from another story of a family who homesteaded in the area. According to legend, one night the father didn't come home from the fields, so the mother sent their son to find him. When the son didn't come home, she sent the other son. When he didn't come home, she sent the daughter and finally went looking herself. In a coulee (deep ravine) not far from their home, she found a band of Sioux warriors scalping her husband and sons and raping her daughter. She began to scream, grasped one of the Sioux tomahawks and started swinging at everything in sight. The fire in her eyes scared the Sioux, and they left the 'crazy woman' with her massacred family. From that day, despite pleading and coaxing from neighbors and the sheriff, she would not leave that spot. She remained there howling and mourning, fed by the passers-by who would leave her food, until she died 20 years later. ■

Corridor below). The journey, along a well-kept dirt road, takes about an hour and skirts the base of the Absarokas. To reach Swingley Rd from Livingston, head east (towards I-90) on Park St and watch for the turnoff about a mile out of town.

The Crazy Mountains

Lying to the north of I-90, the Crazy Mountains are one of Montana's undiscovered gems for hiking, wildlife watching and mountain lake fishing. Accessible by only a few roads and having only one developed campground, the area is relatively unused, even by locals. The **Big Creek Trail** is the highlight of the area, starting off along a series of gentle cascades then plunging through spectacular scenery up to Twin Lakes, set amongst dramatic cirques. From the lakes you can continue up to Conical Pass and make a nontechnical climb up to 10,737-foot Conical Peak. On the south side of the pass, Crazy Peak rises to 11,178 feet.

The trail starts at the east side of the *Half Moon Campground*, which has water, pit toilets and $7 sites. To get to the campground, drive 11 miles north of Big Timber on US 191 and turn west at the sign reading Big Timber Canyon; 3 miles west is another signed turnoff from where a bumpy country road winds 12 miles past a

gated ranch and then continues 3 miles before it dead-ends at the campground.

The gated ranch through which you must pass to reach the campground is the *Lazy K Bar Ranch* (☎ 406-537-4404), PO Box 550, Big Timber, MT 59011, Montana's oldest dude ranch and childhood home to cowboy poet Spike Van Cleeve. The $1000 per-person, per-week price tag includes a horse, planned rides, hikes, campfires, three hearty meals a day and a chance to pitch in with ranch chores.

The alternative access roads, which enter the range from the west, are Cottonwood Rd and Rock Creek Rd, which head east from US 89 near the small community of Clyde Park.

The Boulder River Corridor

The Boulder River flows from the upper reaches of the Absarokas through a narrow limestone valley and out into a wide expanse of ranch land to where it meets the Yellowstone River at Big Timber (called 'Rivers Across' by Lewis and Clark). The hiking trails along the many creeks which drain into the river give quick (and steep) access to the jagged interior peaks of the Absarokas. Two favorite trails are the **Big Creek Trail** and the **Great Falls Creek Trail**, which make good day-hikes or can be combined with other trails for multiple-day loops. It's possible to do a point-to-point hike over one of the passes into the Paradise Valley, which lies on the west side of the mountain's ridge; the South Fork of Deep Creek is a good end point for such a trip. There are also several USFS campgrounds at the river's southern end. At its northern end, about 25 miles south of Big Timber, the **Natural Bridge and Falls** viewing point and loop trail is a very worthwhile destination, even as a side trip when traveling along I-90.

To get to this part of the river, take McCleod St (Big Timber's main drag that runs south from I-90) south until it becomes Boulder River Rd. The pavement ends about 20 miles south of town, though the dirt road is in excellent condition.

There are also trails and a campground 14 miles up the West Fork of the Boulder River, accessible via West Fork Boulder Rd, which turns off Boulder River Rd 16 miles south of Big Timber. Stop at the Big Timber Ranger District Office (☎ 406-932-5155), next to Frosty Freeze on the east side of I-90, for maps and information.

In the 1890s **Big Timber** was one of the largest wool-shipping centers in the country. Montana's first wool mill, still standing on McLeod St, operated here from 1901 to 1930. The town has a few classic bars, a fly-fishing shop as well as the terrific *Grand Hotel* (☎ 406-932-4459), 139 McCloud, which was built in 1890, is on the National Register of Historic Places and charges $55 to $85 for period-decorated rooms and a full breakfast. The *Big Timber KOA* (☎ 406-932-6569), 6 miles west of town on I-90, has tent sites for $18, RV spaces for $23.

Greycliff Prairie Dog Town
Seven miles east of Big Timber off I-90, Greycliff Prairie Dog Town is a true form of entertainment. The little critters, part of the ground squirrel family and unique to North America, peek their heads out of the ground, look around, give a few 'yeep yeep' warnings to their friends and retreat back down into the earth. As soon as one comes into focus, it disappears and

another one pops up somewhere else. Prairie dogs are some of the only vegetarians in Montana: they feed off grasses, roots and bulbs. In their highly organized social system, each 'town' consists of neighborhoods that house one or two adult males and two to four adult females. Their young are born in early spring and can be seen by mid-May. The crater-shaped mounds are back doors, dome-shaped ones are front doors. Almost as fun as watching the animals themselves is watching people watch the animals.

HWY 78
Hwy 78 turns southwest off I-90 at Columbus and briefly follows the Stillwater River before turning south and then east to meet US 212 in Red Lodge. Besides being the best route between Red Lodge and the Bozeman area, the highway leads through some scenic one-bar towns and gives access to the Absaroka-Beartooth Wilderness, which stretches west all the way to the Paradise Valley.

Absarokee
Primarily a wilderness gateway, Absarokee (pronounced 'apsorkee') is the put-in point for raft trips on the Stillwater River. Depending on the snowmelt, most trips run from early June to mid-July. Beartooth Whitewater (☎ 406-446-3142) is one of the few rafting companies that does not penalize half-day trippers; rates are $25 for a half day, $50 for a full day. Adventure Whitewater (☎ 406-446-3061) combines rafting and fishing on half- and full-day excursions, and also runs trips on the Yellowstone River.

Paintbrush Trails Inc (☎ 406-328-4158) offers one-hour ($14), half-day ($40), and all-day ($60) trail rides, overnight pack trips and combined pack/fishing trips into nearby lakes.

Fishtail
Four miles southwest of Hwy 78 on Nye Rd, Fishtail is home of the *Cowboy Bar and Supper Club* (☎ 406-328-4288). The bar's trademark 'Chickenshit Game' is a

MONTANA

pretty hilarious sight, sober or not. Two chickens share a large cage with a numbered grid painted on the bottom. People pick numbers (which correspond to grid numbers) out of a hat, and whichever numbers the chickens grace with their droppings are the lucky winners. Watching the crowd encourage defecation is about as good as it gets. The games start at 1 pm on Sunday (post-church entertainment?) and last until the chickens are pooped-out.

Roscoe

Halfway between Absarokee and Red Lodge at a bend in the highway, Roscoe (population 22) has a statewide reputation as home of the *Grizzly Bar* (☎ 406-328-6789). Not quite as rugged as its name implies (there is a giant stuffed grizzly above the entrance), the bar teems with anglers, backpackers and hunters who make the bar their first re-entry destination upon leaving the backcountry. Basically its reputation rests on fantastic food, strong cocktails and an outdoor beer garden that is extremely lively in the summer months.

Across from the Grizzly Bar on Hwy 78, *Granny & Papa's B&B* (☎ 406-328-6789) charges $40 to $60 for a creekside room and full hearty breakfast. Next door is a wooden-front post office still in full swing.

ABSAROKA-BEARTOOTH WILDERNESS

Bordered by the Paradise Valley and US 89 to the west, I-90 to the north, Hwy 87 and US 212 to the east, and merging with Yellowstone National Park in the south, this 1475-sq-mile wilderness is the third most visited wilderness area in the USA. The thickly forested Absaroka Range dominates the area's west half and is most easily reached from the Paradise Valley or Boulder River Corridor (see Paradise Valley earlier in this section). Smaller in breadth but much higher, the Beartooth Range's jagged peaks and Alpine tundra meadows – results of heavy glacial activity – are best reached from the east off Hwy 78 and US 212 near Red Lodge.

Forests bordering the wilderness area fall under three separate USFS districts: the Gallatin in the west, Custer in the east, and Shoshone (Wyoming) in the southeast.

Because of its proximity to Yellowstone National Park, the Beartooth portion gets two-thirds of the area's traffic – most of it concentrated near the wilderness boundaries. The rugged interior is not nearly as crowded.

East Rosebud Lake

A drainage basin for several high lakes and East Rosebud Creek, this lake sits at the northern butt of the East Rosebud Plateau (a small extension of the Beartooth Plateau) with Sylvan Peak (to the southeast) and Mt Hole-in-the-Wall (southwest) visible on either side. On its northern shore, at the end of East Rosebud Creek Rd 14 miles south of Hwy 78 from Roscoe, is a small USFS campground with fire rings and pit toilets. From the campground trails head south, along the east side of the lake and East Rosebud Creek, into the heart of the wilderness area, and east to Sylvan and Crow lakes and eventually to the West Fork of Rock Creek near Red Lodge. Rainbow Lake, about 4 miles south along the **East Rosebud Creek Trail** is a good day-hike destination.

Five miles before East Rosebud Lake (about 9 miles from Roscoe), USFS *Jimmy Joe Campground* is a good spot to see butterflies from May to July and is popular for birdwatching. This is a good camp spot if you're looking for more solitude than East Rosebud offers.

West Rosebud Lake

Created by the Mystic Lake hydroelectric dam, West Rosebud Lake is a favorite among anglers and day-hikers. The lake is the westernmost of a four-lake chain connected by a 7-mile hiking trail that begins from the parking lot on the lake's north shore. On the south side of West Rosebud Creek is a large campground with fire rings and pit toilets. The lake is 17 miles south of Fishtail at the end of West Rosebud Creek Rd. People with two vehicles can hike from

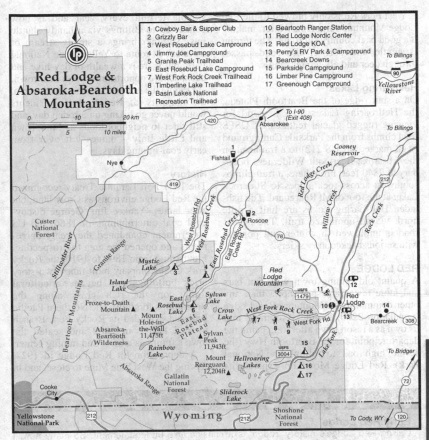

Red Lodge & Absaroka-Beartooth Mountains

1 Cowboy Bar & Supper Club
2 Grizzly Bar
3 West Rosebud Lake Campround
4 Jimmy Joe Campground
5 Granite Peak Trailhead
6 East Rosebud Lake Campground
7 West Fork Rock Creek Trailhead
8 Timberline Lake Trailhead
9 Basin Lakes National Recreation Trailhead
10 Beartooth Ranger Station
11 Red Lodge Nordic Center
12 Red Lodge KOA
13 Perry's RV Park & Campground
14 Bearcreek Downs
15 Parkside Campground
16 Limber Pine Campground
17 Greenough Campground

East to West Rosebud Lake (17 miles), across the northern foothills of Mt Hole-In-The-Wall and Froze-To-Death Mountain.

West Fork Rock Creek

A mile south of town, just north of the Ranger Station, West Fork Rd turns southwest off US 212. The road passes the turnoff to Red Lodge Mountain and several USFS campgrounds along Rock Creek and it continues 12 miles to the West Fork Rock Creek trailhead at road's end. The West Fork trail follows the creek 4 miles to Quinnebaugh Meadows, a popular day-hike picnic spot and good for wildflower

viewing in early July. From here you can take a steep 1-mile trail up to Lake Mary (where unmarked trails continue over to Sylvan, Crow and East Rosebud lakes), or continue along the main trail to Sundance Lake and Sundance Pass, a good multiple-day option which takes you into some very rugged country and has the potential for a loop trip.

Another good day-hike is up the Timberline Lake Trail, which starts on the south side of West Fork Rd, 2 miles before road's end. This trail climbs 4½ miles along Timberline Creek to Gertrude and Timberline lakes, both good for trout fishing.

West Fork Rd is only plowed to the Red Lodge Mountain turnoff in winter, making it a good backcountry ski route. The terrain is gentle and part of the road passes through deer and elk winter range.

Hellroaring Lakes

On a spur ridge of the Beartooth Plateau, the Hellroaring Lakes area is good for viewing rugged glacial features. A USFS road climbs from the Parkside Campground (well marked off US 212) to a trailhead on the Absaroka-Beartooth Wilderness boundary at 9840 feet. From here, a trail climbs southwest across rock slopes to Sliderock Lake, at the foot of Mt Rearguard. The fish-laden Hellroaring Lakes are half a mile north via an unmarked trail. The access road is unplowed in winter and popular with serious backcountry skiers.

RED LODGE

A quaint old mining town with fun bars and more restaurants per capita than any other community in Montana, Red Lodge (population 2200) is quickly coming into its own as a resort town after long being the departure point for the Beartooth Hwy (the scenic 'high road' to Yellowstone National Park). Red Lodge Mountain expands its skiable terrain every year and is now connected to Billings via a handy shuttle bus. Summer brings a steady stream of travelers en route to Yellowstone National Park, but there is a wealth of day-hike and backpacking opportunities right near town.

Despite the many newcomers to the area, the majority of Red Lodge's residents would never go hiking on a rodeo day, and still refer to neighborhoods as Finn Town and Little Italy – names left over from early coal-mining days.

History

The 1851 Fort Laramie Treaty recognized the Red Lodge environs as Crow land, but after James 'Yankee Jim' George discovered coal outcroppings in 1866, the US government abandoned the treaty agreements and opened the area to prospecting. Flourishing from 1896 to 1910, the Rocky Fork Coal Company built fancy two-story brick buildings and began agricultural forays on the rich grass along the Beartooth's foothills. The Northern Pacific Railroad extended its Rocky Fork Branch to Red Lodge in 1889 and sealed the town's future as a trade and mining center.

A depression hit Red Lodge in 1924, forcing the West Side Mine to close, and in

Early Red Lodge

Calling Red Lodge's history 'rough' is a considerable understatement. So many new buildings went up that there was no wood left to build sidewalks; people waded through streets of knee-deep mud as they passed between two dozen bars and a row of brothels known as 'the Castles.' Ambivalent laws failed at keeping peace and justice among the diversity of immigrant and US-born miners: Little Italy, Finn Town and Highburg (where rich mining executives lived) each had its own set of culturally designated rules. In the absence of a common language to solve misunderstandings, guns and fists became the major tools of communication.

John 'Liver-eating' Johnson was an old frontiersman who was the only man in town tough and large enough to enforce law and order without words, and thus was appointed the first town constable in 1881.

There are plenty of stories of how he got his nickname: some say he killed a man and ate pieces of the man's liver; others contend that during a fight with some Sioux, Johnson ripped open a calf and ate its liver. Still others claim he killed, scalped and ate the livers of Crow Indians as revenge for killing his wife, and others say he merely threatened to eat the liver of any Indian that came too close. Whatever the story, he was made all the more notorious by the Robert Redford movie *Jeremiah Johnson*. ∎

turn, half the town's population left. Red Lodge's hard times were relatively short-lived, however, for construction of the Beartooth Hwy began in 1931 and secured economic revitalization, beginning the transition from mining and agriculture to recreation and tourism.

Orientation

On the west bank of Rock Creek, Red Lodge is 60 miles south of Billings and 80 miles north of Cooke City (and the north entrance to Yellowstone National Park). US 212 runs north-south through town as Broadway Ave, the main street, and becomes the Beartooth Hwy south of town. Numbered streets run east to west across Broadway; 1st St is northernmost and 25th St southernmost, a mile below. With the exception of Red Lodge Mountain, 6 miles southwest of town, all of Red Lodge's attractions, accommodations and restaurants are within walking distance of each other.

Information

The Red Lodge Chamber of Commerce (☎ 406-446-1718), 601 N Broadway Ave, has accommodations information, while the Beartooth Ranger Station (☎ 406-446-2103), 3 miles south of Red Lodge on US 212, is the best resource for maps and information on the Absaroka-Beartooth Wilderness, Beartooth Mountains and Beartooth Hwy. The office closes from noon to 1 pm on weekends. There's a large topo map posted out front.

You'll find the bank, hardware store (which sells maps and fishing licenses) and bookstores along Broadway. The post office is on W 13th St at the corner of S Hauser Ave. The Carbon County Memorial Hospital (☎ 406-446-2345), 600 W 20th St, has a 24-hour emergency facility.

Carbon County Museum

The Carbon County Museum, located on Broadway Ave at the south end of town, is worth a look for its collection of rodeo gear. Alice Greenough, the first woman named to the Cowgirl Hall of Fame and one of the few women honored in the Cowboy Hall of Fame, started the museum as a tribute to her father Ben 'Pack-Saddle' Greenough who, among other things, won the first professional bronco-busting contest in the state and chopped wood for Calamity Jane. The museum is free and is open daily from 10 am to 6 pm Memorial Day to Labor Day.

Hiking

The Custer National Forest acts as a green buffer between Red Lodge and the high, glaciated Beartooth Plateau to the south and west. Hiking in this area is magnificent, as it takes relatively little time and effort to reach terrain that resembles the Himalayas (on a smaller scale of course). You can gain about 3000 feet of elevation by car and begin your hike from the Beartooth Hwy, but it's very important to allow a day or two to acclimatize. Also be aware that the barren terrain offers little shade, shelter or wood. With proper preparation, however, it's a stunning place to explore. Backpackers should inquire at the ranger station in Red Lodge about the three- to four-day **Spogen Lake Loop**, which traverses classic Beartooth Plateau scenery – glacial lakes, peaks and knife-edged ridges. An easy day-hike is the 3-mile ramble to **Rock Island Lake**, which begins from a trailhead marker on USFS Rd 306 and meets the Beartooth Hwy about 2 miles east of Cooke City. An excellent book to have is *Hiking the Beartooths*, available at the grocery store and bookstores in Red Lodge.

Hikes closest to Red Lodge begin from Rock Creek and its west fork, which drain the Beartooth Plateau. There are also good trailheads at East and West Rosebud lakes, off Hwy 78. (For more details on these hikes, see the Absaroka-Beartooth Wilderness section above.)

Skiing

Downhill Six miles southwest of downtown, Red Lodge Mountain (☎ 800-444-8977, 406-446-2610 for ski reports) has a 2400-foot vertical drop serviced by eight lifts. Halfway jokingly called 'Sludge Lodge' or 'Crud Lodge,' the northeast-facing mountain gets most of its midwinter sunshine in the morning, so by the afternoon the snow resembles stale meringue, crusty and impossible to get through. By contrast, the higher temperatures and longer days of February and March, plus a higher base elevation (7400 feet) than any other Montana ski hill, give Red Lodge Mountain some of Montana's best spring skiing.

A full-service lodge with a bar, restaurant, rental shop and ski-school program is at the base of the mountain. Tickets for adults/children are $32/12.

Renting equipment downtown instead of on the mountain will save a few bucks, although it is less convenient. Red Lodge Ski Rentals (☎ 406-446-1255), 510 N Broadway Ave, rents snowboards and downhill and cross-country skis.

Cross-Country Numerous hiking, snowmobile and dogsled trails cut through the Beartooth Range, making a vast trail network well-suited for cross-country skiing. Some of the more popular trails include: 6 miles of groomed trails at the base of Red Lodge Mountain; the Parkside Trail, which starts at the Parkside Campground 11 miles south of town on US 212, with 3- and 6-mile loops and access to the Absaroka-Beartooth Wilderness; the Basin Lakes National Recreation Trail, which has 3-, 5- and 7-mile loops, 5 miles southwest of town, up West Fork Rd; and the Palisades Trail, which traverses 2 miles between Red Lodge Mountain and Palisades Campground and offers consistently good wildlife viewing in the Willow Creek Valley.

The Red Lodge Nordic Center (☎ 406-425-1070), 2 miles west of Red Lodge on Hwy 78, is Red Lodge's top cross-country resource and a good place for beginning skiers or those who want to ski on well-maintained tracks. The center has 6 miles of groomed trails of varying degrees of difficulty, a ski school and rental shop; a day pass costs $6.

Special Events
February's festivities revolve around the **Rocky Mountain Winter Games**, held at Red Lodge Mountain in February, while March features the unlikely **Red Lodge Ski-Joring National Finals**. Ski-joring is a modern version of the Scandinavian sport of pulling a skier behind a horse; today's sport includes jumps and gates.

The **Home of Champions Rodeo** has been held since 1924 and takes place over the Fourth of July weekend. In early August, the nine-day **Festival of Nations** celebrates Red Lodge's diverse cultural history with parades, games, music, dancing, exhibits and food.

Places to Stay
Red Lodge Central Reservations (☎ 800-444-8977) arranges ski packages including airfare, car rental, lift tickets and accommodation. Red Lodging (☎ 406-446-1272), PO Box 1477, Red Lodge, MT 59068, rents everything from cabins to cottages to slopeside condos.

Camping South of Red Lodge on US 212, before it begins to ascend the Beartooth Plateau, are 10 USFS campgrounds. With shady creekside locations, the nicest are *Limber Pine* and *Greenough*, both 10 miles south of town. A bit more remote and close to good hiking are the two on West Fork Rd which turns west from US 212, 2½ miles south of town, just north of the Ranger Station.

Perry's RV Park and Campground (☎ 406-446-2722), 2 miles south of Red Lodge on US 212, has 30 sites ($10 per tent, $17 for an RV) and clean laundry and shower facilities.

Most sites are creekside at the *Red Lodge KOA* (☎ 406-446-2364), 4 miles north of Red Lodge on US 212, which also has a pool, playground and small store. Tent sites cost $18, RV spaces $31.

Motels The cheapest of the motels is the family owned *Eagle's Nest* (☎ 406-446-2312), 702 S Broadway Ave, where standard rooms cost $38/42 for a single/double, and 'pre-remodel' rooms (not much different from the others) are a bargain at $26; rooms with kitchenette cost $50, and the Ski Haus – which sleeps up to eight people and includes a kitchenette – costs $108.

The *Red Lodge Inn* (☎ 406-446-2030), 811 S Broadway Ave, has frilly rooms for $46/52. The *Yodeler Motel* (☎ 406-446-1435), 601 S Broadway Ave at the corner of 17th St, charges $43/53 for subterranean rooms that are remarkably light due to large basement windows. Upper-level rooms with balconies and in-room Jacuzzis cost $68. Best Western's *Lu Pine Inn* (☎ 406-446-1321), which is a block west of Broadway Ave at the corner of 18th St and S Hauser St, has a pool, Jacuzzi and ski-repair room. Rooms start at $55/60.

A fun and elegant place to stay is the old *Pollard Hotel* (☎ 406-446-0001), 2 N Broadway Ave, Red Lodge's first brick building. Its cozy lobby and restaurant are hubs of local activity and there's a nice health club with racquetball courts. Prices start at $60/85. The most upscale of Red Lodge's accommodations is the *Rock Creek Resort* (☎ 406-446-1111), 4½ miles south of town. Rooms start at $95 and condos are available for around $200.

Vacation Rentals & B&Bs *Pitcher Guest Houses* (☎ 406-446-2859), 2 S Platt, are no-host, fully furnished vacation homes that sleep up to eight people. A three-night minimum stay is required, and reservations are necessary. Prices are $70 to $135.

Rooms at the *Willows Inn B&B* (☎ 406-446-3913), 224 S Platt, start at $65 and couldn't possibly take any more lace or floral-print material. In back of the main house are two guest cottages with kitchens and laundry facilities that sleep up to six people for $80 to $120 (without breakfast).

Places to Eat
There's an *IGA Supermarket*, 2 blocks west of Broadway at the north end of town. A favorite pastime of locals is driving up to the Grizzly Bar (in Roscoe, see above) for lunch or dinner.

The unexciting beige exterior makes *PD McKinneys*, on the corner of 15th St and Broadway Ave, look more like an old postal building than Red Lodge's favorite breakfast spot; it's open daily from 6 am to 2 pm.

Bogart's Restaurant, 11 S Broadway Ave, has the best margaritas and Mexican food in town, and beautiful single-piece carved mahogany bar. *17 Broadway*, at that address, is a cozy après-ski favorite with good fish and steak dishes for around $10.

Attached to the Mystic Mountain Bar on Broadway Ave, *Mystic Mountain Pizza* may keep you waiting for an eternity, but all anxiety disappears once the food arrives. Pizzas with names like the Road-kill (for carnivores, naturally) cost $8 to $15; pastas cost $6 to $11.

Entertainment
Red Lodge's nightlife pours from the bars along Broadway Ave. A young, outdoorsy crowd congregates for drinking and dancing (to live bands on weekends) at the *Snowcreek Saloon*, 124 S Broadway Ave, where ski instructors moonlight as bartenders. Behind the swinging doors of the *Snag Bar*, 107 S Broadway Ave, a leather-faced crowd wearing cowboy hats and boots drinks cheap domestic beer and talks cattle prices. Formerly the Finnish Opera House, built in 1897, the *Carbon County Coal Co Bar and Casino*, 123 S Broadway Ave, is a rough-and-tumble Western bar with multiple money-eatin' machines and live poker.

Shopping
It's easy to spend an afternoon browsing in Red Lodge's shops and looking at its historical old buildings – many of them on the National Register of Historic Places. Sylvan Peak, 9 S Broadway Ave, has a full line of outdoorsy clothes (mostly fleece) that they make right there in the shop. The handmade wooden toys from Magpie Toymakers, 115 N Broadway Ave, captivate parents as much as kids but always cause a dilemma over where they should go – in the playroom or on the front mantelpiece.

MONTANA

Bearcreek Downs

Imagine pigs with names like Oscar Mayer, Hot Links and Jimmy Dean wearing little numbered jackets and racing around a mud track to a food-laden finish line. Then imagine a crowd of full-grown adults, some of them sober, screaming and cursing over the $3 they won or lost on their porker. Surreal as it sounds, the scene portrays a normal weekend night at the Bearcreek Downs, directly behind the Bearcreek Saloon (☎ 406-446-3481), 7 miles southeast of Red Lodge. In a stroke of Montana genius, bar owners Pit and Lynn DeArmond ditched traditional mariachi band entertainment and began the 'Swine Sweepstakes' as a sideline attraction to their homemade margaritas and Mexican food. The food and drink is as good as ever but definitely takes a back seat to the pig track, which has attracted journalists and television crews from 'Good Morning America' and Japan's Fuji TV.

In 1984, the state declared the races illegal and refused to issue a license that would allow pari-mutuel betting to continue. To remedy the problem, Bearcreek adopted a 'spots pool' method and contributes half of each pool to a local scholarship fund. Races begin at 7 pm on Saturdays and Sundays year-round. ■

Getting There & Away

Flying into Billings (an hour north of Red Lodge) is the cheapest and most direct way to get to this part of Montana. There are numerous car rental agencies at the Billings airport. There's also a shuttle (☎ 406-446-2257, 888-446-2191) that connects Red Lodge to the airports of Billings and Cody, WY, and stops at the Rock Creek Resort, Red Lodge Mountain and Roscoe; prices are $22 one-way, $40 roundtrip for solo travelers, $18 each way per person for two or more.

Getting Around

During the winter a ski shuttle connects accommodations in town to Red Lodge Mountain. The $5 shuttle leaves town at 9 am and returns at 4 pm; contact the mountain or any motel for information.

BEARTOOTH HWY

The Beartooth Hwy (US 212) connects Red Lodge to Cooke City and Yellowstone's north entrance by an incredible 68-mile road that was built in 1932 for $2.5 million. An engineering feat, and the 'most beautiful drive in America' according to the late TV journalist Charles Kuralt, this road is a destination as well as a travel corridor.

From its northern starting point at Red Lodge, the highway climbs Rock Creek Canyon's glaciated walls via a series of gnarled switchbacks, crosses the Wyoming border with a fanfare of billboards and reaches the plateau's twin summits (and the only public toilets along the route) at an elevation of 10,350 feet. Alpine tundra is the only thing that grows up here (where snow can last from October to mid-July), giving the landscape a desolate, otherworldly look. In fact, unless you are an outdoorsy type who makes frequent forays above 10,000 feet, it probably *is* another world – you can't usually reach this kind of terrain by car. There are turquoise blue tarns (glacial lakes), mini glaciers and jagged ridgelines visible on all sides of the highway, but to really experience the surroundings you must get out of the car, even if it's just for a few minutes to breathe the thin, cold air. The bird-like chirps of marmot signal their ubiquity in this terrain.

The grade is gradual from Cooke City to the summit and accessible lakes and trailheads are frequent. A detailed, turn-by-turn Beartooth Hwy map that highlights several hiking trails is available at the Beartooth Ranger District (☎ 406-446-2103), 3 miles south of Red Lodge, before the highway begins to climb.

MONTANA

Cooke City

Set between two forested ridges of the Beartooths, this one-street town (population 85 in winter, 350 in summer) on the northern edge of Yellowstone National Park gets a steady flow of summer visitors passing through en route to Red Lodge and the park. In winter, the road from Yellowstone is only plowed as far as Cooke City, so visitors – mostly backcountry skiers and snowmobilers – tend to check in and stay awhile. There's not much here in the way of shops, sites or even trailheads, but the town's got a backwoods feel and a year-round population that's as rugged as the surrounding peaks.

The tiny Cooke City Bike Shack (☎ 406-838-2412) is a good stop for anyone who wants to hike, bike or ski in the immediate area. They have a good inventory of equipment (from skis to freeze-dried food) and maps, and the owner is a long-time local who is tremendously helpful with trail suggestions. The historic Cooke City Mercantile is a fun browse and has some interesting history on the walls. They also have a good supply of groceries, beer and wine.

If it's not too cold out, the *Yellowstone Yurt Hostel* (☎ 800-364-6242) offers 'yurt-style' accommodations in a big round tent with hot showers and cooking facilities for $12 a person. The hostel is 3 blocks north of the main street from the west end of town (it's well marked from the road). The *High Country Motel* (☎ 406-838-2272) has rooms for $35 to $55, and the *Soda Butte Lodge* (☎ 406-838-2251, 800-527-6462), which has a restaurant, pool and sauna, has rooms starting at $52.)

Montana Plains

Eastern Montana, from the Rocky Mountains to the North Dakota border, resembles its neighboring Plains states more than its mountainous western third. In the north, along US 2, strip farms sprawl across the seemingly endless prairie, interrupted only by water towers and grain elevators. In the southwest corner, cattle ranches and oil deposits have created a wealthy if barren landscape with Billings as its hub. Lewis and Clark traveled along the Missouri River in 1805 and had to portage around

HIGHLIGHTS

- Chief Plenty Coups State Park – a tranquil counterpoint to the nearby popular Little Bighorn Battlefield

- Makoshika State Park – a little-visited park with spectacular rock formations and seemingly endless badlands

- Miles City – watch a live cattle auction each Tuesday and have a drink in one of the town's 100-year-old bars

- Virgelle – an outpost on the designated Wild and Scenic portion of the Missouri River, where you can embark on a raft trip or cross the water in a car ferry

the Great Falls of the Missouri, now a major stopping point for anyone retracing Lewis and Clark's itinerary. There are isolated mountain ranges near Lewistown and breathtaking badlands in Makoshika State Park on the North Dakota border, but this is generally not the Montana envisioned by recreationalists.

Choosing a travel route through this area should be easy as there are only two. US 2 traverses Montana's northern tier along the Hi-Line, well-serviced by small agricultural communities every 40 miles or so; Hwy 200 cuts across the very middle of the state, remote territory where Lewistown stands lonely watch. Indecisive types can bridge the two via US 191, roughly midway between Great Falls – the region's largest city – and the North Dakota border.

GREAT FALLS
Straddling the Missouri River, Great Falls (population 57,758) remains the agricultural and commercial hub that it was meant to be when East Coast entrepreneur Paris Gibson laid the plans for the city in 1885. Home to large grain companies such as Purina and General Mills, major hydroelectric plants run by Montana Power Co and Maelstrom Airforce Base, which has long-term NASA and defense contracts, the town is unquestionably the hub of Montana's northern plains. Though decidedly drab (and terribly cold and windy from October to June), it's a good stopping point between Glacier and Yellowstone National Parks, if only for its selection of cheap accommodation and food which lie near I-15 and Hwy 200.

Anyone interested in Lewis and Clark lore should plan on spending a day along the River's Edge Trail which skirts the southern flank of the Missouri. Here the Lewis and Clark expedition was forced to portage 18 miles around five waterfalls which make the river unnavigable by boat,

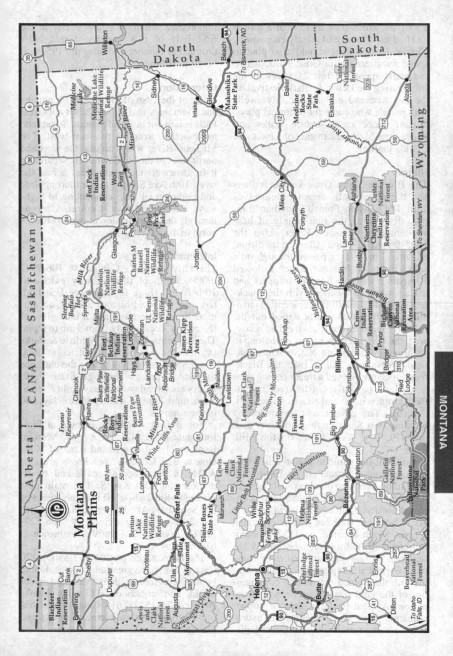

a journey which took more than a month and had its fair share of grizzly encounters. Charlie Russell fans should also plan to spend an afternoon in Great Falls, where the artist spent the last 24 years of his life. During the Lewis & Clark Festival on the last weekend in June, the city swells with people who come for historical plays, dugout canoe races, nature walks and larger-than-life reenactments of Lewis and Clark's journey.

History

The Blackfeet and Gros Ventre Indians had the Great Falls area to themselves until 1743, when French-Canadian trappers discovered the rich supply of beaver along the Missouri River. After the 1805-06 Lewis and Clark expedition, explorer Jim Bridger passed through on a solo trip up the Missouri River, followed 10 years later by a flood of trappers and traders who did business with the Blackfeet. In 1841 a small-pox epidemic (introduced by trappers) nearly wiped out the tribe. By the time the Blackfeet had recovered, the US government was well along in its program of herding Native Americans onto reservations, and, in 1855, the Blackfeet reluctantly signed a treaty ceding their home-land to settlers. Blackfeet resentment erupted in several attacks on new settlements. The government responded by building Fort Shaw on the Sun River and, in 1879, Fort Assiniboine on the Milk River.

Paris Gibson came to the area in 1883, having made a fortune on the East Coast producing woolen blankets. He bought thousands of acres of prairie land, contacted his friend James J Hill, owner of the Great Northern Railroad and incorporated a town which became, by 1887, a major railroad hub (Gibson later became a US senator). As railroads replaced river transport, Great Falls replaced Fort Benton as the link that joined the mining communities of the gold country to the rest of the nation. A meat-packing plant, a copper reduction plant, silver smelters and hydroelectric dams further boosted Great Falls'

importance. Montana's largest city in the first half of this century, Great Falls dropped to number two after the 1950s oil boom in Billings.

Orientation

Lying at the cusp of the Rocky Mountains and Montana's vast plains, the city of Great Falls is laid out in a grid pattern. Streets run north-south, avenues run east-west. The Missouri River wraps around the west and north sides of the old downtown, separating it from newer residential areas across the river. 10th Ave S is the major thoroughfare and commercial strip connecting to highways outside of town. Central Ave runs through the heart of downtown 10 blocks north of 10th Ave S.

Information

The City Visitor's Center (☎ 406-771-0885), south of the highway exits and 10th Ave S (look for the large US flag), has maps, a local history exhibit, accommodation information and a nice view of the city. It's open daily from 9 am to 6 pm. The Department of Fish, Wildlife & Parks (☎ 406-454-3441) has its office at 4600 Giant Springs Rd, just before the entrance to Giant Springs Heritage State Park. Hours are Monday to Friday from 8 am to 5 pm, until 7 pm on weekends, holidays and in the summer.

You'll find ATMs downtown at First Interstate Bank, 421 1st Ave N, Norwest Bank at 21 3rd Ave N and Bank of Montana at 324 Central Ave. There are also ATMs in the shopping malls and supermarkets on 10th Ave S. The main post office (☎ 406-761-4894) is at the corner of 3rd St and 1st Ave N. For fax services, try the 24-hour Insty Prints (☎ 406-727-3291); fax 406-727-9669) downtown at 613 Central Ave.

The Bookmarkit (☎ 406-453-3500), 120 Central Ave, has a great selection, including books by regional authors, Montana guidebooks and cookbooks. Fireside Books (☎ 406-771-1522), 614 Central Ave, has out-of-print Western literature books and vintage maps.

Great Falls

0   250   500 m
0   250   500 yards

PLACES TO STAY
1   Old Oak Inn
4   Mid-Town Motel
6   Best Western
    Ponderosa Inn
15 Holiday Inn
18 Comfort Inn
20 Super 8
21 Town House Inn

PLACES TO EAT
4   Perkins
5   Bookmarkit
9   Penny's
    Gourmet to Go
11 Museum Cafe
17 MacKenzie River
    Pizza Co

OTHER
2   Charles M Russell
    Museum Complex
3   Post Office
7   Insty Prints
8   Fireside Books
10 Knicker Biker
12 River's Edge
    Trailhead
13 Falls Cleaners and
    Laundry Center
14 City Visitor's Center
16 Rent-A-Wreck
19 Enterprise

MONTANA

Benefis Health Care (☎ 406-761-1200), 1101 26th St S, has a 24-hour emergency room.

Falls Cleaners and Laundry Center, 614 9th St S, is open daily from 8 am to 9 pm.

Things To See & Do

The best way to explore Lewis and Clark history is along the **River's Edge Trail**, which covers 7 miles of riverbank from Oddfellows Park (near where 3rd Ave S meets River Drive) to the Rainbow Dam; pick up the free 'A Guide to the River's Edge Trail' newsletter from the visitors center. The trail passes Black Eagle and Rainbow Falls, and is supposed to reach the 'Great Falls of the Missouri' at Ryan Dam by the year 2000 (currently these falls, the first ones encountered by Lewis and Clark, are accessible by taking US 87 north and turning east on Morony Dam Rd for 5 miles, or via a narrow dirt path which continues where the paved trail ends). Though four of the five falls are dammed, the historical interpretation signs along the way are quite good.

The best vehicle access to the trail is 6 miles from downtown at the **Lewis and**

Clark Interpretation Center, which has good quality films and historical exhibits. Adjacent to the center is Giant Springs Heritage State Park, where one of the world's largest freshwater springs pumps out 134,000 gallons of water per minute. The 201-foot Roe River, which runs from the springs to the Missouri River, is the shortest river in the world, according the *Guinness Book of World Records*. The DFWP Headquarters and Visitor's Center (☎ 406-454-3441), a quarter mile from the spring' and on the River's Edge Trail, has books, natural history exhibits and a great three-dimensional map of the Missouri River. Access to the trail in the state park costs $3 per car, 50¢ per cyclist or pedestrian. If you're even marginally inclined towards physical activity, hit the trail by bike. Knicker Biker (☎ 406-454-2912), downtown at 1123 Central Ave, rents bikes for $8 for the first hour ($2 each additional hour) or $19 for 24 hours.

Downtown, at 400 13th St N, the **Charles M Russell Museum Complex** holds the largest collection of the acclaimed artist's work and personal memorabilia in the state. Russell's clapboard house and log cabin studio have been moved to the site and are open for viewing during the summer. Visitors to Montana may be more acquainted with Charles Russell's paintings than they realize – his images of Native Americans, buffalo and the prairies can be seen on everything from coffee cups and greeting cards to the State Capitol in Helena. It's hours are Sunday from 1 to 5 pm year-round, Monday to Saturday from 9 am to 6 pm May to October, and Tuesday to Saturday from 10 am to 5 pm the rest of the year.

Five blocks away at 1400 1st Ave N (at the corner of 14th St N), the **Paris Gibson Square Museum** (☎ 406-727-8255) has contemporary exhibits, an excellent gift shop and a Museum Cafe (lunch by reservation only – call the Arts Center) that serves some of the best food in Great Falls at a very reasonable price. Hours are Tuesday to Friday from 10 am to 5 pm and weekends from noon to 5 pm between Memorial Day and Labor Day.

Places to Stay
Great Falls has basically two pockets of accommodations: downtown and 10th Ave S. Accomodations downtown are handy for people who enjoy exploring on foot, while 10th Ave S motels (most of them chain-owned) offer proximity to highways and shopping malls.

Camping For urban camping year-round, head to the *Great Falls KOA* (☎ 406-727-3191), on the eastern end of 10th Ave S at

Charles M Russell
Born in 1864 to an upper-crust, Yale-educated St Louis family, young Charles whiled away his classroom hours drawing scenes inspired by the exploits of his great-uncle, William Bent, who founded Bent's Fort, CO. Convinced that a trip would cure his boyish daydreams, Russell's parents sent him west for his 16th birthday. Hardly disappointed, Charles took to the cowboy life and spent the next 10 years on the open range learning every aspect of cow-punching, from curing saddle sores to blowing paychecks on whiskey.

During that time, he spent a winter in Canada with the Blood Indians – a time that greatly influenced his painting. He came to know their language and culture, and emerged disillusioned about what the government had done to the Indians and buffalo. Besides being a painter, Russell was also a humorist and storyteller. Historians debate whether his poor grammar and misspelled words were intentional – to perpetuate his 'old cowboy' image – but, contrived or not, they were effective. ■

1500 S 51st St, where grassy tent sites cost $18 and RV spaces are $25.

B&Bs For a nice B&B, the *Old Oak Inn* (☎ 406-727-5782), 709 4th Ave N, charges $50 to $65 per night.

Motels Three motels along 10th Ave S have single/double rooms starting at $31/37: the *Rendezvous Motor Inn* (☎ 406-452-9525), 10th Ave S and Fox Farm Rd; the *Sahara Motel* (☎ 406-761-6150, 800-772-1330), 3466 10th Ave S; and the *Wagon Wheel Motel* (☎ 406-761-1300), 2620 10th Ave S, which has a swimming pool (and a honeymoon suite with a heart-shaped bathtub and bed!). Also along 10th Ave S is the *Highwood Village Motel* (☎ 406-452-8505, 800-253-8505), 4009 10th Ave S, which charges $30/38. Chain-owned motels along 10th Ave S include the *Comfort Inn* (☎ 406-454-2727), the *Holiday Inn* (☎ 406-727-7200, 800-257-1988), the *Town House Inn* (☎ 406-761-4600, 800-442-4667), and, next to the Holiday Village Mall, the *Super 8* (☎ 406-727-7600), all of which have rooms between $40 and $61.

Downtown alternatives are the *Mid-Town Motel* (☎ 406-453-2411, 800-457-2411), at the corner of 6th St and 2nd Ave N, which shares lobby space with a Perkins restaurant and has single/double rooms starting at $37/42, and the *Best Western Ponderosa Inn* (☎ 406-761-3410, 800-528-1234), 220 Central Ave, with rooms for $45/50.

Places to Eat
In the morning head to the *Bookmarkit*, 120 Central Ave, for good coffee and pastries, or *Perkins*, on the corner of 6th St and 2nd Ave N, for a full breakfast. *Penny's Gourmet to Go*, 815 Central Ave, is a good lunch spot and has vegetarian options (closed Sunday). The *Museum Cafe* (☎ 406-727-8255) in the Paris Gibson Arts Center, serves wonderful four-course, fixed-menu lunches for $7.50; reservations are required.

Locals are unanimous that *Eddie's Supper Club*, 3725 2nd Ave N, serves the best steak in town; it's open daily from 5 pm to 11 pm. The best non-meat-intensive meal you'll find in Great Falls is at *MacKenzie River Pizza Co*, next to the Comfort Inn at 1220 9th St, which has a wide variety of pizzas and excellent salads. The adjoining bar has regional microbrews on tap and broadcasts sporting events.

Getting There & Away
Great Falls International Airport (☎ 406-727-3404) is 3 miles southwest of downtown on I-15. Delta Airlines has short hops to Helena and three flights daily to Salt Lake City, UT. Horizon Air routes many of its flights through Missoula. Travelers without a rental car or other means of transportation will have to take a taxi (☎ 406-453-3241) to get into town, which costs around $7 to go to 10th Ave S, and $9 to downtown.

Near the airport baggage claim is Great Falls' bus terminal (☎ 406-454-1982), where Trailways and Rimrock buses service Helena ($16 one-way) and Butte ($22) twice daily, Missoula ($22), Lewistown ($22) and Billings ($31) once a day.

Great Falls is 85 miles from Shelby, 94 miles from Helena and 172 miles from Livingston. I-15 runs north to Canada via Shelby and southwest to Helena. US 87 goes northeast to Havre and southeast with Hwy 200 to Lewistown.

Getting Around
Car rental agencies at the airport include Hertz (☎ 406-761-6641), Avis (☎ 406-761-7610), National (☎ 406-453-4386) and Budget (☎ 406-454-1001). Less expensive are Rent-a-Wreck (☎ 406-761-0722), 617 10th Ave S, and Enterprise (☎ 406-761-1600), 1201 10th Ave S, both of which offer complimentary airport transportation to customers.

AROUND GREAT FALLS
Ulm Pishkun State Monument
About 12 miles south of Great Falls on I-15 and then west from the Ulm exit on a gravel road, steep cliffs rise above the golden prairie grass. Before they had horses to give

them enough speed to hunt buffalo at close range, Assiniboine and Gros Ventre hunters used cliffs or *pishkun* to kill large numbers of buffalo. Hunters made a V-shaped formation behind the herd and drove it toward the steep cliffs; animals that did not die from the fall were immediately dispatched by tribesmen waiting at the bottom. Panels at the top of the cliffs describe the process in detail and map out a trail to follow around the site. There's an adjacent picnic area with an expansive view but no shade, and pit toilets. (For more on buffalo jumps, see the sidebar in the Yellowstone Country chapter.)

Benton Lake National Wildlife Refuge

About 12 miles north of Great Falls, 5000 acres of Missouri River marshlands constitute the Benton Lake National Wildlife Refuge. Spring and fall migration periods are the most exciting times to visit, as tundra swans and snow geese pass en route to and from Canada. Over 200 bird species (mostly waterfowl) live at the refuge year-round. The best wildlife viewing is in the early morning and late afternoon. **Prairie Marsh Drive** makes a 9-mile loop through the refuge and is lined with site markers that correspond to an informative brochure available at the NWR headquarters (☎ 406-727-7400) at the refuge's entrance. A sign on US 87 heading north directs you to **Bootlegger Trail** (which jogs to the left of the highway), which leads to the refuge entrance and headquarters. The refuge is open year-round, daily from dawn to dusk; the headquarters are open Monday to Friday from 7:30 am to 4:30 pm.

KING'S HILL NATIONAL SCENIC BYWAY

Between Great Falls and Livingston, US 89 follows Belt Creek through the Little Belt Mountains and over King's Hill Pass, Montana's highest at 7393 feet. The 71 mile stretch north of White Sulphur Springs is designated the King's Hill National Scenic Byway.

About 12 miles south of where US 89 turns south from US 87, **Sluice Boxes**

State Park extends along the bottom of a canyon that has been inhabited on and off over the past century. Some of the old cabins are still in good shape, including the retreat where Don Bosco, a Catholic missionary and philosopher, spent several years. From the parking lot (which is well signed off US 89), a trail runs along Belt Creek to the cabin and continues (another mile) to where the broad, shallow creek becomes a deep, narrow channel that flows through dramatically steep limestone walls or 'sluice boxes.' The first half mile of the trail is easy, passing old limestone kilns (they look like cave dwellings) and a lovely swimming hole about 300 yards from the trailhead. Further on, it gets brushy. You have to wade across the creek to get to Don Bosco's cabin, twice more to reach the sluice boxes, but the trip is well worth it. As a 'primitive' state park, there's no fee and no running water, just a pit toilet.

South of Sluices Boxes, US 89 ascends into the Little Belts, past pillars and other rock formations of some of the oldest exposed rock in North America. The old mining camp of **Monarch** is now home to the *Cub's Den*, a favorite post-activity watering hole, and miner's cabins turned in to garages and vacation homes.

Approaching **Neihart** from either direction you are greeted by huge old wooden mine shafts and gouged-out mountain sides, testimony to the town's once booming silver industry. The dilapidated yet charming old houses and sheds along the highway support one small grocery store and (of course) a bar. One and a half miles south is a well-marked half-mile trail to **Memorial Falls**, a double waterfall in a narrow limestone canyon. Foot traffic gets heavy in summer, but it's still a nice little jaunt.

The natural 115° F hot springs that surface in **White Sulphur Springs** were once used by the Crow and Gros Ventre tribes and weary stagecoach passengers for medicinal purposes. They're now 'owned' by the *Spa Hot Springs Motel* (☎ 406-547-3366), 202 W Main St, which charges $3 for use of the pool and grounds and $1 for swimsuit and towel rental; rooms start at

$34. The town's bars and graceful old homes – mostly from the 1880s – are worth a look, as is the **Meagher County Historical Museum** (☎ 406-547-2324), housed in an 1892 granite building called 'the castle,' 2 blocks north of Main St (turn up the hill at the Mint bar).

Between White Sulphur Springs and Livingston the scenery is dramatic, with the Big Belt and Bridger Mountains in the west and Crazy Mountains in the east, but the land is divided like a checkerboard into state and private property so that it's hard to access without trespassing. One place worth stopping for a look is the wooden **Ringling Catholic Church**, which has been standing guard over the highway and the little town of Ringling since the beginning of the century.

Activities

South of Monarch you start seeing access roads to the Lewis and Clark National Forest which extends almost all the way to White Sulphur Springs. Stop by the National Forest Service Information Station, south of Monarch, for maps and information on the numerous **hiking** and **mountain biking** trails in the area. Two recommended day-hikes are the **Paine Gulch Trail**, which starts across from National Forest Service Rd 737 (near the Lazy Doe Restaurant on US 87) and goes through a wildlife management research preserve, and the more rugged **Pioneer Ridge Trail**, 2 miles south of the Lazy Doe off Rd 734. For an extended trip, ask the ranger about the **Tenderfoot Trail** which makes a figure-8 through some scenic backcountry.

About 14 miles south of Neihart, the **Kings Hill Winter Recreation Area** has a large network of snowmobile and cross-country ski trails that are free and connect to **Showdown Ski Area** (☎ 406-236-5522), a downhill slope with two lifts and a 1400-foot vertical drop. The cross-country trails are good for mountain biking. The lodge at Showdown has the area's only facilities – sport shop, restaurant, equipment rental – and is closed in summer.

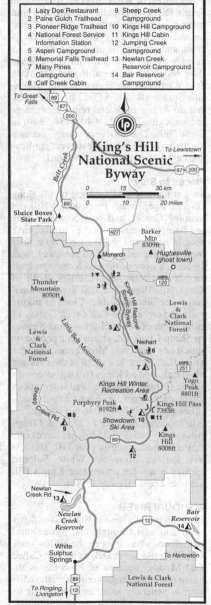

1 Lazy Doe Restaurant	9 Sheep Creek
2 Paine Gulch Trailhead	Campground
3 Pioneer Ridge Trailhead	10 Kings Hill Campground
4 National Forest Service	11 Kings Hill Cabin
Information Station	12 Jumping Creek
5 Aspen Campground	Campground
6 Memorial Falls Trailhead	13 Newlan Creek
7 Many Pines	Reservoir Campground
Campground	14 Bair Reservoir
8 Calf Creek Cabin	Campground

King's Hill National Scenic Byway

MONTANA

Northwest of White Sulphur Springs, the Smith River is popular for **fishing** and **rafting**, especially at the end of June and second week in July when irrigation is down and the river is up. Camp Baker, 15 miles west of White Sulphur Springs via Hwy 360, is the main put-in spot. On Main St in White Sulphur Springs, Castle Mountain Sports (☎ 406-547-2330) can hook you up with a guide and rental equipment or contact the DFWP (☎ 406-454-5840) in Great Falls. Due to its popularity, permits for the river are given by lottery; applications are $15 each (one per person).

Places to Stay
Sites at the four USFS campgrounds along US 89 (Aspen, Many Pines, Kings Hill and Jumping Creek), and near Newlan Creek and Bair reservoirs all cost $7 to $11, have potable water and are available on a first-come first-served basis. To get away from the road, try one of the USFS campgrounds on Sheep Creek Rd, 12 miles south of Kings Hill Pass. Two USFS recreational cabins are also available. Close to hiking trails and creeks, the *Calf Creek Cabin*, 12 miles south of Kings Hill Pass and 8 miles up Sheep Creek Rd, sleeps four people on bunk beds and cots. More accessible, the *Kings Hill Cabin*, just south of the pass and a half mile east on Kings Hill Rd, sleeps six people on bunk beds; required reservations are made through the Forest Supervisor's Office (☎ 406-791-7700) in Great Falls.

In Monarch, *Rocking J Cabins & Campground* (☎ 406-236-5535) has creekside cabins for $42, campsites for $10. The *Spa Hot Springs Motel* in White Sulphur Springs is another option (see King's Hill National Scenic Byway above).

MISSOURI RIVER
From Great Falls the Missouri River flows north and east through vast agricultural expanses to where it meets the Yellowstone River near the North Dakota border. Called 'Old Muddy' because of its coffee-with-cream color and languorous pace, the Missouri is generally more interesting for its history than its white-water opportunities.

The river was the navigation artery for Lewis and Clark, fur traders and, starting in 1831, steamboats that brought people and supplies to Fort Benton where overland travel to the West began.

In 1976 the 149-mile stretch of river between Fort Benton and the Fred Robinson Bridge was designated a National Wild and Scenic River, thus preserved for ecological and historical reasons in its natural free-flowing state. Because its banks are so steep and high, the river is hard to explore at any length unless you embark on a multiple-day float trip (see below). There are, however, a few good river access roads that cross US 87, which runs between Great Falls and Havre.

Fort Benton & Around
Fort Benton (population 1654), 38 miles north of Great Falls, is the most developed spot on this stretch of river. Once the terminus of steamboat travel, this sleepy town was the jumping-off point for just about all homesteaders, prospectors and traders headed west. In the mid-1800s, Front St was home to 150 saloons and deemed the 'roughest block in the West.' It now has a river front walk with sculptures and historical displays, two noteworthy regional museums and the busy BLM Wild & Scenic Upper Missouri Visitor's Center (☎ 406-622-5185) (closed late-September to May). There are a handful of restaurants and bars on Front St, and free camping in the public park which has restrooms and sheltered picnic tables.

North 12 miles is **Loma**, where you can cross the Missouri on the Loma Bridge (turn east at the Red Rose Inn, just before the Loma Bridge Fishing Access point). From the north side of the bridge improved gravel roads wind for about 22 miles through farm and ranch land to the Virgelle Ferry crossing. Here you press a sound signal and wait for the ferry guard to motor across on a large, cable-controlled platform to pick you up and take you across to the small homestead town of Virgelle; ferry service ends when the river starts to freeze, usually in November. You can also get to

Virgelle from US 87 (the turnoff is well signed, 25 miles north of Fort Benton).

The **Virgelle Mercantile** (☎ 406-378-3110, 800-426-2926) was built in 1885 as a river outpost and homestead supplier, and is now run by two creative fellows who restore and sell antiques and operate the Missouri River Canoe Company (see below). Restored cabins and beautifully decorated rooms are available starting at $80, including breakfast.

Floating the Missouri
Travelers who have the time and money should consider a float trip along the Missouri River, through what's known as the 'Missouri River Breaks,' to see the steep white cliffs, caves, pillars and funky rock formations of shale and sandstone that are only accessible by boat. The BLM Upper Missouri Wild and Scenic Visitor's Center in Fort Benton has all the information necessary for experienced floaters to plan their own trip and a list of outfitters that offer guided trips. The BLM publishes the *Upper Missouri National Wild and Scenic River Floater's Guide*, a four-map set ($8) available at the visitors center or through the mail from the US Department of the Interior.

There are no permits or reservations required to float the river, but the BLM has registration boxes at the major launches including Fort Benton, Loma and the James Kipp Recreation Area (see the Charles M Russell National Wildlife Refuge in Around Lewistown later in this chapter). Designated campsites are marked on the Floater's Guide but primitive camping is allowed anywhere (except the islands) on federal land on a first-come, first-served basis.

The very reputable Missouri River Canoe Company (☎ 406-378-3110, 800-426-2926) offers fully guided four- to seven-day trips including meals, accommodation and shuttles to and from Great Falls or Havre for about $300 per person, per day. They also have canoe rentals and van shuttles for do-it-yourselfers; call early in the season to make reservations.

THE HI-LINE
Paralleling the Great Northern Railroad's tracks and the Missouri River, US 2 crosses Montana's northern tier along a transportation corridor traditionally known as the 'Hi-Line.' Travelers accustomed to Western Montana's dramatic mountains, forests and rivers are likely to find this portion of the state dry, desolate and even boring. Green for just two short months during spring, parched brown from June to October and white with snow-drifts the rest of the year, it consists of vast expanses of farm, ranch and reservation land mirrored in the boundless sky overhead.

What towns do exist along the Hi-Line are trade and service centers for surrounding agricultural communities, county seats and highway crossroads. These towns may not offer obvious tourist attractions (often they have little more than a gas station, cafe and grain elevator), but they embody a spirit and way of life which has all but vanished from more cosmopolitan areas.

Havre
Largest of the towns along the Hi-Line and the seat of Hill County, Havre (population 10,232) is a good stopping point, if only for its cheap accommodations and movie theater. The Bears Paw Mountains to the south offer a nice diversion for car-weary travelers who need some fresh air, though the Highland Center Shopping Mall is a more popular playground among locals. Havre's location between the Milk River, which provides irrigation for wheat and hay fields, and the rich grazing lands of the Bears Paw foothills has created a stable and unique economic environment in which many people are both ranchers and farmers. Great Northern officials named the town after the French port Le Havre, but citizens have always pronounced it 'Hav-er.'

Orientation & Information Havre occupies a 4-mile strip of US 2, 102 miles east of Shelby and 88 miles west of Malta. US 87 goes southwest to Great Falls 153 miles

MONTANA

Montana Immigrants & A Hill of Dreams

Following Montana's 1880s gold strikes, railroad companies began vying for land rights, knowing they stood to make a fortune carrying passengers to and from the gold fields. James J Hill, a Canadian who owned a route between St Paul, MN, and Winnipeg, Canada, had dreams of building a northern railroad to the Pacific coast in order to compete with the powerful Union Pacific Railroad Company.

Initially, Hill faced a problem the UP had never encountered: much of his Great Northern route passed through reservation land. President Grover Cleveland had qualms about infringing on any more on Native American lands but, facing economic and political pressure, he legislated a 75-foot right of way – and the use of all adjacent stone and timber for construction purposes – to Hill's Great Northern Railroad in 1887.

Over the following six years, as the railroad crept west towards Everett, WA, Hill did everything he could to ensure that the railcars would be full. In a monumental land campaign, he financed immigrant passage from Europe, offered free transportation west, and assaulted the Midwest and the East with Montana products and propaganda. Whether his tales of Montana's rich soil and mild climate were hopeful conjectures or just plain old lies is debatable, but in any case they worked. By 1910, new settlers – many of them Slavic and Scandinavian – had filed claims on 5 million Montana acres.

Between 1910 and 1917, the weather was unusually mild, farms flourished, wheat prices were high and James J Hill was a national hero. Bustling towns, named after unlikely European cities, sprang up in a matter of weeks. By 1925 however, Montana's climate was back to its old self and even harsher than average. Drought, wind and grasshoppers swept Montana's northern tier, forcing the foreclosure of 20,000 farms, and settlers who had once praised the name of James J Hill now cursed it, even as they rode his trains away from the scene of their ruin. Those who stuck it out, however, learned from their mistakes. Rust- and drought-resistant wheat and strip-farming – in which alternating strips of crops and fallow land conserve moisture and protect against wind – were the main inventions born of the experience and are still in use today. In fact, Montana is the most strip-farmed state in the country. ∎

away and Route 232 goes north 38 miles to the Canadian port of Wild Horse. Sites and services are concentrated along US 2 which is called 1st St within the city limits. Numbered avenues run north-south across 1st St. Those businesses not on 1st St are generally within the 3 blocks south of it.

Havre's chamber of commerce (☎ 406-265-4383) is at 518 1st St; on weekends pick up area brochures at the Duck Inn or the Earl H Clack Memorial Museum (see below). The post office and banks with ATMs are on 3rd Ave. The Highland Park Laundromat and Ice Cream Parlor, 1102 S Washington Ave, is open until 9 pm (7 pm on Sunday).

Things to See & Do Travelers need not put aside a whole day to explore Havre, but several sights and the old downtown pro-

vide good excuses to get out of the car and stretch the legs.

The **Earl H Clack Memorial Museum** (☎ 406-265-4000) is the centerpiece of Havre's new Heritage Center, downtown on 3rd Ave. Exhibits focus on **Fort Assiniboine**, a 'peace-keeping unit' 6 miles southwest of Havre that was occupied from 1897 to 1911. On summer weekends the museum offers tours of the fort's weathered remains; tours cost $5 per person and last about three hours.

Across the highway from the museum, behind the Highland Center Shopping Mall, is the **Wahkpa Chu'qn Archaeological Site**, a pishkun used to kill buffalo about 200 years ago. The site is still being excavated, but you can have a look around on a guided tour ($5 adults, $3.50 students and seniors). From mid-May to September,

MONTANA

hourly tours leave from a booth just inside the Highland Center Mall's south entrance, Tuesday to Sunday from 10 am to 5 pm; closed Monday. There are also special evening tours Tuesday to Saturday at 7 pm. Tours in the off-season are arranged by appointment. For information call ☎ 406-265-6417.

Located at 120 3rd Ave at the corner of Main St, **Havre Beneath the Streets** (☎ 406-265-8888) offers one of Montana's more unique tours: a one-hour trip below ground, past Havre's old saloons, brothels and opium dens. Regularly scheduled tours, which cost $6 ($5 for children and seniors), operate from May to September, leaving at 1:30 pm and 3:30 pm; in July and August tours leave every hour from 9 am to 5 pm, and Sunday evening tours are added. From September to May, tours are given by appointment only.

South of Havre, the **Bears Paw Mountains** – a scattering of dark buttes between 4000 and 5000 feet high – are used for religious ceremonies and vision quests by descendants of the Cree, Chippewa and Metis (a half-Chippewa, half-French tribe) that live on the Rocky Boys Reservation. These Indians came to Montana, led by Stone Child (called Rocky Boy), in the 1880s after a futile rebellion against the Canadian government. The only public access to the mountains is at the Bears Paw Ski Bowl, about 25 miles south of Havre, a beginner hill with one chairlift and an 875-foot vertical drop – as exciting to hike as it is to ski.

Places to Stay & Eat Chain motels and restaurants line US 2 west of downtown. Havre's most prominent lodging and dining facility is the *Duck Inn* (☎ 406-265-9615), on the eastern edge of town at 1300 1st St, which charges $42/45 for single/double rooms. The complex has three restaurants, a lounge and casino, and manages the Conoco gas station and general store across the highway.

The *Havre Budget Inn* (☎ 406-265-8625), south of 1st St at 115 9th Ave, has rooms for $37/40. Buses to/from Great Falls stop in front of the *Park Hotel* (☎ 406-265-7891), 335 1st St at the corner of 4th Ave, which sits atop a decent cafe; rooms start at $28/34, and there's a sleeping room with shared bathroom for $20 per person. Havre's deluxe (in the most relative sense) accommodations are at the *El Toro Inn* (☎ 406-265-5414, 800-422-5414), 521 1st St, which charges $43/47.

Getting There & Away Amtrak (☎ 800-872-7245) stops twice daily in Havre – eastbound at 1:27 pm and westbound at 2:14 pm. The station is at 235 Main St, at the north end of 3rd St.

Rimrock Stages (☎ 406-265-6444) offers daily bus service to Great Falls ($18) from where you can catch buses bound for Canada and most of Montana's larger cities. The bus depot is in the lobby of the Park Hotel, 335 1st St at the corner of 4th Ave.

Bears Paw Battlefield National Monument

South of Chinook, the Bears Paw Battlefield National Monument (also called Chief Joseph Battlefield) marks the tragic end of the Nez Percé 1800-mile flight toward freedom (see the Battle of the Big Hole in the Gold Country chapter). When the Nez Percé stopped in this grassy coulee along

The eloquent and heroic Chief Joseph

MONTANA

Miles Creek, they were only 40 miles away from sanctuary in Canada – a one-day journey. Believing US soldiers to be several days behind them, the tribe set up camp along a protected creek bed and planned to rest for a day. However, General Miles of Fort Keogh learned of their location and decided to head them off in the Bears Paw Mountains. Without warning, US troops descended on the camp and killed many people before the tribe had time to resist. Four days later, on October 5, 1877, after the fierce battle which claimed the lives of chiefs Sitting Bull and Looking Glass, Chief Joseph surrendered to General Nelson A Miles with these famous words:

It is cold and we have no blankets. The little children are freezing to death. My people, some of them, have run away to the hills, and have no blankets, no food; no one knows where they are – perhaps freezing to death. I want to have time to look for my children and see how many I can find. Maybe I shall find them among the dead.

Hear me, my chiefs. I am tired; my heart is sick and sad.

From where the sun now stands, I will fight no more forever.

The site has changed little since then, except for the addition of interpretive panels marking significant points on the battlefield, two pit toilets and a parking lot.

The closest services are on US 2 in **Chinook**, which bears the Indian name for the warm winds that blow off the eastern Rocky Mountain slopes. By melting the snow and allowing cattle to access the rich bunchgrass pasture, these winds have been the saving grace of many a Hi-Line ranch. Along Indiana Ave, which runs south through Chinook to the battlefield, is the chamber of commerce (☎ 406-357-2100), Bank of Montana (with ATM) and the **Blaine County Museum**, whose multimedia presentation on the Battle of the Bears Paw is of interest to anyone heading to the battlefield. The *Chinook Hotel* (☎ 406-357-2231), 2 blocks north of Indiana Ave at 62 3rd St, has the cheapest rooms in town at $15/30 single/double. The *Bear Paw Court* (☎ 406-357-2221) on

US 2 at the east edge of town, has clean, spacious rooms for $43/49.

Nine miles south of the Bears Paw Battlefield, the *Cleveland Bar* is a rough-edged watering hole (a favorite among hunters in the fall) with legendary burgers and baked beans.

Fort Belknap Indian Reservation

Named after US Secretary of War William Belknap, the 1000-sq-mile Fort Belknap Reservation is home to the Assiniboine and Gros Ventre tribes. Once bitter enemies, the two tribes joined in alliance against the Canadian Bloods, with whom they eventually made peace in 1887.

Tribal Headquarters are at the Fort Belknap Agency (☎ 406-353-2205), 8 miles south of Harlem on Hwy 66, and tourist information is in Hays, 30 miles south of Harlem at all-purpose Martin's Grocery, which has a gas pump, general store and information about tribal events.

Hays is also home to **St Paul's Mission**, established in 1887 by Jesuit priests, and its shrine to the Virgin Mary, erected in 1931 by a German immigrant, whose centerpiece is a replica of a holy statue in Einseldn, Switzerland. From the mission a road leads 1 mile south into **Mission Canyon**, a rock gorge cut into the Little Rocky Mountains by fast-flowing Little Peoples Creek. Beyond the narrowest part of the canyon is an open meadow used for powwows and ceremonial dances. You can camp here with permission from the tribe (ask at Tribal Headquarters or Martin's Grocery, listed above), though there are no facilities. Further up the road are several remote campgrounds next to the creek which also require permission for use. After a steep and windy climb, the road ends behind the massive terraced hillside of Pegasus Mining Company's operations (see below).

Little Rocky Mountains

Accessible from Hwy 66, the arduous route between US 2 and US 191, the Little Rocky Mountains are a hotbed of mining activity. Gold strikes in 1884 brought the

MARISA GIERLICH

JOHN ELK

MICHAEL CLARK

MICHAEL CLARK

Montana

Top Left: Traditional dancer, Blackfeet Reservation, Browning
Bottom: Horse trailer, near Little Bighorn

Top Right: Virgelle ferry crossing, Missouri River
Middle Right: Historic Butte, with the Berkeley Pit in the background

JOHN ELK

RIC ERGENBRIGHT

RIC ERGENBRIGHT

Glacier National Park

Top: Going-to-the-Sun Road
Bottom Left: St Mary's Lake

Bottom Right: Lunch Creek

Gros Ventre: Big Bellies or Waterfalls?

The name 'Gros Ventre,' French for 'Big Belly,' has nothing to do with physical appearance. It's not known exactly how the name came into use, but one version of the story has it that French trappers encountered members of the tribe along the Missouri River and tried to find out what lay ahead of them on their journey upriver. Familiar with the waterfalls near present-day Great Falls, the Indians made the hand signal for waterfall – palms toward them and raised eye-level, then brought down to their chests and, just above the belly, outwards in a circular motion. The trappers didn't know what to make of this, but ever afterwards called the tribe Gros Ventre.

The Gros Ventre have their roots in a branch of the Arapahoe, who came to Montana in the early 19th century and lived along the north bank of the Missouri River until the Cree drove them across to the south bank in 1872. The Assiniboine tribe originated in the Dakotas as a mountain-dwelling branch of the Sioux. ∎

first rush of prospectors to the Little Rocky Mountains, but these early miners were 'get rich quick' types who extracted placer gold for a few months and then left. Currently, the Pegasus Mining Company (originally on the scene as the Zortman Mining Company) owns or leases much of the land around Zortman and Landusky. The company is embroiled in a fierce battle with local Indians and several environmental agencies regarding contaminated groundwater and surfacewater resulting from the mines which have extracted over $25 million in gold from these hills.

Home to Pegasus Mining Company headquarters, **Zortman** is a lively little mining settlement which gets weekday activity from Pegasus employees (most of whom live in Malta, Harlem or Dodson), and weekend traffic from photographers with an eye for abandoned miners' sheds.

Once the livelier of the two towns, now **Landusky** has a remote campground with fire rings and tables (no toilets), but otherwise has no businesses, houses or (usually) people.

The only places to eat or stay are in Zortman. The *Miner's Club Cafe and Bar* serves food Monday to Saturday from 5:30 am to 8:30 pm and Sunday from 6 am to 8 pm, though the bar is open nightly to 1 am. The *Buckhorn Store & Cabins* (☎ 406-673-3162) charges $10 for a tent site, $32 for a cabin with bathroom and kitchen and has a decent supply of dry goods. On a forested ridge 3 miles northeast of Zortman, the USFS Camp Creek Campground has 14 tent sites ($7), potable water, restrooms and sheltered picnic areas.

Bowdoin National Wildlife Refuge

The Bowdoin National Wildlife Refuge is a 24-sq-mile haven for waterfowl. A 15-mile loop road, with 11 stops that correspond to a detailed brochure (available at the NWR Headquarters), encircles Lake Bowdoin and provides excellent opportunities to see pelicans, double-crested cormorants and great blue herons nesting on Lake Bowdoin Island. Early morning and late afternoon are the best times for viewing. To reach the refuge, turn southeast off US 2, half a mile east of Malta on to the well signed blacktop road and go 7 miles to the refuge entrance. NWR Headquarters (☎ 406-654-2863) are 100 yards past the entrance and open Monday to Friday from 7:30 am to 4:30 pm; there's a kiosk with maps out front.

The nearest accommodations are on US 2 in Malta, which bears absolutely no resemblance to its Mediterranean namesake and gives no hint of the bustling days gone by when it was the center of a cattle empire that stretched from Havre to Glasgow and from the Missouri River to the Canadian border. The *Edgewater Inn* (☎ 406-654-1302, 800-821-7475 in Montana), on US 2 charges $40/45 for single/double rooms, which includes a dunk in their indoor pool and spa (non-guests pay $2). Their adjacent campground has tent sites for $10 and RV sites for $16. Two blocks east on US 2, the *Sportsman Motel* (☎ 406-654-2300) has rooms for $35/38, and a few kitchenettes for $41. One block south, the *Great Northern Motor Hotel* (☎ 406-654-2100) has a lounge, steakhouse, coffee shop and indoor parking. Rooms are $42 for a single plus $4 each additional person.

Sleeping Buffalo Hot Springs

East of Malta, US 2 enters the ancient Missouri River Valley where the Milk River now flows. Along the highway and throughout the valley, glacial debris and boulders bearing the marks of Native Americans (mostly Assiniboine, Chippewa and Cree) lie scattered across the land. One particularly sacred rock, which resembles a sleeping buffalo, is now a roadside monument (marked by an Historic Site sign), where Native Americans give offerings of tobacco, cigarettes and sage.

One mile north of the monument, Sleeping Buffalo Hot Springs (☎ 406-527-3370) has three natural mineral pools which, because the water's high mineral content makes maintenance tough, are in a pretty bad state of disrepair. The ultra-hot, hot and warm pools, however, are worth the $5 entrance fee after a long day's drive. Motel rooms surrounding a grassy courtyard start at $32, and houses which sleep eight cost $80 per night. Camping costs $5 for tents and $10 for RVs.

Glasgow

Primarily the turnoff and service point en route to Fort Peck Dam, Glasgow (population 3656) has a Pioneer Museum (marked by an F-101 fighter plane on US 2) which has admirable displays (considering the size of the town it's in) regarding Fort Peck Dam and the now-extinct Audubon Bighorn sheep; admission is free. There are also some picturesque brick buildings decorated with colorful Art Deco tile along 2nd Ave, and several lively bars (notably the Montana Bar) on 1st Ave, looking much as they did when they first opened.

If you're looking for a place to stay other than the Fort Peck Hotel or campgrounds while visiting the Fort Peck area, *Koskis Motel* (☎ 406-228-8282, 888-238-8282), on US 2, has rooms for $40/45, $48 for kitchenettes. Just across US 2, the *Cottonwood Inn* (☎ 406-228-8213, 800-321-8213) has a swimming pool, restaurant and lounge and offers many discounts; rooms start at $46/55. The old *Roosevelt Hotel* (☎ 406-228-4341), 412 3rd Ave between 4th and 5th Sts, is a bit of a relic but the cheapest sleep around with $21/24 rooms.

Fort Peck Dam & Reservoir

Established as a trading fort in 1863, the original Fort Peck now lies submerged beneath the waters of Montana's largest 'lake,' created by Fort Peck Dam. Completed in 1937 as a Public Works Administration project, the dam's construction took four years and was a tremendous boost to Montana's Depression-era economy. Fort Peck Dam's original functions were to control floods and make the Missouri River navigable; the dam's 165,000 kilowatt power-making capacity, some-what of an afterthought, was not utilized until 1939.

An oasis in the middle of northeastern Montana's otherwise empty prairie, Fort Peck Lake's 1600 miles of shoreline and 245,000 acre-feet of water are a boater's and angler's paradise. The low, undulating hills that surround the lake are barren except for bunchgrass, sagebrush and (in early summer) yellow wildflowers that cling to its edge in brilliant contrast to the bright blue water.

Tourist services and designated attractions are concentrated on the reservoir's northern shore, around the junction of Hwys 24 and 117. Adventurous types and fossil hounds with a good car (or boat) and a few extra travel days will find the lake's more remote reaches worth exploring.

Orientation & Information Fort Peck's entrance is 20 miles south of Glasgow and 52 miles north of Hwy 200 via Hwy 24. A visitors information booth, open on weekends between Memorial Day and Labor Day from 10 am to 4 pm, is at the entrance. The town of Fort Peck (population 226), which has a bank, post office and well-stocked market, is 2 miles south of the entrance by way of Missouri Rd. Yellowstone Rd turns west off Missouri Rd, descends a hill from the top of the dam, and goes to the Downstream Camp and power plants; turning left at the bottom of the hill leads to several recreational day-use areas and free campsites

Information on the sights, recreation areas and campsites listed below is available from the Corps of Engineers (☎ 406-526-3411), next to the Fort Peck Hotel in Fort Peck, open Monday to Friday from 8:30 am to 4:30 pm. The Charles M Russell National Wildlife Refuge encompasses the whole area of Fort Peck Lake, but is best accessed from Lewistown.

Things to See & Do Free tours of Fort Peck's massive **power plant** leave from inside its front doors hourly from 10 am to 4 pm between Memorial Day and Labor Day. Besides the interesting facts and figures, the tour provides access to the power plant's museum, whose major contributors were amateur photographers and rock hounds who worked on the dam's construction. Four-mile **Fort Peck Dam** is the area's centerpiece. Three miles east of the dam, the **spillway** regulates and discharges overflow, and divides Fort Peck Reservoir from the Missouri River basin. A side road at the spillway's west end leads to an overlook with descriptive signs and a great view.

Built as construction and dam operation headquarters, the 'town' of Fort Peck is a picturesque cluster of woodsy buildings surrounding a nice lawn. The town jewel is the **Fort Peck Theater** (☎ 406-228-9219), whose summer theater productions, performed nightly from June to August, have an excellent reputation statewide. Performance times vary (generally 8 pm Monday to Wednesday, with additional shows Thursday to Saturday night and Sunday afternoon). Tickets cost $8 to $12 and often sell out on summer weekends.

South of Fort Peck, Hwy 24 undulates through ruggedly beautiful badlands, giving access to the Bear Creek, Rock Creek, McGuire Creek and Nelson Creek **recreation areas**. These places are ultra-remote and good for viewing wildlife. The Bear Creek and North Rock Creek areas are basic boat-launch facilities with pit toilets and a few picnic areas. South Rock Creek is home to the **Rock Creek Marina** (☎ 406-485-2560), open from April to October, which maintains a small campground with tables, fire rings, showers and electric hookups. Sites cost $6 and the small store sells bait, beverages and a limited selection of groceries. Farther south, McGuire Creek is recommended for people who want to be surrounded by nothing but natural beauty. There is no boat launch here so traffic is minimal, and the only facilities are pit toilets; camping is free.

To reach *really* wild territory – the lake's southern shore – you must be willing to drive long and dusty roads or hire a boat from Fort Peck Marina (see below). From the southern terminus of Hwy 24, Hwy 200 heads west to Jordan, where a dirt road, impassable with even a splash of rain, heads north to **Hell Creek State Park**. Accessed primarily by boat, the park has a small marina, store and campground with showers and $11 sites. Named for the fossil-rich Hell Creek Formation, this is some of Montana's best fossil-gathering territory.

The **Fort Peck Marina** (☎ 406-526-3442), west of the north Hwy 24 entrance, rents 16-foot power boats for $60 a day (not including gas) and is the base for the area's fishing guides who charge $100 per person for eight hours. Although trolling is best, shore fishing is less expensive. The small bridge north of Downstream Camp has parking on its east side and good fishing from its west.

Places to Stay & Eat The *West End Campground*, west of the north Hwy 24 entrance, has 20 unprotected sites next to the marina on a bluff overlooking the lake, which cost $10. Facilities include showers, picnic shelters, electricity and water hookups. *Downstream Camp* (☎ 406-526-3224

is – you guessed it – downstream from the dam and spillway. It offers a great view of the massive power plant and a boat ramp, and is the only campground on the lake that takes reservations. Tent sites cost $8, RV spaces cost $10 ($3 extra for a reservation). More remote campgrounds around the lake are at the recreation areas along Hwy 24 south of Fort Peck, and at the *Pines Recreation Area*, recommended for its shade; sites here include pit toilets, picnic tables and fire rings, and cost $7.

Non-campers have a good option. Built in 1934 as a guesthouse/construction-crew dormitory, the *Fort Peck Hotel* (☎ 406-526-3266), central to the town, looks like an upscale summer camp lodge; rooms start at $48. Its woodsy dining room is overpriced, except on Sundays, when an enormous all-you-can-eat buffet costs $9.50 per person.

Next to the main marina office is *Fort Peck Houseboat Rentals* (☎ 406-526-3597), which has 36-foot houseboats for $150 a night.

The *Gateway Inn*, 16 miles south of Glasgow just before Fort Peck Dam, is a fun weekend hangout spot with live bands, a much-used dance floor, pool table, dartboards and a few slot machines. The kitchen, known for its home-fried chicken and barbecue beef sandwiches, is open daily from 11 am to 10 pm, while the bar stays open until 2 am.

Wolf Point
Established in 1888, the 3125-sq-mile Fort Peck Reservation is home to Assiniboine and Yanktonai Sioux tribes. The reservation's hub is Wolf Point, a lively bicultural community which, although officially on the reservation, leases most of its surrounding land to farmers and ranchers. Developed around steamboat trade, the original town sat on the Missouri River bank, a mile south of present-day Wolf Point, until the arrival of the railroad in 1912 lured business away. The **Wolf Point Area Historical Society Museum** (☎ 406-653-1912), 220 Second Ave S, chronicles Wolf Point's history. The **Wild Horse Stampede**, Wolf

Point's claim to fame, is held annually during the second weekend in July. Besides being Montana's oldest continuous rodeo, it is one of the few that features Indian dance and drum competitions along with regular rodeo events.

Wolf Point's accommodations are among the cheapest on the Hi-Line. On US 2 at the east edge of town, the *Big Sky Motel* (☎ 406-653-2300) has rooms with coffeemakers and refrigerators for $28/34. One block west, the *Homestead Inn* (☎ 406-653-1300) offers complimentary doughnuts and coffee with their $29/35 rooms. The *Sherman Motor Inn* (☎ 406-653-1100, 800-952-1100) is Wolf Point's 'convention headquarters,' with a pool and the town's fanciest restaurant; rooms cost $35/41.

LEWISTOWN
If you were to arrive directly from New York or even Portland, you'd probably view Lewistown as a small agricultural town with an hour's worth of attractions and nothing to do at night. If, however, you've been traveling in Montana awhile or live in one of the even smaller towns in the area, Lewistown (population 6380) appears a bustling bastion of civilization.

During the cattle rustling and mining days of the 1880s, Lewistown was the place where men armed with Winchesters came to spend their loot on Saturday night. Nowadays people from the Eastern Plains come to shop, eat in restaurants and attend to medical needs. A new medical center and retirement facility have increased the town's older population, while a younger crowd has migrated from the east to be near the mountains. Folks from all over the West come the third weekend in August during the increasingly popular **Montana Cowboy Poetry Gathering**.

History
Trade between trappers and Indians took place at Fort Musselshell, established at the junction of the Missouri and Musselshell rivers in 1860. When gold was discovered in the Judith Mountains the government built Fort Magginis, east of the present-day

town, to protect settlers and keep the Sioux in check. Meanwhile, the Metis (a half-French, half-Chippewa tribe from Canada) settled what is now Lewistown. There are still names like Juneaux, LaFontaine and LeGrand in the phonebook, though full-blood Metis no longer exist here. At the turn of the century, rustlers and outlaws found the Lewistown area much to their liking – few people, abundant cattle and just two days journey to the Canadian border.

Orientation & Information
Main St, the primary thoroughfare and business district, runs southwest-northeast for 1 mile and is intersected by numbered avenues which begin at the north end of town.

Lewistown's Chamber of Commerce (☎ 406-538-5436) is in the same building as the Central Montana Museum (see below) at 408 NE Main St and is open Monday to Friday from 8 am to noon and from 1 to 5 pm, and weekends (summer only) from 10 am to 4 pm. To reach the BLM (☎ 406-538-7462) and CM Russell NWR Headquarters (☎ 406-538-8706), next to each other on Airport Rd, take Main St south until it climbs a hill at the edge of town; Airport Rd is on the left at the top of the hill, across from a Pizza Hut and a gas station.

Also on Main St are a bank with ATM and bookstores. The main post office is at 204 3rd Ave N. The Central Montana Medical Center (☎ 406-538-7711, 800-732-5171) is at 408 Wendell Ave.

Things to See & Do
Lewistown's star attraction is its **downtown**, listed on the National Register of Historic Places. Most of the sandstone structures along Main St were carved by Croatian immigrants (you can often spot the artisan's name somewhere near the door) who arrived with the Central Montana Railroad in 1903. This handiwork carries through to the grand residential homes of

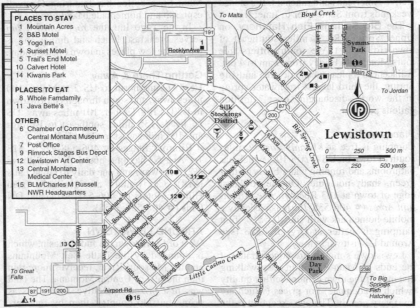

PLACES TO STAY
1 Mountain Acres
2 B&B Motel
3 Yogo Inn
4 Sunset Motel
5 Trail's End Motel
10 Calvert Hotel
14 Kiwanis Park

PLACES TO EAT
8 Whole Famdamily
11 Java Bette's

OTHER
6 Chamber of Commerce, Central Montana Museum
7 Post Office
9 Rimrock Stages Bus Depot
12 Lewistown Art Center
13 Central Montana Medical Center
15 BLM/Charles M Russell NWR Headquarters

Lewistown

0   250   500 m
0   250   500 yards

To Malta
Boyd Creek
Symms Park
To Jordan
Silk Stockings District
To Great Falls
Little Casino Creek
Frank Day Park
To Big Springs Fish Hatchery
Airport Rd

MONTANA

the Silk Stockings District, between Boulevard and Washington Sts at 2nd and 3rd Aves, which was named for its affluence, not immoral character.

The **Lewistown Art Center** (☎ 406-538-8278), 1 block west of Main St at 801 W Broadway, is a piece of art in itself. Its shell is made of the same local sandstone as other buildings, but boards from local farms have been added to it and decorated with wrought-iron fixtures from the old high school. Part of the building is an old bunkhouse where single male employees of Lewistown's largest department store used to board; the other part is an old carriage house that was moved to the site in 1983 to expand the center. Exhibits feature work by local artists and the gift shop sells beautiful pottery and a small selection of Montana Writer's Project books. It's closed Monday; admission is free.

The **Central Montana Museum** (☎ 406-538-5436), 408 NE Main St, has the requisite collection of local memorabilia and relics focusing on homesteaders, Native Americans and ranchers. It's closed weekends from September to June; free.

The **Big Springs Fish Hatchery**, on Upper Springs Rd, 6 miles southeast of town (follow 1st Ave south), offers free tours Monday to Friday from 9 am to 4 pm. Adjacent is a pleasant picnic area and Big Spring, the third largest freshwater spring in the world, discharging over 3 million gallons per hour.

Places to Stay

Camping is free at *Kiwanis Park*, 2 miles south of town on US 87/US 191, which has bathrooms and running water but is neither green, shady nor quiet. On the northeast edge of town at 103 Rocklyn Ave, *Mountain Acres* (☎ 406-538-7591) is basically a mobile home park with sites for $10. Tent camping is better at Crystal Lake (see Around Lewiston below).

Lewistown's motels are concentrated at the ends of Main St within easy walking distance of the town center. Neither quality (which is adequate) nor prices (which are low) vary greatly. The one exception is the historic *Calvert Hotel* (☎ 406-538-5411), 2 blocks from Main St at 216 7th Ave S, whose single/double rooms cost $23/30.

Near the chamber of commerce, the *Sunset Motel* (☎ 406-538-8741), 115 NE Main St, charges $31/36. Across the street, the *Trail's End Motel* (☎ 406-538-5468) has a heated outdoor pool and rooms for $34/41.

The *B&B Motel* (☎ 406-538-5496, 800-341-8000), charges $42/46 for the town's cleanest rooms. Montana's only community-owned motel is also Lewistown's most comfortable: the *Yogo Inn* (☎ 406-538-8721), 211 E Main St, with a restaurant, lounge, pool and $49/65 rooms.

Places to Eat

The *Whole Famdamily*, 206 W Main St, is the hands-down favorite for wholesome, home-cooked food. Sandwiches, soups and dinner specials are served Monday to Friday from 11 am to 8 pm (Saturday until 5 pm). A new addition to Lewistown's culinary scene is the hip *Java Bette's*, at 618 Main St, a coffee bar featuring Caravali espresso and homemade baked goods.

In the Yogo Inn, the *Yogo Garden Inn* serves breakfast, lunch and dinner and is one of the few places in town open Sunday.

Getting There & Away

US 191 runs north to US 2 at Malta, 100 miles away, and south through Harlowtown to I-90 at Big Timber, 101 miles away. US 87 heads 135 miles southeast to Billings and 105 miles west to Great Falls.

Rimrock Stages (☎ 406-538-9227), 513 1st Ave N, has one bus daily to Billings ($21 one-way) and one daily to Great Falls ($18). Car rentals are available from Hilltop Motors (☎ 406-538-4014) and DN Olds (☎ 406-538-3455).

AROUND LEWISTOWN

West of Lewistown the Judith Basin, which is bounded by the Little Belt Mountains and the Missouri River, receives more rain than the rest of Central Montana. The land was first prized by Native Americans as prime buffalo country, then by ranchers and farmers for hay and grain production. It's intersected by US 87, the main route between Lewistown and Great Falls.

The Big Open region, east of Lewistown, is just that – big and open. Inhabitants are few and far between, and shrubs and prairie grass seem to roll endlessly across the land. Its economy relies on oil production from the Cat Creek Anticline, Central Montana's richest concentration of 'black gold,' and open-range cattle ranching, started by Granville Stuart in the 1880s. Few people (even Montanans) venture into the Big Open. When they do, it is usually to visit the Charles M Russell National Wildlife Refuge, or the remote reaches of Fort Peck Reservoir – both good destinations for people seeking space, solitude and an off-the-beaten track experience.

North and south of Lewistown are small, isolated mountain ranges that provide recreation for area locals. The Judith Mountains, in the north, have a wealth of old mine sites, while the Big Snowy Mountains (south) have hiking and camping at and around Crystal Lake.

The Judith Mountains

When Perry McAdow exhibited a gold and silver statue at the 1893 World's Fair, he started a stampede to the Judith Mountains. Ten years later, an estimated $18 million had been extracted from Maiden, Gilt Edge and Kendall, the hubs of mining activity. Roads head into the Judiths from US 191, northeast of Lewistown, and lead past old mine workings and gravel pits. Most of the land is privately owned, making public access a bit tricky, but in general, people up there are friendly towards curious travelers.

The best preserved remains are at **Kendall**, which is not yet privately owned. The biggest crowds you are likely to see are from the nearby KLM Scout Camp. To reach Kendall, take US 191 north for about 9½ miles from Lewistown, and turn west on Hwy 81. Two and a half miles away is a gravel road, marked 'KLM Scout Camp,' which leads straight to Kendall. If you turn east at the Hwy 81 junction, you end up at Maiden, a popular departure point for

mountain biking. There aren't any official trails, but uncrowded secondary roads crisscross the mountains.

Crystal Lake

About 30 miles southwest of Lewistown in the west end of the Big Snowy Mountains, Crystal Lake is surrounded by dense pine forests and, high above the lake, sheer limestone cliffs.

Despite heavy use, the lake remains quiet since no motorized boats are allowed. The fishing here is mainly for rainbow trout, though bass and crappie have been known to get themselves hooked. Hiking trails, most of which start from the campground, offer a closer look at the Big Snowy terrain. The **Crystal Lake Shoreline Trail** makes a level loop (just under 2 miles) around the lake, and the **Crystal Cascades Trail** climbs gently for 6½ miles to Cascade Falls. More challenging is the **Ulhorn Trail**, which climbs steeply to the Big Snowy Crest, a plateau from which you can view the adjacent Little Snowy Mountains and the checkered Central Montana Plains. From here, the trail crosses a saddle ridge and splits: the west fork goes to a not-so-exciting ice cave about a half-mile away, and the east fork crosses Knife Blade Ridge and connects with a trail that heads back to the campground (about a 10-mile trip). Trails are well-marked and a useful map is available at the campground entrance or from the campground host.

The *Crystal Lake Campground*, at the pear-shaped lake's south end, is a favorite weekend and summer destination for hikers and anglers, and acts as the hub of lake activity. Sites cost $8 per night, and the campground is equipped with pit toilets, picnic tables and fire rings. Camping is first-come, first-served and fills quickly on summer weekends.

Charles M Russell National Wildlife Refuge

Remote, awe-inspiring and conspicuously free of access roads, the Charles M Russell National Wildlife Refuge is the country's second-largest refuge outside of Alaska. Technically, the refuge has over 700 miles of roads, but less than 100 miles are paved. As a result, people rarely journey into its wilds. The south side of the Missouri River is especially rugged, though it is possible to get to with an off-road vehicle, a willingness to get lost and a full tank of gas. A 73-mile loop designated by the BLM as the **Missouri Breaks Byway** begins 1 mile south of the Fred Robinson Bridge, 76 miles north of Lewistown on US 191. Camping is permitted anywhere along the route, but water is generally unavailable. There are no developed hiking trails, but the terrain is open and easy to navigate (long off-road journeys require a map and compass). Take caution at the slightest chance of rain – a few drops and the roads around here are pure gumbo.

More cautious travelers should stick to the area around the Fred Robinson Bridge. From the bridge's north side, a 20-mile self-guided loop – for cars, bikes or hearty feet – skirts along the Missouri River and takes about two hours to complete (by car). Even though this is the most traveled part of the refuge, you still have a good chance of viewing elk (reintroduced from Yellowstone National Park in 1951), pronghorn, and bighorn sheep, and, in spring (roughly from May to early June), sharp-tailed grouse courtship rituals.

On the south side of the bridge, the BLM maintains the **James Kipp State Recreation Area**, which has a boat launch, picnic facilities and a campsite with pit toilets, potable water and fire rings; campsites cost $3 per night and are available on a first-come, first-served basis, though they are rarely full.

The refuge does not have a visitors center, but there is a DFWP field station just south of the James Kipp campground which is open Monday to Friday 7 am to 4:30 pm, and has information posted. Maps and information are posted at the campground and are also available in Lewistown (see above), or by writing the Charles M Russell National Wildlife Refuge, PO Box 110, Lewistown, MT 59547.

Harlowton

On the north bank of the Musselshell River at the junction of US 12 and US 191, Harlowtown (population 1127) appears something like Lewistown did 50 years ago. As in Lewistown, most of Harlowton's buildings are made of local sandstone carved by immigrant stonecutters, but because they are not flanked by modern construction, they have more of their original integrity. As a whole, the downtown, which lies along Central Ave east of US 191, is wonderfully intact, and most of it is listed on the National Register of Historic Places. The three-story **Graves Hotel**, built in 1903 during Harlowton's railroad boom, dominates the scene.

The best place to learn about Harlowton's early days as a flour and wool production center is the **Upper Musselshell Historical Society Museum**, 11 S Central Ave, open Tuesday to Saturday from May to November from 10 am to 5 pm, and Sunday from 1 to 5 pm.

The USFS Musselshell Ranger District Office (☎ 406-932-6407) just west of US 12, which is open Monday to Friday from 7:30 am to 4:30 pm, has information about **floating** and **fishing** on the Musselshell River and **hiking** in the Little Belt Mountains. Across the street from the ranger's office, the *Eat Shop Drive Inn* has burgers and such for under $5.

Fourteen miles south of Harlowton along US 191 is a **fossil area** containing pockets of 'gizzard stones' – rocks polished by the digestive process of dinosaurs millions of years ago. This is where, in 1908, Albert Siberling of Harlowton found the remains of a Paleocene mammal *Ptilodus montanus*, now at the American Museum of Natural History in New York.

BILLINGS

Despite its grand title as 'Montana's largest city,' Billings (population 91,195) is essentially friendly and unintimidating. The Yellowstone River, which brushes the east side of town, and the surrounding 400-foot buff sandstone cliffs, known as the Rimrocks or 'rims,' give the city a picturesque

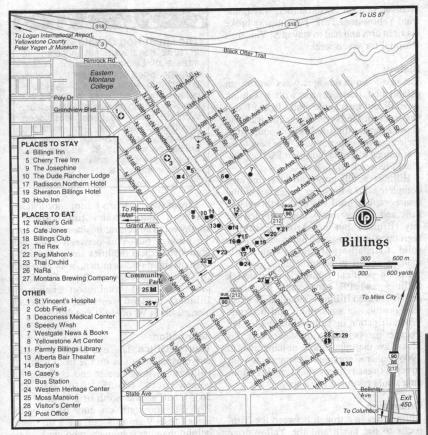

PLACES TO STAY
4 Billings Inn
5 Cherry Tree Inn
9 The Josephine
10 The Dude Rancher Lodge
17 Radisson Northern Hotel
19 Sheraton Billings Hotel
30 HoJo Inn

PLACES TO EAT
12 Walker's Grill
15 Cafe Jones
18 Billings Club
21 The Rex
22 Pug Mahon's
23 Thai Orchid
26 NaRa
27 Montana Brewing Company

OTHER
1 St Vincent's Hospital
2 Cobb Field
3 Deaconess Medical Center
6 Speedy Wash
7 Westgate News & Books
8 Yellowstone Art Center
11 Parmly Billings Library
13 Alberta Bair Theater
14 Barjon's
16 Casey's
20 Bus Station
24 Western Heritage Center
25 Moss Mansion
28 Visitor's Center
29 Post Office

Billings

MONTANA

setting. Originally Billings proper was contained within these natural boundaries, but since the oil boom of the 1950s, the edges have been pushing farther and farther into the country. But the interaction between Billings and its surrounding farm and ranch land has always been a part of the city's character, and the prices of wheat and beef undeniably dictate its mood. The economy is diverse enough, however, that it remains pretty stable. Several large banks have corporate headquarters here and Billings' health care facilities are the largest and best between Seattle and Minneapolis. The

College of the Rockies, which specializes in aviation and equine studies, is also a big attraction.

Travelers usually hit Billings on the way to somewhere else, like the Little Bighorn Battlefield, Red Lodge and Yellowstone National Park. Billings' airport is one of Montana's busiest and there is a myriad of accommodations, so Billings acts as a good hub. At least one day could be dedicated to exploring the city proper.

Ernest Hemingway brought excitement to Billings in November 1930 when he, John Dos Passos, and a local cowboy were involved in a car crash on their way home from Yellowstone Park. Hemingway broke his right arm and had to stay at St Vincent's Hospital for seven weeks.

History

The first town in this area was Coulson, an established trade center with a saloon, sawmill and mercantile store. In 1881 surveyors from the Northern Pacific Railroad chose a more solid site 2 miles southeast as their base for construction. The new town was named after the Northern Pacific president Frederick Billings.

Billings rapidly grew into a thriving city, complete with a horsecar system of public transportation, until 1886, when three large fires and a disastrous winter crippled the city. Bruised but not broken, Billings regrouped and prospered again on the more solid foundation of a growing cattle industry and irrigated agriculture.

Strong political figures like Frederick Billings and PB Moss, and economic activity steered Billings immediately into a lead position in agriculture and banking. When irrigation in Yellowstone Valley led to experiments in growing sugar beets, PB Moss saw the opportunity at hand and, in 1906, gathered enough investments to construct a sugar refinery that remains Montana's only commercial factory.

Orientation

Billings lies in a trough between the Rimrocks to the north and the Yellowstone River to the southeast. Interstate 90 parallels the river through town, then heads east toward Little Bighorn Battlefield. Eight miles east of downtown (exit 450) I-94 branches off I-90 toward Miles City. Sixteen miles west of downtown, US 212 branches southwest off I-90 toward Red Lodge and Yellowstone National Park.

Billings' main thoroughfare is 27th St, which runs from I-90 exit 450 through downtown to Hwy 3 at the airport entrance. The other main thoroughfare begins as Laurel Rd from I-90 exit 446, then crosses downtown perpendicular to 27th St as Montana Ave.

The Great Hog Debate

In 1882 hogs were set loose in the streets of Billings to devour excess garbage. Soon out of control, the hogs busted into several kegs of oysters – neither cheap nor easy to come by – that were sitting on a hotel's back steps. Within a week the hogs were bacon and their owner irate. Throughout the following year, the *Billings Gazette* ran articles on who was 'for' and who was 'against' the hogs, creating a political division in the city. ■

Downtown, streets run northwest-southeast and avenues run northeast-southwest. The central business streets are 1st through 6th Aves between 32nd and 26th Sts; medical facilities are in the northwest quadrant of downtown, on N 28th and N 29th Sts, just below the Rims. The shopping malls and hotel/motel chains of Billings' modern west side are spread along 24th St W, off I-90 exit 466.

Information

Tourist Office The eye-catching Cattle Drive Monument sits on the front lawn of Billings' visitors center and chamber of commerce (☎ 406-252-4016, 800-735-2635), half a mile north of I-90 at 815 S 27th St. The staff, on duty Monday to Friday from 9 am to 5 pm, are a bit more helpful than the volunteers who work after hours. It's open May to September daily from 8:30 am to 7:30 pm, and the rest of the year Monday to Friday from 8:30 am to 5 pm.

Money Banks are clustered on N Broadway (N 28th St) downtown.

Post The main post office is right behind the visitors center, on S 27th St; the downtown branch is next to the Sheraton on 1st Ave.

Bookstores & Libraries Westgate News & Books (☎ 406-656-1616), 511 N 24th St, has international newspapers and a wide selection of Montana travel guides. Barjon's (☎ 406-252-4398, 800-288-4318), 2718 3rd Ave N, is the hip place in town, a New Age bookstore with books on local yoga workshops, massage therapists and alternative goods.

The Parmly Billings Library, on 4th Ave N between 28th and 29th Sts, has an entire Montana Room filled with books, videos, periodicals and early Montana maps and exploration charts. Nonlocals can't borrow materials, but the library facilities are very comfortable and are open Tuesday to Thursday from 10 am to 9 pm, Friday to 5 pm and Saturday 1 to 5 pm.

Publications The *Magic City Monthly* is a free publication that highlights various restaurants, current entertainment and recreation opportunities around Billings. Once a week the *Billings Gazette* publishes *Enjoy*, an entertainment supplement.

Medical Services The Deaconess Medical Center (☎ 406-657-4000), 2800 10th Ave N, is Montana's largest, with a 24-hour emergency center. St Vincent's Hospital (☎ 406-657-8778) is at 1233 N 30th St.

Laundry The Laundry Room (☎ 406-652-2993), south of Rimrock Mall at the corner of W 32nd St and King Ave, is smoke-free (rare for a Montana establishment) and open daily from 7 am to 9 pm. Speedy Wash (☎ 406-248-4177), downtown at 2505 6th Ave N, has same-day drop-off service and is open daily from 7 am to 11 pm.

Things to See & Do
Most of Billings sights are within walking distance of one another downtown. In summer the Billings Trolley has ongoing two-hour tours ($10) that cover everything you'd ever want to see; find out about pick-up and departure points from the visitors center. Fun Adventures (☎ 406-254-7180) works with local guides in organizing any itinerary you want, from horseback riding to golfing to visiting Yellowstone National Park; call at least a week before you arrive.

As far as 'must-sees' go, the two that stand out are the **Western Heritage Center** (☎ 406-256-6809), 2822 Montana Ave, which has changing exhibits and an outstanding artifact collection representing various cultural traditions – Crow, Northern Cheyenne, Hispanic, Japanese, Chinese, Volga German – integral to Yellowstone Valley life, and the **Yellowstone Art Center** (☎ 406-256-6804), housed in the 1916 Yellowstone County Jail building at 401 N 27th St, which exhibits national and regional art. Both museums are free and closed Monday.

Also worth seeing is the **Moss Mansion** (☎ 406-256-5100), 914 Division St at the corner of 2nd Ave N, designed by New York architect RJ Hardenbergh who is noted for his work on the Waldorf Astoria Hotel in Manhattan. The red sandstone home has 28 rooms, an onyx fireplace and silk and gold-leaf wall coverings. Docents lead tours of the mansion June to August, Monday to Saturday from 10 am to 4 pm and Sunday from 1 to 3 pm. Admission is $5 for adults, $4 for seniors and $3 for children under 12.

The **Yellowstone County Peter Yegen Jr Museum** (☎ 406-256-6811), at the entrance to Logan International Airport, is filled with local artifacts including a late 19th-century chuckwagon. It's open weekdays from 10:30 am to 5 pm, weekends from 2 to 5 pm and is free.

Branching off from Hwy 318 near the airport, **Black Otter Trail** skirts the top edge of the Rims, giving an expansive view of Billings and, on clear days, the Bighorn, Pryor, Crazy, Beartooth and Snowy mountains. Black Otter was a Crow chief killed here by a Sioux war party and then given a treetop burial. The trail passes by the grave of Luther S 'Yellowstone' Kelly, one of those classic frontiersmen who left the comforts of the East Coast to live out the wild way, learning Crow and Sioux languages. Further along the trail is all that remains of Coulson – **Boothill Cemetery** – where lies Sheriff 'Muggins' Taylor, who let the world know of Custer's defeat.

MONTANA

Above the Yellowstone River and across from Black Otter Trail is **Sacrifice Cliff**. Crow legend has it that two brothers returned from a battle to find their camp (at the top of the cliff) infested with smallpox. To appease the gods, whom they believed were not happy with their acts in battle, the brothers blindfolded themselves, climbed on their best horse together and rode off the cliff.

Opened in 1997, **Zoo Montana** (☎ 406-652-8100), 2100 S Shiloh Rd at the west end of Billings, has river otters, waterfowl, a children's zoo (rabbits and the like) and plans to add a Siberian tiger and snow monkeys. There are also nature trails around the area and a sensory garden. It is open April 15 to October 15 daily from 10 am to 5 pm. Admission is $3 for adults, $2 for children.

Places to Stay

If you're just passing through on I-90, it's most convenient to stay at one of the big chain motels near the freeway. If you arrive by plane or are going to see some sights and have a meal or two, stay downtown.

Camping Billings boasts America's first KOA, now called the *Billings KOA* (☎ 406-252-3104), started by two brothers to accommodate people traveling to the World's Fair. It's in a beautiful spot next to the Yellowstone River, half a mile south of I-90 (well signed off the interstate). Campsites are grassy, shady and cost $17. RV spaces, packed tightly together, cost $23. Amenities include an outdoor pool, mini-golf course, store, laundry facilities and nightly barbecue for $7.

B&Bs At 514 N 29th St, *The Josephine* (☎ 406-248-5898) is run by super-friendly folks who really know how to cook breakfast. The five flowery rooms cost $48 to $75.

Motels The *Picture Court Motel* (☎ 406-252-8478, 800-523-7379) is in a less than desirable location, next to the busy interstate at 5146 Laurel Rd off I-90 exit 446, but the friendly owner compensates with

nice flower boxes, complimentary coffee and a small lobby with reading materials. Rooms cost $31/35 for a single/double.

A quarter mile north along Laurel Rd at 4808 Underpass Ave, the *Parkway Motel* (☎ 406-245-3044) also tries to compensate for its noisy, urban location by putting a pine tree in front of each room. Rooms cost $32/36.

The *Cherry Tree Inn* (☎ 406-252-5603, 800-237-5882), 823 N Broadway (also known as N 28th St), has a cramped lobby and comfortable, though dull rooms for $35/41 a single/double.

At 880 N 29th St, the *Billings Inn* (☎ 406-252-6800) rooms have microwaves and small refrigerators, and there is a coin-op laundry facility within the motel. A large Continental breakfast is included in the room price of $42/47. Rooms at the centrally located *Dude Rancher Lodge* (☎ 406-259-5561, 800-221-3302), 415 N 29th St, have the most character in Billings, with lassos, oxbows, and light fixtures hanging from wagon wheels. Rooms cost between $40 and $50.

Off I-90 exit 450 at 1001 S 27th St, the *HoJo Inn* (☎ 406-248-4656) has rooms for $52/60.

Hotels A good choice downtown is the *Radisson Northern Hotel* (☎ 406-245-5121) at 19 N 28th St, with a spa and $65/85 rooms. One block away, the *Sheraton Billings Hotel* (☎ 406-252-7400, 800-325-3535), 27 N 27th St, has rooms with great views of the city starting at $85.

Places to Eat

Besides offering the usual meat and potatoes, Billings has some well-trained, innovative chefs and good ethnic restaurants. The pubs around town also serve good, inexpensive food and often have happy hour specials until 6:30 pm. For coffee, pastries and a nice atmosphere, stop by *Cafe Jones*, 2712 2nd Ave.

The outside deck of the *Billings Club*, 2702 1st Ave N, is packed at lunchtime and just after 5 pm on weekdays, when business folk congregate over cold microbrews and appetizers. There's also a full dinner menu, served until 11 pm. *Pug Mahon's*, 3011 1st Ave N, is a friendly Irish bar with darts, cribbage, a great beer list and good food (Irish stew, sandwiches) to match. On Sundays people line up for Pug's brunch, complete with champagne. New in town is the *Montana Brewing Company*, on S 28th St between 2nd and 1st Aves, which brews their own beer and makes wood-fired pizzas.

Billings has a surprisingly decent variety of Asian cuisine on offer. The *Thai Orchid* (☎ 406-256-2206), 2926 2nd Ave N, makes great curries at any spice level and has a nice atmosphere. West of town at 1301 Grand, *Khanthaliy's Eggrolls and Laotian Cuisine* is essentially a take-out joint with a few tables that makes great noodle dishes for under $5. For quite authentic Korean food, and a few Japanese dishes thrown in for good measure, try *NaRa*, on the corner of Division St and 1st Ave N.

At the corner of 3rd Ave and 27th St N, *Walker's Grill* (☎ 406-245-9291) has a cosmopolitan bistro setting, exceptional wine list and very reasonable prices. Signature dishes include rock shrimp pasta with pesto and roasted garlic ($9.50), and grilled pork chops with a mustard and pinenut crust ($11); closed Sunday. In an historic hotel at 2401 Montana Ave, *The Rex* (☎ 406-245-7477) serves aged Montana beef ($11 to $16), prime rib ($15) and seafood flown in from Seattle. Both restaurants are open for dinner only.

Entertainment
Casey's, at 109 N Broadway (28th St), has live jazz and blues performances nightly. Weeknights are free and mellow, but weekend headliners draw boisterous crowds and cost $4 to $7. (For Billings' best bar hangouts, see Places to Eat above.)

A magnet for the whole eastern part of the state, the *Alberta Bair Theater* (☎ 406-256-6052), 103 N Broadway, is Billings' cultural jewel. Productions range from country music to symphony concerts, and from children's theater to musicals. The extensive program ensures there will be entertainment available at least once a week all year long.

The *Billings Studio Theater* (☎ 406-248-1141), 1500 Rimrock Rd, stages six productions by playwrights ranging from Shakespeare to Neil Simon and three children's shows annually.

In summer the Billings Mustangs baseball team, the Cincinnati Reds Pioneer League affiliate, play their home games at Cobb Field only highlight in section; downtown at N 27th St and 9th Ave.

Getting There & Away
Air Logan International Airport, atop the Rims, 2 miles north of downtown, is served primarily by Delta Airlines which flies through Salt Lake City, UT, and is generally the cheapest to the West Coast. Continental and United Airlines both have three flights daily to Denver. Northwest Airlines flies to Minneapolis and the West Coast. Horizon Air flies to/from points west, and Big Sky Airlines flies within Montana.

Bus Greyhound, Rimrock Stages and Powder River Transportation use the bus station (☎ 406-245-5116) at 2502 1st Ave N. Between the three operators there is one bus daily to/from Missoula, Helena, Butte, Bozeman, Livingston and Seattle, and two daily to/from Denver.

Train Though it can't really be considered public transport, given the price, Montana Rockies Rail Tours (☎ 800-519-7245) runs trips between Billings or Bozeman and Sandpoint, ID, along the first route of the Northern Transcontinental Railroad, completed in 1883. The trip includes bus transfers between Spokane, WA, and Sandpoint, meals and accommodation on the *Mon-tana Daylight* in 'Explorer,' 'Big Sky' or 'Gold Nugget' class for $400/600/1050 respectively. Longer trips go through Livingston, the Paradise Valley and Yellowstone National Park.

Getting Around
Bus Billings is one of the few cities in Montana with an efficient bus system. Big

green and white buses stop at most corners and at any of the obvious blue and green MET signs around town. Operating hours are Monday to Friday from 6 am to 7 pm, and Saturday from 10:30 am to 3:45 pm. Tickets, available from the driver, cost 75¢ and include one free transfer; a book of 10 tickets costs $6. If you want more information call Billings Metropolitan Transit System at ☎ 406-657-8218.

Car Major car rental agencies, including Hertz (☎ 406-248-9151), Avis (☎ 406-252-8007), Budget (☎ 406-259-4168) and National (☎ 406-252-7626), can be found at the airport. A cheaper alternative is Thrifty (☎ 406-259-1025) or Enterprise (☎ 406-652-2000). Both of these companies will pick-up and drop-off renters at the airport, bus station or hotels.

Taxi Billings Area City Cab (☎ 406-252-8700) and Billings Area Yellow Cab (☎ 406-245-3033) run 24 hours.

AROUND BILLINGS
Pictograph Cave State Park
Five miles south of I-90 exit 452 on Coburn Rd, Pictograph Cave State Monument is a rich archaeological find. Excavations in the three caves – Pictograph, Ghost and Middle – have yielded over 30,000 Paleo-Indian artifacts left by a succession of cultures who inhabited the area over a period of 10,000 years.

The remarkable highlights of the monument are the cave paintings. The paint, made of ground flowers, roots, bark, clay, charcoal and animal fat, was applied with fingers, twigs, bones and tufts of hair attached to sticks. The pictographs have withstood the ravages of time better, in fact, than the spray paint used by vandals to do some decorating of their own. Pictograph Cave has the best preserved drawings.

The caves are accessible from a central parking lot via a quarter-mile trail. Hours are April 15 to October 15 daily from 8 am to 8 pm.

Pompey's Pillar
Northeast of Billings off I-94, the massive sandstone butte of Pompey's Pillar stands as a natural monument to the Lewis and Clark Expedition. Clark etched his signature on the rock on July 25, 1806. Strangely enough, that is the only remaining physical mark of their expedition. Clark, however, is not the only graffiti artist to have scrawled upon the rock. Crow Indians before him, homesteaders after him and modern-day tourists have all left their mark. Clark named the rock after Sacagawea's son, who was nicknamed 'Pomp,' which, in Shoshone, means 'little chief.'

Little Pomp Charbonneau
Pomp was the son of Toussaint Charbonneau and Sacagawea, who accompanied the Lewis and Clark Expedition between 1805 and 1806. In all those pictures of Sacagawea, young Pomp is the one in the papoose.

Being the youngest member of the expedition was just the beginning of his incredible life. Captain Clark was so taken with the infant that he sent the child to private schools in St Louis at his own expense. At Fort Union in Montana, the teenage Charbonneau met German nobleman Prince Paul von Wurtemberg, who was impressed by the well-educated boy. He took Charbonneau back to Germany with him, where Charbonneau spent the next six years as a courtier. During this time, he learned five languages fluently, and traveled across the Continent and to Africa with the prince.

Charbonneau eventually returned to western USA. He served as a guide through the Montana wilderness, trapped furs, served as alcalde (mayor) at a California mission and prospected for gold in the 1850s California gold rush. In 1866, he hankered to return to Montana, where gold fever had broken out. He got no farther north than Danner, Oregon, then a stage stop, where he died of pneumonia at the age of 61. ■

A wooden walkway leads to the visitors center run by the BLM (which is open daily from 8 am to 8 pm), and continues to the pillar's summit. Behind the visitors center is a large picnic area with plenty of shade and grass, and a short trail that leads to the Yellowstone River. Swimming is prohibited because of strong currents and deep holes.

LITTLE BIGHORN BATTLEFIELD

Southeast of Billings, rolling prairies and low pine-covered hills stretch for mile after endless mile. The Crow Indian Reservation

(Montana's largest) and the Northern Cheyenne Indian Reservation constitute the bulk of land. This is where General George Custer made his famous 'last stand' and where numerous other battles between Native Americans and the US Cavalry were fought.

The Little Bighorn National Monument (called Custer Battlefield up to 1993) is undeniably one of Montana's most popular attractions. As such, it has a wonderful visitors center with interpretive displays and videos, maps of the battlefield, a good book shop and lectures given throughout

The Battle of the Little Bighorn

With the discovery of gold in the Black Hills, President Ulysses S Grant decided that a full attack on the Sioux would be the only way to get the Indians out of the newly prized area. The most famous of all the battles is Custer's Last Stand, or more appropriately called the Battle of the Little Bighorn.

On March 17, 1876, Colonel Joseph J Reynolds, under command of General George Crook, attacked a Sioux camp on the Powder River. The surprised Sioux rallied and counterattacked, causing the soldiers to return to Fort Fetterman. The Oglalas, Miniconjous and Cheyennes who fought Reynolds and his men set forth to the East Fork of the Little Powder River to unite with Crazy Horse, and then 60 miles on to another branch of the Powder River to find Sitting Bull. By early spring, 400 lodges including about 3000 people were joined together.

General Alfred H Terry led an expedition westward from Fort Abraham Lincoln (near present-day Mandan, North Dakota) toward the Yellowstone River. At the mouth of the Rosebud he sent one of his staff officers, General George Armstrong Custer with the Seventh Cavalry forward to find the Sioux encampment believed to be in the Little Bighorn Valley. Terry would then continue up the Yellowstone to meet up with Colonel John Gibbon's forces in order to attack from the north.

On the morning of June 24, Custer's troops encountered a fresh Indian trail, and at the midday stop scouts reported that the Sioux were camped on the lower Little Bighorn. Not aware of the incredible size of the encampment that had formed over the weeks, Custer divided his Seventh Cavalry into three parts to form a three-prong attack. Two columns worked their way upstream to the west, and though Custer was to stay back, he changed his mind and went north. Dust from the running of cavalry horses alerted the Indians and they attacked Reno's (one of the two columns) troops. Custer watched the fight, ordered reinforcements, then charged ahead into the encampment. Over 2000 warriors attacked the cavalry head on, causing the soldiers to flee in pure chaos. Not a single soldier survived.

Word reached the general public of the defeat on July 4, 1876 – the day that marked the centennial of the Declaration of Independence. The annihilation of a unit of the US Army by a force of so-called 'savages' shocked the country and placed the concept of the USA into question – it was clear the government lacked effective control over large sections of territory that it claimed. Only by devoting enormous resources to the defeat of the Sioux and their allies was the government able to overcome such a damaging blow to its prestige. ■

the day on various aspects of the battle and its encompassing history.

It's hard to grasp the full story of the battle in an afternoon's visit, but listening to the lectures and going on one of the free guided tours gives you a good overall view of what happened. For the most part the guides are objective and fair to both sides involved. Tour schedules are posted at the visitors center information desk. The handbook that is passed out at the entrance is also a good information source.

Beyond the visitors center, the battlefield is best suited for visiting by car. There's a 4½-mile tour that begins at the center and winds around the area in a chronological order. Alternately you can get a ride from the center out to the starting point and wind your way back on foot, although all the cars can make the road quite congested.

The entrance to the battlefield is 1 mile east of I-90 on US 212. It's open mid-April to Memorial Day from 8 am to 6 pm, Memorial Day to Labor Day to 8 pm, and the rest of the year to 4:30 pm. The entrance fee is $5 per vehicle, $3 per walk-in. For information contact Little Bighorn Battlefield National Monument (☎ 406-638-2621), PO Box 39, Crow Agency, MT 59022.

Half- and full-day private tours with a Crow guide are available through Custer Battlefield Tours (☎ 406-665-1580), 416 N Cody St, in Hardin.

AROUND LITTLE BIGHORN BATTLEFIELD

Though the area's most famous battle site is that of the Little Bighorn, there are other, less-developed monuments and battlefields in the area. These give a glimpse of what the landscape was like at the time of conflict and help complete the story of why the Battle of the Little Bighorn occurred. They tell the history of the lesser-known battles that occurred at the same time (and because of the same government policies). Best of all, being away from the crowds lets the history of the region sink in. Hardin is the hub and the only major center around.

Hardin

Where summer street dances are family affairs and standard Sunday dress is a cowboy hat and boots, one would expect the population to be made up of descendants of European homesteaders, but such is not the case. On the Crow Reservation's northern border, Hardin (population 3225) is the largest center of commerce in the area and gets much of its local business from the reservation residents. From Memorial Day to Labor Day, however, most people in town are passing through en route to the Little Bighorn Battlefield National Monument (18 miles away) and Bighorn Canyon National Recreation Area.

The town really comes to life during **Little Bighorn Days** held the last Wednesday to Sunday of June. It's easy to see that the event has grown larger than its historical relevance – there's a professional rodeo, carnival, arts and crafts fair, antique show, street dancing, a Scandinavian feast and a parade. More academic is the **Little Big Horn Symposium** and the lectures on Native American interpretation of the battle that occur around town during the event.

The culmination and feature attraction of Little Bighorn Days is **Custer's Last Stand Reenactment**, an hour-long narrated spectacle with a cast of 300 horses, Indians and soldiers. Tickets ($8 for adults, $4.50 for children) are available at the Hardin Chamber of Commerce (☎ 406-665-1672), 21 E 4th St, or at the reenactment grounds (6 miles west of town).

Also of interest are the **Bighorn County Historical Museum**, off I-90 exit 497, which has ammunition, horseshoes and several uniforms from the Little Bighorn Battle, and the **Jailhouse Gallery**, 219 N Center Ave, which has regional painting and photography.

Places to Stay The *Bighorn Valley KOA* (☎ 406-665-1635), half a mile north of I-90 on Hwy 47, is surrounded by cottonwood trees and has tent sites for $18, RV spaces for $26; it's open from April to September.

The *American Inn* (☎ 406-665-1870), 1324 N Crawford Ave one block south of

I-90 exit 495, has nice rooms for $45/63 single/double and an outdoor pool. Next door, *Super 8* (☎ 406-665-1700) has $55 rooms.

A great mom-and-pop operation, the *Lariat Motel* (☎ 406-665-2683), 709 N Center Ave, has homemade cookies and coffee on hand and cozy rooms for $41/47.

Chief Two Moon Monument

In 1936 an Indian trader by the name of Monicre built a monument in memory of Chief Two Moon's participation in the Battle of the Little Bighorn. The simple stone monument sat quietly for many years on US 212 near Busby. Then, in 1990, Congress passed a law allowing bones that had been stored for research in museums throughout the USA to be returned to their homelands for proper burial. The monument has since become a symbol for some of the US government's questionable history regarding Native Americans.

The **Two Moon World Peace Gathering** congregates in late June at the Austin Two Moon Ranch, 5 miles east of Busby on US 212, to pray, feast and discuss current Native American issues. Call tribal headquarters (☎ 406-638-2601) for more information on the events.

St Labre Mission

In 1884, the year that an executive order set aside the present-day Northern Cheyenne Reservation, Bishop Brondel purchased land in the Tongue River valley (the Northern Cheyenne's original homeland) and founded the St Labre Mission. Today the mission revolves around its school and the **Northern Cheyenne Museum**. The museum has a large collection of beadwork, clothing, religious and ceremonial artifacts and jewelry. The teepee-shaped stone church symbolizes the Native American and Ro-man Catholic beliefs of the mission. On a clear day the stained-glass windows are dazzling.

The mission is well-marked off US 212 in the small community of Ashland. Students and staff members are usually on hand to give tours. Hours are June to September daily from 8 am to 4:30 pm, closed weekends September to May.

Rosebud Battlefield State Park

On June 4, 1876, Sitting Bull had moved his people to the area around the Rosebud Creek to perform the traditional Sun Dance. While dancing he had a vision of white soldiers falling down and saw that these soldiers didn't have ears. Soon after, the US government ordered the attack on the Sioux and Cheyenne who had refused to go to the reservations, and three separate columns headed toward the Sioux area

The Crow

Though greatly reduced from its original 59,000 sq miles, the 3400-sq-mile Crow Indian Reservation is Montana's largest. Most of the Crow tribe's 7000 members live on the reservation, and, partly because the US government didn't mandate English-only boarding schools on the reservation, nearly 80% of the residents speak the Crow language.

The Crow call themselves Absaroke, which means 'people of the large-beaked bird' or 'people of the raven.' In the 18th century they migrated west, becoming nomadic buffalo hunters. They settled first in the Black Hills and then south of the Yellowstone River.

When William Clark traveled through their territory in 1806, he noted that the Crow were exceptionally skilled equestrians and the women excelled at quill and beadwork. Initial relations between Crow and whites were friendly. At Fort Remon, at the confluence of the Bighorn and Yellowstone rivers, the Crow traded hides and pelts and protection from the hostile Blackfeet for tobacco, food, guns and liquor. In the 1880s the Crow grew more economically dependent on the settlers as the buffalo disappeared.

Under the 1851 and 1868 Fort Laramie treaties, the Crow received Montana's largest tract of reservation land. Many members of the Crow acted as scouts for the government during the Little Bighorn and Rosebud battles. ■

MONTANA

The Northern Cheyenne

The Northern Cheyenne Reservation is 694 sq miles of prairie and pine-covered sand-stone uplands between the Crow Indian Reservation and the Tongue River. Most of the 3500 residents live in the small towns of Ashland, Busby and Lame Deer. Tribal head-quarters and the Cheyenne Depot, the first tribally owned convenience store in Montana, are in Lame Deer.

Caught in the domino effect of resettlement, the Cheyenne were pushed off their land in the mid-19th century, near present-day Minnesota by the Sioux, who had been moved off their land by tribes from the north. With the decline in their agricultural settlements and the increase of horses available, the Cheyenne moved closer and closer to the Eastern Plains, following the buffalo. They eventually split into two groups: the Northern Cheyenne who stayed in the Dakotas and Montana and the Southern Cheyennes who moved southwest into present-day Colorado. The Northern Cheyenne allied with the Sioux to fight soldiers, settlers and the Crow.

With the discovery of gold in the Black Hills in the 1870s, the US government ordered all western tribes onto reservations, but the Cheyenne and Sioux refused to go. General George Custer and the US cavalry were called in, and thus set the stage for the much discussed Battle of the Little Bighorn. The Cheyenne were sent to Oklahoma Indian Territory, but, determined to return to their homeland, they escaped in 1878 and made a grueling 11-month journey, led by Dull Knife (Morning Star) and Lone Wolf, back to the Tongue River valley.

Conflicts have continued over the reservation's land as the Northern Cheyenne Reservation sits atop the rich coal fields of the Fort Union Formation. In the 1970s developers proposed mining the land, but the tribe voted to preserve it. ■

around Little Bighorn. On June 17, 1876, eight days before the Battle of the Little Bighorn, the army set up camp in the head-waters of the Rosebud. General George Crook's troops stayed at Rosebud, while General Alfred A Terry marched ahead to meet up with Colonel John Gibbon and sent General George A Custer along to find the Sioux encampment. (For more on the Battle of the Little Bighorn, see the sidebar earlier in this chapter.)

On that morning, Crook's men were having coffee when the Sioux and Chey-enne, painted for war, came down the hills and attacked. Crook's Crow and Shoshone scouts held off the warriors long enough for Crook to organize his forces, and the battle raged for six bloody hours before ending with no apparent victor. It did, how-ever, knock Crook's battalion out of any further battles and Crook retired from fighting and took up fishing instead.

The battles at the mouth of Rosebud Creek involved over 10 sq miles and 2500 combatants. Rosebud Battlefield State Park, 23 miles south of Busby on County Rd 314, then 3 miles west on a dirt road, covers 3000 acres of the battlefield.

Elmer E 'Slim' Kobold homesteaded the site of the battle and, with the help of archaeologists, marked the areas of most significance with concrete pyramids. To guard against strip-mining, Rosebud Battlefield was added to the National Register of Historic Places.

Chief Plenty Coups State Park

Inspired by Mt Vernon on a trip to Wash-ington, DC, Crow chief Aleck-chea-ahoosh – or Chief Plenty Coups – decided to preserve his two-story log home as an historic site. At his request, the park stands not as a memorial to him but to the Crow Nation. There is a small museum and his home is open for viewing, left much the way it was when he lived there. On the bank of Pryor Creek, it's a very peaceful place to spend the afternoon; there's a beautiful picnic area with tables, grills, potable water and toilet facilities.

To reach the park head south from Billings 35 miles on Pryor Creek Rd then go 1 mile west from Pryor off Hwy 416 (it's well signed). It's open between May and September daily from 10 am to 5 pm, and October to April by appointment. The park fee is $3 per vehicle, $1 per walk-in.

BIGHORN CANYON NATIONAL RECREATION AREA – NORTH UNIT

The northern unit of the Bighorn Canyon NRA is prized for its fishing along the Bighorn River north of Bighorn Lake and for its boating opportunities, which center around Ok-A-Beh Marina. Besides the weekend anglers and water-skiers who journey down from Hardin, out-of-town visitors (mostly serious anglers) base themselves in the small town of Fort Smith. Ted Turner, former president Jimmy Carter and former secretary of state Dick Cheney are among the more illustrious, though not necessarily luckiest, regular fishing frequenters. (For more on the Bighorn Canyon NRA, see the Bighorn Country chapter in the Wyoming section. This entry covers the NRA that's accessible from Hardin.)

Orientation & Information

The northern unit is 42 miles southwest of Hardin on Hwy 313. Fort Smith Village, which consists of a grocery store, cafe, gas station and some fly-fishing shops, is the first development reached by the highway and is the entrance to the area. From the village, the road branches in three directions: north 2 miles to Afterbay Campground, west 4 miles to Yellowtail Dam and south to Ok-A-Beh Marina 10 miles away.

The Yellowtail Dam Visitors Center (☎ 406-666-3234) sits on the northeast side of the dam, 6 miles from Fort Smith Village. Displays cover some Crow history but center on the construction and engineering of Yellowtail Dam; a narrated informational film is shown on request. Fort Smith rangers are on duty to offer tours and answer questions. It's open Memorial Day to Labor Day daily from 9 am to 6 pm.

Plenty Coups

Crow chief Aleck-chea-ahoosh, which translates to 'Many Achievements' or 'Plenty Coups,' was the last Crow chief to earn his title by 'counting coups,' or earning war honors. After completing the four requisite acts to be considered for chieftainship – being the first to touch an enemy during battle, taking an enemy's weapon without killing him, 'cutting horse' (stealing a horse from the enemy camp) and leading a successful raid or war party – Plenty Coups 'counted coup' at least 80 times until the federal government prohibited 'violent warring activity' on reservation land, thus prohibiting counting coups.

As last warrior chief, Plenty Coups could have left a bitter legacy for generations prohibited from following in his footsteps. Instead, he was a model of transition and a wise leader for the Crow. For practicality's sake, Plenty Coups told his people not to wage war on new settlers, but to accept them; White culture was coming to stay, and the only way for the Crow to survive was to make peace with the settlers. Realizing that education would be his people's most powerful tool, he warned the Crow that 'with education you will be the White man's equal, without it you will be the White man's victim.'

As a spokesman for his people, Plenty Coups traveled frequently to Washington, DC, and was invited to the 1921 dedication of the Tomb of the Unknown Soldier. ■

Yellowtail Dam

Yellowtail Dam backs up the Bighorn River 71 miles into Wyoming, forming the so-called Bighorn Lake, the recreation and water storage area. Downstream are the power plant, spillway and afterbay that constitute the irrigation and power producing zone. A self-taught lawyer and interpreter for Chief Plenty Coups, Robert Yellowtail became the first Native American superintendent of his own reservatio' in 1934. He fought a seven-year battle

MONTANA

save his reservation from homesteaders in 1917, and then against the US government for 10 years to keep a dam from being built on the Bighorn River. The government won, but as a peacemaking 'Band-Aid' named the dam after him.

There are no official tours of the dam, but you can pick up a brochure from the visitors center and follow the concrete path behind the center to an overlook and elevator that goes down to the power plant level.

Fishing Fishing for trout, perch, ling and walleye in Bighorn Lake requires a boat. Ok-A-Beh Marina, 10 miles from Fort Smith Village, rents boats for $21 an hour including gas. The marina also has a limited grocery store and serves hot dogs and burgers on weekends. If you have your own trailer you can rent a boat at the Bighorn Angler (☎ 406-666-2233) in Fort Smith for $18 an hour including gas.

Fort Smith Village has some excellent fly shops, but most people associate fishing on the Bighorn with the area's oldest shop – the Bighorn Angler. It runs guided trips ($280 per day for two people) that include a boat, equipment, guide and big lunch. Other options are Quill Gordon (☎ 406-666-2253) and the Bighorn Trout Shop (☎ 406-666-

2375), which have similar packages and prices.

The four fishing access sites – Two Leggins, Mallard Landing, Big Horn and Three Mile – can be reached from Hwy 313 between Fort Smith and Hardin. Make sure to stay within the high-water mark to avoid trespassing on reservation land.

Hiking The only accessible, developed hiking trail is a 3-mile trail between the Yellowtail Dam Visitors Center and the southeast side of the Ok-A-Beh Marina. It follows a relatively flat, well-marked course along the canyon edge through a pasture filled with wildflowers, muddy natural springs, cow pies and mosquitoes. It does, however, have nice views of the water and surrounding canyon walls.

Places to Stay & Eat
Camping is restricted to *Afterbay Campground*, where tent and RV sites crowd the barren shoreline. They have a campfire program on summer weekend nights that draws a big crowd. All the northern unit's motels are operated by fly shops in Fort Smith Village. The Bighorn Angler charges $55/65 for motel units, $75 to $100 (three to five people) for a two-room cabin with a bathroom and kitchen. They also rent a furnished cabin on the Bighorn River for $185 a night, with a five-person maximum and two-night minimum. The Bighorn Trout Shop has units for $52/67 and rooms in an old cabin with a shared bath for $25/40. *Quill Gordon*'s motel rooms run $50 to $85.

The *River Crow Lodge* serves family-style meals nightly at 8 pm and 10 pm and is a great place to hear about the 'one that got away.' *Polly's Place*, the only other option, serves diner food for around $6.

PRYOR MOUNTAINS
Bordered by Bighorn Canyon in the east and the Clarks Fork of the Yellowstone River in the west, the Pryor Mountains run southwest-northeast from the Wyoming border to the northwest corner of the Crow Indian Reservation. The range is small and

---

How Bighorn Canyon Got Its Name
Crow legend tells of a young boy who lived with his stepfather near Bighorn Canyon. The stepfather was afraid that the boy's mother loved her son more than she loved him, so he took the boy hunting near the canyon and pushed him over the edge. Miraculously, the boy landed on a ledge and was saved by a herd of bighorn sheep.

The herd's leader, called 'Big Metal' because his hooves and horns glistened like steel, gave the boy his wisdom, surefootedness, sharp vision, strong heart and the honorable name of Big Metal on the condition that he return to his tribe and name the canyon and river 'Bighorn.' ■

low – Crown Butte (6885 feet) is the highest point – but has a wide range of scenery. Sedimentary Madison limestone underlies the range and dictates the landscape: at low elevations it's been eroded into desert formations and narrow canyons; thick Douglas fir forests cover the higher elevation plateaus; in between it forms rolling uplands dotted with sage. The nation's first wild horse range spreads over 32,000 acres of the southern hills and is home to stock believed to have been left from the Spanish occupation in the 17th century. There's also a bighorn sheep herd roaming about, but apparently it's very elusive.

Land in the Pryors is governed by the Forest Service, National Park Service, BLM and Crow Tribal Reserve. Roads out here are mostly improved gravel, but some require high-clearance and four-wheel drive; all of them become impassable in wet weather. Due to the lack of development, it's a good idea to have plenty of gas and water, and a good map (which you can pick up in Billings or Red Lodge).

There are no designated hiking trails, but old jeep roads are good for exploring by foot or, better yet, by bike (one with fat, nubby tires and plenty of gears!). Cross-country travel is relatively easy since the area is so open.

A good destination (and departure point for further exploration) is **Dry Head Vista**, where a parking lot atop a barren plateau offers a terrific view. To reach it, turn east off of US 310 on to Pryor Mountain Rd (about 2 miles south of the town of Bridger, 45 miles south of Billings) and go 15 miles to the Sage Creek Junction; continue east (the road is now Forest Service Rd 3085) for 19 miles, past Sage Creek Campground, a USFS campground with pit toilets, no potable water and $7 sites, to the Dry Head Vista parking area. From here you can continue along Rd 3085 to Wyoming Creek for a good short hike (along the creek on an unmarked trail), or turn southeast on Forest Service Rd 3092 and drive 3 miles to **Commissary Ridge** which offers miles of hiking and biking terrain.

MILES CITY

Except for the fast-food restaurants and chain motels near the highway, Miles City (population 8882) hasn't changed much in the past 80 years. Two-story brick facades with bright neon bar signs stand face to face along Main St; sprawling gnarled oaks shade streets of elegantly restored houses with leaded-glass windows and deep porches; and steep bluffs rise above the Yellowstone River on the north side of town. Just outside the town limits the prairie stretches as far as the eye can see.

After the Battle of the Little Bighorn, General Nelson Miles commanded Fort Keogh, from where he continued to launch campaigns to force the Sioux onto reservations. The post grew rapidly into a town sustained by hunters, traders, miners and prospectors on their way to and from gold strikes in the Black Hills. Cattle drives through Montana stopped in Miles City and established the town's position (which exists to this day) as Eastern Montana's primary horse and cattle market.

Orientation & Information

Travelers to Miles City used to know it as the point where the Tongue River meets the Yellowstone, but now it's better known as the halfway point on I-94 between Billings and the North Dakota border. US 12 goes east to the border through the tiny town of Baker, and Hwy 59 goes north to Fort Peck Lake and south to Wyoming. Maneuvering from one highway to another and from the highways to downtown can be tricky. Haynes Ave (Hwy 312), a four-lane avenue lined with strip malls, runs north-south connecting US 12 and I-94. Main St runs west from Haynes Ave, passes beneath the railroad tracks, cuts through the heart of downtown, bridges the Tongue River and becomes I-94/US 12 as it leaves Miles City to the southwest.

You need not look farther than Main St for most things, including banks, a laundromat and the chamber of commerce (☎ 406-232-2890), which has local maps and visitor information. The Department of Fish, Wildlife & Parks (☎ 406-232-1280) just west of the Tongue River Bridge at 3 W Main St, has fishing licenses. The main post office is at 196 N 7th St.

Things to See & Do
Miles City is a good place to stroll around, sit in coffee shops or bars on Main St and absorb Western culture from the people who live it day-to-day. If you're in town on Tuesdays, there's no better place to do this than at the **live cattle auction** at the Sales Yard just past Gerryowen Rd on W Main St.

Worth a look if you enjoy memorabilia, the **Range Riders Museum** (☎ 406-232-4483), west of the Tongue River Bridge on Main St, has an excellent collection of spurs and tack, Native American photos and a reconstructed schoolhouse. Hours are April to October daily from 8 am to 8 pm; admission for adults is $3.50, $1 for seniors and children.

More contemporary are the shows at the **Custer County Art Center** (☎ 406-232-0635), next to the Miles City Waterplant on the west end of Main St, which features regional multimedia art. The 'North American Indian' series of Edward S Curtis, who spent his professional life photographing the main tribes of the world, can be viewed by calling the center in advance. It's open Tuesday to Sunday 1 to 5 pm; free.

Once a military outpost, **Fort Keogh** is now a livestock and range research station funded by the USDA Research Service and the Montana Agricultural Experiment Station. Visitors are welcome to stop by Monday to Friday from 9 am to 5 pm. Take Main St (US 10) southwest of town.

Occupying 269 cottonwood-covered acres in the middle of the Yellowstone River is **Pirogue Island State Park**, 1 mile north of Miles City on Hwy 22, then 2 miles east on Kinsey Rd, a good spot for fishing, agate hunting, picnicking and spotting bald eagles and white-tailed and mule deer.

Special Events
At the **Miles City Bucking Horse Sale**, held the third weekend of May, bucking

horses meet a losing fate – either they are auctioned off to professional rodeo companies or to packing plants. Live bands, parades, street dances and a carnival take place downtown.

The last weekend of June, colorful orbs dance through the sky during the **Hot Air Balloon Festival**, which is growing in size and acclaim each year.

Places to Stay
Accommodations in Miles City are unexciting but cheap, with most along the highway strips. Luckily, a few mom-and-pop operations still stand. There's a *KOA* (☎ 406-232-3991) at 1 Palmer St, walking distance to downtown. Tent sites cost $18, RV spaces $22.

Four miles northeast of downtown on US 10, the *Star Motel* (☎ 406-232-9971) offers dim but comfortable rooms starting at $19/21 a single/double. Tucked among the motels on Haynes Ave, *Custer's Inn* (☎ 406-232-5170, 800-456-5026), 1209 S Haynes Ave, has an indoor pool and rooms for $40/45. Across the street, the *Days Inn* (☎ 406-232-3550, 800-525-6303), 1006 S Haynes Ave, charges $41/47.

The orange brick *Olive Hotel* (☎ 406-232-2450), 501 Main St, is a Miles City landmark, the hub of summer activity and undeniably the best place to stay for a dose of Old West ambiance. Rooms start at $31/41.

Places to Eat
If you're going to eat one steak in Montana, Miles City is the place to do it. *Louie's* (☎ 406-232-2450), in the Olive Hotel, and the *Hole in the Wall*, on Main St, are two good choices. The *600 Cafe*, right next door, is popular with the locals and serves breakfast all day; it's open from 6 am to 9 pm. The bar and tin ceiling here date back to 1883.

A good alternative to meat and potatoes is *New Hunan*, south of US 10 on N Earling St near Otter St. Their big dinner buffet ($8) includes soup and four entrees. Individual dishes are better prepared and cost $6 to $11.

There are several supermarkets open until 10 pm on Haynes Ave.

Entertainment

One of Miles City's most endearing attributes is its concentration of old bars. Lining Main St, the *Bison Inn*, *Trail Inn*, *Montana Bar* and *Range Riders Bar* stand as they have for the past 50 years and serve much the same type of crowd. The Montana Bar, at Main St and 7th Ave N is the best of the bunch with its original 1902 tile floor, printed tin ceiling, carved mahogany back bar and not a Bud Light poster to be seen.

The *Milestown Microbrewery* in the Golden Spur Lounge (☎ 406-232-3544), 1014 S Haynes Ave, produces 104 barrels of Milestown Pale Ale and several seasonal specialty beers per year. The adjacent Golden Spur Casino usually has a few on tap.

GLENDIVE

Glendive's restored downtown block, shaded by oak and chestnut trees, is a welcome respite for travelers making the long dusty drive to the Dakotas. Besides being the undisputed 'Paddlefish Capital of Montana,' Glendive (population 4557) is where people come to hunt for agate along the Yellowstone River and explore Makoshika State Park (see below).

The Merrill Ave Historic District, along Merrill Ave between Douglas and Clement Sts, encompasses most of Glendive's downtown which was built during prosperous railroad days in the early 1900s. The chamber of commerce has a detailed walking-tour map for real history hounds.

The Frontier Gateway Museum, 1 mile from downtown on Belle Frontage Rd off I-94 exit 215, has an exceptional agate collection, found locally on the Yellowstone River, and fossils and dinosaur bones, also found in the immediate area.

Orientation & Information

Glendive straddles the Yellowstone River just south of the Hwy 16 and I-94 intersec-

The Modern Day *Polyodon spathula*

There are only two places in the world where you'll find paddlefish – in the Yangtze River in China and in the Missouri and Yellowstone rivers in the USA. According to fossil evidence these unique fish have been around for 70 million years. And prehistoric they do look, with a paddle-shaped snout measuring up to 2 feet that helps the fish navigate through the murky rivers. An adult paddlefish can weigh from 50 to 160 pounds. ∎

tion. The original town center is on the east side of the river, while a modern shopping center is on the river's west side.

Two auto bridges span the river: the northern one connects Glendive to I-94 via Merrill Ave; the southern one hooks up with Hwy 16. Merrill Ave, which runs northeast-southwest, is Glendive's main thoroughfare.

The Glendive Tourist Information Office (☎ 406-365-5601), 301 S Merrill Ave, is open Monday to Friday from 9 am to 4 pm (to 5 pm in summer). The post office is at 221 N Kendrick Ave.

First Fidelity Bank at 319 N Merrill Ave, First West Bank at 204 W Bell St and Buttrey Food and Drug, 307 Harmon Ave, have ATMs. There's 24-hour medical service at the Glendive Medical Center (☎ 406-365-3306), 202 Prospect Drive.

Paddlefishing

In May and June, the Intake fishing access site, 17 miles north of Glendive on Hwy 16, attracts curious tourists and anglers. Intake continually yields more paddlefish than any other spot in the country. Since catching – or rather, snagging – a paddlefish involves no serious skill, paddlefishing is popular with armchair anglers as well as experts. A heavy line is dropped to the bottom and jerked along until, with some luck, it catches a fish by the snout.

Reeling in the fish is the hard part since they're big and like a good fight.

In order to participate you'll need a fishing license (sold at the site) and a 'tag' (which costs $8). The paddlefish limit is one per person (hard-core anglers can cross into North Dakota, which has a two-fish limit). Workers clean the fish in exchange for the fish roe, which they salt, package and sell as 'Montana caviar.'

Places to Stay

The *Green Valley Campground* (☎ 406-365-4156), a half mile north of Hwy 16 off I-94 exit 213, is dominated by RVs, which pay $14, though there are a few grassy tent spots for $11.

The motels downtown are a bit more ragged than those near the highways, but are convenient to restaurants and shopping. The *Parkwood Motel* (☎ 406-365-8221), 1002 W Bell, next to Eyer Park, is the best deal in town, with rooms starting at $20/22 a single/double. The *Riverside Inn* (☎ 406-365-2349, 800-283-4678), just north of the junction of Hwy 16 and I-94, is part of the Budget Host chain and charges $39/43.

The *Hostetler House B&B* (☎ 406-365-4505), downtown at 113 N Douglas, has two rooms, which cost $35/45 a single/double, in a restored 1912 house. Guests are welcome to use the hot tub, TV and sitting room.

Places to Eat

The standard array of fast food awaits those merely exiting the highway for a brief stop. For more home-style cooking combined with a bit of casino action there's *Twilite* (☎ 406-365-8705), 209 N Merrill Ave, a favorite spot for steaks. *Doc & Eddy's Casino*, in the West Plaza Shopping Mall, serves up burgers, spaghetti and steaks and has a full bar. *CC's Family Cafe*, 1902 N Merrill Ave, is recommended for breakfast and lunch.

MAKOSHIKA STATE PARK

The Sioux called the land 'Ma-ko-shi-ka,' which roughly means 'badlands.' Makoshika State Park, Montana's largest,

encompasses 8100 acres of hogback ridges, fluted hillsides, stratified canyons, pinnacles, caprocks and unique gumbo knobs, which extend east to the Dakotas. Because of its remote location, few tourists visit, but its odd and intriguing landscape thrills photographers, naturalists and hikers.

With the erosion of the Hell Creek Formation, fossils from the Cretaceous Period – 'the age of reptiles' – have been unearthed. The park's largest discovery came in 1991, when archaeologists found a triceratops skull in the southeastern corner. The skull is now on view in the park visitors center. Other fossils have been found of *Tyrannosaurus rex*, crocodiles and turtles.

Vegetation is sparse on the badlands' southern slopes, but those facing north are abundant with juniper and ponderosa pine, jackrabbits, mule deer, bobcats and coyotes. Prairie falcons, golden eagles and turkey vultures are also common – so common, in fact, that there's the annual **Buzzard Days** festival held in spring to honor the turkey vultures.

Orientation & Information

The park entrance is 2 miles southwest of downtown Glendive at the end of a route marked with green and yellow dinosaur footprints that begins where southern Merrill Ave veers left onto Barry St. The day-use fee is $3, while campers pay $8.

An unpaved road loops through the park, giving access to the campground and several picnic areas. The most scenic viewpoints and the real heart of Makoshika, however, are reached by hiking trails and dirt roads that become impassable with the least bit of rain. The park headquarters and visitors center (☎ 406-365-6256) is open daily from 10:30 am to 7 pm. A park guidebook is available for $2.

Hiking

Hiking Makoshika is rewarding but somewhat risky. Water (not enough) and sun (too much), plus the occasional prairie rattlesnake require hikers to be prepared and aware. The **Caprock Nature Trail** is a half-mile loop that skirts canyon walls and passes one exceptionally magnificent natural bridge.

For a good view of all that lies east, hike the first half-mile of the **Kinney Coulee Trail** which descends 300 feet to the badlands bottom. The short descent is a fine hike in itself and good entry route for extended backcountry trips into the seemingly endless maze of canyons and gullies.

Both of these trails begin from the park's main road and are shown on the visitor center map.

Places to Stay

Camping is permitted anywhere in the park, though an abundance of rattlesnakes and lack of water makes extended stays difficult. There is a campground equipped with water, toilets and tables about a mile from the visitors center.

EKALAKA & MEDICINE ROCKS

About 30 miles south of Baker, Ekalaka is the end of the road, in this case Hwy 7. Claude Carter, a buffalo hunter and bartender, was en route to a site near the railroads to set up a saloon when his wagon got stuck in the mud. 'Hell,' he said, 'any place in Montana is a good place to build a saloon.' So without traveling any farther, he built the Old Stand Saloon, still in business today.

David Harrison Russell homesteaded here in 1881 and married Sitting Bull's niece, Ijkalaka – Sioux for 'swift one;' when the post office was established he gave it that name, thus naming the town.

Ekalaka is not on the way to anywhere else: to come this far, you really have to want to be here, whether to visit nearby Medicine Rocks State Park or to view the dinosaur collection at the Carter County Museum. Virtually unchanged in appearance and mentality since the 1930s, Ekalaka embodies all that is lost to modernity – a slow gait, community pride and people who take time to visit.

Carter County Museum

Somewhat improbably, the Carter County Museum (☎ 406-775-6886) houses what is considered to be a world-renowned collection of dinosaur remains, including the world's only found remains of a pachycephalosaurus. The museum curator is a touted authority on US paleontology and plains archaeology. The museum is open Tuesday to Friday from 9 am to noon and 1 to 5 pm, and Saturday from 1 to 5 pm only; $3 admission.

Medicine Rocks State Park

Theodore Roosevelt wrote of what is now Medicine Rocks State Park:

Over an irregular tract of gently rolling sandy hills, perhaps about three quarters of a mile square, were scattered several hundred detached and isolated buttes or cliffs of sandstone, each butte from 15 to 50 feet high, and from 30 to a couple of 100 feet across. Some of them rose as sharp peaks or ridges or as connected chains, but much the greater number had flat tops like little table lands. The sides were cut and channeled by the weather into the most extraordinary forms; caves, columns, battlements, spires, and flying buttresses were mingled in the strangest confusion . . . altogether it was as fantastically beautiful a places as I had ever seen.

These 60-foot cryptic sandstone formations that rise out of southeastern Montana's rolling prairie like fingers clutching for the sky were sacred to Native Americans for their spiritual power and protection or 'big medicine.' Though the rocks are scribbled over by modern graffiti artists, it is still possible to make out engravings from as early as 1889. Most notable are a rosebud and dove carved by Herbert Dalton in 1904 when he lived out here as a shepherd for the Anderson sheep ranch near Ekalaka. Some geologists contend that the Medicine Rocks are sand dunes which turned to stone under their own weight. The most accepted idea, however, is that they are sandstone deposits left by ancient seas and estuaries. Over the past 50 million years, the uplifted rocks have been worn down – by wind, heat, the freeze-thaw cycle, intrusive tree roots – at a slower rate than the rock that has become the surrounding prairie.

The park encompasses 316 acres whose eastern border is Hwy 7. From the entrance gate (on Hwy 7, 25 miles south of Baker), a dirt road, impassable after rain, goes west 4 miles, past several picnic areas, to the park's western boundary. There's no camping permitted, but more than one traveler has managed to witness the light-play on the rocks at sunrise. No developed hiking trails exist, and the land surrounding the formations is flat and open enough to easily navigate.

Places to Stay & Eat
There are USFS campsites south of Ekalaka on US 323 – 3 miles to Ekalaka Park and 7 miles to McNab Pond. Both have toilets and potable water. Ekalaka is primarily just a watering hole, but the *Guest House* (☎ 406-775-6337) has rooms for $30/32. The *B&B Grill*, behind the Old Stand Bar, has good food for under $10 and is open until 10 pm. Across the street and next to the New Life Bar, the *Old Mill Cafe* serves breakfast and has buffalo on the lunch and dinner menus. A small general store has limited groceries and sundries.

Idaho

MAXINE CASS

Facts about Idaho

For many people, Idaho is synonymous with wilderness. More than 18 million acres of federally protected wilderness areas and national forests are in Idaho – only Alaska has more. Idaho's 3100 white-water river miles give it more runnable rivers than any other state; names like the River of No Return and Hells Canyon bring a smile to the faces of white-water enthusiasts around the world. Wildlife rare in other states – woodland caribou, forest wolves and wolverines – are still found here.

The Idaho wilderness may be protected from further mining and logging, but the incredible boom in adventure tourism – and the state's aggressive marketing of its natural beauty – threaten the wilderness ethos just as surely. The woods of central and northern Idaho ring with the sounds of hikers, white-water rafters, mountain bikers and skiers. The arid southern half of the state is a major agricultural area. Idaho's most famous product is the potato, but crops from mint to melons and marigolds grow in the Snake River Plain under mile after mile of rotating sprinklers. Idaho's physical contrasts are mirrored in its population. Social cohesion and a sense of purpose seem largely absent here. People can be suspicious of outsiders and indifferent to issues beyond their community. From the insular Mormon farm towns of south-eastern Idaho, to the trendy crowds on the streets of Boise, to the Aryan Nation headquarters in the Idaho Panhandle, there seems to be little that ties these communities together.

Idaho is not particularly destination-driven, as most visitors are traveling I-84 and US 95, the main east-west and north-south corridors. Those who do get off the interstate and spend some time are usually rewarded. Travelers find unlimited recreational opportunities here, and resorts, outfitters and guides to get you outdoors and

up a hill, through the rapids or down the slopes are everywhere. The scenery is spectacular and diverse, and the cost of travel comparatively inexpensive.

INFORMATION
State Tourist Offices
The Idaho Travel Council, a division of the Idaho Department of Commerce (☎ 800-847-4843, 800-635-7820), 700 W State St, PO Box 83720, Boise, ID 83720-0093, represents several state organizations. Callers can request the 'Official Idaho State Travel Guide,' a state highway map, 'Idaho State Park Guide,' the useful 'Idaho RV & Campground Directory' and information on outdoor adventure vacations, river flows and reservoir elevations. Idaho's state welcome centers are on I-15 near Malad City, I-84 near Payette and I-90 near Post Falls.

Idaho has several regional travel bureaus which provide more detailed information:

Southwest Idaho Travel Association c/o
    Convention & Visitors Bureau of Boise
    168 N 9th St at Idaho St, PO Box 2106,
    Boise, ID 83701 (☎ 208-344-7777,
    800-635-5240)

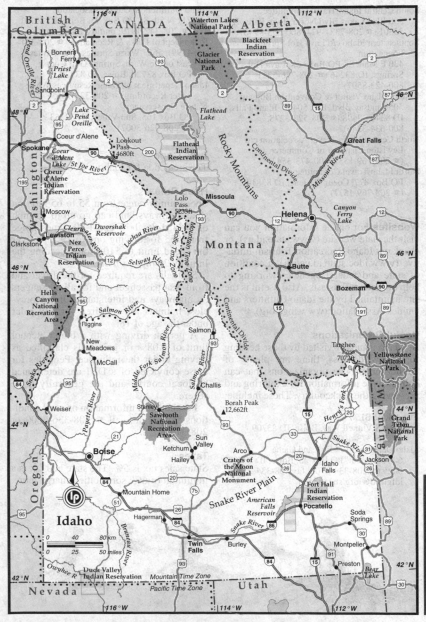

IDAHO

South Central Idaho Travel Committee
858 Blue Lakes Blvd North, Twin Falls, ID
83301 (☎ 208-733-3974, 800-255-8946)

Southeastern Idaho c/o Lava Hot Springs
Foundation
430 E Main St, PO Box 668, Lava Hot
Springs, ID 83246 (☎ 208-776-5221,
800-423-8597)

Eastern Idaho Visitor & Convention Bureau
505 Lindsay Blvd, Box 50498, Idaho Falls,
ID 83405-0498 (☎ 208-523-3278,
800-634-3246)

North Central Idaho Travel Association c/o
Lewiston Chamber of Commerce
(☎ 208-769-1537, 800-473-3543)

North Idaho Travel Committee
PO Box 877, Coeur d'Alene, ID 83814
(☎ 208-769-1537)

Websites For online information you can
visit the state website (www.state.id.us), or
check out Idaho Recreation Tourism Initiative (www.idoc.state.id.us/irti), a coalition
of state and federal agencies working to
help outdoor enthusiasts. Also useful is the
site maintained by the Idaho Outfitters and
Guides Association (www.ioga.org).

Useful Organizations

As Idaho is mostly visited by those heading
for the wilderness, there are plenty of
public and private organizations that can
help provide information for exploring and
preserving the backcountry. These include:

Idaho State BLM
1387 S Vinnell Way, Boise, ID 83709
(☎ 208-373-4000)

Idaho Department of Fish and Game
600 S Walnut, PO Box 25, Boise, ID 83707-
0025 (☎ 208-334-3700; fax 208-334-2148;
idfginfo@idfg.state.id.us)

Idaho Outfitters & Guides Association
711 N 5th St, PO Box 95, Boise, ID 83701
(☎ 208-342-1919; outfitt@aol.com)

Idaho Dept of Parks & Recreation (☎ 208-334-
4199), 5657 Warm Springs Ave, 4 miles
east of the Warm Springs Golf Course,
PO Box 83720, Boise, ID 83720

Idaho Department of Water Resources White-
water Recording (☎ 208-327-7865)

Nature Conservancy
PO Box 165, Sun Valley, ID 83353
(☎ 208-926-3007)

Area Code

The area code for Idaho is 208.

Road Rules

Speed limits range from 55 to 65 mph on
state highways, and can go up to 75 mph
on I-84, I-86, I-15 and I-90. Fines range
from $53 for driving one to 19 mph over
the speed limit to $108 for exceeding the
limit by 20 mph or more.

Seatbelts are required for the driver and
front-seat passenger and for all passengers
on highways and interstates. On motorcycles, helmets are required for any rider
under the age of 18.

A person driving with a blood alcohol
limit of 0.08% or greater is classified as
driving under the influence. Penalties for
those convicted of a DUI are determined
by local courts, and are generally quite
severe.

For the latest information on road conditions state-wide, call ☎ 208-336-6600 or
208-376-8028.

Taxes

State sales tax is 5%. The state bed tax is a
minimum of 6%; some cities charge more.

Snake River Plain

The mighty Snake River, the nation's sixth largest in volume, flows into Idaho from Wyoming at the Palisades Reservoir, and then through the verdant Swan Valley. The renowned Henry's Fork joins the Snake River just north of Idaho Falls. Here the Snake River leaves the forests of eastern Idaho and swings south and west onto the arid plains of southern Idaho, flowing through the American Falls Reservoir near Pocatello. At Twin Falls, it plummets over Shoshone Falls into a dramatic canyon and then flows through the Hagerman Valley. South of Boise it makes a northward turn into north-central Idaho. Following the Idaho-Oregon state line, the Snake River eventually merges with the Columbia River 1036 miles from its source.

Once a barren tract of lava flows, sagebrush and scorpions, this broad basin is now one of America's most important food producing regions. The Snake River Plain contains the majority of Idaho's population and is the center of its economy. Communities along the Snake River Plain serve the needs of area farmers and ranchers, and welcome travelers with inexpensive rooms and wary courtesy. Traveling across southern Idaho can be a long and grueling affair, especially during summer when temperatures regularly rise over 100°F and the pervasive irrigation projects boost the humidity toward 100%.

Southwestern Idaho

Southwestern Idaho is a patchwork of rivers, desert and mountains. Population centers line the Snake River and the vast agricultural region surrounding it. The Treasure Valley, known for producing sugar beets, extends from Caldwell to Mountain Home with Boise at its center. The region's

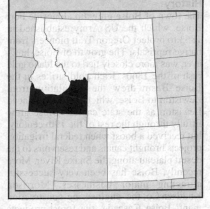

rivers offer world-class whitewater and its lakes brim with trout.

BOISE

Boise (boy-see; population 163,360) is an enjoyable city that manages to meld vestiges of the cowboy Wild West with urban sophistication. Much of Boise's vibrancy derives from the fact that it is the state capital, the state's largest city and home to a university. Boise is a worthy destination for travelers who enjoy a hip, easygoing city focused on outdoor recreation.

At an elevation of 2842 feet, Boise sits at the western end of the vast Snake River

IDAHO

831

Plain, which is backed up to the foothills of the Boise Front. The name Boise derives from the French word *bois* for 'wooded,' and the city does its best to live up to its billing. The Boise River Greenbelt follows the Boise River the length of town; this recreational frontage links the many city parks and civic institutions. Visitors find Boise easy to navigate. It has none of the scruffy, urban stress of big cities, and no undercurrent of crime or hostility. Much of its late 19th-century architectural core remains. Street life abounds: cafes and restaurants remain open late, and on hot summer evenings crowds from nightspots spill onto the sidewalks.

History

The town of Boise grew up alongside Fort Boise, which the US Army established in 1863 to protect Oregon Trail pioneers from native reprisals. The growth of Boise, however, was more closely tied to the Idaho gold rush of the 1860s. Rich gold strikes in the Boise Basin drew the population from Lewiston to Boise, which in 1865 replaced Lewiston as the state capital. Boise grew fitfully through the rest of the 19th century, but received a boost when federal irrigation projects brought canals and reservoirs to the desert plateau along the Snake River. More recently, Boise has been very successful attracting major businesses. Morrison Knudsen Co, the engineering-construction giant; Boise Cascade, the forest-products leader; Ore-Ida Foods; Albertson's, the supermarket chain; JR Simplot, the agricultural chemical manufacturer; and Hewlett Packard are all headquartered or maintain a large corporate presence here.

Orientation

Boise is along the Boise River north of I-84. The east access route from I-84 follows Broadway Ave and enters downtown along Front St. The west access is Hwy 184 (I-84 exit 49), or 'The Connector,' which follows Fairview Ave and enters Boise city center along Main St. Generally, numbered streets run north-south and named streets run east-west. Front St

How the Snake River Got Its Name

An Indian tribe in southern Idaho, now known as the Shoshone, used a hand signal resembling the motion of a snake to identify themselves. The term 'snake' became their tribal name and later the name for the river that flowed through their territory. ∎

divides north and south street addresses. Capitol Blvd, which replaces 7th St, is the main north-south artery. It runs south from the Idaho State Capitol across the Boise River to the base of the hill dominated by the Depot (see below). Downtown has an array of one-way streets. Streets in the older section of downtown Boise are a puzzle of grids that meet at often confusing intersections.

The main business and shopping district is between State and Grove Sts and between 9th and 4th Sts. Many restaurants and nightspots are in the downtown activity centers of Old Boise, The Grove and the 8th St Market Place.

Information

Tourist Offices Accessible and comprehensive tourist information is in the Information Center (☎ 208-344-5338) facing The Grove in Boise Centre, the convention center at 850 Front St. It is run by the Convention & Visitors Bureau of Boise (☎ 208-344-7777, 800-635-5240), 168 N 9th St at Idaho St, PO Box 2106, Boise, ID 83701, open 8:30 am to 5 pm weekdays. They have brochures on nine interesting Boise walking tours. The Boise Area Chamber of Commerce (☎ 208-344-5515; fax 208-344-5849), 300 N 6th St at Bannock St, PO Box 2368, Boise, ID 83702, has the 'Downtown Boise Map & Directory' and other publications. Visitor Information on the 1st-floor rotunda of the Idaho State Capitol is also helpful. The city also has a website (www.boise.org) that provides a wide range of tourist information.

DION GOOD

LEE FOSTER

LEE FOSTER

JOHN ELK

Idaho

Top Left: Snake River Canyon
Bottom: Wheat fields of the Palouse

Top Right: Ernest Hemingway's grave, Ketchum
Middle Right: Basque festivities

Idaho

Top: Storm breaks over Lake Pend Oreille   **Bottom:** Powdery Sun Valley peaks

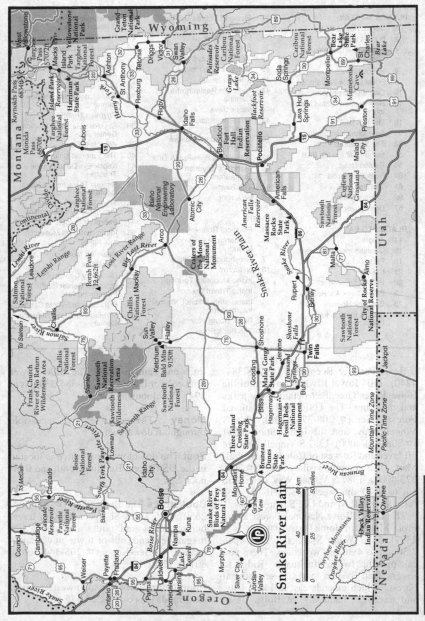

PLACES TO STAY		
1	Burton House B&B	
2	Budget Hotel	
4	Doubletree Downtown	
5	Cabana Inn	
8	Sands Motel	
9	Boise Centre Travelodge	
15	Owyhee Plaza Hotel	
16	Best Western Safari Motor Inn	
18	Idanha Hotel	
31	Americana Kampground	
32	The Statehouse Inn	
51	Idaho Heritage Inn B&B	
56	Reston Hotel	
60	Boulevard Motel	
61	The Boisean	
62	University Inn	
67	Boise River Inn	

PLACES TO EAT
11 Amore
15 Gamekeeper Restaurant
18 Peter Schott's
21 Noodles
22 Pollo Rey
23 Bitter Creek Ale House
25 Bangkok House
26 Louie's Pizza & Italian Restaurant

27 Flying M Espresso & Fine Crafts
34 Coffee-News
35 Brick Oven Beanery
36 The Piper Pub & Grill
42 Milford's Fish House
43 Koffee Klatsch
44 Cafe Ole Restaurant & Cantina
48 Moxie Java
49 The Renaissance Classic Cuisine
50 Rocky Mountain Bagel Bakery
52 TableRock BrewPub & Grill
55 Aladdin's Egyptian Restaurant
64 The Ram
66 Wok King

OTHER
3 Practical Rent-A-Car
6 Sixteenth St Coin-op Laundry
7 Greyhound Bus Depot
10 Neurolux
12 Idaho Mountain Touring
13 Idaho Travel Council
14 Idaho State Capitol, Visitor Information
17 Blues Bouquet
19 The Book Shop

20 Convention & Visitors Bureau of Boise
24 Post Office
28 Boise Area Chamber of Commerce
29 Idaho Outfitters & Guides Association
30 Boise Little Theatre
33 Boise Centre, Information Center
37 Egyptian Theatre
38 St Luke's Regional Medical Center
39 Wheels R Fun
40 The Emerald Club
41 Knock 'Em Dead Dinner Theatre
45 Basque Museum & Cultural Center
46 Tom Grainery's Sporting Pub, Grainey's Basement
47 Pengilly's Saloon
53 Idaho Historical Museum
54 The Flicks
57 Boise Art Museum
58 Zoo Boise
59 Discovery Center of Idaho
63 Morrison Center for the Performing Arts
65 BSU Special Events Center
68 Morrison Knudsen Nature Center

Boise Parks & Recreation (☎ 208-384-4240), 1104 Royal Blvd, has a map of the Boise River Greenbelt detailing its parks and museums. The USFS Boise National Forest office (☎ 208-373-4100), 1249 S Vinnell Way, and the Idaho State BLM (☎ 208-373-4000), 1387 S Vinnell Way, are off Overland Rd west of Cole Rd near Wal-Mart. Their common visitors center (☎ 208-373-4007), 1387 S Vinnell Way, open 7:30 am to 4:30 pm weekdays, sells a good selection of BLM and USFS maps.

The USFS Boise National Forest Boise Front-Mountain Home District (☎ 208-343-2527), 5493 Warm Springs Ave, is open 7:30 am to 4:30 pm weekdays. There you can pick up two useful maps: 'Ridge to Rivers Trail System' and 'Boise National Forest,' which extends east to Idaho City, and excellent handouts on Boise Basin

trails and campgrounds. The BLM Lower Snake River District (☎ 208-384-3300) is at 3948 Development Ave.

Money ATMs are readily accessible throughout downtown.

Post The downtown post office is located in the US Federal Building at 8th and Bannock Sts.

Bookstores The Book Shop (☎ 208-342-2659), 906 Main St, specializes in travel books, maps and books on Idaho. For magazines and out-of-town newspapers head to Coffee-News (☎ 208-344-7661), 801 W Main St.

Road Conditions For southwestern Idaho road conditions call ☎ 208-376-8028.

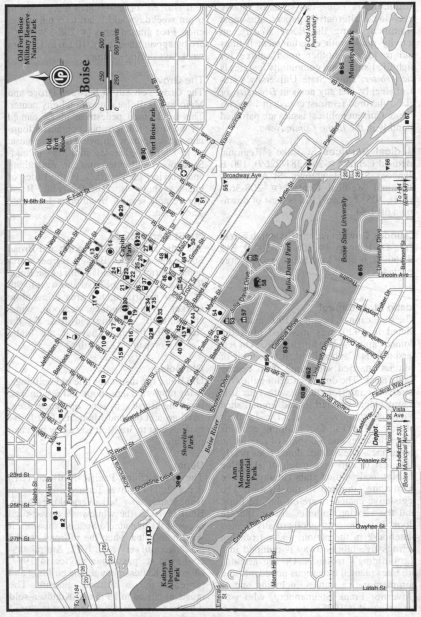

Publications Boise has scads of mostly free, local alternative papers, the most prominent being the *Boise Weekly*, an activity guide with entertainment listings and reviews. Another good source for nightlife listings and community features is the *Arbiter*, Boise State University's student weekly. Get gay news in *Diversity*, or Idaho-flavored feminist essays in *Women's Times*. Current political issues are parodied monthly in the *Idaho Comic News*.

Medical Services St Luke's Regional Medical Center (☎ 208-381-2269), 190 E Bannock St, is downtown. St Alphonsus Regional Medical Center (☎ 208-367-2121), 1055 N Curtis Rd, is west of downtown off I-84.

Laundry Downtown, the Sixteenth Street Coin-Op Laundry (☎ 208-345-3958), 215 N 16th St, is open long hours and has large machines.

Idaho State Capitol

The state capitol, begun in 1905 and completed in 1920, was modeled after the domed capitol in Washington, DC. On Jefferson St at Capitol Blvd, it was built of convict-quarried sandstone from nearby Table Rock. The dowdy exterior belies the handsome interior, faced with four different colors of marble and embellished with mahogany woodwork. The 1st floor of this 201,000-sq-foot building contains epic sculptures and a display of rare Idaho gemstones. The rotunda dome rises nearly 200 feet to end in a patch of sky blue emblazoned with 43 stars (Idaho was the 43rd state admitted to the Union). The legislative chambers are on the 3rd floor, and the viewing galleries are on the 4th floor. It is the only geothermally heated statehouse in the nation; water from hot springs five blocks away is pumped into the building's radiators. On the grounds are trees planted by various presidents and commemorative statues, including one of Governor Frank Steunenberg, who was assassinated in 1905.

It is open for self-guided tours 7 am to 6 pm weekdays and 9 am to 5 pm weekends. Free guided tours (☎ 208-334-2470) are by appointment only, 10 am to 1:30 pm weekdays during summer.

The Grove

The Grove, on 8th St between Grove and Main Sts, is Boise's unofficial city center. This brick-lined pedestrian plaza, named for the street it interrupts, contains a fountain and sculptures. Enjoying free live music (5 to 8 pm Wednesday mid-May to mid-September) and entertainment, sunbathing and playing hackey-sack is the order of business here most of the year. Boise Centre and several restaurants face onto The Grove.

8th St Marketplace

The 8th St Marketplace, at 8th and Broad Sts, is the center of Boise's former warehouse district. It extends south to the Boise River, east to Capitol Blvd and west to 9th St. Now gentrified, the area is a public market selling produce, seafood, wine, cheese, crafts, clothing and gifts. Try the 'Idaho Spud' candy bars at the Idaho Candy Company, 412 S 8th St.

Old Boise

Old Boise is a district of fine old buildings, many renovated into shops and restaurants, recalling Boise's bygone opulence. Centered around 6th and Main Sts, Old Boise extends east to 3rd St. It has a few bars and nightlife.

Depot

The grand Union Pacific Railroad (UP) depot, 2603 Eastover Terrace off Crescent Rim, stands on a hill overlooking Boise. Built in 1925, the whitewashed, red-tiled depot looks like an old Spanish mission. It was mothballed when the railroad ceased passenger rail service in 1971; Amtrak discontinued its passenger service in 1997. Morrison Knudsen bought the building and turned it into a railroad museum. The museum closed in 1996 and Knudsen sold it to the City of Boise. The depot is closed indefinitely, but the city hopes to acquire part of the original collection and reopen the museum.

Julia Davis Park

This lovely park fronts onto the Boise River and contains several important museums and a **rose garden**. The Julia Davis Park Bandstand is a popular venue for concerts; free rock concerts take place every Wednesday during July.

The premier museum in the state is the **Idaho Historical Museum** (☎ 208-334-2120), 610 N Julia Davis Drive, which provides an excellent overview of Idaho's rich heritage. Displays include good coverage of the region's Native Americans, Oregon Trail pioneers and the mining frontier. It is open 9 am to 5 pm Monday to Saturday and 1 to 5 pm Sunday; admission is free. Adjacent to the museum is the **Pioneer Village**, a collection of old pioneer buildings dating from the mid- to late 19th century.

The **Boise Art Museum** (☎ 208-345-8330), 670 S Julia Davis Drive, features permanent and traveling exhibits of visual arts, including an American Realism collection. It is open 10 am to 5 pm Tuesday to Friday, noon to 5 pm weekends; it is also open Mondays from June to August. Admission is $3/2 for adults/seniors and $2/1 for students/children (under 19). Admission is free the first Thursday of each month, when the museum also stays open until 9 pm.

In the middle of the park is **Zoo Boise** (☎ 208-384-4260), 355 N Julia Davis Drive, which boasts a large display of birds of prey as well as moose, elk and Bighorn sheep. In addition to traditional zoo favorites from Africa, there is children's petting zoo. Open 10 am to 5 pm daily, and until 9 pm Thursday Memorial Day to Labor Day, admission is $4/2/1.75 for adults/seniors/children (four to 11). Admission is $2/1 for adults/children Thursday.

The **Discovery Center of Idaho** (☎ 208-343-9895), 131 Myrtle St, is a museum of experiential, hands-on science popular with children. Check out the magnetic sand. It is open 10 am to 5 pm Tuesday to Saturday

and noon to 5 pm Sunday. Admission is $4/3/2.50 for adults/seniors (60+)/children (three to 18).

The **Boise Tour Train** (☎ 208-342-4796) operates city tours in open-air train cars from Julia Davis Park daily during summer, Wednesday to Sunday during September, and weekends only October and May; call for departure times. Admission is $6.50/6/3.50 for adults/seniors/children (four to 12).

The City Arts Celebration (☎ 208-336-4936) fills the month of September with special performances, films and exhibits; its Art in the Park (☎ 208-345-8330), a large arts and crafts festival, is held in Julia Davis Park.

Boise State University (BSU)

Across a footbridge from Julia Davis Park is BSU, Idaho's largest university. Founded in 1932, BSU only joined the state university system in 1974. Little historic or notable architecture is on the 110-acre campus but its setting along the Boise River Greenbelt and the quad-like symmetry of its red-brick buildings make for a pleasant stroll.

Basque Museum & Cultural Center

At Grove St and Capitol Blvd are two sites commemorating Idaho's Basque pioneers. The Basque Museum & Cultural Center (☎ 208-343-2671), 611 Grove St, tells the story of these Pyrenean people who settled in Idaho from the late 19th century onward; southwestern Idaho has one of the largest Basque settlements outside of Europe. The cultural center features language classes and a reading room. The adjacent **Cyrus Jacobs-Uberuaga House**, 607 Grove St, built in 1864 as a boarding house (Boise's first brick building) for Basque immigrants, is part of the museum. Both sites are open 10 am to 4 pm Tuesday to Friday and 11 am to 3 pm Saturday. Admission is by donation.

Morrison Knudsen Nature Center

The Morrison Knudsen Nature Center (☎ 208-334-2225, 208-368-6060), 600 S Walnut St, has a wetlands area and natural history exhibits, the highlight of which is an underwater viewing window into life in a simulated mountain stream. Outdoor paths lead along the stream to a wetland pond and a habitat demonstration area. The museum and underwater viewing area are open 10 am to 5 pm weekdays and noon to 5 pm weekends. Admission is $2.50/1.50 adults/seniors and $1.50/50¢ for students/children (six to 12). The stream area is open daily sunrise to sunset; admission is by donation.

Old Fort Boise
Northeast of Fort St is Old Fort Boise, a 466-acre park whose grounds are scattered with historic buildings.

Idaho Botanical Garden
The Idaho Botanical Garden (☎ 208-343-8649), 2373 N Penitentiary Rd, has nine theme gardens, including a Basque, Heirloom Rose and Butterfly Garden. The Meditation Garden seems an odd place, backed up against the walls of Old Idaho Penitentiary. It is open 9 am to 5 pm weekdays and 10 am to 6 pm weekends mid-April to mid-October. Guided tours are available 11 am Saturday June to August. Admission is $3 for adults, $2 for seniors and children (over five).

Old Idaho Penitentiary
Old Idaho Penitentiary (☎ 208-368-6080), 2445 N Penitentiary Rd, was Idaho's first jail. It was built in 1870 and used until 1974, when it was replaced by a new facility and turned into a museum. On the National Register of Historic Places, this creepy, fascinating and well-curated old prison shows how prison architecture and facilities reflect changing cultural notions of punishment and criminality.

It is open 10 am to 5 pm daily during summer and noon to 5 pm daily the rest of the year. A brochure describes a 90-minute self-guided tour through the prison yard. One-hour guided tours start at 10:30, 11:30 am, 12:30, 1:30, and 2:30 pm. Admission is $4 for adults, $3 for seniors and children (six to 12). From Broadway Ave, follow Warm Springs Rd east 1½ miles to Penitentiary Rd.

Boise River Greenbelt
The Boise River Greenbelt is a 19-mile paved hiking, jogging and biking path along the Boise River. It links many parks in Boise's extensive park system: Kathryn Albertson, Shoreline, Ann Morrison Memorial, Julia Davis, and Municipal parks; the BSU campus; Warm Springs Golf Course; and Discovery State Park outside of Boise. The **Pioneer Walk** near Ann Morrison Park connects the Boise River Greenbelt with downtown's Front St. At the **Natatorium and Hydrotube** (☎ 208-345-9270), 1811 Warms Springs Ave in Municipal Park, waters come from nearby hot springs.

Activities
Just minutes from downtown, the Boise River has a popular fly-fishing stretch for rainbow, brown and, occasionally, steelhead trout. Wheels R Fun (☎ 208-343-8228), on Shoreline Drive at S 13th St in Shoreline Park, rents rollerblades ($18), bikes ($18), rafts ($44) and inner tubes ($5). Idaho River Sports Sales & Rentals (☎ 208-336-4844), 1521 N 13th St, also rents rafts. Idaho Mountain Touring (☎ 208-336-3854), 915 W Jefferson St, rents mountains bikes ($23) and camping gear.

Special Events
The **San Inazio Basque Festival** (☎ 208-343-2671), held the last weekend of July, celebrates Boise's Basque heritage with folk dancing, music, food and special guests from Boise's sister cities in the Pyrenees. The popular **Western Idaho Fair** (☎ 208-376-3247), held in late August at the fairgrounds on Chinden Blvd, is a celebration of the state's agricultural bounty, with a carnival, rodeo and various farm products, livestock and garden competitions.

Places to Stay
Boise has a good selection of moderately priced accommodations. Try to stay close to downtown to enjoy the bustling evening streets. Reservations are helpful, especially when conventions are in town. Boise bed tax is 11%.

Places to Stay – budget

Camping *On the River RV Park* (☎ 208-375-7432, 800-375-7432), 6000 N Glenwood St, offers swimming and fishing in the Boise River. Tent sites cost $14; sites with full hookups $19. Head north 4 miles from I-84 exit 46, then east on US 20/26 another 4 miles, and turn north onto Glenwood St. Also near I-84 exit 46 is the *Fiesta RV Park* (☎ 208-375-8207), 1101 Fairview Ave. Tent sites cost $18; sites with full hookups $22. The attractive *Americana Kampground* (☎ 208-344-5733), 3600 Americana Terrace in Kathryn Albertson Park, has RV-only sites ($17).

Hotels & Motels Older places west of downtown include: *Sands Motel* (☎ 208-343-2533), 1111 W State St (singles/doubles $29/32); *Cabana Inn* (☎ 208-343-6000), 1600 Main St ($30/35); and *Budget Hotel* (☎ 208-344-8617), 2600 Fairview Ave ($35/40), with a sauna and restaurant. The *Econo Lodge* (☎ 208-344-4030), 2155 N Garden between Fairview Ave and W Main St, has singles/doubles for $40/47.

Another budget area is along Capitol Blvd near BSU. *The Boisean* (☎ 208-343-3645, 800-365-3645; fax 208-343-4823), 1300 S Capitol Blvd, has a pool. Rooms start at $32; some have kitchenettes. The *University Inn* (☎ 208-345-7170, 800-345-7170), 2360 University Drive, has a restaurant and pool. Rooms range from $42 to $64. Across the street is the *Boulevard Motel* at Ann Morrison Rd. The *Grandview Motel,* (☎ 208-342-8676), 1315 Federal Way, is a little isolated, but in a scenic spot.

Downtown, the *Boise Centre Travelodge* (☎ 208-342-9351), 1314 Grove St, has a pool ($42/47). Near the airport (I-84 exit 53), singles/doubles cost $47/53 at the *Super 8 Motel* (☎ 208-344-8871), 2773 Elder St at Vista Ave, and at the *Comfort Inn* (☎ 208-336-0077), 2526 Airport Way.

Places to Stay – middle

B&Bs Within walking distance of downtown is the *Idaho Heritage Inn B&B* (☎ 208-342-8066), 109 W Idaho St, a large home on the National Register of Historic Places. Rooms range from $60 to $85; bicycles are available. *Burton House B&B* (☎ 208-342-8033), 1033 W Fort St at N 10th St, is a 1905 Queen Anne home, six blocks north of the capitol. Rooms range from $55 to $65. The *Robin's Nest B&B* (☎ 208-336-9551, 800-717-9551), 2389 W Boise Ave, is a 19th-century Victorian home with rooms ranging from $75 to $95.

Hotels & Motels The *Boise River Inn* (☎ 208-344-9988), 1140 Colorado Ave near the east end of BSU, has a pool. Singles/doubles cost $50/55; some rooms have kitchenettes. The grande dame of Boise properties is the *Idanha Hotel* (☎ 208-342-3611, 800-798-3611 in Idaho), 928 Main St, a lovely 1901 Queen Anne hotel. Renovated without losing its charm, the Idanha boasts a good restaurant. Singles/doubles cost $50/56; ask for one of the turret rooms. The *Best Western Safari Motor Inn* (☎ 208-344-6556, 800-541-6556), 1070 Grove St, has a pool, sauna and Jacuzzi ($55/65). An original Boise hotel, the fully renovated *Owyhee Plaza Hotel* (☎ 208-343-4611, 800-233-4611), 1109 Main St, has a good restaurant and pool; singles/doubles start at $63/73. Singles/doubles at *Quality Inn* (☎ 208-343-7505), 2717 S Vista Ave, cost $50/56.

Near the airport (I-84 exit 53) is the *Best Western Vista Inn* (☎ 208-336-8100, 800-727-5006), 2645 Airport Way; rooms start at $63. They cater to rafters and other backcountry travelers who fly into remote central Idaho destinations. Anyone (including nonguests) can park a vehicle here for a bargain $2.50/day or $15/week.

The *Doubletree Downtown* (☎ 208-344-7691), 1800 Fairview Ave, is not as close to downtown as the name purports but is popular with business travelers and the well-heeled. It has a restaurant, pool and fitness center; rooms start at $77. South of the Boise River near BSU is the *Reston Hotel* (☎ 208-344-7971, 800-264-7377), 1025 S Capitol Blvd. It has a pool, hot tub and restaurant; singles/doubles cost $78/86. *The Statehouse Inn* (☎ 208-342-4622, 800-243-4622), 981 Grove St, is convenient to downtown and has a spa. Singles/doubles cost $80/90. The *Doubletree Riverside* (☎ 208-343-1871), 2900 Chinden Blvd, west of downtown along the Boise River, functions as a small convention hotel and has a restaurant, pool and fitness center. Rooms start at $104. The *Boise Park Suite Hotel* (☎ 208-342-1044, 800-342-1044), 424 E Park Center Blvd, also caters to business travelers and has a pool and fitness center; suites start at $125.

Places to Eat
Restaurants The *Brick Oven Beanery* (☎ 208-342-3456), 8th and Main Sts, offers outdoor seating on The Grove. The food is inexpensive (most dishes are under $5), hearty and quite good, ranging from salads to burgers and pot pies. For good inexpensive Chinese food, go to *Wok King* (☎ 208-345-1779), 2146 Broadway Ave. For Thai food, go to *Bangkok House* (☎ 208-336-0018), 624 W Idaho St. Entrees range from $5 to $8. The *Earth Food Cafe & Juice Bar* (☎ 208-342-7169), 2907 W State St, offers healthy, international vegetarian cuisine.

Cafe Ole Restaurant & Cantina (☎ 208-344-3222), 404 S 8th St in the 8th St Market Place, serves good Mexican food in a pleasant kitschy dining room, where the sound of fountains and the cool basement shade are welcome on a hot summer day. Seafood rellenos are a specialty; most traditional dishes are under $8, and the margaritas are good. Downtown, *Pollo Rey* (☎ 208-345-0323), 222 N 8th St at Idaho, is a good choice for a fast burrito (under $5). *The Ram* (☎ 208-345-2929), 709 E Park Blvd near Broadway Ave, is popular; try the fajitas. *Aladdin's Egyptian Restaurant* (☎ 208-368-0880), 111 Broadway Ave, features Mediterranean cuisine with belly dancing on Friday evenings.

Italian food is popular in Boise. A good inexpensive family place is *Noodles* (☎ 208-342-9300), 800 W Idaho St, with a wide selection of pasta, salads and pizza. Try Boise's favorite pizza at *Louie's Pizza & Italian Restaurant* (☎ 208-344-5200), 620 W Idaho St. *Amore* (☎ 208-343-6435), 921 W Jefferson St, offers outstanding, light Italian food – much of it vegetarian – with a trattoria atmosphere and outdoor seating.

Boise has many fine moderately priced restaurants offering both traditional and trendy food. Traditional Italian meals are served at the cozy *The Renaissance Classic Cuisine* (☎ 208-344-6776), 110 S 5th St at Main St. Favorites include chicken and veal piccata and pesto al pasta. Seafood choices (under $16) change daily. The *Gamekeeper Restaurant*, in the Owyhee Plaza Hotel, is a bastion of traditional American dining with tableside flambé and feats of carving presented in a stately dining room redolent of the 1920s. *Peter Schott's* (☎ 208-336-9100), in the Idanha Hotel, offers an eclectic, locally renowned menu ranging from dishes originating in chef Schott's native Austria to the cutting edge of nouveau cuisine. *Milford's Fish House* (☎ 208-342-8382), S 405 8th St at Broad St, offers a good selection of seafood, including fresh Pacific oysters.

Cafes *Koffee Klatsch* (☎ 208-345-0452), 409 S 8th St, is a central meeting place for caffeine lovers, with live music, a light menu and a friendly crowd. *Coffee-News* (☎ 208-344-7661), 801 W Main St, brews espresso to accompany its stock of print media; half a block off The Grove, it is a late-night hangout for Boise intelligentsia. *Moxie Java* (☎ 208-343-9033), 570 W Main St, is another central Boise gathering place, with lots of outside seating along Main St. *Flying M Espresso & Fine Crafts* (☎ 208-345-4320), 500 W Idaho St at 5th St, both artsy and homey, serves pastries, coffee drinks and light lunch entrees on mismatched thrift-store dinette sets. It hosts music in the evenings and has folk art for sale.

Grocery Stores The *Boise Co-op* (☎ 208-342-6652), 1674 Hill Rd, is Idaho's largest natural foods store and the place to stock up on organic groceries.

Entertainment
Cinemas Sit in the lap of the mummy and see first-run releases at Old Boise's

Egyptian Theatre (☎ 208-342-1441), 700 W Main St, a wildly evocative showcase from the glory days of movie houses. Nearby is the *8th St Market Place Theatre* (☎ 208-342-0229), 8th and Front Sts. For art and foreign films, head to *The Flicks* (☎ 208-342-4222), 646 Fulton St.

Theater The *Idaho Shakespeare Festival* (☎ 208-336-9221), 408 S 9th St, holds outdoor performances in Park Center Park mid-June to early September. The *Boise Little Theatre* (☎ 208-342-5104), 100 E Fort St, the *Stage Coach Theatre* (☎ 208-342-2000), 2000 Kootenai St, and *Knock 'Em Dead Dinner Theatre* (☎ 208-385-0021), 333 S 9th St, are notable regional theater companies.

Performing Arts The ArtsLine (☎ 208-376-2787) offers comprehensive information on Boise arts and entertainment. Select-A-Seat (☎ 208-385-3535) sells tickets for many events.

Most of the following companies perform on the BSU campus at either the *Morrison Center for the Performing Arts* (☎ 208-385-1609), 1910 Campus Drive, or at the *BSU Special Events Center* (☎ 208-345-3531), 1800 University Drive. *Boise Master Chorale* (☎ 208-344-7901) holds concerts in October, December, March and May. The *Oinkari Basque Dancers* (☎ 208-336-8219), an internationally acclaimed Basque dance troupe, performs at festivals and cultural events throughout the year.

The Esther Simplot Performing Arts Academy, 516 S 9th St, is home to: *Ballet Idaho* (☎ 208-343-0556), Boise's professional dance troupe; *Boise Opera* (☎ 208-345-3531); and the *Boise Philharmonic* (☎ 208-344-7849), which accompanies most of the above and performs its own concert series.

Live Music Rock bands perform upstairs and downstairs at *Tom Grainey's Sporting Pub* (☎ 208-345-2505) and *Grainey's Basement* (☎ 208-345-2955), 107 S 6th St. For Boise's punk and grunge scene, go to popular *Neurolux* (☎ 208-343-0886), 111 N 11th St. *Blues Bouquet* (☎ 208-345-6605), 1010 Main St, is the place for the blues. *Pengilly's Saloon* (☎ 208-345-6344), 513 Main St, Boise's oldest bar, goes acoustic on Monday but rocks out the rest of the week.

Pubs & Bars A happening place for drinks is *The Piper Pub & Grill* (☎ 208-343-2444), 8th and Main Sts, on a balcony above this busy downtown intersection. A few blocks away is Boise's best brewery, the *TableRock Brewpub & Grill* (☎ 208-342-0944), 705 Fulton St, offering many German-styled beers and ales and a wide range of good food. *Bitter Creek Ale House* (☎ 208-345-1813), 246 N 8th St between Bannock and Idaho Sts, serves local ales and food. *Harrison Hollow Brew House* (☎ 208-343-6820), 2455 Bogus Basin Rd, on the way to the ski resort, is a favorite for *aprés*-ski snacking and quaffing. Boise's busiest gay bar is *The Emerald Club* (☎ 208-342-5446), 415 S 9th St; the entrance is on Borah St. A happy mix of gay and straight people meet here to dance to old-fashioned disco hits.

Getting There & Away
Air Boise Municipal Airport (☎ 208-383-3110), 3501 Airport Way (I-84 exit 53), Idaho's largest airport, is served by five carriers: Delta Air Lines, Horizon Air, Northwest Airlines, Southwest Airlines and United Airlines. Delta Air Lines serves Boise with a dozen daily flights from Salt Lake City, UT. Horizon Air has several daily flights from Seattle and Spokane, WA, and Portland, OR. Northwest Airlines runs nonstop flights to Minneapolis, MN, while Southwest Airlines has several daily flights to Salt Lake City, Portland, Spokane, Las Vegas, NV, Phoenix, AZ, and St Louis, MO. Daily United Airlines flights depart Boise for Denver.

Bus Greyhound Bus Lines (☎ 208-343-3681), 1212 W Bannock St, serves cities along three principal routes: I-84 between Salt Lake City and Portland via Boise; I-15/ US 20/ US 287/ US 191 between Salt

Lake City and Bozeman, MT, via Pocatello; and US 95 between Reno, NV, and Spokane. Buses depart Boise three times daily for Salt Lake City (12:10, 2:25 and 9:40 am) and Portland (5:55 am, 3:50 and 8:50 pm).

Northwestern Trailways (☎ 208-336-3300), 1105 La Pointe, operates a daily bus route between Boise and Seattle via Spokane. Idaho stops along this route are: Boise (departs 9:15 am), Horseshoe Bend, Cascade, McCall, Riggins, White Bird, Grangeville, Cottonwood, Lewiston and Moscow. Their buses stop at Boise's Greyhound bus depot.

Car Boise is on I-84, which traverses southwestern and south-central Idaho, linking Salt Lake City to eastern Oregon via Burley, Twin Falls, Mountain Home and Boise. US 95 runs north-south along the length of western Idaho linking Reno to Canada via Boise, Lewiston and Coeur d'Alene. Hwy 55, a shorter route, heads north from Boise to New Meadows via McCall, where it joins US 95.

Getting Around
Bus Boise Urban Stages (The BUS; ☎ 208-336-1010), 300 S Ave A, operates local service. Numbered bus shelters are easy to spot on city streets, but those numbers do not correspond to the numbered bus routes. The BUS Transit Mall is along Main and Idaho Sts between 9th St and Capitol Blvd. Not all routes run Saturday and some route numbers are reassigned. Buses do not operate Sunday. Schedules are available at The BUS office, tourist offices and businesses. The one-way fare is 75¢; transfers are free.

A few useful routes follow. Warm Springs Bus No 1 goes to the Idaho State Capitol, St Lukes Hospital, Morrison Knudsen Nature Center and the Natatorium from Shelter No 4 at 9th and Idaho Sts. Vista Bus No 3 goes down 9th St and Vista Ave all the way to the airport. Roosevelt Bus No 13 goes to the downtown post office, airport and BSU from Shelter No 6 at 8th and Main Sts. The BSU Shuttle Bus No 19 loops the campus during spring and fall semesters. Federal Way Bus No 33 goes along Broadway Ave and Federal Way from Shelter No 7 at Main St and Capitol Blvd.

Car Avis (☎ 208-383-3350), Budget (☎ 208-383-3090), Hertz (208-383-3100) and National (☎ 208-383-3210) are at the airport. Alamo (☎ 208-336-1904), 2770 S Orchard St, is near the airport. Sun Valley Express/Idaho Car Rental (☎ 208-342-7795, 800-634-6539), 2393 Airport Way rents cars, vans and 4WD vehicles. Try Dollar (☎ 208-345-9727), Thrifty (208-342-7795) and Payless (208-342-7780) for cheaper rates. Enterprise (☎ 208-375-0004) delivers vehicles to your hotel. Practical (☎ 208-344-3732), 2565 W Main St, is downtown.

Taxi Call Boise City Taxi (☎ 208-377-3333) or Yellow Cab (☎ 208-345-5555) for a taxi.

AROUND BOISE
World Center for Birds of Prey
The World Center for Birds of Prey (☎ 208-362-8687), 5666 W Flying Hawk Lane, founded as a rehabilitation facility for injured birds of prey, also contains fine educational displays. Its three sections include an interpretive center, the California Condor Facility and the Tropical Raptor Building. Exhibits dispel myths about raptors and teach about the complex environmental requirements for healthy populations of birds of prey. Tours of the nursery (where

The endangered California condor

some rare birds like the peregrine falcon are incubated) and the rehabilitation center are given. The outdoor flight display stars trained falcons and an adult harpy eagle, one of the world's largest raptors. It is open 9 am to 5 pm daily March to October, and 10 am to 4 pm November to February; admission is $4/3/2 for adults/seniors/children (four to 16). Follow S Cole Rd (I-84 exit 50B) to W Flying Hawk Lane, 6 miles to the center. (Also see Snake River Birds of Prey Area later in this chapter.)

Boise Front

Northeast of Boise, trails network the mountains of the Boise Front offering many **hikes**, typically up barren gulches. An easily accessible trail begins behind the Old Idaho Penitentiary. The area, however, is usually too hot during summer for midday hiking. A short **scenic drive** up Table Rock Rd leads to the distinctive mesa overlooking Boise called **Table Rock** (3658 feet). Roads and trails also go to **Boise Peak** (6525 feet). The area is popular for **mountain biking**. Bogus Basin Rd continues behind Bogus Basin Resort (see below) to the USFS *Shafer Butte Campground*, the only campground in the Boise Front. A good topographic map for any activity is 'Off-Road Vehicles on the Boise Front,' available from the BLM (see Boise earlier in this chapter).

Fishing

Favorite fishing spots within an easy drive of Boise are: South Fork of the Boise River for rainbow trout; South Fork of the Snake River for cutthroat and brown trout; and Silver Creek for rainbow and brown trout. In Boise, contact Idaho Angler (☎ 208-389-9957, 800-787-9957), 1033 W Bannock St, for tips, gear and guided trips.

BOGUS BASIN RESORT

The Bogus Basin Resort (☎ 208-332-5100 ski area, 800-367-4397 reservations, 208-342-2100 ski report), 2405 Bogus Basin Rd, 16 miles north of Boise, offers downhill and cross-country skiing during winter. The resort (base elevation 6000 feet) has two downhill ski areas, Bogus Creek and Pioneer, with 45 runs and a maximum vertical drop of 1800 feet. The Bogus Creek Area has restaurants, lifts up Deer Point (7070 feet) and services at the Bogus Creek Lodge. Continue to the Pioneer Area for lifts up Shafer Butte (7590 feet) and lodging and restaurants at the *Pioneer Inn Condominiums* (☎ 208-332-5224; fax 208-332-5181); rooms start at $62. The resort has 17 miles of Nordic trails, a public race course, night skiing, sleigh rides, instruction and rentals. It is open 10 am to 10 pm weekdays and 9 am to 10 pm weekends. Full-day lift tickets cost $31/22 for adults/children; tickets for skiing from 4 to 10 pm cost $20/17. During summer, the resort offers lift-served mountain biking and miles of hiking trails. From downtown Boise, take Hays St north to Harrison Blvd north, which leads directly onto Bogus Basin Rd.

NAMPA & AROUND

West of Boise between Nampa (population 37,558) and the Idaho-Oregon state line is Idaho's principal growing region for sugar beets, onions, hops and mint. The area produces commercial vegetable seed, including radish, lettuce, onion, sweet corn and carrot, and has five wineries. Most people zoom through, but Nampa, a quintessential farm town, tempts the traveler to exit I-84. The downtown is dressed up with trees and flower boxes, and old storefronts have been converted into antique shops. The most imposing building in Nampa is the Baroque-style former UP depot, built in 1903, which houses the county museum.

Orientation & Information

Caldwell Blvd (Hwy 55/I-84 Business), the main road leading into Nampa from Caldwell, becomes one-way downtown at 3rd St S and 2nd St S, and turns northeast onto 11th Ave (I-84 exit 38).

Somewhat confusing numbered avenues run southwest to northeast and numbered streets run southeast to northwest. 1st and 2nd Sts are the main downtown streets; 12th Ave is the main cross street. The Nampa

Chamber of Commerce (☎ 208-466-4641, 208-466-4655 24-hour events line), 1305 3rd St S at 12th Ave, is open 8 am to 5 pm weekdays. The Idaho Department of Fish and Game (☎ 208-465-8465, 208-887-6729) is at 3101 S Powerline Rd. The post office is at 123 11th Ave S.

Things to See & Do
Downtown lends itself to a **walking tour**. Begin at the Canyon County Historical Society Museum, 1200 Front St, open 1 to 5 pm Tuesday to Saturday, and wander between 11th and 14th Aves and 3rd and Front Sts. Pick up the 'Farm to Market Agricultural Tours' brochure for self-guided **agricultural tours** with **wine-tasting** stops. Among the wineries around nearby Lowell Lake, the most well-known is **St Chapelle Winery** (☎ 208-459-7222), 19348 Lowell Rd, Caldwell off Hwy 55, 5 miles north of Marsing. Birdwatching and boating are the highlights of the **Deer Flat National Wildlife Refuge** (208-467-9278); take 12th Ave S to Lake Lowell Rd and continue 4 miles west to the refuge.

Places to Stay
The *Mason Creek RV Park* (☎ 208-465-7199), 807 Franklin Blvd (I-84 exit 36), has sites ranging from $13 to $19.

Rooms start at $28 at the *Budget Inn* (☎ 208-466-3594), 908 S 3rd St, and *Starlite Motel* (☎ 208-466-9244), 320 11th Ave N. Next to the fire station, the *Desert Inn Motel* (☎ 208-467-1161), 115 9th Ave S, has a pool; singles/doubles cost $35/39.

Mid-range options include the *Super 8 Motel* (☎ 208-467-2888), 624 Nampa Blvd at I-84 exit 35 ($42/46), and *Sleep Inn* (☎ 208-463-6300), 1315 Industrial Rd ($49/55). Shilo Inn operates two properties: the *Shilo Inn Nampa Blvd* (☎ 466-8993), 617 Nampa Blvd, has rooms from $55 to $59, and the *Shilo Inn Motel* (☎ 208-465-3250), 1401 Shilo Drive, has suites from $68. Both have a pool, spa and hot tub.

Places to Eat
Nampa offers a selection of good breakfast choices. *Say You Say Me* (☎ 208-466-

2728), 820 Caldwell Blvd, produces what surely must be Idaho's largest omelet – made with eight eggs! Fried potato dishes are another favorite. *Little Kitchen Grille & Bistro* (☎ 208-467-9677), 1224 1st St S, serves breakfast anytime. *Ranch House Steakhouse & Saloon* (☎ 208-466-7020), 1809 Karcher Rd, is an old-fashioned supper club with dancing on weekends. *El Rinconcito* (☎ 208-466-6963), 824 1st St S, is one of the better Mexican restaurants.

Getting There & Away
Bus Greyhound Bus Lines (☎ 208-468-8910) stops at 3116 Garrity Blvd, suite 11, east of town near Kings Rd. Daily buses depart Nampa for Salt Lake City, UT, via Boise at 1:25, 8:30 am and 11:10 pm and for Portland, OR, at 6:25 am, 4:20 and 9:20 pm.

Car Nampa is along I-84, 20 miles west of Boise (I-84 exits 38, 36 and 35).

CALDWELL & AROUND
Agricultural Caldwell (population 21,089) lost its town center to the commercial strip along Cleveland Blvd (US 30). Founded in 1891, Albertson's College, formerly the College of Idaho, is Idaho's oldest four-year institute of higher learning and produced many of the state's early leaders. Caldwell is one of the gateways into remote southwestern Idaho, a sparsely populated desert plateau that is home to large cattle ranches, old mining camps and US Air Force bombing ranges. The Caldwell Chamber of Commerce (☎ 208-459-7493; fax 208-454-1284) is at 300 Frontage Rd, PO Box 819, Caldwell, ID 83605. The post office is at 821 Arthur St.

Places to Stay & Eat
The *Caldwell Campground & RV Park* (☎ 208-454-0279) has tent sites ($11) and sites with full hookups ($18). Motels are plentiful near I-84 exits, but try the *Sundowner Motel* (☎ 208-459-1585), 1002 Arthur St at 10th St, for singles/doubles ($39/43) closer to downtown.

US 30 between Nampa and Caldwell is lined with fast-food restaurants and food stalls selling homemade Mexican food to agricultural workers. For tasty Texas-style barbecue, go to *The Armadillo* (☎ 208-459-1226), 4808 E Cleveland Blvd, which serves ribs, steak and smoked prime rib at reasonable prices. Downtown, head upstairs to pleasant *Acapulco Mexican Restaurant* (☎ 208-463-0007), 708 Main St, where the local business crowd has lunch.

Getting There & Away
Bus Greyhound Bus Lines (☎ 208-459-2816) stops at 1017 Arthur St. Daily buses depart Caldwell for Salt Lake City, UT, via Boise at 1:05, 8:10 am and 10:50 pm, and for Portland, OR, at 6:45 am, 4:40 and 9:40 pm.

Car Caldwell is west of Nampa off I-84.

MOUNTAIN HOME & AROUND
Mountain Home (population 8988) is at the western end of the Magic Valley, which extends east to Twin Falls. From Boise, I-84 crosses a flat stretch of native sage and shortgrass desert. Mountain Home, somewhat wistfully named, lies in the middle of this barren plain. It is 9 miles east of Mountain Home Air Force Base and is the trade center for the sprawling ranches that extend to the Idaho-Nevada state line along Hwy 51. Mountain Home has the distinction of having Idaho's highest mean temperature; summer highs hover around 100°F. Contact the Mountain Home Chamber of Commerce (☎ 208-587-4334) at 110 N 3rd St E, PO Box 3, Mountain Home, ID 83647.

CJ Strike Reservoir
The Snake and Bruneau rivers feed the CJ Strike Reservoir and form its neighboring marshes and ponds. Mule deer and white-tailed deer join the thousands of shorebirds, ducks, geese and raptors that migrate here. Marshes are closed during nesting season (February to May) in this popular fishing area. From Bruneau on Hwy 51, head west on Hwy 78 for 4 miles to the entrance, where a map detailing roads, campgrounds (such as *Cove Recreation Site*), boat ramps and shoreline access is available.

Snake River Birds of Prey National Conservation Area
The 755-sq-mile Snake River Birds of Prey National Conservation Area, established in 1980 and administered by the BLM, encompasses North America's densest concentration of nesting birds of prey. Stretching along 80 miles of the basalt cliff-lined Snake River, this desert refuge is home to more than 700 pairs of raptors, as well as red-tailed hawk, golden eagle, prairie falcon and great horned owl. From mid-March to late June is the best viewing season. Ground squirrels, jackrabbits, badgers and songbirds live in the riparian zone along the river.

Access to the refuge is from Kuna, south of Boise, or Grandview. Take Hwy 69 (I-84 exit 44) south 8 miles to Kuna, and follow signs 5 miles south on Swan Falls Rd. Alternatively, Grandview is on Hwy 78 about 17 miles northwest of Hwy 51 and 23 miles south of Mountain Home. The visitors center beyond Kuna and the BLM Lower Snake River District (see Boise – Information earlier in this chapter) has an area map and brochure, which suggests a three- to four-hour 56-mile **driving tour** of the refuge. A 10-mile **hiking** trail follows the north side of the Snake River between Swan Falls Dam and Celebration Point. The nearest campgrounds are along the CJ Strike Reservoir (see above).

This same section of river is popular for **floating**; contact MacKay Wilderness River Trips (☎ 800-635-5336), 3190 Airport Way, Boise, ID 83705, or Birds of Prey Expeditions (☎ 208-922-5285; fax 208-922-5286), 252 N Meridian Rd, Kuna.

Bruneau Dunes State Park
Some of North America's highest sand dunes are the centerpiece of the 4800-acre Bruneau Dunes State Park (☎ 208-366-7919). The dunes were formed in a bend of the Snake River after the Bonneville Flood. The river eventually receded, leaving a high-sided rocky bowl full of sand. The largest dune is about 470 feet high and

overlooks a small lake (the lake is historically recent, the result of an artificially high water table due to the region's ubiquitous irrigation). The area is popular with children and other youthful adventurers, who like to scamper up the dunes and roll back down into the water. By midsummer, the lake is unpleasant and filled with algae, yet children and hardened anglers persist in making the most of this desert lake.

The visitors center has interesting information on natural history and the dunes. A 5-mile hiking trail starts here. A campground ($11) with showers is beside the lake; be aware this is a very hot place in midsummer. The day-use fee is $2 per vehicle. Take Hwy 51 south 15 miles from Mountain Home and head east on Hwy 78 2 miles to a signed road, which leads 1 mile to the entrance.

Three Island Crossing State Park

This state park (☎ 208-366-2394) is where the main branch of the Oregon Trail crossed the Snake River. Three islands divide the wide river into smaller, more easily fordable segments. Pioneers who forded here continued along the more hospitable north bank of the Snake River. Those who did not were consigned to the southern cutoff, a barren and dangerous trail through blistering desert.

The visitors center offers a good overview of the history and hardships of the Oregon Trail and preserves original trail artifacts. The crossing here fostered a deep dread in the emigrants, as a sampling of pioneer diaries in the visitors center makes clear. Floating all one's belongings in a Conestoga wagon across the Snake River – even if it is divided into thirds – was a dangerous enterprise. A Conestoga wagon is on display near the visitors center, and it is hard to believe that people would attempt to cross the Snake – let alone the continent – in such a contraption. A portion of the Oregon Trail winds off through the park to disappear in the sagebrush; the easily visible remnants of the trail descend the steep hill across the Snake River from the park, where the crossing began.

A lovely picnic area overlooks the islands and a pleasant campground ($11) with showers. The day-use fee is $2 per vehicle. Three Island Crossing (2482 feet) is 26 miles southeast of Mountain Home (I-84 exit 120).

Places to Stay

Mountain Home KOA Kampground (☎ 208-587-5111, 800-562-8695), 220 E 10th St N, has laundry and showers. Tent sites cost $14; sites with full hookups $17. The *Towne Center Motel* (☎ 208-587-3373), 410 N 2nd St E, has singles/doubles at $24/40. *Motel Thunderbird* (☎ 208-587-7927), 910 Sunset Strip at US 30 W, has rooms with kitchenettes ranging from $25 to $65. Rooms at the *Hi Lander Motel and Steak House* (☎ 208-587-3311), 615 S 3rd St W, cost $35/40. *Best Western Foothills Motor Inn* (☎ 208-587-8477, 800-604-8477), 1080 US 20, has a hot tub, restaurant and rooms starting at $45. All of the above have pools. *Rose Stone Inn* (☎ 208-587-8866, 800-717-7673), 495 N 3rd St E, has rooms ranging from $45 to $85.

Places to Eat

Stoney's Desert Inn (☎ 208-587-9931), 1500 Sunset Strip, is open 24 hours. Go to the *German Deli* (☎ 208-587-2925), 190 E 2nd St N, for authentic cold cuts and potato salad. Another local favorite for Tex-Mex grills is the *Top Hat Southern BBQ* (☎ 208-587-9223), 145 N 2nd St E. *Chapala Restaurant* (☎ 208-587-6925), 650 N 2nd St E, is the best Mexican restaurant.

Getting There & Away

Bus Greyhound Bus Lines stops at Hiler's Conoco at 5th St N and 2nd St E. Daily buses depart Mountain Home for Salt Lake City, UT, at 1:05, 3:20 and 10:35 am and for Portland, OR, at 4:30 am, 2:25 and 7:15 pm.

Car Mountain Home, 41 miles southeast of Boise, is near I-84 exit 90.

BRUNEAU RIVER

The remote Bruneau River, south of Mountain Home, carves an often very narrow canyon, 60 miles long and 800 feet deep, through vast desert. The 25-mile Cass III-VI section from Indian Hot Springs (3790 feet) to Indian Bathtub (2580 feet) can be rafted in four or five days April to June and has camps amid juniper and cedar. (See BLM in Boise – Information earlier in this chapter.)

To book a white-water trip, contact: Hughes River Expeditions, PO Box 217, Cambridge, ID 83610 (☎ 208-257-3477, 800-262-1882; fax 208-257-3476); or Wilderness River Outfitters & Trail Expeditions, PO Box 871, Salmon, ID 83467 (☎ 208-756-3959, 800-252-6581).

OWYHEE MOUNTAINS & PLATEAU
The rugged and remote Owyhee Mountains give rise to the canyon-cutting rivers of the same name that drain spectacularly into southeastern Oregon. During spring and fall pronghorn antelope and mule deer can be spotted on the sagebrush grasslands. Wild horses roam open rangeland across much of the Owyhee Front. Birds of prey nest in the area, and native redband trout swim its streams. The area offers hiking, camping and in winter cross-country skiing and snowmobiling on maintained trails.

The **Owyhee Uplands National Back Country Byway**, a 140-mile two-day scenic drive, suitable for high-clearance vehicles, begins from Marsing, on Hwy 55 west of Nampa. Head south on US 95 to Jordan Valley, OR. Follow Flint Rd east to Triangle Junction and then head northeast over Toy Pass to Oreana. Take Hwy 78 northwest to Marsing. Hwy 78 follows the route of the southern cutoff of the Oregon Trail, along the south bank of the Snake River.

A mining camp established in the 1860s, Silver City was once a major Idaho town with the usual mining-camp mix of bar, brothel, brewery and bank. The spooky old hotel's dining room and bar are still open for business, though only roads suitable for high-clearance vehicles lead into the town, which is 17 miles north of Jordan Valley and 23 miles south of Hwy 78.

The BLM Lower Snake River District administers the area (see Boise – Information

earlier in this chapter). Rafters and boaters look for the 'Owyhee & Bruneau River Systems Boating Guide' ($5) for sale at BLM and USFS offices. Fill up your gas tank and supply of drinking water before driving through the area.

Rafting
The **Owyhee River** carves its way through the Duck Valley Indian Reservation and west along a high desert plateau into Oregon. The river's many forks, known for their extreme remoteness and wildlife viewing opportunities, are run during April and May:

Upper Fork – a seven-day Class II-V run through a scenic canyon.
South Fork – a run with long Class II-III rapids.
East Fork – begins in Nevada and flows through a deep gorge across southwestern Idaho past Bighorn sheep lambing grounds where mountain lions and raptors can be seen.
Middle Fork – a four-day 53-mile run with challenging Class IV-V rapids; the put-in is at the confluence, Three Forks (3950 feet), and the take-out in Rome, OR (2360 feet).
Lower Fork – a Class II-III five- to six-day run, with hot springs along the way, from Rome, OR to Lake Owyhee.

To book a white-water trip, contact:

River Odysseys West
PO Box 579, Coeur d'Alene, ID 83816 (☎ 208-765-0841, 800-451-6034; fax 208-667-6506)
Hughes River Expeditions
PO Box 217, Cambridge, ID 83610 (☎ 208-257-3477, 800-262-1882; fax 208-257-3476)
Wilderness River Outfitters & Trail Expeditions
PO Box 871, Salmon, ID 83467 (☎ 208-756-3959, 800-252-6581)

Places to Stay & Eat
Campsites range from $5 to $13 at *Givens Hot Springs* (☎ 208-495-2000, 800-874-6046 in Idaho; fax 208-286-0925), about 10 miles south of Marsing in Melba. It offers mineral waters in a pool or small private rooms. In Silver City is the legendary *Idaho Hotel* (☎ 208-583-4104), PO Box 75, Murphy, ID 83650.

IDAHO

Two good restaurants share this unlikely part of Idaho. The *Sandbar* (☎ 208-896-4124), 18 1st St E, on Hwy 78 one block east of Marsing from the junction with US 95, is a lounge and supper club beside the Snake River. The steak, fresh seafood and prime rib (served on weekends only) are excellent. Ten miles northwest of Murphy is the *Blue Canoe* (☎ 208-495-2269), another popular steak and seafood dinner house with a Cajun flair. Both restaurants are open for lunch and dinner.

FRUITLAND & PAYETTE

Fruitland (population 2963) and Payette (population 6647), on US 95 along the true left and right banks of the Payette River, respectively, are east of the Snake River, where I-84 crosses the Idaho-Oregon state line at Ontario, OR. These hardworking farm towns produce most of the country's frozen and processed potatoes and many of its onions. Most motels, restaurants and public transportation options are in Ontario, while campgrounds are in Fruitland and Payette. The Payette Chamber of Commerce (☎ 208-642-2362) is at 700 Center Ave, Payette, ID 83661.

Places to Stay & Eat

The *Neat Retreat* (☎ 208-452-4324), 2701 Alder St, Fruitland, has camp sites starting at $17. The *Lazy River RV Park* (☎ 208-642-9667), 11575 N River Rd, Payette, 4 miles north on US 95, has $10 sites with showers and laundry. The only hotel is the *Montclair Motel* (☎ 208-642-2693), 625 S Main St, Payette; rooms start at $30, some have kitchenettes.

WEISER

Weiser (population 5167; elevation 2120 feet) lies between the Snake River Plain and the foothills of the Rocky Mountains. North of Weiser, the Snake River begins its plunge into Hells Canyon. Surrounded by irrigated orchards, with handsome private homes and civic buildings, Weiser was home to the Intermountain Institute, built for the college preparation of rural Idaho youth. Founded in 1899, with a Christian,

slightly utopian bent, male and female students were educated together, and worked in school dairies, broom factories and bakeries. Discrimination by race or religion was banned. The institute closed during the Great Depression of 1929, and the buildings had many tenants before being developed as the local museum and the festival grounds for the Weiser Fiddlers Festival. The Weiser Chamber of Commerce (☎ 208-549-0452) is at 8 E Idaho St. The post office is at W 1st and W Main Sts.

Special Events

Weiser is known nationwide for the **National Old Time Fiddlers Contest**, which is held the third week of June and attracts folk musicians of all ages from across North America. The highlight is the crowning of the National Grand Champion Fiddler. In conjunction with the festival are a crafts fair, food concessions, a parade, a rodeo and a cowboy-poet gathering.

Places to Stay & Eat

Indian Hot Springs (☎ 208-549-0070), 914 Hot Springs Rd, 6 miles northwest of Weiser, has tent sites ($8) and sites with full hookups ($12) with a mineral-water pool (open to nonguests), a hot tub and showers. *Gateway RV Park* (☎ 208-549-2539), 229 E 7th St at the Weiser River Bridge, has sites with full hookups ($12) with a shower and laundry. *Monroe Creek Campground & RV Park* (☎ 208-549-2026), 822 US 95, 1½ miles north of town, has tent sites ($13) and sites with full-hookups ($16), along with a hot tub, showers and laundry facilities.

Rooms range from $32 to $60 at the *State Street Motel* (☎ 208-549-1390), 1279 State St. *Colonial Motel* (☎ 208-549-0150), 251 E Main St, offers kitchen units; rooms range from $28 to $66. *Indianhead Motel & RV Park* (☎ 208-549-0331), 747 US 95, has showers and laundry. Sites with full hookups cost $14; rooms start at $20.

Open 24 hours a day, *The Beehive* (☎ 208-549-3544), 611 US 95, serves reasonably priced lunch and dinner buffets.

CAMBRIDGE

Unassuming Cambridge (population 442; elevation 3840) is at the junction of US 95 and Hwy 71, which is the only road leading to Hells Canyon Dam (see Hells Canyon National Recreation Area in the Central Idaho Rockies chapter). When traveling north on US 95, Cambridge offers more comfortable and cheaper places than the often-hot Weiser, Payette or Fruitland.

Places to Stay & Eat

Hunters Inn (☎ 208-257-3325) and historic *Cambridge House B&B* (☎ same), along with a bistro and espresso shop are on Superior St. Hotel rooms start at $35 at the hotel; B&B rooms range from $40 to $70. At *Frontier Motel & RV Park* (☎ 208-257-3851), 240 S Superior St, sites cost $12 and rooms start at $28. *Kay's Cafe* (☎ 208-257-3561), on Superior St, serves breakfast all day. Their steak and homemade pies are excellent.

NEW MEADOWS

At the important junction of US 95 and Hwy 55 (and on the 45th parallel, the halfway mark between the equator and the North Pole), New Meadows is an inexpensive and pleasant town in which to spend the night. Contact the Meadows Valley Chamber of Commerce (☎ 208-347-2647) at PO Box 170, New Meadows, ID 83654. The helpful USFS Payette National Forest New Meadows Ranger Station, on Hwy 55, is open 7:30 am to 4:30 pm weekdays.

Popular with cyclists, pleasant *Zim's Hot Springs* (☎ 208-347-2686), 4 miles north of New Meadows west of US 95, has grassy but shadeless tent sites ($8) and sites with hookups ($13). Nonguests can soak for $5. The *Hartland Inn and Motel* (☎ 208-347-2114; fax 208-347-2535), on US 95 at Hwy 55, has singles/doubles for $35/38 and a hot tub.

BOISE BASIN

The timbered Boise Mountains and crystal-clear streams of the Boise Basin are bounded on the west by Hwy 55 between Boise and Banks, on the north by the beautiful South Fork of the Payette River, and on the east by Hwy 21 between Boise and Lowman. Two scenic routes lead out of Boise through the Boise Basin: the **Payette River Scenic Byway** follows Hwy 55 between Boise and New Meadows, via the Long Valley and McCall; and the **Ponderosa Pine Scenic Byway** (Hwy 21) goes northeast from Boise to Lowman, continuing on to the Sawtooth National Recreation Area (see the Central Idaho Rockies chapter).

Information

Contact the Idaho City Chamber of Commerce (☎ 208-392-4290) at Box 7, Idaho City, ID 83631. Contact the USFS Boise National Forest for information on hiking (they have dozens of one-page handouts describing trails), rafting and camping; rafters should ask for their 'Payette River Whitewater' brochure (see Boise – Information earlier in this chapter). The USFS Boise National Forest Lowman Ranger Station, on Hwy 21 east of Lowman, is open 8 am to 4:30 daily.

Idaho City

Along Hwy 21, 38 miles northeast of Boise, is Idaho City. Founded in 1862, Idaho City became a large city due to the large gold strike. Today it has historic buildings and a museum with gold rush memorabilia.

Hot Springs

Enjoy the hot springs with nearby USFS campgrounds along the South Fork Payette River. Six miles west of Lowman on Hwy 17 is **Pine Flats Hot Springs**, ¼ mile from the campground. The popular **Kirkham Hot Springs**, 3 miles east of Lowman, are at the edge of the river near the campground. **Bonneville Hot Springs** are 18 miles east of Lowman along Warm Springs Creek. **Sacajawea Hot Springs**, near Grandjean Campground and Sawtooth Lodge, are 22 miles east of Lowman; go 5 miles down USFS Rd 524 to Wapiti Creek.

Rafting

The Payette River is the nearest river to Boise with challenging whitewater. Its North Fork follows Hwy 55 from Payette Lake in McCall south through Long Valley to Banks on Hwy 55. Its South Fork begins in the Sawtooth Mountains and flows west past Grandjean, Lowman and Garden Valley to Banks. Banks, 42 miles north of Boise on Hwy 55, is on the Main Payette River, just below the confluence of the north and south forks. Several easily accessible white-water runs are listed below.

North Fork – two sections include a 9-mile Class I-III run from Cabarton Bridge (4700 feet) to Smiths Ferry (4490 feet) and the dangerous 16-mile Class IV-VI run from Smiths Ferry (4490 feet) to Banks (2790 feet).
South Fork – two upper sections include Grandjean to Canyon (Class III) and Canyon to Lower (Class IV); a 5-mile Class III lower section runs from Deer Creek (2950 feet) to Banks.
Main Fork – a 7-mile Class II-III run from Banks to Bee Hive Bend (2670 feet).

The South Fork sections can be combined for one- to three-day trips; otherwise all sections are run as day trips. The notoriously difficult North Fork below Smiths Ferry with its 1700-foot vertical drop is one of the world's finest advanced kayak runs; it is not offered commercially. The season is May to September, except on the Upper South Fork from Grandjean, where it is May to mid-July. Scenic campsites line the rivers, and some sites along the South Fork have hot springs nearby.

To book a white-water trip, contact:

OARS
    PO Box 67, Angels Camp, CA
    (☎ 209-736- 4677, 800-328-0290,
    800-346-6277; fax 209-736-2902)
    1127-B Airway Ave, Lewiston, ID 83501
    (☎ 208-743-4201, 800-328-0290,
    800-346-6277)
Cascade Raft Company
    Rt 1, Box 117A Rio, Horseshoe Bend, ID
    83629 (☎ 208-793-2221, 800-292-7238;
    fax 208-939-1899)

Headwaters River Company
    PO Box 1, Banks, ID 83602 (☎ 208-793-
    2348, 800-800-7238)
Bear Valley River Company
    Banks, ID 83602 (☎ 800-235-2327)

Places to Stay

Three USFS campgrounds are along Hwy 55 between Banks and Smiths Ferry. (See Hot Springs above for additional reference to campgrounds in the area.)

Getting There & Away

Bus Northwestern Trailways stops on Hwy 55 in Horseshoe Bend. Daily buses go northbound to Spokane, WA (9:45 am) via McCall, Riggins, Grangeville, Lewiston and Moscow; southbound buses go to Boise (7:05 pm).

Car It is 35 miles from Boise to Banks on Hwy 55, 35 miles between Banks and Lowman, and 71 miles from Lowman to Boise on Hwy 21.

McCALL

At the northern end of Long Valley, McCall (population 2876) sits along Payette Lake's southern shore, where the Payette River begins its course south to the Snake River. This pleasant year-round resort community – unlike others in Idaho – tries to minimize hype and glitz and maintain a relaxing pace of life, while offering water sports, great winter skiing and good restaurants and lodging. During summer, myriad colorful flower boxes line the streets and storefronts. The outdoor decks of bars and restaurants at the lakefront marina offer views of distant forested mountains. Public access to the lake is unfortunately largely limited to Ponderosa State Park (see below). Beware! Payette Lake is rumored to have a tourist-eating monster named Sharlie living in its depths.

Orientation

Hwy 55 enters town from the northwest and becomes east-west Lake St as it follows Payette Lake's south shore. Mission St divides W Lake St and E Lake St. Restau-

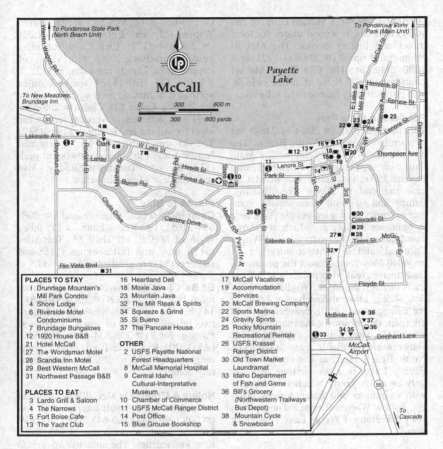

McCall

To Ponderosa State Park (North Beach Unit)

To Ponderosa State Park (Main Unit)

Payette Lake

To New Meadows, Brundage Inn

0   300   600 m
0   300   600 yards

PLACES TO STAY
1 Drunrdage Mountain's Mill Park Condos
4 Shore Lodge
6 Riverside Motel Condominiums
7 Brundage Bungalows
12 1920 House B&B
21 Hotel McCall
27 The Wondsman Motel
28 Scandia Inn Motel
29 Best Western McCall
31 Northwest Passage B&B

PLACES TO EAT
3 Lardo Grill & Saloon
4 The Narrows
5 Fort Boise Cafe
13 The Yacht Club
16 Heartland Deli
18 Moxie Java
23 Mountain Java
32 The Mill Steak & Spirits
34 Squeeze & Grind
35 Si Bueno
37 The Pancake House

OTHER
2 USFS Payette National Forest Headquarters
8 McCall Memorial Hospital
9 Central Idaho Cultural-Interpretative Museum
10 Chamber of Commerce
11 USFS McCall Ranger District
14 Post Office
15 Blue Grouse Bookshop
17 McCall Vacations
19 Accommodation Services
20 McCall Brewing Company
22 Sports Marina
24 Gravity Sports
25 Rocky Mountain Recreational Rentals
26 USFS Krassel Ranger District
30 Old Town Market Laundramat
33 Idaho Department of Fish and Game
36 Bill's Grocery (Northwestern Trailways Bus Depot)
38 Mountain Cycle & Snowboard

McCall Airport

To Cascade

rants and stores are diffused along Lake St. Downtown, Hwy 55 turns south and becomes N 3rd St.

Information

The McCall Chamber of Commerce (☎ 208-634-7631), 1001 State St, is in a log building one block south of W Lake St. The Central Idaho Cultural Center-Interpretative Museum is at this historic site.

The USFS Payette National Forest headquarters (☎ 208-634-0700), 804 W Lakeside Ave, is open 7:30 am to 4:30 pm weekdays. Detailed hiking, fishing and mountain biking information is more readily avail-

able from the two USFS Payette National Forest offices: McCall Ranger District (☎ 208-634-0400), 102 W Lake St at Mission St; and Forest Krassel Ranger District (☎ 208-634-0600), 500 N Mission St. They sell topographic maps ($4) of the McCall and Krassel districts, which include the Frank Church River of No Return Wilderness Area. The Idaho Department of Fish and Game (☎ 208-634-8137) is at 555 Deinhard Lane.

The post office is at 216 Lenora at 2nd St; the zip code is 83638. Mail Boxes Etc (☎ 208-634-5600; fax 208-634-5757) provides fax services. Blue Grouse Bookshop

IDAHO

(☎ 208-634-2434) in McCall Drug, at 2nd and Lenora Sts, is a good source for local travel and history books. The McCall Memorial Hospital (☎ 208-634-2221) is at 1000 State St. The Old Town Market Laundromat, 507 N 3rd St at Colorado St, also issues fishing licenses and sells bait.

Ponderosa State Park

This lakeside park (☎ 208-634-2164) has two units: Main and North Beach. The day-use fee is $3 per vehicle. The Main Unit, on a peninsula extending into Payette Lake, is 2 miles east of McCall near the end of Davis Ave. Boating, fishing and swimming are popular summer pastimes. In winter, people flock here to build ice sculptures, which are showcased during the February Annual Winter Carnival, and to cross-country ski. A graveled loop road crowns the peninsula, leading to great viewpoints and hiking trails through the forest. Wildlife is abundant – deer make themselves at home in the campground, while beavers, fox and elk roam the meadows and marshes. Tent sites ($12), sites with hookups ($16) and showers are available year-round. The North Beach Unit, at the north end of Payette Lake, is a summertime, day-use only area. Its sandy beach is a favorite with swimmers and nonmotorized boaters. Follow Warren Wagon Rd north from Hwy 55 along Payette Lake's western shore.

Activities

Canyons Inc (☎ 208-634-4303), PO Box 823, McCall, ID 83638, provides information on floating and fishing, and offers boating and kayaking trips on Payette Lake. Sports Marina (☎ 208-634-8361), 1300 E Lake St, also rents boats. Gravity Sports (☎ 208-634-8530), 503 Pine St, sells and rents gear, including bicycles, kayaks and canoes. Mountain Cycle & Snowboard (☎ 208-634-6333), 212 N 3rd St, rents mountain bikes. Rocky Mountain Recreational Rentals (☎ 208-634-4646), 1304 Roosevelt Ave, rents kayaks, windsurfers and other boats. Ya-Hoo Corrals

(☎ 208-634-3360, 888-562-5772), Warren Wagon Rd, and Epley's Horse Rides (☎ 208-634-5173), Lick Creek Rd, offer guided horseback rides with views of Payette Lake. Hourly rates start at $12.

Little Ski Hill (5324 feet), 3 miles northwest of McCall on Hwy 55, is run by the Payette Lakes Ski Club (☎ 208-634-5691). Its 405 feet of vertical terrain are ideal for Alpine and telemark skiers ($12). The ski area features 25 km of groomed Nordic trails ($6) and a snowboard park ($12). It is open Tuesday to Sunday. (Also see Brundage Mountain below.)

Places to Stay

Camping McCall Campground (☎ 208-634-5165), 190 Krahn Lane, is 1½ miles south of McCall off Hwy 55. Tent sites ($12), sites with full hookups ($16) and showers ($4) are available year-round.

B&Bs Close to downtown is the three-room 1920 House B&B (☎ 208-634-4661), 143 E Lake St ($70). Nestled amid pines two minutes south of town, Northwest Passage B&B (☎ 208-634-5349, 800-597-6658), 201 Rio Vista Blvd, offers rooms ranging from $65 to $85 in a contemporary home.

Hotels & Motels On McCall's western end is the charming and well-run Brundage Inn (☎ 208-634-2344, 800-643-2009), 1005 W Lake St. Its clean rooms start at $45; some have kitchenettes. The attractive Riverside Motel Condominiums (☎ 208-634-5610, 800-326-5610), 400 W Lake St, is along the banks of the Payette River. Singles/doubles cost $40/45; some have kitchenettes. Condos start at $75. Brundage Bungalows (☎ 208-634-8573), 308 W Lake St, are refurbished cabins set among trees. They come with kitchenettes and range from $55 to $90. Singles/doubles at the friendly and well-shaded Scandia Inn Motel (☎ 208-634-7394), 401 N 3rd St, cost $46/50. Across the street, less-desirable rooms at The Woodsman Motel (☎ 208-634-7671), 402 N 3rd St, cost $42/52. The Best Western McCall (☎ 208-634-6300) is at 415 N 3rd St.

Hotel McCall (☎ 208-634-8105; fax 208-634-8755), 1101 N 3rd St, is a charming remodeled property with a great downtown location near the lake. The individually decorated rooms start at $70. The elegant *Shore Lodge* (☎ 208-634-2244, 800-657-6464), 501 W Lake St, has a beautiful log and stone foyer and dining room with two restaurants, recreational facilities, a hot tub and sauna. Streetside rooms start at $89; lakeside suites start at $149.

Four miles north of McCall is the friendly, peaceful *Bear Creek Lodge* (☎ 208-634-3551, 800-634-2327; fax 208-634-4299), Hwy 55 mile marker 149, with 65 acres adjacent to national forest land. Their fully-equipped lodge rooms cost $120; cabins cost $150. (Also see New Meadows earlier in this chapter.)

Long-Term Rentals McCall Vacations (☎ 208-634-7056, 800-799-3880), 317 E Lake St, and Accommodation Services (☎ 208-634-7766, 800-551-8234; fax 208-634-7766), 1008 N 3rd St, have furnished condominiums and cabins with kitchens starting at $80. Rentals at the lakeside *Brundage Mountain's Mill Park Condos* (☎ 208-634-4151, 800-888-7544), 1410 Mill Rd near Ponderosa State Park, range from $95 to $160. The downtown *Fircrest Condominiums* (☎ 208-634-4528) have kitchens and ski lockers. Some rentals include ski packages.

Places to Eat
Start the day with espresso and pastries at *Mountain Java* (☎ 208-634-2027), 501 Pine St, or *Moxie Java* (☎ 208-632-3607), 312 E Lake St. For a heartier breakfast, head to *The Pancake House* (☎ 208-634-5849), 209 N 3rd St. *Squeeze & Grind* (☎ 208-634-2247), 337 Deinhard Lane, is a relaxing juice and espresso bar with outstanding smoothies, quiches, and desserts. The *Heartland Deli*, on E Lake St in the McCall Mall, serves muffins and bagels, and sandwiches on their terrace overlooking the lake.

The *Fort Boise Cafe* (☎ 208-634-8551), 406 W Lake St, has homestyle family dining. *Lardo Grill & Saloon* (☎ 208-634-

8191), 600 Lake St, serves pasta, steak and hamburgers ($8 to $12); the bar is the local favorite. *The Yacht Club* (☎ 208-634-5649), 203 E Lake St, has a substantial American and Italian menu served in a lakefront dining room. Most pasta dishes are under $10. *Si Bueno* (☎ 208-634-2128), 335 Deinhard Lane, is the place of choice for Mexican food. *McCall Brewing Company* (☎ 208-634-2333), 809 N 3rd St, serves hand-crafted ales, homemade soup and salad, and tasty burgers and sandwiches.

The Mill Steak & Spirits (☎ 208-634-7683), Hwy 55 at Stibnite St, is the premier steak house with prices to match. McCall's finest dining room is the Shore Lodge's *The Narrows* where tables set with linen and crystal overlook Payette Lake. The menu features five unique daily selections, such as loin of elk with forest mushrooms. Seating is on a first-come, first-served basis.

Getting There & Away
Air The McCall airport is south of town at Hwy 55 and Deinhard Lane. Private air transport companies operate one- to eight-passenger, nonscheduled intercity and charter flights from McCall throughout central Idaho. Most charge an hourly rate for charter backcountry flights. Many, however, offer a fixed per-seat fare with a two-passenger minimum for certain intercity flights. McCall Air Taxi (☎ 208-634-7137, 800-992-6559) has fixed per-seat fares for Boise-McCall ($63); charter flights cost $195/hour (for example, McCall-Stanley or McCall-Salmon). Boise-based Access Air (☎ 800-307-4984) also has fixed per-seat fares for Boise-McCall ($65); charter flights cost $155/hour. Pioneer Air Service (☎ 208-634-5445, 208-634-7127) operates Boise-McCall charter flights for about $200.

Bus Northwestern Trailways stops at Bill's Grocery (☎ 208-634-2340), 147 N 3rd St. Daily buses go northbound (11:45 am) to Spokane, WA, via Riggins, Grangeville, Lewiston and Moscow; southbound buses (5:15 pm) go to Boise via Cascade and

IDAHO

Horseshoe Bend. The one-way fare is $15 to Boise and $21 to Lewiston.

Car McCall, on Hwy 55, is 28 miles north of Cascade and 12 miles southeast of New Meadows at the junction of Hwy 55 and US 95.

BRUNDAGE MOUNTAIN

Brundage Mountain (☎ 208-634-4151 or 800-888-7544 office, 208-634-7462 ski area), PO Box 1062, McCall, ID 83638, noted for producing Olympic skiers, has 28 runs with a maximum vertical drop of 1800 feet over 2 miles. Base elevation is 5840 feet. Full-day lift tickets cost $29 for adults; $24 after 1 pm. Full-day tickets cost $24/17 for teens/children (seven to 11); $19/14 after 1 pm. Children under seven ski free. Brundage Mountain Ski Cats (☎ 800-888-7544) offers guided back-country skiing on otherwise inaccessible slopes adjacent to the ski area. The Brundage Mountain Ski School and Brundage Mountain Rental & Ski Shop offer equipment rentals and instruction. The ski season is mid-November to mid-April. Call ☎ 208-634-7669 or 888-255-7669 for a snow report.

Brundage is also popular during summer for its outdoor concerts, hiking and biking. It has 15 miles of single-track mountain bike trails and lift-served mountain biking. The resort is open 9:30 am to 4:30 pm daily. It is 4 miles east of Hwy 55 and 4 miles north of McCall. The *Brundage Mountain Restaurant* (☎ 208-634-7462), in the day lodge, serves breakfast and lunch.

South-Central Idaho

Spectacular natural features are the secret of south-central Idaho's appeal. The region boasts a waterfall taller than Niagara Falls, a prime rock-climbing area, underground rivers issuing forth from canyon walls, expansive grasslands and ancient fossils found nowhere else.

TWIN FALLS

Twin Falls (population 32,660; elevation 3747 feet), the hub of the Magic Valley, is a sprawling farm and ranch center that locals affectionately call 'Twin.' Along the Snake River, which forms the town's northern border, are two remarkable waterfalls: Shoshone Falls; and to the east, the town's namesake, Twin Falls. Perrine Bridge on US 93 (from I-84 exit 173 go south 3 miles on US 93 toward town) is the best place to view the impressive Snake River Canyon. Just east of the bridge was where daredevil Evel Knievel attempted to jump the canyon aboard a rocket-powered motorcycle in 1974. Twin Falls is a convenient jumping-off point for nearby destinations, as well as Craters of the Moon National Monument, Sun Valley and the Sawtooth National Recreation Area (see the Central Idaho Rockies chapter).

Orientation

Twin Falls is 6 miles south of I-84 along US 93, south of the Snake River. In Twin Falls, US 93 follows Blue Lakes Blvd south and turns west onto Addison Ave (US 30). Blue Lake Blvd divides east-west street addresses; Shoshone St divides north-south ones. Twin Falls' easily overlooked older downtown, which is removed from these two commercial strips, follows Shoshone St from the junction of Blue Lakes Blvd and Addison Ave. Downtown's numbered avenues run northwest to southeast, intersecting with numbered streets that run southwest to northeast. Shoshone St replaces 1st St downtown. Washington St (Hwy 74) leads south to the airport.

Information

The Twin Falls Chamber of Commerce and South Central Idaho Travel Committee (☎ 208-733-3974, 800-255-8946), 858 Blue Lakes Blvd N, is open 8 am to 5 pm weekdays. The Buzz Langdon visitors center (☎ 208-734-9531), on the west side of US 93 south of Perrine Bridge at the Snake River Canyon viewing area, is open 8 am to 8 pm daily. One-page South Central Idaho handouts detail hundreds of

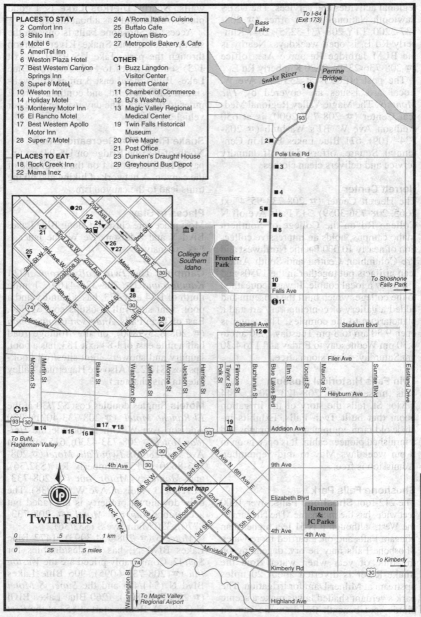

PLACES TO STAY

2 Comfort Inn
3 Shilo Inn
4 Motel 6
5 AmeriTel Inn
6 Weston Plaza Hotel
7 Best Western Canyon
   Springs Inn
8 Super 8 Motel
10 Weston Inn
14 Holiday Motel
15 Monterey Motor Inn
16 El Rancho Motel
17 Best Western Apollo
   Motor Inn
28 Super 7 Motel

PLACES TO EAT

18 Rock Creek Inn
22 Mama Inez

24 A'Roma Italian Cuisine
25 Buffalo Cafe
26 Uptown Bistro
27 Metropolis Bakery & Cafe

OTHER

1 Buzz Langdon
   Visitor Center
9 Herrett Center
11 Chamber of Commerce
12 BJ's Washtub
13 Magic Valley Regional
   Medical Center
19 Twin Falls Historical
   Museum
20 Dive Magic
21 Post Office
23 Dunken's Draught House
29 Greyhound Bus Depot

Twin Falls

IDAHO

regional activities and services. The USFS Sawtooth National Forest office (☎ 208-737-3200, TTY 208-731-3235), 2647 Kimberly Rd E, is open weekdays. Nearby is the BLM Jarbidge Resource Area office (☎ 208-736-2350), 2620 Kimberly Rd E.

The post office is at 253 2nd Ave W. Local arts issues are covered by *The Monthly*. The Magic Valley Regional Medical Center (☎ 208-737-2000) is at 650 Addison Ave W. BJ's Washtub (☎ 208-734-3109), 671 Blue Lakes Blvd in Centennial Square, offers drop-off laundry service and delivers clean clothes.

Herrett Center
The Herrett Center (☎ 208-733-9554 ext 2665, 208-736-3059), 315 Falls Ave off N College Rd on the College of Southern Idaho campus, holds an impressive collection of nearly 10,000 Pacific Northwest and Pre-Columbian Central and South American artifacts put together in the 1950s and 1960s by a local couple. It was bequeathed to the college, which built the museum and added a gallery of contemporary art and a planetarium to the complex. The center is open 9:30 am to 8 pm Tuesday, 9:30 am to 4:30 pm Wednesday to Friday and 1 to 4:30 pm Saturday; admission is free.

Twin Falls Historical Museum
This museum (☎ 208-423-5907), 144 Taylor St, tells the story of the irrigation boom that built Twin Falls. Exhibits include old farm equipment, photographs and a furnished pioneer cabin. It is open noon to 5 pm weekdays May to mid-September. Admission is free.

Shoshone Falls Park
The 212-foot **Shoshone Falls**, over 1000 feet wide, has the nickname 'The Niagara of the West,' although it is 51 feet higher than Niagara Falls and once carried more water. Shoshone Falls may be dry, depending on the time of year when water from the Snake River is diverted about 20 miles upstream at Milner Dam for irrigation. The park's verdant shaded lawns make a scenic picnic spot beneath the dramatic canyon

walls. Nearby **Dierkes Lake** is a good place to swim and has a boat launch.

Access to Shoshone Falls is only on the south side of the Snake River Canyon through the park. Take US 93 (I-84 exit 173) south 3 miles to Falls Ave (off Blue Lakes Blvd), head east 3 miles to a well-signed 3300 East Rd, and continue north 2 miles to the park. The day-use fee is $2 per vehicle.

Snake River Rim Recreation Area
North of Perrine Bridge on US 93, an unpaved road heads east on the north side of the canyon. A network of hiking and biking trails lead to the canyon rim.

Places to Stay
Most places are clustered along Blue Lakes Blvd N and Addison Ave W; the latter is less expensive.

Camping The *Twin Falls/Jerome KOA Kampground* (☎ 208-324-4169), 1 mile north of I-84 exit 173, has a laundry and a pool. Tent sites/full hookups cost $18/24. East of Twin Falls, *Anderson Campground* (☎ 208-825-9800), on the frontage road half a mile east of I-84 exit 183, has a pool, laundry and showers. Tent sites/full hookups cost $18/22. (Also see Hagerman Valley later in this chapter.)

Motels Singles/doubles cost $27/30 at the *El Rancho Motel* (☎ 208-733-4021), 380 Addison Ave W. Others include the *Holiday Motel* (☎ 208-733-4330), 615 Addison Ave W ($28/30), *Twin Falls Motel* (☎ 208-733-8620), 2152 Kimberly Rd ($32/36), and *Monterey Motor Inn* (☎ 208-733-5151), 433 Addison Ave W ($34/38). The only downtown property is the faded but acceptable *Super 7 Motel* (☎ 208-733-8770), 320 Main Ave S ($32/36).

Motel 6 (☎ 208-734-3993), 1472 Blue Lakes Blvd N, has singles/doubles for $37/42. Comparably priced are the *Weston Inn* (☎ 208-733-6095), 906 Blue Lakes Blvd N ($44/48) and the *Super 8 Motel* (☎ 208-734-5801), 1260 Blue Lakes Blvd N ($48/53). Rooms start at $53 at the *Best*

Western Apollo Motor Inn (☎ 208-733-2010), 296 Addison Ave W, and *Comfort Inn* (☎ 208-734-7494), 1893 Canyon Springs Rd. Most have a pool.

Hotels Singles/doubles at the *Weston Plaza Hotel* (☎ 208-733-0650), 1350 Blue Lakes Blvd N are $49/54. All of Twin Falls' higher-end hotels have pools: *AmeriTel Inn* (☎ 208-736-8000, 800-822-8946), 1377 Blue Lakes Blvd N ($70/75); *Best Western Canyon Springs Park Hotel* (☎ 208-734-5000, 800-727-5003), 1357 Blue Lakes Blvd N ($72/82); and *Shilo Inn* (☎ 208-733-7545), 1586 Blue Lakes Blvd N ($85).

Places to Eat
Blue Lakes Blvd leading into Twin Falls is lined with acceptable restaurants. Several locally owned restaurants downtown serve good food in friendly surroundings. Join local ranchers at the *Buffalo Cafe* (☎ 208-734-0271), 218 4th Ave W, for a big, traditional breakfast. The house specialty is buffalo chips, or fried potatoes smothered with gravy. Home to Twin Falls' slightly alternative crowd, *Metropolis Bakery & Cafe* (☎ 208-734-4457), 125 Main Ave E, is a great bakery and espresso bar specializing in delicious European-style pastries. It has live acoustic music Thursday evenings.

The *Uptown Bistro* (☎ 208-733-0900), 117 Main Ave E, is a local favorite. Weekdays sandwiches and light fare (pasta, salads) cost under $9. On Friday and Saturday evenings, Continental dishes ($15 to $20) like beef Wellington or an intriguing chicken Vera (which the menu describes as 'named after a ghost I once worked with') are served. The pleasant *Mama Inez* (☎ 208-734-0733), 164 Main Ave N, features southwestern meals with interesting dishes like crab tacos and various egg creations.

A'Roma Italian Cuisine (☎ 208-733-0617), 147 Shoshone St N, has checkered tablecloths and inexpensive pasta and salads for weekday lunches; on Friday and Saturday evenings only A'Roma is open for dinner, with traditional and Twin Falls' Italian dishes (tenderloin finger steaks with spaghetti) leading the menu. The best steak

house is the *Rock Creek Inn* (☎ 208-734-4151), 200 Addison Ave W, which serves excellent prime rib dinners ($15).

Entertainment
Dunken's Draught House (☎ 208-733-8114), 102 Main Ave N, offers 21 draft beers, including cask-conditioned ales. The old bar is light, airy and a pleasant place on a hot summer afternoon.

Getting There & Away
Air SkyWest/The Delta Connection (☎ 208-734-6232) runs daily flights to Salt Lake City, UT, out of Magic Valley Regional Airport (☎ 208-733-5215), south of town.

Bus Greyhound Bus Lines (☎ 208-733-3002), 461 2nd Ave S, departs Twin Falls daily for Salt Lake City at 2:35, 4:55 am, and 1:05 pm and for Portland, OR, at 2:35 am, 12:10, and 4:30 pm. Another daily bus goes to Pocatello.

Sun Valley Stages (☎ 208-383-3085), 119 S Park Ave W, operates a charter service between Twin Falls and Ketchum during winter; call to inquire about individual seats.

Getting Around
Bus TRANS IV (☎ 208-736-2133, 800-531-2133 in Idaho) operates intracity buses 8 am to 5pm weekdays. TRANS IV also operates two intercity routes: westbound Buhl-Filer-Jerome-Kimberly-Wendell, and eastbound Burley-Rupert-Paul.

Car Avis (☎ 208-733-5527), Budget (☎ 208-734-4067) and National (☎ 208-733-3646) are at the airport. Hertz (☎ 208-733-2668) is at 210 Shoshone St W. Try Used-A-Car Rental (☎ 208-733-2298, 800-481-6637), 1654 Blue Lakes Blvd N, for cheaper rentals.

Taxi For a taxi, call ☎ 208-733-9101.

AROUND TWIN FALLS
Caldron Linn
East of Twin Falls (near I-84 exit 188) is Caldron Linn, where the Snake River

narrows to 40 feet. The resulting swirling waterfalls forced many explorers to abandon their boats and continue on foot.

South Hills
About 25 miles south of Twin Falls are the South Hills, a range of 7000-foot mountains with **hiking**, **horseback riding**, moderate to difficult **mountain biking** and camping. Take Hwy 50 east of Kimberly and head south on Rock Creek Rd (G3 Rd) up Rock Creek Canyon. Two popular trailheads are Third Fork and Harrington Fork. Mountain Magic Resort with downhill and cross-country **skiing** is at the end of the paved road.

Rafting
The 15-mile Murtaugh section of the Snake River begins near the town of Murtaugh, east of Twin Falls, and ends at the eastern end of Twin Falls. This is an excellent Class III-IV day trip. To book a full-day white-water trip ($150), contact High Adventure River Tours (☎ 208-733-0123, 800-286-4123; fax 208-734-6651), 1211 E 2350 S, Hagerman, ID 83332 or PO Box 222, Twin Falls, ID 83303.

Diving
The deserts of Idaho may seem an unlikely place for scuba diving, but Dive Magic (☎ 208-733-8203), 236 Main Ave N, Twin Falls, offers lessons and rentals for use in Snake River reservoirs.

BUHL & AROUND
Buhl (population 3799), 18 miles west of Twin Falls on US 30, offers little to the traveler, but many pass through when visiting the Hagerman Valley (see below). The Buhl visitors center (☎ 208-543-6682), 104 S Broadway, is at the east end of town. Southwest of Buhl is the curious 200-foot **Balanced Rock**, a 40-ton mushroom-shaped rock formation. Buhl's motels are less desirable than those in Twin Falls or the Hagerman Valley. The basic *Siesta Motel* (☎ 208-543-6427), 629 S Broadway Ave, has rooms starting at $28. Singles/

doubles at the well-kept older *Oregon Trail Motel* (☎ 208-543-8814), 510 S Broadway Ave, cost $40/45.

HAGERMAN VALLEY
The verdant Hagerman Valley (elevation 2959 feet) is along a stretch of the Snake River Canyon that contains renowned fossils and Thousand Springs. The Thousand Springs Scenic Byway includes 48 miles on US 30 between Twin Falls and Bliss; the byway continues on Hwy 50 east of Twin Falls. Pleasant campgrounds with hot springs make this scenic area appealing. Fishing and birdwatching are excellent throughout the valley.

Hagerman
US 30 becomes north-south State St in Hagerman. You can contact the Hagerman Chamber of Commerce (☎ 208-837-9131) at PO Box 599, Hagerman, ID 83332. The **Hagerman Valley Historical Society Museum**, open 1 to 4 pm Thursday to Sunday, has a complete skeleton of *Equus simplicidens*. See below for lodging and restaurant information.

Thousand Springs
Streams and rivers from the Rocky Mountains far to the north plunge underneath the basalt, lava-clogged Snake River Plain's porous surface and flow through subterranean aquifers as underground rivers. The Snake River's 400-foot canyon exposes these aquifers, which pour down its walls as springs. The aptly named Thousand Springs are in all likelihood fed by the Lost River, which drains a large mountain valley north of Arco only to disappear beneath the lava flows at Craters of the Moon National Monument. US 30 runs along the stretch of the Snake River where cascades of water gush out of the northern canyon walls, forming a lush green valley. Much of the water is diverted directly into fish hatcheries and trout farms (from where 90% of the nation's farm-raised trout come), and the rest is diverted for irrigation.

The Nature Conservancy (☎ 208-536-6797) owns the **Thousand Springs Preserve**, which includes 2 miles of springs and 3 miles of Snake River frontage and is open to visitors Friday to Monday afternoons, Memorial Day to Labor Day. Trails lead to the springs, and volunteers are available to answer questions. Once a year, the conservancy leads a canoe trip past the springs. To reach the preserve, turn off I-84 exit 155 at Wendell and follow signs toward Hagerman (away from Wendell). After 3 miles, turn south at the sign for Buhl. Follow this road for 2½ miles and turn west at Rd 3200 S. In 2 miles the road comes to a T-junction; turn left onto Thousand Springs Grade. From the south, the site can be reached from US 30 via Clearlakes Rd at Buhl.

Hagerman National Fish Hatchery
This hatchery (☎ 208-837-4896), off US 30 just south of Hagerman, raises more than 1.5 million steelhead annually, which are trucked to the Salmon River each spring, and other game fish for stocking Idaho rivers. Enjoy the outdoor self-guided walking tour, or have a picnic.

Malad Gorge State Park
The dramatic 250-foot Malad Gorge forms the core of Malad Gorge State Park (☎ 208-837-4505), named *rivière aux malades* (sickly river) by French trappers who ate poisonous roots. The river crosses a lava plateau and plunges over a 60-foot waterfall into a narrow gorge, cutting its course 2½ miles downstream to its confluence with the Snake River. The best view of the waterfall and the springs gushing out of the canyon walls is from the Devil's Wash Bowl Overlook (3260 feet). The nearby steel footbridge spans the chasm leading to a 1-mile trail along the gorge's north rim. A road follows the gorge's south rim with stunning views overlooking the Snake River Canyon. The park has a picnic area, but camping is not allowed. To reach the park, take I-84 exit 147 and follow the signs 1 mile to the park. Alternatively from

Hagerman, turn east on the small road immediately north of The Rock Lodge, which climbs 5 miles to the park.

A separate unit of the park, **Niagara Springs** is part of the Thousand Springs area and a national natural landmark. At this major waterfowl wintering site, a huge spring pours from the cliffs at 250 cubic feet per second to fill Crystal Springs Lake, noted for its fishing. Take I-84 exit 157 and follow Rex Leland Hwy south 9 miles. The last mile is steep and narrow, dropping 350 feet; trailers and RVs are not recommended. From the south, take US 30 to Clearlakes Rd in Buhl.

River Cruises
1000 Springs Tours (☎ 208-837-9006, 800-838-1096), US 30 at Hagerman St, operates scenic cruises from three launch sites: Hagerman's Bell Rapids Dock, Sliger's Thousand Springs Resort and Twin Falls. Trips depart according to demand, so call ahead; rates start at $24/17 for adults/children.

Rafting
The Snake River through Hagerman Valley is a popular Class I-III rafting trip, not for white-water, but exploration of canyon wildlife and geology. Most full-day trips put in below Lower Salmon Falls Dam, north of Hagerman, and take out 10 miles downstream near Bliss. Half/full-day trips cost $40/50.

To book a rafting trip, contact: High Adventure River Tours (☎ 208-733-0123, 800-286-4123; fax 208-734-6651), 1211 E 2350 S, Hagerman, ID 83332 or PO Box 222, Twin Falls, ID 83303; or Hagerman Valley Outfitters (☎ 208-837-6100), PO Box 245, Hagerman, ID 83332.

Places to Stay
Three hot springs east of Hagerman offer picnicking, camping, bathing and swimming in the river. Isolated and peaceful *Banbury Hot Springs* (☎ 208-543-4098), off US 30 10 miles north of Buhl and then 2 miles east (follow the signs), has sites

ranging from $10 to $14 and a laundry. *Sligar's 1000 Springs Resort* (☎ 208-837-4987), 5 miles south of Hagerman on US 30, has a pool and riverside tent sites ($10) and sites with full hookups ($16). *Miracle Hot Springs* (☎ 208-543-6002; fax 208-543-6091), on US 30, across from the turnoff to Banbury Hot Springs is OK in a pinch, although it is close to the road.

In the town of Hagerman, the *Hagerman RV Village* (☎ 208-837-4906), 18049 US 30, has shadeless but grassy sites (ranging from $10 to $16) with laundry and showers. Nonguests can shower for $3.50. *The Rock Lodge* (see below) has a few grassy but cramped sites starting at $8.

The Gooding Hotel B&B and AYH Hostel (☎ 208-934-4374, 888-260-6656), 112 Main St, Gooding, ID 83330, is north of the Hagerman Valley at the junction of Hwys 26 and 46 (I-84 exit 157 or 141). The dorm costs $10/13 for members/nonmembers; B&B rooms range from $40 to $55.

One mile north of Hagerman, *The Rock Lodge* (☎ 208-837-4822), 17940 US 30, has creekside rooms and cabins ranging from $41 to $75. Singles/doubles at the bland *Hagerman Valley Inn* (☎ 208-837-6196), at Frog's Landing in Hagerman, cost $37/50.

Places to Eat

In Hagerman, *The Little Bitt* (☎ 208-837-6359, 800-600-6359), 160 S State St, is a pleasant cafe that serves breakfast all day. At the south end of town, *Snake River Grill & Restaurant* (☎ 208-837-6227) at Frog's Landing, boasts hearty country cooking, local catfish and sturgeon, and wild game.

Getting There & Away

To reach the Hagerman Valley, follow US 30 west from Twin Falls or Buhl (US 30 drops into the valley 8 miles north of Buhl), or follow US 30 south (I-84 exit 141) from Bliss.

HAGERMAN FOSSIL BEDS NATIONAL MONUMENT

On a bluff above the Snake River, the Hagerman Fossil Beds National Monument

(☎ 208-837-4793) has the world's best Upper Pliocene terrestrial fossil beds. The fossil beds were created 2 to 3½ million years ago, when this desert canyon was a grassland dotted with lakes and marshes. First excavated by the Smithsonian Institute in 1929, these renowned beds, dubbed the 'horse quarry,' yielded hundreds of skeletons of prehistoric horses, or *Equus simplicidens*, and more than 140 other fossilized species, including ancient camels and eight species found nowhere else. National monument status was conferred in 1988.

A temporary visitors center in Hagerman, 221 N State St, open 8:30 am to 5 pm daily during summer, has informative displays on fossil beds and prehistoric natural history, and slide and video presentations. Pick up the comprehensive self-guided tour handout. Direct access to the fossil beds is prohibited. Visitors can view the fossil beds from a boardwalk overlook; an exhibit is nearby. NPS rangers conduct natural history and guided site tours weekends June to September; call for the schedule. The site is also visible across the river from the Bell Rapids Dock just south of Hagerman off US 30.

To reach the fossil beds, go south 3 miles on US 30 from Hagerman and cross the bridge over the Snake River. Turn west onto an unmarked paved road that follows the river's true left bank. Continue about 12 miles and then follow signs to the monument.

SHOSHONE

The town of Shoshone (population 1365), 21 miles north of Twin Falls at the junction of US 26, US 93 and Hwy 75, is notable for nearby caves. **Mammoth Cave**, 10 miles north of Shoshone on Hwy 75, is a red-colored volcanic lava tube about 1 mile long; it can be explored on a self-guided tour. Seven miles farther north are the **Shoshone Indian Ice Caves**, a glacier beneath lava flows. The largest cave is 1000 feet long, 30 feet wide and 40 feet high, and has been used to supply ice to neighboring towns since the 1930s. Forty-minute tours depart 8 am to 7:15 pm May to September. Admission to the adjacent museum is free. Temperatures in the caves stay below freezing, so dress warmly, wear sturdy shoes and bring a flashlight. Contact the BLM Shoshone District office (☎ 208-886-2206), 400 W F St, PO Box 2B, Shoshone, ID 83352, for more information.

BURLEY

Burley (population 9498), midway across southern Idaho, offers little to travelers except motels and a couple of good cafes.

Orientation & Information Overlook Ave (I-84 exit 208) links Burley to I-84. US 30 becomes Main St downtown. The Mini Cassia Chamber of Commerce (☎ 208-678-7230) is at 1177 7th St in Heyburn, a town west of Burley. The BLM Burley District office (☎ 208-677-6641) is at 15 E 200 S. Rupert is 3 miles north of Burley (I-84 exit 211).

Places to Stay & Eat The *Budget Motel* (☎ 208-678-2200, 800-635-4952), 900 N Overland Ave, is a vast and pleasant place with rooms ranging from $38 to $48. Next door is the *Best Western Burley Inn* (☎ 208-678-3501, 800-599-1849), 800 N Overland Ave, with a pool and rooms ranging from $56 to $80. The attractive, older *Greenwell Motel* (☎ 208-678-5576), 904 E Main St, has rooms ranging from $32 to $64; some have kitchen units.

Burley has two gems for family dining: *Connor's Cafe* (☎ 208-678-9367), just north of I-84 exit 208 at the Philips 66 station, a kind of archetype of truck-stop cafes; and *Price's Cafe* (☎ 208-678-5149), 2444 Overland Ave, with a 36-foot 'smorgasbord' buffet table with inexpensive, all-you-can-eat lunches and dinners daily. *Tio Joe's* (☎ 208-678-9844), 262 Overland Ave, is a good Mexican restaurant.

Getting There & Away Greyhound Bus Lines (☎ 208-678-0477), 510 Oakley Ave, departs Burley daily for Salt Lake City, UT, at 5:45 am and 1:55 pm and for Portland, OR, at 1:25, 10:55 am and 3:30 pm. If you're driving, Burley is off I-84 near the I-86 junction 40 miles east of Twin Falls and 77 miles west of Pocatello. Nine miles east of Burley, I-84 cuts to the southeast toward Salt Lake City.

AROUND BURLEY
Mt Harrison
In the Albion Mountains, **Pomerelle Ski Area** (☎ 208-673-5599, 208-673-555 snow report), has 22 runs on Mt Harrison (9265 feet) with a maximum 1000-foot vertical drop. Half/full-day lift tickets cost $15/20. Lifts are open during July and August offering panoramic views. From Delco-Albion (I-84 exit 216), take Hwy 77 south 25 miles to Howell Canyon Rd. **Hiking** and **mountain biking** trails cover the forested mountain. Two excellent mountain bike rides include the trail from Albion to the summit and the 26-mile ride from Mt Harrison to the City of Rocks. Campgrounds are abundant.

Lake Walcott
Lake Walcott is a reservoir on the Snake River created by Minidoka Dam northeast of Burley. Site of a state park and the **Minidoka National Wildlife Refuge**, it boasts birdwatching fishing, boating, camping and world-class windsurfing.

CITY OF ROCKS NATIONAL RESERVE
Administered jointly by the NPS and Idaho State Parks, the 22-sq-mile City of Rocks (☎ 208-824-5519; fax 208-824-5563), PO Box 169, Almo, ID 83312, is a jumble of granite towers, cliffs and pinnacles in a pinyon pine and juniper forest and contains some of the oldest exposed rock in North America. Named by pioneers to whom it resembled a spired city, the California Cutoff of the Oregon Trail passed through the City of Rocks (elevation 5800 feet). On Register Rock, the names and initials of Oregon Trail travelers, written with axle grease on the rock face, are still visible. Other travelers gave fanciful names to formations, such as Elephant Head, Squaw Papoose, Kaiser's Helmut and King's Throne. The Twin Sisters, two rock spires, are over 62 stories high. The area was established in 1988 as a

IDAHO

national natural landmark. It offers world-class **rock climbing** with hundreds of short, mostly single-pitch, routes ranging from 5.4 to 5.14. For instruction and guided climbs, contact: Exum Mountain Guides (☎ /fax 307-733-2297; fax 307-733-9613), PO Box 56, Moose, WY 83012; and Jackson Hole Mountain Guides (☎ 307-733-4979, 800-239-7642), 165 N Glenwood St, PO Box 7477, Jackson, WY 83002.

Campgrounds ($8), open April to November, are primitive. To reach City of Rocks from Burley, take Hwy 27 south for 17 miles to Oakley and follow the signs on a paved, then maintained-gravel road 19 miles to the park. Alternatively, follow Hwy 77 (I-84 exit 245) west toward Malta, and then follow signs to Elba and Almo, a total of 30 miles. The park begins 2 miles west of Almo.

Southeastern Idaho

During frontier times this region was busy: Hudson's Bay Company trappers explored the river valleys looking for furs, Oregon Trail pioneers traversed mountain passes to reach the Snake River and Mormons moved north from Utah to establish farms and communities. Today the Fort Hall Indian Reservation, home to Shoshone and Bannock, comprises much of the region. The prime attraction of this underpopulated region is the appealing patchwork of farms and ranches along the river valleys and rugged, arid mountains.

Two scenic drives are worthwhile. The 113-mile **Bear Lake-Caribou National Scenic Byway** follows US 89 along the west shore of Bear Lake from the Idaho-Utah state line to Montpelier and continues north on US 30 to Soda Springs. Here it meets the **Pioneer Historic Byway**, which follows Hwy 34 from Preston to Soda Springs. The joint byway continues north on Hwy 34 to Wyoming's Star Valley.

POCATELLO

Pocatello (population 51,340; elevation 4454 feet) is Idaho's second-largest city. Greater Pocatello includes Chubbuck, a town to its north. Both towns were carved out of the Fort Hall Indian Reservation during the 1880s. Pocatello was established as a rail junction in 1884, when the north-south railroads between Montana's gold fields and Salt Lake City were joined with the east-west UP. Pocatello thrived as the center of a vast agricultural area, including Idaho's noted potato fields. Present-day Pocatello, however, is not immediately appealing. The city center is in a decrepit state and the rest of the city sprawls along suburban streets. Pocatello is home to Idaho State University (ISU) which has about 11,000 students and a curriculum emphasizing science and technology.

Orientation

Two roads lead to Pocatello's city center south of the railroad tracks: the underpass at Center St and the overpass at Benton St. Newer businesses are oriented to serve the I-15 and I-86 corridors, which intersect here. The main road is Yellowstone Ave (US 91, I-86 exit 61), which turns into the one-way S 4th and S 5th Aves (US 91/US 30) and provides access to the city center and ISU. Center St divides north-south street addresses; 5th Ave divides east-west ones.

Information

The Greater Pocatello Chamber of Commerce (☎ 208-233-1525; fax 208-233-1527) is at 343 Center. The USFS Caribou National Forest Pocatello Ranger District (☎ 208-236-7500), 250 S 4th Ave, suite 282, is in the US Federal Building. The Idaho Department of Fish and Game (☎ 208-232-4703) is at 1345 Barton Rd.

The post office is at 205 S Main St. Mail Boxes Etc (☎ 208-233-7775), 775 Yellowstone Ave, provides fax services. The Pocatello Regional Medical Center (☎ 208-234-0777) is at 777 Hospital Way (I-15 exit 69). For laundry, head to the Sunshine Laundry Center (☎ 208-237-9960), 1442

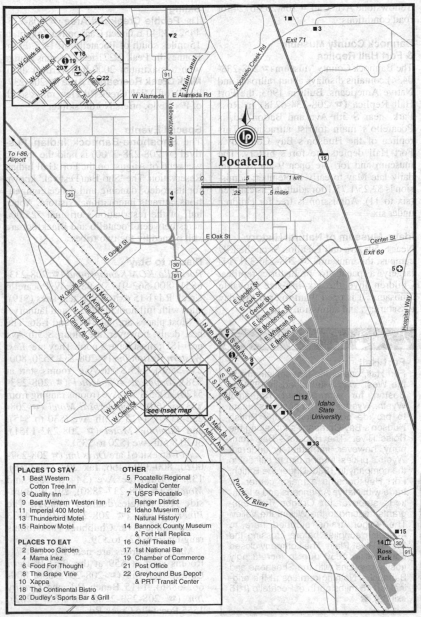

Pocatello

To I-86,
Airport

Exit 71

Pocatello Creek Rd

Exit 69

Idaho
State
University

Portneuf River

Ross
Park

PLACES TO STAY
1   Best Western
    Cotton Tree Inn
3   Quality Inn
9   Best Western Weston Inn
11 Imperial 400 Motel
13 Thunderbird Motel
15 Rainbow Motel

PLACES TO EAT
2   Bamboo Garden
4   Mama Inez
6   Food For Thought
8   The Grape Vine
10 Xappa
18 The Continental Bistro
20 Dudley's Sports Bar & Grill

OTHER
5   Pocatello Regional
    Medical Center
7   USFS Pocatello
    Ranger District
12 Idaho Museum of
    Natural History
14 Bannock County Museum
    & Fort Hall Replica
16 Chief Theatre
17 1st National Bar
19 Chamber of Commerce
21 Post Office
22 Greyhound Bus Depot
    & PRT Transit Center

see inset map

IDAHO

Yellowstone Ave. Call ☎ 208-233-6724 for road conditions.

Bannock County Museum & Fort Hall Replica

The Bannock County Museum (☎ 208-233-0434) contains displays about railroads and Native Americans. Built in 1963, the Fort Hall Replica (☎ 208-234-6238) in Ross Park, near S 5th Ave and Barton Rd, is Pocatello's main tourist attraction. This replica of the Hudson's Bay Company's Fort Hall depicts the fort's history. The museum and fort are open 9 am to 7 pm daily late May to early September; admission is $2.25/1.75/1 for adults/teens/children (six to 11). Admission is free for children under six.

Idaho Museum of Natural History

Near S 5th Ave and E Dillon St on the ISU campus, this museum (☎ 208-236-3317) is largely a paean to prehistoric reptiles. Children love the six life-size movable dinosaurs. It is open 9 am to 5pm Monday to Saturday, and admission is free.

Fort Hall

Fort Hall, one of the first settlements in the West, was established in 1834 by Boston fur entrepreneur Nathaniel Wyeth. Wyeth's trading post was meant to provide competition to the British Hudson's Bay Company's fort along the Boise River. The Hudson's Bay Company, however, immediately undercut Wyeth's prices, forcing him to sell out to the company in 1836. Under the British, Fort Hall became a major center for trade with Native Americans and a fortuitous stopover for Oregon Trail emigrants heading to the Willamette Valley. The wagon trains stopped here to replenish supplies before crossing the Snake River Plain. The company closed Fort Hall in 1856 due to increasingly hostile relations with the Shoshone and Bannocks. Nothing remains at the original fort 15 miles north of Pocatello (I-15 exit 80). ■

Skiing

The **Pebble Creek Ski Area** (☎ 208-775-4452), 3340 E Green Canyon Rd, Inkom, is 15 miles south of Pocatello off I-15. From Bonneville Peak (9271 feet), 24 runs plunge with a maximum 2000-foot vertical drop. **Mink Creek Recreation Area** (☎ 208-237-9922), off Mink Creek Rd a few miles south of Pocatello, offers Nordic skiing.

Special Events

The **Shoshone-Bannock Indian Festival** (☎ 208-238-3700) is held the second weekend of August on the Fort Hall Indian Reservation. The 'Sho-Ban Festival,' known for its rodeo, dancing and dance competitions, attracts international visitors. About half of the reservation's original 525,000 acres between Pocatello and Blackfoot are still owned by the two tribes.

Places to Stay

Pocatello KOA Kampground (☎ 208-233-6851, 800-562-9175), 9815 W Pocatello Creek Rd (I-15 exit 7), has tent sites ($19), sites with full hookups ($24) and laundry.

Most places are near I-15 and I-86. The best deals, however, are along S 5th Ave near ISU; most have a pool. They are: *Best Western Weston Inn* (☎ 208-233-5530, 800-238-5530), 745 S 5th Ave (rooms start at $38); *Imperial 400 Motel* (☎ 208-233-5120), 1055 S 5th Ave (rooms ranging from $23 to $60); *Thunderbird Motel* (☎ 208-232-6330), 1415 S 5th Ave ($30 to $45); and *Rainbow Motel* (☎ 208-232-1451), 3020 S 5th Ave ($20 to $35).

At I-86 exit 61 are *Days Inn* (☎ 208-237-0020, 800-329-7466; fax 208-237-3216), 133 W Burnside Ave ($44 to $55) and *Motel 6* (☎ 208-237-7880), 291 W Burnside Ave (singles/doubles $30/35). The *Pineridge Inn* (☎ 208-237-3100), 4333 Yellowstone Ave, Chubbuck, has rooms ranging from $21 to $39.

Many properties are near I-15 exit 71. Rooms start at $59 at the *Best Western Cotton Tree Inn* (☎ 208-237-7650, 800-662-6886), 1415 Bench Rd, and *Quality Inn* (☎ 208-233-2200, 800-527-5202), 1555 Pocatello Creek Rd.

Places to Eat

For espresso and pastries try *The Grape Vine* (☎ 208-232-5218), 466 S 5th Ave. *Food for Thought* (☎ 208-233-7267), 504 E Center, is a convenient place for soups, salads, sandwiches and dessert. The *Bamboo Garden* (☎ 208-238-2331), 1200 Yellowstone Ave, has good Hunan and Szechuan food, while the *Mama Inez Restaurant* (☎ 208-234-7674), 350 Yellowstone Ave, turns out great Tex-Mex food and is the chain's original restaurant. Go to *Xappa*, 904 S 4th Ave, for smoothies. *Dudley's Sports Bar & Grill* (☎ 208-232-3541), 150 S Arthur Ave, is the most popular microbrewery. *The Continental Bistro* (☎ 208-233-4433), 140 S Main St, with a handsome old bar serving regional microbrews, has a broad menu with daily seafood and steak specials and an impressive wine list. Try a grilled steak and Gorgonzola cheese salad or the veal medallions with wild mushrooms.

Entertainment

The *Chief Theatre*, 215 N Main St, is the performing arts center. Call ☎ 208-232-4433 for current events. On Friday and Saturday nights, local bands tune up at *1st National Bar* (☎ 208-233-1516), 232 W Center St. For information about concerts and other events at ISU call ☎ 208-236-2831 or 208-236-3662.

Getting There & Away

Air Pocatello Municipal Airport, 5 miles west of town (I-86 exit 56), is served by Horizon Air and SkyWest/The Delta Connection. Daily Horizon Air flights connect Pocatello with Boise, while SkyWest/The Delta Connection flies daily to Salt Lake City, UT. It may be more affordable to fly into Salt Lake City and rent a car there or take the shuttle (see below).

Salt Lake City Airport Shuttle Rexburg-based Salt Lake Airport Shuttle Hop (SLASH; ☎ 800-359-6826) runs shuttles between Salt Lake City and Pocatello. The shuttle picks up at the Quality Inn, 1555 Pocatello Creek Rd, at 8 am and noon. The one way/roundtrip fare is $33/62. The trip takes three hours.

Bus Greyhound Bus Lines (☎ 208-232-5365), 215 W Bonneville, operates daily buses along I-15 northbound to Bozeman, MT (1:05 am and 9:30 pm), and southbound to Salt Lake City (12:45 am and 4:15 pm). Another daily bus goes west to Burley.

Car Pocatello is on north-south I-15, which links Salt Lake City to Butte, MT, via Pocatello and Idaho Falls, at the junction of I-86.

Getting Around

Bus Pocatello Regional Transport (PRT) Transit Center (☎ 208-234-2287) shares the Greyhound bus depot. It is open 8 am to 5 pm weekdays and 10 am to 5 pm Saturday.

Car Hertz (☎ 208-233-2970) and Avis (☎ 208-232-3244) are at the airport. U-Save Car Rental (☎ 208-237-9010, 800-426-5299) is at 1407 Yellowstone Ave.

Taxi For a taxi, call ☎ 208-232-1115.

MASSACRE ROCKS STATE PARK

Oregon Trail pioneers dreaded traversing the flat and arid homeland of the warring Shoshone and Bannock tribes. Today Massacre Rocks State Park (☎ 208-548-2672, 208-548-2472), between Burley and Pocatello (I-86 exit 28), is a pleasant place with a visitors center, open 8:30 am to 8:30 pm daily, and lovely campground. The park's name derives from the polished round boulders scattered by the Bonneville Flood and from the Indian and pioneer clashes that took place near here. Two nature trails lead into a sagebrush savanna. The day-use fee is $2 per vehicle. The campground is set amid juniper and sagebrush and overlooks the Snake River. All sites ($11) have full hookups, and there are showers and a boat ramp.

Nearby, south of the park, **Register Rock** is a lump of basalt inscribed with names of passing emigrants. The oldest name dates from 1849. Elaborately protected with Plexiglas shields and a

IDAHO

Killings at Massacre Rocks

The killings that prompted the name of Massacre Rocks occurred several miles east of Massacre Rocks State Park. In 1862, well after the initial emigration of white settlers across the Oregon Trail, the natives along the Snake River became hostile to the wagon trains crossing their plateau. Three separate emigrant groups, in a total of 52 wagons, were progressing west from Fort Hall when the lead wagon train was attacked. In this and the following battles, 10 men and women were killed and brought back to Massacre Rocks to be buried. Revisionist history (along with a solid dose of Hollywood horse dramas) placed the killings at a gatelike passage between two upright pillars near the south end of the park; the killings, however, actually took place far from there. ■

roofed structure, the pioneers' autographs are barely visible.

AMERICAN FALLS

American Falls (population 4341) is a charmless town beside a reservoir of the same name. The 50-foot cascade for which the town was named were obliterated by dams in 1925, and the old town center was flooded by the reservoir. A new town was built higher on the riverbank in 1927. American Falls is along I-86, 10 miles north of Massacre Rocks State Park.

If you need to stay here, the best bet is the *Hillview Motel* (☎ 208-226-5151) at I-86 exit 40, where rooms range from $28 to $42. One of the better places to eat is *Melody Lanes* (☎ 208-226-2815), 152 Harrison St, a bowling alley/cafe that serves hearty breakfasts and good sandwiches. Otherwise, you have a choise of fast-food places near the I-86 on-ramps.

BLACKFOOT

Blackfoot (population 10,406) is Idaho's potato capital. Irrigated potato fields stretch off in all directions; pull off the road to

admire the railroad cars filled with tubers. The good-natured but tacky **Idaho's World Potato Exposition** (☎ 208-785-2517), in the former railroad depot, is devoted to potato history and horticulture. The museum is open 10 am to 7 pm Monday to Saturday and 10 am to 5 pm Sunday; admission is $2/1.50/50¢ adults/seniors/children. The 180-sq-mile **Hells Half Acre Lava Field**, a national natural landmark, is northeast of Blackfoot. About 28,000 years old, the lava beds are visible just west of I-15/US 26. For information contact the Blackfoot Chamber of Commerce (☎ 208-785-0510) at PO Box 801, Blackfoot, ID 83221.

Places to Stay & Eat

Y Motel (☎ 208-785-1550), 1375 S Broadway, at the south end of town, has rooms ranging from $30 to $45. The *Best Western Blackfoot Inn* (☎ 208-785-4144), 750 Jensen Grove Drive, starts at $40. The *Weston Inn* (☎ 208-785-5000), at 1229 Parkway Ave, is comparable. For breakfast and family dining, go to *Homestead Family Restaurant* (☎ 208-785-0700), at 1355 Parkway Drive. For dinner try the *Colonial Inn* (☎ 208-785-1390), 659 S Ash St.

SODA SPRINGS & AROUND

Soda Springs (population 4050; elevation 5839 feet) is nestled between the Wasatch and Aspen ranges in the Cache and Caribou national forests to its west and east, respectively. Oregon Trail pioneers were apparently amused by the area's geysers and effervescent spring water, and allegedly added sugar to the water to make frontier soda pop – although a taste of the springwater suggests otherwise. An enormous phosphorus processing plant north of town, operated by Monsanto, has poured slag into the same area since 1953; it is dumped five times per hour, 24 hours a day. The contorted pile, known as the **Monsanto Slag Pour**, resembles a lava flow, especially when the slag is molten. On the plant's eastern side an attempt has been made to reclaim the slaglands by planting grass.

IDAHO

Information

Contact the Soda Springs Chamber of Commerce (☎ 208-547-4964, 888-399-0888) at PO Box 697, Soda Springs, ID 83276. The USFS Caribou National Forest Soda Springs Ranger District (☎ 208-547-4356), 421 W 2nd St S, is open 8 am to 5 pm weekdays and 9 am to 2 pm Saturday. The post office is at 220 S Main St.

Geyser Park

In 1937, the city was drilling a well, hoping to hit a hot springs for the local pool, when it hit a pocket of water infused with carbon dioxide. The resulting geyser shot 150 feet into the air. The mineral water spray, only a block off Main St, soon began to discolor the city's buildings. The situation was resolved by creating a park and capping the geyser with a timer. Currently, this captive geyser is scheduled to erupt on the half-hour. The park is one block west of downtown.

Hooper Springs Park

Many of the soda springs for which the area is named are currently inundated by Alexander Reservoir, west of town. An example of what fascinated Oregon Trail emigrants can still be seen north of town at Hooper Springs, a natural effervescent spring. Go ahead and taste the water from the pool or fountain. The park is a pleasant place for a picnic with views onto the nearby phosphorus slag heap. Hooper Springs is 2 miles north of Soda Springs on Hwy 34.

Formation Springs & Cave

Ancient cold springs feed these wetlands and crystal clear pools at the base of the Aspen Mountains, which are protected as a Nature Conservancy Preserve. The water bubbling to the surface here is believed to have been in the earth for 13,000 years. The water contains high concentrations of travertine, which have shaped and molded some peculiar geologic formations, the star of which is the 1000-foot-long Formation Cave. The ponds are also popular nesting areas for waterfowl. Follow Hwy 34 4 miles north to Trail Canyon Rd and go east 1½ miles.

Lava Hot Springs

Modern facilities enable bathers to enjoy the soothing hot pools, which are fed by several springs. Lava Hot Springs is east of I-15 and west of Soda Springs off US 30.

Grays Lake National Wildlife Refuge

The shallow marsh-like Grays Lake and its national wildlife refuge has the world's largest concentration of breeding greater sandhill cranes. May and June are the best birdwatching months. The refuge is 33 miles north of Soda Springs on Hwy 34, which continues east to Freedom in Wyoming's Star Valley. Several USFS campgrounds line the road.

Places to Stay & Eat

The BLM *Dike Lake Campground* (☎ 208-236-6880) is 11 miles north on Hwy 34 on the southeast end of Blackfoot Reservoir. The USFS *Eight Mile Campground* is 13 miles south of town on USFS Rd 425 (Eightmile Canyon Rd); either go south on 3rd St E or a few miles east on US 30 to USFS Rd 425. Free camping and drinking water is available at both spots.

Motels and food are simple but pleasant. All the following are along US 30. The *Caribou Lodge & Motel* (☎ 208-547-3377, 800-270-9178), 110 W 2nd St S, has rooms ranging from $25 to $50. At the *Lakeview Motel* (☎ 208-547-4351), 341 W 2nd St S, rooms go for $25 to $50. *J-R Inn* (☎ 208-547-3366), 179 W 2nd St S, is probably the nicest place to stay; rooms range from $32 to $44. The *Trail Motel & Restaurant* (☎ 208-547-0240), 213 E 2nd St S, with rooms ranging from $22 to $35, also has a few RV sites.

For good family dining go to *Ender's Cafe* (☎ 208-547-4980), 76 S Main St.

Getting There & Away

Soda Springs is on US 30, 50 miles southeast of Pocatello, 21 miles east of Lava Hot Springs and 48 miles north of Montpelier.

PRESTON

Preston (population 4191) is part of the earliest settled portion of Idaho. Mormon farmers moved up the Cache Valley from Logan, UT, in 1860 and founded Franklin, 7 miles south of Preston. Preston is along US 91 in the Bear River Valley 8 miles north of the Idaho-Utah state line. The Preston Chamber of Commerce (☎ 208-852-2703) is at 32 West Oneida St, Preston, ID 83263. The post office is at 55 E Oneida St.

Places to Stay & Eat

Rooms at the pleasant *Plaza Motel* (☎ 208-852-2020), 427 S US 91, range from $30 to $42. *Shipley's Country Kitchen* (☎ 208-852-0332), 101 N State St, serves tasty breakfasts and lunches. For steaks and supper-club fare, try the *Main Street Grill* (☎ 208-852-1447), 96 S State St.

Getting There & Away

Greyhound Bus Lines departs Preston daily for Salt Lake City, UT, at 6:55 pm and for Bozeman, MT, at 10:55 am.

MONTPELIER

Montpelier (population 2867), established in 1864 by Mormon pioneer farmers, is along the Oregon Trail, which followed present-day US 30 between Montpelier and Soda Springs. By far the most exciting incident in local history was when Butch Cassidy and his gang robbed the bank in 1896. Montpelier is east of the Bear River in a broad, green basin beneath the Preuss Range and the Caribou National Forest. The USFS Caribou National Forest Ranger Station (☎ 208-847-0375) is at 432 Clay St. The Bear Lake Memorial Hospital (☎ 208-847-1630) is at 164 S 5th St.

Places to Stay & Eat

It is difficult to escape the noise from the railroad anywhere in town. The *Montpelier KOA Kampground* (☎ 208-847-0863, 800-562-7576), 2 miles east on US 89, has a pool and sites starting at $15. In a pinch, camping is free at the overgrown USFS *Montpelier Canyon Campground*, on US 89 near Geneva Summit (6938 feet), about 16 miles east of Montpelier.

Rooms start at $20 at *Michelle Motel* (☎ 208-847-1772, 800-590-1772), 401 Boise St, and at *Budget Motel* (☎ 208-847-1273), 240 N 4th St. At the *Three Sisters Motel* (☎ 208-847-2324), 112 S 6th St at US 89, and *Park Motel* (☎ 208-847-1911), 745 Washington St at 8th St, rooms range from $25 to $50. The nicer places are the *Super 8 Motel* (☎ 208-847-8888), 276 N 4th St, and the *Best Western Clover Creek Inn* (☎ 208-847-1782), 243 N 4th St, with rooms starting at $40. Restaurants are uninspiring, but try the *7M Country Cafe* (☎ 208-847-0208), 24312 US 89, for basic home cooking.

Getting There & Away

Montpelier is at the junction of US 89 from Bear Lake and US 30, which links Pocatello to Kemmerer, WY, via Soda Springs.

BEAR LAKE VALLEY

The Bear Lake Valley (elevation 6000 feet) was discovered in 1812 by fur trappers, and by 1827 had become an important center for trade fairs attended by trappers like Jim Bridger and Donald MacKenzie. At its center is the 112-sq-mile Bear Lake, a fault-block lake 20 miles south of Montpelier that bisects the Idaho-Utah state line. Limestone particles suspended in the

Battle of Bear River

The Battle of Bear River, one of the bloodiest in Idaho history, occurred north of Preston. On a freezing day in January 1863, Colonel Patrick Conner led 300 US Army troops against an encampment of 500 Shoshone Indians. The Shoshone underestimated the resolve and ferocity of the troops and allowed them to breach the swollen Bear River. Infantry and cavalry units moved in on the village, torching all the tepees and indiscriminately killing men, women and children. Contemporary reports claim that up to 400 Shoshone died, while only 22 soldiers died. ∎

IDAHO

shallow water give the lake its deep blue color. It supports four native fish species, which are sought by anglers. Bear River, which once fed Bear Lake, bypasses the lake as it tumbles down out of Wyoming and north toward Soda Springs. The lake is kept from becoming saline by a canal linking Bear River to the lake, where the water is stored until it is needed by downriver farms. Another canal then feeds the water back into the river. The resulting wetlands and marshes north of the lake comprise the **Bear Lake National Wildlife Refuge** (☎ 208-847-1757), a waterfowl preserve with a nesting colony of white-faced ibis; whooping cranes have also been known to visit. A sign west of Montpelier directs you to the refuge.

Along US 89 on west side of the lake are the towns of Paris, St Charles and Fish Haven, settled by Mormon pioneers in the 1860s. Of note are the **Paris Historical Museum** and, across the street, the **Paris Idaho State Tabernacle** (1884-89), designed by the sons of Brigham Young, a central figure in the establishment of the Mormon church. The tabernacle is open for tours 9:30 am to 5:30 pm Memorial Day to Labor Day. St Charles was settled by Gutzon Borglum, who carved Mt Rushmore. Contact the Bear Lake Convention & Visitors Bureau (☎ 208-945-2072, 800-448-2327) at 2661 US 89, PO Box 26, Fish Haven, ID 83287.

Bear Lake State Park
Bear Lake State Park (☎ 208-945-2790) is popular with locals, though little known to the outside world. The park's two units, North Beach and East Beach, have boat ramps and broad, sandy beaches. Camping is allowed, but no established campgrounds exist. The easiest access is Turnpike Rd east of St Charles.

Minnetonka Cave
The half-mile-long limestone Minnetonka Cave (☎ 208-945-2407) winds 1800 feet into the mountainside past colorful formations. The USFS offers one-hour guided tours from 10 am to 5:30 pm June to Labor Day; tours cost $4/3 for adults/children. Contact the USFS in Montpelier (see above) for details. Follow St Charles Creek Rd 10 miles west of St Charles to the cave.

Places to Stay
West of Paris is the USFS *Paris Spring Campground*. The pleasant *Minnetonka RV Park & Campground* (☎ 208-945-2941), in St Charles, has sites ranging from $11 to $14. The USFS *St Charles Canyon Campground*, one of three in the canyon, is near Minnetonka Cave and has sites for $8. In Fish Haven is *Bear Lake RV Park*.

Getting There & Away
US 89, the most direct route between the nearest airport at Salt Lake City, UT, and Jackson, WY, follows the west shore of Bear Lake north to Montpelier. From Montpelier, US 89 continues northeast up the Montpelier Canyon to Wyoming's Star Valley.

Eastern Idaho

Alpine lakes surrounded by meadows, untamed rivers, waterfalls, wildlife, rugged mountains and the backdrop of the Teton Range dazzle Eastern Idaho visitors. Idaho Falls is the gateway to this inviting region.

IDAHO FALLS
Dominated by the spire of its Mormon temple, Idaho Falls (population 49,928; elevation 4600 feet) is a prototypical agricultural and ranching center, with well-heeled farmers lending the city a veneer of sophistication. Within a day's drive of Idaho Falls are Craters of the Moon National Monument to the west (see the Central Idaho Rockies chapter), Yellowstone and Grand Teton national parks to the northeast (see the Greater Yellowstone chapter in the Wyoming section) and Montana to the north.

First called Taylor Bridge, the city began life in the 1860s as a crossing on the Snake River, here no more than 60 feet across. In 1872 the community changed its name to

IDAHO

Eagle Rock and, with the arrival of the railroad, the town was up and running. Thinking the city would attract more settlers with a name other than Eagle Rock, a group of Chicago investors renamed it Idaho Falls in 1891. Only in 1911, however, was a diversion weir for a hydroelectric project built on the Snake River. The cataract, 1500 feet wide and dropping a meager 20 feet, is visible from the bridge on W Broadway St. The **Snake River Greenbelt**, a network of pleasant walking and cycling trails, connects Idaho Fall's riverside parks.

Orientation

Downtown has declined in favor of commercial strips leading out to suburbs. The city center, however, contains some charming architecture, and a few business still struggle on. To reach downtown, take I-15 exit 118 and follow Broadway St across the Snake River to Yellowstone Ave (US 26). The city center is wedged between the Snake River and Yellowstone Ave. The historic district centers on Ridge Ave, three blocks east of and parallel to Yellowstone Ave, between Pine and Birch Sts.

Information

The Greater Idaho Falls Chamber of Commerce (☎ 208-523-1010, 800-634-3246 outside Idaho) and Eastern Idaho Visitor & Convention Bureau (☎ 208-523-3278) are at 505 Lindsay Blvd, PO Box 50498, Idaho Falls, ID 83405-0598. Their impressive visitor information center, open 9 am to 5 pm Monday to Saturday, has exhibits, maps, books and extensive regional travel information.

The USFS Targhee National Forest Palisades Ranger Station (☎ 208-523-1412), 3659 E Ririe Hwy (US 26), open 8 am to 4:30 pm weekdays, has books and maps as well as lists of trails and campgrounds. The BLM Idaho Falls District office (☎ 208-524-7500) is at 1405 Hollipark Drive, Idaho Falls, ID 83401. The Idaho Department of Fish & Game (☎ 208-525-7290) is at 1515 Lincoln Rd.

The post office is at 605 4th St. The Columbia Eastern Idaho Regional Medical Center (☎ 208-529-6111) is at 3100 Channing Way. For laundry, go to Broadway Wash-N-Dry (☎ 208-529-5385), 1711 W Broadway St. Call ☎ 208-745-7278 for road conditions.

Bonneville County Historical Museum

This museum (☎ 208-522-1400), 200 N Eastern Ave at Elm St, in the handsome old Carnegie Library, preserves the history of the old settlement of Eagle Rock – including a recreated main street and Native American artifacts. Another display explains the development of nuclear energy at the Idaho National Engineering Laboratories (see INEL in the Central Idaho Rockies chapter). It is open 10 am to 5 pm weekdays and 1 to 5 pm Saturday; admission is $1/25¢ for adults/children.

Places to Stay

Camping The *Idaho Falls KOA Kampground* (☎ 208-523-3362), 1440 Lindsay Blvd, has a pool and laundry. Tent sites cost $19; sites with full hookups are $24.

Motels Singles/doubles cost $35/45 at the *Evergreen Gables Motel* (☎ 208-522-5410), 3130 S Yellowstone Ave. Some have cooking units. The older *Towne Lodge* (☎ 208-523-2960), 255 E St, has clean, comfortable rooms ($30/43). The *Littletree Inn* (☎ 208-523-5993), 888 N Holmes Ave, near the municipal golf course, has rooms for $33/39. *Motel West* (☎ 208-522-1112), 1540 W Broadway St, costs $38/46.

Most of the mid-range places face the Snake River Greenbelt, are north of W Broadway St and west of the river and have pools and spas. *Super 8 Motel* (☎ 208-522-8880), 705 Lindsay Blvd, has singles/doubles for $44/48. At the *Best Western Stardust Motor Lodge* (☎ 208-522-2910), 700 Lindsay Blvd, rooms cost $51/61. Comparable is the *Comfort Inn* (☎ 208-528-2804), 195 S Colorado Ave (I-15 exit 118). Rooms start at $59 at the *Hampton Inn* (☎ 208-529-9800), 2500 Channing Way and the *Quality Inn* (☎ 208-523-6260), 850 Lindsay Blvd. The *Best Western Driftwood* (☎ 208-523-2242), 575 River Pkwy, and

Shilo Inn (☎ 208-523-0088), 780 Lindsay Blvd, have rooms starting at $69.

Hotels The *Holiday Inn West Bank* (☎ 208-523-8000, 800-432-1005), 475 River Pkwy, has rooms ranging from $85 to $105. Rooms start at $89 at the *Best Western Cotton Tree Inn* (☎ 208-523-6000), 900 Lindsay Blvd, and $99 at *AmeriTel Inn* (☎ 208-523-1400), 645 Lindsay Blvd.

Places to Eat

Oddly, in the middle of Mormon Idaho is a beautiful coffeeshop, the *High Desert Rose Coffee Roasting Company & Cafe* (☎ 208-528-5464), 504 Shoup Ave. This espresso bar and cafe serves light meals in the renovated main gallery of an ornate old department store. Otherwise head to *DD Mudd*, on the 400 block of A St, for an espresso. The *Lost Arts Brew & Breadworks* (☎ 208-528-9288), 298 D St, serves unusual sandwiches, homemade breads and two dozen microbrews. The *BBQ Pit* (☎ 208-523-0255), 235 E St, which serves ribs and Thai food, now competes with nearby *Bubba's Bar-B-Que* (☎ 208-523-2822), 888 E 17th St, part of the well-known chain. *Saigon Restaurant* (☎ 208-529-8799), 3390 S Yellowstone Ave, is good, and lots of Chinese restaurants are around. A night out on the town here means *Jaker's Steak, Ribs & Fish House* (☎ 208-524-5240), 851 Lindsay Blvd, with an eclectic menu of Western favorites. A bit more salt-of-the-earth is *The Loft* (☎ 208-523-1977), N County Line Rd and US 20, an old-fashioned steak house and cocktail lounge in a log cabin.

Getting There & Away

Air Idaho Falls is served by Horizon Air, SkyWest/The Delta Connection and Delta Airlines out of Fanning Field Municipal Airport (☎ 208-529-1221), N Skyline Rd (I-15 exit 119). Daily Horizon Air flights connect Idaho Falls with Boise. SkyWest/The Delta Connection and Delta Airlines offer nine daily flights between Idaho Falls and Salt Lake City, UT. It may be more affordable to fly into Salt Lake City and

rent a car there or take the shuttle (see below).

Salt Lake City Airport Shuttle Rexburg-based Salt Lake Airport Shuttle Hop (SLASH; ☎ 800-359-6826) runs shuttles between Salt Lake City and Idaho Falls. The shuttle picks up at the Flying J, 1490 W Broadway St at Saturn Ave, west of I-15, at 7 and 11 am. The one-way/roundtrip fare is $37/70. The trip takes four hours.

Bus Greyhound Bus Lines (☎ 208-522-0912), 850 Denver St, one block north of W Broadway St, operates daily buses along I-15 northbound to Bozeman, MT (3 and 10:50 am), and southbound to Salt Lake City (2:55 and 11:30 pm).

The Idaho Falls-based Community and Rural Transport (CART; ☎ 208-522-2278), 850 Denver St, operates buses on Tuesday and Friday at 7 am and 4 pm along the Idaho Falls-Arco-Mackay-Challis-Salmon route. The one-way/roundtrip fare Idaho Falls-Salmon costs $22/40. Another CART route goes twice daily to Teton Valley (via Rexburg); buses go to Jackson, WY, as needed.

Car Idaho Falls is on I-15 at the junction of US 20 and US 26: I-15 continues north to Butte, MT; US 20 heads northeast to West Yellowstone, MT; and US 26 heads southeast to Jackson, via Alpine, WY.

Getting Around

Car Avis (208-522-4225), Budget (☎ 208-522-8800), Hertz (☎ 208-529-3101) and National (☎ 208-522-5276) are at the airport. In town are Rent-A-Wreck (☎ 208-529-8411), 720 W Broadway, and Enterprise (☎ 208-523-8111), 1626 Hollipark Drive.

Taxi Call East Way Taxi (☎ 208-525-8344) for a taxi.

CAMAS NATIONAL WILDLIFE REFUGE

Marshland, ponds and lakes comprise the Camas National Wildlife Refuge (☎ 208-662-5423), 36 miles north of Idaho Falls (I-15 exit 150 at Hamer). Spring and fall

IDAHO

migrations bring more than 100,000 ducks and 3000 geese. Other waterfowl, birds, raptors and wildlife are easily spotted year-round. Pick up a brochure and map at the refuge.

REXBURG

Rexburg (population 14,506) is known as the center of the seed-eye potato industry and as the home of Ricks College, founded in 1888, one of the first Mormon academies in Idaho. The Rexburg Chamber of Commerce (☎ 208-356-5700) is at 134 E Main St. The USFS Targhee National Forest Supervisor (☎ 208-624-3151), 420 N Bridge St, St Anthony, ID, is about 7 miles north of Rexburg. The post office is at 140 S Center St.

Teton Flood Museum

Rexburg's beautiful Mormon temple with twin steeples houses the interesting Teton Flood Museum (☎ 208-356-9101), 51 N Center St. The temple was built in 1911 from locally quarried basalt. The city bought it and converted it into a meeting house and museum after the temple sustained considerable damage in the June 1976 flood. Earth-filled Teton Dam, on the Teton River about 20 miles east of Rexburg, gave out, releasing 80 billion gallons of water. The flood lashed through Rexburg, Blackfoot and Idaho Falls before being absorbed into the backwaters of American Falls Dam. Six people and 18,000 livestock died; 25,000 people were driven from their homes. The museum is open 10 am to 5 pm Monday to Saturday; admission is by donation.

Farnsworth TV Pioneer Museum

This museum (☎ 208-745-8423), 118 W 1st St in Rigby, 12 miles south of Rexburg off US 20, would be another unremarkable local collection were it not for the fact that a Rigby local named Philo Farnsworth was the inventor of TV. Born in Rigby in 1906, Philo showed a remarkable talent for science and physics. At the age of 19, he formulated the technical theory behind the cathode-ray tube. In 1934, a London-based company hired Farnsworth to design the prototype of the modern TV. Philo licensed his product with Philco, RCA and later NBC, helping usher in the age of television. The museum maintains a collection of early TVs and charts the history of the broadcast image. It is open 1 to 5 pm Tuesday to Saturday; admission is by donation.

Menan Buttes National Historic Landmark

Southwest of Rexburg are the two Menan Buttes. Large basalt lava buttes are rare. Both have half-mile-wide, 300-foot-deep craters.

Special Events

Rexburg is a happening place from the last weekend of July to the first week in August when Ricks College hosts the **Idaho International Folk Dance Festival** (☎ 208-356-5700), which attracts dance troupes from around the world.

Places to Stay & Eat

At *Rex's Motel* (☎ 208-356-5477, 800-449-5477), 357 W 4th St S, rooms range from $25 to $36. For more comfort, the *Days Inn* (☎ 208-356-9222), 271 S 2nd St W, has a pool; rooms range from $37 to $66. On the edge of town is the *Best Western Cottontree Inn* (☎ 208-356-4646), 450 W 4th St S, with a pool, restaurant and hot tub; rates start at $44. Popular for inexpensive family dining is *Me & Stan's* (☎ 208-356-7300), W Main St at S 2nd St W. *La Fiesta* (☎ 208-359-1984), 136 W Main St, serves Mexican food.

Getting There & Away

Greyhound buses stop in Rexburg and St Anthony on their daily route between Salt Lake City, UT, and Bozeman, MT. CART (☎ 208-356-9033) buses ply between Idaho Falls and Rexburg every two hours, stopping at 74 W Main St.

SWAN VALLEY

The Snake River, coursing between the Caribou and Snake mountains, enters eastern Idaho filling the Palisades Reservoir. The verdant steep-walled Swan Valley runs 60 miles northwest from Palisades Dam to the confluence with Henry's Fork, just north of Idaho Falls. Trout fishing is the main pastime, and river and lake access is abundant along US 26, which runs the length of this lovely rural valley. Most amenities are designed with anglers in mind, cafes often doubling as bait shops. Motels and stores are basic. If you are near Idaho Falls on US 20 and headed toward Yellowstone National Park, detour through Swan Valley and join the **Teton Scenic Byway** through Teton Valley (see below) en route to Henry's Fork and West Yellowstone, MT.

Orientation & Information

The three small towns of Swan Valley, Irwin and Palisades lie west to east on US 26. USFS campgrounds are all east of the dam along the reservoir. Contact the Swan Valley Chamber of Commerce (☎ 208-483-3972) at PO Box 19, Swan Valley, ID 83449. Self-issuing permits ($6) are required for boaters and floaters along the South Fork of the Snake River at six designated launch sites, including Palisades, Palisades Creek, Spring Creek, Conant, Fullmer and Byington (see Idaho Falls for the nearest USFS and BLM offices and regulations).

Fishing

The Snake River west of Palisades Dam is a noted fly-fishing stream for cutthroat, rainbow and German brown trout. For guided fly-fishing trips, contact Mountain Stream Outfitters (☎ 208-483-3332), 3378 US 26, or South Fork Lodge (see below).

Places to Stay & Eat

Try any of the competitive and cheap campgrounds (sites with full hookups cost $12) in Palisades: *Husky's RV Park*, *Palisades Pines* or *Dot E Dot RV Park*. USFS campgrounds along the reservoir include: *Big Elk Creek* ($8), north of US 26 on USFS Rd 262; *Blowout* ($5), with a boat launch; and *Alpine* ($8), at the west end of the town of Alpine, WY. In Swan Valley, the *Fox's*

Corner Inn has campsites. The *South Fork Lodge* (☎ 208-483-2112), on US 26 in Irwin, 4 miles west of Swan Valley, has sites ($13) and lodge rooms (from $75 to $110). The lodge's restaurant is the best place to eat in the valley. In Irwin are *McBride's B&B* and *Swan Valley B&B* (☎ 208-483-4663, 800-241-7926), PO Box 115, Irwin, ID 83428, which has a spa. Nearby is the *Sandy Mite Fly Shop & Cafe* (☎ 208-483-2609).

Getting There & Away

From Swan Valley, Hwy 31 leads north over Pine Creek Pass (6764 feet) to Victor in the Teton Valley (see below). US 26 continues 28 miles along the Snake River from Swan Valley to Alpine in Wyoming's Star Valley (see the Greater Yellowstone chapter in the Wyoming section).

TETON VALLEY

John Colter first stumbled upon the Teton Valley (elevation 6200 feet) in 1808 while searching for beaver. It soon became a favored rendezvous place for mountain men like Jim Bridger to meet and trade with native tribes, and was known as Pierre's Hole. In the late 19th century Mormon families founded the valley's towns. Farming has remained the valley's mainstay, but these once-sleepy ranching towns are now a year-round mecca for outdoor adventure, with fabulous skiing, hiking, mountaineering and mountain biking. The towns boast restaurants, espresso shops, art galleries, stores selling and renting outdoor gear and summer music festivals.

The Teton River descends the west side of the Teton Range and flows northwest into the Henry's Fork of the Snake River near Rexburg. The valley is surrounded on three sides by mountain ranges within the Targhee National Forest: the Teton Range to the west, the Snake River Range to the south and the Big Hole Mountains to the southwest. The west face of the mighty Teton Range soars above this broad, scenic valley, which is warmer, sunnier and more peaceful than its well-known Wyoming neighbor, Jackson Hole (see the Greater Yellowstone chapter in the Wyoming section).

Orientation

Teton Valley's main towns from south to north along Hwy 33 are Victor (population 562), Driggs (population 941), 9 miles north, and Tetonia (population 164), 7 miles from Driggs. Most of the valley lies in Teton County, ID, though a small portion (up to the Teton crest) is in Teton County, WY. Alta, WY, the base village for Grand Targhee Ski & Summer Resort (see below) is 4 miles east of Driggs.

Information

Travelers can find most necessary services in Driggs, where all of the following are located. The Teton Valley Chamber of Commerce (☎ 208-354-2500) is at 10 E Ashley at N Main St. The USFS Targhee National Forest Teton Basin Ranger District (☎ 208-354-2312), 525 S Main St, has information on area trails and campgrounds. The post office is next to Hillman's on S Main St. Dark Horse Books (☎ 208-354-8882), 55 N Main St, has an excellent selection of books and maps. For outdoor activities, pick up *The Hole Outdoors*, a free Driggs monthly. Teton Valley Hospital (☎ 208-354-2383) is at 283 N 1st St E. Laundry N' Lunch (☎ 208-354-2718), 190 N Main St, is more than just a place to clean clothes.

Activities

The Teton River offers great **fishing**. In Driggs, Basin Travel Stop (☎ 208-354-2787), 111 N Main St, and Ye Old Spirits & Beverage Shoppe (☎ 208-354-8414), 52 N Main St, offers fishing licenses and tips. Trails crisscrossing the Big Hole Mountains are excellent for **mountain biking**. Nearby **hiking** trails head east up canyons on the west side of the Tetons, including Darby and Teton canyons. Backcountry hiking trails can be snow-covered as late as July, so plan accordingly. The area around Teton Pass on Hwy 33 is great for backcountry **skiing**. Teton Aviation Center (☎ 208-354-3100, 800-472-6382), 675 Airport Rd, Driggs, offers **glider rides** for an aerial

tour of the Teton Range. Several stores offer advice and rent skis, snowboards, snowmobiles, kayaks, mountain bikes and camping gear.

About 8 miles from Victor, on the Idaho-Wyoming state line, Rendezvous Ski Tours (☎ 208-787-2906) operates three huts accessible for **backcountry skiing**. The huts are at different elevations (8000, 8400 and 8800 feet), but are all reached by 4-mile trails that are skiable by anyone with basic cross-country skills. The huts sleep up to eight people and rent for $150 per night, not including food and sleeping gear, which you must bring yourself. Rendezvous also has guided trips that start at $125 per person, per night, and include food, bedding and meals.

As part of the package (whether you hire a guide or not), Rendezvous provides transportation from either Jackson or Idaho Falls and has a guest house where clients can stay before and/or after their backcountry trip for $40 per person, per night, including breakfast. The huts fill quickly on weekends and holidays, so make reservations at least one month before you want to go. The guest house is also open during summer months, when Rendezvous offers guided nature tours.

Places to Stay

Camping The well-maintained *Teton Valley Campground* (☎ 208-787-2647; fax 208-787-2647), 1 mile south of Victor on Hwy 31, has a pool, showers and a laundry. Grassy, shaded tent sites cost $19; sites with full hookups cost $26. Several USFS campgrounds (starting at $5) are in the area: *Pine Creek Campground* is 5 miles south of Victor on Hwy 31 and *Trail Creek Campground* is 6 miles southeast of Victor on Hwy 33. The USFS *Reunion Flat Campground* (7500 feet) and *Teton Canyon Campground* (7200 feet) are about 10 miles east of Driggs in the forested Teton Canyon; take USFS Rd 025 east past Alta, WY, and turn right onto USFS Rd 009.

B&Bs The *Teton Creek B&B* (☎ 208-354-2584), 41 S Baseline Rd, half a mile south of Driggs, ranges from $55 to $75. The Teton-view rooms at the *Wilson Creekside Inn B&B* (☎ 307-353-2409) in Alta range from $70 to $80. The *Alta Lodge B&B* (☎ 307-353-2582), 590 Targhee Towne Rd, Alta, ranges from $65 (with shared bathroom) to $85.

Hotels & Motels The *Pines Motel & Guest Haus* (☎ 208-354-2774, 800-354-2778), 105 S Main St, Driggs, has singles/doubles for $35/40; those with shared bathroom cost $30/35. *Intermountain Lodge* (☎ 208-354-8153), 34 E Ski Hill Rd, 1 mile east of Driggs, has two-bed log cabins with kitchens for $59. At the *Teton Tepee Lodge & Ski Shop* (☎ 307-353-8176), Alta, rooms start at $60. The *Teton Mountain View Lodge* (☎ 208-456-2741, 800-625-2232), 510 Egbert Ave, Tetonia, costs $61/66. They also rent snowmobiles during winter. *Best Western Teton West* (☎ 208-354-2363, 800-252-2363), 476 N Main St, Driggs, has an indoor pool; rooms range from $63 to $74. The *Super 8 Motel* (☎ 208-354-8888), 133 S Hwy 33, at the north end of Driggs, costs $70. (Also see Grand Targhee Ski & Summer Resort below.)

Places to Eat
Driggs has several decent restaurants. *The Breakfast Shoppe* (☎ 208-354-8294), 95 S Main St, serves hearty breakfasts and lunches. *Java the Hut* is next door. *Stompin' Grounds Cafe & Coffee* (☎ 208-354-3283), 285 N Main St, serves espresso and healthy food throughout the day. *O'Rourke's Fine Food & Beer* (☎ 208-354-8115), 42 E Little Ave, is a sports bar and grill serving sandwiches ($5) and pizza. Across the street, *Mike's Eats* (☎ 208-354-2797), 10 N Main St, serves breakfast, pizza and barbecue 'buf' burgers in a handsome old storefront. Another good choice is *Tony's Pizza & Pasta* (☎ 208-354-8829), 364 N Main. *Barrels & Bins* (☎ 208-354-2307), 36 S Main St, is a well-stocked natural foods store.

Old Dewey House Restaurant (☎ 208-787-2092) is at 37 S Main, Victor. The *Knotty Pine* (☎ 208-787-2866), 58 S Main St, Victor, is a good place for baby back

ribs, steak and seafood with live music on weekends, as well as breakfast and lunch. *Cicero's Sue Casa* (☎ 208-787-2099), on Victor's Main St, serves authentic Mexican food. Try the huckleberry shake at Victor's *Emporium* (☎ 208-787-2221), 45 N Main St, an old-fashioned fountain. For home-style food in Tetonia, go to *Trails End Cafe* (☎ 208-456-2202), 110 N Main St.

Getting There & Away
Bus The CART (☎ 208-354-2240) bus stops at 47 S Main St, Driggs. Buses go twice daily to Idaho Falls via Rexburg (6:30 am and 2 pm). The one-way fare is $7.50. Buses go to Jackson, WY, as needed; the one-way fare is $13.

Car Hwy 33 parallels the Idaho-Wyoming state line; Victor is 23 miles west of Jackson, WY. The accurately-named Teton Scenic Byway follows Hwy 33 north from Victor through Driggs and Tetonia, where Hwy 33 turns sharply west, and turns north onto Hwy 32 and continues to Ashton. Hwy 31 leads southwest from Victor 21 miles to Swan Valley. Hwy 33/Hwy 22 between Victor and Jackson crosses the Teton Pass (8429 feet), which has a 10% grade for several miles on both sides. It is plowed during winter.

GRAND TARGHEE SKI & SUMMER RESORT
On the west side of the Teton Range, Grand Targhee Ski & Summer Resort (☎ 307-353-2300, 800-827-4433; info@ grandtarghee.com), Alta, WY, is revered for its incredible depth of powder snow (over 500 inches of snow falls each winter!), its high-mountain location and its easy-going but professional service and amenities. Base elevation is 8100 feet, and high-speed lifts to the top of Fred's Mountain (10,200 feet) access 1500 acres of runs, with a total vertical drop of 2200 feet in 3.2 miles. The runs are suited for families and intermediate-level skiers. Full-day lift tickets cost $39/24 for adults/children (six to 14); half-day lift tickets (12:30 to 4 pm) cost $24/20. Seniors (62-69) pay $24 for a

IDAHO

full-day ticket and $20 for a half-day ticket. Lift tickets are free to seniors over 70.

Adjacent Peaked Mountain (10,230 feet) is reserved for **snowcat powder skiing**, wherein large snow machines haul skiers 2800 feet to the top for a wilderness ski experience. Half/full-day powder skiing rates are $145/210; lessons are available. Grand Targhee offers a full range of rentals and instruction, and operates a Nordic center. Nearly 10 miles of trails are groomed for skating and classic Nordic skiing. Trail passes cost $8 for adults and $5 for seniors/ children. Snowboards are welcome on all slopes. The ski season is mid-November to mid-April. Other winter activities include snowshoeing, sleigh rides and dog sledding.

Targhee, as it is often called, is a year-round resort with hiking, climbing, horseback riding and lift-served mountain biking during summer. A one-hour hike to the top of Targhee affords a spectacular vista of the Grand Teton itself; ride the lift down free. Their summer **music festival** series includes Rockin' the Tetons in mid-July, the Blues & Microbrew Fest in late July and the Grand Targhee Bluegrass Music Festival in early August.

Places to Stay & Eat
Lodgings, based on a minimum double occupancy, are: *Targhee Lodge* (standard room $101), *Teewinot Lodge* (deluxe room with hot tub $132), or the *Sioux Lodge Condominiums*. Sioux Lodge has four-person studios ($177), six-person lofts ($254) and eight-person two-bedroom units ($315). Rates fluctuate seasonally. (Also see Teton Valley above.)

Getting There & Away
The resort is reached from Driggs. Head 4 miles east on USFS Rd 025 (toward Alta) to the Idaho-Wyoming state line, and, in Wyoming, continue east 8 miles to Targhee. From the second switchback en route to the resort is the first glimpse of the Grand Teton and an overlook of the Teton Basin.

Resort shuttles between Targhee and airports in Idaho Falls and Jackson, WY, cost $60 for one person or $30 per person for two or more people; reservations are required.

Targhee Express (☎ 307-734-9754) operates once-daily winter bus service between Jackson, Teton Village (☎ 307-733-3101) and Targhee. One bus departs Snow King Resort at 7:30 am, making three Jackson stops; another departs Teton Village at 7:40 am, making two stops. Buses depart Targhee at 4:45 pm for Jackson and Teton Village. The roundtrip fare is $12; reservations are required by 9 pm the previous night.

HENRY'S FORK
North of Ashton, US 20 climbs steadily out of the potato-rich plains and onto a plateau covered with lodgepole pine forests. Here the Henry's Fork of the Snake River (elevation 6490 feet), one of loveliest rivers in Idaho, hurries purposefully through meadows and open forests. It is easy to spend a few days in the area.

Along Henry's Fork on US 20 are the small towns of Last Chance and Island Park, and the privately owned 'resort' of Macks Inn, which sits in an 18-by-23-mile-wide caldera, with 1200-foot escarpments on its south and west rims. West of Island Park is the large **Island Park Reservoir**, popular for fishing and kayaking, with campgrounds and several boat launches. Several fly-fishing outfitters, guides and stores are in the area.

Information
For information, contact the Island Park Chamber of Commerce (☎ 208-558-7448), PO Box 83, Island Park, ID 83429, and the very useful USFS Targhee National Forest Island Park Ranger Station (☎ 208-558-7301), off US 20 on the towns' southern outskirts. Macks Inn Laundry & Shower is on USFS Rd 059, 100 yards east of US 20.

Mesa Falls Scenic Byway
The 28-mile Mesa Falls Scenic Byway (Hwy 47) begins at US 20 just east of Ashton and rejoins US 20 one-quarter mile north of the entrance to Harriman State Park of Idaho (see below). Along the drive are Lower and Upper Mesa Falls (65 feet

and 114 feet, respectively) and views of the distant Teton Mountains. Paved Hwy 47 ends beyond Upper Mesa Falls and the byway continues on the unpaved and unmaintained USFS Rd 294. Attractive USFS campgrounds are at *Warm River* and *Lower Falls*.

Harriman State Park of Idaho

In 1902 UP investors bought a 4500-acre ranch on the banks of Henry's Fork. Railroad Ranch, as the holding was known, operated as a working ranch and getaway for the wealthy UP shareholders, including Solomon Guggenheim, Charles Jones and Edward Harriman. The ranch was deeded to the state as Harriman State Park of Idaho (☎ 208-558-7368) in 1961 by Harriman's children. This gift actually spurred the establishment of the state park division. The elaborate old ranch buildings are open to visitors, and 16,000 acres around the ranch are designated as the **Harriman Wildlife Refuge**. Over 5000 trumpeter swans winter on the broad spring-fed Henry's Fork, with several pair resident year-round. The park is one of Idaho's best wildlife viewing areas, with abundant elk, deer, moose, black bear, beaver, otter, eagles, osprey, duck and sandhill cranes. The legendary Henry's Fork rainbow trout lures anglers. The park offers 20 miles of trails for hiking, cycling, horseback riding and cross-country skiing.

The day-use fee is $3. Camping is not allowed, but 9 miles west of the park entrance is the USFS *West End Campground*. The park is west of US 20 19 miles north of Ashton and 8 miles south of Island Park.

Big Springs National Natural Landmark

The South Fork of the Henry's Fork River rises magically out of a cleft in a wooded slope, where Big Springs delivers 120 million gallons per day from sources deep within the volcanic mountain. Enormous rainbow trout feed at the spring and are protected from fishing. Idaho's best population of gray owls lives in the surrounding forest. Turn east onto USFS Rd 059 just

south of Macks Inn and go 5 miles to the parking area. A trail leads to the springs, while another nature trail follows the newborn river for 1 mile. The nearby stark USFS *Big Springs Campground* costs $8.

Henry's Lake State Park

Fishing is the main attraction in the Henry's Lake basin (6596 feet), centered around Henry's Lake State Park (☎ 208-558-7532), 17 miles southwest of West Yellowstone, MT. The park and campgrounds are open Memorial Day to September; sites range from $7 to $10.

Hiking

Northwest of Macks Inn is **Sawtell Peak** (9866 feet). The trail crosses the Continental Divide and offers views of the Yellowstone caldera, then drops into the Rock Creek Basin. Head west from US 20 on USFS Rd 024 to the trailhead.

Places to Stay & Eat

Several private campgrounds (starting at $10) are along US 20, but a few USFS campgrounds (about $8) are lovely and worth the short drive. In addition to those listed above, try the USFS *Box Canyon Campground*, 1½ miles up USFS Rd 134 north of Last Chance, and *Upper Coffee Pot*, on unpaved USFS Rd 311, 2 miles west of US 20 south of Macks Inn, with a lovely riverside hiking trail.

Henry's Fork Landing Cafe & Motel (☎ 208-558-9201) is in Last Chance. A nice place is *Pond's Lodge* (☎ 208-558-7221) in Island Park, with rooms in an attractive log lodge or cabins ranging from $40 to $160. *Macks Inn* (☎ 208-558-7272) has RV sites ($15) and rooms ranging from $27 to $105.

For good fun, go to *Big Jud's Country Diner* (☎ 208-652-7806), on US 20 in Ashton, and order their 1-lb burger; if you eat the whole thing there, they take your picture, hang it on the wall and send you out the door with a waffle ice-cream cone. In Last Chance, at *The Chalet* (☎ 208-558-9953) enjoy tasty hashbrowns and homemade pies amid the ceaseless banter between three generations of family members who run the place.

Getting There & Away

Bus Greyhound buses stop at Macks Inn along their daily route between Salt Lake City, UT, and Bozeman, MT.

Car Island Park is on US 20, 49 miles north of Rexburg and 29 miles southwest of West

Yellowstone, MT, via Targhee Pass (7072 feet) on the Continental Divide and Idaho-Montana state line. US 20 can be congested during summer. The Ashton-Flagg Ranch Rd (USFS Rd 261) leads east from Ashton to the John D Rockefeller Memorial Parkway (see the Greater Yellowstone chapter in the Wyoming section), a seldom-used back way into northwestern Wyoming wilderness areas and national parks.

Central Idaho Rockies

Powerful rivers flowing through mountainous terrain characterizes this region, which contains the largest contiguous wilderness in the lower 48 states. The Salmon River, the USA's longest undammed river, runs 425 miles across central Idaho, beginning in the heart of the Sawtooth National Recreation Area (8000 feet) and ending at its confluence with the Snake River (905 feet) in Hells Canyon National Recreation Area south of Lewiston. The Continental Divide to the east follows the incised ridges of the Bitterroot Mountains along the Idaho-Montana state line. It takes time to drive the few two-lane, winding roads that penetrate this vast wilderness. Much of the region is accessible only by hiking, rafting, horsepacking or driving for miles along unpaved USFS roads. Many recreation enthusiasts fly into the region's numerous remote air strips. To see this vast and wild country requires some planning and initiative. Innumerable outfitters and guide services can ease your trip into the wilderness. Most communities have at least one that handles rafting, fishing, mountain biking, cross-country skiing and/or horseback riding.

Watch for dehydration in this arid terrain. Rattlesnakes and poison ivy are common.

Central Idaho

The aptly named Sawtooth Mountains, the most dramatic range in the central Idaho Rockies, tower above numerous lakes in the broad Stanley Basin. The Salmon River flows north through this valley before continuing its gentle course northeast toward the town of Salmon. North of Salmon, the river pivots to the west and begins its descent through North America's second deepest gorge – a wild canyon nicknamed the River of No Return. Large irrigated

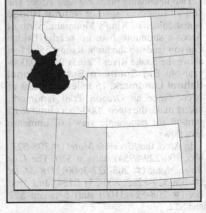

meadows and cattle ranches flank much of the river. To the south, world-renowned Sun Valley Resort nestles in the Big Wood River valley between the Smoky and Pioneer mountains.

IDAHO

ARCO & LOST RIVER VALLEY

Arco (population 1085; elevation 5328 feet), at the northern edge of the Snake River Plain, is the gateway to the Pioneer, Lost River and Lemhi mountains. The Big Lost River flows through the desolate valley between the Pioneer and Lost River ranges only to disappear south of Arco beneath the lava flows of the Craters of the Moon National Monument (see below). Arco is the Butte County seat and has a few basic campgrounds, motels and restaurants. Contact the Butte County Chamber of Commerce (☎ 208-527-8977) at 132 W Grande Ave, PO Box 837, Arco, ID 83213.

US 93 runs north from Arco along the Big Lost River past Mackay, the valley's only other town, crosses Willow Creek Summit (7160 feet) and descends to Challis (see Challis later in this chapter). The Lost River Range contains **Borah Peak** (12,662 feet), the highest peak in Idaho. In October 1983, this arid valley was the scene of a 7.3 earthquake that dropped the valley floor 9 feet and raised the peak 6 inches. Numerous trails and campgrounds are in the region.

Two interesting hikes are near Arco. The 80-foot limestone span of **Natural Bridge** is a shoulder of King's Mountain, north of Arco; a strenuous hike up nearby Bridge Canyon leads to the arch. Rising 2500 feet above the Snake River Plain is the 300,000-year-old **Big Southern Butte National Natural Landmark**, 15 miles southeast of Arco. Once an Oregon Trail landmark, hikers make the steep 2000-foot climb to its summit for panoramic views of immense lava flows.

In Arco, the *Riverside Motel* (☎ 208-527-895, 800-229-8954) starts at $20. The *Lost River Motel* (☎ 208-527-3600), *DK Motel* (☎ 208-527-8282, 800-231-0134) and *Arco Inn* (☎ 208-527-3100) start between $27 and $32.

The Idaho Falls-based Community and Rural Transport (CART; ☎ 208-527-9944) sends twice daily buses twice a week (Tuesday and Friday) from Pickles Place to Idaho Falls (at 9:45 am and 6:45 pm) and north to Salmon via Mackay and Challis (at 8:15 am and 5:15 pm). Arco is on US 20/ US 26 at the junction of US 93, which leads north to Mackay (27 miles) and Challis (54 miles beyond Mackay). Arco is 67 miles west of Idaho Falls and 18 miles east of Craters of the Moon National Monument.

IDAHO NATIONAL ENGINEERING LABORATORY

In a stretch of grim desert, this laboratory (known as INEL) established in 1949 is one of the US government's primary atomic energy and technology test sites. The first electrical generation using nuclear fission took place here in 1951, and in 1955 nearby Arco became the first community in the world to be powered by atomic energy. The world's first nuclear power plant, known as **EBR-1**, is a national historic landmark. This long-ago mothballed breeder reactor now serves as a visitors center (☎ 208-526-2331) for the 890-sq-mile nuclear reservation, with exhibits on the development of nuclear energy in the Idaho desert. The reservation is still the site of major nuclear research and development projects, many of which were done in conjunction with the Pentagon. One major project studies disposal of spent nuclear fuel from power plants and atomic submarines. Lockheed, the aircraft manufacturing giant, currently manages the reservation for the US Department of Energy and employs 6700 people. To reach INEL, take US 26 east of Arco for 20 miles or US 20 west of Idaho Falls for 46 miles. Call ☎ 208-526-0050 to arrange guided tours. The visitors center and EBR-1 reactor are open 8 am to 4 pm daily Memorial Day to Labor Day. Admission is free.

CRATERS OF THE MOON NATIONAL MONUMENT

Craters of the Moon National Monument (☎ 208-527-3257), PO Box 29, Arco, ID 83213, is an 83-sq-mile showcase of volcanism. Part of the Great Rift System, the northern edge of the Snake River Plain meets the base of the Pioneer Mountains here. Lava flows, cinder cones, lava tubes and spatter cones offer glimpses into the volcanic activity that formed the Craters of the Moon 15,000 year ago and ceased only 2000 years

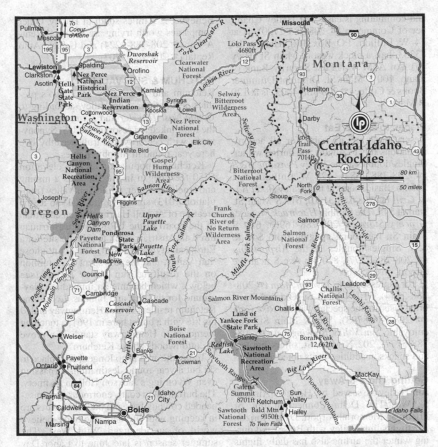

ago. The visitors center, open 8 am to 6 pm daily, has interesting exhibits. The 7-mile **Crater Loop Rd**, open late April to mid-November, is the easiest way to see the area and its unique wildlife by vehicle or bicycle. Allow at least two hours to explore the route. Several short trails lead from Crater Loop Rd to the edge of craters, onto cinder cones, and into undeveloped tunnels and lava caves (bring a flashlight). The barren black basalt absorbs heat, and by mid-morning on a sunny summer day temperatures can be over 100°F. The volcanic rock is sharp, so wear sturdy shoes. During winter, the loop road is excellent for **cross-country skiing**; you

can call ☎ 208-527-3257 for a ski report. The day-use fee is $4 per vehicle and includes a park brochure and map. A surreal campground ($10) near the entrance station is open May to October. The monument is on US 20/US 26 18 miles west of Arco, or a one-hour drive southeast of Ketchum.

HAILEY

Hailey (population 5423; elevation 5342 feet), 12 miles south of Ketchum on Hwy 75, has the airport for Ketchum and Sun Valley (see below) and is the birthplace of poet Ezra Pound (1902). Hailey's accommodations are less expensive than Ketchum's, and commuting is easy. The Hailey Chamber of Commerce (☎ 208-788-2700), is at 14 W Bullion, PO Box 100, Hailey, ID 83333, half a block west of Main St (Hwy 75). An ATM is at First Security Bank of Idaho, 100 S Main St. Different Drummer Books & Coffee (☎ 208-788-4403) is at 120 N Main St.

Places to Stay & Eat
Reservations are advisable for all accommodations July to August and during winter. Singles/doubles at the *Povey Pensione B&B* (☎ 208-788-4682), 128 W Bullion, cost $45/55. Basic rooms at the *Hailey Hotel Bar & Grill* (☎ 208-788-3140), 619 S Main St, start at $45. The humble *Hitchrack Motel & Grocery Store* (☎ 208-788-1696), 619 S Main St, has rooms ranging from $40 to $55. Singles/doubles at the *Airport Inn* (☎ 208-788-2277), 820 4th Ave S near the airport, cost $58/66.

For espresso, go to *Java on Main* (☎ 208-788-2444), 310 N Main St. Old-fashioned breakfasts are the specialty at *Sun Rise Cafe* (☎ 208-788-8793), 106 N Main St. The enjoyable *Sun Valley Brewing Co* (☎ 208-788-5777), 202 N Main St, offers burgers and snacks in addition to its noted ales.

Getting There & Away
Air Hailey is served by Horizon Air and SkyWest/The Delta Connection out of Friedman Memorial Airport. Daily Horizon Air flights link Hailey with Boise, and during winter the airline also has daily flights from Seattle, WA, and weekend flights from Portland, OR. SkyWest/The Delta Connection operates daily flights between Hailey and Salt Lake City, UT. The nearest major airports are in Boise (see Boise in the Snake River Plain chapter) and Salt Lake City.

Car Hailey is on Hwy 75 12 miles south of Ketchum and 69 miles north of Twin Falls. It is a 2½- to three-hour drive west to Boise (about 140 miles).

Getting Around
Avis (☎ 208-788-2382) is at the airport and Budget (☎ 208-788-3660), 118 N Main,

Bellevue, is 3 miles south of Hailey. Other companies worth trying are Practical Rent-A-Car (☎ 208-788-3224) and U-Save Auto Rental (☎ 208-788-9707).

KETCHUM & SUN VALLEY
Ketchum and Sun Valley are Idaho's premier destinations. Sun Valley, according to *Condé Nast Traveler* and *Ski* magazines, is the top-ranked ski resort in the US. Synonymous with celebrity, the truly wealthy live here year-round in 'trophy' homes.

Ketchum (population 3280; elevation 5750 feet) began in the 1880s as a mining and smelting center, while Sun Valley (population 1013) sprang to life in 1936 as the creation of Averell Harriman, then chairman of the board of the UP Railroad. Harriman hired an Austrian count to select a site for a European-style ski resort. The count chose Sun Valley, and the UP spent $1.5 million on the resulting Sun Valley Resort (see below), which became an immediate playground for the rich and famous. Long-time Ketchum resident Ernest Hemingway ended his life with a bullet here in 1961; a touching memorial to Hemingway stands in a grove of cottonwoods above Ketchum.

Today the area is no longer just a place to ski but a year-round destination, surpassing even Wyoming's Jackson Hole in its finery. The buffalo-skin coats, enormous turquoise-banded cowboy hats and buckskin skirts are in keeping with life here, the make-believe world of an idealized Wild West. The summer season is late June to Labor Day and the winter season December to March, depending on snow conditions.

Orientation
Hwy 75 parallels the Big Wood River through this narrow north-south valley, with its discrete communities of Ketchum, Sun Valley and Elkhorn. Ketchum is the main commercial district along Hwy 75 (Main St) and has an abundance of restaurants, hotels and boutiques. In Ketchum, northeast-southwest streets are numbered and northwest-southeast avenues are named and numbered; 3rd St is replaced by Sun Valley Rd, which leads 1 mile northeast to Sun

IDAHO

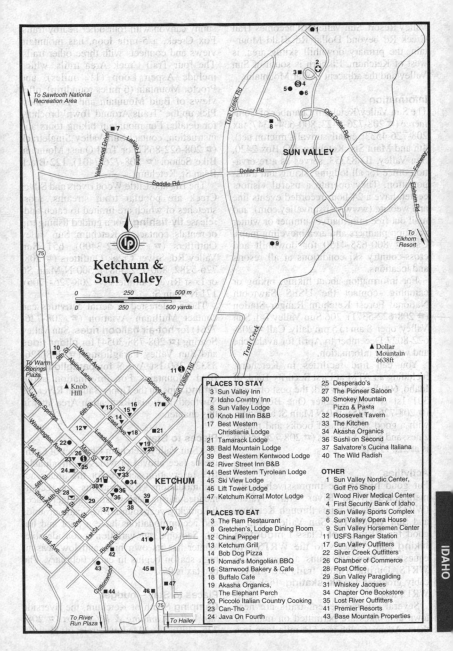

PLACES TO STAY
3 Sun Valley Inn
1 Idaho Country Inn
8 Sun Valley Lodge
9 Knob Hill Inn B&B
17 Best Western
Christiania Lodge
21 Tamarack Lodge
38 Bald Mountain Lodge
39 Best Western Kentwood Lodge
42 River Street Inn B&B
44 Best Western Tyrolean Lodge
45 Ski View Lodge
46 Lift Tower Lodge
47 Ketchum Korral Motor Lodge

PLACES TO EAT
3 The Ram Restaurant
8 Gretchen's, Lodge Dining Room
12 China Pepper
13 Ketchum Grill
14 Bob Dog Pizza
15 Nomad's Mongolian BBQ
16 Starwood Bakery & Cafe
18 Buffalo Cafe
19 Akasha Organics,
The Elephant Perch
20 Piccolo Italian Country Cooking
23 Can-Tho
24 Java On Fourth

25 Desperado's
27 The Pioneer Saloon
30 Smokey Mountain
Pizza & Pasta
32 Roosevelt Tavern
33 The Kitchen
34 Akasha Organics
36 Sushi on Second
37 Salvatore's Cucina Italiana
40 The Wild Radish

OTHER
1 Sun Valley Nordic Center,
Golf Pro Shop
2 Wood River Medical Center
4 First Security Bank of Idaho
5 Sun Valley Sports Complex
6 Sun Valley Opera House
9 Sun Valley Horsemen Center
11 USFS Ranger Station
17 Sun Valley Outfitters
22 Silver Creek Outfitters
26 Chamber of Commerce
28 Post Office
29 Sun Valley Paragliding
31 Whiskey Jacques
34 Chapter One Bookstore
35 Lost River Outfitters
43 Premier Resorts
41 Base Mountain Properties

IDAHO

Valley Resort. Sun Valley Rd becomes Trail Creek Rd beyond Dollar Rd. Bald Mountain, the primary downhill skiing area, is west of Ketchum. Elkhorn is south of Sun Valley and the adjacent Dollar Mountain.

Information

The Sun Valley/Ketchum Chamber of Commerce (☎ 208-726-3423, 800-634-3347; fax 208-726-4533; email sunval@micron.net), 4th and Main Sts, Ketchum, PO Box 2420, Sun Valley, ID 83353, serves as a reservation office for all lodging, skiing and transportation. They operate a useful visitors center, have a 24-hour recorded events line and website (www.visitsunvalley.com), and mail out free informative summer or winter vacation planners and area bicycling maps. Call ☎ 800-635-4150 for downhill and cross-country ski conditions at all resorts and locations.

For information about hiking, biking or camping, contact the USFS Sawtooth National Forest Ketchum Ranger Station (☎ 208-622-5371), 206 Sun Valley Rd, Sun Valley, open 8 am to 5 pm daily. Call ☎ 208-622-8027 December to April for avalanche and weather information.

You can find facilities in Ketchum, including an ATM at First Security Bank of Idaho, 600 Sun Valley Rd; the post office at 301 1st Ave N; Chapter One Bookstore (☎ 208-726-5425), 160 N Main St at 2nd St, with a good selection of books and magazines; and Suds Yer Duds (☎ 208-726-9820) is at 220 Lewis.

Activities

For good **hiking** the impressively well-maintained Wood River Trail System (WRTS) winds 20 miles through Ketchum and Sun Valley. The Sun Valley Trail is good for 10 miles of Class I **mountain biking** and connects to the WRTS. An equestrian lane also runs alongside the WRTS. During winter, trails are impeccably groomed for **ski-skating**. Pick up a WRTS map.

Several other excellent trails are near town and bikes are permitted on many of them. Adams Gulch is a 5½-mile loop in a sunny canyon with four other nearby trails. Fox Creek, a 5-mile loop, has mountain views and connects with three other trails. The four Trail Creek Area trails, which include Aspen Loop (1¾ miles), and Proctor Mountain (6 miles roundtrip), offer views of Bald Mountain and Sun Valley. Pick up the 'Trails Around Town' brochure for details. For mountain biking tours and instruction, contact Sun Valley Singletrack (☎ 208-622-8687) or Trail Quest Mountain Bike School (☎ 208-726-7401), 122 Black Bean St, Ketchum.

The Big and Little Wood rivers and Silver Creek are popular trout streams, most stretches of which are limited to catch-and-release **fly-fishing**. For a guided fishing trip or rentals, contact, in Ketchum: Sun Valley Outfitters (☎ 208-622-3400), 651 Sun Valley Rd; Silver Creek Outfitters (☎ 208-726-5282, 800-732-5687), 500 N Main St; or Lost River Outfitters (☎ 208-726-1706), 171 N Main St.

Those interested in aerial activities can contact Mulligan Aviation (☎ 208-726-7261) for **hot-air balloon rides**, Sun Valley Soaring (☎ 208-788-3054) for **glider rides** and Sun Valley Paragliding (☎ 208-726-3332), 260 1st Ave N for **paragliding** off Bald Mountain. For information about **rafting** trips on the Upper Salmon River see Sawtooth National Recreation Area later in this chapter.

Places to Stay

The Sun Valley/Ketchum Chamber of Commerce (see above) provides an invaluable, free reservation service for the area's accommodations. Reservations are recommended during peak seasons; budget places fill quickly year-round. Most campgrounds and accommodations have a pool and hot tub. Seasonal rate variation is considerable. Winter has its own high and low season; high season begins in early February. The bed tax is 9%.

Places to Stay – budget

Camping South of Ketchum, the riverside *Sun Valley Camping & RV Resort* (☎ 208-726-3429), 106 Meadow Circle, off Hwy 75 north of the Elkhorn Rd junction, has a Jacuzzi and pool. Sites start at $19. Showers cost $5 for nonguests. The USFS *Boundary Campground*, on Trail Creek Rd 3 miles east of the USFS Ketchum Ranger Station, is free, and sites fill quickly.

Motels & Hotels Several options are along Ketchum's S Main St within walking distance of downtown. The *Ski View Lodge* (☎ 208-726-3441), 409 S Main St, has multicolored two-bed log cabins ranging from $40 to $70. The *Lift Tower Lodge* (☎ 208-726-5163, 800-462-8646), 703 S Main St, faces Bald Mountain. Rooms start at $56. *Ketchum Korral Motor Lodge* (☎ 208-726-3510, 800-657-2657), 310 S Main St, has nice older log cabins ($58 to $85), which are off the road surrounded by trees. Rooms at the slightly faded *Bald Mountain Lodge* (☎ 208-726-9963, 800-892-7407), 151 S Main St, start at $70. Convenient to Ketchum's restaurants and nightlife is the *Best Western Christiania Lodge* (☎ 208-726-3351, 800-535-3241), 651 Sun Valley Rd. Rooms range from $64 to $79, and there is a pool.

Places to Stay – middle
Convenient to Warm Springs Plaza, the pleasant *Heidelberg Inn* (☎ 208-726-5361, 800-284-4863; fax 208-726-2084), 1908 Warm Springs Rd, has rooms starting at $65. The *Tamarack Lodge* (☎ 208-726-3344, 800-521-5379), 500 E Sun Valley Rd, has a pool and rooms with fireplaces ranging from $89 to $139. The *Best Western Tyrolean Lodge* (☎ 208-726-5336, 800-333-7912), 260 Cottonwood St, has beautiful views of Bald Mountain and is within walking distance of River Run Plaza. It has a spa and exercise room; singles/doubles cost $80/90.

Places to Stay – top end
B&Bs The *River Street Inn B&B* (☎ 208-726-3611, 800-954-8585; fax 208-726-2439; riverst@sprynet.com), 100 Rivers St W, has large, comfortable rooms starting at $130. The attractive European-style *Knob Hill Inn B&B* (☎ 208-726-8010, 800-526-

8010; fax 208-726-2712), 960 N Main St, has sumptuous rooms, a pool, a spa, a sauna and two restaurants. Rooms range from $160 to $300.

Hotels At the modern *Best Western Kentwood Lodge* (☎ 208-726-4114, 800-805-1001), 180 S Main St, rooms range from $105 to $145. The small and luxurious *The Idaho Country Inn* (☎ 208-726-1019, 800-250-8341), 134 Latigo Lane, has hot tubs, outstanding views and spacious sunny rooms ranging from $125 to $185. *Pinnacle Inn at the Mountain* (☎ 208-726-5700, 800-255-3391; fax 208-726-2877), is at the Warm Springs Plaza. Rooms range from $100 to $150 during summer and $195 to $350 during winter.

Long-Term Rentals If you're interested in renting a private home or condominium, contact these Ketchum-based property management firms: Base Mountain Properties (☎ 208-726-5601, 800-521-2515, bmp@sunvalley.net), 200 Rivers St W; Premier Resorts (☎ 208-727-4000, 800-635-4404, premier-resorts@sunvalley.net), 333 S Main St; and High Country Property Rentals (☎ 208-726-1256, 800-726-7076, highctry@micron.net). A property's proximity to the lift areas affects rates dramatically.

Places to Eat
Ketchum boasts over 80 restaurants and offers good values for the budget conscious. *Java on Fourth* (☎ 208-726-2882), 191 4th St, serving espresso and gourmet coffees, is also open at night for homemade desserts. *Buffalo Cafe* (☎ 208-726-9795), 320 East Ave N, makes omelets and serves buffalo burgers ($6) for lunch. At *The Kitchen* (☎ 208-726-3856), 200 Main St, an omelet with hashbrowns ($6) is a breakfast favorite. *Bigwood Bakery* (☎ 208-726-2034), 270 Northwood Way, bakes organic, naturally leavened bread and operates a cafe. For wholesome homemade food, go to *Starrwood Bakery & Cafe* (☎ 208-726-2253), 591 4th St E. Try *Akasha Organics*, at The Elephant Perch on Sun Valley Rd and downstairs in Chapter One Bookstore

IDAHO

(☎ 208-726-4777), 160 N Main St, for organic juices and vegetarian soups.

Two popular pizza places are *Bob Dog Pizza* (☎ 208-726-2358), 451 4th St E, and *Smokey Mountain Pizza & Pasta* (☎ 208-622-5625), 200 Sun Valley Rd. *Sushi on Second* (☎ 208-726-5181), 260 2nd St at Main St, serves traditional dishes as well as Idaho-inspired ones like crispy trout. *Desperado's* (☎ 208-726-3068), 4th St at Washington Ave, serves inexpensive Mexican food on their outdoor deck. For something lighter, go to *Can-Tho* (☎ 208-726-6207), 460 Washington Ave N, a Vietnamese restaurant.

You do not need to dress up or spend a lot to eat out in style. *Piccolo Italian Country Cooking* (☎ 208-726-9251), 220 East Ave N, serves three-course pasta meals ($13). The *Ketchum Grill* (☎ 208-726-4460, 208-726-7434), 520 East Ave, offers a friendly welcome and good values in a converted old home; vegetarian dishes make up half the menu. *Nomad's Mongolian BBQ* (☎ 208-726-0556), 571 4th St E, serves affordable hearty authentic stir-fry dishes. *The Wild Radish* (☎ 208-726-8468), 200 S Main St, offers international cuisine at lunch and dinner (entrees start at $10).

For superior Asian food, go to *China Pepper* (☎ 208-726-0959), 511 Leadville Ave; try chili prawns with coriander. *Roosevelt Tavern* (☎ 208-726-5083), 280 N Main St, serves steak, sushi and seafood; trout is $14. The best Italian restaurant is *Salvatore's Cucina Italiana* (☎ 208-726-3111), 111 Washington Ave N, with pasta and traditional veal dishes. *The Pioneer Saloon* (☎ 208-726-3139), 308 N Main St, a nationally ranked restaurant, is the ultimate choice for prime rib, steak and seafood.

Entertainment
Thunder Mountain Brewery, 251 Northwood Way E, is a lively place to quaff a pint and talk about snow conditions. A steady stream of musicians passes through the area. Most bars and lounges have music on weekends. A good place to catch the local scene is *Whiskey Jacques* (☎ 208-726-3200), 206 N Main St.

Getting There & Away
Air See Hailey above for local air service. Boise Municipal Airport and Salt Lake City International Airport are the nearest major airports.

Boise Municipal Airport Shuttle Sun Valley Stages (☎ 800-574-8661) operates winter shuttles between Sun Valley and the Boise Municipal Airport, with stops at the Sun Valley Inn, the Sun Valley/ Ketchum Chamber of Commerce and the Chevron station in Hailey. Shuttles depart the Sun Valley Inn at 7 and 9 am; they depart Boise at 1:45, 3:30 and 5 pm. The trip takes three hours and costs $40/70 one-way/roundtrip.

Bus Sun Valley Stages (☎ 208-733-3921) also operates a charter service between Twin Falls and Ketchum during winter; call to inquire about individual seats.

Car Ketchum is on Hwy 75, 12 miles north of Hailey and 61 miles south of Stanley. Sun Valley is just 1 mile northeast of Ketchum.

Getting Around
Bus Ketchum Area Rapid Transit (KART; ☎ 208-726-7140, 208-726-7576) operates free bus service to River Run Plaza, Warm Springs Plaza, Ketchum, Sun Valley and Elkhorn.

Car U-Save Auto Rental (☎ 208-622-9312) and Practical Rent-A-Car (☎ 208-622-4525), 512 N Main St, are in Ketchum. Others car rental companies are at the airport in Hailey.

Taxi Call A-1 Taxicab (☎ 208-726-9351) or Bald Mountain Taxi & Limo (☎ 208-726-2650) for a taxi.

SUN VALLEY RESORT
The doyen of Ketchum and Sun Valley is undoubtedly the Sun Valley Resort. The grand old Sun Valley Lodge has a princely lobby with a photographic display of the glitterati on skis – from Mary Pickford to

Gary Cooper, Lucille Ball, the Kennedys and Marilyn Monroe.

Orientation & Information

The resort is centered east of Sun Valley Rd and north of Dollar Rd, 1 mile northeast of Ketchum and east of Hwy 75. The resort operates separate facilities at Bald Mountain, west of Ketchum, and Dollar Mountain, on Elkhorn Rd south of the junction of Fairway, Dollar and Old Dollar Rds in Sun Valley. Within the resort is the Sun Valley Mall with several restaurants, sports outfitters and other stores, a movie theater and a post office along an outdoor pedestrian boardwalk.

Contact the Sun Valley Resort (☎ 208-622-4111, 800-786-8259 reservations; fax 208-622-3700) for accommodation and Bald Mountain reservations; ask for the resort recreation guide. Call the Sun Valley Sports Information Line (☎ 208-622-2231) for information on all resort activities and for Dollar Mountain reservations. First Security Bank of Idaho has an ATM here. Wood River Medical Center (Moritz Hospital; ☎ 208-622-3333) is adjacent to the resort.

Bald Mountain

The forested slopes of Bald Mountain (9150 feet), known locally as Baldy, catch tons of dry powdery snow, making this a world-class mountain for downhill skiing. From the summit, 64 diverse runs descend a maximum of 3400 vertical feet and are served by 13 lifts; almost two-thirds of the runs are rated for advanced skiers. Snowboarding is welcomed. Bald Mountain has two lift areas, each with a day lodge, restaurant and ski school (☎ 208-622-2248): **River Run Plaza**, south of Ketchum off 3rd St, and **Warm Springs Plaza**, northwest of Ketchum on Warm Springs Rd. A day lodge, also with a restaurant, is on Seattle Ridge (8600 feet). Two other restaurants on the mountain, Lookout and Roundhouse, are served by lifts. Full-day lift tickets cost $52/29 for adults/children; half-day $37/21. Multiple-day lift tickets are available at a discount.

Mid-June to mid-September, lifts operate 9 am to 4 pm; tickets cost $12/5 for adults/children. The **Bald Mountain Trail** has great views; take the lift one-way, walk the other. Trails traverse the mountain; Broadway Trail connects the summit to Seattle Ridge, and the Cold Springs Trail links with the WRTS and the Warm Springs Trail. Lifts from River Run Plaza are open for lift-served mountain biking. Pick up the Sun Valley 'Mountain Biking, Hiking, Sightseeing Trail Map' for details. The 8-mile **Baldy Perimeter Trail** is the ultimate for experienced mountain bikers.

Dollar Mountain

Dollar Mountain (6638 feet) is Sun Valley's original ski area. Its sage-covered arid slopes contrast dramatically to Baldy's higher elevation and forested slopes. Dollar Mountain has five lifts serving 13 easy runs with a 628-foot maximum vertical drop, making it a favorite of beginners and families. Snowboarding is welcomed. Full-day lift tickets cost $24/17 for adults/children; half-day $16/10. During summer, the area is popular for mountain biking and horseback riding.

Sports Center

The resort's Sports Complex offers almost every activity imaginable. The Nordic center offers ski rentals, instruction and access to 25 miles of groomed trails, and the resort has one of country's 100 best golf courses (reservations are necessary). Also popular are tennis; the skating center, open for ice skating 10 am to 9 pm daily year-round; winter sleigh rides to a log cabin in the woods, where lunch or dinner is served; and guided horseback rides on Dollar Mountain from the horsemen center (☎ 208-622-2387 reservations only) on Sun Valley Rd south of Dollar Rd.

Places to Stay

Sun Valley Resort has four accommodations: *Sun Valley Lodge*, where rooms range from $139 to $204 and suites start at $264; *Sun Valley Inn*, with rooms from $99 to $169; *Lodge Apartments*, offering one-to three-bedroom units from $139 to $399; and *Sun Valley Condominiums*, which has studio to four-bedroom units ranging from $119 to $299.

Places to Eat

Try *The Konditorei* in the mall for breakfast and lunch, featuring grilled sandwiches like bratwurst and chicken schnitzel (about $7). *The Ram Restaurant* (☎ 208-622-2225), at Sun Valley Inn, serves steak, pasta and seafood; entrees range from $14 to $22. *Gretchen's*, at the Sun Valley Lodge, serves breakfast, lunch and dinner. The *Lodge Dining Room* (☎ 208-622-2150) is the area's most exclusive restaurant, serving traditional French cuisine accompanied by live music; the Sunday brunch is popular.

Entertainment

Internationally renowned figure skaters perform in the popular *Sun Valley Ice Show*, held Saturday evenings during summer at the outdoor ice arena (☎ 208-622-8020) behind Sun Valley Lodge; admission includes an outdoor buffet. The *Sun Valley Opera House* (☎ 208-622-2244) shows films and has occasional musical events. The *Sun Valley Summer Symphony* (☎ 208-622-5607) presents free classical music concerts during August in an open-air tent.

Getting There & Away

Hailey airport transfers are complimentary for resort guests.

AROUND KETCHUM & SUN VALLEY

A mile south of Sun Valley on Elkhorn Rd, **Elkhorn Resort** (☎ 208-622-4511, 800-355-4676) has a golf course, sports facilities and restaurants. Elkhorn, as it is commonly called, also offers groomed cross-country trails, instruction and rentals. Accommodations are in the lodge or condominiums. Rates range from $95 to $295 in summer; $89 to $275 in winter. During summer, the Jazz on the Green concert series is held in the courtyard Thursday evenings. Elkhorn Village Stables (☎ 208-622-8503) are off Village Loop Rd.

East of Ketchum is **Hyndman Peak**, a 12,000-foot mountain. The stiff 5000-foot climb to the summit is popular. Much of it is cross-country, and many hikers stop at Hyndman Saddle, short of the summit. Access is from USFS Rd 203; from Ketchum, go south on Hwy 75 to Gimlet and turn east onto Fork Wood River Rd, which connects with USFS Rd 203.

Sun Valley Helicopter Ski Guides (☎ 208-622-3108, 800-872-3108), 260 1st Ave N, Ketchum, offers **heli-skiing** trips into the Pioneer Mountains, northeast of Ketchum, mid-December to April.

SAWTOOTH NATIONAL RECREATION AREA

Established in 1972, the 400-sq-mile USFS-administered SNRA spans parts of the Sawtooth, Smoky, Boulder and Salmon River mountains. These timbered slopes, with 42 peaks over 10,000 feet, are home to four major rivers (Salmon, South Fork Payette, Boise and Big Wood), 1000 lakes, 100 miles of streams and 700 miles of trails. The broad spring-fed meadows beneath these peaks are collectively known as the Stanley Basin. The adjacent 340-sq-mile Sawtooth Wilderness Area centers around the rugged Sawtooth Range. Pockets of privately owned land, including the town of Stanley, dot the area, primarily along Hwy 75. The region, visited by 1.5 million people annually, offers easy access to endless recreational activities and supports commercial timber harvesting, grazing and mining.

Recreation in the SNRA and Stanley (see below) has two short seasons: winter and July through August (although some residents argue it is only July). It can snow any month of the year. Summer activities include hiking, fishing, rafting, horseback riding, boating and camping. Snowmobiling is the most popular winter activity, followed by cross-country skiing.

Orientation

North-south Hwy 75 runs through the SNRA parallel to the Salmon River and offers access to most of the lakes, trailheads and campgrounds. Alturas, Pettit and

River Trips
Rafting and kayaking are big business in Idaho, and with good reason: the state is blessed with some gorgeous and exciting rivers. The best way to enjoy these is to try an overnight or multiple-day trip. Some good choices are listed below.

Main Fork Salmon National Wild & Scenic River
The largest undammed river in the US offers camping on sandy beaches, wildlife viewing opportunities, hiking, fishing, and visiting historical buildings, pictographs and hot springs. Class III-III+

Middle Fork Salmon National Wild & Scenic River
This premium Alpine river bisects the Frank Church River of No Return Wilderness Area, the largest wilderness area in the lower 48 states. The 3000-foot vertical drop offers more than 100 Class III-IV rapids. Highlights include the canyon's geologic diversity, picturesque hikes to waterfalls, hot springs and pictographs and superb fly-fishing. The Middle Fork is combinable with Main Fork Salmon River.

Lower Fork Salmon River
This fork passes through four gorges and is at lower elevations. It has fun Class III rapids, warmer water and great beaches, making it desirable for families. This can be done as an overnight trip.

Snake National Wild & Scenic River through Hells Canyon
The classic Class III-IV river has all things big – waves, views, cliffs – as well as offering great wildlife viewing, fishing and swimming.

Middle Fork Clearwater National Wild & Scenic River
The Selway and Lochsa rivers, tributaries of the Middle Fork Clearwater, offer tough Class III-V rapids. ∎

Redfish lakes, all west of Hwy 75, are popular activity centers. Many USFS roads branch off Hwy 75. At Stanley, Hwy 75 turns sharply east toward Challis, and Hwy 21 heads northwest. The only western access to the SNRA is from Grandjean on Hwy 21 via remote USFS Rd 524.

Information
Entrance Pass All SNRA and Sawtooth National Forest visitors are required to have a Recreation User Pass. Vendors include the SNRA headquarters and USFS Stanley and Lowman ranger stations. A day pass costs $2; an annual pass $5.

Tourist Offices The SNRA headquarters (☎ 208-726-7672, 800-260-5970), Hwy 75 (Star Route), 8½ miles north of Ketchum, is open 8:30 am to 5 pm daily and 9 am to 4:30 pm daily during winter. During spring and fall it is closed Sunday. The 'Your Guide to the Sawtooth National Recreation Area' brochure is only available here. They sell books, USGS topographical maps, the 'USFS Sawtooth National Forest Travel Map,' Earthwalk Press' *Sawtooth Wilderness Hiking Map & Guide* and 'Bike Routes to the Sawtooths.' The SNRA Stanley Ranger Station (☎ 208-774-3681), on Hwy 75 3 miles south of Stanley, open daily mid-June to Labor Day, and weekdays the rest of the year, has extensive information on day hikes and campgrounds. They sell USGS topographical and Idaho Department of Transportation maps. The Redfish Lake visitors center (☎ 208-774-3376), open 9 am to 5 pm Wednesday to Sunday mid-June to Labor Day, offers guided tours and evening programs Wednesday to Saturday July 4 to Labor Day.

Useful Organizations The Sawtooth Wildlife Council (☎ 208-774-3426), PO Box 92, Stanley, ID 83278, works to protect wildlife and their habitat, emphasizing

IDAHO

education and recovery of salmon populations, and publishes a quarterly newsletter.

Laundry & Showers At Redfish Lake near the gas station are laundry and showers ($1 for three minutes). Showers are also available at Easley Hot Springs.

Galena Summit
Galena Summit (8701 feet), on Hwy 75 north of the SNRA headquarters, marks the watershed between the Salmon and Big Wood rivers. Alexander Ross discovered this pass in 1824 while searching for beaver. The overlook has breathtaking views of the Stanley Basin to the north. At the southern base of Galena Summit is the old silver and lead mining town of Galena, founded in 1879.

Historic Ghost Towns
Six and a half miles north of Galena Summit, **Vienna** was a thriving town with 2000 buildings after Levi Smiley discovered gold there, but by 1900 it had became a ghost town. Follow USFS Rd 077 (Smiley Creek Rd) 10 miles west from Hwy 75. A mile farther north on Hwy 75, USFS Rd 204 (Beaver Creek Rd) leads 2 miles west to **Sawtooth City**, which flourished in the 1880s; site excavation is ongoing.

Sunbeam Dam & Hot Springs
Remnants of Sunbeam Dam, the only dam ever built on Salmon River, are visible from Hwy 75 11 miles east of Lower Stanley. The hydropower dam, built in the 1900s, supplied power for gold mining. The hot springs are a favorite stop for rafters, drivers

along Hwy 75 and visitors heading to/from the Land of the Yankee Fork State Park (see Challis & Around later in this chapter).

Sawtooth Fish Hatchery
Self-guided tours of the Sawtooth Fish Hatchery (☎ 208-774-3684), which works to restore salmon and steelhead trout populations, are possible during summer.

Scenic Flights
Stanley Air Taxi (see Stanley later in this chapter) offers scenic half-hour/one-hour flights ($86/160).

Rafting
Half-day rafting trips (7 to 12 miles) on the Upper Main Salmon River (Class II-III) are ideal for beginners and families. Half-day trips start at $63; trips with a riverside meal start at $80. To book a trip, contact:

The River Company
    PO Box 2329, Sun Valley, ID 83353
    (☎ 208-726-8890, 800-398-0346;
    fax 208-726-8895)
    Hwy 21, Stanley (☎ 208-774-2244,
    800-398-0346)
Triangle C Ranch Whitewater Expeditions
    PO Box 69, Stanley, ID 83278
    (☎ 208-774-2266, 800-303-6258)
White Otter Outdoor Adventures
    211 Sun Valley Rd (☎ 208-726-4331,
    208-838-2406 summer only, 800-438-4331)

From June to mid-July the put-in is usually Basin Creek, which is 8½ miles east of Stanley and offers a longer run with two Class IV rapids. Mid-July to August the put-in is Elk Creek downstream of Sunbeam Dam, 13½ miles east of Stanley. The take-out is near Torrey's Hole, 21½ miles east of Stanley.

Independent rafters need self-issuing permits to raft this section of the Upper Salmon River; permit instructions are obvious along Hwy 75 at the put-ins. Controlled launch times are usually 9 am to 3 pm daily. Mid-August to mid-September rafters must portage the salmon spawning beds at Indian Riffles and Torrey's Hole. From the shore the nests of salmon eggs, called 'redd,' which lie covered by a layer of gravel, are

Launch Reservations for Access-Controlled Rivers

Private (noncommercial) rafters need to have launch reservations for access-controlled sections of four National Wild & Scenic Rivers:

Main Fork Salmon River
North Fork Ranger District
100 River Rd, PO Box 100, North Fork, ID 83466 (☎ 208-865-2725 application requests, 208-865-2700 information; fax 208-865-2739)

Middle Fork Salmon River
Middle Fork Ranger District
US 93 N, PO Box 750, Challis, ID 83226-0750 (☎ 208-879-4112 application requests, 208-879-4101 information; fax 208-879-4198)

Snake River
Hells Canyon NRA
PO Box 699, Clarkston, WA 99403 (☎ 509-758-1957; fax 509-758-1963)

Selway River
West Fork Ranger District
6735 West Fork Rd, Darby, MT 59829 (☎ 406-821-3269; fax 406-821-1211)

Advance planning is required because more applications are submitted each year than there are permits to be allocated. Even though almost 1100 trip permits are issued annually for more than 10,000 rafters on these rivers, not everyone gets a launch reservation or receives a permit for their preferred river and launch date. Contact any of the above offices after October 1 for an information packet and application form for any of these rivers. They accept applications with a nonrefundable $6 fee only between December 1 and January 31. A February computer lottery determines who gets launch reservations. To inquire about unassigned, canceled or unconfirmed launches, which are reassigned on a first-come, first-served basis, call the above offices 8 am to 4:30 pm weekdays after February. On commercial rafting trips, the outfitter handles these details. (See the listing for each river later in this chapter for more details.) ■

---

visible. Authorities close the river when rafters violate these regulations.

Hiking

The SNRA trails offer great day hikes and backpacking trips. The most popular trails lead into the Sawtooth Wilderness Area. The Sawtooth National Forest provides free brochures describing most hikes.

South of Galena Summit For hikes into the Boulder Mountains, turn north off Hwy 75 at the SNRA headquarters onto USFS Rd 146 (North Fork Rd), and go 5.2 miles to the North Fork trailhead. For nice lake hikes, turn west off Hwy 75 onto Prairie Creek Rd, 10 miles north of the SNRA headquarters, and drive 2½ miles to the Prairie and Miner lakes trailhead.

North of Galena Summit For hikes into the very popular Sawtooth Valley and Sawtooth Wilderness Area, turn west off Hwy 75 at milepost 170.3 onto Pettit Lake Rd and drive 2 miles to the Tin Cup trailhead. To hike into the White Cloud Mountains, Hwy 75 at milepost 174.6, turn east onto unpaved 4th of July Creek Rd. Champion Creek trailhead is 5 miles east, and 4th of July Lake trailhead is 10 miles east. Hikes in the Redfish Lake Area lead into the Sawtooth Wilderness Area. Turn southwest off Hwy 75 at milepost 185.1 onto Redfish Lake Rd and go 2 miles to the Redfish Lake trailhead. Most hikers then take the shuttle boat across the lake (see Boating below). To reach Sawtooth Lake, turn off Hwy 21 at milepost 128.4, west of Stanley, and go south on unpaved Iron Creek Rd

IDAHO

4 miles to the Iron Creek trailhead. The very popular 5-mile hike to Sawtooth Lake beneath Mt Regan (10,190 feet) climbs 1700 feet.

Mountain Biking
Mountain biking is very popular. Easy rides are on Decker Flat Rd, west of Hwy 75 at milepost 174.7; and Nip and Tuck Rd, half a mile up Valley Creek Rd, north of Hwy 21 at milepost 125.9. More difficult rides are the Galena Loop, starting from Galena Lodge, and the Fisher Creek-Williams Creek Loop, starting at Fisher Creek Rd east of Hwy 75 at milepost 176.3. Galena Lodge has 25 miles of dirt-and single-track mountain bike trails. Mountain bikes are for rent at the gas station near Redfish Corrals. Backroads (☎ 510-527-1555, 800-462-2848; fax 510-527-1444), 801 Cedar St, Berkeley, CA 94710-1800, offers six-day cycling trips.

Climbing & Mountaineering
The White Cloud and Boulder mountains, east of Hwy 75, offer many nontechnical mountaineering routes. The granite Sawtooth Range, west of Hwy 75, offers fine wilderness Alpine climbs. Idaho's finest high-standard long routes (grade III-V, rated 5.8 to 5.11) are on Elephant Perch, west of Redfish Lake, as is popular Mt Heyburn. The Redfish Lake Lodge serves as a climbing information center for the area.

Skiing
South of Galena Summit are the two **cross-country skiing** areas of Prairie Creek, west of Hwy 75, and Galena Lodge (☎ 208-726-4010), east of Hwy 75. Galena Lodge offers world-class Nordic skiing with rentals, lessons, groomed trails and hut skiing. Backcountry **ski touring** is possible throughout the SNRA.

Boating
Shuttle boats cross Redfish Lake with a minimum of four passengers, departing the far end of the lake at 9 am, 2, 5 and 7 pm. The one-way fare is $5/2.50 for adults/children (under six). *Lady of the Lake* offers one-hour scenic tours of Redfish Lake at 10 am, noon and 3 pm. Tours cost $6.50/4.50 for adults/children.

Fishing
Trout-fishing is seasonally good in Redfish, Stanley and Alturas lakes. Visit McCoy's Tackle & Gift Shop (☎ 208-774-3377), Niece Ave at Ace of Diamonds Ave, Stanley, to ask where the fish are biting.

Horseback Riding
Galena Stage Stop Corrals (☎ 208-726-1735), at the southern base of Galena Summit, and Redfish Corrals (☎ 208-774-3311), near Redfish Lake, offer 1½-hour ($28), half-day ($56) and full-day ($85) horseback rides mid-June to Labor Day.

Places to Stay & Eat
Camping The SNRA has 37 campgrounds in five regions: Wood River Corridor, south of Galena Summit; Alturas Lake Area, on Hwy 75 north of Galena Summit; Redfish Lake Area, south of Stanley; Stanley Lake Area, off Hwy 21 west of Stanley; and Salmon River Canyon, on Hwy 75 east of Stanley. Reservations (made at least five days in advance) are possible at the following campgrounds: *Easley* in the Wood River Corridor; *Point* and *Glacier View* in the Redfish Lake Area; and *Elk Creek*, *Sheep Trail* and *Trap Creek* in the Stanley Lake Area. Sites at other campgrounds are on a first-come, first-served basis; most start at $9. Wheelchair-accessible campsites are at Wood River and Alturas and Redfish lakes. Evening programs are held at the Redfish Lake amphitheater and Wood River Campground. The popular *Easley Campground*, 12 miles north of SNRA headquarters, has hot springs. Three miles south of Stanley, Redfish Lake, on Redfish Rd west of Hwy 75, has six campgrounds; *Sockeye*, the most remote, has quiet sites above the lake. Campgrounds along the lake's east side have the best mountain views. Along Stanley Lake, on USFS Rd 455, 4 miles west of Stanley and 3½ miles off Hwy 21,

are the picturesque *Stanley Lake* and *Lakeview* campgrounds.

Lodges *Galena Lodge* serves breakfast and lunch daily and dinner on weekends. The year-round *Smiley Creek Lodge* (☎ 208-774-3547), north of Galena Summit, has tent sites ($10), sites with full hookups ($20), tepees ($35), cabins ($40) and lodge rooms ($50). Food is mediocre, but their ice cream parlor and smoothies are good. *Redfish Lake Lodge* (☎ 208-774-3536), on Redfish Lake, has lodge rooms with shared bathroom, cabins, motel rooms and a restaurant. It is open Memorial Day to Labor Day. (Also see Stanley below.)

Getting There & Away
Three scenic byways access the SNRA. From the south, the 116-mile Sawtooth Scenic Byway follows Hwy 75 between Shoshone and Stanley. From the west, the 131-mile Ponderosa Pine Scenic Byway follows Hwy 21 between Stanley and Boise. From the east, the 162-mile Salmon River National Scenic Byway follows Hwy 75 between Stanley and Challis, and continues on US 93 between Challis and Salmon.

STANLEY
The old ranching and mining community of Stanley (population 96) sits at 6300 feet amid breathtaking scenery. The first gold strike in the Stanley Basin was in 1863, and mining continued until 1879. Today Stanley is an enclave of the SNRA (see above) and an excellent base for exploring the area. Tourism is definitely well-established, but remote Stanley retains a low-key demeanor.

Orientation & Information
Upper Stanley sprawls along Hwy 21, while Lower Stanley is on Hwy 75, 1 mile north of the Hwy 21/Hwy 75 junction. The rustic old town is along the unpaved Ace of Diamonds Ave, one block south of and parallel to Hwy 21. The Stanley-Sawtooth Chamber of Commerce (☎ 208-774-3411, 800-878-7950) in the community building

on Hwy 21, PO Box 8, Stanley, ID 83278, is open 9 am to 5 pm daily. The Sawtooth Hotel & Cafe has a small bookstore. Jerry's Country Store has an ATM.

Things to See & Do
The **Stanley Museum** (☎ 208-774-3517), Hwy 75 about half-mile north of the Hwy 21 junction, is in a former ranger station. On the National Register of Historic Places, the museum recounts Stanley Basin history and is open 11 am to 5 pm daily late May to Labor Day; admission is by donation.

The Mountain Village Mercantile issues fishing licenses. Contact Sawtooth Guide Service (☎ 208-774-9947) for guided steelhead **fishing**. Sawtooth Rentals (☎ 208-774-3409, 208-734-4060), 13 River Rd, rents snowmobiles during winter, offering guided trips and instruction. They rent float-trip gear, ATVs, Jet skis and mountain bikes the rest of the year.

Places to Stay
Most places are log-cabin style and have kitchenettes. Rates are highest July to August; reservations are recommended. Spring and fall are the least expensive seasons.

Open May to mid-October, *Elk Mountain RV Resort* (☎ 208-774-2202), 4 miles west of Stanley on Hwy 21, has a few tent sites ($12), sites with hookups ($18), laundry, showers and a cafe (known for its barbecue ribs and chicken).

A charming place and the best deal in town is *The Cole's Sawtooth Hotel & Cafe* (☎ 208-774-9947), at the west end of Ace of Diamonds Ave. Singles/doubles cost $45/50; those with a shared bathroom cost $27/30. All other Stanley accommodations are along Hwy 21 west of the Hwy 75 junction. The well-appointed and -maintained *Valley Creek Motel* (☎ 208-774-3606) has Sawtooth-view rooms ($76) and its enthusiastic owner is a welcoming host. The newer and cute *Stanley Outpost* (☎ 208-774-3646) starts at $80. The rustic *Danner's Log Cabin Motel* (☎ 208-774-3539) has rooms with one bed ($45) and two beds ($60). Rooms with private decks and good views at the

Creek Side Lodge (☎ 208-774-2213, 800-523-0733) start at $59. The Triangle C Ranch Log Cabins (☎ /fax 208-774-2266, 800-303-6258) has small cabins ranging from $75 to $95. The attractive, large Mountain Village Lodge (☎ 208-774-3661, 800-843-5475; fax 208-774-3761) starts at $65/70 and has a natural hot spring. The least exciting of the bunch is the Meadow Creek Motel (☎ 208-774-3611); rooms range from $40 to $55.

All Lower Stanley accommodations are on Hwy 75 north of the Hwy 21 junction. The Salmon River Lodge (☎ 208-774-3422), off Hwy 75 east of the Salmon River, offers privacy and panoramic views; rooms range from $55 to $60. Sawtooth Rentals & Motel (☎ 208-774-3409, 800-284-3185), has rooms along the road for $65; riverfront rooms with private decks start at $85. Jerry's Motel (☎ 208-774-3566, 800-972-4627), at Jerry's Country Store, has clean riverfront rooms starting at $53. Gunter's Salmon River Cabins (☎ 208-774-2290, 888-574-2290) has rooms without kitchenettes ($60) and riverfront rooms ($105). Woolley's Lodging (☎ 208-774-2208) is less inspiring. The only non-log cabin in town is the Redwood Motel (☎ 208-774-3531), a well-maintained older property. Rooms without kitchenettes start at $46; other cottages start at $53. It is open late May to October.

Places to Eat

The Sawtooth Hotel & Cafe (☎ 208-774-9947) is open for breakfast and lunch; try their homemade soups and breads. They also serve espresso and desserts until 7 pm and prepare picnic lunches. Peaks & Perks in Lower Stanley has espresso and specialty coffees, homebaked goods and ice cream. Sawtooth Luce's Pizza & Suds (☎ 208-774-3361) serves what the name says. The Mountain Village Restaurant & Saloon (☎ 208-774-3317) features homestyle ranch cooking for breakfast, lunch and dinner. Kasino Club (☎ 208-774-3516), 21 Ace of Diamonds Ave, only open for drinks and dinner (starting at $11) on a first-come, first-served basis, promises 'service with a snarl.'

The only microbrew pub in the Stanley Basin, it offers a wide menu selection.

Getting There & Away

Air Stanley Airport is south of Hwy 21. Private air transport companies operate one- to eight-passenger nonscheduled intercity and charter flights from Stanley throughout central Idaho. Most charge an hourly rate for charter backcountry flights. Many, however, offer a fixed per-seat fare with a twopassenger minimum for certain intercity flights. Stanley Air Taxi (☎ 208-774-2276, 800-228-2236) is at the airport. McCall & Wilderness Air (☎ 208-774-2221 in Stanley summer only; other times 208-634-7137, 800-992-6559 in McCall or 208-756-4713, 800-235-4713 in Salmon) has fixed per-seat/charter fares for Boise-Stanley ($63/253, 35 minutes). Boise-based Access Air (☎ 800-307-4984) also has fixed per-seat fares for Boise-Stanley ($65); charter flights cost $155 per hour.

Car Stanley is at the junction of Hwy 75 and Hwy 21 at the northern end of the SNRA. It is 61 miles north of Ketchum, 52 miles southwest of Challis and 129 miles northeast of Boise.

Vehicle Shuttles River Rat Express (☎ 208-774-2265 in summer, 800-831-8942 year-round), PO Box 301, Stanley, ID 83278, operates a shuttle service. The put-in and take-out on several Idaho rivers are scores of miles apart, necessitating shuttling rafters, their vehicles and occasionally their nonriver gear back to where they started from. Rafters park their vehicles in designated lots near the put-in and River Rat Express drives rafters' vehicles to designated lots near the take-out. They also charter old school buses to shuttle rafters from these parking lots or nearby towns (from which you fly in or out) to the put-in and take-out points, which can be up to 50 miles away. Rates vary widely depending on individual needs; call for details. Sample rates for vehicle shuttles on the Salmon River are: Lower Fork $100, Middle Fork $135, Main Fork $195. They provide a crucial service for the rafting industry, but with no competition, their service is not the friendliest and their record, though long established, is somewhat dubious.

Getting Around
Contact the Mountain Village Lodge for car rental.

MIDDLE FORK SALMON NATIONAL WILD & SCENIC RIVER
Ranked one of the top 10 white-water rivers in world, the Middle Fork Salmon River has over 100 Class III-IV rapids in 100 miles. The river can be run May to September in four to eight days; most rafters do it in six. Bounded by Frank Church River of No Return Wilderness Area, it boasts hot springs, waterfalls, pictographs and riverside ranches and lodges.

A launch reservation is required June to September for rafting its 96 miles (see the Launch Reservations for Access-Controlled Rivers sidebar earlier in this chapter). Permits are still required for launch dates outside the controlled-access period. Starting in 1999, a $5 per person per day fee will be charged.

Daily commercial rates range from $205/185 to $262/207 for adults/children. To book a white-water trip, contact:

OARS
    PO Box 67, Angels Camp, CA (☎ 209-736-
    4677, 800-328-0290, 800-346-6277;
    fax 209-736-2902)
    1127-B Airway Ave, Lewiston, ID 83501
    (☎ 208-743-4201, 800-328-0290,
    800-346-6277)
Middle Fork Rapid Transit
    160 2nd St W, Twin Falls, ID 83301
    (☎ 208-734-7890, 208-774-3440 summer,
    800-342-9728; fax 208-733-0883)
Middle Fork River Expeditions
    PO Box 199, Stanley, ID 83278
    (☎ 208-774-3659 summer, 800-801-5146)
    1615 21st Ave E, Seattle, WA 98112
    (☎ 206-324-0364 winter, 800-801-5146)
Aggipah River Trips
    Box 425 E5, Salmon, ID 83467
    (☎ 208-756-4167)

Triangle C Ranch Whitewater Expeditions
    PO Box 69, Stanley, ID 83278
    (☎ 208-774-2266, 800-303-6258)
Echo: The Wilderness Company
    6529 Telegraph Ave, Berkeley, CA 94609-
    1113 (☎ 510-652-1600, 800-652-3246;
    fax 510-652-3987)
River Odysseys West
    PO Box 579, Coeur d'Alene, ID 83816
    (☎ 208-765-0841, 800-451-6034;
    fax 208-667-6506)

The Middle Fork combined with Main Fork Salmon makes an 11- to 12-day trip (see Main Fork Salmon National Wild & Scenic River later in this chapter). Daily commercial rates for combined Middle-Main trips range from $162/139 to $181/159 for adults/children.

Getting There & Away
At high water, the put-in is Boundary Creek (5640 feet), a two-hour drive northwest of Stanley. Take Hwy 21 northwest of Stanley to Bear Valley Rd (USFS Rd 198, which turns into USFS Rd 579). Head west to Dagger Falls Rd and continue north to the river. During early June when snow blocks access and late August when water is low, rafters put in downstream of Boundary Creek. The intermediate put-in, Indian Creek (4662 feet), about 20 miles downstream, has no road access and requires flying in; on a busy day, dozens of flights are not unheard of. (See Stanley for the nearest airport to the put-ins.) The take-out is at Cache Bar (3000 feet) on the Main Fork Salmon, 5 miles upstream from Corn Creek, the Main Fork Salmon put-in. (See Salmon later in this chapter for the nearest airport to the Cache Bar take-out. Also see Stanley for information about vehicle shuttles.)

CHALLIS & AROUND
Challis (population 1123; elevation 5280 feet), along the Salmon River, is in the broad, agricultural Round Valley between the Salmon River Mountains and Lost River Mountains, and is the trade town for a widespread ranching and mining community. During the 1960s, a large open-pit molybdenum mine opened southwest of town;

IDAHO

other area mines tap tungsten, copper and cobalt.

Orientation & Information

Challis is just west of US 93, north of the US 93/Hwy 75 junction. The Challis Area Chamber of Commerce (☎ 208-879-2771) is at 700 Main St, PO Box 1130, Challis, ID 83226. The USFS Challis National Forest Middle Fork Ranger District (☎ 208-879-4101), US 93 N, PO Box 750, Challis, ID 83226-0750, administers parts of four major mountain ranges: Pioneer, Salmon River, Lost River and Lemhi. The Land of the Yankee Fork is jointly administered by the USFS Challis National Forest Yankee Fork Ranger District (☎ 208-838-2201), Clayton, ID, and Idaho Department of Parks & Recreation (☎ 208-879-5244), PO Box 1086, Challis, ID 83226. The Land of Yankee Fork Historic Area visitors center (☎ 208-879-5244) is off Hwy 75 south of Challis.

Custer Motorway

The Custer Motorway, once a miners' toll road, links Challis to Custer. From Challis head west on Main Ave and Garden Creek Rd (west of 7th St). Turn north onto narrow unpaved USFS Rd 070 (Mill Creek Rd), crossing Mill Creek Summit to the Yankee Fork Rd and Custer. One campground is along Mill Creek Rd. This 35-mile route, usually open May to mid-October, is suited to high-clearance vehicles.

Land of the Yankee Fork State Park

Jordan Creek and the Yankee Fork were rich gold-mining centers in the 1870s, but by 1888 the General Custer mine closed. Nearby **Custer City** (6456 feet), now on the National Register of Historic Places, became a ghost town by 1910. Today, visitors can take a self-guided tour of the town's many restored buildings and the interesting **Custer Museum**. The museum is open 10 am to 5:30 pm mid-June to Labor Day, and admission is by donation. Admission to the site is free.

One mile west of Custer are the dilapidated remains of Bonanza, another former settlement. Nearby is the **Yankee Fork Gold Dredge**. Tours ($2.50) run from 10 am to 5 pm daily July to Labor Day. From Bonanza, USFS Rd 172 (Jordan Creek Rd) leads 9 miles north into the Frank Church River of No Return Wilderness Area.

Take Hwy 75 east of Stanley to Sunbeam, turn north onto paved USFS Rd 013 (Yankee Fork Rd), and continue 10 miles to Custer. Alternatively, follow the Custer Motorway (see above) from Challis to Custer. Several campgrounds north of Sunbeam on USFS Rd 013 are along the river.

Places to Stay

South of Challis, *Challis Hot Springs* (☎ 208-879-4442), 4½ miles west of US 93, has sites ranging from $11 to $15 with hot springs access. Several BLM campgrounds are on US 93 along the Salmon River between Challis and Salmon. The *Challis All Valley RV Park* (☎ 208-879-2393) has sites ranging from $10 to $15, showers and a laundry.

The Village Inn (☎ 208-879-2239, 208-879-4295), on US 93, offers kitchenettes and rooms ranging from $38 to $64. Comparably priced is the *Challis Motor Lodge & Lounge* (☎ 208-879-2251), US 93 at Main St. Overlooking the river, singles/doubles at the *Northgate Inn* (☎ 208-879-2490, 208-879-5767) cost $36/38.

Getting There & Away

Air Challis is served by Challis Aviation (☎ 208-879-2372), owned by Mountain Bird Inc (see Salmon below), out of Challis Municipal Airport.

Bus The Idaho Falls-based Community and Rural Transport (CART; ☎ 208-879-2448) operates twice daily buses twice a week (Tuesday and Friday) southbound to Idaho Falls via Mackay and Arco (8:05 am and 5:05 pm) and northbound to Salmon (10:05 am and 7:05 pm).

Car Challis is on US 93 north of the US 93/Hwy 75 junction 52 miles northeast of Stanley, 81 miles north of Arco, and 58 miles southwest of Salmon.

SALMON & AROUND

Salmon (population 3233, elevation 4000 feet) was just another ranch and lumber town in this wide and fertile valley until tourism along the Salmon River spurred new life. Today, Salmon caters to the throngs who come to raft and fish. Numerous shops sell outdoor gear.

Orientation & Information

US 93 becomes Main St downtown. The Salmon Valley Chamber of Commerce (☎ 208-756-2100; fax 208-756-4840) is at 200 Main St. On US 93 South are the USFS Salmon & Challis National Forest Ranger District (☎ 208-756-2215, 208-756-5100), and the BLM Salmon District office (☎ 208-756-5400, 208-756-2201). The Idaho Department of Fish and Game (☎ 208-756-2271) is at 1215 US 93 N.

Storyteller (☎ /fax 208-756-6121), 519 Main St, sells newspapers and books and provides fax services. Cyclists beware! On Main St you must walk your bike; many unwary cyclists have gotten tickets.

Things to See & Do

The **Lemhi County Historical Museum**, on Main St, is open 10 am to 5 pm daily. Salmon Air Taxi (see Getting There & Away below) offers **scenic flights** around Salmon for $145 per hour.

To book half-day and full-day **rafting** and **fishing** trips on the Salmon River near the town of Salmon, contact:

Idaho Adventures River Trips
    913 US 93 N, PO Box 834-B9, Salmon, ID 83467 (☎ 208-756-2986; fax 208-756-6373)
Warren River Expeditions
    PO Box 1375, Salmon, ID 83467
    (☎ 208-756-6387)
Wilderness River Outfitters & Trail Expeditions
    Hwy 28, PO Box 871, Salmon, ID 83467
    (☎ 208-756-3959)

Places to Stay

Camping The convenient *Salmon Meadows Campground* (☎ 208-756-2640), 400 N St Charles St, two blocks off Main St, has tent sites ($12) and sites with hookups ($15). *Century II Campground* (☎ 208-756-2063), 603 US 93 N, has $15 sites. Both have laundry and showers.

B&Bs Rooms start at $35 at the *Heritage Inn* (☎ 208-756-3174), 510 Lena St, and *Solaas B&B* (☎ 208-756-3903), Hwy 28. *Syringa Lodge B&B* (☎ 208-756-4424), 2000 Syringa Drive, has singles/doubles for $40/60. *Country Cottage Inn* (☎ 208-756-4319), 401 S St Charles St, costs $45/55.

Motels At the south end of town, the pleasant, clean *Suncrest Motel* (☎ 208-756-2294, 208-756-2299), 705 S Challis St (US 93 S) has singles/doubles for $31/33. Rooms at the *Motel DeLuxe* (☎ 208-756-2231), 112 Church St, cost $35/39. Two blocks north of the Salmon River Bridge is *Wagons West Motel* (☎ 208-756-4281, 800-756-4281), 503 US 93 N, with rooms for $42/46. Rooms at the inviting *Stagecoach Inn* (☎ 208-756-4251, 208-756-2919), 201 US 93 N, north of the bridge, costs $50/60. They have laundry and cater to rafters and other backcountry travelers who fly into remote central Idaho destinations. Anyone can park a vehicle here for free.

Places to Eat

HG's Place, Main St at S Andrew St, a great deli with microbrews on tap, is named for the building's original owner HG Redwine. The excellent *Food for Thought Eatery* (☎ 208-756-3950), 317B US 93 N, is one block north of Stagecoach Inn. Both have reasonable vegetarian selections. Try breakfast or lunch at the *Smokehouse Cafe* (☎ 208-756-4334), 312 Main St. The *Salmon River Coffee Shop* (☎ 208-756-3521), 606 Main St, serves basic but well-prepared chops, steak, chicken and burgers, and has a salad bar. For pizza, try *Garbonzo's Pizza* (☎ 208-756-4565), Hwy 28 South, or *Last Chance Pizza* (☎ 208-756-4559), 605 Lena St. *Nature's Pantry* (☎ 208-756-6067), Main St at N St Charles St, sells natural and freeze-dried camping foods.

Getting There & Away

Air Salmon Airport is 4 miles south on US 93 S. Private air transport companies

IDAHO

operate one- to eight-passenger nonscheduled intercity and charter flights throughout central Idaho. Most charge an hourly rate for charter backcountry flights. However, many offer a fixed per-seat fare with a two-passenger minimum for certain intercity flights. Salmon Air Taxi (☎ 208-756-6211, 800-448-3413; fax 208-756-6219), owned by Mountain Bird Inc, has fixed per-seat fares from Salmon to Stanley ($65), Salmon to Hailey ($80), Salmon to Boise ($100), Salmon to McCall ($85) and Salmon to Grangeville ($90). Wilderness Air (☎ 208-756-4713, 800-235-4713) also has fixed per-seat/charter fares for Boise-Salmon ($105/460). Boise-based Access Air (☎ 800-307-4984) also has fixed per-seat fares for Boise-Salmon ($99); charter flights cost $155/hour.

Bus The Idaho Falls-based Community and Rural Transport (CART; ☎ 208-756-2191), 402 Van Dreff St at S St Charles St, one block off Main St across from the fire station, operates twice daily (6:30 am and 4 pm) buses twice a week (Tuesday and Friday) along the Salmon-Challis-Mackay-Arco-Idaho Falls route. Buses return to Salmon the same day. One-way/roundtrip fares between Salmon-Idaho Falls are $22/40.

Car Salmon is on US 93 at Hwy 28, 58 miles northeast of Challis and 46 miles south of the Idaho-Montana state line.

NORTH FORK & AROUND

North Fork is 21 miles north of Salmon on US 93. Here rafters head west following the Main Fork Salmon River, and US 93 continues north 25 miles, where it crosses Lost Trail Pass (6995 feet) at the Idaho-Montana state line. Just over the border in Montana looms Lost Trail Powder Mountain, a popular downhill ski area (see the Bitterroot Valley section in the Montana chapters). The USFS Salmon National Forest North Fork Ranger District (☎ 208-865-2383, 208-865-2700) is at 100 River Rd. *Wagonhammer Campground* (☎ 208-865-2477) has sites ranging from $8 to $16. The *North Fork Motel & Campground* (☎ 208-865-2412; fax 208-865-2214) has both sites ($8 to $13) and motel rooms ($36 to $46) as well as showers. Rooms at *River's Fork Inn* (☎ 208-865-2301) range from $48 to $53.

MAIN FORK SALMON NATIONAL WILD & SCENIC RIVER

Bounded by five national forests, the Main Fork Salmon River flows through the second deepest canyon in North America. The Class III-IV river is run June to September in five to seven days. Along the river are hot springs, pictographs, historic sites and homesteads, including the interesting Buckskin Bill Museum at Five Mile Bar. Rafters can camp on beautiful beaches or stay at comfortable lodges.

A launch reservation is required from mid-June to mid-September if you want to raft the 79 river miles between Corn Creek (2920 feet) and Vinegar Creek (1960 feet) near Long Tom Bar (see the Launch Reservations for the Access-Controlled Rivers

Salmon of the Salmon River

Three species of salmon participate in one of the world's longest-known fish migrations, the 900-mile eight-month journey between the Upper Salmon River spawning beds and the Pacific Ocean. As of 1997 only 350 of the threatened Chinook, or king, salmon (*Oncorhynchus tschawytscha*) and a few endangered bright-red sockeye salmon (*Oncorhynchus nerka*) remain, along with 1200 steelhead (*Oncorhynchus mykiss gairdncri*), the ocean-going rainbow trout. Eight huge hydropower dams on the Lower Snake and Columbia rivers block the route between the spawning beds and ocean and are the greatest factor in the decline of these once abundant fish. None of the proposed solutions – barging fish around the dams or the large hatchery program – have halted the steady decline in the fish run. It now appears that unless the dams are removed the salmon of the Salmon River will vanish. ∎

Jet Boats on National Wild & Scenic Rivers?

The 1976 Wild & Scenic Rivers Act gave federal protection to designated rivers. The Central Idaho Wilderness Act of 1980, however, stripped Idaho's National Wild & Scenic Rivers of basic protection conferred by the 1976 Act as well as the more restrictive provisions of the Wilderness Act of 1964. How did this happen? Congress specifically directed that the requirements of the 1976 Act would take precedence. But in the 1980 Act Congress granted an allowance for jet boats, recognizing an 'historic use' of jet boats as an integral part of the transportation system on the Salmon River.

Today white-water rafters compete with jet boats on the Main Fork Salmon River and Snake River through Hells Canyon. Ironically, permits are required and access is controlled on National Wild & Scenic Rivers for rafters and kayakers, but not for jet boaters who have free rein to terrorize the waterways.

A 'jet back' is when a jet boat transports rafters back upstream after rafting, avoiding shuttles to return to their vehicles. Jet backs, however, are an intrusion whose frequency, especially on the Main Fork Salmon River, is escalating. Unfortunately jet boat use is not going to go away. Considered 'essential' to transport guests and supplies to private lodges along these rivers, their use is entrenched in local mentality. Rafters can avoid booking a trip with a company that uses jet backs or supports nonessential jet boat use, and so help preserve the wild and scenic nature of these amazing rivers. ■

sidebar earlier in this chapter). Reservations are not required at other times. Starting in 1999, a $5 per person per day fee will be charged. Daily commercial rates range from $170/157 to $216/186 for adults/children. To make a booking for a white-water trip, contact:

OARS
  PO Box 67, Angels Camp, CA (☎ 209-736-4677, 800-328-0290, 800-346-6277; fax 209-736-2902)
  1127-B Airway Ave, Lewiston, ID 83501 (☎ 208-743-4201, same 800 numbers as above)
Warren River Expeditions Inc
  PO Box 1375, Salmon, ID 83467 (☎ 208-756-6387, 800-765-0421; fax 208-756-4495)
Wilderness River Outfitters & Trail Expeditions
  PO Box 871, Salmon, ID 83467 (☎ 208-756-3959, 800-252-6581)
Aggipah River Trips
  Box 425 E5, Salmon, ID 83467 (☎ 208-756-4167)
Echo: The Wilderness Company
  6529 Telegraph Ave, Berkeley, CA 94609-1113 (☎ 510-652-1600, 800-652-3246; fax 510-652-3987)
Holiday River Expeditions Inc
  126 W Main St, PO Box 86, Grangeville, ID 83530 (☎ 208-983-1518, 800-628-2565; fax 208-983-1695)

Getting There & Away

The put-in is Corn Creek 27 miles west of Shoup, which is 19 miles west of North Fork. (See Salmon earlier in this chapter for the nearest airport to the put-in.) The take-out is east of Riggins at Carey Creek boat ramp. See McCall in the Snake River Plain chapter for the nearest airport to the take-out; see Stanley earlier in this chapter for information about vehicle shuttles.

North-Central Idaho

North-central Idaho is the mountainous midsection of Idaho, cleaved by the Salmon, Clearwater and Snake rivers to the south, north and west, respectively. The Snake River incises a deep gorge along the Idaho-Oregon state line. Few roads pass through this rugged area; US 95 and US 12 are the only north-south and east-west roads.

LEWISTON & CLARKSTON

The twin cities of Lewiston, ID, and Clarkston, WA, sprawl across the flood plain at the confluence of the Clearwater and Snake rivers. These friendly towns (elevation 736 feet) are at the southern edge of the

IDAHO

Palouse, a vast agricultural area producing peas, lentils, wheat and livestock. Lewiston (population 31,430) is referred to as the 'Inland Port,' as the Columbia and Snake rivers' dam and lock system allows barges to travel between Lewiston and Portland, OR. The Potlatch Lumber Mill on the Clearwater River is one of the state's largest timber-product facilities; its sour, sulfurous odor is immediately noticeable, but to locals it smells like jobs. Massive, bare canyon walls enclose these hardworking towns. Despite the desert-like aridity, their location at this great confluence has made Lewiston and Clarkston (population 7120) north-central Idaho's commercial center. Relatively new to the subtleties of tourism, Lewiston's and Clarkston's amenities are basic and inexpensive.

History

The towns' namesakes, Lewis and Clark (see The Lewis & Clark Expedition sidebar in Facts about the Rocky Mountains), passed through here in 1805 and 1806. The area, however, was first settled in 1860 at the beginning of Idaho's gold rush. The confluence was the head of steamboat navigation from Portland and the area boomed as a transport and trade center, but the land was part of the Nez Percé Indian Reservation and the Indian Agent would not allow permanent settlement. Thus, for two years Lewiston was a tent settlement of 2000. In 1863, Lewiston, the first incorporated town, was named territorial capital. In 1865, however, partisans of Boise stole the state seal and decamped to the south. Lewiston filed suit to regain the capital, to no avail.

Lewiston and Clarkston continued to grow as trade and transport hubs, especially as federal irrigation projects brought orchards along the protected and temperate canyon bottoms. The biggest change for the area, however, came in 1955 when the US Army Corps of Engineers began to build Washington state's four Snake River dams, which brought slackwater to the Port of Lewiston in 1975. Lewiston is the country's most inland port: vessels drawing less than 14 feet and weighing less than 12,000 tons journey upriver 470 miles from the mouth of the Columbia River to Lewiston's loading docks.

Orientation

Lewiston lies south of the Clearwater River and east of the Snake River; Clarkston is south and west of the Snake River. The effect is that of a huge T with a city tucked under each 'arm.' Two bridges cross the Snake River linking Lewiston and Clarkston: the Interstate Bridge (US 12); and the Southway Bridge. US 95/US 12 crosses Memorial Bridge over the Clearwater River at Lewiston's northeast end. North of Lewiston, US 95 climbs the 7% to 8% 2000-foot grade over Lewiston Hill.

Lewiston's downtown, below an imposing rock bluff, is along Main St between 1st and 9th Sts; US 12 bypasses downtown. Many newer businesses are along 21st St and Thain Rd, which lead south to the suburbs. Lewiston's numbered streets run north-south and numbered avenues run east-west. US 12 E north of Memorial Bridge is also called North & South Hwy.

Clarkston's downtown is along 5th and 6th Sts, although many businesses are on Bridge St (US 12). 6th St (Hwy 129) leads 5 miles south of Clarkston along the Snake River past the enormous basalt outcrop called Swallows Crest to Asotin, WA.

Information

The Lewiston Chamber of Commerce (☎ 208-743-3531, 800-473-3543) is at 111 Main St, Lewiston. The Clarkston Chamber of Commerce (☎ 509-758-7712, 800-933-2128) is at 502 Bridge St, Clarkston. The Idaho Department of Fish and Game (☎ 208-799-5010) is at 1540 Warner Ave, Lewiston.

Lewiston's post office is at 1613 Idaho St (zip 83501). Clarkston's is at 949 6th St. Kling's Book Store (☎ 208-743-8501), 704 Main St, Lewiston, sells books and regional maps. St Joseph Regional Medical Center (☎ 208-743-2511) is at 415 6th St, Lewiston. Tri-State Memorial Hospital (☎ 509-758-5511), is at 1221 Highland Ave, Clarkston. Do laundry at Express Mart (☎ 509-758-6927), 5th and Bridge Sts, Clarkston.

IDAHO

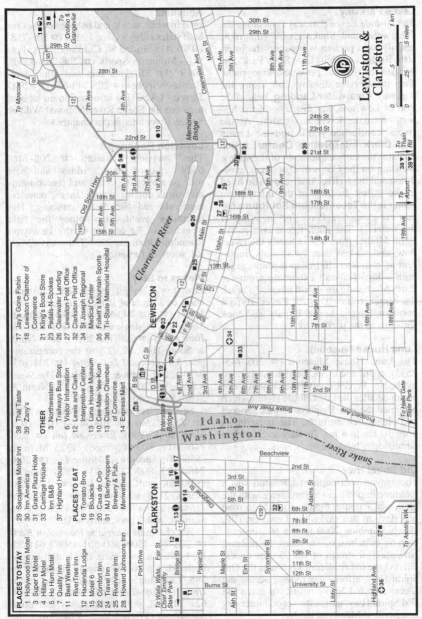

Lewiston & Clarkston

1 km
.5 miles
0   .5
0   .25   .5

PLACES TO STAY
1 Hollywood Inn Motel
3 Super 8 Motel
4 Hillary Motel
5 Ho Hum Motel
7 Quality Inn
11 Best Western
    River Tree Inn
12 Hacienda Lodge
15 Motel 6
22 Comfort Inn
24 Travel Inn
25 Riverview Inn
28 Howard Johnsons Inn

29 Sacajawea Motor Inn
30 Inn America
31 Grand Plaza Hotel
33 Carriage House
    Inn B&B
37 Highland House

PLACES TO EAT
16 Tomato Bros
19 BoJacks
20 Casa de Oro
31 MJ Barleyhoppers
    Brewery & Pub;
    Meriwethers

38 Thai Taste
39 Zany's

OTHER
6 Northwestern
    Trailways Bus Stop
9 Visitor Information
12 Lewis and Clark
    Interpretive Center
13 Luna House Museum
10 Cee-Mee-Nee-Kum
13 Clarkston Chamber
    of Commerce
14 Express Mart

17 Jay's Gone Fishin
18 Lewiston Chamber of
    Commerce
21 King's Book Store
23 Pedals-N-Spokes
26 Clearwater Landing
27 Lewiston Post Office
32 Clarkston Post Office
34 St Joseph Regional
    Medical Center
35 Follett's Mountain Sports
36 Tri-State Memorial Hospital

IDAHO

Levee Parkway

The 20-mile Levee Parkway runs along the Clearwater and Snake rivers (the most heavily used portion is between the Interstate Bridge and Hells Gate State Park) and is a source of local pride and enjoyment. Two interpretive displays are along the parkway. **Clearwater Landing**, behind the Port of Lewiston, has displays on the history of Snake River navigation. At the rivers' confluence you'll find the **Lewis and Clark Interpretive Center**, which explains the early exploration of the valley, focusing on the Corps of Discovery expedition and the Native Americans who lived in the valley. In front of the interpretive center is the **Tsceminicum Sculpture** *(si-min-eye-kum,* Nez Percé for 'meeting of the waters'). The main figure is a native Earth Mother from whose hands the rivers flow, and no less than 79 animals, representing characters in Indian legends, grace both sides of a wall extending from the Earth Mother figure's wild mane. To reach the center, follow D St or Levee Bypass between 1st and Levee Bypass and look for signs to the parking lot.

Luna House Museum

The Luna House Museum (☎ 208-743-2535), at 3rd and C Sts, Lewiston, operated by the Nez Percé County Historical Society, is named after the Luna House Hotel, which occupied the site. Displays include pioneer and Nez Percé artifacts. The museum is open 10 am to 4 pm Tuesday to Saturday; admission is by donation.

Old Spiral Hwy

The canyon wall north of Lewiston was a longtime impediment to commerce with the grain-rich Palouse. Finally, in 1914, a road was devised that snaked up Lewiston Hill, slowly climbing 2000 feet in 9½ miles – with 64 switchbacks – to reach the plateau. Nowadays, a stretch of US 95 zips up the hill, but the old road, now known as the Old Spiral Hwy, affords great views across the Clearwater and Snake rivers. To catch the Old Spiral Hwy, turn at the second intersection north of Memorial Bridge.

Activities

Find live bait, tackle and fishing licenses for both states at Jay's Gone Fishin (☎ 509-758-8070), 118 Bridge St, Clarkston, WA. Follett's Mountain Sports (☎ 208-743-4200), 1019 21st St, rents skis and other gear. Pedals-N-Spokes (☎ 208-743-6567), 829 D St, rents bikes. (For information on jet boat trips see the Snake River National Wild & Scenic River later in this chapter.)

Lewiston Roundup

The Lewiston Roundup (☎ 208-746-6324), one of Idaho's oldest and best rodeos, attracts top stars and the community turns out for street dances, parades, carnivals and Nez Percé dancing. The three-day event takes place the first weekend in September at the Lewiston Roundup Grounds, 7000 Tammany Creek Rd, south of Lewiston.

Places to Stay

Lewiston's budget motels are clustered north of Memorial Bridge. Try the *Hillary Motel* (☎ 208-743-8514), 2030 North & South Hwy (singles/doubles $26/32); *Ho Hum Motel* (☎ 208-743-2978), 2015 North & South Hwy, $23/27; or the comparably priced *Hollywood Inn Motel* (☎ 208-743-9424), 3001 North & South Hwy. The *Super 8 Motel* (☎ 208-743-8808), 3120 North & South Hwy, costs $41/48.

Several places are along Lewiston's Main St: *Travel Inn* (☎ 208-743-4501), 1021 Main St ($30/40); *Riverview Inn* (☎ 208-746-3311, 800-806-7666), 1325 Main St ($36/44); *Sacajawea Motor Inn* (☎ 208-746-1393, 800-333-1393), 1824 Main St ($38/46); and *Comfort Inn* (☎ 208-798-8090), 2128 8th Ave ($53/60). *Howard Johnson's Inn* (☎ 208-743-9526), 1716 Main St, with a pool, starts at $62.

The charming *Carriage House Inn B&B* (☎ 208-746-4506, 800-501-4506), 611 5th St, Lewiston, in a quiet residential neighborhood, has rooms ranging from $75 to $85. Lewiston's best is the *Grand Plaza Hotel* (☎ 208-799-1000, 800-232-6730), 621 21st St, with river views and good restaurants ($76/86). Across the street, the pleasant *Inn America* (☎ 208-746-4600, 800-469-4667), 702 21st St, is a good value at $42/52.

Clustered along Bridge St in Clarkston, WA, are a few budget properties including the nice but older *Hacienda Lodge* (☎ 509-758-5583), 812 Bridge St ($30/34). Nearby, the *Motel 6* (☎ 509-758-1631), 222 Bridge St, has a pool ($36/42). The *Best Western River Tree Inn* (☎ 509-758-9551, 800-597-3621), 1257 Bridge St, has rooms for $59/69, a pool, exercise room and sauna; some rooms have kitchenettes. The *Quality Inn* (☎ 509-758-9500), 700 Port Drive, with a pool, starts at $63/68. *Highland House B&B* (☎ 509-758-3126), 707 Highland Ave, Clarkston, is an 1890s Victorian done up English-style. Rooms range from $35 to $80.

Places to Eat
The choice of restaurants is rather limited and uninspiring. For burgers and 1950s atmosphere, go to *Zany's* (☎ 208-746-8131), 21st St at 19th Ave. *Thai Taste*, 1410 21st St, is a bit pricey but a good change of pace. *BoJacks* (☎ 208-746-9532), 311 Main St, serves 'broiler-pit' steaks. The best Mexican food is at *Casa de Oro* (☎ 208-798-8681), 504 Main St. The Grand Plaza Hotel's *MJ Barleyhoppers Brewery & Pub* and *Meriwethers* offer the best quality and selection in town. Clarkston's best choice is *Tomato Bros* (☎ 509-758-7902), 200 Bridge St, for the wood-fired pizzas, pasta and salads.

Shopping
North Lewiston shops sell local Nez Percé-made jewelry and artifacts. Cee-Mee-Nee-Kum (☎ 208-743-3989), 2317 1st Ave N, has Nez Percé beadwork, seed and cut beads. Marsha's Trading Post (☎ 208-743-5778), 1105 36th St N, has Native American-made goods, beads and some antiques. The Nez Percé Express II (☎ 208-746-6225), 7411 North & South Hwy, looks like a convenience store but also sells jewelry.

Getting There & Away
Air Lewiston and Clarkston are served by Horizon Air and United Express out of the Lewiston-Nez Percé County Regional Air-

port (☎ 208-746-7962), the only airport in north-central Idaho with regularly scheduled flights. It's located off 17th St (which turns into 5th St) south of Lewiston.

Horizon Air (☎ 208-743-9293), 406 Burrell Ave, serves Lewiston with several daily nonstop flights from Seattle, WA, and Portland, OR. United Express (☎ 208-746-9516) flies to Portland daily.

Bus Northwestern Trailways (☎ 208-746-8108) stops at the Hollywood Inn Motel, 3001 North & South Hwy. Daily buses go northbound to Spokane, WA, at 6 am and 3:10 pm via Moscow, and southbound to Boise at 12:10 pm, via US 95 to New Meadows and Hwy 55. The one-way/round-trip fare to Spokane is $20/35; the fare to Boise is $33/59.

Car Lewiston and Clarkston are along US 12 just west of US 95, 75 miles northwest of Grangeville and 110 miles south of Coeur d'Alene. US 12 leads east to Orofino (44 miles), and US 195 leads north to Spokane (89 miles).

Getting Around
Car Hertz (☎ 208-746-0411), Budget (☎ 208-746-0488) and National Car Rental (☎ 208-743-0176) are at the airport. In Lewiston are Enterprise (☎ 208-746-2878), 625 21st St, Rent-A-Wreck (☎ 208-746-9585), 102 Thain Rd, and Valley Car Rental (☎ 208-743-9371), 18th and Main Sts.

Taxi Call Valley Cab (☎ 208-299-4840) or A-1 Cab Service (☎ 208-743-9478) for a taxi.

AROUND LEWISTON & CLARKSTON
Hells Gate State Park
Along the true right bank of the Snake River, 4 miles south of Lewiston, is the 960-acre Hells Gate State Park (☎ 208-799-5015), 3620A Snake River Ave. A popular antidote for hot summer days, it offers a swimming beach, campground with showers and a picnic area. Short hiking trails access the Levee Parkway. Five miles of bridal paths wind through the park to an overlook; Hells Gate Stables

IDAHO

(☎ 208-743-3142) rents horses during summer. Hells Gate Marina (☎ 208-799-5016) is the departure point for most jet boat trips (see Snake National Wild & Scenic River later in this chapter) and some charter fishing trips. The Williams Memorial visitors center has well-designed displays explaining Snake River geology and history and central Idaho's flora and fauna. The day-use fee is $2 per vehicle. Tent sites cost $12; sites with full hookups cost $16. The park accepts campground reservations 15 days in advance for an additional fee.

Asotin County Historical Society Museum

This gem of a museum (☎ 509-243-4659), 215 Filmore St at 3rd St, Asotin, WA, was built in 1922 and served as a funeral home for 50 years. Its historic buildings include a one-room school, a log cabin, a pioneer home and a blacksmith shop. It's open 1 to 5 pm Tuesday to Saturday; admission is by donation.

Buffalo Eddy Pictographs

Twelve miles south of Asotin, WA, a jumble of rocks constrict the Snake River into a fast-moving channel. On the rocks are well-preserved pictographs of warriors brandishing weapons. Perhaps these images once warned of a prehistoric territorial boundary some 7000 years ago. The area is easy to find, although it is not signed. From Asotin continue on 1st St until it becomes graveled Snake River Rd. Follow Snake River Rd as it winds through an increasingly sheer canyon until it passes through a narrow crevice between two rock faces. The pictographs are on the rocks near the river. As Snake River Rd continues toward the confluence of the Snake and Grande Ronde rivers, the stark canyon walls get higher and increasingly striated by basalt lava flows. The road joins Hwy 3 in Oregon, 31 miles south of Buffalo Eddy.

NEZ PERCÉ NATIONAL HISTORICAL PARK

This amorphous NPS-administered park is comprised of 24 distinct sites in four coun-

ties linked by 400 miles of road. The park brochure describes it as 'as much an idea as it is actual physical property.' Sites are inside and outside the 137-sq-mile Nez Percé Indian Reservation (☎ 208-843-2253), PO Box 305, Lapwai, ID 83540, established in 1855 and downsized in 1877. Most of the land south of the Clearwater River between Lewiston and Kooskia is part of the reservation. The **Nez Percé National Historic Trail**, which crosses Oregon, Idaho, Wyoming and Montana, passes many park sites. The park honors Nez Percé legend and battle sites, as well as locations significant to the history of white exploration, but visiting more than a few of the widely scattered sites is time consuming.

The Nez Percé National Historical Park visitors center (☎ 208-843-2261), PO Box

---

Nez Percé Creation Myth

According to Nez Percé myth, Meadowlark told Coyote that a monster was devouring all the other creatures. Coyote put five knives and some firemaking tools in his pack, swung it over his back and set off to confront the monster. After exchanging challenges with each other, the monster inhaled Coyote, and Coyote tumbled inside the belly of the monster, where all the other animals were waiting. Coyote found the monster's heart, lit a fire and began to carve off portions. Finally, he cut the heart free and the monster died, allowing the captured animals to escape. Coyote butchered the monster and scattered all the parts of its body to the winds; the bits were transformed into various Native American tribes. Fox reminded Coyote that he had neglected to leave a portion of the body to create a tribe for the valleys of the Clearwater and Snake rivers. Coyote washed his hands, and with the monster's blood created the Nee-Me-Poo, 'The People,' or the Nez Percé. **The Heart of the Monster**, a site on US 12 between Kamiah and Kooskia, is a stone mound that is believed to be the heart of the monster that died in the process of giving rise to this tribe. ■

93, US 95, Spalding, ID 83551, 11 miles east of Lewiston, houses an excellent museum devoted to the Nez Percé, and a bookstore and gift shop. It is open 8 am to 5:30 pm daily. Pick up a park brochure and map to decide what sites to visit. Those within 5 miles of the visitors center give a sense of what the rest of the park is like. A loop drive along the **Clearwater Canyons Scenic Byway** (US 12), Hwy 13 and US 95 takes about three hours, and passes many sites.

RIGGINS & AROUND

Riggins (population 530; elevation 1800 feet) is a narrow strip of land in a desolate, deep canyon at the confluence of the Main Salmon and Little Salmon rivers. Nestled along US 95 above the true left bank of the Salmon River, Riggins prides itself as Idaho's white-water capital and is the base for rafting on the Lower Salmon River (see below) and Snake National Wild & Scenic River through Hells Canyon (see below). Steelhead, trout and small-mouth bass attract anglers to these rivers. Arid and sparsely vegetated hills rise above the canyon floor. USFS roads near Riggins provide limited access to the Hells Canyon National Recreation Area (see below).

Orientation & Information

Riggins is basically a one-street town with businesses stretching along Main St (US 95); street numbers are scarce. Contact the Salmon River Chamber of Commerce (☎ 208-628-3778), PO Box 289, Riggins, ID 83549 for a list of outfitters (many handle rafting, fishing and horsepacking); a kiosk (☎ 208-628-3440), in a gravel lot at the center of town, is open during summer. The Salmon River Motel has a laundry and provides fax services.

Rafting

Half-day and full-day rafting trips on the Lower Salmon River, which put in at or near Riggins and take out near Lucille, run May to September. Half-day trips (about 10 miles) range from $30 to $44 for adults, and start at $25 for children. Full-day trips

(about 20 miles) start at $60/44 for adults/children. To book a day trip, contact:

Discovery River Expeditions
    PO Box 465, Riggins, ID 83549
        (☎ 208-628-3319, 800-755-8894)
Epley's Whitewater Adventures
    1512 N Main, Riggins, ID 83549
        (☎ 800-233-1813)
    PO Box 987, McCall, ID 83638
        (☎ 208-628-3533, 800-233-1813)
Salmon River Experience
    1513 N Main, Riggins, ID 83549
        (☎ 208-628-3014, 800-892-9223)
    812 Truman St, Moscow, ID 83843
        (☎ 208-882-2385, 800-892-9223)
Wapiti River Guides – Folklore wilderness trips
    led by a modern-day mountain man
    126 N Main St (next to the Riggins City
    Center), PO Box 1125, Riggins, ID 83459
        (☎ 208-628-3523, 800-488-9872)
Salmon River Challenge, Inc
    PO Box 1299, Riggins, ID 83549
        (☎ 208-628-32640, 800-732-8574)

Places to Stay

At the north end of Riggins is the small and pleasant *River Village RV Park* (☎ 208-628-3441), 1434 N US 95, with laundry and shower. Grassy shady tent sites above the river cost $10; sites with full hookups cost $15. The grassy and shady *Riverside RV Park* (☎ 208-628-3390, 208-628-3698), at Salmon River Rd, has $15 sites with full hookups. Tent campers are not allowed unless they have their own toilet facilities.

Rooms at the uninspiring *Bruce Motel* (☎ 208-628-3005), N Main St, start at a negotiable $30. Clean, riverview rooms at the *River View Motel* (☎ 208-628-3041; fax 208-628-3908), 708 N US 95 north of town, start at $42. In town try the well-maintained older *Riggins Motel* (☎ 208-628-3001, 800-669-6739), 615 S Main St, with shady trees and hot tub. Singles/doubles cost $35/42. The *Salmon River Motel* (☎ 208-628-3231), 1203 S US 95, has rooms starting at $38/40.

The Lodge at Riggins Hot Springs (☎ 208-628-3785), PO Box 1247, Riggins, ID 83549, is 9 miles east of Riggins off Salmon River Rd. Rooms are in the main lodge or in triplex cabins. Rates range from $225 to $300 including meals and access to the hot springs.

IDAHO

Places to Eat

Glenna's Deli (☎ 208-628-3997) offers sandwiches, salad, soup and pastries, and packs picnic lunches for rafting trips. *Cattlemen's Restaurant* (☎ 208-628-3915), 601 S Main St, serves breakfast and family-style lunch and dinner.

Getting There & Away

Bus Northwestern Trailways stops at city hall, a brick building on US 95. Daily buses go northbound to Spokane, WA (12:50 pm) via Grangeville, Lewiston and Moscow; southbound buses go to Boise (4:10 pm) via US 95 to New Meadows and then Hwy 55.

Car Riggins is on US 95, 44 miles south of Grangeville and 90 miles north of McCall.

CLEARWATER MOUNTAINS

The arid, rugged and remote **Gospel Hump Wilderness Area** is not as well known as Idaho's other wilderness areas. Its curious name comes from Gospel Hill and Buffalo Hump, former mining areas in the Clearwater Mountains. The area, primarily used by horsepackers out of lodges, is underutilized by hikers and backpackers. Access to the Gospel Hump Wilderness Area is from the north side of the Salmon River east of Riggins, east of US 95 between Lucile and White Bird and south of Grangeville off Hwys 13 and 14.

HELLS CANYON NATIONAL RECREATION AREA

As early as 1895, the term 'Hells Canyon' was applied to the Snake River's passage through North America's deepest gorge, thousands of feet deeper than the Grand Canyon. From He Devil Peak (9393 feet) on the east rim, the canyon drops 8913 feet to the Snake River at Granite Creek. The average depth is 6600 feet. Hat Point (6982 feet) in Oregon's Eagle Gap Mountains is the west rim's highest point. The remote and wild 652,000-acre Hells Canyon NRA offers hiking, fishing, swimming, camping and dramatic views of the gorge and surrounding mountains. (For white-water rafting and jet boat trips see Snake River Wild & Scenic River below.)

Orientation

Hells Canyon NRA spans the Idaho-Oregon state line, but the Oregon section is not readily accessible from Idaho. From Cambridge (see Southwestern Idaho in the Snake River Plain chapter), Hwy 71 leads north to Hells Canyon Dam Rd and the dam at its south end. US 95 parallels its eastern boundary; a few unpaved roads lead from US 95 between Riggins and White Bird into Hells Canyon NRA, crossing parts of the Nez Percé National Forest and Hells Canyon Wilderness Area. Only one road leads from US 95 to the Snake River itself at Pittsburg Landing.

Information

The Hells Canyon NRA Riggins office (☎ 208-628-3916), has excellent information and maps on campgrounds along the Snake and Salmon rivers, as well as road, trail and fishing conditions in the Hells Canyon Wilderness Area. Located on US 95 in Riggins' southern outskirts, it is open 8 am to 5 pm weekdays.

The USFS Hells Canyon NRA Wallowa-Whitman National Forest Snake River office (☎ 509-758-0616), 2535 Riverside Drive, Clarkston, WA, on Hwy 129 south of the Southway Bridge, is open 7:45 to 11.30 am and 12:30 to 4:30 pm weekdays. They list outfitters and river flows. (Also see the Launch Reservations for Access-Controlled Rivers sidebar earlier in this chapter.)

A significant distance away, not readily accessible from Idaho, are the Hells Canyon NRA headquarters (☎ 503-426-4978), 88401 Hwy 82, Enterprise, OR, and the USFS Wallowa-Whitman National Forest (☎ 503-523-6391), 1550 Dewey Ave, Baker City, OR.

Hells Canyon Lookouts

Travelers with a little time can drive to the canyon rim on unpaved fair-weather roads for dramatic views. The most popular drive is USFS Rd 517 (Seven Devils Rd). Go about one-fourth of a mile south of the Hells Canyon NRA Riggins office on US 95 and turn west on USFS Rd 517 (open July to mid-October). The gravel road climbs steadily 17 miles (the first 10 miles are single lane with steep grades and turnouts; high-clearance vehicles are recommended for the next 7 steep and rough miles), crossing Windy Saddle and arriving at the rim and Seven Devils Campground after about one hour. The road continues 2 miles north to **Heaven's Gate Lookout** (8430 feet), one of the most breathtaking view points in the Hells Canyon area.

4WD vehicles can follow the rough, steep USFS Rd 241 west from US 95, one-fourth of a mile north of Riggins, 15 miles to **Iron Phone Junction** (1½ hours). The road is open mid-June to October. From Iron Phone Junction, USFS Rd 2060 continues west to **Sawpit Saddle** or USFS Rd 1819 to **Low Saddle**. A 17-mile loop trip along the rim follows other USFS roads before descending again on USFS Rd 241, or by continuing along the rim on dry-weather-only USFS Rd 420 (USFS Rd 672 is the better choice in wet weather) for 25 miles to USFS Rd 493 (Deer Creek Rd).

The promontory of **Sheep Rock** (6847 feet), on USFS Rd 106 at the NRA's south end, is a national natural landmark with outstanding Hells Canyon views.

Seven Devils Mountains

The 8000-foot Seven Devils Mountains separate the Little Salmon River and Salmon River valleys from the Snake River canyon. Dozens of lakes brimming with brook trout are east of the crest. Miles of **hiking** trails crisscross the slopes with spectacular canyon views. One lovely trail follows the little-known Rapid National Wild & Scenic River, which tumbles down the eastern slopes. **Windy Saddle** is the main trailhead for the Seven Devils Mountains, Hells Canyon Wilderness Area and the Heavens Gate Scenic National Recreation Trail. Anywhere camping is free, but there is no piped water. Take USFS Rd 517 from Riggins to trailheads.

Lower Pittsburg Landing

The unpaved rough USFS Rd 493 (Deer Creek Rd) leaves US 95 at White Bird, heading west over Pittsburg Saddle to the Snake River at Lower Pittsburg Landing (17 miles, 1½ hours). The grade is not suitable for large RVs or vehicles pulling trailers. Lower Pittsburg Landing has a boat launch, a swimming beach, fishing area and campground; drinking water is not reliable. The sandy terrain here was a longtime Nez Percé camp and popular during the brief 1910s homesteading boom, when 21 homesteads clung to life along this stretch of Hells Canyon.

Snake River National Recreation Trail

Upper Pittsburg Landing, 2 miles before Lower Pittsburg Landing, is the trailhead for the 30-mile long Snake River National Recreation Trail, suited to **hiking** and **horseback riding**, along the river to Hells Canyon Dam. A few walk-in campsites are at Upper Pittsburg Landing, but there's no drinking water.

SNAKE RIVER NATIONAL WILD & SCENIC RIVER

The Snake National Wild & Scenic River through Hells Canyon is popular with rafters and jet boaters. Rafters run this Class III-IV section May to September in three to five days. Known for all things big – waves, views, cliffs – the river is lined with historic sites like the Kirkland Ranch and other homesteads, pictographs, hiking trails and wildlife like bighorn sheep and mountain goats. Steelhead and sturgeon fishing begins during fall. Its warm waters are great for swimming.

Rafting

A launch reservation is required late May to mid-September for rafting the designated 'wild' 31.5 river miles between Hells Canyon Dam and Pittsburg Landing (see the Launch Reservations for Access-Controlled Rivers sidebar earlier in this chapter). Self-issuing permits are required for launch dates outside the controlled-access period on this section and year-round for launches at or

IDAHO

downstream of Pittsburg Landing, where the 36-mile designated 'scenic' section begins. The daily commercial rates range from $160/125 to $210/192 for adults/children. To book a white-water trip, contact:

OARS
    PO Box 67, Angels Camp, CA (☎ 209-736-4677, 800-328-0290, 800-346-6277; fax 209-736-2902,)
    1127-B Airway Ave, Lewiston, ID 83501 (☎ 208-743-4201, 800-328-0290, 800-346-6277)
Holiday River Expeditions Inc
    126 W Main St, PO Box 86, Grangeville, ID 83530 (☎ 208-983-1518, 800-628-2565; fax 208-983-1695)
Salmon River Experience
    1513 N Main, Riggins, ID 83549 (☎ 208-628-3014, 800-892-9223)
    812 Truman St, Moscow, ID 83843 (☎ 208-882-2385, 800-892-9223)
Northwest Voyageurs
    PO Box 373, 1 Salmon River Route, Lucile, ID 83542-0373 (☎ 208-628-3021, 800-727-9977; fax 208-628-3780)
River Odysseys West
    PO Box 579, Coeur d'Alene, ID 83816 (☎ 208-765-0841, 800-451-6034; fax 208-667-6506)

Jet Boat Trips

Half-day jet boat trips usually go to Dug Bar-Nez Percé Crossing (118 miles roundtrip). Half-day trips start at $50/35 for adult/children. Full-day jet boat trips go to: Rush Creek (182 miles roundtrip, $80/45); Granite Creek (200 miles, $100/55); or Hells Canyon Dam (216 miles, $150/80). Full-day trips usually include lunch. Dinner cruises to Hellar Bar Lodge (70 miles roundtrip) start at $42. The river is renowned for its white sturgeon, the world's largest freshwater fish, rainbow and steelhead trout and smallmouth bass. Full-day guided fishing trips range from $125 to $150.

Two-day one-night trips range from $195 to $260; an additional day costs $125. Beamers Hells Canyon Tours (see below) is well known for its historic 'mail run,' delivering the US mail to outlying canyon ranches. Two-day one-night fishing trips range from $265 to $365; an additional day

costs $185. Camping and lodging are available.

To book a jet boat trip, contact:

Beamers Hells Canyon Tours
    PO Box 1243, Lewiston, ID 83501 (☎ 208-743-4800, 800-522-6966)
    1451 Bridge St, Clarkston, WA (☎ 509-758-4800, 800-522-6966)
High Roller Excursions
    1718 7th Ave N, Lewiston, ID (☎ 208-746-5740, 800-456-2779)
River Quest Excursions
    3665-A Snake River Ave, Lewiston, ID (☎ 208-746-8060, 800-589-1129)
Snake Dancer Excursions
    614 Lapwai Rd, Lewiston, ID (☎ 208-743-0890, 800-234-1941; fax 208-743-3117)
    PO Box 635, Clarkston, WA 99403
Snake River Adventures
    227 Snake River Ave, Lewiston, ID (☎ 208-746-6276, 800-262-8874; fax 208-746-9906)

To book a fishing-oriented jet boat trip, contact: Scenic River Charters (☎ 208-746-6808, 208-746-6443), 1209 Main St, Lewiston; or Mainstream Outdoor Adventures (☎ 208-983-2261, 208-743-0512, 800-800-8382), 5700 Tammany Creek Rd, Lewiston.

Getting There & Away

For rafters, the put-in is below the Hells Canyon Dam (1475 feet) in Oregon. The three-day take-out is Pittsburg Landing (1120 feet); the five-day at Hellar Bar (1080 feet). (See McCall in the Snake River Plain chapter for the nearest airport to both the put-in and Pittsburg Landing take-out. See Lewiston & Clarkston earlier in this chapter for the nearest airport to the Hellar Bar take-out. See Stanley for information about vehicle shuttles.)

Most jet boat trips depart from Lewiston's Hells Gate Marina or Clarkston's Swallows Crest Park boat launch (see Around Lewiston & Clarkston earlier in this chapter).

LUCILE & AROUND

Lucile, 10 miles north of Riggins on US 95, has a few nice campgrounds. Northwest Voyageurs (☎ 208-628-3021, 800-727-9977), on Salmon River Rt 1, Lucile, ID

IDAHO

83542-0373, offers steelhead trips and rents rafts, kayaks, mountain bikes and other gear. The pleasant *Prospectors Gold RV & Campground* along the true right bank of the Salmon River offers shady tent sites ($3) and sites with electricity ($10). North of Lucile, the well-maintained *Riverfront Gardens RV Park* has riverside sites on manicured lawns. *Swiftwater RV Campground*, on US 95 south of White Bird and Hammer Creek, is also pleasant.

LOWER FORK SALMON RIVER

About 15 million years ago, the Lower Fork Salmon River carved its canyon through Miocene lava flows. The Snake River created Hells Canyon, 8 miles to the west, in a similar way. The river has big sandy beaches for camping and warm water, great for swimming. Trails lead to nearby pictographs. Steelhead fishing begins in late September. This 40-mile Class III river is usually run in three to five days June to September. Its status as a National Wild & Scenic River is pending, meanwhile self-issuing permits are required year-round. Contact the BLM (☎ 208-962-3245), Route 3, Cottonwood, ID, for details.

Daily commercial rates range from $145/120 to $181/154 for adults/children. To book a white-water trip, contact:

OARS
 PO Box 67, Angels Camp, CA (☎ 209-736-4677, 800-328-0290, 800-346-6277; fax 209-736-2902)
 1127-B Airway Ave, Lewiston, ID 83501 (☎ 208-743-4201, 800-328-0290, 800-346-6277)
Aggipah River Trips
 Box 425 E5, Salmon, ID 83467 (☎ 208-756-4167)
Holiday River Expeditions Inc
 126 W Main St, PO Box 86, Grangeville, ID 83530 (☎ 208-983-1518, 800-628-2565; fax 208-983-1695)
Northwest Voyageurs
 PO Box 373, 1 Salmon River Route, Lucile, ID 83542-0373 (☎ 208-628-3021, 800-727-9977; fax 208-628-3780)
River Odysseys West
 PO Box 579, Coeur d'Alene, ID 83816 (☎ 208-765-0841, 800-451-6034; fax 208-667-6506)

Getting There & Away

The put-in is at Hammer Creek (1410 feet), adjacent to a BLM campground ($8), where US 95 leaves the valley at White Bird, about 28 miles north of Riggins. (See McCall in the Snake River Plain chapter for the nearest airport to the put-in.) The take-out is at Hellar Bar (1080 feet) on the Snake River below the confluence of the Salmon and Snake rivers, about 35 miles south of Lewiston. (See Lewiston & Clarkston for the nearest airport to the take-out. See Stanley for information about vehicle shuttles.)

WHITE BIRD & AROUND

Between Riggins and White Bird, US 95 follows the Salmon River through a narrow canyon. At White Bird US 95 leaves the river and climbs the 4245-foot White Bird Grade. The current US 95 was built in 1975, but history enthusiasts should take the winding 16-mile-long old highway. Built in 1915, it is designated the **White Bird Battlefield Auto Tour**, after the first real battle of the so-called Nez Percé War, fought on this steep escarpment in 1877. Battle sites are keyed to a tour brochure available from the information post at the beginning of the route. It is on the National Register of Historic Places.

The USFS Nez Percé National Forest Salmon River Ranger District (☎ 208-839-2211), on US 95, near **Slate Creek** south of White Bird, is open 7 am to 4 pm weekdays. They sell excellent river guides and the 'Nez Percé National Forest' topographic map. Ask for the free Clearwater Nez Percé Country Travel Planner. The site also houses the interesting **Forest Ranger Museum**.

GRANGEVILLE & AROUND

Surrounded by wheat farms and cattle ranches, Grangeville (population 3666) is an old agricultural trade town now changing to accommodate tourism. The Camas Prairie (elevation 3390 feet), a broad volcanic plateau cut on each side by deep canyons, sprawls northwest of Grangeville. Grangeville is the gateway to Idaho's Northwest Passage and is a jumping-off point for the Gospel Hump and Selway-

IDAHO

Bitterroot wilderness areas. The **Clearwater Canyons Scenic Byway** heads east and north on Hwy 13 down Harpster Grade Rd to Kooskia. Hwy 14 leads southeast to Elk City, one of Idaho's most remote towns, from where more obscure USFS roads dead-end at distant wilderness trailheads.

Orientation & Information

Hwy 13 is Main St in town. Idaho Ave runs north-south and divides east-west street addresses. The Grangeville Area Chamber of Commerce (☎ 208-983-0460; fax 208-983-9188), 201 E Main St, PO Box 212, Grangeville, ID 83850, is open 10 am to 2 pm weekdays. The USFS Nez Percé National Forest Clearwater Ranger Station (☎ 208-983-1950), 319 E Main St, has very useful information. The post office is on E Main St at Idaho Ave. Syringa General Hospital (☎ 208-983-1700) is at 607 W Main St.

The Priory of St Gertrude & St Gertrude Museum

A satisfying side trip from the small town of Cottonwood, 14 miles north of Grangeville off US 95, leads to a Benedictine nunnery and an eclectic museum of early Idaho history; follow the signs from Cottonwood. Established in 1920, the Priory of St Gertrude, with its Romanesque-style stone chapel and convent, was completed in 1925; the nuns did much of the labor. The chapel, marked by twin 90-foot towers, is open to visitors. Next door, St Gertrude Museum (☎ 208-962-3224) began as a collection of relics gathered by Sister Alfreda Elsensohn, an expert in Idaho pioneer history. Highlights include the personal belongings of Main Salmon River homesteaders Sylvan Hart (Buckskin Bill) and former Chinese slave Polly Bemis, Nez Percé artifacts and cultural items of the Montagnard (Mountain) people of Vietnam. The museum is open 9:30 am to 4:30 pm Monday to Saturday and 1:30 to 4:30 pm Sunday; or make an appointment (☎ 208-962-7123). Admission is by donation.

Skiing

The Snowhaven Ski Area (☎ 208-983-2299), 7 miles south of Grangeville, offers Alpine skiing on three runs with a base elevation of 5200 feet and maximum 400-foot vertical drop. A trail connects it to Fish Creek Meadows Nordic Park 'n Ski, with 10 miles of groomed cross-country trails. Cottonwood Butte Ski Area (☎ 208-962-3624), 5 miles west of Cottonwood, has four runs with a maximum 845-foot vertical drop. The ski season is mid-December to March.

Places to Stay & Eat

Harpster RV Park (☎ 208-983-2312), on Hwy 13, has sites ranging from $9 to $12. At the clean *Monty's Motel* (☎ 208-983-2500), 700 W Main St, and *Elkhorn Lodge* (☎ 208-983-1500), 822 SW 1st, rooms start at $36. The Victorian *Meadows House B&B* (☎ 208-983-0718, 983-4350), 306 S Meadow, costs $65/75. On a 300-acre Camas Prairie farm is *Mariel's B&B* (☎ 208-962-5927), Rt 1, Box 207, Cottonwood, ID 83522, with singles/doubles at $40/46.

Grangeville offers cafes, but *Oscar's Restaurant* (☎ 208-983-2106), 101 E Main St, noted for its 12 different cuts of steak, stands out. They also serve espresso, Mexican food, sandwiches, chicken and seafood. For organic groceries, go to *The Health Food Store* (☎ 208-873-1276), 709 W North St.

Getting There & Away

Bus Northwestern Trailways stops on US 95 N at the Highway Station, the first easily visible gas station. Daily buses go northbound to Spokane, WA (1:30 pm) via Lewiston and Moscow; southbound buses go to Boise (1:30 pm) via US 95 to New Meadows and then Hwy 55.

Car Grangeville is on US 95 at Hwy 13, 72 miles southeast of Lewiston and 44 miles north of Riggins.

KOOSKIA

The South and the Middle forks of the Clearwater River meet at Kooskia (popula-

Battle of White Bird

The Nez Percé traditionally lived peaceably with white settlers around eastern Oregon's Wallowa Mountains, even though the land was not a protected reservation. Relations, however, deteriorated across the West in the aftermath of the Battle of the Little Bighorn in 1876. The US Army ordered the Nez Percé to comply with a treaty they had not signed, moving them from their Oregon homeland to a parcel of land in Idaho (the current Nez Percé Indian Reservation). Eventually, the Nez Percé chiefs reluctantly agreed to move on the reservation, and they gathered their people and camped at Tolo Lake west of Grangeville.

Several young braves, however, impetuously decided to settle scores with some settlers along the Salmon River (one of the settlers had murdered the elderly father of two of the braves). On June 13, 1877, three braves left the camp and killed three settlers. The next day, a larger party of Nez Percé left camp and raided further settlements, killing 15 more whites. The chiefs realized that if they moved onto the reservation the army would exact a terrible revenge. Instead, they decided to flee to freedom in Canada. The entire encampment – over 800 people and 2500 horses – moved off the Camas Prairie and dropped into the White Bird Canyon to prepare for their journey. An army force of about 100 men, under the command of Captain David Perry, rode south from Fort Lapwai to apprehend the Nez Percé.

On June 17, the army inched down the steep ravine toward the Nez Percé camp. A contingent of warriors rode out to parley under a white flag, but trigger-happy soldiers fired upon the delegation. Battle was initiated, and the Nez Percé and army troops clashed at several points along the steep hillside. In a decisive one-hour battle, 34 soldiers were killed, with no Nez Percé casualties. The chiefs, however, realized they had no choice but to flee. The Nez Percé, led by Chief Joseph, were eventually captured just a few miles short of Canada. ■

---

tion 756; elevation 1653 feet), a rustic town on the west and north flanks of Mt Stuart. The informative Kooskia Service Directory Kiosk, with useful maps, is at the junction of US 12 and Hwy 13. The USFS Clearwater National Forest Lochsa Ranger District (☎ 208-926-4274/5), 502 Lowry St south of the Clearwater Bridge, has information about Lochsa Valley (see below) trails and campgrounds.

Singles/doubles at the *Mount Stuart Inn* (☎ 208-926-0166), 006 S Main St, cost $35/45. The *Rivers Cafe* (☎ 208-926-4450), 018 N Main St, is an appealing, backwoodsy restaurant serving homestyle meals. *Idaho Backroads Cafe* (☎ 208-926-4488), 118 Main St, serves burgers and steaks, and has a salad bar and tasty huckleberry shake. *Kooskia Herbs N' Things* (☎ 208-926-4372) sells organic and bulk foods and produce.

LOCHSA VALLEY

US 12, the only east-west road across northern Idaho, links Kooskia to Missoula, MT, via the Lochsa Valley. At the head of the valley is Lolo Pass (5235 feet) on the Idaho-Montana state line and the Continental Divide. This 99-mile stretch of US 12 mostly follows the Lochsa River, which descends from the Bitterroot Mountains and offers good fly-fishing. Footbridges across the Lochsa River access the northern side of the 2095-sq-mile **Selway-Bitterroot Wilderness Area**. One of Idaho's best-known wilderness areas, its 2000 miles of trails are used primarily by horsepackers, rather than hikers or backpackers, and by snowmobilers and cross-country skiers during winter. Apart from the tiny settlements of Syringa (16 miles east of Kooskia), Lowell (7 miles east of Syringa) and Powell, near Lolo Pass, no other towns exist.

Hot Springs

The upper Lochsa River is fed by hot springs in the midst of green forested meadows. Short walks lead to two popular undeveloped soaking pools. **Weir Hot Springs** is east of milepost 142 at Weir Creek Bridge. Follow a trail on the west side of the stream one-half mile to the pool. The highly popular **Jerry Johnson Hot Springs**, west of Powell, has three sets of pools. The USFS limits camping at the springs to preserve the area. Go east of milepost 152 to the parking area for the Warm Springs Pack Bridge. Cross the bridge and hike 1 mile to the hot springs.

Lochsa Historical Ranger Station

On US 12 near Boulder Creek is the Lochsa Historical Ranger Station, open 9 am to 4 pm daily Memorial Day to Labor Day. These log buildings, constructed in the 1930s, represent life in a remote USFS station, where over 200 men once lived and worked to manage the vast forest.

Places to Stay & Eat

Many USFS campgrounds are along US 12; the best is *Wilderness Gateway*, 25 miles east of Lowell. The pleasant riverside *Three Rivers Resort* (☎ 208-926-4430), on US 12 at Lowell, has tent sites ($5 per person), RV sites ($18), motel rooms (singles/doubles $39/49) and river-view cabins (starting at $72), along with a pool and hot tubs. The rustic *Lochsa Lodge* (☎ 208-942-3405), 12 miles west of the Idaho-Montana state line, has unplumbed cabins ($28) and motel rooms ($45). Both have cafes. Favorites for good homecooked meals and huckleberry pie are the *Syringa Cafe* (☎ 208-926-0057) and *Middlefork Cafe* (☎ 208-926-0169), both in Syringa.

Getting There & Away

US 12, heavily traveled during summer, follows the winding Lochsa River; allow sufficient time to reach your destination. Gas stations at Syringa, Lowell and Lolo Hot Springs (7 miles into Montana) close early in the evening. The Lolo Pass can be snowy and dangerous during winter; call ☎ 208-746-3005 for road conditions.

MIDDLE FORK CLEARWATER NATIONAL WILD & SCENIC RIVER

The Selway and Lochsa rivers, tributaries of the Middle Fork Clearwater National Wild & Scenic River, flow through the Selway-Bitterroot Wilderness Area and meet below the town of Lowell. Here they become known as the Middle Fork Clearwater, which flows west to Kooskia to join the main Clearwater River.

Selway River Section

A pristine wilderness of fern-carpeted fir and cedar forests surrounds the Selway River. Known for its big Class III-V whitewater, the river is usually run in three to five days May to June. A launch reservation is required mid-May to July for rafting the 46 miles between Paradise Guard Station (3050 feet) and Meadow Creek (1720 feet) above Selway Falls (see the Launch Reservations for Access-Controlled Rivers sidebar earlier in this chapter). Reservations are not required at other times. Snow may block access for May launch dates, while late launch dates may encounter low water.

Lochsa River Section

The aptly named Lochsa ('lock-saw,' meaning 'rough water' in Nez Percé) River is a challenging white-water run that is popular with kayakers. The 26-mile Class III-V section with over 50 rapids between Grave Creek (about 2500 feet) and Split Creek (1720 feet) is usually run in two or three days mid-May to mid-July. Wetsuits and helmets are recommended, as is prior white-water experience. No permit is necessary; bring your own gear as outfitters do not rent gear for use on this river. Contact the USFS in Orofino (see Orofino later in this chapter) for their 'Lochsa White Water Rafting' brochure. Daily commercial rafting rates start at $150/138 for adults/children. To book a white-water trip, contact:

Holiday River Expeditions Inc
    126 W Main St, PO Box 86, Grangeville, ID 83530 (☎ 208-983-1518, 800-628-2565; fax 208-983-1695)

River Odysseys West
   PO Box 579, Coeur d'Alene, ID 83816
   (☎ 208-765-0841, 800-451-6034;
   fax 208-667-6506)
Three Rivers Rafting
   HC 75, Box 61, Kooskia, ID 83539
   (☎ 208-926-4430; fax 208-926-7526)

Getting There & Away

Elk City on Hwy 14 east of Grangeville is the nearest town to the Selway's put-in and take-out; from Elk City head north on USFS Rd 443, or from Lowell head southeast on USFS Rd 223. The Lochsa's 10 put-ins and take-outs are along US 12 east of Lowell, as are nine USFS campgrounds. (See Lewiston & Clarkston earlier in this chapter for the nearest airport to both put-ins and take-outs.)

KAMIAH

Kamiah (population 1314; elevation 1194 feet), a major Nez Percé center along US 12 in a wide bend of the Clearwater River valley, has a pleasantly old-fashioned one-street downtown. The townsfolk have been welcoming strangers since Lewis and Clark camped here with the Nez Percé for four weeks in 1806, at aptly named Long Camp. Today gambling and the Empire Lumber company are the economic mainstays. More recently, the militia movement has come to stay. Libertarian 'Bo' Gritz established Almost Heaven, an antigovernment community of so-called Christian patriots, near Kamiah.

The Kamiah Chamber of Commerce (☎ 208-935-2290) is at 516 Main St, PO Box 1124 Kamiah, ID 83536. The USFS Clearwater National Forest Pierce Ranger District (☎ 208-935-2513), on the south side of US 12, is open 7:30 am to 4:30 pm weekdays. A kiosk displays a topographic map and tourist brochures.

Places to Stay & Eat

The enormous, well-shaded *Lewis-Clark Resort* (☎ 208-935-2556, 800-264-9943), 2 miles east of Kamiah on US 12, has tent sites ($10), sites with full hookups ($15), a few log cabins (ranging from $40 to $59)

and a pool. Rooms at the well-kept, older *Kamiah Inn Motel* (☎ 208-935-0040), 216 3rd St, range from $30 to $50. The newer *Clearwater 12 Motel* (☎ 208-935-2671, 800-935-2671), on US 12 next to a logging operation, has some kitchenettes; singles/doubles cost $40/50. *Jilinda's Family Dining*, at Bill's Conoco, 5 miles east of Kamiah, serves better-than-usual family fare with a good salad bar. *Clearwater Valley Natural Foods* (☎ 208-935-0695) is at 501 4th St.

OROFINO & AROUND

Orofino (population 3122; elevation 1027 feet), the largest town in the Clearwater River valley, marks the transition point from the eastern forested slopes to the western high desert canyons. As the town's name indicates (it means 'fine gold' in Italian), Orofino was born of the gold rush. The state's first strike in 1860 was east of here, near Pierce. The town now serves as a center for logging operations in the Clearwater National Forest. Orofino prides itself as the steelhead capital of the world, and can be a busy place during summer due to Dworshak Reservoir (see below).

Information

The Orofino Chamber of Commerce (☎ 208-476-4335; fax 208-476-3634) is at 217 1st St, PO Box 2221, Orofino, ID 83544. The USFS Clearwater National Forest headquarters (☎ 208-476-4541), 12730 US 12, open 8 am to 4:30 pm weekdays and 8:30 am to 5 pm weekends, offers useful information and maps of Dworshak Reservoir.

Dworshak Dam & Reservoir

Built in 1973, the Dworshak Dam, 7 miles west of Orofino on Ahsahka Rd on the North Fork Clearwater River, is the largest dam ever built by the US Army Corps of Engineers. The visitors center (☎ 208-476-1255), on the west side of the dam, conducts free guided tours during summer; call for schedules. The 53-mile-long reservoir is a haven for boating, water sports, fishing and camping; the section along upper Elk

Creek is open to nonmotorized vessels. Along the reservoir's banks are 80 primitive campsites, accessible by boat only. The US Army Corps of Engineers-operated *Dent Acres* has a picnic area, a boat launch, swimming and sites with hookups ($18).

Below the dam at the confluence of the North Fork Clearwater and Clearwater rivers is the **Dworshak National Fish Hatchery** (☎ 208-476-4591), in Ahsahka, the largest producer of steelhead trout and spring Chinook in the world. This massive facility is open 7:30 am to 4:30 pm daily for self-guided tours.

Dworshak State Park

Dworshak State Park (☎ 208-476-5994), on the west shore of Dworshak reservoir, 45 minutes from Orofino, has picnic areas, boat launches, swimming beaches and *Freeman Creek Campground*, with waterfront tent sites ($9), sites with hookups ($18) and showers. The day-use fee is $2 per vehicle.

Skiing

Six miles north of Pierce, off Hwy 11, is **Bald Mountain Ski Area** (☎ 208-464-2311); 15 runs with a maximum vertical drop of 975 feet descend from its 5036-foot summit.

Places to Stay & Eat

Helgeson Place Hotel (☎ 208-476-5729, 800-404-5729), 125 Johnson Ave at Michigan Ave, has remodeled singles/doubles for $37/41. Nearby, on a less-busy road, is the attractive *White Pine Motel* (☎ 208-476-7093, 800-874-2083), 222 Brown Ave, with rooms ranging from $33 to $55. *Riverside Motel* (☎ 208-476-5711), 10560 US 12, 2 miles west of the bridge, starts at $24.

Clearwater Bakery & Cafe (☎ 208-476-3025), 214 Johnson Ave, serves breakfast and lunch Monday to Saturday. The *Ponderosa Restaurant* (☎ 208-476-4818), 220 Michigan Ave, offers hearty steaks, chops and potatoes. Clearwater Valley Natural Foods (☎ 208-476-4091) is in the VFW Building on Michigan Ave.

Getting There & Away

Orofino is on US 12, 23 miles northwest of Kamiah and 44 miles east of Lewiston.

MOSCOW & AROUND

The rolling wheat and lentil fields and forests of the windswept Palouse Hills span the Idaho-Washington state line, centering around Moscow (population 20,100; elevation 2720 feet) and Pullman, WA. At the east edge of the Palouse, Moscow is home to the University of Idaho. The town's year-round population is boosted during the academic year by 11,000 students. Moscow has more of an alternative bent than its academic sister-city Pullman, which is home to Washington State University.

Orientation

US 95 (Main St) runs north-south through downtown. For 10 blocks, however, US 95 is divided into two one-way streets: northbound Washington St; southbound Jackson St. Hwy 8 is the main east-west road; west of Main St it is Pullman Rd, east of Main St it is Troy Hwy.

Information

The Moscow Chamber of Commerce (☎ 208-882-1800, 800-380-1801), 411 S Main St, is open 8 am to 5 pm weekdays. The USFS Clearwater National Forest, Forest Service Information and Intermountain Research Station (☎ 208-882-3557), is at 1221 S Main St.

The post office is at 220 E 5th St (the entrance is on Jefferson St); another branch is at the university. Book People of Moscow (☎ 208-882-7957), 512 S Main St, is packed with books and a great place to browse. The University of Idaho bookstore (☎ 208-885-6469) is on Deakin St across from the student union. The Gritman Medical Center (☎ 208-882-4511) is at 700 S Main St. Homestyle Laundry (☎ 208-882-1241) is in the Palouse Empire Mall, east of downtown.

Latah County Historical Society

The Latah County Historical Society (☎ 208-882-1004) offices and library, with a

IDAHO

special emphasis on genealogy, is at 327 E 2nd St. It is open 9 am to noon and 1 to 5 pm Tuesday to Friday. The **McConnell Mansion Museum**, a Victorian at 110 S Adams St, is open 1 to 4 pm Tuesday to Saturday or by appointment. Their bookstore has regional history books and a walking tour brochure of historic Moscow homes.

University of Idaho
The university, near 6th and Rayburn Sts, has somewhat of a reputation as a party school. Academically, natural resource fields are strong at this land-grant university. Perhaps its finest feature for the casual visitor is the **Shattuck Arboretum and Botanical Garden**, along Nez Percé Drive behind the administration building. The visitor information (☎ 208-885-6424) is at 645 Pullman Rd.

Camas Winery
Stop by the downtown Camas Winery (☎ 208-882-0214, 800-616-0214), 110 S Main St, for a sip of its Hog Heaven Red (a sherry-grape blend), Palouse Gold (a muscat-riesling blend) or a dry chardonnay. The tasting room is open noon to 6 pm Tuesday to Saturday. Upstairs is a wine bar, also serving premium beers.

Appaloosa Museum & Heritage Center
The Appaloosa Museum & Heritage Center, 5070 Hwy 8 W, near the Idaho-Washington state line, details the interesting history of the horse breed developed by Nez Percé and Palouse Indians. The Appaloosa Horse Club (☎ 208-882-5578), which sponsors **trail rides** and other events, also has their headquarters here. It is open 8 am to 5 pm weekdays and 9 am to 3 pm Saturday June to August; admission is by donation.

Places to Stay
Singles/doubles at the *Royal Motor Inn of Moscow* (☎ 208-882-2581), 120 W 6th St, cost $29/34. The *Mark IV Motor Inn* (☎ 208-882-7557, 800-833-4240), 414 N Main St, offers airport shuttles and has a pool and hot tub; rooms start at $35/40.

The *Hillcrest Motel* (☎ 208-882-7579, 800-368-6564), 706 N Main St, costs $46/49. The above have convenient downtown locations. Off Pullman Rd west of the downtown area are: the *Palouse Inn* (☎ 208-882-5511), at 101 Baker St ($32/37); the *Super 8 Motel* (☎ 208-883-1503), 175 Peterson Drive ($33/41); and the *Best Western University Inn* (☎ 208-882-0550), at 1516 W Pullman Rd ($73/83), which has a pool. Rates are higher during the academic year.

Beau's Butte B&B (☎ 208-882-4061), 702 Public Ave, is north of downtown. Rooms range from $55 to $60, with an indoor hot tub. Rooms start at $60 at the *Paradise Ridge B&B* (☎ 208-882-5292), 3377 Blaine Rd. The *Peacock Hill B&B* (☎ 208-882-1423), 1245 Joyce Rd, 5 miles north of Moscow, looks down onto Moscow and the Palouse. Rooms range from $75 to $85, and they offer horseback riding and cross-country skiing.

Places to Eat
Eateries are on Main St between 1st and 6th Sts. *Upper Crust Bakery* (☎ 208-883-1024), 310 W 3rd St, is a place to sprawl with the morning paper, a muffin and some coffee. The *Main St Deli* (☎ 208-882-0743) and *West 4th Bar & Grill* (same ☎) are set in the atmospheric old Moscow Hotel, 313 S Main St. The *Moscow Food Cooperative*, (☎ 208-882-8537), 310 W 3rd St, is an excellent grocery store with a good bakery and deli serving vegetarian sandwiches.

Entertainment
The Treaty Grounds Brew Pub (☎ 208-882-3807), 2124 W Pullman Rd, proffers good beer and conviviality.

Getting There & Away
Air Moscow is served by Horizon Air out of the Pullman-Moscow Regional Airport (☎ 509-334-4555, 800-547-9308), 3200 Airport Complex North off Hwy 270 in Pullman, WA. Horizon Air operates several daily flights from Seattle, WA, and Portland, OR.

Airport Shuttle Link Transportation
(☎ 208-882-1223, 800-359-4541) provides
airport transfers.

Bus Northwestern Trailways (☎ 208-882-
5521) stop at the Royal Motor Inn, 120 W
6th St at Jackson St. Daily buses go
northbound to Spokane, WA (6:50 am,
4 pm); $15/27 one-way/roundtrip. A daily
southbound bus to Lewiston (8:40 pm) costs
$5/9; another to Boise (8 pm), via US 95 to
New Meadows then on Hwy 55, is $37/65.

Car Moscow is on US 95 some 25 miles
north of Lewiston and 85 miles south of
Coeur d' Alene. Pullman is 10 miles west
of Moscow.

Getting Around

Bus The local transit company, Moscow/
Latah Public Transit (☎ 208-882-8313),
operates buses from 8 am to 4 pm on weekdays, but not along any established route.
Call at least 24 hours in advance to schedule a ride to somewhere in the area. The
one-way fare is $1.25.

Car Budget (☎ 509-332-3511) and Hertz
(☎ 509-332-4485) have locations at the airport. Also worth trying are Sears Rent-A-
Car (☎ 509-332-5230) and U-Save Auto
Rental (☎ 509-334-5195).

Taxi Call Moscow/Pullman Taxi Service
(☎ 208-883-4744) for a taxi.

Idaho Panhandle

Wedged between Washington, Montana and Canada, Idaho's Panhandle evokes two images. This largely unpopulated sliver, with dense forests, deep glacier-carved lakes and mighty rivers, is where locals head for family fishing and boating vacations. But the Panhandle's remoteness has also attracted right-wing survivalist and white supremacist groups. Though media coverage emphasizes their presence, few people are associated with these movements. The average traveler is more likely to confront a moose or a bear than a civilian militia unit in this beautiful, lake-gemmed area, speckled with resorts and old mining towns. Coeur d'Alene and Sandpoint are major destinations for skiers, anglers and water sport enthusiasts. The old silver-mining town of Wallace preserves the Western flavor of its historic town center, and nearby Kellogg offers scenic gondola rides. Sixty lakes within 60 miles of Coeur d'Alene, including Priest, Pend Oreille and Coeur d'Alene, serve as playgrounds for residents of nearby Spokane, WA. Outdoor activities are everywhere; from white-water rafting near Bonners Ferry to jet skiing on Coeur d'Alene Lake and backpacking through the primeval forest around Priest Lake.

COEUR D'ALENE

Coeur d'Alene (population 31,076; elevation 2125 feet), at the head of a deep blue lake between low, green-laden mountains, has been a tourist destination since the 1910s. Coeur d'Alene began as a civilian community alongside the US Army's Fort Sherman, which was founded in 1878 by Civil War General William Sherman. The town boomed when gold prospectors reached the South Fork Coeur d'Alene River. Steamboats provided transport and hauled freight until the 1920s. Today, Coeur d'Alene is the most popular of northern Idaho's lakefront resorts. Catering more to Idaho residents looking to splurge than to

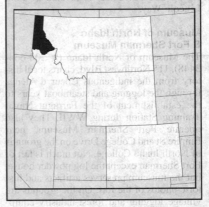

international jet-setters, Coeur d'Alene is a great place for family vacations. During summer water-skiers and Jet skiers rule.

Orientation

The town has two commercial districts. The newer strip, along US 95 at I-90, is lined with hotels, fast-food emporia and shopping malls. In the now-gentrified downtown, old storefronts and motels now house restaurants and shops for vacationers. The most prominent building on the shore and skyline is the Coeur d'Alene Resort, known to most

IDAHO

people simply as the Resort. The Coeur d'Alene Indian Reservation wraps around the lake's south end.

Information

The Coeur d'Alene and Post Falls Convention & Visitors Bureau (☎ 208-773-4080, 800-292-2553), PO Box 908, Post Falls, ID 83854, is on River Bend Rd in the factory outlets and is open 10 am to 4 pm Monday to Saturday and 11 am to 4 pm Sunday. The USFS Idaho Panhandle National Forest's office (☎ 208-765-7223) is at 3815 Schreiber Way. The BLM Coeur D'Alene District office (☎ 208-769-5000) is at 1808 N 3rd St. The Idaho Department of Fish and Game (☎ 208-769-1414) is at 2750 Kathleen Ave.

The post office is at 111 N 7th St; the zip code is 83814. The Kootenai Medical Center (☎ 208-667-6441) is located at 2003 Lincoln Way.

Museum of North Idaho & Fort Sherman Museum

The Museum of North Idaho (☎ 208-664-3448), 115 Northwest Blvd, charts local history from the indigenous Coeur d'Alenes through the logging and steamboat years to the establishment of the Farragut Naval Training Station during WWII. They also operate Fort Sherman Museum, near Empire St and College Drive on the grounds of North Idaho College. Not much is left of Fort Sherman except the log powder house, but the museum preserves artifacts and historic photos of the fort. On the grounds are vintage logging and forest-industry equipment and memorabilia, including a 1924 smoke-chaser's cabin. The Museum of North Idaho is open 11 am to 5 pm Tuesday through Saturday, April through October; admission is $1.50/50¢ for adults/children (six to 16), or $4 per family. The Fort Sherman Museum is open 1 to 4:30 pm Tuesday through Saturday, May through September; donations accepted.

City Park & Beach

The city's recreational heart is the popular lakeside park and beach at the edge of downtown. During the summer, a crush of people swimming, sailing, Jet skiing and windsurfing enjoy the sun and lake. Concessions and rental companies operate from the park, Independence Point city dock and the nearby Resort marina.

Activities

The 2-mile **hiking** trail, Tubbs Hill Trail, starts from the Resort's northernmost parking lot, crosses McEuen Park, then climbs through forests in Tubbs Hill Park to a viewpoint over the lake before looping back.

The 18-hole **golf** course (☎ 208-667-4653) at the Coeur d'Alene Resort (see below) features a floating green on an offshore island. For guests of the resort, tee time can be reserved immediately; the day rate is $140 during the summer. For nonguests, tee time must be reserved at least three days in advance; the day rate is $180 during the summer.

Lake Coeur d'Alene Parasail (☎ 208-756-5367), at the Independence Point city dock, takes people **parasailing** 500 feet above the lake for a quick spin and a lovely view. Brooks Seaplane (☎ 208-664-2842), at Independence Point, offers **seaplane rides** above Coeur d'Alene and Pend Oreille lakes. A 20-minute flight costs $40/20 for adults/children; they also offer longer flights.

Lake Cruises

For decades the only way to get around Coeur d'Alene Lake was by boat. Today Lake Coeur d'Alene Cruises (☎ 208-765-4000), at the Adventure Center in the Resort, relives that era. The most popular of their many cruises is the 90-minute cruise along the northern end of the lake, offered at least once daily early May to mid-October. Cruises depart the Resort's marina and cost $12/11/7 for adults/seniors/children (three to 10).

Art on the Green

Art on the Green is a three-day arts and crafts gathering that combines music, theater, visual arts and food. The festival takes over the lakefront area of North Idaho Col-

IDAHO

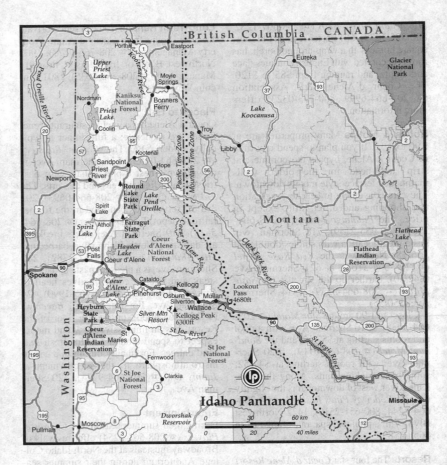

lege and it is usually held on the first weekend of August.

Places to Stay

The Coeur d'Alene Central Reservations (☎ 800-876-8921) offers a free reservation service.

Camping The attractive *Wolf Lodge Campground* (☎ 208-664-2812), 12425 E I-90 (I-90 exit 22), east of town, sports a swimming hole on the river and grassy sites ($14 to $20) near the lake. It is open April to November. Closer to town, grassy sites ($17 to $19) are available year-round at *Robin RV Park & Campground* (☎ 208-664-2306), at 703 Lincoln Way. The *Coeur d'Alene KOA Kampground* (☎ 208-664-4471, 800-562-2609), 10700 Wolf Lodge Bay Rd (I-90 exit 22 off Hwy 97), has a pool; sites start at $21.

B&Bs *Blackwell House* (☎ 208-664-0656, 800-899-0656), 820 Sherman Ave, is a 1904 mansion; rooms (some with shared bathroom) range from $75 to $119. *Gregory's*

IDAHO

McFarland House B&B (☎ 208-667-1232, 800-335-1232), 601 Foster Ave, an old four-square home with a wrap-around porch, has rooms decorated with English antiques, lace and chintz, and ranging from $85 to $120. The Coeur d'Alene B&B Association (☎ 208-664-6999, 800-773-0323) offers more information.

Hotels & Motels Many properties are at I-90 exit 12. If you plan to spend any time in Coeur d'Alene, bypass the commercial strip and head for the older, well-maintained terrace-style motels downtown. They are convenient to beaches, recreation and shopping and differ little, except in price. The *Flamingo Motel* (☎ 208-664-2159, 800-955-2159), 718 Sherman Ave, has a great location with singles/doubles at $66/78. Nearby is the *Red Rose Motel* (☎ 208-664-3167), at 621 Sherman Ave ($42/50). Farther up the street is the *State Motel* (☎ 208-664-8239), 1314 Sherman Ave ($50/55).

Closer to I-90 are the *Star Motel* (☎ 208-664-5035), 1516 Sherman Ave, with a pool and rooms starting at $57/62, and the *Sandman Motel* (☎ 208-664-9119), 1620 Sherman Ave, with rooms starting at $47/52; some have cooking units. Along the Spokane River west of downtown is the slightly upscale *Rodeway Pines Resort Inn* (☎ 208-664-8244, 800-651-2510), 1422 Northwest Blvd, with a pool and spa; rates range from $65 to $89.

Resorts The four-star *Coeur d'Alene Resort* (☎ 208-765-4000, 800-688-5253; fax 208-667-2707; resortinfo@cdaresort.com), Front Ave at 2nd St, puts Coeur d'Alene on the tourism map. Among other luxuries, it has three lounges, two restaurants (one with an 18-foot salad bar) and recreation center, complete with a private bowling alley and racquetball court. The lakefront setting overlooks a marina and a floating boardwalk 3.3 miles long. During winter, the Resort offers Ski & Stay packages in conjunction with the Silver Mountain Resort (see Wallace & Silver Valley later in this chapter). Rooms start at $80; suites can cost as much as $325.

Long-Term Rentals You can rent a private vacation home from Coeur d'Alene Property Management (☎ 208-765-0777), 1900 Northwest Blvd, or from Resort Property Management (☎ 208-765-6035), 1801 Lincoln Way, suite 4.

Places to Eat
Coeur d'Alene has a lively restaurant scene. Prices are moderate; a full dinner is typically under $12. The *Coffee Roastery* (☎ 208-664-0452), 511 Sherman Ave, is downtown's best espresso bar, with pastries, salads, light entrees and desserts. The *3rd Street Cantina* (☎ 208-664-0693), 201 3rd St, serves Mexican food in the former railroad depot. *Rustler's Roost* (☎ 208-664-5513), 819 Sherman Ave, offers breakfast all day and 'North Idaho-style barbecue.' *Tito Macaroni's* (☎ 208-667-2782), 210 Sherman Ave, is a pleasant pasta house. For steak and Pacific coast bivalves head to *Crickets Oyster Bar* (☎ 208-765-1990), 424 Sherman Ave. For fine dining, *Beverly's* (☎ 208-765-4000), on the 7th floor of the Resort, has an impressive view and menu; expect to spend around $20 for fresh seafood entrees. For quality dining in a casual bistro atmosphere, try the eclectic menu at *Jimmy D's* (☎ 208-664-9774), 320 Sherman Ave.

Entertainment
During their summer season, the *Carrousel Players* (☎ 208-667-0254) offer revivals of Broadway musicals at the North Idaho College Auditorium during their summer season. The *Northwest Summer Playhouse* (☎ 208-667-1323), 1320 E Garden Ave, an

---

Gettin' Hitched
Coeur d'Alene is the region's wedding capital; chapels abound. No blood test, witnesses or waiting are necessary. Some B&Bs and the Resort host so many ceremonies that they have clergy on staff. You must be 18, or have a parent's permission; licenses cost $28 to $33. ∎

Coeur d'Alene

PLACES TO STAY
2 Rodeway Pines
   Resort Inn
3 Robin RV Park
   & Campground
6 Gregory's McFarland
   House B&B
14 Red Rose Motel
16 Coeur d'Alene Resort
20 Flamingo Motel
21 Blackwell House
22 State Motel
23 Star Motel
24 Sandman Motel

PLACES TO EAT
10 3rd St Cantina
11 Jimmy D's

12 Coffee Roastery
15 Rustler's Roost
18 Tito Macaroni's
19 Crickets Oyster Bar

OTHER
1 Greyhound Bus Depot
4 Fort Sherman Museum
5 YMCA Pool
7 Northwest Summer
   Playhouse
8 Museum of North Idaho
9 TW Fishers
13 Post Office
17 Visitors Center
25 Coeur d'Alene Resort
   Golf Course

Equity theater group, mounts three shows each season, one of which is staged at the outdoor amphitheater at Silver Mountain Resort (see Wallace & Silver Valley later in this chapter).

TW Fishers (☎ 208-664-2739), 204 2nd St, offers pub grub to complement its fine selection of ales. Brewery tours are available between 1:30 and 5:30 pm daily; call for an appointment.

Getting There & Away
Air The nearest airport is the Spokane International Airport in Spokane, WA, 33 miles west of Coeur d'Alene.

Bus Greyhound Bus Lines (☎ 208-664-3343), 1527 Northwest Blvd, follows I-90 between Spokane and Missoula, MT. Daily buses depart Coeur d'Alene for Spokane (12:30, 8:05 am and 4:30 pm) and Missoula (2, 10 am and 7:30 pm).

North Idaho Community Express (NICE; ☎ 208-664-9769), which stops at the Greyhound bus depot, operates four daily buses between Coeur d'Alene and Sandpoint. The one-way fare is $7.

Car I-90 runs east-west along the northern edge of the lake, linking Coeur d'Alene to Missoula, MT, 163 miles east, and Spokane,

IDAHO

33 miles west. US 95 is the main north-south route: Sandpoint is 44 miles north and Lewiston is 121 miles south.

Getting Around
Auto Rental of Coeur d'Alene (☎ 208-667-4905), 120 Anton Ave, rents cars. Call Sunset Taxi (☎ 208-664-8000) for a taxi. NICE (☎ 208-664-9769) offers curb-to-curb service; call ahead to arrange a pick-up.

AROUND COEUR D'ALENE
Silverwood Theme Park
This may not be the reason you came to Idaho, but Silverwood (☎ 208-683-3400), 15 miles north of Coeur d'Alene on US 95, will get the attention of any kids in your entourage. It features a full battery of amusement rides; an idealized recreation of a mining camp, complete with sing-alongs, silent films and live stage shows; an authentic steam train that transports passengers around the 500-acre site and is menaced by desperadoes in the backwoods; and an air show. The daring can ride in a vintage biplane (Silverwood was once a private airport). One admission fee covers all rides and activities (food is extra). Admission is $21 for those eight to 64 and $13 for seniors and children (three to seven). It is open daily mid-June to Labor Day, and weekends from late May to mid-June and during September.

Emerald Creek Garnet Area
The star garnet, found only in Idaho and India, is accessible at one of the world's only public garnet-digging areas. The site is south of Coeur d'Alene Lake and 5 miles south of Fernwood; take Hwy 3 to USFS Rd 447. It is administered by the USFS St Maries Ranger District (☎ 208-245-2531), PO Box 407, St Maries, ID 83861, and open Memorial Day to Labor Day. A $10 permit, available at the site, is required. Bring your own shovel, bucket and (ideally) a screen; be prepared to get muddy.

Hobo Cedar Grove Botanical Area
Northeast of Clarkia is the Hobo Cedar Grove Botanical Area, a national natural landmark. This 240-acre grove has old-growth western red cedar trees with trunks five to eight feet in diameter. A self-guided nature trail goes through the area. Another trail leads south up Marble Creek from St Joes Valley.

Rafting
The **St Joe National Wild & Scenic River** southeast of Coeur d'Alene, flows into Coeur d'Alene Lake. This one-day Class III run of 12 to 14 miles is best done from May to June. To book a rafting trip, contact River Odysseys West (☎ 208-765-0841, 800-451-6034; fax 208-667-6506), PO Box 579, Coeur d'Alene, ID 83816. Full-day trips start at $80.

WALLACE & SILVER VALLEY
The upper reaches of the South Fork Coeur d'Alene River contain some of the world's richest silver and lead veins, and have been the focus of intensive mining from the 1880s to the present. Most old mining centers are now ghost towns, and the environmental damage caused by mining is apparent. The well-preserved town center of Wallace (population 954; elevation 2800 feet) is a delight to anyone interested in historic architecture. (Wallace also served as backdrop for the film *Dante's Peak).* The area also has an interesting trail: decades ago railroads snaked their way around steep mountainsides and across narrow valleys to reach the Silver Valley mines, and today this engineering marvel – including the most expensive single sections of rail line ever laid – has been restored for use as a hiking and biking path.

Orientation & Information
Wallace and Kellogg are 9 miles apart along I-90. Both ends of Silver Valley are mountain passes. Above Coeur d'Alene Lake on I-90 is Fourth of July Pass (3070 feet). Lookout Pass is on I-90 at the Idaho-Montana state line. Both can be icy during winter. For a winter road report, call ☎ 208-772-0531.

The Wallace Chamber of Commerce (☎ 208-753-7151) is at 509 Bank St. The mailing address is: PO Box 1167, Wallace, ID 83873. The USFS Panhandle National

The Road to Ruin
An ongoing battle over logging in the Coeur d'Alene National Forest in the Bitterroot Mountains, east of Coeur d'Alene, pits the US government against the timber industry. The USFS has, at a financial loss, been reimbursing timber companies for road construction in national forests. The cost of logging roads in national forests is the reason national forests lose money on timber sales. The national forest system now has 2½ times more road miles than the national highway system, and in the Coeur d'Alene National Forest 20 road miles exist per 1 sq mile of forest. Logging roads are devastating to water quality in watersheds when erosion fills streams and rivers with silt, causing floods, loss of habitats and devastation to fish populations. Legislation is now pending in the US Congress which would prevent future taxpayer revenue from being used to build logging roads in national forests. ∎

Forest Wallace Ranger District (☎ 208-752-1221), in Silverton west of Wallace, offers hiking, camping and mountain-biking information. The Wallace post office (☎ 208-753-3435) is at 403 Cedar St.

Wallace National Historic District
Wallace, a late 19th-century mining town, is on the National Register of Historic Places. Stop to look at the architecture and get a sense of life on the Idaho mining frontier. The **Wallace District Mining Museum** (☎ 208-556-1592), 509 Bank St, chronicles the history of the area's mines and the techniques of extracting silver and lead ore from mile-deep shafts. It is open 8:30 am to 7 pm weekdays (until 6 pm on weekends) daily Memorial Day to Labor Day, and 9 am to 5 pm weekdays and 10 am to 5 pm Saturday the rest of the year. Admission is $1.50 for adults, 50¢ for seniors and children.

At 6th and Bank Sts, **ornate buildings** house shops and businesses. Note the pressed-tin turrets on the White & Bender Building. A block north on 6th St at Cedar St, the Art Deco Civic Center Building is fronted with terra-cotta brick. Several old hotels, including The Jameson (1900), are on the next block north.

The **Northern Pacific Depot Railroad Museum** (☎ 208-752-0111) sits at 6th and Pine Sts, beneath I-90. The 1st floor of this handsome Queen Anne is constructed of Chinese bricks, and the 3rd floor sports a chateau-esque tower. The museum is open 9 am to 7 pm daily Memorial Day to Labor Day, 10 am to 3 pm the rest of the year. Admission is $2/1.50 for adults/seniors and students.

Several grandiose structures, once home to fraternal organizations, are on Cedar St. The Eagles Building now houses the **Wallace District Arts Center** (☎ 208-753-8381), 515 Cedar St, which has an espresso bar, performance space and small gallery dedicated to local artists.

Sierra Silver Mine Tour
At the Sierra Silver Mine (☎ 208-752-5151), 420 5th St, Wallace, you can ride a trolley to the mine entrance for an underground tour. Tours depart every 30 minutes 9 am to 4 pm mid-May to October; in June and July hours are extended to 6 pm. Admission is $7.50 for adults, $6.50 for seniors and children; children under four are not allowed.

Old Mission State Park
The Mission of the Sacred Heart, now a state park (☎ 208-682-3814) in Cataldo (I-90 exit 39) is the state's oldest building, offering a glimpse into the meeting of Christianity and Native America. The park has a visitors center and picnic area, and guided tours are offered. A self-guided half-mile nature path leads to the river. The park is open from 8 am to 6 pm; the day-use fee is $3 per vehicle. Annually on August 15, members of the Coeur d'Alene tribe make a pilgrimage to the mission to celebrate the **Feast of the Assumption**. After Mass, members enact a pageant called 'The Coming of the Black Robes.'

Silver Mountain Resort

Silver Mountain Resort (☎ 208-783-1111, 800-204-6428; info@silvermt.com) sprawls across Kellogg (6300 feet) and Wardner (6200 feet) peaks. The centerpiece of winter and summer activities is the gondola, which goes from the valley floor to Mountain Haus (5700 feet), the ski lodge. The gondola is billed as the world's longest single-stage carrier, transporting passengers 3.1 miles and gaining 3400 feet in 19 minutes. During winter the ski area offers lots of dry powder snow, 50 runs and a maximum 2200-foot vertical drop. Weekend lift tickets cost $29/23 for adults/seniors and students; midweek tickets cost $32/21. Lessons and rentals are available. For a snow report call ☎ 208-666-8822.

During summer, the gondola carries passengers to the lodge. A series of outdoor concerts and plays take place in the band shell. The lodge restaurant and a barbecue concession are also open. Hiking trails lead to remote meadows and overlooks, and a network of mountain bike trails leads back to Kellogg. The ski lifts continue to the top for panoramic views of three states and Canada. The summer program runs on weekends only from Memorial Day weekend to mid-June and for the first two weekends of October; the lifts run daily mid-June to September. Gondola rides cost $7/6/4 for adults/seniors/children (seven to 12).

To reach Silver Mountain, take I-90 exit 49. Base Village is at 610 Bunker Ave, Kellogg.

Taft Tunnel Bike Trail

The Taft Tunnel Bike Trail project converted 15 miles of old Chicago, Milwaukee and St Paul Railroad track, tunnel and trestle into an exhilarating recreation trail. The centerpiece is the 8771-foot Taft Tunnel, built in 1909, through solid rock from the Montana side of Lookout Pass to Idaho. The trail winds through nine tunnels and over seven wooden trestles before reaching the valley floor.

For years, the abandoned tunnel and railroad tracks were popular with hikers and mountain bikers. Then liability concerns in the face of increased usage forced the USFS

The First Idaho Mission

In the early 1800s, as the first European explorers and traders crossed the Rocky Mountains, Native Americans in Idaho and Montana began hearing about Christianity. The Flatheads, a Salish tribe living in western Montana and northern Idaho, became so intrigued by stories of the 'Black Robes' that in the 1830s four delegations of Flatheads journeyed to St Louis, MO, to ask for missionaries. In 1841, Father Pierre De Smet, a Jesuit, came west, establishing missions and farms among the Salish.

Father De Smet promised the Coeur d'Alene Indians their own mission and Black Robes, who in 1848 began building a mission on a bluff above the Coeur d'Alene River. In charge of construction was Father Anthony Ravalli, an Italian-born Jesuit who was also a physician, scientist, mechanic, artist, architect and sculptor. Using only local products, Ravalli, another Brother and the enthusiastic Coeur d'Alenes set to work. The 3600-sq-foot church was built from a framework of mortised and tenoned beams, with dowels strung between. Straw and grass were woven through the dowels and then faced with river mud. The resulting walls were over a foot thick; no nails were used in any part of the structure. In fact, the only tools available to the Brothers and the Indians at the time were an axe, pulleys, pocket knives and rope. To outfit the church, Ravalli turned to local goods: old tin cans became chandelier sconces, the rough pine altar was faux painted to resemble marble and the walls were covered with newsprint, which was whitewashed and then painted with floral designs.

The mission remained in operation until 1924. The church and the parish house next door were declared a state park in 1974 and restored. Both can be visited at Old Mission State Park near Cataldo. ■

to close the Taft tunnel and dissuade activity along the neglected trestles. But grassroot support and back-room politics persuaded the USFS to allocate funds to clear the tunnel and make the trestles safe for recreational use.

The trail requires a headlamp for bikers and strong flashlights for hikers; be prepared to get a little wet and chilly. The grade never exceeds 1.7%, but several vertigo-inducing trestles traverse sheer cliffs and steep rocky canyons.

To reach the trail, drive over Lookout Pass to Montana's I-90 exit 5 and look for the Taft Area. Turn south and follow Rainy Creek Rd 2 miles. At the Y-junction go toward East Portal. The parking area is immediately ahead, and beyond it is the gate to the tunnel. The trail follows the contours of Loop Creek until it meets Moon Pass Rd, which leads in 20 miles to Wallace (via Placer Creek Rd).

Contact Taft Tunnel Preservation Society (☎ 208-556-1523) at PO Box 1222, Wallace, ID 83873; for a $1 donation, they send a letter and map. The Lookout Pass Ski Area (see below) and Excelsior Bikes (☎ 208-786-3751), 10 W Portland Ave, Kellogg, also offers information and rent mountain bikes.

Lookout Pass Ski Area
The small family-oriented Lookout Pass Ski Area (☎ 208-744-1392), on the Idaho-Montana state line (I-90 exit 0), offers rentals. No cross-country trails are groomed but USFS roads are popular for Nordic skiing.

Places to Stay
Motels cluster at Kellogg's I-90 exit 49, but local hotels and B&Bs offer more character.

Camping *Kellogg/Silver Valley KOA Kampground* (☎ 208-682-3612, 800-562-0799), 801 Division St (I-90 exit 45), offers streamside sites, pool and laundry. Tent sites cost $20; sites with full hookups are $25.

Hostels *Kellogg Hostel* (☎ 208-783-4171), at 834 W McKinley Ave, Kellogg, is the former HI/AYH hostel. Dorm rooms with kitchen access range from $12 to $15.

B&Bs *The Jameson* (☎ 208-556-1554), at 304 6th St, PO Box 869, Wallace, ID 83873, is a restored landmark hotel; rooms range from $55 to $60. Two Wallace Victorian mansions have become classy B&Bs. Rooms at *Beale House B&B* (☎ 208-752-7151, 888-752-7151), 107 Cedar St, range from $75 to $95. *Twenty-one Bank Street* (☎ 208-752-7292), 21 Bank St, has rooms starting at $70.

In Kellogg, an older hotel with a colorful past is *The McKinley Inn* (☎ 208-786-7771, 800-443-3505), 210 McKinley Ave. It has comfortable renovated rooms ranging from $50 to $65.

Hotels & Motels The *Brooks Hotel* (☎ 208-556-1571), 500 Cedar St, Wallace, an old behemoth of a hotel, was gutted and room sizes doubled. It is now one of northern Idaho's best lodging options with rooms starting at $40. At the *Stardust Motel* (☎ 208-752-1213), 410 Pine St, singles/doubles cost $44/54. The upscale *Best Western Wallace Inn* (☎ 208-752-1252), 100 Front St, offers a pool and spa; rooms range from $70 to $82.

Places to Eat
An abundance of roadside cafes and drive-ins insure no one starves in these old mining towns. The brass-and-wainscot-rich restaurant at *The Jameson* (see above) is a good choice for a burger at lunch or a steak dinner ($10 to $15).

Entertainment
Towns on the National Register of Historic Places always seem to have a summer theater group specializing in melodrama, and Wallace is no exception. *Sixth St Melodrama* (☎ 208-752-8871), 212 6th St, offers campy diabolical theater from the first weekend of July to Labor Day. Shows are mounted in the Lux Building, one of Wallace's oldest structures and formerly one of the city's many brothels.

IDAHO

Getting There & Away

Missoula, MT, is 121 miles to the east of Wallace, and Coeur d'Alene is 42 miles west of Kellogg. Greyhound Bus Lines offers three daily buses along the I-90 corridor between Missoula and Spokane, WA.

SANDPOINT & LAKE PEND OREILLE

Sandpoint (population 6748; elevation 2126 feet) is the largest resort community on Lake Pend Oreille. Nestled between forested hills, this beautiful 90,000-acre lake is the largest in Idaho and the second-deepest in the nation, next to Oregon's Crater Lake.

During WWII the US Navy developed a huge inland naval base here that trained nearly 300,000 sailors. The navy still maintains a small submarine base for design testing. Sandpoint, with interesting shops and good restaurants, is a pleasant place. Winter brings abundant snow and energetic skiers to Schweitzer Mountain Resort, just north of town. A second resort area lies on the eastern shore of Lake Pend Oreille at Hope and East Hope. A profusion of camgrounds and marinas make it preferable for campers and boaters. Drive to Hope on a summer's evening to watch the sun set over the lake.

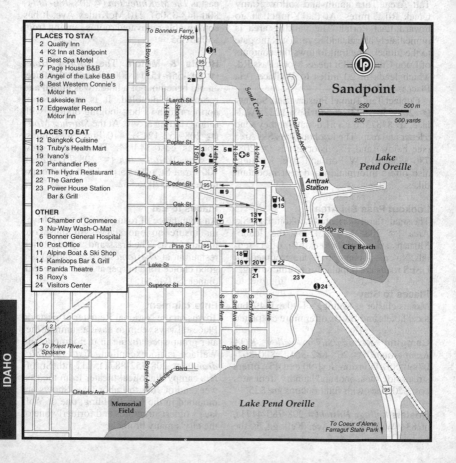

PLACES TO STAY
2 Quality Inn
4 K2 Inn at Sandpoint
5 Best Spa Motel
7 Page House B&B
8 Angel of the Lake B&B
9 Best Western Connie's
   Motor Inn
16 Lakeside Inn
17 Edgewater Resort
   Motor Inn

PLACES TO EAT
12 Bangkok Cuisine
13 Truby's Health Mart
19 Ivano's
20 Panhandler Pies
21 The Hydra Restaurant
22 The Garden
23 Power House Station
   Bar & Grill

OTHER
1 Chamber of Commerce
3 Nu-Way Wash-O-Mat
6 Bonner General Hospital
10 Post Office
11 Alpine Boat & Ski Shop
14 Kamloops Bar & Grill
15 Panida Theatre
18 Roxy's
24 Visitors Center

Sandpoint

Lake Pend Oreille

Orientation

A one-way counterclockwise loop circles Sandpoint's downtown. 1st Ave follows the lakefront; Bridge St turns off 1st Ave and leads to City Beach. Public parking is available on N 3rd Ave between Oak and Church Sts. East of Sandpoint on Hwy 200 is Ponderay, followed by Kootenai. Across the lake from Sandpoint are Hope and East Hope. At the south end of Lake Pend Oreille is Farragut State Park, formerly the naval training base.

Information

The Greater Sandpoint Chamber of Commerce (☎ 208-263-2161, 800-800-2106 24 hours; chamber@netw.com) is at 100 US 95 N, PO Box 928, Sandpoint, ID 83864. The USFS Idaho Panhandle National Forest office (☎ 208-263-5111) is at 1500 US 2. The post office is at 210 N 4th Ave. The Bonner General Hospital (☎ 208-263-1441) is at 520 N 3rd Ave. To do laundry, head to Nu-Way Wash-O-Mat (☎ 208-263-6332), 502 5th Ave. There's a visitors center on US 95 going south.

City Beach

The lake is the place to be in Sandpoint during summer. Most people make the easy stroll from downtown to City Beach for swimming and sunbathing. See Activities below for more information.

Farragut State Park

At the beginning of WWII, Eleanor Roosevelt, while flying across the northern USA, noted Lake Pend Oreille glimmering in the Idaho forests. She knew that the US Navy and her husband President FD Roosevelt were looking for a large, remote inland lake to develop as a naval training camp. She reported back and, after a quick exploratory trip by the president, work commenced in 1942 on Farragut Naval Training Center, which for four years was the second-largest naval training base in the world.

It was decommissioned in 1946 and in 1964 became Farragut State Park (☎ 208-683-2425), E 13400 Ranger Rd, Athol, ID 83801. The 4000-acre park, at the south end of Lake Pend Oreille 4 miles east of Athol (which is 24 miles south of Sandpoint) and 18 miles north of Coeur d'Alene on US 95, is very popular. The $3 day-use fee per vehicle allows access to 16,000 feet of the Lake Pend Oreille shoreline, 20 miles of trails and a 9-mile designated mountain-bike path. (See Places to Stay – Camping below.)

Activities

Directly across from City Beach is Windbag Sailboat Rentals (☎ 208-263-7811) where sailboats, windsurfing equipment, paddle boats and canoes can be rented. For **boating** and **water sports**, resorts along Lake Pend Oreille have marinas offering moorage, rental and charter services. In addition to the marina at City Beach in Sandpoint, there are East Hope Marina (☎ 208-263-3083) and the adjacent Holiday Shores Marina (☎ 208-264-5515), 1165 Hwy 200, East Hope.

The best **fishing** access is along the eastern end of Lake Pend Oreille. Eagle Charters (☎ 208-264-5274), at the Holiday Shores Marina in Hope, and Diamond Charters (☎ 208-264-5283), at the Pend Oreille Resort along Hwy 200 in Hope, are the main charter businesses.

The nearby Clark Fork River is popular for **rafting**. To book a rafting trip, contact River Odysseys West (☎ 208-765-0841, 800-451-6034; fax 208-667-6506), PO Box 579, Coeur d'Alene, ID 83816. The Alpine Boat & Ski Shop (☎ 208-263-5157), 213 Church St, does double duty as a ski shop and marina. Western Pleasure Inc (☎ 208-263-9066), 4675 Upper Gold Creek Rd, about 4½ miles outside of Kootenai off Gold Creek Rd, offers guided **horseback rides**.

Lake Cruises

During summer, a two-hour boat tour departs from the boat ramp at the beach at 1:30 pm daily. Purchase tickets upon boarding for $13/11/8 for adults/seniors/children. Lake Pend Oreille Cruises (☎ 208-263-4598) has more information.

Festival at Sandpoint

The Festival at Sandpoint (☎ 208-265-4554, 888-265-4554), held the first two weeks in August, presents music ranging from country to jazz and classical, with such artists as Tony Bennett, the Robert Cray Band, Al Jarreau, John Hiatt and The Pretenders. The main stage is under the stars at Memorial Field; other events are held at Schweitzer Mountain Resort.

Places to Stay

Camping The woods are full of campgrounds. *Alpine Trailer Park* (☎ 208-265-0179), 5 miles south of Sandpoint at US 95 and Sagle Rd, has RV-only sites with hookups starting at $14.

West of Sandpoint along the Pend Oreille River is *Springy Point Recreation Area* (☎ 208-437-3133), with tent camping ($12) and no hookups. It has showers and offers river swimming. Take US 95 south across the bridge to Lakeshore Rd, the first road to the west, and continue 3 miles.

On the eastern shores of Lake Pend Oreille are several lovely campgrounds. The USFS *Samowen Campground* (☎ 208-263-5111), 2 miles west of Hwy 200 on Spring Creek Rd in East Hope, is a thrifty alternative to the area's expensive resorts. Sites are on a peninsula and cost $11; reservations are recommended. For a more pampered camping experience, go to *Beyond Hope Resort* (☎ 208-264-5251), 3 miles down Samowen Rd off Hwy 200 E. Sites with hookups start at $23.

Farragut State Park (see above) has two campgrounds, with showers and a swimming beach, which are favorites of vacationing families: *Whitetail Campground* has tent sites ($12), and *Snowberry Campground* has sites with full hookups ($15). Write the park for campground reservations; do not call.

Round Lake State Park (☎ 208-263-3489), on Dufort Rd 10 miles south of Sandpoint, is a year-round campground with sites starting at $11. During summer the small lake is popular for picnicking, swimming, fishing and hiking.

B&Bs *Page House B&B* (☎ 208-263-6584, 800-500-6584), 502 N 2nd Ave, in downtown Sandpoint, is an historic home built in 1918 by the town's first mayor; rooms cost $75. The beautiful *Angel of the Lake B&B* (☎ 208-263-0816, 800-872-0816), 410 Railroad Ave, is on the lake near downtown. Rooms range from $65 to $85.

Hotels & Motels Stay close enough to downtown to walk to shops and City Beach. Make reservations as many places are booked months in advance, especially on weekends. *Best Spa Motel* (☎ 208-263-3532, 800-286-1818), 521 N 4th Ave at Poplar St, offers hot tubs and large singles/doubles for $60/69. Next door is *K2 Inn at Sandpoint* (☎ 208-263-3441), 501 N 3rd Ave, with rooms for $45/49. *Best Western Connie's Motor Inn* (☎ 208-263-9581), 323 Cedar St, is a large complex with a pool, spacious rooms ($91/97) and convention facilities.

For comparatively inexpensive lake access, the *Lakeside Inn* (☎ 208-263-3717, 800-543-8126), 106 Bridge St, is unsurpassed ($68/84). The *Edgewater Resort Motor Inn* (☎ 208-263-3194, 800-635-2534), 56 Bridge St, is the lodging of choice in Sandpoint, on the marina next to the beach; it has a spa and golf and ski packages. Rates are $110/119 with substantial off-season discounts.

Without reservations, you may end up staying farther from town. The *Quality Inn* (☎ 208-263-2111), 807 N 5th Ave, usually has rooms available ($58/60). The *Super 8 Motel* (☎ 208-263-2210), 3245 US 95 N, just north of Sandpoint in Ponderay, costs $52/65.

Resorts Along Lake Pend Oreille, the word 'resort' signifies marinas and access to the water. One of the nicest is *Pend Oreille Shores Resort* (☎ 208-264-5828), 1250 Hwy 200 in Hope, with condos and suites overlooking a busy marina. One-bedroom units start at $138; two-bedroom units are $170. The resort's Floating Restaurant is a favorite for a sunset meal or cocktail.

Long-Term Rentals Contact Tamarack Knoll Enterprises (TKE Vacation Rentals; ☎ 208-263-5539), 395 Garfield Bay Rd, for information on lakefront cabins and condominiums, and for cabin cruisers and other watercraft.

Places to Eat

Sandpoint has many good restaurants. If you are on a budget, 1st Avenue is lined with espresso stands, pubs, bagel shops and various ethnic restaurants. For something healthy or organic, head for *Truby's Health Mart* (☎ 208-263-6513), 113 Main St. Popular for breakfast and family dining, *Panhandler Pies* (☎ 208-263-2912), at 120 S 1st Ave, serves affordable homestyle cooking. Light, airy *Hydra Restaurant* (☎ 208-263-7123), 115 Lake St, is popular with good values on everything from sandwiches to chicken and steak.

Fine dining in Sandpoint means going Continental. *Ivano's* (☎ 208-263-0211), 124 S 2nd Ave, is a good northern Italian restaurant with pasta dishes and veal and chicken specialties ($15). *The Garden* (☎ 208-263-5187), 15 E Lake St near the lake, has outdoor seating during summer and a greenhouse dining room year-round, emphasizing fresh seafood and old-fashioned European favorites like beef Stroganoff ($16).

Popular for fresh fish, pasta and sandwiches is *Power House Station Bar and Grill* (☎ 208-265-2449), at 120 E Lake Ave. Find excellent Thai food at *Bangkok Cuisine* (☎ 208-265-4149), 202 N 2nd Ave.

Tressle Creek Inn (☎ 208-264-9017), 555 Hwy 200 East, Hope, is popular for pasta, steak and cocktails, and has a charming setting over a small marina where a creek enters the lake. The renowned *Floating Restaurant* at the Pend Oreille Shores Resort (☎ 208-264-5311), 1250 Hwy 200, offers a stunning pageant of color over the lake when the sun sets; the steak and fresh seafood are good, too.

Entertainment

On weekend nights, downtown bars offer live music and dancing. Two of the best are

Roxy's (☎ 208-263-6696), at 215 Pine St, and *Kamloops Bar & Grill* (☎ 208-263-6715), 302 N 1st Ave.

Getting There & Away

Bus North Idaho Community Express (NICE; ☎ 208-664-9769), which stops at Yokes Pac'n Save, 3295 US 95 N, operates four daily buses between Sandpoint and Coeur d'Alene. The one-way fare is $7.

Train Amtrak's *Empire Builder* line goes daily between Chicago and Seattle, WA. The eastbound train departs at 2:33 am; the westbound one at 11:09 pm. The depot is on Railroad St behind the Cedar St Public Market. For the luxury-minded, there's also Montana Rockies Rail Tours (☎ 800-519-7245), which runs trips to Sandpoint and between Bozeman or Billings, MT, along the first route of the Northern Transcontinental Railroad. Fares includes bus transfers between Spokane, WA, and Sandpoint, and meals and accommodation on the *Montana Daylight* in 'Explorer,' 'BigSky' or 'Gold Nugget' class for $400/600/1050, respectively. Longer trips go through Livingston, MT, the Paradise Valley and Yellowstone National Park.

Car East-west US 2 and Hwy 200 intersect at Sandpoint along US 95, which is 44 miles north of Coeur d'Alene and 64 miles south of the US-Canada border.

Getting Around

Car Agency Rent A Car (☎ 208-263-4155) is at 315 S Ella Ave. Dealerships such as Evergreen Ford Mercury Nissan (☎ 208-263-3127), at 3215 US 95 N, also rent cars.

Taxi Call Bonner Cab Co (☎ 208-263-7626) for a taxi.

SCHWEITZER MOUNTAIN RESORT

Northern Idaho's best ski area is Schweitzer Mountain Resort (☎ 208-263-9555, 800-831-8810), 11 miles north of Sandpoint off US 2 and US 95, with downhill and cross-country skiing, and night skiing Thursday to Saturday. From a maximum elevation of 6400 feet, 48 runs drop a maximum of 2400 vertical feet. Annual snowfall usually exceeds 300 inches. Full-day lift tickets (including night skiing) start at $34/17/17 for adults/seniors/children (seven to 17). During summer, the chairlift provides rides for hikers and mountain bikers who want to explore the high country.

Accommodations are available, as are lessons and rentals. During ski season, rooms at *Green Gables Lodge* (☎ 208-263-0257, 800-831-8810) start at $129. Rates drop up to 50% during summer, when the lodge becomes the focus of mountain biking, llama treks, hiking and festival events.

BONNERS FERRY & AROUND

Bonners Ferry (population 2491; elevation 2180 feet) began as a ferry crossing on the Kootenai River during Canada's Wild Horse Creek gold rush in the 1860s. Since then, Bonners Ferry has gone through several incarnations, especially as a mill town. With lumbering on the skids, this town situated in a deep canyon straddling the large and turbulent Kootenai River is now trying to make a living by tourism. Recreation, such as great fishing and rafting, abounds, though it is the sometimes unsettlingly dense forests that most travelers recall.

Orientation & Information

Downtown Bonners Ferry is north of the Kootenai River, with newer development to its south. A cluster of businesses sit on the plateau above the canyon, near the junction of US 95 and US 2. The Bonners Ferry Chamber of Commerce (☎ 208-267-5922), PO Box X, Bonners Ferry, ID 83805, has a summer information center at 7198 US 95. The USFS Kaniksu National Forest Bonners Ferry Ranger Station (☎ 208-267-5561), on US 95 just south of Bonners Ferry, offers information on area camping and recreation. The Boundary County Community Hospital (☎ 208-267-3141) is at 551 Kaniksu St. The two US-Canada border crossings are: Eastport (☎ 208-267-3966) on US 95, open 24

hours; and Porthill (☎ 208-267-5309) on Hwy 1, only open during daylight.

Moyie Bridge & Falls

The 1223-foot Moyie Bridge carries US 2 450 feet above the Moyie River Canyon 11 miles east of Bonners Ferry. For a closer look at the river and its impressive double-drop falls, turn toward Moyie Springs at the west end of the bridge and follow the paved road south until a side road leads back under the bridge. This road overlooks the churning 100-foot and 40-foot falls. In Idaho tradition, the falls are dammed at the top for hydropower.

Rafting

Two nearby rivers are popular for rafting: a 15-mile Class III stretch of the lower Moyie River is usually run May to June, and the enormous and powerful Kootenai River is run during summer. Day trips, including lunch, start at $55. To book a rafting trip, contact: River Odysseys West (☎ 208-765-0841, 800-451-6034; fax 208-667-6506), PO Box 579, Coeur d'Alene, ID 83816; Moyie River Outfitting Guide Service (☎ 208-267-2108); or Twin Rivers Canyon Resort (see Places to Stay below).

Places to Stay

Camping *Bonners Ferry Resort* (☎ 208-267-2422), 2 miles south of town on US 95, has tent sites ($14), sites with full hookups ($17), motel rooms ($59), a pool and laundry. In a spectacular setting, where the Moyie and Kootenai rivers meet, the 160-acre *Twin Rivers Canyon Resort* (☎ 208-267-5932), 1 mile east of Moyie Springs, has access to fishing, hiking trails and river swimming. Tent sites cost $11; sites with full hookups are $17.

Hotels & Motels *Kootenai Valley Motel* (☎ 208-267-7567), on US 95 just south of Bonners Ferry, is an attractive well-kept motel in a grove of trees. Singles/doubles cost $60/95. *Bonners Ferry Log Inn* (☎ 208-267-3986), 2 miles north of Bonners Ferry on US 95, is a new log motel with nicely furnished rooms ($45/64). The *Best Western*

Kootenai River Inn (☎ 208-267-8511), across from downtown in the Kootenai River Plaza, offers dramatic riverfront rooms starting at $76/88. This large complex houses the local casino.

Places to Eat
Grab an early-morning espresso or a sandwich for lunch at *Deli Delite* (☎ 208-267-2241), 1106 S Main St. *Three Mile Junction Cafe* (☎ 208-267-3513), at the junction of US 2 and US 95, 3 miles north of Bonners Ferry, has great breakfasts and a daily sandwich-and-homemade-pie lunch special. *Alberto's Mexican Restaurant* (☎ 208-267-7493), 222 E Riverside, serves the area's best Mexican food. Go to *The Springs Restaurant* (☎ 208-267-8511), in the Kootenai River Inn, for pasta, steak and fish in a river-front dining room; full dinners run $12 to $15.

Getting There & Away
Bonners Ferry is on US 95, 32 miles north of Sandpoint and 32 miles south of Eastport.

PRIEST LAKE
If you are searching for isolation and wilderness, then Priest Lake (2800 feet) is for you: this area is remote even for Idaho. Traveling the lone road through dense wilderness along the surging Priest River is like heading back into the forest primeval. From the shores of Priest Lake north into Canada, the forest spreads for hundreds of miles. Priest Lake, an Ice Age relic gouged out between peaks of the Selkirk Mountains, is actually two separate lakes linked by a wide, 2½-mile-long channel called the Thoroughfare; the combined length of the lakes is over 25 miles. The area around Priest Lake is home to woodland caribou, grizzly bears, gray wolves, moose and wolverines. You will be lucky, however, to sight these north woods denizens, in part due to the dense forests.

Orientation
Hwy 57 divides at Coolin, 22 miles north of the little town of Priest River. Hwy 57 continues 17 miles to Nordman, about halfway up the west side of the lake. Three miles east

of Nordman is Reeder Bay. North from Nordman, a rough gravel road, maintained during summer only, continues over the Selkirk Mountains to Metaline Falls, WA. The other fork off Hwy 57 leads to Coolin, where the road turns to gravel and winds up the east side of the lake to the Lionshead and Indian Creek units of Priest Lake State Park.

To call any of the little settlements along Priest Lake a town is to exaggerate. Coolin and Nordman are the largest, and each has a few shops, restaurants and accommodations. Most lodges offer a basic selection of groceries, camping goods and a restaurant. Otherwise, you are on your own.

Information
Contact the Priest Lake Chamber of Commerce (☎ 208-443-3191, 888-774-3785) at PO Box 174, Coolin, ID 83821. The USFS Kaniksu National Forest Priest Lake Ranger Station (☎ 208-443-2512), in Nordman, has information on camping, hiking and other outdoor recreation around Priest Lake.

Places to Stay
Camping There are plenty of campgrounds along Priest Lake. *Priest Lake State Park* (☎ 208-443-2200), Indian Creek Bay No 423, Coolin, ID 83821, has three units. Dickensheet Unit is near Coolin, on the Priest River just below the lake; its primitive sites ($7) are popular with rafters. Indian Creek Unit, 16 miles north of Coolin, is the most developed, offering lakefront tent sites ($12), sites with hookups ($18) and showers. The Lionhead Unit is 8 miles north. No hookups make this preferable for tent camping ($9). Write to the park for reservations; no phone calls.

Of the many USFS campgrounds near Priest Lake, the most popular is probably *Reeder Bay*, 3 miles east of Nordman on the lake, with a boat slip and swimming beach; sites cost $10. The USFS maintains two primitive campgrounds on Kalispell Island. To reach them bring your own boat or rent one from the Priest Lake Marina (☎ 208-443-2405), off W Lake Shore Rd, about 8 miles north of the Coolin junction on Hwy 57.

Resorts Rustic lakeside resorts offer cabins, condominiums and lodge rooms. *Hill's Resort* (☎ 208-443-2551), on Luby Bay, has cabins and motel units for $80 to $250, a marina, restaurant and lounge. Go north 6 miles on Hwy 57 and take USFS Rd 1337 1 mile east to the lake. *Elkins on Priest Lake* (☎ 208-443-2432), on Reeder Bay 3 miles east of Nordman, has cabins ($85 to $235) in the woods overlooking the lake, a lodge, restaurant and moorage for boats. The *Grandview Resort* (☎ 208-443-2433), at Reeder Bay, has lodge rooms, cabins and suites ($75 to $165), with a pool, restaurant and store.

Places to Eat

Most restaurants along Priest Lake are associated with lodges and resorts, and some offer good homestyle cooking. An especially good place is *Patton's at the Marina* (☎ 208-443-2405), at the Priest Lake Marina at Kalispell Bay, with pasta, pizza and Italian entrees. Overlooking the lake is the dining room at *Cavanaugh Bay Resort* (☎ 208-443-2095), 4 miles east of Coolin. Burgers, steaks and chicken are cooked over an outdoor grill. Otherwise, the selection is limited to a few restaurants at Coolin and Nordman.

Getting There & Away

There is no public transportation available to Priest Lake. Your only option is to drive. From Coeur d'Alene (95 miles) take I-90 to Hwy 41. At Priest River, take Hwy 2 north to Priest Lake. Spokane, WA, is 90 miles away, and Sandpoint is 63 miles away.

Glossary

14er or Fourteener – Local Colorado term for a mountain whose elevation is 14,000 feet or more.

AAA – American Automobile Association, a private organization that provides information (including maps) and road services for motorists.

acequia – Spanish word meaning irrigation ditch.

adobado – Marinated meat used in Mexican cooking.

Anasazi – A group of Native Americans that inhabited southern Colorado and parts of Arizona, New Mexico and Utah from 100 to 1300 AD. The term comes from a Navajo word meaning 'enemy ancestors' but misinterpreted as 'ancient ones.'

BIA – Bureau of Indian Affairs, an organization under the Department of the Interior responsible for dealings with indigenous peoples in the continental USA.

bison – The term 'buffalo' is used interchangeably. This bovine (*Bison bison*) once freely roamed North America's Great Plains but was hunted to near extinction. Under federal protection bison recovered slightly and are maintaining stable numbers in Montana and Wyoming, and have reached larger numbers in Colorado, where they are raised commercially.

BLM – Bureau of Land Management, an agency of the Department of the Interior which controls substantial portions of public lands in the Rocky Mountain states and elsewhere in the West.

brown & white cooking – Slang for 'meat and potatoes.'

buffalo – See bison.

caldera – A giant circular basin-like depression resulting from the cataclysmic explosion or collapse of the center of a volcano.

C&W – Country & Western music; an amalgamation of rock music and folk music of the southern and western USA. Line dancing and the two-step are dances associated with C&W music.

CB&Q – Chicago, Burlington & Quincy Railroad.

DOW – Colorado Department of Wildlife.

D&RG – Denver & Rio Grande Railroad.

full hookup – Facility equipped for the hookup of a Recreational Vehicle (see RV).

glacial erratic – A large rock fragment that has been transported by moving ice from its place of origin.

Gold Medal streams – Waters designated by the Colorado Wildlife Commission for having a (naturally or artificially) high density of large trout.

GOP – The Grand Old Party; the Republican Party.

hard-shell camping – Term for camping in an enclosed RV unit (excludes canvas pop-up trailers).

HI/AYH – Hostelling International/American Youth Hostels, a term given to hostels affiliated with Hostelling International, which is a member group of IYHF (International Youth Hostel Federation).

horno – A conical outdoor oven built of adobe.

kiva – A subterranean circular room initially built by the Anasazi.

KOA – Kampgrounds of America, a private RV-oriented organization that provides moderate- to high-priced camping with substantial amenities throughout the USA.

krummholz – German for 'crooked wood,' referring to stunted trees, shaped by wind and snow, at mountainous treeline margins.

Lakota – Plains Indians, also commonly known as Teton Sioux, who were the most effective opponents of the US Army in the wars of the mid- to late-19th century.

maverick – An unbranded calf; one who dissents from a group.

mavericking – The unauthorized branding of calves, undertaken by cowboys trying to build their own herds on the open range. Cattle barons considered such activities rustling and took both legal and illegal steps to eliminate the practice.

metate – A stone with a concave indent used by Native Americans and Hispanics to grind grain with a handheld 'mano' stone.

moradas – Lodges in which the Penitente Brotherhoods of southern Colorado and New Mexico practiced their once secretive rites, including self-flagellation.

NASTAR – National Standard Race, a recreational ski program created in 1969 that offers timed races at Alpine ski areas for amateurs.

National Register of Historic Places – Listing of historic buildings, as designated by the NPS on nomination of property owners and local authorities. Determination is based on supporting evidence supplied by them regarding the significance in the development of a community. Being listed on the National Register restricts property owners from making major structural changes to the buildings, but also provides tax incentives for preservation. Often referred to as the 'National Register.'

NPR – National Public Radio, a noncommercial listener-supported broadcast organization that produces and distributes news, public affairs and cultural programming via a network of loosely affiliated radio stations throughout the USA.

NPS – National Park Service, a division of the Department of the Interior which administers US national parks and monuments.

NRA – National Recreation Area, term used to describe National Park Service units in areas of considerable scenic or ecological importance that have been modified by human activity, most often major dam projects; some of these, like Flaming Gorge NRA in Utah and Wyoming, are now administered by the USFS.

NRA – National Rifle Association, the influential Washington, DC-based organization that zealously lobbies against gun controls of any kind and has many members in the West.

PBS – Public Broadcasting System, a noncommercial television network that produces and distributes news, public affairs and cultural programming via a network of loosely affiliated television stations throughout the USA.

Penitente Brotherhood – Roman Catholic religious group with mainly Hispanic followers that formerly practiced such rites as self-flagellation and fasting.

petroglyph – A carving or inscription on a rock.

pictograph – A drawing or painting on a rock.

Plains Indians – A group of tribes, including the Lakota, Cheyenne, Arapaho, Comanche and Sioux, that was hostile to settlement, and the Crow and Shoshone, who were cooperative with the US government.

PRCA – Professional Rodeo Cowboys Association, an organization based in Colorado Springs that coordinates and sanctions rodeos throughout the West.

res – slang for reservation, frequently used by Native Americans.

riparian – Relating to, living or located on a stream or river bank.

rustler – One who steals stock, especially cattle.

rut – The fall mating period for male moose, elk and bighorn sheep. The word comes from the Latin term for roar, referring to the deep resonant sound made by the animals when they are 'in rut.'

RV – Recreational vehicle; a large moving object from which vacationers can see the USA in comfort akin to that enjoyed while staying home. (Also see full-hookup.)

santos – Carved wooden religious figurines used in small Catholic shrines, including those of the Penitente. Associated with these are *retablos* (altarpieces or religious pictures) and *bultos* (sculptures).

smokejumpers – Firefighters who parachute into forest fires.

sopaipilla – A pillow-like flatbread often served with honey.

Superfund sites – Toxic land sites identified and slated for federally funded cleanup.

sutler – A civilian provisioner to an army post.

SWA – State Wildlife Area designated in Colorado.

TNM&O – Texas-New Mexico & Oklahoma Coaches Inc.

Uncle Pete – The Union Pacific Railroad, so nicknamed for the power it exercises in the towns of Wyoming's Southern Tier.

UP – The Union Pacific Railroad Corporation.

USFS – United States Forest Service, a division of the Department of Agriculture which implements policies on federal forest lands on the principles of 'multiple use,' including timber-cutting, watershed management, wildlife management, and camping and recreation. Many of the most scenic areas in the Rockies are under USFS jurisdiction.

USFWS – United States Fish & Wildlife Service, an agency of the Department of the Interior with responsibility for fish and wildlife habitat and related matters.

USGS – United States Geological Survey, an agency of the Department of the Interior responsible for, among other things, detailed topographic maps of the entire country. Widely available at outdoor-oriented businesses, USGS maps are particularly popular with hikers and backpackers.

WPA – Works Progress Administration, a federal government program established under Franklin Delano Roosevelt's administration during the Depression of the 1930s; throughout the country, WPA programs employed writers who produced exceptional guidebooks with great cultural and historical depth, and artists who left many notable monuments like murals in federal government buildings.

WSGA – Wyoming Stock Growers Association.

yurt system – A system of huts maintained for use in the summer by hikers and mountain bikers and in the winter by cross-country (Nordic) skiers. Different systems maintain the huts for use from a simple stopover to overnight and week-long stays.

Climate Charts

Denver, CO

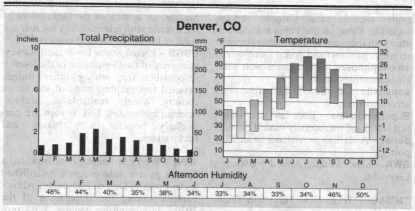

Total Precipitation

Temperature

Afternoon Humidity

J	F	M	A	M	J	J	A	S	O	N	D
48%	44%	40%	35%	38%	34%	33%	34%	33%	34%	46%	50%

Cheyenne, WY

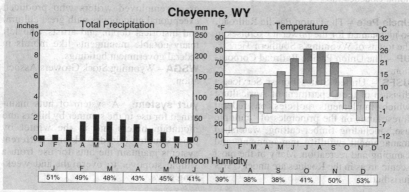

Total Precipitation

Temperature

Afternoon Humidity

J	F	M	A	M	J	J	A	S	O	N	D
51%	49%	48%	43%	45%	41%	39%	38%	38%	41%	50%	53%

Butte, MT

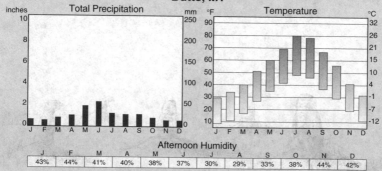

Total Precipitation

Temperature

Afternoon Humidity

J	F	M	A	M	J	J	A	S	O	N	D
43%	44%	41%	40%	38%	37%	30%	29%	33%	38%	44%	42%

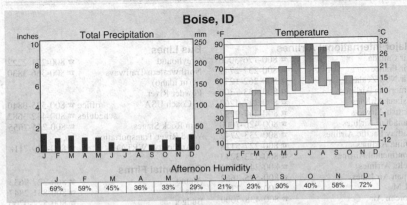

Boise, ID

Total Precipitation

Temperature

Afternoon Humidity

J	F	M	A	M	J	J	A	S	O	N	D
69%	59%	45%	36%	33%	29%	21%	23%	30%	40%	58%	72%

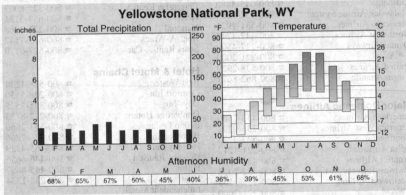

Yellowstone National Park, WY

Total Precipitation

Temperature

Afternoon Humidity

J	F	M	A	M	J	J	A	S	O	N	D
68%	65%	67%	50%	45%	40%	36%	39%	45%	53%	61%	68%

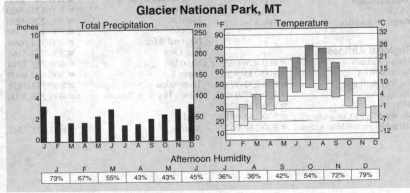

Glacier National Park, MT

Total Precipitation

Temperature

Afternoon Humidity

J	F	M	A	M	J	J	A	S	O	N	D
73%	67%	55%	43%	43%	45%	36%	36%	42%	54%	72%	79%

Toll-Free Telephone Numbers

Major International Airlines

Air Canada	☎ 800-776-3000
Air France	☎ 800-237-2747
Air New Zealand	☎ 800-262-1234
American Airlines	☎ 800-433-7300
Asiana Airlines	☎ 800-227-4262
British Airways	☎ 800-247-9297
Canadian Airlines	☎ 800-426-7000
Cathay Pacific Airlines	☎ 800-233-2742
China Airlines	☎ 800-227-5118
Continental Airlines	☎ 800-523-3273
Delta Airlines	☎ 800-241-4141
Japan Air Lines	☎ 800-525-3663
KLM	☎ 800-374-7747
Korean Air	☎ 800-438-5000
Lufthansa	☎ 800-645-3880
Malaysian Airline System	☎ 800-552-9264
Mexicana Airlines	☎ 800-531-7921
Northwest Airlines	☎ 800-447-4747
Qantas Airways	☎ 800-227-4500
TWA	☎ 800-221-2000
United Airlines	☎ 800-538-2929
Virgin Atlantic	☎ 800-862-8621

Major Domestic Airlines

American Airlines	☎ 800-433-7300
America West Airlines	☎ 800-235-9292
Continental	☎ 800-523-3273
Delta Air Lines	☎ 800-221-1212
Frontier Airlines	☎ 800-432-1359
Midwest Express Airlines	☎ 800-452-2022
Northwest Airlines	☎ 800-225-2525
TWA	☎ 800-221-2000
United Airlines	☎ 800-241-6522
USAir	☎ 800-428-4322
Vanguard Airlines	☎ 800-826-4827

Regional Airlines

Alaska Airlines	☎ 800-426-0333
America West	☎ 800-235-9292
Big Sky Airlines	☎ 800-237-7788
Horizon Air	☎ 800-547-9308
Reno Air	☎ 800-736-6247
SkyWest/Delta Connection	☎ 800-453-9417
United Express/Mesa Airlines	☎ 800-241-6522

Bus Lines

Greyhound	☎ 800-231-2222
Northwestern Trailways (in Idaho)	☎ 800-366-3830
Powder River Coach USA	office ☎ 800-525-0840
	schedules ☎ 800-442-3682
Rim Rock Stages	☎ 800-255-7655
Wind River Transportation Authority (WRTA)	☎ 800-439-7118

Car Rental Firms

Alamo	☎ 800-327-9633
Avis	☎ 800-831-2847
Budget	☎ 800-527-0700
Enterprise Rent-A-Car	☎ 800-325-8007
Hertz	☎ 800-654-3131
National	☎ 800-227-7368
Rent-A-Wreck	☎ 800-637-7147
Sears Rent-A-Car	☎ 800-527-0770

Hotel & Motel Chains

Best Western	☎ 800-528-1234
Comfort Inn	☎ 800-228-5150
Days Inn	☎ 800-325-2525
Doubletree Hotels	☎ 800-222-8733
Econo Lodge	☎ 800-553-2666
Hampton Inn	☎ 800-426-7866
Holiday Inn	☎ 800-465-4329
Howard Johnson	☎ 800-446-4656
Hilton	☎ 800-445-8667
Hyatt	☎ 800-233-1234
Independent Motels of America (IMA)	☎ 800-341-8000
La Quinta Inn	☎ 800-531-5900
Marriott	☎ 800-228-9290
Motel 6	☎ 800-440-6000
National 9 Inn	☎ 800-524-9999
Red Lion	☎ 800-733-5466
Shilo Inn	☎ 800-222-2244
Super 8	☎ 800-800-8000
Travelodge	☎ 800-578-7878
Westin Hotels & Resorts	☎ 800-228-3000

Train

Amtrak	☎ 800-872-7245

Index

SIDEBARS

LONELY PLANET PRODUCTS

Lonely Planet is known worldwide for publishing practical, reliable and no-nonsense travel information in our guides and on our web site. The Lonely Planet list covers just about every accessible part of the world. Currently there are nine series: *travel guides, shoestring guides, walking guides, city guides, phrasebooks, audio packs, travel atlases, Journeys*–a unique collection of travel writing–and *Pisces Books* (diving and snorkeling guides.)

EUROPE

Amsterdam • Austria • Baltic States & Kaliningrad • Baltic States phrasebook • Britain • Central Europe on a shoestring • Central Europe phrasebook • Czech & Slovak Republics • Denmark • Dublin • Eastern Europe on a shoestring • Eastern Europe phrasebook • Finland • France • French phrasebook • Germany • German phrasebook • Greece • Greek phrasebook • Hungary • Iceland, Greenland & the Faroe Islands • Ireland • Italy • Italian phrasebook • Lisbon • London • Mediterranean Europe on a shoestring • Mediterranean Europe phrasebook • Paris • Poland • Portugal • Portugal travel atlas • Prague • Romania & Moldova • Russia, Ukraine & Belarus • Russian phrasebook • Scandinavian & Baltic Europe on a shoestring • Scandinavian Europe phrasebook • Slovenia • Spain • Spanish phrasebook • St Petersburg • Switzerland • Trekking in Greece • Trekking in Spain • Ukrainian phrasebook • Vienna • Walking in Britain • Walking in Italy • Walking in Switzerland • Western Europe on a shoestring • Western Europe phrasebook

NORTH AMERICA

Alaska • Backpacking in Alaska • Baja California • Bermuda • California & Nevada • Canada • Chicago • Deep South • Florida • Hawaii • Honolulu • Los Angeles • Mexico • Mexico City • Miami • New England • New Orleans • New York City • New York, New Jersey & Pennsylvania • Pacific Northwest USA • Rocky Mountains USA • San Francisco • Seattle • Southwest USA • USA phrasebook • Washington, DC & The Capital Region

CENTRAL AMERICA & THE CARIBBEAN

Bahamas, Turks & Caicos • Central America on a shoestring • Costa Rica • Cuba • Eastern Caribbean • Guatemala, Belize & Yucatán: La Ruta Maya • Jamaica • Panama

SOUTH AMERICA

Argentina, Uruguay & Paraguay • Bolivia • Brazil • Brazilian phrasebook • Buenos Aires • Chile & Easter Island • Chile travel atlas • Colombia • Ecuador & the Galápagos Islands • Latin American Spanish phrasebook • Peru • Quechua phrasebook • Rio de Janeiro • South America on a shoestring • Trekking in the Patagonian Andes • Venezuela

Travel Literature: Full Circle: A South American Journey

AFRICA

Arabic (Moroccan) phrasebook • Africa on a shoestring • Africa –The South • Cape Town • Cairo • Central Africa • East Africa • Egypt & the Sudan • Egypt travel atlas • Ethiopian (Amharic) phrasebook • Kenya • Kenya travel atlas • Malawi, Mozambique & Zambia • Morocco • North Africa • South Africa, Lesotho & Swaziland • South Africa travel atlas • Swahili phrasebook • Trekking in East Africa • Tunisia • West Africa • Zimbabwe, Botswana & Namibia • Zimbabwe, Botswana & Namibia travel atlas

Travel Literature: The Rainbird: A Central African Journey • Songs to an African Sunset: A Zimbabwean Story

ISLANDS OF THE INDIAN OCEAN

Madagascar & Comoros • Maldives & Islands of the East Indian Ocean • Mauritius, Réunion & Seychelles

Also Available: Brief Encounters • Travel with Children • Traveller's Tales

Lonely Planet products are distributed worldwide. They are also available by mail order from Lonely Planet, so if you have difficulty finding a title please write to us. North American and South American residents should write to 150 Linden St, Oakland CA 94607, USA; European and African residents should write to 10A Spring Place, London NW5 3BH, UK; and residents of other countries to PO Box 617, Hawthorn, Victoria 3122, Australia.

NORTH-EAST ASIA

Beijing • Cantonese phrasebook • China • Hong Kong • Hong Kong, Macau & Canton • Japan • Japanese phrasebook • Japanese audio pack • Korea • Korean phrasebook • Mandarin phrasebook • Mongolia • Mongolian phrasebook • North-East Asia on a shoestring • Seoul • Taiwan • Tibet • Tibet phrasebook • Tokyo

Travel Literature: Lost Japan

MIDDLE EAST & CENTRAL ASIA

Arab Gulf States • Arabic (Egyptian) phrasebook • Cairo • Central Asia • Central Asia phrasebook • Iran • Israel & the Palestinian Territories • Israel & the Palestinian Territories travel atlas • Istanbul • Jerusalem • Jordan & Syria • Jordan, Syria & Lebanon travel atlas • Lebanon • Middle East • Turkey • Turkey travel atlas • Turkish phrasebook • Trekking in Turkey • Yemen

Travel Literature: The Gates of Damascus • Kingdom of the Film Stars: Journey into Jordan

INDIAN SUBCONTINENT

Bengali phrasebook • Bangladesh • Delhi • Goa • Hindi/Urdu phrasebook • India • India & Bangladesh travel atlas • Indian Himalaya • Karakoram Highway • Nepal • Nepali phrasebook • Pakistan • Rajasthan • Sri Lanka • Sri Lanka phrasebook • Trekking in the Indian Himalaya • Trekking in the Karakoram & Hindukush • Trekking in the Nepal Himalaya

Travel Literature: In Rajasthan • Shopping for Buddhas

SOUTH-EAST ASIA

Bali & Lombok • Bangkok • Burmese phrasebook • Cambodia • Ho Chi Minh • Indonesia • Indonesian phrasebook • Indonesian audio pack • Jakarta • Java • Laos • Lao phrasebook • Laos travel atlas • Malay phrasebook • Malaysia, Singapore & Brunei • Myanmar (Burma) • Philippines • Pilipino phrasebook • Singapore • South-East Asia on a shoestring • Thailand • Thailand's Islands & Beaches • Thai phrasebook • Thailand travel atlas • Thai audio pack • Thai Hill Tribes phrasebook • Vietnam • Vietnamese phrasebook • Vietnam travel atlas

ANTARCTICA

Antarctica

AUSTRALIA & THE PACIFIC

Australia • Australian phrasebook • Bushwalking in Australia • Bushwalking in Papua New Guinea • Fiji • Fijian phrasebook • Islands of Australia's Great Barrier Reef • Melbourne • Micronesia • New Caledonia • New South Wales & the ACT • New Zealand • Northern Territory • Outback Australia • Papua New Guinea • Papua New Guinea phrasebook • Queensland • Rarotonga & the Cook Islands • Samoa • Solomon Islands • South Australia • Sydney • Tahiti & French Polynesia • Tasmania • Tonga • Tramping in New Zealand • Vanuatu • Victoria • Western Australia

Travel Literature: Islands in the Clouds • Sean & David's Long Drive

THE LONELY PLANET STORY

...blished its first book in 1973 in response to the numerous 'How did you do it?' questions Maureen and ...er were asked after driving, bussing, hitching, sailing and railing their way from England to Australia.

Written at a kitchen table and hand collated, trimmed and stapled, *Across Asia on the Cheap* became an instant local best seller, inspiring thoughts of another book.

Eighteen months in South-East Asia resulted in their second guide, *South-East Asia on a shoestring*, which they put together in a backstreet Chinese hotel in Singapore in 1975. The 'yellow bible', as it quickly became known to back-packers around the world, soon became the guide to the region. It has sold well over half a million copies and is now in its 9th edition, still retaining its familiar yellow cover.

Today there are 350 titles, including travel guides, walking guides, language kits & phrasebooks, travel atlases, diving guides and travel literature. The company is the largest independent travel publisher in the world. Although Lonely Planet initially specialized in guides to Asia, today there are few corners of the globe that have not been covered.

The emphasis continues to be on travel for independent travelers. Tony and Maureen still travel for several months of each year and play an active part in the writing, updating and quality control of Lonely Planet's guides.

They have been joined by over 100 authors and 300 staff at our offices in Melbourne (Australia), Oakland (USA), London (UK) and Paris (France). Travelers themselves also make a valuable contribution to the guides through the feedback we receive in thousands of letters each year and on our website.

The people at Lonely Planet strongly believe that travelers can make a positive contribution to the countries they visit, both through their appreciation of the countries' culture, wildlife and natural features, and through the money they spend. In addition, the company makes a direct contribution to the countries and regions it covers. Since 1986 a percentage of the income from each book has been donated to ventures such as famine relief in Africa; aid projects in India; agricultural projects in Central America; Greenpeace's efforts to halt French nuclear testing in the Pacific; and Amnesty International.

'I hope we send people out with the right attitude about travel. You realize when you travel that there are so many different perspectives about the world, so we hope these books will make people more interested in what they see. Guidebooks can't really guide people. All you can do is point them in the right direction.'

– Tony Wheeler

LONELY PLANET PUBLICATIONS

Australia
PO Box 617, Hawthorn 3122, Victoria
☎ (03) 9819 1877 fax (03) 9819 6459
email talk2us@lonelyplanet.com.au

USA
150 Linden Street
Oakland, California 94607
☎ (510) 893 8555, TOLL FREE (800) 275 8555
fax (510) 893 8572
email info@lonelyplanet.com

UK
10A Spring Place,
London NW5 3BH
☎ (0171) 428 4800 fax (0171) 428 4828
email go@lonelyplanet.co.uk

France
1 rue du Dahomey, 75011 Paris
☎ 01 55 25 33 00 fax 01 55 25 33 01
email bip@lonelyplanet.fr

World Wide Web: www.lonelyplanet.com or *AOL* keyword: lp